The American System of Criminal Justice

About the Authors

George F. Cole is Professor Emeritus of Political Science at the University of Connecticut. A specialist in the administration of criminal justice, he has published extensively on such topics as prosecution, courts, and corrections. George Cole is also coauthor with Christopher Smith of *Criminal Justice in America*, coauthor with Todd Clear and Michael Reisig of *American Corrections*, and coauthor with Marc Gertz and Amy Bunger of *The Criminal Justice System: Politics and Policies*. He developed and directed the graduate corrections program at the University of Connecticut and was a Fellow at the National Institute of Justice (1988). Among his other accomplishments, he has been granted two awards under the Fulbright-Hays Program to conduct criminal justice research in England and the former Yugoslavia. In 1995 he was named a Fellow of the Academy of Criminal Justice Sciences for distinguished teaching and research.

Trained as a lawyer and social scientist, Christopher E. Smith, J.D., Ph.D., is Professor of Criminal Justice at Michigan State University, where he teaches courses on criminal justice policy, courts, corrections, and law. In addition to writing more than 100 scholarly articles, he is the author of 20 books, including several other titles with Wadsworth: *Criminal Procedure; Law and Contemporary Corrections; Courts, Politics, and the Judicial Process; The Changing Supreme Court: Constitutional Rights and Liberties* with Thomas R. Hensley and Joyce A. Baugh; *Courts and Public Policy; Politics in Constitutional Law;* and *Courts and the Poor.*

The American System of Criminal Justice

TWELFTH EDITION

George F. Cole
University of Connecticut

Christopher E. Smith
Michigan State University

 **WADSWORTH**
CENGAGE Learning

Australia • Brazil • Japan • Korea • Mexico • Singapore • Spain • United Kingdom • United States

The American System of Criminal Justice
Twelfth Edition
George F. Cole and Christopher E. Smith

Senior Acquisitions Editor, Criminal Justice: Carolyn Henderson Meier

Development Editor: Shelley Murphy

Assistant Editor: Meaghan Banks

Editorial Assistant: John Chell

Technology Project Manager: Bessie Weiss

Marketing Manager: Michelle Williams

Marketing Assistant: Jillian Myers

Marketing Communications Manager: Tami Strang

Project Manager, Editorial Production: Jennie Redwitz

Creative Director: Rob Hugel

Art Director: Maria Epes

Print Buyer: Becky Cross

Permissions Editor: Bob Kauser

Production Service: Greg Hubit

Text Designer: Liz Harasymczuk

Photo Researcher: Sarah Evertson

Copy Editor: Tricia Lawrence

Illustrator: Lotus Art

Cover Designer: Tim Heraldo, Riezebos Holzbaur Design Group

Cover Image: Tim Laman, Getty Images; istockphoto

Compositor: Newgen

For product information and technology assistance, contact us at **Cengage Learning Customer & Sales Support, 1-800-354-9706.**

For permission to use material from this text or product, submit all requests online at **www.cengage.com/permissions.** Further permissions questions can be e-mailed to **permissionrequest@cengage.com.**

Library of Congress Control Number: 2008933882

Student Edition:
ISBN-13: 978-0-495-59965-4
ISBN-10: 0-495-59965-4

Loose-leaf Edition:
ISBN-13: 978-0-495-60088-6
ISBN-10: 0-495-60088-1

Wadsworth
10 Davis Drive
Belmont, CA 94002-3098
USA

Cengage Learning is a leading provider of customized learning solutions with office locations around the globe, including Singapore, the United Kingdom, Australia, Mexico, Brazil, and Japan. Locate your local office at **www.cengage.com/international.**

Cengage Learning products are represented in Canada by Nelson Education, Ltd.

To learn more about Wadsworth, visit **www.cengage.com/wadsworth**

Purchase any of our products at your local college store or at our preferred online store **www.ichapters.com.**

Printed in Canada
1 2 3 4 5 6 7 12 11 10 09 08

Brief Contents

Contents

PART TWO

Police 157

CHAPTER 5

Police 158

CHAPTER 6

Police Officers and Law Enforcement Operations 200

PART THREE

Courts 319

PART FOUR

Corrections 461

CHAPTER 15

Incarceration and Prison Society   532

CHAPTER 16

Reentry into the Community   574

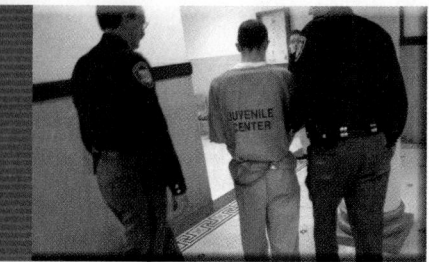

PART FIVE

The Juvenile Justice System   601

Preface

Most students come to the introductory course in criminal justice intrigued by the prospect of learning about crime and the operation of the criminal justice system. Many of them look forward to the roles they may one day fill in allocating justice, either as citizens or in careers with the police, courts, or corrections. All have been exposed to a great deal of information—and misinformation—about criminal justice through the news and entertainment media. Whatever their views, few are indifferent to the subject they are about to explore.

Like all newcomers to a field, however, introductory students in criminal justice need, first, *content mastery*—a solid foundation of valid information about the subject—and second, *critical understanding*—a way to think about this information. They need conceptual tools that enable them not only to absorb a large body of factual content but also to process that information critically, reflect on it, and extend their learning beyond the classroom. This text aims at providing both the essential content and the critical tools involved in understanding criminal justice.

This edition also includes a new, unifying emphasis on citizens' varied and important roles in influencing criminal justice policies and processes. Social commentators and political scientists have long noted that young Americans seem insufficiently interested and engaged in public affairs. Participation rates for youthful voters lag behind those of older demographic groups. Surveys indicate that many young people lack knowledge about both current events and the operation of their country's governing system. Such trends raise questions about the vibrancy of the American democracy and the range of values and opinions that inform decisions about public policies.

Young Americans are certainly entitled to make their own choices about whether and how they become involved in public affairs. If, however, their lack of participation is due to insufficient knowledge about their important potential roles in democratic processes then the study of criminal justice—a high-interest subject for college students—presents an opportunity to make clearer to them all citizens' inevitable and unavoidable roles in affecting criminal justice.

The American public is accustomed to seeing officials in the criminal justice system—legislators, prosecutors, judges, defense attorneys, and corrections officials—as constituting the decision makers who shape criminal justice policies and processes. Students who aspire to careers in these positions undoubtedly recognize their potential importance for the system. Less well recognized, however, are the influence and importance of all citizens in their roles as voters, members of neighborhood associations and community organizations, and even renters and homeowners. In these roles, all Americans influence criminal justice through a variety of activities, ranging from formal decisions about voting or buying security systems for businesses and churches to less formal actions in personal crime prevention decisions (e.g., locking cars, reporting suspicious activity) that guide the nature and extent of crime problems as well as the allocation of law enforcement resources. The influence of all Americans on criminal justice will be highlighted throughout the book, especially in a new feature, "Civic Engagement: Your Role in the System," that gives students concrete opportunities to analyze and make decisions about real-life examples. This unifying emphasis draws from all three of the book's major themes because active and informed citizens must use knowledge of the *system's characteristics* and

American values in order to understand and improve their own actions that influence *public policy.*

THE APPROACH OF THIS TEXT: THREE KEY THEMES

Criminal justice is a complex subject encompassing an array of topics that cannot be evaluated through a limited or narrow focus. To understand what happens to people who are drawn into the American system of criminal justice, one must analyze such varied subjects as societal problems, determinants of individuals' behavior, government processes, and conceptions of morality and justice. This text tackles the challenge of this complexity by drawing from an interdisciplinary foundation of research, with contributions from criminology, law, history, sociology, psychology, and political science. The interdisciplinary approach supplies the analytical tools and information needed to evaluate the varied institutions, processes, and social phenomena of criminal justice. Although breadth of perspective is necessary for understanding criminal justice, it does not automatically provide an appropriate basis for explaining the American system of justice to students. Information and analysis must be organized and presented in ways that highlight the key elements that shape and drive criminal justice in the United States. We use three organizing themes to bring the complexity of criminal justice into focus and to highlight continuing issues and controversies that affect this dynamic subject:

1. *Criminal justice involves public policies* that are developed within the political framework of the democratic process.

2. *The concept of social system is an essential tool* for explaining and analyzing the way criminal justice is administered and practiced.

3. *American values provide the foundation on which criminal justice is based.* With concerns about terrorism and civil liberties at the forefront of the national agenda, an awareness of basic American values—individual liberty, equality, fairness, and the rule of law—is as vital today as it has ever been in our history.

Over the years the approach of *The American System of Criminal Justice* has enjoyed broad acceptance as it addresses new challenges. Instructors at hundreds of colleges and universities throughout the nation have chosen this book, and during its more than 30 years of use in their classrooms, more than a half million of their students have used it. Yet, textbook authors cannot afford to rest on their laurels, particularly in a field as dynamic as criminal justice. The social scene changes, research multiplies, theories are modified, and new policies are proposed and implemented while old ones become unpopular and fade away. Students and their needs change as well. Accordingly, we have made this twelfth edition of the "Eagle" even more current, vital, cohesive, and appealing to students and instructors alike.

HIGHLIGHTS OF THE TWELFTH EDITION

This edition encompasses major revisions in content and presentation. Users of the eleventh edition will find many significant changes. We have also provided a new focus on the various important roles of citizens in affecting criminal justice in their states, communities, and neighborhoods. This focus draws together the book's themes concerning American values, public policy, and system conception of criminal justice. The remainder of this section considers the major content changes and expanded discussions in the book and then examines the new elements in each chapter.

Focus on Civic Engagement and Citizens' Influence over Criminal Justice

Citizens influence criminal justice through formal roles as justice system professionals; lay participation as voters, jurors, and members of governmental advisory committees; and everyday actions as decision makers for neighborhood associations, community groups, churches, businesses, and their own families and homes. In a democracy, criminal justice policies are not merely imposed by higher authorities. Actions by citizens within their communities influence both the nature of crime and the government's response to it. In each chapter, students' attention will be directed to examples that highlight both the inevitability and importance of all Americans' influence over criminal justice policies and processes.

Focus on Crime and Justice in a Multicultural Society

Issues of race and equal treatment are continuing sources of problems and debates in the American system of criminal justice. Disparities in the treatment of African Americans, Hispanics, and other minorities are pervasive in the criminal justice system. This issue is addressed in Chapter 3 and reexamined in succeeding chapters in discussions of what minority group members experience when they come in contact with the police, the courts, and corrections. The twelfth edition includes new data and examples as well as expanded discussion.

Expanded Coverage of Homeland Security and the War on Terrorism

Since 2001, homeland security and terrorism have become top policy priorities for Americans. These issues affect criminal justice through the reorganization of federal law enforcement agencies, reallocations of resources, expanded efforts to improve law enforcement intelligence and international cooperation, and less federal assistance for local agencies in dealing with many traditional crimes (e.g., bank robbery). New discussions illuminate the changing role of the FBI and issues related to border security and immigration. In addition, there is expanded coverage of the tension between civil liberties issues, such as expectations of privacy, and the push for expanded law enforcement authority.

Expanded Coverage of Cybercrime

The expansion of Americans' reliance on computers and advances in technology create new opportunities for criminals to engage in cybercrime activities. The nature of cybercrime changes over time, partly due to ingenious innovations by thieves and hackers, and partly due to the development of new activities by seemingly ordinary Americans, such as the rise in cyber-bullying among teenagers. The international nature of cybercrime poses significant challenges for American law enforcement officials. Thus each new cohort of students in criminal justice needs knowledge about the rapidly evolving nature of threats related to computer usage.

Expanded Coverage of Policing

The threat of terrorism creates new challenges for emergency response planning and coordination with agencies at all levels of government. Rapid technological changes provide new tools for law enforcement while simultaneously empowering offenders to develop new techniques to break the law and avoid capture. New technology also raises unanticipated issues and questions about use of force, citizens' privacy in an era of expanding databases, and productivity measures for police. All of these changes are occurring in an increasingly diverse and complex society that requires experimentation and adaptation by police.

Expanded Coverage of Immigration-Related Issues

In conjunction with the country's increased emphasis on border security as part of homeland security efforts, law enforcement agencies give greater attention to immigration law issues. In the chapters on corrections, there is increased attention to the legal and systemic issues that arise when people are taken into custody under immigrations laws rather than under traditional criminal justice processes.

More In-Depth Coverage of Juvenile Delinquency

Despite overall reductions in crime rates, youth crime remains a major national problem. This edition features expanded coverage of juvenile justice, including drug abuse, gangs, waiver, and detention issues.

Updated Discussion of the Consequences of Crime Control Policies

We examine emerging questions about the "broken windows thesis," the use of aggressive stop-and-frisk tactics, and the consequences of expanded incarceration and attendant reentry issues.

Key Chapter-by-Chapter Changes

Chapter 1, Crime and Justice in America

A new section introduces the book's civic engagement emphasis and explains the important and inevitable influence of all citizens on crime and criminal justice policy. The chapter also contains a more in-depth analysis of crime data, including discussions of the rise and fall of crime, the measurement of crime, and future trends in crime. There is also newly expanded discussion of cybercrime. New Civic Engagement exercises encourage students to analyze a candidate's criminal justice proposals and college students' advising of senior citizens on computer security for personal computing.

Chapter 2, Victimization and Criminal Behavior

The most recent data on the victimization costs of crime have been added. The discussion of women as offenders and related explanatory theories has been revised and updated. New Civic Engagement exercises encourage students to analyze citizen involvement in victim assistance programs and local juvenile delinquency prevention councils.

Chapter 3, The Criminal Justice System

There is additional material on the expansion of federal involvement in criminal justice following the attacks of 9/11. There is expanded discussion and updated statistics for understanding racial disparities in the criminal justice system. New Civic Engagement exercises encourage students to analyze citizen-initiated neighborhood anticrime efforts and police advisory committees on racial profiling.

Chapter 4, Criminal Justice and the Rule of Law

There is updated material in the Comparative Perspective feature on Islamic law. The chapter contains new examples for such topics as "mistake of fact" and cruel and unusual punishment (*Baze v. Rees* [2008], concerning lethal injections; *Uttecht v. Brown* [2008], capital jury selection). New Civic Engagement exercises encourage students to analyze statewide ballot issues on criminal justice issues and criminal libel laws.

Chapter 5, Police

There is extended coverage of federal law enforcement agencies, especially with respect to the FBI's and law enforcement's roles in the era of homeland security. There are updated data and examples of cities' crime rates, domestic violence, and police-community relations. New Civic Engagement exercises encourage students to analyze police reorganization into public service departments and citizen input on neighborhood crime prevention.

Chapter 6, Police Officers and Law Enforcement Operations

We have updated information on the use of communications technology in policing. There is new material on aggressive stop-and-frisk tactics, the impact of immigration on crime, and volunteer auxiliary police officers. New Civic Engagement exercises encourage students to analyze volunteer auxiliary police units and citizen input for community policing.

Chapter 7, Twenty-First Century Challenges in Policing

The new title reflects expanded emphases on contemporary developments. There are new examples of police use of force and corruption. There is expanded coverage of new technologies used by the police, especially criminal justice databases, crime mapping, and DNA testing. The section on homeland security has been extended to include discussion of fusion centers and debates about the renewal of the USA Patriot Act. In the security management section you'll find new discussion of the government's use of private police and contracting for related private security services. New Civic Engagement exercises encourage students to analyze civilian review boards and citizens' roles in homeland security efforts.

Chapter 8, Police and Constitutional Law

A new Close Up feature discusses judges' skepticism about justifications for aggressive stop-and-frisk searches by the New York City Police Department. An updated New Directions in Criminal Justice Policy feature on constitutional rights of terrorism suspects is included. New Civic Engagement exercises encourage students to analyze citizens' knowledge about legal protections against property damage by the police and the legal basis for stop-and-frisk searches.

Chapter 9, Courts and Pretrial Processes

A new section discusses risks of corruption in the business operations of bail bondsmen. In addition, a new Close Up presents a comparative perspective on the role of bail bondsmen. New Civic Engagement exercises encourage students to analyze ballot issues on judicial tenure and legislative proposals on the regulation of bail agents.

Chapter 10, Prosecution and Defense

New material on prosecutorial misconduct and updated information on compensation rates for indigent defense counsel are included. New Civic Engagement exercises encourage students to analyze citizen input on community prosecution programs and ballot issues affecting provision of legal counsel for indigents.

Chapter 11, Determination of Guilt: Plea Bargaining and Trials

This chapter includes new data on plea bargaining as well as new examples, such as the trial of singer R. Kelly. There is added material on the difficulty of understanding expert testimony and scientific evidence. New Civic Engagement exercises encourage students to analyze the abolition of plea bargaining and citizens' attitudes toward jury duty.

Chapter 12, Punishment and Sentencing

Updated material on sentencing guidelines reform, the impact of three-strikes laws, and community restorative justice boards has been added. The chapter includes the 2008 Supreme Court decisions concerning capital punishment, including lethal injection, child rapists, and the impact of international law. New Civic Engagement exercises encourage students to analyze restorative justice as well as jurors' roles in capital cases.

Chapter 13, Corrections

There is a major new section on the detention and incarceration of immigrants that includes examination of the role of the U.S. Immigration and Customs Enforcement (ICE) agency of the Department of Homeland Security. There is also updated information on incarceration trends and community corrections policies. New Civic Engagement exercises encourage students to analyze the role of citizen-volunteers in corrections and legal protections for people in jail.

Chapter 14, Community Corrections: Probation and Intermediate Sanctions

This chapter contains updated data on trends in probation and other sanctions. New Civic Engagement exercises encourage students to analyze the placement of drug offenders on probation and the operation of community corrections programs.

Chapter 15, Incarceration and Prison Society

This chapter contains expanded coverage on prison rape and other forms of violence. New Civic Engagement exercises encourage students to analyze reentry challenges for female offenders and rehabilitation programs in corrections.

Chapter 16, Reentry into the Community

This chapter contains new discussion of reentry problems and programs, such as the Second Chance Act of 2007, to assist those returning to the community. New Civic Engagement exercises encourage students to analyze lay citizen participation on parole boards and the placement of halfway houses within the community.

Chapter 17, Juvenile Justice

New to this edition is a more in-depth coverage of juvenile justice, including the problems of gangs, drug abuse, and adolescents' developmental maturity. Attention is placed on juvenile detention and waiver provisions for juveniles to be adjudicated in the adult system. New Civic Engagement exercises encourage students to analyze the prosecution of juveniles as adults as well as delinquency prevention.

STUDY AND REVIEW AIDS

To help students identify and master core concepts, the text provides several study and review aids.

- **Chapter outlines** preview the structure of each chapter.

- **Chapter-opening vignettes** introduce the chapter topic with a high-interest, real-life episode. For example, as a means of introducing the criminal justice system, Chapter 1 opens with a new vignette describing the capture in Mexico of U.S. Marine Cesar Laurean who fled the country when he was suspected of murdering a pregnant Marine in North Carolina. The case raises questions about the news media's coverage of crimes and Americans' perceptions of the nation's crime problem. And Chapter 4 begins with a new vignette on the case of U.S. Navy Captain Colleen Shipman, the NASA shuttle astronaut who drove from Texas to Florida to apparently carry out a planned assault on another officer, a case that provides an example of claims concerning the insanity defense. Other chapters open with new vignettes concerning such cases as a highly publicized murder and dismemberment trial in Michigan, the tax evasion trial of movie actor Wesley Snipes, and the sentencing of actress Lindsay Lohan. In all, there are 13 new chapter-opening vignettes in this edition.

- **Chapter Learning Objectives** highlight the chapter's key topics and themes. The numbered Learning Objectives have been carefully matched to individual bullet points in the end-of-chapter Summary for maximum learning reinforcement.

- **Checkpoints** throughout each chapter allow students to test themselves on content as they proceed through the chapter.

- **Going Online** provides students with a set of exercises they can use to expand their knowledge using the World Wide Web.

- **Chapter Summaries and Questions for Review** reinforce key concepts and provide further checks on learning.

- **Key Terms and Cases** are defined throughout the text in the margins of each chapter and can also be located in the Glossary.

- **An appendix on understanding statistical figures and tables** helps readers interpret the data presented in this text and research in other fields as well.

Promoting Critical Understanding

Aided by the features just described, diligent students can master the essential content of the introductory course. While such mastery is no small achievement, most instructors aim higher. They want students to complete this course with the ability to take a more thoughtful and critical approach to issues of crime and justice. *The American System of Criminal Justice,* Twelfth Edition, provides several features that help students learn how to think about the field.

- **Civic Engagement: Your Role in the System** In order to gain a clear understanding of the inevitable, important, and varied ways that citizens influence criminal justice policy and process, two Civic Engagement features in each chapter pose scenarios and questions drawn from real-life examples. Students are asked to place themselves in roles as voters, members of neighborhood organizations, jurors, members of citizen advisory committees, and other real-life contexts in which Americans make decisions that impact criminal justice. For each situation they are asked to use their analytical skills in order to present reasons for a decision or other suggestions related to policy problems. At the conclusion of each feature, students are guided to a website that describes what actually happened in a particular city or state when Americans were confronted with this specific problem or issue.

- **Close Ups and Other Real-Life Examples** Understanding criminal justice in a purely theoretical way does not give students a balanced understanding of the field. The wealth of examples in this book shows how theory plays out in practice and what the human implications of policies and procedures are. In addition to the many illustrations in the text, the Close Up features in each chapter draw on newspapers, court decisions, first-person accounts, and other current sources.

- **New Directions in Criminal Justice Policy** To illustrate criminal justice policies that have been proposed or are being tested, we include a box called "New Directions in Criminal Justice Policy" in many of our chapters. Policies concerning restorative justice, direct supervision jails, and the changing role of federal law enforcement are discussed so that students will be prepared to face the new realities of criminal justice.

- **Doing Your Part** Many Americans have contributed to criminal justice through voluntary activities or by promoting reforms. In selected chapters the roles played by individuals who are assisting the police, crime victims, courts, and prisoners are described in Doing Your Part. Consistent with the theme of Civic Engagement, we hope that these illustrations will encourage students to consider how they might contribute to a just society.

- **A Question of Ethics** Criminal justice requires that decisions be made within the framework of law but also be consistent with the ethical norms of American society. At the end of each chapter A Question of Ethics activities place students in the role of decision makers faced with ethical dilemmas, promoting critical thinking and analysis and offering students a more well-rounded view of what is asked of criminal justice professionals every day.

- **What Americans Think** Public opinion plays an important role in the policy-making process in a democracy. As such, we present the opinions of Americans on controversial criminal justice issues as collected through surveys. Students are encouraged to compare their own opinions with the national perspective.

- **Comparative Perspective** With the move toward more global thinking in academia and society at large, students are showing new interest in learning more about criminal justice in other parts of the world. Several chapters of this edition include a Comparative Perspective feature that describes a component of the criminal justice system in another country. In addition to broadening students' conceptual horizons, these sections encourage a more critical appreciation of the system many Americans take for granted. By learning about others, we learn more about ourselves.

SUPPLEMENTS

The most extensive package of supplemental aids available for a criminal justice text accompanies this edition. Many separate items have been developed to enhance the course and to assist instructors and students. Available to qualified adopters. Please consult your local sales representative for details.

For the Instructor

Instructor's Edition

Designed just for instructors, the *Instructor's Edition* includes a visual walk-through that illustrates the key pedagogical features of the text, as well as the media and supplements that accompany it. Use this handy tool to learn quickly about the many options this text provides to keep your class engaging and informative.

Instructor's Resource Manual with Test Bank

An improved and completely updated *Instructor's Resource Manual with Test Bank* has been developed by Christina DeJong of Michigan State University. The manual includes learning objectives, a chapter summary, detailed chapter outlines, key terms, an explanation of the chapter's themes, class discussion exercises, and worksheets. Each chapter's test bank contains questions in multiple-choice, true-false, fill-in-the-blank, and essay formats, with a full answer key. The test bank is coded to the learning objectives that appear in the main text, and includes the page numbers in the main text where the answers can be found. Finally, each question in the test bank has been carefully reviewed by experienced criminal justice instructors for quality, accuracy, and content coverage. Our Instructor Approved seal, which appears on the front cover, is our assurance that you are working with an assessment and grading resource of the highest caliber.

PowerLecture with JoinIn™ and ExamView®

This one-stop digital library and presentation tool includes preassembled Microsoft® PowerPoint® lecture slides. In addition to the full *Instructor's Resource Manual with Test Bank*, PowerLecture also includes JoinIn and video and image libraries.

Lesson Plans

New to this edition, the instructor-created Lesson Plans bring accessible, masterful suggestions to every lesson. Each lesson plan includes a sample syllabus, learning objectives, lecture notes, discussion topics, in-class activities, tips for classroom presentation of chapter material, a detailed lecture outline, and assignments. Lesson plans are available on the PowerLecture resource and the instructor website, or by emailing your local representative and asking for a download of the eBank files.

WebTutor™ ToolBox on Blackboard® and WebCT®

Jumpstart your course with customizable, rich, text-specific content within your Course Management System. Whether you want to Web-enable your class or put an entire course online, WebTutor delivers. WebTutor offers a wide array of resources including media assets, test bank, practice quizzes, and additional study aids. Visit http://www.cengage.com/webtutor to learn more.

Companion Website

The book-specific website at academic.cengage.com/criminaljustice/cole offers students a variety of study tools and useful resources such as quizzing, web links, Internet exercises, glossary, flash cards, and more.

The Wadsworth Criminal Justice Video Library

So many exciting, new videos—so many great ways to enrich your lectures and spark discussion of the material in this text. Your Cengage Learning representative will be happy to provide details on our video policy by adoption size. The library includes these selections and many others:

- *ABC® Videos:* ABC videos feature short, high-interest clips from current news events as well as historic raw footage going back 40 years. Perfect for discussion starters or to enrich your lectures and spark interest in the material in the text, these brief videos provide students with a new lens through which to view the past and present, one that will greatly enhance their knowledge and understanding of significant events and open up to them new dimensions in learning. Clips are drawn from such programs as *World News Tonight, Good Morning America, This Week, PrimeTime Live, 20/20,* and *Nightline,* as well as numerous ABC News specials and material from the Associated Press Television News and British Movietone News collections. Your Wadsworth representative will be happy to provide a complete listing of videos and policies.

- *The Wadsworth Custom Videos for Criminal Justice:* Produced by Wadsworth and Films for the Humanities, these videos include short five- to ten-minute segments that encourage classroom discussion. Topics include white-collar crime, domestic violence, forensics, suicide and the police officer, the court process, the history of corrections, prison society, and juvenile justice.

- *Oral History Project:* Developed in association with the American Society of Criminology, the Academy of Criminal Justice Society, and the National Institute of Justice, these videos will help you introduce your students to the scholars who have developed the criminal justice discipline. Compiled over the last several years, each video features a set of Guest Lecturers—scholars whose thinking has helped build the foundation of present ideas in the discipline. Vol. 1: Moments in Time; Vol. 2: Great Moments in Criminological Theory; Vol. 3: Research Methods.

- *Court TV Videos:* One-hour videos presenting seminal and high-profile cases such as the interrogation of Michael Crowe and serial killer Ted Bundy, as well as crucial and current issues such as cybercrime, double jeopardy, and the management of the prison on Riker's Island.

- *A&E American Justice:* Forty videos to choose from on topics such as deadly force, women on death row, juvenile justice, strange defenses, and Alcatraz.

- *Films for the Humanities:* Nearly 200 videos to choose from on a variety of topics such as elder abuse, supermax prisons, suicide and the police officer, the making of an FBI agent, domestic violence, and more.

For the Student

CengageNOW™

CengageNOW is an easy-to-use online resource that helps students study in less time to get the grade they want—NOW. Featuring CengageNOW Personalized Study (a diagnostic study tool containing valuable text-specific resources), students focus on just what they don't know. If the textbook does not include an access code card, students can go to www.ichapters.com to purchase CengageNOW.

Audio Study Tools

Now students have a quick, convenient, and enjoyable way to study—and they can do it while doing all the other things they need to do. In just ten minutes, students can review each chapter of the textbook assigned, and audio practice quizzes help students figure out what they know and what they don't. Audio Study Tools will be available for sale at www.ichapters.com; both in complete versions and by the chapter/ by the concept.

Study Guide

An extensive student guide has been developed and updated for this edition by Christina DeJong of Michigan State University. Because students learn in different ways, the guide includes a variety of pedagogical aids to help them, as well as integrated art and figures from the main text. Each chapter is outlined and summarized, major terms and figures are defined, and worksheets and self-tests are provided.

Current Perspectives: Readings from InfoTrac® College Edition

These readers, designed to give students a closer look at special topics in criminal justice, include free access to InfoTrac College Edition. The timely articles are selected by experts in each topic from within InfoTrac College Edition. They are available for free when bundled with the text and include the following titles:

- *Cyber Crime*
- *Victimology*
- *Juvenile Justice*
- *Racial Profiling*
- *White-Collar Crime*
- *Terrorism and Homeland Security*
- *Public Policy and Criminal Justice*
- *New Technologies and Criminal Justice*
- *Ethics in Criminal Justice*
- *Forensics and Criminal Investigation*

Terrorism: An Interdisciplinary Perspective

Available for bundling with each copy of *The American System of Criminal Justice*, Twelfth Edition, this 80-page booklet (with companion website) discusses terrorism in general and the issues surrounding the events of September 11, 2001. Information-packed, the book examines the origins of terrorism in the Middle East, focusing on Osama bin Laden in particular, as well as issues involving bioterrorism, the specific role played by religion in Middle Eastern terrorism, globalization as it relates to terrorism, and the reactions to and repercussions of terrorist attacks.

Crime Scenes: An Interactive Criminal Justice CD-ROM, Version 2.0

Recipient of several *New Media Magazine* Invision Awards, this interactive CD-ROM allows students to take on the roles of investigating officer, lawyer, parole officer, and judge in excitingly realistic scenarios. Available FREE when bundled with every copy of *The American System of Criminal Justice,* Twelfth Edition. An instructor's manual for the CD-ROM is also available.

Mind of a Killer CD-ROM

Voted one of the top 100 CD-ROMs by an annual *PC Magazine* survey, *Mind of a Killer* gives students a chilling glimpse into the realm of serial killers, with over 80 minutes of video, 3-D simulations, an extensive mapping system, a library, and much more.

Internet Guide for Criminal Justice, Second Edition

Internet beginners will appreciate this helpful booklet. With explanations and the vocabulary necessary for navigating the web, it features customized information on criminal justice–related websites and presents Internet project ideas.

Internet Activities for Criminal Justice, Second Edition

This completely revised 96-page booklet shows how to best utilize the Internet for research through searches and activities.

A GROUP EFFORT

No one can be an expert on every aspect of the criminal justice system. Authors need help in covering new developments and ensuring that research findings are correctly interpreted. This revision has greatly benefited from the advice of two groups of criminal justice scholars (see the inside front endpapers for a complete list). The first group of reviewers teach at a wide range of colleges and universities throughout the country and have used previous editions of the text, so their comments concerning presentation, levels of student abilities, and the requirements of introductory courses at their institutions were especially useful. Reviewers in the second group we consulted are nationally recognized experts in the field; they focused their attention on the areas in which they specialize. Their many comments helped us avoid errors and drew our attention to points in the literature that had been neglected.

The many criminal justice students and instructors who used the eleventh edition also contributed abundantly to this edition. Their comments provided crucial practical feedback. Others gave us their comments personally when we lectured in criminal justice classes around the country.

Others have helped us as well. Chief among them was Senior Editor Carolyn Henderson Meier, who has supported our efforts. Our Development Editor, Shelley Murphy, provided invaluable comments as we revised the book. The project has benefited much from the attention of Project Manager Jennie Redwitz, and Meaghan Banks was invaluable in helping us develop the supplements. Tricia Lawrence used her effort and skill to contribute to the copyediting process. As always, Greg Hubit used his managerial skills to oversee the project from manuscript submission to bound books. Liz Harasymczuk designed the interior of the book.

Finally, the following reviewers for this twelfth edition contributed valuable comments and suggestions for our revision:

Michael T. Brady, Salve Regina University

Geriann M. Brandt, Maryville University

Ron Davis, Mayland Community College

William Ralph Garris, University of South Carolina Lancaster

Robert D. Hanser, University of Louisiana at Monroe

Brian K. Harte, State University of New York at Canton

James L. Jengeleski, Shippensburg University

Jeffrey D. Lane, Georgia State University

Jimmy J. Williams, University of Alabama

Ultimately, however, the full responsibility for the book is ours alone. We hope you will benefit from it, and we welcome your comments.

George F. Cole
(gcole281@earthlink.net)

Christopher E. Smith
(smithc28@msu.edu)

Crime and the Criminal Justice System

© David R. Frazier/The Image Works

The American system of criminal justice is a response to crime—a problem that has demanded the attention of all societies throughout history. To understand how the system works and why crime persists in spite of our efforts to control it, we need to examine both the nature of criminal behavior and the functioning of the justice system itself. As we shall see, the reality of crime and justice involves much more than "cops and robbers," the details of legal codes, and the penalties for breaking laws. From defining which behavior counts as criminal to deciding the fate of offenders who are caught, the process of criminal justice is a social process subject to many influences other than written law.

By introducing the study of this process, Part 1 provides a broad framework for analyzing how our society—through its police, courts, and corrections—tries to deal with the age-old problem of crime.

CHAPTER 1

Crime and Justice in America

CHAPTER LEARNING OBJECTIVES

→ Understand how public policies on crime are formed

→ Recognize how the crime control and due process models of criminal justice help us understand the system

→ Be able to explain: "What is a crime?"

→ Describe the major types of crime in the United States

→ Analyze how much crime there is and understand how it is measured

The bearded man appeared tired and dazed as he stood with his wrists locked together by handcuffs under the watchful eye of armed law enforcement officers in April 2008. The jagged tattoos from his elbows to his shoulders on both arms undoubtedly attracted the attention of people throughout the world who saw his photograph. With his vacant stare, unruly beard, and disheveled hair, he looked like what he was—a man with only one dollar in his pocket who had been sleeping in fields and eating fruit from trees and vines. Despite his apparent similarity to a downtrodden, homeless man, he was actually a notorious fugitive, and newspapers and television reports throughout the United States trumpeted the news of the capture of 21-year-old U.S. Marine Corporal Cesar Laurean in Tacambaro, Mexico (CBS News, 2008a).

Laurean fled to Mexico shortly before North Carolina police found the charred remains of 20-year-old U.S. Marine Corporal Maria Lauterbach buried in his backyard. Lauterbach had been missing for a month before a note that Laurean left for his wife when he fled finally led authorities to the body. The Marine Corps was investigating Lauterbach's complaint that she had been raped by Laurean. Because of that complaint, Laurean was considered as a suspect in the young woman's disappearance.

Tragically, police also found the charred remains of the fetus that Lauterbach was carrying: she was eight months pregnant at the time of her death (McKinley, 2008). Once he returned to North Carolina, Laurean faced the prospect of spending the rest of his life in prison if he were to be convicted of the murder.

Why did the Lauterbach murder receive so much national attention? Why did CNN's headline proclaim "Pregnant Marine Missing from North Carolina Base" when other pregnant women who are murdered receive nothing more than brief attention in their local news? (CNN, 2008; CBS News, 2008b). Does the attention directed at this case tell us anything about the image of crime in the minds of Americans? It is possible that the disappearance of a pretty, blond, young pregnant woman aroused public fear about the kinds of crimes that could strike any of us without warning, including people in comfortable suburban neighborhoods. It is also possible that Americans have developed a fascination with shocking criminal events—a fascination fed by sensational news stories, sustained media attention to murder trials, and numerous television shows such as the popular dramas *Law and Order* and *CSI* (Crime Scene Investigation) that generate spinoffs and copycat programs.

Similarly, the murder of Eve Carson, the University of North Carolina student body president and also a young blond woman, by a carjacker in March 2008 generated significant attention in the national news media (CBS News, 2008c). Meanwhile, a male graduate student from India at Duke University who was murdered by an intruder in his apartment did not receive widespread attention until it was discovered that the same assailant had participated in Eve Carson's murder (*USA Today*, 2008). Do differences in media coverage reflect bias on the part of newspaper reporters and television producers? Do the media cover stories with the greatest interest to the public or do they shape the public's knowledge and perceptions by their own choices concerning what stories to cover? To what extent are Americans knowledgeable about the realities of crime? Alternatively, is our understanding of crime determined by highly publicized cases that make us fearful of random victimization rather than by facts about what really happens in our society? These are important questions because our understanding of crime—or lack of understanding—can determine the way that we use our power as voters, members of community organizations, and, for some college students, future justice system officials to shape public policies concerning criminal justice.

All Americans influence criminal justice policy. We make judgments about political candidates, in part, based on their views on gun control, capital punishment, and other criminal justice issues. We express our views and fears to city councils, school boards, state legislatures, and other policy-making bodies that decide whether and how to spend money on safety and security in our communities. We make choices about the neighborhoods where we will reside, the schools where we will send our children, and the stores where we will shop based, in part, upon our perceptions about risk and crime. Even these decisions can have important impacts on economic development and neighborhood stability within communities. Moreover, many college students who study criminal justice will eventually become professionals in the justice system and thereby have even more influence over how policies develop and how policies are applied to the lives of others within American society. In light of the importance of criminal justice to all Americans—and, conversely, the important contributions that all Americans play in shaping criminal justice policy—it is essential that Americans develop realistic understandings of the nature of crime and justice in their society.

Murder trials, sensational news stories, and television dramas certainly do not reflect an accurate picture of crime in the United States. As we shall see in the chapters that follow, a typical criminal case tends to be a minor theft charge that leads a young offender to be placed on probation after quickly pleading guilty without a trial. Yet the attention paid by the media and public to the murders of Maria Lauterbach and Eve Carson reflects the nature of Americans' often-intense concern about crime, public safety, and justice—issues most see as significant problems facing the United States.

Public opinion polls indicate that Americans are keenly aware that crime is a problem in U.S. society. A Gallup Poll taken in October 2007 revealed that 57 percent of Americans describe crime in the United States as "extremely or very serious," and an additional 39 percent see crime as a "moderately serious" problem (Gallup Poll, 2008). The same poll also revealed that only 15 percent of Americans believe that crime is "extremely or very serious" in the area in which they live, and 51 percent view crime as "not too serious" or "not serious at all" in their own neighborhoods. Thus, although Americans see crime as an important problem for the nation, most people are not preoccupied with fears about crime when they are in their own neighborhoods.

Even so, these results provide only a glimpse of Americans' viewpoints—not the complete picture. Americans live within a mobile society in which people travel for work, shopping, and recreation. Additional survey questions would likely reveal that Americans' fears and concerns about crime depend on the context in which they find themselves. Their sense of safety and security while at home may disappear when they drive to work in city centers or when they leave a shopping mall after dark.

Examine the March 2008 national survey results reported in "What Americans Think." In this particular poll, the largest number of respondents cited the economy, with its housing crisis, unemployment, and rising gas prices, as the most important issue. With American military personnel fighting and dying abroad, people predictably regard the war in Iraq as the "nation's most important non-economic problem." As described by the Gallup Poll officials, "Crime tends to rate much more highly as a national problem in the eyes of Americans when the international stage is calm and the economy is in good shape. Otherwise, those concerns tend to overshadow crime" (Gallup Poll, 2008). In light of the Iraq war, housing crisis, and rising gas prices in 2008, it is no surprise that Americans are less focused on crime. There are indications, however, that American still view crime as a serious problem, including the fact that 70 percent of Americans believed that crime was worse in the United States than it was in 2007 (Gallup Poll, 2008).

If we look beyond the war, several factors indicate that people still see crime as an especially important problem. Although only 2 percent cited "crime/violence" as the most important problem, an additional 6 percent focused on "immigration/illegal aliens," an issue concerning people violating our country's laws. Another 1 percent cited "guns/control" and another 1 percent named "judicial system/courts/law." We must also recognize that the 5 percent of Americans who named "terrorism or national security" as the most important problem are talking about issues intimately connected to crime, public safety, and justice. Acts labeled as "terrorism" are themselves crimes. Hijackings, bombings, and murders violate criminal laws. Investigations and prosecutions resulting from such acts involve the Federal Bureau of Investigation (FBI), local police, prosecutors, and judges. Even some of the 4 percent of respondents who cited ethics, dishonesty, and family decline may have been thinking about crime-related issues such as Internet scams and juvenile delinquency.

Given Americans' concerns about criminal justice issues, politicians attempt to gain favor with voters by proposing policies to address crime. These proposals do not always reflect careful analysis of the costs and benefits of different policy choices. In fact, politicians often try to outdo one another in being "tough on crime" without fully understanding the costs and consequences of such policies. This toughness has led to many shifts in public policies: adding 100,000 police officers nationwide, building more prisons, extending the death

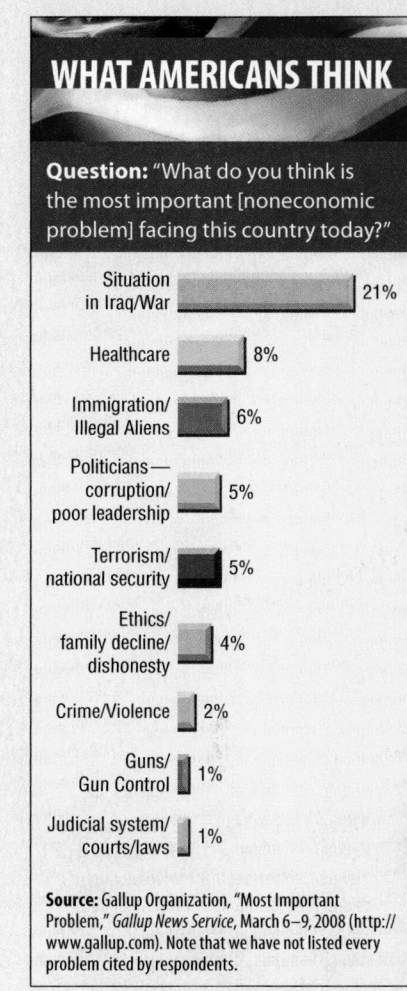

WHAT AMERICANS THINK

Question: "What do you think is the most important [noneconomic problem] facing this country today?"

Situation in Iraq/War	21%
Healthcare	8%
Immigration/ Illegal Aliens	6%
Politicians— corruption/ poor leadership	5%
Terrorism/ national security	5%
Ethics/ family decline/ dishonesty	4%
Crime/Violence	2%
Guns/ Gun Control	1%
Judicial system/ courts/laws	1%

Source: Gallup Organization, "Most Important Problem," *Gallup News Service*, March 6–9, 2008 (http://www.gallup.com). Note that we have not listed every problem cited by respondents.

penalty to cover 60 federal offenses, mandating longer sentences, and requiring parolees to register with the police. The public's perception of crime tends to encourage the government to spend millions of dollars in ways that affect individuals drawn into the criminal justice system for punishment.

In the face of public opinion polls and the politicians' desire to appear "tough," an important question arises: Are concerns about crime justified? Polls indicate that many Americans do not realize that serious crime declined steadily from the record-setting years of the early 1980s through 2000. Additional drops in crime occurred for various crimes during the early years of the twenty-first century. However, the nation's view of crime as a serious problem may continue to validate one reporter's observation in the early 1990s: "It is as though the country were confronting a devastating new wave of theft and violence" (Blonston, 1993). In fact, however, there is no national crime wave. Violent crime rates decreased each year from 1990 (729 per 100,000 people) through 2005 (469 per 100,000 people) with only a slight rise to 473 per 100,000 people in 2006 (BJS, 2007a). The homicide rate was 9.8 per 100,000 people in 1991. By 2006, the homicide rate was 5.7 per 100,000 people (BJS, 2007a).

Despite these declines, as indicated by the earlier discussion of the Gallup Poll, most Americans regard crime to be a "serious" problem. Because this concern about crime seems to ignore the actual drops in crime rates, many critics believe that people in the United States are unduly preoccupied with crime as a policy issue.

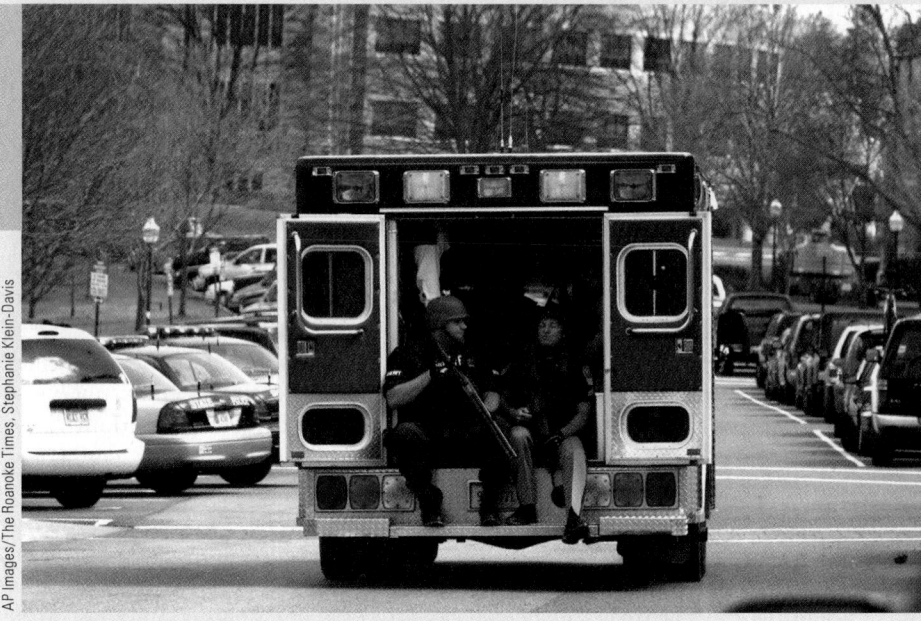

Police officers head across the Virginia Tech campus in response to the April 2007 shootings by a troubled student who killed 32 students and professors in a classroom building and dormitory. How does the publicity surrounding such events affect Americans' view of crime?

AP Images/The Roanoke Times, Stephanie Klein-Davis

THE MAIN THEMES OF THIS BOOK

The study of criminal justice offers a fascinating view of a crucial social problem. Drawing from the perspectives of such academic disciplines as economics, history, law, political science, psychology, and sociology, the field of criminal justice aims at supplying knowledge and developing policies to deal with criminality. This aim, however, poses a fundamental challenge in a democratic society: how to develop policies that deal with crime while still preserving individual rights, the rule of law, and justice.

Democracy in the United States is defined and guided by historic American values, including individual liberty, the preservation of constitutional rights, an expectation of personal privacy, and the protection of private property and free enterprise. These American values guide the development of public policy in all areas of government, including criminal justice. The application of American values, however, creates special tensions and problems in criminal justice. For example, people's sense of liberty may depend on how freely they can walk the streets without fearing crime; therefore, they want tough crime-control policies. On the other hand, other aspects of American values emphasize the protection of the criminal defendant's rights in order to ensure that no one is improperly denied his or her liberty. Finding the proper balance between conflicting values may pose an even greater challenge during the current era, in which fears about terrorism have enhanced citizens' concerns about crime and public safety. In the aftermath of the September 11, 2001, terrorist attacks on the World Trade Center in New York and the Pentagon in Washington, DC, 78 percent of Americans indicated their willingness to give up some freedom in order to gain greater security (Gallup Poll, 2002). Thus the nation may be facing an era in which a new balance will develop between individual rights and protection from crime.

To facilitate the exploration of these issues and others, this book presents three major themes: (1) crime and justice are public policy issues, (2) criminal justice can best be seen as a social system, and (3) the criminal justice system embodies society's effort to fulfill American values, such as liberty, privacy, and individuals rights. As we shall see, these values can come into conflict as choices are made about how to operate the system and define public policies. These themes are important for all Americans because of people's involvement in shaping criminal justice policy through their roles as voters, members of community organizations, and, for many students of criminal justice, future criminal justice professionals. All Americans are affected by criminal justice issues through perceptions that guide their choices about how to behave, where to live, and how to protect themselves and their families from victimization. All Americans also influence criminal justice when they vote on statewide ballot issues, vote for specific political candidates, make suggestions to their neighborhood associations, and express their views to elected officials. Knowledge of criminal justice from a public policy perspective and an understanding of the operation of the criminal justice system are essential tools for Americans to use in making decisions about their own behavior and for guiding their voting decisions and other involvement in shaping public policy. In asserting their influence over criminal justice, Americans also need to bear in mind the third theme: the need to uphold and strike an appropriate balance between our nation's values, including personal privacy and due process, and the necessary government authority for maintaining safety and security in society.

This chapter focuses on the first theme concerning crime and justice as public policy issues. The third theme, American values, is also presented in this chapter and will appear in each chapter throughout the book. Chapter 1 also examines the nature and definition of **crime**. As you learn about crime and the criminal justice system, take note of the many different academic disciplines that contribute to our knowledge in these areas. For example, the study of criminal justice requires psychologists to analyze the thinking and behavior of individuals. Criminologists develop and test theories about the causes of criminal behavior. Sociologists and economists examine the impact of society on crime as well as crime's impact on society. Political scientists explore the development of public policy and the operations of criminal justice agencies. Increasingly, chemists, biologists, and engineers play important roles in criminal justice because of the development of new scientific methods for investigating crimes and new technologies for weapons, surveillance, databases, and other essential aspects of law enforcement administration. Clearly, criminal justice provides a

crime
A specific act of commission or omission in violation of the law, for which a punishment is prescribed.

multidisciplinary area of study that appeals to people with varied interests and expertise.

An understanding of the crime problem and U.S. society's definition of this problem as a public policy issue will give you the groundwork for later discussions about criminal justice as a social system in which actors and agencies interact and make decisions. To guide your study, we address the following themes.

CRIME AND JUSTICE AS PUBLIC POLICY ISSUES

Who bears responsibility for addressing issues of crime and justice? The answer to this question depends on the organization of a society and the nature of its governing system. Looking back at human history, one can see many approaches to crime and punishment. For example, in a sparsely populated rural society that lacked effective control by government, crime and justice were often viewed as private matters. When one individual harmed another through violence or theft, a measure of justice could be obtained through vengeful acts by the victim's 's family or through the payment of compensation by the perpetrator. Such approaches were common in the centuries before central governments became dominating forces in modern nations. Alternatively, local leaders could rely on religious values or cultural traditions to impose punishments upon wrongdoers.

Such approaches still exist in some communities that are isolated or otherwise guided by nongovernment leaders and organizations. For example, in 2002, news stories emerged about a young woman in Pakistan who was sexually assaulted by tribal leaders as punishment for her brother's association with a woman from a higher-status tribe, a violation of local customs (Tanveer, 2002). In doing this, the leaders violated Pakistani law, but they asserted significant control over the community in a region where Pakistani officials did not always have enough authority to enforce the rules of the criminal justice system. In the United States, by contrast, crime and justice are public policy issues, because the government addresses them. Institutions and processes of government produce laws to define crimes; create and operate agencies to investigate, prosecute, and punish criminals; and allocate resources to address the problems of crime and justice. Moreover, these institutions and processes are influenced by the actions of American citizens, as they cast their votes for specific candidates, bring issues and problems to the attention of elected officials, and publicly protest against those policies that they see as unfair, inappropriate, or ineffective.

public policy
Priorities and actions developed by government to use public resources as a means to deal with issues affecting society.

Crime and justice are important and difficult **public policy** issues in the United States. In a democracy, we struggle to strike a balance between maintaining public order and protecting individual freedom. Both sides of this equation represent American values. To enjoy the liberty that we value so highly, we want to feel safe to move freely in society. On the other hand, if we push too strongly to ensure safety, we could limit individual rights and liberty by unnecessarily restricting, detaining, or punishing too many individuals. For example, we could impose policies that make us feel safe from crime, such as placing a police officer on every street corner and executing suspected criminals. Such severe practices have been used elsewhere in the world. Although they may reduce crime, they also fly in the face of democratic values. If we gave law enforcement officers a free hand to work their will on the public, we would be giving up individual freedom, due process, and our conception of justice. Liberty and legal rights are so important that they are enshrined in the nation's founding document, the U.S. Constitution. However, the protection of these democratic values can impede the ability of criminal justice officials to catch and punish offenders. Thus we continually struggle to find the proper balance between stopping crime and preventing government officials from violating individuals' rights.

NEW DIRECTIONS in CRIMINAL JUSTICE POLICY

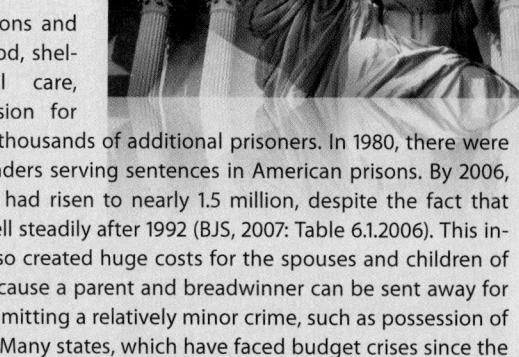

Questioning the Benefits of Imprisonment

FOR THREE DECADES, states employed tough crime-control policies, including building many new prisons and imprisoning larger numbers of offenders. These policies reflected a desire to increase the severity of punishment applied to lawbreakers. It also reflected a belief that crime could be reduced by holding offenders behind bars for longer periods. Every year that an offender is kept in prison is a year in which that offender will not commit crimes against the public. Moreover, some states undertook efforts to make prison life more difficult by eliminating opportunities for prisoners to take college courses and other educational programs and by removing weightlifting equipment and other specific recreational activities.

In 2005, new proposals emerged from political leaders, including conservative Republicans, that called into question the use of tough imprisonment policies. Arnold Schwarzenegger, the governor of California, a state with tens of thousands of prisoners, proposed that prisons shift to an emphasis on rehabilitating offenders, providing them with education and skills, and helping them to reenter society after their release from custody. U.S. Senator Sam Brownback, a conservative Republican from Kansas, proposed that Congress allocate millions of dollars to the task of assisting ex-prisoners with jobs, housing, and treatment for substance abuse (Warren, 2005).

Do these new proposals indicate that current imprisonment policies have failed? In evaluating public policies, one of the big issues is how one defines success. Advocates of tough imprisonment policies argue that criminal offenders must receive tough, predictable punishments so that they do not believe that they can get away with merely a slap on the wrist. These advocates also argue that imprisonment policies of the past few decades have caused the drop in crime rates because so many repeat offenders were behind bars and kept away from criminal activity. Advocates of tough policies also typically believe that crime is caused by the choices that criminals make and not by people's experiences with poverty, unemployment, and unstable families.

By contrast, the new reformers believe that imprisonment has been enor-mously expensive with respect to building and staff-ing new prisons and supplying food, shelter, medical care, and supervision for hundreds of thousands of additional prisoners. In 1980, there were 320,000 offenders serving sentences in American prisons. By 2006, that number had risen to nearly 1.5 million, despite the fact that crime rates fell steadily after 1992 (BJS, 2007: Table 6.1.2006). This increase has also created huge costs for the spouses and children of prisoners, because a parent and breadwinner can be sent away for years for committing a relatively minor crime, such as possession of illegal drugs. Many states, which have faced budget crises since the early 2000s, look at curbing expensive prison systems as a potential source of financial savings. In addition, the new reformers believe that society will gain greater benefits by preparing offenders to be successful citizens upon release rather than simply holding them in cells for years on end.

Did tough imprisonment policies lower the crime rate? That question generates many debates. Do correctional officials actually understand how to prepare prisoners for success in society? Rehabilitation of prisoners fell out of favor with policy makers in the 1980s because of a belief that no one really knows how to reform individual criminal offenders. Policy makers' views on these two questions will in part determine the direction of criminal punishment.

What do you think the United States should do? Do you fear that crime rates will rise with diminished use of imprisonment? Do you believe that society will benefit by educating prisoners and helping them find jobs after release from custody?

Researching the Internet

 You can read a brief discussion by two of the nation's leading experts about the connection between imprisonment and crime rates by going to *American System of Criminal Justice* 12e companion site at academic.cengage.com/criminaljustice/cole.

Some critics of criminal justice, such as Jeffrey Reiman, argue that our system is designed not to reduce crime or to achieve justice but to project to the American people a visible image of the threat of crime (Reiman, 1996: 1). This is done by maintaining a sizable population of criminals while at the same time failing to reduce crime. Reiman argues that we need to move away from a system of *criminal* justice to one of criminal *justice*. He urges policies that

- End crime-producing poverty
- Criminalize the harmful acts of affluent and white-collar offenders
- Create a corrections system that promotes human dignity
- Make the exercise of police, prosecution, and judicial power more just
- Establish economic and social justice

If adopted, Reiman's thought-provoking critical perspective would revolutionize not only the criminal justice system but also many of the attitudes and customs of U.S. society.

Dealing with the crime problem concerns not only the arrest, conviction, and punishment of offenders; it also requires the development of policies to deal with a host of issues such as gun control, stalking, hate crimes, computer crime, drugs, child abuse, and global criminal organizations. Many of these issues are controversial; policies must be hammered out in the political arenas of state legislatures and Congress. (To learn about debates concerning the use of imprisonment to punish offenders and reduce crime, see "New Directions in Criminal Justice Policy.") Any policy choice carries with it costs and consequences as well as potential benefits. Predicting consequences can be difficult. Moreover, values in society may change and a particular policy choice that enjoyed widespread popularity at one moment may become unpopular just a few years later, especially if it does not deliver the benefits intended by the policy's advocates.

The Role of Public Opinion

In a democracy, public opinion greatly influences political leaders. They know that if they develop policies contrary to what the public thinks, they may lose the next election and diminish the legitimacy of those policies. As a result, these leaders often enact policies on crime that are thought by researchers to have little potential impact on crime but that nonetheless allay the general public's anxiety about crime and safety.

Throughout this book, you will find marginal items labeled "What Americans Think." These present the results of public opinion surveys on issues concerning crime and the administration of justice. As you read each chapter, consider these expressions of public opinion. Do you agree with the majority of Americans on each issue? Or does your understanding of criminal justice give you a different perspective on the policies that might better address these problems? See, for example, "What Americans Think" about the criminal justice system.

Do your opinions differ from those of other criminal justice students?

To find out the opinions of other criminal justice students, go to *The American System of Criminal Justice* 12e companion site at academic.cengage.com/criminaljustice/cole. Click on "Survey" and answer the questionnaire. Your responses will be collated with those of other students so that you can review the results by clicking on the website again. You may want to download and print out your responses as well as those of students throughout the country. Compare your opinion, student opinion, and the general public's opinion.

Contemporary Policies

Over the past several decades, both conservatives and liberals have promoted policies for dealing with crime. Each group has its own perspective on what works best to advance justice. Conservatives believe that solutions will come from stricter enforcement of the law through the expansion of police forces and the enactment of laws that require swift and certain punishment of criminals (Logan and DiIulio, 1993: 486). Advocates of such policies have dominated since the early 1980s. They argue that we must strengthen crime control, which they claim has been hindered by certain decisions of the U.S. Supreme Court and by programs that substitute government assistance for individual responsibility.

In contrast, liberals argue that stronger crime-control measures endanger the values of due process and justice (S. Walker, 1993). They claim that strict measures are ineffective because progress will come from reshaping the lives of offenders and changing the social and economic conditions from which criminal behavior springs. Thus they advocate programs to reduce poverty, increase educational opportunities for poor youths, and provide counseling and drug rehabilitation.

WHAT AMERICANS THINK

Question: "I am going to read you a list of institutions in American society. Please tell me how much confidence you, yourself, have in each one—a great deal, quite a lot, some, or very little: the criminal justice system?"

- Great deal/quite a lot 19%
- None 2%
- Very little 33%
- Some 44%

Source: Bureau of Justice Statistics, *Sourcebook of Criminal Justice Statistics, 2007* (Washington, DC: U.S. Government Printing Office, 2008), Table 2.11.2007.

As you consider these arguments, think about how they relate to crime trends. In the 1960s, when we were trying the liberal approach of rehabilitating offenders, crime increased. Does this mean that the approach does not work? Perhaps it was merely overwhelmed by the sheer number of people who were in their crime-prone years (between the ages of 16 and 24). Perhaps there would have been even more crime if not for the efforts to rehabilitate people. On the other hand, crime rates decreased when tough policies were implemented in the 1980s and thereafter. But was that because of the conservative policies in effect, or because there were fewer people in the crime-prone age group? If conservative policies are effective, then why did violent crime rates rise in the early 1990s, when tough policies were still in force? Clearly, there are no easy answers. Nonetheless, we cannot avoid making choices about how to use the police, courts, and corrections system most effectively.

Crime and Justice in a Democracy

Americans agree that criminal justice policies should control crime by enforcing the law and should protect the rights of individuals. But achieving both objectives is difficult. They involve questions such as the amount of power police should have to search people without a warrant, the rules judges must follow in deciding if certain types of evidence may be used, and the power of prison wardens to punish inmates. These questions are answered differently in a democracy than they would be in an authoritarian state.

The administration of justice in a democracy also differs from that in an authoritarian state in the nature and extent of the protections provided for an accused person while guilt is determined and punishment imposed. The police, prosecutors, judges, and correctional officials are expected to act according to democratic values—especially respect for the rule of law and the maintenance of civil rights and liberties. Further, citizens must view the criminal justice system as legitimate and have confidence in its actions.

Laws in the United States begin with the premise that all people—the guilty as well as the innocent—have rights. Moreover, unlike laws in some other countries, U.S. laws reflect the desire to avoid unnecessarily depriving people of

Many organizations seek to influence the development of criminal justice policy; for one example, read about the Criminal Justice Policy Foundation. To link to this website, go to *The American System of Criminal Justice* 12e companion site at academic.cengage.com/criminaljustice/cole.

In a democracy, citizens must take an interest in the criminal justice system, as they are doing here in this demonstration against drug use and killings in East Los Angeles. As a citizen, how can you become involved in criminal justice issues?

© Joseph Sohm;ChromoSohm Inc./Corbis

liberty, either by permitting the police to arrest people at will or by punishing a person for a crime that he or she did not commit.

Although all Americans prize freedom and individual rights, they often disagree about the policies that deal with crime. Our greatest challenge as we move through the twenty-first century may be to find ways to remain true to the principles of fairness and justice while operating a system that can effectively protect, investigate, and punish.

checkpoint

1. What criminal justice policies are advocated by conservatives?
2. What are liberals' criticisms of contemporary policies?
3. What two criminal justice goals do Americans agree on? (Answers are at the end of the chapter.)

Crime Control versus Due Process

In one of the most important contributions to systematic thought about criminal justice, Herbert Packer (1968) describes two competing models of criminal justice administration: the **crime control model** and the **due process model**. These are contrasting ways of looking at the goals and procedures of the criminal justice system. The crime control model is much like an assembly line, whereas the due process model is like an obstacle course.

In reality, of course, no criminal justice official or agency functions according to one model or the other. Elements of both models appear throughout the system. However, the two models reveal key tensions within the criminal justice process, as well as the gap between how we describe the system and the way most cases are actually processed. Table 1.1 presents the main elements of each model.

crime control model
A model of the criminal justice system that assumes freedom is so important that every effort must be made to repress crime; it emphasizes efficiency, speed, finality, and the capacity to apprehend, try, convict, and dispose of a high proportion of offenders.

due process model
A model of the criminal justice system that assumes freedom is so important that every effort must be made to ensure that criminal justice decisions are based on reliable information; it emphasizes the adversarial process, the rights of defendants, and formal decision-making procedures.

Crime Control: Order as a Value

The crime control model assumes that every effort must be made to repress crime. It emphasizes efficiency and the capacity to catch, try, convict, and punish a high proportion of offenders; it also stresses speed and finality. This model places the goal of controlling crime uppermost, putting less emphasis on protecting individuals' rights. As Packer points out, the crime control model calls for efficiency in screening suspects, determining guilt, and applying sanctions to the convicted; this will achieve liberty for all citizens. High rates of crime and the limited resources of law enforcement make speed and finality necessary. All of these elements depend on informality, uniformity, and few challenges by defense attorneys or defendants.

In this model, police and prosecutors decide early on how likely the suspect is to be found guilty. If a case is unlikely to end in conviction, the prosecutor

TABLE 1.1	Due Process Model and Crime Control Model Compared				
What other comparisons can be made between the two models?					
	Goal	**Value**	**Process**	**Major Decision Point**	**Basis of Decision Making**
Due Process Model	Preserve individual liberties	Reliability	Adversarial	Courtroom	Law
Crime Control Model	Repress crime	Efficiency	Administrative	Police, pretrial processes	Discretion

may drop the charges. At each stage—from arrest to preliminary hearing, arraignment, and trial—established procedures are used to determine whether the accused should be passed on to the next stage. Rather than stressing the combative aspects of the courtroom, this model promotes bargaining between the state and the accused. Nearly all cases are processed through such bargaining, and they typically end with the defendant pleading guilty. Packer's description of this model as an assembly-line process conveys the idea of quick, efficient decisions by actors at fixed stations that turn out the intended product—guilty pleas and closed cases.

Due Process: Law as a Value

If the crime control model looks like an assembly line, the due process model looks more like an obstacle course. This model assumes that freedom is so important that every effort must be made to ensure that criminal justice decisions stem from reliable information. It stresses the adversarial process, the rights of defendants, and formal decision-making procedures. For example, because people are poor observers of disturbing events, police and prosecutors may well be wrong in presuming a defendant to be guilty. Thus, people should be labeled as criminals only on the basis of conclusive evidence. To reduce error, the government must prove beyond a reasonable doubt that the defendant is guilty of the crime. Therefore, the process must give the defense every opportunity to show that the evidence is not conclusive, and an impartial judge and jury must decide the outcome. According to Packer, the assumption that the defendant is innocent until proved guilty has a far-reaching impact on the criminal justice system.

In the due process model, the state must prove that the person is guilty of the crime as charged. Prosecutors must prove their cases while obeying rules dealing with such matters as the admissibility of evidence and respect for defendants' constitutional rights. Forcing the state to prove its case in a trial protects citizens from wrongful convictions. Thus the due process model emphasizes justice as protecting the rights of individuals and reserving punishment for those who unquestionably deserve it. These values are stressed even though some guilty defendants may go free because the evidence against them is not conclusive enough. By contrast, the crime control model values efficient case processing and punishment over the possibility that innocent people might get swept up in the process.

checkpoint

4. What are the main features of the crime control model?
5. What are the main features of the due process model?

The Politics of Crime and Justice

Criminal justice policies are developed in national, state, and local political arenas. There is always a risk that politicians will simply do what they believe voters want to hear rather than think seriously about whether those policies will achieve their goals. For example, the crime bill passed by Congress in 1994 expanded the death penalty to cover 60 additional offenses, including the murder of members of Congress, the Supreme Court, and the president's 's staff. These are tough provisions, but will they actually accomplish anything? Many criminologists doubt it.

Frequently, "knee-jerk" reactions inform the political process. A problem occurs and captures significant public attention. Calls to do something arise.

Criminal justice policies are decided by legislators who respond to voters' concerns and perceptions about crime. Legislators also determine priorities for government spending on various policy issues. Do you think your state and local government spends too little, too much, or just enough on criminal justice as compared to issues such as education and transportation?

© Bob Daemmerich/PhotoEdit

Politicians respond with (1) outrage, (2) a limited examination of the problem, and (3) a law—often poorly thought out and with little regard for unintended consequences. Politicians often propose laws without carefully studying the nature and extent of the problem they claim to address (Gest, 2001).

If not written carefully, laws may affect more people than the original targets of the law. In one example, a 12-year-old Boy Scout and honors student in Texas forgot to remove a small pocketknife from his jacket pocket after a weekend camping trip. When he found the knife in his pocket at school, he placed it in his locker. Another student reported him to school officials. Because the state's Safe Schools Act of 1995 imposed a "zero tolerance" policy for weapons in schools, the boy was arrested and taken to a juvenile detention facility without officials informing his parents. After being expelled from school and spending weeks in a school for juvenile offenders, he began contemplating suicide (Axtman, 2005c). In another example, a 14-year-old suburban youth in Michigan was charged with the crime of threatening terrorism, based on a law enacted by the Michigan legislature in the aftermath of September 11. Teased and bullied by classmates, the boy responded by making a list of people that he would like to kill. Although critics contended that this case of an angry, immature bullying victim did not fit the legislature's intent in creating an antiterrorism law, the county prosecutor charged the boy anyway. If convicted, he could spend five years in a juvenile detention facility. If he had been an adult, he would have faced up to 20 years in prison (Mask and Witsil, 2005). Ultimately, he successfully served a term on probation and had his record cleared (Frye, 2005).

Other examples of laws with unanticipated consequences might include sex offender registration statutes intended to keep the public informed about the names and home addresses of violent offenders who have been released from prison. If not carefully worded, such laws can require a lifetime of registration and public humiliation for a broad array of "sex offenders" such as teenagers convicted of indecent exposure when caught making out in a car or someone convicted of urinating in the bushes at a public park.

The clearest link between politics and criminal justice shows up in the statements of Republicans and Democrats who try to outdo each other in showing how tough they can be on crime (Estrich, 1998). Just as important are the more "routine" links between politics and the justice system. The creation of new crimes and the budgets of criminal justice agencies are decided by legislators responding to the demands of voters. Look at the survey presented in "What

Americans Think." How might a politician react to these results? Do you think the public has accurately identified the country's most pressing problems?

Many other types of political decisions affect criminal justice, some of which create undesirable consequences. For example, Congress appropriates millions of dollars to help states and cities wage the "war on drugs" by arresting more people but allocate no additional funds to provide attorneys for poor defendants. A legislature may create a budget crisis for local police agencies by requiring the collection of DNA samples from everyone in local jails without providing the funds for technicians and labs to gather, store, and test samples. At the state and local levels, many criminal justice authorities—including sheriffs, prosecutors, and judges—are also elected officials. There are no elected justice officials in the federal system except the president of the United States, who appoints federal prosecutors throughout the country. The decisions of state and local elected officials will be influenced by the concerns and values of their communities, because these officials want to please the public in order to be reelected. When the decisions of prosecutors, sheriffs, and judges are affected by their efforts to please voters, there are concerns that these officials will lose sight of other important values, such as equal treatment for all defendants. "A Question of Ethics," at the end of this chapter, illustrates one dilemma arising from such influences.

As you learn about each part of the criminal justice system, keep in mind the ways that decision makers and institutions are connected to politics and government. Criminal justice is closely linked to society and its institutions, and to understand it fully we must be aware of those links.

checkpoint

6. At what level of government are many justice officials elected to office?
7. How do politics influence criminal justice policies?

Citizens and Criminal Justice Policy

Americans should not view themselves as passive observers of criminal justice policy. In fact, they are intimately involved in the processes that produce public policy. Most obviously, citizens vote for the elected officials who create criminal laws, run the criminal justice system, and implement criminal justice policies. Often, votes are based on concerns about issues, such as economic problems or wars, that are regarded as more pressing than criminal justice at a given moment in time. At other times, citizens may vote based on loyalty to a political party or perceptions about a candidate's leadership abilities. Americans who move beyond simple beliefs and assumptions about criminals in order to learn about crime and the criminal justice system can position themselves to incorporate consideration of these issues into their decisions about whom to support on election day.

Because the United States is a democracy, there are opportunities for citizens to go beyond merely voting and act to directly affect policy decisions. For example, a specific, tragic criminal event can lead individual Americans to devote time and energy toward shaping justice policy. Candy Lightner, whose teenage daughter was killed by a hit-and-run drunk driver, founded Mothers Against Drunk Driving (MADD), an organization that became very influential throughout the United States in shaping the development and enforcement of criminal laws concerning drunken driving. Similarly, Sarah Brady, whose husband James was seriously injured in a 1981 assassination attempt on President Ronald Reagan, founded the Brady Center to Prevent Gun Violence, an organization that pursues her vision of sensible gun control laws. In another example, Carolyn McCarthy became dedicated to influencing criminal justice policy after a random shooting

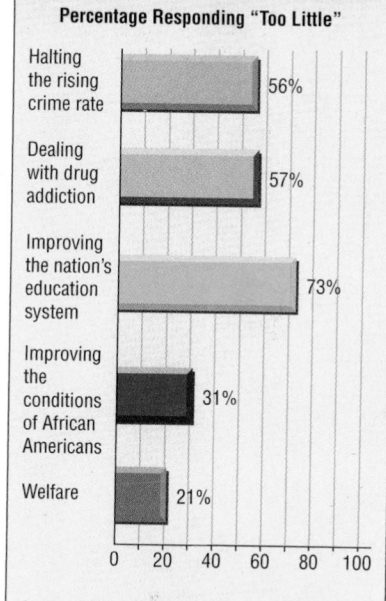

WHAT AMERICANS THINK

Question: "We are faced with many problems in this country, none of which can be solved easily or inexpensively. I'm going to name some of the problems and for each one I'd like you to tell me whether you think we're spending too much money on it, too little money, or about the right amount."

Percentage Responding "Too Little"

Halting the rising crime rate	56%
Dealing with drug addiction	57%
Improving the nation's education system	73%
Improving the conditions of African Americans	31%
Welfare	21%

0 20 40 60 80 100

Source: Bureau of Justice Statistics, *Sourcebook of Criminal Justice Statistics, 2002* (Washington, DC: U.S. Government Printing Office, 2003), Table 2.40.

by a mentally ill man killed her husband and seriously injured her son. She successfully ran for a seat in Congress and represents a New York district. Other individuals have used their personal motivation to mobilize other people and thereby influence capital punishment, sex offender registration laws, and other aspects of criminal justice policy.

Individual Americans also influence criminal justice policy through their involvement in community organizations, such as neighborhood associations, parent-teacher organizations, and church groups. They often must make decisions about how to keep their homes, schools, and churches safe and secure. This often requires communication and cooperation with police agencies as well as decisions about policies regarding lighting, alarms, public education, and other matters that affect people's vulnerability to criminal victimization.

It is important for Americans to become knowledgeable about criminal justice issues. In our daily lives, we cannot escape making decisions that impact the risk of victimization for ourselves and others. Do we click a link in an unsolicited email message and risk becoming a victim of cybercrime? Do we approach an ATM machine at night in a dark, isolated corner? What do we teach our children about how to handle situations when they are approached by strangers? We also face other questions about how we will influence public policy. How will we vote on ballot issues that will change laws concerning criminal sentences, drug rehabilitation, gambling, and other policy issues? Do we remain silent and passive if our elected officials in local, state, or national government pursue criminal justice policies with which we disagree? Because criminal justice issues affect the lives of all Americans, there are important reasons for educated citizens to recognize their role and impact.

checkpoint

8. Who are examples of individual Americans who have influenced criminal justice policy?
9. How do average citizens affect criminal justice?

DEFINING CRIME

Why does the law label some types of behavior but not others as criminal? For example, many young people ask, "Why is it illegal to smoke marijuana but legal to consume alcohol?" If the answer is that marijuana might be addictive, could lead to the use of more potent drugs, and may have negative effects on health, then the questioner might point out that alcoholism is a major social problem, drinking beer can create a thirst for hard liquor, and overuse of alcohol leads to heart and liver disorders as well as many auto accidents. A parent facing such arguments from a teenager may find it difficult to explain why the parent drinks alcohol but forbids the teenager to smoke marijuana. Frequently, the parent may cut the argument short by simply declaring, "You cannot use marijuana, because pot smoking is against the law, and that's that!" Criminal laws are not necessarily developed through consistent logical reasoning. Instead, they reflect societal values, some of which may be inconsistent, as well as the preferences of politicians.

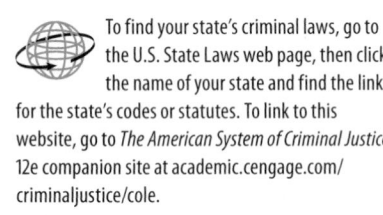 To find your state's criminal laws, go to the U.S. State Laws web page, then click the name of your state and find the link for the state's codes or statutes. To link to this website, go to *The American System of Criminal Justice* 12e companion site at academic.cengage.com/criminaljustice/cole.

Criminal law is defined by elected representatives in state legislatures and Congress who make choices about the behaviors that government will punish. Some of those choices reflect a broad consensus in society that certain actions, such as rape, assault, and murder, are so harmful that they must be punished. Such crimes have traditionally been called ***mala in se***—wrong in themselves. However, legis-

mala in se
Offenses that are wrong by their very nature.

latures also create criminal laws concerning certain acts whose harm the public is still debating. These crimes are referred to as *mala prohibita*—they are crimes because they are prohibited by the government and not because they are wrong in themselves. Everyone does not agree, for example, that gambling, prostitution, drug use, and assisted suicide should be punished. Today, some people view these behaviors as free choices that adults should be able to make themselves (see "What Americans Think"). Indeed, these behaviors have not been illegal at all times and in all places. Gambling, for example, is illegal in many states, but it represents an important legitimate business in Nevada, New Jersey, Michigan, Native American reservations, and other locations in the United States. Regulated prostitution is legal in Nevada and in many countries of the world, but not in most U.S. states. Although the federal government has blocked the implementation of state laws that relax drug regulations, voters in several U.S. states have expressed their views on the subject by voting to permit people to smoke marijuana for medicinal purposes. Thus the designation of such activities as crimes does not reflect values that are universally shared throughout the United States.

Evidence from a national survey helps show the extent to which Americans agree about the behaviors that should be defined as crimes (BJS, 1988: 16). In this study, respondents were asked to rank the seriousness of 204 illegal events. The results (Table 1.2) showed wide agreement on the severity of certain crimes. However, crime victims scored those acts higher than did nonvictims. The ratings assigned by minority group members tended to be lower than those assigned by whites. Thus there is disagreement about which behaviors to punish as crimes. Examine your own views by considering the proposed "hate crime" legislation in "Civic Engagement: Your Role in the System."

civic engagement
your role in the system

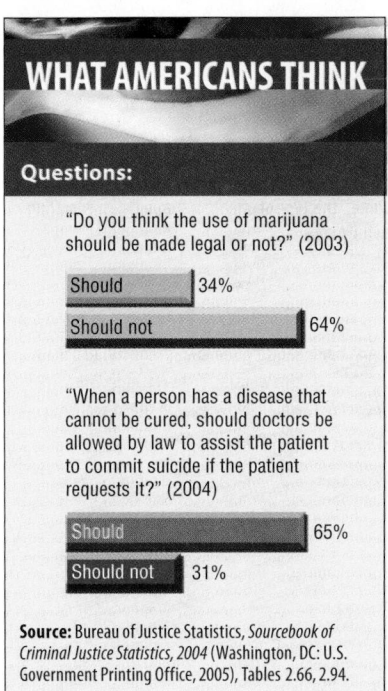

As part of a state legislator's campaign for reelection, she proposes a new criminal law: it will be a crime, carrying a punishment of up to three years of imprisonment, to place a noose or a swastika on someone's else property or public property for the purposes of intimidation or harassment. How do you evaluate this "hate crime" proposal? *Make a list of three arguments that are important for your evaluation of the issue.* Will you vote for this legislator? Such a proposal was actually considered in the Maryland state legislature in 2008. Examine the proposal online and find out what happened to it. To link to this website, go to *The American System of Criminal Justice* 12e companion site at academic.cengage.com/criminaljustice/cole.

mala prohibita
Offenses prohibited by law but not wrong in themselves.

---

checkpoint

10. Who defines certain behaviors as criminal?
11. What is meant by *mala in se* and by *mala prohibita*?

TYPES OF CRIME

Crimes can be classified in various ways. As we have seen, scholars often use the distinction between *mala in se* and *mala prohibita*. Crimes can also be classified as either felonies or misdemeanors. **Felonies** are serious crimes punishable by incarceration for more than one year in prison or the death penalty. **Misdemeanors** are less serious offenses that are punishable by jail sentences of less than one year, probation, fines, or other intermediate sanctions. A third scheme classifies crimes by the nature of the act. This approach produces six types of crime: visible crime, occupational crime, organized crime, victimless crime, political crime, and cybercrime. Each type has its own level of risk and reward, each arouses varying degrees of public disapproval, and each is committed by a certain kind of offender. New types of crime emerge as society changes. Cybercrimes committed through the use of computers over the Internet are becoming a major global problem.

WHAT AMERICANS THINK

Questions:

"Do you think the use of marijuana should be made legal or not?" (2003)

Should	34%
Should not	64%

"When a person has a disease that cannot be cured, should doctors be allowed by law to assist the patient to commit suicide if the patient requests it?" (2004)

Should	65%
Should not	31%

Source: Bureau of Justice Statistics, *Sourcebook of Criminal Justice Statistics, 2004* (Washington, DC: U.S. Government Printing Office, 2005), Tables 2.66, 2.94.

felonies
Serious crimes usually carrying a penalty of incarceration for more than one year or the death penalty.

misdemeanors
Offenses less serious than felonies and usually punishable by incarceration of no more than one year, probation, or intermediate sanctions.

TABLE 1.2 How Do People Rank the Severity of a Crime?

Respondents to a survey were asked to rank 204 illegal events ranging from school truancy to planting a deadly bomb. A severity score of 40 indicates that people believe the crime is twice as bad as a crime receiving a severity score of 20.

Severity Score	Ten Most Serious Offenses	Severity Score	Ten Least Serious Offenses
72.1	Planting a bomb in a public building. The bomb explodes and twenty people are killed.	1.3	Two persons willingly engage in a homosexual act.
52.8	A man forcibly rapes a woman. As a result of physical injuries, she dies.	1.1	Disturbing the neighborhood with loud, noisy behavior.
		1.1	Taking bets on the numbers.
43.2	Robbing a victim at gunpoint. The victim struggles and is shot to death.	1.1	A group continues to hang around a corner after being told by a police officer to break up.
39.2	A man stabs his wife. As a result, she dies.	0.9	A youngster under 16 runs away from home.
35.7	Stabbing a victim to death.	0.8	Being drunk in public.
35.6	Intentionally injuring a victim. As a result, the victim dies.	0.7	A youngster under 16 breaks a curfew law by being on the street after the hour permitted by law.
33.8	Running a narcotics ring.	0.6	Trespassing in the backyard of a private home.
27.9	A woman stabs her husband. As a result, he dies.	0.3	A person is vagrant. That is, he has no home and no visible means of support.
26.3	An armed person skyjacks an airplane and demands to be flown to another country.		
25.8	A man forcibly rapes a woman. No other physical injury occurs.	0.2	A youngster under 16 is truant from school.

Source: Bureau of Justice Statistics, *Report to the Nation on Crime and Justice*, 2nd ed. (Washington, DC: U.S. Government Printing Office, 1988), 16.

Visible Crime

visible crime
An offense against persons or property that is committed primarily by members of the lower social classes. Often referred to as "street crime" or "ordinary crime," this type of offense is the one most upsetting to the public.

Visible crime, often called "street crime" or "ordinary crime," ranges from shoplifting to homicide. For offenders, such crimes are the least profitable and, because they are visible, the least protected. These are the acts that the public regards as "criminal." The majority of law enforcement resources are used to deal with them. We can divide visible crimes into three categories: violent crimes, property crimes, and public order crimes.

 For an example of a state's sex offender registry, see Iowa's registry. To link to this website, go to *The American System of Criminal Justice* 12e companion site at academic.cengage.com/criminaljustice/cole.

Violent Crimes

Acts against people in which death or physical injury results are *violent crimes*. These include criminal homicide, assault, rape, and robbery. The criminal justice system treats these as the most serious offenses and punishes them accordingly. Although the public is most fearful of violence by strangers, many of these offenses are committed by people who know their victim.

Property Crimes

Property crimes are acts that threaten property held by individuals or by the state. Many types of crimes fall under this category, including theft, larceny, shoplifting, embezzlement, and burglary. Some property offenders are amateurs who occasionally commit these crimes because of situational factors such as financial need or peer pressure. In contrast, professional criminals make a significant portion of their livelihood from committing property offenses.

Public Order Crimes

Acts that threaten the general well-being of society and challenge accepted moral principles are defined as *public order crimes*. They include public drunkenness, aggressive panhandling, vandalism, and disorderly conduct. Although the police tend to treat these behaviors as minor offenses, there is concern that this type of disorderly behavior instills fear in citizens, leads to more-serious crimes, and hastens urban decay (Kelling and Coles, 1996). The definition and enforcement of such behaviors as crimes highlights the tensions between different interpretations of American values. Many people see such behavior as simply representing the liberty that adults enjoy in a free society to engage in offensive and self-destructive behavior that causes no concrete harm to other people. By contrast, other people see their own liberty limited by the need to be wary and fearful of actions by people who are drunk or out of control.

Those charged with visible crimes are disproportionately young, male, poor, and members of minority groups. Some argue that this is due to the class bias of a society that has singled out visible crimes for priority enforcement. They note that law enforcement officials do not focus as much attention on other kinds of crimes.

Occupational Crime

Occupational crimes are committed in the context of a legal business or profession. Often viewed as shrewd business practices rather than as illegal acts, they are crimes that, if done right, are never discovered. An important American value is economic liberty. Each person is presumed to have the opportunity to make his or her own fortune through hard work and innovative ideas. The success of the American economic system is built, in part, on the creativity of people who invent new products, develop new technologies, or discover new ways to market goods. Although we admire entrepreneurial activities, some individuals go too far in using their creativity within our free enterprise system. The freedom to make financial transactions and other decisions in fast-moving private businesses also creates opportunities to steal from employers or defraud customers and investors. These crimes cost society billions of dollars each year. Many estimates indicate that the money stolen through occupational crime far exceeds the total amounts stolen through visible crimes such as robbery and larceny (Center for Corporate Policy, 2005).

Crimes committed in the course of business were first described by criminologist Edwin Sutherland in 1939, when he developed the concept of white-collar crime. He noted that such crimes are committed by respectable offenders taking advantage of opportunities arising from their business dealings. He forced criminologists to recognize that criminal behavior was not confined to lower-class people (so-called blue-collar crime) but reached into the upper levels of society (Shover, 1998: 133; Sutherland, 1949).

The white-collar/blue-collar distinction has lost much of its meaning in modern society. Since the 1970s, research on white-collar crime has shifted from the individual to the organization (Friedrichs, 1996: 38). Gary Green has described four types of occupational crimes (Green, 1997: 17–19):

1. *Occupational crimes for the benefit of the employing organizations.* Employers rather than offenders benefit directly from these crimes. They include price fixing, theft of trade secrets, and falsification of product tests. In these cases an employee may commit the offense but will not benefit personally, except perhaps through a bonus or promotion. It is the company that benefits. These crimes are "committed in the suites rather than in the streets."

   In 2002, many Americans became more keenly aware of the impact of occupational crimes when news reports focused on corporate misconduct that produced significant detrimental consequences for investors and pension funds. Arthur Andersen, the international accounting firm, was convicted of obstruction of justice for interfering with the federal investigation of Enron, the energy company whose collapse cost investors and employees

occupational crime
Criminal offense committed through opportunities created in a legal business or occupation.

Multimillionaire Conrad Black, owner of many media businesses, leaves the Chicago federal courthouse in December 2007 after being sentenced to 6½ years in prison for swindling investors out of millions of dollars. Do Americans view such occupational crimes as serious matters that deserve the attention of police and prosecutors?

AP Images/Jerry Lai

Some organizations attempt to monitor crimes and other socially harmful activities by government officials, corporations, and executives. For one example, see the website of CorpWatch. To link to this website, go to *The American System of Criminal Justice* 12e companion site at academic.cengage.com/criminaljustice/cole.

millions of dollars (Torriero and Manor, 2002). The company faced a potential fine of $500,000 for the crime. As in the case of communications giant WorldCom, Xerox, Tyco, and other companies, Enron and its accountants relied on deceptive practices to inflate earnings reports and the value of its stock (Kadlec, 2002). These actions, some of which may have violated criminal laws, advanced the interests of the company as well as the bank accounts of many high-level corporate officials.

2. *Occupational crimes through the exercise of government authority.* In these crimes the offender has the legal power to enforce laws or command others to do so. Examples include removal of drugs from the evidence room by a police officer, acceptance of a bribe by a public official, and falsification of a document by a notary public. For example, in July 2002 a U.S. Army colonel stationed in South Korea was charged with accepting bribes from Korean construction businesses that sought contracts to build military barracks at American bases. The colonel was responsible for approving more than $300 million annually in government contracts. Investigators found more than $700,000 in cash hidden in the colonel's home (Carter, 2002).

3. *Occupational crimes committed by professionals in their capacity as professionals.* Doctors, lawyers, and stockbrokers may take advantage of clients by, for instance, illegally dispensing drugs, using funds placed in escrow, or using "insider" stock-trading information for personal profit or, if their offices are not prospering, to keep their businesses going (Willott, Griffin, and Torrance, 2001). In 2004, for example, a psychiatrist in Houston admitted

guilt in a scheme to defraud the federal government out of millions of dollars by approving ineligible people for motorized wheelchairs paid for by Medicare and Medicaid and then accepting kickbacks from wheelchair companies (U.S. Department of Justice, 2004). From the late 1990s onward, fraud crimes increased as financial services professionals and corporate executives took advantage of Americans' interest in investments and used that interest as a means to obtain money illegally (Labaton, 2002).

Many commentators believe that the American value of economic liberty led the government to reduce the regulation of business. As a result, some individuals exploited the lack of government control to manipulate corporate stock values in ways that gave them great profits but ultimately harmed millions of investors. As a result of the scandals involving Enron and other corporations, Congress is moving toward new public policy choices that will reduce corporate executives' freedom to make decisions without supervision and accountability.

4. *Occupational crimes committed by individuals as individuals, where opportunities are not based on government power or professional position.* Examples of this type of crime include thefts by employees from employers, filing of false expense claims, and embezzlement (Wright and Cullen, 2000). Employee crime is believed to account for about 1 percent of the gross national product and causes consumer prices to be 10 to 15 percent higher than they would be otherwise. Employee theft is involved in about a third of business failures. The total loss due to employee theft therefore is greater than all business losses from shoplifting, burglary, or robbery (Friedrichs, 1996: 115).

Although they are highly profitable, most types of occupational crime do not come to public attention. Regulatory agencies, such as the Federal Trade Commission and the Securities and Exchange Commission, often do not enforce the law effectively. Many business and professional organizations "police" themselves, dropping employees or members who commit offenses.

The low level of criminal enforcement of occupational crimes may result from the fact that the general public does not always view them as threatening or serious. Such crimes usually do not involve violence or threats to public safety, although some may involve selling unsafe food or defective products. Many people may not realize, however, the huge costs of such crimes to society. In addition, the complex nature of financial transactions and executive decisions may make these cases difficult to investigate and prosecute. In the words of one criminologist, "Many of these cases lack jury appeal: that is, the sexiness of other cases, in which it is easier to identify the harm that was caused and how it was caused" (Eitle, 2000: 830).

Organized Crime

The term **organized crime** refers to a framework within which criminal acts are committed, rather than referring to the acts themselves. A crime syndicate has an organizational structure, rules, a division of labor, and the capacity for ruthless violence and corrupting law enforcement, labor and business leaders, and politicians (Jacobs and Panarella, 1998: 160). Organized criminals provide goods and services to millions of people. They will engage in any activity that provides minimum risk and maximum profit. Thus organized crime involves a network of activities, usually cutting across state and national borders, that range from legitimate businesses to shady deals with labor unions to providing "goods"—such as drugs, sex, and pornography—that cannot be obtained legally. In recent years organized crime has been involved in new services such as

organized crime
A framework for the perpetration of criminal acts—usually in fields, such as gambling, drugs, and prostitution—providing illegal services that are in great demand.

money laundering
Moving the proceeds of criminal activities through a maze of businesses, banks, and brokerage accounts in order to disguise their origin.

 The FBI's website describes the nature of organized crime challenges faced by the United States as well as the agency's activities to counteract crime groups. To link to this website, go to *The American System of Criminal Justice* 12e companion site at academic.cengage.com/criminaljustice/cole.

commercial arson, illegal disposal of toxic wastes, and **money laundering**. Few organized criminals are arrested and prosecuted.

Investigations of the crime "families," which are known as the Mafia and Cosa Nostra, have yielded detailed accounts of their structure, membership, and activities. The FBI and the media give the impression that the Mafia is a unified syndicate, but scholars tend to believe that the "families" are fairly autonomous local groups (Abadinsky, 2003; Albanese, 1991). The June 2002 death of John Gotti, the imprisoned boss of New York's Gambino crime family, led to numerous news stories reviewing the activities of "the most important gangster since Al Capone" (Pyle, 2002). Gotti's death was also treated as the end of an era, because criminal organizations no longer neatly fit the image of falling under exclusive control of the families of European immigrants.

Although the public often associates organized crime with Italian Americans—indeed, the federal government indicted 73 members of the Genovese New York "crime family" in 2001 (Worth, 2001)—other ethnic groups have dominated at various times. Thirty-five years ago, one scholar noted the strangeness of America's "ladder of social mobility," in which each new immigrant group uses organized crime as one of the first rungs of the climb (Bell, 1967: 150). However, debate about this notion continues, because not all immigrant groups have engaged in organized crime (Kenney and Finckenauer, 1995: 38).

Some believe that the pirates of the seventeenth century were an early form of organized crime in America. But in the 1820s the "Forty Thieves," an Irish gang in New York City, were the first to organize on a large scale. They were followed by Jews who dominated gambling and labor rackets at the turn of the century. The Italians came next, but they did not climb very far up the ladder until the late 1930s (Ianni, 1973: 1–2).

Over the last few decades, law enforcement efforts have greatly weakened the Mafia. Beginning in 1978 the federal government mounted extraordinary efforts to eradicate the group. Using electronic surveillance, undercover agents, and mob turncoats, as well as the FBI, the federal Organized Crime Task Forces, and the U.S. attorneys' offices, law enforcement launched investigations and prosecutions. As J. B. Jacobs notes, "The magnitude of the government's attack on Cosa Nostra is nothing short of incredible." By 1992, 23 bosses were convicted, and the leadership and soldiers of five New York City families (Bonanno, Colombo, Gambino, Genovese, Lucchese) were decimated (Jacobs, Panarella, and Worthington, 1994: 4). In addition, an aging leadership, lack of interest by younger family members, and pressures from new immigrant groups contributed to the fall of the Mafia.

Today African Americans, Hispanics, Russians, and Asians have formed organized crime groups in some cities. Drug dealing has brought Colombian and Mexican crime groups to U.S. shores, and Vietnamese-, Chinese-, and Japanese-led groups have formed in California. In recent years, there has been increased concern about criminal gangs from Eastern Europe and Central America. Specific gangs from El Salvador, which have thousands of members there and in the United States, have gained reputations for horrific violence. As a result, the U.S. government has sought to establish formal links with police in El Salvador and elsewhere in order to make a coordinated international effort against criminal organizations (Archibold, 2007).

Just as multinational corporations have emerged during the past 20 years, organized crime has also developed global networks. Increasingly transnational criminal groups "live and operate in a borderless world" (Zagaris, 1998: 1402). Senator John Kerry describes a "global criminal axis" involving the drug trade, money laundering, and terrorism (Kerry, 1997). In addition, organized crime groups are also involved in sexual slavery in which women and children are lured or transported across international borders and held as prisoners while being forced to sell their bodies in the sex trade for the benefit of their captors.

 Several organizations attempt to assist people who are victimized by human traffickers. The Freedom Network is a coalition of organizations focused on human trafficking and sexual slavery. To link to this website, go to *The American System of Criminal Justice* 12e companion site at academic.cengage.com/criminaljustice/cole.

In the aftermath of September 11, American law enforcement and intelligence officials increased their efforts to monitor and thwart international organizations that seek to attack the United States and its citizens. Many of these organizations use criminal activities, such as drug smuggling and stolen credit card numbers, to fund their efforts. Because the flow of money and weapons to organizations that employ terrorist tactics for political purposes is so closely connected to international crime networks, the United States will undoubtedly devote additional personnel and resources to this issue. The American government seeks to cut off the supply of money and weapons to these organizations as well as to avoid the worst-case scenario of a transfer of nuclear material or weapons from a Russian crime organization to Al-Qaida or other groups intent on using such materials to attack the United States.

Crimes without Victims

Crimes without victims involve a willing and private exchange of goods or services that are in strong demand but illegal—in other words, offenses against morality. Examples include prostitution, gambling, and drug sales and use. These are called "victimless crimes" because those involved do not feel that they are being harmed. Prosecution for these offenses is justified on the grounds that society as a whole is harmed because the moral fabric of the community is threatened. However, using the law to enforce moral standards is costly. The system is swamped by these cases, which often require the use of police informers and thus open the door for payoffs and other kinds of corruption.

The "war on drugs" is the most obvious example of policies against one type of victimless crime. Possession and sale of drugs—marijuana, heroin, cocaine, opium, amphetamines—have been illegal in the United States for over a hundred years. Especially during the past 40 years, extensive government resources have been used to enforce these laws and punish offenders. In "One Man's Journey Inside the Criminal Justice System" (go to *The American System of Criminal Justice* 12e companion site at academic.cengage.com/criminaljustice/cole), Chuck Terry describes his love of heroin and the consequences as he traveled inside the criminal justice system.

crimes without victims
Offenses involving a willing and private exchange of illegal goods or services that are in strong demand. Participants do not feel they are being harmed, but these crimes are prosecuted on the ground that society as whole is being harmed.

political crime
An act, usually done for ideological purposes, that constitutes a threat against the state (such as treason, sedition, or espionage) or a criminal act by a state.

Political Crime

Political crime refers to criminal acts either by the government or against the government that are carried out for ideological purposes (F. E. Hagan, 1997: 2). Political criminals believe they are following a morality that is above the law. Examples include James Kopp—arrested for the murder of Dr. Barnett Slepian near Buffalo, New York, and of other doctors who performed abortions—and Eric Rudolph, wanted for the bombing of abortion clinics in Atlanta and Birmingham and the pipe bomb explosion at the Atlanta Olympics. Similarly, shocking acts of violence that are labeled as terrorism, including the 1995 bombing of the federal building in Oklahoma City by Timothy McVeigh and the 2001 attacks on the World Trade Center and Pentagon, spring from political motivations.

Sex workers such as this prostitute provide a service that is in demand but illegal. Are these willing and private exchanges truly "victimless"?

© Lynsey Addario/Corbis

In some authoritarian states, merely criticizing the government is a crime that can lead to prosecution and imprisonment. In Western democracies today, there are few political crimes other than treason, which is rare. Although many illegal acts, such as the World Trade Center and Oklahoma City bombings, can be traced to political motives, they are prosecuted as visible crimes under laws against bombing, arson, and murder rather than as political crimes per se.

Political crimes against the government include activities such as treason, sedition (rebellion), and espionage. Since the nation's founding, many laws have been passed in response to perceived threats to the established order. The Sedition Act of 1789 made it a crime to utter or publish statements against the government. The Smith Act of 1940 made it a crime to call for the overthrow of the government by force or violence. During the Vietnam War, the federal government used charges of criminal conspiracy to deter those who opposed its military policies. The foregoing examples became obsolete as federal judges' interpretations of the Constitution expanded the definition of free speech and thereby limited the government's authority to pursue prosecutions based on an individual's expression of political beliefs and policy preferences. However, in the aftermath of September 11, the U.S. government entered a new era in which people were detained or prosecuted based on their alleged connections to organizations employing terror tactics.

Cybercrime

As new technologies emerge, so do people who take advantage of them for their own gain. One has only to think of the impact of the invention of the automobile to realize the extent to which the computer age will lead to new kinds of criminality. Today, the justice system is facing the ramifications of cybercrimes on criminal law.

cybercrimes
Offenses that involve the use of one or more computers.

Cybercrimes involve the use of computers and the Internet to commit acts against people, property, public order, or morality. Thus, cybercriminals have learned "new ways to do old tricks." Some use computers to steal information, resources, or funds. These thefts can be aimed at simply stealing money or they can involve the theft of companies' trade secrets, chemical formulas, and other information that could be quite valuable to competing businesses. Others use computers for malicious, destructive acts, such as releasing Internet viruses and "worms" to harm computer systems. In addition, there are widespread problems with people illegally downloading software, music, videos, and other copyrighted materials (Hinduja, 2007). Although such acts, which are done by millions of Americans every day, are actually federal crimes, they are seldom prosecuted unless the government identifies individuals or organizations with substantial involvement in such activities. In addition, new issues continually arise that produce suggestions about criminalizing new forms of cyber behavior, such as cyberbullying between teens that leads to psychological harms and behavioral problems (Hinduja and Patchin, 2007; Patchin and Hinduja, 2006).

identity theft
The theft of social security numbers, credit card numbers, and other information in order to secure loans, withdraw bank funds, and purchase merchandise while posing as someone else, the unsuspecting victim, who will eventually lose money in these transactions.

Identity theft has become a huge problem affecting many middle-class and affluent Americans who would otherwise seldom find themselves victimized by criminals (Collins, 2005). Perpetrators of identity theft use other people's credit card numbers and social security numbers to secure fraudulent loans and steal money and merchandise. Other offenders use the Internet to disseminate child pornography, to advertise sexual services, or to stalk the unsuspecting. Police departments have given special emphasis to stopping computer predators who establish online relationships with juveniles in order to manipulate those children into sexual victimization. Thus officers often pretend to be juveniles in online conservations in "chat rooms" in order to see if sexual predators will attempt to cultivate a relationship and set up a personal meeting (Eichenwald, 2006).

In attacking these problems, the FBI's National Computer Crime Squad lists its responsibilities as covering the following:

- Intrusions of the Public Switched Network (the telephone company)
- Major computer network intrusions
- Network integrity violations
- Privacy violations
- Industrial espionage
- Pirated computer software
- Other crimes where the computer is a major factor in committing the criminal offense

The global nature of the Internet presents new challenges to the criminal justice system. For example, in 2008, a Colombian man was sentenced to nine years in prison by a U.S. district court for installing keystroke logging software on computers in hotel business centers and other public-access computer locations. He collected personal information, such as bank account numbers and passwords, from 600 people who used those computers. Subsequently, the personal and financial information enabled him to steal $1.4 million. The FBI arrested him during one of his trips to the United States (U.S. Dept. of Justice, 2008). In another example, stolen credit card numbers are sold on the Internet, primarily by dealers based in countries that were formerly part of the Soviet Union. Computer hackers steal large numbers of credit card numbers from the computer systems of legitimate businesses and sell the numbers in bulk to dealers who sell them throughout the world via members-only websites. Credit card fraud costs online merchants more than $1 billion each year (Richtel, 2002).

It is extremely difficult to know how many cybercrimes occur and how much money is lost through identity theft, auction fraud, investment fraud, and other forms of financial computer crime. The federal government's Internet Crime Complaint Center (IC3) publishes an annual report that provides perspective on the question by compiling information on complaints filed each year. In 2007, the IC3 received nearly 207,000 complaints about cybercrime financial losses totaling more than $239 million (Internet Crime Complaint Center, 2008). These cybercrimes primarily were committed by perpetrators in the United States (63 percent), but people in other countries also victimized Americans regularly. The other leading countries of origin for cybercriminal enterprises were Great Britain (15 percent), Nigeria (6 percent), Canada (6 percent), and Romania (2 percent) (Internet Crime Complaint Center, 2008).

Efforts to create and enforce effective laws that will address such activities have been hampered by the international nature of cybercrime. Agencies in various countries are seeking to improve their ability to cooperate and share information. However, law enforcement officials throughout the world are not equally committed to and capable of catching cyberthieves and hackers. Criminals in some countries may have better computer equipment and expertise than do the officials trying to catch them. However, the FBI and other law enforcement agencies have made a concerted effort to improve their equipment, hire computer experts, and train their officers to investigate cybercrime. The FBI uses Cyber Action Teams or CATs to act quickly in addressing large-scale or especially damaging cybercrimes. The FBI describes CATs as "small, highly trained teams of FBI agents, analysts, and computer forensics and malicious code experts who travel around the world on a moment's notice to respond to cyber intrusions" (FBI, 2006). For example, in 2006 an FBI CAT team traveled to Morocco and Turkey to help those governments apprehend cybercriminals who were unleashing

The FBI describes its priorities and efforts in fighting computer crime on its cybercrime page. To link to this website, go to *The American System of Criminal Justice* 12e companion site at academic.cengage.com/criminaljustice/cole.

CLOSE UP

Hate Crimes: A Threatening Version of Visible Crime

AFRICAN AMERICAN CHURCHES are set afire in the Southeast; the home of the mayor of West Hartford, Connecticut, is defaced by swastikas and anti-Semitic graffiti; gay Wyoming student Matthew Shepard is murdered; an African American woman in Maryland is beaten and doused with lighter fluid in a race-based attack. These are just a few of the more than 7,500 hate crimes reported to the police each year. The U.S. Department of Justice said that threats, assaults, and acts of vandalism against Arab Americans and people of South Asian ancestry increased in the months following the events of September 11. Crimes based on the victims' ethnicity may become more diversified as Americans react to their anger and fear about the threat of terrorism from foreign organizations.

Hate crimes have been added to the penal codes of 46 states and the District of Columbia. These are violent acts aimed at individuals or groups of a particular race, ethnicity, religion, sexual orientation, or gender. The laws also make it a crime to vandalize religious buildings and cemeteries or to intimidate another person out of bias. Although the Ku Klux Klan, the World Church of the Creator, and Nazi-style "skinhead" groups represent the most visible perpetrators, most hate crimes are committed by individuals acting alone. For example, analysts believe that a single individual sent threatening letters to African American actor Taye Diggs and his wife, white Broadway actress Idina Menzel, in 2004. In 2008, an Ohio man was arrested by the FBI for sending threatening letters to Supreme Court Justice Clarence Thomas and other African American men who are married to white women.

Hate crime laws have been challenged on the ground that they violate the right of free speech. Some argue that racial and religious slurs must be allowed on this basis. In response, supporters of hate crime laws say that limits must be placed on freedom of speech and that some words are so hateful that they fall outside the free speech protection of the First Amendment.

In *Wisconsin v. Mitchell* (1993), the U.S. Supreme Court upheld a state law providing for a more severe sentence in cases "in which the offender intentionally selects the person against whom the crime [is committed] because of the race, religion, color, disability, sexual orientation, national origin or ancestry of that person."

In a society that is becoming more diverse, hate crimes hurt not only their victims but the social fabric itself. Democracy depends on people sharing common ideals and working together. When members of groups are pitted against one another or fear each other, the entire community suffers. But is criminal law the way to attack this problem?

Researching the Internet

 The American Psychological Association provides information about hate crimes on its web page "Hate Crimes." To link to this website, go to *The American System of Criminal Justice* 12e companion site at academic.cengage.com/criminal justice/cole.

Sources: Drawn from Associated Press, "Menzel Takes Stage Despite Racist Threats," December 6, 2004 (http://www.boston.com); J. Jacobs, "Should Hate Be a Crime?" *Public Interest*, Fall 1993, pp. 1–14; C. Newton, "Crimes against Arabs, South Asians Up," *Washington Post*, June 26, 2002 (http://www.washingtonpost.com); "Ohio Man Accused of Threat to Justice," *New York Times*, April 10, 2008 (http://www.nytimes.com).

malicious codes on the Internet and engaging in the theft of credit card numbers (FBI, 2006).

Differences in legal principles and social values also impact the effectiveness of pursuing cybercrime. For instance, in the United States, some laws intended to punish people involved in online pornography have been struck down for violating First Amendment rights to free expression.

Since the events of September 11, many countries' law enforcement agencies have increased their communication and cooperation in order to thwart terrorist activities. As these countries cooperate in investigating and monitoring the financial transactions of groups that employ terror tactics, it seems likely that they will also improve their capacity to discover and pursue cybercriminals. For example, the FBI has also joined forces with the national police agencies of Australia, Canada, New Zealand, and the United Kingdom to form the Strategic Alliance Cyber Crime Working Group, an international organization for sharing information and cooperating in cybercrime investigations (FBI, 2008).

Law enforcement agencies cannot prevent cybercrimes from occurring. Normally they react to such harmful activities in order to limit theft and damage. People cannot rely on law enforcement efforts to protect them from harm. The first defense against some forms of cybercrime is citizen awareness and caution.

How much do you know about cybercrime? Consider how you would address the problem presented in "Civic Engagement: Your Role in the System."

Which of these six main types of crime is of greatest concern to you? If you are like most people, it is visible crime. Thus, as a nation, we devote most of our criminal justice resources to dealing with such crimes. To develop policies to address these crimes, however, we need to know more about the amount of crime and all the types of crimes that occur in the United States. Within the various categories of crime, new types of offenses can emerge as society evolves and changes. As discussed in the Close Up box, hate crimes represent a category of visible crime based on specific motives that target individuals because of their race or ethnicity. Further, new types of offenses can arise within a given category of crime. As we have seen, creative thieves continually find new ways to exploit technology for profit in various forms of cybercrime. For example, criminals have become increasingly skilled at creating phony websites that look identical to websites of legitimate businesses as well as stealing information from laptop computers that are connected to wireless networks. Because of the dynamic and innovative nature of contemporary criminal activities, law enforcement officials must attempt to match the creativity and resources of lawbreakers in order to protect society.

civic engagement your role in the system

Your elderly grandparents have finally decided to buy a computer, sign up with an Internet service provider, and begin participating in the cyberuniverse through email, online banking, and all of the computer activities that they have seen described in newspapers and television. They say to you, "How do we protect ourselves from this identity theft stuff that we've heard about?" *Make a list of suggestions to help these newcomers avoid becoming victims of cybercrime.* How do your suggestions compare to the advice provided for the public by the federal government? To link to this website, go to *The American System of Criminal Justice* 12e companion site at academic.cengage .com/criminaljustice/cole.

checkpoint

12. What are the six main types of crime?
13. What groups are overrepresented among those arrested for visible or street crimes?
14. Why is the term *occupational crime* more useful today than the term *white-collar crime*?
15. What is the function of *organized crime*?
16. What is meant by the term *crimes without victims*?
17. What are political crimes?
18. What types of criminal activities are labeled as cybercrime?

THE CRIME PROBLEM TODAY

Although the crime rate generally declined from the 1990s through the initial years of the twenty-first century, 71 percent of respondents to a national survey in 2007 expressed the belief that crime was increasing, and an additional 8 percent believed that crimes rates had remained unchanged (BJS, 2008: Table 2.34.2007). The gaps between the public's perceptions and available information highlight several important questions for students of criminal justice. How much crime actually exists in the United States? Is the United States the most crime-ridden nation of the world's industrial democracies? How do we measure the amount of crime? What are the current and future trends? By trying to answer these questions, we can gain a better understanding of the crime problem and the public's beliefs about it.

A wealth of statistical information on crime and the justice system can be found in the Sourcebook of Criminal Justice Statistics. To link to this website, go to *The American System of Criminal Justice* 12e companion site at academic.cengage.com/criminaljustice/cole.

The Worst of Times?

There has always been too much crime. Ever since the nation's founding, people have felt threatened by it. Outbreaks of violence erupted after the Civil War, after World War I, during Prohibition, and during the Great Depression (Friedman, 1993). But the nation has also seen extended periods, such as the 1950s,

FIGURE 1.1

A century of murder

The murder rate per 100,000 people in the United States has risen, fallen, and (since 1960) risen again. Data from the last several years show a significant decline from the peak in 1980. What causes these trends?

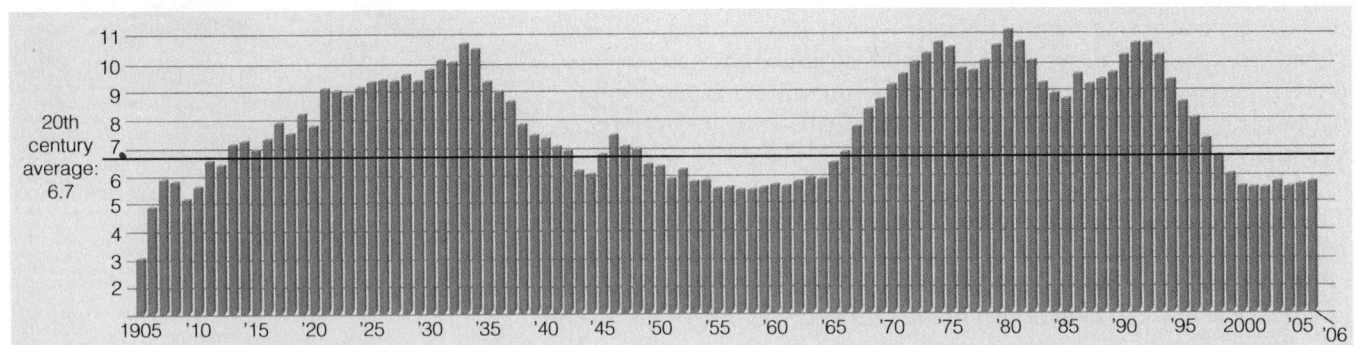

Sources: Bureau of Justice Statistics, *Sourcebook of Criminal Justice Statistics, 1999* (Washington, DC: U.S. Government Printing Office, 2000), Table 3.146; Bureau of Justice Statistics, *Sourcebook of Criminal Justice Statistics, 2007* (Washington, DC: U.S. Government Printing Office, 2000), Table 3.106.2006 (http://www.albany.edu/sourcebook).

marked by comparatively little crime. Thus, ours is neither the best nor the worst of times.

Although crime is an old problem, the amount and types of crime do not remain consistent. During both the 1880s and the 1930s, pitched battles took place between strikers and company police. Race riots causing deaths and property destruction occurred in Chicago, Omaha, Tulsa, and other cities between 1919 and 1921. These riots typically occurred when white mobs attacked African Americans because of a rumored crime, such as Omaha's riot after an African American was accused of attacking a white woman. Organized crime was rampant during the 1930s. The murder rate, which reached a high in 1933 and a low during the 1950s, rose to a new high in 1980 of 10.2 per 100,000 people and then declined to 5.7 per 100,000 in 2006. As illustrated in Figure 1.1, the trends show a steady decline since 1993.

What if we examine crimes other than murder? Overall rates for violent crimes and property crimes have dropped since 1991, but the rates for 2006 remained well above the crime rates experienced by Americans at the close of the relatively peaceful 1950s. The rate of violent crime was 158 offenses per 100,000 people in 1961. That rate rose over the next three decades until it peaked in 1991 and 1992 at 758 violent offenses per 100,000 (Figure 1.2). However, from 1992 to 2004, the violent crime rate dropped steadily to 463 offenses per 100,000, a rate lower than any year since 1977, followed by a slight uptick to 469 in 2005 and 474 in 2006 (BJS, 2007a: Table 3.106.2006).

Rates of property crimes show a similar pattern: rising dramatically from 1960 through 1991 before falling each year through 2006 (see Figure 1.3 for an overview). Property crimes rates went from 1,748 per 100,000 people in 1961 to more than 5,000 per 100,000 in the first years of the 1980s. Although there was a small drop during the mid-1980s, with a low point of 4,498 per 100,000 in 1984, the rate pushed back up toward 5,000 in the first years of the 1990s. After falling steadily through the rest of the 1990s, the property crime rate was only 3,335 in 2006. Although this figure was nearly double the rate of 1961, it returned property crime rates to a level not seen since 1969 (BJS, 2003f: Table 3.103). Americans may not accurately recognize that crime rates have fallen for more than a decade, yet they may be justified in labeling crime as a serious national problem, especially if they are comparing today's crime rates with those of the early 1960s.

The drop in crime rates raises interesting questions about why crime has declined in the United States. You will recall from "New Directions in Criminal

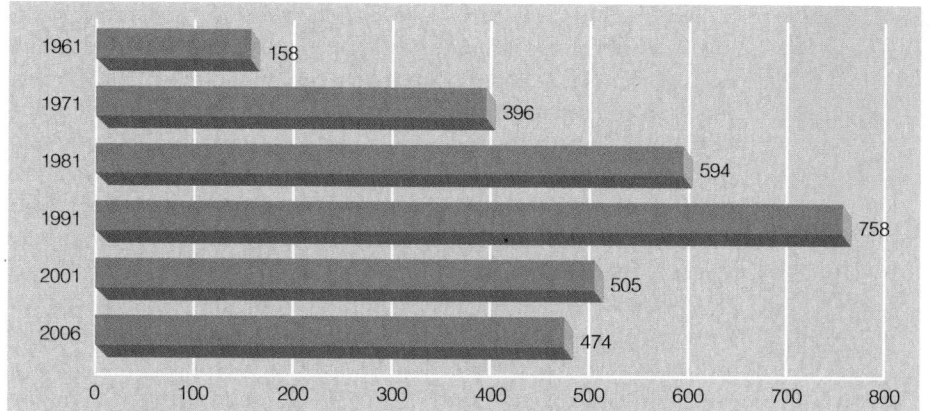

FIGURE 1.2
Violent crime rates per 100,000 people

Source: Bureau of Justice Statistics, *Sourcebook of Criminal Justice Statistics, 2006* (Washington, DC: U.S. Government Printing Office, 2007), Table 3.106.2006 (http://www.albany.edu/sourcebook).

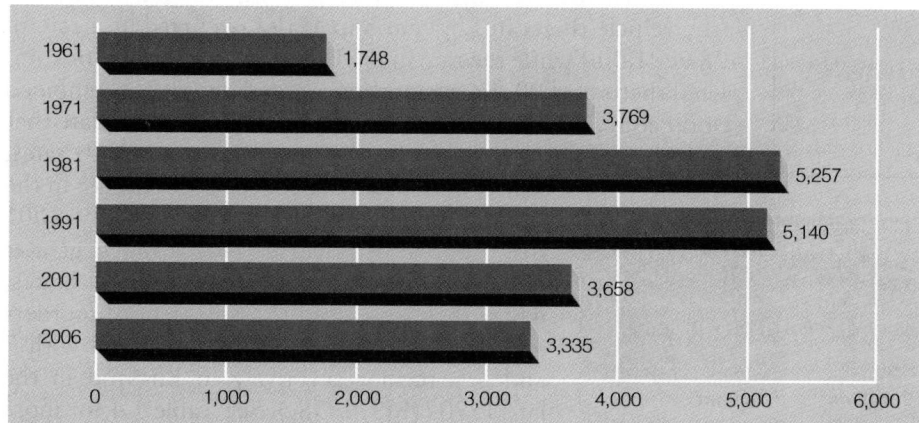

FIGURE 1.3
Property crime rates per 100,000 people

Source: Bureau of Justice Statistics, *Sourcebook of Criminal Justice Statistics, 2006* (Washington, DC: U.S. Government Printing Office, 2007), Table 3.106.2006 (http://www.albany.edu/sourcebook).

Justice Policy," earlier in this chapter, that some observers argue that reductions in crime occurred as a result of the policy of increasing the number of offenders held in prison and holding them for longer sentences. The debate over imprisonment illustrates the continuing disagreements about which factors shape crime rates. As you read subsequent chapters in the book, you will encounter other possible explanations for changes in crime rates. For example, demographic changes over time affect the number of young men who are in their crime-prone years (ages 16–24) at any given moment in history. Economic changes affect the number of people who are unemployed and living in poverty from year to year. In addition, police officials constantly experiment with new law enforcement strategies, some of which may have affected crime rates in the past decade. As you consider subsequent chapters concerning theories of crime and law enforcement policies, think about how various factors can affect trends in crime rates.

The Most Crime-Ridden Nation?

How does the amount of crime in the United States compare with that in other countries? It is often said the United States has more crime than do other modern industrial nations. But as James Lynch argues, this belief is too simple to be useful (1995: 11). He points out that comparing crime rates in different nations is difficult. First, one must choose nations that are similar to the United States—nations with democratic governments, similar levels of economic development, and the same kinds of legal systems (MacCoun et al., 1993). Second, one must get data from reliable sources. The two main sources of cross-national crime data are Interpol (the international police agency based in Europe) and the International Crime Survey.

TABLE 1.3 — Comparative Homicide Rates per 100,000 People; Average Rates, 1999–2001

Homicide rates in the United States exceed those of industrialized democracies, but some developing countries have higher rates.

Nation	Homicide Rate
United States	5.6
Finland	2.9
France	1.7
England and Wales	1.6
Spain	1.1
Russia	22.0
South Africa	55.9

Source: G. Barclay and C. Tavares, *International Comparisons of Criminal Justice Statistics 2001*, October 2003, British Home Office Report, Table 1.1 (http://www.csdp.org/research/hosb1203.pdf.).

TABLE 1.4 — Percentage of Respondents Victimized by Specific Crimes During 2000

These data from the International Crime Victimization Surveys indicate that the United States does not lead the world in rates of non-homicide offenses.

Nation	Auto Theft	Burglary	Robbery
United States	0.5	1.8	0.6
Australia	1.9	3.9	1.2
Canada	1.4	2.3	0.9
Denmark	1.1	3.1	0.7
England and Wales	2.1	2.8	1.2
France	1.7	1.0	1.1
Japan	0.1	1.1	0.1
Sweden	1.3	1.7	0.9
Switzerland	0.3	1.1	0.7

Source: United Nations Interregional Crime and Justice Research Institute (UNICRI), *The International Crime Victimization Surveys*, 2001, Appendix 4, pp. 178–79 (http://www.unicri.it/icvs/index.htm).

Lynch compares early 1990s crime rates in the United States and in Australia, Canada, England and Wales, West Germany, France, the Netherlands, Sweden, and Switzerland. Both police and victim data show that the homicide rate in the United States was more than twice that in Canada, the next highest country, and many times that in the other countries. The same was generally true at that time for robbery, but American robbery rates subsequently declined in the later 1990s to levels below that of several other countries.

Other studies examine the data concerning property crimes, with surprising results. The victim surveys show that rates of property crime are lower in the United States than in several other industrialized countries. In 2003, for example, the household burglary rate in England and Wales was 34 per 1,000 households, whereas in the United States it was only 30. Similarly, vehicle thefts in England and Wales occurred at a rate of 108 per 1,000 while the rate in the United States was 67 for completed thefts and 90 for attempts and completed thefts combined (Dodd et al., 2004). Like Lynch's study, other data indicate that the main difference between the countries lay in homicide rates, which were more than three times higher in the United States than in England in 1999–2001 (see Table 1.3). Firearms play a much greater role in violent crimes in the United States, where they were used in 68 percent of murders and 41 percent of robberies, compared with 7 and 5 percent respectively in England in the late 1990s (BJS, 1998c). See Table 1.4 for more on non-homicide offenses.

In sum, the risk of lethal violence is much higher in the United States than in other well-established industrial democracies, but it is much lower than in industrialized countries, such as Russia and South Africa, that have sought to move from authoritarian governments to democracy in the past two decades. However, the risk of minor violence is not greater in the United States than in several other countries. Moreover, the United States has lower rates of serious property crime, even compared with many of those countries thought to be safer (J. Lynch, 1995: 17).

Interestingly, crime rates in Western countries besides the United States may have begun to decline (Tonry, 1998b: 22–23). Crime rates in Canada fell for a decade before rising 6 percent in 2003 from increases in counterfeiting and property crime. The rates subsequently declined again in 2004 and 2005. Canada experienced continued declines for most violent crimes (Gannon, 2006). According to the British Crime Survey, crime in England and Wales fell 42 percent from 1995 to 2007, with burglaries reduced by nearly 60 percent and violent crimes dropping by 40 percent (Nicholas et al., 2007). Significant declines in crime appeared in crime data from many of the 11 industrial countries in the International Crime Victimization Surveys during the 1990s (Mayhew and van Dijk, 1997). We can gain more insight into the nature and extent of crime in the United States by looking at countries, such as Iceland, where there is little crime. Some might say that because Iceland is small, homogeneous, and somewhat isolated, we cannot

COMPARATIVE PERSPECTIVE

Iceland: A Country with Little Crime

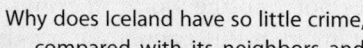

Why does Iceland have so little crime, compared with its neighbors and other developed countries? Is it the size of the population? The homogeneity of the people? The physical isolation from the major centers of Europe? What is it like to live in a country where there are only two homicides per year, and where the first bank robbery with a firearm occurred in 1984?

Iceland is an island republic the size of Virginia. It has a population of 297,000. The country retains strong cultural ties to Denmark, which ruled it from 1380 until 1944, and to the rest of Scandinavia. The Icelandic population is ethnically homogeneous, and policies have been instituted to restrict immigration. There are relatively small differences along class lines, literacy is very high, and about 95 percent of the people there belong to the Evangelical Lutheran Church. The people enjoy a high standard of living, an extensive health and welfare system, and a low unemployment rate.

Even though 90 percent of the Icelandic people live in urban areas, the society is one where extended families, strong community ties, and a homogeneous culture seem to act as effective agents of social control. Iceland is also relatively equalitarian: There are no slums, and education and health care are provided to all, thus further reducing social disparities.

After centuries of isolation, Iceland first came into extensive contact with European and North American countries at the end of World War II. The result has been a cultural lag in the shift to industrialization and urbanization. Iceland has retained many aspects of an agrarian society.

When compared with those of the United States, Icelandic crime rates are extremely low. For example, the assault rate per 100,000 people is 14, whereas in the United States it is 310; the rate for homicide is 0.73 in Iceland and 5.60 in the United States; the rate for rape is 16.35 in Iceland and 33.00 in the United States. The country's homogeneous population, geographic isolation, and prohibition of handgun ownership all may contribute to its low level of violence.

The Icelandic public has become most concerned by the increase in drug use during the past two decades, but such use remains minuscule compared with that of other Western countries. Marijuana use increased during the 1970s but has declined since then. Still, a study conducted in 1997 found a greater percentage of Icelanders than citizens of other Nordic nations had used marijuana at least once, with the exception of Denmark. However, only 1.6 percent admitted using marijuana during the last six months. This is similar to the other Nordic countries.

Although Icelanders express much concern about the use of hard drugs, the problem seems minor when compared with drug use in the United States. In 1984, about 4 percent of Icelanders aged 16–36 said they had consumed amphetamines. Not until 1983 did police find cocaine; the first seizure of a significant amount (one kilo) took place in 1987. Yet scholars believe that drug use has increased considerably during the past decade.

Undoubtedly the size of Iceland's 's population and its isolation from the major drug supply routes account for the low level of drug abuse. However, special drug police were established in the 1970s. Today, the Reykjavik police allocate a greater portion of their budget to drug control than do the police in Copenhagen and Oslo. But containing the drug problem is enhanced by the ease with which the country may be "sealed" because import routes are few, and it is difficult for drug users to hide their habit in such a tightly knit community. There seem to be no organized drug rings in Iceland.

Whereas most Western countries are preoccupied with the "war on drugs," this social problem is overshadowed in Iceland by concern over the abuse of alcohol. Alcohol abuse correlates strongly with the crime rate, particularly drunken driving. Overall consumption of alcohol has increased during recent decades, and public drunkenness is the most common violation of the criminal law.

With the highest number of automobiles per capita in the world, Iceland strictly enforces its drunken-driving rules, resulting in a high arrest rate (1,400 per 100,000 people versus 386 per 100,000 in the United States). Most arrests occur as a result of intensive routine highway checks. When blood tests reveal a level of 0.5 to 1.2 per milliliter alcohol, drivers lose their licenses for one month. When tests show a level of more than 1.2 per milliliter, drivers lose their licenses for a year. A third offense means a prison sentence. Low levels of serious crime and a policy of treating alcohol offenses severely have resulted in the fact that 20 percent of prisoners in Iceland have been committed for drunken driving.

The number of crimes reported to the Icelandic police reflects the rapid transformation of the society during the past 40 years. As in other countries, the crime rate increased after World War II but leveled off during the past decade. Several factors can account for the increases in crime compared with that of a generation ago. For example, the growth in economic crime seems to be a consequence of more-complex business activities. Concern over the abuse of alcohol has resulted in proactive law enforcement policies that have increased the number of arrests. But these "increases" must be viewed in the context of the comparatively low levels of criminality in Iceland. As in other Scandinavian countries, as well as such low-crime countries as Switzerland, cultural, geographic, economic, and public policy factors appear to explain the relative absence of crime in Iceland.

Sources: Drawn from Helgi Gunnlaugsson, "Icelandic Sociology and the Social Production of Criminological Knowledge," in *From a Doll's House to the Welfare State: Reflections on Nordic Sociology*, ed. Margareta Bertilsson and Goran Therborn (Montreal: International Sociological Association, 1998), 83–88; Omar H. Kristmundsson, "Crime and the Crime Control System of Iceland," unpublished paper, University of Connecticut, 1999.

compare the two countries. But as we can see in the Comparative Perspective on page 31, other factors help explain differences in the amount and types of crime in different countries.

The preceding discussions indicate that, contrary to public perceptions, crime rates in the United States have declined since the early 1990s and that the United States does not lead the world in crime. This information warns us to avoid accepting an image of the contemporary United States as an especially crime-ridden nation. According to the data, we must recognize that the level and nature of crime in the United States can change over time and that other countries have crime problems of their own. Bear in mind, however, that all the conclusions rest on one factor: our reliance on data about crime and crime rates. What if our data are not accurate? Can we really know for sure that crime declined or that our country compares favorably with other countries in the world? Further, the development of public policies in criminal justice often rests on crime statistics. Thus we work hard to identify ways to improve our knowledge about and measurement of crime. We know, however, that crime data can be flawed. Let's look closely at the sources of crime data and ask ourselves if they give us a true picture of crime in the United States.

Keeping Track of Crime

One of the frustrations in studying criminal justice is the lack of accurate means of knowing the amount of crime. Surveys reveal that much more crime occurs than is reported to the police. This is referred to as the **dark figure of crime**.

Most homicides and auto thefts are reported to the police. In the case of a homicide, a body must be accounted for, and insurance companies require a police report before they will pay for a stolen car. However, according to surveys of victims, a majority of rape or sexual assault victims do not report the attack; almost one-half of robbery victims and nearly 60 percent of victims of simple assault do not do so. Figure 1.4 shows the percentage of victimizations not reported to the police.

Crimes go unreported for many reasons. Some victims of rape and assault do not wish to be embarrassed by public disclosure and police questioning; the most common reason for not reporting a violent crime is that it was viewed by the victims as a personal, private matter. In the case of larceny, robbery, or bur-

dark figure of crime
A metaphor referring to the dangerousness dimension of crimes that are never reported to the police.

FIGURE 1.4
Percentage of victimizations not reported to the police
Why do some people not report crimes to the police? What can be done to encourage reporting?

Source: Bureau of Justice, *Criminal Victimization in the United States, 2005 Statistical Tables*, NCJ 215244, Table 91 (http://www.ojp.usdoj.gov).

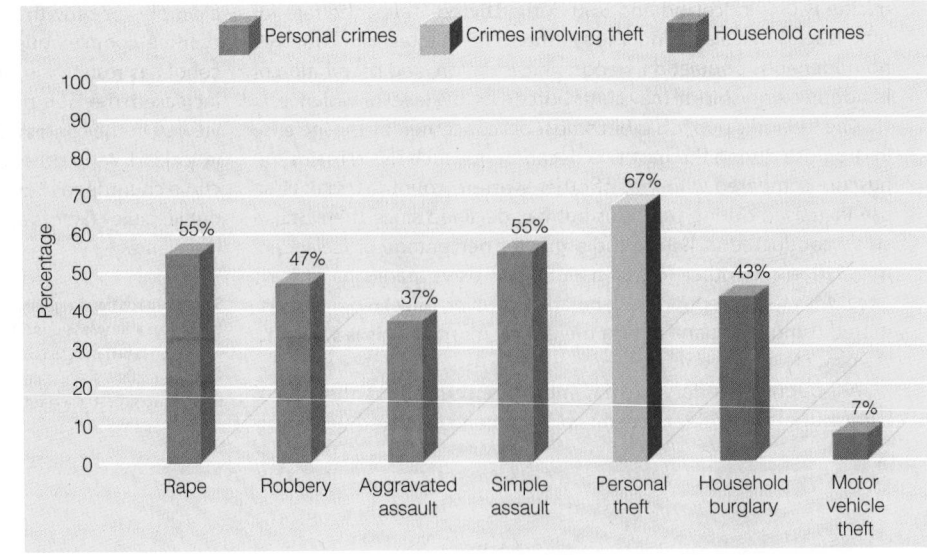

glary, the value of the property lost may not be worth the effort of calling the police. Many people refrain from reporting crimes because they do not want to become involved, fill out papers at the station house, perhaps go to court, or appear at a police lineup. They may not want police to come to their homes to ask questions if they have stolen property, drugs, unregistered guns, or other evidence of their own illegal activities there. In some neighborhoods, people may fear retaliation from gangs or individual criminals if they go to the police. As these examples suggest, many people feel the costs and risks of reporting crimes outweigh the gains.

Until 1972, the only crimes counted by government were those that were known to the police and that the police reported to the Federal Bureau of Investigation for the FBI's Uniform Crime Reports (UCR). Since then, the Department of Justice has sponsored the National Crime Victimization Surveys (NCVS), which pose questions to a sample of the public to find out how much victimization has occurred. One might hope that the data from these two sources would give us a clear picture of the amount of crime, crime trends, and the characteristics of offenders. However, the picture remains blurred and imperfect because of differences in the way crime is measured by the UCR and the NCVS as well as flaws contained in the data reported by each of these sources.

Uniform Crime Reports

Annually published statistical summary of crimes reported to the police, based on voluntary reports to the FBI by local, state, and federal law enforcement agencies.

The Uniform Crime Reports

Issued each year by the FBI, the **Uniform Crime Reports (UCR)** are a statistical summary of crimes reported to the police. At the urging of the International Association of Chiefs of Police, Congress in 1930 authorized this system for compiling crime data (Rosen, 1995). The UCR come from a voluntary national network of some 16,000 local, state, and federal law enforcement agencies, policing 93 percent of the U.S. population. The main publication of the UCR is an annual volume, *Crime in the United States*.

 The FBI's Uniform Crime Reports are available online under the "Reports & Publications" link. To link to this website, go to *The American System of Criminal Justice* 12e companion site at academic.cengage.com/criminaljustice/cole.

With the drop in crime in recent years, police executives have faced new pressures to show that their cities are following the national trend. Some officials have even falsified their crime statistics as promotions, pay raises, and department budgets have become increasingly dependent on positive data. For example, an audit of the Atlanta police released in 2004 found that they had underreported crimes as part of an effort to make the city appear safer when it was competing to be the host city for the 1996 Summer Olympics (Niesse, 2004). In 2005 leaders of police unions in New York City alleged that officers were pressured to report felonies as merely misdemeanors or treat a series of crimes as a single event in order to help the city show favorable results in its efforts to combat crime (Moses, 2005). Because the FBI relies on reports from local police departments, the UCR are inaccurate when police agencies underreport crime in order to advance the organizational self-interest of their city government and agency.

The UCR use standard definitions to ensure uniform data on the 29 types of crimes listed in Table 1.5. For 8 major crimes Part I—(Index Offenses)—the data show factors such as age,

TABLE 1.5	**Uniform Crime Reports Offenses**

The UCR present data on 8 index offenses and 21 other crimes for which there is less information. A limitation of the UCR is that they tabulate only crimes that are reported to the police.

Part I (Index Offenses)	**Part II (Other Offenses)**
1. Criminal homicide	9. Simple assaults
2. Forcible rape	10. Forgery and counterfeiting
3. Robbery	11. Fraud
4. Aggravated assault	12. Embezzlement
5. Burglary	13. Buying, receiving, or possessing stolen property
6. Larceny/theft	14. Vandalism
7. Auto theft	15. Weapons (carrying, possession, etc.)
8. Arson	16. Prostitution and commercialized vice
	17. Sex offenses
	18. Violation of narcotic drug laws
	19. Gambling
	20. Offenses against the family and children
	21. Driving under the influence
	22. Violation of liquor laws
	23. Drunkenness
	24. Disorderly conduct
	25. Vagrancy
	26. All other offenses (excluding traffic)
	27. Suspicion
	28. Curfew and loitering (juvenile)
	29. Juvenile runaways

Source: Federal Bureau of Investigation, *Crime in the United States*, 2000 (Washington, DC: U.S. Government Printing Office, 2001).

race, and number of reported crimes solved. For the other 21 crimes Part II—(Other Offenses)—the data are less complete.

The UCR present crime data in three ways: (1) as *aggregates* (a total of 447,403 robberies were reported to the police in 2006), (2) as *percentage changes* over different periods (there was a 10.3 percent decrease in robberies from 1997 to 2006), and (3) as a *rate per 100,000 people* (the robbery rate in 2006 was 160.4) (FBI, 2007a).

The UCR provide a useful but incomplete picture of crime levels. The UCR fail to provide an accurate picture of crime in the United States for many reasons, including the following:

- They count only crimes reported to the police.

- They count and classify crimes but do not provide complete details about offenses.

- They rely on voluntary reports from local police departments.

- Local police may adjust the classification of crimes in order to protect the image of a police department or community.

- The definitions of specific crime categories can be interpreted inconsistently.

- They count only a specific set of crimes and do not focus on corporate, occupational, and computer crime.

- Seven percent of Americans live in jurisdictions where police agencies do not make reports to the UCR.

National Incident-Based Reporting System (NIBRS)
A reporting system in which the police describe each offense in a crime incident, together with data describing the offender, victim, and property.

In response to criticisms of the UCR, the FBI has made some changes in the program that are now being implemented nationwide. Some offenses have been redefined, and police agencies are being asked to report more details about crime events. Using the **National Incident-Based Reporting System (NIBRS)**, police agencies are to report all crimes committed during an incident, not just the most serious one, as well as data on offenders, victims, and the places where they interact. For example, the NIBRS seeks to gather detailed information on such matters as the race, sex, and age of the victim and offender; types of weapons used; value of property stolen; victim injuries; and relationship, if any, between the victim and offender. While the UCR now count incidents and arrests for the 8 index offenses and count arrests for other crimes, the NIBRS provides detailed incident data on 46 offenses in 22 crime categories. The NIBRS distinguishes between attempted and completed crimes as well. In 2004 the FBI reported that the UCR Program is continually converting to the more comprehensive and detailed NIBRS (FBI, 2004b: 502).

The National Crime Victimization Surveys

National Crime Victimization Surveys (NCVS)
Interviews of samples of the U.S. population conducted by the Bureau of Justice Statistics to determine the number and types of criminal victimization and thus the intent of unreported as well as reported crime.

A second source of crime data is the **National Crime Victimization Surveys (NCVS)**. Since 1972, the Census Bureau has done surveys to find out the extent and nature of crime victimization. Thus data have been gathered on unreported as well as reported crimes. Interviews are conducted twice each year with a national probability sample of approximately 76,000 people in 43,000 households. The same people are interviewed twice a year for three years and asked if they have been victimized in the last six months.

Each person is asked a set of screening questions (for example, did anyone beat you up, attack you, or hit you with something such as a rock or a bottle?) to determine whether he or she has been victimized. The person is then asked questions designed to elicit specific facts about the event, the offender, and any financial losses or physical disabilities caused by the crime.

Besides the household interviews, separate studies are also done to find out about the victimization of businesses. These data allow us to estimate how many crimes have occurred, learn more about the offenders, and note demographic patterns. The results show that for the crimes measured (rape, robbery, assault, burglary, theft), there were 23 million victimizations in 2005 (down from 43 million in 1973). This level is much higher than the number of crimes actually reported to the police suggests.

In reporting data from the NCVS, the Bureau of Justice Statistics often emphasizes households as the unit of analysis in order to present a more accurate picture of the dispersion of crime. All households do not experience the same risks of victimization. Most households are not victimized at all during a given year, whereas others experience multiple victimizations. For 2003, for example, the 24 million crimes were experienced by only 17 million households, according to the assessment developed from the survey (Klaus, 2004).

Although the NCVS provide a more complete picture of the nature and extent of crime than do the UCR, they too have flaws. Because government employees administer the surveys, the people interviewed tend not to report crimes in which they or members of their family took part. They also may not want to admit that a family member engages in crime, or they may be too embarrassed to admit that they have allowed themselves to be victimized more than once.

The NCVS are also imperfect because they depend on the victim's *perception* of an event. The theft of a child's lunch money by a bully may be reported by one person but not by another. People may say that their property was stolen when in fact they lost it. Moreover, people's memories of dates may fade, and they may misreport the year in which a crime occurred even though they remember the event itself clearly. In addition to the problem of victims' perceptions, Clayton Mosher, Terance Miethe, and Dretha Phillips (2002: 168), have identified other problems in relying on victim surveys:

- Surveys only cover a limited range of crimes.

- Surveys are based on a relatively small sample of people; there are risks that they will not be representative of the national population or that errors in data analysis will lead to erroneous conclusions about the nation as a whole.

- The identification of victimization can depend on how the survey questions are phrased.

The FBI describes the UCR and NCVS as complementary. Each is intended to supply information that is missing through the other's approach to measuring crime. Table 1.6 (p. 36) compares the Uniform Crime Reports and the National Crime Victimization Surveys.

In describing the two approaches, the FBI acknowledges that they do not provide a complete picture of crime in the United States. For example, the NCVS do not interview children under the age of 12 and do not include questions about certain crimes, such as arson and crimes against businesses. If such crimes are not reported to the police, and therefore not recorded in the UCR, they are therefore not included in the two main sources of crime data used by government policy makers.

Because there is no perfect way to measure crime, government agencies work to keep improving the available methods for counting, classifying, and analyzing the occurrence of crime each year. Students of criminal justice must recognize the limitations of crime data, so that they can discuss crime with the awareness that a complete and accurate picture of criminal offenses and victimization does not exist.

Trends in Crime

Experts agree that, contrary to public opinion and the claims of politicians, crime rates have not been steadily rising. The NCVS show that the victimization rate peaked in 1981 and has declined since then. The greatest declines are

TABLE 1.6	The UCR and the NCVS

Compare the data sources. Remember that the UCR tabulate only crimes reported to the police, while the NCVS are based on interviews with victims.

	Uniform Crime Reports	National Crime Victimization Surveys
Offenses Measured	Homicide	
	Rape	Rape
	Robbery (personal and commercial)	Robbery (personal)
	Assault (aggravated)	Assault (aggravated and simple)
	Burglary (commercial and household)	Household burglary
	Larceny (commercial and household)	Larceny (personal and household)
	Motor vehicle theft	Motor vehicle theft
	Arson	
Scope	Crimes reported to the police in most jurisdictions; considerable flexibility in developing small-area data	Crimes both reported and not reported to police; all data are for the nation as a whole; some data are available for a few large geographic areas
Collection Method	Police department reports to Federal Bureau of Investigation	Survey interviews: periodically measures the total number of crimes committed by asking a national sample of 43,000 households representing 76,000 people over the age of 12 about their experiences as victims of crime during a specific period
Kinds of Information	In addition to offense counts, provides information on crime clearances, persons arrested, persons charged, law enforcement officers killed and assaulted, and characteristics of homicide victims	Provides details about victims (such as age, race, sex, education, income, and whether the victim and offender were related) and about crimes (such as time and place of occurrence, whether or not reported to police, use of weapons, occurrence of injury, and economic consequences)
Sponsor	Department of Justice's Federal Bureau of Investigation	Department of Justice's Bureau of Justice Statistics

in property crimes, but crimes of violence have also dropped, especially since 1993. The violent crime victimization rate in the NCVS decreased by more than 50 percent for nearly all demographic categories, men, women, African Americans, and Hispanics. The only categories to experience lesser drops in violent crime victimization, primarily people with household incomes below $25,000, still experienced victimization rate drops in excess of 40 percent (Catalano, 2004: Table 6).

The UCR show similar results, revealing a rapid rise in crime rates beginning in 1964 and continuing until 1980, when the rates began to level off or decline. In fact, according to the UCR, property crimes have gone from a peak rate of 5,353 per 100,000 people in 1980 to a rate of 3,624 in 2002. Violent crime fell steadily from its peak of 758 per 100,000 in 1991 and 1992 to 495 in 2002 (BJS, 2003f: Table 3.103).

Figure 1.5 displays four measures of violent crime, adjusted for changes made in the NCVS in 1992. The top two measures are based on the victimization survey, while crimes recorded by the police and arrests are from the UCR and are presented below these. Remember that the differences in the trends indicated by the NCVS and the UCR are explained in part by the different data sources and different populations on which their tabulations are based. The UCR are based on crimes reported to the police, while the NCVS record crimes experienced by victims. Apparent inconsistencies in the two sources of data are likely to stem from a combination of problems with victims' memories, inaccuracies in crime records in individual police agencies, and inconsistencies in the data projections used to produce the NCVS and UCR.

Earlier in the chapter, we saw that the reasons for the decline in crime in the United States produce much debate. Among the reasons given by analysts are the aging of the baby boom population, the increased use of security sys-

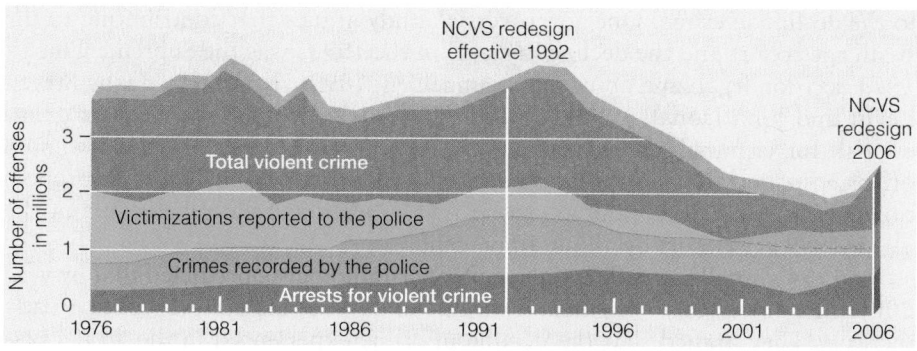

FIGURE 1.5
Four measures of serious violent crime

Note: The violent crimes included are rape, robbery, aggravated assault, and homicide. The shaded area at 1992 indicates that, because of changes made to the victimization survey, data prior to 1992 are adjusted to make them comparable to data collected under the redesigned methodology. Questions about homicides are not included in the NCVS, so the data here include the assumption that the 15,854 homicides in 2006 were reported to the police.

Sources: Michael Rand and Shannan Catalano, "Criminal Victimization, 2006," *Bureau of Justice Statistics Bulletin*, December 2007; FBI, *Crime in the United States, 2006* [Uniform Crime Reports], http://www.fbi.gov.

tems, the aggressive police efforts to keep handguns off the streets, and the dramatic decline in the use of crack cocaine. Other factors may include the booming economy of the 1990s and the quadrupling of the number of people incarcerated since 1970. There are concerns about the final two factors, in that economic downturns could fuel an increase in crime, as could the release from prison of hundreds of thousands of parolees and offenders who complete their sentences each year. For now, though, let's look more closely at two other factors—age and crack cocaine—as a means of assessing future crime levels.

Age

Changes in the age makeup of the population are key to the analysis of crime trends. It has long been known that men aged 16 to 24 are the most crime-prone group. The rise in crime in the 1970s has been blamed on the post–World War II baby boom. By the 1970s the boomers had entered the high-risk crime group of 16- to 24-year-olds. They made up a much larger portion of the U.S. population than ever before. Between 40 and 50 percent of the total arrests during that decade resulted from the growth in the total population and in the size of the crime-prone age group. Likewise, the decline in most crime rates that began during the 1980s has been attributed to the maturing of the post–World War II generation.

During the 1990s the 16- to 24-year age cohort was smaller than it had been at any time since the early 1960s, and many people believe that this contributed

Trends in crime rates are associated with the number of young people in the population, especially males aged 16 to 24, during any given year. Why are young people more likely than older people to commit crimes? When teenagers gather in a park or on a street corner, should people be worried about those youths engaging in criminal behavior?

to the decline in crime. One controversial study argues that contributing to the small age cohort and the decline in crime in the 1990s was the Supreme Court's 1973 decision legalizing abortions (Samuelson, 1999: 76). The study, by Steven Levitt and John Donahue, suggests that those who would have been at greatest risk for criminal activity during their crime-prone years—"the unwanted offspring of teenage, poor and minority women—were aborted at disproportionately high rates" (Brandon, 1999: A5). Abortions reduced the size of the 1973–1989 age cohort by about 40 percent.

In 1994 a small but influential group of criminologists predicted that by year 2000 the number of young men in the 14- to 24-year-old cohort would greatly increase. They argued that the decline in crime experienced in the 1990s was merely the "lull before the storm" (Steinberg, 1999: 4WK). In the words of James Fox, "To prevent a blood bath in 2005, when we will have a flood of 15-year-olds, we have to do something today with the 5-year-olds" (Krauss, 1994: 4). However, this link between increases in the juvenile population and a rise in violent crime has not occurred. For most years since the prediction was made, the homicide rate among teenage offenders has been falling, although individual cities have experienced increases in homicides during specific years.

Crack Cocaine

The huge increase in violent crime, especially homicide, in the late 1980s and early 1990s is now generally attributed to killings by young people aged 24 and under. These killings were driven by the spread of crack cocaine and the greater use of high-powered semiautomatic handguns by young people in that market (Blumstein, 1996; Butterfield, 1998a). During this period hundreds of thousands of unskilled, unemployed, young men from poor urban neighborhoods became street vendors of crack. To protect themselves, because they were carrying valuable merchandise (drugs and money), they were armed. They felt they needed this protection, because drug dealers cannot call for police assistance if threatened. As shootings increased among sellers engaged in turf battles over drug sales, others began to arm themselves, and the resulting violence continued to skyrocket (Blumstein, 1996). The sharp drop in violent crime in the 1990s followed the sudden decline in the use of crack as more and more people saw the devastation that the drug brought (Egan, 1999: A1).

Crime Trends: What Do We Really Know?

Pointing to specific factors that cause an increase or decrease in crime rates is difficult. Once people thought that, with the proper tools, they could analyze and solve the crime problem. However, crime is complex. Key questions remain: Do changes in crime rates occur because of demography, unemployment rates, housing conditions, and changes in family structure? Or do crime rates result from interactions among these and other factors? How do the policies of law enforcement, sentencing, and corrections affect criminality? Until we know more about the causes of criminal behavior, we can neither blame nor praise government policies for shifts in crime rates.

checkpoint

19. Has crime in the United States reached record levels?
20. For which crimes does the crime rate in the United States exceed that of most industrialized democracies?
21. What are the two main sources of crime data?
22. What are key factors in crime trends?

A QUESTION OF ETHICS

YOU ARE A new police officer, fresh from the police academy. While riding with your training officer during your first weeks on the job, you are called to a home where an irate mother wants to press charges against three teenagers who beat her son and stole his bike. She presents the boy to you and you can see that his arm is in a sling, he has a puffy lip, and there are visible bruises on his face. You carefully write out a complete report under the watchful eye of the training officer who listens but asks no questions.

When you return to the patrol car, the training officer says to you, "By the way, don't file this as an assault and theft. It just increases our crime statistics for no good reason. The prosecutor isn't going to charge these kids anyway. Plus we have to help the chief show that the department is reducing crime. We'll just go find these kids, scare the hell out of them, and get the bike back."

Critical Thinking and Analysis

What would you do if a superior officer said such things to you? Do you have any choice, or are you obligated to obey without objecting? Now imagine that you are the police chief in a community where the mayor has just said to you, "If you can't reduce the crime rate this year, we'll find a new chief of police who can handle the job." Write a memo for your police department instructing your officers on how to handle reports of fistfights at school and thefts among kids on the playground.

SUMMARY

Understand how public policies on crime are formed

- Crime and justice are high on the agenda of national priorities.
- Crime and justice are public policy issues.
- Public opinion and citizen involvement affect criminal justice.
- Criminal justice can best be seen as a social system.
- As a democracy, the United States faces a struggle to strike a balance between maintaining public order and protecting individual freedom, especially because of the tensions between conflicting American values.

Recognize how the crime control and due process models of criminal justice help us understand the system

- The crime control model and the due process model are two ways of looking at the goals and procedures of the criminal justice system.
- The crime control model focuses on efficiency in an administrative process that relies on discretionary decisions.
- The due process model focuses on reliable decisions in an adversarial process that relies on law.

Be able to explain: "What is a crime?"

- Politics affect the development of laws concerning criminal justice at the national, state, and local levels.
- Politicians define crimes through laws that they enact and they do not always anticipate the consequences of laws.
- Criminal laws may reflect a consensus in society or may reflect conflicts about values and morality in contexts in which the preferences of the majority of legislators will prevail.

Describe the major types of crime in the United States

- There are six broad categories of crime: visible crime, occupational crime, organized crime, crimes without victims, political crime, and cybercrime.
- Each type of crime has its own level of risk and profitability, each arouses varying degrees of public disapproval, and each has its own group of offenders with their own characteristics.

Analyze how much crime there is and understand how it is measured

- Today's crime problem is not unique. Throughout the history of the United States, crime has reached high levels at various times.
- Homicide is the primary type of crime that occurs at higher rates in the United States than in other industrialized democracies.
- The amount of crime is difficult to measure. The Uniform Crime Reports and the National Crime Victimization Surveys are the best sources of crime data.
- The complexity of crime statistics makes monitoring trends in crime a challenge.
- Crime rates are affected by changes in social factors, such as the size of the cohort of young males in their crime prone years (16–24) and the introduction of new drugs or other criminal activities that affect social contexts in certain communities.

QUESTIONS FOR REVIEW

1. What are the goals of criminal justice in a democracy?
2. What are the major elements of Packer's due process model and crime control model?

3. What are the six types of crime?

4. What are the positive and negative attributes of the two major sources of crime data?

KEY TERMS

crime (p. 7)
crime control model (p. 12)
crimes without victims (p. 23)
cybercrimes (p. 24)
dark figure of crime (p. 32)
due process model (p. 12)
felonies (p. 17)
identity theft (p. 24)
mala in se (p. 16)
mala prohibita (p. 17)
misdemeanors (p. 17)
money laundering (p. 22)

National Crime Victimization Surveys (NCVS) (p. 34)
National Incident-Based Reporting System (NIBRS) (p. 34)
occupational crime (p. 19)
organized crime (p. 21)
political crime (p. 23)
public policy (p. 8)
Uniform Crime Reports (UCR) (p. 33)
visible crime (p. 18)

FOR FURTHER READING

Gest, Ted. 2001. *Crime and Politics: Big Government's Erratic Campaign for Law and Order.* New York: Oxford University Press. An experienced journalist provides analytical descriptions of the political interests and events that shaped federal crime policy on such issues as gun control and narcotics laws.

Reiman, Jeffrey. 2000. *The Rich Get Richer and the Poor Get Prison: Ideology, Crime, and Criminal Justice.* 6th ed. Boston: Allyn and Bacon. A stinging critique of the system. Argues that the system serves the powerful by its failure to reduce crime.

Walker, Samuel. 2001. *Sense and Nonsense about Crime and Drug Policy.* 5th ed. Belmont, CA: Wadsworth. A provocative look at crime policies.

Wilson, James Q., and Joan Petersilia, eds. 2002. *Crime.* Rev. ed. San Francisco: Institute for Contemporary Studies Press. Essays by 28 leading experts on crime and justice.

Windlesham, David. 1998. *Politics, Punishment, and Populism.* New York: Oxford University Press. A distinguished British scholar who served as a visiting researcher in the United States provides a detailed analysis of the political interactions that produced the Violent Crime Control and Law Enforcement Act of 1994 during President Clinton's first term in office.

GOING ONLINE

For an up-to-date list of web links, go to *The American System of Criminal Justice* 12e companion site at academic .cengage.com/criminaljustice/cole.

1. Using the Internet, access a leading national or state newspaper. Count the number of crime and noncrime stories appearing on the front page for a typical week. What percentage of crime stories do you find? What types of crimes are described? Should readers be concerned about crime in their community?

2. Find the Uniform Crime Reports. What are the crime rates for the most recent year? Is there anything surprising about the level of crime reported?

3. Go to the U.S. Justice Department's primary website on cybercrime. Read about people recently convicted of cybercrimes and the specific activities in which they were engaged. Are you vulnerable to any of these crimes? Are there any cybercrime activities that surprised you?

CHECKPOINT ANSWERS

1. *What criminal justice policies are advocated by conservatives?*

   Stricter enforcement of the law through the expansion of police forces and the enactment of laws that require swift and certain punishment of offenders.

2. *What are liberals' criticisms of contemporary policies?*

   Stronger crime measures endanger the values of due process and justice.

3. *What two criminal justice goals do Americans agree on?*

   That criminal justice policies should both control crime by enforcing the law and protect the rights of individuals.

4. *What are the main features of the crime control model?*

   Every effort must be made to repress crime through efficiency, speed, and finality.

5. *What are the main features of the due process model?*

   Every effort must be made to ensure that criminal justice decisions are based on reliable information. It stresses the adversarial process, the rights of defendants, and formal decision-making procedures.

6. *At what level of government are many justice officials elected to office?*

   State and local levels of government.

7. *How do politics influence criminal justice policies?*

   Penal codes and budgets are passed by legislatures, many criminal justice officials are elected, and criminal justice policies are developed in political arenas.

8. *Who are examples of individual Americans who have influenced criminal justice policy?*

   Cindy Lightner, founder of MADD; Sarah Brady, founder of Brady Center for Gun Control; Congresswoman Carolyn McCarthy.

9. *How do average citizens affect criminal justice?*

   Voting, participating in community organizations, taking steps to impact their own potential vulnerability to victimization.

10. *Who defines certain behaviors as criminal?*

Elected representatives in state legislatures and Congress.

11. *What is meant by* mala in se *and by* mala prohibita?

Mala in se: offenses that are wrong in themselves (murder, rape, assault).
Mala prohibita: acts that are crimes because they are prohibited (vagrancy, gambling, drug use).

12. *What are the six main types of crime?*

Visible crime, occupational crime, organized crime, crimes without victims, political crime, cybercrime.

13. *What groups are overrepresented among those arrested for visible or street crimes?*

Young, male, poor.

14. *Why is the term occupational crime more useful today than the term white-collar crime?*

Workplace-related crimes are committed by all occupational groups.

15. *What is the function of organized crime?*

To provide goods and services that are in high demand but are illegal.

16. *What is meant by the term crimes without victims?*

These are crimes against morality in which the people involved do not believe they have been victimized.

17. *What are political crimes?*

Crimes such as treason committed for a political purpose.

18. *What types of criminal activities are labeled as cybercrime?*

Using computers to steal valuable information and assets, identity theft, illegal downloading, malicious viruses.

19. *Has crime in the United States reached record levels?*

No, there have been other eras when crime was high.

20. *For which crimes does the crime rate in the United States exceed that of most industrialized democracies?*

Violent crimes such as murder.

21. *What are the two main sources of crime data?*

Uniform Crime Reports, National Crime Victimization Surveys.

22. *What are key factors in crime trends?*

Demography (e.g., age cohorts), changing social contexts that may impact jobs, neighborhoods, and families, such as the spread of new drugs or other criminal activities (e.g., crack, gangs, business closures).

CHAPTER **2**

Victimization and Criminal Behavior

CHAPTER LEARNING OBJECTIVES

→ Understand who becomes victims of crime

→ Recognize the impacts of crime on society

→ Identify the justice system's responses to the needs of crime victims

→ Understand the theories put forward to explain criminal behavior

→ Analyze crime causation theories and apply them to different groups of offenders

For the 100 students in the lecture hall, it was business as usual. Instructor Joseph Peterson illustrated his geosciences lecture with Power-Point slides as they took notes and cast glances at the clock, awaiting the approaching end of the class period. Then the first shot rang out and nightmarish chaos immediately followed. A man jumped out from behind the curtain on the stage and began firing into the auditorium. "He's got a gun!" "Call 911!" Screams and commotion erupted as dozens of students ran for the exits while others dove to the floor and attempted to hide beneath their seats. Just as quickly, the auditorium became eerily silent, except for the sound of the black-clad gunman firing randomly into the audience, reloading, and then emptying his guns again on that tragic day in February 2008. (Saulny and Davey, 2008).

The police at Northern Illinois University (NIU) arrived at the Cole Hall auditorium within two minutes. They found the gunman dead of a self-inflicted gunshot wound. He had brought a shotgun into the building in a guitar case and he also had three handguns. The police counted six empty shotgun shells and 48 shell casings for handgun ammunition scattered around the body. They also found themselves in the middle of an urgent medical emergency as dead and wounded students lay scattered among the seats. The tragic tally for

the brief event was five homicide victims and 16 others suffering from gunshot wounds—plus the death of the perpetrator, Steven Kazmierczak, a former honors student at NIU who received awards for his criminal justice research (Henizmann and St. Clair, 2008).

The event was highly publicized because the nature of the crime and location of the incident differed so greatly from those of most crimes, which involve the loss of property or some other less dramatic event. The case embodies one of the worst fears of Americans: that they or their children will be trapped within the sights of a suicidal gunman, intent on killing as many people as possible without caring at all about the suffering of others or the consequences for himself. Despite the fact that the NIU campus shooting did not represent a "typical crime," the case provides an excellent illustration of the factors that shape the subject of crime victimization and the questions about victimization that are raised as a result.

For example, who are the crime victims in this case? Obviously, the students who were killed and wounded. But what about their families? Aren't they also victims of this crime because they suffered psychological and emotional harm? What about the university? Has its reputation as a safe place to attend college been destroyed? Will fewer students apply for admission in the future? What about members of the victims' hometown communities throughout Illinois? They lost relatives, friends, and neighbors while churches lost parishioners— and society lost future educated citizens who might have made significant contributions to the well-being of their communities, the nation, or the world. Would it be proper to say that all people in society are also victims of the crime? The shooter's actions cost the public thousands of dollars to pay for law enforcement officers to investigate the case and refine plans at NIU—and other universities throughout the country that watched the news reports in horror—to make sure that their emergency response planning and training could appropriately address such situations. Moreover, members of the public may feel less safe as a result of hearing about this shocking crime, which could have happened to anyone. Does that make each of us—individually—a victim? We might feel as if we have lost a bit of our security and liberty if this event enhances our fears, nervousness, and discomfort when we wonder if any strangers around us—at the movies, at the ballpark, or in the mall—might turn out to have similar murderous plans.

These are important questions to consider, because how we answer them will define the scope of the subject of criminal victimization. In other words, when we talk about the victimizing consequences of crime, should we only talk about the individuals most directly harmed by a crime or should we also consider people who suffer less direct, but equally real, consequences? These questions actually have practical consequences under circumstances in which we speak of "victims' rights," such as crime victims being entitled to compensation. We need to define what we mean by a "victim" before we can implement any such policy.

In other kinds of crimes, we may also consider additional questions about criminal victimization. When two young women were kidnapped in California in 2002, their names were broadcast on the news during the search effort. After their rescue, in violation of the rules and ethical standards for many news outlets and law enforcement agencies, a law enforcement officer told news reporters that the women had been sexually assaulted (NBC News, 2002). Does the publicizing of such personal information intensify the women's pain and humiliation? Does it violate their right to privacy? As you can see, the responses of the news media and officials in the criminal justice system can affect the issue of crime victimization.

A further question arises when we ask whether people bear any responsibility for their own victimization. If young women sit in parked cars in dark, out-of-the-way places, do they place themselves at risk of victimization? The women in the California kidnapping case were parked with their boyfriends at 1:00 A.M. on an empty country road. Does such a context raise the risk of kidnapping, date rape, or other crimes? Before answering that question, we might also take one step back and ask whether raising issues about victims' responsibility for the harms they have suffered is ethical in the first place. Is such a line of inquiry unfair and inhumane? Yet, as we study criminal events, we cannot help but notice that some crimes occur when victims make themselves more vulnerable or when they take actions that appear to trigger a violent response from the wrongdoer. Do such questions imply that victims are at fault for the crime directed at them? No. Clearly, people who commit criminal acts must be punished as the ones responsible for those acts. However, an understanding of criminal events and victim behavior may help us discover how to teach people to reduce their risk of criminal victimization.

An additional important question looms in this and every other criminal case: Why did the perpetrator do what he or she did? Criminal behavior is the main cause of criminal victimization. Scholars, policy makers, and the public have long pondered questions such as "What causes crime?" and "Why do criminal offenders cause harm to other human beings?" These questions have significant implications for the subject of criminal victimization. Theories about crime causation often influence government policies for controlling and punishing violations of criminal laws.

In this chapter, we examine the many facets of crime victimization, including aspects that the general public does not generally recognize. In addition, we discuss the causes of crime. Many complex and controversial theories center on why people commit crimes. In considering this subject, we need to bear in mind that no single theory can be expected to explain all crimes. Remember that "crimes" are whatever actions a legislature defines as deserving punishment at a particular moment in history. Thus, we should not assume that a corporate official who employs deceptive accounting practices in order to skim off millions of dollars in business profits has the same motives as the man who shot the students at NIU. The fact that crime has many causes, however, does not mean that all proposed theories about crime causation are equally useful or valid. We need to look closely at theories about crime and evaluate what evidence supports them.

CRIME VICTIMIZATION

Until the past few decades, researchers paid little attention to crime victims. The field of **victimology**, which emerged in the 1950s, focused attention on four questions: (1) Who is victimized? (2) What is the impact of crime? (3) What happens to victims in the criminal justice system? (4) What role do victims play in causing the crimes they suffer? We discuss these questions in the following sections.

Who Is Victimized?

Not everyone has an equal chance of becoming a crime victim. Moreover, recent research shows that people who are victimized by crime in one year are also more likely to be victimized by crime in a subsequent year (Menard, 2000). Research shows that members of certain demographic groups are more likely to be victimized than others. As Andrew Karmen notes, "Victimization definitely does not appear to be a random process, striking people just by chance" (Karmen, 2001: 87). Victimologists have puzzled over this fact and come up with several

victimology
A field of criminology that examines the role the victim plays in precipitating a criminal incident and the impact of crimes on victims.

 The National Center for Victims of Crime provides information about services for crime victims. To link to this website, go to *The American System of Criminal Justice* 12e companion site at academic.cengage.com/criminaljustice/cole.

According to the lifestyle exposure model, demographic factors (age, gender, income) and exposure to dangerous places, times, and people influence the probability of being victimized. Based on this model, how would you assess your own risk of victimization?

AP Images/Kevork Djansezian

answers. One explanation is that demographic factors (age, gender, income) affect lifestyle—people's routine activities such as work, home life, and recreation. Lifestyles, in turn, affect people's exposure to dangerous places, times, and people (Varano et al., 2004). Thus, differences in lifestyles lead to varying degrees of exposure to risks (R. F. Meier and Miethe, 1973: 466). Figure 2.1 shows the links among the factors used in the lifestyle-exposure model of personal victimization. Using this model, think of a person whose lifestyle includes going to nightclubs in a "shady" part of town. Such a person runs the risk of being robbed if she walks alone through a dark high-crime area at two in the morning to her luxury car. By contrast, an older person who watches television at night in her small-town home has a very low chance of being robbed. But these cases do not tell the entire story. What other factors make victims more vulnerable than nonvictims?

Men, Youths, Nonwhites

The lifestyle-exposure model and survey data shed light on the links between personal characteristics and the chance that one will become a victim. Figure 2.2 shows the influence of gender, age, and race on the risk of being victimized by a violent crime such as rape, robbery, or assault. If we apply these findings to the lifestyle-exposure model, we might suggest that African American teenagers are most likely to be victimized because of where they may live (urban, high-crime areas), how they may spend their leisure time (outside late at night), and the people with whom they may associate (violence-prone youths). Lifestyle factors may also explain why elderly white women are least likely to be victimized by a violent crime. Perhaps it is because they do not go out at night, do not associate with people who are prone to crime, carry few valuables, and take precautions such as locking their doors. Thus, lifestyle opportunities and choices directly affect the chance of victimization.

Race is a key factor in exposure to crime. African Americans and other minorities are more likely than whites to be raped, robbed, and assaulted. The rate of violent crime victimization for whites is 20 per 1,000 people, compared with 27 per 1,000 for African Americans. For Hispanic men, the rate is 28 per 1,000 and for Hispanic women it is 22 per 1,000 (BJS, 2006). White Americans are fearful of being victimized by African American strangers (Skogan, 1995: 59). However, most violent crime is intraracial: Three of every four victims are of the same race as the attacker (Figure 2.3). These figures do not reveal that there

FIGURE 2.1

Lifestyle-exposure model of victimization

Demographic and subcultural factors determine personal lifestyles, which in turn influence exposure to victimization.

Source: Adapted with permission from Robert F. Meier and Terance D. Miethe, "Understanding Theories of Criminal Victimization," in *Crime and Justice: A Review of Research,* ed. Michael Tonry (Chicago: University of Chicago Press, 1973), 467.

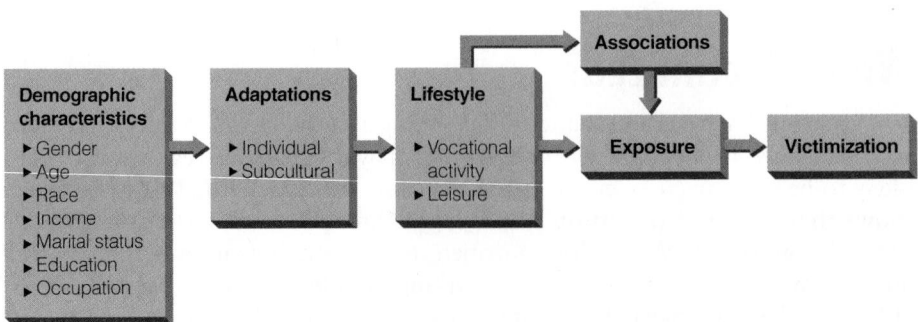

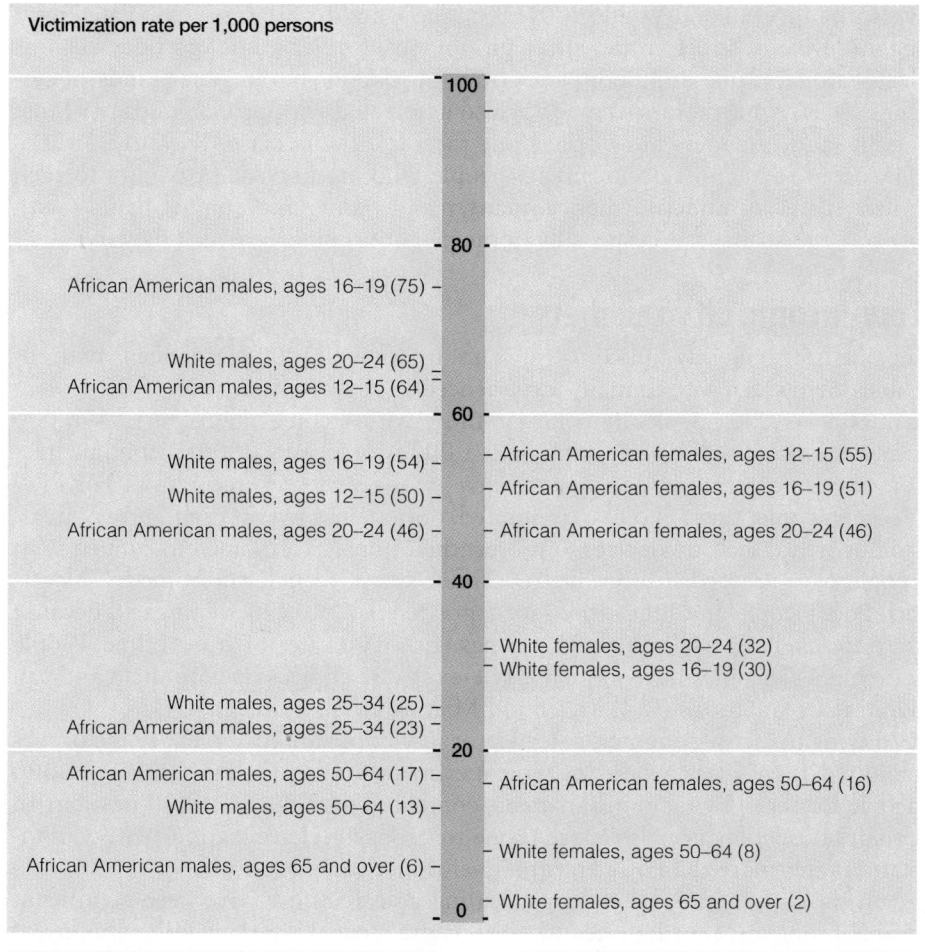

FIGURE 2.2
Victimization rates for violent crimes
African American male teenagers have the highest victimization rate for violent crimes. Why are they more likely than other age, gender, and racial groups to be robbed or assaulted?

Source: Bureau of Justice Statistics, *Criminal Victimization in the United States—Statistical Tables* (Washington, DC: U.S. Department of Justice, 2006) Table 10—Violent Crimes, 2005 (http://www.ojp.gov/bjs/pub/pdf/cvus/current/cv0510.pdf).

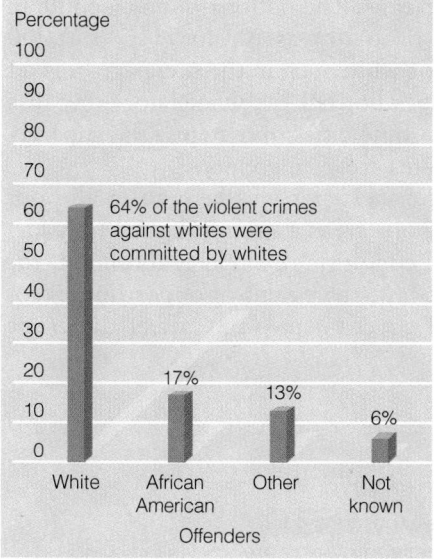

a   White victims

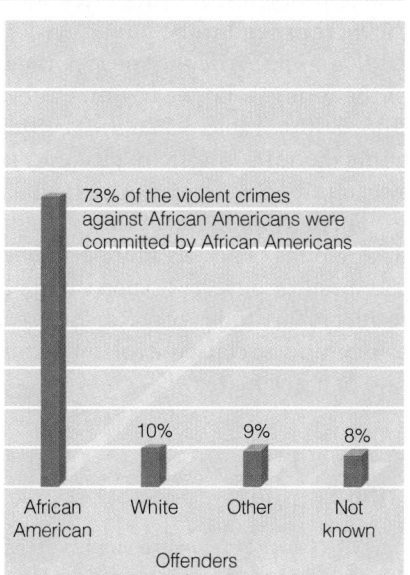

b   African American victims

FIGURE 2.3
Victims and offenders are of the same race in three out of four violent crimes
Although whites seem most fearful of being victimized by African Americans, most violent crime is intraracial. Why do people have such misperceptions?

Note: Figures do not equal 100% because of rounding.

Source: Bureau of Justice Statistics, *Criminal Victimization in the United States—Statistical Tables* (Washington, DC: U.S. Department of Justice, 2006) Table 42—Personal Crimes of Violence, 2005, (http://www.ojp.gov/bjs/pub/pdf/cvus/current/cv0510.pdf).

is a direct connection between race and crime. To the contrary, these numbers simply reflect that African Americans and whites often live in separate neighborhoods in this country. And, most importantly, African American neighborhoods are much more likely to be those experiencing what scholars call "high levels of socioeconomic disadvantage" with respect to unemployment, quality of schools, quality of housing, and other factors associated with income and wealth (Lauritsen and White, 2001: 53). These factors are often associated with higher levels of street crime, although obviously other kinds of crime, such as occupational crime and computer crime, appear mostly in other kinds of settings. These same factors of race are also associated with property crimes: Most victims and offenders are of the same race and social class. The street crimes that people fear most occur among people who are in close proximity to each other. Again, in modern America, many people come into contact mainly with others of the same race, especially in the neighborhoods in which they live.

Low-Income City Dwellers

Income is also closely linked to exposure to crime. In 2005 Americans with incomes below $7,500 annually experienced a victimization rate of 38 violent crimes per 1,000 people. By contrast, those with incomes in excess of $75,000 experienced only 16 violent crimes per 1,000 people (BJS, 2006). Economic factors largely determine where people live, work, and seek recreation. For low-income people, these choices are limited. Some must live in crime-prone areas, cannot afford security devices to protect their homes, cannot avoid contact with people who are prone to crime, or cannot spend their leisure time in safe areas. Poor people and minorities face a greater risk of being victimized, because they are likely to live in inner-city zones with high rates of street crime. People with higher incomes have more lifestyle-exposure choices open to them and can avoid risky situations (R. F. Meier and Miethe, 1993: 468).

Living in a city is, in fact, a key factor in victimization. Violent crime occurs mainly in large cities, where the violent crime victimization rate is 30 per 1,000 people for those living in urban areas, compared with 20 per 1,000 in suburbs. Urban households are also more prone to property victimization, with victimization rates more than 50 percent higher than those in suburbs.

In the inner cities, where drug dealing and drug use have been significant visible problems, murder rates have risen the most. Like their killers, many of the victims tend to be young African Americans. The national homicide rate in 2005 among African American men aged 18 to 24 was 102 for every 100,000 of the same group, nearly nine times that for white men in the same age bracket (BJS, 2006: Table 3.126.2005). But this does not tell the whole story, because homicide rates differ by city and state. In some cities and states, the gaps between rates for African Americans and whites are even greater.

Furthermore, we cannot conclude that crime rates will be high in all poor urban areas. There is more crime in some poor areas than in others. Many factors besides poverty—such as the physical condition of the neighborhood, the residents' attitudes toward society and the law, the extent of opportunities for crime, and social control by families and government—may affect the crime rate of a given area.

checkpoint

1. What are the main elements of the lifestyle-exposure model?
2. What are the characteristics of the group that is most victimized by violent crime? Of the least-victimized group? (Answers are at the end of the chapter.)

Acquaintances and Strangers

The frightening image of crime in the minds of many Americans is the familiar scene played out in many movies and television shows in which a dangerous stranger grabs a victim on a dark street or breaks into a home at night.

Many crimes are committed by strangers against people whom they have never seen before. However, most Americans do not realize the extent to which violent crimes occur among acquaintances, friends, and even relatives. In 2005, for example, female victims of violent crimes were victimized by strangers in only 34 percent of those crimes. That means acquaintances or relatives committed two-thirds of the violent crimes against female victims. Although only 46 percent of male victims suffered violent crimes at the hands of acquaintances and relatives, that figure still constitutes a significant percentage of violent crimes (BJS, 2006). Table 2.1 shows the number and percentages of crimes committed by strangers, intimates (spouses, boyfriends, and girlfriends), other relatives, and friends and acquaintances.

As indicated by Table 2.1, victims tend to suffer different kinds of crimes, depending on whether strangers or nonstrangers are the perpetrators. Robbery victims tend to be victimized by strangers, but female sexual assault victims are more likely to be victimized by someone they know. These differences reflect, in part, the contexts in which these crimes occur. Robbers take valuables from an individual by force and then typically run away. Thus, the scenario fits situations in which robbers hope to escape without being caught or identified. This result is much more difficult for a robber who is known to the victim. By contrast, sexual assaults often take place in isolated or private locations. People are most likely to place themselves in isolated or private locations, such as inside a house or apartment, with someone they know.

Although Americans often fear violent victimization at the hands of strangers, most violence against women is perpetrated by those with whom they are intimate—husbands, boyfriends, and former lovers. What policies could address this problem?

© Janine Wiedel Photolibrary/Alamy

As we have seen, people's odds of being victimized depend in part on the people with whom they associate. An element of the lifestyle-exposure model includes consideration of the places that people frequent and the people with whom they interact. Some people increase their vulnerability to victimization by spending time with people who steal property and commit acts of violence. In the case of female victims, who suffer nearly 20 percent of their violent victimizations from husbands and boyfriends, this may mean that they misjudged their partners or that they could not anticipate how marital conflicts and other interpersonal stress would affect interactions and behavior. This does not mean, however, that these victims have necessarily chosen to place themselves at risk. Our legal system, at least theoretically, does not blame victims for the harms they suffer. The individuals who commit crimes, including domestic violence, are responsible for their own behavior.

There are other contexts in which people's risk of victimization is high because of the people with whom they associate, yet they cannot readily prevent

TABLE 2.1 Victim and Offender Relationships

Look at the differences in crimes by strangers and nonstrangers for various kinds of offenses. Are you surprised by the frequency with which crime victims experience harm at the hands of people whom they know?

| | Percentage of Perpetrators | | | |
Relationship to Victim	Violent Crime	Rape/Sexual Assault	Robbery	Simple Assault
All Victims				
Intimate	9	26	5	10
Other Relative	6	6	2	6
Friend/Acquaintance	37	35	24	39
Stranger	46	31	67	42
Female Victim				
Intimate	18	28	9	20
Other Relative	8	7	2	8
Friend/Acquaintance	39	38	39	38
Stranger	34	26	48	33
Male Victim				
Intimate	3	0	3	3
Other Relative	5	0	2	8
Friend/Acquaintance	36	0	18	40
Stranger	54	100	74	49

Note: Percentages do not total 100% because the table omits offenses committed by offenders whose relationship with the victim is unknown.
Source: Bureau of Justice Statistics, *Criminal Victimization in the United States—Statistical Tables* (Washington, DC: U.S. Department of Justice, 2006) Table 43a—Personal Crimes of Violence, 2005 (http://www.ojp.gov/bjs/pub/pdf/cvus/current/cv0510.pdf).

The office of the Attorney General of Florida provides advice about how to protect yourself from crime. Were you aware of all of these specific suggestions? To link to this website, go to *The American System of Criminal Justice* 12e companion site at academic.cengage.com/criminaljustice/cole.

such situations from arising. For example, people who live in neighborhoods with active drug trafficking may be acquainted with neighbors, former schoolmates, and even relatives who rob and steal because they have become dependent on illegal drugs and they need money to support their drug habits. When these acquaintances commit crimes, people who live nearby may find avoiding victimization difficult. They cannot stop walking down the streets or leaving their homes empty and vulnerable to burglary when they go to work or school. Moreover, they may be reluctant to report some crimes, because they fear that the offenders will take revenge. People may also be reluctant to report theft committed by a relative with a drug habit. They may be upset about losing their valuables, but they do not want to see their son, daughter, or cousin arrested and sent to prison. If the perpetrators of such crimes know that their relatives will not report them, they may feel encouraged to victimize these people further in order to support a drug habit. Prior relationships among people may facilitate some crimes and keep victims from seeking police assistance. In effect, life circumstances that are separate from lifestyle choices can be important for exposing individuals to increased risk of victimization (Armstrong and Griffin, 2007). As you read the accompanying Close Up box, think about what you would do if you had a relative involved in criminal activities.

checkpoint

3. Which crime against which victim is the most likely to be committed by nonstrangers?
4. Which type of crime is the most likely to be committed by strangers?

CLOSE UP

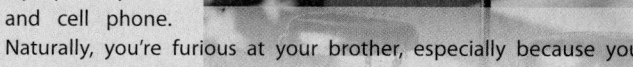

Victimization in the Family?

AS A BUSY college student working two part-time jobs and living with your parents, you spend very little time at home. Your younger brother, who decided to work full-time rather than enroll in college after high school, is hanging around with people who supposedly use and sell drugs. Whenever you try to talk to your brother about his friends' reputations, he gets angry and leaves the room. You notice that household items regularly disappear and your parents immediately buy new ones. The vacuum cleaner, the lawn mower, the snowblower, a gas grill, and the stereo have all been replaced. You can't help noticing your brother's increasingly suspicious behavior, so you lock your bedroom door whenever you leave the house. When you overhear your parents discussing missing jewelry, you ask them whether they recognize that your brother is apparently stealing items in order to support a drug habit. You then ask, "What are you going to do about it?"

"Your brother has some problems right now. But he'll only be hurt worse if we call the police or do anything like that. We just need to give him some time to get himself together." You shake your head and think to yourself, "I wouldn't put up with this stuff in my own house." Shortly thereafter, you return home one evening to find your bedroom door open and several expensive items missing, including your personal MP3 player, laptop computer, and cell phone. Naturally, you're furious at your brother, especially because you know that you can't afford to replace these items.

If this happened to you, what would you do? Would you call the police? Would you think that your brother should be sent into the criminal justice system? Could you stand the thought that your brother is likely to steal even more items from you and your parents? Are there alternative courses of action that you could take?

Researching the Internet

Go to the website of the Partnership for a Drug-Free America. Read the materials that advise parents about how to teach their children about drugs and determine whether their children are using drugs. Does this information help you to decide how you would handle the foregoing situation? To link to this website, go to *The American System of Criminal Justice* 12e companion site at academic.cengage.com/criminaljustice/cole.

The Impact of Crime

Crime affects not only the victim but all members of society. We all pay for crime through higher taxes, higher prices, and fear. These factors impinge on key American values such as individual liberty and protection of private property and personal wealth. As such, many people advocate crime-control policies as a means to restore American values.

As we have seen, crime can diminish our sense of liberty by making us fearful about going certain places, being out after dark, and trusting strangers. In addition, the money that we work so hard to earn is reduced by the costs of increased insurance premiums to cover thefts throughout society and increased taxes to pay for police and other government services. There may be other costs, too. For example, research shows an increased probability of people deciding to move to a new home after being victimized by a crime in their neighborhood (Dugan, 1999). Moving produces financial costs, personal costs in the loss of friendships and the social isolation of arriving in a new location, and the hassles of becoming settled in a new neighborhood, especially for a family with children. Estimating the precise impact of crime is difficult; clearly, however, we all share the burdens of crime, and these burdens clash with long-held American values.

Costs of Crime

Crime has many kinds of costs. First, there are the economic costs—lost property, lower productivity, and the cost of medical care. Second, there are psychological and emotional costs—pain, trauma, and lost quality of life. Third, there are the costs of operating the criminal justice system.

It is extremely difficult to get a firm estimate of the costs of crime. Periodic studies by the government, industry, or university researchers tend to focus on only certain aspects of costs or certain kinds of crime. When one looks at the various surveys, however, it is clear that the costs of crime to society are staggering. A Justice Department study from the mid-1990s estimated the total annual cost of tangible losses from crime (medical expenses, damaged or lost property, work time) at $105 billion. The intangible costs (pain, trauma, lost quality of life) to victims came to $450 billion (NIJ, 1996). Operating the criminal justice system costs taxpayers more than $185 billion a year to pay for police, courts, and corrections (BJS, 2006: Table 1.4.2003). Further, in the aftermath of the September 11 tragedy, government costs increased as more money was spent on airport security, border patrols, and counterterrorism activities. These figures do not include the costs of occupational and organized crime to consumers. Businesses' losses from hackers' attacks on their computers stood at $660 million in 2003 (McGuire, 2004). Overall losses from economic crimes alone were estimated to be $200 billion in 2000, and private businesses spent more than $103 billion on consultants, services, and products to combat these economic crimes (Security Industry Association, 2000). In 2006, an annual survey of 150 corporate retail chains by Professor Richard Hollinger of the University of Florida found that retailers had more than $40 billion in annual losses from theft. Employee theft accounted for $19 million, shoplifting caused $13 billion in losses, and the rest was from vendor fraud ("Survey Estimates," 2007). Other costs arise from crime prevention measures by individual citizens who install locks and alarms or employ guards and security patrols.

Fear of Crime

One impact of crime is fear. Fear limits freedom. Because they are fearful, many people limit their activities to "safe" areas at "safe" times. Fear also creates anxieties that affect physiological and psychological well-being. What are the costs to the quality of people's lives if they spend time worrying about victimization every day? What is the cost of human suffering if people cannot get a good night's sleep because they awaken at every sound, fearing that an intruder is breaking in? The very people who face the least chance of being victimized, such as women and the elderly, are often the most fearful (Miethe, 1995: 14). All Americans do not experience the same fears (Lee and Ulmer, 2000), but many do adjust their daily activities to avoid being victimized.

Since 1965, public opinion polls have asked Americans whether they "feel more uneasy" or "fear to walk the streets at night" (see "What Americans Think"). From 1972 to 1993, more than 40 percent of respondents indicated that fear of crime limited their freedom. Coinciding with the declining crimes rates during the 1990s, the percentage of respondents who were fearful of walking near their homes dropped to 30 percent in 2001. Despite the improvement in quality of life indicated by the lower figure, this number still represents a significant segment of the American public. Further, the figure had risen to 37 percent by 2007. Figure 2.4 shows the results of a 12-city study of perceptions of community safety. The percentage of fearful residents differs not only by city but also by the extent to which they fear crime in their city, in their neighborhood, or on the street. In some large cities, more than 60 percent of residents say they are afraid to walk through their neighborhoods at night, while in small towns and rural areas fewer than 30 percent express this concern.

A 2007 survey indicated nearly identical levels of fear among whites and African Americans concerning their risk of victimization for burglary, vehicle theft, and sexual assault (BJS, 2007a). For some crimes, however, higher levels of fear are found among nonwhites and people with low incomes, the groups that are most likely to be victimized. In the 2007 survey, for example, 62 percent of African Americans feared that their children could be physically harmed at school but only 28 percent of whites expressed the same fear. Forty percent of

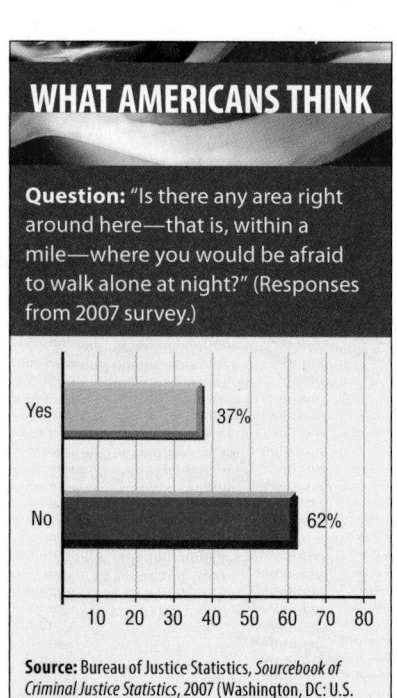

WHAT AMERICANS THINK

Question: "Is there any area right around here—that is, within a mile—where you would be afraid to walk alone at night?" (Responses from 2007 survey.)

Yes   37%

No   62%

10 20 30 40 50 60 70 80

Source: Bureau of Justice Statistics, *Sourcebook of Criminal Justice Statistics,* 2007 (Washington, DC: U.S. Government Printing Office, 2008), Table 2.37.2007.

African Americans frequently or occasionally feared being murdered, while the same was true for only 31 percent of whites. The most significant gap was evident for the 57 percent of African Americans who feared being victimized by a hate crime when only 37 percent of whites had similar fears (BJS, 2007a: Table 2.39.2007). In 2002, the most recent year with race-specific data available on this question, 41 percent of African Americans but only 30 percent of whites expressed fears about walking at night in their own neighborhoods. In another study, 50 percent of those with incomes below $20,000 expressed these fears, while only 28 percent of those with incomes over $50,000 made such statements. These differences may reflect what people actually observe in their own neighborhoods. In addition, researchers suggest that the degree to which certain crimes are feared depends on two factors: the seriousness of the offense and the chances that it will occur. However, not all fears are based on realistic assessments of risk. For example, women and the elderly are more fearful than the average citizen, despite lower-than-average rates of victimization (BJS, 2006: Table 2.38; Warr, 1993: 25).

Although crime rates are down, Americans' fears seem to exceed the actual victimization risks. People do not have a clear picture of the true risk of crime in their lives. They gain perceptions about crime from talk at their workplace and from politicians' statements and campaign promises. Their views about crime also seem to be shaped more by what they see on television than by reality (Chiricos, Padgett, and Gertz, 2000). Although fewer than 8 percent of victimizations are due to violent crime, such crimes are the ones most frequently reported by the media. In the mid-1990s, although violent crime decreased, television and newspaper coverage of violent crime increased more than 400 percent. One result was a jump in the percentage of Americans ranking crime as the nation's foremost problem—from 9 percent to 49 percent between January 1993 and January 1994 (Chiricos, Escholz, and Gertz, 1997: 342).

The amount of news coverage of crime, compared with coverage of the economy or government, can be startling (Chermak, 1995: 48). Crime stories sell newspapers, build viewership, and appeal to certain types of audiences. Data from the National Opinion Survey on Crime and Justice reveal that the regular viewers of television crime programs such as *Cops* and *America's Most Wanted* showed a higher degree of fear "about the probability of being sexually assaulted, beaten, knifed, and getting killed" than did other viewers (Haghighi and Sorensen, 1996: 29).

Most people do not experience crime directly but instead learn about it indirectly (Skogan and Maxfield, 1981: 157). Local television news has a major impact on attitudes about crime (Kurtz, 1997). In addition, television shows such as *The FBI Files* (1998–), *Unsolved Mysteries* (1989–2003), *Hard Copy* (1989–1999), and *A Current Affair* (1986–1996; revived March 2005) presented reports of actual heinous crimes almost daily (Kappeler, Blumberg, and Potter, 1996: 47). Fictional television dramas, such as the various *Law and Order* and *CSI* programs, may enhance the effect. Researchers believe that

FIGURE 2.4
Fear of crime in 12 cities
Percentage of residents who said they were fearful of crime in their city or neighborhood, or of being a victim of street crime.

Source: Bureau of Justice Statistics, *Criminal Victimization and Perceptions of Community Safety in 12 Cities, 1998* (Washington, DC: U.S. Government Printing Office, 1999), 10.

TABLE 2.2 Rates of Crime Compared with Rates of Other Events

Crime is a major concern to many Americans, but what are the risks of victimization compared with other kinds of risks?

Events	Rate per 1,000 Adults per Year
Accidental injury, all circumstances	220
Accidental injury at home	66
Personal theft	61
Accidental injury at work	47
Violent victimization	31
Assault (aggravated and simple)	25
Injury in motor vehicle accident	22
Death, all causes	11
Victimization with injury	11
Serious (aggravated) assault	8
Robbery	6
Heart disease death	5
Cancer death	3
Rape (women only)	1
Accidental death, all circumstances	0.4
Pneumonia/influenza death	0.4
Motor vehicle accident death	0.2
Suicide	0.2
HIV infection death	0.1
Homicide	0.1

Source: Bureau of Justice Statistics, *Highlights from 20 Years of Surveying Crime Victims* (Washington, DC: U.S. Government Printing Office, 1993), 4.

 The problem of fear of crime is not unique to the United States. In Britain, the government's Home Office has developed information and programs to address the problem in their country. To link to this website, go to *The American System of Criminal Justice* 12e companion site at academic.cengage.com/criminaljustice/cole.

conversations with friends also tend to magnify the perception of local violence. Such conversations often focus on crimes against women, the elderly, and children. Stories about defenseless victims create a feeling that violent crime lurks everywhere.

Fear of crime may also be linked to disorderly conditions in neighborhoods and communities (Skogan, 1990; Wilson and Kelling, 1982). As discussed by George Kelling and Catherine Coles, in urban areas, disorderly behavior—public drunkenness, urination, aggressive panhandling, and menacing behavior—offends citizens and instills fear. Unregulated disorderly behavior may signal to citizens that an area is unsafe. Because of this fear, they "will stay off the streets, avoid certain areas, and curtail their normal activities and associations" (Kelling and Coles, 1996: 20). Avoidance of "unsafe" business areas may lead to store closings, decline in real estate value, and flight to more orderly neighborhoods.

In any case, among all groups, the fear of crime outstrips the real risk of it. People do not assess the risk of crime as they do other risks, such as those caused by nature or by accident (see Table 2.2).

Actions that might reduce the fear of crime are costly, and those who can best afford to protect themselves are those who are least threatened by crime. Some responses to the perceived risk of crime may not seem costly, such as staying at home after dark. Yet even such a simple measure is often far easier for the rich than for the poor. The rich tend to work during the day, with some control over their hours of work. Poorer people are more likely to work evenings and nights as waiters, security guards, or convenience store clerks. Other measures, such as moving to the suburbs, installing home security systems, and hiring private security companies, are also most available to the rich.

checkpoint

5. What are some of the impacts of crime?
6. How is fear of crime shaped, and how does it relate to actual crime rates?
7. Why are poor people often less likely than others to take actions to reduce the risk of crime?

The Experience of Victims within the Criminal Justice System

After a crime has occurred, the victim is often forgotten. Although victims may have suffered physical, psychological, and economic losses, the criminal justice system focuses on finding and prosecuting the offender.

A Houston police officer comforts Velma Jones after she arrived at the scene where her daughter was fatally shot by a robber. Do justice system officials provide enough support for crime victims?

AP Images/David J. Phillip

Too often the system is not sensitive to the needs of victims. For example, defense attorneys may ask them hostile questions and attempt to paint them, rather than the defendant, as causing the crime to occur. Likewise, although victims provide key evidence, the police may question them closely—and in a hostile fashion—to find out if they are telling the truth. Often the victim never hears the outcome of a case. Sometimes a victim comes face-to-face with the assailant, who is out on bail or on probation. This can be quite a shock, especially if the victim assumed that the offender was in prison.

Victims may be forced to miss work and lose pay in order to appear at judicial proceedings. They may be summoned to court again and again, only to learn that the arraignment or trial has been postponed. Any recovered property may be held by the court for months as the case winds its way through the system. In short, after cases have been completed, victims may feel that they have been victimized twice, once by the offender and once by the criminal justice system.

During the past two decades, justice agencies have become more sensitive to the interests of crime victims. This has happened partly because victims often are the only witnesses to the crime and their help is needed. Many victims are not willing to provide such help if it involves economic and emotional costs. Some research indicates that victims are more likely to cooperate with the prosecutor if victims' assistance workers meet with them to provide comfort as well as information about how the court system operates (Dawson and Dinovitzer, 2001). Many victims' assistance workers are volunteers from the community. As you think about the issue presented in "Civic Engagement: Your Role in the System," consider what assistance you think should be provided to someone who has been traumatized by a criminal event.

civic engagement
your role in the system

Your roommate is having nightmares after witnessing a robbery in which the victim was seriously injured by a blow to the head. Your roommate rushed to aid the fallen victim and came home with his shirt soaked with the victim's blood. *Make a list of symptoms that you might look for as indicators of serious problems affecting someone who has witnessed or been victimized by a crime. Then make a list of things that might help such people recover from the event. Then see how* victims' assistance volunteers in Sacramento deal with such situations. See the Special Victims' Recovery Project. To link to this website, go to *The American System of Criminal Justice* 12e companion site at academic.cengage.com/criminaljustice/cole.

For an example of state services provided to crime victims, see the website of the New York State Crime Victims Board. To link to this website, go to *The American System of Criminal Justice* 12e companion site at academic .cengage.com/criminaljustice/cole.

In October 2004, President Bush signed into law the Justice for All Act of 2004. The statute contains provisions concerning a variety of matters, such as DNA testing of offenders and compensation for people wrongly convicted of federal crimes. The statute also includes rights for crime victims in federal criminal cases. These rights include the following:

1. The right to be reasonably protected from the accused
2. The right to notice of any court proceeding, parole proceeding, release, or escape of the accused
3. The right not to be excluded from any court proceeding unless attendance might affect the victim's testimony
4. The right to be reasonably heard at any public proceeding regarding release, plea, sentencing, or parole
5. The reasonable right to confer with the federal prosecutor
6. The right to full and timely restitution as provided by law
7. The right to proceedings free of unreasonable delay
8. The right to be treated with fairness and with respect for the victim's dignity and privacy

The rights for victims contained in the statute resemble those in a proposed constitutional amendment called the Crime Victims' Bill of Rights. However, because Congress never took action to initiate the constitutional amendment process, these provisions were placed into a statute instead. At least 20 states have amended their constitutions in order to provide similar protections for crime victims. As you read the Close Up box, consider how a federal constitutional amendment concerning victims' rights might affect the criminal justice system. It is not yet clear how the Justice for All Act will affect the system. It is notable, however, that the act does not authorize crime victims to file lawsuits if government officials fail to fulfill the rights provided by the statute. Only in limited circumstances will violations of these rights permit the victim to request that a plea bargain be rescinded or that an offender be resentenced. In effect, crime victims might have no way to make prosecutors and other court officials obey the statute.

Many states have implemented programs that give information, support, and compensation to victims. Information programs are designed (1) to sensitize justice officials to the need to treat crime victims courteously and (2) to let victims know what is happening at each stage of a case. In some states the investigating officer gives the victim a booklet listing the steps that will be taken and telephone numbers that can be called should questions arise.

Support matters most when the victim faces medical, emotional, or financial problems as a result of a crime. Such support comes from rape crisis centers, victim assistance programs, and family shelters. These programs may be administered by courts, prosecutors' offices, or private agencies. Often these programs rely heavily on volunteers, who may not know enough to recognize the full range of victims' needs, especially the need for psychological assistance to deal with lingering emotional harm. In most states, compensation programs help victims of violent crime by paying the medical expenses of those who cannot afford them. When property has been stolen or destroyed, compensation programs encourage judges to order restitution by the offender as part of the sentencing. Some states also have victim–offender mediation programs to permit victims to express themselves and help offenders to learn about the harmful consequences of their behavior (Lightfoot and Umbreit, 2004).

Crime victims can also file civil lawsuits against the offenders who injured them. Such lawsuits are not difficult to win, especially after an offender's guilt

CLOSE UP

Victims' Rights

IN 1996 A PROPOSED constitutional amendment was introduced in Congress. To become part of the Constitution, the proposed amendment would need to be approved by two-thirds of both chambers of Congress and then ratified by three-fourths of the states through action by their state legislatures or state constitutional conventions. One version of the proposed amendment says, in part:

> To ensure that the victim is treated with fairness, dignity, and respect, from the occurrence of a crime of violence and other crimes as may be defined by law pursuant to section 2 of this article, and throughout the criminal, military, and juvenile justice processes, as a matter of fundamental rights to liberty, justice, and due process, the victim shall have the following rights: to be informed of and given the opportunity to be present at every proceeding in which those rights are extended to the accused or convicted offender; to be heard at any proceeding involving sentencing, including the right to object to a previously negotiated plea, or a release from custody; to be informed of any release or escape; and to a speedy trial, a final conclusion free from unreasonable delay, full restitution from the convicted offender, reasonable measures to protect the victim from violence or intimidation by the accused or convicted offender, and notice of the victim's rights.

The proposed amendment raises many questions. For example, are family members or friends of a murder victim considered "victims" under the proposal? Does the right to be present and object to pleas and sentences really constitute a significant entitlement? Further, the proposed amendment does not guarantee that prosecutors and judges will follow the wishes of crime victims. Indeed, criminal justice officials retain the discretionary authority to ignore crime victims and do what they would have done anyway. They merely have to make sure that victims are notified and permitted to speak.

Should the criminal justice system really accommodate the wishes of victims with respect to sentencing? Would this create increased risks of unequal treatment for convicted offenders? For example, a purse-snatching victim who lost treasured family photographs may be so upset and angry that she demands a maximum sentence of incarceration for the offender. By contrast, another person who is seriously injured in a violent assault may have religious beliefs that emphasize forgiveness and therefore ask the court to send the offender to a counseling program rather than to prison. In theory, criminal punishment reflects society's sense of the appropriate punishment rather than that of an individual victim. In a victim-centered system that caters to the desires of individuals, "justice" may be defined in ways that treat offenders in an unequal manner.

Finally, do any of the proposed rights of victims conflict with existing rights for defendants? The victim's right to a speedy trial stands out as one possible source of problems. Could a victim force a defendant to go to trial before the defendant's attorney is completely prepared? Alternatively, would judges merely define the victim's right to a speedy trial in such a vague manner that the right would be more symbolic than substantive?

Look again at the numbered list of rights created in federal cases by the Justice for All Act of 2004. How does the wording of this statute compare with the wording of the proposed constitutional amendment? Did Congress select wording for the statute that seeks to avoid some of the questions raised by the proposed constitutional amendment?

Researching the Internet

 Although politicians and the public generally support the idea of crime victims' rights, potential problems could arise with the creation of such rights. Using the Internet, find the legal provisions defining crime victims' rights in two different states. How are these laws similar? How are they different?

---

has been proven in a criminal case. However, most offenders cannot afford to pay restitution, especially if they are sitting in prison. Thus, victims typically do not receive full compensation for their losses and the continuing emotional harms that they suffer. See "Doing Your Part" for more on victims' rights; see also "A Question of Ethics," at the end of this chapter.

checkpoint

8. Why do some crime victims feel mistreated by the justice system?
9. What rights have been provided in federal criminal cases by the Justice for All Act?

The Role of Victims in Crime

Victimologists study the role victims play in some crimes. Researchers have found that many victims behave in ways that invite the acts committed against them. This does not mean that it is the victim's fault that the crime occurred. It

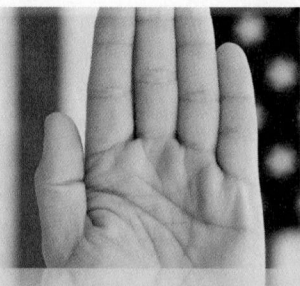

DOING YOUR PART

Crime Victims Assistance Volunteer

WHEN THE PROSECUTOR'S office in Washington County, Oregon, sought to initiate a crime victims' assistance program in 2002, Rita and Vern Strobel became the first volunteers. The Strobels assist victims by accompanying them to court hearings, keeping them informed of the schedule for hearings and trials, explaining how the court system operates, and assisting with the paperwork necessary to get victims' compensation and other benefits.

In Lafayette, Georgia, a court-established program assists both victims and witnesses. Volunteers help to fulfill the provisions of Georgia's Victims' Bill of Rights by informing victims of their rights and educating them about how the court system works. Local victims' assistance programs throughout the country rely on volunteers to provide comfort, support, and assistance to victims of crime. These programs are often administered by local prosecutors' offices. Other programs develop in neighborhood centers. In Buffalo, New York, Linda Kowalewski helped to found the East Side's Neighborhood Information Center in order to assist crime victims. Eventually, the center's activities expanded to include a food pantry and home energy assistance program.

Agencies that administer victims' assistance program are constantly searching for dedicated volunteers interested in serving their communities by helping their fellow citizens who are experiencing the trauma and crisis that accompanies crime victimization.

Researching the Internet

The website for the federal government's Office for Victims of Crime provides information about and links to victims' assistance programs. To link to this website, go to *The American System of Criminal Justice* 12e companion site at academic.cengage.com/criminal justice/cole.

Sources: D. Bonilla, "At East Side Neighborhood Center, Assistance Comes in Many Forms," *Buffalo News*, August 25, 2002, p. C4; S. Martin, "Victim Witness Assistance Program a Big Help to Those Affected by Crime in Georgia," *Chattanooga Times*, April 29, 2002, p. B3; "Meet Your Neighbor: Shepherding Crime Victims," *Portland Oregonian*, April 4, 2002, p. 12.

means instead that the victim's behavior may have increased the risk of the crime through consent, provocation, enticement, risk taking, or carelessness with property.

What do studies tell us about these situations? First, some people do not take proper precautions to protect themselves. For example, they leave keys in their cars or enter unsafe areas. Using common sense may be a requirement of living in modern society. Second, some victims provoke or entice another person to commit a crime. Third, some victims of nonstrangers are not willing to help with the investigation and prosecution. Although these behaviors do not excuse criminal acts, they do force us to think about other aspects of the crime situation.

Karmen points out that some victims are partly to blame for motor vehicle theft (2001: 118). In some cases the victims are legally blameless, while in others they have posed as victims to commit insurance fraud. Victim contributions to motor vehicle theft can include *negligence* (leaving the keys in the vehicle), *precipitation* (leaving the car in a vulnerable location so it can be stolen), and *provocation* (arranging to have a vehicle damaged or destroyed). According to Karmen, survey research indicates that 75 percent of vehicle owners have not installed alarms, 30 percent do not always lock their car doors, and 10 percent admit that they sometimes leave their keys in parked cars (2001: 119).

Victimologists now recognize that victims play a key role—positive or negative—in many crimes. Research shows that their behavior may facilitate crimes. On the other hand, resistance by some victims may prevent offenders from completing robberies and other crimes (Tark and Kleck, 2004).

Clearly, victims affect and are affected by crime in many ways. But victims represent only one of the many factors that help explain crime. We now turn to the major theories of the causes of crime.

checkpoint

10. What behaviors of victims can invite crime?

CAUSES OF CRIME

Whenever news of a crime hits the headlines, whether the crime is a grisly murder or complex bank fraud, the first question is "Why did he (or she) do it?" Do people commit crimes because they are poor, greedy, mentally ill, or just plain stupid? If you look at any newspaper on a single day, you can see reports on a variety of crimes. For example, on March 19, 2005, newspapers reported on the former governor of Connecticut being sentenced to prison for accepting money and gifts from contractors; New York City detectives accused of being "hit men" working for organized-crime leaders; and the government's concerns about preventing terrorist attacks on public transportation (Feuer, 2005; Lipton, 2005b; Yardley and Stowe, 2005). Can we link all of these crimes to a single cause? Are there differences between these crimes and other offenses, such as a young man who sells illegal drugs or a repeat sex offender who kidnaps and murders a young child? These and similar difficult questions serve as the focus of the field of academic study known as criminology.

Criminology centers on learning about criminal behavior, the nature of offenders, and how crime can be prevented. Research focuses mainly on the offender. Fewer questions are asked about how factors such as the economy, government policy, family, and education affect crime (Messner and Rosenfeld, 1994: 45–47). In this section we look at the two major schools of criminological thought—classical and positivist. We then examine biological, psychological, sociological, and life course theories of the causes of criminal behavior. Finally, we explore women and crime and assess the various theories.

Classical and Positivist Theories

Two major schools of criminological thought are the classical and positivist schools. Each was pioneered by scholars influenced by the dominant intellectual ideas of their times.

The Classical School

Until the eighteenth century, most Europeans explained criminal behavior in supernatural terms—as the work of the devil. Those who did wrong were "possessed" by the devil. Some Christians believed that all humanity had fallen with Adam and had remained in a state of total depravity ever since. Indictments often began, "[John Doe], not having the fear of God before his eyes but being moved and seduced by the instigation of the devil, did commit [a certain crime]." Such approaches to crime stemmed from a clear differentiation between good people and evil people. In addition, by attributing crime to the devil, this viewpoint did not see possibilities for lawbreakers to control their own behavior.

Before the eighteenth century, defendants had few rights. The accused had little chance to put forth a defense, confessions were obtained through torture, and the penalty for most offenses was physical punishment or death.

In 1764 Cesare Beccaria published his *Essays on Crime and Punishments.* This was the first attempt to explain crime in secular, or worldly, terms instead of religious terms. The book also pointed to injustices in the administration of criminal laws. Beccaria's ideas prompted reformers to try to make criminal law and procedures more rational and consistent. From this movement came **classical criminology,** whose main principles are as follows:

1. Criminal behavior is rational, and most people have the potential to engage in such behavior.

2. People may choose to commit a crime after weighing the costs and benefits of their actions.

3. Fear of punishment is what keeps most people in check. Therefore, the severity, certainty, and speed of punishment affect the level of crime.

4. The punishment should fit the crime, not the person who committed it.

5. The criminal justice system must be predictable, with laws and punishments known to the public.

classical criminology
A school of criminology that views behavior as stemming from free will, that demands responsibility and accountability of all perpetrators, and that stresses the need for punishments severe enough to deter others.

Classical ideas declined in the nineteenth century, partly because of the rise of science and partly because its principles did not take into account differences between individuals or the way the crime was committed.

Neoclassical Criminology After remaining dormant for almost a hundred years, classical ideas took on new life in the 1980s, when America became more conservative. Some scholars argue that crimes may result from the *rational choice* of people who have weighed the benefits to be gained from the crime against the costs of being caught and punished. But they also recognize that the criminal law must take account of differences among individuals. To a large extent, sentencing reform, criticisms of rehabilitation, and greater use of incarceration stem from this renewed interest in classical ideas, or *neoclassicism*. However, the positivist school of thought has dominated American criminology since the start of the twentieth century.

Positivist Criminology

positivist criminology
A school of criminology that views behavior as stemming from social, biological, and psychological factors. It argues that punishment should be tailored to the individual needs of the offender.

By the middle of the nineteenth century, as the scientific method began to take hold, the ideas of the classical school seemed old-fashioned. Instead, **positivist criminology** used science to study the body, mind, and environment of the offender. Science could help reveal why offenders committed crimes and how they could be rehabilitated. Here are the key features of this approach:

1. Human behavior is controlled by physical, mental, and social factors, not by free will.
2. Criminals are different from noncriminals.
3. Science can be used to discover the causes of crime and to treat deviants.

Positivism has served as the foundation for many types of theories, which we explore in the following sections. Understanding the main theories of crime causation is important because they affect how laws are enforced, guilt is determined, and crimes are punished. As we describe each of the theories, consider its implications for crime policies. For example, if biological theories are viewed as sound, then the authorities might try to identify potential offenders through genetic analysis and then segregate or supervise them. On the other hand, the acceptance of sociological theories might lead to efforts to end poverty, improve education, and provide job training.

checkpoint

11. What were the main assumptions of the classical school?
12. What are the main assumptions of the positivist school?

Biological Explanations

criminogenic
Factors thought to bring about criminal behavior in an individual.

The medical training of Cesare Lombroso (1836–1909) led him to suppose that physical traits distinguish criminals from law-abiding citizens. He believed that some people are at a more primitive state of evolution and hence are born criminal. These "throwbacks" have trouble adjusting to modern society. Lombroso's ideas can be summarized as follows (Lombroso, 1968 [1912]):

1. Certain people are born criminals with **criminogenic** traits.
2. They have primitive physical traits such as strong canine teeth, huge jaws, and high cheekbones.
3. These traits are acquired through heredity or through alcoholism, epilepsy, or syphilis.

Around the turn of the century, interest shifted from physical traits to inherited traits that affect intelligence. Some scholars believed that criminals commit crimes to alleviate pathological urges inherited from mentally defective ancestors. They studied genealogies to find the links between these traits and the criminal records of family members.

Two studies, first published in 1875 and 1902, of families with the fictitious names of Jukes and Kallikak, presented evidence that genetic defects passed on to offspring could condemn them to lives of crime. Richard Dugdale studied more than 1,000 descendants of the woman he called Ada Jukes, whom he dubbed the "mother of criminals." Among them were 280 paupers, 60 thieves, 7 murderers, 140 criminals, 40 people with venereal diseases, and 50 prostitutes (Dugdale, 1910). Similar data collected by Henry H. Goddard (1902) supported the belief that the Kallikak family, whose members were all related to the illegitimate son of Martin Kallikak, contained more criminals than did the descendants of Martin's later marriage into a "good" family.

These early studies may no longer seem credible to us, but they were taken seriously in their time and affected criminal justice for decades. For example, many states passed laws that required repeat offenders to be sterilized. It was assumed that crime could be controlled if criminal traits were not passed from parents to children. Not until 1942 did the U.S. Supreme Court declare required sterilization unconstitutional (*Skinner v. Oklahoma*).

Renewed Interest in Biological Explanations

Although **biological explanations** of crime were ignored or condemned as racist after World War II, they have attracted renewed interest. *Crime and Human Nature*, by James Q. Wilson and Richard Herrnstein, reviews the research on this subject (Wilson and Herrnstein, 1985). Unlike the early positivists, the authors do not claim that any one factor explains criminality. Instead, they argue that biological factors predispose some people to a crime. Genetic makeup, body type, and IQ may outweigh social factors as predictors of criminality. The findings of research on nutrition, neurology, genetics, and endocrinology give some support to the view that these factors may contribute to violent behavior in some people (Brennan, Mednick, and Volavka, 1995: 65). Other researchers have identified physiological factors associated with antisocial behavior, which they see as a step toward considering a possible link between biology and offending (Cauffman, Steinberg, and Piquero, 2005).

These new findings have given biological explanations a renewed influence and reduced the dominance of sociological and psychological explanations. Scientists are doing further research to see if they can find biological factors that make some people prone to violence and criminality (Fishbein, 1990: 27). For example, a study published in 2002 found that a single gene can help predict which abused children will become violent or antisocial adults. Although most abused children do not commit crimes, studies indicate that abused children are twice as likely as other children to commit crimes later in life. Abused children with a specific gene identified in the study were twice as likely as other abused children to commit acts of violence (Hathaway, 2002). The study does not prove that possession of the gene causes a person to commit crimes, because 15 percent of the abused children with the gene did not do so. However, it provides an interesting indication of how genetic factors (such as a specific gene) may interact with life experiences (such as victimization by child abuse) to trigger or facilitate later criminal behavior.

Contemporary research does not merely look at genes as providing a biological basis for behavior that can lead to crime. Researchers also examine specific physical and environmental conditions that affect the human body and thereby potentially influence behavior. In one obvious example, individuals who receive certain kinds of head injuries or suffer from tumors in particular locations of the brain can experience impairments affecting their knowledge, perception, and behavior. Other people may have abnormal levels of certain chemicals in

biological explanations
Explanations of crime that emphasize physiological and neurological factors that may predispose a person to commit crimes.

their brains that affect hyperactivity, irritability, and risk-taking behavior. If such conditions are diagnosed and people have access to treatment, doctors may prescribe certain drugs to counteract the chemical imbalance. People who suffer from specific medical conditions, such as Attention Deficit Hyperactivity Disorder (ADHD), may be prone to aggressiveness and impulsive behavior that can lead to the violation of criminal laws, such as fighting, substance abuse, and improper operation of motor vehicles. Their problems may be compounded if they come from poor families in which they lacked opportunities for diagnosis, treatment, and supervision.

Other studies examine links between nutrition and behavior. Many studies explore possible connections between sugar consumption or vitamin deficiencies and aggressiveness, intelligence, or specific psychological problems. For example, one study found that consumption of fish rich in omega-3, such as salmon, is associated with lower levels of hostility in young adults (Iribarren et al., 2004). A study of young offenders in a British prison found a decrease in antisocial behavior among those who received vitamins and nutritional supplements (Gesch et al., 2002). Such studies raise interesting possibilities for affecting some potential offenders through greater understanding of the links between diet and behavior.

Studies also examine environmental influences on brain development and behavior. Herbert Needleman, a medical researcher who has studied the effects of lead on children for 30 years, stated in a 2005 report to the American Association for the Advancement of Sciences that "when environmental lead finds its way into the developing brain, it disturbs neural mechanisms responsible for regulation of impulse. That can lead to antisocial and criminal behavior" (University of Pittsburgh Medical Center, 2005). Medical researchers have long known that children's exposure to lead paint affects brain development, but Needleman's research has found a link between lead exposure and juvenile delinquency. Because people in modern society are exposed to lead and other chemicals through polluted air and water, factory operations, and other sources, additional research on exposure to environmental contaminants may lead to greater understanding of the connections between chemical effects on the human body and antisocial behavior.

Policy Implications of Biological Explanations

A policy based on biological theories of crime would attempt to identify people who have traits that make them prone to crime and then treat or control those people. This might lead to selective incarceration, intensive supervision, or drug therapies. Special education might be required for those with learning disabilities. In addition, research concerning environmental influences on the human body, such as excessive exposure to lead or the need for better nutrition, could lead to policies that attempt to limit environmental harms and provide better nutrition and medical care for targeted populations. Because modern research has never established a simple connection between biology and criminality, however, these policy approaches are highly problematic. As indicated by the recent study connecting a genetic marker in some abused children with higher rates of subsequent violent behavior, not all of the child-abuse victims with the gene committed crimes. Moreover, there appears to be an interaction between life experiences and the gene. Thus, basing policies merely on the gene or some other biological connection would lead to the treatment or punishment of too many people.

checkpoint

13. What were the main elements of Lombroso's theory?

Dennis Rader, the serial killer self-named "BTK" (for "bind, torture, kill") was convicted in August 2005 of brutally killing 10 people in Wichita, Kansas. Does criminological theory help us understand what motivated him to commit these terrible acts?

© Bo Rader-Pool/Getty Images

Psychological Explanations

People have often viewed criminal behavior as being caused by a mental condition, a personality disturbance, or limited intellect. **Psychological explanations** of crime center on these ideas.

Before the eighteenth century, as we have seen, those who engaged in such behavior were thought to be possessed by demons. However, some scholars suggested that defects in the body and mind caused people to act "abnormally." One early advocate of this idea was Henry Maudsley (1835–1918), an English psychologist who believed that criminals were "morally insane." Moral insanity, he argued, is an innate characteristic, and crime is a way of expressing it. Without crime as an outlet, criminals would become insane (Maudsley, 1974).

Sigmund Freud (1856–1939), now seen as one of the foremost thinkers of the twentieth century, proposed a *psychoanalytic theory* that crime is caused by unconscious forces and drives. Freud also claimed that early childhood experiences greatly affected personality development. Freud's followers expanded his theory, saying that the personality is made up of three parts: the id, ego, and superego. The id controls drives that are primarily sexual, the ego relates desires to behavior, and the superego (often referred to as the conscience) judges actions as either right or wrong. Psychoanalytic theory explains criminal behavior as resulting from either an undeveloped or an overdeveloped superego. For example, a person who commits a violent sex crime is thought to have an undeveloped superego, because the urges cannot be controlled. Alternatively, a person with an overdeveloped superego may suffer from guilt and anxiety. To reduce the guilt, the person may commit a crime, knowing that punishment will follow. To ensure punishment, the offender will unconsciously leave clues at the crime scene. Psychoanalysts say this occurred in the famous Loeb-Leopold murder of Bobby Franks in 1924 (Regoli and Hewitt, 1994).

Psychiatrists have linked criminal behavior to such concepts as innate impulses, psychic conflict, and the repression of personality. Such explanations propose that crime is a behavior that takes the place of abnormal urges and desires. Although the psychological approach takes many different forms, all are based on the idea that early personality development influences later behavior.

psychological explanations
Explanations of crime that emphasize mental processes and behavior.

NEW DIRECTIONS in CRIMINAL JUSTICE POLICY

Dealing with Sex Offenders

SEX OFFENSES ARE among the most shocking of crimes, especially when children are victimized by repeat offenders. Yet some sex offenders repeatedly gained opportunities in recent years to commit crimes because, after being convicted for a crime, they served their complete prison sentences and then gained release from custody.

Because many criminal justice officials concluded that repeat sex offenders are motivated by deep-seated psychological problems that are difficult, if not impossible, to cure, efforts emerged to find ways to keep repeat sex offenders confined in secure treatment centers. Many state legislatures enacted laws to provide for such custody and treatment, even for offenders who had already served their prison sentences.

People who were confined to such facilities filed legal actions claiming that, by punishing them twice for their offenses, these laws violated their constitutional right against double jeopardy. The first punishment was the prison term and the second punishment was the civil commitment and mandatory residential treatment of indefinite duration. The U.S. Supreme Court, however, rejected those claims and approved state laws that provide for repeat sex offend-

ers' potentially indefinite confinement in secure treatment facilities (*Kansas v. Hendricks*, 1997). This policy is based on the presumption that repeat sex offenders suffer from severe psychological problems that require continuing confinement and treatment.

By choosing specific individuals for confinement, presumably for long periods and perhaps even for life, such policies have a selective incapacitation effect. Selective incapacitation always creates risks that someone will be confined who really would not have committed another crime. It is extremely difficult, and probably impossible, to make perfectly accurate predictions about people's future behavior. Thus, the Supreme Court has warned states to be careful in defining which people are eligible for civil confinement and treatment as well as determining the nature of proof required before a person can be placed in custody.

Researching the Internet

  To investigate the laws in your state and other states concerning sex offenders, find the links to various states' statutes at Findlaw. For example, see Washington's law on sexually violent predators in Title 71.09. To link to this website, go to *The American System of Criminal Justice* 12e companion site at academic .cengage.com/criminaljustice/cole.

Psychopathology

For an example of policies based on psychological theories of crime causation, see the website of the Texas Council on Sex Offender Treatment. To link to this website, go to *The American System of Criminal Justice* 12e companion site at academic.cengage.com/criminaljustice/cole.

The terms *psychopath, sociopath,* and *antisocial personality* refer to a person who is unable to control impulses, cannot learn from experience, and does not feel emotions, such as love. This kind of person is viewed as psychologically abnormal, as a crazed killer or sex fiend.

During the 1940s, after several widely publicized sex crimes, many state legislatures passed "sexual psychopath laws" designed to place "homicidal sex fiends" in treatment institutions. Such laws were later shown to be based on false assumptions. They reveal the political context within which the criminal law is fashioned (Sutherland, 1950).

Psychological theories have been widely criticized. Some critics point to the fact that measuring emotional factors is difficult, as is identifying people thought to be prone to crime. Others note the wide range of theories—some contradicting one another—that take a psychological approach to crime.

Policy Implications of Psychological Explanations

Despite the criticisms, psychological explanations have played a major role in criminal justice policy during the twentieth century and beyond. The major implication of these theories is that people with personality disorders should receive treatment, while those whose illegal behaviors stem from learning should be punished so that they will learn that crime is not rewarded.

Policies that stress rehabilitation attempt to change the offender's personality and hence behavior. From the 1940s to the mid-1970s, psychotherapy, counseling, group therapy, behavior modification, and moral development programs were used in efforts to rehabilitate criminals. However, the past three decades have seen less reliance on these policies, except as a justification to confine repeat sex offenders even after they have served their full criminal sentences. As you read about these programs in "New Directions in Criminal Justice Policy," consider whether you think this is an appropriate application of psychological theory.

checkpoint

14. What is a psychopath?

Sociological Explanations

In contrast to psychological approaches, **sociological explanations** focus on the way that belonging to social groups shapes people's behavior. Sociologists believe that criminality is caused by external factors rather than being inborn. Thus, sociological theories of crime assume that contact with the social world, as well as such factors as race, age, gender, and income, mold the offender's personality and actions.

Social theorist Emile Durkheim (1858–1917) argued that when a simple rural society develops into a complex urbanized one, traditional standards decline. Some people cannot adjust to the new rules and will engage in criminal acts.

In the 1920s a group of researchers at the University of Chicago looked closely at aspects of urban life that seemed linked to crime: poverty, bad housing, broken families, and the problems faced by new immigrants. They found high levels of crime in those neighborhoods that had many opportunities for delinquent behavior and few legitimate means of earning a living.

From a sociological perspective, criminals are made, not born. Among the many theories stressing the influence of societal forces on criminal behavior, three types deserve special mention: social structure theories, social process theories, and social conflict theories.

sociological explanations
Explanations of crime that emphasize the social conditions that bear on the individual as causes of criminal behavior.

Social Structure Theories

Social structure theories suggest that criminal behavior is related to social class. People in various social classes have quite different amounts of wealth, status, and power. Those in the lower class suffer from poverty, poor education, bad housing, and lack of political power. Therefore, members of the lower class, especially the younger members, are the most likely to engage in crime. Crime thus is created by the structure of society.

Sociologist Robert Merton extended Durkheim's ideas about the role of social change and urbanization on crime. He stressed that social change often leads to a state of **anomie,** in which the rules or norms that guide behavior have weakened or disappeared. People may become anomic when the rules are unclear or they are unable to achieve their goals. Under such conditions, antisocial or deviant behavior may result.

It is said, for example, that American society highly values success but makes it impossible for some of its members to succeed. It follows that those who are caught in this trap may use crime as a way out. Theorists believe that this type of situation has led some ethnic groups into organized crime. Others argue that social disorganization brings about conditions in which, among other things, family structure breaks down, alcohol or drug abuse becomes more common, and criminal behavior increases. They assert that poverty must be ended and the social structure reformed if crime is to be reduced.

social structure theories
Theories that attribute crime to the existence of a powerless lower class that lives with poverty and deprivation and often turns to crime in response.

anomie
A breakdown in and disappearance of the rules of social behavior.

Contemporary Theories Contemporary theorists have drawn from social structure concepts and Merton's anomie theory to develop certain theories of crime causation. Prominent among modern approaches is the general theory of strain.

According to this approach, negative relationships can lead to negative emotions. These emotions, particularly anger, are expressed through crime and delinquency. *Strain* results from the failure to achieve valued goals, which may particularly affect poor people in a society that values financial success. Strain is also produced by negative experiences, including unemployment, child abuse, criminal victimization, and family problems, which also may prevail in poor communities. Under the theory, those who cannot cope with negative experiences may be predisposed to criminal behavior (Liska and Messner, 1999: 36–37).

As these ideas have become more refined, they have been applied to white-collar crime. Although one may assume that the affluent would benefit most from American social structure, theorists have raised this question: Do business people measure their success against the wealth and power of those that they see above them in their corporate settings and affluent communities? To achieve even higher levels of success in a structure that values ever-increasing wealth, individuals may break rules and violate laws in order to enhance their personal success. Thus, structure theories have been used to explain the behavior of corporate leaders who manipulate stock prices and take other actions to add to their wealth despite already being millionaires (Liska and Messner, 1999: 37).

Policy Implications of Social Structure Theories If crime is caused by social conditions, then actions should be taken to reform the conditions that breed crime. Such actions include policies to combat the effects of poverty, including education and job training, urban redevelopment, better health care, and economic development. Theorists who apply structural theories to white-collar crime are likely to see such criminality as an inevitable component of a society with a free-market economy that equates wealth with success.

Social Process Theories

Many criminologists believe that the social structure approach does not adequately explain criminality by middle-class and affluent people. They fear that a focus on social structure erroneously presents crime as a problem mainly of the poor. **Social process theories**, which date from the 1930s but did not gain recognition until the 1960s and 1970s, assume that any person, regardless of education, class, or upbringing, has the potential to become a criminal. However, some people are likely to commit criminal acts because of the circumstances of their lives. Thus, these theories try to explain the processes by which certain people become criminals.

Three Social Process Theories There are three main types of social process theories: learning theories, control theories, and labeling theories.

Learning theories hold that criminal activity is learned behavior. Through social relations, some people learn how to be a criminal and acquire the values associated with that way of life. This view assumes that people imitate and learn from one another. Thus, family members and peers are viewed as major influences on a person's development.

In 1939 Edwin Sutherland proposed a type of learning theory called the **theory of differential association**, which states that people learn behavior through interactions with others, especially family members (Sutherland, 1947). Criminal behavior occurs when a person encounters others who are more favorable to crime than opposed to it. If a boy grows up in a family where, say, an older brother is involved in crime, he will tend to learn criminal behavior. If people in the family, neighborhood, and gang believe that illegal activity is not shameful, this belief increases the chance that the young person will engage in crime.

Control theories hold that social links keep people in line with accepted norms (M. Gottfredson and Hirschi, 1990; Hirschi, 1969). In other words, all

social process theories
Theories that see criminality as normal behavior. Everyone has the potential to become a criminal, depending on (1) the influences that impel one toward or away from crime and (2) how one is regarded by others.

learning theories
Theories that see criminal behavior as learned, just as legal behavior is learned.

theory of differential association
The theory that people become criminals because they encounter more influences that view criminal behavior as normal and acceptable than influences that are hostile to criminal behavior.

control theories
Theories holding that criminal behavior occurs when the bonds that tie an individual to society are broken or weakened.

members of society have the potential to commit crime, but most are restrained by their ties to family, church, school, and peer groups. Thus, sensitivity to the opinion of others, commitment to a conventional lifestyle, and belief in the standards or values shared by friends all influence a person to abide by the law. A person who lacks one or more of these influences may engage in crime.

Finally, **labeling theories** stress the social process through which certain acts and people are labeled as deviant. As Howard Becker notes, society creates deviance—and, hence, criminality—"by making the rules whose infraction constitutes deviance, and by applying those rules to particular people and labeling them outsiders" (Becker, 1963).

Becker studied the process through which people become deviant. Social control agencies, such as the police, courts, and corrections, are created to label certain people as outside the normal, law-abiding community. When they have been labeled, those people come to believe that the label is true. They take on a deviant identity and start acting in deviant ways. Once labeled, the person is presumed by others to be deviant, and they react accordingly. This reinforces the deviant identity.

Labeling theory has generated criticism and debate. Many scholars question whether evidence exists to support the theory, especially when one looks broadly at the various kinds of activities and types of people involved in acts that constitute crimes.

Policy Implications of Social Process Theories If crime is a learned behavior, it follows that people need to be treated in ways that build conventional bonds, develop positive role models, and avoid labeling. Policies to promote stable families and develop community agencies to help those in need are based on this view. Examine the issue in "Civic Engagement: Your Role in the System" and consider whether social process theories—or other theories about the causes of criminal behavior—would provide the basis for suggestions that you make about how to reduce crimes committed by juveniles.

Social Conflict Theories

In the mid-1960s, the then-current biological, psychological, and sociological explanations of criminal behavior were challenged by **social conflict theories**. These theories assume that criminal law and the justice system are designed mainly to control the poor. The rich commit as many crimes as do the poor, it is argued, but the poor are more likely to be caught and punished. Those in power use the law to impose their version of morality on society in order to protect their property and safety. They use their power to change the definitions of crime to target acts they view as threatening.

Types of Social Conflict Theories There are different types of social conflict theories. One type, proposed by critical, radical, or Marxist criminologists, holds that the class structure causes certain groups to be labeled as deviant. In this view, "deviance is a status imputed to groups who share certain structural characteristics (e.g., powerlessness)" (Spitzer , 1975: 639). Thus, the criminal law is aimed at the behavior of specific groups or classes. One result is that the poor are deeply hostile toward the social order, and this hostility is one factor in criminal behavior. Moreover, when the status quo is threatened, legal definitions of crime are changed in order to trap those who challenge the system. For example, vagrancy laws have been used to arrest labor union organizers, civil rights workers, and peace activists when those in power believed that these groups threatened their interests.

labeling theories
Theories emphasizing that the causes of criminal behavior are not found in the individual but in the social process that labels certain acts as deviant or criminal.

civic engagement
your role in the system

Imagine that your state's governor identified you as a local community leader and asked you to serve on your county's juvenile crime prevention council to help suggest and plan programs to prevent youth crime. *Which theories of crime causation would provide the basis for your suggestions? Make a list of three suggestions to prevent youth crime and identify which theory or theories of crime causation relate to each suggestion.* Then examine the website of the North Carolina Juvenile Crime Prevention Councils to see what programs are actually being advanced in that state. To link to this website, go to *The American System of Criminal Justice* 12e companion site at academic.cengage .com/criminaljustice/cole.

social conflict theories
Theories that assume criminal law and the criminal justice system are primarily a means of controlling the poor and the have-nots.

 Go to the website of the National Check Fraud Center and read about different kinds of white-collar crime. Which theories of crime provide the most plausible explanations for the various kinds of offenses? To link to this website, go to *The American System of Criminal Justice* 12e companion site at academic.cengage.com/criminaljustice/cole.

Policy Implications of Social Conflict Theories Conflict theories require policies that would reduce class-based conflict and injustice. Policies to help women, the poor, and minorities deal with government agencies would follow. Criminal justice resources would focus on crimes committed by upper-class as well as lower-class offenders.

Like other theories about the causes of criminal behavior, sociological theories have met with criticism. Their critics argue that these theories are imprecise, unsupported by evidence, and based on ideology. Even so, sociological theories have served as the basis for many attempts to prevent crime and rehabilitate offenders.

checkpoint

15. What is the main assumption of social structure theories?
16. What is the main assumption of social process theories?
17. What is the main assumption of social conflict theories?

Life Course Explanations

life course theories
Theories that identify factors affecting the start, duration, nature, and end of criminal behavior over the life of an offender.

Life course theories seek to identify factors that shape criminal careers, in order to explain when and why offenders begin to commit crimes and to see what factors lead individuals to stop their participation in crimes.

Studies in this area often try to follow individuals from childhood through adulthood in order to identify the factors associated with beginning, avoiding, continuing, or ceasing criminal behavior. Criminal careers often begin at an early age; people who eventually become involved with crime often exhibit disruptive behavior, lack family support, and experiment with drinking and drugs as youths. Some theorists discuss *pathways* into crime, which may begin with minor habits of lying and stealing that lead to more serious offenses. However, pathways into crime are not identical for all kinds of offenders (Maxwell and Maxwell, 2000). For example, those youths who engage in bullying and fighting may begin a pathway toward different kinds of crimes and criminal careers than do those who start out using and selling drugs.

What factors might shape the future behavior of these children? How do life course explanations contribute to our understanding of why some people commit crimes?

AP Images/Kathy Willens

The factors identified by life course theorists that can impact criminal careers overlap with factors discussed in psychological, social structure, and social process theories, such as unemployment, failure in school, impulsiveness, and unstable families. In other words, life course theorists' ideas about factors associated with criminal behavior are consistent with factors identified in other theories. However, these theorists study criminal behavior from a broader perspective as something that develops, evolves, changes, and sometimes ends over the course of a person's life.

The research of Robert Sampson and John Laub is among the most influential in examining the life course and criminal careers (Sampson and Laub, 1993; Laub and Sampson, 2003). They reanalyzed and built on the famous studies of Sheldon and Eleanor Glueck that had followed the lives of 1,000 Boston-area boys from 1940 through the 1960s (Glueck and Glueck, 1950). The Gluecks' studies had matched and compared the lives of 500 delinquent boys with those of 500 nondelinquent boys from the same neighborhoods who possessed similar backgrounds and characteristics. Sampson and Laub gathered data on the same men in the 1990s, by which time the surviving "boys" from the original study were becoming senior citizens.

Based on their research, Sampson and Laub discuss informal and formal social controls over the life course. Unlike some researchers, who see youthful criminality as setting into place behavior patterns that continue into adulthood, Sampson and Laub emphasize *turning points* in life that move individuals away from criminal careers. For example, their study showed that military service, employment, and marriage served as particularly important factors leading away from criminal careers, while incarceration and alcohol abuse were associated with continued lawbreaking. Other researchers have tested the theory by, for example, examining how the experience of incarceration may diminish an offender's prospects for positive life course developments, such as marriage and employment (Huebner, 2005). In another example, researchers examined whether the development of religiosity may be another turning-point factor, but the evidence in that regard is weak and requires further long-term studies (Giordano et al., 2008). As indicated by this summary, life course explanations do not seek to identify a single or primary factor as the cause of criminal behavior. Instead, they try to identify and evaluate the timing, interaction, and results of complex factors that affect people's lives.

Policy Implications of Life Course Theories Although life course theories highlight the complex factors and situations that can affect individuals differently throughout their lives, several elements emerge for policy makers. They might, for instance, try to diminish the use of incarceration for young offenders, because such experiences are associated with criminal careers that continue into adulthood. Policies might also be developed to encourage and support key turning points, such as marriage and stable employment, that are associated with individuals' moves away from criminal activities.

checkpoint

18. What are potential turning points for criminal careers in life course theories?

Women and Crime

Theories about causes of crime are almost all based on observations of men. The fact that women commit crime less often than men (and the fact that most criminologists have historically been male) has helped to explain this fact (Klein, 1973). Many people assumed that most women, because of their nurturing and

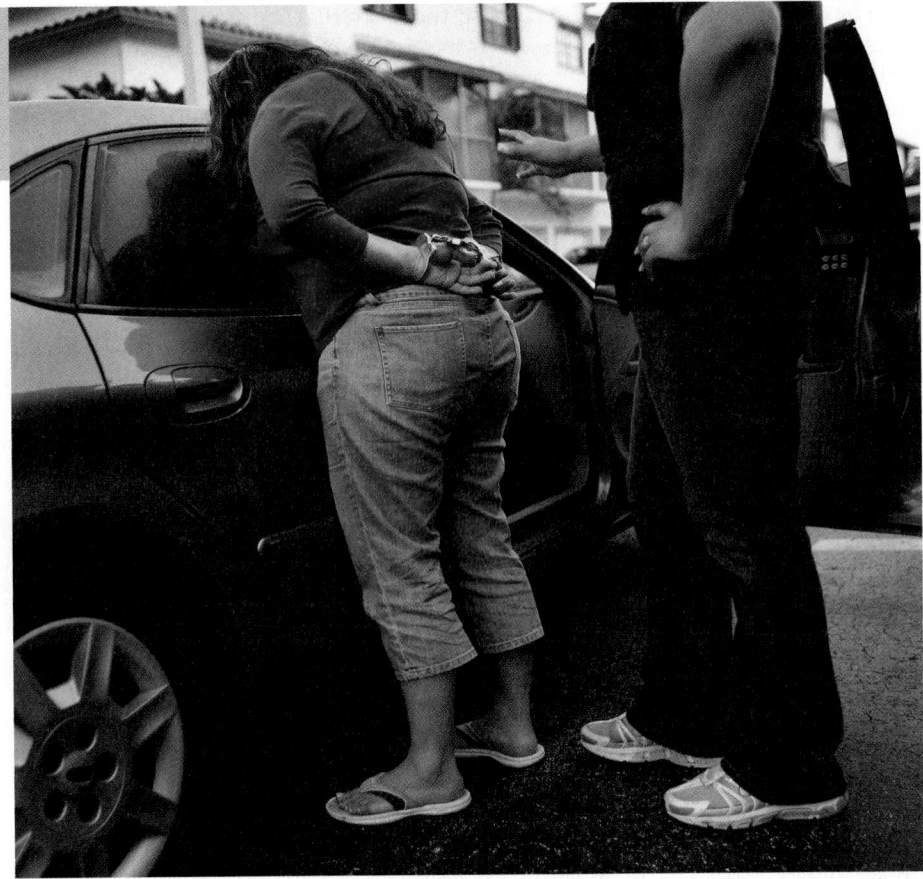

A Miami police officer arrests Josephine Martinez in 2008 as part of a crackdown on mortgage fraud scams. How has women's participation in crime changed in recent decades?

© Joe Raedle/Getty Images

dependent nature, could not commit serious crimes. Those who did commit crimes were labeled as "bad" or "fallen" women. Unlike male criminals, then, female criminals were viewed as moral offenders.

Most traditional theories of crime cannot explain two important facts about gender and offending. First, a theory that purports to explain crime causation must explain why women are less likely to commit crime than men (the "gender gap"). Women accounted for approximately 24 percent of all arrests in 2006, with men responsible for the remaining 76 percent (FBI, 2006). Second, an effective theory must explain why women commit different kinds of crime than men do—women are less likely to be arrested for violent crimes than men, and are more likely to be arrested for crimes such as embezzlement and prostitution (FBI, 2006). Although it is a challenge to explain these differences, criminologists must also remind themselves to avoid overgeneralizing about the behavior of men versus the behavior of women. Individual offenders who are male or female may have similar motivations or personal circumstances that shape their criminal behavior (Kruttschnitt and Carbone-Lopez, 2006).

Figure 2.5 displays the differences in offending between men and women for serious crimes. Female offenders are less likely to be arrested for any type of offense than male offenders. In addition, women are mostly likely to be arrested for larceny/theft than any other offense (approximately 38 percent of all arrests for theft were women), but men are still twice as likely as women to be arrested for larceny/theft.

Two books published in 1975 attempted to explain these facts about female offending. Rita Simon's *Women and Crime* and Freda Adler's *Sisters in Crime* both hypothesized that women's liberation would result in increases in female offending. Although Adler and Simon disagreed about how the *types* of crime

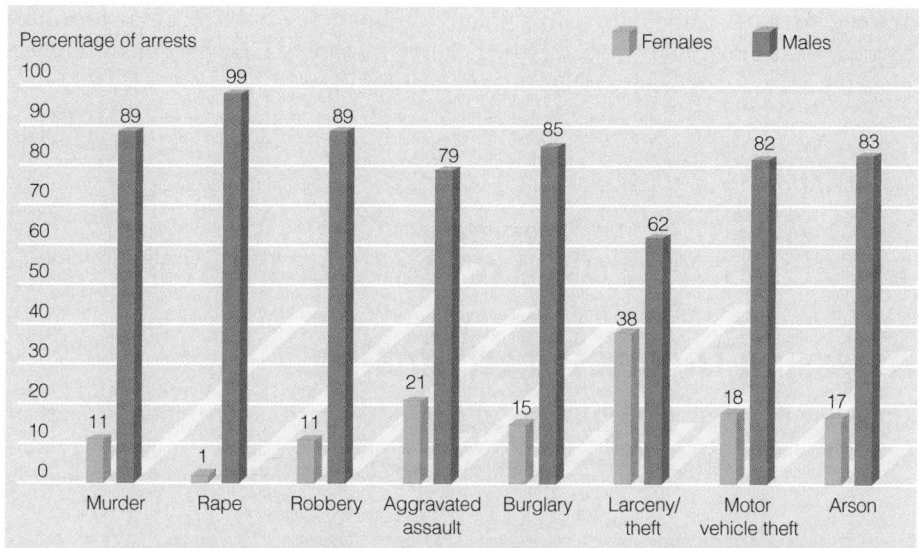

FIGURE 2.5

How do the types of crimes committed by men and women differ?
While most arrests are of men, women make up a relatively high percentage of arrests for larceny/theft.

Source: Federal Bureau of Investigation, *Crime in the United States, 2006* (Washington, DC: U.S. Government Printing Office, 2007), Table 42.

committed by women would be affected by women's liberation, both agreed the gender gap would be reduced significantly. It can be a challenge, however, to test predictions with complete accuracy. For example, an apparent increase in violence by women as measured by arrests might also be affected by changing police policies, such as the adoption of "zero tolerance" for any domestic violence situation, rather than an actual widespread change in offending by women (Steffensmeier et al., 2005).

Beginning in the 1990s, theorists recognized the importance of *social structure* in explaining female criminality. These theorists posit that our society is structured in such a way as to create different opportunities for men and women in the workforce, that power differentials exist between men and women, and that important differences in sexuality shape the behavior of men and women (Messerschmidt, 1993). Behavioral differences between male and female offenders can have adverse consequences for women. For example, corrections officials may apply predictive tools for the risk of re-offending that do not accurately account for differences in offending patterns by some women and thereby disadvantage women in classification processes and in the allocation of resources in corrections programs (Reisig, Holtfreter, and Morash, 2006.)

In recent decades, scholars also increased their attention to testing various crime causation theories using data about women suspects and offenders. For example, the impact of "strain" from sociological theory has been found to affect changes in offending and drug use patterns among a sample of female subjects (Slocum, Simpson, and Smith, 2005). Recent developments related to women and crime include life course theories, which focus on the paths taken by individuals through life and identify important turning points in people lives—these "transitions" can affect individual behavior and lead people either to or away from criminal activity (Sampson and Laub, 1990). To better explain gender and crime, feminist pathways researchers focus on the impact of critical life events, such as victimization, to determine why some women engage in criminal behavior. It is well known, for example, that many women working as prostitutes were sexually abused as children (Widom, 1995).

As the status of women changes and as more women pursue careers in business and industry, some scholars believe that women will commit more economic and occupational crimes, such as embezzlement and fraud. However, research continues to show that arrested women, like male offenders, tend to come from poor families in which physical and substance abuse are present (Rosenbaum, 1989: 31). Other researchers believe that the rising crime rates among women are due in part to a greater willingness of police and prosecutors to treat them like men. Thus far, the findings of research on gender differences in crime are not conclusive (Decker et al., 1993: 142).

Checkpoint

19. What have feminist researchers contributed to theories of female criminality?
20. How do the number and trends in arrests compare for male and female arrestees?

Assessing Theories of Criminality

Undoubtedly, many of the theories of crime described here contain at least an element of truth (see Table 2.3). However, none is powerful enough to predict criminality or establish a specific cause for an offender's behavior. The theories

TABLE 2.3	Major Theories of Criminality and Their Policy Implications

Scholars and the public support various types of policies. We know little about the real causes of crime, but note how many people think they have the answers!

Theory	Major Premise	Policy Implications	Policy Implementation
Biological	Genetic, biochemical, or neurological defects cause some people to commit crime.	Identification and treatment or control of persons with crime-producing biological factors. Selective incapacitation, intensive supervision.	1. Use of drugs to inhibit biological urges of sex offenders. 2. Use of controlled diet to reduce levels of antisocial behavior caused by biochemical imbalances. 3. Identification of neurological defects through CAT scans. Use of drugs to suppress violent impulses. 4. Special education for those with learning disabilities.
Psychological	Personality and learning factors cause some people to commit crime.	Treatment of those with personality disorders to achieve mental health. Those whose illegal behavior stems from learning should have their behavior punished so they will realize that crime is not rewarded.	1. Psychotherapy and counseling to treat personality disorders. 2. Behavior modification strategies, such as electric shock and other negative impulses, to change learned behavior. 3. Counseling to enhance moral development. 4. Intensive individual and group therapies.
Social Structure	Crime is the result of underlying social conditions such as poverty, inequality, and unemployment.	Actions taken to reform social conditions that breed crime.	1. Education and job-training programs. 2. Urban redevelopment to improve housing, education, and health care. 3. Community development to provide economic opportunities.
Social Process	Crime is normal learned behavior and is subject to either social control or labeling effects.	Individuals to be treated in groups, with emphasis on building conventional bonds and avoiding stigmatization.	1. Youth programs that emphasize positive role models. 2. Community organizing to establish neighborhood institutions and bonds that emphasize following society's norms. 3. Programs designed to promote family stability.
Social Conflict	Criminal definitions and punishments are used by some groups to control other groups.	Fundamental changes in the political and social systems to reduce class conflict.	1. Development of programs to remove injustice in society. 2. Provision of resources to assist women, minorities, and the poor in dealing with the criminal justice system and other government agencies. 3. Modification of criminal justice to deal similarly with crimes committed by upper-class members and crimes committed by lower-class members.
Life Course	Offenders have criminal careers that often begin with pathways into youth crime but can change and end through turning points in life	Foster positive turning points such as marriage and stable employment	1. Policies to reduce entry pathways associated with youth incarceration and substance abuse 2. Policies to promote educational success, full employment, successful marriages, and stable families

are limited in other ways as well. They tend to focus on visible crimes and the poor. They have less to say about upper-class or organized crime. Most of the theories also focus on male behavior. What is missing, and truly needed, is a verifiable theory that merges these disparate ideas about the causes of crime. Once we have a complete and testable account of what causes crime, we can develop better policies to deal with it.

A QUESTION OF ETHICS

IMAGINE THE FOLLOWING scenarios: Two women, who live in different cities, arise early one morning to prepare to leave for their jobs at different insurance companies. As single parents, they both bear the responsibility of providing financial support as well as parental guidance to their children. After one woman parks in the underground garage next to her office building, an unfamiliar man sneaks up behind her, places a handgun against her face, and demands her purse and the keys to her car. Because she is startled and frightened, she drops her keys and reflexively bends to retrieve them. When she moves, the gun goes off and she is killed. In the other city, the woman is sitting at her desk in her office tower when suddenly her entire office suite bursts into flames in an explosion. She is killed instantly. The date is September 11, 2001. One woman has been killed in a parking garage in the Midwest and the other has died in the hijackers' attack on the World Trade Center in New York City.

In the aftermath of the September 11 tragedy, Congress enacted legislation to compensate terrorism victims with financial awards that exceed those of victim compensation programs and instead match the kinds of significant awards that someone might win in a wrongful death lawsuit. Thus the family of the woman killed at the World Trade Center would be eligible for significant financial support from the federal government to replace the income that she would have provided for her family. By contrast, the family of the woman killed in the parking garage would receive very little. If the state's law provided for compensation, it would probably be a modest amount that might not even cover the cost of the funeral. Both women were killed in sudden attacks by strangers. Both women left behind children who had relied on them for financial support as well as emotional support and parental guidance.

Critical Thinking and Analysis

Is it ethical for the federal government to provide financial support for one victim's family but not for the other? Are there any persuasive reasons to treat the two families differently? Stage a pro–con debate with a classmate. One of you should represent the views of the federal government in justifying the compensation program, and the other should provide the perspective of crime victims' families whose loved ones died in situations other than the terrorist attack of September 11.

Researching the Internet

 You can find information on the compensation program and other services for September 11 victims on the "September 11" web page of the National Center for Victims of Crime. To link to this website, go to *The American System of Criminal Justice* 12e companion site at academic.cengage.com/criminaljustice/cole.

SUMMARY

Understand who becomes victims of crime

▪ Young residents of lower-income communities are among those most likely to be victimized by crime.

▪ Because of the connection between race and social status in the United States, African Americans are more frequently victimized by crime than are whites.

▪ A significant percentage of crimes, especially those against women, are committed by acquaintances and relatives of victims.

Recognize the impacts of crime on society

▪ Because of the financial and other costs it produces, crime significantly affects all of society.

▪ Financial costs from white-collar crime, employee theft, and fraud lead to huge financial losses for businesses.

▪ Medical costs and lingering psychological effects impose heavy burdens on victims.

▪ Fear of crime may make everyone in society feel less free to go to certain places or to live their daily lives without being nervous and fearful.

Identify the justice system's responses to the needs of crime victims

▪ Government agencies have begun to be more sensitive to the needs of crime victims. Thus, many states support programs to provide services and compensation.

■ State and federal legislation has provided new rights for crime victims, including compensation, forms of assistance, and information about the offender who victimized them.

■ Scholars have begun to study the role that victims may play in facilitating crimes.

Understand the theories put forward to explain criminal behavior

■ The classical school of criminology emphasized reform of criminal law, procedures, and punishments.

■ The rise of science led to the positivist school, which viewed behavior as stemming from social, biological, and psychological factors.

■ Positivist criminology has dominated the study of criminal behavior since the beginning of the twentieth century.

■ Biological theories of crime claim that physiological and neurological factors may predispose a person to commit crimes. Some of these factors may be associated with genes but others may be affected by nutrition, environmental pollution, medical conditions, or brain injuries.

■ Psychological theories of crime propose that mental processes and behavior hold the key to understanding the causes of crime.

■ Sociological theories of crime emphasize the social conditions that bear on the individual as causes of criminal behavior. Three types of sociological theory are social structure theories, social process theories, and social conflict theories.

■ Life course theories are based on long-term studies and identify factors associated with pathways into criminal careers and turning points away from criminal activity.

Analyze crime causation theories and apply them to different groups of offenders

■ All criminal theories have implications for policy decisions.

■ The criminality of women has only recently been studied. Some argue that, as women become more equal with men in society, the number of crimes committed by women will increase.

■ Theories of criminality are criticized for focusing too exclusively on lower-class and male perpetrators.

QUESTIONS FOR REVIEW

1. Who is most likely to be victimized by crime?

2. What are the costs of crime?

3. How does the criminal justice system treat victims?

4. What are the major theories of criminality?

5. What have scholars learned about criminal behavior by women?

KEY TERMS

anomie (p. 65)
biological explanations (p. 61)
classical criminology (p. 59)
control theories (p. 66)
criminogenic (p. 60)
labeling theories (p. 67)
learning theories (p. 66)
life course theories (p. 68)
positivist criminology (p. 60)
psychological explanations (p. 63)

social conflict theories (p. 67)
social process theories (p. 66)
social structure theories (p. 65)
sociological explanations (p. 65)
theory of differential association (p. 66)
victimology (p. 45)

FOR FURTHER READING

Butterfield, Fox. 1996. *All God's Children: The Bosket Family and the American Tradition of Violence*. New York: Avon. A detailed account of the transmission of a culture of violence through multiple generations of one family.

Erikson, Kai T. 1966. *Wayward Puritans*. New York: Wiley. A famous analysis of three "crime waves" in Puritan New England.

Heidensohn, Frances M. 1985. *Women and Crime*. New York: New York University Press. An account and critique of criminological and sociological writings on women and criminality.

Karmen, Andrew. 2003. *Crime Victims: An Introduction to Victimology*, 5th ed. Belmont, CA: Wadsworth. A thorough overview of issues and research concerning crime victims.

Laub, John H., and Robert J. Sampson. 2003. *Shared Beginnings, Divergent Lives: Delinquent Boys to Age 70*. Cambridge, MA: Harvard University Press. Most recent follow up on the senior citizens who were the "boys" studied since 1940 in the long-term study of criminal careers. Uses reflective interviews with the subjects to explain details of life course theory.

Messner, Steven F., and Richard Rosenfeld. 2001. *Crime and the American Dream*. 3rd ed. Belmont, CA: Wadsworth. Argues that high levels of serious crime result from the normal functioning of the American social system.

GOING ONLINE

For an up-to-date list of web links, go to *The American System of Criminal Justice* 12e companion site at academic .cengage.com/criminaljustice/cole.

1. Access Victims Assistance Online and examine the kinds of victims' assistance programs that are provided in countries outside of the United States. Do you think any of the services provided elsewhere but not here should also be supplied to American crime victims?

2. Access the Crime Victims' Bill of Rights for the State of New Jersey. Do you see any potential problems in implementing these rights effectively?

3. Access Crimetheory.com. Read about two theories of crime causation. Which theory do you believe helps explain a larger number of crimes or the behavior of a larger number of offenders?

CHECKPOINT ANSWERS

1. *What are the main elements of the lifestyle-exposure model?*

Demographic characteristics, adaptations, lifestyle, associations, exposure.

2. *What are the characteristics of the group that is most victimized by violent crime? Of the least-victimized group?*

Most victimized: teenage African American men. Least victimized: elderly white women.

3. *Which crime against which victim is the most likely to be committed by nonstrangers?*

Rape/sexual assault against female victims.

4. *Which type of crime is the most likely to be committed by strangers?*

Robbery.

5. *What are some of the impacts of crime?*

Fear, financial costs, emotional costs, lifestyle restrictions.

6. *How is fear of crime shaped, and how does it relate to actual crime rates?*

People gain perceptions about crime through the news media, movies, and television shows; thus, perceptions and fears about crime often exceed the actual risks of victimization.

7. *Why are poor people often less likely than others to take actions to reduce the risk of crime?*

Poor people often reside in higher-crime areas without being able to afford home security systems. They are also more likely to travel to and from work in the evening if they work third shifts or have service occupations.

8. *Why do some crime victims feel mistreated by the justice system?*

The system focuses on finding and punishing the offender; police and lawyers often question victims closely, in an unsympathetic manner; victims do not always receive assistance that covers their medical expenses and other losses.

9. *What rights have been provided in federal criminal cases by the Justice for All Act?*

Receive notice about hearings, attend hearings, consult with the federal prosecutor, gain restitution, and avoid unnecessary delays.

10. *What behaviors of victims can invite crime?*

Failing to take precautions; taking actions that may provoke or entice; refusing to assist police with investigations.

11. *What were the main assumptions of the classical school?*

Criminal behavior is rational, and the fear of punishment keeps people from committing crimes.

12. *What are the main assumptions of the positivist school?*

Criminal behavior is the product of social, biological, and psychological factors.

13. *What were the main elements of Lombroso's theory?*

Offenders are born criminals and have traits that mark them.

14. *What is a psychopath?*

A person who is unable to control impulses, cannot learn from experience, and does not have normal human emotions.

15. *What is the main assumption of social structure theories?*

Crime is caused by people's negative reactions to social inequality, lack of opportunity, and the success of others that does not seem to be attainable in a society that values wealth and status.

16. *What is the main assumption of social process theories?*

Everyone has the potential of becoming a criminal, depending on the influences, such as learning or labeling, that move one toward or away from crime and on how one is regarded by others.

17. *What is the main assumption of social conflict theories?*

Criminal law and the criminal justice system are primarily a means of controlling the poor and the have-nots.

18. *What are potential turning points for criminal careers in life course theories?*

Marriage, military service, and stable employment are associated with moving away from criminal careers.

19. *What have feminist researchers contributed to theories of female criminality?*

The idea that women would commit more crimes as they became liberated and achieved greater equality in the workplace and elsewhere in society.

20. *How do the number and trends in arrests compare for male and female arrestees?*

Women constitute a small percentage of arrestees for all crimes except larceny/theft, although arrests of women for violent crimes rose recently even as arrests of men declined.

CHAPTER 3

The Criminal Justice System

CHAPTER LEARNING OBJECTIVES

→ Understand the goals of the criminal justice system

→ Recognize the different responsibilities of federal and state criminal justice operations

→ Analyze criminal justice from a system perspective

→ Identify the authority and relationships of the main criminal justice agencies, and understand the steps in the decision-making process for criminal cases

→ Understand the criminal justice "wedding cake" concept

→ Recognize the possible causes of racial disparities in criminal justice

The defendant stood quietly in front of the judge. A tall, muscular man wearing a baggy, black-and-white striped prison uniform. He hoped that the judge would follow the prosecutor's recommendation and impose a prison sentence of 12 to 18 months. When the judge began to speak, however, it was obvious that the judge was angry that the defendant had not been more cooperative with law enforcement officials. Moreover, the judge clearly believed that the defendant had not fully taken responsibility for his actions. Thus, on December 10, 2007, football star Michael Vick, the quarterback of the Atlanta Falcons, found himself sentenced to 23 months in prison for operating an illegal dog-fighting ring (Rankin and Ledbetter, 2007).

At the start of 2007, football star Michael Vick stood at the top of the world. He was two years into a 10-year, $130 million contract to play football for the Falcons and he made millions more by endorsing Nike shoes, EA Sports video games, Coca-Cola, and other products. Everything changed for Vick on July 18, 2007, when a federal grand jury issued an indictment—a formal criminal charge—against the star athlete for his involvement in an illegal dog-fighting ring. Based on information provided by federal prosecutors, the members of the public who served on the grand jury in

Richmond, Virginia, concluded that sufficient evidence existed to prosecute Vick for attending dog fights, placing bets, and even participating in the killing of dogs that did not fight well in these brutal, bloody events (Maske, 2007). As with other Americans who are drawn into the criminal justice system, Michael Vick suddenly needed to focus his attention, energy, and money on the task of defending himself against charges that could lead him to spend years of his life in prison. In addition, like other criminal defendants who lose their jobs and friends, Vick's reputation was instantly tarnished and he suffered personal costs, including suspension from his football team and the cancellation of endorsement contracts. He immediately lost millions of dollars without yet being convicted of a crime. Even if he were eventually to be found "not guilty" of the charges, there was no guarantee that he would regain the money and career opportunities that disappeared when he was indicted.

The criminal charges against Vick did not come as a complete surprise. As in other cases, the events leading to charges against Vick began with decisions and actions by law enforcement officers who investigated allegations by searching a home owned by Vick and by interviewing various witnesses. When news reporters and football officials asked Vick about his rumored involvement in illegal dog fighting, he always denied any wrongdoing.

In the days after the announcement of formal charges on July 18, Vick hired one of the nation's most prominent criminal defense attorneys, Billy Martin, a Washington, D.C. lawyer who had previously represented professional athletes and other prominent people. Some observers interpreted Martin's involvement as a sign that Vick intended to maintain his claim of innocence and fight the charges all the way through a courtroom trial (Lupica, 2007).

Five weeks later, Vick's case turned in a new direction. He appeared at a hearing in federal court in order to plead guilty. He admitted that he was deeply involved in the dog-fighting operation. He also apologized for his actions. The prosecution agreed to recommend a sentence of 12 to 18 months in federal prison, but the judge made no promises about what the actual sentence would be (Markson and Mummolo, 2007). Thus the ultimate punishment rested in the hands of a single judge. The judge would determine the specific length of Vick's sentence from within the range of prison terms established by the American people's elected representatives in Congress.

One month after pleading guilty, a state court grand jury in Virginia indicted Vick on state criminal charges for dog fighting. He was charged with two felony counts, each one punishable by a sentence of up to five years in state prison (*Associated Press*, "Vick Is Indicted," 2007b). His trial in state court was scheduled for spring 2008.

Knowing that he would receive a federal prison sentence of some length for pleading guilty, Vick voluntarily reported for prison in November 2007, even though the judge would not announce the specific sentence until December. He wanted to get started on serving his sentence. When U.S. District Court Judge Henry E. Hudson imposed the more severe 23-month sentence, he sternly told Vick, "You need to apologize to the millions of young people who looked up to you." At the close of the hearing, before he was led away by U.S. marshals, Vick apologized to the judge and to his family (Rankin and Ledbetter, 2007). Later, Vick agreed to prosecutors' demands that he create a $928,000 fund to care for the pit bulls that were seized from his dog-fighting operation (Geroux, 2007).

Because he tested positive for marijuana prior to his sentencing, Judge Hudson declared that Vick was eligible for substance abuse treatment in prison. At the minimum security federal prison in Leavenworth, Kansas, where Vick was initially sent to serve his sentence, he waited to gain a spot in the federal prison system's drug abuse program. If he gained admission to the program and completed it successfully, it was possible that he could be transferred to a halfway house located in a community where he could work at a job during the day and return to the facility to be supervised during evenings and nights (Munson, 2008).

Michael Vick's case is not typical, especially with respect to the wealth that permitted him to hire prominent defense lawyers and the news media attention generated by the case. However, his case illustrates the operation of the criminal justice system. Like the overwhelming majority of criminal convictions, Vick's case ended when he entered a guilty plea. Jury trials are relatively unusual despite their prominence in television shows and movies that portray the operation of the criminal justice system.

As in other cases, the path of Vick's case depended on a series of decisions made by law enforcement officers, the prosecutor, the defense attorney, and the judge. In Vick's case, the prosecutor depended on information produced through the police investigation in order to develop the evidence to be presented at trial or to force the defendant to negotiate a plea. Federal agents used specific investigative techniques to gather evidence against Vick. They sought a search warrant from a judge to permit them to search the house owned by Vick where the dog-fighting operation was located. They interviewed witnesses who reportedly saw Vick at dog fights. Law enforcement officials also worked with the prosecutor to get other defendants involved in the case to cooperate by providing evidence against Vick in exchange for leniency in their own cases. The prosecutor subsequently made decisions about what evidence to present to the grand jury and what specific charges to ask the grand jury to approve.

The prosecutor and defense attorney negotiated an agreement through which Vick admitted guilt in exchange for the prosecutor's recommendation of a less-than-maximum sentence. Later, the prosecutor and defense attorney each used their own independent judgments in crafting strategies for presenting their arguments to the judge at the sentencing hearing.

The conclusion of Vick's court case moved him to the corrections segment of the criminal justice system. Even in corrections, officials use their judgment to determine what will happen to a specific individual. Will the individual be sent to a high-security prison? Will the sentence be served in a facility that is close to the offender's family so that it is easier to see visitors on a regular basis? Will the offender be enrolled in education courses, vocational training, or substance abuse programs while serving the sentence? The American system of criminal justice can be unpredictable because its processes depend on the combined actions and decisions of so many different people. In addition, rules and processes may vary from state to state and courthouse to courthouse. In Vick's case, many state court prosecutors would be satisfied with Vick's federal prison sentence and therefore would avoid spending their own limited time and resources on pursuing additional state charges against the quarterback. However, the Virginia prosecutor responsible for the county where the dog fighting occurred decided to seek an additional conviction and additional punishment for Vick under state criminal law. This later prosecution in state court could produce very different results, such as a lengthier sentence to be served under more difficult conditions in a higher-security Virginia prison.

Police, prosecutors, and judges make individual decisions about whom to investigate, what charges to file, and in the case of poor defendants, which attorney will represent the defense. Each of these decisions can lead a defendant to be treated differently from a similarly situated individual being prosecuted in another state or county. The fates of criminal defendants depend on human decision makers who may be influenced by different beliefs, sources of information, and societal pressures. In Vick's case, did the Virginia prosecutor seek additional charges because he believed that the federal prison sentence was "too light" for the crimes? Did he feel pressured to bring additional charges because pet owners and animal rights activists were so vocal and outraged about Vick's crime? Did he feel obligated to make sure that a prosecution is pursued whenever there is evidence that a state law was broken? Or was he tempted to be in the public spotlight because he knew that any additional prosecution of Vick would generate tremendous attention from the news media? We can never know exactly what factor or combination of factors led to this decision, or to many other decisions made by officials in the criminal justice system.

In this chapter, we examine the goals of criminal justice and how American criminal justice operates as a system. Moreover, we shall see how that system's processes are shaped by scarce resources, individual decision makers, and other factors that can lead to divergent treatment for similar criminal cases. In the United States, our history has taught us that differences in the treatment of suspects, defendants, and offenders may be related to issues of race, ethnicity, and social class and the interaction of these demographic factors with the criminal justice system's processes. Thus this chapter will also examine controversies about whether discrimination in criminal justice processes exists and, if so, in what ways.

THE GOALS OF CRIMINAL JUSTICE

To begin our study of the criminal justice system, we must ask, What goals does the system serve? Although these goals may seem straightforward in theory, saying exactly what they mean in practice can be difficult.

In 1967 the President's Commission on Law Enforcement and Administration of Justice described the criminal justice system as an apparatus that society uses to "enforce the standards of conduct necessary to protect individuals and the community" (U.S. President's Commission, 1967: 7). This statement will form the basis for our discussion of the goals of the system. Although there is much debate about the purposes of criminal justice, most people agree that the system has three goals: (1) doing justice, (2) controlling crime, and (3) preventing crime.

Doing Justice

"Doing justice" is the foundation of the rules, procedures, and institutions that make up the American criminal justice system. Without the principle of justice, there would be little difference between criminal justice in the United States and

Thousands of St. Louis residents participated in a unity march against crime in June 2008. Their theme of a "Call to Oneness" was intended to make people think about social problems and crime in their communities. How can the interest and energy generated by such public events be translated into concrete actions to prevent crime?

AP Images/Jeff Roberson

that in authoritarian countries. Fairness is essential: We want to have fair laws. We want to investigate, judge, and punish fairly. Doing justice also requires upholding the rights of individuals and punishing those who violate the law. All of these elements reflect American values and appear in the U.S. Constitution. Thus, the goal of doing justice embodies three principles: (1) offenders will be held fully accountable for their actions, (2) the rights of persons who have contact with the system will be protected, and (3) like offenses will be treated alike and officials will take into account relevant differences among offenders and offenses (DiIulio, 1993: 10).

Doing justice successfully is a tall order, and we can easily identify situations in which criminal justice agencies and processes fall short of this ideal. In authoritarian political systems, criminal justice clearly serves the interests of those in power, but in a democracy people can try to improve the capacity of their institutions to do justice. Thus, however imperfect they may be, criminal justice institutions and processes can maintain public support. In a democracy, a system that makes doing justice a key goal is viewed as legitimate and can therefore pursue the secondary goals of controlling and preventing crime.

Controlling Crime

The criminal justice system is designed to control crime by arresting, prosecuting, convicting, and punishing those who disobey the law. A major constraint on the system, however, is that efforts to control crime must be carried out within the framework of law. This reflects a central tension within American values, in that we do not fully enjoy our liberty if we live in fear of crime, yet the value that we place on rights may inhibit our effectiveness in controlling crime. The criminal law not only defines what is illegal but also outlines the rights of citizens and the procedures officials must use to achieve the system's goals.

In any city or town, we can see the goal of crime control being actively pursued: police officers walking a beat, patrol cars racing down dark streets, lawyers speaking before a judge, probation officers visiting clients, or the wire fences of a prison stretching along a highway. Taking action against wrongdoers helps to control crime, but the system must also attempt to keep crimes from happening.

Preventing Crime

Crime can be prevented in various ways. Perhaps most important is the deterrent effect of the actions of police, courts, and corrections. These entities not only punish those who violate the law but also provide examples that will likely keep others from committing wrongful acts. For instance, a racing patrol car responding to a crime also serves as a warning that law enforcement is at hand.

Crime prevention depends on the actions of criminal justice officials and citizens. Unfortunately, many people do not take even the basic steps necessary to protect themselves and their property, as we saw in Chapter 2. For example, they leave their homes and cars unlocked, do not use alarm systems, and walk in dangerous areas.

Citizens do not have the authority to enforce the law. Society has assigned that responsibility to the criminal justice system. Thus, citizens must rely on the police to stop criminals; they cannot take the law into their own hands. Still, they can and must be actively engaged in preventing crime. Examine "Civic Engagement: Your Role in the System" to consider what concrete steps people can take to address a specific crime problem within a neighborhood. Also read "A Question of Ethics"

**civic engagement
your role in the system**

You live in a neighborhood in which a convenience store appears to serve as the central location where illegal drugs are bought and sold. There are frequent fights and disturbances outside the store. Once there was even a shooting. Your neighbors ask you to lead a neighborhood effort to reduce crime and disorder around the store. *Make a list of suggestions that you would take to a neighborhood meeting about this problem.* Then read about what happened when such a situation arose in a Minneapolis neighborhood. To link to this website, go to *The American System of Criminal Justice* 12e companion site at academic.cengage.com/criminaljustice/cole.

The National Crime Prevention Council provides information and programs on preventing crime. You can learn about their activities and resources by going to *The American System of Criminal Justice* 12e companion site at academic.cengage.com/criminaljustice/cole.

at the end of this chapter as you consider how far citizens should be permitted to go in trying to prevent crime.

Any decision made in the justice system—whether in doing justice, controlling crime, or preventing crime—will reflect particular legal, political, social, and moral values. As we study the system, we must be aware of the possible conflicts among these values and the implications of choosing one value over another. The tasks assigned to the criminal justice system are most easily performed when they are clearly defined, so that citizens and officials can act with precise knowledge of their duties.

checkpoint

1. What are the three goals of the criminal justice system?
2. What is meant by doing justice? (Answers are at the end of the chapter.)

CRIMINAL JUSTICE IN A FEDERAL SYSTEM

federalism
A system of government in which power is divided between a central (national) government and regional (state) governments.

Like other aspects of American government, criminal justice is based on **federalism**, in which power is divided between a central (national) government and regional (state) governments. States have a great deal of authority over their own affairs, but the federal government handles matters of national concern. Because of federalism, no single level of government is solely responsible for the administration of criminal justice.

The structure of the U.S. government was created in 1789 with the ratification of the U.S. Constitution. The Constitution gives the national government certain powers—to raise an army, to coin money, to make treaties with foreign countries—but all other powers, including police power, were retained by the states. No national police force with broad powers may be established in the United States.

The Constitution does not include criminal justice among the federal government's powers. However, the government participates in criminal justice in many ways. For example, the Federal Bureau of Investigation (FBI) is a national law enforcement agency. In addition, certain criminal cases are tried in U.S. district courts, which are federal courts, and there are federal prisons throughout the nation. Most criminal justice activity, however, occurs at the state rather than the national level.

Two Justice Systems

Both the national and state systems of criminal justice enforce laws, try criminal cases, and punish offenders, but their activities differ in scope and purpose. The vast majority of criminal laws are written by state legislatures and enforced by state agencies. However, Congress has enacted a variety of national criminal laws, which the FBI, the Drug Enforcement Administration, the Secret Service, and other federal agencies enforce.

Except in the case of federal drug offenses, relatively few offenders break federal criminal laws, compared with the large numbers who break state criminal laws. For example, only small numbers of people violate the federal law against counterfeiting and espionage, while large numbers violate state laws against assault, larceny, and drunken driving. Even in the case of drug offenses, which during the 1980s and 1990s swept large numbers of offenders into federal prisons, many violators end up in state correctional systems because such crimes violate both state and federal laws. Recall from Michael Vick's case at the beginning of this chapter that certain crimes, such as running a dog-fighting operation, that violate laws in both systems may lead to additional convictions and punishment for offenders who violate these laws.

The role of criminal justice agencies after the assassination of President John F. Kennedy in November 1963 illustrates the division of jurisdiction between federal and state agencies (Johnson, 2007). Because Congress had not made killing the president a federal offense, the suspect, Lee Harvey Oswald, would have been charged under Texas laws had he lived (Oswald was shot to death by Jack Ruby shortly after his arrest). The U.S. Secret Service had the job of protecting the president, but apprehending the killer was the formal responsibility of the Dallas police and other Texas law enforcement agencies. Subsequently, new laws made such offenses federal crimes.

Expansion of Federal Involvement

Since the 1960s the federal government has expanded its role in dealing with crime, a policy area that has traditionally fallen to state and local governments. As Willard Oliver notes, the federal role has become much more active in "legislating criminal activity, expanding [the] federal law enforcement bureaucracy, widening the reach and scope of the federal courts, and building more federal prisons" (2002: 1).

The report of the U.S. President's Commission on Law Enforcement and Administration of Justice (1967: 613) emphasized the need for greater federal involvement in local crime control and urged that federal grants be directed to the states to support criminal justice initiatives. Since then, Congress has allocated billions of dollars for crime control efforts and passed legislation, national in scope, to deal with street crime, the "war on drugs," violent crime, terrorism, and juvenile delinquency. Although most criminal justice expenditures and personnel remain at the local level, over the past 40 years the federal government has increased its role in fighting street crime (Oliver, 2002; Gest, 2001).

Because many crimes span state borders, we no longer think of some crimes as being committed at a single location within a single state. For example, crime syndicates and gangs deal with drugs, pornography, and gambling on a national level. Thus, Congress has expanded the powers of the FBI and other federal agencies to pursue criminal activities that were formerly the responsibility of the states. In addition, new crimes, such as computer fraud schemes, have also spurred new laws from Congress because they can cross both state and international borders.

Congress enacts laws designed to allow the FBI to investigate situations in which local police forces will likely be less effective. Under the National Stolen Property Act, for example, the FBI may investigate thefts worth over $5,000 when the offenders have probably transported the stolen property across state lines. As a

Federal law enforcement agencies bear special responsibility for certain crimes. Here, FBI and ATF investigators sift through the ruins of the Morning Star Missionary Baptist Church near Boligee, Alabama. Officials initially suspected this fire and those that destroyed other nearby African American churches might be the work of racial hate groups. Eventually, three white college students pleaded guilty to arson and received prison sentences in 2007 for what they described as misguided pranks that got out of control. What should be the role, if any, of federal law enforcement agencies in local arson cases?

© Gary Tramontina/Getty Images

national agency, the FBI is better able than any state agency to pursue criminal investigations across state borders.

Disputes over jurisdiction may occur when an offense violates both state and federal laws. If the FBI and local agencies do not cooperate, they may each seek to catch the same criminals. This can have major implications if the agency that makes the arrest determines which court tries the case. Usually, however, law enforcement officials at all levels of government seek to cooperate and to coordinate their efforts.

After the September 11 attacks on the World Trade Center and the Pentagon, the FBI and other federal law enforcement agencies focused their resources and efforts on investigating and preventing terrorist threats against the United States, including tightening security at airports and national borders. As a result, the role of the FBI as a law enforcement agency may be changing. One month after the attacks, 4,000 of the agency's 11,500 agents were dedicating their efforts to the aftermath of September 11. So many FBI agents were switched from their traditional law enforcement activities to antiterror initiatives that some observers claimed that other federal crimes, such as bank robberies, were no longer being vigorously investigated (Kampeas, 2001). Federal resources are increasingly applied to other specific priorities, such as the illegal importation and employment of foreign workers who lack proper visas and work permits (Rich, 2006). The federal government's response to potential threats to national security and other priorities may ultimately diminish the federal role in traditional law enforcement and thereby effectively transfer responsibility for many criminal investigations to state and local officials.

The reorientation of the FBI's priorities is just one aspect of changes in federal criminal justice agencies to address the threat of terrorism. Congress and President George W. Bush sought to increase the government's effectiveness by creating new federal agencies. The Transportation Security Administration (TSA), a new agency within the Department of Transportation, assumed responsibility for protecting travelers and interstate commerce. Most importantly, federal employees of the TSA took over the screening of passengers and their luggage at airports throughout the country. In light of the ease with which the September 11 hijackers brought box cutters onboard commercial airliners, there were grave concerns that employees of private security agencies were neither adequately trained nor sufficiently vigilant to protect the traveling public.

The biggest change in federal criminal justice occurred in November 2002, when Congress enacted legislation to create a new Department of Homeland Security (DHS). They created this department in order to centralize the administration and coordination of many existing agencies that were previously scattered throughout various departments. The Secretary of Homeland Security oversees the Coast Guard, the Immigration and Naturalization Service, the Border Patrol, the Secret Service, the Federal Emergency Management Agency, and other agencies (including the new TSA) concerned with protecting our food supply, nuclear power facilities, and other potential terrorism targets. The Department of Homeland Security will train emergency first responders, coordinate federal agencies' actions with those of state and local agencies, and analyze domestic intelligence information obtained by the CIA, FBI, and other sources (Table 3.1).

The Secretary of Homeland Security faces an enormous challenge in seeking to integrate departments that previously operated separately. In its first years, it faced accusations that it gave grants to local communities based on political considerations rather than actual security needs. Thus, during the 2005 confirmation hearings for Judge Michael Chertoff, the second secretary of DHS, Chertoff pledged to reevaluate the programs and policies of the gigantic agency (Lipton, 2005a).

Because both state and federal systems operate in the United States, criminal justice here is highly decentralized. As Figure 3.1 shows, almost two-thirds

The Transportation Security Administration, the new agency responsible for security at airports and seaports, maintains an informative website concerning security issues, job opportunities, and related matters. To link to this website, go to *The American System of Criminal Justice* 12e companion site at academic.cengage.com/criminaljustice/cole.

For information about the responsibilities and activities of the FBI and the Department of Homeland Security, as well as job opportunities with those agencies, visit their websites. To reach these sites, go to *The American System of Criminal Justice* 12e companion site at academic.cengage.com/criminaljustice/cole.

TABLE 3.1   Department of Homeland Security

Congress approved legislation to create a new federal agency dedicated to protecting the United States from terrorism. The legislation merges 22 agencies and nearly 170,000 government workers.

	Agencies Moved to the Department of Homeland Security	Previous Department or Agency
Border and Transportation Security	Immigration and Naturalization Service enforcement functions	Justice Department
	Transportation Security Administration	Transportation Department
	Customs Service	Treasury Department
	Federal Protective Services	General Services Administration
	Animal and Plant Health Inspection Service (parts)	Agriculture Department
Emergency Preparedness and Response	Federal Emergency Management Agency	(*Independent agency*)
	Chemical, biological, radiological, and nuclear response units	Health and Human Services Department
	Nuclear Incident response teams	Energy Department
	National Domestic Preparedness Office	FBI
	Office of Domestic Preparedness	Justice Department
	Domestic Emergency Support Teams	(*From various departments and agencies*)
Science and Technology	Civilian biodefense research program	Health and Human Services Department
	Plum Island Animal Disease Center	Agriculture Department
	Lawrence Livermore National Laboratory (parts)	Energy Department
Information Analysis and Infrastructure Protection	National Communications System	Defense Department
	National Infrastructure Protection Center	FBI
	Critical Infrastructure Assurance Office	Commerce Department
	National Infrastructure Simulation and Analysis Center	Energy Department
	Federal Computer Incident Response Center	General Services Administration
Secret Service	Secret Service including presidential protection units	Treasury Department
Coast Guard	Coast Guard	Transportation Department

Source: *New York Times*, November 20, 2002, p. A12.

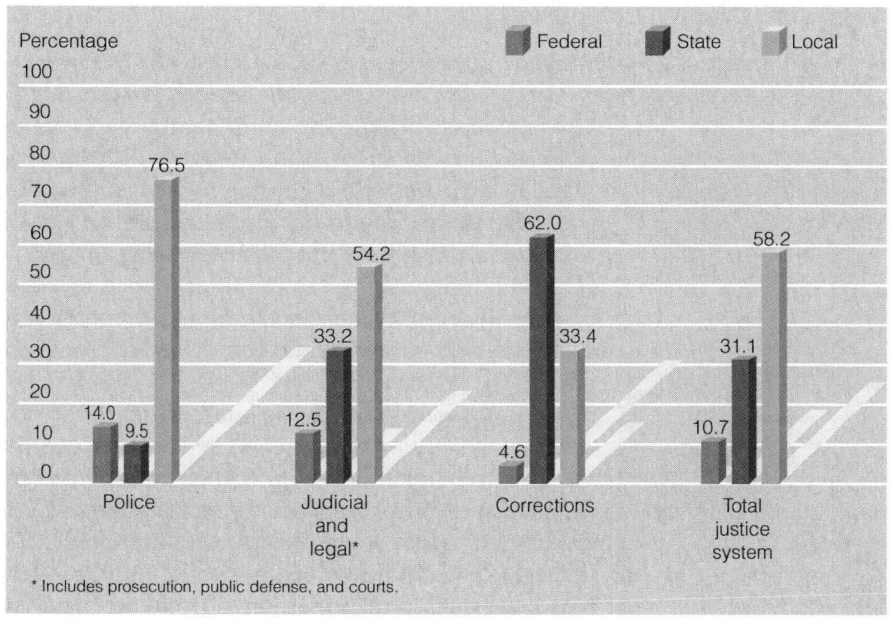

* Includes prosecution, public defense, and courts.

FIGURE 3.1

Percentage (rounded) of criminal justice employees at each level of government, 2001

The administration of criminal justice in the United States is very much a local affair, as these employment figures show. Only in corrections do states employ a greater percentage of workers than do municipalities.

Source: Bureau of Justice Statistics, *Sourcebook of Criminal Justice Statistics, 2004* (Washington, DC: U.S. Government Printing Office, 2004), Table 1.17.

of all criminal justice employees work for local governments. The majority of workers in all of the subunits of the system—except corrections—are tied to local government. Likewise, the costs of criminal justice are distributed among the federal, state, and local governments.

Laws are enforced and offenders are brought to justice mainly in the states, counties, and cities. As a result, local traditions, values, and practices shape the way criminal justice agencies operate. Local leaders, whether members of the city council or influential citizens, can help set law enforcement priorities by putting pressure on the police. Will the city's police officers crack down on illegal gambling? Will juvenile offenders be turned over to their parents with stern warnings, or will they be sent to state institutions? The answers to these and other important questions vary from city to city.

checkpoint

3. What are the key features of federalism?
4. What power does the national government have in the area of crime and justice?
5. What main factor has caused federal involvement in criminal justice to expand?

CRIMINAL JUSTICE AS A SYSTEM

To achieve the goals of criminal justice, many kinds of organizations—police, prosecution, courts, corrections—have been formed. Each has its own functions and personnel. We might assume that criminal justice is an orderly process in which a variety of professionals act on each case on behalf of society. To know how the system really works, however, we must look beyond its formal organizational chart. In doing so, we can use the concept of a **system**: a complex whole made up of interdependent parts whose actions are directed toward goals and influenced by the environment in which they function.

system
A complex whole consisting of interdependent parts whose operations are directed toward goals and are influenced by the environment within which they function.

The System Perspective

Criminal justice is a system made up of parts or subsystems. The subsystems—police, courts, corrections—have their own goals and needs but are also interdependent. When one unit changes its policies, practices, or resources, this change will affect other units as well. An increase in the number of people arrested by the police, for example, will affect not only the judicial subsystem but also the probation and correctional subsystems. For criminal justice to achieve its goals, each part must make a unique contribution; each must also have contact with at least one other part of the system.

In coming to understand the nature of the entire criminal justice system and its subsystems, we must see how individual actors play their roles. The criminal justice system comprises a great many people doing specific jobs. Some, such as police officers and judges, are well-known to the public. Others, such as bail bondsmen and probation officers, are less well-known. A key concept here is **exchange**, meaning the mutual transfer of resources among individual actors,

exchange
A mutual transfer of resources; a balance of benefits and deficits that flow from behavior based on decisions about the values and costs of alternatives.

The system perspective emphasizes that criminal justice is made up of parts or subsystems, including police, courts, and corrections. Here, Judge Orlando Hudson confers with prosecutors and defense attorneys during the Durham, North Carolina, trial of Michael Peterson, who was convicted of murdering his wife, Kathleen. Each participant brings his or her own perspective to the system.

AP Images/Chuck Liddy

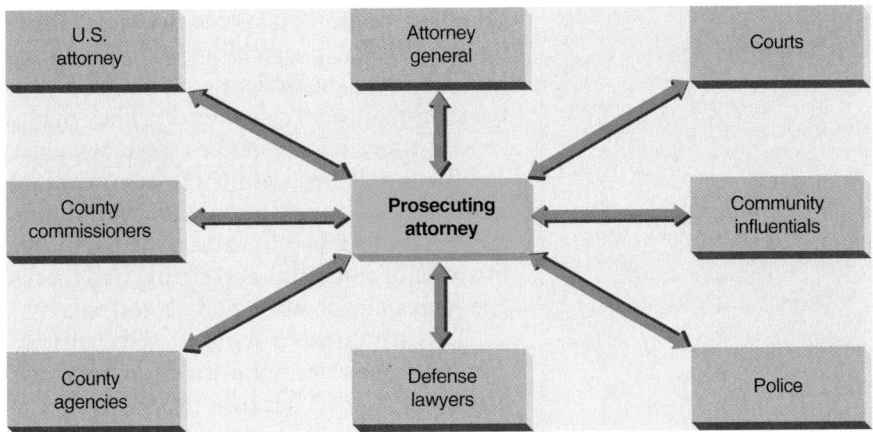

FIGURE 3.2
Exchange relationships between prosecutors and others
The prosecutor's decisions are influenced by relationships with other agencies and members of the community.

each of whom has goals that he or she cannot accomplish alone. Each needs to gain the cooperation and assistance of other actors by helping those actors achieve their own goals. The concept of exchange allows us to see interpersonal behavior as the result of individual decisions about the benefits and costs of different courses of action.

There are many kinds of exchange relationships in the criminal justice system, some more visible than others. Probably the most obvious example is the **plea bargain,** in which the defense attorney and the prosecutor reach an agreement: The defendant agrees to plead guilty in exchange for a reduction of charges or a lighter sentence. As a result of this exchange, the prosecutor gains a quick, sure conviction; the offender receives a shorter sentence; and the defense attorney can move on to the next case. Thus, the cooperation underlying the exchange promotes the goals of each participant.

The concept of exchange reminds us that decisions are the products of interactions among individuals and that the subsystems of the criminal justice system are tied together by the actions of individual decision makers. Figure 3.2 presents selected exchange relationships between a prosecutor and other individuals and agencies involved in the criminal justice process.

The concepts of system and exchange are closely linked. In this book, these concepts serve as an organizing framework to describe individual subsystems and actors and help us see how the justice process really works. Let's turn now to the main characteristics of the system, all of which shape the decisions that determine the fates of defendants.

plea bargain
A defendant's plea of guilty to a criminal charge with the reasonable expectation of receiving some consideration from the state for doing so, usually a reduction of the charge. The defendant's ultimate goal is a penalty lighter than the maximum punishment formally warranted by the original charge.

Characteristics of the Criminal Justice System

The workings of the criminal justice system have four major characteristics: (1) discretion, (2) resource dependence, (3) sequential tasks, and (4) filtering.

Discretion

All levels of the justice process reveal a high degree of **discretion.** This term refers to officials' freedom to act according to their own judgment and conscience (see Table 3.2). For example, police officers decide how to handle a crime situation, prosecutors decide which charges to file, judges decide how long a sentence will be, and parole boards decide when an offender will be released from prison.

The extent of such discretion may seem odd, given that the United States is ruled by law and has created procedures to ensure that decisions are made in accordance with law. However, instead of being a mechanical system in which the law dominates decisions, criminal justice is a system in which actors may take various factors into account and exercise many options as they dispose of a case. The

discretion
The authority to make decisions without reference to specific rules or facts, using instead one's own judgment; allows for individualization and informality in the administration of justice.

TABLE 3.2   Who Exercises Discretion?

Discretion is exercised by various actors throughout the criminal justice system.

These Criminal Justice Officials ...	Must Often Decide Whether or How to ...
Police	Enforce specific laws
	Investigate specific crimes
	Search people, vicinities, buildings
	Arrest or detain people
Prosecutors	File charges or petitions for adjudication
	Seek indictments
	Drop cases
	Reduce charges
Judges or Magistrates	Set bail or conditions for release
	Accept pleas
	Determine delinquency
	Dismiss charges
	Impose sentence
	Revoke probation
Correctional Officials	Assign to [which] type of correctional facility
	Award privileges
	Punish for infractions of rules
	Determine date and conditions of parole
	Revoke parole

Source: Bureau of Justice Statistics, *Report to the Nation on Crime and Justice*, 2nd ed. (Washington, DC: U.S. Government Printing Office, 1988), 59.

role of discretion opens the door for individual police officers, prosecutors, defense attorneys, and judges to make decisions based, at least in part, on their own self-interest. They may want to save time, save resources, or move a case to completion. Whenever people base criminal justice decisions on self-interest, however, they run the risk that American values, such as individual liberty and constitutional rights, will receive inadequate consideration and protection.

Two arguments are often used to justify discretion in the criminal justice system. First, discretion is needed because the system lacks the resources to treat every case the same way. If every violation of the law were pursued through trial, for example, the costs would be immense. Second, many officials believe that discretion permits them to achieve greater justice than rigid rules would produce. However, the second justification can only be true when officials emphasize justice in their decisions. If they emphasize other considerations, such as efficiency or cost, their use of discretion may clash with justice and other important American values that supposedly form the foundation of the criminal justice system.

Resource Dependence

 Many police departments make their budget information available on the Internet; check out, for example, the budget for the Madison, Wisconsin, police. To link to this website, go to *The American System of Criminal Justice* 12e companion site at academic.cengage.com/criminaljustice/cole.

Criminal justice agencies do not generate their own resources; rather, they depend on other agencies for funding. Therefore, actors in the system must cultivate and maintain good relations with those who allocate resources—that is, political decision makers, such as legislators, mayors, and city council members. Some police departments gain revenue through traffic fines and property forfeitures, but these sources generate too little to sustain their budgets.

Because budget decisions are made by elected officials who seek to please the public, criminal justice officials must also maintain a positive image and good relations with voters. If the police have strong public support, for example, the mayor will be reluctant to reduce the law enforcement budget. Criminal justice officials also seek positive coverage from the news media. Because the media often provide a crucial link between government agencies and the public, criminal justice officials may announce notable achievements while trying to limit publicity about controversial cases and decisions.

Sequential Tasks

Decisions in the criminal justice system follow a specific sequence. The police must make an arrest before a defendant is passed along to the prosecutor; the prosecutor's decisions determine the nature of the court's workload; and so forth. If officials act out of sequence, they cannot achieve their goals. For example, prosecutors and judges cannot bypass the police by making arrests, and correctional officials cannot punish anyone who has not passed through the earlier stages of the process.

The sequential nature of the system is a key element in the exchange relationships among decision makers who depend on one another to achieve their goals. It thus contributes to the strong interdependence within the system.

Filtering

The criminal justice system also serves as a **filtering process**. At each stage, some defendants are sent on to the next stage, while others are either released or processed under changed conditions. As shown in Figure 3.3, people who have been arrested may be filtered out of the system at various points. Note that few suspects who are arrested are then prosecuted, tried, and convicted. Some go free because the police decide that a crime has not been committed or that the evidence is not sound. The prosecutor may decide that justice would be better served by sending the suspect to a substance abuse clinic. Although many defendants will plead guilty, the judge may dismiss charges against others, and the jury may acquit a few defendants. Most of the offenders who are actually tried, however, will be convicted. Thus, the criminal justice system is often described as a funnel—many cases enter it, but only a few result in conviction and punishment.

To summarize, the criminal justice system is composed of a set of interdependent parts (subsystems). This system has four key attributes: (1) discretion, (2) resource dependence, (3) sequential tasks, and (4) filtering. Within this

filtering process
A process by which criminal justice officials screen out some cases while advancing others to the next level of decision making.

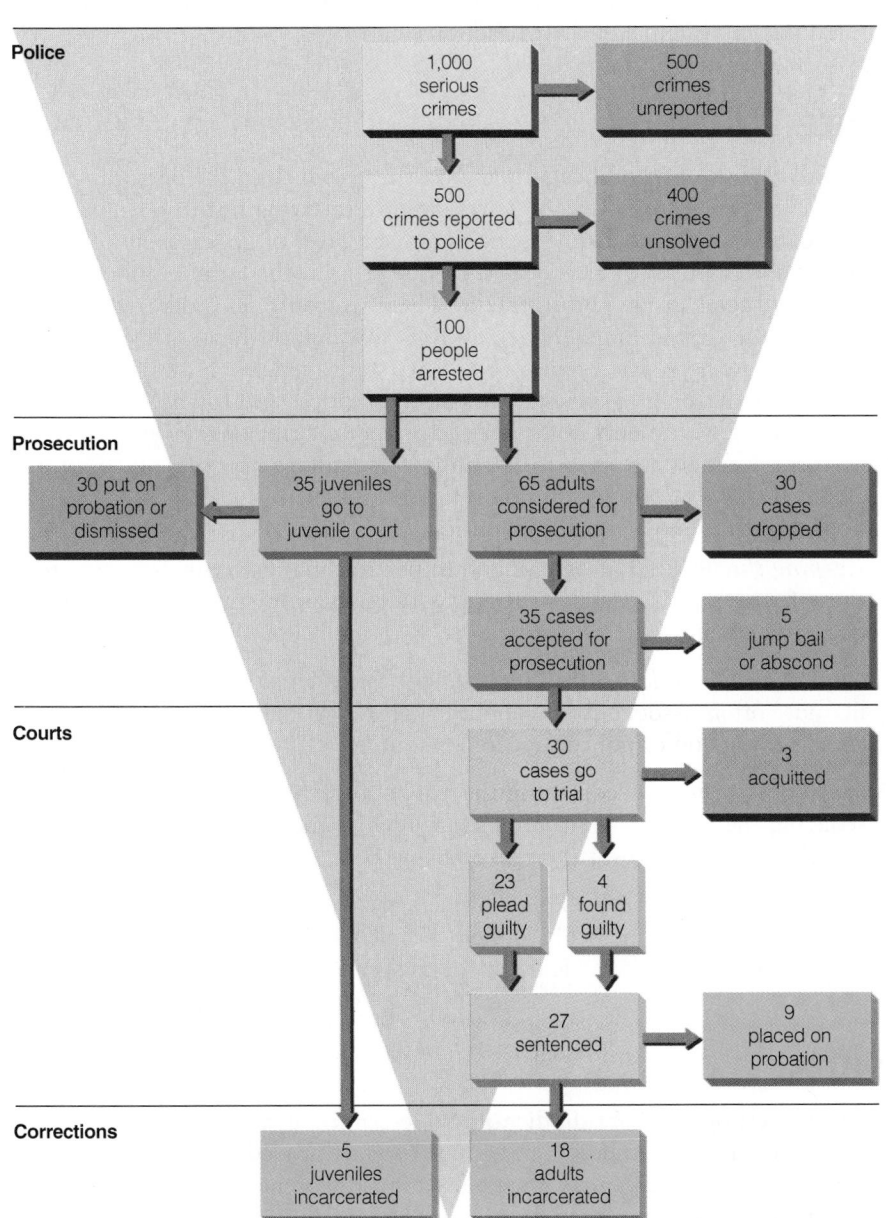

FIGURE 3.3

Criminal justice as a filtering process
Decisions at each point in the system result in some cases being dropped while others are passed to the next point. Are you surprised by the small portion of cases that remain?

Sources: Data from this figure have been drawn from many sources, including Bureau of Justice Statistics, *Sourcebook of Criminal Justice Statistics, 1998* (Washington, DC: U.S. Government Printing Office, 1999) and Bureau of Justice Statistics, Bulletin, February 1988.

framework, we look next at the operations of criminal justice agencies and then examine the flow of cases through the system.

checkpoint

6. What is a system?
7. What is one example of an exchange relationship?
8. What are the major characteristics of the criminal justice system?

OPERATIONS OF CRIMINAL JUSTICE AGENCIES

The criminal justice system has been formed to deal with people accused of violating the criminal law. Its subsystems consist of more than 60,000 public and private agencies with an annual budget of more than $185 billion and nearly 2.4 million employees (Hughes, 2006). Here we review the main parts of the criminal justice system and their functions.

Police

We usually think of the police as being on the "front line" in controlling crime. When we use the term *police*, however, we are referring not to a single agency or type of agency but to many agencies at each level of government. The complexity of the criminal justice system can be seen in the large number of organizations engaged in law enforcement. There are only 50 federal government agencies in the United States, whereas 17,876 state and local law enforcement agencies operate here. Forty-nine of these are state agencies (Hawaii has no state police). The remaining agencies serve counties, cities, and towns, reflecting the fact that local governments dominate the police function. At the state and local levels, these agencies have nearly one million full-time employees and a total annual budget that exceeds $68 billion (Hughes, 2006).

Police agencies have four major duties:

1. *Keeping the peace.* This broad and important mandate involves the protection of people and rights in situations ranging from street-corner brawls to domestic quarrels.

2. *Apprehending violators and combating crime.* This task is the one the public most often associates with police work, although it accounts for only a small proportion of police time and resources.

3. *Preventing crime.* By educating the public about the threat of crime and by reducing the number of situations in which crimes are likely to be committed, the police can lower the rate of crime.

4. *Providing social services.* Police officers recover stolen property, direct traffic, give emergency medical aid, help people who have locked themselves out of their homes, and provide other social services.

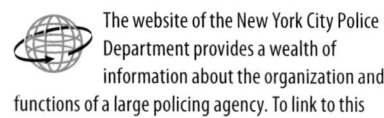

The website of the New York City Police Department provides a wealth of information about the organization and functions of a large policing agency. To link to this website, go to *The American System of Criminal Justice* 12e companion site at academic.cengage.com/criminaljustice/cole.

Courts

adjudication
The process of determining whether the defendant is guilty or not guilty.

Courts are responsible for **adjudication**—determining whether the defendant is guilty or not guilty. In so doing, they must use fair procedures that will produce just, reliable decisions. Courts must also impose sentences that are appropriate to the behavior being punished.

The United States has a **dual court system** that consists of a separate judicial system for each state in addition to a national system. Each system has its own series of courts; the U.S. Supreme Court can correct certain errors made in all other court systems. Although the Supreme Court can review cases from both the state and federal courts, it will hear only criminal justice cases involving federal law or constitutional rights.

With a dual court system, the law may be interpreted differently in different states. Although the wording of laws may be similar, state courts have the power to interpret and define their own laws for application within their own states. To some extent, these variations reflect regional differences in social and political conditions; that is, although a common set of American values concerning liberty and rights exists throughout the country, the interpretation and weight of those values may vary in the minds of citizens and judges in various regions. For example, the nature of expectations about personal privacy, equal treatment, and the role of private gun ownership as elements of liberty are viewed differently in the northeastern and Great Lakes states than in the southern and mountain states. For example, the New Jersey Supreme Court ruled that, under its state's constitution, motorists stopped by the police cannot have their cars searched merely because police officers ask them to consent to a search (*State v. Carty*). Instead, they must have a "reasonable and articulable suspicion" of criminal activity in order to conduct a search. By contrast, the U.S. Supreme Court and all other states, except Hawaii, permit automobile searches based on the driver's consent alone (Mansnerus, 2002).

Such variations can also exist within federal courts in different regions of the country. For example, a federal court in Texas interpreted the Second Amendment to the U.S. Constitution, which refers to both a "well-regulated Militia" and "the right of the people to keep and bear arms," as guaranteeing a right for individuals to own firearms (*United States v. Emerson*, 2001). Meanwhile, a different federal court in California interpreted the same words but concluded that the Amendment guarantees to states the ability to have an armed militia in the form of the National Guard (*Silveira v. Lockyer*, 2002). When federal courts in different regions announce divergent interpretations of the U.S. Constitution and federal statutes, the U.S. Supreme Court often acts to provide a common interpretation for the entire country. For this issue, the Supreme Court later clarified matters by identifying a constitutional right for individuals to own handguns and keep them within their own homes (*District of Columbia v. Heller*, 2008). This right, as currently defined, only prevents bans on handgun ownership by Congress and federal entitites, such as Washington, D.C. The Court's decision did not clarify, however, the extent to which state laws may impose limitations on gun ownership. The U.S. Supreme Court does not possess the authority to provide a final interpretation of all state laws. Each state's supreme court can define its own laws as long as those definitions are not inconsistent with the U.S. Constitution. Thus the U.S. Supreme Court will not strike down state gun regulations unless it eventually concludes that the U.S. Constitution protects gun owners against limitations imposed by state legislatures. In the immediate future, there will continue to be variation in gun control laws enforced by the country's many states as well as differences in the conclusions that various state and federal judges reach about the meaning of those state laws.

dual court system
A system consisting of a separate judicial structure for each state in addition to a national structure. Each case is tried in a court of the same jurisdiction as that of the law or laws broken.

Corrections

On any given day, more than seven million (one of every 31) American adults fall under the supervision of local, state, and federal correctional systems. There is no typical correctional agency or official. Instead, a variety of agencies and programs are provided by private and public organizations—including federal, state, and local governments—and carried out in many different community and closed settings.

While the average citizen may equate corrections with prisons, less than 30 percent of convicted offenders are in prisons and jails; the rest are being supervised in the community. Probation and parole have long been important aspects of corrections, as have community-based halfway houses, work release programs, and supervised activities.

The federal government, all the states, most counties, and all but the smallest cities engage in corrections. Nonprofit private organizations such as the YMCA have also contracted with governments to perform correctional services. In recent years, for-profit businesses have also entered into contracts with governments to build and operate correctional institutions.

The police, courts, and corrections are the main agencies of criminal justice. Each is a part, or subsystem, of the criminal justice system. Each is linked to the other two subsystems, and the actions of each affect the others. These effects can be seen as we examine the flow of decision making within the criminal justice system.

checkpoint

9. What are the four main duties of police?
10. What is a dual court system?
11. What are the major types of state and local correctional agencies?

THE FLOW OF DECISION MAKING IN THE CRIMINAL JUSTICE SYSTEM

The processing of cases in the criminal justice system involves a series of decisions by police officers, prosecutors, judges, probation officers, wardens, and parole board members. At each stage in the process, they decide whether a case will move on to the next stage or be dropped from the system. Although the flowchart shown in Figure 3.4 appears streamlined, with cases entering at the top and moving swiftly toward the bottom, the actual route may be quite long, with many detours. At each step, officials have the discretion to decide what happens next. Many cases are filtered out of the system, others are sent to the next decision maker, and still others are dealt with by informal means.

Moreover, the flowchart does not show the influences of social relations or the political environment. For example, questions always arise about whether members of prominent families receive preferential treatment. Such cases can involve Republicans or Democrats. President George W. Bush, for example, violated federal securities laws by failing to file required reports on at least three occasions in the late 1980s when he profited handsomely from the timing of the purchase and sale of stock for a company where he served on the board of directors and had access to inside information about the company's plans and prospects. Other company shareholders lost money, but Bush sold his stock at a profit just before news became public that made the stock price drop (Leopold, 2002). However, the government investigated the case and declined to pursue any action against him; his father was serving as president of the United States at the time. In another example, reports surfaced in 1997 indicating that the late Michael Kennedy, then a 39-year-old lawyer and nephew of the late President John F. Kennedy, had carried on an affair with his children's 14-year-old babysitter. If true, Kennedy would have been guilty of statutory rape, because having sexual relations with an underage girl, even if she willingly participates,

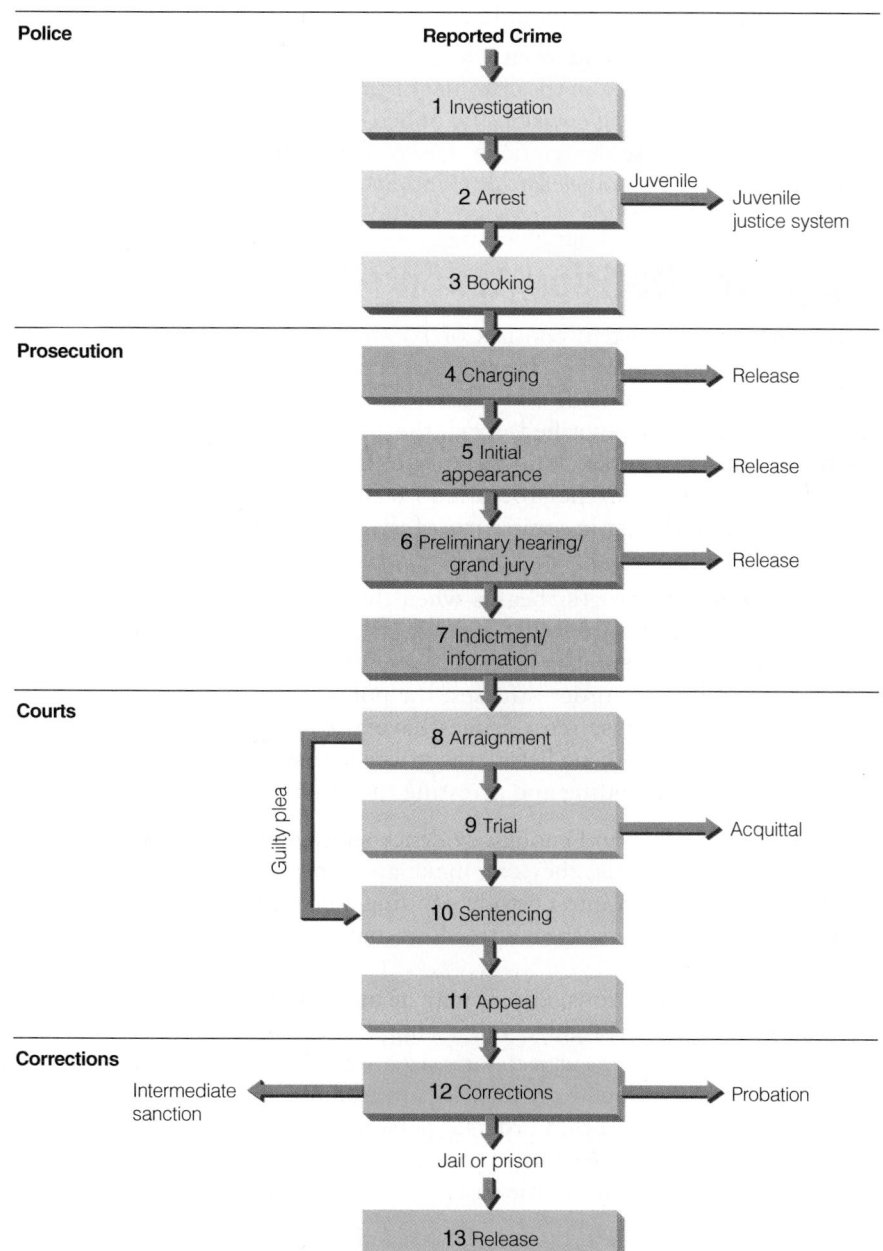

Police

Reported Crime

1 Investigation

2 Arrest → Juvenile → Juvenile justice system

3 Booking

Prosecution

4 Charging → Release

5 Initial appearance → Release

6 Preliminary hearing/ grand jury → Release

7 Indictment/ information

Courts

8 Arraignment

9 Trial → Acquittal

Guilty plea

10 Sentencing

11 Appeal

Corrections

Intermediate sanction ← 12 Corrections → Probation

Jail or prison

13 Release

FIGURE 3.4

The flow of decision making in the criminal justice system

Each agency is responsible for a part of the decision-making process. Thus the police, prosecution, courts, and corrections are bound together through a series of exchange relationships.

is a serious felony. Amid reports that Kennedy's lawyers were negotiating a quiet financial settlement with the girl and her family, the local prosecutor announced that no criminal charges would be filed because the girl—by that time a college student—refused to provide any evidence against Kennedy (Kenworthy, 1998). Did prosecutors decline to pursue these cases because the suspects were members of prominent, politically powerful families? We cannot know for sure. But political considerations or behind-the-scenes negotiations may very well have influenced these decisions.

Prosecutors can use their power to pursue cases even when victims refuse to testify. Both prosecutors and judges may pressure witnesses to testify, sometimes even jailing reluctant witnesses for contempt of court. In 2005, for example, a federal judge ordered two news reporters to be jailed for refusing to disclose their sources concerning an investigation to find the government official who revealed the identity of a CIA officer. One reporter avoided jail by testifying, but the other refused to reveal confidential sources and was locked up. Many factors can influence prosecutors' decisions to use their full powers or, alternatively, to decline to prosecute even when evidence of wrongdoing exists. Thus, as we describe the 13 steps in the criminal justice process, we must bear in mind that other factors affecting decisions by police, prosecutors, and judges may not be fully evident in these descriptions. Discretion, political pressure, and other factors can alter the outcomes for different defendants.

Steps in the Decision-Making Process

The criminal justice system consists of 13 steps that cover the stages of law enforcement, adjudication, and corrections. The system looks like an assembly line where decisions are made about defendants—the raw material of the process. As these steps are described, recall the concepts discussed earlier: system, discretion, sequential tasks, filtering, and exchange. Be aware that the terms used for different stages in the process may differ from state to state, and the sequence of the steps differs in some parts of the country, but the flow of decision making generally follows this pattern.

1. *Investigation.* The process begins when the police believe that a crime has been committed. At this point, an investigation is begun. The police normally depend on a member of the community to report the offense. Except for traffic and public order offenses, the police rarely observe illegal behavior themselves. Because most crimes have already been committed and offenders have left the scene before the police arrive, the police are at a disadvantage in quickly finding and arresting the offenders.

2. *Arrest.* If the police find enough evidence showing that a particular person has committed a crime, they can make an arrest. An **arrest** involves physically taking a person into custody pending a court proceeding. This action not only restricts the suspect's freedom, but it is also the first step toward prosecution.

   Under some conditions, arrests may be made on the basis of a **warrant**—a court order issued by a judge authorizing police officers to take certain actions, such as arresting suspects or searching premises. In practice, most arrests are made without warrants. In some states, police officers may issue a summons or citation that orders a person to appear in court on a certain date. This avoids the need to hold the suspect physically while waiting for decisions to be made about the case.

3. *Booking.* After an arrest, the suspect is usually transported to a police station for booking, in which a record is made of the arrest. When booked, the suspect may be fingerprinted, photographed, interrogated, and placed in a lineup to be identified by the victim or witnesses. All suspects must also be warned that they have the right to counsel, that they may remain silent, and that any statement they make may be used against them later. Bail may be set so that the suspect learns what amount of money must be paid or what other conditions must be met to gain release from custody until the case is processed.

4. *Charging.* Prosecuting attorneys are the key link between the police and the courts. They must consider the facts of the case and decide whether there is reasonable cause to believe that an offense was committed and that the suspect committed the offense. The decision to charge is crucial because it sets in motion the adjudication of the case.

5. *Initial appearance.* Within a reasonable time after arrest, the suspect must be brought before a judge. At this point, suspects are given formal notice of the charge(s) for which they are being held, advised of their rights, and, if approved by the judge, given a chance to post bail. At this stage, the judge decides whether there is enough evidence to hold the suspect for further

arrest
The physical taking of a person into custody on the grounds that probable cause exists to believe that he or she has committed a criminal offense. Police may use only reasonable physical force in making an arrest. The purpose of the arrest is to hold the accused for a court proceeding.

warrant
A court order authorizing police officials to take certain actions; for example, to arrest suspects or to search premises.

criminal processing. If enough evidence has not been produced, the judge will dismiss the case.

The purpose of bail is to permit the accused to be released while awaiting trial and to ensure that he or she will show up in court at the appointed time. The concept of bail is connected to the important American value of liberty. Bail represents an effort to avoid depriving presumptively innocent people of liberty before their guilt has been proven in court. Bail requires the accused to provide or arrange a surety (or pledge), usually in the form of money or a bond. The amount of bail is based mainly on the judge's view of the seriousness of the crime and the defendant's prior criminal record. Suspects may also be released *on their own recognizance*—a promise to appear in court at a later date. In a few cases bail may be denied and the accused held because he or she is viewed as a threat to the community or there is a high risk that the individual will flee.

6. *Preliminary hearing/grand jury.* After suspects have been arrested, booked, and brought to court to be informed of the charge and advised of their rights, a decision must be made as to whether there is enough evidence to proceed. The preliminary hearing, used in about half the states, allows a judge to decide whether there is probable cause to believe that a crime has been committed and that the accused person committed it. If the judge does not find probable cause, the case is dismissed. If there is enough evidence, the accused is bound over for arraignment on an **information**—a document charging a person with a specific crime. In the federal system and in some states, the prosecutor appears before a grand jury, which decides whether there is enough evidence to file an **indictment** or true bill charging the suspect with a specific crime. The preliminary hearing and grand jury are designed to prevent hasty and malicious prosecutions, to protect people from mistakenly being humiliated in public, and to decide whether there are grounds for prosecution. The use of the grand jury reinforces the American value of limited government. By giving citizens the authority to overrule the police and prosecutor in determining whether criminal charges should be pursued, the grand jury represents an effort to reduce the risk that government officials will use their power to deprive people of liberty in unjustified circumstances.

7. *Indictment/information.* If the preliminary hearing leads to an information or the grand jury vote leads to an indictment, the prosecutor prepares the formal charging document and presents it to the court.

8. *Arraignment.* The accused person appears in court to hear the indictment or information read by a judge and to enter a plea. Accused persons may plead guilty or not guilty or, in some states, stand mute. If the accused pleads guilty, the judge must decide whether the plea is made voluntarily and whether the person has full knowledge of the consequences. When a guilty plea is accepted as knowing and voluntary, there is no need for a trial, and the judge imposes a sentence. Plea bargaining can take place at any time in the criminal justice process, but it tends to be completed before or after arraignment. Very few criminal cases proceed to trial. Most move from the entry of the guilty plea to the sentencing phase.

9. *Trial.* For the small percentage of defendants who plead not guilty, the Sixth Amendment guarantees the right to a trial by an impartial jury if the charges are serious enough to warrant a prison sentence of more than six months. In many jurisdictions, lesser charges do not entail a right to a jury trial. Most trials are summary or bench trials—that is, they are conducted without a jury. Because the defendant pleads guilty in most criminal cases, only about 10 percent of cases go to trial and only about 5 percent are heard by juries. Whether a criminal trial is held before a judge alone or before a judge and jury, the procedures are similar and are set out by state law and Supreme

information
A document charging an individual with a specific crime. It is prepared by a prosecuting attorney and presented to a court at a preliminary hearing.

indictment
A document returned by a grand jury as a "true bill" charging an individual with a specific crime on the basis of a determination of probable cause from evidence presented by a prosecuting attorney.

Court rulings. A defendant may be found guilty only if the evidence proves beyond a reasonable doubt that he or she committed the offense.

10. *Sentencing.* Judges are responsible for imposing sentences. The intent is to make the sentence suitable to the offender and the offense within the limits set by the law. Although criminal codes place limits on sentences, the judge often still has leeway. Among the judge's options are a suspended sentence, probation, imprisonment, or other sanctions such as fines and community service.

11. *Appeal.* Defendants who are found guilty may appeal convictions to a higher court. An appeal can be based on the claim that the trial court failed to follow the proper procedures or that the defendant's constitutional rights were violated by the actions of police, prosecutors, defense attorneys, or judges. The number of appeals is small compared with the total number of convictions, and in about 80 percent of appeals, trial judges and other officials are ruled to have acted properly. Even defendants who win appeals do not necessarily go free. Normally the defendant is given a second trial, which may result in an acquittal, a second conviction, or a plea bargain to lesser charges.

12. *Corrections.* The court's sentence is carried out by the correctional subsystem. Probation, intermediate sanctions such as fines and community service, and incarceration are the sanctions most often imposed. Probation allows offenders to serve their sentences in the community under supervision. Youthful offenders, first offenders, and those convicted of minor violations are most likely to be sentenced to probation rather than incarceration. The conditions of probation may require offenders to observe certain rules—to be employed, maintain an orderly life, or attend school—and to report to their supervising officer from time to time. If these requirements are not met, the judge may revoke the probation and impose a prison sentence. Many new types of sanctions have been used in recent years. These intermediate sanctions are more restrictive than probation but less restrictive than incarceration. They include fines, intensive supervision probation, boot camp, home confinement, and community service. Whatever the reasons used to justify them, prisons exist mainly to separate criminals from the rest of society. Those convicted of misdemeanors usually serve their time in city or county jails, while felons serve time in state prisons. Isolation from the community is one of the most painful aspects of incarceration. Not only are letters and visits restricted, but supervision and censorship are ever present. To maintain security, prison officials make unannounced searches of inmates and subject them to strict discipline.

13. *Release.* Release may occur when the offender has served the full sentence imposed by the court, but most offenders are returned to the community under the supervision of a parole officer. Parole continues for the duration of the sentence or for a period specified by law. Parole may be revoked and the offender returned to prison if the conditions of parole are not met or if the parolee commits another crime.

The case of Christopher Jones is described on page 97. Jones, a then 31-year-old man from Battle Creek, Michigan, was arrested, charged, and convicted of serious crimes arising from the police investigation of a series of robberies. His case illustrates how the steps just discussed can play out in the real world.

checkpoint

12. What are the steps of the criminal justice process?

THE CRIMINAL JUSTICE PROCESS

The State of Michigan versus Christopher Jones

Investigation

In October 1998, police in Battle Creek, Michigan, investigated a string of six robberies that occurred in a ten-day period. Assaults occurred during some of the robberies. One victim was beaten so badly with a power tool that he required extensive reconstructive surgery for his face and skull. The police received an anonymous tip on their Silent Observer hotline, which led them to put together a *photo lineup*—an array of photographs of local men who had criminal records. Based on the anonymous tip and photographs identified by the victims, the police began to search for two men who were well-known to them, Christopher Jones and his cousin Fred Brown.

Arrest

Christopher Jones had shut himself into a bedroom at his parents' house. He was a 31-year-old African American man whose life was in shambles. A dozen years of struggles with cocaine addiction had cost him his marriage and several jobs in local factories. In addition, he had a criminal record, stretching back several years, from pleading guilty to charges of attempted larceny and attempted breaking and entering in separate incidents. Thus he had a record of stealing to support his drug habit, and he had previously spent time on probation and done a short stretch in a minimum-security prison and a boot camp. But he had never been caught with drugs, and he had never been accused of committing an act of violence.

Because his family feared that he would be injured or killed by the police if he tried to run or resist arrest, his parents called the police and told them where he was. At approximately 10:00 P.M. on October 28, as officers surrounded the house, the family opened the door and showed the officers the way to the bedroom. When Jones heard the knock on the door, he knew he had to face the inevitable. He surrendered peacefully and was led to the waiting police car in handcuffs.

The officers took him to the police station. A detective with whom Jones was acquainted offered him a cup of coffee and then read him his *Miranda* rights, including his right to remain silent and his right to an attorney. The detective then informed Jones that he was looking at the possibility of a life sentence in prison unless he helped the police by providing information about Fred Brown. Jones said that he did not want to talk to the police yet, and he asked for an attorney. Because arrested suspects are entitled to have an attorney present during questioning if they ask for one, the police ceased questioning Jones. He was taken next door to the jail.

Booking

At the jail, Jones was strip-searched. After removing all of his clothes so that officers could make sure he had not hidden weapons or drugs in his clothing or on his body, he was given a bright-orange jumpsuit to wear. He was photographed and fingerprinted. He was told that he would be arraigned the next morning. The police handed him a blanket and locked him in the *holding cell*—a large cell where people are placed immediately upon arrest. The holding cell was big enough to hold approximately ten people and it had four cement benches to serve as beds. As Jones looked for a space to lie down on the floor

2 charged in violent robberies

TRACE CHRISTENSON
The Enquirer

Two Battle Creek men arraigned Thursday on charges stemming from a series of recent robberies are facing sentences of up to life in prison if convicted.

Fred Brown, 31, is charged with assault with intent to murder, armed robbery and breaking and entering. Christopher R. Jones, also 31, is charged with unarmed robbery and home invasion.

Battle Creek police believe the men are responsible for six robberies in 10 days at Battle Creek businesses and homes.

One of the victims must have reconstructive surgery after he was hit in the face with either an electric drill or hammer, police said.

Charges read in court Thursday involve two of the robberies, but after the hearing, assistant prosecutor Justin McCarthy said the investigation is ongoing and charges in other robberies could be filed later.

Brown and Jones were arrested about 10 p.m. Wednesday at separate locations – Brown near Hamlin Avenue and Angell Street and Jones on Irving Park Drive.

Fred Brown   **Christopher R. Jones**

Police learned of their possible involvement in the robberies from an anonymous call.

"We got a Silent Observer tip that they were the ones doing it, and we put together a photo lineup," Sgt. Carter Bright said.

Jones' charges are connected to an Oct. 26 robbery at K-D Slot Car Racing, 21 N. 20th St. A man there was injured when he was hit in the face and some toy cars and parts were taken.

Brown is charged in the Oct. 25 robbery of a home at 383 Truth Drive, where cash was taken.

District Court Magistrate Jill Booth set a cash bond at $200,000, and both men remain in the Calhoun County jail.

A preliminary examination for Jones was scheduled for Nov. 3 and for Brown on Nov. 6.

---

with his blanket, he estimated that 16 men were sleeping in the crowded cell that night.

Arraignment

The next morning, the men in the holding cell were taken to a neighboring room for video arraignment. A two-way camera system permitted Jones to see the district courtroom in the neighboring courthouse at the same time that the judge and others in the courtroom could view him on a television screen. The judge informed Jones that he was being charged with breaking and entering, armed robbery, and assault with intent to commit murder. The final charge alone could draw a life sentence. Under Michigan law, these charges can be filed directly by the prosecutor without being presented to a grand jury for indictment as required in federal courts and some other states. The judge set bond (bail) at $200,000, an amount that an unemployed, penniless person like Jones would have no hope of obtaining.

At a second video arraignment several days later, Jones was informed that he faced seven additional counts of assault with intent to commit murder, armed robbery, unarmed robbery, and home invasion for four additional robberies. Bond was set at $200,000 for each alleged robbery. Thus he faced ten felony charges for the five robberies, and his total bail was $1 million.

Jail

After arraignment, jail officers examined Jones's current charges and past record in order to determine the level of security and supervision he would need in the jail. Prisoners charged with violent offenses or who have substantial criminal records are kept in areas separate from people charged with property crimes. Jones was placed in a medium-security area with 55 others who were charged with serious felonies. Jones would eventually spend nine months at the jail before his case concluded.

Defense Attorney

Under state court procedures, Jones was supposed to have a preliminary hearing within two weeks after his arraignment. At the preliminary hearing, the prosecution would be required to present enough evidence to justify the charges. If the evidence was inadequate, the district judge could dismiss the charges. If there was enough evidence to raise the possibility of guilt, the district judge would send the case up to the Calhoun County Circuit Court, the court that handled felony trials.

Jones received a letter informing him of the name of the private attorney appointed by the court to represent him, but he did not get to meet the attorney until he was taken to court for his first preliminary hearing. Minutes before the hearing, the attorney, David Gilbert, introduced himself to Jones. Jones wanted to delay any preliminary hearing until a lineup could be held to test the victims' identification of him as a robber. According to Jones, Gilbert said they must proceed with the preliminary hearing for one of the charges, because the victim had traveled from another state in order to testify. The preliminary hearing covering the rest of the charges was postponed, but the out-of-town witness's testimony led the district judge to conclude that sufficient evidence existed to move one of Jones's cases to the circuit court on an armed robbery charge.

Lineup

Jones waited for weeks for the lineup to be scheduled. When he was taken to his rescheduled preliminary hearing, his attorney complained to the judge that the lineup had never been conducted. The judge ordered that the lineup be held as soon as possible.

Jones and the other men were told to stand and turn around in front of a one-way mirror. One by one, the victims of each robbery looked at the men in the room and attempted to determine if any of them were the robbers. At the end of each identification, one of the men in the lineup was asked to step forward, and Jones presumed this meant that the victim had identified that man as one of the robbers. Jones was only asked to step forward twice, and other men were asked to step forward at other times. Jones guessed that he was picked out by two of the victims, but that the other three victims either picked other men or were unable to identify anyone.

Jones's defense attorney was unable to attend the lineup. Another attorney arrived and informed Jones that he would take Mr. Gilbert's place. Although Jones protested that the other men in the lineup were much shorter and older, he was disappointed that the substitute attorney was not more active in objecting that the men looked too different from Jones to adequately test the victims' ability to make an identification. He later discovered that his substitute attorney had just entered private practice after serving as an assistant prosecutor at Jones's first preliminary hearing.

Preliminary Hearing

At the next preliminary hearing, the victims in each case provided testimony about what happened. Because the testimony generally focused on Brown as the perpetrator of the assaults and robberies, the defense attorney argued that many of the charges against Jones should be dropped. The judge determined that the victims' testimony provided enough evidence to send most of the charges against Jones to the circuit court.

Plea Bargaining

Jones waited for weeks in jail without hearing much from his attorney. Although he didn't know it, the prosecutor was formulating a plea agreement and communicating to the defense attorney the terms under which charges would be dropped in exchange for a guilty plea from Jones. Outside the courtroom a few minutes before a hearing on the proposed plea agreement, Gilbert told Jones that the prosecutor had offered to drop all of the other charges if Jones would plead guilty to one count of unarmed robbery for the incident in which the victim was seriously injured by Brown and one count of home invasion for another robbery. Jones did not want to accept the deal, because he claimed that he was not even present at the robbery for which he was being asked to plead guilty for home invasion. According to Jones, the attorney insisted that this was an excellent deal compared with all of the other charges that the prosecutor could pursue. Jones still resisted. In the courtroom, Judge James Kingsley read the offer to Jones, but Jones refused to enter a guilty plea. Like the defense attorney, the judge told Jones that this was a favorable offer compared with the other serious charges that the prosecutor could still pursue against Jones. Jones again declined.

Jones was worried that he was making a mistake by turning down the plea offer. He wondered if he could end up with a life sentence, even for a crime he did not commit, if one of the victims identified him by mistake as having done a crime that was actually committed by Brown. Outside the courtroom, he told his attorney that he had changed his mind. They went right back into the courtroom and told the judge that he was ready to enter a guilty plea. As they prepared to enter the plea, the prosecutor said that they also expected Jones to provide information about the five robberies and testify against Brown as part of the plea agreement. The defense attorney protested that this condition had not been part of the plea agreement offered by prosecution. Jones told the judge that he could not provide any information about the home invasion to which he was about to plead guilty because he was not present at that robbery and had no knowledge of what occurred. Judge Kingsley declared that he would not accept a guilty plea when the defendant claimed to have no knowledge of the crime.

After the hearing, the prosecutor and defense attorney renewed their discussions about a plea agreement. Jones agreed to take a polygraph (lie detector) test so that the prosecutor could find out which robberies he actually knew about. Although Jones waited for weeks for the polygraph test in hopes that it would show prosecutors that his criminal involvement with Brown was limited, no test was ever administered.

Scheduled Trial and Plea Agreement

Jones waited for several more weeks in jail. According to Jones, when Gilbert came to visit, he informed Jones that the armed robbery trial was scheduled for the following day. In addition, the prosecutor's plea offer had changed. Fred Brown pleaded guilty to armed robbery and assault with intent less than murder and he was facing a sentence of 25 to 50 years in prison. Because Brown pleaded guilty, the prosecutor no longer needed Jones as a potential witness in any trial against Brown. Thus the prosecutor no longer offered the unarmed robbery and home invasion pleas. He now wanted Jones to plead to the same charges as Brown in exchange for dropping the other pending charges. According to Jones, Gilbert claimed the prosecutor would be very angry if he did not take the plea, and the attorney encouraged Jones to accept the plea by arguing that the prosecutor would otherwise pursue all of the other charges, which could bring a life sentence. Jones refused to plead guilty.

The next day, Jones was given his personal clothes to wear instead of the orange jail jumpsuit, because he was going to court for trial instead of for a hearing. Prior to entering the court, Gilbert again encouraged Jones to consider the plea agreement. He raised the possibility of a life sentence if the prosecutor pursued all of the pending charges and, according to Jones, he said that the guilty plea could be withdrawn if the sentencing recommendation made by the probation office was too high. Because he did not want to risk getting a life sentence and he believed he could later withdraw the plea if he wanted, Jones decided to accept the offer.

With his attorney's advice, he entered a plea of no contest to the two charges. A no contest plea is treated the same as a guilty plea for punishment purposes. However, the plea means that crime victims must prove their case in any subsequent civil lawsuit against the defendant for injuries suffered in the alleged crime rather than automatically winning the lawsuit because the offender admitted guilt.

Before taking the plea, Judge Kingsley informed Jones that by entering the plea he would be waiving his right to a trial, including his right to question witnesses and to have the prosecutor prove his guilt beyond a reasonable doubt. After Judge Kingsley read the charges of armed robbery and assault with intent to do great bodily harm and asked, "What do you plead?" Jones replied, "No contest." Then the judge asked Jones a series of questions.

> Judge Kingsley: Mr. Jones, has anyone promised you anything other than the plea bargain to get you to enter this plea?
> Jones: No.
> Judge Kingsley: Has anyone threatened you or forced you or compelled you to enter the plea?
> Jones: No.
> Judge Kingsley: . . . Are you [entering this plea] of your own free will?
> Jones: Yes.

The judge reminded Jones that there had been no final agreement on what the ultimate sentence would be and gave Jones one last opportunity to change his mind about pleading no contest. Jones repeated his desire to enter the plea, so the plea was accepted.

Immediately after the hearing, Jones had second thoughts about pleading no contest. According to Jones, "I was feeling uneasy about being pressured [by my attorney] to take the plea offer . . . [so I decided] to write to the Judge and tell him about the pressures my attorney put upon me as well as [the attorney] telling me I had a right to withdraw my plea. So I wrote the Judge that night." Jones knew he was guilty of stealing things at one robbery, but he had been unarmed. He felt as if he had been pressured into pleading guilty to an armed robbery and assault that he did not commit because the prosecutor threatened him with so many other charges and his own attorney seemed so eager for him to accept the plea agreement. He subsequently learned that the law did not permit him to withdraw the plea.

Presentence Investigation

Probation officers are responsible for conducting presentence investigations in which they review offenders' records and interview the offenders about their education, work history, drug use, and family background before making recommendations to the judge about an appropriate punishment. Jones felt that his interview with the probation officer went well, but he was dismayed to discover that his file erroneously stated that he had three prior criminal convictions instead of two. The extra conviction would mean additional years tacked on to his sentence unless he could get his file corrected. When the errors were eventually corrected, the presentence report prepared by the probation office ultimately recommended 5 to 25 years for armed robbery and 4 to 7 years for assault.

When Gilbert learned that Jones had written the letter to Judge Kingsley that was critical of Gilbert's performance in the case, he asked the judge to permit him to withdraw as Jones's attorney. Judge Kingsley initially refused to permit him to withdraw. However, when Jones spoke in open court at the first scheduled sentencing hearing about his criticisms of Gilbert as well as his complaints about the prosecution's handling of the lineup and the failure to administer the polygraph test, the judge decided to appoint a new defense attorney to handle sentencing at a rescheduled hearing. It was clear that the relationship between Gilbert and Jones had deteriorated to the point that it would be difficult for them to cooperate in preparing for the sentencing hearing.

Sentencing Preparation

The new defense attorney, Virginia Cairns, encouraged Jones's parents, siblings, ex-wife, and minister to write letters to the judge describing Jones's positive qualities and his prospects for successful rehabilitation after prison. Jones was pleased with his attorney. According to Jones, "She came to visit me within a week or so . . . . She said she would fight for me to get a lesser sentence than what was recommended."

Sentencing

Although he was arrested in October 1998, Jones's case did not complete its processing until the sentencing hearing in July 1999. When his case was called, Jones was led into the courtroom wearing an orange jail jumpsuit and escorted by a deputy sheriff. Judge Kingsley called on Jones to make his statement first. Jones faced the judge as he spoke, glancing occasionally at his family and at the victim when he referred to them in his remarks.

> First and foremost, I would like to say what happened to the victim was a tragedy. I showed great remorse for that. He is in my prayers along with his family. Even though, your Honor, I'm not making any excuses for what I'm saying here today, the injuries

the victim sustained were not at the hands of myself and nor did I actually rob this victim. I was present, your Honor, as I told you once before, yes, I was. And it's a wrong. Again I'm not making any kind of excuse whatsoever....

Your Honor, I would just like to say that drugs has clouded my memory, and my choices in the past. I really made some wrong decisions. Only times I've gotten into trouble were because of my drug use.... One of the worst decisions I really made was my involvement of being around the co-defendant Fred Brown. That bothers me to this day because actually we didn't even get along. Because of my drug use again I chose to be around him.

Jones also used his statement to talk about his positive record as a high school student and athlete, his work with the jail minister, and his desire to talk to young people about his experiences in order to steer them away from drugs.

Cairns spoke next. She called the court's attention to several errors in the presentence report, such as the fact that Jones had only two prior convictions rather than three. She emphasized the letters of support from Jones's family and argued that this support system would help him to become rehabilitated after serving his prison term. She argued that Jones should receive a less severe sentence than the long prison term imposed on the co-defendant Brown.

The courtroom was completely silent as the victim spoke about his severe injuries and how his $40,000 worth of medical bills had driven him to bankruptcy.

I went from having perfect vision to not being able to read out of my left eye any more. I got steel plates in my head.... They left me to die that morning. He took the keys to my car.... So today it's true, I don't think Mr. Jones should be sentenced same as Brown. That's who I want—I want to see him sentenced to the maximum. He's the one that crushed my skull with a drill. But Jones did hit me several times while Mr. Brown held me there to begin with. It's true that I did hit him with a hammer to get them off me. But he still was there. He still had the chance of not leaving me without keys to my car so I could get to a hospital. He still had the choice to stop at least and phone on the way and say there's someone that could possibly be dead, but he didn't.... You don't treat a human being like that. And if you do you serve time and pretty much to the maximum. I don't ask the Court for 25 years. That's a pretty long time to serve. And I do ask the Court to look at 15 to 20. I'd be happy. Thank you.

Gary Brand, the assistant prosecutor, recommended a 20-year sentence and noted that Jones should be responsible for $35,000 in restitution to the victim and to the state for medical expenses and lost income.

After listening to the presentations, Judge Kingsley spoke sternly to Jones. He agreed that Jones's drug problem had led to his involvement in this crime and the crimes that led to Jones's prior convictions. He also noted that Jones's family support was much stronger than that of most defendants appearing in circuit court. He chastised Jones for falling into drugs when life got tougher after enjoying a successful career in high school. Judge Kingsley then proceeded to announce his sentencing decision.

You are not in my view as culpable as Mr. Brown. I agree with [the victim] that you were there. When I read your handwritten letter, Mr. Jones, I was a bit disturbed by your unwillingness to confront the reality of where you found yourself with Mr. Brown. You were not a passive observer to everything that went on in my view. You

were not as active a participant as Mr. Brown, but you were not an innocent victim in the sense that "I simply walked into the store. I had no idea what was going on. I just stood there in amazement as my acquaintance brutalized this man." I don't think that's the case. But what I'm going to do, Mr. Jones, is as follows: Taking everything into consideration as it relates to the armed robbery count, it is the sentence of the Court that you spend a term of not less than 12 years nor more than 25 years with the Michigan Department of Corrections. I will give you credit for the [261 days] that you have already served.

The judge also ordered the payment of $35,000 in restitution as a condition of parole. He also noted that the sentence was within the state's new sentencing guidelines and remarked that the cost to the taxpayers would be approximately $500,000 to hold Jones in prison during the sentence. He concluded the hearing by informing Jones of his right to file an application for a leave to appeal.

Prison

After spending a few more weeks in jail awaiting transfer to the state prison system, Jones was sent to the state correctional department's classification center at a state prison in Jackson. At the center, newly incarcerated prisoners are evaluated. Based on their criminal history, presentence report, psychological and medical problems, and age, they are assigned to one of 40 correctional facilities in the state. Jones spent one month in the center in which he was confined to a cell with one other prisoner. Because there was no mirror in the cell, he shaved by looking at his reflection in the pipes on back of the toilet. Each day the prisoners were released from their cells for ten minutes at each meal and one hour in the recreation yard.

He was eventually assigned to a Level IV prison, where he lived with a cellmate in a space designed to house one prisoner. Prisons' security classifications range from Level I for minimum security to Level VI for "super maximum," high security. At prison, conditions were better than at the classification center. They were given more time at each meal and more choices of foods. There were longer periods in the morning and the afternoon for recreation, prison jobs, and school. Because Jones was a high school graduate who had previously attended a community college—and therefore was one of the most highly educated prisoners in his institution—he became head clerk in the prison library. Over the years, he was transferred to seven different prisons for both medical reasons and to move him into lower-security facilities as he proved himself to be well-behaved. He eventually moved to a Level I prison where, as the tenth anniversary of his arrest approached, he prepared for his first meeting with the parole board to be considered for possible release into the community under parole supervision.

For Critical Analysis

Were any aspects of the processes and decisions in the Jones case unfair or improper? Did the outcome of the case achieve "justice"?

Sources: T. Christenson, "Two Charged in Violent Robberies," *Battle Creek Inquirer*, October 30, 1998, p. 1A; Interview with Christopher Jones, St. Louis Correctional Facility, St. Louis, Michigan, October 19, 1999; Letters to author from Christopher Jones, October and November 1999; Calhoun County Circuit Court transcripts for plea hearing, May 20, 1999, and sentencing hearing, July 16, 1999.

The Criminal Justice Wedding Cake

Although the flowchart shown in Figure 3.4 is helpful, we must note that not all cases are treated equally. The process applied to a given case, as well as its outcome, is shaped by the importance of the case to decision makers, the seriousness of the charge, and the defendant's resources.

Some cases are highly visible either because of the notoriety of the defendant or victim or because of the shocking nature of the crime. At the other extreme are "run-of-the-mill cases" involving unknowns charged with minor crimes.

As shown in Figure 3.5, the criminal justice process can be compared to a wedding cake. This model shows clearly how different cases receive different kinds of treatment in the justice process.

Layer 1 of the "cake" consists of celebrated cases that are highly unusual, receive much public attention, result in a jury trial, and often drag on through many appeals. These cases embody the ideal of an adversary system of justice in which each side actively fights against the other, either because the defendant faces a stiff sentence or because the defendant has the wealth to pay for a strong defense. Further, Layer 1 cases in a sense serve as morality plays. People see the carefully crafted arguments of the prosecution and defense as expressing key issues in society or tragic flaws in individuals. The trial of singer Michael Jackson on child molestation charges in 2005 and the tax evasion trial of movie star Wesley Snipes in 2008 illustrate the kinds of cases at the top of the "cake." Not all cases in Layer 1 receive national attention, however. Local crimes, especially cases of murder and rape, can go to trial because of the long prison sentences at stake for the defendants if they are convicted.

The Layer 1 cases fit the ideals of American values concerning liberty, due process, and constitutional rights. In such cases, attorneys work vigorously to make sure that the defendant's rights are protected and that the trial process produces a careful, fair decision about the defendant's guilt and punishment. The drawn out, dramatic procedures of such trials fulfill the picture of the American justice process that is taught to schoolchildren and reinforced in movies and television shows. When people in other countries ask Americans to describe the U.S. legal system, they are most likely to draw from their idealized image of American values and describe the Layer 1 process. Too often, however,

Joe Francis, the wealthy producer of the *Girls Gone Wild* video series, arrives at a press conference after being released on bail in March 2008 after spending 11 months in a Nevada jail awaiting trial on federal tax evasion charges. Unlike most Americans, Francis can afford to hire attorneys who will fight vigorously against the prosecutors and, if a favorable plea cannot be negotiated, take the case through an expensive trial. Does the United States achieve its motto of "equal justice under law" if not all defendants have the resources to battle prosecution effectively at trial?

© Jonathan Alcorn/ ZUMA Press

FIGURE 3.5

The criminal justice wedding cake

This figure shows that different cases are treated in different ways. Only a very few cases are played out as "high drama"; most are handled through plea bargaining and dismissals.

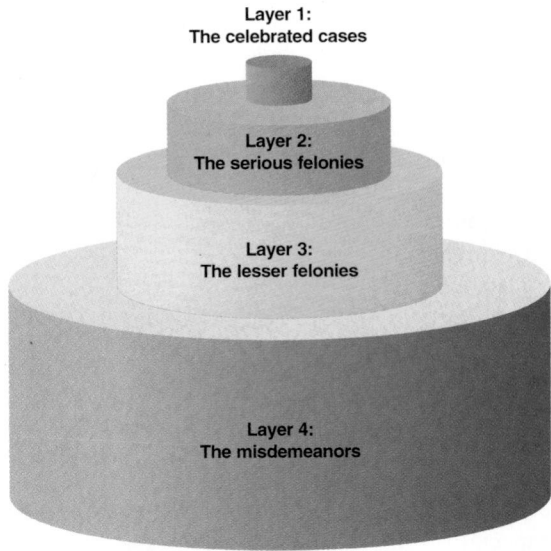

Source: Drawn from Samuel Walker, *Sense and Nonsense about Crime and Drugs*, 4th ed. (Belmont, CA: Wadsworth, 1998), 30–37.

the public's belief in the prevalence of idealistic American values leads to the erroneous conclusion that most criminal cases follow this model.

Layer 2 consists of serious *felonies:* violent crimes committed by people with long criminal records, against victims unknown to them. Police and the prosecutors speak of these as "heavy" cases that should result in "tough" sentences. In such cases the defendant has little reason to plead guilty and the defense attorney must prepare for trial.

Layer 3 also consists of felonies, but the crimes and the offenders are seen as less important than those in Layer 2. The offenses may be the same as in Layer 2, but the offender may have no record, and the victim may have had a prior relationship with the accused. The main goal of criminal justice officials is to dispose of such cases quickly. For this reason, many are filtered out of the system prior to trial, usually through plea bargaining.

Layer 4 is made up of *misdemeanors.* About 90 percent of all cases fall into this category. They concern such offenses as public drunkenness, shoplifting, prostitution, disturbing the peace, and traffic violations. Looked on as the "garbage" of the system, these cases are handled by the lower courts, where speed is essential. Prosecutors use their discretion to reduce charges or recommend probation as a way to encourage defendants to plead guilty quickly. Trials are rare, processes are informal, and fines, probation, or short jail sentences result.

The wedding cake model provides a useful way of viewing the criminal justice system. Cases are not treated equally: Some are seen as quite important, others as merely part of a large number that must be processed. When one knows the nature of a case, one can predict fairly well how it will be handled and what its outcome will be.

---

checkpoint

13. What is the purpose of the wedding cake model?
14. What types of cases are found on each layer?

CRIME AND JUSTICE IN A MULTICULTURAL SOCIETY

One important aspect of American values is the principle of equal treatment. The American value of equality is prominently announced and displayed in important national documents. The Declaration of Independence speaks of every American being "created equal," and the Fourteenth Amendment to the Constitution guarantees the right to "equal protection." Critics of the criminal justice system argue that discretionary decisions and other factors produce racial discrimination. Discrimination calls into question the country's success in fulfilling the values that it claims to regard as supremely important. As such, we should look closely at whether or not discrimination exists in various criminal justice settings.

Disparity and Discrimination

African Americans, Hispanics, and other minorities are subjected to the criminal justice system at much higher rates than are the white majority (Cole, 1999: 4–5; J. Hagan and Peterson, 1995:14). For example:

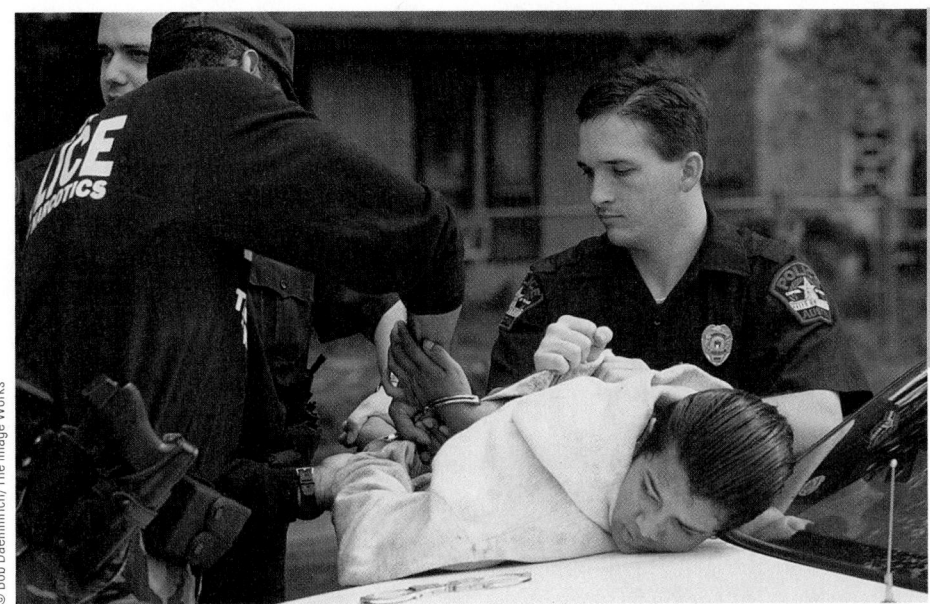

© Bob Daemmrich/The Image Works

- African Americans account for one-third of all arrests and one-half of all incarcerations in the United States, although only 12 percent of the people in the United States are African American.

- The per capita incarceration rate for African Americans is seven times greater than that for whites.

- Since 1980 the proportion of Hispanics among all inmates in U.S. prisons has risen from 7.7 percent to 16.0 percent.

- About one-third of all African American men in their twenties are under criminal justice supervision.

- The rate of unfounded arrests of Hispanics in California is double that of whites.

- Among 100,000 African American men aged 15–19, 68 will die as the result of a homicide involving a gun, compared with about 6 among 100,000 white men in the same age group.

- The robbery victimization rate for African Americans is 150 percent of that for whites, and they are victimized by rapes and aggravated assaults at similar rates that exceed those for whites.

- The crime victimization rate is 260 per 1,000 Hispanic households versus 144 per 1,000 non-Hispanic households.

- The violent crime victimization rate for Native Americans is more than twice the rate for the nation.

The experiences of minority group members with the criminal justice system may contribute to differences in their views about the system's fulfillment of the goal of equal treatment (Lundman and Kaufman, 2003). See "What Americans Think" on page 104 for more on this topic.

A central question is whether racial and ethnic disparities like those just listed result from discrimination or from some other cause (Mann, 1993: vii–xiv; Wilbanks, 1987). A **disparity** is a difference between groups that legitimate factors can explain. For example, the fact that 18- to 24-year-old men are arrested out of proportion to their numbers in the general population is a disparity explained by the fact that they commit more crime. It is not thought to be the result of a public policy that singles out young men for arrest. **Discrimination**

disparity
The unequal treatment of one group by the criminal justice system, compared with treatment accorded other groups.

discrimination
Differential treatment of individuals or groups based on race, ethnicity, sexual orientation, or economic status, instead of on their behavior or qualifications.

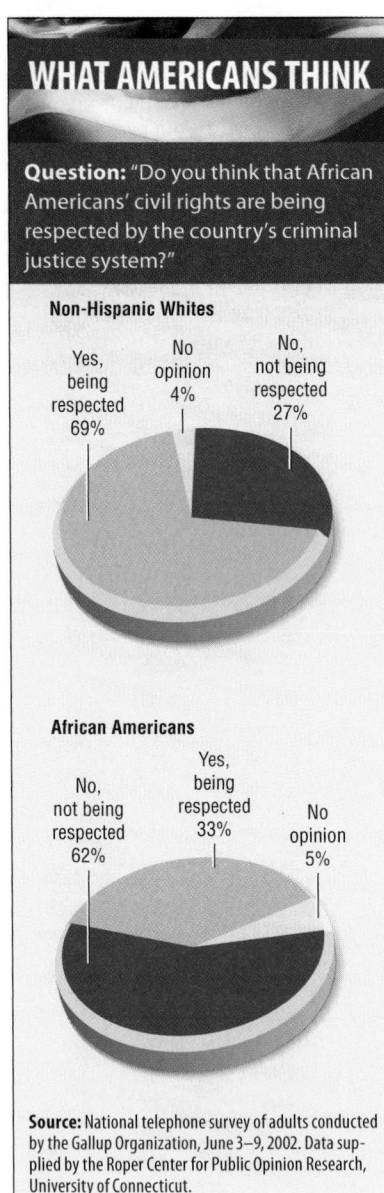

The NAACP Legal Defense Fund is an organization that uses lawsuits as a means to combat racial discrimination, including discrimination in the justice system. To link to this website, go to *The American System of Criminal Justice* 12e companion site at academic.cengage.com/criminaljustice/cole.

occurs when groups are differentially treated without regard to their behavior or qualifications: for example, if people of color are routinely sentenced to prison regardless of their criminal history.

Explanations for Disparities

Three differing theories can be examined as possible explanations for the existence of racial disparities in criminal justice: (1) people of color commit more crimes, (2) the criminal justice system is racist, with the result that people of color are treated more harshly, or (3) the criminal justice system expresses the racism found in society as a whole. We consider each of these views in turn.

Explanation 1: People of Color Commit More Crimes

Nobody denies that the proportion of minorities arrested and placed under correctional supervision (probation, jail, prison, parole) exceeds the proportion of minorities in the general population. However, people disagree over whether bias accounts for the disparity.

Disparities in arrests and sentences may be due to legitimate factors. For example, prosecutors and judges are supposed to take into account differences between serious and petty offenses, and between repeat and first-time offenders. It follows that more people of color will end up in the courts and prisons if they are more likely to commit more serious crimes and have more serious prior records than are whites (S. Walker, Spohn, and DeLone, 2003).

But why would minorities commit more crimes? The most extreme answer is that they are more predisposed to criminality. This assumes that people of color make up a "criminal class." The available evidence does not support this view. Behavior that violates criminal laws is prevalent throughout all segments of society. For example, studies of illicit drug use find that young adults, men, whites, and those with less than a high school education are more likely to use drugs than are others. As the Clinton Administration's "Drug Czar" General Barry McCaffrey, the former director of the U.S. Office of National Drug Control Policy, said, "The typical drug user is not poor and unemployed" (*New York Times*, September 9, 1999: A14). Furthermore, self-report studies, in which people are asked to report on their own criminal behavior, have shown that nearly everyone has committed a crime, although most are never caught. Other offenses committed by large segments of affluent people, whites, and other population groups include drunken driving, misreporting income for taxation purposes, and falsifying reimbursement forms for business expenses. Indeed, both President George W. Bush and Vice President Dick Cheney have had drunken driving convictions; further, in secretly taped conversations released in 2005, President Bush indicated that he had used marijuana and said, "I haven't denied anything" with respect to questions about whether he had used cocaine (Kirkpatrick, 2005b).

Many of these kinds of crimes are difficult to detect or are low priorities for law enforcement agencies. In other instances, affluent perpetrators are better positioned to gain dismissals or light sentences because of their status within the community, social networks, or access to high-quality legal representation.

In evaluating theories about possible links between race and crime, we must be aware that many commentators may be focusing on only specific kinds of crimes, such as burglaries, robberies, and murders. In addition, analysts may focus only on crimes that resulted in prosecutions. Such limitations may distort an accurate understanding of this important issue. Race itself is not causally linked to crime. Instead, any apparent associations between crime and race relate to subcategories of people within racial and ethnic groups, such as poor, young men, as well as certain categories of crimes that are commonly investigated and prosecuted. Research links crime to social contexts, not to race (Bruce, 2003).

Crime problems evolve and change over time. An examination of new problems and trends helps demonstrate that criminal behavior is not linked to race. Identity theft and computer crime, for example, cause economic harms and losses in the billions of dollars, yet no one has claimed a link between these crimes and race. Even if we look at developments affecting "street crimes," we can see that factors other than race appear to create the contexts for criminal behavior. For example, one of the most significant crime problems to hit the United States at the dawn of the twenty-first century is the "meth crisis": the spread of highly addictive methamphetamine that can be "cooked" in homemade labs out of over-the-counter medicines and readily available chemicals. Americans use this inexpensive, dangerous drug more often than crack cocaine or heroin. Moreover, according to reports, the "crisis has spread among white, often poor, usually rural Americans . . . [and] is rampant in small communities" (Bonne, 2001). According to U.S. Senator Tom Harkin, meth addiction accounts for up to 50 percent of the thefts and burglaries in Iowa, as addicts try to support their habits, and methamphetamine played a role in the crimes of 26 percent of that state's prison population (Harkin, 2005).

The link between crime and economic disadvantage is significant (McNulty and Bellair, 2003). The "meth crisis" has spread among poor whites in rural areas and small towns. Other kinds of crimes prevail among the poor in urban areas. Further, minority groups suffer greatly from poverty. Only 10 percent of whites live in poverty, compared with 24 percent of African Americans and 20 percent of Hispanics (U.S. Census Bureau, 2007). Unemployment rates are highest among people of color, and family income is lowest. In 2007, 4.2 percent of white males over age 16 were unemployed, while the unemployment rate for African American men was nearly 9.1 percent (Bureau of Labor Statistics, 2008). The gap may actually be even larger if minorities are overrepresented among the half-million people classified as "discouraged workers" who do not count in government unemployment statistics because they have given up trying to find a job.

Poor people do not have the same opportunities that affluent Americans do to acquire money unlawfully through tax cheating, employee theft, and illegal stock transactions. If poor people seek to steal, they tend to do so through means available to them, whether they be burglaries at farmhouses by white meth addicts in rural areas or such crimes as shoplifting, street-corner drug sales, and robbery by minority offenders in urban areas. Further, police and prosecutors can more easily detect such crimes and emphasize them as enforcement priorities than they can white-collar crimes, identity theft, or computer offenses. In light of the association between race and poverty as well as the criminal opportunities associated with economic status, it would not be surprising to find Native Americans, Hispanics, and African Americans to be overrepresented among perpetrators of certain categories of crimes.

Related to the link between crime and disadvantage is the fact that most crime in America is intraracial, not interracial. Victimization rates, especially homicide and robbery, are higher for minorities than for whites. In 2005, the victimization rate (crimes per 1,000 people) was 44 for African Americans with family income between $15,000 and $24,999 but only 27.5 for whites in the same income category. The rate was 38 for African Americans in the $25,000 to $34,999 income category but only 23.2 for their counterparts among whites (BJS, 2006). As John DiIulio points out, "No group of Americans suffers more when violent and repeat criminals are permitted to prey upon decent, struggling, law-abiding inner city citizens and their children than . . . 'black America's silent majority'" (1994: 3). The poor cannot move away from the social problems of the inner cities. As a result, many poor people face victimization by neighbors, and this burden falls disproportionately on minority group members who are overrepresented among the poor.

One way to explain racial disparities in the criminal justice system, then, is to point out that African Americans and Hispanics are arrested more often and for more serious offenses than are whites. These factors are tied to the types of crimes investigated and enforced by criminal justice officials rather than to behavioral patterns linked to race. Some analysts argue that the most effective crime-control policies would be those that reduce the social problems, such as poverty and unequal educational opportunities, that appear to contribute to higher crime rates among the poor (Tonry, 1995).

Explanation 2: The Criminal Justice System Is Racist

Other explanations focus on the possible existence of racism in the criminal justice system. Many writers have discussed and analyzed evidence concerning biased attitudes among criminal justice officials, the system's perpetuation of inequalities created by discrimination throughout American history, and other facets of racism. These explanations are particularly disturbing because they violate important American values about equality and fairness. These values are embodied in the Fourteenth Amendment, which purports to guarantee equal protection for people of different races when they are subjected to government laws, policies, and procedures. The contemporary Supreme Court has not been active in evaluating and supporting claims concerning alleged violations of equal protection in the criminal justice system. Its inaction has left open more opportunities for discrimination to be a source of racial disparities (C. E. Smith, DeJong, and Burrow, 2002).

Racial disparities may result if people who commit similar offenses are treated differently by the criminal justice system because of their race or ethnicity. From this perspective, the fact that people of color are arrested more often than whites does not mean that they are more crime prone. For example, although African Americans make up 13 percent of monthly drug users, they represent 35 percent of those arrested for drug possession, 55 percent of convictions, and 74 percent of prison sentences (Butterfield, 1995b). One study found that the police make unfounded arrests of African Americans four times as often as of whites (Donziger, 1996: 109). Critics point to *racial profiling* as evidence of unequal treatment. For example, if law enforcement officials single out people for traffic stops because of their race, then African Americans, Hispanics, Arabs, and others are subjected to discriminatory treatment that critics regard as evidence of racism. Evidence of racial profiling by officers in many law enforcement agencies has led to new laws and policies that require police to keep records about their traffic law enforcement patterns (Engel, Calnon, and Bernard, 2002).

Despite efforts to monitor and prevent such activities, evidence that some police officers use race as the basis for stopping, searching, and arresting individuals persists (Alpert, 2007). Obviously, racial profiling activities—or the lack thereof—can vary from officer to officer and police department to police department (Warren et al, 2006). A 2005 study of Texas law enforcement agencies reported, for example, that the Houston Police Department searched 12 percent of African American drivers and 9 percent of Hispanic drivers stopped by its officers but searched only 3.7 percent of the white drivers who were pulled over (Steward and Totman, 2005). A national study of traffic stops by Engel and Calnon (2004: 78) found that

> after controlling for other relevant factors, the odds that black drivers would receive a citation were 47% greater compared to the odds for white drivers, and the odds for Hispanic drivers were 82% higher.... After controlling for arrest, the odds of being searched were 50% higher for black drivers and 42% higher for Hispanic drivers than for white drivers.

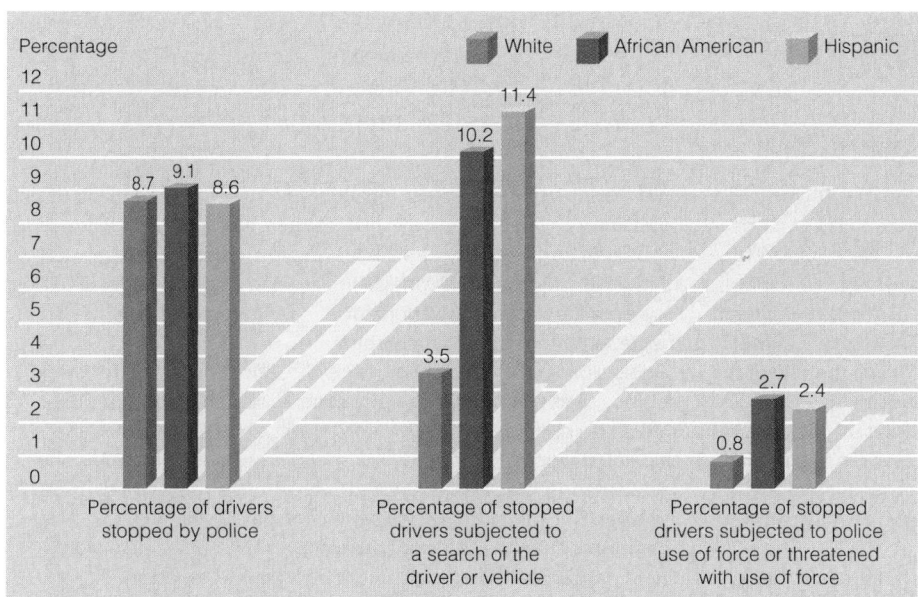

FIGURE 3.6
Differences in vehicle searches and police use of force against motorists, 2002

Source: Matthew R. Durose, Erica L. Schmitt, and Patrick Langan, *Contracts between Police and the Public: Findings from the 2002 National Survey,* Washington, DC. Bureau of Justice Statistics, April 2005, pp. 4, 8.

These actions took place despite a finding that white drivers were more likely than minority drivers to be carrying contraband. Figure 3.6 shows the results of a separate government study that found more frequent searches and police use of force against Hispanic and African American motorists (Durose, Schmitt, and Langan, 2005). If minority group members are stopped, searched, and arrested at higher rates than whites, even if they do not have higher rates of committing offenses, then they will be overrepresented among those drawn into the criminal justice system. Read the Close Up box to examine additional aspects of this problem.

The disparities among crime rates, arrest rates, and rates of incarceration are central to the claim by some that the criminal justice system is biased against minority groups. The arrest rate of minority citizens is indeed greater than their offense rates justify. According to data from the Bureau of Justice Statistics for 2005, victims of aggravated assault identified their assailants as African Americans in 25 percent of cases, yet African Americans comprised 34 percent of suspects arrested for aggravated assault. African Americans constituted 56 percent of suspects arrested for robbery although robbery victims reported that the robbers were African Americans in only 41 percent of cases (BJS, 2006). In sum, the odds of arrest are higher for African American suspects than for white suspects. With respect to sentencing, research indicates that African American and Hispanic men are less likely to receive the benefit of prosecutors' discretionary recommendations for lesser sentences in federal cocaine prosecutions (Hartley, Madden, and Spohn, 2007). A similar finding of racial disparities emerged in a study of who benefits from Florida judges' discretionary authority to "withhold adjudication" for people sentenced to probation so that they can avoid having a felony record if they successfully complete the terms of their probation (Bontrager, Bales, and Chiricos, 2005). African Americans and Hispanics were less likely than whites to benefit from these discretionary decisions.

Logic alone suggests that higher arrest rates and prosecutions will lead minority group members to be overrepresented among those receiving criminal punishment, including prison sentences. Further, research has found that judges' discretion in sentencing produces longer sentences for African Americans in some jurisdictions, even when studies control for other factors (Bushway and Piehl, 2001). These factors lead critics to point to the following fact as evidence of a racist system: 50 percent of the prison population is African American.

CLOSE UP

Racial Profiling

DR. ELMO RANDOLPH'S commute to his office near Newark, New Jersey, usually takes only 40 minutes, but the African American dentist is often late. Since 1991 Randolph has been stopped by state troopers on the New Jersey Turnpike more than 50 times. After stopping his gold BMW by the side of the road, the officer approaches and asks him the same question: "Do you have any drugs or weapons in your car?" One time when he refused to let police search his car, they seized his license and made him wait on the side of the highway for 20 minutes. Randolph asks, "Would they pull over a white middle-class person and ask the same question?" He has sold the BMW.

Profiling—the use of race and ethnicity as clues to criminality—has become a highly charged issue in recent years because of the rising number of complaints that minority drivers were being pulled over by the police in disproportionate numbers. After the terrorist attacks of September 11, concerns about profiling expanded as people of Middle Eastern ancestry found themselves singled out for searches at airports or for investigations of their financial records and social networks. In traffic and airport investigations, police have often justified stops on the grounds that people fit the profile of a drug runner. Studies give credence to the complaints of African Americans and Hispanics that they are so frequently stopped on highways and frisked on city streets that only their race can explain the pattern. For example, a study by the U.S. Government Accountability Office (formerly known as the General Accounting Office), the research agency that provides reports to Congress, revealed that African American women returning from abroad were nine times as likely as white women to be subjected to X-ray searches at airports, even though white women were found to be carrying illegal contraband twice as often as African American women.

The police argue that race is only one characteristic used to determine if a person should be stopped for questioning. They say they are trained to develop a "sixth sense," the instinctive ability to sniff out situations or isolate individuals who seem potentially unsafe. From this viewpoint the police often act against individuals who seem "out of place"—a shabbily dressed youth in a upscale part of town or a man in a pinstriped suit prowling a gritty ghetto. Often, however, a person's furtive look or uneasy gait may give officers a vague sense that something is not right.

Determining when and how the police should use race to assess suspects and situations involves a complicated balancing of public safety and civil liberties. Law enforcement experts insist that effective police work depends on quick analysis and that skin color is one factor among many—like dress or demeanor—that officers must consider. But minority leaders say that racial profiling is based on the presumption that African Americans and Hispanics are linked to crime or that Arab Americans might be linked to terrorism. This has led to the humiliation and physical abuse of innocent citizens. As a result, some police agencies have attempted to develop specific policies to steer their officers away from improper use of race and ethnicity as factors in their decisions to make stops and conduct searches.

Researching the Internet

 To read reports on allegations of racial profiling by officers in some police departments, see the Racial Profiling web page of the ACLU. To link to this website, go to *The American System of Criminal Justice* 12e companion site at academic.cengage.com/criminaljustice/cole.

Sources: Drawn from American-Arab Anti-Discrimination Committee, "ADC Reiterates Objection to Government Investigations Based on Racial Profiles," Press Release, March 20, 2002 (http://www.adc.org); American Civil Liberties Union, "Driving While Black: Racial Profiling on our Nation's Highways," June 1999 (http://www.aclu.org); Ralph Blumenthal, "Study in Texas Sees Race Bias in Searches," *New York Times*, February 25, 2005 (http://www.nytimes.com); *New York Times*, April 9, 1999, p. A21; Newsweek, May 17, 1999, p. 34; Frederick Schauer, *Profiles, Probabilities, and Stereotypes* (Cambridge, MA: Harvard University Press, 2003); U.S. General Accounting Office, *U.S. Customs Service: Better Targeting of Airline Passengers for Personal Searches Could Produce Better Results* (Washington, DC: U.S. Government Printing Office, March 2000).

Criminal justice officials need not act in racist ways to cause disparities in arrest and incarceration rates. At each stage of the process, the system itself operates in ways that may put minority group members at a disadvantage. The number of minority arrests may be greater because police patrols are more heavily concentrated in areas where nonwhites live, where drug use is more open, and where users are more likely to be observed by police. Further, a study of 150,000 cases in Connecticut found that on average an African American or Hispanic man must pay double the bail that would be paid by a white man for the same offense (Donziger, 1996: 111). Most pretrial release practices take into account factors such as employment status, living arrangements, and prior criminal record. Poor offenders are less likely to be able to make bail and hire their own lawyer. Prosecutors may be less likely to dismiss charges against a poor, unemployed African American or Hispanic offender. These offender characteristics may further skew sentencing as well.

For example, a recent study of sentencing of women convicted of misdemeanors found that race and ethnicity did not directly affect sentencing. Instead, African American and Hispanic women were more likely than their white counterparts to receive jail sentences because of other factors, including socio-economic status, prior criminal record, and the severity of charges pursued against them (Brennan, 2006). These factors create racial and ethnic disparities, but we cannot attribute them to a single decision maker.

Is the criminal justice system racist? The result of the system's decisions cannot be disputed—African American and Hispanic men end up in prison and jails in higher proportions than their crime and arrest rates can explain. Research finds that Hispanic defendants are at greater risk of receiving severe sentences than are other offenders (Steffensmeier and Demuth, 2001). A review of 38 studies found that more than two-thirds of them had uncovered biases in the system that were disadvantageous to African Americans. The authors concluded that "race is a consistent and frequently significant disadvantage when [imprisonment] decisions are considered . . . [but] race is much less of a disadvantage when it comes to sentence length" (Chiricos and Crawford, 1995). These conclusions do not mean that every minority defendant is treated disadvantageously compared with whites. Instead, the existence, nature, and extent of discrimination can vary by community (Britt, 2000). Thus, racial discrimination may be limited to certain types of cases, circumstances, and defendants (Walker, Spohn, and DeLeone, 2003).

Explanation 3: America Is a Racist Society

Some people claim that the criminal justice system is racist because it is embedded in a racist society. In fact, some accuse the system of being a tool of a racist society.

Evidence of racism appears in the way society asks the criminal justice system to operate. For example, federal sentencing guidelines punish users of crack cocaine far more harshly than users of powder cocaine, even though the drugs are virtually identical in their chemical composition and effect on users. A primary difference is that whites tend to use cocaine in its powder form, while people of color in the inner cities tend to use crack cocaine. Thus, the imposition of significantly harsher punishments for one form of the drug produces racial disparities in imprisonment rates (Tonry, 1995).

In addition, sentencing studies find a stronger link between unemployment rates and rates of imprisonment than between crime rates and rates of imprisonment. This suggests that prisons are used to confine people who cannot find jobs—and many of the unemployed are African American men (Chiricos and Bales, 1991). In addition, the country's history of racial discrimination that produced high-minority populations in impoverished neighborhoods that lack economic development may contribute to increased re-imprisonment of minority ex-offenders who face more difficult challenges in succeeding within these communities (Reisig et al., 2007). Moreover, according to law professor Michael Tonry, the war on drugs was "foreordained to affect disadvantaged black youths disproportionately [and was based on] the willingness of the drug war's planners to sacrifice young black Americans" (Tonry, 1995: 123). Others point out that enforcement of drug laws focuses almost exclusively on low-level dealers in minority neighborhoods (Donziger, 1996: 115). Yet federal health statistics define the typical drug addict as a white male in his twenties who lives in a suburb where drug busts rarely happen (*New York Times*, May 10, 1999: A26).

Other evidence of racism in American society shows up in the stereotyping of offenders. As Coramae Richey Mann points out, such stereotyping varies among racial and ethnic groups, depending on the crime and the section of the country. Americans, including police officers and other criminal justice officials, may make assumptions about the criminal tendencies of African Americans, Native Americans, and members of other minority groups (Mann, 1993: vii). Conditioned to think of social ills as minority problems, readers of a *Hartford*

civic engagement
your role in the system

Imagine that you are the president of your homeowners' association. The police chief calls you and asks, "Will you come to a meeting of leaders from community organizations to provide advice about how the police can reach out to citizens and provide reassurance that the department wants to examine and address any concerns about racial profiling?" *Make a list of suggestions that you would give to the police so that they could demonstrate to the community their commitment to prevent racial profiling in traffic stops and other police activities.* Then read about the process used in Cincinnati to get citizens involved in providing information and advice to the police on the issue of racial profiling. To link to this website, go to *The American System of Criminal Justice* 12e companion site at academic .cengage.com/criminaljustice/cole.

Courant series on drug-addicted prostitutes were stunned to learn that 70 percent were white (*New York Times*, May 10, 1999: A26).

That racist stereotyping affects police actions can be seen in cases of African American and Hispanic professionals who have been falsely arrested when the police were looking for a person of color and these individuals happened to be out of place. Judge Claude Coleman was handcuffed and dragged through crowds of shoppers in Short Hills, New Jersey, while protesting his innocence; Princeton University professor Cornel West was stopped on false cocaine charges while traveling to Williams College; and law student Brian Roberts was pulled over by the police as he drove through an affluent St. Louis neighborhood on his way to interview a judge for a class project (Tonry, 1995: 51).

If people of color are overrepresented in the justice system because the larger society is racist, the solution may seem daunting. Nobody knows how to quickly rid a society of racist policies, practices, and attitudes.

As you consider these three potential sources of racial disparities, consider whether citizens can play a role in diminishing any of these causes. Individuals can try to be educated about issues of race and be self-conscious about their own attitudes and behavior. However, controlling one's self is not going to change how justice system officials act or reshape the nature of society. Does that mean the problem of racial disparities is beyond the reach of citizen action? Consider the problem of racial profiling presented in "Civic Engagement: Your Role in the System." How can citizens help to educate or monitor or change law enforcement officials?

checkpoint

15. What is meant by racial or ethnic disparities in criminal justice?
16. What three alternative explanations are used to account for such disparities?

A QUESTION OF ETHICS

WHAT ACTIONS CAN citizens take in seeking to prevent crime? This is not always an easy question to answer. In 1986, Prentice Rasheed, a storeowner in Miami, attached an extension cord to metal grates in his store because he wanted to give a jolt of electricity to intruders in order to prevent burglaries. A would-be burglar was electrocuted, and Rasheed was prosecuted for manslaughter. The general doctrine brought from English common law into American law is that one cannot take a life in order to protect property, and the Florida Supreme Court had endorsed this principle as a component of that state's laws. Despite the law, a grand jury refused to indict Rasheed for the crime, because the store-owner said that he knew little about electricity and had no idea that the contraption could kill someone.

In November 2004, Eric Griffin seriously wounded a dog owned by his neighbor, Richard Hammock, by firing a pellet gun because he was angry about the dog's barking. After rushing his dog to the veterinary hospital, Hammock did not know if the dog would live.

He returned to his house, picked up a two-foot piece of wood, and went to Griffin's front porch to confront his neighbor about shooting the dog. When Hammock broke the glass in Griffin's front door, Griffin fired a shotgun blast through the door and killed Hammock. The country prosecutor declined to press any charges against Griffin because Colorado law permits the use of lethal force to defend one's home.

Critical Thinking and Analysis

If you were a juror, would you have voted to acquit Rasheed if the case had gone to trial? Does an acquittal or failure to file charges send a message to property owners that they can aggressively defend their property, in spite of what the law may say? What if a firefighter or police officer had been electrocuted while checking the store? Was Rasheed's action different than Griffin's action? How? Which law is better for society Florida's or Colorado's?

Sources: Richard Lacayo, "Trouble with Fighting Back," *Time*, November 10, 1986 (*Time* magazine online archives); "DA Says Make My Day Law Protects Man Who Shot, Killed Neighbor in Barking Dog Dispute," KUSA-TV Denver, November 13, 2004 (http://www.9news.com).

SUMMARY

Understand the goals of the criminal justice system

- The three goals of criminal justice are doing justice, controlling crime, and preventing crime.

- Doing justice concerns the foundation of rules, procedures, and institutions of the system.

- Controlling crime involves arresting, prosecuting, and punishing those who commit offenses.

- Preventing crime requires the efforts of citizens as well as justice system officials.

Recognize the different responsibilities of federal and state criminal justice operations

- Both the national and state systems of criminal justice enforce laws, try cases, and punish offenders.

- Federal officials enforce crimes defined by Congress.

- Federal involvement in criminal justice has expanded in recent decades.

- Federal justice agencies shifted their priorities in the aftermath of 9/11.

- Most criminal laws and criminal cases are under the authority of state criminal justice systems.

Analyze criminal justice from a system perspective

- Criminal justice is composed of many organizations that are interdependent and interact as they seek to achieve their goals.

- The primary subsystems of criminal justice are police, courts, and corrections.

- Key characteristics of the criminal justice system influence activities within the system.

- The key characteristics of the criminal justice system are discretion, resource dependence, sequential tasks, and filtering.

- Discretion occurs at all levels of the system and gives freedom to justice system officials in some aspects of their decision making.

- Resource dependence requires justice system agencies to maintain good relationships with government officials.

- Decisions and tasks in the criminal justice system occur in a sequential manner.

- Discretionary decisions in the criminal justice system create a filtering process that moves suspects and convicted offenders out of the system at different points.

Identify the authority and relationships of the main criminal justice agencies, and understand the steps in the decision-making process for criminal cases

- Police possess authority over the investigation, arrest, and booking steps in the criminal justice process.

- Prosecutors possess authority over charging, initial appearances and arraignments, plea bargaining and trials.

- Judges are involved in preliminary hearings, bail, plea agreements, and sentencing.

- Corrections officials administer punishments and release decisions.

- Criminal justice officials must interact and cooperate in the sequential process in order to achieve the system's goals.

Understand the criminal justice "wedding cake" concept

- The criminal justice "wedding cake" concept provides a way to describe the frequency through which certain processes and outcomes occur in the criminal justice system.

- The small top of the wedding cake represents the relatively small number of very serious cases that are processed through trials.

- The lower, larger portions of the wedding cake represent the increasing frequency of plea bargaining for larger numbers of cases as one moves downward toward less serious offenses.

Recognize the possible causes of racial disparities in criminal justice

- Research does not support any theories about race causing criminal behavior.

- Race in the United States can be associated with poverty and evidence exists that some kinds of crimes can be associated with poverty and neighborhood contexts.

- Evidence exists concerning differential treatment of members of various racial groups by criminal justice officials in some contexts.

- More frequent stops, searches, and arrests of minority group members can explain disparities in outcomes even without a greater frequency of criminal behavior by members of minority groups.

- Evidence of differential treatment exists in some studies of judges' sentencing decisions.

- The existence of racial attitudes in American society can affect how laws are written and enforced, such as the imposition of more severe sentences for crack cocaine offenses that are more frequently committed by members of minority groups and less severe treatment of meth offenders, who are usually white.

QUESTIONS FOR REVIEW

1. What are the goals of the criminal justice system?

2. What is a system? How is the administration of criminal justice a system?

3. What are the 13 steps in the criminal justice decision-making process?

4. Why is the criminal justice wedding cake a better depiction of reality than is a linear model of the system?

5. What is the challenge of criminal justice in a multicultural society?

KEY TERMS

adjudication (p. 90)
arrest (p. 94)
discretion (p. 87)
discrimination (p. 103)
disparity (p. 103)
dual court system (p. 91)
exchange (p. 86)

federalism (p. 82)
filtering process (p. 89)
indictment (p. 95)
information (p. 95)
plea bargain (p. 87)
system (p. 86)
warrant (p. 94)

FOR FURTHER READING

Friedman, Lawrence M. 1993. *Crime and Punishment in American History*. New York: Basic Books. A historical overview of criminal justice from colonial times. Argues that the evolution of criminal justice reflects transformations in America's character.

Martinez, Ramiro, Jr. and Abel Valenzuela. Eds. 2006. *Immigration and Crime: Race, Ethnicity, and Violence*. New York: New York University Press. A selection of articles by major scholars on the intersections of immigration, race, ethnicity and crime in the American criminal justice system. Gives attention to Hispanics in the criminal justice system, an issue of increasing interest in light of their place as the largest minority group in the country.

Peterson, Ruth, Lauren Krivo, and John Hagan. 2006. *The Many Colors of Crime: Inequalities of Race, Ethnicity, and Crime in America*. New York: New York University Press. A variety of prominent scholars address issues of race and ethnicity, including perceptions of crime and the operation of the criminal justice system.

Smith, Christopher E., Christina DeJong, and John D. Burrow. 2002. *The Supreme Court, Crime, and the Ideal of Equal Justice*. New York: Peter Lange. An examination of how U.S. Supreme Court decisions have alleviated, facilitated, or tolerated discrimination by race, gender, social class, and offender status in the American criminal justice system.

Walker, Samuel, Cassia Spohn, and Miriam DeLeone. 2006. *The Color of Justice: Race, Ethnicity and Crime in America*. 4th ed. Belmont, CA: Wadsworth. An excellent overview of the links between crime, race, and ethnicity.

GOING ONLINE

For an up-to-date list of web links, go to *The American System of Criminal Justice* 12e companion site at academic .cengage.com/criminaljustice/cole.

1. Using the Internet, access leading state or national newspapers and look for articles about criminal cases. How many articles are about trials and how many are about plea bargains? For the cases that went to trial, what kinds of charges were pressed and who were the defendants?

2. Type "police discretion" into any search engine. In the articles that you find, what kinds of concerns are raised about the nature and consequences of police discretion? What suggested remedies are provided?

3. Look for reports and articles on racial profiling. Is there strong evidence that such activities occur? Is it widespread or only in certain locations? Based on these articles, do you believe that racial profiling is a problem? If so, can it be eliminated?

CHECKPOINT ANSWERS

1. *What are the three goals of the criminal justice system?*
Doing justice, controlling crime, preventing crime.

2. *What is meant by doing justice?*
Offenders are held fully accountable for their actions, the rights of people who have contact with the system will be protected, and like offenses will be treated alike and officials will take into account relevant differences among offenders and offenses.

3. *What are the key features of federalism?*
A division of power between a central (national) government and regional (state) governments.

4. *What power does the national government have in the area of crime and justice?*
Enforcement of federal criminal laws.

5. *What main factor has caused federal involvement in criminal justice to expand?*
The expansion of criminal activities across state and national borders.

6. *What is a system?*
A complex whole made up of interdependent parts whose actions are directed toward goals and influenced by the environment within which it functions.

7. *What is one example of an exchange relationship?*
Plea bargaining.

8. *What are the major characteristics of the criminal justice system?*
Discretion, resource dependence, sequential tasks, filtering.

9. *What are the four main duties of police?*
Keeping the peace, apprehending violators and combating crime, preventing crime, providing social services.

10. *What is a dual court system?*
A separate judicial system for each state in addition to a national system.

11. *What are the major types of state and local correctional agencies?*

Prisons, jails, probation, parole, community programs. Public, nonprofit, and for-profit agencies carry out correctional programs on behalf of state and local governments.

12. *What are the steps of the criminal justice process?*

(1) investigation, (2) arrest, (3) booking, (4) charging, (5) initial appearance, (6) preliminary hearing/grand jury, (7) indictment/information, (8) arraignment, (9) trial, (10) sentencing, (11) appeal, (12) corrections, (13) release.

13. *What is the purpose of the wedding cake model?*

To show that all cases are not treated alike.

14. *What types of cases are found on each layer?*

Layer 1: celebrated cases in which the adversarial system is played out in full; Layer 2: serious felonies committed by people with long criminal records against victims unknown to them; Layer 3: felonies in which the crimes and the offenders are viewed as less serious than in Layer 2; Layer 4: misdemeanors.

15. *What is meant by racial or ethnic disparities in criminal justice?*

That racial and ethnic minorities are subjected to the criminal justice system at much higher rates than are the white majority.

16. *What three alternative explanations are used to account for such disparities?*

Minorities commit more crime; the criminal justice system is racist; U.S. society is racist.

CHAPTER 4

Criminal Justice and the Rule of Law

CHAPTER LEARNING OBJECTIVES

→ Recognize the bases and sources of American criminal law

→ Understand how substantive criminal law defines a crime and the legal responsibility of the accused

→ Understand how procedural criminal law defines the rights of the accused and the processes for dealing with a case

→ Recognize the United States Supreme Court's role in interpreting the criminal justice amendments to the Constitution

After arriving at the Orlando, Florida, airport on a late night flight in February 2007, U.S. Navy Captain Colleen Shipman hurried toward her car in the parking lot. When she became aware that someone was following her, she rushed to her car and locked the door. A woman standing outside her car tapped on her window and asked for a ride. Shipman told the woman that she would send someone to help her. When the woman began to cry, Shipman rolled down the window a few inches—when suddenly the woman pulled out a canister and sprayed Shipman with pepper spray. Shipman quickly drove away and notified police about the attack (CNN, 2007).

Police quickly found the alleged attacker, who had thrown a wig and a BB gun into a nearby trash container. The police also found a steel mallet, folding knife, and rubber tubing. Further investigation revealed latex gloves and driving directions from Houston to the Orlando airport. These items aroused suspicions that a crime more significant than a mere assault had been planned (CNN, 2007). Was it an attempted kidnapping? Might the perpetrator have even intended to kill the victim?

Normally, an assault with minor injuries would attract attention only from the local news media. In this case, however, the event triggered weeks of national news coverage

when the suspect was identified as U.S. Navy Captain Lisa Nowak, an astronaut who orbited the earth on the space shuttle. Her arrest in this case came just a few short months after her professional high point when the space shuttle Discovery landed smoothly at Cape Canaveral, Florida, in July 2006 and NASA officials celebrated the mission's success. Among the smiling heroes welcomed home was Nowak, who had operated the shuttle's robot arm during spacewalks in order to transfer tons of cargo from the Discovery to the International Space Station that orbits the earth (Schwartz, 2006).

According to news reports, Nowak had been involved in an affair with another shuttle astronaut who subsequently dropped Nowak and began to date Shipman. When questioned by the police, Nowak reportedly said that she drove from Houston to Orlando to find Shipman just because she wanted to talk. Her use of pepper spray as well as the other items found in her possession at the airport led law enforcement officials to conclude that she had more sinister intentions for harming Shipman. Thus Nowak was charged with assault, kidnapping, and attempted murder (Schwartz, 2007b).

As the case worked its way through preliminary hearings in the Florida courts, Nowak's attorney submitted a document to inform the judge and the prosecutor that Nowak would be asserting the insanity defense at trial. By making a claim of insanity, Nowak hoped to avoid any finding of guilt or imposition of punishment for her actions. According to Donald Lykkebak, Nowak's defense attorney, she suffered from manic-depressive disorder, obsessive-compulsive disorder, and other serious psychological problems (Schwartz, 2007a).

A criminal defendant's claim of insanity raises difficult questions for the justice system. Two psychiatrists reportedly planned to testify that Nowak was legally insane at the time she committed the assault. In these cases, however, the psychiatrists' testimony does not decide the issue. Prosecutors typically present other psychiatrists who testify that the defendant was not insane. Moreover, the judge or jury must apply the law that defines insanity and reach its own conclusion about the conflicting testimony and evidence.

legal responsibility
The accountability of an individual for a crime because of the perpetrator's characteristics and the circumstances of the illegal act.

Claims of insanity frequently cause observers to question whether such a defense should be available to permit people to avoid **legal responsibility** and punishment for their criminal acts. In this case, can we avoid wondering how a military officer could claim to be insane after undergoing careful psychological screening in order to become an astronaut? Could a U.S. Naval Academy graduate with advanced degrees in engineering who recently played a key role in the success of a space shuttle mission really be insane? Moreover, how can someone claim to be insane when she carefully plans the details of a trip from Houston to Orlando in order to confront, if not physically harm, someone for whom she holds feelings of anger and jealousy? Criminal law must address difficult questions for which there are not always easy answers.

In this chapter, we shall examine the primary components of criminal law. Substantive criminal law is developed through statutes enacted by the American people's elected representatives in state legislatures and Congress. It addresses the specific acts for which people will be punished as well as the circumstances in which people may not be held fully responsible for their actions. We shall also introduce procedural criminal law, which defines the procedures used in legal processes and the rights possessed by criminal suspects and defendants. Even though Nowak acknowledged that she attacked Shipman with pepper spray, she was still entitled to a trial and representation by an attorney as she attempted to show why she should not be held fully responsible for her actions. The right to counsel and the right to trial by jury are two of the elements provided by procedural criminal law. The precise nature of individuals' rights under procedural criminal law is determined by judges' interpretations of the U.S. Constitution, state constitutions, and relevant statutes enacted by Congress and state legislatures.

FOUNDATIONS OF CRIMINAL LAW

Like most Americans, you probably realize that law and legal procedures are key elements of the criminal justice system. Americans are fond of saying that "we have a government of laws, not of men (and women)." According to our American values, we do not have a system based on the decisions of a king or dictator. Our judges and elected representatives in legislatures create laws that shape the rules for society, and those rules are supposed to apply to everyone. Does that mean that every citizen, police officer, and member of Congress obeys those rules? No. But the rules of law set the standards for their behavior, and they can face consequences for their failure to comply.

Historically, presidents, governors, and mayors have not had the power to legally punish people they dislike. Instead, even our most powerful leaders have had to make decisions within limits imposed by law. The government could only seek to punish people who violated defined laws, and their guilt had to be determined through procedures established by law. After the attacks on the World Trade Center and Pentagon on September 11, however, some commentators have expressed fears that the federal government has moved away from traditional constitutional values by jailing suspected terrorists without charging them with any crimes or presenting any evidence in court to prove their involvement in wrongdoing (C. E. Smith, 2004). Thus we find ourselves in a new era that raises challenges to the traditional operation of American criminal law.

Laws tell citizens what they can and cannot do. Laws also tell government officials when they can seek to punish citizens for violations and how they must go about it. Government officials who take actions according to their own preferences run the risk that judges will order them to take different actions that comply with the law. The president of the United States is no exception. In 2004, for example, the U.S. Supreme Court ordered President George W. Bush's administration to permit a U.S. citizen being held as a suspected terrorist to meet with an attorney and have opportunities to make arguments in court (*Hamdi v. Rumsfeld*). Government officials are expected to follow and enforce the law. Thus, in a democracy, laws provide a major tool to prevent government officials from seizing too much power or using power improperly.

Substantive Law and Procedural Law

Criminal law is only one category of law. Peoples' lives and actions are also affected by **civil law**, which governs business deals, contracts, real estate, and the like. For example, if you harm other people in an automobile collision or damage their property, they may sue you to pay for the harm or damage. By contrast, the key feature of criminal law is the government's power to punish people for damage they have done to society.

Of the two categories of criminal law, **substantive criminal law** defines actions that the government can punish. It also defines the punishments for such offenses. Often called the *penal code*, substantive law answers the question "*What* is illegal?" Elected officials in Congress, state legislatures, and city councils write the substantive criminal laws. These legislators decide which kinds of behaviors are so harmful that they deserve to be punished. They also decide whether each violation should be punished by imprisonment, a fine, probation, or another kind of punishment. When questions about the meaning of substantive criminal laws arise, judges interpret the laws by seeking to fulfill the legislators' intentions.

Criminal laws can also be created and changed through ballot issues in those states that permit statewide voting as a means to create law. Here citizens are directly involved in shaping their own criminal laws, although this process

civil law
Law regulating the relationships between or among individuals, usually involving property, contract, or business disputes.

substantive criminal law
Law defining acts that are subject to punishment and specifying the punishments for such offenses.

civic engagement
your role in the system

In several states, voters made decisions about ballot proposals to remove criminal penalties for the personal possession and use of marijuana. *Make a list of contrasting arguments for and against the legalization of marijuana for personal use (not for selling). How would you vote on the issue?* Then look at the wording and the competing arguments for such a ballot issue that was presented to voters in Alaska. To link to this website, go to *The American System of Criminal Justice* 12e companion site at academic.cengage.com/criminaljustice/cole.

procedural criminal law
Law defining the procedures that criminal justice officials must follow in enforcement, adjudication, and corrections.

 To see an example of substantive criminal law, see sections on criminal law in Title XL and Title L of the Kentucky Revised Statutes. To link to this website, go to *The American System of Criminal Justice* 12e companion site at academic.cengage.com/criminaljustice/cole.

common law
The Anglo-American system of uncodified law, in which judges follow precedents set by earlier decisions when they decide new but similar cases. The substantive and procedural criminal law was originally developed in this manner but was later codified—set down in codes—by state legislatures.

typically affects only a small number of laws. Usually a petition drive is required to obtain the required number of signatures to place a specific proposal on the ballot. Criminal law ballot issues often concern the issues of gambling and drug use. Ballot issues may also be aimed at sentencing and other aspects of criminal justice. Think about whether the general population of voters is sufficiently knowledgeable to create criminal laws as you consider the issue in "Civic Engagement: Your Role in the System."

By contrast, **procedural criminal law** defines the rules that answer the question, "*How* shall the law be enforced?" It protects the constitutional rights of defendants and provides the rules that officials must follow in all areas of the criminal justice system. It embodies the American values of liberty and individual rights by seeking to ensure that no one will be incarcerated or otherwise punished unless the government proves criminal guilt through proper procedures that respect constitutional rights. Legislatures define many aspects of procedural criminal law, such as how bail will be set and which kind of preliminary hearing will take place before a trial. However, the U.S. Supreme Court and state supreme courts also play a key role in defining procedural criminal law. These courts define the meaning of rights in the U.S. Constitution and in state constitutions. Their interpretations of constitutional provisions create rules on such issues as when and how police officers can question suspects and when defendants can receive advice from their attorneys.

checkpoint

1. What is contained in a state's penal code?
2. What is the purpose of procedural criminal law? (Answers are at the end of the chapter.)

Sources of Criminal Law

The earliest known codes of law appeared in the Sumerian law of Mesopotamia (3100 B.C.) and the Code of Hammurabi (1750 B.C.). These written codes were divided into sections to cover different types of offenses. Other important ancestors of Western law are the Draconian Code, produced in the seventh century B.C. in Greece, and the Law of the Twelve Tables created by the Romans (450 B.C.) However, the main source of American law is the common law of England.

Common Law

Common law was based on custom and tradition as interpreted by judges. In continental Europe, a system of *civil law* developed in which the rules were set down in detailed codes produced by legislatures or other governing authorities. By contrast, the common law of England was not written down as a list of rules. Rather, it took its form from the collected opinions of the judges, who looked to custom in making their decisions. The judges created law when they ruled on specific cases. These rulings, also known as *precedents*, established legal principles to be used in making decisions on similar cases. When such cases arose, judges looked to earlier rulings to find principles that applied to the type of case they were deciding. Over time, as new kinds of situations emerged, judges had to create new legal principles to address them. As more rulings on various kinds of legal issues were written down, they grew into a body of law—composed of principles and reasoning—that other judges could use in deciding their own cases. The use of a common set of precedents made the application of law more stable and consistent. Moreover, the judges' ability to adjust legal principles when new kinds of situations arose made the common law flexible enough to respond to changes in society.

The American colonies maintained the English precedents and procedures, but after independence the states began to make some changes in the law. For example, state legislatures often formalized the definitions of crimes and punishments in the English common law by enacting statutes that placed these definitions into the penal code. These statutes then became subject to interpretation by judges. American judges still create precedents when they interpret statutes, state constitutions, the U.S. Constitution, and prior judicial opinions. These judicial rulings guide the decisions of other courts on issues concerning both substantive and procedural criminal law.

Written Law

Most people would agree that having a document that clearly states the criminal law, both substantive and procedural, would be helpful. It would allow citizens to know definitively when they might be in danger of committing an illegal act and to be aware of their rights if official action is taken against them. If such a document could be written in simple language, society would probably need fewer lawyers. However, writing such a document is impossible. Our criminal laws and procedures are too complex to be reduced to simple terms. In part, the complexity stems from the unpredictable array of individual circumstances that can arise in criminal cases. If you pick up someone's wallet in the fitness center locker room because you mistakenly thought it was yours, should we treat that act the same as when a person intentionally runs away with someone else's wallet? Further, we are constantly expanding the scope and complexity of criminal law. When we try to define new illegal acts, such as secretly photographing people with camera-equipped cell phones or intercepting information from wireless Internet connections, we see how the law must constantly respond to new, unforeseen problems. Moreover, any effort to reduce rules to words on a page creates opportunities for those words to be interpreted in different ways. If we have a crime called negligent homicide, for example, how will we define *negligence*? The need for interpretation means that lawyers and judges will always have a role in shaping and changing the meaning of both substantive and procedural law.

Because we cannot compile a single, complete document that provides all the details of criminal law, we continue to rely on four sources of law: constitutions, statutes, court decisions (also known as case law), and administrative regulations.

Constitutions contain basic principles and procedural safeguards. The Constitution of the United States was written in Philadelphia in 1787 and went into effect in 1789 after the required number of states ratified it. This document sets forth the country's governing system and describes the institutions (legislature, courts, and president) that will make its laws. The first ten amendments to the Constitution, known together as the Bill of Rights, were added in 1791. Most of these amendments provide protections against government actions that would violate basic rights and liberties. Several have a direct bearing on criminal law, because they guarantee the rights of due process, jury trial, and representation by counsel, as well as protection against unreasonable searches and cruel and unusual punishments. Most state constitutions also contain protections against actions by state and local governments. During the 1960s the U.S. Supreme Court decided to require state and local governments to respect most of the rights listed in the Bill of Rights. (Before that time most criminal justice provisions of the Bill of Rights protected citizens only against actions by the federal government.) As a result of court decisions, the power of police officers, prosecutors, and judges is

constitution
The basic laws of a country or state defining the structure of government and the relationship of citizens to that government.

The New Hampshire Constitution provides an example of a state's constitution that is nearly as old as the U.S. Constitution. To link to this website, go to *The American System of Criminal Justice* 12e companion site at academic.cengage.com/criminaljustice/cole.

statutes
Laws passed by legislatures. Statutory definitions of criminal offenses are found in penal codes.

case law
Court decisions that have the status of law and serve as precedents for later decisions.

administrative regulations
Rules made by government agencies to implement specific public policies in areas such as public health, environmental protection, and workplace safety.

 You can read provisions of the *Model Penal Code* and compare them with provisions of states' laws by going to *The American System of Criminal Justice* 12e companion site at academic.cengage.com/criminaljustice/cole.

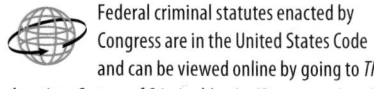 Federal criminal statutes enacted by Congress are in the United States Code and can be viewed online by going to *The American System of Criminal Justice* 12e companion site at academic.cengage.com/criminaljustice/cole.

limited by the U.S. Constitution as well as the constitution of the state in which they work.

Statutes are laws passed by legislative bodies; the substantive and procedural rules of most states are found in their statutes. Although state legislatures write the bulk of criminal law, Congress and local governments play a role in shaping it. Federal criminal laws passed by Congress deal mainly with violations that occur on property of the U.S. government (such as national parks, military bases) or with actions that involve the national interest (such as terrorism, counterfeiting) or more than one state (such as taking a kidnap victim across state lines). State constitutions and legislatures give cities and towns limited authority to create laws dealing with local problems, including minor offenses. National, state, and local rules governing certain kinds of criminal conduct do overlap. Possession or sale of drugs, for example, may violate criminal laws at all three levels of government. In such situations, law enforcement agencies must decide which one will prosecute the offender.

If we want to know the definition of a crime covered by a statute, we consult a state's penal code. This code clearly specifies the acts that constitute a crime and the penalty to be imposed. Although the laws of most states are similar, differences inevitably arise in the lawmaking process. To make state laws more uniform, the American Law Institute has developed the *Model Penal Code*, which it urges legislatures to follow when creating states criminal laws.

Court decisions, often called **case law**, provide a third source of criminal law. As noted earlier, the main characteristic of the common law system is that judges look to earlier decisions to guide their rulings. Although statutes have replaced much of the common law of crime, precedent remains an important aid to lawyers and judges in interpreting penal codes.

Administrative regulations are laws and rules made by federal, state, and local agencies. The legislature, president, or governor has given those agencies the power to make rules governing specific policy areas such as health, safety, and the environment. Most regulations produced since the mid-twentieth century deal with modern concerns, such as wages and work hours, pollution, traffic, workplace safety, and pure food and drugs. Many of the rules are part of the criminal law, and violations are processed through the criminal justice system.

As you can see, the criminal law is more than just a penal code written by a state legislature or Congress. Figure 4.1 summarizes the sources of criminal law.

checkpoint

3. How does the common law shape criminal law?
4. What are the forms of written law?

Felony and Misdemeanor

Crimes are classified by how serious they are. The distinction between a felony and a misdemeanor is one of the oldest in the criminal law. Most laws define felonies and misdemeanors in terms of punishment. Conviction on a felony charge usually means that the offender may be given a prison sentence of more than a year of imprisonment. The most serious felonies, such as planned murders, may draw the death penalty. Those who commit misdemeanors are dealt with more leniently; the sentence might be a fine, probation, or a jail sentence of less than a year. Some states define the seriousness of the offense according to the place of punishment: prison for felonies, jail for misdemeanors. Be aware, however, that if someone is convicted of multiple misdemeanors, he can receive a sentence of one year for each crime and thereby serve a longer sentence. For example, movie

FIGURE 4.1
Sources of criminal law
Although codes of law existed in ancient times, American criminal law is derived mainly from the common law of England. The common law distinguishes English-speaking systems from the civil-law systems of the rest of the world.

CONSTITUTIONAL LAW	**STATUTORY LAW**	**CASE LAW**	**ADMINISTRATIVE LAW**
The Constitution of the United States and the state constitutions define the structure of government and the rights of citizens.	The substantive and procedural criminal laws are found in laws passed by legislative bodies such as the U.S. Congress and state legislatures.	Consistent with the common law heritage, legal opinions by judges in individual cases have the status of law.	Also having the status of law are some decisions of federal and state governmental agencies that have been given the power to regulate such areas as health, safety, and the environment in the public interest.

star Wesley Snipes was convicted of three misdemeanors for willfully failing to file tax returns and in 2008 a federal judge sentenced him to three years in prison, one year for each misdemeanor (*New York Times*, 2008).

Whether a defendant is charged with a felony or a misdemeanor determines not only how the person is punished, but also how the criminal justice system will process the defendant. Certain rights and penalties follow from this distinction. The seriousness of the charge in part determines the conditions under which the police may make an arrest and the court level where the charges will be heard. For example, although the Sixth Amendment to the U.S. Constitution says criminal defendants are entitled to a right to trial by jury, in 1996 the U.S. Supreme Court declared that this provision only applies to people accused of serious offenses. People who face less than six months in jail for a charge are not entitled to a jury trial. The Constitution requires only that they be tried in front of a judge (*Lewis v. United States*).

The distinction between types of crimes also can affect a person's future. People with felony convictions may be barred from certain professions, such as law and medicine, and in many states they are also barred from certain other occupations, such as bartender, police officer, and barber. Depending on a state's laws, felony convictions may also keep people from ever voting, serving on juries, or running for election to public office (Olivares, Burton, and Cullen, 1996).

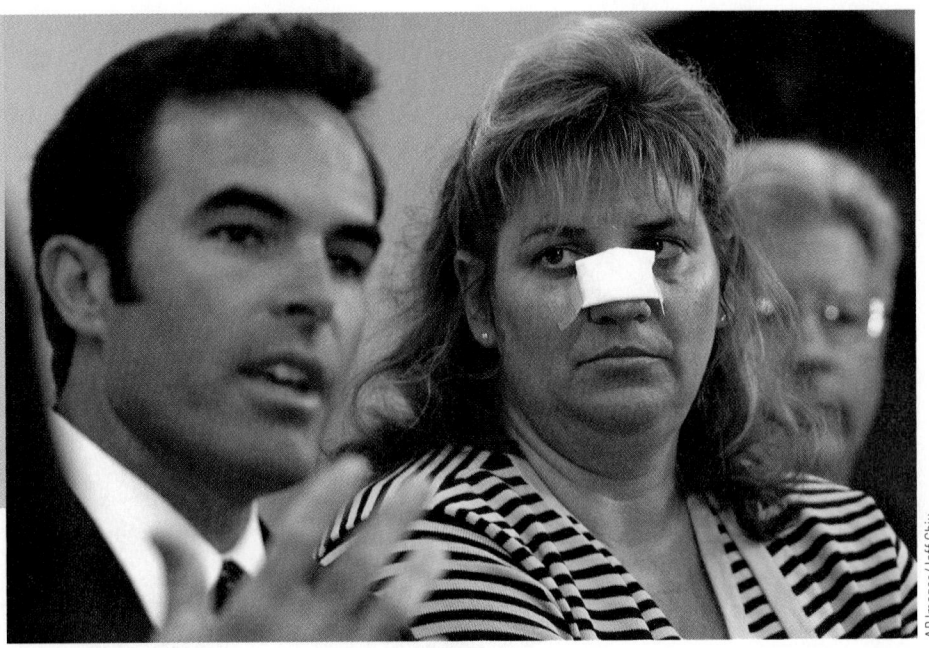

Appearing at a news conference, Oakland A's baseball fan Jennifer Bueno and her attorney announce their lawsuit against the Texas Rangers and pitcher Frank Francisco. Francisco struck Bueno in the face with a chair during a game as he tried to hit her husband who was heckling the Rangers from a seat near the dugout. The Rangers apologized, settled the case, and paid Bueno an undisclosed amount of money in 2007. Francisco pleaded no context to misdemeanor assault and was sentenced to a brief work program and anger management classes. Do civil lawsuits impose an unfair double punishment on people convicted of crimes?

AP Images/Jeff Chiu

Criminal versus Civil Law

As mentioned earlier, the legal system makes basic distinctions between criminal and civil law. A violation of criminal law is an offense against society as a whole, while civil law regulates relations between individuals. Criminal law focuses on the intent of the wrongdoer. We view intentional acts as most deserving of punishment, but we may decide to press criminal charges even when a harmful event was an "accident." By contrast, civil law centers on fixing the blame for the damage or harm.

In some cases, both criminal and civil proceedings arise from the same event. When hunting, if you carelessly fire a shot that crashes through the window of a home and wounds the homeowner, the homeowner may bring a civil lawsuit against you to recover the cost of the damage you caused. The cost could include medical bills and the price of fixing the window. This legal action falls within the area of civil law known as *torts*, which deals with compensation for damage to property or people's injuries. In a separate action, the state may charge you with a violation of the criminal law because your actions violated society's rules for the lawful use of firearms. Although criminal and civil law are distinct, both attempt to control human behavior by steering people to act in a desired manner and by imposing costs on those who violate social rules.

Increasingly, civil lawsuits are being brought against offenders who previously were subject only to criminal charges. For example, some department stores now sue shoplifters for large amounts, and some rape victims bring civil lawsuits against their attackers. Other rape victims successfully sue apartment complexes for failing to maintain secure conditions that would prevent criminal attacks. Victims can win civil lawsuits even against defendants who have been acquitted of criminal charges. Such was the case when the families of murder victims Nicole Brown Simpson and Ronald Goldman won a lawsuit worth millions of dollars against O. J. Simpson, despite the retired football star's acquittal after a highly publicized murder trial. To gain a criminal conviction, prosecutors must persuade the jury or judge that the evidence proves the defendant's guilt beyond a reasonable doubt. The Simpson jury in the criminal case did not believe that the evidence met this high standard of proof. In the later civil trial, however, a different jury believed that the evidence satisfied the lower civil-law standard of showing by a "preponderance of evidence" that Simpson was most likely responsible for the two deaths.

Civil law is also important for the criminal justice system because citizens can file lawsuits against police officers, correctional officers, and other government actors if they believe those actors have violated their constitutional rights. Such lawsuits can result in multimillion dollar verdicts, especially when innocent citizens are seriously injured or killed through improper high-speed driving or the use of weapons by the police. These civil lawsuits help shape police training and departmental policies, because government agencies want to avoid the high costs of defending and losing civil rights litigation (C. E. Smith and Hurst, 1997).

Civil lawsuits also provide the vehicle for citizen involvement in shaping criminal law by challenging whether a law enacted by a legislature is proper. If a citizen believes that a criminal law clashes with a legal right that is guaranteed by the U.S. Constitution or a state constitution, the individual can use court processes to challenge that law by filing a lawsuit against the government. For example, residents of Washington, D.C. filed a lawsuit and took their case all the way to the U.S. Supreme Court in 2008 to challenge whether the city's laws regulating private gun ownership violate individuals' constitutional rights (Savage, 2008). Such laws can also be challenged through the criminal process if someone is charged with a crime and challenges the legality of the criminal law. As you read "Civic Engagement: Your Role in the System," consider what you would do if you thought one of your state's statutes or one of your city's ordinances was unconstitutional.

Another example of a link between criminal and civil law is **civil forfeiture**. This concept, derived from English common law, allows for government to take privately owned property, and it has frequently been applied in drug law enforcement (Stahl, 1992). Forfeiture can even affect property owners who are not guilty of any crime. In 1996 the U.S. Supreme Court decided that, despite her innocence, a wife lost her ownership rights to a car when her husband used the vehicle to pick up a prostitute (*Bennis v. Michigan*). Forfeiture laws frequently permit law enforcement agencies to sell seized property and use the money for themselves. The use of forfeiture by law enforcement agencies has generated controversy, especially when applied against people who have never been convicted of any crime. In 2000, an unusual coalition of conservatives and liberals persuaded Congress to enact legislation limiting the federal government's authority to seize property. Under the law, the federal government must show by a preponderance of evidence that property it seeks to seize is linked to crimes. Previously, owners of seized property bore the difficult burden of proving that their property was not linked to criminal conduct (Abrams, 2000). The passage of the law reflected the fact that Americans across the political spectrum had come to believe that government forfeiture practices violated American values about the protection of private property and individuals' entitlement to due process of law before losing property or receiving punishment.

In summary, the bases of American criminal law are complex. English common law and the laws found in such written sources as constitutions, statutes, case law, and administrative regulations all contribute to what most people call "criminal law." Within this body of law, there is a major division between substantive criminal law and procedural criminal law.

 Opportunities for crime victims to file lawsuits against offenders are explained on a website of former prosecutors who later represented victims in civil cases. To link to this website, go to *The American System of Criminal Justice* 12e companion site at academic.cengage.com/criminaljustice/cole.

civil forfeiture
The confiscation of property by the state because it was used in or acquired through a crime. In recent years the police have used civil forfeiture to seize property that they believe was purchased with drug profits.

civic engagement
your role in the system

Imagine that you live in a state with criminal libel laws that permit prosecutions for making false statements about other individuals. If someone called the police on you for posting criticisms of a professor on your personal website, what would you do? *Make a brief list of your options for protecting yourself and resolving the controversy.* Then read about what happened to a high school student in Utah who posted negative comments about his school's principal on his website. To link to this website, go to *The American System of Criminal Justice* 12e companion site at academic.cengage.com/criminaljustice/cole.

 Information about forfeiture is available at the website of the U.S. Treasury Department's Executive Office for Asset Forfeiture. To link to this website, go to *The American System of Criminal Justice* 12e companion site at academic.cengage.com/criminaljustice/cole.

checkpoint

5. What is the difference between a felony and a misdemeanor?
6. What types of legal issues arise in civil-law cases?

SUBSTANTIVE CRIMINAL LAW

As we have seen, substantive criminal law defines acts that are subject to punishment and specifies the punishments. It is based on the doctrine that no one may be convicted of or punished for an offense unless the offense has been defined by the law. In short, people must know in advance what is required of them. Thus, no act can be regarded as illegal until it has been defined as punishable under the criminal law. While this sounds like a simple notion, the language of law is often confusing and ambiguous. As a result, judges must interpret the law so that the meaning intended by the legislature can be understood.

FIGURE 4.2

The seven principles of criminal law

These principles of Western law are the basis for defining acts as criminal and defining the conditions required for successful prosecution.

A crime is	
1 legally proscribed	(legality)
2 human conduct	(*actus reus*)
3 causative	(causation)
4 of a given harm	(harm)
5 which conduct coincides	(concurrence)
6 with a blameworthy frame of mind	(*mens rea*)
7 and is subject to punishment	(punishment)

Seven Principles of Criminal Law

The major principles of Western criminal law were summarized in a single statement by legal scholar Jerome Hall (1947). To convict a defendant of a crime, prosecutors must prove that all seven principles have been fulfilled (Figure 4.2).

1. *Legality.* There must be a law that defines the specific action as a crime. Offensive and harmful behavior is not illegal unless it was already prohibited by law before it was committed. The U.S. Constitution forbids *ex post facto* laws, or laws written and applied after the fact. Thus, when the legislature defines a new crime, people can be prosecuted only for violations that occur after the new law has been passed.

2. *Actus reus.* Criminal laws are aimed at human acts, including acts that a person failed to undertake. The U.S. Supreme Court has ruled that people may not be convicted of a crime simply because of their status. Under this *actus reus* requirement, for a crime to occur a person must perform an act of either commission or omission. In *Robinson v. California* (1962), for example, the Supreme Court struck down a California law that made being addicted to drugs a crime. States can prosecute people for using, possessing, selling, or transporting drugs when they catch them performing these acts, but states cannot prosecute them merely for the status of addiction.

3. *Causation.* For a crime to have been committed, there must be a causal relationship between an act and the harm suffered. In Ohio, for example, a prosecutor tried to convict a burglary suspect on a manslaughter charge when a victim, asleep in his house, was killed by a stray bullet as officers fired at the unarmed, fleeing suspect. The burglar was acquitted on the homicide charge because his actions in committing the burglary and running away from the police were not the direct cause of the victim's death (Bandy, 1991). However, states can write their criminal statutes to account for specific situations by attributing causation to lawbreakers. For example, Oklahoma state law permits murder convictions for those involved in a crime that results in a collaborator being killed by the police. In one case, after three men robbed a restaurant, one of them fired at a police dog. The police returned fire and killed the shooter. Subsequently, the other two robbers were convicted of murder for the death of their accomplice at the hands of the police (News Channel 8, 2005). Under Oklahoma law, the crime committed by the three robbers caused the death.

4. *Harm.* To be a crime, an act must cause harm to some legally protected value. The harm can be to a person, property, or some other object that a legislature deems valuable enough to deserve protection through the government's power to punish. This principle is often questioned by those who feel

that in causing harm only to themselves they are not committing a crime. Laws that require motorcyclists to wear helmets have been challenged on this ground. Such laws, however, have been written because legislatures see enough forms of harm to require protective laws. These forms of harm include injuries to helmetless riders, tragedy and loss for families of injured cyclists, and the medical costs imposed on society for head injuries that could have been prevented.

An act can be deemed criminal if it might lead to harm that the law seeks to prevent; this is called an **inchoate offense**. Thus, criminal law includes conspiracies and attempts, even when the lawbreaker does not complete the intended crime. For example, people can be prosecuted for planning to murder someone or hiring a hit man to kill someone. The potential for grave harm from such acts justifies the application of the government's power to punish.

inchoate offense
Conduct that is criminal even though the harm that the law seeks to prevent has been merely planned or attempted but not done.

5. *Concurrence*. For an act to be considered a crime, the intent and the act must be present at the same time (J. Hall, 1947: 85). Let's imagine that Joe is planning to murder his archenemy, Bill. He spends days planning how he will abduct Bill and carry out the murder. While driving home from work one day, Joe accidentally hits and kills a jogger who suddenly—and foolishly—has run across the busy street without looking. The jogger turns out to be Bill. Although Joe had planned to kill Bill, he is not guilty of murder, because the accidental killing was not connected to Joe's intent to carry out a killing.

6. Mens rea. The commission of an act is not a crime unless it is accompanied by a guilty state of mind. This concept is related to intent. It seeks to distinguish between harm-causing accidents, which generally are not subject to criminal punishment, and harm-causing crimes, which involve some level of intent. Certain crimes require a specific level of intent; examples include first-degree murder, which is normally a planned, intentional killing, and larceny, which involves the intent to permanently and unlawfully deprive an owner of his or her property. Later in this chapter we examine several defenses, such as necessity and insanity, that can be used to assert that a person did not have a *mens rea*—"guilty mind" or blameworthy state of mind—and hence should not be held responsible for a criminal offense. The element of *mens rea* becomes problematic when there are questions about an offender's capability of understanding or planning harmful activities, as when the perpetrator is mentally ill or is a child. The defense attorneys in shuttle astronaut Lisa Nowak's case, described at the beginning of the chapter, sought to attack the *mens rea* element by claiming she was legally insane at the time that the crime was committed.

mens rea
"Guilty mind" or blameworthy state of mind, necessary for legal responsibility for a criminal offense; criminal intent, as distinguished from innocent intent.

Exceptions to the concept of *mens rea* are strict liability offenses involving health and safety, in which showing intent is not necessary. Legislatures have criminalized certain kinds of offenses in order to protect the public. For example, a business owner may be held responsible for violations of a toxic waste law whether or not the owner actually knew that his employees were dumping polluting substances into a river. Other laws may apply strict liability to the sale of alcoholic beverages to minors. The purpose of such laws is to put pressure on business owners to make sure that their employees obey regulations designed to protect the health and safety of the public. Courts often limit the application of such laws to cases that involve recklessness or indifference.

7. *Punishment*. There must be a provision in the law calling for punishment of those found guilty of violating the law. The punishment is enforced by the government and may carry with it loss of freedom, social stigma, a criminal record, and loss of rights.

The seven principles of substantive criminal law allow authorities to define certain acts as being against the law and provide the accused with a basis for mounting a defense against the charges. During a criminal trial, defense attorneys often try to show that one of the seven elements either is unproven or can be explained in a way that is acceptable under the law.

These seven principles are by no means adopted throughout the world; other countries base their laws on different principles (Souryal, Potts, and Alobied, 1994). Laws typically reflect the values and traditions of a society. Criminal law may stem from religious tenets, for example, rather than laws enacted by legislatures. The values protected by the law may also differ. In the United States, *defamation*—slander or libel by making false statements that harm someone else's reputation—is addressed by civil tort law. A person can sue to gain compensation from someone who harms his or her reputation. By contrast, under Islamic law, society may punish certain kinds of defamation as criminal offenses. As they do between countries, differences in traditions, values, and social structures also create variations among the state laws within the United States. For example, although many states sponsor lotteries as a means to raise money for public education, Utah's state constitution says that the "legislature shall not authorize any game of chance, lottery or gift enterprise." Utah's laws make gambling a crime while other states have casinos and other forms of legalized gambling. As you read the next section, think about differences in the definitions of crimes and punishments in the United States, as well as throughout the world, that also reflect the way in which law is shaped by values and traditions.

checkpoint

7. What are the seven principles of criminal law?

Elements of a Crime

Legislatures define certain acts as crimes when they fulfill the seven principles under certain attendant circumstances while the offender is in a certain state of mind. These three factors—the act (*actus reus*), the attendant circumstances, and the state of mind (*mens rea*)—are together called the elements of a crime. They can be seen in the following section from a state penal code:

> Section 3502. Burglary Offense defined: A person is guilty of burglary if he enters a building or occupied structure, or separately secured or occupied portion thereof, with intent to commit a crime therein, unless the premises are at the time open to the public or the actor is licensed or privileged to enter.

The elements of burglary are, therefore, entering a building or occupied structure (*actus reus*) with the intent to commit a crime therein (*mens rea*) at a time when the premises are not open to the public and the actor is not invited or otherwise entitled to enter (attendant circumstances). For an act to be a burglary, all three elements must be present.

Even if it appears that the accused has committed a crime, prosecution will succeed only if the elements match the court's interpretations of the law. For example, Pennsylvania judges have interpreted the *actus reus* of burglary to include entering a building that is open to the public, such as a store or tavern, so long as the entry was "willful and malicious—that is, made with the intent to commit a felony therein." Thus, in Pennsylvania one can be convicted of burglary for entering a store with the intent to steal even though the entry was made during business hours and without force.

The elements of crimes and required proof before punishment in the American system differ from those in other systems. The definitions of crimes and punishments reflect the values of a particular system of justice. An act committed in one country may not be a crime, yet if that same act were committed elsewhere, it might be punished harshly. The Comparative Perspective on traditional Islamic criminal law provides examples of approaches that differ from those in the United States. These traditional approaches are not advocated by all Muslims and they are not followed in all countries in which Muslims constitute the majority of the population. However, these approaches operate in several locations around the world and they are advocated by many fundamentalists who seek to have their interpretation of Islam control law and government.

Statutory Definitions of Crimes

Federal and state penal codes often define criminal acts somewhat differently. To find out how a state defines an offense, one must read its penal code; this will give a general idea of which acts are illegal. To understand the judge's interpretations of the code, one must analyze the judicial opinions that have sought to clarify the law.

In the following discussion we focus on two of the eight index crimes of the Uniform Crime Reports (UCR), homicide and rape. The elements of these crimes are interpreted differently in different states.

Murder and Nonnegligent Manslaughter

The common-law definition of criminal homicide has been subdivided into degrees of murder and voluntary and involuntary manslaughter. In addition, some states have created new categories, such as reckless homicide, negligent homicide, and vehicular homicide. Each of these definitions involves slight variations in the *actus reus* and the *mens rea*. Table 4.1 on page 130 defines these offenses according to the Uniform Crime Reports, which count murder and nonnegligent manslaughter as index offenses.

In legal language, the phrase *malice aforethought* is used to distinguish murder from manslaughter. This phrase indicates that murder is a deliberate, premeditated, and willful killing of another human being. Most states extend the

Philadelphia police gather evidence at the scene of an October 2007 armored car robbery in which two guards were killed. What will the prosecutor need to prove in order to convict the robbers of murder?

© Ed Hille/MCT/Landov

COMPARATIVE PERSPECTIVE

Islamic Criminal Law

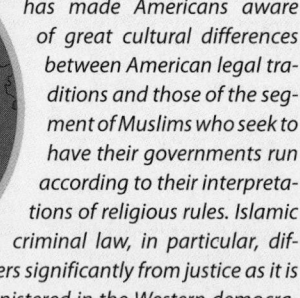

THE RISE OF fundamentalist Islamic thought throughout the world has made Americans aware of great cultural differences between American legal traditions and those of the segment of Muslims who seek to have their governments run according to their interpretations of religious rules. Islamic criminal law, in particular, differs significantly from justice as it is administered in the Western democracies. Countries that define their crimes and punishments according to Shari'a, the law of Islam, appear harsh in the eyes of many Americans. Bear in mind, however, that there are different Islamic sects and differing perspectives on religious-based commands. Therefore not all Muslim countries interpret and apply Shari'a in the same way. What are some of the major differences that exist between the American system and the elements of Islamic law described here?

The U.S. State Department, the federal government agency responsible for foreign affairs, publishes annual reports on human rights in countries around the world. The 2007 report on Saudi Arabia provided a glimpse of stark differences between that country's approach to crime and punishment and the approach taken in the United States. According to the Country Reports on Human Rights Practices (U.S. Department of State, 2008):

> There are two types of courts: Shari'a and special. The legal system is based on the government's interpretation of Islamic law in all courts. . . . During the year according to Human Rights Watch (HRW), the press reported 153 beheadings of individuals who were convicted of murder, narcotics-related offenses, and armed robbery, as well as rape, sorcery, and adultery. The government also punished persons for various offenses with amputations for theft and lashings, including for alcohol-related offenses or for being alone in the company of an unrelated person of the opposite sex. . . . In a Shari'a court, the testimony of one man equals that of two women. Under the Hanbali interpretation of Shari'a, judges may discount the testimony of persons who are nonpracticing Muslims or who do not adhere to the Hanbali doctrine.

Very few countries actually follow Islamic law to define their crimes and punishments. Although Saudia Arabia and Sudan do, for example, Iran suspended the religion-based use of amputation and execution by stoning in December 2002, although the government can still enforce crimes defined by Islamic law. In 2008, there were reports that officials in a region of southern Iran were, in fact, using amputation as criminal punishment for robbers. Pakistan defines some crimes and punishments according to the *Shari'a*, but over the past 20 years it has emphasized ordinary punishments, such as imprisonment, rather than amputation and other religious punishments. However, in following religious laws, Pakistan can create difficult issues of proof of a crime. As described by one *New York Times* reporter after a Pakistani court overturned a rape conviction in a case that drew international attention and outrage: "In Pakistan, if a woman reports a rape, four Muslim men must generally act as witnesses before she can prove her case. Otherwise, she risks being charged with fornication or adultery—and suffering a public whipping and long imprisonment" (Kristof, 2005). In 2006, the Pakistani government pushed the national legislature to reform the rape law and move such cases from Islamic courts to criminal courts.

Despite its infrequent use by national governments, Islamic law may be applied in local villages in places such as Pakistan and Afghanistan. In various other countries, including Nigeria and Iraq, advocates are pushing for its use throughout society, although many of the Islamic-dominated states of northern Nigeria actually moderated their enforcement of Islamic law in 2007. Because the use of Islamic law is one focal point for activists seeking to turn these countries into religion-based governments, it is useful to compare aspects of *Shari'a* with those of the American approach.

Such practices as stoning for adultery and amputation for theft give Americans the perception that Islamic law is exceptionally harsh. What most Americans do not realize is that there are judicial and evidentiary safeguards within the *Shari'a*. One reason that the national government of Pakistan has not imposed punishments from the *Shari'a* is that conviction for these crimes requires the presentation of specific evidence and a higher standard of proof than in nonreligious systems. Islamic criminal law is concerned with (1) the safety of the public from physical attack, insult, and humiliation; (2) the stability of the family; (3) the protection of property against theft, destruction, or unauthorized interference; and (4) the protection of the government and the Islamic faith against subversion.

Criminal acts are divided into three categories. *Hudud* offenses are crimes against God, and punishment is specified in the Koran and the Sunna, a compilation of Muhammad's statements. *Quesas* and *Tesarsare* are crimes against others such as those that threaten a family's livelihood, including physical assault and murder, which are punishable by retaliation—"the return of life for a life in case of murder." As shown here for the seven *Hudud* offenses, the Koran defines the crime, specifies the elements of proof required, and sets the punishment.

Theft

Theft is the taking of property belonging to another, the value of which is equal to or exceeds a prescribed amount, usually set at ten dirhams or about 75 cents. The property must be taken from the custody of another person in a secret manner, and the thief must obtain full possession of the property. "Custody" requires that the property should have been under guard or in a place of safekeeping.

By contrast, American criminal law focuses on ownership rather than custody, so that stealing something left in the open, including items sitting unattended in public places, clearly fall under laws against theft if the offender intends to take items known to be owned by others.

Extramarital Sexual Activity

Sexual relations outside marriage are believed to undermine marriage and lead to family conflict, jealousy, divorce, litigation, and the spread of disease.

Islamic *Hudud* offenses, required proofs, and punishments

Crime	Proof	Punishment
Adultery	Four witnesses or confessions	Married person: stoning to death. Convict is taken to a barren site. Stones are thrown first by witnesses, then by the *qadi* (judge), and finally by the rest of the community.
		For a woman, a grave is dug to receive the body.
		Unmarried person: 100 lashes. Maliki school also punishes unmarried men with one year in prison or exile.
Defamation	Unsupported accusation of adultery	Free person: 80 lashes.
		Slave: 40 lashes.
		Convict is lightly attired when whipped.
Apostasy	Two witnesses or confessions	Man: death by beheading.
		Woman: imprisonment until repentance.
Highway robbery	Two witnesses or confessions	With homicide: death by beheading. The body is then displayed in a crucifixion-like form.
		Without homicide: amputation of right hand and left foot.
		If arrested before commission: imprisonment until repentance.
Use of alcohol	Two witnesses or confessions	Free person: 80 lashes (*Shafi'i*, 40).
		Slave: 40 lashes.
		Public whipping is applied with a stick, using moderate force without raising the hand above the head so as not to lacerate the skin. Blows are spread over the body and are not to be applied to the face and head. A man stands, and a woman is seated. A doctor is present. Flogging is inflicted by scholars well versed in Islamic law, so that it is justly meted out.
Theft	Two witnesses or confessions	First offense: amputation of hand at wrist, by an authorized doctor.
		Second offense: amputation of second hand at wrist, by an authorized doctor.
		Third offense: amputation of foot at ankle, by an authorized doctor, or imprisonment until repentance.
Rebellion	Two witnesses or confessions	If captured: death. If surrendered or arrested: *Ta'azir* punishment.

Sources: From A. A. Mansour, "Hudud Crimes," in *The Islamic Criminal Justice System,* ed. M. C. Bassiouni (Dobbs Ferry, NY: Oceana, 1982), 195. Copyright © 1982 by Oceana Publications. Reprinted by permission.

Some American states continue to criminalize adultery and premarital cohabitation through old laws that remain on the books. However, these laws are rarely enforced, and many prosecutors doubt whether juries will convict people of such offenses, because society has become more tolerant of such commonplace behavior.

Defamation

In addition to false accusations of fornication, this offense includes impugning the legitimacy of a woman's child. Defamation by a husband of his wife leads to divorce and is not subject to punishment.

Defamation under American law can lead to civil lawsuits concerning harmful falsehoods spoken or written about a person that significantly harm that person's reputation.

Highway Robbery

This crime interferes with commerce and creates fear among travelers and is therefore subject to punishment.

American robbery statutes typically apply in all contexts and do not focus on travelers. The primary exception is carjacking statutes enacted by Congress and state legislatures in response to highly publicized incidents of drivers being killed and injured by robbers who forcibly stole their vehicles as they sat at traffic lights or stop signs.

Use of Alcohol

Drinking wine and other intoxicating beverages is prohibited because it brings about indolence and inattention to religious duties.

By contrast, alcoholic beverages are legal in the United States, subject to regulations concerning the legal drinking age and criminal statutes concerning the operation of vehicles while a person is under the influence of alcohol.

Apostasy

This is the voluntary renunciation of Islam. The offense is committed by any Muslim who converts to another faith, worships idols, or rejects any of the tenets of Islam. Enforcement varies by country. For example, in 2008 an Egyptian court ruled that Christians who converted to Islam in order to more easily obtain a divorce were permitted to later convert back to Christianity again.

In the United States, the First Amendment protections for freedom of religion and freedom of speech permit people to change religions and to criticize the religions of others without fear of criminal prosecution.

continued

Rebellion

Rebellion is the intentional, forceful overthrow or attempted overthrow of the legitimate leader of the Islamic state.

In the United States, the government can change only through the process of democratic elections. Any effort to use force as the means to overthrow the government will result in criminal prosecution.

Sources: From Nadim Audi, "Egyptian Court Allows Return to Christianity," *New York Times*, February 11, 2008 (http://www.nytimes.com); Nazila Fathi, "Spate of Executions and Amputations in Iran," *New York Times*, January 11, 2008 (http://www.nytimes.com); Noah Feldman, "Why Shariah?" *New York Times*, March 16, 2008 (http://www.nytimes.com); Lydia Polgreen, "Nigeria Turns From Harsher Side of Islamic Law," *New York Times*, December 1, 2007 (http://www.nytimes.com); Salman Masood, "Pakistan Moves Toward Altering Rape Law," *New York Times*, November 16, 2006 (http://www.nytimes.com); Nicholas D. Kristof, "When Rapists Walk Free," *New York Times*, March 5, 2005 (http://www.nytimes.com); U.S. Department of State, *Country Reports on Human Rights Practices, 2007* (http://www.state.gov); Council of Foreign Relations, "Governing under Sharia," March 14, 2003 (http://www.cfr.org); *Islamic Criminal Law and Procedure: An Introduction*, by M. Lippman, S. McConville, and M. Yerushalmi, 42–43. Copyright © 1988 by Praeger Publishers. Reprinted by permission of Greenwood Publishing Group, Inc., Westport, CT; A.A. Mansour, "Hudud Crimes," in *The Islamic Criminal Justice System*, ed. M. C. Bassiouni (Dobbs Ferry, NY: Oceana, 1982), 195. Copyright © 1982 by Oceana Publications . Reprinted by permission.

definition of murder to these two circumstances: (1) defendants knew their behavior had a strong chance of causing death, showed indifference to life, and thus recklessly engaged in conduct that caused death, or (2) defendants caused death while committing a felony. Mitigating circumstances, such as the heat of passion or extreme provocation, would reduce the offense to manslaughter because the requirement of malice aforethought would be absent or reduced. Likewise, manslaughter would include a death resulting from an attempt to defend oneself that was not fully excused as self-defense. It might also include a death resulting from recklessness or negligence.

Rape

In recent decades, pressure mounted, especially from women's groups, for stricter enforcement of laws against rape and for greater sensitivity toward victims. Successful prosecution of suspected rapists is difficult because proving *actus reus*

 You can see the definitions of murder, manslaughter, and other offenses in the codes of the states as well as the codes of other countries by going to *The American System of Criminal Justice* 12e companion site at academic .cengage.com/criminaljustice/cole.

TABLE 4.1   Definitions of Offenses in the Uniform Crime Reports (Part I)

The exact descriptions of offenses differ from one state to another, but these UCR definitions provide a national standard that helps us distinguish among criminal acts.

1   Criminal homicide:

   a. Murder and nonnegligent manslaughter: the willful (nonnegligent) killing of one human being by another. Deaths caused by negligence, attempts to kill, assaults to kill, suicides, accidental deaths and justifiable homicides are excluded. Justifiable homicides are limited to (1) the killing of a felon by a law enforcement officer in the line of duty and (2) the killing of a felon by a private citizen.

   b. Manslaughter by negligence: the killing of another person through gross negligence. Excludes traffic fatalities. While manslaughter by negligence is a Part I crime, it is not included in the Crime Index.

2   Forcible rape:

   The carnal knowledge of a female forcibly and against her will. Included are rapes by force and attempts or assaults to rape. Statutory offenses (no force used—victim under age of consent) are excluded.

3   Robbery:

   The taking or attempting to take anything of value from the care, custody, or control of a person or persons by force or threat of force of violence and/or by putting the victim in fear.

4   Aggravated assault:

   An unlawful attack by one person upon another for the purpose of inflicting severe or aggravated bodily injury. This type of assault usually is accompanied by the use of a weapon or by means likely to produce death or great bodily harm. Simple assaults are excluded.

5   Burglary—breaking or entering:

   The unlawful entry of a structure to commit a felony or a theft. Attempted forcible entry is included.

6   Larceny/theft (except motor vehicle theft):

   The unlawful taking, carrying, leading, or riding away of property from the possession or constructive possession of another. Examples are thefts of bicycles or automobile accessories, shoplifting, pocket picking, or the stealing of any property or article that is not taken by force and violence or by fraud. Attempted larcenies are included. Embezzlement, "con" games, forgery, worthless checks, and so on, are excluded.

7   Motor vehicle theft:

   The theft or attempted theft of a motor vehicle. A motor vehicle is self-propelled and runs on the surface and not on rails. Specifically excluded from this category are motorboats, construction equipment, airplanes, and farming equipment.

8   Arson:

   Any willful or malicious burning or attempt to burn, with or without intent to defraud, a dwelling house, a public building, a motor vehicle or an aircraft, the personal property of another, and so on.

Source: Federal Bureau of Investigation, *Crime in the United States, 2001* (Washington, DC: U.S. Government Printing Office, 2002).

and *mens rea* may not be possible (Hickey, 1993). Because the act usually takes place in private, prosecutors may have difficulty showing that sexual intercourse took place without the victim's consent. These issues are compounded by the desire of many victims to avoid reliving the trauma of the event by talking about it in court and facing tough questioning from defense attorneys.

Force is a necessary element in the definition of rape. In some courts, the absence of injury to the victim's body was taken to show that there was no resistance, which may imply that consent was given. Since the 1970s, many jurisdictions have either eliminated the traditional requirements of corroborating evidence and resistance by the victim or interpreted those requirements as demanding only minimal substantiation (Horney and Spohn, 1991).

Another problem in prosecuting rape is that rape victims often feel humiliated when their identities are revealed and they are questioned in court about actions that could indicate consent to engage in sex. Many victims therefore are reluctant to press charges (Bast, 1995). In 2004, for example, Colorado prosecutors dropped rape charges against NBA basketball star Kobe Bryant after the alleged victim decided that she did not want to endure the experience of a trial. Thus, jurors never faced the difficult matter of determining whether to believe Bryant's claim that the woman consented to the sexual encounter. Some victims are unwilling to report rape because of the insensitive way victims have been treated. In recent decades many states have enacted laws that limit the kinds of questions that can be asked of rape victims in courts, especially questions concerning the victim's reputation or past sexual history.

If a state's laws divide sex offenses by degrees, as is typically done with murder and manslaughter, rape is the most serious or first-degree offense. Lesser sex offenses typically lack all of the elements of rape. Michigan's criminal code, for example, uses the phrase *sexual penetration* for first-degree criminal sexual conduct and *sexual contact* for the second-degree offense. States that do not divide their sex offenses by degrees may use other terms, such as *sexual assault,* to designate lesser crimes.

From this review of the crimes of murder and rape, we can see that substantive criminal law defines the conditions that must be met before a person can be convicted of an offense. The seven principles of Western law categorize these doctrines, and the penal code of each of the states and the laws of the United States define offenses in specific terms. However, the crafting of precise definitions for criminal offenses does not necessarily enable us to determine when a crime has been committed. Often, difficult issues arise concerning evidence and the reliability of witnesses that will ultimately determine whether an individual is punished for a specific act. With respect to sex crimes, for example, many questions can arise no matter how carefully legislators write their states statutes. How can the court system determine if rape occurred when the defendant claims that the victim consented to have sex? Does the task of reaching judgment become even more difficult when the victim and alleged assailant are dating and have previously engaged in consensual sex? It is difficult for the criminal justice process to reach accurate conclusions in every case.

checkpoint

8. What is the difference between murder and manslaughter?

Responsibility for Criminal Acts

Thus far we have described the elements of crime and the legal definition of offenses; we now need to look at the question of responsibility. Of the seven principles of criminal law, *mens rea* is crucial in establishing responsibility for the act.

To obtain a conviction, the prosecution must show that the offender not only committed the illegal act but also did so in a state of mind that makes it appropriate to hold him or her responsible for the act. In February 2005, a 12-year-old girl in St. Louis reportedly confessed to a social worker that she had strangled her 9-year-old sister during a quarrel over a hamburger. Prior to the confession, officials did not know what had caused the death of the younger girl, who was found lying lifeless on the floor of the family's home (MSNBC News, 2005). Was this young girl old enough to control her anger and understand the consequences of her actions? This case raises the question of whether a child can form the same criminal intent as an adult. The analysis of *mens rea* is difficult because the court must inquire into the defendant's mental state at the time the offense was committed. In other words, it must determine what someone was thinking when he or she performed an act.

Many defendants who admit they committed the harmful act still plead not guilty. They do so not only because they know that the state must prove them guilty but also because they—or their attorneys—believe that *mens rea* was not present. Accidents provide the clearest examples of such situations: The defendant argues that it was an accident that the gun went off and the neighbor was killed, or that the pedestrian suddenly crossed into the path of the car. As U.S. Supreme Court Justice Oliver Wendell Holmes (1841–1935) once said, "Even a dog distinguishes between being stumbled over and being kicked" (O. W. Holmes, 1881: 3).

The courts say that events are "accidents" when responsibility is not fixed; *mens rea* is not present, because the event was not intentional. But a court may not accept the claim that an event was an accident. In some cases the offender is so negligent or reckless that the court holds him or her responsible for some degree of the resulting harm. If a passing pedestrian was killed as the result of a game of throwing a loaded gun into the air and watching it fire when it hit the ground, the reckless gun-tossers could be held responsible. If a pedestrian was killed by a car in which the driver was preoccupied with speaking on a cellular phone, the reckless driver could be charged with a crime. The court holds people accountable for irresponsible actions that cause serious harms; such actions are not easily justified as being "mere accidents" for which no one should be punished.

Note that *mens rea*, or criminal responsibility, may occur even when the defendant had no motive or specific intention to cause harm. In other words, motives do not establish *mens rea*; rather, the nature and level of one's intent do. The *Model Penal Code* lists four mental states that can be used to meet the requirement of *mens rea*: the act must have been performed intentionally, knowingly, recklessly, or negligently. Some offenses require a high degree of intent. For example, larceny requires a finding that the defendant intentionally took property to which she knew she was not entitled, intending to deprive the rightful owner of it permanently.

strict liability
An obligation or duty that when broken is an offense that can be judged criminal without a showing of *mens rea*, or criminal intent; usually applied to regulatory offenses involving health and safety.

As we have seen, a major exception to the *mens rea* principle has to do with public welfare offenses or **strict liability** offenses—criminal acts that require no showing of intent. Most of these offenses are defined in a type of law first enacted in England and the United States in the late 1800s. This sort of law dealt with issues arising from urban industrialization, such as sanitation, pure food, decent housing, and public safety. Often the language of the law did not refer to *mens rea*. Some courts ruled that employers were not responsible for the carelessness of their workers, because they had no knowledge of the criminal offenses being committed by them. An employer who did not know that the food being canned by his employees was contaminated, for example, was not held responsible for a violation of pure food laws, even if people who ate the food died. Other courts, however, ruled that such owners were responsible to the public to ensure the quality of their products, and therefore they could be found criminally liable if they failed to meet the standards set forth in the law. Some experts believe that the principle should be applied only to violations of health and safety regulations that carry no prison sentence or stigma. In practice, the penalty in such cases is usually imposed on business owners only after many failed attempts to persuade them to obey the law.

The absence of *mens rea*, then, does not guarantee a verdict of not guilty in every case. In most cases, however, it relieves defendants of responsibility for acts that would be labeled criminal if they had been intentional. Besides the defense of accidents, there are eight defenses based on lack of criminal intent: entrapment, self-defense, necessity, duress (coercion), immaturity, mistake of fact, intoxication, and insanity.

Entrapment

Entrapment is a defense that can be used to show lack of intent. The law excuses a defendant when it is shown that government agents have induced the person to commit the offense. That does not mean the police may not use undercover agents to set a trap for criminals, nor does it mean the police may not provide ordinary opportunities for the commission of a crime. But the entrapment defense may be used when the police have actually encouraged the criminal act.

During the twentieth century, the defense of entrapment evolved through a series of court decisions. In earlier times, judges were less concerned with whether the police had baited a citizen into committing an illegal act and were more concerned with whether or not the citizen had taken the bait. Today when the police implant the idea for a crime in the mind of a person who then commits the offense, judges are more likely to consider entrapment. This issue raises tough questions for judges, who must decide whether the police went too far toward making a crime occur that otherwise would not have happened (D. D. Camp, 1993). In addition, it raises difficult problems for defendants who may be reluctant to assert entrapment or other defenses for fear that such efforts will be held against them if, after conviction, the court's sentencing guidelines lead to harsher punishments for defendants who did not admit their guilt (Bridges, 2004).

The key question is the predisposition of the defendant. In 1992 the Supreme Court stressed that the prosecutor must show beyond a reasonable doubt that a defendant was predisposed to break the law before he or she was approached by government agents. The case involved Keith Jacobson, a Nebraska farmer who had ordered, from a California bookstore, magazines containing photographs of nude boys. The material did not violate the law at that time, but a few months later Congress passed the Child Protection Act, and the U.S. Postal Service and the Customs Service began enforcing it. These agencies set up five fictional organizations with names such as the American Hedonist Society and sent letters to Jacobson and others whose names were on the California bookstore's mailing list. The letters urged Jacobson to fight the new law by ordering items that "we believe you will find to be both interesting and stimulating." One postal inspector, using a pseudonym, even became Jacobson's "pen pal." Jacobson ordered the material and was arrested by federal agents. No other pornographic material was found in his home.

The Court accepted Jacobson's entrapment defense. In the majority opinion, Justice Byron White wrote that government officials may not "originate a criminal design, implant in an innocent person's mind the disposition to commit a criminal act, and then induce commission of the crime so that the government may prosecute" (*Jacobson v. United States*).

Self-Defense

A person who has a reasonable fear that he or she is in immediate danger of being harmed by another person may ward off the attack in self-defense. The laws of most states also recognize the right to defend others from attack, to protect property, and to prevent a crime. For example, in August 2002, T. J. Duckett,

entrapment
The defense that the police induced the individual to commit the criminal act.

an African American football player for the NFL's Seattle Seahawks, was attacked by three white men who yelled racial slurs at him as he walked toward his car after a concert. Duckett lost a tooth and suffered a cut, which required four stitches, when he was struck with a bottle in the surprise attack. The 250-pound running back then defended himself, knocking one attacker unconscious and causing a second attacker to be hospitalized with injuries. The third attacker ran away. Although the attackers received the most serious injuries, they faced criminal charges because Duckett was entitled to defend himself with reasonable force against an unprovoked criminal assault (Winkeljohn, 2002).

The level of force used in self-defense cannot exceed the person's reasonable perception of the threat. Thus, a person may be justified in shooting a robber who is holding a gun to her head and threatening to kill her, but not justified in doing so if the robber is clearly unarmed. A Kentucky woman who was nine months pregnant killed another woman in 2005 when the woman lured her into an apartment and attacked her with a knife in an apparent effort to cut her open and steal her baby. She struck her attacker with an ashtray, wrestled the knife away, and stabbed the assailant (CNN, 2005b). Because the pregnant woman was attacked with a lethal weapon, she was justified in killing her attacker. By contrast, homeowners generally are not justified in shooting an unarmed burglar who has left the house and is running across the lawn.

Necessity

Unlike self-defense, in which a defendant feels that he or she must harm an aggressor to ward off an attack, the necessity defense is used when people break the law in order to save themselves or prevent some greater harm. A person who speeds through a red light to transport an injured child to the hospital or breaks into a building to seek refuge from a hurricane could claim to be violating the law out of necessity.

The English case *The Queen v. Dudley and Stephens* (1884) offers a famous example of necessity. After their ship sank, four sailors found themselves adrift in the ocean without food or water. Twenty days later, two of the sailors, Thomas Dudley and Edwin Stephens, killed the youngest sailor, the cabin boy, and ate his flesh. Four days later, a passing ship rescued them. When they returned to England, they were tried for murder. The court found that

> if the men had not fed upon the body of the boy they would . . . within the four days have died of famine. That the boy, being in a much weaker condition, was likely to have died before them. That at the time of the act there was no sail in sight, nor any reasonable prospect of relief. That under these circumstances there appeared to the prisoners that unless they then fed or very soon fed upon the boy or one of themselves they would die of starvation. That there was no appreciable chance of saving life except by killing some one for the others to eat.

Despite these findings, the court did not accept their defense of necessity. Lord Coleridge, the chief justice, argued that regardless of the degree of need, standards had to be maintained and the law not weakened. Dudley and Stephens were convicted and sentenced to death, but the Crown later reduced the sentence to 6 months in prison.

Duress (Coercion)

The defense of duress arises when someone commits a crime because another person coerces him or her. During a bank robbery, for instance, if an armed robber forces one of the bank's customers at gunpoint to drive the getaway car, the customer would be able to claim duress. However, courts generally do not accept this defense if people do not try to escape from the situation. After heiress Patty Hearst was kidnapped by a radical political group and held for many months in the 1970s, she took part in some of the group's armed robberies. She could not use the defense of duress because, in the court's view, she took part in the crimes without being directly coerced by her captors. Despite claiming that she had been psychologically coerced and physically abused while in captivity, she was convicted and ultimately served 21 months in prison before her sentence was commuted by President Jimmy Carter.

Immaturity

Anglo-American law excuses criminal acts by children younger than age seven on the grounds of their immaturity and lack of responsibility for their actions—*mens rea* is not present. Although common law has presumed that children aged 7 to 14 are not liable for their criminal acts, prosecutors have been able to present evidence of a child's mental capacity to form *mens rea*. Juries can assume the presence of a guilty mind if it can be shown, for example, that the child hid evidence or tried to bribe a witness. As a child grows older, the assumption of immaturity weakens. Since the development of juvenile courts in the 1890s, children above age seven generally have not been tried by the same rules as adults. In some situations, however, children can be tried as adults if, for example, they are repeat offenders or are charged with a particularly heinous crime. Indeed, fear about perceived increases in violent crimes by youths led many states to rewrite their laws in order to give prosecutors or judges greater authority to prosecute youths as adults. In 2008 the U.S. Supreme Court declined to hear an appeal from Christopher Pittman, who as a 12-year-old killed his grandparents, was tried as an adult, and sentenced to 30 years in prison, despite debates about whether his antidepressant medication may have contributed to his violent behavior (Greenhouse, 2008).

Mistake of Fact

The courts have generally upheld the view that ignorance of the law is no excuse for committing an illegal act. But if an accused person has made a mistake of fact in some crucial way, that may serve as a defense (Christopher, 1994). For example, suppose some teenagers ask your permission to grow sunflowers in a vacant lot behind your home. You help them weed the garden and water the plants. Then it turns out that they are growing marijuana. You were not aware of this because you have no idea what a marijuana plant looks like. Should you be convicted for growing an illegal drug on your property? The answer depends on the specific degree of knowledge and intent that the prosecution must prove for that offense. The success of such a defense may also depend on the extent to which jurors understand and sympathize with your mistake.

For example, in 2008 a college professor attending a professional baseball game bought his 7-year-old son a bottle of "lemonade." Because he and his family seldom watch television, however, he had no idea that "hard lemonade" even existed. Thus he made a mistake of fact by purchasing an alcoholic beverage for his very underage son. When police officers spotted the child with the beverage, the boy was taken from the custody of his parents for a few days until officials decided that it was unintentional mistake. If prosecutors had pursued criminal charges against the professor, his fate would have depended on whether the jury believed his claim of making an ignorant mistake of fact in purchasing the alcoholic "lemonade" for a child (Dickerson, 2008).

Intoxication

The law does not relieve an individual of responsibility for acts performed while voluntarily intoxicated. There are, however, cases in which intoxication can be used as a defense, as when a person has been tricked into consuming a substance without knowing that it may cause intoxication. People may try to argue, for example, that an expected side effect of prescription medication caused violent behavior. Other complex cases arise when the defendant must be shown to have had a specific, rather than a general, intent to commit a crime. For example, someone may claim that they were too drunk to realize that they had left a restaurant without paying the bill. Drunkenness can also be used as a mitigating factor to reduce the seriousness of a charge. In 1996 the U.S. Supreme Court narrowly approved a Montana law that barred defendants from using evidence of voluntary intoxication to attempt to show that they lacked the *mens rea* element of criminal offenses (*Montana v. Egelhoff*). Thus states can enact laws that prevent the use of the intoxication defense.

Insanity

As illustrated by the case of Lisa Nowak that opened this chapter, the defense of insanity provides an opportunity to avoid responsibility for a crime. Debates about insanity have become more complicated as we gain increased medical knowledge about such conditions as postpartum depression (Manchester, 2003). The public believes that many criminals "escape" punishment through the skillful use of psychiatric testimony. Yet only about 1 percent of incarcerated offenders are held in mental hospitals because they were found "not guilty by reason of insanity." The insanity defense is rare, generally used only in serious cases or where there is no other valid defense. In four states (Idaho, Montana, Nevada, Utah), defendants cannot use the insanity defense to gain acquittal (Rottman et al., 2000). Instead, juries may find defendants to be "guilty but insane" or "guilty but mentally ill." In other American jurisdictions, defendants found to be "not guilty by reason of insanity are not automatically released." They are typically confined to a mental institution until doctors determine that they have recovered enough to be released. Some people acquitted of crimes may be confined to such institutions for a longer time than if they had been convicted and sent to prison.

Over time American courts have used five tests of criminal responsibility involving insanity: the *M'Naghten* Rule, the Irresistible Impulse Test, the *Durham* Rule, the *Model Penal Code*'s Substantial Capacity Test, and the test defined in the federal Comprehensive Crime Control Act of 1984. These tests are

In 2007 a New Jersey court found Denise Volpicelli "not guilty by reason of insanity" for first-degree murder charges after she suffocated her 12-year-old son and then repeatedly stabbed herself. The judge ordered that she be committed to a secure psychiatric facility. Should severe mental problems enable people who kill others to avoid prison sentences?

TABLE 4.2   Insanity Defense Standards

The standards for the insanity defense have evolved over time.

Test	Legal Standard Because of Mental Illness	Final Burden of Proof	Who Bears Burden of Proof
M'Naghten (1843)	"Didn't know what he was doing or didn't know it was wrong."	Varies from proof by a balance of probabilities on the defense to proof beyond a reasonable doubt on the prosecutor	
Irresistible Impulse (1897)	"Could not control his conduct."		
Durham (1954)	"The criminal act was caused by his mental illness."	Beyond a reasonable doubt	Prosecutor
Model Penal Code (1972)	"Lacks substantial capacity to appreciate the wrongfulness of his conduct or to control it."	Beyond a reasonable doubt	Prosecutor
Present federal law	"Lacks capacity to appreciate the wrongfulness of his conduct."	Clear and convincing evidence	Defense

Source: National Institute of Justice, *Crime File*, "Insanity Defense," a film prepared by Norval Morris (Washington, DC: U.S. Government Printing Office, n.d.).

FIGURE 4.3
Standards for insanity used by the states
State laws differ in the standards used to determine insanity.

Sources: National Mental Health Association, NMHA Policy Positions: In Support of the Insanity Defense, March 7, 2004 (http://www.nmha.org); David B. Rottman, Carol R. Flango, Melissa T. Cantrell, Randall Hansen, and Neil LaFountain, *State Court Organization 1998* (Washington, DC: U.S. Department of Justice, 2000).

Map legend:
- *M'Naghten* Rule
- *M'Naghten* Rule and Irresistible Impulse Test
- *Model Penal Code*
- *Durham* Rule
- No insanity acquittals

summarized in Table 4.2, and the tests used in the various states are shown in Figure 4.3.

Before 1843 the insanity defense could be used only by those who were so lacking in understanding that they could not know what they were doing. In that year Daniel M'Naghten was acquitted of killing Edward Drummond, a man he had thought was Sir Robert Peel, the prime minister of Great Britain. M'Naghten claimed that he had been delusional at the time of the killing, but the public outcry against his acquittal caused the House of Lords to ask the court to define the law with regard to delusional persons. The judges of the Queen's Bench answered by saying that a finding of guilt cannot be made if,

> at the time of the committing of the act, the party accused was laboring under such a defect of reason, from disease of the mind, as not to know the nature and quality of the act he was doing, or if he did know it that he did not know he was doing what was wrong.

This test, often referred to as the "right-from-wrong test," is accepted by many states today.

Over the years many have criticized the *M'Naghten* Rule as not in keeping with modern concepts of mental disorder. Some have argued that people may be able to distinguish right from wrong and still be insane in the psychiatric sense, and that terms such as *disease of the mind, know,* and *nature and quality of the act* have not been defined adequately. Some states allow defendants to plead that, while they knew what they were doing was wrong, they could not control an urge to commit the crime. The Irresistible Impulse Test excuses defendants when a mental disease was controlling their behavior even though they knew that what they were doing was wrong. Five states use this test along with the *M'Naghten* Rule.

The *Durham* Rule, originally developed in New Hampshire in 1871, was adopted by the Circuit Court of Appeals for the District of Columbia in 1954 in the case of *Durham v. United States.* Monte Durham had a long history of criminal activity and mental illness. When he was 26, he and two companions broke into a house. He was found guilty, and an appeals court judge, David Bazelon, rejected the *M'Naghten* Rule, stating that an accused person is not criminally responsible "if an unlawful act is the product of mental disease or mental defect." The *Durham* Rule defined insanity more broadly than did the *M'Naghten* Rule by assuming that insanity is caused by many factors, not all of which may be present in every case.

The *Durham* rule aroused controversy. It was argued that the rule offered no useful definition of "mental disease or defect." By 1972 (*United States v. Brawner*) the federal courts had overturned the *Durham* Rule in favor of a modified version of a test proposed in the *Model Penal Code.* By 1982 all federal courts and about half of the state courts had adopted the *Model Penal Code*'s Substantial Capacity Test, which states that a person is not responsible for criminal conduct "if at the time of such conduct as a result of mental disease or defect he lacks substantial capacity either to appreciate the criminality [wrongfulness] of his conduct or to conform his conduct to the requirements of law." The Substantial Capacity Test broadens and modifies the *M'Naghten* and Irresistible Impulse rules. Key terms have been changed to conform better with modern psychological concepts, and the standards lacking in *Durham* have been supplied. By stressing substantial capacity, the test does not require that a defendant be unable to distinguish right from wrong.

All of the insanity tests are difficult to apply. Moreover, as the Close Up box shows, significant difficulties arise in deciding what to do with someone who has been found not guilty by reason of insanity. Jurors' fears about seeing the offender turned loose might even affect their decisions about whether the person was legally insane at the time of the crime.

John Hinckley's attempt to assassinate President Ronald Reagan in 1981 reopened the debate on the insanity defense. Television news footage showed that Hinckley had shot the president. Yet, with the help of psychiatrists, Hinckley's lawyers counteracted the prosecution's efforts to persuade the jury that Hinckley was sane. When Hinckley was acquitted, the public was outraged, and several states acted to limit or abolish the insanity defense. Twelve states introduced the defense of "guilty but mentally ill" (Klofas and Yandrasits, 1989). This defense allows a jury to find the accused guilty but requires that he or she be given psychiatric treatment while in prison (L. A. Callahan et al., 1992). As indicated in the Close Up box, Hinckley gained permission to take supervised day trips away from the hospital in 1999. In 2003 a judge granted Hinckley permission to make six *unsupervised* day trips within Washington, D.C., with his parents as well as two overnight stays at a local hotel with his family (CBS News, 2004b). The fact that the man who shot the president of the United States could walk among other members of the public aroused new debates about the insanity defense.

In 1997 a Pennsylvania jury found multimillionaire John du Pont guilty of third-degree murder but mentally ill in the shooting of Olympic wrestler David Schultz. Under Pennsylvania law, a verdict of guilty but mentally ill means the defendant was sane enough to understand right from wrong. Third-degree murder is defined as killing without premeditation. Psychiatrists had testified that

CLOSE UP

The Insanity Defense and Its Aftermath

DEFENDANTS WHO ARE judged "not guilty by reason of insanity" are typically committed to mental hospitals. If medical experts subsequently determine that they are not a danger to themselves or the community, they may be released. New York law provides the opportunity for a jury trial if a person acquitted through the insanity defense wants to challenge a judge's decision to extend the length of confinement in a mental hospital. In April 1999 Albert Fentress, a former schoolteacher, sought such a jury trial. Twenty years earlier, he had tortured, killed, and cannibalized a teenager, but he had been found not guilty by reason of insanity. The jury listened to four expert witnesses, presented by the prosecution, who asserted that Mr. Fentress had not changed during two decades in the hospital. They also listened to four expert witnesses, including doctors from the state's psychiatric facility, who said that Mr. Fentress no longer posed a danger to society. How could the average juror know which set of experts presented the most accurate diagnosis? In the end, the jury voted 5 to 1 that although Fentress was still mentally ill, he no longer needed to be confined to the hospital.

Undoubtedly, many members of the public would be shocked to think that someone who has committed an outrageous, gruesome murder could be released to walk freely in society. Many members of the public were probably equally shocked in 2003 when John Hinckley, Jr., the man who shot President Ronald Reagan in 1981, was allowed to take unsupervised outings, away from the mental hospital where he had been confined after successfully presenting an insanity defense. Some states have sought to prevent the release of mentally ill, violent offenders by enacting statutes that permit the state to hold such people in mental hospitals after they have finished serving prison sentences. In 1997 the U.S. Supreme Court approved the use of such laws for people diagnosed as "sexually violent predators" (*Kansas v. Hendricks*). However, such laws apply only to people who are convicted of crimes, not to those found not guilty by reason of insanity.

The jury's decision in the Fentress case led the governor of New York to complain that "individuals like Albert Fentress can hide behind an insanity plea to avoid the prison time they deserve" (LeDuff, 1999: B1). However, an insanity acquittal does not always lead to more-lenient treatment for people committed to mental hospitals. In Virginia, for example, one-quarter of the 239 people confined to mental hospitals after asserting the insanity defense were accused only of misdemeanors. Thus, if they had been convicted, they would have served a jail sentence of a year or less. Instead, some of them may serve much longer commitments in the hospital. A man named Leroy Turner has spent more than 13 years in Virginia's Central State Hospital after having been found not guilty by reason of insanity for breaking a window. His doctors say that his substance abuse problems are in remission and he is not psychotic. Even though some mental health experts estimate that as many as 40 percent of Virginia's sanity acquittees no longer need to be hospitalized, the state's Forensic Review Panel approves relatively few petitions for release. Is it fair for people to lose their liberty for long periods when they have been acquitted of minor crimes?

In the case of Albert Fentress, a judge blocked the jury's release decision. Fentress later withdrew his petition for release when new victims came forward to contradict his claim that the murder was a one-time psychotic event and he had never before victimized anyone with sex abuse or violence.

As the foregoing examples show, the insanity defense presents significant problems. How can we follow our tradition of reserving criminal convictions for people with sufficient mental capacity yet also protect society from dangerous people and avoid unduly long hospital commitments for insanity acquittees charged with minor offenses?

These problems may be especially difficult when decision-making responsibilities land in the hands of jurors who lack knowledge about psychiatry and mental illness. In 2002, a jury in Houston, Texas, convicted Andrea Yates of murdering her five young children by drowning them in the bathtub. The prosecution and the defense agreed that she was mentally ill, but the prosecutors claimed that she understood right from wrong. By contrast, a jury in Tyler, Texas, in 2004 acquitted Deanna Laney, whom they found to be insane when she claimed to follow God's orders by beating her sons to death with rocks in her front yard. In Laney's case, all five mental health experts for the prosecution and defense testified that she suffered from psychotic delusions. In the case of Yates, one expert claimed she knew what she was doing. A portion of that expert's testimony was later found to be erroneous because he said Yates might have copied the plot of a specific episode from a television show—but that episode never existed. Thus a court of appeals overturned Yates's conviction. Can jurors accurately determine if someone was insane when a crime was committed? Are decisions by different juries consistent? When experts contradict each other in their assessments, will jurors tend to play it safe by convicting the defendant? If there are so many problems, then why do we keep the insanity defense? What would you do about this issue?

Sources: Drawn from CNN, "Yates Attorneys Won't Seek Release," January 6, 2005 (http://www.cnn.com); FOX News, "Laney Acquitted of All Charges," April 3, 2004 (http://www.foxnews.com); David M. Halbfinger, "Verdict in Cannibalism Case Is Set Aside," *New York Times*, June 11, 1999, p. B4; "In Virginia, Insanity Plea Can Bring Long Incarceration," *Washington Post*, June 21, 1999, p. B3; Charlie LeDuff, "Jury Decides Hospitalized Killer in Cannibalism Case Can Go Free," *New York Times*, April 22, 1999, p. B1; Man Gets Life Sentence in Killing, *Lansing State Journal*, August 4, 1999, p. 3B; Bill Miller, "Judges Let Stand Hinckley Ruling; St. Elizabeths Officials Have Right to Decide on Day Trips," *Washington Post*, April 28, 1999, p. A7; Press Release of N.Y. Attorney General Eliot Spitzer, December 11, 2001 (http://www.oag.state.ny.us).

Researching the Internet

 See how the American Psychiatric Association explains its position on the insanity defense by going to *The American System of Criminal Justice* 12e companion site at academic.cengage.com/criminaljustice/cole.

du Pont was a paranoid schizophrenic and that this mental illness contributed to the murder. The verdict means that du Pont will first go to a mental institution and then, if medical authorities say he is well enough, go to prison to serve his sentence.

Norval Morris (1982) suggests that the defendant's condition after the crime should be taken into account in deciding whether he or she should be confined in a hospital or a prison. Illness at the time of the crime should be considered also in deciding the charge on which the defendant may be convicted. For example, a defendant found to have diminished mental capacity would be convicted of manslaughter rather than murder.

The Comprehensive Crime Control Act of 1984 changed the federal rules on the insanity defense by limiting it to those who cannot, because of severe mental disease or defect, understand the nature or the wrongfulness of their acts. This change means that the Irresistible Impulse Test cannot be used in the federal courts. It also shifts the burden of proof from the prosecutor, who in some federal courts had to prove beyond a reasonable doubt that the defendant was not insane, to the defendant, who has to prove his or her insanity. The act also creates a new procedure whereby a person who is found not guilty only by reason of insanity must be committed to a mental hospital until he or she no longer poses a danger to society. Although these rules originally applied only to federal courts, they are spreading to several states.

The movement away from the insanity defense reduces the importance of *mens rea*. Many reform efforts have aimed at punishing crimes without regard for the knowledge and intentions of the offender.

The U.S. Supreme Court has reminded states that they cannot do away with all considerations of mental competence, because it affects many phases of the criminal justice process. The insanity defense focuses on the mental state of people at the moment that they commit crimes. A second issue arises concerning their mental state at the time of trial. In the past, people who lacked the mental competence to understand the charges against them and to assist in their own defense were committed to mental hospitals until they were able to stand trial (T. Ho, 1998; Winick, 1995). In 1996 the justices unanimously declared that states cannot require defendants to meet an excessively high standard in proving incompetence to stand trial. Such standards would result in too many trials of people who lack the necessary mental competence to face charges (*Cooper v. Oklahoma*).

In practice, the outcomes of the various insanity tests frequently depend on jurors' reactions to the opinions of psychiatrists presented as expert witnesses by the prosecution and defense. For example, the prosecution's psychiatrist will testify that the defendant does not meet the standard for insanity, while the defendant's psychiatrist will testify that the defendant does meet that standard. The psychiatrists themselves do not decide whether the defendant is responsible for the crime. Instead, the jurors decide, based on the psychiatrists' testimony and other factors. They may take into account the seriousness of the crime and their own beliefs about the insanity defense. The rules for proving insanity thus clearly favor wealthy defendants who can afford to hire psychiatrists as expert witnesses.

There is nothing automatic about the insanity defense, even for defendants who engage in highly abnormal behavior (Steury, 1993). In fact, it is rare for anyone to present a successful insanity defense. In 1991, for example, Jeffrey Dahmer was arrested for drugging and killing more than a dozen men and boys whom he had lured to his Milwaukee apartment. He had sex with the corpses, cut up and ate the bodies, and saved body parts in his refrigerator. Despite his shocking behavior, a Wisconsin jury rejected his insanity defense, perhaps because they feared that he might be released some day if he were not held fully responsible for the crimes.

The few defendants acquitted by reason of insanity are nearly always committed to a mental hospital (P. H. Robinson, 1993). Although the criminal justice system does not consider hospitalization to be "punishment," commitment to a psychiatric ward results in loss of liberty and often a longer period of confinement than if the person had been sentenced to prison. A robber may have faced only ten years in prison, yet an acquittal by reason of insanity may lead to a lifetime of hospital confinement if the psychiatrists never find that he has recovered enough to be released. Thus the notion that those acquitted by reason of insanity have somehow "beaten the rap" may not reflect reality.

checkpoint

9. What kind of offense has no *mens rea* requirement?
10. What are the defenses in substantive criminal law?
11. What are the tests of criminal responsibility used for the insanity defense?

PROCEDURAL CRIMINAL LAW

Procedural law defines how the state must process cases. According to **procedural due process**, accused people must be tried in accordance with legal procedures. The procedures include providing the rights granted by the Constitution to criminal defendants. As we saw in Chapter 1, the due process model is based on the premise that freedom is so valuable that efforts must be made to prevent erroneous decisions that would deprive an innocent person of his or her freedom. Rights are not only intended to prevent the innocent from being wrongly convicted; they also seek to prevent unfair police and prosecution practices aimed at guilty people, such as conducting improper searches, using violence to pressure people to confess, and denying defendants a fair trial.

The concept of due process dates from the thirteenth century, when King John of England issued the Magna Carta, promising that "no free man shall

procedural due process
The constitutional requirement that all people be treated fairly and justly by government officials. An accused person can be arrested, prosecuted, tried, and punished only in accordance with procedures prescribed by law.

The Magna Carta, signed by England's King John in 1215, is the first written guarantee of due process. It established the principle that people must be arrested and tried according to the processes outlined in the law. What might the American criminal justice system look like if it lacked procedural rights?

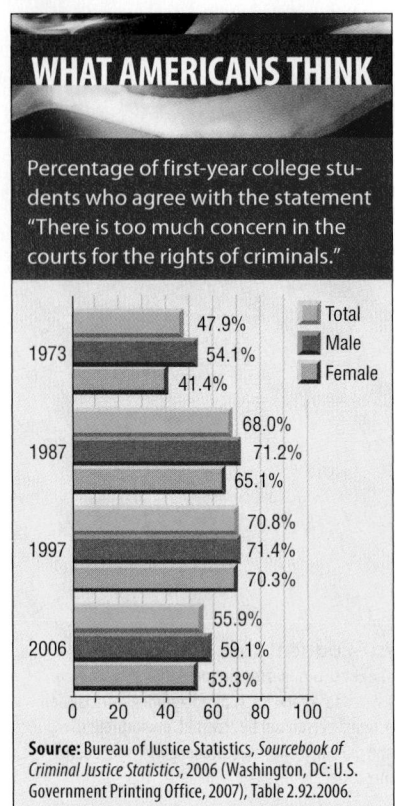

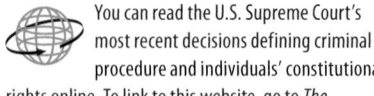

You can read the U.S. Supreme Court's most recent decisions defining criminal procedure and individuals' constitutional rights online. To link to this website, go to *The American System of Criminal Justice* 12e companion site at academic.cengage.com/criminaljustice/cole.

be arrested, or imprisoned, or disseized, or outlawed, or exiled, or in any way molested; nor will we proceed against him unless by the lawful judgment of his peers or by the law of the land." This rule, that people must be tried not by arbitrary procedures but according to the process outlined in the law, became a basic principle of procedural law.

The importance of procedural law has been evident for centuries. American history contains many examples of police officers and prosecutors harassing and victimizing those who lack political power, including poor people, racial and ethnic minorities, and unpopular religious groups. The development of procedural safeguards through the decisions of the U.S. Supreme Court has helped protect citizens from such actions. Because of the weight it places on protecting procedural rights and preventing police misconduct, the Supreme Court may favor guilty people by ordering new trials or may even release them from custody.

Individuals' rights and the protection against improper deprivations of liberty represent central American values. However, the protection of rights for the criminally accused can clash with competing American values that emphasize the control of crime as an important component of protecting all citizens' freedom of movement and sense of security. Because the rules of procedural criminal law can sometimes lead to the release of guilty people, some observers believe that it is weighted too heavily in favor of American values emphasizing individuals' rights rather than equally valid American values that emphasize the protection of the community.

Public opinion does not always support the decisions by the Supreme Court and other courts that uphold the rights of criminal defendants and convicted offenders. Many Americans would prefer that other goals for society, such as stopping drugs and ensuring that guilty people are punished, would come before the protection of rights. Such opinions raise questions about Americans' commitment to the Bill of Rights. According to public opinion data, most first-year college students believe that courts have placed too much emphasis on the rights of criminal defendants. Moreover, this sentiment has grown over the past 30 years. In addition, although male and female students' support for rights differed in 1973, the two groups show less difference today. Do you agree that there are too many rights? Can you identify specific rights that give too much protection to criminal defendants? Would reducing the rights available in the criminal justice process create any risks? See "What Americans Think."

Unlike substantive criminal law, which is defined by legislatures through statutes, procedural criminal law is defined by courts through judicial rulings. Judges interpret the provisions of the U.S. Constitution and state constitutions, and these interpretations establish the procedures that government officials must follow. Because it has the authority to review cases from state supreme courts as well as from federal courts, the U.S. Supreme Court has played a major role in defining procedural criminal law. The Supreme Court's influence stems from its power to define the meaning of the U.S. Constitution, especially the Bill of Rights. Although public opinion may clash with Supreme Court rulings, the Supreme Court can make independent decisions because the voters cannot remove its members from office.

The Bill of Rights

When it was ratified in 1789, the U.S. Constitution contained few references to criminal justice. Because many people were concerned that the document did not set forth the rights of individuals in enough detail, in 1791 ten amendments were added that list legal protections against actions of the government. These are the Bill of Rights. Four of these amendments concern criminal justice issues. The Fourth Amendment bars unreasonable searches and seizures. The Fifth

Amendment outlines basic due process rights in criminal cases. For example, consistent with the assumption that the state must prove the defendant's guilt, protection against **self-incrimination** means that people cannot be forced to respond to questions whose answers may reveal that they have committed a crime. The protection against **double jeopardy** means that a person may be subjected to only one prosecution or punishment for a single offense within the same jurisdiction. The Sixth Amendment provides for the right to a speedy, fair, and public trial by an impartial jury, as well as the right to counsel. The Eighth Amendment bars excessive bail, excessive fines, and cruel and unusual punishments.

For most of U.S. history, the Bill of Rights did not apply to most criminal cases, because it was designed to protect people from abusive actions by the federal government. Specifically, it did not seek to protect people from state and local officials, who handled nearly all criminal cases. This view was upheld by the U.S. Supreme Court in the 1833 case of *Barron v. Baltimore*. However, as we shall see shortly, this view gradually changed in the middle of the twentieth century.

The Fourteenth Amendment and Due Process

After the Civil War, three amendments were added to the Constitution. These amendments were designed to protect individuals' rights against infringement by state and local government officials. Two of the amendments had little impact on criminal justice: The Thirteenth Amendment abolished slavery and the Fifteenth Amendment attempted to prohibit racial discrimination in voting. The other amendment, however, profoundly affected criminal justice.

The Fourteenth Amendment, ratified in 1868, barred states from violating people's right to due process of law. It states that "no State shall . . . deprive any person of life, liberty, or property without due process of law; nor deny to any person within its jurisdiction the equal protection of the laws." These rights to due process and equal protection served as a basis for protecting individuals from abusive actions by local criminal justice officials. However, the terms *due process* and *equal protection* are so vague that it was left to the U.S. Supreme Court to decide if and how these new rights applied to the criminal justice process.

For example, in *Powell v. Alabama* (1932), the Supreme Court ruled that the due process clause required states to provide attorneys for poor defendants facing the death penalty. This decision stemmed from a notorious case in Alabama in which nine African American men, known as the "Scottsboro boys," were quickly convicted and condemned to death for allegedly raping two white women, even though one of the alleged victims later admitted that she had lied about the rape (Goodman, 1994).

In these early cases, the justices had not developed clear rules for deciding which specific rights applied against state and local officials as components of the due process clause of the Fourteenth Amendment. They implied that procedures must meet a basic standard of **fundamental fairness**. In essence, the justices simply reacted against brutal situations that shocked their consciences. In doing so, they showed the importance of procedural criminal law in protecting individuals from abusive and unjust actions by government officials.

The Due Process Revolution

From the 1930s to the 1960s, a majority of the Supreme Court justices supported the fundamental fairness doctrine. Even so, they applied it on a case-by-case basis, not always in a consistent way. After Earl Warren became chief justice in 1953, he led the Supreme Court in a revolution that changed the meaning and scope of constitutional rights for criminal justice. Instead of requiring state and local officials merely to uphold fundamental fairness, the Court began

self-incrimination
The act of exposing oneself to prosecution by being forced to respond to questions whose answers may reveal that one has committed a crime. The Fifth Amendment protects defendants against compelled self-incrimination. In any criminal proceeding, the prosecution must prove the charges by means of evidence other than the involuntary testimony of the accused.

double jeopardy
The subjecting of a person to prosecution more than once in the same jurisdiction for the same offense; prohibited by the Fifth Amendment.

Barron v. Baltimore (1833)
The protections of the Bill of Rights apply only to actions of the federal government.

 The Bill of Rights is housed in the National Archives in Washington, DC, and the National Archives has a description of the history and content of the document. To link to this website, go to *The American System of Criminal Justice* 12e companion site at academic.cengage.com/criminaljustice/cole.

Powell v. Alabama (1932)
An attorney must be provided to a poor defendant facing the death penalty.

fundamental fairness
A legal doctrine supporting the idea that so long as a state's conduct maintains basic standards of fairness, the Constitution has not been violated.

Security officials at airports, as well as police patrol units, use dogs that can sniff for bombs, drugs, or large amounts of cash. Should such dogs be used to investigate anyone selected by police officers or should they only be used when people engage in suspicious behavior?

© Joel Nito/AFP/Getty Images

incorporation
The extension of the due process clause of the Fourteenth Amendment to make binding on state governments the rights guaranteed in the first ten amendments to the U.S. Constitution (the Bill of Rights).

to require them to abide by the specific provisions of the Bill of Rights. Through the process of **incorporation**, the Supreme Court during the Warren Court era declared that elements of the Fourth, Fifth, Sixth, Eighth, and other amendments were part of the due process clause of the Fourteenth Amendment. Up to this point, states could design their own criminal justice procedures so long as those procedures passed the fairness test. Under Warren's leadership, however, the Supreme Court's new approach imposed detailed procedural standards on the police and courts. As it applied more and more constitutional rights against the states, the Court made decisions that favored the interests of many criminal defendants. These defendants had their convictions overturned and received new trials, because the Court believed that it was more important to protect the values underlying criminal procedure than to single-mindedly seek convictions of criminal offenders.

In the eyes of many legal scholars, the Warren Court's decisions made criminal justice processes consistent with the American values of liberty, rights, and limited government authority. To critics, however, these decisions made the community more vulnerable to crime and thereby harmed American values by diminishing the overall sense of liberty and security in society. Politicians, police chiefs, and members of the public strongly criticized Warren and the other justices. These critics believed that the Warren Court was rewriting constitutional law in a manner that gave too many legal protections to criminals who harm society. In addition, Warren and his colleagues were criticized for ignoring established precedents that defined rights in a limited fashion. Some people alleged that the justices were advancing their own political views rather than following the true meaning of the Constitution.

From 1962 to 1972 the Supreme Court, led by Chief Justices Earl Warren (1953–1969) and Warren Burger (1969–1986), applied most criminal justice rights in the U.S. Constitution against the states. By the end of this period, the process of incorporation was nearly complete. Criminal justice officials at all levels—federal, state, and local—were obligated to respect the constitutional rights of suspects and defendants.

checkpoint

12. What is incorporation?
13. Prior to incorporation, what test was used by the Supreme Court to decide which rights applied to the states?
14. Which Supreme Court era (named for the chief justice) most significantly expanded the definitions of constitutional rights for criminal defendants?

The Fourth Amendment: Protection against Unreasonable Searches and Seizures

The right of the people to be secure in their persons, houses, papers, and effects, against unreasonable searches and seizures, shall not be violated, and no Warrants shall issue, but upon probable cause, supported by Oath or affirmation, and particularly describing the place to be searched, and the persons or things to be seized.

The Fourth Amendment limits the ability of law enforcement officers to search a person or property in order to obtain evidence of criminal activity. It also limits the ability of the police to detain a person without justification (Perkins and Jamieson, 1995). When police take an individual into custody or prevent an individual from leaving a location, such detentions are considered to be seizures under the Fourth Amendment. As we shall examine in greater detail in Chapter 8, the Fourth Amendment does not prevent the police from conducting searches or making arrests; it merely protects people's privacy by barring unreasonable searches and arrests. It is up to the Supreme Court to define the situations in which a search or seizure is "reasonable" or "unreasonable."

The justices also face challenges in defining such words as *searches* and *seizures*. For example, in 2005 the Supreme Court ruled that no issues concerning Fourth Amendment rights arose when a K-9 officer had a trained police dog sniff the exterior of a vehicle that was stopped for a traffic violation. The dog indicated to the officer that the car's trunk contained marijuana, and that discovery led to a criminal conviction. However, unlike a *search*, for which officers must have proper justifications, the use of the dog did not require any justification, because the dog's scent-based examination of the vehicle's exterior did not invade the driver's right to privacy (*Illinois v. Caballes*). Because different Supreme Court justices do not always agree on the Constitution's meaning, the definitions of these words and the rules for police searches can change as the makeup of the Court changes.

The wording of the Fourth Amendment makes clear that the authors of the Bill of Rights did not believe that law enforcement officials should have the power to pursue criminals at all costs. The Fourth Amendment's protections apply to suspects as well as law-abiding citizens. Police officers are supposed to follow the rules for obtaining search warrants, and they are not permitted to conduct unreasonable searches even when trying to catch dangerous criminals. As we shall see in Chapter 8, improper searches that lead to the discovery of criminal evidence can lead judges to bar police and prosecutors from using that evidence to prove the suspect's guilt. Thus, police officers need to be knowledgeable about the rules for searches and seizures and to follow those rules carefully in conducting criminal investigations.

Police face challenges in attempting to respect Fourth Amendment rights while also actively seeking to prevent crimes and catch offenders. There are risks that officers may be tempted to go too far in investigating crimes without an adequate basis for suspicion and thereby violate Fourth Amendment rights. The discussion of racial profiling in Chapter 3 illustrates one aspect of the risk that officers will use their authority in ways that collide with the Fourth Amendment, by conducting stops and searches without an appropriate basis.

The Fifth Amendment: Protection against Self-Incrimination and Double Jeopardy

> No person shall be held to answer for a capital, or otherwise infamous crime, unless on a presentment or indictment of a Grand Jury, except in cases arising in the land or naval forces, or in the Militia, when in actual service in time of war or public danger; nor shall any person be subject for the same offense to be twice put in jeopardy of life or limb; nor shall be compelled in any criminal case to be a witness against himself, nor be deprived of life, liberty, or property, without due process of law; nor shall private property be taken for public use, without just compensation.

The Fifth Amendment clearly states some key rights related to the investigation and prosecution of criminal suspects. For example, the protection against compelled self-incrimination seeks to prevent authorities from pressuring people into acting as witnesses against themselves. Presumably, this right also helps to protect against torture or other rough treatment when police officers question criminal suspects. In Chapter 8, we shall discuss the Fifth Amendment rules that guide officers in questioning criminal suspects. The right against double jeopardy seeks to keep prosecutors from putting defendants on trial over and

grand jury
A body of citizens that determines whether the prosecutor possesses sufficient evidence to justify the prosecution of a suspect for a serious crime.

over again in repeated efforts to convict them of the same offense. One of the rights in the Fifth Amendment, the entitlement to indictment by a grand jury before being prosecuted for a serious crime, applies only in federal courts. This is one of the few rights in the Bill of Rights that the Supreme Court never applied to the states. A **grand jury** is a body of citizens drawn from the community to hear evidence from the prosecutor in order to determine whether there is a sufficient basis to move forward with a criminal prosecution. Some states use grand juries by their own choice; they are not required to do so by the Fifth Amendment. Other states simply permit prosecutors to file charges directly against criminal suspects.

Because of the limit imposed by the Fifth Amendment, a person charged with a criminal act may be subjected to only one prosecution or punishment for that offense in the same jurisdiction. As interpreted by the Supreme Court, however, the right against double jeopardy does not prevent a person from facing two trials or receiving two sanctions from the government for the same criminal acts (Henning, 1993; Hickey, 1995; Lear, 1995). Because a single criminal act may violate both state and federal laws, for example, a person may be tried in both courts. Thus, when Los Angeles police officers were acquitted of assault charges in a state court after they had been videotaped beating motorist Rodney King, they were convicted in a federal court for violating King's civil rights. The Supreme Court further refined the meaning of double jeopardy in 1996 by ruling that prosecutors could employ both property forfeiture and criminal charges against someone who grew marijuana at his home. The Court did not apply the double jeopardy right in the case, because the property forfeiture was not a "punishment" (*United States v. Ursery*). In yet another case, the Supreme Court permitted Alabama to pursue kidnapping and murder charges against a man who had already been convicted for the same murder in Georgia when the victim was kidnapped in one state and killed in the other (*Heath v. Alabama*, 1985). Thus, the protection against double jeopardy does not prevent two different trials based on the same criminal acts as long as the trials are in different jurisdictions and based on different charges.

checkpoint

15. What rights are protected by the Fourth Amendment?
16. What rights are protected by the Fifth Amendment?

The Sixth Amendment: The Right to Counsel and a Fair Trial

In all criminal prosecutions, the accused shall enjoy the right to a speedy and public trial, by an impartial jury of the State and district wherein the crime shall have been committed, which district shall have been previously ascertained by law, and to be informed of the nature and cause of the accusation; to be confronted with the witnesses against him; to have compulsory process for obtaining witnesses in his favor, and to have the assistance of counsel for his defense.

The Sixth Amendment includes several provisions dealing with fairness in a criminal prosecution. These include the right to counsel, to a speedy and public trial, and to an impartial jury.

The Right to Counsel

Gideon v. Wainwright (1963)
Indigent defendants have a right to counsel when charged with serious crimes for which they could face six months or more incarceration.

Although the right to counsel in a criminal case had prevailed in federal courts since 1938, not until the Supreme Court's landmark decision in *Gideon v. Wainwright* (1963) was this requirement made binding on the states when indigent

With Judge Roger Klein presiding, Michelle Moore testifies in February 2008 at the murder trial of Shawna Nelson in Ft. Collins, Colorado. Do the formal proceedings of a criminal trial truly protect the rights of defendants or do they just create opportunities for attorneys to obscure the truth by manipulating the presentation of evidence?

AP Images/Brian Brainerd,pool

defendants faced serious criminal charges. **Indigent defendants** are those who cannot afford to hire their own attorney. Many states already provided attorneys for indigents, but the Court forced all of the states to meet Sixth Amendment standards. In previous cases the Court, applying the doctrine of fundamental fairness, had ruled that states must provide poor people with counsel only when this was required by the special circumstances of the case. A defense attorney had to be provided when conviction could lead to the death penalty, when the issues were complex, or when a poor defendant was either very young or mentally handicapped. After the *Gideon* decision and the later case of *Argersinger v. Hamlin* (1972), all indigent defendants facing the possibility of a jail or prison sentence were entitled to be provided with attorneys. Defendants who have enough money to hire their own defense attorneys must do so without any assistance from the government.

Although the *Gideon* ruling directly affected only states that did not provide poor defendants with attorneys, it set in motion a series of cases that affected all the states by deciding how the right to counsel would be applied in various situations. Beginning in 1963, the Court extended the right to counsel to preliminary hearings, initial appeals, postindictment identification lineups, and children in juvenile court proceedings. Later, however, the Burger Court declared that attorneys need not be provided for discretionary appeals or for trials in which the only punishment is a fine (*Ross v. Moffitt*, 1974; *Scott v. Illinois*, 1979).

The Right to a Speedy and Public Trial

The nation's founders were aware that in other countries accused people often languished in jail awaiting trial and faced conviction in secret proceedings. At the time of the American Revolution, the right to a speedy and public trial was recognized in the common law and included in the constitutions of six of the original states. But the word *speedy* is vague, and the Supreme Court has recognized that the desire for quick processes may conflict with other interests of society (such as the need to collect evidence) as well as with interests of the defendant (such as the need for time to prepare a defense).

The right to a public trial is intended to protect the accused against arbitrary conviction. The Constitution assumes that judges and juries will act in accordance with the law if they must listen to evidence and announce their decisions in public. Again, the Supreme Court has recognized that there may be cases in

indigent defendants
People facing prosecution who do not have enough money to pay for their own attorneys and court expenses.

 You can read about a non profit organization that provides attorneys for indigent criminal defendants in Seattle at the website of the Defender Association. To link to this website, go to *The American System of Criminal Justice* 12e companion site at academic.cengage.com/criminaljustice/cole.

which the need for a public trial must be balanced against other interests. For example, the right to a public trial does not mean that all members of the public have the right to attend. The courtroom's seating capacity and the interests of a fair trial, free of outbursts from the audience, may be considered. In hearings on sex crimes when the victim or witness is a minor, courts have barred the public in order to spare the child embarrassment. Alternatively, in some states trials have become even more public than the authors of the Sixth Amendment ever imagined, because court proceedings are televised, with some carried on the Internet and national cable systems through CNN.COM/CRIME and truTV (formerly known as COURT-TV).

These Sixth Amendment rights obviously represent important American values related to liberty and fair judicial proceedings. In the aftermath of the September 11 tragedy, however, the federal government's antiterrorism efforts have challenged these values (C. E. Smith, 2004). The Bush administration sought to limit the rights available for American citizens suspected of involvement in terrorism. Foreign citizens taken into custody by U.S. military forces in Afghanistan and elsewhere who are labeled as "unlawful combatants" are being held at the U.S. Navy base in Cuba and other American military installations around the world. In the case of one jailed American, the U.S. Supreme Court said that he was entitled to meet with an attorney and file court actions to challenge the basis for his detention (*Hamdi v. Rumsfeld*, 2004). The Supreme Court also said that the foreign citizens being held in Cuba may file legal actions in U.S. courts to challenge their continued confinement (*Rasul v. Bush*, 2004). By early 2008 none of the terrorism suspects held without charges had yet received the full benefits of the Sixth Amendment as the U.S. government planned to hold military hearings with limited defendants' rights rather than criminal trials (Associated Press, 2008). It remains to be seen whether judges will take further action to force the government to respect the values embodied in the Sixth Amendment or whether competing concerns about national security and related matters will receive a higher priority. The Bush administration's determined efforts to gain convictions without providing full procedural rights may be one element behind the American public's expressed concerns about inadequate protection for civil liberties. See "What Americans Think" and consider how you would answer the question.

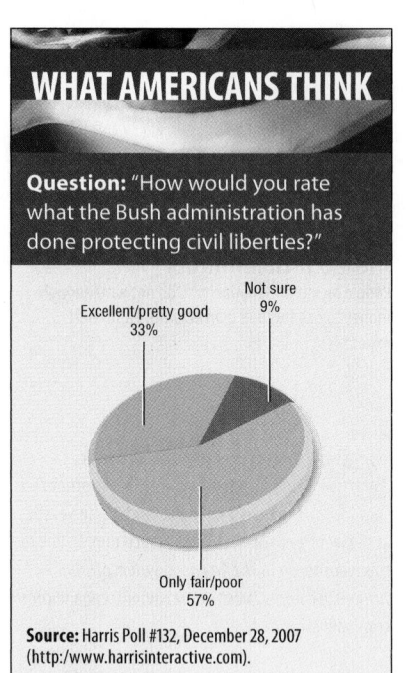

WHAT AMERICANS THINK

Question: "How would you rate what the Bush administration has done protecting civil liberties?"

Not sure
9%

Excellent/pretty good
33%

Only fair/poor
57%

Source: Harris Poll #132, December 28, 2007 (http://www.harrisinteractive.com).

The Right to an Impartial Jury

The right to a jury trial was well established in the American colonies at the time of the Revolution. In their charters, most of the colonies guaranteed trial by jury, and it was referred to in the First Continental Congress's debates in 1774, the Declaration of Independence, the constitutions of the 13 original states, and the Sixth Amendment to the U.S. Constitution. Juries allow citizens to play a role in courts' decision making and to prevent punishments in cases that do not have enough evidence for a proper conviction.

Several Supreme Court decisions have dealt with the composition of juries. The Magna Carta required that juries be drawn from "peers" of the accused person who live in the area where the crime was committed. However, the Sixth Amendment does not refer to a jury of one's peers. Instead, the Supreme Court has held that the amendment requires selection procedures that create a jury pool made up of a cross section of the community. Most scholars believe that an impartial jury can best be achieved by drawing jurors at random from the broadest possible base (Hans and Vidmar, 1986; Levine, 1992). The jury is expected to represent the community, and the extent to which it does is a central concern of jury administration (C. E. Smith, 1994). Prospective jurors are usually summoned randomly from voter registration lists or drivers' license records. After the jury pool has been formed, attorneys for each side may ask potential jurors questions and seek to exclude specific jurors (C. E. Smith and Ochoa,

1996). Thus, the final group of jurors may not, in fact, reflect the diversity of a particular city or county's residents (N. J. King, 1994). In addition, a specific jury may be even less representative of the community because of the ability of lawyers to influence its composition in the jury selection process, such as prosecutors' ability to exclude capital punishment opponents from juries in death penalty cases (*Uttecht v. Brown*, 2007).

The Eighth Amendment: Protection against Excessive Bail, Excessive Fines, and Cruel and Unusual Punishments

Excessive bail shall not be required, nor excessive fines imposed, nor cruel and unusual punishments inflicted.

The briefest of the amendments, the Eighth Amendment, deals with the rights of defendants during the pretrial (bail) and correctional (fines, punishment) phases of the criminal justice system.

Release on Bail

The purpose of bail is to allow for the release of the accused while he or she is awaiting trial. The Eighth Amendment does not require that all defendants be released on bail, only that the amount of bail not be excessive. Despite these provisions, many states do not allow bail for those charged with particular offenses, such as murder, and there seem to be few limits on the amounts that can be required. In 1987 the Supreme Court, in *United States v. Salerno and Cafero*, upheld provisions of the Bail Reform Act of 1984 that allow federal judges to detain without bail suspects who are considered dangerous to the public.

Excessive Fines

The Supreme Court ruled in 1993 that the forfeiture of property related to a criminal case can be analyzed for possible violation of the excessive fines clause (*Austin v. United States*). In 1998 the Court declared for the first time that a forfeiture constituted an impermissible excessive fine. In that case, a man failed to comply with the federal law requiring that travelers report if they are taking $10,000 or more in cash outside the country (C. E. Smith, 1999a). There is no law against transporting any amount of cash. The law only concerns filing a report to the government concerning the transport of money. When one traveler at the Los Angeles airport failed to report the money, which was detected in his suitcase by a cash-sniffing dog trained to identify people who might be transporting money for drug dealers, he was forced to forfeit all of the $357,000 that he carried in his luggage. Because there was no evidence that the money was obtained illegally and because the usual punishment for the offense would only be a fine of $5,000, a slim, five-member majority on the Supreme Court ruled that the forfeiture of all the traveler's money constituted an excessive fine (*United States v. Bajakajian*). It remains to be seen whether the Court's recent interest in violations of the excessive fines clause will limit law enforcement agencies' practices in forcing criminal defendants to forfeit cash and property.

Cruel and Unusual Punishments

Because the nation's founders were concerned about the barbaric punishments that had been inflicted in seventeenth- and eighteenth-century Europe, where offenders were sometimes burned alive or stoned to death, they banned "cruel and unusual punishments." The Warren Court set the standard for judging issues of

FIGURE 4.4

Relationship of the Bill of Rights and the Fourteenth Amendment to the rights of the accused

For most of U.S. history, the Bill of Rights protected citizens only against violations by officials of the federal government. The Warren Court used the process of incorporation so that portions of the Fourteenth Amendment were interpreted as protecting citizens from unlawful actions by state officials.

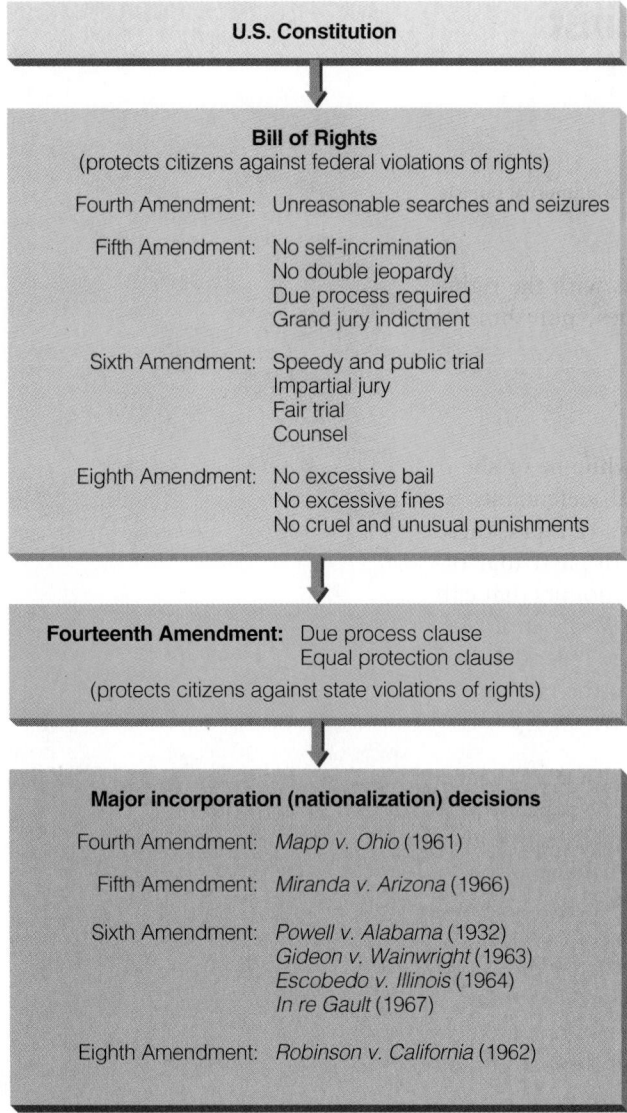

cruel and unusual punishment in a case dealing with a former soldier who was deprived of U.S. citizenship for deserting his post during World War II (*Trop v. Dulles*, 1958). Chief Justice Earl Warren declared that judges must use the values of contemporary society to determine whether a specific punishment is cruel and unusual. This test has been used in death penalty cases; however, the justices have strongly disagreed over the values of American society concerning the death penalty. For example, only a few justices concluded that society's contemporary values have developed to the point that the death penalty violates the Eighth Amendment's ban on cruel and unusual punishments in all circumstances. Justices William Brennan and Thurgood Marshall advanced that viewpoint from the 1970s through their retirements at the beginning of the 1990s. Justice Harry Blackmun reached the same conclusion just prior to his retirement in the early 1990s. Most recently, Justice John Paul Stevens announced in 2008 that he had reached the same conclusion, but he was the only member of the contemporary Court to express that viewpoint (*Baze v. Rees,* 2008).

The use of the contemporary standards test caused controversy when a slim majority of justices applied it to declare that states violate the cruel and unusual punishments clause when they apply the death penalty for murders committed by youths under the age of eighteen (*Roper v. Simmons,* 2005) and for murders committed by mentally retarded offenders (*Atkins v. Virginia,* 2002). They declined, however, to reach the same conclusion about the use of lethal injection as a method of execution (*Baze v. Rees,* 2008). We shall examine these and other death penalty issues in greater detail in Chapter 12.

The test from *Trop v. Dulles* is also used to evaluate whether the conditions of confinement in prisons constitute cruel and unusual punishment. If, for example, prison officials deprived incarcerated offenders of medical care, food, or shelter, such actions could violate the Eighth Amendment. (For another look at this issue, see "A Question of Ethics" at the end of this chapter.)

Since the 1950s the rights of defendants in state criminal trials have greatly expanded. The Supreme Court has incorporated most of the Fourth, Fifth, Sixth, and Eighth Amendments, as shown in Figure 4.4. Figure 4.5 shows the amendments that protect defendants at various stages of the criminal justice process.

checkpoint

17. What are the main criminal justice rights set forth in the Sixth Amendment?
18. What are the main criminal justice rights set forth in the Eighth Amendment?

THE SUPREME COURT TODAY

After a remarkable 12-year period (1993–2005) in which the same nine men and women served on the Supreme Court together, in 2005 Justice Sandra Day O'Connor announced her retirement and Chief Justice William Rehnquist died.

FIGURE 4.5
Protections of the Bill of Rights
The Bill of Rights protects defendants during various phases of the criminal justice process.

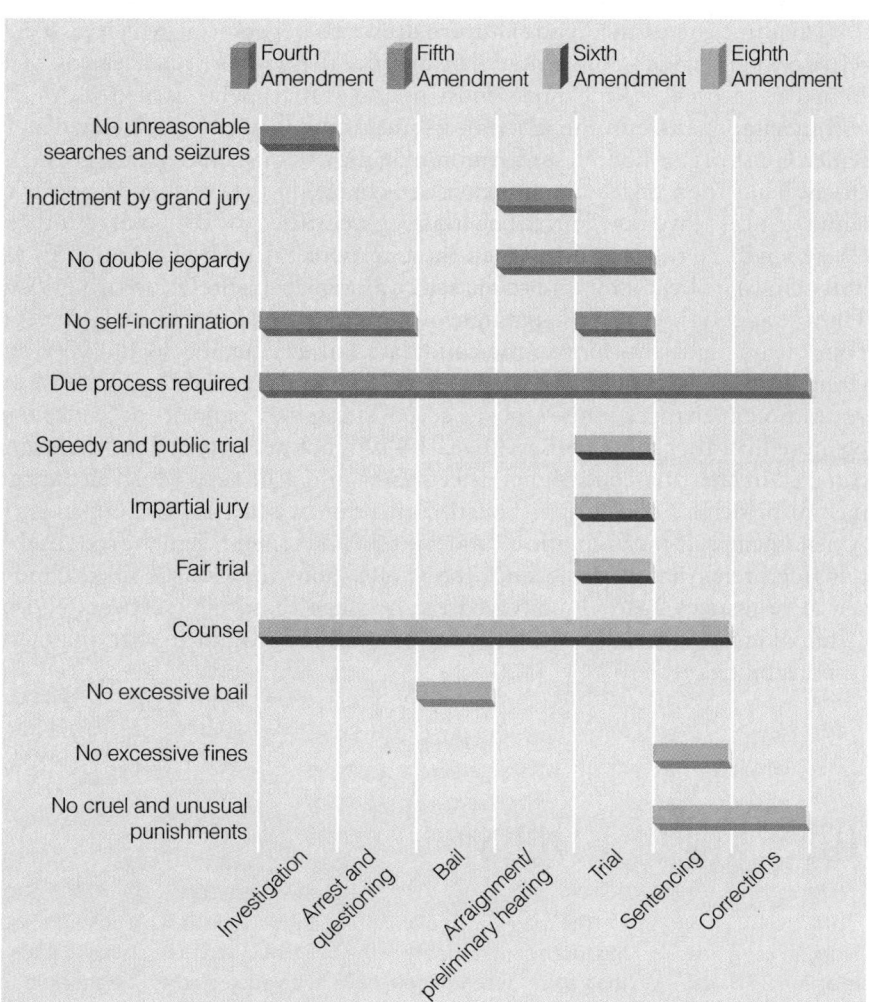

John Roberts, a federal judge, was appointed to serve as the new Chief Justice. Because Roberts, a former Rehnquist law clerk, seems similar to the late Chief Justice, his initial performance did not dramatically alter the Court's decision-making trends (Hensley, Baugh and Smith, 2007).

President Bush appointed federal appellate judge Samuel Alito to replace Justice O'Connor. Consistent with Alito's advocacy of expanded law enforcement authority during his previous career as a government lawyer (Kirkpatrick, 2005a), his initial performance as Supreme Court justice demonstrated that he was generally less likely than O'Connor to support maintaining current definitions of rights for criminal suspects and defendants (Greenhouse, 2007). Alito solidified the conservative majority on the Court and his contributions to decision making may lead to changes in decisions affecting criminal justice through new and different interpretations of the Bill of Rights. Although O'Connor generally favored the prosecution's arguments in criminal justice cases, she and Justice Anthony Kennedy provided the deciding votes for several liberal decisions that narrowed the scope of capital punishment, limited certain kinds of searches, and barred states from criminalizing aspects of adults' private sexual conduct (*Lawrence v. Texas*, 2003). Alito's initial performance indicates that he is less likely to support liberal decisions that endorse individuals' claims about constitutional rights.

The direction of the Court's future decisions depends on which justices will retire next and which president will be in office to nominate replacements. Justice John Paul Stevens, the Court's most liberal justice, who turned 88 in 2008, will inevitably retire in the not-too-distant future. Other justices, such as Ruth Bader Ginsburg, a liberal, and Antonin Scalia, a conservative, are in their seventies. Thus the Court's composition will change in the coming decade as these aging justices leave the Court. The looming questions for the Court's future are: (1) who will be the president when these retirements take place? and (2) which individuals will the new president select as replacements for retiring justices? The presidential election campaign of 2008 made it very clear that new appointments made by Democratic candidate Barack Obama would be very different individuals than those appointed by Republican candidate John McCain.

Although changes in the Court's composition may make its decisions tend to be more liberal or more conservative, this will not necessarily produce dramatic changes in the rules and rights affecting criminal justice. Most of the fundamental principles concerning Fourth Amendment searches and seizures, Fifth Amendment self-incrimination, and Sixth Amendment right to counsel have remained remarkably stable since the 1960s. Thus the Court's liberal and conservative justices have all conveyed the message that police officers and other criminal justice officials must be aware of the Bill of Rights in carrying out their responsibilities.

A QUESTION OF ETHICS

AT A JUNE 1998 sentencing hearing in Long Beach, California, Ronnie Hawkins, a petty thief, served as his own attorney as he faced a possible sentence of 25 years to life under the state's three-strikes law. In the courtroom he had to wear chains and shackles to prevent him from escaping. He also wore a stun belt designed to deliver a high-voltage electric shock if he disobeyed law enforcement officers. When Hawkins interrupted Judge Joan Comparet-Cassani, she warned him not to interrupt again or he would receive an electric shock. When he repeatedly interrupted the judge, she ordered the bailiff to activate the belt. Hawkins was zapped with a painful 8-second jolt of 50,000 volts of electricity.

Is the use of electric shock devices proper under the Supreme Court's test that applies contemporary standards of society to define cruel and unusual punishment? Do electric shocks constitute the sort of torture that the framers of the Eighth Amendment intended to ban? Technically, the Supreme Court applies the Eighth Amendment only to punishments inflicted on convicted offenders. Defendants who have not yet been convicted of a crime are protected against abuses by the due process clause, but the courts apply the Eighth Amendment test to determine if pretrial detainees' due process rights have been violated. Stun belts are placed on both pretrial detainees and convicted offenders, especially when they are being transported and there are fears that they might try to escape. As such, the belts might be regarded as violating both the Eighth Amendment and the due process clause.

The mere threat of painful electric shocks is likely quite frightening for prisoners, because the belt's manufacturer claims that fewer than three dozen people have been subjected to the shock in the 50,000 times that the belt has been used. In fact, a federal court of appeals overturned one man's robbery conviction because it concluded that the belt interfered with his ability to focus on and participate in his trial proceedings. The human rights group Amnesty International argues that electroshock stun belts are inhumane. Should such devices be used on offenders like Hawkins who, chained and shackled in a courtroom chair, were not attempting to escape or threatening public safety? Even if it does not violate the Eighth Amendment to use such stun belts (the courts have not yet decided the issue), is it ethical to use such painful techniques in order to force defendants and offenders to cooperate?

Critical Thinking and Analysis

Place yourself in the position of a justice on the U.S. Supreme Court. You are considering Ronnie Hawkins's claim that the use of the stun belt violated his right against cruel and unusual punishments. How would you decide the case? Does the use of the stun belt violate contemporary standards? Is your decision affected by the fact that he was seated, wearing chains and shackles? Would you make a different decision if the belt had been activated while he attempted to escape from the courtroom?

Sources: Drawn from Minerva Canto, "Federal Government Investigates Use of Stun Belt," *Lansing State Journal*, August 7, 1998, p. 4A; "Commission Investigating Judge Who Shocked Inmate," *Lansing State Journal*, August 27, 1998, p. 4A; "Noisy Defendant Shocks Judge with Security Belt," *National Law Journal*, July 27, 1998; Catherine Wilson, "Court Rules Stun Belt Violated Rights," *Miami Herald*, April 6, 2002 (http://www.miami.com/mld/miamiherald/news/state).

SUMMARY

Recognize the bases and sources of American criminal law

- Criminal law focuses on state prosecution and punishment of people who violate specific laws enacted by legislatures, while civil law concerns disputes between private citizens or businesses.

- Criminal law is divided into two parts: substantive law, which defines offenses and penalties, and procedural law, which defines individuals' rights and the processes that criminal justice officials must follow in handling cases.

- The common-law tradition, which was inherited from England, involves judges shaping law through their decisions.

- Criminal law is found in written constitutions, statutes, judicial decisions, and administrative regulations.

Understand how substantive criminal law defines a crime and the legal responsibility of the accused

- Substantive criminal law involves seven important elements that must exist and be demonstrated by the prosecution in order to obtain a conviction: legality, *actus reus*, causation, harm, concurrence, *mens rea*, and punishment.

- The *mens rea* element, concerning intent or state of mind, can vary with different offenses, such as various degrees of murder or sexual assault. The element may also be disregarded for strict liability offenses that punish actions without considering intent.

- Criminal law provides opportunities to present several defenses based on lack of criminal intent: entrapment, self-defense, necessity, duress (coercion), immaturity, mistake of fact, intoxication, and insanity.

- Standards for the insanity defense vary by jurisdiction, with various state and federal courts using several different tests: the *M'Naghten* Rule, the Irresistible Impulse Test, the *Durham* Rule, the Substantial Capacity Test (from the *Model Penal Code*), and the federal Comprehensive Crime Control Act.

Understand how procedural criminal law defines the rights of the accused and the process for dealing with a case

- The U.S. Supreme Court did not apply the provisions of the Bill of Rights to state and local officials until the mid-twentieth century, when the Court incorporated most of the specific provisions in the Bill of Rights into the due process clause of the Fourteenth Amendment.

- The Fourth Amendment prohibition on unreasonable searches and seizures provides guidance to police about what actions they may take in looking for evidence of a crime or carrying out an arrest.

- The Fifth Amendment provides protections against compelled self-incrimination and double jeopardy. The protection against double jeopardy does not always prevent a person from being tried twice for the same criminal act.

- The Sixth Amendment includes the right to counsel, the right to a speedy and public trial, and the right to an impartial jury.

- The Eighth Amendment includes protections against excessive bail, excessive fines, and cruel and unusual punishments. Decisions concerning cruel and unusual punishment affect the death penalty as well as conditions in prisons.

Recognize the United States Supreme Court's role in interpreting the criminal justice amendments to the Constitution

- Changes in the Supreme Court's composition will affect decisions concerning specific legal issues as a new president will replace retiring justices with new appointees who may interpret rights in new ways.

- Both liberal and conservative justices convey the message that criminal justice officials must be aware of the Bill of Rights in carrying out their responsibilities, so future decisions affecting criminal justice will not necessarily produce many dramatic changes.

QUESTIONS FOR REVIEW

1. What two functions does law perform? What are the two major divisions of the law?

2. What are the sources of criminal law? Where would you find it?

3. What are the seven principles of criminal law?

4. What is meant by *mens rea*? Give examples of defenses that defendants can use to deny that *mens rea* existed when the crime was committed.

5. What is meant by the incorporation of the Bill of Rights into the Fourteenth Amendment?

6. Which amendments in the Bill of Rights protect people in the criminal justice system?

KEY TERMS AND CASES

administrative
  regulations (p. 120)
case law (p. 120)
civil forfeiture (p. 123)
civil law (p. 117)
common law (p. 118)

constitution (p. 119)
double jeopardy (p. 143)
entrapment (p. 133)
fundamental fairness (p. 143)
grand jury (p. 146)
inchoate offense (p. 125)

3. Find New Hampshire's statute defining the nature and consequences of the insanity defense in the New Hampshire Criminal Code, Chapter 651 (651:8-b). Then find the law governing the insanity defense in one other state. Compare the two statutes. How are they different? Can you think of specific kinds of mentally ill offenders whose situations might be overlooked by these statutes?

FOR FURTHER READING

Katz, Leo. 1998. *Ill-Gotten Gains: Evasion, Blackmail, Fraud, and Kindred Puzzles of the Law*. Chicago: University of Chicago Press. An examination of the relationship between substantive criminal law and morality, using many thought-provoking examples.

Lewis, Anthony. 1964. *Gideon's Trumpet*. New York: Vintage Books. A classic examination of the case of *Gideon v. Wainwright* showing the process by which the issues came to the U.S. Supreme Court.

Moran, Richard. 2000. *Knowing Right from Wrong: The Insanity Defense of Daniel McNaughtan*. New York: Free Press. Examination of the insanity defense through study of the first English case that stands as the guiding precedent for the rules in many contemporary American states.

Morris, Norval. 1982. *Madness and the Criminal Law*. Chicago: University of Chicago Press. A stimulating and controversial examination of the insanity defense, by a leading criminal justice scholar.

Simpson, A. W. Brian. 1984. *Cannibalism and the Common Law*. Chicago: University of Chicago Press. Exciting study of the case of *The Queen v. Dudley and Stephens* showing that there were many such incidents during the age of sailing in which punishment did not follow.

Smith, Christopher E. 2004. *Constitutional Rights: Myths and Realities*. Belmont, CA: Wadsworth. Examination of the provisions of the Bill of Rights affecting criminal justice, including consideration of how those rights are applied in cases to provide less protection than most Americans expect.

GOING ONLINE

For an up-to-date list of web links, go to *The American System of Criminal Justice* 12e companion site at academic .cengage.com/criminaljustice/cole.

1. Read the Michigan statute defining the crime of seduction. You can find it by going to the Michigan Legislature website or to Findlaw: Michigan Compiled Laws for section 750.532. Is this crime out of step with contemporary society? Does the law embody assumptions about men and women that effectively treat the sexes differently?

2. At the Cornell Law School website find a U.S. Supreme Court decision from the past several years that has clarified or changed the rights possessed by suspects and defendants. How will this decision affect the behavior

of police officers, prosecutors, and other officials in the criminal justice system?

CHECKPOINT ANSWERS

1. *What is contained in a state's penal code?*

   Penal codes contain substantive criminal law that defines crimes and also punishments for those crimes.

2. *What is the purpose of procedural criminal law?*

   Procedural criminal law specifies the defendant's rights and tells justice system officials how they can investigate and process cases.

3. *How does the common law shape criminal law?*

   Based on English tradition, judges make decisions relying on the precedents of earlier cases.

4. *What are the forms of written law?*

   Constitutions, statutes, judicial decisions, and administrative regulations.

5. *What is the difference between a felony and a misdemeanor?*

   A felony usually involves a potential punishment of a year or more in prison; a misdemeanor carries a shorter term of incarceration, probation, fines, or community service.

6. *What types of legal issues arise in civil-law cases?*

   Civil law includes tort lawsuits (for example, personal injury cases), property law, contracts, and other disputes between two private parties.

7. *What are the seven principles of criminal law?*

   Legality, *actus reus*, causation, harm, concurrence, *mens rea*, punishment.

8. *What is the difference between murder and manslaughter?*

   Murder requires malice aforethought while manslaughter involves homicides that are not planned or that result from recklessness.

9. *What kind of offense has no* mens rea *requirement?*
   Strict liability offense.

10. *What are the defenses in substantive criminal law?*

    Entrapment, self-defense, necessity, duress (coercion), immaturity, mistake of fact, intoxication, insanity.

11. *What are the tests of criminal responsibility used for the insanity defense?*

    M'Naghten Rule (right-from-wrong test), Irresistible Impulse Test, *Durham* Rule, *Model Penal Code*, federal Comprehensive Crime Control Act.

12. *What is incorporation?*

Taking a right from the Bill of Rights and applying it against state and local officials by making it a component of the due process clause of the Fourteenth Amendment.

13. *Prior to incorporation, what test was used by the Supreme Court to decide which rights applied to the states?*

Fundamental fairness.

14. *Which Supreme Court era (named for the chief justice) most significantly expanded the definitions of constitutional rights for criminal defendants?*

Warren Court.

15. *What rights are protected by the Fourth Amendment?*

Protection against unreasonable searches and seizures.

16. *What rights are protected by the Fifth Amendment?*

The right against compelled self-incrimination and against double jeopardy; the right to due process.

17. *What are the main criminal justice rights set forth in the Sixth Amendment?*

The right to counsel, to a speedy and fair trial, to a jury trial, and to confrontation and compulsory process.

18. *What are the main criminal justice rights set forth in the Eighth Amendment?*

The right to protection against excessive bail, excessive fines, and cruel and unusual punishments.

Police

© Jack Sullivan/Alamy

Although the police are the most visible agents of the criminal justice system, our images of them come mainly from fiction, especially movies and television. The reality of police experiences, however, differs greatly from the dramatic exploits of the cops in *Law and Order*, *Without a Trace*, and other television shows.

In Part 2 we examine the police as the key unit of the criminal justice system: the one that confronts crime in the community. Chapter 5 traces the history of policing and looks at its function and organization. Chapter 6 explores the recruitment of officers and the daily operations of the police. Chapter 7 analyzes current issues and trends in policing. Chapter 8 examines the relationship between the police and constitutional law. As we shall see, police work is often done in a hostile environment in which life and death, honor and dishonor are at stake. Police officers have discretion to deal with many situations; how they use it greatly affects the way society views policing.

CHAPTER 5

Police

CHAPTER LEARNING OBJECTIVES

→ Understand how policing evolved in the United States

→ Recognize the main types of police agencies

→ Comprehend the functions of the police

→ Understand how the police are organized

→ Analyze influences on police policy and styles of policing

→ Understand how police officers balance actions, decision making, and discretion

→ Recognize the importance of connections between the police and the community

As their cars sped along the highway on August 1, 2007, drivers felt the roadway shake beneath them as concrete and steel loudly groaned and cracked—before giving way. Some cars tumbled into the swiftly flowing Mississippi River. Others dropped straight down into the twisted remnants of the bridge that had collapsed. Because the shocking event occurred on a major highway in broad daylight in the middle of a major city— Minneapolis, Minnesota—the emergency call center instantly received dozens of 911 calls from witnesses and victims reporting the catastrophe. Police officers were on the scene within minutes. Officers immediately took charge of the rescue effort, including trying to ensure the safety of civilian bystanders who had jumped into the river and climbed through the wreckage in their own individual efforts to find survivors (Levy, 2007). When emergencies occur, police officers serve as first responders. Along with firefighters and emergency medical personnel, law enforcement officers are expected to rush to the scene, restore order, and assist in rescue operations.

The rescue and recovery effort was coordinated by the Minneapolis Police Department and the Hennepin County Sheriff's Office, but they were joined by other police agencies that provided specialized assistance. The Federal

Bureau of Investigation (FBI) sent its Evidence Response Team, which possessed special expertise in gathering information to help determine the cause of the bridge collapse. The FBI also sent its Underwater Search team with divers and special submersible cameras to try to find any bodies submerged in the river. In addition, officers from the U.S. Marshals came to the scene to try to provide perimeter security and prevent onlookers from interfering or being endangered. Similarly, other local, state, and federal agencies sent personnel to assist in the initial rescue efforts as well as the subsequent recovery work. Although the tragic event cost 13 lives and injured an additional 145 people, the federal government's report on the event in 2008 praised the cooperation and communication among the law enforcement officers, firefighters, and emergency medical personnel (Karnowski, 2008).

Before the terrorist attack on the World Trade Center on September 11, 2001, and the courageous response of police officers and firefighters, many of whom lost their lives in the collapse of the twin towers, many Americans had had little reason to recognize the importance of law enforcement agencies at all levels of government in serving society in numerous ways. Now, as illustrated by the Minneapolis bridge collapse, there is much wider recognition that police officers are not merely crime fighters. They are essential civil servants who can act quickly and professionally to coordinate responsive efforts in the face of disasters. Moreover, the swift actions of so many different law enforcement agencies in Minneapolis demonstrated the importance of the network of relationships among national, state, and local police forces.

When they picture law enforcement operations, many Americans think immediately of their local police department. If pressed to name other agencies, many people could undoubtedly cite the state police officers who patrol interstate highways, and the FBI, whose agents have appeared widely in books, television, and movies. Few people, however, have any inkling about the large number of separate law enforcement agencies, in various levels of government, that have specific responsibilities for criminal investigations and other aspects of police work. People will hear about the Drug Enforcement Administration (DEA), Secret Service, and other agencies, but it is difficult for the average citizen to grasp the size and complexity of law enforcement operations in the United States.

The uniformed men and women who patrol American streets are the most visible presence of government in the United States. They are joined by thousands of plainclothes officers who share various law enforcement responsibilities. Whether they are members of the local or state police, sheriff's departments, or federal agencies, the more than 700,000 sworn officers in the country play key roles in U.S. society. Citizens look to them to perform a wide range of functions: crime prevention, law enforcement, order maintenance, and community services.

However, the public's expectations of the police are not always clear. Citizens form judgments about the police, and those judgments have a strong impact on the way the police function. In a free society the police are required to maintain order. In performing this task, police officers are given a great deal of authority. Using their powers to arrest, search, detain, and use force, they can interfere with the freedom of any citizen. If they abuse such powers, they can threaten the basic values of a stable, democratic society.

In this chapter we examine several aspects of policing. A brief history of the police precedes discussions of the types of law enforcement agencies; their functions, organization, and policies; and their actions and interactions with citizens and the community as a whole.

he organized a small group of "thief-takers" to pursue and arrest lawbreakers. The government was so impressed with Fielding's Bow Street Amateur Volunteer Force (known as the Bow Street Runners) that it paid the participants and attempted to form similar groups in other parts of London.

After Henry Fielding's death in 1754, these efforts declined. As time went by, however, many saw that the government needed to assert itself in enforcing laws and maintaining order. London, with its unruly mobs, had become an especially dangerous place.

In the early 1800s, several attempts were made to create a centralized police force for London. While people saw the need for social order, some feared that a police force would threaten the freedom of citizens and lead to tyranny. Finally, in 1829 Sir Robert Peel, home secretary in the British Cabinet, pushed Parliament to pass the Metropolitan Police Act, which created the London police force. This agency was organized like a military unit, with a 1,000-man force commanded by two magistrates, later called "commissioners." The officers were called "bobbies" after Sir Robert Peel. In the British system, cabinet members who oversee government departments are chosen from the elected members of Parliament. Thus, because it was supervised by Peel, the first police force was under the control of democratically elected officials.

Under Peel's direction, the police had a four-part mandate:

1. To prevent crime without using repressive force and to avoid having to call on the military to control riots and other disturbances

2. To maintain public order by nonviolent means, using force to obtain compliance only as a last resort

3. To reduce conflict between the police and the public

4. To show efficiency through the absence of crime and disorder rather than through visible police actions (Manning, 1977: 82)

In effect, this meant keeping a low profile while maintaining order. Because of fears that a national force would threaten civil liberties, political leaders made every effort to focus police activities at the local level. These concerns soon came to the United States.

checkpoint

1. What three main features of American policing were inherited from England?
2. What was the frankpledge and how did it work?
3. What did the Statute of Winchester (1285) establish?
4. What did the Metropolitan Police Act (1829) establish?
5. What were the four mandates of the English police in the nineteenth century? (Answers are at the end of the chapter.)

Policing in the United States

As with other institutions and areas of public policy, the development of formal police organizations reflected the social conditions, politics, and problems of different eras in American history. The United States drew from England's experience but implemented policing in its own way.

The Colonial Era and the Early Republic

From the earliest colonies through the westward expansion of the nineteenth century, those Americans who pushed the boundaries of the expanding frontier inevitably needed to take care of themselves. As settlers moved westward from

THE DEVELOPMENT OF POLICE IN THE UNITED STATES

Law and order is not a new concept; it has been a subject of debate since the first police force was formed in London in 1829. Even further back, the Magna Carta of 1215 placed limits on constables and bailiffs. Reading between the lines of that historic document reveals that the modern problems of police abuse, maintenance of order, and the rule of law also existed in thirteenth-century England. Further, current remedies—recruiting better-qualified people to serve as police, stiffening the penalties for official misconduct, creating a civilian board of control—were suggested even then to ensure that order was kept in accordance with the rule of law.

The English Roots of the American Police

The roots of American policing lie in the English legal tradition. Three major aspects of American policing evolved from that tradition: (1) limited authority, (2) local control, and (3) fragmented organization. Like the British police, but unlike police in continental Europe, the police in the United States have limited authority; their powers and duties are specifically defined by law. England, like the United States, has no national police force; instead, 43 regional authorities are headed by elected commissioners who appoint the chief constable. Above these local authorities is the home secretary of the national government, which provides funding and can intervene in cases of police corruption, mismanagement, and discipline. In the United States, policing is fragmented: There are many types of agencies—constable, county sheriff, city police, FBI—each with its own special jurisdiction and responsibilities.

Systems for protecting citizens and property existed before the thirteenth century. The **frankpledge** system required that groups of ten families, called *tithings,* agree to uphold the law, keep order, and bring violators to a court. By custom, every male person above the age of 12 was part of the system. When a man became aware that a crime had occurred, he was obliged to raise a hue and cry and to join others in his tithing to track down the offender. The tithing was fined if members did not perform their duties.

Over time, England developed a system in which individuals within each community were chosen to take charge of catching criminals. The Statute of Winchester, enacted in 1285, set up a parish constable-watch system. Members of the community were still required to pursue criminals, just as they had been under the frankpledge system, but now a constable supervised those efforts. The constable was a man chosen from the parish to serve without pay as its law enforcement officer for one year. The constable had the power to call the entire community into action if a serious disturbance arose. Watchmen, who were appointed to help the constable, spent most of their time patrolling the town at night to ensure that "all's well" and to enforce the criminal law. They were also responsible for lighting street lamps and putting out fires.

Not until the eighteenth century did an organized police force evolve in England. With the growth of commerce and industry, cities expanded while farming declined as the main source of employment and the focus of community life. In the larger cities these changes produced social disorder.

In the mid-eighteenth century, the novelist Henry Fielding and his brother, Sir John Fielding, led efforts to improve law enforcement in London. They wrote newspaper articles to inform the public about crime, and they published flyers describing known offenders. After Henry Fielding became a magistrate in 1748,

frankpledge
A system in old English law in which members of a *tithing,* a group of ten families, pledged to be responsible for keeping order and bringing violators of the law to court.

the East Coast, they relied on each other for assistance and protection in all matters, from weather disasters to conflicts with Native Americans. They also needed to protect themselves and their neighbors from those who might cause harm through theft or other crimes. Although we are accustomed to seeing police officers in every contemporary American community, early settlements needed every able-bodied person to devote themselves to clearing land, farming, and contributing to survival. Governing institutions and occupational specialization developed more fully after communities and the economic basis for their survival became more firmly established.

Along the East Coast, the colonists drew from their experiences in England in adopting the English offices of constable, sheriff, and night watchman as the first positions with law enforcement responsibilities. Before the Revolution, American colonists shared the English belief that members of a community had a duty to help maintain order. The watch system served as the primary means of keeping order, warning of danger, and responding to reports of crime. Boston's watch system began before 1640. Each citizen was required to be a member of the watch, but paid watchmen could be hired as replacements. Although the watch system originally operated at night, cities eventually began to have day-time watchmen, too. Over time, cities began to hire paid, uniformed watchmen to deal with public danger and crime (S. Walker, 1999).

After the formation of the federal government in 1789, police power remained with the states, in response to fear of centralized law enforcement. However, the American police developed under conditions that differed from those in England. Unlike the British, police in the United States had to deal with ethnic diversity, local political control, regional differences, the exploration and settling of the West, and a generally more violent society.

For example, in the South, slave patrols developed as organized forces to prevent slave revolts and catch runaway slaves. These patrols had full power to break into the homes of slaves who were suspected of keeping arms, to physically punish those who did not obey their orders, and to arrest runaways and return them to their masters. Under the watch system in northern cities, watchmen reacted to calls for help. By contrast, the mobility of slave patrols positioned them to operate in a proactive manner by looking for African Americans whom whites feared would disrupt society, especially the economic system of slavery. Samuel Walker (1999) describes the slave patrols as a distinctly American form of law enforcement and the first modern police forces in the United States.

Beginning in the 1830s and continuing periodically for several decades, many American cities experienced violent riots. Ethnic conflict, election controversies, hostility toward nonslave blacks and abolitionists, mob actions against banks during economic declines, and violence in settling questions of morality, such as the use of alcohol—all these factors contributed to fears that a stable democracy would not survive. The militia was called in to quell large-scale conflicts, because constables and watchmen proved ineffective in restoring order (Uchida, 2005). These disorders, along with perceptions of increased problems with serious crimes, helped push city governments to consider the creation of professional police forces.

American policing after this early period is often described in terms of three subsequent historical periods: the political era (1840–1920), the professional model era (1920–1970), and the community policing era (1970–present) (Kelling and Moore, 1988). This description has been criticized because it applies only to the urban areas of the Northeast while largely ignoring the very different development of the police in rural areas of the South and West. Still, it remains a useful framework for exploring the organization of the police, the focus of police work, and the strategies employed by police (H. Williams and Murphy, 1990).

During the political era, the officer on a neighborhood beat dealt with crime and disorder as it arose. Police also performed various social services, such as providing beds and food for the homeless. Should today's police officers devote more time to providing social services for the public?

Culver Pictures

The Political Era: 1840–1920

The period from 1840 to 1920 is called the political era because of the close ties between the police and local political leaders at that time. In many cities the police seemed to work for the mayor's political party rather than for the citizens. This relationship served both groups in that the political "machines" recruited and maintained the police while the police helped the machine leaders get out the vote for favored candidates. Ranks in the police force often went for sale to the highest bidder, and many officers took payoffs for not enforcing laws on drinking, gambling, and prostitution (S. Walker, 1999: 26).

In the United States, as in England, the growth of cities led to pressures to modernize law enforcement. Social relations in cities differed from those in towns and the countryside.

In 1845, New York City established the first full-time, paid police force. Boston and Philadelphia were the first to add a daytime police force to supplement the night watchmen; other cities—Chicago, Cincinnati, New Orleans—quickly followed. By 1850 most major U.S. cities had created police departments organized on the English model. A chief, appointed by the mayor and city council, headed each department. The city was divided into precincts, with full-time, paid patrolmen assigned to each. Early police forces sought to prevent crimes and keep order through the use of foot patrols. The officer on the beat dealt with crime, disorder, and other problems as they arose.

In addition to foot patrols, the police performed service functions, such as caring for derelicts, operating soup kitchens, regulating public health, and handling medical and social emergencies. In cities across the country, the police provided beds and food for homeless people. In station houses, overnight "lodgers" might sleep on the floor or in clean bunkrooms (Monkkonen, 1981: 127). Because they were the only government agency that had close contact with life on the streets of the city, the police became general public servants as well as crime control officers. Because of these close links with the community and service to it, they had the citizens' support (Monkkonen, 1992: 554).

Police developed differently in the South because of the existence of slavery and the agrarian nature of that region. As noted previously, the first organized police agencies with full-time officers developed in cities with large numbers of slaves (Charleston, New Orleans, Richmond, and Savannah), where white owners feared slave uprisings (Rousey, 1984: 41).

Westward expansion in the United States produced conditions quite different from those in either the urban East or the agricultural South. The frontier became settled before order could be established. Thus, those who wanted to maintain law and order often had to take matters into their own hands by forming vigilante groups.

One of the first official positions created in rural areas was that of sheriff. Although the sheriff had duties similar to those of the "shire reeves" of seventeenth-century England and the sheriffs appointed by British governors in the early New England colonies, American sheriffs took on a different role: They were elected and had broad powers to enforce the law. As elected officers, sheriffs had close ties to local politics. They also depended on the men of the community for assistance. This is how the *posse comitatus* (Latin for "power of the county"), borrowed from fifteenth-century Europe, came into being. Local men above the age of 15 were required to respond to the sheriff's call for assistance, forming a body known as a *posse*.

After the Civil War, the federal government appointed U.S. marshals to help enforce the law in the western territories. Some of the best-known folk heroes of American policing were U.S. Marshals Wyatt Earp, Bat Masterson, and Wild Bill Hickok, who tried to bring law and order to the "Wild West" (Calhoun, 1990). While some marshals did extensive law enforcement work, most had mainly judicial duties, such as keeping order in the courtroom and holding prisoners for trial.

During the twentieth century, urban centers developed throughout the country. This change blurred some of the regional differences that had helped define policing in the past. In addition, growing criticism of the influence of politics on the police led to efforts to reform the nature and organization of the police. Specifically, reformers sought to make police more professional and to reduce their ties to local politics.

The Professional Model Era: 1920–1970

American policing was greatly influenced by the Progressive movement. The Progressives were mainly upper-middle-class, educated Americans with two goals: more efficient government and more government services to assist the less fortunate. A related goal was a reduction of the influence of party politics and patronage (favoritism in handing out jobs) on government. The Progressives saw a need for professional law enforcement officials who would use modern technology to benefit society as a whole, not just local politicians.

© Jeff Shere/Stockphoto.com

During the professional era, the police saw themselves as crime fighters. Yet many inner-city residents saw them as a well-armed, occupying force that did not support efforts to advance civil rights and racial equality. If the police see themselves as crime fighters, how might that orientation interfere with efforts to gain citizens' cooperation and improve police-community relationships?

The key to the Progressives' concept of professional law enforcement is found in their slogan, "The police have to get out of politics, and politics has to get out of the police." August Vollmer, chief of police of Berkeley, California, from 1909 to 1932, stood as one of the leading advocates of professional policing. He initiated the use of motorcycle units, handwriting analysis, and fingerprinting. With other police reformers, such as Leonhard Fuld, Raymond Fosdick, Bruce Smith, and O. W. Wilson, he urged that the police be made into a professional force, a nonpartisan agency of government committed to public service. This model of professional policing has six elements:

1. The force should stay out of politics.

2. Members should be well trained, well disciplined, and tightly organized.

3. Laws should be enforced equally.

4. The force should use new technology.

5. Personnel procedures should be based on merit.

6. The main task of the police should be fighting crime.

Refocusing attention on crime control and away from maintaining order probably did more than anything else to change the nature of American policing. The narrow focus on crime fighting broke many of the ties that the police had formed with the communities they served. By the end of World War I, police departments had greatly reduced their involvement in social services. Instead, for the most part, police became crime fighters.

O. W. Wilson, a student of Vollmer, was a leading advocate of professionalism. He earned a degree in criminology at the University of California in 1924 and became chief of police in Wichita, Kansas, in 1928. He came to national attention by reorganizing the department and fighting police corruption. He promoted the use of motorized patrols, efficient radio communication, and rapid response. He believed that one-officer patrols were the best way to use personnel and that the two-way radio, which allowed for supervision by commanders, made officers more efficient (Reiss, 1992: 51). He rotated assignments so that officers on patrol would not become too familiar with people in the community (and thus prone to corruption). In 1960, Wilson became superintendent of the Chicago Police Department with a mandate to end corruption there.

The new emphasis on professionalism spurred the formation of the International Association of Chiefs of Police (IACP) in 1902 and the Fraternal Order of Police (FOP) in 1915. Both organizations promoted the use of new technologies, training standards, and a code of ethics.

Advocates of professionalism urged that the police be made aware of the need to act lawfully and to protect the rights of all citizens, including those suspected of crimes. They sought to instill a strong—some would even say rigid ("Just the facts, ma'am")—commitment to the law and to equal treatment (Goldstein, 1990: 7).

By the 1930s the police were using new technologies and methods to combat serious crimes. They became more effective against crimes such as murder, rape, and robbery—an important factor in gaining citizen support. By contrast, efforts to control victimless offenses and to maintain order often aroused citizen opposition. As Mark Moore and George Kelling have noted, "The clean, bureaucratic model of policing put forth by the reformers could be sustained only if the scope of police responsibility was narrowed to 'crime fighting'" (1983: 55).

In the 1960s the civil rights and antiwar movements, urban riots, and rising crime rates challenged many of the assumptions of the professional model. In their attempts to maintain order during public demonstrations, the police in many cities seemed to be concerned mainly with maintaining the status quo. Thus, police officers found themselves enforcing laws that tended to discriminate against African Americans and the poor. The number of low-income racial

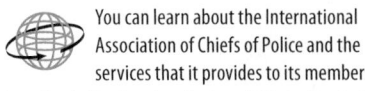 You can learn about the International Association of Chiefs of Police and the services that it provides to its members by going to *The American System of Criminal Justice* 12e companion site at academic.cengage.com/criminaljustice/cole.

minorities living in the inner cities was growing, and the professional style kept the police isolated from the communities they served. In the eyes of many inner-city residents, the police were an occupying army keeping them at the bottom of society, not public servants helping all citizens.

Although the police continued to portray themselves as crime fighters, citizens became aware that the police often were not effective in this role. Crime rates rose for many offenses, and the police could not change the perception that the quality of urban life was declining.

The Community Policing Era: 1970–Present

Beginning in the 1970s, calls were heard for a move away from the crime-fighting focus and toward greater emphasis on keeping order and providing services to the community. Research studies revealed the complex nature of police work and the extent to which day-to-day practices deviated from the professional ideal. The research also questioned the effectiveness of the police in catching and deterring criminals.

Three findings of this research are especially noteworthy:

1. Increasing the number of patrol officers in a neighborhood had little effect on the crime rate.

2. Rapid response to calls for service did not greatly increase the arrest rate.

3. Improving the percentage of crimes solved is difficult.

Such findings undermined acceptance of the professional crime-fighter model (Moore, 1992: 99). Critics argued that the professional style isolated the police from the community and reduced their knowledge about the neighborhoods they served, especially when police patrolled in cars. Use of the patrol car prevented personal contacts with citizens. Instead, it was argued, police should get out of their cars and spend more time meeting and helping residents. This would permit the police to help people with a range of problems and in some cases to prevent problems from arising or growing worse. For example, if the police know about conflicts between people in a neighborhood, they can try to mediate and perhaps prevent the conflict from growing into a criminal assault or other serious problem. Reformers hoped that closer contact with citizens would not only permit the police to help them in new ways but would also make them feel safer, knowing that the police were available and interested in their problems.

Community policing encourages personal contact between officers and citizens, especially interactions that facilitate citizens' cooperation with and support for the police. Is your own involvement in criminal justice affected by your view of police officers and interactions with them?

In a provocative article titled "Broken Windows: The Police and Neighborhood Safety," James Q. Wilson and George L. Kelling argued that policing should work more on little problems such as maintaining order, providing services to those in need, and adopting strategies to reduce the fear of crime (1982: 29). They based their approach on three assumptions:

1. Neighborhood disorder creates fear. Areas with street people, youth gangs, prostitution, and drunks are high-crime areas.

2. Just as broken windows are a signal that nobody cares and can lead to worse vandalism, untended disorderly

behavior is a signal that the community does not care. This also leads to worse disorder and crime.

3. If the police are to deal with disorder and thus reduce fear and crime, they must rely on citizens for assistance.

Advocates of the community policing approach urge greater use of foot patrols so that officers will become known to citizens, who in turn will cooperate with the police. They believe that through attention to little problems, the police may not only reduce disorder and fear but also improve public attitudes toward policing. When citizens respond positively to police efforts, the police will have "improved bases of community and political support, which in turn can be exploited to gain further cooperation from citizens in a wide variety of activities" (Kelling, 1985: 299).

Closely related to the community policing concept is problem-oriented policing (see Chapter 6). Herman Goldstein, the originator of this approach, argued that instead of focusing on crime and disorder the police should identify the underlying causes of such problems as noisy teenagers, battered spouses, and abandoned buildings used as drug houses. In doing so they could reduce disorder and fear of crime (Goldstein, 1979: 236). Closer contacts between the police and the community might then reduce the hostility that has developed between officers and residents in many urban neighborhoods (Sparrow, Moore, and Kennedy, 1990).

In *Fixing Broken Windows*, a book written in response to the Wilson and Kelling article, George L. Kelling and Catherine Coles (1996) call for strategies to restore order and reduce crime in public spaces in U.S. communities. In Baltimore, New York, San Francisco, and Seattle, police are paying greater attention to "quality-of-life crimes"—by arresting subway fare-beaters, rousting loiterers and panhandlers from parks, and aggressively dealing with those who are obstructing sidewalks, harassing others, and soliciting. By handling these "little crimes," the police not only help restore order but also often prevent worse crimes. In New York, for example, searching fare-beaters often yielded weapons, questioning a street vendor selling hot merchandise led to a fence specializing in stolen weapons, and arresting a person for urinating in a park resulted in discovery of a cache of weapons.

Although reformers argue for a greater focus on order maintenance and service, they do not call for an end to the crime-fighting role. Instead, they want a shift of emphasis. The police should pay more attention to community needs and seek to understand the problems underlying crime, disorder, and incivility. These proposals have been adopted by police executives in many cities and by influential organizations such as the Police Foundation and the Police Executive Research Forum.

The high point for community policing came in the 1990s. The federal government created the Office of Community Oriented Policing Services, more commonly known as the "COPS Office," which provided grants to local police agencies for hiring new officers and developing community policing programs. Between 1995 and 2003, the COPS Office supplied nearly $7 billion to 13,000 state and local agencies to hire 118,000 new officers and implement training and programs for community policing (Uchida 2005: 37).

The new focus for the police did not go unchallenged (Reichers and Roberg, 1990: 105). Critics question whether the professional model really isolated police from community residents (S. Walker, 1984). Taking another view, Carl Klockars doubted whether the police would give higher priority to maintaining order and wondered whether Americans want their police to be something other than crime fighters (1985: 300). Others wonder whether the opportunity to receive federal money and hire new officers led departments to use the language of community policing in portraying their activities even though they never fully adopted the new methods.

 Look at the website of the Department of Homeland Security in order to see how much activity and organizational change has occurred since September 2001. To link to this website, go to *The American System of Criminal Justice* 12e companion site at academic.cengage.com/criminaljustice/cole.

Homeland Security: The Next Era for Policing?

The hijackers' attacks against the World Trade Center and Pentagon on September 11, 2001, made homeland security and antiterrorism efforts among the highest priorities for the U.S. government. As we shall see in Chapter 7, this event shifted the federal government's funding priorities for law enforcement and led to a reorganization of federal agencies. According to Craig Uchida, "Priorities for training equipment, strategies, and funding have transformed policing once again—this time focusing on homeland security" (2005: 38). Instead of focusing funds on community policing, federal money shifted toward supplying emergency response training, hazardous materials gear, and equipment for detecting bombs and other weapons of mass destruction, and collection of intelligence data. In public comments, a few police officials have made reference to "terrorist-oriented policing," but it is not clear how such a concept or emphasis would be defined at the local level (Kerlikowske, 2004). Some observers believe that a shift toward homeland security may appeal to traditionalists in law enforcement who prefer to see themselves as heroically catching "bad guys" rather than solving problems within neighborhoods. Yet, a by-product of the increased emphasis on homeland security may be better coordinated services for society in non-crime-fighting situations, such as public emergencies. For example, police officials in Minneapolis credited their training in a course on Integrated Emergency Management, conducted by the federal government, as one of the reasons that they could respond so quickly and effectively when the I-35W bridge collapsed, as described in the opening of this chapter (Karnowski, 2008).

Community policing will not disappear. Many police executives remain committed to its purposes and principles. However, federal agencies have clearly made homeland security their top priority, and federal funding for local police departments has shifted as well. Further development of a homeland security focus throughout policing may depend on whether American cities suffer additional terror attacks. Thus, whether the early years of the twenty-first century will be regarded as the dawn of a new era for all levels of policing remains to be seen.

Whichever approach the police take—professional, crime fighting, or community policing—it must be carried out through a bureaucratic structure. We therefore turn to a discussion of police structure, function, and organization in the United States.

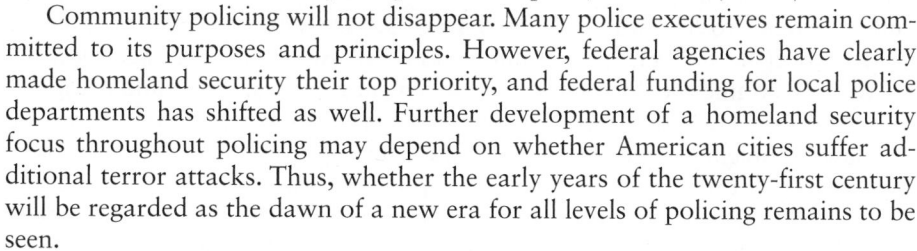

checkpoint

6. What are the major historical periods of American policing?
7. What was the main feature of the political era?
8. What were the major recommendations of the Progressive reformers?
9. What are the main criticisms of the professional model era?
10. What is community policing?

LAW ENFORCEMENT AGENCIES

As discussed in Chapter 3, the United States has a federal system of government with separate national and state structures, each with authority over certain functions. Police agencies at the national, state, county, and municipal levels are responsible for carrying out three functions: (1) maintaining order, (2) enforcing the law, and (3) providing services to the community. Each of these functions contributes to the prevention of crime. They together employ more than one million people, both sworn and unsworn personnel. Nearly 800,000 full-time

TABLE 5.1	Personnel in Federal, State, County, and Local Law Enforcement Agencies

The decentralized nature of U.S. law enforcement is shown by the fact that 53 percent of all full-time sworn officers are in local departments.

Type of Agency	Number of Full-Time Sworn Officers	Percentage of Total
Local Police	446,974	53%
County Police	175,018	21%
State Police	58,190	7%
Special Police*	49,398	6%
Federal	104,884	13%

*Officers in state and local parks, transportation, animal control, housing, and so forth.

Source: Bureau of Justice Statistics, "Law Enforcement Statistics—2004," (http://www.ojp.usdoj.gov/bjs/lawenf.htm).

sworn officers serve in state and local agencies, and an additional 88,000 sworn officers operate in federal agencies. Police agencies include the following (BJS, 2007; Reaves, 2006):

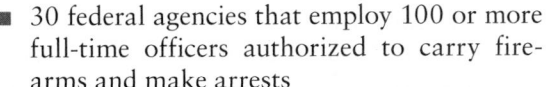

- 12,766 local police departments
- 3,070 sheriff's departments
- 49 state police departments (all states except Hawaii)
- 135 Native American tribal police agencies
- 30 federal agencies that employ 100 or more full-time officers authorized to carry firearms and make arrests

In addition, there are 1,481 special police agencies (jurisdictions limited to transit systems, parks, schools, and so on) as well as additional federal agencies each with fewer than 100 sworn officers.

This list shows both the fragmentation and the local orientation of American police. Seventy percent of expenditures for policing are spent at the local level. Each level of the system has different responsibilities, either for different kinds of crimes, such as the federal authority over counterfeiting, or for different geographic areas, such as state police authority over major highways. The broadest authority tends to lie with local units. Table 5.1 shows the number of full-time sworn officers in federal, state, county, and local law enforcement agencies.

As we examine the differing law enforcement agencies, we should recognize that 9-11 has triggered an expansion and reorganization, especially among federal law enforcement agencies. The creation of the Department of Homeland Security, the reordering of crime control policies away from street crime and drugs to international and domestic terrorism, and the great increase in federal money to pursue the war against terrorism are greatly affecting law enforcement at all levels of government. (See "New Directions in Criminal Justice Policy" for more on the war on terrorism.)

Federal Agencies

Federal law enforcement agencies are part of the executive branch of the national government. They investigate a specific set of crimes defined by Congress. Recent federal efforts against drug trafficking, organized crime, insider stock trading, and terrorism have attracted attention to these agencies, even though they handle relatively few crimes and employ only 104,884 full-time officers authorized to make arrests.

The FBI

The Federal Bureau of Investigation (FBI) is an investigative agency within the U.S. Department of Justice with the power to investigate all federal crimes not placed under the jurisdiction of other agencies. Established as the Bureau of Investigation in 1908, it came to national prominence under J. Edgar Hoover, its director from 1924 until his death in 1972. Hoover made major changes in the bureau (renamed the Federal Bureau of Investigation in 1935) to increase its professionalism. He sought to remove political factors from the selection of agents, established the national fingerprint filing system, and oversaw the development of the Uniform Crime Reporting System. Although Hoover has been criticized for many things, such as FBI spying on civil rights and antiwar activ-

NEW DIRECTIONS in CRIMINAL JUSTICE POLICY

Federal Law Enforcement and the War on Terrorism

IN THE WAKE of the events of 9-11, a dramatic reordering of priorities and responsibilities has taken place among federal law enforcement agencies. As a result of this shift, many federal agencies have had to reorient their focus toward addressing the issues of terrorism and away from the street crime and drug cases they had been handling prior to 9-11.

One key sign of this change is the creation of the Department of Homeland Security (DHS) as a central government agency to oversee and coordinate law enforcement agencies that were previously scattered throughout other departments of government. For example, DHS includes the U.S. Secret Service, the U.S. Coast Guard, Customs and Border Protection, and the Transportation Security Administration.

Equally important are changes in the Department of Justice, home to the FBI, Drug Enforcement Agency, and, since January 2003, the law enforcement functions of the Bureau of Alcohol, Tobacco, Firearms, and Explosives. FBI Director Robert Mueller has said that "while we remain committed to our other important national security and law enforcement responsibilities, the prevention of terrorism takes precedence in our thinking and planning" (http://www.fbi.gov/aboutus.htm). In testimony before Congress in 2008, Director Mueller said that "we have roughly a 50/50 balance between national security and criminal programs." He also said that "Public corruption is the top priority of the [FBI's] Criminal Investigative Division," meaning that this emphasis on catching public officials taking bribes limits the FBI's attention on other kinds of crimes.

The shift in the FBI's emphasis creates new challenges for state and local law enforcement. Director Mueller acknowledged as much in a 2007 speech before the International Association of Chiefs of Police (IACP). Mueller said, "I know that our reallocation of resources has impacted your work. Some of you may have less daily contact with FBI agents on drug cases, bank robberies, and smaller white collar crime cases." Thus local police may find themselves with greater responsibility for a variety of offenses that previously received significant attention from the FBI. However, few local governments can afford to increase police agencies' budgets, even when those agencies find themselves with additional crime control responsibilities.

In addition, state and local law enforcement officials must increase their own attention to homeland security issues, including emergency response training. Local police chiefs have complained that the FBI and other federal agencies do not share information about terrorism suspects being monitored in their communities and thus local communities feel insufficiently informed about the risks and threats that they may face.

Police agencies at all levels of government face new challenges in developing mechanisms for communication and coordination. The FBI has responded by creating Joint Terrorism Task Forces (JTTFs) in more than 100 of its field offices to coordinate teams of federal, state, and local officers who investigate and prevent acts of terrorism. The FBI has also created an Office of Law Enforcement Coordination to improve communication and cooperation with other police agencies. More initiatives may be necessary to face the challenge of effective policing in an era of threats from terrorism.

Sources: Robert S. Mueller, "Statement Before the House Judiciary Committee," April 23, 2008 (http://www.fbi.gov); Robert S. Mueller, "Speech Before International Association of Chiefs of Police," October 15, 2007, New Orleans, LA (http://www.fbi.gov); "About Us: Director Robert Mueller and the FBI and War on Terrorism" (http://www.fbi.gov); "Govt-wide Security Rises while Other Spending Falls," *Government Security News*, February 3, 2005 (http://www.gsnmagazine.com); Henry Stern, "Portland May Pull Out of FBI Task Force," *Portland Oregonian*, December 21, 2004 (http://www.oregonlive.com).

Researching the Internet

You can read online about the FBI's counterterrorism efforts by going to *The American System of Criminal Justice* 12e companion site at academic.cengage.com/criminaljustice/cole.

---

ists during the 1960s, his role in improving police work and the FBI's effectiveness is widely recognized.

Within the United States, the FBI's 12,590 special agents work out of 56 field offices and 400 additional satellite offices known as "resident agencies." In 2002 the FBI announced a new list of priorities that describes its work:

1. Protect the United States from terrorist attack.

2. Protect the United States against foreign intelligence operations and espionage.

3. Protect the United States against cyber-based attacks and high-technology crimes.

4. Combat public corruption at all levels.

5. Protect civil rights.

6. Combat transnational and national criminal organizations and enterprises.

The FBI's website contains a wealth of information about the agency, its various areas of emphasis, career opportunities, and national crime statistics. To link to this website, go to *The American System of Criminal Justice* 12e companion site at academic.cengage.com/criminaljustice/cole.

FBI evidence technicians helped local police gather evidence when the remains of four dead babies were found at a home in Ocean City, Maryland, in July 2007. As the FBI increasingly devotes its attention to counterterrorism efforts, will local police departments be able to effectively investigate complex crimes despite less assistance from FBI experts?

© Shawn Thew/epa/Corbis

7. Combat major white-collar crime.

8. Combat significant violent crime.

9. Support federal, state, county, municipal, and international partners.

10. Upgrade technology to successfully perform the FBI's mission.

The advancement of the FBI's mission requires skilled professionals in addition to the traditional law enforcement-trained special agents. The emphasis on counterterrorism led to an increase in intelligence analysts within the agency, from 1,023 in September 2001 to more than 2,100 in April 2008. In addition, the number of foreign-language specialists increased from 784 to more 1,300 in the same time period (Mueller, 2008).

As indicated by its priority list, the FBI has significant responsibilities for fighting terrorism and espionage against the United States. In addition, it continues its traditional mission of enforcing federal laws, such as those aimed at organized crime, corporate crime, corrupt government officials, and violators of civil rights laws. The bureau also provides valuable assistance to state and local law enforcement through its crime laboratory, training programs, and databases of fingerprints, stolen vehicles, and missing persons. With the growth of cybercrime, the FBI has become a leader in using technology to counteract crime as well as to prevent terrorism and espionage.

Specialization in Federal Law Enforcement

The FBI is the federal government's general law enforcement agency. Other federal agencies, however, enforce specific laws. Elsewhere in the Department of Justice, for example, the Drug Enforcement Administration (DEA) investigates illegal importation and sale of controlled drugs. The DEA's activities range from investigations of individual drug traffickers to monitoring of organized crime's involvement in the drug trade to coordinating drug enforcement efforts with state and local police as well as foreign governments. The DEA has more than 4,400 special agents who made nearly 28,000 arrests in 2007 (http://www.usdoj.gov/dea/statisticsp.html).

In January 2003 the law enforcement functions of the Bureau of Alcohol, Tobacco, Firearms, and Explosives (ATF) were transferred to the Department of Justice. Previously, the agency had been part of the Department of the Treasury. The ATF targets smuggling and illegal sales of guns and cigarettes. It also investigates bombings through the work of its field agents and laboratory scientists.

The Department of Justice also contains the U.S. Marshals Service. Federal marshals provide security at courthouses, transport federal prisoners, protect witnesses, and pursue fugitives within the United States who are wanted for domestic criminal charges or who are sought by police officials in other countries. Because of the FBI's increased emphasis on terrorism, its agents are now less involved in the pursuit of fugitives. This development increased the marshals' responsibilities for this duty. In 2007, U.S. marshals apprehended more than 36,000 fugitives on federal warrants and assisted in the capture of 56,600 individuals wanted by local police departments (U.S. Marshals Service, 2008). At the same time, the shooting of a state judge in an Atlanta courthouse and the murders of the husband and mother of a federal judge in Chicago in 2005 increased pressure on the marshals to evaluate and strengthen security for federal judges and their courtrooms.

As described in Chapter 3, several federal law enforcement agencies were reorganized and relocated in conjunction with the creation of the Department of Homeland Security. These agencies include those responsible for Customs and Border Protection, formerly known as the Customs Service and the Border Patrol, the Secret Service, and the Transportation Security Administration. The Secret Service was created in 1865 to combat counterfeit currency. After the assassination of President William McKinley in 1901, it received the additional duty of providing security for the president of the United States, other high officials, and their families. The Secret Service has 2,100 special agents in Washington, D.C., and field offices throughout the United States. It also has 1,200 uniformed police officers who provide security at the White House, the vice president's residence, and foreign embassies in Washington.

Many other federal agencies include law enforcement personnel. Some of these agencies are well recognized, but others are not. Within the Department of the Interior, for example, officers responsible for law enforcement serve as part of the National Park Service. Other officers in the Fish and Wildlife Service protect wildlife habitats, prevent illegal hunting, and investigate illegal trafficking of wildlife. Many people know about conservation officers and other law enforcement officials, such as postal inspectors in the Office of Inspector General of the U.S. Postal Service. By contrast, few people realize that special agents in the U.S. Department of Education investigate student loan fraud, and similar officers in the U.S. Department of Health and Human Services investigate fraud in Medicare and Medicaid programs. Law enforcement functions exist in many federal agencies, including those whose overall mission has little to do with the criminal justice system.

The responsibilities and activities of the U.S. Secret Service, including career opportunities at the agency, are described at their web page. To link to this website, go to *The American System of Criminal Justice* 12e companion site at academic.cengage.com/criminaljustice/cole.

Internationalization of U.S. Law Enforcement

Law enforcement agencies of the U.S. government have increasingly stationed officers overseas, a fact little known by the general public (Nadelmann, 1993). In a shrinking world with a global economy, terrorism, electronic communications, and jet aircraft, much crime is transnational, giving rise to a host of international criminal law enforcement tasks. American law enforcement is being "exported" in response to increased international terrorism, drug trafficking, smuggling of illegal immigrants, violations of U.S. securities laws, and money laundering, as well as the potential theft of nuclear materials.

To meet these challenges, U.S. agencies have dramatically increased the number of officers stationed in foreign countries. The FBI has 70 overseas offices known as Legal Attaches or Legats. These offices focus on coordination with law enforcement personnel in other countries. Their activities are limited by the formal agreements negotiated between the United States and each host country. In many other countries, American agents are authorized only to gather information and facilitate communications between countries. American agencies are especially active in working with other countries on counterterrorism, drug trafficking, and cybercrime. As described by FBI Director Mueller (2008):

> These Legats are the FBI's first responders on the global front, from assisting our British counterparts in the London bombings to finding the man responsible for the attempted assassination of President Bush in Tbilisi, Georgia. We train together; we work hand-in-hand on multinational task forces and investigations.

According to Mueller (2008), these international partnerships help the United States find people who help to finance terrorism, help prevent terrorists from getting access to nuclear materials, and contribute to investigations of child pornography and human trafficking.

Interpol, the International Criminal Police Organization, was created in 1946 to foster cooperation among the world's police forces. Based today in Lyon, France, Interpol maintains an intelligence databank and serves as a clearinghouse for information gathered by agencies of its 186 member nations. Interpol officially describes its four core functions providing:

1. Secure global police communications
2. Data services and databases for police
3. Support to police services
4. Police training and development

In 2008, Interpol's six priority crime areas were: (1) drugs and criminal organizations, (2) public safety and terrorism, (3) financial and high-tech crime, (4) trafficking in human beings, (5) fugitive apprehension, and (6) corruption (http://www.interpol.int). Many criminal suspects and prison escapees have been caught after fleeing to a different country because Interpol is able to disseminate information about fugitives. Despite the benefits of international cooperation, Interpol's secretary-general has complained that individual countries have not shared enough information with Interpol in a timely manner (Noble, 2006). It appears that countries may be wary of sharing information about terrorism and other investigations or they are too inclined to think of specific events as "local" and not even consider whether it would be worthwhile to explore whether there are international connections behind a specific incident of criminal or terrorist activity.

The U.S. Interpol unit, the U.S. National Central Bureau, is a division of the Department of Justice. Based in Washington, DC, this bureau facilitates communication with foreign police agencies. It has a permanent staff plus officers assigned by 13 federal agencies including the FBI, the Secret Service, and the DEA. Interpol has also formed links with state and local police forces in the United States.

International involvement by American law enforcement officials extends beyond the activities of federal agencies. Since the end of the cold war, American police organizations have assisted United Nations peacekeeping operations in Bosnia, Cyprus, Haiti, Kosovo, Panama, and Somalia. In these countries more than 3,000 police officers from around the world "have engaged in monitoring, mentoring, training, and generally assisting their local counterparts." Effective policing and following the rule of law are considered essential elements for achieving peace, safety, and security within a society. In countries that are developing democratic systems of government, trainers emphasize that policing is to be conducted by civilian police forces whose officers are trained in basic law enforcement skills and who display respect for the law and for human rights. The U.S. government relied on private companies to supply police trainers and training facilities in Iraq and Afghanistan. Evaluation reports have questioned whether these private companies have been effective in providing the needed

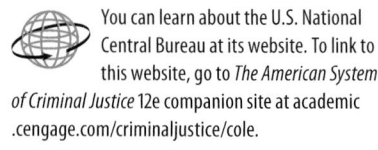
You can learn about the U.S. National Central Bureau at its website. To link to this website, go to *The American System of Criminal Justice* 12e companion site at academic.cengage.com/criminaljustice/cole.

To learn about the mission and accomplishments of Interpol, the international policing organization, see its website. To link to this website, go to *The American System of Criminal Justice* 12e companion site at academic.cengage.com/criminaljustice/cole.

training for countries that desperately need professional police in order to achieve stability and order (Glanz and Rohde, 2006; Schmitt and Rohde, 2007).

State Agencies

Every state except Hawaii has its own law enforcement agency with statewide jurisdiction. In about half of the states, state police agencies carry out a wide range of law enforcement tasks. The others have state highway patrols with limited authority, primarily the task of enforcing traffic laws. The American reluctance to centralize police power has generally kept state police forces from replacing local ones.

Before 1900 only Texas had a state police force. The Texas Rangers, a quasi-military force, protected white settlers from bandits and Native American raids. It had already been established by 1836, when Texas declared its independence from Mexico. Modern state police forces were organized after the turn of the century, mainly as a wing of the executive branch that would enforce the law when local officials did not. The Pennsylvania State Constabulary, formed in 1905, was the first such force. By 1925 almost all of the states had police forces.

All state forces regulate traffic on main highways, and two-thirds of the states have also given them general police powers. In only about a dozen populous states such as Massachusetts, Michigan, New Jersey, New York, and Pennsylvania can these forces perform law enforcement tasks across the state. For the most part, they operate only in areas where no other form of police protection exists or where local officers ask for their help. In many states, for example, the crime lab is run by the state police as a means of assisting local law enforcement agencies.

You can learn about the responsibilities and activities of the California Highway Patrol at its website. Like the websites of other law enforcement agencies, the Highway Patrol's site also provides information on career opportunities. To link to this website, go to *The American System of Criminal Justice* 12e companion site at academic.cengage.com/criminaljustice/cole.

County Agencies

Sheriffs are found in almost every one of the 3,100 counties in the United States (except those in Alaska), employing 175,018 full-time sworn officers. Sheriffs' departments are responsible for policing rural areas, but over time, especially in the Northeast, the state or local police have assumed many of these criminal justice functions. In parts of the South and West, however, the sheriff's department is a well-organized force. In 33 states, sheriffs are elected and hold the position of chief law enforcement officer in the county. Even when the sheriff's office is well organized, however, it may lack jurisdiction over cities and towns. In these situations, the sheriff and his or her deputies patrol unincorporated parts of the county or small towns that do not have police forces of their own.

In addition to performing law enforcement tasks, the sheriff often serves as an officer of the court; sheriffs may operate jails, serve court orders, and provide bailiffs, who maintain order in courtrooms. In many counties, politics mix with law enforcement, in that sheriffs may be able to appoint their political supporters as deputies and bailiffs. In other places, such as Los Angeles County and Oregon's Multnomah County, the sheriff's department is staffed by professionals who are hired through competitive civil service processes.

Native American Tribal Police

Through treaties with the United States, Native American tribes are separate, sovereign nations that maintain a significant degree of legal autonomy. They have the power to enforce tribal criminal laws against everyone on their lands, including non–Native Americans (Mentzer, 1996). The last national census found 2.4 million Native Americans and Alaska Natives belonging to approximately five hundred tribes (Ogunwole, 2006). However, many tribes are not recognized by the federal government, and many Native Americans do not live on reservations. Traditionally, Native American reservations have been policed either by federal officers of the Bureau of Indian Affairs (BIA) or by their own tribal police. The Bureau of Justice Statistics identified 171 tribal law enforcement agencies with a total of 2,303 full-time sworn officers (Hickman, 2003). An additional 320 full-time sworn officers of the BIA provide law enforcement services on other reservations (Reaves, 2006). As the number of non–Native Americans entering reservations for recreational purposes (such as gambling) has increased, criminal jurisdiction disputes have as well. Tribal police agencies often face difficult challenges with inadequate resources (Wakeling, Jorgensen and Michaelson, 2001).

Municipal Agencies

The police departments of cities and towns have general law enforcement authority. City police forces range in size from nearly 36,000 full-time sworn officers in the New York City Police Department to only one sworn officer in 561 small towns. There are 446,974 full-time sworn local police officers. Sworn personnel are officers with the power to make arrests. Nearly three-quarters of municipal police departments employ fewer than 25 sworn officers. Nearly 90 percent of local police agencies serve populations of 25,000 or less, but half of all sworn officers work in cities of at least 100,000. The five largest police departments—New York, Chicago, Los Angeles, Philadelphia, and Houston—together employ nearly 16 percent of all local police officers (Hickman and Reaves, 2006).

In a metropolitan area composed of a central city and many suburbs, policing is usually divided among agencies at all levels of government, giving rise to conflicts between jurisdictions that may interfere with efficient use of police resources. The city and each suburb buys its own equipment and deploys its officers without coordinating with those of nearby jurisdictions. In some areas with large populations, agreements have been made to enhance cooperation between jurisdictions.

In essence, the United States is a nation of small police forces, each of which is authorized, funded, and operated within the limits of its own jurisdiction. This is in direct contrast to the centralized police forces found in many other countries. For example, in France the police are a national force divided between the Ministry of Interior and the Ministry of Defense. All police officers report to these national departments, as the Comparative Perspective shows.

Because of the fragmentation of police agencies in the United States, each jurisdiction develops its own enforcement goals and policies. For example, 90 percent of municipal police departments serving cities with population of 100,000 or more have a written policy on conducting strip searches but only 43 percent of departments serving communities of 2,500 or smaller have such written policies. Similarly 68 percent of communities with populations from 250,000 to 500,000 have formal, written plans for community policing while fewer than 30 percent of departments serving cities of 50,000 or smaller have such plans (Hickman and Reaves, 2006). These differences may reflect the varied contexts of particular jurisdictions, such as urban neighborhoods instead of rural areas. But they also may reflect the different philosophies and goals of these agencies leaders. Each agency must make choices about how to organize itself and use its resources to achieve its goals.

Despite this fragmentation, law enforcement agencies often seek to coordinate their efforts. Most recently, issues of homeland security and emergency preparedness have drawn agencies together to plan their coordinated responses to large-

COMPARATIVE PERSPECTIVE

Organization of the Police in France

France has a population of about 59 million and a unitary form of government. Political power and decision making are highly centralized in bureaucracies located in Paris. The entire country has a single criminal code and standardized criminal justice procedures. The country is divided into 96 territories known as departments and further divided into districts and municipalities. In each district, a commissaire of the republic represents the central government and exercises supervision over the local mayors.

Police functions are divided between two separate forces under the direction of two ministries of the central government. With more than 200,000 personnel employed in police duties, France has a ratio of law enforcement officers to the general population that is greater than that of the United States or England.

The older police force, the Gendarmerie Nationale, with nearly 90,000 officers, is under the military and is responsible for policing about 95 percent of the country's territory. The gendarmerie patrols the highways, rural areas, and those communities with populations of less than 10,000. Members are organized into brigades or squads collectively known as the Departmental Gendarmerie. They operate from fixed points, reside in their duty area, and constitute the largest component of the force. A second agency, the Mobile Gendarmerie, may be deployed anywhere in the country. These are essentially riot police; their forces are motorized, have tanks, and even have light aircraft. The Republican Guard, the third component of the Gendarmerie, is stationed in Paris, protects the president, and performs ceremonial functions.

The Police Nationale is under the Ministry of the Interior and operates mainly in urban centers with populations greater than 10,000. The Police Nationale is divided into the Directorate of Urban Police, which is responsible for policing the cities with patrol and investigative functions, and the Directorate of Criminal Investigation, which provides regional detective services and pursues cases beyond the scope of the city police or the gendarmerie. Another division, the Air and Frontier Police, is responsible for border protection. The Republican Security Companies are the urban version of the Mobile Gendarmerie but without the heavy armament.

In addition to traditional patrol and investigative functions, the Police Nationale also contains units responsible for the collection of intelligence information and for the countering of foreign subversion. The Directorate of General Intelligence and Gambling has 2,500 officers and has as its purpose the gathering of "intelligence of a political, social, and economic nature necessary for the information of government." This includes data from public opinion surveys, mass media, periodicals, and information gathered through the infiltration of various political, labor, and social groups. The Directorate of Counterespionage has the mission of countering the efforts of foreign agents on French soil intent on impairing the security of the country.

The police system of the central government of France is powerful; the number, armament, legal powers, and links to the military are most impressive. The turbulent history of France before and after the revolution of 1789 gave rise to the need for the government to be able to assert authority. Since the 1930s France has had to deal not only with crime but also with political instability. The Nazi invasion of 1940, weak governments following World War II, the Algerian crisis in 1958, and student rioting in 1968 all brought conditions that nearly toppled the existing regime. The need to maintain order in the streets would seem to be a major concern of the government. This concern has continued in recent years as police officers have faced civil disturbances by protesting students as well as riots by poor, disaffected youths in the Paris suburbs. In the latter case, dozens were wounded by shotgun pellets, gasoline bombs, and rocks.

Source: Adapted from Philip John Stead, The Police of France (New York: Macmillan, 1983), 1–12. Copyright © 1983 by Macmillan Publishing Company, a division of Macmillan, Inc. Reprinted by permission of The Gale Group. Also "European Police and Justice Systems: France" (2008) http://www.interpol.int; Ariane Bernard, "Youths Clash With the Police in France," New York Times, November 27, 2007, www.nytimes.com; Elaine Sciolino, "Paris Suburbs Riots Called 'A Lot Worse' Than in 2005," International Herald Tribune, November 27, 2007, http://www.int.com.

scale emergencies. Agencies also work together through such initiatives as "Amber Alerts," the plan used in increasing numbers of metropolitan areas to notify all police agencies and media outlets immediately if a child has been abducted.

checkpoint

11. What is the jurisdiction of federal law enforcement agencies?
12. Why are some law enforcement agencies of the U.S. government located overseas?
13. What are the functions of most state police agencies?
14. Besides law enforcement, what functions do sheriffs perform?
15. What are the main characteristics of the organization of the police in the United States?

POLICE FUNCTIONS

The police are expected to maintain order, enforce the law, and provide services as they seek to prevent crime. However, they perform other tasks as well, many of them having little to do with crime and justice and more to do with community service. They direct traffic, handle accidents and illnesses, stop noisy parties, find missing persons, enforce licensing regulations, provide ambulance services, take disturbed people into protective custody, and so on. The list is long and varies from place to place. Some researchers have suggested that the police have more in common with social service agencies than with the criminal justice system.

The American Bar Association has published a list of police goals and functions that includes the following (Goldstein, 1977: 5):

1. Prevent and control conduct considered threatening to life and property (serious crime).

2. Aid people who are in danger of harm, such as the victim of a criminal attack.

3. Protect constitutional rights, such as the right of free speech and assembly.

4. Facilitate the movement of people and vehicles.

5. Aid those who cannot care for themselves: the drunk or the addicted, the mentally ill, the disabled, the old, and the young.

6. Resolve conflict, whether between individuals, groups of individuals, or individuals and government.

7. Identify problems that could become more serious for the citizen, for the police, or for government.

8. Create a feeling of security in the community.

How did the police gain such broad responsibilities? In many places the police are the only public agency that is available 7 days a week and 24 hours a day to respond to calls for help. They are usually best able to investigate many kinds of problems. Moreover, the power to use force when necessary allows them to intervene in problematic situations.

We can classify the functions of the police into three groups, each of which can contribute to crime prevention: (1) order maintenance, (2) law enforcement, and (3) service. Police agencies divide their resources among these functions on the basis of community need, citizen requests, and departmental policy.

Order Maintenance

order maintenance
The police function of preventing behavior that disturbs or threatens to disturb the public peace or that involves face-to-face conflict among two or more people. In such situations, the police exercise discretion in deciding whether a law has been broken.

The **order maintenance** function is a broad mandate to prevent behavior that either disturbs or threatens to disturb the peace or involves face-to-face conflict among two or more people. A domestic quarrel, a noisy drunk, loud music in the night, a beggar on the street, a tavern brawl—all are forms of disorder that may require action by the police.

Unlike most laws that define specific acts as illegal, laws regulating disorderly conduct deal with ambiguous situations that different police officers could view in different ways. For many crimes, determining when the law has been broken is easy. However, order maintenance requires officers to decide not only whether a law has been broken but also whether any action should be taken and, if so, who should be blamed. In a bar fight, for example, the officer must decide who started the fight, whether an arrest should be made for assault, and whether to arrest other people besides those who started the conflict.

Patrol officers deal mainly with behavior that either disturbs or threatens to disturb the peace. They confront the public in ambiguous situations and have wide discretion in matters that affect people's lives. If an officer decides to arrest someone for disorderly conduct, that person could spend time in jail and lose his or her job even without being convicted of the crime.

Officers often must make judgments in order maintenance situations. They may be required to help people in trouble, manage crowds, supervise various kinds of services, and help people who are not fully accountable for what they do. The officers have a high degree of discretion and control over how such situations will develop. Patrol officers are not subject to direct control. They have the power to arrest, but they may also decide not to make an arrest. The order maintenance function is made more complex by the fact that the patrol officer is normally expected to "handle" a situation rather than to enforce the law, usually in an emotionally charged atmosphere. In controlling a crowd outside a rock concert, for example, the arrest of an unruly person may restore order by removing a troublemaker and also serving as a warning to others that they could be arrested if they do not cooperate. However, an arrest may cause the crowd to become hostile toward the officers, making things worse. Officers cannot always predict precisely how their discretionary decisions will promote or hinder order maintenance.

To uphold important American values of equal treatment and respect for constitutional rights, police officers must make decisions fairly and within the boundaries of their authority. Officers may face a difficult, immediate situation that leads them to use force or target specific individuals for restraint. The volatile context of order maintenance situations, where emotions are running high and some people may be out of control, can produce anger and hostility toward officers. If officers must stop a disturbance in a bar, for example, they will inevitably seek to restrain individuals who are contributing to the disturbance. However, if they cannot restrain everyone, they may choose specific individuals or focus their attention on the people standing close at hand. As a result, some citizens may believe that officers are applying unequal treatment or targeting individuals because of their race or ethnicity. Thus the immediacy of order maintenance problems and the need to make quick decisions can create risks that officers will be viewed as acting in a manner contrary to American values.

Police in East Lansing, Michigan, used tear gas and arrested more than 50 people in April 2008 when an outdoor party adjacent to Michigan State University's campus attracted several thousand participants and turned into a civil disturbance with property damage and bottle throwing. In such situations, police officers must control their own emotions and avoid escalating the conflict even as they risk injury from thrown objects. Because each situation can take on a life of its own, is it possible to train officers to make appropriate decisions in all situations?

© Kevin W. Fowler/Lansing State Journal

Law Enforcement

The **law enforcement** function applies to situations in which the law has been violated and the offender needs to be identified or located and then apprehended. Police officers who focus on law enforcement serve in specialized branches such as the vice squad and the burglary detail. Although the patrol officer may be the first officer at the scene of a crime, in serious cases a detective usually prepares the case for prosecution by bringing together all the evidence for the prosecuting attorney. When the offender is identified but not located, the detective conducts the search. If the offender is not identified, the detective must analyze clues to find out who committed the crime.

The police often portray themselves as enforcers of the law, but many factors interfere with how effectively they can do so. For example, when a property crime is committed, the perpetrator usually has some time to get away. This limits the ability of the police to identify, locate, and arrest the suspect. Burglaries, for instance, usually occur when people are away from home. The crime may not be discovered until hours or days have passed. The effectiveness

law enforcement
The police function of controlling crime by intervening in situations in which the law has clearly been violated and the police need to identify and apprehend the guilty person.

of the police also decreases when assault or robbery victims cannot identify the offender. Victims often delay in calling the police, reducing the chances that a suspect will be apprehended.

As in the case of order maintenance, the important American values of equal treatment and respect for rights can be threatened if officers do not make their law enforcement decisions professionally and try to be objective. If people believe that such decisions target specific neighborhoods or particular ethnic groups, police actions might generate suspicion and hostility. People in some communities have complained that police enforce narcotics laws primarily in poor neighborhoods populated by members of minority groups. Such perceptions of the police clash with the American values of equal treatment and respect for rights.

Service

service
The police function of providing assistance to the public, usually in matters unrelated to crime.

Police perform a broad range of services, especially for lower-income citizens, that are not related to crime. This **service** function—providing first aid, rescuing animals, helping the disoriented, and so on—has become a major police function. Crime prevention has also became a major component of police service to the community. Through education and community organizing, the police can help the public take steps to prevent crime.

Research has shown how important the service function is to the community. Analysis of more than 26,000 calls to 21 police departments found that about 80 percent of requests for police assistance do not involve crimes; the largest percentage of calls, 21 percent, were requests for information (Scott, 1981). Because the police are available 24 hours a day, people turn to them in times of trouble. Many departments provide information, operate ambulance services, locate missing persons, check locks on vacationers' homes, and intervene in suicide attempts. For example, if one looks at the records of calls to police in San Jose, California, during April 2008, the categories of frequent calls include such service categories as automobile collisions, requests to check on the welfare of someone, and complaints about someone parking illegally. Even in the category labeled "disturbances," many of the calls are likely to result in the police discovering that a brief argument between spouses has ended, police asking someone to turn down loud music, or another situation that does not relate to a crime (http://www.sjpd.org/).

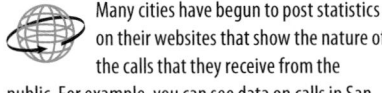 Many cities have begun to post statistics on their websites that show the nature of the calls that they receive from the public. For example, you can see data on calls in San Jose, California, at their web page. See the city's figures and examine how many of the calls are for service matters rather than order maintenance and law enforcement. To link to this website, go to *The American System of Criminal Justice* 12e companion site at academic.cengage.com/criminaljustice/cole.

Critics claim that valuable resources are being inappropriately diverted from law enforcement to services. However, performing service functions can help police control crime. Through the service function, officers gain knowledge about the community, and citizens come to trust the police. Checking the security of buildings clearly helps prevent crime, but other activities—dealing with runaways, drunks, and public quarrels—may help solve problems before they lead to criminal behavior.

Implementing the Mandate

Although people may depend most heavily on the order maintenance and service functions of the police, they act as though law enforcement—the catching of lawbreakers—is the most important function. According to public opinion polls, the crime-fighter image of the police remains firmly rooted in citizens' minds and is the main reason given by recruits for joining the force.

Public support for budgets is greatest when the crime-fighting function is stressed. This emphasis appears in the organization of big-city departments. The officers who perform this function, such as detectives, have high status. The focus on crime leads to the creation of special units to deal with homicide, burglary, and auto theft. All other tasks fall to the patrol division. In some departments, this pattern creates morale problems because extra resources are allocated and prestige devoted to a function that is concerned with a small percentage of the problems brought to the police. In essence, police are public servants who keep the peace, but their organization reinforces their own law enforcement image and the public's focus on crime fighting.

But do the police prevent crime? David Bayley claims that they do not. He says that "the experts know it, the police know it, but the public does not know it" (Bayley, 1994: 3). He bases this claim on two facts. First, no link has been found between the number of police officers and crime rates. For example, Philadelphia and Baltimore are major cities with a relatively high number of police officers for their respective populations. Philadelphia has 46 officers per 10,000 residents and Baltimore has 52 officers for every 10,000 residents. Yet, in 2006 these cities had relatively high rates of violent crime: 152 violent crimes per 10,000 people for Philadelphia and 170 violent crimes per 10,000 residents for Baltimore. By contrast, San Antonio, Texas (17 officers per 10,000 residents) and Indianapolis (15 officers per 10,000 residents) have significantly fewer police officers for the populations of their respective cities and they also had much lower rates of violent crime: 61 violent crimes per 10,000 residents for San Antonio and 96 violent crimes per 10,000 residents for Indianapolis (FBI, 2007; Hickman and Reaves, 2006).

Second, the main strategies used by modern police have little or no effect on crime. Those strategies are street patrolling by uniformed officers, rapid response to emergency calls, and expert investigation of crime by detectives. Bayley says that the police believe these strategies are essential to protect public safety, yet no evidence exists that they achieve this goal (1994: 5).

Peter Manning's observation of many years ago remains valid today: The police have an impossible mandate:

> To much of the public the police are seen as alertly ready to respond to citizen demands, as crime fighters, as an efficient, bureaucratic, highly organized force that keeps society from falling into chaos. The policeman himself considers the essence of his role to be the dangerous and heroic enterprise of crook-catching and the watchful prevention of crimes.... They do engage in chases, in gunfights, in careful sleuthing. But these are rare events. (Manning, 1971: 157)

checkpoint

16. What is the order maintenance function? What are officers expected to do in situations where they must maintain order?
17. How do law enforcement situations compare with order maintenance situations?

ORGANIZATION OF THE POLICE

Most police agencies are organized in a military manner with a structure of ranks and responsibilities. But police departments are also bureaucracies designed to achieve objectives efficiently. Bureaucracies are characterized by a division of labor, a chain of command with clear lines of authority, and rules to guide the activities of staff. Police organization differs somewhat from place to place, depending on the size of the jurisdiction, the characteristics of the population, and the nature of the local crime problems. However, the basic characteristics of a bureaucracy appear in all sizeable departments.

Bureaucratic Elements

The police department in Phoenix, Arizona, reveals the elements of bureaucracy in a typical urban police force. Figure 5.1 shows the Phoenix Police Department's organizational chart, which we refer to in the following discussion.

FIGURE 5.1

Organization of the Phoenix, Arizona, Police Department

This is a typical structure. Note the major divisions of headquarters, management and support services, investigation, and field operations (patrol).
Specialized and geographic divisions are found within these divisions.

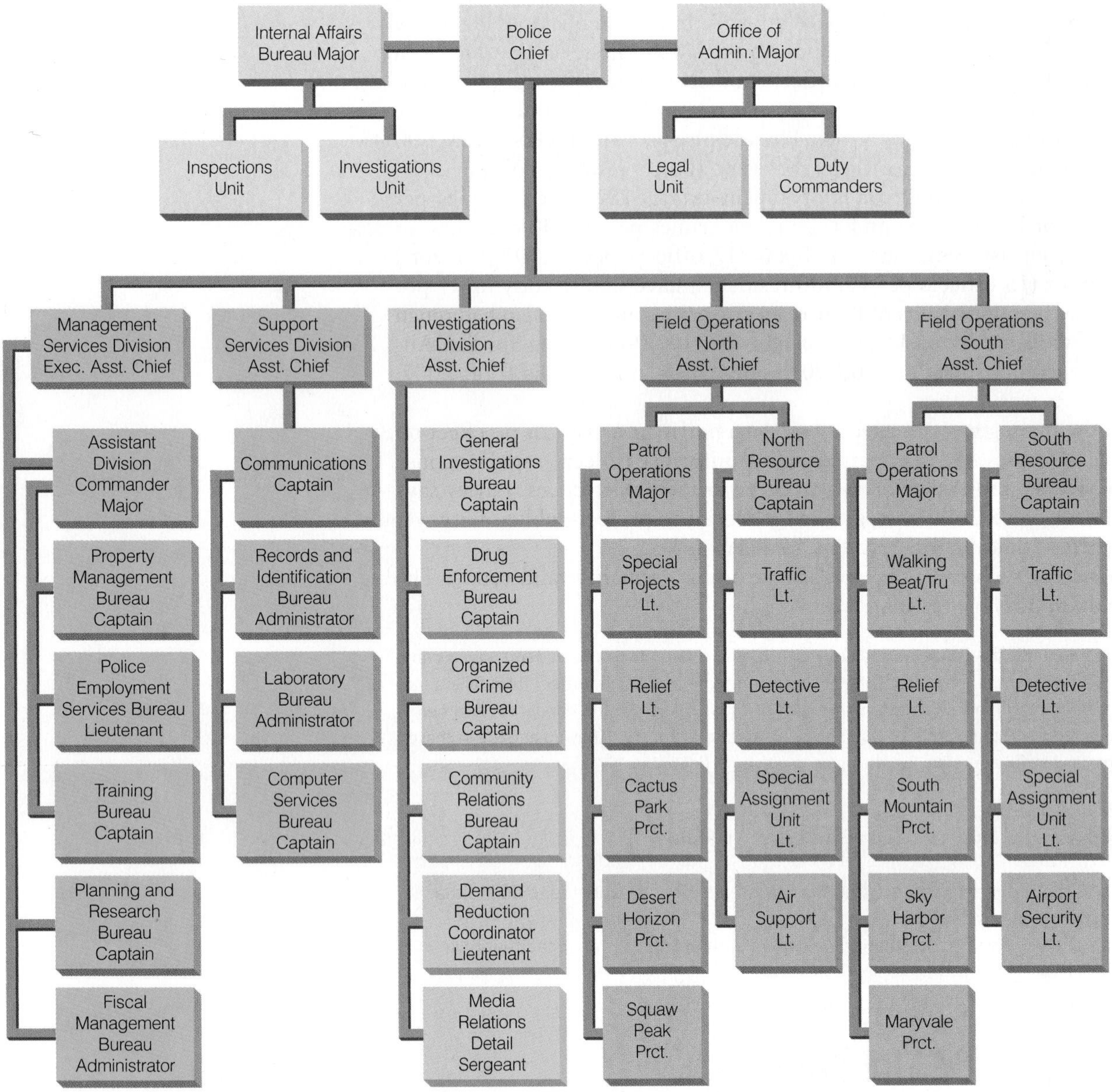

Internal Affairs Bureau Major — Police Chief — Office of Admin. Major

Inspections Unit

Investigations Unit

Legal Unit

Duty Commanders

Management Services Division Exec. Asst. Chief

- Assistant Division Commander Major
- Property Management Bureau Captain
- Police Employment Services Bureau Lieutenant
- Training Bureau Captain
- Planning and Research Bureau Captain
- Fiscal Management Bureau Administrator

Support Services Division Asst. Chief

- Communications Captain
- Records and Identification Bureau Administrator
- Laboratory Bureau Administrator
- Computer Services Bureau Captain

Investigations Division Asst. Chief

- General Investigations Bureau Captain
- Drug Enforcement Bureau Captain
- Organized Crime Bureau Captain
- Community Relations Bureau Captain
- Demand Reduction Coordinator Lieutenant
- Media Relations Detail Sergeant

Field Operations North Asst. Chief

- Patrol Operations Major
  - Special Projects Lt.
  - Relief Lt.
  - Cactus Park Prct.
  - Desert Horizon Prct.
  - Squaw Peak Prct.
- North Resource Bureau Captain
  - Traffic Lt.
  - Detective Lt.
  - Special Assignment Unit Lt.
  - Air Support Lt.

Field Operations South Asst. Chief

- Patrol Operations Major
  - Walking Beat/Tru Lt.
  - Relief Lt.
  - South Mountain Prct.
  - Sky Harbor Prct.
  - Maryvale Prct.
- South Resource Bureau Captain
  - Traffic Lt.
  - Detective Lt.
  - Special Assignment Unit Lt.
  - Airport Security Lt.

Source: City of Phoenix, Arizona, Police Department, *Annual Report,* 1990.

Division of Labor

The Phoenix department is divided into four divisions, marked in Figure 5.1 by different colors: Headquarters, Management and Support Services, Investigation, and Field Operations (patrol). Within the Management and Support Services division and the Investigations division, authority is further delegated to bureaus and units that have special functions (for example, property management, training, laboratory, organized crime). The Field Operations divisions are further divided into geographic units for patrol in precincts and into specialized units to deal, for example, with traffic or special projects.

The bureaucratic organization of an urban police department such as Phoenix allows the allocation of resources and the supervision of personnel, taking into account the needs and problems of each district.

Chain and Unity of Command

The military character of police departments is illustrated by the chain of command according to ranks—officer, commander, sergeant, lieutenant, captain, major, and chief (see Figure 5.1). These make clear the powers and duties of officers at each level. Relationships between superiors and subordinates emphasize discipline, control, and accountability. Each officer has an immediate supervisor who has authority and responsibility for the actions of those below. These values help officers mobilize resources. They also ensure that civil liberties are protected; if police officers are accountable to their superiors, they are less likely to abuse their authority by needlessly interfering with the freedom and rights of citizens.

Rules and Procedures

Complex bureaucracies such as police departments depend on clearly stated rules and procedures to guide officers. These rules are usually found in operations manuals so that officers will know the procedures they should take when confronted by particular types of incidents. In some departments the rules are so detailed that they tell officers when they may unholster their gun, what precautions to take when stopping a vehicle, arrest procedures, and actions to take in domestic squabbles. Obviously, rules cannot define all police actions, and the specificity of some rules detract from law enforcement effectiveness. Critics say that the rules of too many departments are hidebound and cannot possibly cover all circumstances. They argue that officers must be encouraged to use discretion without fear of sanctions for not strictly following the rules.

Operational Units

All but the smallest police departments assign officers to operational units that focus on specific functions: patrol, investigation, traffic, vice, and juvenile. These units perform the basic tasks of crime prevention and control. The patrol and investigation (detective) units form the core of the modern department. The patrol unit handles a wide range of functions, including preventing crime, catching suspects, mediating quarrels, helping the ill, and giving aid at accidents. The investigation unit identifies, apprehends, and collects evidence against lawbreakers who commit serious crimes. Because of their overlapping duties, the separation of patrol and investigation can cause problems. While the investigation unit usually focuses on murder, rape, and major robberies, the patrol unit has joint responsibility for investigating those crimes but is also solely responsible for investigating the more numerous lesser crimes.

The extent to which departments create specialized units may depend on the size of the city and its police force. Many departments have traffic units, but only those in midsized to large cities also have vice and juvenile units. Large departments usually have an internal affairs section to investigate charges of corruption against officers, as well as other problems associated with the staff and officers. The juvenile unit works with young people, focusing mainly on crime prevention. All special units depend on the patrol officers for information and assistance.

Because of the traditional top-down military structure of the police, with designated ranks and superior officers who have command authority over inferior officers, as well as the development of specific law enforcement specializations,

civic engagement
your role in the system

A new mayor has proposed that the police department be reorganized by merging it with the fire department and the emergency medical response department. The proposal would require that every front-line officer be trained to work as a police officer, firefighter, and emergency medical technician. Thus they could all perform any safety service needed by the public. *Make a list of the arguments supporting and opposing this proposal. Do you support the proposal?* Then look at the description of the combined police-fire department in Amberley Village, Ohio, and investigate such departments in other cities such as Kalamazoo, Michigan. To link to this website, go to *The American System of Criminal Justice* 12e companion site at academic.cengage.com/criminaljustice/cole.

citizens may feel as if they have little influence over the organization of the police in their communities. It is possible that they can lobby the city council to create a new, specialized division to deal with a specific problem, such as juvenile delinquency, traffic, or vice, but it is generally difficult to think about a drastic restructuring of police organization and functions. Consider the issue in "Civic Engagement: Your Role in the System" and think about whether you have any ideas to improve police organization.

The Police Bureaucracy and the Criminal Justice System

The police play an important role as a bureaucracy within the broader criminal justice system. Three issues arise in the organizational context within which the police operate.

First, the police are the gateway through which information and individuals enter the justice system. Police have the discretion to determine which suspects will be arrested. Cases that are sent to the prosecutor for charging and then to the courts for adjudication begin with an officer's decision that there is probable cause for an arrest. The care taken by the officer in making the arrest and collecting evidence greatly affects the ultimate success of the prosecution. The outcome of the case, whether through plea bargaining by lawyers or through a trial with a judge and jury, hinges on the officer's judgment and evidence-gathering activities.

Second, police administration is influenced by the fact that the outcome of a case is largely in the hands of others. The police bring suspects into the criminal justice process, but they cannot control the decisions of prosecutors and judges. In some cases, the police officers feel that their efforts have been wasted. For example, the prosecutor sometimes agrees to a plea bargain that does not, in the eyes of the officer, adequately punish the offender. The potential for conflict between police and other decision makers in the system is increased by the difference in social status between police officers, who often do not have college degrees, and lawyers and judges, who have graduate degrees.

Third, as part of a bureaucracy, police officers are expected to observe rules and follow the orders of superiors while at the same time making independent, discretionary judgments. They must stay within the chain of command yet also make choices in response to events on the streets. The tension between these two tasks affects many aspects of their daily work, which we shall explore further later in this chapter and in Chapter 6.

checkpoint

18. What are three characteristics of a bureaucracy?
19. What are the five operational units of police departments with sufficient size for specialization?

POLICE POLICY

The police cannot enforce every law and catch every lawbreaker. Legal rules limit the ways officers can investigate and pursue offenders. For example, the constitutional ban on unreasonable searches and seizures prevents police from investigating most crimes without a search warrant.

Because the police have limited resources, they cannot have officers on every street at all times of the day and night. This means that police executives must develop policies regarding how the members of their department will implement their mandate. These policies guide officers in deciding which offenses to address most and which tactics to use. They develop policies, for example, on whether to have officers patrol neighborhoods in cars or on foot. Changes in policy—such as increasing the size of the night patrol or tolerating prostitution and other public order offenses—affect the amount of crime that gets official attention and the system's ability to deal with offenders.

Police frequently emphasize their role as crime fighters. As a result, police in most communities focus on the crimes covered by the FBI's Uniform Crime Reports. These crimes make headlines, and politicians point to them when they call for increases in the police budget. They are also the crimes that poor people tend to commit. Voters pressure politicians and the police to enforce laws that help them feel safe in their daily lives. They see occupational crimes, such as forgery, embezzlement, or tax fraud, as less threatening. Because these crimes are less visible and more difficult to solve, they receive less attention from the police.

Decisions about how police resources will be used affect the types of people who are arrested and passed through the criminal justice system. Think of the hard choices you would have to make if you were a police chief. Should more officers be sent into high-crime areas? Should more officers be assigned to the central business district during shopping hours? What should the mix of traffic control and crime fighting be? These questions have no easy answers. Police officials must answer them according to their goals and values.

American cities differ in racial, ethnic, economic, and government characteristics as well as in their degree of urbanization. These factors can affect the style of policing expected by the community. In a classic study, James Q. Wilson found that citizen expectations regarding police behavior affect the political process in the choice of the top police executive. Chiefs who run their departments in ways that antagonize the community tend not to stay in office very long. Wilson's key finding was that a city's political culture, which reflects its socioeconomic characteristics and its government organization, had a major impact on the style of policing found there. Wilson described three different styles of policing—the watchman, legalistic, and service styles (Wilson, 1968). Table 5.2 documents these styles of policing and the types of communities in which they appear.

Departments with a *watchman* style stress order maintenance. Patrol officers may ignore minor violations of the law, especially those involving traffic and juveniles, as long as there is order. The police exercise discretion and deal with many infractions in an informal way. Officers make arrests only for flagrant violations and when order cannot be maintained. The broad discretion exercised by officers can produce discrimination when officers do not treat members of different racial and ethnic groups in the same way.

In departments with a *legalistic* style, police work is marked by professionalism and an emphasis on law enforcement. Officers are expected to detain a high proportion of juvenile offenders, act vigorously against illicit enterprises, issue traffic tickets, and make a large number of misdemeanor arrests. They act as if a single standard of community conduct exists (as prescribed by the law) rather than different standards for juveniles, minorities, drunks, and other groups. Thus, although officers do not

TABLE 5.2　Styles of Policing

James Q. Wilson found three distinct styles of policing in the communities he studied. Each style emphasizes different police functions, and each is linked with the specific characteristics of the community.

Style	Defining Characterisics	Community Type
Watchman	Emphasis on maintaining order	Declining industrial city, mixed racial/ethnic composition, blue collar
Legalistic	Emphasis on law enforcement	Reform-minded city government, mixed socioeconomic composition
Service	Emphasis on service with balance between law enforcement and order maintenance	Middle-class suburban community

Source: Drawn from James Q. Wilson, *Varieties of Police Behavior* (Cambridge, MA: Harvard University Press, 1968).

discriminate in making arrests and issuing citations, the strict enforcement of laws, including traffic laws, can seem overly harsh to some groups in the community.

Suburban middle-class communities often experience a *service* style. Residents feel that they deserve individual treatment and expect the police to provide service. Burglaries and assaults are taken seriously, while minor infractions tend to be dealt with by informal means such as stern warnings. The police are expected to deal with the misdeeds of local residents in a personal, nonpublic way so as to avoid embarrassment.

In all cases, before officers investigate crimes or make arrests, each police chief decides on policies that will govern the level and type of enforcement in the community. Given that the police are the entry point to the criminal justice system, the decisions made by police officials affect all segments of the system. Just as community expectations shape decisions about enforcement goals and the allocation of police resources, they also shape the cases that prosecutors and correctional officials will handle.

checkpoint

20. What are the characteristics of the watchman style of policing?
21. What is the key feature of the legalistic style of policing?
22. Where are you likely to find the service style of policing?

POLICE ACTIONS

We have seen how the police are organized and which three functions of policing—law enforcement, order maintenance, and service—compose their mandate. We have also recognized that police officers must be guided by policies developed by their superiors as to how policing is to be implemented. Now let us look at the everyday actions of the police as they deal with citizens in often highly discretionary ways. We shall then discuss domestic violence to show how the police respond to serious problems.

Encounters between Police and Citizens

To carry out their mission, the police must have the public's confidence, because they depend on the public to help them identify crime and carry out investigations (see "What Americans Think"). Each year one in five Americans age 16 and older has face-to-face contact with law enforcement officers. In 2005, 40 percent of these contacts involved drivers stopped by a patrol officer. A third of the contacts occurred when police responded to a call for assistance or came to the scene of an automobile collision. Less than 6 percent of the contacts occurred when police were investigating a crime and less than 3 percent were the result of police suspecting a specific individual of criminal activity. Overall, 90 percent of people who had contact with the police believed that the police acted properly. However, among drivers stopped by the police, African Americans were less likely than whites or Hispanics to believe that the police had stopped them for a legitimate reason (Durose, Smith, and Langan, 2007). People's contacts with the police may shape their perceptions of the police and could affect their willingness to cooperate.

Although most people are willing to help the police, fear, self-interest, and other factors keep some from cooperating. Many people avoid calling the police, because they think it is not worth the effort and cost. They do not want to spend time filling out forms at the station, appearing as a witness, or confront-

WHAT AMERICANS THINK

Question: "I am going to read you a list of institutions in American society. Please tell me how much confidence you, yourself, have in each one—a great deal, quite a lot, some, or very little: the police?

Very little 12%

Some 33%

None 1%

Great deal/quite a lot 54%

Source: Bureau of Justice Statistics, *Sourcebook of Criminal Justice Statistics, 2007* (Washington, DC: U.S. Government Printing Office, 2008), Table 2.12.2007.

ing a neighbor or relative in court. In some low-income neighborhoods, citizens are reluctant to assist the police because their past experience has shown that contact with law enforcement "only brings trouble." Without information about a crime, the police may decide not to pursue an investigation. Clearly, then, citizens have some control over the work of the police through their decisions to call or not to call them.

Officers know that developing and maintaining effective communication with people is essential to their job. As Officer Marcus Laffey of the New York Police Department says, "If you can talk a good game as a cop, you're halfway there." He says that police use of "confrontation and force, of roundhouse punches and high speed chases makes the movies and the news, but what you say and how you say it come into play far more than anything you do with your stick or your gun, and can even prevent the need for them" (Laffey, 1998: 38).

Citizens expect the police to act both effectively and fairly—in ways consistent with American values. Departmental policy often affects fairness in encounters between citizens and police. When should the patrol officer frisk a suspect? When should a deal be made with the addict-informer? Which disputes should be mediated on the spot and which left to more formal procedures? Surprisingly, these conflicts between fairness and policy are seldom decided by heads of departments but fall largely to the officer on the scene. In many areas the department has little control over the actions of individual officers.

Police Discretion

Police officers have the power to deprive people of their liberty—to arrest them, take them into custody, and use force to control them. In carrying out their professional responsibilities, officers are expected to exercise discretion—to make choices in often ambiguous situations as to how and when to apply the law. Discretion can involve ignoring minor violations of the law or holding some violators to rule-book standards. It can mean arresting a disorderly person or taking that person home.

In the final analysis, the officer on the scene must define the situation, decide how to handle it, and determine whether and how the law should be applied. Five factors are especially important:

1. *The nature of the crime.* The less serious a crime is to the public, the more freedom officers have to ignore it.

2. *The relationship between the alleged criminal and the victim.* The closer the personal relationship, the more variable the use of discretion. Family squabbles may not be as grave as they appear, and a spouse may later decide not to press charges, so police are wary of making arrests.

3. *The relationship between the police and the criminal or victim.* A polite complainant will be taken more seriously than a hostile one. Likewise, a suspect who shows respect to an officer is less likely to be arrested than one who does not.

4. *Race/ethnicity, age, gender, class.* Although contested by many, research shows that officers are more likely to strictly enforce the law against young, minority, and poor men while being more lenient to the elderly, whites, and affluent women.

5. *Departmental policy.* The policies of the police chief and city officials promote more or less discretion.

Patrol officers—who are the most numerous, the lowest-ranking, and the newest to police work—have the most discretion. For example, if they chase a young thief into an alley, they can decide, outside of the view of the public, whether to make an arrest or just recover the stolen goods and give the offender a stern warning.

As we have seen, patrol officers' primary task is to maintain order and enforce ambiguous laws such as those dealing with disorderly conduct, public drunkenness, breach of the peace, and other situations in which it is unclear if a law has been broken, who committed the offense, and whether an arrest should be made. Wilson describes a patrol officer's role as "unlike that of any other occupation . . . one in which subprofessionals, working alone, exercise wide discretion in matters of utmost importance (life and death, honor and dishonor) in an environment that is apprehensive and perhaps hostile" (Wilson, 1968: 30).

Although some people call for detailed guidelines for police officers, such guidelines would probably be useless. No matter how detailed they were, the officer would still have to make judgments about how to apply them in each situation. At best, police administrators can develop guidelines and training that, one hopes, will give officers shared values and make their judgments more consistent.

Domestic Violence

How the police deal with domestic violence can show the links between police–citizen encounters, the exercise of discretion, and actions taken (or not taken) by officers. Domestic violence, also called "battering" and "spouse abuse," is assaultive behavior involving adults who are married or who have a prior or an ongoing intimate relationship.

Violence by an intimate (husband, ex-husband, boyfriend, or ex-boyfriend) accounted for about 21 percent of all violence experienced by female victims in 2006, compared with 5 percent for male victims. In that year, nearly 600,000 women were victims of intimate partner violence (Rand and Catalano, 2007). The highest rates of victimization from nonlethal violence by an intimate occur among African American women, women aged 20 to 24, and women in households in the lowest income categories. In addition, from 2001 through 2005, 30 percent of female homicide victims were killed by intimate partners while the comparable figure for men was only 5 percent (Catalano, 2007).

Until the 1970s most citizens and criminal justice agencies viewed domestic violence as a "private" matter best settled within the family or between intimate partners. Today police agencies typically have developed policies and training that direct officers to treat assaults between intimate partners or family members as crimes. Should the police also be responsible for providing assistance and services to the victims of such assaults?

© Viviane Moos/Corbis

Before 1970 most citizens and criminal justice agencies viewed domestic violence as a "private" affair best settled within the family. It was thought that police involvement might make the situation worse for the victim because it raised the possibility of reprisal. Even today, though a large number of calls to the police involve family disturbances, about half go unreported. (See "A Question of Ethics," at the end of the chapter.)

From the viewpoint of most police departments, domestic violence was a "no-win" situation in which one or both disputants often challenged or attacked the officers responding to calls for help. If an arrest was made, the police found that the victim often refused to cooperate with a prosecution. In addition, entering a home to deal with an emotion-laden incident was thought to be more dangerous than investigating "real" crimes. Many officers believed that trying to deal with family disputes was a leading cause of officer deaths and injury. However, this belief has been challenged by researchers who have found that domestic violence cases are no more dangerous to officers than are other incidents (Garner and Clemmer, 1986; Stanford and Mowry, 1990).

Police response to domestic violence can be a highly charged, uncertain, and possibly dangerous encounter with citizens in which officers must exercise discretion. In such a situation, how does an officer maintain order and enforce the law in accordance with the criminal law, departmental policies, and the needs of the victim? This question is addressed in the Close Up box on page 190, which presents the stories of Joanne Tremins and Tracey Thurman—two women who suffered years of abuse by their husbands without any action by the police.

In the past, most police departments advised officers to try to calm the parties and refer them to social service agencies rather than arrest the attacker. This policy of leniency toward male spouse abusers was studied in Chester, Pennsylvania. Researchers found that the police were less likely to arrest a man who attacked a female intimate than they would men who had committed similar violent acts against other victims (Felson and Ackerman, 2001; Fyfe, Klinger, and Flavin, 1997: 455–73).

Prodded by the women's movement, police departments began to rethink this policy of leniency when research in Minneapolis found that abusive spouses who are arrested and jailed briefly are much less likely to commit acts of domestic violence again (Sherman and Berk, 1984: 261). Although studies in other cities (Charlotte, Milwaukee, and Omaha) did not produce similar results (N. T. Ho, 2000), the research led some departments to order officers to make an arrest in every case in which evidence of an assault existed (Sherman et al., 1991: 821). Police officers may have supported the arrest policy because it gave them a clear directive regarding what to do (Friday, Metzger, and Walters, 1991). Officers in Minneapolis, though, told researchers they preferred to retain the discretion to do what was necessary (Steinman, 1988).

Some people argue that if arrests reduce domestic violence in some cases, arrests followed by prosecution will have an even greater impact. If so, pursuing all cases of spouse abuse seems to be the best course. However, a study of prosecutorial discretion in domestic violence cases in Milwaukee shows that factors such as the victim's injuries and the defendant's arrest record influence the decision to charge, not just the fact of spouse abuse (Schmidt and Steury, 1989).

In many states, policies have changed as a result of lawsuits by injured women who claimed that the police ignored evidence of assaults and in effect allowed the spouse to inflict serious injuries (Robinson, 2000). In addition, there is a growing sense that domestic violence can no longer be left to the discretion of individual patrol officers. Today, two dozen states require the arrest without a warrant of suspects in violent incidents, even if the officer did not witness the crime but has probable cause to believe that the suspect committed it. Most large departments and police academies have programs to educate officers about domestic violence.

 The website of the National Coalition Against Domestic Violence provides resources for victims of domestic violence. To link to this website, go to *The American System of Criminal Justice* 12e companion site at academic.cengage.com/criminaljustice/cole.

CLOSE UP

Battered Women, Reluctant Police

AS JOANNE TREMINS was moving some belongings out of her ramshackle house on South Main Street [in Torrington, Connecticut], her 350-pound husband ran over, grabbed the family cat and strangled it in front of Tremins and her children.

For more than three years, Tremins said, she had complained to Torrington police about beatings and threats from her husband. Instead of arresting him, she said, the police acted "like marriage counselors." The cat attack finally prompted police to arrest Jeffrey Tremins on a minor charge of cruelty to animals. But four days later, outside a local cafe, he repeatedly punched his wife in the face and smashed her against a wall, fracturing her nose and causing lacerations and contusions to her face and left arm.

That Joanne Tremins is suing this New England town of 34,000 is not without historical irony. For it was here that Tracey Thurman . . . won a $2 million judgment against the police department in a federal civil rights case that has revolutionized law enforcement attitudes toward domestic violence.

The Thurman case marked the first time that a battered woman was allowed to sue police in federal court for failing to protect her from her husband. The ruling held that such a failure amounts to sex discrimination and violates the Fourteenth Amendment.

The resulting spate of lawsuits has prompted police departments nationwide to reexamine their long-standing reluctance to make arrests in domestic assault cases, particularly when the wife refuses to press charges. State and local lawmakers, facing soaring municipal insurance costs, are also taking notice.

Here in hilly Torrington . . . Police Chief Mahlon C. Sabo said [the Thurman case] had a "devastating" effect on the town and his seventy-member force. "The police somehow, over the years, became the mediators," said Sabo. "There was a feeling that it's between husband and wife. In most cases, after the officer left, the wife usually got battered around for calling the police in the first place." Although the law now requires them to make arrests, police officers here said, the courts toss out many domestic cases for the same reason that long hampered police.

"Unfortunately, many women just want the case dropped and fail to recognize they're in a dangerous situation," said Anthony J. Salius, director of the family division of Connecticut Superior Court. "If she really doesn't want to prosecute, it's very difficult to have a trial because we don't have a witness." Nearly five years after the attack by her estranged husband, Tracey Thurman remains scarred and partially paralyzed from multiple stab wounds to the chest, neck, and face. Charles Thurman was sentenced to 14 years in prison.

For eight months before the stabbing, Thurman repeatedly threatened his wife and their two-year-old son. He worked at Skee's Diner, a few blocks from police headquarters, and repeatedly boasted to policemen he was serving that he intended to kill his wife, according to the lawsuit.

In their defense, police said they arrested Thurman twice before the stabbing. The first charges were dropped, and a suspended sentence was imposed the second time. Tracey Thurman later obtained a court order barring her husband from harassing or assaulting her.

On June 10, 1983, Tracey Thurman called police and said her husband was menacing her. An officer did not arrive for twenty-five minutes and, although he found Charles Thurman holding a bloody knife, he delayed several minutes before making an arrest, giving Thurman enough time to kick his wife in the head repeatedly.

Less than a year after police were found liable in the attack on Thurman, Joanne Tremins also found that a restraining order obtained against her husband was worthless. . . . Tremins recounted how she made about sixty calls to police to complain about her husband, a cook. But she acknowledges that, on most of the occasions, when the police asked if she wanted him arrested, she said no.

"How could I say that?" she asked. "He's threatening to kill me if I have him arrested. He's threatening to kill my kids if I have him arrested. He'd stand behind the cops and pound his fist into the palm of his hand."

Hours before Tremins strangled the cat, . . . he beat and kicked his wife and her son, Stanley Andrews, fourteen. When an officer arrived, Joanne Tremins said, he told her that he could not make an arrest unless she filed a complaint at the police station.

"My son was all black and blue," Tremins said. "But [the officer] refused to come into my room and look at the blood all over the walls and the floor."

After Tremins was taken into custody for the cat incident, police did charge him with assaulting the son. He was released on bond, and his wife was issued a restraining order.

When her husband approached Tremins days later at a cafe in nearby Winsted, police refused to arrest him, despite the order. After the beating, Jeffrey Tremins was charged with assault and sentenced to two years in prison.

Source: Howard Kurtz, "Battered Women, Reluctant Police," *Washington Post*, February 28, 1988, p. A1. Copyright © 1988, *The Washington Post*. Reprinted with permission.

Researching the Internet

 The Nashville Police Department provides detailed information about domestic violence on its web page. To link to this website, go to *The American System of Criminal Justice* 12e companion site at academic.cengage.com/criminaljustice/cole.

Even though we can point to policy changes imposed to deal with domestic violence, the officer in the field remains the one who must handle these situations. Laws, guidelines, and training can help; however, as is often true in police work, the discretion of the officer inevitably determines what actions will be taken.

checkpoint

> 23. Why do patrol officers have so much discretion?
> 24. Why have police in the past failed to arrest in domestic violence situations?

POLICE AND THE COMMUNITY

The work of a police officer in an American city can be very difficult, involving hours of boring, routine work interrupted by short spurts of dangerous crime fighting. Although police work has always been frustrating and dangerous, officers today must deal with situations ranging from helping the homeless to dealing with domestic violence to confronting shoot-outs at drug deals gone sour. Yet police actions are sometimes mishandled by officers or misinterpreted by the public, making some people critical of the police.

Special Populations

Urban police forces must deal with a complex population. City streets contain growing numbers of people suffering from mental illness, homelessness, alcoholism, drug addiction, or serious medical conditions such as acquired immunodeficiency syndrome (AIDS). In addition, they may find youthful runaways and children victimized by their parents' neglect. Several factors have contributed to increasing numbers of "problem" people on the streets. These factors include overcrowded jails, cutbacks in public assistance, and the closing of many psychiatric institutions, which must then release mental health patients. Although most of these "problem" people do not commit crimes, their presence disturbs many of their fellow citizens and thus they may contribute to fear of crime and disorder. Clearly, dealing with special populations poses a major challenge for police in most cities (Finn, 2002).

Patrol officers cooperate with social service agencies in helping individuals and responding to requests for order maintenance. The police must walk a fine line when requiring a person to enter a homeless shelter, obtain medical assistance, or be taken to a mental health unit (McCoy, 1986; Melekian, 1990). Police departments have developed various techniques for dealing with special populations. Memphis, Houston, Atlanta, and Chicago use "crisis intervention teams" composed of selected officers who receive 40 hours of special training and who coordinate their efforts with social service agencies and families (Twyman, 2005). Each community must develop policies so that officers will know when and how they are to intervene when a person has not broken the law but is upsetting residents.

Policing in a Multicultural Society

Carrying out the complex tasks of policing efficiently and according to the law is a tough assignment even when the police have the support and cooperation of the public. But policing in a multicultural society like the United States presents further challenges.

In the last half-century, the racial and ethnic composition of the United States has changed. During the mid-twentieth century, many African Americans moved from rural areas of the South to northern cities. In recent years, people from Puerto Rico, Cuba, Mexico, and South America have become the fastest-growing minority groups in many cities. Immigrants from Eastern Europe, Russia, the Middle East, and Asia have entered the country in greater numbers

In multicultural America, police officers must be sensitive to the perspectives and customs of many groups. They must uphold civil liberties and treat people equally while upholding the law. These responsibilities can be difficult in highly emotional situations in which people are engaged in conflicts or treat the police in an uncooperative and disrespectful manner. Have you ever observed or heard about situations in which police officers' emotions, such as anger or frustration, affected their decisions or behavior?

AP Images/Nick Ut

A newspaper's analysis of persons stopped by police in New York City at each stop in the subway system provided indications that police suspicions may be disproportionately focused on members of minority groups. To link to this website, go to *The American System of Criminal Justice* 12e companion site at academic.cengage.com/criminaljustice/cole.

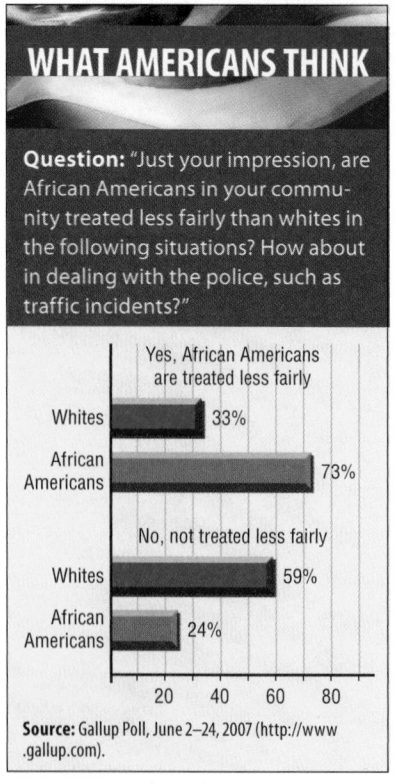

WHAT AMERICANS THINK

Question: "Just your impression, are African Americans in your community treated less fairly than whites in the following situations? How about in dealing with the police, such as traffic incidents?"

Yes, African Americans are treated less fairly

Whites	33%
African Americans	73%

No, not treated less fairly

Whites	59%
African Americans	24%

20   40   60   80

Source: Gallup Poll, June 2–24, 2007 (http://www.gallup.com).

than before. Since 1980 the United States has witnessed a huge increase in immigration, rivaling the stream of foreigners that arrived in the early 1900s.

Policing requires trust, understanding, and cooperation between officers and the public. People must be willing to call for help and provide information about wrongdoing. But in a multicultural society, relations between the police and minorities are complicated by stereotypes, cultural variations, and language differences. Most of the newer immigrants come from countries around the world with cultural traditions and laws that differ from those in the United States. American police officers may know little about these traditions, especially if the immigrants they serve cannot communicate easily in English. Moreover, after the tragedy of September 11, law enforcement officials may have increased caution and suspicion when encountering people who they believe to be, accurately or not, Middle Eastern or Muslim. Lack of familiarity, difficulties in communicating, and excessive suspicion can create risks that officers will violate the American value of equal treatment of all people.

Like other Americans who have limited personal experience and familiarity with people from different backgrounds, officers may attribute undesirable traits to members of minority groups. Historically, many Americans have applied stereotypes to their fellow citizens. These stereotypes may include assumptions that certain people are prone to involvement with drugs or other criminal activities. Treating people according to stereotypes, rather than as individuals, creates tensions that harden negative attitudes.

Very few officers can speak a language other than English. Often, only large urban departments have officers who speak any of the many languages used by new immigrants. People who speak little English and who report crimes, are arrested, or are victimized may not be understood. Language can be a barrier for the police in responding to calls for help and dealing with organized crime. Languages and cultural diversity make it harder for the FBI or local police to infiltrate the Russian, Vietnamese, and Chinese organized-crime groups now found in East and West Coast cities.

Public opinion surveys have shown that race and ethnicity are key factors shaping attitudes toward the police. As seen in "What Americans Think," questions of fair treatment by the police differ among racial groups. Young, low-income racial-minority men have the most negative attitudes toward the police (S. Walker, Spohn, and DeLeone, 2007). As discussed in the Close Up box, these attitudes may stem from experiences gained through encounters with police officers.

Inner-city neighborhoods—the areas that need and want effective policing—often significantly distrust the police; citizens may therefore fail to report crimes and refuse to cooperate with the police. Encounters between officers and members of these communities are often hostile and sometimes lead to public protests or large-scale disorders. For example, in April 2001 three nights of violent protests erupted in Cincinnati, Ohio, after a police officer shot and killed an unarmed African American teenager whom police sought for outstanding misdemeanor and traffic violations. In January 2008, hundreds of protesters

CLOSE UP

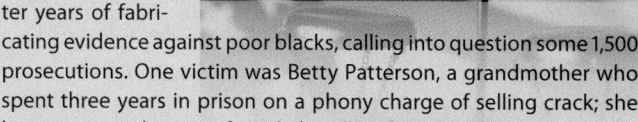

Living under Suspicion

IN 1995, AFTER one of the most highly publicized criminal trials in American history, Hall of Fame football legend O. J. Simpson, an African American, was found "not guilty" of murdering his ex-wife and a man outside of her home. The trial revealed that Detective Mark Fuhrman, who claimed that he had found a bloody glove in Simpson's backyard, had previously made derogatory, racist remarks about African Americans. Fuhrman was later convicted of committing perjury when he denied ever making racist comments. In a subsequent civil lawsuit, a jury found Simpson liable for the deaths by applying a "preponderance of evidence" standard rather than the stricter "beyond a reasonable doubt" standard used in criminal cases. Public opinion polls showed that African Americans and whites were deeply divided in their views about Simpson's guilt.

If you're white and confused about why so many blacks think O. J. Simpson is innocent of murder, try a simple exercise. Take a few minutes to sit down with an African American, preferably a male, and ask whether he has ever been hassled by the police. Chances are you'll get an education. . . .

He may have been pulled over for the offense of driving after dark through a white neighborhood, for the misdemeanor of driving with a white woman or for the felony of driving too fancy a car. He may have been questioned for making a suspicious late-night call from a public phone in a suburban mall or, as a boy, for flagrantly riding his new bike on his own street.

He may have been a student or a lawyer—even an off-duty policeman, threatened with drawn guns before he could pull out his badge. Some black parents warn their children never to run out of a store or a bank: Better to be late than shot dead.

When you grow up in vulnerability and live at the margins of society, the world looks different. That difference, starkly displayed after Mr. Simpson's acquittal in the criminal trial, has been less passionate but no less definitive since he was found liable in his civil trial. . . .

For many African Americans, Mr. Simpson has become more symbol than individual. He is every black man who dared to marry a white women, who rose from deprivation to achievement, who got uppity and faced destruction by the white establishment that elevated him. He is every black man who has been pulled over by a white cop, beaten to the ground, jailed without evidence, framed for a crime he didn't commit.

Given that legacy, it is difficult for blacks not to doubt the police, and the doubts undermine law enforcement. In 1995 five Philadel-

phia policemen were indicted and pleaded guilty after years of fabricating evidence against poor blacks, calling into question some 1,500 prosecutions. One victim was Betty Patterson, a grandmother who spent three years in prison on a phony charge of selling crack; she later won a settlement of nearly $1 million from the city.

The indictments came as the Simpson jurors were hearing tapes of antiblack remarks by Detective Mark Fuhrman that reflected the endemic racism of the Los Angeles Police Department. As documented by the Christopher Commission, which investigated the department after the Rodney King beating in 1991, officers felt so comfortable in their bigotry that they typed racist computer messages to one another, apparently confident that they would face no punishment.

This is precisely the lesson of the black-white reactions to the Simpson case. Most policemen are not racist or corrupt, but most departments do not combat racism as vigorously as they do corruption. Many blacks have come to see the police as just another gang. Alarm bells should be going off, for the judicial system cannot function without credibility.

Of the country's institutions, police departments are probably furthest behind in addressing racism in their ranks. Some corporations are learning that a diverse work force enhances profits. The military knows that attracting volunteers and maintaining cohesion requires racial harmony. Police departments ought to understand that their bottom line is measured in legitimate convictions. They need to retrain officers and screen applicants for subtle bigotry. If morality is not argument enough, try pragmatism.

Source: David K. Shipler, "Living under Suspicion," *New York Times*, February 7, 1997, p. A33.

Researching the Internet

Read about the O. J. Simpson trial at the Famous Trials website located at the University of Missouri–Kansas City Law School by going to *The American System of Criminal Justice* 12e companion site at academic.cengage.com/criminaljustice/cole.

---

marched in Lima, Ohio, to express their outrage that police officers shot and killed a young African American woman and wounded her toddler when entering a home to look for a male drug suspect. Twenty-seven percent of Lima's 38,000 residents are African American, yet only two of the city's 77 police officers are African Americans (Maag, 2008).

Same-race policing may lead to a greater willingness of residents of minority neighborhoods to report crimes and to assist investigations. Such policing may also reduce unjustified arrests, misuse of force, and police harassment. The limited research on this question found that same-race policing leads to a greater reduction of property crime. The researchers argue that a given number of officers will have a greater impact on crime while requiring fewer arrests, if deployed in a same-race setting (Donohue and Levitt, 1998).

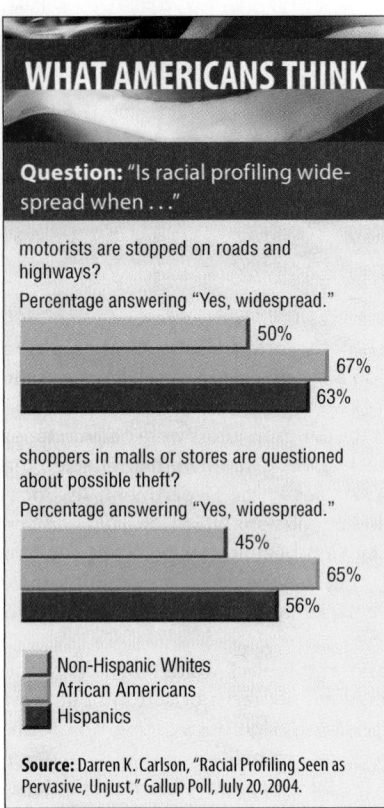

Source: Darren K. Carlson, "Racial Profiling Seen as Pervasive, Unjust," Gallup Poll, July 20, 2004.

The American Civil Liberties Union has filed several successful lawsuits to challenge racial profiling by police in traffic stops and automobile searches. The organization's website contains a variety of reports about the issue. To link to this website, go to *The American System of Criminal Justice* 12e companion site at academic.cengage.com/criminaljustice/cole.

The National Sheriffs' Association maintains a separate website devoted exclusively to neighborhood watch programs. To link to this website, go to *The American System of Criminal Justice* 12e companion site at academic.cengage.com/criminaljustice/cole.

Why do some urban residents resent the police? John DiIulio argues that this resentment stems from permissive law enforcement and police abuse of power (DiIulio, 1993: 3). The police are charged with failure in giving protection and services to minority neighborhoods and, as we shall see in a later chapter, with abusing residents physically or verbally. The police are seen as permissive when an officer treats an offense against a person of the same ethnic group as the offender more lightly than a similar offense in which the offender and victim are members of different groups. The police say that such differences occur because they are working in a hostile environment. The white patrol officer may fear that breaking up a street fight among members of a minority group will provoke the wrath of onlookers, while community residents may in fact view inaction as a sign that the police do not care about their neighborhood. It is said that the police do not work effectively on crimes such as drug sales, gambling, petty theft, and in-group assault, although these are the crimes that are most common in urban neighborhoods and that create the greatest insecurity and fear among residents.

Studies raise questions about whether some police officers harbor prejudices against the poor and racial minorities. Such attitudes can lead these officers to see African Americans or Hispanics as potential criminals; as a result, these officers can possess exaggerated perceptions about the extent of minority crime. It should be noted, however, that the possession of prejudicial attitudes does not necessarily mean that an officer will behave in a discriminatory manner (Walker, Spohn and DeLeone, 2007). However, as indicated by "What Americans Think," many African Americans and Hispanics perceive themselves as targeted for suspicion when they are engaging in routine activities such as driving their cars or shopping. If both police and citizens view each other with suspicion or hostility, then their encounters will be strained and the potential for conflict will increase.

As noted by Jerome Skolnick and James Fyfe, the military organization of the police and a "war on crime" attitude can lead to violence against inner-city residents, whom the police see as the enemy (1993: 160). It is little wonder, therefore, that urban ghetto dwellers may think of the police as an army of occupation and that the police may think of themselves as combat soldiers.

Ultimately, stereotypes, tensions, and conflicts make it much more difficult for police officers to do their jobs effectively. All aspects of officers' responsibilities, including service, order maintenance, and crime control, can suffer when police officers and the communities they serve lack cooperation and trust.

Community Crime Prevention

There is a growing awareness that the police cannot control crime and disorder on their own. Social control requires involvement by all members of the community. When government agencies and neighborhood organizations cooperate, community crime prevention can improve. As one expert says, "Voluntary local efforts must support official action if order is to be preserved within realistic budgetary limits and without sacrificing our civil liberties" (Skogan, 1990: 125). Across the country, community programs to help the police have proliferated. We now look at several such approaches.

Citizen crime-watch groups have been formed in many communities. More than 6 million Americans belong to such groups, which often have direct ties to police departments. Read about Jaci Woods, an Irvine, California, volunteer, in "Doing Your Part." One of the challenges for community prevention programs is to include young people as participants rather than treat youths as targets of surveillance and suspicion (Forman, 2004).

One of the most well-known programs is Neighborhood Watch, a program that developed in the 1960s and that the National Sheriffs' Association (NSA) adopted as a nationwide initiative in 1972. The NSA provides information and technical assistance for groups that want to start Neighborhood Watch groups in their communities. Reflecting the changing themes of contemporary policing, the NSA's website touts Neighborhood Watch as important for homeland security as well as for crime prevention.

The Crime Stoppers Program is designed to enlist public help in solving crimes. Founded in Albuquerque, New Mexico, in 1975, it has spread across the country. Television and radio stations present the "unsolved crime of the week," and cash rewards are given for information that leads to conviction of the offender. Although these programs help solve some crimes, the numbers of solved crimes remain small compared with the total number of crimes committed.

In 1991 the federal government initiated the Operation Weed and Seed Program as a means to coordinate citizens' and agencies' efforts in community crime prevention and to encourage neighborhood revitalization. The program is administered by the Community Capacity Development Office of the U.S. Department of Justice. The government awards grants to local programs designed to address problems in targeted neighborhoods. Under the "Weed" segment of the program, the local U.S. Attorney's Office works with law enforcement agencies and state prosecutors to crack down on violence, drugs, and gang activity. At the same time, human services agencies work with neighborhood associations in the "Seed" activities designed to clean up neighborhoods, repair homes, encourage small businesses to develop, and institute delinquency prevention programs for youths. By 2005, Weed and Seed programs existed at 300 sites around the nation. In the Providence, Rhode Island, program, for example, residents of the targeted neighborhood are directly involved in Neighborhood Watch, mentoring programs for youths, and community cleanup and home repair projects.

As the federal budget deficit grows and the federal government shifts funding toward homeland security, state and local governments may face decisions about whether to continue community initiatives such as Operation Weed and Seed. The Pennsylvania Commission on Crime and Delinquency (PCCD), for example, has taken a leading role in facilitating the development and continuation of community-based programs. The PCCD has expanded the Weed and Seed concept to smaller Pennsylvania communities that were not targeted for federal grants. The PCCD also provides funding and technical assistance for other community prevention programs that seek to build coalitions of citizens who will work to improve the quality of life within their neighborhoods (Feinberg, Greenwood, and Osgood, 2004).

Successful community-based crime prevention programs typically work with the police and other government agencies to restore order and control crime. Many police chiefs and community leaders work continuously to develop new ways to involve citizens in crime prevention and to increase participation in existing programs (Christensen,

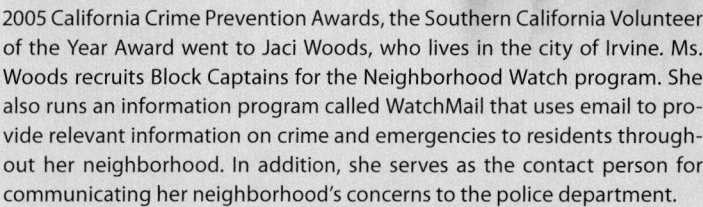

DOING YOUR PART

Crime Prevention Volunteer

Jaci Woods

When the California Crime Prevention Officers' Association handed out its 2005 California Crime Prevention Awards, the Southern California Volunteer of the Year Award went to Jaci Woods, who lives in the city of Irvine. Ms. Woods recruits Block Captains for the Neighborhood Watch program. She also runs an information program called WatchMail that uses email to provide relevant information on crime and emergencies to residents throughout her neighborhood. In addition, she serves as the contact person for communicating her neighborhood's concerns to the police department.

According to her award citation, she actively helped to solve local problems of identity theft and mail theft that occurred when thieves took items from local residents' mailboxes. She analyzed the problem and then worked with the U.S. Postal Service and city government to replace people's older mailboxes with more secure types of mailboxes.

As a community volunteer, she is doing her part.

Source: "2005 California Crime Prevention Awards," California Crime Prevention Officer's Association (http://www.safestate.org).

Researching the Internet

To learn about opportunities in Volunteers in Police Service (VIPS), see the organization's website. To link to this website, go to *The American System of Criminal Justice* 12e companion site at academic.cengage.com/criminaljustice/cole.

civic engagement
your role in the system

Your local police chief has asked you to lead a citizens' committee to develop a "neighborhood policing plan" that will include specific commitments by neighbors and specific expectations for police. *Make a list of citizen activities that should be part of the plan.* Then look at the Neighborhood Policing Plans developed by residents of Minneapolis. To link to this website, go to *The American System of Criminal Justice* 12e companion site at academic.cengage.com/criminaljustice/cole.

Information on the Weed and Seed Program is available at the website of the U.S. Office of Justice Programs. To link to this website, go to *The American System of Criminal Justice* 12e companion site at academic .cengage.com/criminaljustice/cole.

2008). Scholars say that the citizens of a community must take responsibility for maintaining civil and safe social conditions. Experience has shown that "while police might be able to retake a neighborhood from aggressive drug dealers, police could not hold a neighborhood without significant commitment and actual assistance from private citizens" (Kelling and Coles, 1996: 248). Think about what strategies you would suggest for preventing and reducing crime in your home neighborhood as you read "Civic Engagement: Your Role in the System."

checkpoint

25. What "special populations" pose challenges for policing?
26. What factors make policing in a multicultural society difficult?
27. What are the two basic reasons that urban residents sometimes resent the police?
28. How are citizen watch groups and similar programs helpful to the police?

A QUESTION OF ETHICS

YOU ARE A police officer responding to a call from neighbors about a loud argument in a home. You hear a man and a woman shouting at each other as you ring the doorbell. The voices go silent at the sound of the bell. When a woman answers the door, you notice a large bruise on her cheek and it appears that she has been crying.

"Are you all right?" you ask. She nods her head silently but looks at the floor rather than meeting your gaze.

Suddenly the door swings open and you recognize the man in the doorway as a police dispatcher whom you encounter at the po-lice station nearly every day. His voice contains a note of urgency as he speaks. "Look, man. You know who I am. My girlfriend and I were just having a little argument. Can't you just leave it alone? If you write this up or anything, I could lose my job. Everything's okay. Please just leave it alone."

Critical Thinking and Analysis

Does the bruise indicate that an assault occurred? Should you ask additional questions? Should you make an arrest? Write a memo describing what you would do if the woman remained silent and declined to answer any questions about what occurred.

SUMMARY

Understand how policing evolved in the United States

- The police in the United States owe their roots to early nineteenth-century developments in policing in England.

- Like their English counterparts, the American police have limited authority, are under local control, and are organizationally fragmented.

- The three eras of American policing are the political era (1840–1920), the professional model era (1920–1970), and the community policing era (1970–present).

Recognize the main types of police agencies

- In the U.S. federal system of government, police agencies are found at the national, state, county, and municipal levels.

- Federal agencies include the FBI, DEA, Secret Service, and sworn officers in dozens of other agencies.

- Most states have a state police force and sheriff's departments are the primary county-level policing agencies.

Comprehend the functions of the police

- The functions of the police are order maintenance, law enforcement, and service.

- Police have cultivated an image as crime fighters preoccupied with the law enforcement function.
- The service function is actually the basis for most calls to police departments.

Understand how the police are organized

- The police are organized along military lines so that authority and responsibility can be located at appropriate levels.
- Larger police departments have specialized units.

Analyze influences on police policy and styles of policing

- Police executives develop policies on how they will allocate their resources according to one of three styles: the watchman, legalistic, or service styles.
- The development of differing styles can be affected by the nature of the community and political context.
- Suburban middle-class communities often have a service style; the legalistic style emphasizes law enforcement; the watchman style emphasizes order maintenance.

Understand how police officers balance actions, decision making, and discretion

- Discretion is a major factor in police actions and decisions. Patrol officers exercise the greatest amount of discretion.
- The problem of domestic violence illustrates the links between encounters with citizens by police, their exercise of discretion, and the actions they take.

Recognize the importance of connections between the police and the community

- Police face challenges in dealing with special populations, such as the mentally ill and homeless, who need social services yet often disturb or offend other citizens as they walk the streets.
- Policing in a multicultural society requires an appreciation of the attitudes, customs, and languages of minority group members.
- To be effective, the police must maintain their connection with the community.

QUESTIONS FOR REVIEW

1. What principles borrowed from England still underlie policing in the United States?
2. What are the eras of policing in the United States and what are the characteristics of each?
3. What are the functions of the police?
4. How do communities influence police policy and police styles?
5. How does the problem of domestic violence illustrate basic elements of police action?
6. What problems do officers face in policing a multicultural society?

KEY TERMS

frankpledge (p. 161)
law enforcement (p. 178)

order maintenance (p. 179)
service (p. 180)

FOR FURTHER READING

Conlon, Edward. 2005. *Blue Blood*. New York: Riverhead. An insider's view of the New York City Police Department by a Harvard-educated officer from a family of police officers.

Goldstein, Herman. 1990. *Problem-Oriented Policing*. New York: McGraw-Hill. Examination of the move toward problem-oriented, or community, policing. Argues for a shift to this focus.

Nadelmann, Ethan. 1993. *Cops across Borders: The Internationalization of U.S. Criminal Law Enforcement*. University Park: Pennsylvania State University Press. A major work describing the increased presence of American law enforcement agencies in foreign countries.

Skolnick, Jerome H. 1966. *Justice without Trial: Law Enforcement in a Democratic Society*. New York: Wiley. One of the first books to examine the subculture of the police and the exercise of discretion.

Tonry, Michael, and Norval Morris, eds. 1992. *Modern Policing*. Chicago: University of Chicago Press. An outstanding collection of essays by leading scholars examining the history, organization, and operational tactics of the police.

Wilson, James Q. 1968. *Varieties of Police Behavior*. Cambridge, MA: Harvard University Press. A classic study of the styles of policing in different types of communities. Shows the impact of politics on the operations of the force.

GOING ONLINE

For an up-to-date list of links, go to *The American System of Criminal Justice* 12e companion site at academic.cengage.com/criminaljustice/cole.

1. Go to the U.S. Secret Service website and obtain information on entry requirements and the application process for becoming a special agent. What types of people is the Secret Service seeking? Do you qualify?
2. Go to the Citizen Corps website and read about the federal government's initiative to organize citizen participation in community safety and homeland security. What role can citizens play in preventing violence and threats to community safety?

3. Can an average citizen play a role in addressing problems of domestic violence? Search the Internet for the kinds of volunteer opportunities that exist for citizens to provide needed help to domestic violence programs.

CHECKPOINT ANSWERS

1. *What three main features of American policing were inherited from England?*

Limited authority, local control, organizational fragmentation.

2. *What was the frankpledge and how did it work?*

A rule requiring groups of ten families to uphold the law and maintain order.

3. *What did the Statute of Winchester (1285) establish?*

Established a parish constable system. Citizens were required to pursue criminals.

4. *What did the Metropolitan Police Act (1829) establish?*

Established the first organized police force in London.

5. *What were the four mandates of the English police in the nineteenth century?*

To prevent crime without the use of repressive force, to manage public order nonviolently, to minimize and reduce conflict between citizens and the police, and to demonstrate efficiency by the absence of crime.

6. *What are the major historical periods of American policing?*

Political era, professional model era, community policing era.

7. *What was the main feature of the political era?*

Close ties between the police and local politicians, leading to corruption.

8. *What were the major recommendations of the Progressive reformers?*

The police should be removed from politics, police should be well trained, the law should be enforced equally, technology should be used, merit should be the basis of personnel procedures, the crime-fighting role should be prominent.

9. *What are the main criticisms of the professional model era?*

The professional, crime-fighting role isolated the police from the community. The police should try to solve the problems underlying crime.

10. *What is community policing?*

The police should be close to the community, provide services, and deal with the little problems.

11. *What is the jurisdiction of federal law enforcement agencies?*

Enforce the laws of the federal government.

12. *Why are some law enforcement agencies of the U.S. government located overseas?*

Because of the increase in international criminality in a shrinking world.

13. *What are the functions of most state police agencies?*

All state police agencies have traffic law enforcement responsibilities, and in two-thirds of the states they have general police powers.

14. *Besides law enforcement, what functions do sheriffs perform?*

Operate jails, move prisoners, and provide court bailiffs.

15. *What are the main characteristics of the organization of the police in the United States?*

Local control, fragmentation.

16. *What is the order maintenance function? What are officers expected to do in situations where they must maintain order?*

Police have a broad mandate to prevent behavior that either disturbs or threatens to disturb the peace or involves face-to-face conflict among two or more people. Officers are expected to handle the situation.

17. *How do law enforcement situations compare with order maintenance situations?*

The police in order maintenance situations must first determine if a law has been broken. In law enforcement situations, that fact is already known; thus, officers must only find and apprehend the offender.

18. *What are three characteristics of a bureaucracy?*

A bureaucracy has (1) division of labor, (2) chain of unity and command, and (3) rules and procedures.

19. *What are the five operational units of police departments with sufficient size for specialization?*

Patrol, investigation, traffic, vice, and juvenile.

20. *What are the characteristics of the watchman style of policing?*

Emphasis on order maintenance, extensive use of discretion, and differential treatment of racial and ethnic groups.

21. *What is the key feature of the legalistic style of policing?*

Professionalism and using a single standard of law enforcement throughout the community.

22. *Where are you likely to find the service style of policing?*

Suburban middle-class communities.

23. *Why do patrol officers have so much discretion?*

They deal with citizens, often in private, and are responsible for maintaining order and enforcing laws. Many of these laws are ambiguous and deal with situations in which the participants' conduct is in dispute.

24. *Why have police in the past failed to arrest in domestic violence situations?*

These situations were often viewed as family problems rather than criminal events; police also feared making the situation worse.

25. *What "special populations" pose challenges for policing?*

Runaways and neglected children; people who suffer from homelessness, drug addiction, mental illness, or alcoholism.

26. *What factors make policing in a multicultural society difficult?*

Stereotyping, cultural differences, and language differences.

27. *What are the two basic reasons that urban residents sometimes resent the police?*

Permissive law enforcement and police abuse of power.

28. *How are citizen watch groups and similar programs helpful to the police?*

They assist the police by reporting incidents and providing information.

CHAPTER 6

Police Officers and Law Enforcement Operations

CHAPTER LEARNING OBJECTIVES

→ Identify why people become police officers and how they learn to do their jobs

→ Understand the elements of the police officer's "working personality"

→ Recognize factors that affect police response

→ Understand the main functions of police patrol, investigation, and special operations units

→ Analyze patrol strategies that police departments employ

In the early morning hours of October 18, 2007, police officers in Rialto, California, assisted by federal agents from the Drug Enforcement Administration (DEA) and Bureau of Alcohol, Tobacco, Firearms, and Explosives (ATF) were carrying out search warrants in a neighborhood troubled by drug-dealing and drive-by shootings. The officers were members of Rialto's SWAT team—the Special Weapons and Tactics team that carries out especially risky missions. In large departments, some officers are full-time SWAT team specialists, but in smaller cities, such as Rialto, SWAT team members also spend part of their time as regular patrol officers (Arballo, 2007).

When the officers entered one residence and ordered everyone to the floor, a man ran to the back of the duplex. Rialto police officer Sergio Carrera, Jr., followed the suspect. Suddenly, the other officers and the suspect's girlfriend in the front room heard shots (Reston and Kelly, 2007). Apparently, Officer Carrera and the suspect struggled over a gun. When the gun discharged, Carrera was fatally wounded in the upper torso. The young officer, a 29-year-old married man with two children, was only the second Rialto officer ever to be killed in the line of duty (Brooks et al., 2007).

Sadly, police officers' deaths in the line of duty, such as that of Officer Carrera, occur with troubling regularity. During 2006, 48 law enforcement officers were killed throughout the United States through the felonious actions of lawbreakers and another 66 died as a result of accidents while on duty (FBI, 2007b). Obviously, police officers face significant potential risks in their jobs and they never know when they may be called upon to courageously save a life—or put their own lives on the line while protecting society.

In this chapter, we focus on the actual work of the police as they pursue suspects, prevent crimes, and otherwise serve the public. The police must be organized so that patrol efforts can be coordinated, investigations carried out, arrests made, evidence gathered, crimes solved, and violators prosecuted. At the same time, patrol officers must be prepared to maintain

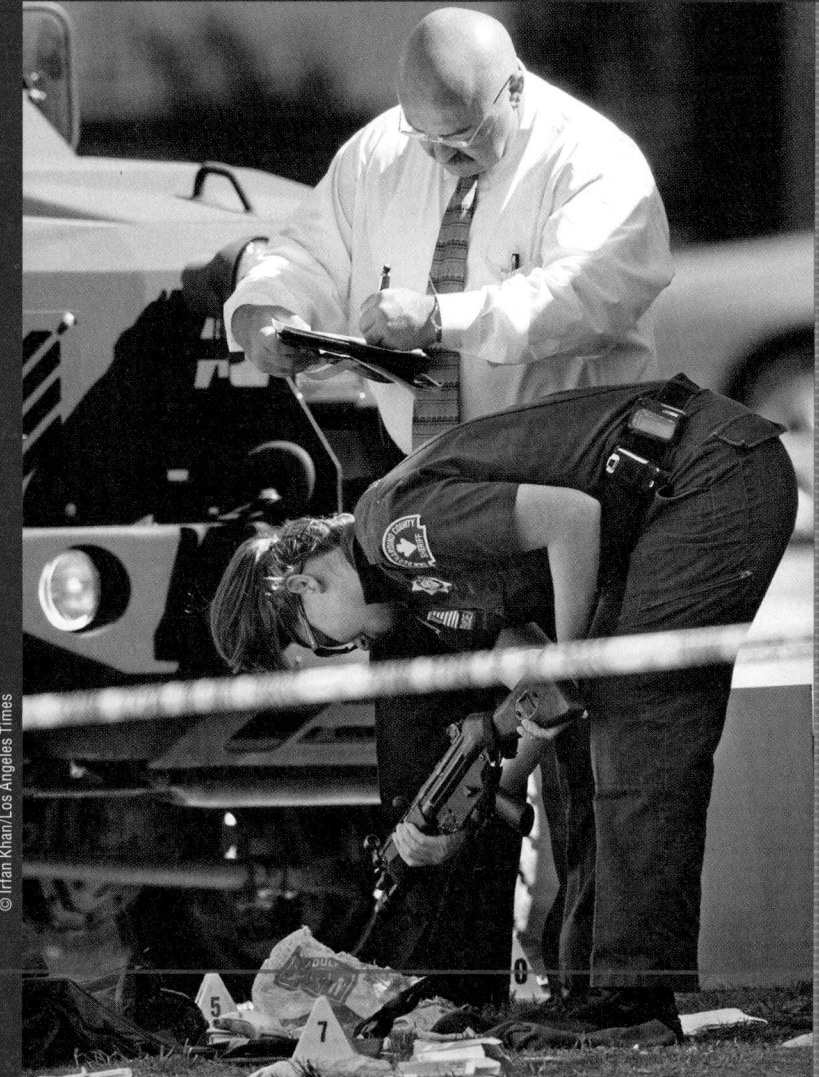

order and provide needed services for the citizens in a community. Much of the time, police work may seem quite boring as officers drive for hours along quiet streets, direct traffic, and respond to complaints about noisy teenagers or illegally parked cars. At any moment, however, grave dangers may arise and officers may be called upon to make quick decisions that will profoundly affect the lives of others as well as their own. Because American society depends so much on police officers for service, order maintenance, and crime control, it is important to understand who they are and what they do in their jobs every day.

WHO ARE THE POLICE?

Police officers never know what they might encounter around the next corner as they walk or drive on patrol. What if an armed fugitive surprised an officer by opening fire? What motivates someone to choose such a career? These questions are important because they help to determine which people will be granted the authority to carry firearms and make discretionary decisions about arrests, searches, and even ending the lives of other human beings by pulling the trigger during stressful, fast-moving, and dangerous scenarios.

Because policing is such an important occupation, society would obviously benefit from recruiting its most thoughtful, athletic, and dedicated citizens as police officers. Happily, many such individuals are attracted to this field. Yet, many other people who would make fine law enforcement officers turn to other occupations, because policing is such a difficult job. The modest salaries, significant job stress, and moments of danger involved in police work can deter some individuals from choosing this public service occupation.

If you or someone you know plans a career in law enforcement, ask yourself what aspects of the job make it more appealing than other kinds of work. Some people might want the adventure and excitement of investigating crimes and catching suspects. Others might be drawn to the satisfactions that come from being a public servant. Still others may be attracted to a civil service job with good benefits. Table 6.1 presents the reasons people give for choosing police work as a career.

Recruitment

How can departments recruit well-rounded, dedicated public servants who will represent the diversity of contemporary America? All agencies require recruits to pass physical fitness tests, and they check to see if applicants have criminal records. Agencies increasingly require recruits to undergo psychological evaluations, because each officer will ultimately make important discretionary decisions, including those that may determine life and death in stressful situations (Langworthy, Hughes, and Sanders, 1995: 26).

Besides these requirements, what other factors determine who is hired by specific law enforcement agencies? One factor is compensation. The average starting salary in 2003 was $35,500 plus the likelihood of overtime pay (Hickman and Reaves, 2006). Federal agencies and others that provide good compensation and benefits tend to attract larger numbers of applicants. Because of limited budgets, rural sheriffs' departments, by contrast, may have a more difficult time recruiting a competitive applicant pool. Such departments may recruit outstanding officers who want to live in a particular rural community, but more attractive compensation packages in other agencies may also lure their current employees away.

Another factor is the educational level of potential recruits. Most departments require only a high school diploma, but they actually may seek to re-

TABLE 6.1	Reasons for Choosing Police Work as a Career		
To what extent do the reasons for choosing police work differ from those that might be given for choosing other careers? What explains the different responses given by men and women?			
Reason	**Male**	**Female**	**Total**
Variety	62.2%	92.1%	69.4%
Responsibility	50.4	55.3	51.6
Serve public	48.7	50.0	49.0
Adventure	49.6	39.5	47.1
Security	46.2	34.2	43.3
Pay	43.7	42.1	43.3
Benefits	36.1	31.6	35.0
Advancement	31.9	34.2	32.5
Retirement	27.7	5.3	22.3
Prestige	16.0	13.2	15.3

Source: Harold P. Slater and Martin Reiser, "A Comparative Study of Factors Influencing Police Recruitment," *Journal of Police Science and Administration* 16 (1988): 170.

cruit people with at least some college education. In the largest cities, with populations greater than 500,000, about one-quarter of departments require at least some college education and a small percentage require either a two-year or a four-year degree (Hickman and Reaves, 2006). The percentage of state and local law enforcement agencies that required education beyond high school doubled between 1990 and 2000 and is likely to continue to increase over time (Reaves and Hickman, 2004). The expansion of criminal justice programs at community colleges and universities throughout the United States has produced increasing numbers of law enforcement officers who have taken college courses in criminology, law, sociology, and psychology. Competitive entry-level positions in the most sought-after agencies, including federal law enforcement agencies, state police departments, and those in the cities and suburbs (which provide the most generous pay and benefits), now often require college education. Fortunately, the expansion of college criminal justice programs has helped provide qualified applicants. Increasingly, college-educated officers seek advanced degrees in evening and Internet-based programs.

Debate continues about whether college-educated officers perform better than those who lack advanced education (Roberg and Bonn, 2004). The idea that college-educated officers would be better decision makers and make more effective officers helped to spur the creation of the federal Police Corps program (Gest, 2001). Although some researchers found that a college education makes little difference for police performance, other scholars concluded that employment of college-educated officers reduces disciplinary problems and citizens' complaints while it improves report writing and other aspects of performance (Krimmel, 1996; Lersch and Kunzman, 2001). Obviously, education alone does not determine performance; departmental training, supervision, and other factors also shape it.

In recent years, many police departments have had difficulty finding enough qualified recruits. Police departments face competition from the stepped-up recruiting efforts by the military as well as better pay and benefits in many private sector occupations. In addition, while the military has loosened its requirements with respect to criminal records and education, police departments typically maintain strict requirements for their recruits regarding education, ab-

Look at the qualifications for becoming a New York City police officer on the department's recruitment website. To link to this website, go to *The American System of Criminal Justice* 12e companion site at academic.cengage.com/criminaljustice/cole. Are the requirements necessary and appropriate? Do you fulfill the requirements?

sence of a criminal record, physical and psychological fitness, and passing drug tests (Heredia, 2007).

The Changing Profile of the Police

For most of the nation's history, almost all police officers were white men. Today, women and minorities represent a growing percentage of officers within police departments in many areas (see Figure 6.1). There are several reasons for this. In 1968, the National Advisory Commission on Civil Disorders found that poor police–minority relations contributed to the ghetto riots of the 1960s. The Equal Employment Opportunity Act of 1972 bars state and local governments from discriminating in their hiring practices. Pressured by state and federal agencies as well as by lawsuits, most city police forces have mounted campaigns to recruit more minority and female officers (Martin, 1991). Since the 1970s the percentage of minority group members and women has doubled. Nearly 24 percent of local police officers nationwide belong to minority groups. The percentage is even larger—38 percent—in big-city police departments in cities with populations greater than 500,000 (Hickman and Reaves, 2006).

The advancement of diversity within police forces reflects the American value of equal opportunity. Although the United States has a long history of racial and gender discrimination, such actions clash with the Constitution's equal protection clause. In addition to promoting equality, the expansion of employment opportunities to additional groups may provide significant benefits for law enforcement officials. If people in neighborhoods composed largely of members from a specific ethnic or racial group see the police as "outsiders" who are different and hostile, developing the community cooperation needed to prevent and investigate crimes can be difficult. When a force employs police officers from all demographic groups, the police gain legitimacy because they are seen as reflecting the interests of all people and there may be reductions in race-based disparities affecting who is stopped, searched, or arrested (Brown and Frank, 2006). Further, they may gain concrete benefits in communication and cooperation.

Unfortunately, many of the minority and female officers who served as trailblazers to desegregate many departments faced hostility and harassment

Examine the job description for "Police and Detectives" under Service Occupations described by the U.S. Department of Labor. To link to this website, go to *The American System of Criminal Justice* 12e companion site at academic.cengage.com/criminaljustice/cole. Does anything about the description surprise you?

The police are no longer exclusively made up of white males. Women and minorities now represent an increasing portion of the force, especially in urban areas. Are women or minority group members visible among the police officers that you see where you live?

© REUTERS/Chip East/Landov

from their colleagues as they attempted to prove themselves. Many of these courageous officers also faced disrespect and hostility from citizens who did not believe that they could be effective. Although the employment discrimination lawsuits that arise periodically indicate that some officers believe racial and gender discrimination still exists, especially with respect to promotions, female and minority officers have become well accepted as capable and valuable law enforcement professionals throughout the country.

Minority Police Officers

Before the 1970s many police departments did not hire nonwhites. As this practice declined, the makeup of police departments changed, especially in large cities. A study of the nation's 62 local police departments serving a population of 250,000 or more found that from 1990 to 2000 the percentage of African American officers rose to 20 percent of the force, Hispanics rose to 14 percent, and Asian/Pacific Islander/Native Americans to 3.2 percent (Reaves and Hickman, 2002). There was an additional 7 percent increase in minority representation from 2000 to 2003. The fact that minority officers now constitute 38 percent of the officers in the nation's largest cities represents a dramatic change in staff composition over the past two decades (Hickman and Reaves, 2006).

As the population and political power shift toward minorities in some American cities, the makeup of their police forces reflects this change. Three-quarters of Detroit's population is now African American, as is about 63 percent of the city's police officers. In El Paso and San Antonio, Texas, which have large Hispanic populations, 72 percent and 42 percent of those police departments are Hispanic, respectively. The extent to which the police reflect the racial composition of a city is believed to affect police–community relations and thus the quality of law enforcement. A survey of Detroit residents found that African Americans held more favorable attitudes toward the police than did whites. As researchers note, "In Detroit, the people who perform the police function are not alien to African Americans; instead they represent an indigenous force" (Frank et al., 1996: 332).

Women on the Force

Women have been police officers since 1905, when Lola Baldwin became an officer in Portland, Oregon. Prior to that time, many cities had "police matrons" to assist in handling women and children in jails but they did not have the power to arrest or engage in investigative and patrol activities (Horne, 2006). After Baldwin became the trailblazing first officer, the number of women officers remained small for most of the twentieth century because of the belief that policing was "men's work." This attitude changed as the result of federal and state laws against employment discrimination as well as court decisions enforcing those laws. Court decisions opened up police work for women by prohibiting job assignments by gender; changing minimum height, weight, and physical fitness requirements; and insisting that departments develop job classification and promotion criteria that were nondiscriminatory (*Blake v. Los Angeles*, 1979; *Griggs v. Duke Power Company*, 1971).

The percentage of female officers rose from 1.5 percent of local police officers in 1970 to over 11 percent by 2003 (Hickman and Reaves, 2006). In-

FIGURE 6.1

The changing profile of the American police officer

Today about one in ten officers is female and one in five belongs to a racial or ethnic minority.

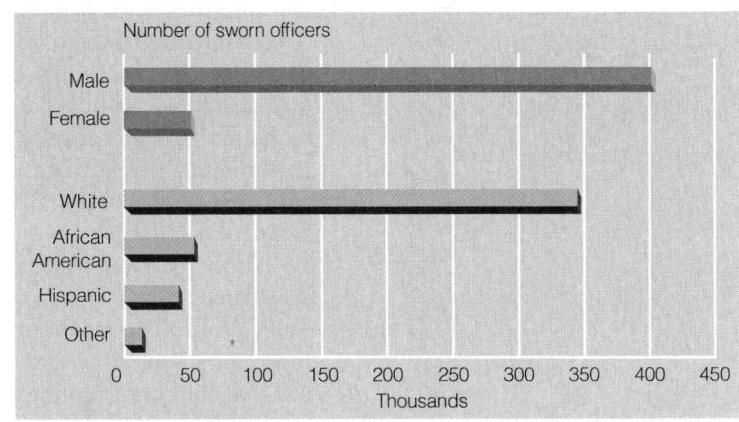

*Includes Asian, Pacific Islander, Native American, and Native Alaskan.

Source: Matthew J. Hickman and Brian A. Reaves, *Local Police Departments, 2003* (Washington, DC: Bureau of Justice Statistics, U.S. Government Printing Office, 2006), 7.

terestingly, the larger the department, the higher the proportion of women as sworn officers. In cities of more than 1 million inhabitants, women make up 17 percent of officers, but women make up only 6 percent of officers, on average, in cities with fewer than 10,000 residents (Hickman and Reaves, 2006). A study of 800 police departments by the International Association of Chiefs of Police (IACP) found that almost 20 percent of the departments surveyed had no women officers, and of the nation's 17,000 departments, only 123 had women serving as chiefs (IACP, 1998: 5). In large police agencies, women hold less than 10 percent of the supervisory positions and only 7 percent of the top command spots (ranks of captain and higher) are held by women (Horne, 2006).

Although some male police officers still question whether women can handle dangerous situations and physical confrontations, most policewomen have easily met the expectations of their superiors. However, the IACP survey found that 25 percent of top law enforcement officials expressed concerns that female officers could not handle physical conflicts (IACP, 1998: 23). Yet, studies done by the Police Foundation and other researchers have found that, in general, male and female officers perform in similar ways. Alissa Worden's research (1993) found few differences in the ways male and female officers viewed "their role, their clientele, or their departments." Research has also found that most citizens have positive things to say about the work of policewomen (Bloch and Anderson, 1974; Grennan, 1987; Sichel, 1978; Worden, 1993). Some researchers believe that women have generally superior performance in avoiding excessive use of force and interviewing crime victims, especially in cases of sexual assault and domestic violence (Prussel and Lonsway, 2001). Rape victims may also specifically request to be interviewed by a female officer, so gender diversity on a police force may be valuable for investigating specific types of crimes or dealing with specific victims and witnesses (Jordan, 2002).

Despite these findings, women still have trouble breaking into police work. Cultural expectations of women often conflict with ideas about the proper behavior of officers. Many people do not think women are tough enough to confront dangerous suspects. Especially with regard to patrol duty, questions like the following often come up:

- Can women handle situations that involve force and violence?
- What changes must be made in training and equipment in order to accommodate women?
- Should women and men have equal opportunities to be promoted?
- Does assigning men and women as patrol partners tend to create tension with their spouses?

As these questions reveal, women must work hard to overcome resistance from their fellow officers and citizens. In particular, they encounter resistance when they assert their authority. They must often endure sexist remarks and worse forms of sexual harassment. Originally, many male officers were upset by the entry of women into what they viewed as a male world. They complained that if their patrol partner was a woman, they could not be sure of her ability to provide necessary physical help in times of danger. The challenges for female officers from minority groups may be even more difficult if they perceive others to doubt their qualifications and ability because of their race as well as their gender (Dodge and Pogrebin, 2001).

According to Susan Martin, the statistics on women in policing provide both "good news and bad news. . . . because the steady numerical and proportional gains [are counterbalanced] by the concentrat[ion] of women at the bottom of the police hierarchy" (2005: 352). In a few cities, such as Atlanta, Boston, Detroit, and Portland, Oregon, a small number of women have risen to the top ranks of police departments. Elsewhere, employment discrimination lawsuits have helped open promotion opportunities for women. In many other departments, however, few women have been promoted to supervisory jobs. Thus, identifying and combating any remaining barriers to the recruitment, retention, and promotion of female officers usually falls to male administrators (S. Walker and Turner, 1992).

The role of women in police work will undoubtedly evolve along with changes in the nature of policing, in cultural values, and in the organization of law enforcement. As citizens become accustomed to women on patrol, female officers will find gaining their cooperation easier.

Training

The performance of the police is not based solely on the types of people recruited; it is also shaped by their training. Most states require preservice training for all recruits. This is often a formal course at a police academy, but in some states candidates for police jobs must complete a basic training program, at their own expense, before being considered for employment. Large departments generally run their own programs, while state police academies may train their own officers as well as recruits from municipal units. Candidates for positions in rural and small-town units may have to pay their own way through training programs at community colleges in order to receive the necessary certification to become a law enforcement officer. The courses range from two-week sessions that stress the handling of weapons to academic four-month programs followed by fieldwork. Recruits hear lectures on social relations, learn foreign-language phrases, and study emergency medical treatment.

Recruits need formal training in order to gain an understanding of legal rules, weapons use, and other aspects of the job. However, the police officer's job also demands social skills that cannot be learned from a lecture or a book. Much of the most important training of police officers takes place during a probationary period when new officers work with and learn from experienced officers. When new officers finish their classroom training and arrive for their first day of patrol duty, experienced officers may tell them, "Now, I want you to forget all that stuff you learned at the academy. You really learn your job on the streets."

The process of **socialization**—in which members learn the symbols, beliefs, and values of a group or subculture—includes learning the informal rather than the rule-book ways of law enforcement. New officers must learn how to look "productive," how to take shortcuts in filling out forms, how to keep themselves safe in dangerous situations, how to analyze conflicts so as to maintain order, and a host of other bits of wisdom, norms, and folklore that define the subculture of a particular department. Recruits learn that loyalty to other officers, esprit de corps, and respect for police authority are highly valued.

In police work, the success of the group depends on the cooperation of its members. All patrol officers operate under direct supervision, and their performance is measured by their contribution to the group's work. Besides supervisors, the officers' colleagues also evaluate and influence them. Officers within a department may develop strong, shared views on the best way to "handle" various situations.

How officers use their personal skills and judgment can mean the difference between defusing a conflict and making it worse so that it endangers citizens and

socialization
The process by which the rules, symbols, and values of a group or subculture are learned by its members.

Much of the most important police training occurs during the first months on patrol when "rookies" work with senior officers and are socialized into the police subculture. Are there any risks created by this method of training that may undercut a police chief's expectations about how police officers should perform?

other officers. In tackling their "impossible mandate," new recruits must learn the ways of the world from the other officers, on whom they depend and vice versa.

---

checkpoint

1. What are the main requirements for becoming a police officer?
2. How has the profile of American police officers changed?
3. What type of training do police recruits need?
4. Where does socialization to police work take place?
   (Answers are at the end of the chapter.)

THE POLICE SUBCULTURE

subculture
The symbols, beliefs, and values shared by members of a subgroup of the larger society.

A **subculture** is made up of the symbols, beliefs, values, and attitudes shared by members of a subgroup within the larger society. The subculture of the police helps define the "cop's world" and each officer's role in it. Like the subculture of any occupational group that sees itself as distinctive, police develop shared values that affect their view of human behavior and their role in society. For example, recent research indicates that officers' use of coercive methods, such as physical force, is associated with alignment between those officers' attitudes and the elements of the police subculture (Terrill, Paoline, and Manning, 2003).

As we just saw, the recruit learns the norms and values of the police subculture through a process of socialization. This begins at the training academy but really takes hold on the job through the interactions with experienced officers. The characteristics of a subculture are not static; they change as new members join the group and as the surrounding environment changes. For example, the composition of the police has changed dramatically during the past 30 years in terms of race, gender, and education. We should thus expect that these "new" officers will bring different attitudes and cultural values to the police subculture (S. Walker, 1999: 332).

Four issues are key to understanding the police subculture: the concept of the "working personality," the role of police morality, the isolation of the police, and the stressful nature of much police work.

The Working Personality

working personality
A set of emotional and behavioral characteristics developed by a member of an occupational group in response to the work situation and environmental influences.

Social scientists have demonstrated that there is a relationship between one's occupational environment and the way one interprets events. The police subculture produces a **working personality**—that is, a set of emotional and behavioral characteristics developed by members of an occupational group in response to the work situation and environmental influences. The working personality of the police thus influences the way officers view and interpret their occupational world. Two elements of police work define this working personality: (1) the threat of danger and (2) the need to establish and maintain one's authority (Skolnick, 1966: 44).

Danger

Because they often face dangerous situations, officers are keenly aware of clues in people's behavior or in specific situations that indicate that violence and lawbreaking are imminent. As they drive the streets, they notice things that seem amiss—a broken window, a person hiding something under a coat—anything that looks suspicious. As sworn officers, they are never off duty. People who know that they are officers will call on them for help at any time, day or night.

Throughout the socialization process, experienced officers warn recruits to be suspicious and cautious. Rookies are told about officers who were killed while trying to settle a family squabble or writing a traffic ticket. The message is clear: Even minor offenses can escalate into extreme danger. Constantly pressured to recognize signs of crime and be alert to potential violence, officers may become suspicious of everyone, everywhere. Thus, police officers maintain a constant state of "high alert," always on the lookout and never letting down their guard.

Being surrounded by risks creates tension in officers' lives. They may feel constantly on edge and worried about possible attack. This concern with danger can also affect their interactions with citizens and suspects. Citizens who come into contact with them may perceive their caution and suspicion as hostility, and officers' evident suspicion may generate angry or uncooperative reactions from suspects. As a result, on-the-street interrogations and arrests may lead to confrontations.

New York City police had to be ready for any threat while providing security for a meeting of the city's mayor, the state's governor, and the U.S. Secretary of Homeland Security during a heightened terrorism alert in 2004. Do the danger and stress police officers face create a risk that they will overreact when citizens fail to cooperate with their requests and instructions?

© Jeff Zelevansky/Reuters/Corbis

Authority

The second aspect of the working personality is the need to exert authority. Unlike many professionals, such as doctors, psychiatrists, and lawyers, whose clients recognize and defer to their authority, police officers must establish authority through their actions. Although the officer's uniform, badge, gun, and nightstick are symbols of his or her position and power, the officer's demeanor and behavior are what determine whether people will defer to him or her.

Victims are glad to see the police when they are performing their law enforcement function, but the order maintenance function puts pressure on officers' authority. If they try too hard to exert authority in the face of hostile reactions, officers may cross the line and use excessive force. For example, when sent to investigate a report of a fight, drunken neighbor, or domestic quarrel, they usually do not find a cooperative complainant. Instead, they must contend not only with the perpetrators but also with onlookers who might escalate the conflict. In such circumstances the officers must "handle the situation" by asserting authority without getting emotionally involved. Even when citizens challenge the conduct of police and their right to enforce the law, they expect the police to react in a detached or neutral manner. For officers who feel burdened with the twin pressures of danger and authority, this may not be easy. Thus, in the daily work of policing, the rules and procedures taught at the academy may affect officers' actions less than does the need to preserve and exert authority in the face of potential danger.

At times, officers must give orders to people with higher status. Professionals, businesspeople, and others sometimes respond to the officer not as a person working for the benefit of the community but as a public servant whom they do not respect. Poor people may also challenge officers' authority when, for example, they are angry about a situation or believe officers are targeting them unfairly. Police officers present themselves in the best light to the public when they perform their jobs in ways that demonstrate a commitment to fair treatment for everyone (Tyler and Wakslak, 2004). In stressful, conflict-laden situations, this may be difficult to do.

Researchers have studied expressions of disrespect by officers toward members of the public and vice versa (Reisig et al., 2004). One finding indicates that police officers' own expressions of disrespect in encounters with citizens, such as name-calling and other kinds of derogatory statements, occur most often when those citizens had already shown disrespect to the officers (Mastrofski, Reisig, and McCluskey, 2002).

In sum, working personality and occupational environment are closely linked and constantly affect the daily work of the police. Procedural rules and the structure of policing come second to the need to exert authority in the face of potential danger in many contexts in which citizens are angry, disrespectful, or uncooperative.

Police Morality

In his field observations of Los Angeles patrol officers, Steve Herbert found a high sense of morality in the law enforcement subculture. He believes that three aspects of modern policing create dilemmas that their morality helps them overcome. These dilemmas include (1) the contradiction between the goal of preventing crime and the officers' inability to do so, (2) the fact that officers must use their discretion to "handle" situations in ways that do not strictly follow procedures, and (3) "the fact that they invariably act against at least one citizen's interest, often with recourse to coercive force that can maim or kill" (Herbert, 1996: 799).

Herbert believes that justifying their actions in moral terms, such as upholding the law, protecting society, and chasing "bad guys," helps officers lessen the dilemmas of their work. Thus use of force may be condoned as necessary for "ridding evil from otherwise peaceable streets." It is the price we pay to cleanse society of the "punks," "crazies," and "terrorists." But police morality can also be applauded: Officers work long hours and are genuinely motivated to help people and improve their lives, often placing themselves at risk. Nonetheless, to the extent that police morality crudely categorizes individuals and justifies insensitive treatment of some community members, it contributes to police–citizen tensions.

Police Isolation

Police officers' suspicion of and isolation from the public may increase when they believe that the public is hostile to them. Many officers feel that people regard them with suspicion, in part because they have the authority to use force to gain compliance. Some scholars argue that this attitude increases officers' desire to use force on citizens (Regoli, Crank, and Culbertson, 1987). Public opinion polls have found that a majority of people have a high opinion of the police; however, as shown in "What Americans Think," various groups of people have different opinions regarding the police officers' ethical standards. Research shows that young people in high-crime neighborhoods may develop negative attitudes based on their own experiences in being watched and questioned by the police (Carr, Napolitano and Keating, 2007).

Police officers' isolation from the public is made worse by the fact that many officers interact with the public mainly in moments of conflict, emotion, and crisis. Victims of crimes and accidents are often too hurt or distraught to thank the police. Citizens who are told to stop some activity when the police are trying to keep order may become angry at the police. Even something as minor as telling someone to turn down the volume on a stereo can turn the police into the "bad guy" in the eyes of people who believe that the officers' authority limits citizens' entitlement to personal freedom. Ironically, these problems may be at their worst in poor neighborhoods where effective policing is needed most. There, pervasive mistrust of the police may keep citizens from reporting crimes and cooperating with investigations.

Because they believe that the public is hostile to them and that the nature of their work makes the situation worse, the police tend to separate themselves from the public and to form strong in-group ties. The police culture also encourages the bonding that often occurs among people who deal with violence. This solidarity "permits fallible men to perform an arduous and difficult task, and . . . places the highest value upon the obligation to back up and support a fellow officer" (Brown, 1981: 82).

One result of the demands placed on the police is that officers often cannot separate their job from other aspects of their lives. From the time they obtain badges and guns, they must always carry these symbols of the position—the tools of the trade—and be prepared to use them. Their obligation to remain vigilant even when off duty and to work at odd hours reinforces the values shared with other officers. Strengthening this bond is officers' tendency to socialize mainly with their families and other officers; indeed, they may have little social contact with people other than police officers. Further, their contacts with citizens can reinforce their perceptions that members of the public view them narrowly as police officers and not as neighbors, friends, and fellow community members. Wherever they go, the police are recognized by people who want to "talk shop"; others harangue them about what is wrong with police service. These incidents can also contribute to isolation.

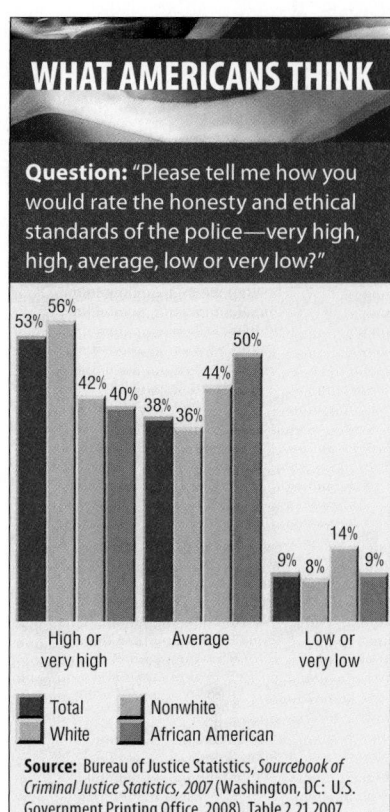

WHAT AMERICANS THINK

Question: "Please tell me how you would rate the honesty and ethical standards of the police—very high, high, average, low or very low?"

Source: Bureau of Justice Statistics, *Sourcebook of Criminal Justice Statistics, 2007* (Washington, DC: U.S. Government Printing Office, 2008), Table 2.21.2007.

Job Stress

Not only isolation but stress often results from the work environment and subculture of the police. This stress, stemming from the elements of danger and authority, can affect not only the way officers treat the citizens they encounter but also the officer's own health (G. Anderson, Litzenberger, and Plecas, 2002). Stress can also affect how officers interact with one another (Haarr and Morash, 1999). Scholars have found that work environment, work-family conflict, and individual coping mechanisms are the most significant predictors of stress for individual officers (Zhao, He, Loverich, and Cancino, 2003).

Always on alert, police sometimes face grave danger and yet feel unappreciated by a public they perceive to be hostile. Thus, that their physical and mental health suffers at times comes as no surprise. In fact, one study found police officers just behind coal miners as carrying out one of the most stressful occupations ("Most Stress," 2006). The effects of stress are compounded by the long hours many officers work, including double shifts that deprive them of sleep and make them work under conditions of severe fatigue (Vila and Kenney, 2002). The stress of police work may help explain why officer suicide poses a problem for some law enforcement agencies (Hackett and Violanti, 2003). However, there are debates among researchers about whether police officers' suicide rates are actually higher than those of other individuals who are similarly affected by factors, such as marital problems and alcohol abuse, that can be associated with higher rates of suicide (Goode, 2002).

In 2002, many Americans were shocked when a Nebraska state trooper killed himself after botching a background check on a man who later participated in killing five people during a bank robbery. When checking the serial number of a gun that he found on the man during a traffic stop, the trooper inadvertently typed the wrong numbers into the computer and failed to discover that the gun was stolen. Apparently, he blamed himself because he believed the homicides would have been prevented if he had arrested the man after doing a proper background check (Lorentzen, 2002). Because of their important duties and self-image as guardians of society, some police officers suffer severe stress when they cannot prevent tragic crimes from occurring.

Psychologists have identified four kinds of stress to which officers are subjected and the factors that cause each (Cullen et al., 1985):

1. *External stress.* This is produced by real threats and dangers, such as the need to enter a dark and unfamiliar building, to respond to "man with a gun" alarms, and to chase lawbreakers at high speeds.

2. *Organizational stress.* This is produced by the nature of work in a paramilitary structure: constant adjustment to changing schedules, irregular work hours, and detailed rules and procedures.

3. *Personal stress.* This can be caused by an officer's racial or gender status among peers, which can create problems in getting along with other officers and adjusting to group values that differ from one's own. Social isolation and perceptions of bias also contribute to personal stress.

4. *Operational stress.* This reflects the total effect of dealing with thieves, derelicts, and the mentally ill; being lied to so often that all citizens become suspect; being required to face danger to protect a public that seems hostile; and always knowing that one may be held legally liable for one's actions.

Although police executives have been slow to deal with the problems of stress, psychological and medical counseling have become more available. Some departments now have stress prevention, group counseling, liability insurance, and family involvement programs. Many states have more liberal disability and retirement rules for police than for other public employees, because police jobs are more stressful (Goolkasian, Geddes, and DeJong, 1989).

As we have seen, police officers face special pressures that can affect their interactions with the public and even harm their physical and mental health. How would you react to the prospect of facing danger and being on the lookout for crime at every moment, even when you were not actually working? It seems understandable that police officers become a close-knit group, yet their isolation from society may decrease their understanding of other people. It may also strengthen their belief that the public is ungrateful and hostile. As a result, officers' actions toward members of the public may be hostile, gruff, or even violent.

In sum, the effects of the police subculture on the behavior of officers are stronger in situations that produce conflict between the police and society. To endure their work, the police find they must relate to the public in ways that protect their own self-esteem. If the police view the public as hostile and police work as adding to that hostility, they will isolate themselves by developing strong values and norms to which all officers conform. In the rest of this chapter, we examine the contexts in which police officers work. Bear in mind how the elements of the police subculture could impact officers' behavior in these contexts.

checkpoint

5. What are the two key aspects of the police officer's working personality?
6. What are the four types of stress felt by the police?

reactive
Acting in response, such as police activity in response to notification that a crime has been committed.

proactive
Acting in anticipation, such as an active search for potential offenders that is initiated by the police without waiting for a crime to be reported. Arrests for crimes without victims are usually proactive.

POLICE RESPONSE AND ACTION

In a free society, people do not want police on every street corner asking them what they are doing. Thus, the police are mainly **reactive** (responding to citizen calls for service) rather than **proactive** (initiating actions in the absence of citizen requests). Studies of police work show that 81 percent of actions result from citizen telephone calls, 5 percent from citizens who approach an officer, and only 14 percent from officers in the field. These facts affect the way departments are organized and the way the police respond to cases.

Because they are mainly reactive, the police usually arrive at the scene only after the crime has been committed and the perpetrator has fled. This means that the police are hampered by the time lapse and sometimes by inaccurate information given by witnesses. For example, a mugging may happen so quickly that victims and witnesses cannot accurately describe what happened. In about a third of cases in which police are called, no one is present when the police arrive on the scene.

Citizens have come to expect that the police will respond quickly to every call, whether it requires immediate attention or can be handled in a more routine manner. This expectation has produced **incident-driven policing**, in which primarily calls for service instigate the response. Studies have shown, though, that less than 30 percent of calls to the police involve criminal law enforcement—most calls concern order maintenance and service (S. Walker, 1999: 80). To a large extent, then, reports by victims and observers define the boundaries of policing.

The police do use proactive strategies such as surveillance and undercover work to combat some crimes. When addressing crimes without victims, for example, they must rely on informers, stakeouts, wiretapping, stings, and raids. Police resources in many cities have been assigned to proactive efforts to apprehend people who use or sell illegal drugs. Because calls from victims reporting these crimes are few, crime rates for such offenses are nearly always reported as rates of arrest rather than rates of known criminal acts. Police efforts with respect to terrorism and homeland security also have a proactive emphasis. Law enforcement personnel attempt to intercept communications, monitor financial transactions and travel patterns, keep suspects under surveillance, and cultivate relationships with potential informers.

incident-driven policing
A reactive approach to policing emphasizing a quick response to calls for service.

Organizational Response

The organization of the police bureaucracy influences how the police respond to citizens' calls. Factors that affect the response process include the separation of police into various functional groups (patrol, vice, investigation, and so on), the quasi-military command system, and the techniques used to induce patrol officers to respond in desired ways.

Police departments are being reshaped by new communications technology, which tends to centralize decision making. The core of the department is the communications center, where commands are given to send officers into action. Patrol officers are expected to remain in constant touch with headquarters and must report each of their actions. Two-way radios, cell phones, and computers are the primary means by which administrators monitor the decisions of officers in the field. In the past, patrol officers might have administered on-the-spot justice to a mischievous juvenile, but now they must file a report, take the youth into custody, and start formal proceedings. Because officers must contact headquarters by radio or computer with reports about each incident, headquarters is better able to guide officers' discretion and ensure

New high-tech tools, connected to high-speed wireless communications, have become widely available to officers in the field. Here, Officer Mike Frome of Portland, Oregon, uses a mobile device that can scan a person's fingerprints and compare them with others in a database.

© John Klicker/The New York Times/Redux

that they comply with departmental policies. Among departments with more than 100 sworn officers, the percentage of state agencies using in-vehicle computers increased from 14 percent to 59 percent between 1990 and 2000. The use of such computers and nonmounted laptops in cars over the same time period increased from 19 percent to 68 percent for local police agencies (Reaves and Hickman, 2004). By 2003, nearly 90 percent of departments in cities with 25,000 or more inhabitants used in-vehicle computers (Hickman and Reaves, 2006). Police had access to computers in their vehicles in only 58 percent of towns with populations from 2,500 to 10,000 and in 36 percent of towns with populations below 2,500 (Hickman and Reaves, 2006). From these figures we can see that the availability of communications and information technology varies, depending on departmental resources.

Most residents in urban and suburban areas can now call 911 to report a crime or obtain help or information. The 911 system has brought a flood of calls to police departments—many not directly related to police responsibilities. In many places, the number of calls increased significantly as the spread of cell phones made it easier for people to make reports as incidents arose. In 1997, the Federal Communications Communication (FCC) set aside the 311 number for cities to use, if they choose, as a nonemergency number. Baltimore was the first city to implement the new number and it soon experienced a 42 percent reduction in 911 calls as many nonemergency calls were placed to 311 instead. Other cities, such as Detroit and New York, followed in Baltimore's footsteps, but not all cities have implemented a 311 call system. The FCC later set aside the 211 number for social services information and the 511 number for traffic information, but relatively few cities have yet implemented call centers to make use of those other numbers (McMahon, 2002). Although 911 systems can automatically trace the location of calls made from landlines, many cities are struggling to upgrade their 911 systems so that they can trace wireless calls to the vicinity of the nearest cell phone tower (Dewan, 2007). Such efforts to upgrade equipment, procedures, and training become more visible in the aftermath of tragedies. One such example was the murder of a University of Wisconsin student in 2008 who dialed 911 from her cell phone, apparently when confronted by an intruder in her apartment, yet the operator did not know her precise location or the nature of the emergency (Arnold, 2008). The 911 system remains the primary means for callers to reach their local government, but there are always concerns that those lines may become too tied up with emergency calls and thereby disrupt the ability of police and other emergency responders to receive quick reports about urgent situations.

The website of the Tukwila, Washington, Police Department provides guidance to citizens about when to call 911. To link to this website, go to *The American System of Criminal Justice* 12e companion site at academic.cengage.com/criminaljustice/cole.

differential response
A patrol strategy that assigns priorities to calls for service and chooses the appropriate response.

To improve efficiency, police departments use a **differential response** system that assigns priorities to calls for service. This system assumes that it is not always necessary to rush a patrol car to the scene when a call is received. The appropriate response depends on several factors—such as whether the incident is in progress, has just occurred, or occurred some time ago, as well as whether anyone is or could be hurt. A dispatcher receives the calls and asks for certain facts. The dispatcher may (1) send a sworn officer to the scene right away, (2) give the call a lower rank so that the response by an officer is delayed, (3) send someone other than a sworn officer, or (4) refer the caller to another agency. Evaluations of differential response policies have found that they contribute to effective use of police resources and satisfying public expectations about an agency's responsiveness.

The policy of differential response clearly saves police resources. It provides other benefits as well. For example, with trained officers answering "911," (1) more-detailed information is gathered from callers, (2) callers have a better sense of when to expect a response, and (3) patrol officers have more information about the case when they respond.

Some experts criticize centralized communications and decision making. Many advocates of community policing believe that certain technologies tend to isolate the police from citizens. By contrast, community-policing strategies attempt to enhance interaction and cooperation between officers and citizens (Morash and Ford, 2002). Widespread use of motorized patrols has meant that residents get only a glimpse of the officers cruising through their neighborhoods. Community-oriented policing attempts to overcome some of the negative aspects of centralized response, often by placing officers on foot or on bicycles or by dedicating specific officers' time to particular neighborhoods.

Productivity

Following the lead of New York's Compstat program, police departments in Baltimore, New Orleans, Indianapolis, and even smaller cities now emphasize precinct-level accountability for crime reduction (Santos, 2008). Through twice-weekly briefings before their peers and senior executives, precinct commanders must explain the results of their efforts to reduce crime. In the Compstat approach, they are held responsible for the success of crime control efforts in their precincts as indicated by crime statistics (Weisburd et al., 2003). Essential to this management strategy is timely, accurate information. Computer systems have been developed to put up-to-date crime data into the hands of managers at all levels (Willis, Mastrofski, and Weisburd, 2004). This allows discussion of department-wide strategies and puts pressure on low producers (Sherman 1998: 430; Silverman, 1999). This innovation has brought major changes to police operations and raised questions as to how police work should be measured. It has also raised questions about whether measures of performance based on data tend to move departments away from community policing by emphasizing a centralized hierarchy focused on accountability and control (Walsh and Vito, 2004).

Quantifying police work is difficult in part because of the wide range of duties and day-to-day tasks of officers (Coutts and Schneider, 2004). In the past, the crime rate and the clearance rate have been used as measures of "good" policing. A lower crime rate might be cited as evidence of an effective department, but critics note that other factors beside policing affect this measure.

The **clearance rate**—the percentage of crimes known to police that they believe they have solved through an arrest—is a basic measure of police performance. The clearance rate varies by type of offense. In reactive situations, this rate can be low. For example, the police may first learn of a burglary hours or even days later; the clearance rate for such crimes is only about 13 percent. Police find more success in handling violent crimes, in which victims often tend to know their assailants; the clearance rate is 44 percent (BJS, 2007a).

In proactive situations, the police are not responding to the call of a crime victim; rather, they seek out crimes. Hence, at least in theory, arrests for prostitution, gambling, and drug selling have a clearance rate of 100 percent, because every crime known to the police is matched with an arrest.

The arrest of a person often results in the clearance of other reported offenses, because the police can link some arrested persons with similar, unsolved crimes. Interrogation and lineups are standard procedures, as is the lesser-known operation of simply assigning unsolved crimes to the suspect. When an offender enters a guilty plea, the bargain may include an admission that he or she committed prior crimes. Professional thieves know that they can gain favors from the police in exchange for "confessing" to unsolved crimes that they may not have committed.

These measures of police productivity are sometimes supplemented by other data, such as the numbers of traffic citations issued, illegally parked cars ticketed, and suspects stopped for questioning, as well as the value of stolen goods recovered. These additional ways of counting work done reflect the fact that an officer may work hard for many hours yet have no arrests to show for his or her efforts (Kelling, 1992: 23). Some of these measures, however, may have adverse consequences for police-community relations. Citizens are usually not happy

clearance rate
The percentage rate of crimes known to the police that they believe they have solved through an arrest; a statistic used to measure a police department's productivity.

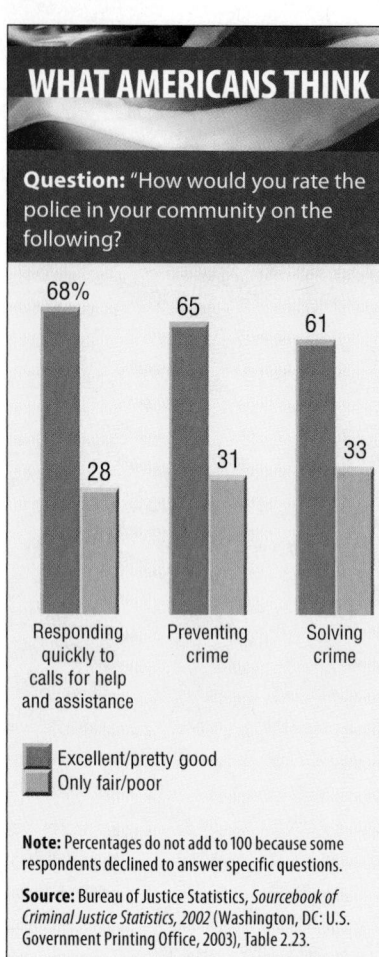

with the perception that officers may be expected to issue a specific number of traffic citations each day, since it leads residents to believe that officers make unjustified traffic stops simply to impress superiors. In New York City, lawsuits about improper searches of pedestrians led to a requirement that the police disclose publicly their statistics on stopping, questioning, and frisking people. In 2008, those statistics caused controversy both because their numbers were increasing and because police disproportionately stopped and questioned African Americans. African Americans constitute one-quarter of the city's population but were subjected to one-half of the stops by police officers (Baker, 2008b). In January through March 2008, New York City police made 145,098 street stops leading to 8,711 arrests, primarily for outstanding warrants or for possession of drugs or weapons (Baker 2008b). The police point to the number of arrests to justify the value of such stops, but critics point to the much larger number of innocent people who experienced an intrusion on their liberty and privacy to question whether the stops are actually used only when people's suspicious behavior creates a justification for police investigation. How do we weigh the costs and benefits of using such stops as a productivity measure that may effectively encourage officers to employ this strategy too frequently?

Society may benefit even more when officers spend their time in activities that are hard to measure, such as calming disputes, becoming acquainted with people in the neighborhood, and providing services to those in need. Some research indicates that officers who engage in activities that produce higher levels of measurable productivity, such as issuing citations or making arrests, also receive higher numbers of citizen complaints about alleged misconduct (Lersch, 2002). Would officers better serve the community by spending time in difficult-to-measure activities? Only further research can provide an answer. As indicated in "What Americans Think," many people seem satisfied by the responsiveness and effectiveness of the police.

One might think that police effectiveness would depend on a city's population, its crime level, and the size of its police force. As seen in Figure 6.2, however, these variables are not always related. The size of San Jose's police force is small relative to the population, but its rates of index offenses are low. In contrast, index offenses in Washington, D.C., rank in the middle range of the cities studied, but its force is the largest. The issue grows even more compli-

FIGURE 6.2

Sworn officers and UCR violent crime index offenses per 1,000 population in 10 U.S. cities (2004)

These major cities have varying numbers of police officers and crimes for every 1,000 residents. As you can see, the amount of crime and numbers of police do not correlate.

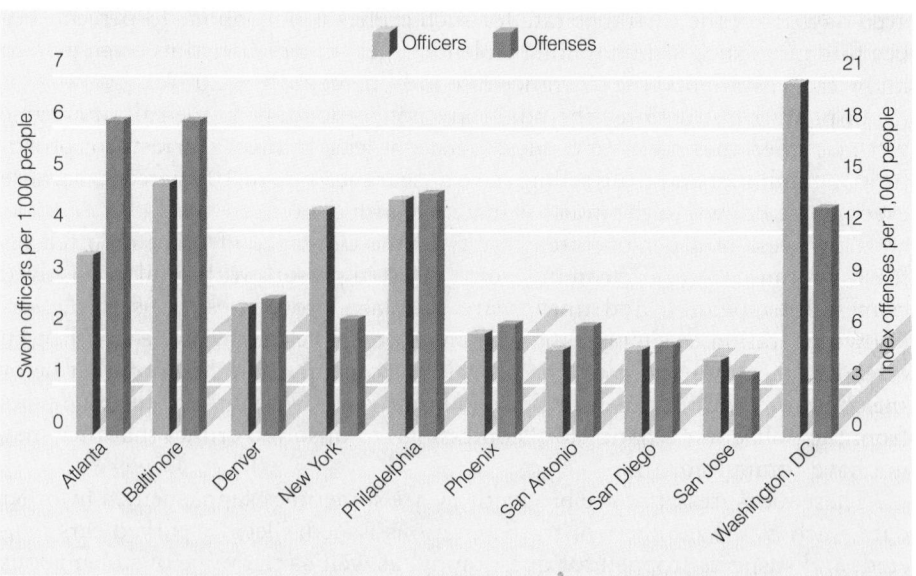

Source: Brian A. Reaves, "Census of State and Local Law Enforcement Agencies, 2004," *Bureau of Justice Statistics Bulletin*, (Washington, DC: Bureau of Justice Statistics, 2007), Appendix Table 4; Federal Bureau of Investigation, *Uniform Crime Reports, 2004*, (Washington, DC: U.S. Department of Justice, 2005), Section II, Table 8.

cated: Police productivity is governed in part by population density, the number of nonresidents who spend part of their day working or visiting in the area, local politics, and other factors. In sum, like other public agencies, the police have trouble gauging the quantity and quality of their work.

checkpoint

7. What is "incident-driven policing"?
8. What is "differential response"?
9. What is the basic measure of police productivity?

DELIVERY OF POLICE SERVICES

In service bureaucracies like the police, a distinction is often made between line and staff functions. **Line functions** are those that directly involve field operations such as patrol, investigation, traffic control, vice, juvenile crimes, and so on. By contrast, *staff functions* supplement or support the line functions. Staff functions are based in the chief's office and the support or services bureau, as well as in the staff inspection bureau. An efficient department maintains an appropriate balance between line and staff duties. Figure 6.3 shows the allocation of line personnel in the nation's six largest departments.

line functions
Police components that directly perform field operations and carry out the basic functions of patrol, investigation, traffic, vice, juvenile, and so on.

FIGURE 6.3

Distribution of sworn police personnel in the nation's six largest departments
What does the distribution of officers tell us about the role of the police in urban areas? How might smaller departments differ from these large urban departments?

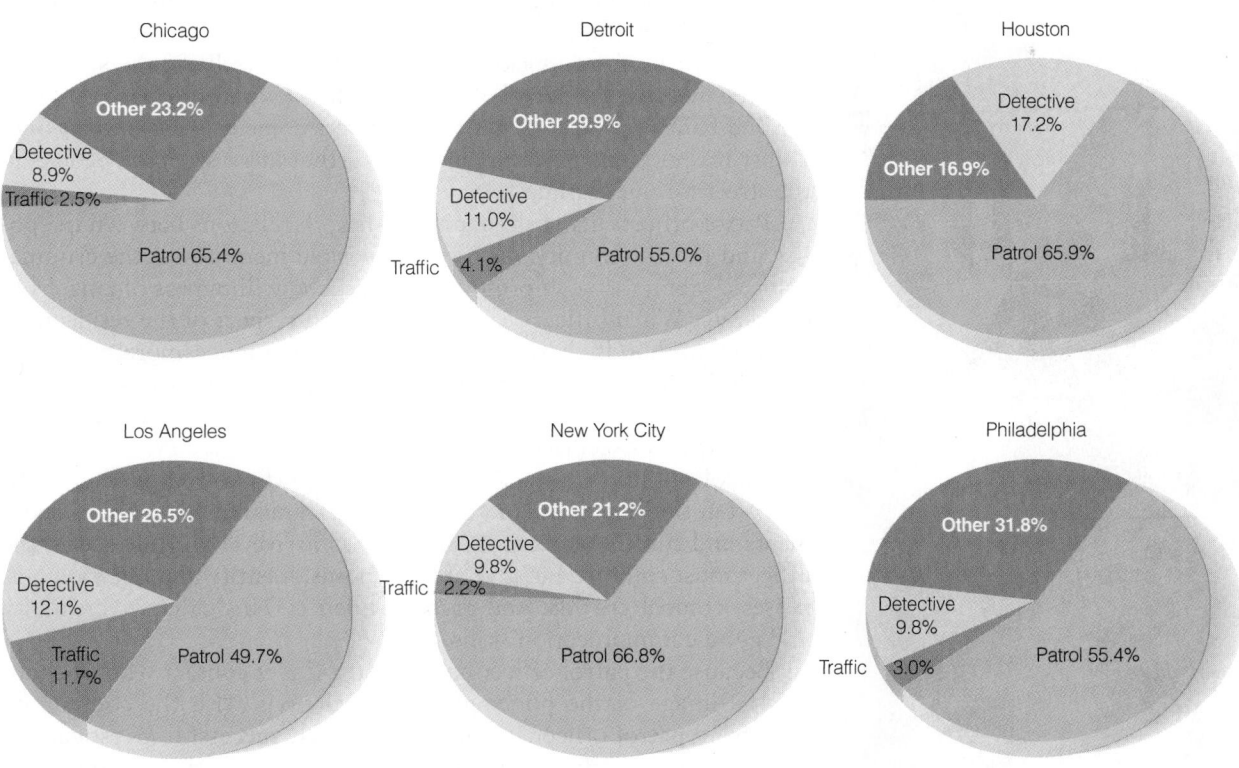

Note: *Other* refers to specialized units such as communications, antiterrorism, administration, and personnel.

Source: Adapted from Anthony Pate and Edwin Hamilton, *The Big Six: Policing America's Largest Departments* (Washington, DC: Police Foundation, 1990), 60.

Patrol Functions

Patrol is often called the backbone of police operations. The word *patrol* is derived from a French word, *patrouiller*, which once meant "to tramp about in the mud." This is an apt description of a function that one expert describes as "arduous, tiring, difficult, and performed in conditions other than ideal" (Chapman, 1970: ix). For most Americans the familiar sight of a uniformed and armed patrol officer, on call 24 hours a day, is what they would call "policing."

Every local police department has a patrol unit. Even in large departments, patrol officers account for up to two-thirds of all **sworn officers**—those who have taken an oath and been given the powers to make arrests and use necessary force in accordance with their duties. In small communities, police operations are not specialized, and the patrol force is the entire department. The patrol officer must be prepared for any imaginable situation and must perform many duties.

Television portrays patrol officers as always on the go—rushing from one incident to another and making several arrests in a single shift. A patrol officer may indeed be called to deal with a robbery in progress or to help rescue people from a burning building. However, the patrol officer's life is not always so exciting, often involving routine and even boring tasks such as directing traffic at accident scenes and road construction sites.

Most officers, on most shifts, do not make even one arrest (Bayley, 1994: 20). To better understand patrol work, note in Figure 6.4 how the police of Wilmington, Delaware, allocate time to various activities.

The patrol function has three parts: answering calls for help, maintaining a police presence, and probing suspicious circumstances. Patrol officers are well suited to answering calls, because they usually are near the scene and can move quickly to provide help or catch a suspect. At other times, they engage in **preventive patrol**—that is, making the police presence known in an effort to deter crime and to make officers available to respond quickly to calls. Whether walking the streets or cruising in a car, the patrol officer is on the lookout for suspicious people and behavior. With experience, officers come to trust in their own ability to spot signs of suspicious activity that merit stopping people on the street for questioning.

Patrol officers also help maintain smooth relations between the police and the community. As the most visible members of the criminal justice system, they can profoundly affect the willingness of citizens to cooperate. When officers earn the trust and respect of the residents of the neighborhoods they patrol, people become much more willing to provide information about crimes and suspicious activities. Effective work by patrol officers can also help reduce citizens' fear of crime and foster a sense of security.

Patrol officers' duties sound fairly straightforward, yet these officers often find themselves in complex situations requiring sound judgments and careful actions. As the first to arrive at a crime scene, the officer must comfort and give aid to victims, identify and question witnesses, control crowds, and gather evidence. This calls for creativity and good communication skills.

Because the patrol officer has the most direct contact with the public, the image of the police and their relations with the community stem from patrol officers' actions. Moreover, successful investigations and prosecutions often depend on patrol officers' actions in questioning witnesses and gathering evidence after a crime.

sworn officers
Police employees who have taken an oath and been given powers by the state to make arrests and use necessary force, in accordance with their duties.

preventive patrol
Making the police presence known, in order to deter crime and to make officers available to respond quickly to calls.

San Antonio, Texas, police officers question a man about a reported disturbance. Patrol officers must be skilled at interacting with all kinds of people in order to do their jobs effectively. They must also make quick decisions in dangerous situations. Which job requires a wider array of skills—a patrol officer dealing with a variety of daily situations or a detective investigating a crime?

FIGURE 6.4

Time allocated to patrol activities by the police of Wilmington, Delaware

The time spent on each activity was calculated from records for each police car unit. Note the range of activities and the time spent on each.

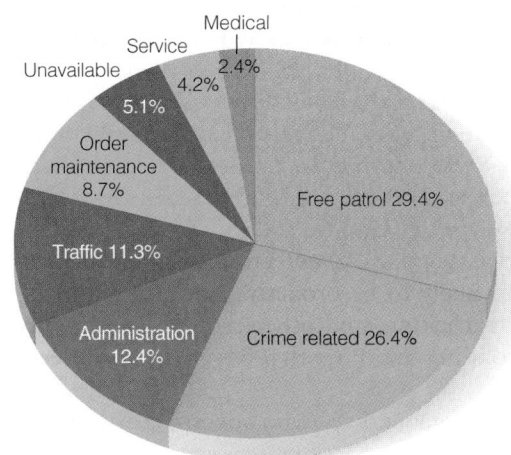

Free patrol: park and walk

Crime related: officer in trouble, suspicious person/vehicle, crime in progress, alarm, investigate crime not in progress, service warrant/subpoena, assist other police

Administration: meal break, report writing, firearms training, police vehicle maintenance, at headquarters, court related

Traffic: accident investigation, parking problems, motor vehicle driving problems, traffic control, fire emergency

Order maintenance: order maintenance in progress, animal complaint, noise complaint

Service: service related

Medical: medical emergency, at local hospital

Source: Jack R. Greene and Carl B. Klockars, "What Police Do," in *Thinking about Police*, 2nd ed., ed. Carl B. Klockars and Stephen D. Mastrofski (New York: McGraw-Hill, 1991), 279.

Is there a role for citizen-volunteers in the important patrol function of policing? Many cities have police auxiliary units, composed of uniformed volunteers, who assist with police functions including working as unarmed officers on patrol. For example, New York City has 4,500 volunteer auxiliary officers. Eight auxiliary officers in New York have been killed in the line of duty in the last fifty years. In a highly publicized tragedy in 2007, two auxiliary officers were killed by a shooting suspect that they were following down the street. One victim was a 19-year-old sophomore at New York University who was intent on a career as a prosecutor and the other was a 27-year-old aspiring novelist (Wilson, 2007). Consider the benefits and risks of using citizen-volunteers on police patrols as you examine "Civic Engagement: Your Role in the System."

Because the patrol officer's job involves the most contact with the public, the best-qualified officers should be chosen to perform it. However, because of the low status of patrol assignments, many officers seek higher-status positions such as that of detective. A key challenge facing policing is to grant to patrol officers a status that reflects their importance to society and the criminal justice system.

civic engagement
your role in the system

Your town's mayor has asked you to lead a community committee to study whether a volunteer auxiliary police unit should be established to assist the regular police. *Make a list of the benefits and risks of using citizen-volunteers. Would you support or oppose the creation of the unit?* Then look at the description of the police auxiliary unit in Baltimore County, Maryland. To link to this website, go to *The American System of Criminal Justice* 12e companion site at academic.cengage.com/criminaljustice/cole.

checkpoint

10. What is the difference between line and staff functions?
11. What are the three parts of the patrol function?

Investigation

All cities with a population of more than 250,000, and 90 percent of smaller cities, have officers called *detectives* assigned to investigative duties. Detectives make up 15 percent of police personnel. Compared with patrol officers, they have a higher status in the department. Their pay is higher, their hours are more flexible, and they are supervised less closely. Detectives do not wear uniforms, and their work is considered more interesting than that of patrol officers. In addition, they engage solely in law enforcement rather than in order maintenance or service work; hence, their activities conform more closely to the image of the police as crime fighters.

Within federal law enforcement agencies, the work of special agents is similar to that of detectives. Several federal agencies, such as Customs and Border Protection and the Fish and Wildlife Service, have uniformed officers. However, the work in many other agencies, such as the FBI, DEA, and Secret Service, is primarily carried out by plainclothes officers who focus on investigations. One key difference between federal special agents and detectives in local departments is that federal agents are more likely to be proactive in initiating investigations to prevent terrorism, drug trafficking, and other crimes. Local police detectives are typically reactive, responding to crimes that have been discovered or reported.

Detectives in small departments are generalists who investigate whatever crimes occur, but in large departments they are assigned to special units such as homicide, robbery, auto theft, forgery, and burglary. In recent decades, because of public pressures, some departments have set up new special units to deal with bias crimes, child abuse, sexual assault, and computer crime (Bayley, 1994: 26).

Most investigative units are separated from the patrol chain of command. Many argue that this results in duplication of effort and lack of continuity in handling cases. It often means that vital information known by one branch is not known by the other.

Like patrol, criminal investigation is largely reactive. Detectives become involved after a crime has been reported and a patrol officer has done a preliminary investigation. The job of detectives is mainly to talk to people—victims, suspects, witnesses—in order to find out what happened. On the basis of this information, detectives develop theories about who committed the crime and then set out to gather the evidence that will lead to arrest and prosecution. David Bayley notes that detectives do not maintain an open mind about the identity of the offender. They know that if people on the scene cannot identify the suspect, they are not likely to find him or her on their own. Detectives collect physical evidence not to find a suspect but rather to support testimony that identifies a suspect (Bayley, 1994: 26).

Herman Goldstein (1977: 55) outlines the process of investigation as follows:

■ When a serious crime occurs and the suspect is identified and caught right away, the detective prepares the case to be presented to the prosecuting attorney.

■ When the suspect is identified but not caught, the detective tries to locate him or her.

■ When the offender is not identified but there is more than one suspect, the detective conducts investigations to determine which one committed the crime.

■ When there is no suspect, the detective starts from scratch to find out who committed the crime.

In performing an investigation, detectives depend not only on their own experience but also on technical experts. Much of the information they need comes from criminal files, lab technicians, and forensic scientists. Many small departments turn to the state crime laboratory or the FBI for such information. Detectives are often pictured as working alone, but in fact they are part of a team.

Although detectives focus on serious crimes, they are not the only ones who investigate crimes. Patrol, traffic, vice, and juvenile units may also do so. In small towns and rural areas, patrol officers must conduct investigations because police departments are too small to have separate detective bureaus. In urban areas, because they tend to be the first police to arrive at the scene of a crime, patrol officers must do much of the initial investigative work. As we have seen, the patrol unit's investigation can be crucial. Successful prosecution of many kinds of cases, including robbery, larceny, and burglary, is closely linked to the speed with which a suspect is arrested. If patrol officers cannot obtain information from victims and witnesses right away, the chance of arresting and prosecuting the suspect greatly decreases.

Apprehension

The discovery that a crime has been committed sets off a chain of events leading to the capture of a suspect and the gathering of the evidence needed to convict that person. It may also lead to several dead ends, such as a lack of clues pointing to a suspect or a lack of evidence to link the suspect to the crime.

The process of catching a suspect has three stages: detection of a crime, preliminary investigation, and follow-up investigation. Depending on the outcome of the investigation, a fourth step may follow: clearance and arrest. As shown in Figure 6.5, these actions are designed to use criminal justice resources to arrest a suspect and assemble enough evidence to support a charge. Here is a fuller description of each step.

1. *Detection of a crime.* Although patrol officers sometimes discover crimes, information that a crime has been committed usually comes in a call to the police. For example, automatic alarms linked to police headquarters could alert the police to a crime on business premises. Such direct communications help shorten response time and increase the chances of catching the suspect.

FIGURE 6.5
The apprehension process
Apprehension of a felony suspect results from a sequence of actions by patrol officers and detectives. Coordination of these efforts is key to solving major crimes.

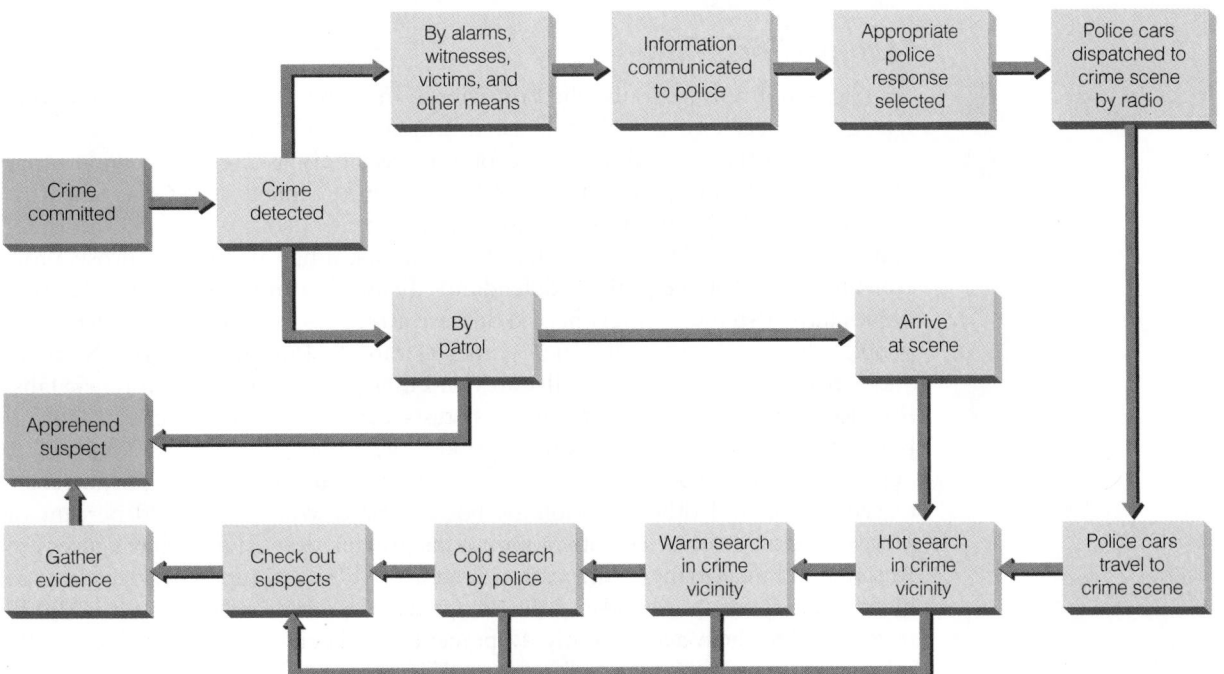

2. *Preliminary investigation.* The first law enforcement official on the scene is usually a patrol officer who has been dispatched by radio. The officer helps the victim, secures the crime scene for investigation, and documents the facts of the crime. If a suspect is present or nearby, the officer conducts a "hot" search and may apprehend the suspect. This initial work is crucial. The officer must gather the basic facts, including the name of the victim, a description of the suspect, and the names of witnesses. After the information is collected, it is sent to the investigation unit.

3. *Follow-up investigation.* After a crime has been brought to the attention of the police and a preliminary investigation has been made, the detective decides what course of action to pursue. In big-city departments, incident reports from each day are analyzed the next morning. Investigators receive assignments based on their specialties. They study the information, weigh each factor, and decide whether the crime can likely be solved.

    Some departments have guidelines for making these decisions so that resources will be used efficiently. If the detectives decide there is little chance of solving the crime quickly, the case may be dropped. Steven Brandl found that in burglary and robbery follow-up investigations, the value of the lost property and the detective's belief that the case could be resolved through an arrest were the main factors affecting how much time and effort were spent in solving the crime (1993: 414).

    When detectives decide that a full-scale investigation is warranted, a wider search—known as a "cold" search—for evidence or weapons is carried out. Witnesses may be questioned again, informants contacted, and evidence gathered. Because of the pressure of new cases, however, an investigation may be shelved so that resources can support "warmer" cases.

4. *Clearance and arrest.* The decision to arrest is a key part of the apprehension process. In some cases, further evidence or links between suspects and others are not discovered if arrests are made too soon. A crime is considered *cleared* when the evidence supports the arrest of a suspect. If a suspect admits having committed other unsolved crimes, those crimes are also cleared. However, when a crime is cleared in police files, the suspect will not necessarily be found guilty in court.

Forensic Techniques

 American police have long relied on science in gathering, identifying, and analyzing evidence. Through the television drama *CSI* (*Crime Scene Investigation*) and its spin-offs, the public has become increasingly aware of the wide range of scientific testing techniques used for law enforcement purposes. Scientific analysis of fingerprints, blood, semen, hair, textiles, soil, weapons, and other materials has helped the police identify criminals. It has also helped prosecutors convince jurors of the guilt of defendants. Beginning in the 1990s, these techniques have also increasingly helped defense attorneys establish the innocence of people who are in prison for such crimes as rape and murder (Dwyer, Neufeld, and Scheck, 2001). Although all states and many large cities have forensic labs, this does not guarantee that the latest tests can be used in all cases. Not all labs have the same technical equipment and personnel. In addition, some police departments, especially those in small towns and rural areas, have little access to crime labs and other technology. For example, while nearly 90 percent or more of agencies in cities with populations greater than 25,000 have access to Automated Fingerprint Identification Systems (AFIS)—computerized systems to match fingerprints, only 64 percent of agencies in towns with 2,500 to 10,000 residents have such access. Only 47 percent of agencies with fewer than 2,500 inhabitants have access to such systems (Hickman and Reaves, 2006). We shall examine issues concerning forensic techniques in greater detail in Chapter 7.

A police officer in Santa Ana, California, dusts the door of a stolen car in order to look for fingerprints. Police departments use various forensic techniques to discover evidence. Some techniques are used at crime scenes and others involve tests in scientific laboratories. Which techniques are likely to be most effective?

© Spencer Grant/PhotoEdit

Research on Investigation

The results of several studies raise questions about the value of investigations and the role detectives play in apprehension. This research suggests that the police have attached too much importance to investigation as a means of solving crimes and shows that most crimes are cleared because of arrests made by the patrol force at or near the scene. Response time is key to apprehension, as is the information given by the victim or witnesses.

A classic study of 153 large police departments found that a key factor in solving crimes was identification of the perpetrator by the victim or witnesses. Of those cases that were not solved right away but were cleared later, most were cleared by routine procedures such as fingerprint searches, tips from informants, and mug-shot "show-ups." The report found that actions by the investigative staff mattered in very few cases. In sum, about 30 percent of the crimes were cleared by on-scene arrest and another 50 percent through identification by victims or witnesses when the police arrived. Thus, only about 20 percent could have been solved by detective work. Even among this group, however, the study found that most crimes "were also solved by patrol officers, members of the public who spontaneously provide further information, or routine investigative practices" (Greenwood, Chaiken, and Petersilia, 1977: 227).

In many cities, the amount of serious crime has gone down during the past decade, but the percentage of unsolved cases has remained relatively stable. In part this may be due to the lack of resources allocated to pursuing "cold cases." Detectives emphasize that although forensic tools are important, solving crimes "the old fashioned way" through much street work is still effective.

Does this research show that detectives are not important? No. Some cases are weak with little evidence, some are strong with a lot of evidence. Police need not devote a great deal of effort in these polar cases. However, in between lie cases with moderate evidence. These do require additional effort by detectives, and, as one researcher found, this "is extremely important with respect to subsequent making of follow-up arrests" (Bayley, 1998: 149). A study of a Midwestern department's follow-up investigations of burglary and robbery backs up this finding (Brandl and Frank, 1994: 163).

The detective's role is important in at least two ways besides solving crimes. First, the status of detective provides a goal to which patrol officers can aspire and thereby gives them an incentive to excel in their work. Second, the public expects the police to conduct investigations. Citizens may have more trust in the police or feel more willing to cooperate with them when they see investigations being conducted, even if those investigations do not always lead to arrests.

checkpoint

12.   What is the job of the detective?
13.   What are the four steps of the apprehension process?

Special Operations

Patrol and investigation are the two largest and most important units in a police department. In metropolitan areas, however, special units are set up to deal with specific types of problems. The most common such units concern traffic, vice, and juveniles. Some cities also have units to deal with organized crime and drugs. Even with special units in place, however, patrol officers and investigators continue to deal with the same problems.

Traffic

Traffic regulation is a major job of the police. On average, 7 percent of officers work in traffic units (Bayley, 1994: 94). The police regulate the flow of vehicles, investigate accidents, and enforce traffic laws. This work may not seem to have much to do with crime fighting or order maintenance, but in fact it does. Besides helping maintain order, enforcement of traffic laws educates the public by promoting safe driving habits and provides a visible service to the community.

Traffic duty can also help the police catch criminals. In enforcing traffic laws, patrol officers can stop cars and question drivers. Stolen property and suspects linked to other criminal acts are often found this way. Most departments can now automatically check license numbers against lists of wanted vehicles and suspects.

Enforcement of traffic laws offers a good example of police discretion. When officers stop drivers for traffic violations, they choose from among various options that include issuing a citation, giving a warning, making an arrest for drunk driving or other offense, or letting the driver go. An officer's specific decision in any situation may depend on a number of factors including department policies, the attitude of the driver, and the amount of time involved in processing paperwork for a citation or arrest.

Traffic work is mostly proactive, and the level of enforcement depends in part on departmental policies. Guided by these policies, officers target certain kinds of violations or certain highways. Some departments expect officers to issue a prescribed number of citations during each shift. Although these norms may be informal, they offer a way of gauging the productivity of traffic officers. For the most part, selective enforcement is the general policy, because the police have neither the desire nor the resources to enforce all traffic laws.

Vice

Enforcement of vice laws depends on proactive police work, which often involves the use of undercover agents and informers. Most big-city police departments have a vice unit. Vice officers often must engage in degrading activities, such as posing as prostitutes or drug dealers, in order to catch lawbreakers. The special nature of vice work requires members of the unit to be well trained in the legal procedures that must be followed if arrests are to lead to convictions.

The potential for corruption in this type of police work presents administrative problems. Undercover officers are in a position to blackmail gamblers and drug dealers and may also be offered bribes. In addition, officers must be transferred when their identities become known.

The growth of undercover work and electronic surveillance, common in vice patrols, troubles critics who favor more open policing. They fear that the use of these tactics violates civil liberties and increases government intrusion into the private lives of citizens, whether or not those citizens commit crimes.

Drugs

Many large cities have a bureau to enforce drug laws. More than 80 percent of cities with populations larger than 100,000 have such units, but it is much less common in smaller cities (Hickman and Reaves, 2006). Many city police departments also participate in multiagency task forces focused on drugs. These agencies may also be linked to task forces that deal with organized crime or with gangs involved in drug dealing. They may use sting operations to arrest drug sellers on the street or to provide drug education in the community.

Drug enforcement sometimes reflects the goal of *aggressive patrol*, or assigning resources so as to get the largest number of arrests and stop street dealing. Police executives believe that they must show dealers and the community that drug laws are enforced.

The police use various strategies to attack drug dealing. One of these involves inspections of houses and buildings used by drug dealers. Those that do not meet city standards can be boarded up in order to rid the neighborhood of dealers. Streets where drugs are dealt openly can be flooded with officers who engage in proactive stops and questioning.

Another strategy is to disrupt the drug market. By flooding an area with officers and closing off abandoned buildings, the police can shut down drug sales in a specific location. This approach has been used in other parts of New York, in Los Angeles, and in other cities. But how effective is it? Do these efforts simply shift the drug market to another area, or do they actually reduce the availability of drugs?

Although some officers prefer patrolling a beat rather than being a drug cop, other officers enjoy the work. As Officer Marcus Laffey of the NYPD explained, moving to narcotics from being a beat cop was refreshing. "For one thing, you deal only with criminals. No more domestic disputes, barricaded schizophrenics, or D.O.A.s, the morass of negotiable and nonnegotiable difficulties people have with their neighbors or boyfriends or stepchildren." Laffey says that patrol cops deal with the "fluid whole of people's lives, but usually when the tide's going out." On the narcotics squad, he notes that "now all I do is catch sellers of crack and heroin, and catch their customers to show that they sold it. Patrol is politics, but narcotics is pure technique" (Laffey, 1999: 29).

Although arrests for drug sale or possession have increased dramatically, some observers believe that this is not the best way to deal with the problem. Many public officials argue that drugs should be viewed as a public health problem rather than as a crime problem. Critics of current policies believe that society would benefit if more resources went to drug treatment programs than to police actions that fill prisons without doing much to reduce drug use.

checkpoint

14. What are three kinds of special operations units that police departments often employ?

ISSUES IN PATROLLING

Patrol officers are the frontline personnel who bear the primary responsibility for all of the major functions of policing, including law enforcement, order maintenance, and service. The effectiveness of patrol officers relies in part on the strategies that police administrators use to distribute personnel throughout a city or county and to instruct officers about practices and priorities. For each specific problem that arises, police agencies instruct their officers to perform in ways tailored to each problem; different problems require different modes of operation.

For example, when police departments throughout metropolitan Washington, D.C., desperately hunted for the sniper who assassinated random victims during October 2002, they instructed officers to scrutinize light-color vans and trucks similar to those reportedly near several shootings, to remain in a high state of readiness for quick response to any reported shooting, and to be a highly visible, mobile presence in commercial areas. The police employed a "swarming strategy" by attempting to close every road and highway in the vicinity of a shooting as quickly as possible after a sniper attack was reported (Weil and Dvorak, 2002). Similar strategies have been used to reduce problems in certain New York City precincts by sending "waves of rookies, teamed with seasoned officers, into high-crime areas" (Hauser, 2008). By contrast, departments that can focus on long-term trends in crime control or service instead of an immediate crisis may be able to establish specific patterns of patrol that emphasize having officers walk within neighborhoods and build personal relationships with individual citizens.

In the last 30 years, many studies been done on police methods of assigning tasks to patrol officers, mobilizing them, and communicating with them. In spite of their mixed conclusions, these studies have caused experts to rethink some aspects of patrolling. However, even when researchers agree on which patrol practices are the most effective, those practices often run counter to the desires of departmental personnel. For example, foot patrol may be important for some community-policing strategies, but many officers would prefer to remain in squad cars rather than pound the pavement. Police administrators therefore must deal with many issues in order to develop and implement effective patrol strategies.

Assignment of Patrol Personnel

In the past it has been assumed that patrol officers should be assigned where and when they will be most effective in preventing crime, keeping order, and serving the public. For the police administrator, the question has been "Where should the officers be sent, when, and in what numbers?" There are no guidelines to answer this question, and most assignments seem to be based on the notion that patrols should be concentrated in "problem" neighborhoods or in areas where crime rates and calls for service are high. Thus, the assignment of officers is based on factors such as crime statistics, 911 calls, degree of urbanization, pressures from business and community groups, ethnic composition, and socioeconomic conditions.

Patrol officers are assigned to shifts and to geographic areas. Demands on the police differ according to the time of day, day of the week, and even season of the year. Most serious crimes occur during the evening hours, and the fewest occur in the early morning. Police executives try to allocate their patrol resources according to these variables. Read the Close Up box about patrol officers in San Francisco to get a sense for the variety and unpredictability of events

CLOSE UP

The Day Has Just Gone from Zero to 60

OFFICERS RAY VARGAS and Nate Steger are on patrol. It's another sunny afternoon in the Mission District, and dead quiet. Vargas and Steger don't usually ride together, but their regular partners are off today, so they share a radio car and prowl Mission Street spine, waiting for a call, or something to happen.

The in-car computer lights up, and shows a call for service on Bryant Street near 18th. Someone has left a bus illegally parked on the street for several days, and the caller wants it towed.

Police work can be very glamorous. Just not today....

Vargas, a 38-year-old former bike messenger, spots a Toyota with no front license plate and decides to pull it over. The car turns into 26th Street from Mission. Vargas follows and notices that the car has picked up speed. Instinct tells him something is amiss. The day has just gone from zero to 60.

He hits the flashing lights as the car makes a right on Capp. He hits the gas and takes the corner fast. The car leans hard to the left.... Up ahead, the Toyota is moving fast, and the driver is now making an illegal turn through heavy traffic....

The cruiser flies down Capp. The siren screams. Flashing red-and-blue lights flicker across graffiti-smeared walls. Adrenaline pumps and the heart beats wildly. The street is narrow and lined with cars. Tunnel vision sets in, making the street seem to be an inch wide as the big police cruiser picks up speed....

It looks like the Toyota's going to jackrabbit, but the driver pulls over halfway down Cesar Chavez.... From behind, three young men are visible inside the car, two in front and one in the back.

Vargas gets out and approaches the driver's side. His .40 caliber semiautomatic pistol is holstered, but his hand hovers over it.

"Put your hands where I can see them," he says, then slaps the rear passenger window and barks to the man inside: "Let me see your hands now."

Vargas reaches into the car and takes the keys. He places them on the car roof....

Steger is on the passenger side. He orders the men to get out of the car one at a time. They're all wearing baggy pants and flat-billed baseball caps turned sideways.... By now, two other cop cars have arrived. The officers handcuff the men and lean them against a chain-link fence that runs along the sidewalk. The driver and passengers say they've done nothing wrong. But one of them is on proba-

tion, so the cops have the authority to search the car. Steger checks the trunk while Vargas looks under the seats. He pulls out a tire jack and holds it aloft, about 30 feet from where the driver and passengers sit.

"What's this?," he asks. "It looks like the slide for a shotgun. You got any weapons? Anything I should know about?"

"That's a jack handle," the driver responds with an angry laugh. "I used it to change my tire.... Why you hassling me?"

Vargas ducks back inside the car and keeps searching. But there are no weapons, no drugs, no contraband. He returns to the cruiser and takes out his ticket book. The driver's going to get a citation for making an illegal left turn.

The men are uncuffed. They massage their wrists as they get back into the Toyota. The Toyota pulls into traffic and slows down. In the other lane, facing the opposite direction of the Toyota, is a white Chevy Caprice. The man in the backseat of the Toyota leans out the window and makes hand gestures at the man in the Caprice.

"He's flashing gang signs," Steger says. It's unclear whether the people in the two cars are friends or enemies....

"I was pretty sure we were going to find drugs in there," Vargas says. "I think they probably tossed it when they were going down Capp."

Steger gets in the car. He calls the dispatch to say they've cleared the incident. It's quiet again in the Mission—until the next call.

Source: John Coopman, "The Day Has Just Gone From Zero to 60," *San Francisco Chronicle*, May 14, 2007 (http://www.sfgate.com).

Researching the Internet

Think about the knowledge needed and kinds of decisions made by the San Francisco officers while on patrol Then look at the curriculum of the Los Angeles Police Academy by going to *The American System of Criminal Justice* 12e companion site at academic.cengage.com/criminaljustice/cole. Are officers receiving the training that they really need?

that may occur during a patrol officer's shift. Also take note of the forms of communication employed by the patrol officers.

The assignment of officers to specific locations is only one aspect of patrol strategies. Law enforcement officials must also decide how police will travel on patrol and what activities the officers will emphasize. Experimentation with different strategies in various cities has led to numerous choices for police leaders. In addition, research on these strategies sheds light on the strengths and weaknesses of various options. We shall examine several options in greater detail: (1) preventive patrol, (2) hot spots, (3) rapid response time, (4) foot versus motorized patrol, (5) one-person versus two-person patrol units, and (6) aggressive patrol.

Preventive Patrol

Preventive patrol has long been thought to help deter crime. Since the days of Sir Robert Peel, experts have argued that a patrol officer's moving through an area will keep criminals from carrying out illegal acts. In 1974 this assumption was tested in Kansas City, Missouri. The surprising results shook the theoretical foundations of American policing (Sherman and Weisburd, 1995).

In the Kansas City Preventive Patrol Experiment, a 15-beat area was divided into three sections, each with similar crime rates, population characteristics, income levels, and numbers of calls to the police. In one area, labeled "reactive," all preventive patrol was withdrawn, and the police entered only in response to citizens' calls for service. In another section, labeled "proactive," preventive patrol was raised to as much as four times the normal level; all other services were provided at the same levels as before. The third section was used as a control, with the usual level of services, including preventive patrol, maintained. After observing events in the three sections for a year, the researchers concluded that the changes in patrol strategies had had *no* major effects on (1) the amount of crime reported, (2) the amount of crime as measured by citizen surveys, or (3) citizens' fear of crime (Kelling et al., 1974). Neither a decrease nor an increase in patrol activity had any apparent effect on crime.

Despite contradictory findings of other studies using similar research methods, the Kansas City finding "remains the most influential test of the general deterrent effects of patrol on crime" (Sherman and Weisburd, 1995: 626). Because of this study, many departments have shifted their focus from law enforcement to maintaining order and serving the public. Some have argued that if the police cannot prevent crime by changing their patrol tactics, they may serve society better by focusing patrol activities on other functions while fighting crime as best they can.

Those who support the professional crime-fighting model of policing have criticized this and other studies that question the effectiveness of preventive patrol. They claim that the research attacks the heart of police work. But the research simply calls into question the inflexible aspects of preventive patrol.

Hot Spots

In the past, patrols were organized by "beats." It was assumed that crime can happen anywhere, and the entire beat must be patrolled at all times. Research shows, however, that crime is not spread evenly over all times and places. Instead, direct-contact predatory crimes, such as muggings and robberies, occur when three elements converge: motivated offenders, suitable targets, and the absence of anyone who could prevent the violation. This means that resources should center on "hot spots," places where crimes are likely to occur (L. E. Cohen and Felson, 1979: 589).

In a study of crime in Minneapolis, researchers found that a small number of hot spots—3 percent of streets and intersections—produced 50 percent of calls to the police. By analyzing the places from which calls were made, administrators could identify those that produced the most crime (Sherman, Gartin, and Buerger, 1989: 27). Because research casts doubt on the ability of officers to identify hot spots for themselves, departments need to gather data about crimes and order maintenance problems (Bichler and Gaines, 2005).

With this knowledge, officers can be assigned to **directed patrol**—a proactive strategy designed to direct resources to known high-crime areas. Re-

The Police Foundation has a summary of the Kansas City study on its website as well as a link to a complete report on the study's findings. To link to this website, go to *The American System of Criminal Justice* 12e companion site at academic.cengage.com/criminaljustice/cole.

directed patrol
A proactive form of patrolling that directs resources to known high-crime areas.

search indicates that directed patrol activities focused on suspicious activities and locations can reduce violent gun crime (McGarrell et al., 2001). However, the extra police pressure may simply cause lawbreakers to move to another neighborhood. The premise of this argument is that "there are only so many criminals seeking outlets for the fixed number of crimes they are predestined to commit" (Sherman and Weisburd, 1995: 629). Although some public drug markets may participate in this shifting of "the action," it does not fit all crime or even all vice—such as prostitution (Sherman, 1990; Weisburd and Green, 1995).

Police administrators know that the amount of crime varies by season and time. Rates of predatory crimes such as robbery and rape increase in the summer months, when people are outdoors. By contrast, domestic violence occurs more frequently in winter, when intimates spend more time indoors in close proximity to one another.

There are also "hot times," generally between 7:00 P.M. and 3:00 A.M. A year-long study done in Minneapolis found that 51.9 percent of crime calls to the police came during this period, while the fewest calls were made between 3:00 A.M. and 11:00 A.M. With this knowledge, the department increased patrol presence in hot spots and at hot times (Koper, 1995). Although this strategy resulted in less crime, many officers disliked the new tactics. Being a "presence" in a hot spot might deter criminals, but the officers grew bored. Preventing crime is not as glamorous as catching criminals (Sherman and Weisburd, 1995: 646).

Rapid Response Time

Most departments are organized so that calls for help come to a central section that dispatches the nearest officers by radio to the site of the incident. Because most citizens have access to phones, most cities have 911 systems, and because most officers patrol in squad cars linked to headquarters by two-way radios, cell phones, and computers, police can respond quickly to calls. But are response times short enough to catch offenders?

Several studies have measured the impact of police response time on the ability of officers to intercept a crime in progress and arrest the criminal. In a classic study, William Spelman and Dale Brown (1984) found that the police succeeded in only 29 of 1,000 cases. It made little difference whether they arrived 2 minutes or 20 minutes after the call. What did matter, however, was how soon the police were called. Figure 6.6 presents these findings.

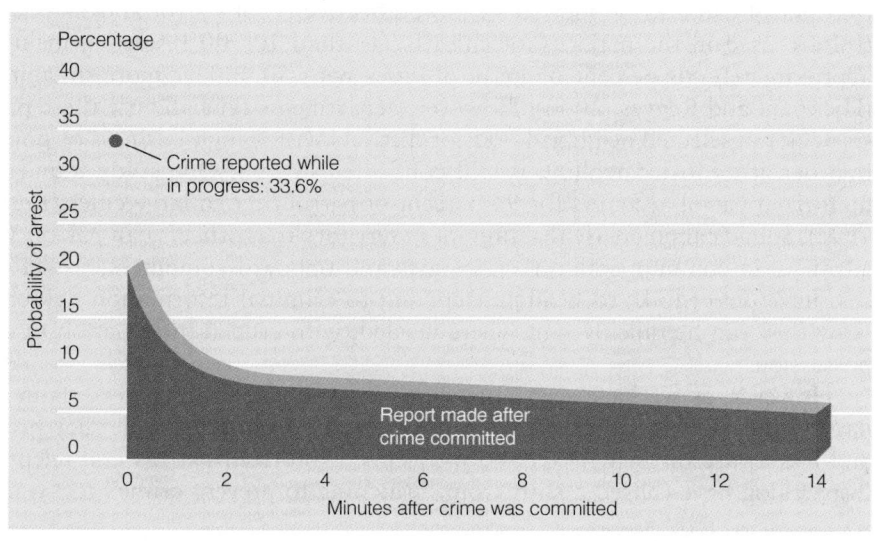

FIGURE 6.6

Probability of arrest as a function of elapsed time after crime

The probability of arrest declines sharply when the police are not called within seconds. What does this imply for patrol policies?

Source: William G. Spelman and Dale K. Brown, *Calling the Police: Citizen Reports of Serious Crime* (Washington, DC: Police Executive Research Forum, 1984), 65. Reprinted by permission.

Although delayed arrival of the police is often due to slowness in calling, it seems unlikely that one could improve arrest rates merely by educating the public about their key role in stopping crime. As Spelman and Brown (1984) point out, three decision-making delays slow the process of calling the police:

1. *Ambiguity delays.* Some people are not sure whether the police should be called, because the situation seems ambiguous. They might see an event but not know whether it is a robbery or two young men "horsing around."

2. *Coping delays.* Other people are so busy coping—taking care of the victim or directing traffic—that they cannot leave the scene to call the police.

3. *Conflict delays.* Still other people must first resolve conflicts before they call the police. For example, they may call someone else for advice about whether to call the police.

Although delay is a major problem, reducing delay would only slightly increase arrest rates. In about three-quarters of crime calls, the police are reactive, in that the crimes (burglary, larceny, and the like) are discovered long after have they have occurred. A much smaller portion are "involvement" crimes (robbery, rape, assault) that victims know about right away and for which they can call the police promptly (Spelman and Brown, 1984: 4). Rapid response time helps in only a small fraction of all calls. In sum, the costs of police resources and the danger created by high-speed response may outweigh any increase in effectiveness due to faster response times (Sherman, 1995: 334).

checkpoint

15. What factors affect patrol assignments?
16. What did the Kansas City study show about preventive patrol?
17. What is a hot spot?
18. What is directed patrol?
19. What types of delays reduce response time?

Foot versus Motorized Patrol

One of the most frequent citizen requests is for officers to be put back on the beat. This was the main form of police patrol until the 1930s, when motorized patrol came to be viewed as more effective. Foot patrol and bicycle patrol are used in the majority of cities larger than 10,000 residents, including approximately 90 percent or more of cities with 50,000 or more inhabitants (Hickman and Reaves, 2006). However, departments typically use these patrol strategies in selected neighborhoods or districts with a high business or population density. Most patrolling is still conducted in cars. One study found that motorized patrol accounts for 94 percent of patrol time in large cities (Reaves, 1992). Squad cars increase the amount of territory that officers can patrol. With advances in communication technologies and onboard computers, patrol officers have direct links to headquarters and to criminal information databases. Now they can be quickly sent where needed, with crucial information in their possession.

However, as we have seen, many citizens and some researchers claim that patrol officers in squad cars have become remote from the people they protect and less aware of their needs and problems. Motorized patrols and telephone dispatching have caused a shift from "watching to prevent crime" to "waiting to respond to crime" (Sherman, 1983: 149). Because officers rarely leave the patrol car, they cannot easily anticipate and mediate disputes, investigate suspected criminal activities, and make residents feel that the police care about their well-being. When officers are distant from the people they serve, citizens may be less inclined to call for help or provide information. Indeed, some departments are keenly aware of the risks of too much distance from the public and the benefits from cultivating communications and relationships. Thus, for example, the Community Affairs division of the New York City police department makes a special effort to include meetings with neighborhood religious leaders and visits to meet residents in housing projects as part of officers' training (Hauser, 2008).

Because of citizens' demands for a familiar figure walking through the neighborhood, the past two decades have seen a revived interest in foot patrol. Studies have shown that although foot patrols are costly and do not greatly reduce crime, they reduce people's fear of crime. In addition, citizen satisfaction with the police increases, and the officers gain a greater appreciation of neighborhood values (M. Cohen, Miller, and Rossman, 1990; Kelling, 1991). In terms of the cost and benefit, foot patrols are effective in high-density urban neighborhoods and business districts.

One-Person versus Two-Person Patrol Units

The debate over one-person versus two-person patrol units has raged in police circles for years. Patrolling is costly, and two one-officer units can cover twice as much territory and respond to as many calls as can a single two-officer unit. A 1991 study of large cities found that 70 percent of patrol cars are staffed by one officer, but the cities use one-person patrol in different ways. For example, Los Angeles uses one-person cars for about half of its units during the day, but only 9 percent at night. Philadelphia, however, uses only one-officer cars (Pate and Hamilton, 1991).

Officers and their union leaders support the two-person squad car. They claim that police are safer and more effective when two officers work together in dangerous or difficult situations. However, police administrators contend that the one-person squad car is much more cost-effective and permits them to deploy more cars on each shift. With more cars to deploy, each can be assigned to a smaller area and response time can be decreased. They also contend that an officer working alone is more alert and attentive because he or she cannot be distracted by idle conversation with a colleague.

Aggressive Patrol

Aggressive patrol is a proactive strategy designed to maximize police activity in the community. It takes many forms, such as "sting" operations, firearms confiscation, raids on crack houses, programs that encourage citizens to list their valuables, and the tracking of high-risk parolees. James Q. Wilson and Barbara Boland (1979) have shown the link between lower crime rates and patrol tactics that increase the risk of arrest. They argue that the effect of the police on crime depends less on how many officers are deployed in an area than on what they do while they are there.

The study showed that officers in an "anticrime patrol" in New York worked the streets of high-crime areas in civilian clothes. Although they accounted for only 5 percent of the officers assigned to each precinct, during one year they made more than 18 percent of the felony arrests, including more than half of

aggressive patrol
A patrol strategy designed to maximize the number of police interventions and observations in the community.

The website of the City of Santa Barbara, California, provides a detailed description of police department's patrol division. To link to this website, go to *The American System of Criminal Justice* 12e companion site at academic .cengage.com/criminaljustice/cole.

Many police chiefs credit aggressive take-back-the-streets tactics with reducing urban crime rates in the past two decades. In some cities, however, there are questions about whether such tactics have harmed police-community relations through searches and arrests that neighborhood residents view as unjustified. If you were a police chief, what patrol strategy would you choose and what specific goals would you seek to advance?

© Lou Dematteis/The Image Works

the arrests for robbery and about 40 percent of the arrests for burglary and auto theft (Wilson and Boland, 1979).

The zero-tolerance policing of the 1990s in New York City is an example of aggressive patrol linked to the "broken windows" theory. This theory asserts "that if not firmly suppressed, disorderly behavior in public will frighten citizens and attract predatory criminals, thus leading to more serious crime problems" (Greene, 1999: 172). Thus, the police should focus on minor, public order crimes such as aggressive panhandling, graffiti, prostitution, and urinating in public. By putting more police on the streets, decentralizing authority to the precinct level, and instituting officer accountability, the zero-tolerance policy was judged to be a major factor in reducing New York City's crime rate (Silverman, 1999). However, the end of the decade saw increasing cries of outrage from citizens, especially those living in low-income, minority neighborhoods, that the police were being too aggressive (*Newsweek*, June 21, 1997: 65). Thus the surge in police stop-and-frisks on New York City's streets in 2008 raised concerns that the police had expanded tactics that are perceived to be overly intrusive and discriminatory (Baker, 2008).

In the 1990s, some police departments began to seize illegally possessed firearms as a way of getting guns off the street. The police may legally seize firearms when they are carried without a permit, when they are illegally concealed, and when the person carrying one is on probation or parole. In Kansas City, Missouri, aggressive traffic enforcement was used as a way to seize firearms in a beat with a high homicide rate. The police seized one gun for every 28 traffic stops (Sherman and Rogan, 1995b: 673). Aggressive patrol tactics were also used to seize firearms in raids on crack houses (Sherman and Rogan, 1995a: 755). The result was a doubling of the gun recovery rate and a major reduction in gun violence (Sherman, 1995: 340). By contrast, in Indianapolis directed patrol aimed at specific locations was found to be more effective than aggressive patrol that maximized traffic stops as a means to reduce gun violence (McGarrell et al., 2001).

Aggressive, zero-tolerance police practices reduced gang-related crime in targeted precincts in Detroit (Bynum and Varano, 2002). Police departments also use aggressive patrol strategies to track high-risk parolees and apprehend them if they commit new offenses.

The most cost-effective of the aggressive patrol strategies seem to be those that encourage officers to carry out more field questioning and traffic stops. To implement such a strategy, the department must recruit certain kinds of officers, train them, and devise requirements and reward systems (traffic ticket quotas, required numbers of field interrogations, chances for promotion) that will encourage them to carry out the intended strategy.

Although aggressive patrol strategies reduce crime, they may also lead to citizen hostility. In New York, Pittsburgh, Charlotte, and other cities, polls show support for the strategy. However, some neighborhoods complain that aggressive patrol has gone too far and is straining police relations with young African Americans and Hispanics. This issue pits the need to balance the rights of individuals against the community's interest in order (Kolbert, 1999: 50). "Put another way, it's whose son is being hassled" (Reibstein, 1997: 66). See "New

NEW DIRECTIONS in CRIMINAL JUSTICE POLICY

Aggressive Patrol and Effective Policing

In "Broken Windows: The Police and Neighborhood Safety," James Q. Wilson and George Kelling (1982) argue that disorderly behavior that remains unregulated and unchecked is a signal to residents that the area is unsafe. Disorder makes residents fearful. They then avoid certain areas and withdraw to the safety of their homes. This retreat of fearful citizens undermines the fabric of urban life, increasing a neighborhood's vulnerability to an influx of disorderly behavior, serious crime, and urban decay.

Wilson and Kelling urge the police and the community to pay attention to public order offenses: aggressive panhandling, public drunkenness, soliciting by prostitutes, urinating in public, rowdiness, and blocking of sidewalks. These "little crimes," they say, can lead to more serious offenses. They believe the police must deal with public order offenses in an aggressive, proactive manner to prevent crime. Based on Wilson and Kelling's thesis, many police departments use aggressive enforcement of public order offenses as part of their version of community policing.

Subsequent research challenges Wilson and Kelling's argument. Robert Sampson and Stephen Raudenbush (2001) draw from a study of Chicago neighborhoods to conclude that both disorder and crime flow from a lack of "collective efficacy" in neighborhoods as well as from structural disadvantages, such as high unemployment rates. *Collective efficacy* is defined as cohesion among residents combined with shared expectations. The study found that where collective efficacy is strong, rates of violence are low, regardless of the economic characteristics and amount of disorder observed in the area. Although Sampson and Raudenbush concede that aggressive enforcement of public order may indirectly reduce crime by helping to stabilize neighborhoods, they argue that a focus on public order is misdirected because it does not address structural disadvantages and low levels of collective efficacy, the two elements that actually cause both disorder and crime.

Advocates of aggressive enforcement believe that several benefits flow from showing zero-tolerance for "little problems," such as public order offenses:

- Reduction of fear of crime, serious crime, and urban decay
- Opportunities to discover people wanted for other crimes or possessing weapons and drugs
- Improved quality of life for neighborhood residents
- Support for citizens who wish to uphold neighborhood standards for behavior

- Improved citizen cooperation and officer familiarity with offenders in the community

According to critics, aggressive enforcement brings risks as well. For example, officers might generate resentment by being perceived as interfering with the liberty of poor people.

When it was first introduced, the "broken windows thesis" became so well-known, widely quoted, and generally accepted that aggressive order maintenance remains one of the most frequently used strategies in community-oriented policing (Reitzel, Piquero, and Piquero, 2005). A major challenge for policing is the recognition and adoption of principles from new research that casts doubts on widely accepted ideas. Will police shift their focus from aggressive order maintenance to thinking more broadly about problem solving within neighborhoods? Addressing issues of structural disadvantages in neighborhoods is difficult for the police, because such issues relate to larger policy issues affected by city and state government decisions concerning poverty, employment, housing, and education. However, police may be able to encourage the development of collective efficacy. As described by Sampson and Raudenbush (2001: 5-6):

> Informally mobilizing a neighborhood cleanup, for example, would reduce physical disorder while building collective efficacy by creating and strengthening social ties and increasing awareness of the residents' commitment to their neighborhood. . . . By contrast, a police-led crackdown on disorder would probably produce a very different response by residents.

If you were a police chief, how would you incorporate newer research into your plans for patrolling neighborhoods? Are police capable of encouraging collective efficacy in neighborhoods, or should they just go back to focusing on reported crimes?

Researching the Internet

To read criticisms of the "broken windows thesis," see "Policing Disorder," an article in the *Boston Review*. To link to this website, go to *The American System of Criminal Justice* 12e companion site at academic.cengage.com/criminaljustice/cole.

Directions in Criminal Justice Policy" for more on the pros and cons of aggressive enforcement. (See also "A Question of Ethics" at the end of this chapter.)

Community Policing

As we saw in Chapter 5, the concept of community policing has taken hold in many cities. To a great extent, community policing has been seen as the solution to problems with the crime-fighter stance that prevailed during the professional era (Murphy, 1992). In addition, many cities have turned to community policing because the federal government has provided funding for the development of community-policing strategies and programs. Community policing consists of attempts by the police to involve residents in making their own neighborhoods safer. Based on the belief that citizens may be concerned about local disorder as well as crime in general, this strategy emphasizes cooperation between the police and citizens in identifying community needs and determining the best ways to meet them (Moore, 1992).

Community policing has four components (Skolnick and Bayley, 1986):

1. Community-based crime prevention
2. Changing the focus of patrol activities to nonemergency services
3. Making the police more accountable to the public
4. Including residents in decision making

As indicated by these four components, community policing requires a major shift in the philosophy of policing. In particular, police officials must view citizens as customers to be served and partners in the pursuit of social goals rather than as a population to be watched, controlled, and served reactively (Morash et al., 2002). Although crime control may still be a priority in community policing, the change in emphasis can strengthen police effectiveness for order maintenance and service (Zhao, He, and Loverich, 2003).

Departments that view themselves as emphasizing community policing do not necessarily implement identical patrol strategies and initiatives (Thurman, Zhao, and Giacomazzi, 2001). Some departments emphasize identifying and solving problems related to disorder and crime. Other departments work mainly on strengthening local neighborhoods. A department's emphasis can affect which activities become the focus of officers' working hours.

Organizational factors can also affect the implementation of community policing. For example, community policing may be carried out by patrol officers assigned to walk neighborhood beats so that they can get to know residents better. It may entail creating police ministations in the community and police-sponsored programs for youth and the elderly. Police departments may also survey citizens to find out about their problems and needs (Reisig, 2002). The common element in community policing programs is a high level of interaction between officers and citizens and the involvement of citizens in identifying problems and assisting the development of solutions. As such, departments need to provide training in problem identification and give officers greater authority to make decisions (Giacomazzi, Riley, and Merz, 2004). As you read "Civic Engagement: Your Role in the System," consider the problem of encouraging public involvement in community policing.

A central feature of community policing for many departments is **problem-oriented policing**, a strategy that seeks to find out what is causing citizen calls for help (Goldstein, 1990). The police seek to identify, analyze, and respond to the conditions underlying the events that prompt people to call the police (DeJong, Mastrofski, and Parks, 2001). Knowing those conditions, officers can enlist community agencies and residents to help resolve them (Braga, 1999). Recent research indicates that problem-solving approaches can impact homicide rates (Chermak and McGarrell, 2004). Police using this approach do not just fight crime; they address a broad array of problems that affect the quality of life in the community.

Many departments train their officers to use the SARA strategy for problem solving (Thurman, Zhao, and Giacomazzi, 2001: 206). SARA stands for a four-step process:

problem-oriented policing
An approach to policing in which officers routinely seek to identify, analyze, and respond to the circumstances underlying the incidents that prompt citizens to call the police.

civic engagement
your role in the system

You attend a neighborhood meeting in which police officers ask community residents for help in implementing and improving community policing. *Make a list of specific things that neighborhood residents can do to assist in the effectiveness of community policing.* Then look online at a report on public involvement in community policing in Chicago. To link to this website, go to *The American System of Criminal Justice* 12e companion site at academic.cengage.com/criminaljustice/cole.

1. Scanning the social environment to identify problems
2. Analysis of the problem by collecting information
3. Response to the problem by developing and employing remedies
4. Assessment of the remedies to evaluate the extent to which the problem has been solved

Regardless of whether the police focus their resources on order maintenance, law enforcement, or service, they tend to respond to specific incidents. In most cases, a citizen's call or an officer's field observation triggers a police response. The police are often asked to respond to a rash of incidents in the same location. Because the police traditionally focus on incidents, they do not try to identify the roots of these incidents. By contrast, those engaged in problem-oriented policing seek to address the underlying causes.

Community policing has spread across the country and gained a great deal of support from citizens, legislators, and Congress (Bayley, 1994). This support appears in the emphasis on community policing in the Violent Crime Control and Law Enforcement Act passed by Congress in 1994. Portions of the act call for increases in the numbers of officers assigned to community policing and for the development of new community policing programs.

Although community policing has won support from police executives, the Police Foundation, the Police Executive Research Forum, and police researchers, it may be difficult to put into effect. As with any reform, change might not come easily (Schafer, 2002). Police chiefs and midlevel managers, who usually deal with problems according to established procedures, may feel that their authority is decreased when responsibility goes instead to precinct commanders and officers on the streets (Alley, Bonello, and Schafer, 2002). Another problem with implementing community policing is that it does not reduce costs; it requires either additional funds or redistribution within existing budgets. Measuring the success of this approach in reducing fear of crime, solving underlying problems, maintaining order, and serving the community is also difficult. In addition, debate centers on how far the police should extend their role beyond crime fighting to remedying other social problems. Police officers may resist committing themselves to daily activities that emphasize goals other than the crime-fighting role that may have attracted them to a career in law enforcement (Mastrofski, Willis, and Snipes, 2002).

Crime and the Impact of Patrol

As previously discussed, the famous Kansas City experiment raised questions about whether and how police patrol impacts crime and crime rates. Thus police departments have tried various means to use patrol in order to provide service, order maintenance, and, hopefully, improvements in crime prevention and crime control. As indicated by the debates about the best approach to police patrol, experimentation with patrol will continue, especially as technological advances may increase the resources and efficiency of patrol officers as they walk a beat or drive through a neighborhood.

In recent decades, as discussed in Chapter 1, crime rates have generally declined in the United States. Many observers have attributed the decrease in crime, at least in part, to aggressive patrol strategies that flow from the "broken windows" thesis. According to these observers, police officers' attention to small matters and more frequent questioning of citizens helped to catch wanted suspects, discover criminal activity, deter potential criminal activity, and reduce the fear of crime within communities. However, even research that finds a crime-reduction impact from these patrol strategies concedes that they explain only a portion of the reduction in crime (Rosenfeld, Fornango and Rengifo, 2007; Messner et al., 2007). As you saw in "New Directions in Criminal Justice Policy" on page 233, other scholars have questioned whether "broken windows" policing works.

Other observers see the development and spread of community policing as an important element in crime reduction as officers became more closely connected to neighborhoods and received greater cooperation from residents. Indeed, the federal government actively encouraged the spread of community policing principles and even provided substantial funding for local communities to hire nearly 100,000 new police officers and carry out community policing programs. Yet, recent research analyses of crime trends have questioned whether community policing and the introduction of additional police officers across the nation actually had any effect on crime rates (Worrall and Kovandzic, 2007).

If we cannot demonstrate that crime rates declined because of new policing strategies, then what explains the reduction in crime? This is a complex question that is subject to debate. We might like to believe that we can address crime problems by simply adjusting the resources devoted to policing and the methods of deploying the police, but we lack strong evidence to support such a belief. Crime rates may have complex connections to the state of the American economy, employment opportunities, family stability, neighborhood cohesion, and other factors. Recently new debates have emerged about how changing social conditions in the United States may affect crime rates. For example, although some political commentators claim that the infusion of illegal immigrants into the United States contributes to increases in street crime, several prominent scholars have reached the opposite conclusion (Sampson, Morenoff, and Raudenbush, 2005). Despite highly publicized criminal activities by Central American–based gangs, these scholars argue that illegal immigrants typically add to stability in poor neighborhoods by gaining employment, promoting marriage and family stability, and avoiding behaviors that will draw the attention of police (Press, 2006; Bermudez, 2008). This is a subject that will undoubtedly be studied by scholars and debated by social commentators.

Other debates surround the impact of stiff sentences, high incarceration rates, and the subsequent reentry each year of nearly 700,000 ex-prisoners into American communities. For example, did ex-prisoners who brought prison society's values back into the community—such as a belief in responding violently to any indications of disrespect by others—contribute to the rise in murders and other violent crimes experienced by some American cities in 2007? Or, alternatively, is there simply a problem of too few resources and programs devoted to reintegrating ex-offenders into society? Research and debates about these issues will also become part of the complex picture of crime and the limited ability of criminal justice agencies to know precisely how to deal with it (Zernike, 2007; Fields, 2008; Solomon et al., 2008). There is certainly an important role for police patrol in providing service and order maintenance. And patrol officers also are essential in responding to and investigating criminal events. It is less clear, however, how patrol can prevent crime and reduce crime rates.

The Future of Patrol

Preventive patrol and rapid response to calls for help have been the hallmarks of policing in the United States for the past half-century. However, research done in the past 35 years has raised many questions about which patrol strategies police should employ. The rise of community policing has shifted law enforcement

COMPARATIVE PERSPECTIVE

Patrol in Japan

MANY COMMUNITY POLICING strategies now being used in the United States have been the tradition in Japan for many years. Patrol officers walking through their assigned neighborhoods and working out of local offices are a hallmark of Japanese policing.

Japanese policemen are addressed by the public as Omawari-san—Mr. Walkabout. This is an accurate reflection of what the public sees the police doing most of the time. Foot patrolling is done out of kobans [mini police stations in urban neighborhoods], usually for periods of an hour. Patrols are more common at night, when officers work in pairs. . . . Patrolmen amble at a ruminative pace that allows thorough observation. . . . Patrolling by automobile, which is much less common than foot patrolling, can be frustrating too. Due to the narrow congested streets of Japanese cities . . . patrol cars are forced to move at a snail's pace. . . .

Patrolling is by no means a matter of high adventure. For the most part it consists of watching and occasionally answering questions. Patrolmen rarely discover genuine emergencies; the chance of coincidence between patrolmen and sudden need are simply too great. Patrolling does not reduce reaction time or particularly enhance availability. What patrolling does is to demonstrate the existence of authority, correct minor inconveniences . . . such as illegally parked cars . . . and generate trust through the establishment of familiar personal relations with a neighborhood's inhabitants. On patrol, policemen are alert for different kinds of problems in different places. In a residential area they watch for people who appear out of place or furtive. In public parks they give attention to loitering males. Around major railroad stations they look for runaway adolescents, lured by the glamour of a big city, who could be victimized by criminal elements. They also watch for teyhaishi . . . labor contractors . . . who pick up and sell unskilled laborers to construction companies. In a neighborhood of bars and cabarets, patrolmen stare suspiciously at stylishly dressed women standing unescorted on street corners. They determine whether wheeled carts piled with food or cheap souvenirs are blocking pedestrian thoroughfares. Throughout every city they pay particular attention to illegally parked cars and cars that have been left with their doors unlocked. . . .

When a Japanese policeman is out on patrol he makes a special point of talking to people about themselves, their purposes, and their behavior. These conversations may be innocent or investigatory. The law provides that policemen may stop and question people only if there is reasonable ground for suspecting they have com-

mitted or are about to commit a crime or have information about a crime. Nevertheless, standard procedure on patrol is to stop and question anyone whenever the policeman thinks it may be useful. One reason for doing so is to discover wanted persons. And the tactic has proved very effective; 40 percent of criminals wanted by the police have been discovered by patrolmen on the street. Not only do officers learn to question people adroitly on the street, they become adept at getting people to agree to come to the koban so that more extended, less-public inquiries can be made. People are under no obligation to do so, any more than they are to stop and answer questions. The key to success with these tactics is to be compelling without being coercive. This in turn depends on two factors: the manner of the police officer and a thorough knowledge of minor laws. The first reduces hostility, the second provides pretexts for opening conversations justifiably. People who park illegally, ride bicycles without a light, or fail to wear helmets when riding a motorcycle are inviting officers to stop them and ask probing questions. The importance with which the police view on-street interrogation is indicated by the fact that prefectural and national contests are held each year to give recognition to officers who are best at it. . . . Senior officers continually impress upon new recruits the importance of learning to ask questions in inoffensive ways so that innocent people are not affronted and unpleasant scenes can be avoided. . . .

The most striking aspect of the variety of situations confronted by policemen is their compelling, unforced naturalness. The police see masses of utterly ordinary people who have been enmeshed in situations that are tediously complex and meaningful only to the persons immediately involved. The outcomes are of no interest to the community at large; the newspapers will not notice if matters are sorted out or not; superior officers have no way of recording the effort patrolmen expend in trying to be helpful; and the people themselves are incapable by and large of permanently escaping their predicaments. Policemen are responsible for tending these individuals, for showing that they appreciate—even when they are tired, hurried, bored, and preoccupied—the minute ways in which each person is unique. It is perhaps, the greatest service they render.

Source: David H. Bayley, Forces of Order: Police Behavior in Japan and the United States (Berkeley: University of California Press, 1979), 33–34, 37, 41, 51–52. Copyright © 1976 The Regents of the University of California. Reprinted by permission.

Researching the Internet

To learn more about policing in Japan, see the English-language website of Japan's National Police Agency. To link to this website, go to *The American System of Criminal Justice* 12e companion site at academic.cengage.com/criminal justice/cole.

toward problems that affect the quality of life of residents. Police forces need to use patrol tactics that fit the needs of the neighborhood. Neighborhoods with crime hot spots may require different strategies than do neighborhoods where residents are concerned mainly with order maintenance. Many researchers believe that traditional patrol efforts have focused too narrowly on crime control, neglecting the order maintenance and service activities for which police departments were originally formed. Critics have urged that the police become more community oriented and return to the first principle of policing: "to remain in close and frequent contact with citizens" (Williams and Pate, 1987). To see this policy in action, we look to Japan, where most patrolling is done on foot, as described in the Comparative Perspective.

How the national effort to combat terrorism will affect local police patrol operations remains uncertain. Since the attacks of September 11, state and local police have assumed greater responsibility for investigating bank robberies and other federal crimes as the FBI and other federal agencies devote significant attention to catching people connected with terrorist organizations. In addition, even local police officers in a neighborhood must be ready to spot suspicious activities that might relate to terrorist activity. They are the first responders in a bombing or other form of attack. Obviously, federal law enforcement officials must work closely with local police in order to be effective. Yet many local police chiefs have criticized the FBI for failing to share important information about local suspects (Bowers, 2002). The new concerns about terrorism will not alter traditional police responsibilities for crime fighting, order maintenance, and service, but they will provide an additional consideration as police administrators plan how to train and deploy their personnel.

checkpoint

20. What are the advantages of foot patrol? Of motorized patrol?
21. How do one-person and two-person patrol units compare?
22. What is aggressive patrol?
23. What are the major elements of community policing?

A QUESTION OF ETHICS

"WE'RE GOING to increase the pressure on the punk kids in that neighborhood," said the sergeant with a determined look on his face. "Whenever you see a teenager standing still or see one with some other teenagers, you are to stop them, frisk them, and make sure that they understand that we won't tolerate any more noise, vandalism, or fooling around that disturbs the older people on the block."

One officer raised his hand and asked a question. "Don't we need some kind of reasonable suspicion about them being armed or planning a crime before we can do a stop-and-frisk search?"

"Don't worry about that. This is our version of aggressive patrolling. They can file a complaint with the department if they want to, but it won't go anywhere. Reasonable suspicion is only going to matter if you find some drugs or a weapon on a kid. If that happens, you can make up some reasons for the stop later so the evidence won't be excluded."

Critical Thinking and Analysis

How will people in the targeted neighborhood react to the sergeant's order? Is there anything that can prevent the officers from using this method of aggressive patrol? If you were an officer who received this order, what would you do?

SUMMARY

Identify why people become police officers and how they learn to do their jobs

- To meet current and future challenges, the police must recruit and train individuals who will uphold the law and receive citizen support.

- Improvements have been made during the past quarter-century in recruiting more women, racial and ethnic minorities, and well-educated people as police officers.

Understand the elements of the police officer's "working personality"

- The police work in an environment greatly influenced by their subculture.

- The concept of the working personality helps us understand the influence of the police subculture on how individual officers see their world.

- The isolation of the police strengthens bonds among officers but can also add to job stress.

Recognize the factors that affect police response

- The police are mainly reactive rather than proactive, which often leads to incident-driven policing.

- The organization of the police bureaucracy influences how the police respond to citizens' calls.

- The productivity of a force can be measured in various ways, including the clearance rate; however, measuring proactive approaches is more difficult.

Understand the main functions of police patrol, investigation, and special operations units

- Police services are delivered through the work of the patrol, investigation, and specialized operations units.

- The patrol function has three components: answering calls for assistance, maintaining a police presence, and probing suspicious circumstances.

- The investigative function is the responsibility of detectives in close coordination with patrol officers.

- The felony apprehension process is a sequence of actions that includes crime detection, preliminary investigation, follow-up investigation, clearance, and arrest.

- Large departments usually have specialized units dealing with traffic, drugs, and vice.

Analyze patrol strategies that departments employ

- Police administrators must make choices about possible patrol strategies, which include directed patrol, foot patrol, and aggressive patrol.

- Community policing seeks to involve citizens in identifying problems and working with police officers to prevent disorder and crime.

- Research has raised questions about the effectiveness of police patrol techniques and community policing for reducing crime.

QUESTIONS FOR REVIEW

1. How do recruitment and training practices affect policing?

2. What is meant by the police subculture, and how does it influence an officer's work?

3. What factors in the police officer's "working personality" influence an officer's work?

4. What issues influence police administrators in their allocation of resources?

5. What is the purpose of patrol? How is it carried out?

6. Why do detectives have so much prestige on the force?

7. What has research shown about the effectiveness of patrol?

KEY TERMS

aggressive patrol (p. 231)	proactive (p. 212)
clearance rate (p. 215)	problem-oriented
differential response (p. 214)	policing (p. 234)
directed patrol (p. 228)	reactive (p. 212)
incident-driven	socialization (p. 207)
policing (p. 213)	subculture (p. 208)
line functions (p. 217)	sworn officers (p. 218)
preventive patrol (p. 218)	working personality (p. 208)

FOR FURTHER READING

Bayley, David H. 1994. *Police for the Future.* New York: Oxford University Press. Examination of policing in five countries—Australia, Canada, Great Britain, Japan, and the United States. Includes a suggested blueprint for the future.

Bratton, William. 1998. *Turnaround: How America's Top Cop Reversed the Crime Epidemic.* New York: Random House. Description by former Police Commissioner William Bratton of the efforts he took to reduce crime in New York City.

Brown, Michael K. 1981. *Working the Street.* New York: Russell Sage Foundation. A classic study of patrol work by officers of the San Diego Police Department.

Harcourt, Bernard. 2001. *The Illusion of Order: The False Promise of Broken Windows Policing.* Cambridge, MA: Harvard University Press. A critical examination of the assumptions and consequences of the "broken windows thesis."

Morash, Merry, and J. Kevin Ford, eds. 2002. *The Move to Community Policing: Making Change Happen.* Thousand Oaks, CA: Sage. Recent research on community policing and the challenges of implementing a new philosophy within police agencies.

Skolnick, Jerome H., and David H. Bayley. 1986. *The New Blue Line.* New York: Free Press. A look at modern policing by two major criminal justice scholars.

GOING ONLINE

For an up-to-date list of web links, go to *The American System of Criminal Justice* 12e companion site at academic.cengage.com/criminaljustice/cole.

1. At the Riley County (Kansas) Police Department website, read the qualifications required of applicants who wish to become police officers. Are these qualifications appropriate? Should any additional qualifications be required?

2. Read the description of one city's police patrol methods on the City of Pottsville (Pennsylvania) Bureau of Police website. Can you tell whether this city emphasizes community policing?

3. Read the federal government's definition of community policing. How difficult would it be to implement all of the elements of this approach to policing?

CHECKPOINT ANSWERS

1. *What are the main requirements for becoming a police officer?*

   High school diploma, good physical condition, absence of a criminal record.

2. *How has the profile of American police officers changed?*

   Better educated, more female and minority officers.

3. *What type of training do police recruits need?*

   Preservice training, usually in a police academy.

4. *Where does socialization to police work take place?*

   On the job.

5. *What are the two key aspects of the police officer's working personality?*

   Danger, authority.

6. *What are the four types of stress felt by the police?*

   External stress, organizational stress, personal stress, operational stress.

7. *What is "incident-driven policing"?*

   Citizen expectation that the police will respond quickly to every call.

8. *What is "differential response"?*

   Policy that prioritizes calls according to whether an immediate or delayed response is warranted.

9. *What is the basic measure of police productivity?*

   Clearance rate—the percentage of crimes known to the police that they believe they have solved through an arrest.

10. *What is the difference between line and staff functions?*

    Personnel assigned to line functions are directly involved in field operations; those assigned to staff functions supplement and support the line function.

11. *What are the three parts of the patrol function?*

    (1) Answering calls for assistance, (2) maintaining a police presence, and (3) probing suspicious circumstances.

12. *What is the job of the detective?*

    Detectives examine the crime scene, question witnesses and victims, and focus on gathering evidence to solve crimes.

13. *What are the four steps of the apprehension process?*

    (1) Detection of crime, (2) preliminary investigation, (3) follow-up investigation, and (4) clearance and arrest.

14. *What are three kinds of special operations units that police departments often employ?*

    Traffic, vice, narcotics.

15. *What factors affect patrol assignments?*

    Crime rates, "problem neighborhoods," degree of urbanization, pressures from business people and community groups, and socioeconomic conditions.

16. *What did the Kansas City study show about preventive patrol?*

    Crime rates do not seem to be affected by changes in patrolling strategies, such as assigning more officers.

17. *What is a hot spot?*

    A location that generates a high number of calls for police response.

18. *What is directed patrol?*

    A proactive patrol strategy designed to direct resources to known high-crime areas.

19. *What types of delays reduce response time?*

    Decision-making delays caused by ambiguity, coping activities, and conflicts.

20. *What are the advantages of foot patrol? Of motorized patrol?*

    Officers on foot patrol have greater contact with residents of a neighborhood, thus gaining their confidence and assistance. Officers on motorized patrol have a greater range of activity and can respond speedily to calls.

21. *How do one-person and two-person patrol units compare?*

One-person patrols are more cost-efficient; two-person patrols are thought to be safer.

22. *What is aggressive patrol?*

A proactive strategy designed to maximize the number of police interventions and observations in a community.

23. *What are the major elements of community policing?*

Community policing emphasizes order maintenance and service. It attempts to involve members of the community in making their neighborhoods safe. Foot patrol and decentralization of command are usually part of community-policing efforts.

CHAPTER 7

Twenty-First Century Challenges in Policing

CHAPTER LEARNING OBJECTIVES

→ Recognize the ways police can abuse their power and the challenges of controlling this abuse

→ Identify the methods that can be used to make police more accountable to citizens

→ Understand the new technologies that assist police investigations and how these technologies affect citizens' rights

→ Identify the issues and problems that emerge from law enforcement agencies' increased attention to homeland security

→ Understand the policing and related activities undertaken by private-sector security management

The spectators, lawyers, and defendants waited in anxious silence as the judge prepared to deliver the verdict. These were no ordinary defendants whose lives hung in the balance on this day in April 2008. The defendants were three New York City police detectives—Gescard Isnora, Michael Oliver, and Marc Cooper—who collectively fired 46 bullets at three unarmed men, killing one and wounding two others. The case attracted national media attention because the dead man, Sean Bell, was killed on his wedding day in November 2006 as he left a nightclub in the early morning hours after his bachelor party. After Bell had a

confrontation with a stranger outside the club, one of the plainclothes detectives thought he heard one of Bell's friends claim to have a gun. A chaotic scene ensued. As Bell, who had been drinking, attempted to drive away, he struck one of the detectives on the leg as well as the unmarked police car. The officers pulled their weapons and fired repeatedly on the vehicle when one detective thought he saw one of Bell's friends reach toward his waistband and presumed that the friend was reaching for a weapon (Wilson, 2008). In fact, Bell's surviving friends later claimed that they did not even know that the plainclothes men were police

officers. They were just trying to get away from threatening strangers who seemed intent on becoming involved with the argument outside the nightclub.

Did the police use force appropriately in this case? Should they have been more certain that they were actually about to be threatened with a weapon? Should they have fired fewer shots? A total of 50 shots were fired by five police officers, although only three officers were ultimately charged with crimes from the incident, including one officer who fired 31 of the shots (Wilson, 2008). Moreover, how do we hold officers accountable for their actions when they choose to use lethal force? Criminal charges and trials are one mechanism for after-the-fact accountability and control, and that was the mechanism that the three officers faced as they awaited the verdict.

Judge Arthur Cooperman delivered the verdicts on the various counts of manslaughter, assault, and reckless endangerment faced by the detectives: "not guilty" on all charges. Many in the courtroom were shocked. How could police officers fire so many shots into a stopped vehicle containing unarmed men and not have committed a crime? As a news reporter observed, "[R]ather than call the shooting justified, the judge said that the prosecution failed to prove it was unjustified, as was its burden" (Wilson, 2008). So the police may have been guilty of crimes, but the prosecution's evidence failed to prove it beyond a reasonable doubt.

Did the verdict demonstrate that police officers can escape consequences for using lethal force on unarmed citizens? Not necessarily. The verdict showed that the United States faces significant challenges in evaluating what circumstances constitute the improper use of force by police officers. We must give the police the authority to use force in order to protect themselves and society, yet the use of force can be triggered in many different kinds of situations, including those involving misperceptions and reasonable fears. To what extent do we want to second-guess and punish police officers who must make quick, on-the-spot decisions that may make the difference between life and death for themselves and others? On the other hand, how do we prevent officers from using force excessively and inappropriately?

When issues of excessive force or corruption affect the police, they can affect the bonds that connect the police to the community they serve and rely on for information, assistance, and support. These bonds are often fragile, especially when racial, gender, or class bias comes into play. How can we make sure that those with authority do not misuse their power?

In this chapter we discuss several new developments and continuing issues about the police and their role in society. For each topic, questions emerge about the role of police in a democratic society. Any police shooting or other use of force that injures a citizen raises concerns that officers may have disregarded the constitutional rights guaranteed to people under the U.S. Constitution. Constitutional issues also arise in less stark form with respect to a variety of other issues. For example, technological developments and the shifting emphasis toward homeland security raise concerns about the surveillance and searches of citizens who have done nothing wrong. In a democratic society, police must act within legal guidelines, remain under the control of elected officials, and be accountable for their actions. These principles can be violated when law enforcement personnel exhibit unethical and illegal behavior. Problems also arise if legislators permit police powers to expand too far because of public fear, a situation that some critics believe is developing with respect to certain aspects of homeland security policies.

We first look at troubling issues that arise when police abuse their power. We also examine what is being done to make police more accountable. Second, we examine how technological changes have given police new abilities to investigate criminal activity and monitor people's behavior and how these new technologies have also raised new questions about the role of police and the preservation of citizens' rights. Third, we discuss the expansion of police activities related to homeland security, especially with respect to federal agencies. Finally, we look at private-sector policing, which falls under the title of security management, a growing industry that is increasingly affecting police operations and requiring unprecedented cooperation between public and private agencies.

POLICE ABUSE OF POWER

The controversy surrounding the police use of force against Sean Bell and his friends is not unique. The beating of Rodney King by Los Angeles police officers drew worldwide attention in 1991 and eventually contributed to a major riot that took dozens of lives. In May 2008, fifteen Philadelphia police officers were suspended from duty after a television news helicopter videotaped them repeatedly kicking and beating three suspects as they lay on the ground being handcuffed (Slobodzian, 2008). Although such scandals have occurred throughout U.S. history, only in the past quarter-century has the public become keenly aware of the problems of police misconduct, especially the illegal use of violence by law enforcement officers and the criminal activities associated with police corruption. For example, as indicated in "What Americans Think" on the next page, as compared to 40 years ago, many more Americans today believe that police brutality occurs in the area where they live. Ironically, there is strong reason to believe that excessive force may have been used more freely 40 years ago because of subsequent improvements in training and implementation of various mechanisms for accountability and control. Police actions are more highly publicized today and can be widely disseminated through videos on YouTube and other means that did not exist in prior decades. Although most officers do not engage in misconduct, these problems deserve study because they raise questions about how much the public can control and trust the police.

Police grab a protester off his bike after he taunted them at a protest against free trade policies during a meeting of international leaders in Miami, Florida. Does this appear to be an appropriate use of force? Is there a risk that police officers use force out of anger rather than out of necessity?

AP Images/David Adame

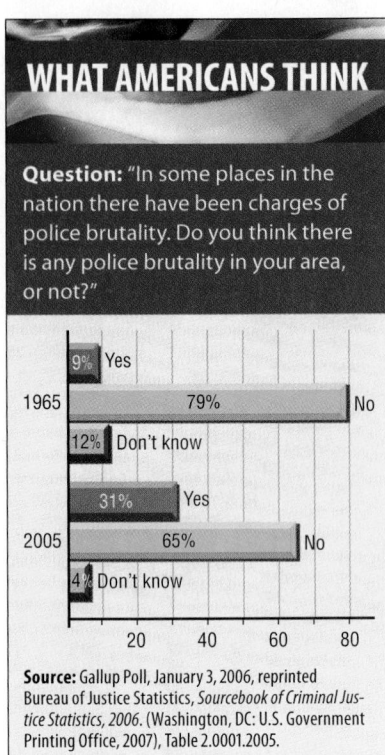
Use of Force

Most people cooperate with the police, yet officers must at times use force to arrest, control disturbances, and deal with the drunken or mentally ill (Thompson, 2001). As noted by Jerome Skolnick and James Fyfe (1993: 37),

> As long as some members of society do not comply with the law and resist the police, force will remain an inevitable part of policing. Cops, especially, understand that. Indeed, anybody who fails to understand the centrality of force in police work has no business in a police uniform.

Thus police may use legitimate force to do their job. It is when they use excessive force that they violate the law. But what is excessive force? Both officers and experts debate this question.

In cities where racial tensions are high, conflicts between police and residents often result when officers are accused of acting in unprofessional ways. Citizens use the term *police brutality* to describe a wide range of practices, from the use of profane or abusive language to physical force and violence.

Stories of police brutality are not new. However, unlike the untrained officers of the early 1900s, today's officers are supposed to be professionals who know the rules and understand the need for proper conduct. Thus, reports of unjustified police shootings and beatings are particularly disturbing (Ogletree et al., 1995). Moreover, when abusive behavior by police comes to light, the public cannot know how often police engage in such actions, because most violence is hidden from public view (Weitzer, 2002). If a person looking on from a nearby window had not videotaped the beating of Rodney King, the officers could have claimed that they had not used excessive force, and King would have had no way to prove that they had. If the TV news helicopter had not been flying above the scene, would we know that the Philadelphia police officers were kicking and beating suspects who were not resisting arrest in 2008? How can we prevent such incidents, especially when they occur without witnesses?

The concept "use of force" takes many forms in practice. We can arrange the various types of force on a continuum ranging from most severe (civilians shot and killed) to least severe ("come-alongs," or being grasped by an officer) (Terrill, 2005). Table 7.1 lists many of these forms of force according to their frequency of use. How often must police use force? Most research has shown that in contacts with suspects, police use force infrequently and the type of force used is usually at the low end of the continuum—toward the less severe. Research in Phoenix found that the single largest predictor of police use of force was use of force by the suspect to which the police then responded (Garner et al., 1995). For example, resistance by a suspect can contribute to the officers' decision to use force (Garner, Maxwell, and Heraux, 2002). On the other hand, other research shows that police used increasing levels of force in 20 percent of encounters in which the individuals offered no resistance (Terrill, 2005). Research in six urban jurisdictions in which 7,512 arrests were examined showed that police used no weapons in 97.9 percent of contacts with the public (Garner and Maxwell, 1999: 31). Again, excessive use of force, in violation of department policies and state laws, is what constitutes abuse of police power.

A report by the National Institute of Justice (Adams, 1999) summarizes knowledge about use of force:

1. Police use force infrequently.

2. Police use of force typically occurs in the lower end of the force spectrum, involving grabbing, pushing, or shoving.

3. Use of force typically occurs when police are trying to make an arrest and the suspect is resisting.

Although more studies are needed, research indicates that use of force is not linked to an officer's personal characteristics such as age, gender, and ethnicity. However, a small percentage of officers may be disproportionately involved in use-of-force situations. In addition, some studies indicate that police may use force more often when dealing with people affected by drugs, alcohol, or mental illness (Adams, 1999). At this point, there is a dire need for additional research to tell us how frequently wrongful use of force by police occurs and whether specific departmental policies concerning hiring, training, and supervision affect officers' decisions to use force (Adams, 1999).

By law, the police have the authority to use force if necessary to make an arrest, keep the peace, or maintain public order. But just how much force is necessary and under what conditions it may be used are complex and debatable questions. In particular, the use of deadly force in apprehending suspects has become a deeply emotional issue with a direct connection to race relations. Research has shown that the greatest use of deadly force by the police is found in communities with high levels of economic inequality and large minority populations (M. D. Holmes, 2000; Sorensen, Marquart, and Brock, 1993).

When the police kill a suspect or bystander while trying to make an arrest, their actions may produce public outrage and hostility. This

TABLE 7.1	Reported Uses of Force by Big-City Police

Police have the legal right to use force to make an arrest, keep the peace, and maintain order. Of the many types of force available to police, the less severe types are used most often.

Type of Force	Rate per Thousand Sworn Officers
Handcuff/leg restraint	490.4
Bodily force (arm, foot, or leg)	272.2
Come-alongs	226.8
Unholstering weapon	129.9
Swarm	126.7
Twist locks/wrist locks	80.9
Firm grip	57.7
Chemical agents (Mace or Cap-Stun)	36.2
Batons	36.0
Flashlights	21.7
Dog attacks or bites	6.5
Electrical devices (TASER)	5.4
Civilians shot at but not hit	3.0
Other impact devices	2.4
Neck restraints/unconsciousness-rendering holds	1.4
Vehicle rammings	1.0
Civilians shot and killed	0.9
Civilians shot and wounded but not killed	0.2

Source: Drawn from Bureau of Justice Statistics, *National Data Collection on Police Use of Force* (Washington, DC: U.S. Government Printing Office, 1996), 43.

was the case in November 1996 when a white officer in St. Petersburg, Florida, killed a black motorist who had refused to lower his window and appeared to be trying to drive away after a routine traffic stop. The riot that followed left more than a dozen people injured and caused $5 million in property damage. A second round of rioting flared up after a predominantly white grand jury cleared the officer of wrongdoing (*USA Today,* November 11, 1996). In the Sean Bell case, more than 200 people were arrested in New York City for intentionally blocking traffic on major roads during organized, public demonstrations against the "not guilty" verdicts issued in 2008.

Fears about the possibility of similar public disorders arose in 2005 when a Los Angeles police officer fired ten shots that killed a 13-year-old boy who was driving a stolen car. The officer fired in the aftermath of a chase, when the boy skidded across a sidewalk and then struck a police car while backing up (Chavez, 2005). The incident led Los Angeles police officials to revise their policies for firing at moving vehicles.

In another example of use of force, New Yorkers were outraged by the killing of Amadou Diallo, an unarmed West African immigrant, who died in a fusillade of 41 bullets fired by four members of New York City's Street Crime Unit. Unarmed and standing alone, Diallo was killed in the vestibule of his apartment building. The officers were looking for a rapist-murderer when they came upon Diallo. As they approached him, they said, they thought he was reaching for a gun. The killing resulted in massive protests and the indictment of the officers on second-degree murder charges. During their trial the officers said that they "reasonably believed" that Diallo was about to use deadly force against them

The San Antonio Police Department conducted a study of the use of force by its officers and the report is available online. To link to this website, go to *The American System of Criminal Justice* 12e companion site at academic.cengage.com/criminaljustice/cole.

Tennessee v. Garner (1985)
Deadly force may not be used against an unarmed and fleeing suspect unless necessary to prevent the escape and unless the officer has probable cause to believe that the suspect poses a significant threat of death or serious injury to the officers and others.

(*New York Times,* February 26, 2000: A13). As in the Bell case, the police officers were acquitted of criminal charges after a trial in the New York courts. The Diallo killing raised questions about New York's zero-tolerance policies and the aggressive tactics of the Street Crime Unit.

There are no accurate data on the number of people shot by the police. Estimates show that the police shoot about 3,600 people each year, with fatal results in as many as 1,000 of these incidents (Cullen et al., 1996: 449). Although these numbers are alarming, it is important to remember that force (hit, held, choked, threatened) is used against 500,000 people each year (BJS, 1997a: 12). The number of police killings should not obscure the fact that many of those killed are young African American men. However, the ratio of blacks to whites killed has declined, in part because of new police policies (Sherman and Cohn, 1986; S. Walker, Spohn, and DeLeone, 2007).

In 2008, an analysis of New York City's detailed records on police shootings showed drops in use of firearms that coincided with the drop in crime rate over the preceding decade. Police opened fire at people only 60 times in 2006 as compared to 147 times in 1996. New York City police fatally shot only 13 people in 2006, while they shot and killed 30 people in 1996. One troubling question that lingers is whether the New York City police are more inclined to use firearms against members of minority groups. Nearly 90 percent of those shot by the police in late 1990s were African American or Hispanic but the police department has refused to release information on the race of the individuals involved for later years. The police department has also stopped providing information on injuries to innocent bystanders from police shootings (Baker, 2008a). The selective release of information raises questions about whether the public is fully informed about use of force and is certain to lead to further legal and political battles as advocacy groups seek additional information.

Until the 1980s the police had broad authority to use deadly force in pursuing suspected felons. Police in about half the states were guided by the common-law principle that allowed the use of whatever force was necessary to arrest a fleeing felon. In 1985 the Supreme Court set a new standard in ***Tennessee v. Garner*** (1985), ruling that the police may not use deadly force in apprehending fleeing felons "unless it is necessary to prevent the escape and the officer has probable cause to believe that the suspect poses a significant threat of death or serious physical injury to the officer or others."

The case dealt with the killing of Edward Garner, a 15-year-old eighth grader who was shot by a member of the Memphis Police Department. Officers Elton Hymon and Leslie Wright were sent to answer a "prowler-inside" call. When they arrived at the scene, they saw a woman standing on her porch and gesturing toward the adjacent house. She told them she had heard glass breaking and someone was inside. While Wright radioed for help, Hymon went to the back of the house, heard a door slam, and saw someone run across the backyard toward a 6-foot chain-link fence. With his flashlight, Hymon could see that Garner was unarmed. He called out, "Police! Halt!" but Garner began to climb the fence.

Convinced that Garner would escape if he made it over the fence, Hymon fired, hitting him in the back of the head. Garner died in the operating room, the ten dollars he had stolen still in his pocket. Hymon had acted under Tennessee law and Memphis Police Department policy.

The standard set by *Tennessee v. Garner* presents problems because judging a suspect's dangerousness can be difficult. Because officers must make quick decisions in stressful situations, creating rules that will guide them in every case is impossible. The Court tried to clarify its ruling in the case of *Graham v. Connor* (1989). Here, the justices established the standard of "objective reasonableness," saying that the officer's use of deadly force should be judged in terms of the "reasonableness at the moment." This means that the use of the deadly force should be judged from the point of view of the officer on the scene. The

Court's decision says that it must be recognized that "officers are often forced to make split-second judgments—in circumstances that are tense, uncertain, and rapidly evolving—about the amount of force that is necessary in a particular situation."

The risk of lawsuits by victims of improper police shootings looms over police departments and creates a further incentive for administrators to set and enforce standards for the use of force. For example, after the Diallo shooting in New York City, the victim's family sued the city and the police officers, eventually leading to a $3 million settlement payment and an apology from the city (Feuer, 2004). Sean Bell's family also filed a lawsuit after his shooting. However, as long as officers carry weapons, some improper shootings will occur. Training, internal review of incidents, and disciplining or firing of quick-trigger officers may help reduce the use of unnecessary force (M. Blumberg, 1989: 442; Fyfe, 1993: 128).

The risk of deaths, injuries, and subsequent lawsuits does not stem from police shootings alone. For example, in 2007, the U.S. Supreme Court blocked a lawsuit by a man who was paralyzed by a police officer's use of force: the police car rammed the claimaint's car off the road when he was speeding and would not pull over when pursued by the police. In this case, the videotape of the chase from the police cruiser's camera convinced a majority of justices that the driver was responsible for creating the necessity of this particular form of police use of force (*Scott v. Harris*, 2007). Police officers have also caused deaths by using chokeholds and striking people in the head with batons. Injuries also result from other forms of physical force, including such seemingly routine procedures as placing a suspect in handcuffs if the handcuffs are too tight.

As a result of lawsuits by people injured at the hands of the police, departments have sought new means of applying force in ways that will not produce injuries. Some of the new methods are taught through training about specific holds and pressure points that officers can use to incapacitate people temporarily without causing permanent harm. In addition, police departments seek new weapons that use less-than-lethal force. Later in this chapter, when we discuss the impact of technology on police, we examine new weapons that use electrical shocks, projectiles, and chemical sprays. Advocates claim that the use of these weapons has saved the lives of citizens and officers by permitting officers to restore order without resorting to the use of guns. Critics have raised concerns about deaths and injuries produced by less-than-lethal weapons. They also point to the risk that officers will resort too quickly to such weapons when situations could be solved through patience and persuasion rather than force (Adang and Mensink, 2004).

Although progress has been made in reducing improper and excessive use of force by police, corruption remains a major problem. We turn to this issue next.

Corruption

Police corruption has a long history in America. Early in the twentieth century, city officials organized liquor and gambling businesses for their personal gain. In many cities, ties between politicians and police officials assured that favored clients would be protected and competitors harassed. Much of the Progressive movement to reform the police aimed at combating such corrupt arrangements.

Although these political ties have diminished in most cities, corruption still exists. In 2008, for example, a New Haven, Connecticut, police detective was sentenced to three years in prison for taking bribes and stealing money seized in drug cases (Orson, 2008). Other New Haven detectives pleaded guilty to related charges stemming from an undercover investigation by the FBI (WFSB, 2007). In April 2005, two police officers in Chicago stood among the 14 reputed

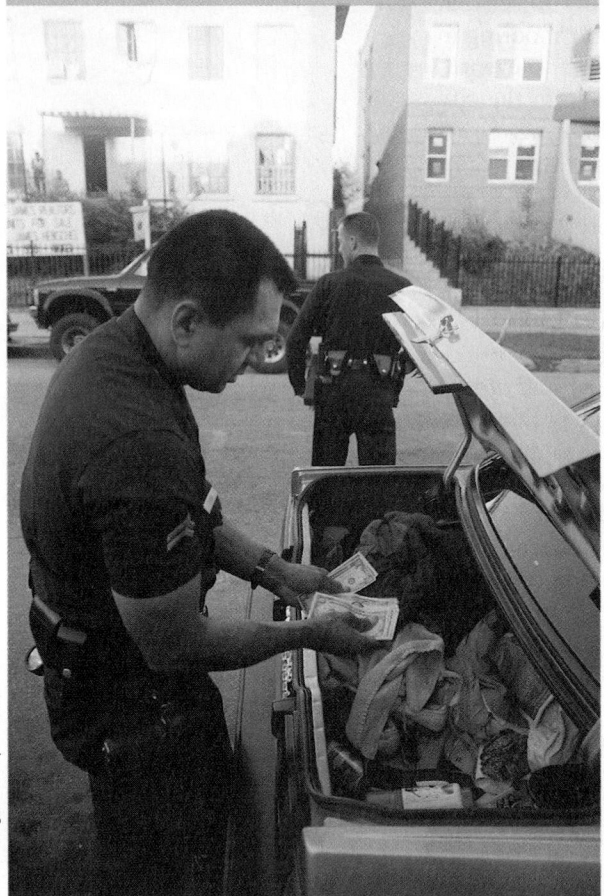

Officers are often placed in situations where they can be tempted to enrich themselves by stealing money, property or drugs, or by accepting favors, gifts, and bribes. If you were a police chief, how would you reduce the risks of police corruption?

organized crime figures indicted in a major investigation of unsolved mob murders. One officer was accused of being a spy for organized crime within the police department and the other officer reportedly passed information to mob leaders who were in jail (Lighty, 2005).

Sometimes corruption is defined so broadly that it ranges from accepting a free cup of coffee to robbing businesses or beating suspects. Obviously, corruption is not easily defined, and people disagree about what it includes. As a useful starting point, we can focus on the distinction between corrupt officers who are "grass eaters" and those who are "meat eaters."

Grass Eaters and Meat Eaters

Grass eaters are officers who accept payoffs that the routines of police work bring their way. *Meat eaters* are officers who actively use their power for personal gain. Although meat eaters are few, their actions make headlines when discovered. By contrast, because grass eaters are numerous, they make corruption seem acceptable and promote a code of secrecy that brands as a traitor any officer who exposes corruption. Grass eaters make up the heart of the problem and are often harder to detect than meat eaters.

In the past, low salaries, politics, and poor hiring practices have been cited as factors contributing to corruption. However, these arguments fall short of explaining today's corruption. Whereas some claim that a few rotten apples should not taint an entire police force, corruption in some departments has been so rampant that the rotten-apple theory does not fully explain the situation. Some explanations center on the structure and organization of police work. Much police work involves enforcement of laws in situations in which there is no complainant or it is unclear whether a law has been broken. Moreover, most police work takes place under the officer's own discretion, without direct supervision. Thus, police officers may have many opportunities to gain benefits by using their discretion to protect people who engage in illegal conduct.

Los Angeles Chief of Police William Bratton has noted disturbing developments related to police corruption:

> It used to be cops took payoffs to look the other way, for what was a more benign activity like gambling, prostitution. What we're seeing now is the insidious aspect caused by the drug problem. There is more and more crossing the line to get involved in that business. (*New York Times,* January 1, 1998: A16)

In cities such as Miami, New Orleans, and Cleveland, officers have been convicted of actively assisting drug dealers or illegally stealing drugs and money from dealers for their own profit.

If police administrators judge success merely by the maintenance of order on the streets and a steady flow of arrests and traffic citations, they may not have any idea what their officers actually do while on patrol. Officers therefore may learn that they can engage in improper conduct without worrying about supervisors' investigations as long as they maintain order on the streets and keep their activities out of the public spotlight.

When police administrators do not monitor the activities of officers, opportunities for corruption will always arise. Enforcement of vice laws, especially drug laws, creates major problems for police agencies. In many cities the rewards for vice offenders are so high that they can easily afford to make large

payments to unethical officers for protection against prosecution. That police operations against victimless crimes are proactive makes the problem worse. Unless drugs are being sold openly, upsetting the residents of a neighborhood, there are no victims to complain if officers ignore or even profit from the activities of drug dealers.

Over time, illegal activity may become accepted as normal. Ellwyn Stoddard, who studied "blue-coat crime," says that it can become part of an "identifiable informal 'code.'" He suggests that officers are socialized to the code early in their careers. Those who "snitch" on other officers may be ostracized (Stoddard, 1968: 205). Recent research shows that officers risk retaliation from peers if they break the code (Cancino and Enriquez, 2004). When corruption comes to official attention, officers protect the code by distancing themselves from the known offender rather than stopping their own improper conduct. Activities under this blue-coat code may include the following (Stoddard, 1968: 205):

- *Mooching*: Accepting free coffee, cigarettes, meals, liquor, groceries, or other items, which are thought of as compensation either for being underpaid or for future favoritism to the donor.

- *Bribery*: Receiving cash or a "gift" in exchange for past or future help in avoiding prosecution. The officer may claim to be unable to identify a criminal, may take care to be in the wrong place when a crime is to occur, or may take some other action that can be viewed as mere carelessness.

- *Chiseling*: Demanding discounts or free admission to places of entertainment, whether on duty or not.

- *Extortion*: Demanding payment for an ad in a police magazine or purchase of tickets to a police function; holding a "street court" in which minor traffic tickets can be avoided by the payment of cash "bail" to the arresting officer, with no receipt given.

- *Shopping*: Picking up small items such as candy bars, gum, and cigarettes at a store where the door has been left unlocked at the close of business hours.

- *Shakedown*: Taking expensive items for personal use during an investigation of a break-in or burglary. Shakedown is distinguished from shopping by the value of the items taken and the ease with which former ownership of items can be determined if the officer is caught.

- *Premeditated theft*: Using tools, keys, or other devices to force entry and steal property. Premeditated theft is distinguished from shakedown by the fact that it is planned, not by the value of the items taken.

- *Favoritism*: Issuing license tabs, window stickers, or courtesy cards that exempt users from arrest or citation for traffic offenses (sometimes extended to family members and friends of recipients).

- *Perjury*: Lying to provide an alibi for fellow officers engaged in unlawful activity or otherwise failing to tell the truth so as to avoid sanctions.

- *Prejudice*: Treating members of minority groups in a biased fashion, especially members of groups that lack political influence in City Hall to cause the arresting officer trouble.

Police corruption has three major effects on law enforcement: (1) suspects are left free to engage in further crime, (2) morale is damaged and supervision becomes lax, and (3) the image of the police suffers. The image of the police agency is very important in light of the need for citizen cooperation. When people see the police as not much different from the "crooks," effective crime control falls even further out of reach. Indeed, recent research has identified connections between violent crime and compromised police legitimacy in disadvantaged communities (Kane, 2005).

Surprisingly, many people do not equate police corruption with other forms of crime. Some believe that police corruption is tolerable as long as the streets

CLOSE UP

Police and Outside Compensation

TASER INTERNATIONAL, the company that manufactures and markets Tasers, a less-lethal, electroshock weapon for police, employs 263 police officers as part-time master instructors who train police departments in the use of the device. Tasers deliver a 50,000-volt shock that causes individuals to collapse in pain. Debate centers on whether the devices may inflict serious harm on some people, such as those with weak hearts. In Minneapolis, an officer paid by Taser International to train officers in various departments was also involved in making the decision about whether to purchase Tasers for use in his own department. An officer in Arizona made a presentation to his city's council advocating the purchase of 300 Tasers. At the time, neither the council members nor his superiors knew that he had received stock options as a form of compensation by Taser International. In both cases, the officers resigned and went to work as sales managers for Taser International when their respective cities began conflict-of-interest investigations.

Sources: "Taser's Use of Police Officers Questioned," *Toledo Blade*, March 27, 2005 (http://www.toledoblade.com); Thor Valdmanis, "Taser Gave Four Officers Stock Options," *USA Today*, January 11, 2005 (http://www.usatoday.com).

Researching the Internet

Go to the website of the International Association of Chiefs of Police (IACP) and examine the Oath of Honor for police officers. To link to this website, go to *The American System of Criminal Justice* 12e companion site at academic.cengage.com/criminaljustice/cole.

Do the actions of the police officers working for Taser International violate this oath? If not, do their actions raise any other ethical issues? If you were a police chief and learned that one of your officers worked for Taser International, what would you do?

remain safe (see "A Question of Ethics" at the end of this chapter). This attitude ignores the fact that corrupt officers are serving only themselves and are not committed to serving the public.

Controlling Corruption

The public has a role to play in stopping police corruption. Scandals attract the attention of politicians and the news media, but it is up to citizens to file complaints about improper actions. Once a citizen files a complaint, however, questions remain about how best to respond. All departments have policies about proper police behavior and ways of dealing with complaints, but some departments tend to sweep corruption complaints under the rug. The most effective departments often have strong leaders who clearly demonstrate to the public and to officers that corruption will not be tolerated and that complaints will be investigated and pursued seriously. Specific innovations are possible. Because of its highly publicized scandals, for example, the city of New York in 1995 created the Commission to Combat Police Corruption, a permanent agency with a full-time staff that is completely separate from the New York City Police Department that it monitors. Read the Close Up on off-duty compensation for police officers from a manufacturer that sells equipment to the police. Does this activity create any risks of corruption?

checkpoint

1. What kinds of practices may be viewed as police abuse?
2. When may the police use force?
3. How did the Supreme Court rule in *Tennessee v. Garner*?
4. What is the difference between grass eaters and meat eaters?
5. What are five of the ten practices cited by Stoddard as blue-coat crime?
   (Answers are at the end of the chapter.)

CIVIC ACCOUNTABILITY

Relations between citizens and the police depend greatly on citizen confidence that officers will behave in accordance with the law and departmental guidelines. Rapport with the community is enhanced when citizens feel sure that the police will protect their persons and property and the rights guaranteed by the Constitution. Making the police responsive to citizen complaints without burdening them with a flood of such complaints is difficult. The main challenge in making the police more accountable is to use citizen input to force police to follow the law and departmental guidelines without placing too many limits on their ability to carry out their primary functions. At present, four less-than-perfect techniques are used in efforts to control the police: (1) internal affairs units, (2) civilian review boards, (3) standards and accreditation, and (4) civil liability lawsuits. We now look at each of these in some detail.

Internal Affairs Units

Controlling the police is mainly an internal matter that administrators must give top priority. The community must be confident that the department has procedures to ensure that officers will protect the rights of citizens. Many departments have no formal complaint procedures, and when such procedures do exist, they often seem designed to discourage citizen input (Figure 7.1). Rumor has it, for example, that several years ago the Internal Affairs Bureau of the San Francisco Police Department posted a sign that said "Write your complaints here." Under the sign was a pile of 1-inch-square scraps of paper.

Depending on the size of the department, a single officer or an entire section can serve as an **internal affairs unit** that receives and investigates complaints against officers. An officer charged with misconduct can face criminal prosecution or disciplinary action leading to resignation, dismissal, or suspension. Officers assigned to the internal affairs unit have duties similar to those of the inspector general's staff in the military. They must investigate complaints against other officers. Hollywood films and television dramas depict dramatic investigations of drug dealing and murder, but investigations of sexual harassment, alcohol or drug problems, misuse of force, and violations of departmental policies are more common.

internal affairs unit
A branch of a police department that receives and investigates complaints alleging violations of rules and policies on the part of officers.

The internal affairs unit must be given enough resources to carry out its mission, as well as direct access to the chief. Internal investigators who assume that a citizen complaint is an attack on the police as a whole will shield officers against such complaints. When this happens, administrators do not get the information they need to correct a problem. The public, in turn, may come to believe that the department condones the practices they complain of and that filing a complaint is pointless. Moreover, even when the top administrator seeks to attack misconduct, he or she may find it hard to persuade police to testify against other officers.

The Internal Affairs Group of the Los Angeles Police Department is described on the LAPD website. To link to this website, go to *The American System of Criminal Justice* 12e companion site at academic.cengage.com/criminaljustice/cole.

Internal affairs investigators find the work stressful, because their status prevents them from maintaining close relationships with other officers. A wall of silence rises around them. Such problems can be especially severe in smaller departments where all the officers know each other well and regularly socialize together.

Civilian Review Boards

If a police department cannot show that it effectively combats corruption among officers, the public will likely demand that a civilian review board investigate the department. These boards allow complaints to be channeled through a committee

FIGURE 7.1
Path of citizen complaints
Compare the actions taken when a citizen is assaulted by a police officer in the course of dealing with a traffic violation and when a citizen is assaulted by a neighbor.

Source: *Hartford Courant*, September 30, 1991, p. A6.

of people who are not sworn police officers. The organization and powers of civilian review boards vary, but all oversee and review how police departments handle citizen complaints. The boards may also recommend remedial action. They do not have the power to investigate or discipline individual officers, however (S. Walker and Wright, 1995).

During the 1980s, as minorities gained more political power in large cities, a revival of civilian review boards took place. A survey of the 50 largest cities found that 36 had civilian review boards, as did 13 of the 50 next-largest cities (S. Walker and Wright, 1995).

The main argument made by the police against civilian review boards is that people outside law enforcement do not understand the problems of policing. The police contend that civilian oversight lowers morale and hinders performance and that officers will be less effective if they are worried about possible disciplinary actions. In reality, however, the boards have not been harsh. Indeed, research on the public's views on appropriate punishment for police misconduct reveals that "the public brings a temperate lens, or one that does not demonstrate a propensity toward harsh punishments" when examining police behavior and the circumstances in which that behavior occurred (Seron, Pereira, and Kovath, 2006: 955).

Review of police actions occurs some time after the incident has taken place and usually comes down to the officer's word against that of the complainant. Given the low visibility of the incidents that lead to complaints, a great many complaints are not substantiated (Skolnick and Fyfe, 1993: 229). The effectiveness of civilian review boards has not been tested; their presence may or may not improve police–citizen relations. Even so, filing a complaint against the police can be quite frustrating, as shown in Figure 7.1. As you read "Civic Engagement: Your Role in the System," consider the best way for a civilian review board to approach complaints against the police.

civic engagement
your role in the system

Imagine that you are a member of a Civilian Review Board that has received a complaint about an off-duty police officer who beat up a female bartender when she refused to serve him more drinks. Moreover, the beating was recorded on a security camera. The officer's lawyer claims that the board should not consider the case until after the criminal assault case against the officer has been completed. *Make a list of arguments—pro and con—regarding postponing the board's review until after the criminal case is completed.* Then see what happened when authorities in Chicago faced just such a case. To link to this website, go to *The American System of Criminal Justice* 12e companion site at academic.cengage.com/criminaljustice/cole.

 To see an example of an active citizen review board, see the website of the Pittsburgh Citizen Police Review Board. To link to this website, go to *The American System of Criminal Justice* 12e companion site at academic.cengage.com/criminaljustice/cole.

Standards and Accreditation

One way to increase police accountability is to require that police actions meet nationally recognized standards. The movement to accredit departments that meet these standards has gained momentum during the past decade. It has the support of the Commission on Accreditation for Law Enforcement Agencies (CALEA), a private nonprofit corporation formed by four professional associations: the International Association of Chiefs of Police (IACP), the National Organization of Black Law Enforcement Executives (NOBLE), the National Sheriffs Association (NSA), and the Police Executive Research Forum (PERF).

The CALEA *Standards*, first published in 1983, have been updated from time to time. The fourth edition, published in 1999, has 439 specific standards. Each standard is a statement, with a brief explanation, that sets forth clear requirements. For example, under Limits of Authority, Standard 1.2.2 requires that "a written directive [govern] the use of discretion by sworn officers." The explanation states, "In many agencies, the exercise of discretion is defined by a combination of written enforcement policies, training and supervision. The written directive should define the limits of individual discretion and provide guidelines for exercising discretion within those limits" (Commission on Accreditation for Law Enforcement Agencies, 1989: 1). Because police departments traditionally have said almost nothing about their use of discretion, this statement represents a major shift. However, the standard still is not specific enough. For example, it does not cover stop-and-frisk actions, the handling of drunks, and the use of informants.

Police accreditation is voluntary. Departments contact CALEA, which helps them in their efforts to meet the standards. This process involves self-evaluation by departmental executives, the development of policies that meet the standards, and the training of officers. The CALEA representative acts like a military inspector general, visiting the department, examining its policies, and seeing if the standards are met in its daily operations. Departments that meet the standards receive certification. Administrators can use the standards as a management tool, training officers to know the standards and be accountable for their actions. By 1998 over 460 agencies had been accredited (S. Walker, 1999: 285).

Obviously, the standards do not guarantee that police officers in an accredited department will not engage in misconduct. However, they are a major step toward providing clear guidelines to officers about proper behavior. Accreditation can also show the public that the department is committed to making sure officers carry out their duties in an ethical, professional manner.

You can learn about CALEA and the accreditation process by going to *The American System of Criminal Justice* 12e companion site at academic.cengage.com/criminaljustice/cole.

Civil Liability Lawsuits

Civil lawsuits against departments for police misconduct can increase civic accountability. In 1961 the U.S. Supreme Court ruled that Section 1983 of the Civil Rights Act of 1871 allows citizens to sue state and local officials for violations of their civil rights. The high court extended this opportunity in 1978 when it ruled that individual officials and local agencies may be sued when a person's civil rights are violated by an agency's "customs and usages." If an individual can show that a rights violation was caused by employees whose wrongful acts were the result of these "customs, practices, and policies, including poor training and supervision," then he or she can win the lawsuit (*Monell v. Department of Social Services of the City of New York*, 1978).

Lawsuits charging brutality, false arrest, and negligence are being brought in both state and federal courts. In several states people have received damage awards in the millions of dollars, and police departments have settled some suits out of court. For example, the Chicago City Council paid nearly $20 million in 2008 to settle a lawsuit by four former death row inmates who were wrongly convicted of murder after Chicago police used electric shocks and beatings to torture them into falsely confessing (CBS2-TV, 2008). Omaha, Nebraska, paid $8 million between 1993 and 2005 to innocent victims of police chases (Hicks, 2005). New York City paid more than $140 million in claims for police actions between 1994 and 1999 (Flynn, 1999).

Civil liability rulings by the courts tend to be simple and severe: Officials and municipalities are ordered to pay a sum of money, and the courts can enforce that judgment. The potential for costly judgments gives police departments an incentive to improve the training and supervision of officers (Vaughn, 2001). One study asked a sample of police executives to rank the policy issues most likely to be affected by civil liability decisions. The top-ranked issues were use of force, pursuit driving, and improper arrests (C. E. Smith and Hurst, 1996). Most departments have liability insurance, and many officers have their own insurance policies.

The courts have ruled that police work must follow generally accepted professional practices and standards. The potential for civil suits seems to have led to some changes in policy. For instance, a $2-million judgment won by Tracey Thurman against the Torrington, Connecticut, police had a profound impact (see the Close Up box "Battered Women, Reluctant Police" in Chapter 5). Plaintiffs' victories in civil suits have spurred accreditation efforts because police executives believe that liability can be avoided or reduced if they can show that their officers are meeting the highest professional standards. In fact, insurance companies that provide civil liability protection now offer discounts for accreditation.

Now that we have considered traditional problems that perpetually arise to challenge law enforcement officials, let's turn our attention to newer developments. In the next section, we examine the impact of new technologies on policing. Technology can increase the capacity of law enforcement officials to fulfill their responsibilities effectively. New developments can also raise new issues and problems.

checkpoint

6. What are the four methods used to increase the civic accountability of the police?
7. What is an internal affairs unit?
8. Why are civilian review boards relatively uncommon?
9. What is the importance of the decision in *Monell v. Department of Social Services of the City of New York*?

POLICING AND NEW TECHNOLOGY

Policing has long made use of technological developments. As discussed in Chapter 5, police departments adopted the use of automobiles and radios in order to increase the effectiveness of their patrols, including better response time to criminal events and emergencies. Technology has affected the investigation of crime as well. As early as 1911, fingerprint evidence was used to convict an offender. Police officers seek to collect fingerprints, blood, fibers, and other crime-scene materials to be analyzed through scientific methods in order to identify and convict criminal offenders.

Police officers also use polygraphs, the technical name for "lie detectors," that measure people's heart rates and other physical responses as they answer questions. Although polygraph results are typically not admissible as evidence, police officers have often used these examinations on willing suspects and witnesses as a basis for excluding some suspects or for pressuring others to confess.

In recent years, scientific advances have enabled police and prosecutors to place greater reliance on DNA "fingerprinting." This technique identifies people through their distinctive gene patterns (also called genotypic features). DNA, or deoxyribonucleic acid, is the basic component of all chromosomes; all the cells in an individual's body, including those in skin, blood, organs, and semen, contain the same unique DNA. The characteristics of certain segments of DNA vary from person to person and thus form a genetic "fingerprint." Forensic labs can analyze DNA from, for example, samples of hair and compare them with those of suspects. Table 7.2 compares DNA and various other forms of forensic evidence that are used in criminal cases. As described by several law enforcement officials, the increasing effectiveness of DNA testing as an investigative tool stems from "improved technology, better sharing of DNA databases among states and a drop in crime . . . that allowed detectives more time to work on unsolved cases" (Yardley, 2006).

Several issues arise as police adopt new technologies. First, questions about the accuracy and effectiveness of technological developments persist, even though the developments were originally embraced with great confidence. For example, despite the long and confident use of fingerprint evidence by police and prosecutors, its accuracy has been questioned. In 2002 a federal judge ruled that expert witnesses could compare crime-scene fingerprints with those of a defendant, but they could not testify that the prints definitely matched. The judge

TABLE 7.2	The Frontiers of Forensics			

Analysis of fingerprints, blood, hair, and DNA are four of the main forensic tools used by the police.

How it Works	Fingerprint	Blood	Hair	DNA
	Experts compare the pattern of ridges and whorls.	Serologists compare proteins and antigens that can vary from person to person.	A crime lab compares the color, shape, and microsopic characteristics.	Technicians compare 3 to 6 regions of DNA obtained from blood, semen, or hair.
Theoretical Accuracy	Perfect: no two fingerprints are identical.	Varies: 1 out of 2 people are type O. But only 1 in 1,000 share all 9 proteins typically tested.	Poor: can identify race but not individuals.	Hotly debated: only 1 in millions may have the same patterns.
Admissibility	In all states, but recently challenged in court	In all states	In all states	Varies by state

Source: *Newsweek*, July 11, 1994, p. 25. © 1994 Newsweek, Inc. All rights reserved. Reprinted by permission.

pointed out that, unlike DNA evidence, fingerprint evidence processes have not been scientifically verified, the error rate for such identifications has never been measured, and there are no scientific standards for determining when fingerprint samples "match" (Loviglio, 2002). Prosecutors later persuaded the judge to reverse his original decision and admit the expert testimony about a fingerprint match, but the judge's first decision raises the possibility that other judges will scrutinize fingerprint evidence more closely.

Second, some worry that new technologies will create new collisions with citizens' constitutional rights. As police gain greater opportunities for sophisticated electronic surveillance, for example, new questions arise about what constitutes a "search" that violates the reasonable expectations of privacy of citizens. The development of technology for the interception of email messages by law enforcement agencies provides an illustration of new situations that were not foreseeable in prior decades. In another example, in several cities police officers with DNA evidence from a rape have asked all of the men in a particular community to submit a DNA sample from a swab of saliva and cells inside the cheek in order to try to find a match with DNA of the perpetrator. Many critics believe that innocent citizens who have done nothing suspicious should not be pressured to provide the government with a sample of their DNA.

Investigative Tools

Computers

One of the most rapidly spreading technological tools for law enforcement officers is the computer, especially portable ones in patrol cars. Computers enable instant electronic communication that permits the radio airwaves to be reserved for emergency calls rather than for requests to check license numbers and other routine matters. Computers also give officers quick access to databases and other information sources that help identify suspects. Depending on the software used and the organization of databases, many officers can make quick checks of individuals' criminal histories, driving records, and outstanding warrants (A. Davis, 2001). With more-advanced computers and software, some officers can even receive mug shots and fingerprint records on their computer screens. Advances in technology provide a variety of possibilities for improving officers' ability to evaluate evidence at the scene of an event. With mobile scanners, officers can potentially run a quick check of an individual's fingerprints against the millions of fingerprint records stored in the FBI's database (Pochna, 2002). The Seal Beach, California, Police Department has worked with high-tech companies to develop streaming video capabilities that can permit officers to view live video from crime-scene cameras as they approach the location of an incident.

For example, if officers can use their computers to access surveillance cameras in banks and convenience stores, they can see the details of a robbery in progress as they approach the scene of an emergency call ("Law Enforcement Solution," 2002). Thus, technology can improve the safety and effectiveness of police officers, especially in their crime-fighting role.

Computers have become very important for investigating specific types of crimes, especially cybercrimes (Hinduja, 2004). Many police departments have begun to train and use personnel to investigate people who use computers to meet children online in order to lure them into exploitative relationships. Computer investigations also involve pursuing people who commit identity theft, steal credit card numbers, and engage in fraudulent financial transactions using computers (Collins, 2005).

Computers are also essential for crime analysis and "crime mapping," methods used with increasing frequency by local police departments. Through the use of Geographic Information System (GIS) technology and software, police departments can analyze hot spots, crime trends, and other crime patterns with a level of previously unavailable sophistication and precision. By analyzing the locations and frequencies of specific crimes, such as burglary, or the nature of calls for service in various neighborhoods, police are better able to deploy their personnel effectively and plan targeted crime-prevention programs (Stroshine, 2005).

One example of promising innovations is the Los Angeles Police Department's development of a "smart car" that incorporates various cutting-edge computer and video technologies. The car contains a camera that can scan license plates at high speed and then the car's computer tells the officers if the car was stolen or if the owner of the vehicle is wanted. The camera-computer system can process 8,000 license plates during a 10-hour shift. By contrast, an officer could manually process only about 100 license plates during the same time period. When the system detects a stolen car, another camera photographs the car and records the GPS location. In addition to the commonly used dashboard video camera, the car also has a rear-facing video camera to monitor any prisoners being transported. The car's computer system can also receive streaming video from surveillance cameras located in housing projects and commercial areas in order to permit officers to spot suspicions persons or crimes in-progress. Finally, the car also contains a launcher in the front grill which can shoot a small GPS-tracking device that will attach itself to a car that officers are following. Even if the officers lose the vehicle in a chase, the car's location will be known through GPS tracking. The LAPD has high hopes for adding a fleet of cars with these technologies to the few "smart cars" that already exist, but there are issues about handling the high cost of adding expensive technological devices to hundreds of police vehicles (Cheung, 2007; Valencia-Martinez, 2006).

Databases

Police departments throughout the country can submit fingerprints from a crime scene in hope of finding the criminal's identity from among the more than 47 million sets of fingerprints stored in the FBI computers. Local and federal law enforcement officials routinely submit the fingerprints of everyone arrested for a serious charge so that the prints can be added to the database. If a suspect

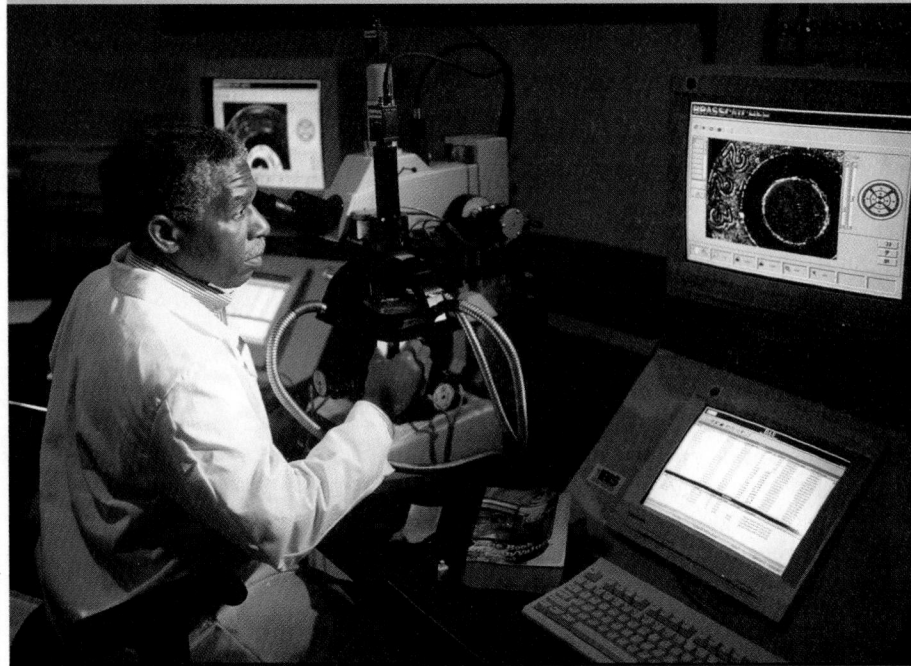

The development of databases and improvements in nationwide computer access to those databases help investigators identify suspects through DNA samples, fingerprints, tattoos, and other markers. Here, the FBI's Lead Ballistics Examiner Walter Dandridge studies the grooves of a .223 slug through a developing database of ballistics signatures from guns used in crimes. Is there any information about Americans that should *not* be centralized in database collections?

© Brooks Kraft/Corbis

latent fingerprints
Impressions from the ridges on the fingertips that are left behind on objects due to natural secretions from the skin or contaminating materials, such as ink, blood, or dirt, that were present on the fingertips at the time of their contact with the objects.

 The FBI describes its fingerprint records and matching processes on its website. To link to this website, go to *The American System of Criminal Justice* 12e companion site at academic.cengage.com/criminaljustice/cole.

is found not guilty, the prints are supposed to be removed from the system (Engber, 2005). These databases may also be used for background checks on people who work in regulated industries such as casinos and banks (Engber, 2005).

A few years ago, matching fingerprints was time consuming because fingerprints had to be sent to the FBI on cards. Since 1999, however, the Integrated Automated Fingerprint Identification System (IAFIS) has enabled police to send fingerprints electronically and then have those prints matched against the millions of prints in the database. The FBI can also provide electronic images of individuals' fingerprints to local law enforcement agencies upon request. Finally, the FBI provides training for state and local police on taking fingerprints and transmitting those prints to the IAFIS for evaluation.

The Department of Homeland Security has developed its own fingerprint database from two primary sources. New post–9-11 rules require the collection of fingerprints from every noncitizen entering the Uniied States. This has created a database of more than 64 million fingerprints that can be linked to the FBI database containing an additional 40 million sets. Military and intelligence officials are also collecting unidentified **latent fingerprints** from cups, glasses, firearms, ammunition, doorknobs, and any other objects that they find overseas in abandoned Al-Qaida training camps, safehouses, and battle sites. The hope is that terrorists will be identified if their fingerprints match to those of visitors to the United States in the database (Richey, 2006).

New debates emerged about whether there should be a national database of ballistic evidence. Advocates argued that every gun sold should undergo a firing test so that its ballistic fingerprint could be stored in the database, just in case the weapon was later used in a crime. Opponents claimed that this was an undesirable step toward national gun registration and that such a database would be useless because the ballistic characteristics of a gun's fired bullets change as the gun is used over time (Chaddock, 2002). The usefulness of these databases depends on the accuracy of technology to match evidence with stored information and the accessibility of database information to police departments and individual officers. In addition, as indicated by the debate about ballistic evidence, the nature and use of evidence databases rely in part on public policy debates about what information can be gathered and how it will be used.

DNA Testing

In spite of questions about which offenders should be required to submit DNA samples, many states and the federal government are building a national database of DNA records that is maintained by the FBI. Known as CODIS, which stands for Combined DNA Index System, the project began in 1990 as a pilot

project serving a few state and local laboratories. CODIS has now grown to include 137 laboratories in 47 states and the District of Columbia.

The federal Justice for All Act, enacted in October 2004, greatly expanded the number of offenders in the federal justice system who must submit DNA samples. Previously, samples were taken only from those who had committed specific violent crimes. Now, samples are taken from offenders convicted of any felony, violent act, or conspiracy. In the federal correctional system, the Bureau of Prisons obtains DNA through blood samples from *all* incoming offenders. In addition, federal probation offices must now obtain samples under the new law. Federal probation offices are scrambling to find qualified phlebotomists (people trained to draw blood samples), as well as to acquire enough test kits for thousands of additional offenders. Moreover, Congress mandated that the samples be collected but did not provide any funds for the probation offices within federal courts to collect these samples (Administrative Office of the U.S. Courts, 2005). Thus, the new requirement is causing budget problems in the justice system.

States have their own laws governing DNA and which people are required to submit a sample. Efforts are underway to expand the collection of samples. In 2007, for example, New York officials proposed expanding required sample collection beyond those convicted of serious crimes so that samples would also be collected from those convicted of misdemeanors (McGeehan, 2007). In 2008, Maryland joined a dozen other states in collecting samples from people arrested, but not yet convicted, for murder, rape, and assault (Arena and Bohn, 2008). California will begin taking samples from everyone arrested on felony charges in 2009, whether or not they are ultimately convicted of a crime (Felch and Dolan, 2008). Georgia instituted a new law in 2008 to permit investigators to compare DNA evidence with samples collected from suspects when a search warrant is obtained to require a subject to provide a sample. Previously, DNA evidence in Georgia could only be compared to samples taken from convicted felons ("Perdue OK's Bill," 2008).

Another proposal to expand the use of DNA testing and evidence concerns searches that look for relatives rather than the exact person whose DNA was left at the crime scene. Although only exact matches of crime-scene evidence and an individual's DNA are supposed to be used in court, it is possible to identify other suspects through wider comparisons. For example, DNA comparisons may indicate that a convicted felon whose sample is in the database is not the perpetrator of a rape, but that he is a relative of the rapist. Thus police would have reason to undertake further investigations of the convicted felon's close male relatives. So-called "kinship-based DNA searching" is already used in Great Britain but is not used as widely in the United States (Wade, 2006).

By taking samples from people convicted of specific crimes in the state and federal systems, officials hope that CODIS will enable them to close unsolved crimes that involve DNA evidence. Unfortunately, problems and delays in collecting and processing the samples persist. Nonetheless, the use of DNA testing and databases has led to arrests in a growing number of unsolved cases. Examples from 2005 illustrate both the possibilities and problems involved in DNA identifications. In April 2005, DNA tests linked a man in Georgia with 25 unsolved rapes in three states, including a rape committed in New York in 1973. The man had fled New York nearly 20 years earlier when facing different rape charges. He was eventually located when Georgia conducted a routine background check when the man attempted to purchase a gun. At the time, officials did not know he was linked to the other unsolved rapes, but the matches emerged when his sample was run through the national database (Preston, 2005). The successful use of the DNA database to close an old case raised officials' optimism about solving other cold cases by testing evidence that had been saved from many years ago. Such was the case, for example, of an imprisoned man in Georgia whose DNA analysis in 2006 indicated that he was responsible for four unsolved murders in Connecticut in the late 1980s and early 1990s (Yardley, 2006) and a serial murderer-rapist in Buffalo, New York, whose unsolved crimes spanned two decades (Staba, 2007).

The arrest of the rapist illustrates the benefit of using DNA testing and databases, but other cases demonstrate problems that need to be addressed. In Truro, Massachusetts, a writer was raped and murdered in her home in 2002. Her bloody body was found on the floor with her two-year-old daughter, who was clinging to it when a friend came to check on her whereabouts. The police sought DNA samples from all men in the small community. Their efforts to obtain these samples led to protests by civil liberties advocates who believed the rights of innocent men were threatened, especially when police said that they would look closely at men who refused to provide a sample. In April 2005, police arrested a man after his sample matched DNA from the crime scene. The suspect was the trash collector who went to the victim's house each week. Unfortunately, although the suspect had volunteered to provide a sample in April 2002, the police did not collect the sample until March 2004. Further, because of a backlog of DNA samples to be tested at the state crime lab, the sample was not evaluated until April 2005 (Belluck, 2005). Did the suspect commit additional crimes during the long delay? That possibility exists. The lack of adequate resources for prompt tests always raises the risk that crimes could have been prevented if a suspect had been identified and arrested earlier in the process.

The problem of too few laboratories and inadequate staff and equipment plagues many states and the federal government. It only took police five days to learn that a man's DNA sample in Vermont identified him as a murder suspect. Unfortunately, however, five years had already passed from the time that the man provided the DNA sample to the time when Vermont crime lab officials could put the sample in the state's database (Ring, 2005). Thus, the long delay prevented quick identification and arrest after he provided the sample. A report from the Bureau of Justice Statistics estimates that we would need 1,900 additional laboratory staff members at a cost of more than $70 million to reduce backlogs in DNA labs throughout the nation (Peterson and Hickman, 2005).

Another potential problem with DNA testing, along with other aspects of forensic science, concerns the ethics and competence of scientists and technicians. Such problems have emerged in the FBI crime lab as well as in various states. For example, crime laboratories in Houston and Fort Worth, Texas, were investigated and shut down after improper handling and analyzing of DNA evidence led to the convictions of people who were actually innocent. For instance, a man sent to prison because of the Houston lab's DNA analysis was exonerated when a private lab retested the sample. Scandals involving improper lab procedures and erroneous testimony by forensic scientists have led states such as Oklahoma and Texas to enact laws requiring crime labs to meet national accreditation standards (Kimberly, 2003). The federal government now requires crime labs to meet accreditation standards in order to receive federal funds, but many labs have not yet gone through the accreditation process. Moreover, critics contend that accreditation will not prevent mistakes and erroneous testimony by scientists and technicians with questionable ethics, skills, or knowledge. This is especially true in the worst cases, such as that of a West Virginia forensic scientist who falsified test results and provided false testimony in order to help prosecutors gain convictions (Roane and Morrison, 2005). Scientists have an obligation to present truthful analyses, and they must avoid seeing themselves as part of the law enforcement team that seeks to convict people of crimes.

The expansion of DNA databases is raising a new issue that ultimately may become viewed as related to ethics. Sometimes genetic material preserved from a crime scene in an unsolved case has deteriorated over the years. By the time it is tested in an effort to match the sample with individuals in a database, forensic scientists may be able to identify fewer markers than the 13 that are usually

The federal government provides a wealth of information on DNA testing and its benefits at a special website. To link to this website, go to *The American System of Criminal Justice* 12e companion site at academic .cengage.com/criminaljustice/cole.

used to match individuals. However, using fewer markers creates risks that the person matched to the sample really is not guilty. In one case in Britain, a man's DNA sample matched six markers from criminal evidence, but when officials identified and tested four more markers, his DNA no longer matched (Felch and Dolan, 2008). This issue creates risks that the growing public belief in the infallibility of DNA testing may lead to erroneous convictions if the DNA sample is incomplete. For example, when evidence from an unsolved 1972 rape-murder in California was tested in 2004, the degraded sample provided only five and a half markers to use in seeking to identify the perpetrator. The scientists used evidence from additional makers that were too faint to be considered conclusive in order to produce the seven markers necessary for the computer search. These markers matched a man who had been convicted of rape in the late 1970s and were the basis for his prosecution and conviction for the 1972 case. The prosecution told the jury the remote odds that the match was a coincidence, but the defense was barred from telling the jury that there was also a 1 in 3 risk that the match was in error because of the small number of genetic markers and the hundreds of thousands of people in the database whose samples were compared. A juror later said that the verdict would likely have been different if the jury had been given complete information about how this DNA match differed from those that match a complete set of 13 markers (Felch and Dolan, 2008).

DNA is an investigative tool for police, but it can also be used to prevent and correct grave errors by exonerating wrongly convicted people. However, it can only serve this aspect of justice when evidence is properly preserved and available for later testing as DNA technology steadily improves. Fewer than half of the states require that evidence be preserved and errors by court clerks and lab technicians have led to the disposal of relevant evidence, even in states with laws that require preservation. A more uniform and structured system of evidence preservation is necessary in order for DNA to provide its full potential benefits for the justice system.

Surveillance and Identification

Police have begun using surveillance cameras in many ways. American cities increasingly use surveillance cameras at intersections to monitor and ticket people who run red lights or exceed speed limits. In Scotland, England, and Australia, law enforcement officials have adopted the use of surveillance cameras that permit police to monitor activities that occur in downtown commercial areas or other selected locations. Officials in a control room can watch everyone who passes within the cameras' fields of exposure. Advances in camera technology can enable these officials to see clearly the license plate numbers of cars and other specific information. American cities, such as New York and Washington, have made moves toward experimenting with this approach to combating crime in specific areas.

Chicago, in particular, has moved forward with plans for the widespread use of surveillance cameras in public places. Using a $5 million grant from the U.S. Department of Homeland Security, Chicago's 2,000 cameras will rotate 360 degrees, possess night-vision capability, and use software designed to detect suspicious activity, such as someone leaving a suitcase or other potential bomb container in a busy, public place (Howlett, 2004). City officials hope that surveillance will help them fight crime as well as improve their ability to identify and prevent potential acts of terrorism. Thus the increased use of surveillance cameras in cities may become one element of local police department's increased emphasis on homeland security.

Critics complain that constant surveillance by government intrudes on the privacy of innocent, unsuspecting citizens and that there is insufficient evidence that this surveillance leads to reduced crime rates (Taifa, 2002). Judges and lawyers, including civil liberties advocates, see no problem with public surveillance; these cameras do not infringe on any rights, because people do not have a reasonable expectation of privacy when they are in public places (Howlett, 2004). There may be other problems, however. For example, there are allegations in some British cities that bored officers in the control booth spend their time engaged in close-up monitoring of attractive women and ignore or hide evidence of police misconduct that is caught on camera. Training, supervision, and the establishment of clear procedures will be necessary to avoid such problems. Despite these allegations, the 500,000 surveillance cameras in London proved especially valuable in the aftermath of the July 2005 subway and bus terrorist bombings when officials used recorded images to identify the bombing suspects (Stecklow, Singer, and Patrick, 2005).

American law enforcement officials have experimented with other surveillance and detection technologies. The National Institute of Justice provides funding to help scientists develop devices that will assist the police. For example, scanners are being developed that will permit officers to detect whether individuals are carrying weapons, bombs, or drugs. Some of these devices detect foreign masses hidden on the human body, while others detect trace particles and vapors that are differentiated from those associated with human bodies and clothing (Business Wire, 2001b; PR Newswire, 2001). The first versions of such scanners are undergoing testing as security measures at airports, prisons, schools, and stadiums. However, officers on the streets could eventually use smaller, more mobile versions, especially if they could point a handheld device at an individual passerby to detect whether the person is carrying weapons or contraband.

Not all technological innovations have yet proven to be effective. At the Super Bowl in 2001, police officers used a surveillance system with facial-recognition technology in an attempt to identify people being sought on outstanding warrants. Casinos in Atlantic City also use facial-recognition technology with surveillance cameras to identify people whom they know to be skilled at cheating. Conceivably, the system could also be used to identify suspected terrorists attempting to enter the country at airports (Meyer and Gorman, 2001). This technology poses problems, however, so that some cities have abandoned their initial experiments. It cannot identify faces and match them with database pictures quickly enough to prevent suspects from disappearing into a crowd and thus requiring officers to search for them. In addition, questions persist about the accuracy of the facial-recognition technology. According to one researcher who has tested some systems, "One out of every 50 people looks like Carlos the Jackal, [the infamous terrorist], and the real Carlos the Jackal has only a 50 percent chance of looking like himself" (Meyer and Gorman, 2001: 1). Whether facial recognition technology will become an effective tool for police remains to be seen.

Researchers claim that iris-recognition technology, which examines the interior of the eye and matches its unique characteristics with information in a database, is much more accurate than facial-recognition technology or technologies that attempt to match voices, fingerprints, or the palm of the hand (Business Wire, 2001a). Such iris-recognition technology appeared throughout the fictional futuristic world in the Stephen Spielberg film *Minority Report*. It is not clear, however, that such technology could be developed for use in police surveillance work. Moreover, such a technology would require the development of an entirely new type of database containing records of people's eyes. As with other developing technologies, significant questions arise about the costs of developing and producing new scientific devices for wide distribution. Even if the scientific community develops new technologies that might benefit policing, the expense of implementing these devices may be far more than individual cities and counties can afford.

Scientists are working to develop technology to detect deceptions that suspects may use when questioned by police. Polygraph tests are considered insufficiently reliable, because some liars are very calm when they lie, and thereby avoid detection, while some truthful people are quite nervous when asked questions. Thus truthful people may look like liars on a polygraph test if their palms sweat and their heart rates increase as they answer. One approach under investigation is the use of a thermal-imaging camera that can detect faint blushing in the faces of people who answer questions in an untruthful manner. Critics warn, however, that this technology may simply reproduce the problems with polygraphs by looking only at physical responses that vary by individual (R. Callahan, 2002).

An alternative technology detects people's brain-wave responses to words and images. The subject wears an electronic headband while being shown words or images flashed on a screen. If the person shows a brain-wave response to words or pictures that would be familiar only to the witness or perpetrator of a crime, then law enforcement officials might be able to move forward with an investigation that ultimately solves the crime (Paulson, 2004). Other scientists have taken this approach a step further by subjecting volunteers to an examination of the brain through magnetic resonance imaging (MRI) while asking questions. The research indicates that specific areas of the brain show activity when someone is telling a lie (American Society of Neuroradiology, 2003). These approaches have not yet been fully tested, nor have the courts yet accepted them. Moreover, they raise concerns that a court would regard this technique as violating the Fifth Amendment privilege against compelled self-incrimination.

The U.S. Supreme Court has already given a sign that it will look critically at some new police technologies. In *Kyllo v. United States* (2001), law enforcement officials pointed a thermal-imaging device at a house to detect unusual heat sources that might indicate marijuana being cultivated under grow lights. Their efforts led to a search of the home and the discovery of 100 marijuana plants. In the majority opinion, Justice Antonin Scalia declared the use of the device in this manner to be an illegal search. According to Scalia, "Obtaining by sense-enhancing technology any information regarding the interior of the home that could not otherwise have been obtained without physical intrusion into a constitutionally protected area constitutes a search" and is therefore covered by the limitations of the Fourth Amendment, especially the warrant requirement (*Kyllo v. United States*, 2001: 2043). Thus it is not clear how judges may evaluate the constitutionally permissible uses of new technologies.

Kyllo v. United States (2001)
Law enforcement officials cannot examine a home with a thermal-imaging device unless they obtain a warrant.

checkpoint

10. What kinds of new technologies are assisting police with their investigative functions?
11. What problems are associated with the use of new technology?

Weapons Technology

Police officers have been sued in many cases when they injured or killed people without proper justification. Some of these lawsuits have resulted in cities and counties paying millions of dollars to people who were injured when police used guns or nightsticks improperly or in an inappropriate situation. To avoid future lawsuits, departments have given greater attention to the training of officers. They have also sought nonlethal weapons that could be used to incapacitate or control people without causing serious injuries or deaths. Traditional **less-lethal weapons,** such as nightsticks and pepper spray, can be used only when officers are in close contact with suspects, and they are not suitable for all situations that officers face.

less-lethal weapons
Weapons such as pepper spray and air-fired beanbags or nets that intend to incapacitate a suspect without inflicting serious injuries.

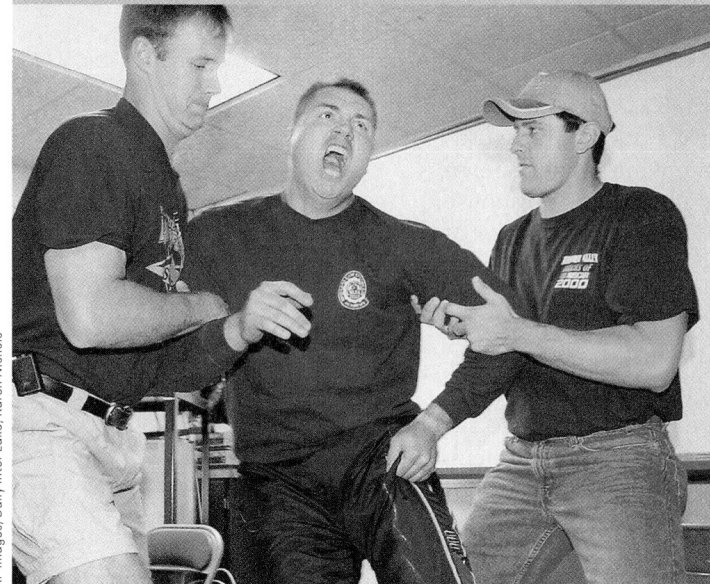

Kalispell, Montana, Police Officer Mike Whitcher reacts as he receives a jolt from a Taser. The Taser fires two wire filaments that send an incapacitating electric jolt into the body. Whitcher had to endure the jolt for a second or two in order to become certified in the use of the weapon. Should such incapacitating weapons also be available for ownership and defensive use by the public?

AP Images/Daily Inter Lake, Karen Nichols

Police officers need to have the ability to incapacitate agitated people who are threatening to harm themselves or others. This need arises when they confront someone suspected of committing a serious crime as well as when they are attempting to control a crowd causing civil disorder. They also seek to enhance their ability to stop criminal suspects from fleeing. A variety of less-lethal weapons have been developed to accomplish these goals. Police use some of them widely, while others are still undergoing testing and refinement.

Projectile weapons shoot objects at people whom the police wish to subdue. Some projectiles, such as rubber bullets, can travel a long distance. Others are employed only when suspects are within a few yards of the officers. Rubber bullets have been used for many years. Although they are generally nonlethal, they can cause serious injuries or death if they hit someone in the eye or elsewhere in the head. Many departments have turned to the use of beanbags, small canvas bags containing tiny lead beads, fired from a shotgun (Spencer, 2000). They are intended to stun people on impact without causing lasting injury. Several police departments in the Los Angeles area, however, have abandoned the use of beanbags because of concerns about injuries and a few deaths caused by these projectiles as well as dissatisfaction with their accuracy when fired at a target (Leonard, 2002).

Other departments have begun to use airguns that shoot *pepperballs,* small plastic pellets filled with a peppery powder that causes coughing and sneezing on release after the suspect is stunned by the impact of the pellet. This weapon drew increased scrutiny after an Emerson College student died when she was hit in the eye by a projectile that disperses pepper spray as police officers attempted to disperse a crowd of revelers who were celebrating a Boston Red Sox victory (CNN, 2004a). Officers can also fill the pellets with green dye in order to mark and later arrest individuals in an out-of-control crowd (Randolph, 2001). Other weapons under development include one that shoots nets that wrap around individual suspects and another that sprays a fountain of foam that envelops the suspect in layers of paralyzing ooze. Law enforcement agencies may also eventually have versions of new weapons being developed for the military, such as devices that send out incapacitating blasts of heat or blinding flash explosions (Hambling, 2005). For example, a new military weapon called "Silent Guardian" shoots a focused beam of radiation that is tuned precisely to stimulate human pain nerves. It inflicts unbearable, incapacitating pain, but, according to the inventors, does not cause injuries (Hanlon, 2007). A law enforcement version, if it worked as intended, could be an alternative to using lethal firearms in some situations.

For suspects who are close at hand, many police departments use the Taser, a weapon with prongs that sends an incapacitating electric jolt of 50,000 volts into people on contact (Ith, 2001). More than 12,000 law enforcement agencies in the United States use these devices. However, the human rights organization Amnesty International has documented more than 150 cases since 2001 in which people died after police used a Taser on them. The manufacturer of Tasers as well as some researchers dispute whether the device actually caused the deaths. Issues have also arisen about whether officers are too quick to use Tasers when they could use persuasion or other means to calm agitated or uncooperative people. The controversy reached a high point when Miami police officers used a Taser on a six-year-old child who was threatening to harm himself (CNN, 2004b). A related controversy expanded in 2008 when lawsuits by Taser International, the device's manufacturer, succeeded in persuading a judge to throw out a county medical examiner's conclusion that the device had caused the death of a jail inmate. Some critics fear that such lawsuits may have a chilling effect on doctors and deter them from reporting findings about any links between the Taser and injuries or deaths experienced by those who receive electrical shocks with the device (Anglen, 2008).

The development of less-lethal weapons has undoubtedly saved officers from firing bullets in many situations in which they previously would have felt required to shoot threatening suspects. However, as with all technologies, these weapons do not magically solve the problem of incapacitating suspects safely. Mechanical problems or misuse by the officer may make the new weapons ineffectual. In addition, officers may act too quickly in firing a less-lethal weapon during inappropriate situations. In such circumstances, needless minor injuries may be inflicted, or the targeted person may become more enraged and thus more threatening to the officers who later must transport the person to jail. Moreover, an officer can carry only so many weapons in his or her arms. The existence of less-lethal weapons will not ensure that such weapons are actually handy when officers must make difficult, on-the-spot decisions about how to handle a threatening situation.

checkpoint

12. What kinds of new weaponry have police employed?

HOMELAND SECURITY

In prior chapters, we have seen how the recent emphasis on homeland security has changed policing. The federal government reorganized various agencies, including law enforcement agencies, in creating the Department of Homeland Security (DHS). Shifts in the FBI's priorities and in the availability of federal funds created new burdens, opportunities, and objectives for local law enforcement agencies. Even traditional programs, such as Neighborhood Watch, now include discussions of moving beyond crime prevention toward contributing more to homeland security. Note, however, that both the FBI and the DHS have been criticized for failing to do enough to make the country fully prepared. For example, in 2008 the U.S. Senate Intelligence Committee issued a report criticizing the FBI's failure to fill key supervisory positions responsible for Al-Qaida-related cases, inadequate training of newly hired intelligence analysts, and delays in the development of a program to collect intelligence on foreign powers operating in the United States (Schmitt, 2008). The FBI has also been criticized for its arguments with ATF over which agency will take charge of specific cases. The competition and lack of cooperation between the agencies was so bad in 2008 that the FBI has refused to merge its bomb database with the ATF's database, even though the U.S. Attorney General ordered both agencies to cooperate on the matter (Markon, 2008).

Although the emphasis on homeland security accelerated and generated a sense of urgency after the hijackers' attacks on September 11, 2001, many police departments gained awareness about their role in homeland security prior to that date. On February 26, 1993, radical Muslims set off a car bomb in the parking garage under the World Trade Center in New York City. Five people were killed and dozens more suffered injuries. In Oklahoma City, Timothy

Sheriff's deputies practice loading an injured victim into an armored vehicle during a training exercise at the Playas Homeland Security Training Center in New Mexico. Since the terrorist attacks of 2001, police officers throughout the nation have increased their training in emergency response procedures. Do local police have the time and resources to effectively add homeland security responsibilities to their traditional duties of law enforcement, service, and order maintenance?

McVeigh, an antigovernment radical, detonated a truck bomb in front of the Federal Building on April 19, 1995. The bomb killed 168 people and injured hundreds more. In both of these examples, local police officers, as well as firefighters, were first responders who rescued survivors, rendered first aid, and began to collect criminal evidence that would be used to identify and punish the perpetrators.

The events of September 11 served to teach Americans that terrorist attacks could not be treated as isolated incidents and rare events. Instead, government officials and citizens alike needed to recognize that specific groups around the world were making plans to inflict large-scale damage on the United States and harm Americans on U.S. soil. This lesson altered the priorities of government agencies and pushed law enforcement agencies at the federal, state, and local levels to make plans for the possibility of future significant threats to homeland security.

Although this section focuses on law enforcement agencies' efforts to combat terrorism, bear in mind that the government needs assistance from citizens in order to identify suspicious activities and respond to emergencies. As you read about the contributions of regular citizens to homeland security in "Doing Your Part," think about whether there may be a role for you.

Preparing for Threats

As discussed in prior chapters, the FBI and DHS make concerted efforts to identify and combat risks in order to reduce the threat of additional attacks. The FBI switched a significant portion of its personnel away from traditional crime control activities in order to gather intelligence on people within the United States who may pose a threat to the nation. The FBI also received budget allocations to enable it to expand the number of special agents and intelligence analysts working on counterterrorism issues. The creation of Joint Terrorism Task Forces (see Chapter 5) reflects the agency's desire to coordinate efforts with state and local officials. Federal officials also seek cooperation and coordination with their counterparts in many countries around the world.

At the same time, the creation of DHS reflected a desire to have better coordination among agencies that were previously scattered throughout the federal government. The DHS also instituted new security procedures at airports and borders as a means of seeking to identify individuals and contraband that pose threats. Many critics believe that the federal government has not done enough to protect ports and critical infrastructure, including nuclear power plants, information systems, subway systems, and other elements essential for the functioning of American society. Attacks with devastating consequences could range from computer hackers disabling key military information systems or computerized controls at energy companies to a suicide airline hijacker hitting a nuclear power or chemical plant. If an attack should target and disable any of these entities, it would fall to local police to maintain order and rescue victims.

Police agencies have traditionally gathered **law enforcement intelligence** information about criminal activities and organizations especially in their efforts to monitor motorcycle gangs, hate groups, drug traffickers, and organized crime. The new emphasis on homeland security broadens the scope of information that agencies need to gather. According to Jonathan White (2004: 73), police must be trained to look for and gather information about such things as

■ Emergence of radical groups, including religious groups

■ Suspicious subjects observing infrastructure facilities

■ Growth of phony charities that may steer money to terrorists

■ Groups with links to foreign countries

■ Unexpected terrorist information found during criminal searches

■ Discovery of bomb-making operations

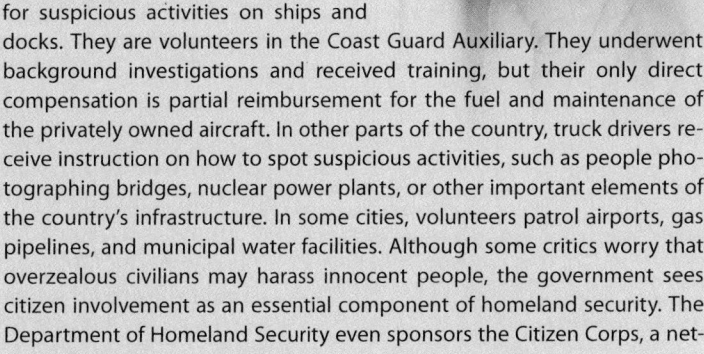

DOING YOUR PART

Homeland Security

IN A SINGLE-ENGINE plane flying along the northern coast of California, three retirees use binoculars to look for suspicious activities on ships and docks. They are volunteers in the Coast Guard Auxiliary. They underwent background investigations and received training, but their only direct compensation is partial reimbursement for the fuel and maintenance of the privately owned aircraft. In other parts of the country, truck drivers receive instruction on how to spot suspicious activities, such as people photographing bridges, nuclear power plants, or other important elements of the country's infrastructure. In some cities, volunteers patrol airports, gas pipelines, and municipal water facilities. Although some critics worry that overzealous civilians may harass innocent people, the government sees citizen involvement as an essential component of homeland security. The Department of Homeland Security even sponsors the Citizen Corps, a network of volunteer organizations. As stated on its website,

> Citizen Corps asks you to embrace the personal responsibility to be prepared; to get training in first aid and emergency skills; and to volunteer to support local emergency responders, disaster relief, and community safety.

What contribution could you make to the homeland security effort?

Source: Based on Dean E. Murphy, "Retirees Answer the Call to Hunt for Terrorists," *New York Times*, May 4, 2005, p. A12.

Researching the Internet

 Read about the Citizen Corps online and for other information for citizens, check the Department of Homeland Security. To link to this website, go to *The American System of Criminal Justice* 12e companion site at academic.cengage.com/criminaljustice/cole.

Local police agencies need training about what to look for and whom to contact if any suspicious activities or materials are discovered. One of the disconcerting aspects of the September 11 tragedy was that specific agencies and officers possessed suspicions about unusual students at flight schools and individuals who had entered the country. If the agencies had shared information more effectively, some people believe that at least some of the September 11 hijackers would have been apprehended and questioned. In light of this lesson, law enforcement agencies at all levels are working harder to coordinate their efforts and share information. Local police officials still complain that the FBI and other federal agencies do not share enough information with them about potential threats within their communities.

Some initiatives to gather and share information have proven unsuccessful. For example, the federal government funded the Multistate Anti-Terrorism Information Exchange, known as MATRIX, that was to collect driver's license, criminal history, and other information from participating states so that they could access this information. Initially, 13 states representing nearly half of the country's population indicated a willingness to participate. However, all but four of these states eventually dropped out of the project amid criticism about

law enforcement intelligence
Information, collected and analyzed by law enforcement officials, concerning criminal activities and organizations, such as gangs, drug traffickers, and organized crime.

the threat to privacy rights as governments created larger and larger databases containing information about people who have done nothing to raise suspicions about their activities. California and Texas, for example, dropped out because of concerns that the MATRIX database, including its sensitive files, was housed in computers at a private company (Krane, 2003). Michigan dropped amid lawsuits alleging that its participation violated a state statute forbidding the state police from participating in interstate intelligence-gathering without legislative approval or outside oversight ("Michigan State Police Drop Out of Anti-Terrorism Network," 2005).

Subsequent efforts to share information emerged in the form of *"fusion centers."* These are state and local intelligence operations that "use law enforcement analysts and sophisticated computer systems to compile, or fuse, disparate tips and clues and pass along the refined information to other agencies" (O'Harrow, 2008). The federal government has provided nearly $250 million for the development and operation of these centers. In addition, the Department of Homeland Security has assigned its personnel to work at these centers. According to the DHS website, "As of March 2008, there were 58 fusion centers around the country. The Department has deployed 23 officers as of March 2008 and plans to have 25 professionals deployed by the end of [fiscal year] 2008" ("State and Local Fusion Centers," www.dhs.gov, 2008). Nineteen of the centers have security clearances that permit them to access information classified as "secret" from the federal government's National Counterterrorism Center ("State and Local Fusion Centers," www.dhs.gov, 2008). It is hoped that the gathering, processing, and sharing of information can help prevent plots from being executed. In retrospect, many wonder if 9-11 might have been preventable if the FBI had access to the CIA's reports on suspicions about the presence in the United States of two of the hijackers. Would the attack have been thwarted if officials in different states had been able to share their suspicions about the behavior of foreigners taking flying lessons in different parts of the country? If information can be passed down to local law enforcement officers, then they may be able to discover suspected terrorists in their everyday activities of making traffic stops or encountering unusual behavior of people in photographing bridges and government buildings (Sheridan and Hsu, 2006).

There are lingering public suspicions about fusion centers and other law enforcement intelligence operations that stem from revelations about government agents spying on American citizens during the 1960s and 1970s for merely expressing their views about civil rights and the Vietnam War. For example, as fusion centers in various states create massive databases that include such information as citizens' credit reports, car rental records, unlisted cell phone numbers, drivers' license photographs, and identity theft reports, there are concerns that the government is unnecessarily intruding too broadly into the lives of all Americans, including those who are not suspected of any wrongdoing (O'Harrow, 2008; German and Stanley, 2007). In addition, the accumulation of so much information into databases and connected networks raises concerns about the risk of a security breach, either through the work of an ingenious hacker or through a government employee losing a laptop computer on a business trip, that will create massive problems with identity theft and computer crime. As law enforcement agencies in the United States continue to develop methods to combat terrorism and protect homeland security, many people will reexamine the balance between providing the government with appropriate tools and safeguarding the rights of Americans against government intrusions.

The emphasis on information analysis and coordination among agencies at all levels of U.S. government, as well as with foreign governments, also impacts law enforcement operations concerning other major problems, such as drug trafficking, money laundering, gun smuggling, and border security. Many of these problems are directly related to threats from terrorism as organizations hostile to the United States seek to finance themselves and gain entry into the country. In addition, the heightened security and increased vigilance creates opportunities to detect and apprehend people involved in these criminal activities who have no connection to terrorist plots. For example, homeland security efforts overlap with initiatives to combat transnational street gangs, such as the MS-13 gang from Central America that has spread from Los Angeles to such places as Washington, D.C., and Charlotte, North Carolina, and brought with it various criminal activities including a series of gang-related homicides (Axtman, 2005a).

Within local police departments, the emphasis on homeland security has led to changes in training, equipment, and operations to prepare first responders to deal with the possibility of weapons of mass destruction and terrorist attacks. The police must also develop regional coordination with neighboring communities and state governments, because large-scale emergencies require the resources and assistance of multiple agencies. Communities need plans for conducting evacuations of buildings and neighborhoods. Police officials must work more closely with firefighters, public health officials, and emergency medical services to prepare for anything from a bomb to a bioterror attack using anthrax, smallpox, or other harmful agents (Hintin, 2002). Some of these threats require the acquisition of new equipment, such as protective suits for suspected biological or chemical hazards or communications equipment that can be used to contact multiple agencies. Many police departments are giving renewed attention to training specialized teams, such as bomb squads and SWAT teams, that will intervene in emergency situations. In addition, they must give all officers additional training on hazardous materials, coordination with outside agencies, and evacuation procedures for malls, central business districts, and hospitals.

The federal government has shifted its funding priorities away from community-oriented policing in order to provide grants for state and local agencies to obtain equipment and training for emergency response and homeland security purposes. One criticism of the funding process is that funds were distributed without careful planning for which locations had the greatest homeland security needs. For example, although many experts regard New York City as one of the top terrorist targets, as evidenced by two major attacks on the World Trade Center and several foiled plots, New York City's Fire Department had only one fully deployable hazardous materials unit for a city of 8 million people. Meanwhile, Grand Forks, North Dakota, reportedly received funds for more biochemical protective suits than they actually have officers to wear them. As a top recipient of homeland security money, Wyoming received funds equal to $38.31 per person in the state, whereas New York received the equivalent of $5.47 per person and was 49th in per-capita funding (Kates, 2003). The skewed distribution of homeland security funds led critics to conclude that politics received too much emphasis and actual threat assessment and demonstrated needs too little. Many observers hoped that planning would become more effective as DHS became better organized and more cohesive.

Just as the development of better communication and coordination among agencies can help combat drug trafficking, gun smuggling, and other crimes unrelated to terrorism, so new training and equipment can serve dual purposes. For example, new equipment for detecting and defusing bombs obtained under homeland security grants can be used for pipe bombs and other explosive devices created by people unconnected to terrorism. Similarly, training in the detection and dismantling of chemical weapons threats has applications in police efforts to find and destroy meth labs and thereby address one of the nation's growing problems with illegal drugs.

A key element of homeland security planning is the development of the Incident Command System (ICS). The principles of ICS were first developed to help

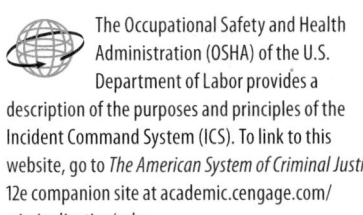 The Occupational Safety and Health Administration (OSHA) of the U.S. Department of Labor provides a description of the purposes and principles of the Incident Command System (ICS). To link to this website, go to *The American System of Criminal Justice* 12e companion site at academic.cengage.com/criminaljustice/cole.

multiple agencies coordinate their efforts in addressing large wildfires in western states. ICS strategies include planning to determine what individual will take charge of managing resources and operations in response to a critical incident. They also include the development of an Incident Action Plan that coordinates the resources, activities, and responsibilities of various agencies and individuals involved in responding to an emergency. By using ICS, agencies are not taken by surprise when emergencies arise and they can spring into action with well-coordinated efforts to maintain order, address primary threats such as fires or bombings, evacuate endangered people, and provide medical aid. The awareness of homeland security needs after September 11 has encouraged police departments to work closely with state officials, firefighters, public health officials, hospitals, and others to develop local and regional ICS plans. Also consider the role of citizens in homeland security as you read "Civic Engagement: Your Role in the System."

checkpoint

13.   What have law enforcement officials done to enhance the protection of homeland security?

New Laws and Controversies

The hijackers' devastating attacks on September 11, 2001, spurred a variety of government actions intended to protect homeland security and combat terrorism. The Bush administration asserted new presidential powers to arrest and detain indefinitely without trial Americans whom it accused of terrorist activities. In 2004, however, the U.S. Supreme Court ruled that the president does not possess unlimited authority and that American detainees are entitled to challenge their confinement through court procedures (*Hamdi v. Rumsfeld*, 2004). The Supreme Court's decision illustrated one aspect of the challenge facing the United States—how to provide government with sufficient power to fight terrorism while also protecting individuals' constitutional rights.

Other controversies arose concerning new state and federal statutes created after September 11. Both Congress and state legislatures enacted new laws aimed at addressing various aspects of homeland security. More than 30 states added new terrorism-related laws. These laws ranged from narrow to broad—from statutes addressing a specific problem to broad authorizations of new powers for law enforcement officials and the definition of new crimes. At the narrow end of the spectrum, for example, after it was discovered that several of the September 11 hijackers had Virginia driver's licenses, Virginia passed a new law to make it more difficult for foreign nationals to obtain a driver's license without possession of specific legal documents.

An example of a broader law is Arizona's statute concerning money laundering, weapons of mass destruction, terrorism and terrorism hoaxes, eavesdropping on communications, and a prohibition of bail for people accused of violent terrorist acts. Some of the purposes and uses of these laws raise questions about whether government powers will grow beyond appropriate boundaries in a democracy that is supposed to place a high value on the protection of individuals' rights.

Because new laws provide tools for justice system officials, controversies can arise when those officials apparently stretch their authority beyond the intentions of the relevant statutes. For example, prosecutors in several cases have used new terrorism laws as a means to prosecute people for criminal acts that are not commonly understood to be related to terrorism. In New York, for example, one of the first prosecutions under the state's antiterrorism laws enacted after September 11 arose when the Bronx district attorney charged street gang members for various crimes. There was no allegation that the gang members had connections to any foreign terrorist networks. Instead, the prosecutor used the state's antiterrorism law to charge gang members with shootings "committed with the intent to intimidate or coerce a civilian population" (Garcia, 2005). Virginia used nearly identical language under its post–September 11 statute as one basis for applying the death penalty to John Muhammad, one of the infamous D.C. snipers who frightened the nation's capital in October 2002, even though there was no proof that he pulled the trigger in any of the shootings (Hegsted, 2005). In other examples, a North Carolina prosecutor charged the operator of a small meth lab under a terrorism statute for "manufacturing a nuclear or chemical weapon" and a Michigan prosecutor used the state's antiterrorism law to charge a high school student for writing up a "hit list" of classmates and school officials ("Charging Common Criminals under Terrorism Laws Doesn't Fit in America's Justice Values," 2003; "Concern Mounts over Anti Terrorism Law," 2005). These two cases generated criticism in newspaper editorials and raised concerns that government officials would exploit terrorism laws for improper purposes. The language of many terrorism laws is sufficiently vague to give prosecutors greater flexibility in seeking convictions. The severe penalties for terrorism-related acts can also give prosecutors more leverage to pressure defendants to plead guilty to lesser charges.

USA Patriot Act

The most controversial legislation came from Congress in the form of the "Uniting and Strengthening America by Providing Appropriate Tools Required to Intercept and Obstruct Terrorism Act." It is best known by its shorthand name, the **USA Patriot Act**. The Patriot Act moved quickly through Congress after the September 11 attacks and covered a wide range of topics including the expansion of government authority for searches and surveillance and the expansion of definitions and penalties for crimes related to terrorism. Critics raised concerns about many provisions because of fears that the government's assertions of excessive power would infringe individuals' rights (Dority, 2005). The Patriot Act made it easier for law enforcement officials to monitor email and obtain "sneak-and-peek" warrants in which they secretly conduct searches without informing a home or business owner until much later that the premises have been searched (Sullivan, 2003). The Patriot Act also authorizes warrantless searches of third-party records, such as those at libraries, financial institutions, phone companies, and medical facilities. This provision sparked an outcry from librarians and booksellers who argued that government monitoring of the reading habits of citizens without sufficient evidence to obtain a warrant violates their rights of privacy and free expression. This provision, in particular, was cited by many of the 150 communities across the country that passed resolutions protesting the excessive authority granted to government by the Patriot Act (Gordon, 2005).

Some of the concerns about the Patriot Act arose because it sailed through Congress in the aftermath of September 11 with very little close examination or debate. Because the law is several hundred pages long, members of Congress had not likely studied the entire law before voting on it. Some of the provisions in the Patriot Act, such as those expanding powers for searches and wiretaps, had been sought by some federal law enforcement officials prior to September 11. Critics claim that the terrorist attacks provided the momentum for powers that these officials had sought to use for crime control purposes unrelated to homeland security. Moreover, some people fear that the Patriot Act authorizes

USA Patriot Act
A federal statute passed in the aftermath of the terrorist attacks of September 11, 2001, that broadens government authority to conduct searches and wiretaps and that expands the definitions of crimes involving terrorism.

CLOSE UP

Swift Action Based on Limited Evidence

POWERFUL BOMBS ROCKED the train station in Madrid, Spain, on March 11, 2004, killing 191 people and injuring 2,000 others. Authorities suspected Muslim radicals who were targeting a country allied with the United States in the invasion of Iraq. FBI experts examined evidence in the bombing, including a partial fingerprint found on a bag of detonators. The FBI officials used their department's automated searching system for the fingerprint database and determined that the print matched Brandon Mayfield's. The fingerprints of Mayfield, a lawyer from Portland, Oregon, who had converted to Islam 20 years earlier, were in the FBI database because he had once been a U.S. Army officer and military fingerprints are included in the FBI computer. Although Spanish authorities cast doubt on the FBI's conclusions, Mayfield was arrested as a material witness and held in jail. The FBI searched his home, examined his telephone records, and analyzed his relationships with other Muslims who they believed had ties to terrorist organizations.

After he spent two weeks in jail, Mayfield was released because Spanish authorities matched the fingerprint to a man from Algeria. The FBI subsequently apologized to Mayfield for the error and paid him $2 million to settle the lawsuit that he filed against the agency.

Sources: MSNBC, "U.S. Lawyer Freed in Madrid Bombing Case," May 20, 2004 (http://www.MSNBC.com); *New York Times*, "Editorial: The F.B.I. Messes Up," May 26, 2004, p. A22; Susan Jo Keller, "Judge Rules Provision in Patriot Act to Be Illegal," *New York Times*, September 27, 2007 (http://www.nytimes.com).

Researching the Internet

 Read the article "Fingerprints: Not a Gold Standard" in *Issues in Science and Technology Online*. To link to this website, go to *The American System of Criminal Justice* 12e companion site at academic.cengage.com/criminaljustice/cole. Should the government rely on a single, partial fingerprint for placing someone in jail? Would the FBI have acted so swiftly against Mayfield if he had belonged to a different religion? How much evidence should the government possess before taking someone into custody?

law enforcement officials to undertake investigatory activities that cannot be readily supervised or monitored by judges and legislators.

In light of their new powers, will law enforcement officials act too swiftly in investigating and even arresting people without an adequate basis for suspicion? Read the Close Up on the arrest of an Oregon lawyer and see whether you think these risks are real.

The Patriot Act received criticism from both liberals and conservatives. Politicians expressed concern that law enforcement officials could too easily search people's homes, obtain their personal records, and intercept their communications without a firm basis for suspicion of wrongdoing. Further, the Patriot Act defined "domestic terrorism" as criminal acts dangerous to human life that appear intended to intimidate civilians or influence public policy by intimidation. Conservatives feared the law could be used against antiabortion protesters who block entrances at abortion clinics, whereas liberals feared that it could be used against environmental activists who take direct actions to prevent the destruction of forests and wildlife. Other critics of the Patriot Act pointed to provisions making it a crime to provide material support for terrorism; they raised concerns that people who donate money to the antiabortion movement or environmental causes could unwittingly find themselves prosecuted for serious terrorism offenses (Lithwick and Turner, 2003).

 The American Library Association's website includes the organization's criticisms of the Patriot Act as well as links to many sources of information about the Act. To link to this website, go to *The American System of Criminal Justice* 12e companion site at academic.cengage.com/criminaljustice/cole.

The Patriot Act faced reexamination in Congress in 2005 because several of its provisions were set to expire. U.S. Attorney General Alberto Gonzales and FBI Director Robert Mueller defended the law in testimony before Congress, calling it essential to the country's security. However, because many of the investigatory and counterintelligence activities of federal agencies remain secret, they would not detail how the government's authority under the Patriot Act had been utilized. Despite criticism and controversy, Congress renewed the Patriot Act with largely the same expanded powers for government in 2006 (Stolberg, 2006).

After the renewal of the Patriot Act, problems emerged. First, federal judges struck down specific provisions of the Act. For example, a federal judge invalidated the provision that authorized the FBI to use informal secret demands, called "national security letters," to compel phone companies and other businesses to provide customer records (Liptak, 2007). Another federal judge struck down the provision that permitted warrantless surveillance and searches of Americans based on the government's claim that "a significant purpose" of such searches is to gather foreign intelligence. The judge concluded that this provision granted too much discretion to the executive branch when government officials should really follow the warrant requirements of the Fourth Amendment (Keller, 2007). In addition, government reports revealed in 2008 that the FBI had improperly used national security letters to make blanket demands for phone records instead of requesting specific phone records (Lichtblau, 2008a). In addition, the FBI improperly obtained other personal information on Americans that was not consistent with the authority granted under the Patriot Act. In response, the FBI instituted a new tracking system for national security letters and increased training and supervision for its agents (Lichtblau, 2008b).

The debates about new laws enacted as part of homeland security and counterterrorism efforts illustrate the struggle to maintain American values of personal liberty, privacy, and individual rights while simultaneously ensuring that law enforcement personnel have sufficient power to protect the nation from catastrophic harm. There are no easy answers for the questions raised about whether the government has too much power and whether Americans' rights have been violated.

Now that we have considered the government's role in homeland security, we turn our attention to the private sector. Corporations and other entities must safeguard their assets, personnel, and facilities. They, too, have heightened concerns about terrorism and other homeland security issues. For example, nuclear power plants, chemical factories, energy companies, and other private facilities make up part of the nation's critical infrastructure. Because terrorists might target such facilities, private-sector officials must address these concerns, just as they have long needed to address other security issues such as employee theft, fires, and trade secrets.

checkpoint

14. What are the criticisms directed at the USA Patriot Act?

SECURITY MANAGEMENT AND PRIVATE POLICING

Only a few years ago, the term *private security* called to mind the image of security guards, people with marginal qualifications for other occupations who ended up accepting minimal wages to stand guard outside factories and businesses. This image reflected a long history of private employment of individuals who served limited police patrol functions. Private policing existed in Europe and the United States before the formation of public police forces. Examples include Fielding's Bow Street Runners in England and the bounty hunters of the American West. In the late nineteenth century, the Pinkerton National Detective Agency provided industrial spies and strikebreakers to thwart labor union activities, and Wells, Fargo and Company was formed to provide security for banks and other businesses.

In recent years, by contrast, private-sector activities related to policing functions have become more complex and important. Today, if one speaks of people employed in "private security," it would be more accurate to envision a variety of occupations ranging from traditional security guards to computer security experts to high-ranking corporate vice presidents responsible for planning and

Contemporary security managers are well-educated professionals with administrative experience and backgrounds in management and law. Here, Hemanshu Nigam, a former federal prosecutor, poses at the offices of Fox Interactive Media where he is the chief security officer. Nigam is responsible for online safety and security at MySpace.com, the popular social networking site. Can you think of any business enterprises or industries that do not need professional security managers in today's ever-changing world of computer technology and international criminal organizations?

overseeing safety and security at a company's industrial plants and office complexes around the world. The aftermath of September 11 has brought a heightened awareness of the importance of security management and private-sector employees in handling police functions.

Retail and industrial firms spend nearly as much for private protection as all localities spend for police protection. Many government entities hire private companies to provide security at specific office buildings or other facilities. In addition, private groups, such as residents of wealthy suburbs, have hired private police to patrol their neighborhoods. Precise figures are difficult to obtain, but about ten years ago an estimated 60,000 private agencies employed more than 1.9 million people in security operations (T. Carlson, 1995: 67). Each year businesses, organizations, and individuals together spend about $100 billion on private security. There are now three times as many officers hired by private-security companies as there are public police (see Figure 7.2).

Private agencies have gained success for several reasons. Private companies recognize the need to be conscientious about protecting their assets, including buildings, financial resources, and personnel. They must be prepared for fires and other emergencies as well as for criminal activity. Next, many threats have spurred an expansion in security management and private policing; these include (1) an increase in crime in the workplace; (2) an increase in fear (real or perceived) of crime; (3) the fiscal crises of the states, which have limited public police protection; and (4) increased public and business awareness and use of more cost-effective private security services (Cunningham, Strauchs, and Van Meter, 1990: 236).

Functions of Security Management and Private Policing

Top-level security managers have a range of responsibilities that require them to fulfill multiple roles that separate individuals would handle in the public sector. For their corporations, they simultaneously function as police chiefs, fire chiefs, emergency management administrators, and computer security experts. They hire, train, and supervise expert personnel to protect corporate computer systems that may contain credit card numbers, trade secrets, confidential corpo-

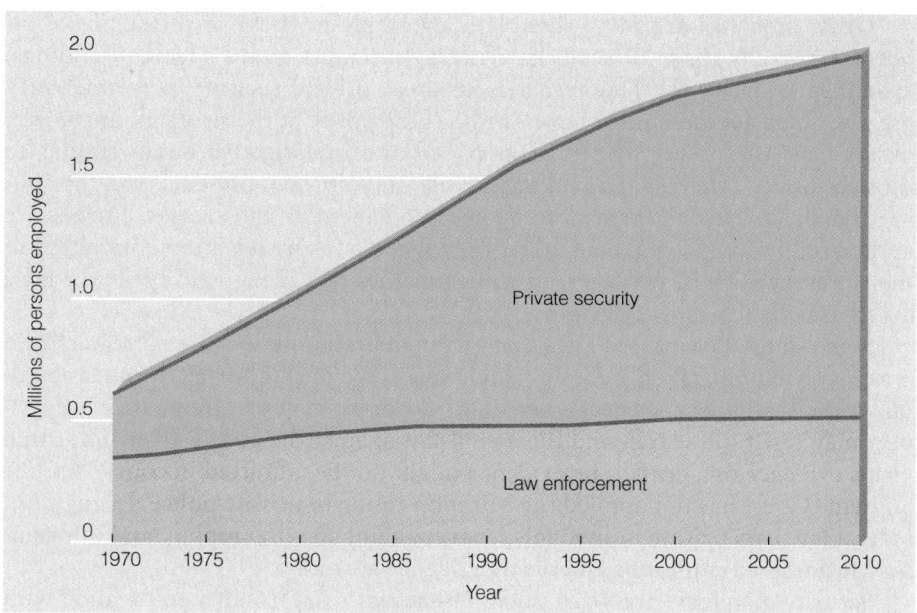

FIGURE 7.2

Employment in private and public protection, 1970–2010 (projected)

The number of people employed by private security firms has surpassed the number employed by the public police and is growing. Such a large private force presents questions for the criminal justice system.

Source: Adapted from William Cunningham, John Strauchs, and Clifford Van Meter, *Private Security: Patterns and Trends* (Washington, DC: National Institute of Justice, U.S. Government Printing Office, 1991), 3. Trend line projection to 2010 by the authors.

rate financial information, and other data sought by hackers intent on causing destruction or stealing money. Frequently they combat cybercriminals who are attacking their computer resources from overseas and are therefore beyond the reach of U.S. law enforcement officials. They also plan security systems and fire and other disaster-response plans for buildings. Such plans include provisions for evacuating large buildings and coordinating their efforts with local police and fire departments in a variety of locales. In addition, they develop security systems to prevent employee theft that may involve sophisticated schemes to use company computer systems to transfer financial assets in improper ways. Because so many American companies own manufacturing plants and office buildings overseas, security companies must often implement their services in diverse countries around the globe.

Security managers are responsible for risk management in their facilities. They need a clear understanding of the assets that must be protected in their corporations, hospitals, and other institutional settings. They must also identify the potential vulnerabilities that they face. Effective risk management depends on identifying specific threats ahead of time and considering how those threats will be minimized or avoided. Some security managers conduct their own risk assessments by inspecting facilities and developing a checklist of assets to be protected, vulnerabilities, and resources for surveillance, asset protection, and emergency response. Other security managers hire outside consultants to undertake such security studies, especially because many professionals believe that an "outsider" may spot vulnerabilities that people who work in a facility every day minimize, take for granted, or ignore (Garvey, 2002).

At lower levels, specific occupations in private security compare more closely to those of police officers. Many security personnel are the equivalent of private-sector detectives. They must investigate "attacks" on company computer systems or activities that threaten company assets. Thus, for example, credit card companies have large security departments that use computers to monitor unusual activity on individual customers' credit cards, which may signal that a thief is using the card. Private-sector detectives must also investigate employee theft. Because this criminal activity extends beyond simple crimes such as stealing money from a store's cash register, investigations might examine whether people are making false reports on expense accounts, using company computers to run private businesses, or misspending company money.

Other activities are more directly comparable to those of police patrol officers, especially those of security officers who must guard specific buildings, apartments, or stores. The activities of these private security personnel vary greatly: Some act merely as guards and call the police at the first sign of trouble, others have the power to carry out patrol and investigative duties similar to those of police officers, and still others rely on their own presence and the ability to make a "citizen's arrest" to deter lawbreakers. In most cases, citizens are authorized by law to make an arrest only when a felony has been committed in their presence. Thus, private security companies risk being held liable for false arrest and violation of civil rights.

Some states have passed laws that give civil immunity to store personnel who reasonably but mistakenly detain people suspected of shoplifting. More ambiguous is the search of a suspect's person or property by a private guard. The suspect may resist the search and file a civil suit against the guard. If such a search yields evidence of a crime, the evidence might not be admitted in court. Yet, the Supreme Court has not applied the *Miranda* ruling to private police. In any case, federal law bars private individuals from engaging in wiretapping, and information so gathered cannot be entered as evidence at trial.

Security managers are often willing to accept responsibility for dealing with minor criminal incidents that occur on their employer's premises. They might perform such tasks as responding to burglar alarms, investigating misdemeanors, and carrying out preliminary investigations of other crimes. Some law enforcement administrators have indicated that they might be willing to transfer some of these tasks to private security firms. They cite several police tasks—such as providing security in public buildings and enforcing parking regulations—that private security might perform more efficiently than the police. In some parts of the country, personnel from private firms already perform some of these tasks.

Private Police and Homeland Security

Private-sector corporations control security for vital facilities in the United States, including nuclear power plants, oil refineries, military manufacturing facilities, and other important sites (Nalla, 2002). Fires, tornadoes, or earthquakes at such sites could release toxic materials into the air and water. Thus, emergency planning is essential for public safety. Moreover, because these sites are now recognized as potential targets of terrorist attacks, the role and effectiveness of security managers matter more than ever to society. They must work closely with law enforcement executives and other government officials to institute procedures that reduce known risks as well as participate in emergency preparedness planning.

Unfortunately, significant problems have emerged in delegating essential homeland security responsibilities to private companies. For example, private security personnel guard the headquarters of the U.S. Department of Homeland Security. Yet security guards assigned to the building claim that they do not have proper training or equipment to handle the job. In 2005, guards at the building opened an envelope containing a mysterious white powder. A well-trained security force would have known to don hazardous materials clothing and carefully seek to dispose of a potentially dangerous chemical or biological hazard. Instead, the private security personnel "carried [the envelope] by the office [of Homeland Security] Secretary Michael Chertoff, took it outside and then shook it outside Chertoff's window without evacuating people nearby" (Margasak, 2006). Because of the improper handling of the situation, if it had been a deadly chemical or biological agent, it might have been inhaled by and consequently killed a number of important officials, including the Secretary of Homeland Security. Fortunately, it turned out to be harmless. Other guards at the same building failed tests conducted by the Secret Service, which sent personnel into the building with fake identification cards. Other guards could not tell what to do when a fire alarm sounded; without radios they could not learn if it was real or a test. And yet another guard said, "I didn't have a clue what to do" when a suspicious bag was reported to be abandoned in the parking lot (Margasak, 2006).

As indicated by the foregoing examples, the federal government has become increasingly dependent on private contractors for a variety of functions, including safety and security (Shane and Nixon, 2007). Private security firms handle a variety of tasks for government, from guarding military bases, nuclear power plants, and government buildings to providing personal security for diplomats traveling in Iraq and other dangerous locations. In guarding buildings and other sites within the United States, the private guards are often paid less than half of what a police officer would be paid. Moreover, they often do not have the same training, equipment, or qualifications as police or military personnel. There have been a number of scandals when private guards are caught sleeping while on duty at nuclear power plants or when companies hire guards with criminal records who then commit crimes. Because of the problems and risks of even greater problems, a number of large private security companies actually lobby the government to seek more rules and regulations for their industry (Margasak, 2007).

Private Employment of Public Police

The officials responsible for asset protection, safety, and security at the top levels of major corporations are often retired police administrators or former military personnel. For example, New York Police Commissioner Raymond Kelly served as Senior Managing Director of Global Corporate Security for a Wall Street financial firm after he left his position as Director of the U.S. Customs Service and before he was appointed to serve as police commissioner. The reliance on people with public-sector experience for important positions in private security management reflects the fact that asset protection and security management have only recently become emphasized as topics in college and university programs. Thus, relatively few professionals have yet gained specific educational credentials in this important area. As a result, the placement of retired law enforcement officials in high-level positions has often created opportunities for strategic communication and coordination between top-level security managers and public-sector police administrators. Both entities have reason to seek cooperation throughout the hierarchy of their respective organizations. Unfortunately, however, they cannot always ensure that individual police officers and lower-level security personnel will sufficiently communicate and coordinate with each other when incidents arise.

At operational levels of security management, private security and local police often make frequent contact. Private firms are usually eager to hire public police officers on a part-time basis. About 20 percent of departments forbid their officers from "moonlighting" for private employers. By contrast, some departments simultaneously facilitate and control the hiring of their officers by creating specific rules and procedures for off-duty employment. For example, the New York City police department coordinates a program called the Paid Detail Unit. Event planners, corporations, and organizations can hire uniformed, off-duty officers for $30 per hour. The police department must approve all events at which the officers will work, and the department imposes an additional 10 percent administrative fee for the hiring of its officers. Thus the department can safeguard against officers working for organizations and events that will cause legal, public relations, or other problems for the police department. The department

The New York City police have a website focused on their efforts to partner with private security managers in order to enhance the city's counterterrorism efforts. To link to this website, go to *The American System of Criminal Justice* 12e companion site at academic.cengage.com/criminaljustice/cole.

can also monitor and control how many hours its officers work so that private, part-time employment does not lead them to be exhausted and ineffective during their regular shifts.

These officers retain their full powers and status as police personnel even when they work for a private firm while off duty. New York and other cities have specific regulations requiring an on-duty officer to be called when a situation arises in which an arrest will be made. While the use of off-duty officers expands the number and visibility of law enforcement officers, it also raises questions, two of which are discussed here.

Conflict of Interest

Police officers must avoid any appearance of conflict of interest when they accept private employment. They are barred from jobs that conflict with their public duties. For example, they may not work as process servers, bill collectors, repossessors, or preemployment investigators for private firms. They also may not work as investigators for criminal defense attorneys or as bail bondsmen. They may not work in places that profit from gambling, and many departments do not allow officers to work in bars or other places where regulated goods, such as alcohol, are sold. No department can know the full range of situations in which private employment of an officer might harm the image of the police or create a conflict with police responsibilities. Thus, departments need to keep tabs on new situations that might require them to refine their regulations for private employment of off-duty officers.

Management Prerogatives

Another issue concerns the impact of private employment on the capabilities of the local police department. Private employment cannot be allowed to tire officers and impair their ability to protect the public when they are on duty. Late-night duties as a private security officer, for example, can reduce an officer's ability to police effectively the next morning.

Departments require that officers request permission for outside work. Such permission can be denied for several reasons. Work that lowers the dignity of the police, is too risky or dangerous, is not in the home jurisdiction, requires more than eight hours of off-duty service, or interferes with department schedules is usually denied.

Several models have been designed to manage off-duty employment of officers. The *department contract model* permits close control of off-duty work, because firms must apply to the department to have officers assigned to them. New York City's system fits this model. Officers chosen for off-duty work are paid by the police department, which is reimbursed by the private firm, along with an overhead fee. Departments usually screen employers to make sure that the proposed use of officers will not conflict with the department's needs. When the private demand for police services exceeds the supply, the department contract model provides a way of assigning staff so as to ensure that public needs are met.

The *officer contract model* allows each officer to find off-duty employment and to enter into a direct relationship with the private firm. Officers must apply to the department for permission, which is granted if the employment standards listed earlier are met. Problems can arise when an officer acts as an employment "agent" for other officers. This can lead to charges of favoritism and nepotism, with serious effects on discipline and morale.

In the *union brokerage model*, the police union or association finds off-duty employment for its members. The union sets the standards for the work and bargains with the department over the pay, status, and conditions of the off-duty employment.

Each of these models has its backers. Albert Reiss notes another complication: The more closely a department controls off-duty employment, the more liability it assumes for officers' actions when they work for private firms (Reiss, 1988).

What remains unknown is how uniformed off-duty patrol affects crime prevention and the public's perception of safety. Public fears may decrease because of the greater visibility of officers whom citizens believe to be acting in their official capacity.

The Public–Private Interface

The relationship between public and private law enforcement is a concern for police officials. Because private agents work for the people who employ them, their goals might not always serve the public interest. Questions have arisen about the power of private security agents to make arrests, conduct searches, and take part in undercover investigations. A key issue is the boundary between the work of the police and that of private agencies. Lack of coordination and communication between public and private agencies has led to botched investigations, destruction of evidence, and overzealousness.

Growing awareness of this problem has led to efforts to have private security agents work more closely with the police. Current efforts to enhance coordination involve emergency planning, building security, and general crime prevention. In other areas, private security managers still tend to act on their own without consulting the police.

One such area is criminal activity within a company. Many security managers in private firms tend to treat crimes by employees as internal matters that do not concern the police. They report UCR index crimes to the police, but employee theft, insurance fraud, industrial espionage, commercial bribery, and computer crime tend not to be reported to public authorities. In such cases the chief concern of private firms is to prevent losses and protect assets. Most of these incidents are resolved through internal procedures (private justice). When such crimes are discovered, the offender may be convicted and punished within the firm by forced restitution, loss of the job, and the spreading of information about the incident throughout the industry. Private firms often bypass the criminal justice system so they do not have to deal with prosecution policies, administrative delays, rules that would open the firms' internal affairs to public scrutiny, and bad publicity. Thus, the question arises: To what extent does a parallel system of private justice exist with regard to some offenders and some crimes (M. Davis, Lundman, and Martinez, 1991)?

Recruitment and Training

Higher-level security managers are increasingly drawn from college graduates with degrees in criminal justice who have taken additional coursework in such subjects as business management and computer science to supplement their knowledge of policing and law. These graduates are attracted to the growing private-sector employment market for security-related occupations, because the jobs often involve varied, complex tasks in a white-collar work environment. In addition, they often gain corporate benefits such as quick promotion, stock options, and other perks unavailable in public-sector policing.

By contrast, the recruitment and training of lower-level private security personnel present a major concern to law enforcement officials and civil libertarians. These personnel handle the important responsibility of guarding factories, stores, apartments, and other buildings. Often on the scene when criminal activity occurs, they are the private security personnel most likely to interact with

Today's security personnel must be aware of numerous potential threats and have the necessary training and equipment to communicate with law enforcement officials. If security guards are merely hourly minimum-wage employees, are they likely to have the qualifications and commitment to provide adequate security at important private enterprises such as chemical factories and nuclear power plants?

© Jeff Greenberg/PhotoEdit

the public in emergency situations. Moreover, any failure to perform their duties could lead to a significant and damaging event, such as a robbery or a fire. In spite of these important responsibilities, which parallel those of police patrol officers, studies have shown that such personnel often have little education and training. Because the pay is low, the work often attracts people who cannot find other jobs or who seek temporary work. This portrait has been challenged by William Walsh (1989), who argues that differences between private and public police are not that striking. However, private security firms in San Francisco reported annual staff turnover rates as high as 300 percent because their low pay and benefits led employees continually to seek higher-paying jobs, especially when better-paid public-sector security work opened up, such as jobs as airport screeners (Lynem, 2002). City police departments and other public law enforcement agencies do not experience these kinds of staffing problems, because they have better pay and benefits.

The growth of private policing has brought calls for the screening and licensing of its personnel. Fewer than half of the states require background checks or examine private security applicants' criminal records from states other than the one in which they currently reside. Twenty-two states have no certification or licensing requirements, and only 17 states have regulatory boards to oversee the private security industry. More than half of the states have no training requirements whatsoever for people who will assume important responsibilities in guarding buildings and other private security tasks (PR Newswire, 2002). Several national organizations, such as the National Council on Crime and Delinquency, have offered model licensing statutes that specify periods of training and orientation, uniforms that permit citizens to distinguish between public and private police, and a ban on employment of people with criminal records.

The regulations that do exist tend to focus on contractual, as opposed to proprietary, private policing. Contractual security services are provided for a fee by locksmiths, alarm specialists, polygraph examiners, and firms such as Brink's, Burns, and Wackenhut, which provide guards and detectives. States and cities often require contract personnel to be licensed and bonded. Similar services are sometimes provided by proprietary security personnel, who are employed directly by the organization they protect, for example, retail stores, industrial plants, and hospitals. Except for those who carry weapons, proprietary security personnel are not regulated by the state or city. Certainly, the importance of private security and its relation to public policing demands further exploration of these and related issues in the years to come.

checkpoint

15. What has caused the growth of security management and private policing?
16. What are the three models for private employment of police officers?

A QUESTION OF ETHICS

BIANCO'S RESTAURANT IS a popular, noisy place in a tough section of town. Open from 6:30 A.M. until midnight, it is usually crowded with regulars who like the low prices and ample portions, teenagers planning their next exploit, and people grabbing a quick bite to eat.

Officer Buchanan has just finished his late-night "lunch" before going back on duty. As he walks toward the cash register, Cheryl Bianco, the manager, takes the bill from his hand and says, "This one's on me, John. It's nice to have you with us."

Officer Buchanan protests, "Thanks, but I'd better pay for my own meal."

"Why do you say that? The other cops don't object to getting a free meal now and then."

"Well, they may feel that way, but I don't want anyone to get the idea that I'm giving you special treatment," Buchanan replies.

"Come off it. Who's going to think that? I don't expect special treatment; we just want you to know we appreciate your work."

Critical Thinking and Analysis

What issues are involved here? If Buchanan refuses to accept Bianco's generosity, what is he saying about his role as a police officer? If he accepts the offer, what does that say? Might people who overhear the conversation draw other meanings from it? Is turning down a free $6.50 meal that important? Write a memo as if you were an officer to whom Buchanan came for advice. What advice would you give?

SUMMARY

Recognize the ways police can abuse their power and the challenges of controlling this abuse

- Police corruption and misuse of force erode community support.

- Police use of deadly force occurs infrequently and can no longer be applied to unarmed fleeing felons.

- Police corruption includes "meat eaters" who actively seek corrupt activities and "grass eaters" who accept favors and payoffs that come their way.

Identify the methods that can be used to make police more accountable to citizens

- Internal affairs units, civilian review boards, standards and accreditation, and civil liability lawsuits increase police accountability to citizens.

Understand the new technologies that assist police investigations and how these technologies affect citizens' rights

- The development of new technologies has assisted police investigations through the use of computers, databases, surveillance devices, DNA testing and other identity tests, and methods to detect deception.

- Questions arise concerning the reliability of technology, the adequacy of resources for using technology, and the ethics and competence of personnel using new technology.

- Police departments are seeking to identify less-lethal weapons that can incapacitate suspects and control unruly crowds without causing serious injuries and deaths.

Identify the issues and problems that emerge from law enforcement agencies' increased attention to homeland security

- Homeland security has become an important priority for law enforcement agencies at all levels of government since September 11, 2001.

- Agencies need planning and coordination in order to gather intelligence and prepare for possible threats and public emergencies.

- The federal government provides funding for state and local fusion centers and emergency preparedness equipment.

- New laws, such as the USA Patriot Act, have caused controversy about the proper balance between government authority and citizens' rights.

Understand the policing and related activities undertaken by private-sector security management

- The expansion of security management and private policing reflects greater recognition of the need to protect private assets and to plan for emergencies.

- Security management produces new issues and problems including concerns about the recruitment, training, and activities of lower-level private security personnel.

- Public-private interaction affects security through such means as joint planning for emergencies, hiring private firms to guard government facilities, and hiring police officers for off-duty private security work.

QUESTIONS FOR REVIEW

1. What are the major forms of police abuse of power?

2. What has the Supreme Court ruled regarding police use of deadly force?

3. What are the pros and cons of the major approaches to making the police accountable to citizens?

4. What controversies exist concerning new technologies employed by the police?

5. What have law enforcement agencies done to enhance homeland security?

6. What problems are associated with private policing?

KEY TERMS AND CASES

internal affairs unit (p. 253)
latent fingerprints (p. 260)
law enforcement
 intelligence (p. 269)
less-lethal weapons (p. 265)
USA Patriot Act (p. 273)

*Kyllo v. United
 States* (2001) (p. 265)
Tennessee v. Garner
 (1985) (p. 248)

FOR FURTHER READING

Leone, Richard C., and Greg Anrig, Jr., eds. 2003. *The War on Our Freedoms: Civil Liberties in an Age of Terrorism.* New York: Public Affairs Press. A series of articles by leading scholars that raise questions about the impact of the USA Patriot Act and other government responses to the threat of terrorism.

Murano, Vincent. 1990. *Cop Hunter.* New York: Simon & Schuster. The story of an undercover cop who for ten years worked for the Internal Affairs Division of the New York City Police Department. Emphasizes the moral dilemmas of policing other officers.

Reiss, Albert J., Jr. 1971. *The Police and the Public.* New Haven, CT: Yale University Press. A classic study of the relationship of police officers to the public they serve.

Shearing, Clifford, and Philip C. Stenning, eds. 1987. *Private Policing.* Newbury Park, CA: Sage. An excellent volume that explores various aspects of the private security industry.

Skolnick, Jerome H., and James J. Fyfe. 1993. *Above the Law: Police and the Excessive Use of Force.* New York: Free Press. Written in light of the Rodney King beating and the riots that followed. The authors believe that only by recruiting and supporting police chiefs who will uphold a policy of strict accountability can brutality be eliminated.

GOING ONLINE

For an up-to-date list of web links, go to *The American System of Criminal Justice* 12e companion site at academic .cengage.com/criminaljustice/cole.

1. Read online reports by American Civil Liberties Union about police abuse cases in major American cities. After reading examples from several cities, think about the best approach to handling these problems. Is a particular approach likely to be most effective? Why?

2. Look at the website of the International Security Management Association. Read the press releases. What issues are of greatest concern to top-level security managers?

3. Read the Electronic Privacy Information Center's online report on *facial-recognition technology*. Do you have concerns about how the technology might be used?

CHECKPOINT ANSWERS

1. *What kinds of practices may be viewed as police abuse?*

 Profanity, abusive language, physical force, and violence.

2. *When may the police use force?*

 The police may use force if necessary to make an arrest, to keep the peace, or to maintain public order.

3. *How did the Supreme Court rule in* Tennessee v. Garner?

 Deadly force may not be used in apprehending a fleeing felon unless it is necessary to prevent the escape and unless the officer has probable cause to believe that the suspect poses a significant threat of death or serious physical injury to the officer or others.

4. *What is the difference between grass eaters and meat eaters?*

 Grass eaters are officers who accept payoffs that police work brings their way. Meat eaters are officers who aggressively misuse their power for personal gain.

5. *What are five of the ten practices cited by Stoddard as blue-coat crime ?*

 Mooching, bribery, chiseling, extortion, shopping, shakedown, premeditated theft, favoritism, perjury, and prejudice.

6. *What are the four methods used to increase the civic accountability of the police?*

Internal affairs units, civilian review boards, standards and accreditation, and civil liability suits.

7. *What is an internal affairs unit?*

A unit within the police department designated to receive and investigate complaints alleging violation of rules and policies on the part of officers.

8. *Why are civilian review boards relatively uncommon?*

Opposition by the police.

9. *What is the importance of the decision in* Monell v. Department of Social Services of the City of New York?

Allows citizens to sue individual officers and the agency when an individual's civil rights are violated by the agency's customs and usages.

10. *What kinds of new technologies are assisting police with their investigative functions?*

Laptop computers in patrol cars connect to various databases, Geographic Information Systems, and DNA testing.

11. *What problems are associated with the use of new technology?*

Questions about the accuracy and reliability of the technology, inadequate resources to utilize technology fully, and ethics and competence of personnel.

12. *What kinds of new weaponry have police employed?*

Less-lethal weapons, including beanbag projectiles, Tasers, and pepperball projectiles.

13. *What have law enforcement officials done to enhance the protection of homeland security?*

Planning and coordinating with other agencies, new equipment and training, and Incident Command System.

14. *What are the criticisms directed at the USA Patriot Act?*

Permits too much government authority for searches and wiretaps, defines domestic terrorism in ways that might include legitimate protest groups.

15. *What has caused the growth of security management and private policing?*

Companies' recognition of the need to protect assets and plan for emergencies, problems with employee theft, computer crime, and other issues that require active prevention and investigation.

16. *What are the three models for private employment of police officers?*

Department contract model, officer contract model, and union brokerage model.

CHAPTER 8

Police and Constitutional Law

CHAPTER LEARNING OBJECTIVES

→ Know the extent of police officers' authority to stop and search people and their vehicles

→ Understand when and how police officers seek warrants in order to conduct searches and make arrests

→ Know whether police officers can look in people's windows or their backyards to see if evidence of a crime exists there

→ Analyze the situations in which police officers can conduct searches without obtaining a warrant

→ Understand the purpose of the privilege against compelled self-incrimination

→ Understand the exclusionary rule and the situations in which it applies

A Baltimore County police officer stopped a car for speeding. Within the car were three men: Donte Partlow, the driver; Joseph Pringle, the front-seat passenger; and Otis Smith, the rear passenger. When Partlow opened the glove compartment to retrieve the vehicle registration, the officer noticed a large amount of money in the glove compartment. The officer asked Partlow if he could search the vehicle. Partlow consented and the officer found five baggies of cocaine jammed between the backseat armrest and the backseat. None of the men would admit to owning the cocaine or provide any information about its ownership. The officer warned them that they all would be arrested if someone did not admit to owning the cocaine. No one spoke, so he arrested all three men.

Is it fair to arrest everyone? What if one passenger had been offered a ride by his friend's cousin, someone he had just met, and he had no knowledge of anyone else's involvement with drugs? Could such a situation ever happen to you? Have you ever ridden in a car with someone who is merely a casual acquaintance? Do you have any legal rights that could protect you from being arrested under such circumstances?

As you recall from Chapter 4, the Fourth Amendment provides protection against

"unreasonable searches and seizures." In the cocaine case, the Fourth Amendment is relevant because all three men in the car were "seized" and therefore a court could examine whether their seizure was "unreasonable." Fundamentally, the case is about whether police officers possess the authority to arrest everyone in a vehicle if they find guns or weapons there. Does the discovery of illegal items in a car make arresting everyone in the vehicle "reasonable"?

After the arrests, Pringle, the front-seat passenger, made incriminating statements that led prosecutors to convict him for possession of cocaine and he was sentenced to a 10-year prison term. Pringle appealed his conviction by claiming that his Fourth Amendment rights were violated when the officer arrested him for the presence of drugs that were located next to Smith in the rear seat and that were traditionally considered the responsibility of Partlow, the driver who is presumed to be in control of the vehicle and its contents. The Maryland Court of Appeals agreed with Pringle. The state court ruled that the officer did not have a sufficient basis for believing that Pringle knew about or had control over the cocaine in the rear seat. Therefore, the arrest of Pringle, as well as his subsequent questioning by the police, occurred as the result of an "unreasonable seizure" in violation of the Fourth Amendment. Because Maryland prosecutors disagreed with their state court of appeals, they asked the U.S. Supreme Court to review the case.

The case of Joseph Pringle demonstrates the potential power of law as a limitation on police officers' efforts to investigate and combat criminal behavior. As we shall see in this chapter, when police officers violate the law by improperly obtaining evidence, they risk being denied permission to use that evidence. As a result, guilty people could be set free and society's efforts to control crime thwarted. The decision of the Maryland Court of Appeals demonstrates that we sometimes place a higher priority on protecting individuals' rights than on pursuing criminal prosecutions.

As you think about the Pringle case, remember that the words of the Fourth Amendment do not provide an answer to the question of whether the arrest was "unreasonable." Indeed, the eighteenth-century men who wrote "unreasonable searches and seizures" could not anticipate that drugs would be a significant social problem or that motor vehicles could be used to transport and hide drugs. Thus, today's judges must make their own decisions about how each situation falls within the intended purposes of the Fourth Amendment.

In December 2003, the U.S. Supreme Court provided its answer to the question raised in the case of *Maryland v. Pringle*. The justices of the U.S. Supreme Court unanimously overturned the decision of the Maryland Court of Appeals. The justices ruled that the discovery of illegal items in a vehicle can justify the arrest of everyone riding in the vehicle. Are you surprised by the U.S. Supreme Court's decision? Do you agree with it? Do you think this decision could ever apply to you? As we examine other Supreme Court decisions, think about the challenge presented by the necessity of applying brief phrases from the Bill of Rights to actual situations, thereby determining which people can be searched and questioned and, more importantly, whether certain individuals will spend many years in prison.

In this chapter we examine individual rights and how those legal protections define the limits of police officers' powers of investigation and arrest. In particular, we look closely at two rights that were introduced in Chapter 4: the Fourth Amendment protection against unreasonable searches and seizures and the Fifth Amendment privilege against compelled self-incrimination (see Appendix A for the complete text).

LEGAL LIMITATIONS ON POLICE INVESTIGATIONS

In our democracy, the rights of individuals contained in the Bill of Rights embody important American values (see Chapter 4). They reflect the historic belief that we do not want to give government officials absolute power to pursue criminal investigations and prosecutions, because that approach to crime control would impose excessive costs on the values of individual liberty, privacy, and due process. If police could do whatever they wanted to do, then people would lack protections against arbitrary searches and arrests. On the other hand, crime control is an important policy goal. We do not want individuals' expectations about legal protections to block the ability of law enforcement officers to protect citizens from crime and punish wrongdoers. Judges must therefore interpret the Constitution in ways that seek to achieve a proper balance between crime control and the protection of individual rights.

Many police actions fall under the Fourth Amendment because they involve searches, seizures, and warrants. If officers exceed their authority by conducting an improper search of a person or a home, judges may release the arrestees or forbid certain evidence from being used. Officers might also be disciplined by their superiors or even sued by people whose rights were violated if investigatory activities violate the rules of law. Clearly, police officers need to know the legal rules that apply to their investigative activities, such as searches, arrests, and the questioning of suspects.

How can an officer know when his or her actions might violate the Fourth Amendment? The officer must depend on information and training provided at the police academy and subsequent updates from city and state attorneys who monitor court decisions. Individual police officers do not have time to follow the details of the latest court decisions. That responsibility rests with those who train and supervise law enforcement officers. Thus, police officers' compliance with the law depends on their own knowledge and decisions as well as the supervision and training provided by their departments.

Search and Seizure

The Fourth Amendment prohibits police officers from undertaking "unreasonable searches and seizures." The Supreme Court defines **searches** as actions by law enforcement officials that intrude on people's **reasonable expectations of privacy**. For example, someone who places a personal diary in a locked drawer within a bedroom of his or her home has demonstrated a reasonable expectation. Police officers cannot simply decide to enter the home and bedroom in order to open the locked door and read the diary.

Many situations raise questions about people's reasonable expectations. For example, should people reasonably expect a police officer to reach into their pockets in order to see if they have guns? Should people reasonably expect a police officer not to walk up to their houses and peer into the windows? Although judges do not always answer these questions in clear, consistent ways, people's reasonable expectations about their privacy are important elements in judges' determinations about legal guidelines for police investigations.

In defining **seizure**, the Supreme Court focuses on the nature and extent of officers' interference with people's liberty and freedom of movement. If an officer who is leaning against the wall of a building says to a passing pedestrian, "Where are you going?" and the person replies, "To the sandwich shop down the street" as she continues to walk without interference by the officer, there is virtually no intrusion on her liberty and freedom of movement. Thus, officers are free to speak to people on the street. If people voluntarily stop in order to speak with the officer, they have not been "seized," because they are free

search
Officials' examination of and hunt for evidence in or on a person or place in a manner that intrudes on reasonable expectations of privacy.

reasonable expectation of privacy
Standard developed for determining whether a government intrusion of a person or property constitutes a search because it interferes with individual interests that are normally protected from government intrusion.

seizure
Any use by the police of authority to deprive people of their liberty or property.

to move along whenever they choose. However, if people are not free to leave when officers assert their authority to halt someone's movement, then a seizure has occurred, and the Fourth Amendment requires that the seizure be reasonable. One form of seizure is an arrest, which involves taking a suspect into custody. In 2005, the Supreme Court endorsed another form of seizure: holding an individual in handcuffs for three hours while officers conduct a search of a home (*Muehler v. Mena*). The detention was reasonable because the individual was present on property where officers searched for weapons and drugs. Property can also be subject to seizure, especially if it is evidence in a criminal case.

When a seizure is very brief, it is called a **stop**, defined as a brief interference with a person's freedom of movement with a duration that can be measured in minutes. When police require a driver to pull over in order to receive a traffic citation, that is a stop. To be permissible under the Fourth Amendment, stops must be justified by **reasonable suspicion**—a situation in which specific aspects of the person's appearance, behavior, and circumstances lead the officer to conclude that the person should be stopped in order to investigate the occurrence of a crime. Officers cannot make stops based solely on hunches.

As we shall see, courts permit police officers to make stops without reasonable suspicion in many kinds of situations. For example, these stops can occur in locations where preventing illegal activities is especially important, such as border-crossing points where smuggling and drug trafficking often occur. Thus, everyone can be stopped in these special situations even if there is no specific basis to suspect them of wrongdoing.

stop
Government officials' interference with an individual's freedom of movement for a duration that can be measured in minutes.

reasonable suspicion
A police officer's belief, based on articulable facts, that criminal activity is taking place, so that intruding on an individual's reasonable expectation of privacy is necessary.

The University of Wisconsin's police department has placed online its pamphlet explaining police stops and providing advice on what to do if you are stopped by an officer. To link to this website, go to *The American System of Criminal Justice* 12e companion site at academic.cengage.com/criminaljustice/cole.

checkpoint

1. What is a search?
2. What justification do police officers need to make a stop?
   (Answers are at the end of the chapter.)

Arrest

An *arrest* is a significant deprivation of liberty, because a person is taken into police custody, transported to the police station or jail, and processed into the criminal justice system. A seizure need not be lengthy to be an arrest. Indeed,

Arrest is the physical taking of a person into custody. What legal requirements must be met to make this a valid arrest? What, if anything, prevents officers from making improper arrests?

© Bill Pugliano/Getty Images

some "stops" may be longer than "arrests" if, for example, a person taken to the police station is released on bail within an hour but a person stopped along a roadside must wait a longer period for the officer to write out a slew of traffic citations. Typically, however, arrests last much longer than stops.

Because arrests involve a more significant intrusion on liberty, they necessitate a higher level of justification. Unlike stops, which require only reasonable suspicion, all arrests must be supported by probable cause. **Probable cause** requires that sufficient evidence exist to support the reasonable conclusion that a person has committed a crime. In order to obtain an arrest warrant, police officers must provide a judicial officer with sufficient evidence to support a finding of probable cause. Alternatively, police officers' on-the-street determinations of probable cause can produce discretionary warrantless arrests. A judge subsequently examines such arrests for the existence of probable cause, in a hearing that must occur shortly after the arrest, typically within 48 hours. If the judge determines that the police officer was wrong in concluding that probable cause existed to justify the arrest, then the suspect is released from custody.

Officers may make arrests when they see people commit criminal acts or when witnesses provide them with sufficient information so that they believe probable cause exists to arrest an individual. Arrest authority is not limited to felonies and misdemeanors, however. The Supreme Court has expanded the discretionary authority of police officers to make arrests. In 2001, the justices decided that police officers can make a warrantless arrest for a fine-only traffic offense, such as a failure to wear a seat belt, which would draw only a fine upon conviction (*Atwater v. City of Lago Vista*, 2001).

Warrants and Probable Cause

Imagine that you are a judge. Two police officers come to your chambers to ask you to authorize a search warrant. They swear that they observed frequent foot traffic of suspicious people going in and out of a house. Moreover, they swear that a reliable informant told them that he was inside the house two days earlier and saw crack cocaine being sold. Does this information rise to the level of "probable cause," justifying issuance of a search warrant? Can you grant a warrant based purely on the word of police officers, or do you need other concrete evidence?

Search Warrant Requirements

The Fourth Amendment requires that "no Warrants shall issue, but upon probable cause, supported by Oath or affirmation, and particularly describing the place to be searched, and the persons or things to be seized." These particular elements of the Amendment must be fulfilled in order to issue a warrant. If they are not fulfilled, then a defendant can later challenge the validity of the warrant. The important elements are, first, the existence of probable cause. Second, the evidence that police officers present to the judicial officer must be supported by "oath or affirmation," which typically means that police officers say "yes" when the judicial officer asks them if they swear or affirm that all the information presented is true to the best of their knowledge. Officers can also fulfill this requirement by presenting an **affidavit**, which is a written statement confirmed by oath or affirmation. Third, the warrant must describe the specific place to be searched; a "general warrant" to search many locations cannot be issued. Fourth, the warrant must describe the person or items to be seized. Thus, if the warrant authorizes a search for a person suspected of robbery, the officers should not open small dresser drawers or other places where they know a person could not be hiding.

The U.S. Supreme Court has attempted to guide judicial officers in identifying the existence of probable cause. Mere suspicion cannot constitute probable

probable cause
Reliable information indicating that evidence will likely be found in a specific location or that a specific person is likely to be guilty of a crime.

affidavit
Written statement of fact, supported by oath or affirmation, submitted to judicial officers to fulfill the requirements of probable cause for obtaining a warrant.

civic engagement
your role in the system

Imagine that your credit card is stolen and someone uses it to purchase child pornography on the Internet. Police officers identify the credit card, search your house, and seize your computer. When they conclude that you are innocent and return the computer, you discover that the computer is now broken. *Make a list of the actions that you could take to seek to have the police repair or replace the broken computer.* Then read the facts of the Hallock's family lawsuit in a similar case that ultimately went all the way to the U.S. Supreme Court. To link to these websites, go to *The American System of Criminal Justice* 12e companion site at academic.cengage.com/criminaljustice/cole.

The *Seattle Times* newspaper provides a legal guide for other newspapers that includes information on how to deal with police officers who arrive with a warrant. To link to this website, go to *The American System of Criminal Justice* 12e companion site at academic.cengage.com/criminaljustice/cole.

totality of circumstances test
Flexible test established by the Supreme Court for identifying whether probable cause exists to justify the issuance of a warrant.

cause, yet the level of evidence to establish it need not fulfill the high level of proof needed to justify a criminal conviction. In essence, probable cause is a level of evidence sufficient to provide a reasonable conclusion that the proposed objects of a search will be found in a location that law enforcement officers request to search. For an arrest warrant, the essential issue is whether sufficient evidence is presented to lead reasonably to the conclusion that a specific person should be prosecuted for an arrestable criminal offense. There is no hard-and-fast definition of *probable cause* that judicial officers can apply to every situation; rather, it serves as a flexible concept that judicial officers can apply in different ways.

During the 1960s the Supreme Court established a two-part test for probable cause in the cases of *Aguilar v. Texas* (1964) and *Spinelli v. United States* (1969). Under the so-called *Aguilar-Spinelli* test, the evidence presented to justify a warrant must (1) provide the basis for the law enforcement officer's knowledge about the alleged criminal activity and (2) provide substantiation for the truthfulness and reliability of the information's source. In other words, law enforcement officers could not simply say that they heard certain information about the existence of criminal activity or seizable objects at a certain location; they were required to provide enough information to convince the judicial officer about the circumstances in which the source gained the information. The police also had to provide information to convince the judicial officer of the truthfulness and reliability of the information's source. In *Illinois v. Gates* (1983), however, the Supreme Court turned away from the two-part test in order to embrace the more flexible **totality of circumstances test**. Thus, rather than requiring that each of the two components be fulfilled, judicial officers can now make a more generalized determination about whether the evidence is both sufficient and reliable enough to justify a warrant.

What happens if police officers damage someone's property while carrying out a search? Not all searches lead to criminal charges. Sometimes innocent citizens are subject to searches if witnesses are mistaken about the identity of someone conducting criminal activity or mistaken about which house is the location of criminal activity. As you read "Civic Engagement: Your Role in the System," consider what someone can do if they suffer losses as the result of a search.

checkpoint

3. What is the difference between an arrest and a stop?
4. What do police officers need to demonstrate in order to obtain a warrant?

PLAIN VIEW DOCTRINE

plain view doctrine
Officers may examine and use as evidence, without a warrant, contraband or evidence that is in open view at a location where they are legally permitted to be.

Although the warrant requirement is a central feature of the Fourth Amendment, the Supreme Court has identified situations in which warrants are not required. What if a police officer is walking down the street and sees a marijuana plant growing in the front window of a home? Has the officer conducted a search by looking into the window? If so, is the search legal even though it took place by chance but was not supported by reasonable suspicion or probable cause? In *Coolidge v. New Hampshire* (1971), the Court discussed the **plain view doctrine**, which permits officers to notice and use as evidence items that are visible to them when the officers are where they are permitted to be. Officers may not break into a home and then claim that the drugs found inside were in plain view on a table. However, if a homeowner invited officers into his home in order to file a report about a burglary, the officers do not need to obtain a warrant in order to seize drugs that they see lying on the kitchen table. Because the drugs were in plain view and the officers had a legal basis for their presence in the house, the owner lost any reasonable expectation of privacy that would otherwise require officers to demonstrate probable cause for a search.

Open Fields Doctrine

Related to the plain view doctrine is the **open fields doctrine**. Under this doctrine, first announced by the Supreme Court in *Hester v. United States* (1924), property owners have no reasonable expectation of privacy in open fields on and around their property. Thus, if criminal evidence is visible, then probable cause has been established for its seizure. The Court has approved cases in which police officers, acting without a warrant, walked past "no trespassing" signs and found marijuana plants in fields on private property (*Oliver v. United States*, 1984). The Court limited this doctrine by refusing to apply it to the *curtilage*, or the yard area immediately surrounding the home. Although protected against physical intrusion by officers, that area remains subject to the plain view doctrine if evidence of criminal activity is clearly visible from the vantage point of a location where officers can lawfully stand. For example, the plain view doctrine includes any areas visible from the air when police officers hover above property in a helicopter.

Plain Feel and Other Senses

If law enforcement officers may conduct a warrantless search under the plain view doctrine, what about using other senses to detect criminal evidence? If officers smell the distinctive odor of an illegal substance, such as marijuana, they are justified in investigating further. Bear in mind that the sense of smell may be employed by a trained police dog, too. Court decisions have established that police dogs who sniff luggage in public places are not conducting searches and therefore are not subject to the requirements of the Fourth Amendment.

Does an officer's sense of "feel" apply to searches of property? As we shall see in the discussion of stop-and-frisk searches, a police officer with reasonable suspicion may conduct a pat-down search of a person's outer clothing. If the officer feels something that is immediately recognizable as a weapon, crack pipe, or other contraband, the item may be seized (*Minnesota v. Dickerson*, 1993). However, police officers cannot aggressively feel and manipulate people's property, such as a duffel bag, in an attempt to detect criminal evidence, unless the luggage examination is part of a standard search in boarding a commercial airliner or crossing an international border into the United States (*Bond v. United States*, 2000).

Table 8.1 reviews selected cases concerning the Fourth Amendment's protection for reasonable expectations of privacy involving searches by sight and feel.

 Residence hall contracts at the University of Massachusetts contain an explanation of the plain view doctrine and officials' responsibility to take notice of contraband that is out in the open. To link to this website, go to *The American System of Criminal Justice* 12e companion site at academic.cengage.com/criminaljustice/cole.

open fields doctrine
Officers are permitted to search and to seize evidence, without a warrant, on private property beyond the area immediately surrounding the house.

checkpoint

5. What is the plain view doctrine?
6. May officers use senses other than sight to find evidence of crime without a warrant?

TABLE 8.1	Searches by Sight and Feel
The Fourth Amendment's protection for reasonable expectations of privacy does not cover criminal evidence that can be seen or felt by officers in specific situations.	
Case	**Decision**
Plain View	
Coolidge v. New Hampshire (1971)	Officers are permitted to notice and use as evidence items in plain view when the officers are where they are legally permitted to be.
Open Fields	
Oliver v. U.S. (1984)	Officers are permitted to intrude on private lands that are open areas, such as fields and pastures, but they may not search the yard area immediately surrounding a house (*curtilage*) without a warrant or a specific justification for a warrantless search.
Plain Feel	
Minnesota v. Dickerson (1993)	While conducting a pat-down search of a suspect's outer clothing, police may seize items in pockets or clothing as evidence if they are immediately identifiable by touch as weapons or contraband.

WARRANTLESS SEARCHES

The U.S. Supreme Court has identified specific categories of searches that do not require warrants. The Court has decided that society's law enforcement needs are so significant in these situations that police officers must have the authority to undertake searches without taking the time to seek a warrant. In the rest of this section, we examine six of these categories: (1) special needs beyond the normal purposes of law enforcement, (2) stop and frisk on the streets, (3) search incident to a lawful arrest, (4) exigent circumstances, (5) consent, and (6) automobile searches.

Special Needs beyond the Normal Purposes of Law Enforcement

Law enforcement officials have a justified need to conduct warrantless searches of every individual in certain specific contexts. The use of metal detectors to examine airline passengers, for example, is a specific context in which the need to prevent hijacking justifies a limited search of every passenger. Here the Court does not require officers to have any suspicions, reasonable or otherwise, about the illegal activities of any individual.

Permissible warrantless searches also take place at the entry points into the United States—border crossings, ports, and airports. The government's interests in guarding against the entry of people and items (such as weapons, drugs, toxic chemicals) that are harmful to national interests outweigh the individuals' expectations of privacy. Typically, these border stops take only a few moments as customs officers check required documents, such as passports and visas, inquire about where the person traveled, and ask what the person is bringing into the United States. The customs officers may have a trained dog sniff around people and their luggage, checking for drugs or large amounts of cash. At the Mexican and

Kansas City, Missouri, police officers conduct a sobriety checkpoint in June 2008. All vehicles were stopped in order to detect whether any drivers had been drinking too much alcohol. Do you think such roadblocks interfere with the rights of drivers who have done nothing to raise suspicions about improper behavior?

© Rich Sugg/MCT/Landov

Canadian borders and at international airports, people may be chosen at random to have their cars and luggage searched. They may also be chosen for such searches because their behavior or their answers to questions arouse the suspicions of U.S. Customs and Border Protection (CBP) officers.

The handbook for CBP officers permits an officer to base some types of searches on suspicion alone, even though mere suspicion does not meet the standard of "reasonable suspicion," which requires the support of articulable facts. The CBP instructs its personnel to consider six categories of factors in determining if suspicion exists to justify searching a traveler at a border crossing or an airport:

1. *Behavioral analysis.* Signs of nervousness, such as flushed face, avoidance of eye contact, excessive perspiration

2. *Observational techniques.* Unexplained bulges in clothing or awkwardness in walking

3. *Inconsistencies.* Discrepancies in answers to questions posed by customs officers

4. *Intelligence.* Information provided to customs officers by informants or other law enforcement officials

5. *K-9.* Signals from law enforcement trained dogs who sniff around people and luggage

6. *Incident to a seizure or arrest.* The discovery of contraband in one suitcase, which can justify the search of the person and the rest of the person's property

As part of its intelligence-based searches, the CBP also relies on the Interagency Border Inspection System (IBIS), a database used by 20 federal agencies to track information on suspected individuals, businesses, vehicles, and vessels. Computer checks on individuals and vehicles at border points may provide the basis for searches. Table 8.2 contains the CBP's policies for personal searches, including the level of suspicion required for each search and whether supervisory approval is required. Do you believe these guidelines strike a proper balance between individuals' rights and societal interests in stopping the flow of contraband?

The Supreme Court has expanded the checkpoint concept by approving systematic stops along highways within the nation's interior in order to look for drunken drivers. Specifically, they approved a sobriety checkpoint program in Michigan. State police had set up a checkpoint at which they stopped every vehicle and briefly questioned each driver. The checkpoint program was challenged as a violation of the Fourth Amendment right to be free from unreasonable seizures, but the Court found no constitutional violation (*Michigan Department of State Police v. Sitz*, 1990). The Court approved checkpoints to ask drivers whether they had witnessed an accident (*Illinois v. Lidster*, 2004). A drunken driver caught at the checkpoint claimed that he was stopped improperly. However, the Court said that police can systematically stop drivers in order to seek information.

Although the U.S. Supreme Court has approved vehicle checkpoints that combat drunken driving and seek information as contexts for permissible warrantless stops and searches, this does not mean that these checkpoints are permissible everywhere in the United States. State supreme courts can interpret their own states' constitutions to provide greater limitations on police than those imposed by the U.S. Supreme Court through the U.S. Constitution. For example, the Michigan Supreme Court ruled that sobriety checkpoints used to identify drunken drivers violate the provisions of the Michigan Constitution concerning searches and seizures (*Sitz v. Department of State Police*, 1993). Decisions of the U.S. Supreme Court provide the baseline of rights for everyone in the country, and a state supreme court cannot give its citizens fewer or weaker

 On its website, U.S. Customs and Border Protection (CBP) provides an explanation of its authority to conduct searches. To link to this website, go to *The American System of Criminal Justice* 12e companion site at academic.cengage.com/criminaljustice/cole.

TABLE 8.2   U.S. Customs and Border Protection Policies for Personal Searches

Search Type	Suspicion	Level Approval
1. Immediate pat-down (frisk): A search necessary to ensure that a person is not carrying a weapon	Suspicion that a weapon may be present	None required
2. Pat-down for merchandise: A search for merchandise, including contraband, hidden on a person's body	One articulable fact	On-duty supervisor
3. Partial body search: The removal of some clothing by a person to recover merchandise reasonably suspected to be concealed on the body	Reasonable suspicion, based on specific, articulable facts	On-duty supervisor
4. X-ray: Medical X-ray by medical personnel to determine the presence of merchandise within the body	Reasonable suspicion, based on specific, articulable facts	Port director and court order, unless person consents
5. Body-cavity search: Any visual or physical intrusion into the rectal or vaginal cavity	Reasonable suspicion, based on specific, articulable facts	Port director and court order, unless person consents
6. MBM (monitored bowel movement): Detention of a person for the purpose of determining whether contraband or merchandise is concealed in the alimentary canal	Reasonable suspicion, based on specific, articulable facts	Port director

Source: U.S. General Accounting Office, *U.S. Customs Service: Better Targeting of Airline Passengers for Personal Searches Could Produce Better Results* (Washington, DC: U.S. Government Printing Office, March 2000).

rights. However, a state court can provide broader rights and stronger limitations on police authority.

The U.S. Supreme Court has not given blanket approval for every kind of checkpoint or traffic stop that police might wish to use. The Court specifically forbids officers on patrol to conduct random stops of vehicles (*Delaware v. Prouse*, 1979). Officers must have a basis for a vehicle stop, such as an observed violation of traffic laws. The Court has also ruled that a city cannot set up a checkpoint in order to check drivers and passengers for possible involvement in drugs. In *City of Indianapolis v. Edmond* (2000), even though police officers stopped vehicles only briefly in order to ask a few questions and circle the car with a drug-sniffing dog, the Court declared that checkpoints cannot be justified by a general search for criminal evidence. Such stops must focus narrowly on a specific objective, such as checking for drunken drivers.

checkpoint

7. In what situations do law enforcement's special needs justify stopping an automobile without reasonable suspicion?

Stop and Frisk on the Streets

Terry v. Ohio (1968)
Supreme Court decision endorsing police officers' authority to stop and frisk suspects on the street when there is reasonable suspicion that they are armed and involved in criminal activity.

Police officers possess the authority to make stops and limited searches of individuals on the streets when specific circumstances justify such actions. The U.S. Supreme Court endorsed this authority in the landmark case of *Terry v. Ohio*

(1968). The Court's decision recognized that seizures short of arrest could be "reasonable" under the Fourth Amendment. In this case, the suspects were not free to leave, yet the officer would presumably have released them if he had not found the weapons. Thus the stop and search occurred as part of the investigation process before any arrest occurred. The justices were clearly concerned about striking an appropriate balance between Fourth Amendment rights and necessary police authority to investigate and prevent crimes.

Although the justices in *Terry* supported law enforcement authority, they struck the balance by carefully specifying the circumstances in which this sort of pat-down search—more commonly known as a **stop-and-frisk search**—can occur. The Court appeared to demand that several specific facts exist in each situation in which a permissible stop and frisk can occur. If we break apart the Court's own words, we can see that the justices explicitly say "We merely hold today that

The stopping and frisking of an individual must be carried out according to the standards first established by the U.S. Supreme Court in *Terry v. Ohio*. What are the standards? Are the standards clear enough to guide police officers and provide appropriate protection for citizens' liberty and privacy?

AP Images/Gregory Bull

[1] where a police officer observes unusual conduct

[2] which leads him reasonably to conclude in light of his experience

[3] that criminal activity may be afoot and

[4] that the persons with whom he is dealing may be armed and presently dangerous,

[5] where in the course of investigating this behavior

[6] he identifies himself as a policeman and makes reasonable inquiries,

[7] and where nothing in the initial stages of the encounter serves to dispel his reasonable fear for his own or others' safety,

[8] he is entitled for the protection of himself and others in the area to conduct a carefully limited search of the outer clothing of such persons in an attempt to discover weapons which might be used to assault him.

These specified factors imposed an obligation on police officers to make observations, draw reasonable conclusions, identify themselves, and make inquiries before conducting the stop-and-frisk search. In addition, the reasonableness of the search was justified by a reasonable conclusion that a person was armed and therefore the officer needed to act in order to protect him- or herself and the public.

Court decisions have given officers significant discretion to decide when these factors exist. For example, if officers see someone running at the sight of police in a high-crime neighborhood, their observation in that context can provide the basis for sufficient suspicion to justify a stop and frisk (*Illinois v. Wardlow*, 2000). Thus, officers need not actually see evidence of a weapon or interact with the suspect prior to making the stop.

The Supreme Court also expanded police authority by permitting officers to rely on reports from reliable witnesses as the basis for conducting the stop and frisk (*Adams v. Williams*, 1972). However, an unverified anonymous tip is not an adequate basis for a stop-and-frisk search. In *Florida v. J. L.* (2000), police officers received an anonymous tip that a young African American man standing at a specific bus stop and wearing a plaid shirt was carrying a gun. Police

stop-and-frisk search
Limited search approved by Supreme Court in *Terry v. Ohio* that permits officers to pat down clothing of people on the streets if there is reasonable suspicion of dangerous criminal activity.

Florida v. J. L. (2000)
Police officers may not conduct a stop-and-frisk search based solely on an anonymous tip.

CLOSE UP

Determining Justification for Police Searches

AFTER LISTENING CARE-FULLY to the two police-men, the judge had a problem: he did not be-lieve them.

The officers, who had stopped a man in the Bronx and found a .22-caliber pistol in his fanny pack, testified that they had several reasons to search him—he was loitering, sweating nervously, and had a bulge under his jacket.

But the judge, John E. Sprizzo of United States District Court in Manhattan, concluded that the police had simply reached into the pack without cause, found the gun, then "tailored" testimony to jus-tify the illegal search. "You can't have open season on searches," said Judge Sprizzo, who refused to allow the gun as evidence, prompting prosecutors to drop the case last May.

Yet for all his disapproval of what the police had done, the judge said he hated to make negative rulings about officers' credibility. "I don't like to jeopardize their career and all the rest of it," he said.

He need not have worried. The police department never learned of his criticism, and the officers—like many others whose word has been called into question—faced no disciplinary action or inquiry.

Over the last six years, the police and prosecutors have cooper-ated in a broad effort that allows convicted felons found with a fire-arm to be tried in federal court, where sentences are much harsher than in state court. Officials say the initiative has taken hundreds of armed criminals off the street, mostly in the Bronx and Brooklyn, and turned some into informers who have helped solve more seri-ous crimes.

But a closer look at those prosecutions reveals something that has not been trumpeted—more than 20 cases in which judges found

police officers' testimony to be unreliable, inconsistent, twisting the truth, or just plain false. The judges' language was often withering: "patently incredible," "riddled with exaggerations," "unworthy of belief."

The outrage usually stopped there. With few exceptions, judges did not ask prosecutors to determine whether the officers had bro-ken the law, and prosecutors did not notify police authorities about the judges' findings. The police department said it did not monitor the rulings and was aware of only one of them; after it learned about the cases recently from a reporter, a spokesman said the department would decide whether further review was needed.

Though the number of cases is small, the lack of consequences for officers may seem surprising, given that a city commission on police corruption in the 1990s pinpointed tainted testimony as a problem so pervasive that the police even had a word for it—"testilying."

And these cases may fuel another longtime concern that flared up again in recent days—suspicions that the police routinely subject people to unjustified searches, frisks, or stops. Last week, the [New York City] Police Department reported a spike in street stops, which it said were "an essential law enforcement tool"—145,098 from Janu-ary through March [2008], more than during any quarter in six years.

The judges' rulings emerge from what are called suppression hearings, in which defendants, before trial, can argue that evi-dence was seized illegally. The Fourth Amendment sets limits on the conditions that permit a search; if they are not met, judges must exclude the evidence, even if that means allowing a guilty person to go free.

Prosecutors and police officials say many of the suppressions stem from difficult, split-second judgments that officers must make

officers went to the bus stop and frisked a young man matching the description. They found a gun and arrested the young man for unlawfully carrying a con-cealed weapon. The justices unanimously ruled that the gun must be excluded from evidence because the officers did not have reliable information as the basis for the search. The Court did not rule out the possibility that an anonymous tip alone might be sufficient in extraordinary circumstances in which a greater societal interest is at stake, such as a report that someone is carrying a bomb—a device with greater risk and likelihood of harm than a handgun. In the post–September 11 effort to combat terrorism, such stops may become more com-mon.

Police officers possess the discretionary authority to make on-the-spot deci-sions to conduct searches. They provide justifications for those searches only when evidence of a crime is discovered and an arrested suspect uses a later court hearing to challenge the legality of the search. By that time, however, officers have had time to prepare an explanation for their actions. If officers are not completely honest and ethical, there are risks that they will manufacture jus-tifications to fit the requirements of stop-and-frisk or other warrantless search categories. Because of the need to grant police the discretion to do certain kinds of searches without obtaining a judge's approval through the warrant process, in potentially dangerous situations about whether to search someone for a weapon—decisions that are not always easy to reconstruct in a courtroom.

But one former federal judge, John S. Martin Jr., said the rulings are meant to deter serious abuses by the police. "The reason you suppress," he said, "is to stop cops from going up to people and searching them when they don't have reason."

Federal judges rarely suppress evidence, Judge Martin said, and the unusual number of suppressions in New York City gun cases raises questions about whether such tactics may be common. "We don't have the statistics for all the people who are hassled, no gun is found, and they never get into the system," he said.

Whatever one makes of the legal debate, these cases offer a revealing glimpse into some police practices—in the street and on the witness stand—that have gone largely unexamined outside the courtroom.

"A Dismal Record"

In one case, the officer explained that he had a special technique for detecting who was hiding a gun. He had learned it from a newspaper article that described certain clues to watch for—a hand brushing a pocket, a lopsided gait, or a jacket or sweater that seems mismatched or out of season.

That was one reason, he told a judge, that he was certain the man he saw outside a Brooklyn housing project last September was concealing a gun. The man, Anthony McCrae, had moved his hand along the front of his waistband, as if moving a weapon, the officer said. Sure enough, a search turned up a gun.

The judge, John Gleeson of Brooklyn federal court, asked the officer, Kaz Daughtry, how successful his method had been in other cases.

Officer Daughtry replied that over a three-day period, he and his partner had stopped 30 to 50 people. One had a gun.

Calling that a "dismal record," the judge said the officer's technique was "little more than guesswork."

Moreover, Judge Gleeson said he did not believe that Officer Daughtry could even have seen the gesture he found so suspicious—Mr. McCrae's hand was in front of him and the officer was about 30 feet behind.

The judge would not allow the gun as evidence, and on April 24, federal prosecutors dropped the charges. A law enforcement official said the Brooklyn district attorney's office learned of the ruling and was reviewing Officer Daughtry's other cases to see if there were problems.

Source: Benjamin Weiser, "Police in Gun Searches Face Disbelief in Court," *New York Times*, May 12, 2008, p. 1.

Researching the Internet

Read the Supreme Court's decision in *Terry v. Ohio* at the website of Cornell University Law School. To link to this website, go to *The American System of Criminal Justice* 12e companion site at academic.cengage.com/criminaljustice/cole. Have police officers and judges stretched the justification for stop-and-frisk searches so that the search authority is much broader than indicated by the reasoning of the Supreme Court in the original case?

---

we place great faith in the honesty and professionalism of police officers. Sometimes, however, officers do not fulfill their professional obligations because they are too intent on finding criminal evidence. It is very difficult for judges to know whether police officers are telling the truth about what happened before and during a search. Thus judges typically accept the police officer's version of events rather than that of the suspect who was arrested. This raises questions about whether we are able to adequately supervise police officers and hold them accountable for errors and rule violations. As you read the Close Up about judges examining police officers' justifications for searches, think about whether officers should face punishment—and what that punishment should be—if judges conclude that their justifications are inaccurate or untruthful.

Search Incident to a Lawful Arrest

The authority to undertake a warrantless search incident to a lawful arrest is not limited by the crime for which the arrestee has been taken into custody. Even someone arrested for a traffic offense can be searched. Although there is no reason to suspect the person has a weapon or to believe that evidence related to the offense will be found in the person's pockets, the arrestee is subject to the same arrest scene search as someone taken into custody for murder *(United States v. Robinson*, 1973).

The justification for searches of arrestees emerged in the Supreme Court's decision in ***Chimel v. California*** (1969). The officers must make sure that the arrestee does not have a weapon that could endanger the officers or others in the vicinity. The officers must also look for evidence on the person of the arrestee that the arrestee might destroy or damage before or during transportation to jail.

Officers can search the arrestee and the immediate area around the arrestee. Officers can also make a protective sweep through other rooms where the suspect may recently have been. However, the arrest would not justify opening drawers and conducting a thorough search of an entire house. If, after the arrest, officers have probable cause to conduct a more thorough search, they must obtain a warrant that specifies the items they seek and the places they will search.

Although a lawful arrest justifies a limited search and protective sweep, the Court has been unwilling to permit thorough warrantless searches at crime scenes, even when a murder victim is discovered. Officers should obtain a warrant to open luggage, packages, and filing cabinets at the murder scene *(Flippo v. West Virginia*, 1999).

Chimel v. California, (1969)
Supreme Court decision that endorsed warrantless searches for weapons and evidence in the immediate vicinity of people who are lawfully arrested.

checkpoint

8. What knowledge must an officer possess in order to conduct a stop-and-frisk search on the streets?
9. Where can officers search when conducting a warrantless search incident to a lawful arrest?

Exigent Circumstances

exigent circumstances
When there is a threat to public safety or the risk that evidence will be destroyed, officers may search, arrest, or question suspects without obtaining a warrant or following other usual rules of criminal procedure.

Officers can make an arrest without a warrant when there are **exigent circumstances**. This means that officers are in the middle of an urgent situation in which they must act swiftly and do not have time to go to court to seek a warrant. With respect to arrests, for example, when officers are in hot pursuit of a fleeing suspected felon, they need not stop to seek a warrant and thereby risk permitting the suspect to get away *(Warden v. Hayden*, 1967). Similarly, exigent circumstances can justify warrantless searches. When the ex-wife of Football Hall-of-Famer O. J. Simpson was stabbed to death in front of her home, police officers went to Simpson's house and climbed the wall to gain entry to his backyard. They claimed that they found a bloody glove in the backyard, and that glove was admitted into evidence against Simpson because a judge was persuaded that the officers made the warrantless entry and search based on the urgency of their need to make sure that no one at the Simpson house was injured or in danger. Ultimately, however, the glove did not help the prosecution's case as Simpson was acquitted.

In *Cupp v. Murphy* (1973), a man voluntarily complied with police officers' request that he come to the police station to answer questions concerning his wife's murder. The couple resided in separate homes at the time. At the station, officers noticed a substance on the man's fingernails that they thought might be dried blood. Over his objections, they took a sample of scrapings under his fingernails and ultimately used that tissue as evidence against him when he was convicted of murdering his wife. The Supreme Court said the search was properly undertaken under exigent circumstances. If officers had taken the time to seek a warrant, the suspect may have gone to the bathroom to wash his hands and the evidence would have been lost.

In other cases, the Supreme Court approved warrantless blood tests because of the need for fast action. For example, evidence of alcohol in the blood will dissipate and disappear if not retrieved immediately through a blood test (*Breihaupt v. Abram*, 1957).

Police officers can use the exigent circumstances justification for warrantless searches for the purpose of seeking evidence. To justify such searches, they do not need to show that there was a potential threat to public safety. As a practical matter, police officers make quick judgments about undertaking certain searches. If incriminating evidence is discovered, courts may be asked to make an after-the-fact determination of whether the urgency of the situation justified a warrantless search and whether the nature and purpose of the search were reasonable. Judges are usually quite reluctant to second-guess a police officer's on-the-spot decision that the urgency of a situation required an immediate warrantless search.

State legislatures may use statutes to define officers' authority to search incident to an arrest. You can read the Illinois statute online at Article 108 within the Code of Criminal Procedure of 1963. To link to this website, go to *The American System of Criminal Justice* 12e companion site at academic.cengage.com/criminaljustice/cole.

Consent

If people consent to a search, officers do not need probable cause or even any level of suspicion to justify the search. The consent effectively absolves law enforcement officers of any risk that evidence will be excluded from use at trial or that they will be found liable in a civil lawsuit alleging a violation of Fourth Amendment rights. Individuals can waive their constitutional rights; a voluntary consent to search effectively waives the legal protections of the Fourth Amendment.

Consent searches provide a valuable investigatory tool for officers who wish to conduct warrantless searches. Officers in many police departments are trained to ask people if they will consent to a search. Thus, some officers ask every motorist during a traffic stop, "May I search your car?" Or, if called to the scene of a domestic dispute or a citizen complaint about noise, the officers may say, "Do you mind if I look around in the downstairs area of your house?" Criminal evidence is often uncovered in such consent searches, a fact which may indicate that many citizens do not know they have the option to say "no" when officers ask for permission to search. Moreover, some citizens may fear that they will look more suspicious to the officers if they say "no," so they agree to searches in order to act as if they have nothing to hide. In addition, in ***United States v. Drayton*** (2002), the Supreme Court said very clearly that police officers do not have to inform people of their right to say "no" when asked if they wish to consent to a search.

One must address two key issues in deciding if a permissible consent search has occurred. First, the consent must be voluntary. Police officers could not have used coercion or threats in order to obtain consent. Even subtler tricks, such as dishonestly telling someone that there is a search warrant and thereby implying that the person has no choice but to consent, will result in the search being declared improper (*Bumper v. North Carolina*, 1968). Second, the consent must be given by someone who possesses authority to give consent and thereby waive the right. Someone cannot, for example, consent to have his or her neighbor's house searched.

United States v. Drayton (2002)
Police officers are not required to inform people of their right to decline when police ask for consent to search.

checkpoint

10. What are "exigent circumstances"?
11. What two elements must be present for a valid consent to permit a warrantless search?

Warrantless searches of automobiles may be conducted when there is probable cause to suspect criminal activity or the presence of evidence related to a crime. California Highway Patrol Sgt. Hal Rosendahl dismantles the dashboard of a car allegedly used to smuggle drugs. Should we require officers to seize vehicles and then seek a warrant from a judge before conducting such searches?

AP Images/Rich Pedroncelli

Automobile Searches

We began a discussion of automobile searches in the section on special needs; here we look at such searches in greater detail. The U.S. Supreme Court first addressed searches of automobiles in *Carroll v. United States* (1925), a case in which federal agents looking for illegal alcohol searched a car. The *Carroll* case, in which the warrantless search was approved, provided an underlying justification for permitting such searches of automobiles. In essence, because cars are mobile, they differ greatly from houses and other buildings. Automobiles can be driven away and disappear in the time that it would take officers to ask a judicial officer for a search warrant.

Police officers have significant authority to search automobiles and to issue commands to people riding in vehicles. For example, during a traffic stop, officers can order passengers as well as the driver to exit the vehicle, even if there is no basis for suspicion that the passengers engaged in any wrongdoing (*Maryland v. Wilson*, 1997). If officers use evidence found in an unjustified traffic stop to convict a passenger of a crime, passengers can use the courts to challenge the legality of the search (*Brendlin v. California*, 2007).

The two key questions that arise in automobile searches are (1) When can an officer stop a car? and (2) How extensively can they search the vehicle? Many automobile searches arise as a result of traffic stops. A stop can occur when an officer observes a traffic violation, including defective safety equipment, or when there is a basis for reasonable suspicion concerning the involvement of the car, its driver, or its passengers in a crime. Police officers are free to make a visible inspection around a car's interior as they question a driver and ask for identification when preparing a citation for a traffic violation. All sworn officers can make traffic stops, even if they are in unmarked vehicles and serving in special vice or detective bureaus that do not normally handle traffic offenses (*Whren v. United States*, 1996). A traffic violation by itself, however, does not provide an officer with the authority to search an entire vehicle (*Knowles v. Iowa*, 1998). Specific factors must create reasonable suspicion or probable cause in order to authorize officers to do anything more than look inside the vehicle.

For example, the lawful arrest of a driver justifies a search of the entire passenger compartment of the automobile for evidence or weapons (*New York v. Belton*, 1981). Moreover, such an arrest justifies the search of a passenger's property (*Wyoming v. Houghton*, 1999). In addition, the Court has expanded officers' authority to search automobiles even when no formal arrest has yet occurred. In *Michigan v. Long* (1983), the Court approved a search of the car's interior around the driver's seat after officers found the car in a ditch and the driver standing outside the car appearing intoxicated. The Supreme Court justified the search as an expansion of the *Terry* doctrine. In effect, the officers were permitted to "frisk" the car in order to protect themselves and others by making sure no weapon was available to the not-yet-arrested driver. Such a search requires that the officers have reasonable suspicion that the person stopped may be armed and poses a potential danger to the officers.

Initially the Court treated containers and closed areas in automobiles differently from the passenger compartment. Even when officers had probable

TABLE 8.3	**Warrantless Searches**
The Supreme Court has ruled that there are circumstances when a warrant is not required.	

Case	Decision
Special Needs	
Michigan Department of State Police v. Sitz (1990)	Stopping motorists systematically at roadblocks designed for specific purposes, such as detecting drunken drivers, is permissible.
City of Indianapolis v. Edmond (2000)	Police traffic checkpoints cannot be justified as a generalized search for criminal evidence; they must be narrowly focused on a specific objective.
Stop and Frisk	
Terry v. Ohio (1968)	Officers may stop and frisk suspects on the street when there is reasonable suspicion that they are armed and involved in criminal activity.
Adams v. Williams (1972)	Officers may rely on reports from reliable witnesses as the basis for conducting a stop and frisk.
Illinois v. Wardlow (2000)	When a person runs at the sight of police in a high-crime area, officers are justified in using that person's flight as a basis for forming reasonable suspicion to justify a stop and frisk.
Incident to an Arrest	
Chimel v. California (1969)	To preserve evidence and protect the safety of the officer and the public after a lawful arrest, the arrestee and the immediate area around the arrestee may be searched for weapons and criminal evidence.
United States v. Robinson (1973)	A warrantless search incident to an arrest is not limited by the seriousness of the crime for which the arrestee has been taken into custody.
Exigent Circumstances	
Warden v. Hayden (1967)	When officers are in hot pursuit of a fleeing suspect, they need not stop to seek a warrant and thereby risk permitting the suspect to get away.
Cupp v. Murphy (1973)	Officers may seize evidence to protect it if taking time to seek a warrant creates a risk of its destruction.
Consent	
Bumper v. North Carolina (1968)	Officers may not tell falsehoods as a means of getting a suspect to consent to a search.
United States v. Drayton (2002)	An officer does not have to inform people of their right to refuse when he or she asks if they wish to consent to a search.
Automobiles	
Carroll v. United States (1925)	Because by their nature automobiles can be easily moved, warrantless searches are permissible when reasonable suspicion of illegal activity exists.
New York v. Class (1986)	An officer may enter a vehicle to see the vehicle identification number when a car has been validly stopped pursuant to a traffic violation or other permissible justification.
California v. Acevedo (1991)	Officers may search throughout a vehicle when they believe they have probable cause to do so.
Maryland v. Wilson (1997)	During traffic stops, officers may order passengers as well as the driver to exit the vehicle, even if there is no basis for suspicion that the passengers engaged in any wrongdoing.
Knowles v. Iowa (1998)	A traffic violation by itself does not provide an officer with the authority to search an entire vehicle. There must be reasonable suspicion or probable cause before officers can extend their search beyond merely looking inside the vehicle's passenger compartment.

cause to search a car's trunk, they were expected to obtain a warrant for any containers found within the trunk. However, this rule changed in the Court's decision in *California v. Acevedo* (1991). Now police officers can search anywhere in the car for which they have probable cause to search. Further, unlike the situations with warrants, the officers themselves, rather than a judge, determine

whether probable cause exists before conducting the warrantless search of the vehicle. If, however, a judge later disagrees with the officer's conclusion about the existence of probable cause, any evidence found in the search of the automobile will likely be excluded from use at trial.

Even if officers lack probable cause to believe that the vehicle has been stolen, an officer may enter the vehicle to see the vehicle identification number by the windshield when a car has been validly stopped pursuant to a traffic violation or other permissible justification (*New York v. Class*, 1986). In addition, the Court permits thorough searches of vehicles, without regard to probable cause, when police officers inventory the contents of impounded vehicles (*South Dakota v. Opperman*, 1976). Containers found within the course of the inventory search may also be opened and searched when the examination of such containers is consistent with a police department's inventory policies.

Table 8.3 reviews selected Supreme Court cases concerning those circumstances in which the police do not need a warrant to conduct a search or to seize evidence.

checkpoint

12.   What defines the scope of officers' authority to search containers in automobiles?

QUESTIONING SUSPECTS

As we saw in Chapter 4, the Fifth Amendment contains various rights, including the one most relevant to police officers' actions in questioning suspects. The relevant words of the Amendment are "No person shall . . . be compelled in any criminal case to be a witness against himself." The privilege against compelled self-incrimination should not be viewed as simply a legal protection that seeks to assist individuals who may be guilty of crimes. By protecting individuals in

A Santa Ana, California, police officer questions a suspect about a knife that was found by police. In such a confined setting, are you confident that suspects will truly understand the nature of their rights before consenting to be questioned without an attorney present?

© Spencer Grant/PhotoEdit

this way, the Fifth Amendment discourages police officers from using violent or otherwise coercive means to push suspects to confess.

In addition to discouraging the physical abuse of suspects, the privilege against compelled self-incrimination also diminishes the risk of erroneous convictions. When police officers use coercive pressure to seek confessions, some innocent people will succumb to the pressure by confessing to crimes that they did not commit. The worst-case scenario is illustrated by the film *In the Name of the Father* (1993), based on a true story in England in which police officers gain a confession from a bombing suspect, whom they know to be innocent, by placing a gun in the suspect's mouth and threatening to pull the trigger.

In the past, because of the Fifth Amendment protection against compelled self-incrimination, the validity of confessions hinged on their being voluntary. Under the doctrine of fundamental fairness, which was applied before the 1960s, the Supreme Court was unwilling to allow confessions that were beaten out of suspects, that emerged after extended questioning, or that resulted from the use of other physical tactics. Such tactics can impose inhumane treatment on suspects and create risks that innocent people will be wrongly convicted.

In *Miranda v. Arizona* (1966), the Warren Court outraged politicians, law enforcement officials, and members of the public by placing limits on the ability of police to question suspects without following specific procedures. The justices ruled that, prior to questioning, the police must inform detained suspects of their right to remain silent and their right to have an attorney present. In response, many police officers argued that they depended on interrogations and confessions as a major means of solving crimes (Cassell and Fowles, 1998). However, nearly four decades later, many suspects continue to confess for various reasons, such as feelings of guilt, inability to understand their rights, and the desire to gain a favorable plea bargain (Leo, 1996a; 1996b). Moreover, surveys indicate that many police officials accept the existence of the *Miranda* rules and do not want to see the Supreme Court reverse its original decision (Zalman and Smith, 2007).

Miranda v. Arizona (1966)
Before questioning a suspect held in custody, police officers must inform the individual of the right to remain silent and the right to have an attorney present during questioning.

Miranda Rules

Suspects in police custody must be told four things before they can be questioned:

1. They have the right to remain silent.

2. If they decide to make a statement, it can and will be used against them in court.

3. They have the right to have an attorney present during interrogation or to have an opportunity to consult with an attorney.

4. If they cannot afford an attorney, the state will provide one.

Prior to the *Miranda* decision, police officers in some places solved crimes by picking up poor people or African Americans and torturing them until a confession was produced. In *Brown v. Mississippi* (1936), the Supreme Court ruled that statements produced after police beat suspects were inadmissible, but it did not insist that counsel be available at the early stages of the criminal process.

Two rulings in 1964 laid the foundation for the *Miranda* decision. In *Massiah v. United States* (1964), the Supreme Court declared that an indicted defendant's rights were violated when he was questioned without his attorney present by someone secretly working for the police. In *Escobedo v. Illinois* (1964), the Court made the link between the Fifth Amendment right against self-incrimination and the Sixth Amendment right to counsel. Danny Escobedo was questioned at the police station for 14 hours without counsel even though he asked to see his attorney. He finally made incriminating statements that the police

Escobedo v. Illinois (1964)
Police cannot refuse access to an attorney for arrested suspects who ask to see one.

CLOSE UP

Miranda v. Arizona, 384 U.S. 436 (1966)

ERNEST MIRANDA, a loading dock worker with a prior history of sex offenses, was arrested for rape. Two detectives took him into a private interrogation room for questioning. Eventually they emerged with his signed confession. Miranda's lawyer challenged the confession, because the questioning took place before the attorney had been appointed to provide representation. Chief Justice Warren delivered the opinion of the Court, as follows.

* * *

Our holding will be spelled out with some specificity in the pages which follow but briefly stated it is this: the prosecution may not use statements . . . stemming from custodial interrogation of the defendant unless it demonstrates the use of procedural safeguards effective to secure the privilege against self-incrimination. By custodial interrogation, we mean questioning initiated by law enforcement officers after a person has been taken into custody or otherwise deprived of his freedom of action in any significant way. As for the procedural safeguards to be employed, unless other fully effective means are devised to inform accused persons of their right to silence and to assure a continuous opportunity to exercise it, the following measures are required. Prior to any questioning, the person must be warned that he has a right to remain silent, that any statement he does make may be used as evidence against him, and that he has the right to the presence of an attorney, either retained or appointed.

The defendant may waive effectuation of these rights, provided the waiver is made voluntarily, knowingly, and intelligently. If, however, he indicates in any manner and at any stage of the process that he wishes to consult with an attorney before speaking there can be no questioning. Likewise, if the individual is alone and indicates in any manner that he does not wish to be interrogated, the police may not question him. The mere fact that he may have answered some questions or volunteered some statements on his own does not deprive him of the right to refrain from answering any further inquiries until he has consulted with an attorney and thereafter consents to be questioned.

The constitutional issue we decide . . . is the admissibility of statements obtained from a defendant questioned while in custody or otherwise deprived of his freedom of action in any significant way. . . .

An understanding of the nature and setting of this in-custody interrogation is essential to our decisions today. The difficulty in depicting what transpires at such interrogations stems from the fact that in this country they have largely taken place incommunicado. From extensive factual studies undertaken in the early 1930's, including the famous Wickersham Report to Congress by a Presidential Commission, it is clear that police violence and the "third degree" flourished at that time.

In a series of cases decided by this Court long after these studies, the police resorted to physical brutality—beatings , hanging, whipping—and to sustained and protracted questioning incommunicado in order to extort confessions. . . . The use of physical brutality and violence is not, unfortunately, relegated to the past or to any part of the country. Only recently in Kings County, New York, the police brutally beat, kicked, and placed lighted cigarette butts on the back of a potential witness under interrogation for the purpose of securing a statement incriminating a third party. . . .

The examples given above are undoubtedly the exception now, but they are sufficiently widespread to be the object of concern. Unless a proper limitation upon custodial interrogation is achieved—such as these decisions will advance—there can be no assurance that practices of this nature will be eradicated in the foreseeable future. . . .

* * *

In dealing with statements obtained through interrogation, we do not purport to find all confessions inadmissible. Confessions remain a proper element in law enforcement. Any statement given freely and voluntarily without any compelling influences is, of course, admissible in evidence. . . . There is no requirement that police stop a person who enters a police station and states that he wishes to confess to a crime, or a person who calls the police to offer a confession or any other statement he desires to make. Volunteered statements of any kind are not barred by the Fifth Amendment and their admissibility is not affected by our holding today. . . .

* * *

In announcing these principles, we are not unmindful of the burdens which law enforcement officials must bear, often under trying circumstances. We also fully recognize the obligation of all citizens to aid in enforcing the criminal laws. This Court, while protecting individual rights, has always given ample latitude to law enforcement agencies in the legitimate exercise of their duties. The limits we have placed on the interrogation process should not constitute an undue interference with a proper system of law enforcement. . . .

Researching the Internet

An online FBI publication provides a history of the events that led to the *Miranda* decision as well as a description of subsequent Supreme Court decisions that have clarified the obligation to provide warnings in different situations. To link to this website, go to *The American System of Criminal Justice* 12e companion site at academic.cengage.com/criminaljustice/cole.

---

said were voluntary. The Court's ruling specified that defendants have a right to counsel when

the investigation is no longer a general inquiry into an unsolved crime, but has begun to focus on a particular suspect, the suspect has been taken into police custody, [and] the police carry out a process of interrogations that lends itself to eliciting incriminating statements.

The Court effectively expanded the right to counsel to apply at an early point in the criminal justice process as a means to guard against law enforcement officers' actions that might violate the Fifth Amendment privilege against compelled self-incrimination.

As you read the Close Up box containing the excerpt from *Miranda v. Arizona* (1966), think about why so many law enforcement officials harshly criticized the decision at first. (See also "A Question of Ethics" at the end of this chapter.)

The *Miranda* warnings apply only to custodial interrogations. If police officers walk up to someone on the street and begin asking questions, they do not need to inform the person of his or her rights. The justices say that people know they can walk away when an officer asks them questions in a public place. When police have taken someone into custody, however, the Supreme Court sees it as an inherently coercive situation. The loss of liberty and isolation experienced by detained suspects can make them vulnerable to abusive interrogation techniques, especially when interrogations take place out of view of anyone other than police officers. When a suspect has been alone in a room with police officers, if the suspect claims to have been beaten, will anyone believe it, even if it is true? If the police say that the suspect confessed, will anyone believe the suspect who says that no confession was ever given? The *Miranda* warnings and presence of counsel during questioning are meant to prevent such risks.

One circumstance in which the Court has permitted police officers to forgo *Miranda* warnings is when taking the time to provide the warnings would create a threat to public safety. This exception is similar to the exigent circumstance justification for warrantless searches. The underlying premise is that in some urgent situations, a larger social need outweighs individuals' rights. In the case that created the **"public safety" exception**, police officers chased an armed man into a supermarket after a reported assault. When they found him with an empty shoulder holster, they asked, "Where's the gun?" after he was handcuffed but before he had been informed of his *Miranda* rights (*New York v. Quarles*, 1984). His response to the question could be used against him in court because the public's safety might have been threatened if the police took the time to read him his rights before asking any questions.

The Fifth Amendment protection against compelled self-incrimination applies only to testimonial evidence, which normally means incriminating statements made by suspects. The Fifth Amendment does *not* protect against the admission into evidence of nontestimonial evidence, such as objects or descriptions of behaviors manifested by the suspect. Thus, police could use evidence of a drunken driving suspect's slurred speech and inability to answer questions, because such evidence was nontestimonial. By contrast, the police could not use as evidence a statement made by the same arrested suspect in response to a question that was posed prior to the delivery of *Miranda* warnings (*Pennsylvania v. Muniz*, 1990).

Although some legal commentators and police officials have criticized *Miranda* warnings, the Supreme Court strongly repeated its endorsement of the *Miranda* requirement in 2000 (*Dickerson v. United States*).

"public safety" exception
When public safety is in jeopardy, police may question a suspect in custody without providing the *Miranda* warnings.

checkpoint

13. What are *Miranda* rights?
14. What is the "public safety" exception?

The Consequences of *Miranda*

During oral arguments at the Supreme Court, the opponents of *Miranda* assumed that every subject would cease to talk upon being informed that there is a right to silence. However, in practice, this has not occurred. Police officers have adapted their techniques in order to question suspects without any impediment from the warnings.

Miranda rights must be provided before questions are asked during custodial interrogations. Many departments train their officers to read the *Miranda* warnings to suspects as soon as an arrest is made. This is done in order to make sure the warnings are not omitted as the suspect is processed in the system. The warnings may be read off a standard "*Miranda* card" to make sure that the rights are provided consistently and correctly. However, the courts do not require that police inform suspects of their rights immediately after arrest. The warnings do not have to be provided until the police begin to ask questions. Thus, after taking a suspect into custody, some officers may use their discretion to delay providing *Miranda* warnings in order to see if the suspect will talk on his or her own. The suspect may be kept in the backseat of a car as officers drive around town, or the suspect may be left alone in a room at the police station. Some suspects will take the initiative to talk to officers because of feelings of guilt. Other suspects may start conversations with officers because they are eager to convince the officers that they have an alibi or that they want to cooperate. The suspect might thus provide contradictory statements that will help build the case.

After suspects in custody have been informed of their *Miranda* rights, officers may attempt to defuse the potential impact of the rights by presenting them in a manner intended to encourage suspects to talk. For example, officers may inform suspects of their rights but then add, "But if you don't have anything to hide, why would you ask for an attorney or stay silent?"

Officers are also trained in interrogation techniques intended to encourage suspects to talk despite *Miranda* warnings. Officers may pretend to be sympathetic to the suspect (Leo, 1996b). They may say, for example, "We understand how bad stuff can happen that you never want to have happen. We know that you had a good reason to get mad and go after that guy with your knife. We probably would have done the same thing if we were in your situation. We know that you never really planned to stab him." Such statements are dishonest, but police officers are allowed to use deception to induce suspects to talk. It is not uncommon for officers to say, untruthfully, "We have five witnesses that saw you do it. If you tell us everything right now, we may be able to get you a good deal. If you don't help us, we don't know what we can do for you." Do such statements constitute coercion that would be regarded as improper pressure in violation of *Miranda*? Probably not—as long as the officers do not threaten suspects in ways that make them fear for their physical safety or the safety of their loved ones.

Miranda rights have become very familiar to the American public through television shows and movies in which police officers inform arrested suspects of their rights. By the time television-watching Americans reach adulthood, they probably will have heard the *Miranda* warnings delivered hundreds of times on these shows. Many Americans can recite the warnings along with the television detectives. Ironically, this very familiarity with the warnings may impede the effective implementation of *Miranda*, because it interferes with suspects' ability to think about what the warnings actually mean. Obviously, rights are most protective for people who have actually thought about the meaning of those rights. As you read "Civic Engagement: Your Role in the System," consider what you would do if stopped and questioned by the police.

Training material supplied to police officers teaches them to use psychological techniques to develop the appearance of sympathy and trust with the suspect. To link to this website, go to *The American System of Criminal Justice* 12e companion site at academic.cengage.com/criminaljustice/cole.

civic engagement
your role in the system

Based on what you know about police authority to stop and question people, how would you advise your friends to behave during encounters with police officers. *Make a list of what to do and what not to do when stopped by the police.* Then look at the advice that the American Civil Liberties Union provides about how to handle encounters with police officers. To link to this website, go to *The American System of Criminal Justice* 12e companion site at academic.cengage.com/criminaljustice/cole.

TABLE 8.4	Questioning Suspects
The Supreme Court has ruled that suspects' rights against self-incrimination are protected by the Fifth Amendment.	

Case	Decision
Miranda Rules	
Miranda v. Arizona (1966)	Before suspects in police custody may be questioned, they must be told that they have the right to remain silent, that anything they say may be used against them, and that they have the right to counsel during questioning.
Public Safety Exception	
New York v. Quarles (1984)	Officers may direct questions to arrested suspects prior to reading the *Miranda* warnings if concerns about public safety require immediate questioning.

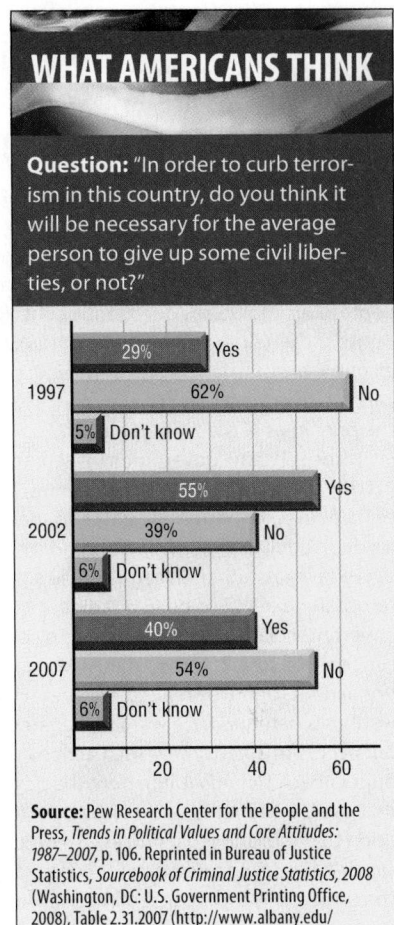

WHAT AMERICANS THINK

Question: "In order to curb terrorism in this country, do you think it will be necessary for the average person to give up some civil liberties, or not?"

1997
- 29% Yes
- 62% No
- 5% Don't know

2002
- 55% Yes
- 39% No
- 6% Don't know

2007
- 40% Yes
- 54% No
- 6% Don't know

Source: Pew Research Center for the People and the Press, *Trends in Political Values and Core Attitudes: 1987–2007*, p. 106. Reprinted in Bureau of Justice Statistics, *Sourcebook of Criminal Justice Statistics, 2008* (Washington, DC: U.S. Government Printing Office, 2008), Table 2.31.2007 (http://www.albany.edu/sourcebook/).

Many suspects talk to the police despite being informed of their right to remain silent and their right to have an attorney present during questioning. Some suspects do not fully understand the rights. They may believe that they will look guilty by remaining silent or by asking for an attorney. Therefore they feel that they must talk to officers in order to have any hope of claiming innocence. Other suspects may be overly confident about their ability to fool the police and therefore talk to officers, despite the warnings, in an effort to act as if they have nothing to hide. More importantly, many suspects believe (often accurately) that they will gain a more favorable charge or plea bargain if they cooperate with officers as fully as possible and as early as possible. Thus, a trio of suspects arrested together after a robbery who are read their *Miranda* rights and who are placed in separate interrogation rooms may, in effect, race to be the first one to tell a version of events in order to pin greater responsibility on the other arrestees and to seek police assistance in gaining a favorable deal with the prosecutor.

This incentive to cooperate can completely negate many of the fears about *Miranda*'s potentially detrimental effect on law enforcement's effectiveness. It can also create problems of its own, however. There are many cases in which the guiltiest suspect, for example, the one who pulled the trigger and killed a store owner during a robbery, is the most eager to cooperate with the police. If the police are not sufficiently skeptical and careful, the most serious offender may get the most favorable deal by having his or her version of events accepted by authorities, and the least culpable defendant, such as the driver of the getaway car, can sometimes end up with the severest punishment if he or she loses the "race" to confess.

Table 8.4 presents selected cases concerning Supreme Court decisions on how the Fifth Amendment protects suspects' rights against self-incrimination. "New Directions in Criminal Justice Policy" examines how 9-11 has engendered debates about the applicability of many of the rights just discussed.

checkpoint

15. How have police officers changed their practices in light of *Miranda*?

THE EXCLUSIONARY RULE

A primary remedy applied for rights violations by police officers is the exclusion of evidence from court. Thus, police may see evidence excluded when they conduct improper stops and searches as well as improper interrogations. Such exclusions of evidence are known as the **exclusionary rule**.

exclusionary rule
The principle that illegally obtained evidence must be excluded from a trial.

NEW DIRECTIONS in CRIMINAL JUSTICE POLICY

Reduction of Rights in a Time of Terrorism

THE U.S. GOVERNMENT'S response to the terrorist attacks on New York City and Washington, D.C., in September 2001 raises questions about the nature of constitutional rights and whether the principles of the Constitution actually govern all of the arrests made by the American government. In other words, can the "war on terrorism" serve as a justification for setting aside the principles of the Bill of Rights?

After 9-11, the government jailed several U.S. citizens without initially charging them with any crimes, giving them access to court proceedings, or permitting them to meet with an attorney. For example, Abdullah al-Muhajir, an American formerly known as Jose Padilla, was arrested in Chicago on the suspicion that he was seeking to obtain material to build a radioactive "dirty bomb." Because the government labeled him as an "enemy combatant" and jailed him in a military prison, it claimed that al-Muhajir is not entitled to constitutional rights and that it need not present any evidence to a court to justify his detention. He was interrogated for months in secret without access to an attorney. Such actions would appear to violate the principles of *Miranda*. Ultimately, the government apparently feared that the U.S. Supreme Court was about to rule that he should be entitled to rights and legal process, so officials transferred him to civilian custody, prosecuted him for conspiracy, and ended up getting a conviction and a 17-year-sentence for him. However, as recently as October 2007, the federal government still claimed that holding him for three years and seven months in isolation in a military jail, where he was reportedly subjected to harsh interrogation techniques that have left him with continuing psychological problems, "did not violate any clearly established constitutional rights" (Richey, 2007).

He was not the only U.S. citizen being held without the provision of the constitutional rights usually available in the criminal justice process. There were at least two other citizens who have been held under similar circumstances. One of those detainees, Yaser Hamdi, was released and deported to Saudi Arabia upon renouncing his U.S. citizenship after the Supreme Court ruled that the government must give him access to the courts to challenge the legality of his detention (*Hamdi v. Rumsfeld*, 2004). Another U.S. citizen, Ahmed Omar Abu Ali, who was born and raised in the United States, was convicted of plotting to assassinate President Bush and sentenced to 30 years in prison. His conviction was widely criticized, however, because he was arrested and initially detained for many months in Saudi Arabia, where he was studying, and there are reports that his confession emerged during a detention period that included being tortured by his Saudi jailers.

Ali Almarri, a legal resident of the United States who is a citizen of Qatar, was arrested in December 2001 while working on a graduate degree at Bradley University in Illinois. He was initially charged with credit card fraud but was transferred to military custody in 2003 when President Bush declared him to be an "enemy combatant" and the government claimed that he was providing financial assistance to terrorist organizations. A U.S. Court of Appeals ruled that the president does not have the power to detain and hold indefinitely without trial people who are arrested within the United States, but the decision was subsequently appealed. As of May 2008, Almarri remained in military custody within the United States as he awaited further court rulings on whether he is entitled to rights under the Bill of Rights.

The government's actions raise interesting questions. Does the government really have the authority to ignore the Bill of Rights by holding people in detention within the United States for indefinite periods? Non-U.S. citizens captured overseas and treated as "enemy combatants" were intentionally sent to a prison at the U.S. Navy base in Guantanamo Bay, Cuba, specifically to claim that that the Bill of Rights should not apply outside of the United States. Therefore the government has asserted that they are not entitled to rights under the Bill of Rights. But the same argument is not available for those being held in military custody within the United States. Should the principles of the Constitution not apply when the U.S. government is detaining accused terrorists within the United States? Do expanded law enforcement powers to conduct searches and surveillance, such as those under the USA Patriot Act, violate basic principles of the Fourth Amendment? In light of the fact that the U.S. government criticizes China and other countries for not providing human rights, is it hypocritical of the United States to reduce the scope of rights and hold people indefinitely in detention without being convicted of a crime? Is there a risk that people who are innocent of terrorism might be erroneously searched or detained because they did not receive the full benefits of rights that were previously available?

These questions are especially interesting because public opinion polls indicate that Americans are divided on the need to sacrifice constitutional rights in the fight against terrorism. They are also divided on the need to use torture against suspected terrorists, an action which would be regarded as violating the right to due process in normal criminal justice processes (see "What Americans Think").

Sources: "Justice Kept in the Dark," *Newsweek*, December 10, 2001, pp. 37–43; Adam Liptak, Neil A. Lewis, and Benjamin Weiser, "After Sept. 11, a Legal Battle on the Limits of Civil Liberty," *New York Times*, August 4, 2002, pp. 1, 16; "Editorial: The Case of Ahmed Omar Abu Ali," *New York Times*, February 24, 2005 (www.nytimes.com); Warren Richey, "U.S. Defends Its Harsh Treatment of an American Citizen," *Christian Science Monitor*, October 19, 2007 (www.csmonitor.com); Adam Liptak, "Court Takes Second Look at Enemy Combatant Case," *New York Times*, November 1, 2007 (www.nytimes.com).

Researching the Internet

Human rights organizations, such as Human Rights Watch, have documented many instances in which the United States has criticized other countries for the very kinds of actions that it appears to be undertaking. To reach the organization's webpage, go to *The American System of Criminal Justice* 12e companion site at academic.cengage.com/criminaljustice/cole.

In *Weeks v. United States* (1914), the U.S. Supreme Court first endorsed the exclusion of evidence from trial as a remedy for improper searches conducted by federal law enforcement officials. The Court clearly declared that if prosecutors were permitted to use improperly obtained evidence, then the Fourth Amendment would lose all meaning and people's rights under the Amendment would disappear. According to Justice William Day's opinion,

> If letters and private documents can thus be seized and held and used in evidence against a citizen accused of an offense, the protection of the 4th Amendment, declaring his right to be secure against such searches and seizures, is of no value, and, so far as those thus placed are concerned, might as well be stricken from the Constitution.

The exclusionary rule does not necessarily require that cases against defendants be dismissed when constitutional rights have been violated. The prosecution can continue, but it may not use improperly obtained evidence. In some cases, other valid evidence of guilt may exist in the form of witness testimony or confessions. Without such alternative evidence, however, the exclusionary rule can lead to charges being dropped. The rule clearly accepts the possibility that a guilty person may go free despite the fact that evidence, although illegally obtained, exists to demonstrate his or her guilt.

Application of the Exclusionary Rule to the States

In *Wolf v. Colorado* (1949), the Supreme Court incorporated the Fourth Amendment. However, the justices declined to apply the exclusionary rule to the states, because they believed states could develop their own remedies to handle improper searches by police. The situation changed when the appointment of Earl Warren as Chief Justice in 1953 ushered in an era in which the Supreme Court expanded the definitions of constitutional rights affecting a variety of issues, including criminal justice. During the Warren era (1953–1969), the Court incorporated most of the criminal justice–related rights in a way that required state law enforcement officials to adhere to the same rules that federal law enforcement officials had to follow. Because the Warren Court justices decided to incorporate various Fifth, Sixth, and Eighth Amendment rights, they not surprisingly also applied the exclusionary rule to the actions of all law enforcement officials, including those in state and local agencies. The Supreme Court applied the exclusionary rule throughout the country in the famous case of ***Mapp v. Ohio*** (1961).

Why did the Supreme Court see the exclusionary rule as necessary? Several reasons emerge in such cases as *Weeks* and *Mapp*. First, *Weeks* declared that the exclusionary rule is essential to making the Fourth Amendment meaningful. In essence, the justices believed that constitutional rights are nullified if government officials are permitted to benefit by violating those rights. Second, the *Mapp* decision indicates that the Constitution requires the exclusionary rule. Third, the majority opinion in *Mapp* concluded that alternatives to the exclusionary rule do not work. Justice Tom Clark's majority opinion noted that many states had found that nothing short of exclusion of evidence would work to correct constitutional rights violations and limit the number of violations that occur. Previously, some states had sought to prevent improper searches by permitting lawsuits against police officers rather than by excluding illegally obtained evidence. Fourth, the *Mapp* opinion argued that the use of improperly obtained evidence by officials who are responsible for upholding the law only serves to diminish respect for the law. In Clark's words, "Thus the State, by admitting evidence unlawfully seized, serves to encourage disobedience to the Federal Constitution which it is bound to uphold." Fifth, the *Mapp* decision indicates that the absence of an exclusionary rule diminishes the protection of all rights because it would permit all constitutional rights "to be revocable at the whim of any police

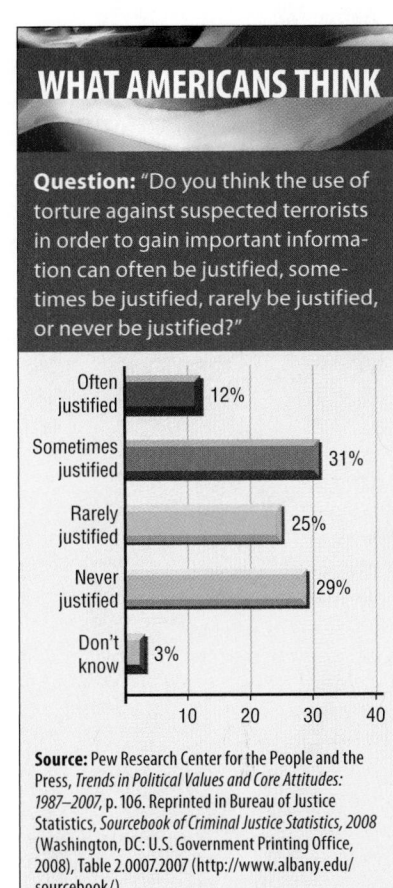

WHAT AMERICANS THINK

Question: "Do you think the use of torture against suspected terrorists in order to gain important information can often be justified, sometimes be justified, rarely be justified, or never be justified?"

Response	%
Often justified	12%
Sometimes justified	31%
Rarely justified	25%
Never justified	29%
Don't know	3%

Source: Pew Research Center for the People and the Press, *Trends in Political Values and Core Attitudes: 1987–2007*, p. 106. Reprinted in Bureau of Justice Statistics, *Sourcebook of Criminal Justice Statistics, 2008* (Washington, DC: U.S. Government Printing Office, 2008), Table 2.0007.2007 (http://www.albany.edu/sourcebook/).

Mapp v. Ohio (1961)
Evidence obtained through illegal searches by state and local police must be excluded from use at trial.

 You can listen to an actual recording of the lawyers' arguments to the Supreme Court in *Mapp v. Ohio* and read the Court's decision by going to *The American System of Criminal Justice* 12e companion site at academic.cengage.com/criminaljustice/cole.

officer who, in the name of law enforcement itself, chooses to suspend . . . [the] enjoyment [of rights]." Sixth, the exclusionary rule is justified as an effective means of deterring police and prosecutors from violating constitutional rights.

checkpoint

16. Why was the exclusionary rule created and eventually applied to the states?

Exceptions to the Exclusionary Rule

The exclusionary rule has many critics, including justices on the Supreme Court. Earl Warren's successor, Chief Justice Warren Burger, who served from 1969 to 1986, criticized the rule as ineffective and misguided. He joined many law enforcement officials, commentators, and politicians in harshly criticizing the Court's decision in *Mapp*. Burger and his allies complained that the Court's decision would hamper police investigations and allow guilty criminals to go free. In Burger's view, there was no proof that the rule prevented officers from conducting improper searches. Moreover, he saw the rule as punishing prosecutors and society rather than the officers who violated people's rights.

Research has not clearly supported claims about the negative consequences of the exclusionary rule. Studies of the rule's impact have produced two consistent findings. First, only a small minority of defendants file a "motion to suppress," which is used to ask a judge to exclude evidence that has allegedly been obtained in violation of the defendant's rights. Second, only a small fraction of motions to suppress evidence are granted (Davies, 1983; Uchida and Bynum, 1991; S. Walker 2001: 90–91). Amid continuing debates about the rule's impact and effectiveness, the Supreme Court began creating exceptions to the exclusionary rule after Burger became chief justice.

"good faith" exception
When police act in honest reliance on a warrant, the evidence seized is admissible even if the warrant is later proved to be defective.

The Supreme Court created a **"good faith" exception** to the exclusionary rule when officers use search warrants *(United States v. Leon,* 1984). When officers have acted in "good faith" reliance on a warrant, the evidence will not be excluded even if the warrant was issued improperly. *Good faith* means that the officers acted with the honest belief that they were following the proper rules. In addition, the reliance and honest belief must be reasonable. If officers knew that a judge had issued a warrant based on no evidence whatsoever, officers could not claim that they reasonably and honestly relied on the warrant. However, if the officers had presented evidence of probable cause to the judge and the judge had made the error by issuing a warrant based on information that actually fell below the standard of probable cause, the officers could use evidence found in the resulting search.

Importantly, the Supreme Court never created a general "good faith" exception to permit the admissibility of improperly obtained evidence whenever police officers make an honest mistake. In *Leon*, there was "good faith" reliance on a warrant, meaning that the fundamental error was made by the judge who issued the warrant. Evidence can still be excluded if officers undertook an improper warrantless search based on their own discretionary decision, even if they honestly (but wrongly) believed that a warrantless search was permitted.

Over the years the Supreme Court has recognized other circumstances where a "good faith" exception is applied to the exclusionary rule. For example,

1. *Reliance on a warrant found to be incorrect (Maryland v. Garrison,* 1987). Police relied on a warrant that incorrectly designated the wrong apartment to search. They were able to use evidence found in the apartment, even though there had been no probable cause to search that apartment in the first place.

2. *Reliance on statutes later declared unconstitutional (Illinois v. Krull,* 1987). Officers conducted a search of a junkyard based on a state statute that au-

thorized warrantless searches of such regulated locations. Although the statute was later declared unconstitutional, the evidence found during the improper search could be used against the defendant.

3. *Reliance on records maintained by justice system employees (Arizona v. Evans, 1995).* Officers stopped a man for a traffic violation. A computer check of his license indicated that there was an outstanding warrant for his arrest. They arrested him and found marijuana in the car, which they had searched in conjunction with the arrest. Although it later turned out that there was no warrant and a court employee had failed to clear the warrant from his record, and therefore the arrest justifying the search was invalid, the marijuana could be used against him.

4. *Reasonable reliance on a consent to search provided by someone who lacked the authority to grant such consent (Illinois v. Rodriguez, 1990).* A suspect's girlfriend provided the police with a key and granted permission to search an apartment even though she did not live in the apartment and she was not supposed to have a key. Evidence was admissible against the defendant because the officers reasonably believed that the girlfriend lived in the apartment.

One important exception to the exclusionary rule is the **"inevitable discovery" exception**. This rule arose from a case involving the tragic abduction and murder of a young girl. The police sought an escapee from a psychiatric hospital who was seen carrying a large bundle. The man being sought contacted an attorney and arranged to surrender to police in a town 160 miles away from the scene of the abduction. The Supreme Court subsequently found that the police improperly questioned the suspect outside of the presence of his attorney while driving him back to the city where the abduction occurred (*Brewer v. Williams*, 1977). The Supreme Court declared that the girl's body and the suspect's statements had to be excluded from evidence because they were obtained in violation of his rights. Thus, his murder conviction was overturned and he was given a new trial. At the second trial, at which he was convicted again, the prosecution used the body in evidence against him based on the claim that search parties would have found the body eventually even without his confession. There was a search team within two and one-half miles of the body at the time that it was found. In **Nix v. Williams (1984)**, the Supreme Court agreed that the improperly obtained evidence can be used when it would later have been inevitably discovered without improper actions by the police.

Table 8.5 summarizes selected Supreme Court decisions regarding the exclusionary rule as it applies to the Fourth and Fifth Amendments.

"inevitable discovery" exception
Improperly obtained evidence can be used when it would later have inevitably been discovered without improper actions by the police.

Nix v. Williams (1984)
Decision in which the Supreme Court created the "inevitable discovery" exception to the exclusionary rule.

TABLE 8.5 Exclusionary Rule	
The Supreme Court has ruled that improperly obtained evidence must be excluded from use by the prosecution, although the Court also created several exceptions to this general rule.	
Case	**Decision**
Exclusionary Rule	
Mapp v. Ohio (1961)	Because the Fourth Amendment protects people from unreasonable searches and seizures by all law enforcement officials, evidence found through improper searches or seizures must be excluded from use at state and federal trials.
"Good Faith" Exception	
United States v. Leon (1984)	When officers act in good faith reliance on a warrant, the evidence will not be excluded even if the warrant was issued improperly.
"Inevitable Discovery" Exception	
Nix v. Williams (1984)	Improperly obtained evidence can be used when it would later have inevitably been discovered without improper actions by the police.

TABLE 8.6	Contexts Outside of the Standard Criminal Prosecution in Which the Exclusionary Rule Does Not Apply
Case	**Decision**
Grand Jury Proceedings	
United States v. Calandra (1974)	A witness summoned to appear before a grand jury cannot refuse to answer questions simply because the questions were based on evidence obtained from an improper search.
Parole Revocation Hearings	
Pennsylvania Board of Pardons and Parole v. Scott (1998)	Improperly obtained evidence can be used at parole revocation proceedings.
Immigration Deportation Hearings	
Immigration and Naturalization Service v. Lopez-Mendoza (1984)	Improperly obtained evidence can be used at deportation hearings.
Impeachment of Defendant	
Harris v. New York (1971)	Improperly obtained statements can be used to impeach the credibility of defendants who take the witness stand and testify in their own trials.

The Supreme Court also created exceptions to the exclusionary rule by identifying stages in the criminal justice process in which the rule does not apply. Table 8.6 lists contexts outside of the standard criminal prosecution in which evidence is not excluded even if officials commit rights violations in the course of gathering evidence.

When the Supreme Court created the exclusionary rule in *Weeks v. United States* (1914) and later expanded its coverage to state and local criminal cases in *Mapp v. Ohio* (1961), it appeared to make strong statements against the use of improperly obtained evidence. As the Court refined the application of the rule from the 1970s onward, it became clear that the exclusion of evidence would arise only in specific situations. The justices have clarified their intention to apply the rule in criminal trials but not in other kinds of proceedings, such as grand jury proceedings and parole revocation hearings, that are not direct criminal prosecutions to determine guilt and punishment. In addition, the specific exceptions to the rule created by the Supreme Court show that the justices changed their approach to determining when evidence should be excluded.

When the Court issued its decisions in *Weeks* and *Mapp*, it appeared that the exclusion of evidence would be guided by a trial judge's answer to the question "Did police violate the suspect's rights?" By contrast, through the development of exceptions to the rule, the Court shifted its focus to the question "Did the police make an error that was so serious that the exclusion of evidence is required?" For example, the "good faith" exception established in *United States v. Leon* (1984) emphasizes the fact that officers did what they thought they were supposed to do. The decision did not rest on the fact that the suspect's Fourth Amendment rights were violated by a search conducted with an improper warrant. Thus, the Supreme Court's creation of exceptions to the exclusionary rule has given police officers the flexibility to make specific kinds of errors without jeopardizing the admissibility of evidence that will help establish a defendant's guilt.

checkpoint

17. What are some of the criticisms of the exclusionary rule?
18. What are the exceptions to the exclusionary rule?

A QUESTION OF ETHICS

YOU ARE A detective in a city police department. The chief detective tells you that a robbery suspect is in an interrogation room and that you should begin questioning the suspect. As you head toward the interrogation rooms, you ask at the front desk whether the suspect has already been informed of his *Miranda* rights. The desk sergeant tells you that the suspect has signed a form waiving his right to the presence of counsel after being informed of his *Miranda* rights.

You notice that the suspect is sweating and shaking, as if experiencing drug withdrawal symptoms, while you ask him about why he was caught with an unlicensed gun and $600 in cash. The suspect talks freely in response to your questions.

"Yeah, I robbed that guy at the ATM machine on Broadway and Second Avenue. It isn't the first time. I need money and I don't know what else to do. I wish I didn't shoot that guy last month by the First National Bank on Main Street. It was an accident. He tried to run and that made me mad so . . ."

The suspect stopped talking in mid-sentence. "Hey, aren't you supposed to tell me about my right to remain silent and all that stuff from TV?" He suddenly glares at you.

"You were already told about those rights and you signed a paper saying that you understood all that and that you wanted to talk."

"No , I didn't."

"Yes, you did. Here I'll show you." When you leave the interrogation room to get the form from the desk sergeant, the suspect yells after you, "I'm not saying anything else without a lawyer."

"Hey, Sarge. This guy not only confessed to the robbery, he also confessed to that unsolved Main Street shooting last month. Give me his sheet. I need to wave it in his face because he's claiming that he was never Mirandized and now he wants to lawyer up."

At the front desk, the sergeant looks surprised. His voice has a note of panic, "It wasn't the robbery guy in room two who signed the sheet. It was the rape suspect in room one. I thought you were going to room one. But look, the arresting officer or somebody else must have read him his rights before he got here. He has already confessed. No one is going to believe a drug addict who claims that he wasn't read his rights when we say otherwise."

Critical Thinking and Analysis

What would you do? Would you start the questioning over again after reading him his rights or would you try to use his confession against him? What if the previous shooting was an unsolved murder for which there was no evidence other than the confession that you just heard? Imagine that you are explaining your decision to your best friend in the police department. What would you say?

Researching the Internet

 To read about a Supreme Court decision concerning a case in which officers obtained a confession without providing *Miranda* warnings and then gave the warnings before seeking to get the suspect to repeat the confession, see *Missouri v. Seibert (2004)* by going to *The American System of Criminal Justice* 12e companion site at academic.cengage.com/criminaljustice/cole.

SUMMARY

Know the extent of police officers' authority to stop and search people and their vehicles

- The Supreme Court has defined rules for the circumstances and justifications for stops, searches, and arrests in light of the Fourth Amendment's prohibition on "unreasonable searches and seizures."

- Most stops must be supported by reasonable suspicion; arrests, like search warrants, must be supported by enough information to constitute probable cause.

Understand when and how police officers seek warrants in order to conduct searches and make arrests

- In order to obtain a warrant, police officers present an affidavit (sworn statement) verifying the information that they present to the judge that they believe constitutes probable cause to search or make an arrest.

Know whether police officers can look in people's windows or their backyards to see if evidence of a crime exists there

- The plain view doctrine permits officers to examine visually and use as evidence anything that is in open sight when they are in a place where they are legally permitted to be.

Analyze the situations in which police officers can conduct searches without obtaining a warrant

- Searches are considered "reasonable" and may be conducted without warrants in specific "special needs" circumstances that have purposes beyond those of normal law enforcement. For example, borders and airports often require searches without warrants.

- Limited searches may be conducted without warrants when officers have reasonable suspicions to justify a stop and frisk for weapons on the streets; when officers make a lawful arrest; under exigent circumstances; when people voluntarily consent to searches of their persons or property; and in certain situations involving automobiles.

Understand the purpose of the privilege against compelled self-incrimination

▪ The Fifth Amendment privilege against compelled self-incrimination helps protect citizens against violence and coercion by police as well as maintain the legitimacy and integrity of the legal system.

▪ The Supreme Court's decision in *Miranda v. Arizona* requires officers to inform suspects of specific rights before custodial questioning, although officers have adapted their practices to accommodate this rule and several exceptions have been created.

Understand the exclusionary rule and the situations in which it applies

▪ In barring the use of illegally obtained evidence in court, the exclusionary rule is designed to deter police from violating citizens' rights during criminal investigations.

▪ The Supreme Court has created several exceptions to the exclusionary rule, including the "good faith" and "inevitable discovery" exceptions.

QUESTIONS FOR REVIEW

1. What are the requirements for police officers with respect to stops, searches, arrests, and warrants?

2. What are the plain view doctrine and the open fields doctrine?

3. Under what circumstances are warrantless searches permissible?

4. How have police officers adapted to the requirements of *Miranda v. Arizona*?

5. What are the exceptions to the exclusionary rule?

KEY TERMS AND CASES

affidavit (p. 291)
exclusionary rule (p. 310)
exigent circumstances (p. 300)
"good faith" exception (p. 312)
"inevitable discovery" exception (p. 313)
open fields doctrine (p. 293)
plain view doctrine (p. 292)
probable cause (p. 291)
"public safety" exception (p. 307)

reasonable expectation of privacy (p. 289)
reasonable suspicion (p. 290)
search (p. 289)
seizure (p. 289)
stop (p. 290)
stop-and-frisk search (p. 297)
totality of circumstances test (p. 292)
Chimel v. California (1969) (p. 300)
Escobedo v. Illinois (1964) (p. 305)

Florida v. J. L. (2000) (p. 297)
Mapp v. Ohio (1961) (p. 311)
Miranda v. Arizona (1966) (p. 305)

Nix v. Williams (1984) (p. 313)
Terry v. Ohio (1968) (p. 296)
United States v. Drayton (2002) (p. 301)

FOR FURTHER READING

Amar, Akhil Reed. 1997. *The Constitution and Criminal Procedure: First Principles*. New Haven, CT: Yale University Press. A detailed examination of the Fourth and Fifth Amendments, with suggestions for remedies other than the exclusionary rule.

Grano, Joseph D. 1996. *Confessions, Truth, and the Law*. Ann Arbor: University of Michigan Press. An analysis of the law related to police interrogation and confessions, including criticisms of *Miranda* rights.

Smith, Christopher E. 2003. *Criminal Procedure*. Belmont, CA: Wadsworth. A detailed review of constitutional rights affecting police investigations and trial processes.

Uviller, H. Richard. 1996. *Virtual Justice: The Flawed Prosecution of Crime in America*. New Haven, CT: Yale University Press. A critical evaluation of the exclusionary rule and other aspects of rights in the criminal justice process, with an emphasis on assessing how legal rules work in the actual processes conducted by police and prosecutors.

White, Welsh S. *Miranda's Waning Protections*. Ann Arbor, MI: University of Michigan Press, 2003. An analysis of police officers' adaptations that facilitate effective interrogation in a manner that avoids interference by *Miranda* as well as a discussion of Supreme Court decisions that give police officers more flexibility in questioning suspects.

GOING ONLINE

For an up-to-date list of web links, go to *The American System of Criminal Justice* 12e companion site at academic .cengage.com/criminaljustice/cole.

1. Read online advice posted on the Internet by defense lawyers concerning how to handle police officers' requests that you consent to do a search. What, if anything, did you learn from this advice? Is it proper for lawyers to provide information to the public that might limit the ability of police officers to do the searches that they want to do?

2. Go to the website of the Criminal Justice Legal Foundation to read the written arguments its lawyers submitted to the Supreme Court that were critical of the *Miranda* rule when the Court decided the *Dickerson* case (2000). Do you think that there are reasons for the Supreme Court to reconsider imposing the *Miranda* requirement on police?

3. Read Professor Yale Kamisar's defense of the exclusionary rule. How do you evaluate Kamisar's defense of the rule? He criticizes proposed changes to the rule. Do you agree with any proposed changes? Why?

CHECKPOINT ANSWERS

1. *What is a search?*

A government intrusion into an individual's reasonable expectation of privacy.

2. *What justification do police officers need to make a stop?*

Reasonable suspicion of wrongdoing based on articulable facts.

3. *What is the difference between an arrest and a stop?*

An arrest requires probable cause and involves taking someone into custody for prosecution, while a stop is a brief deprivation of freedom of movement based on reasonable suspicion.

4. *What do police officers need to demonstrate in order to obtain a warrant?*

The existence of probable cause by the totality of circumstances in the case.

5. *What is the plain view doctrine?*

Officers can examine and use as evidence anything that is in open sight at a place where they are legally permitted to be.

6. *May officers use senses other than sight to find evidence of crime without a warrant?*

Officers may use their sense of smell, especially for distinctive odors such as that of marijuana, but the Supreme Court has limited the authority to feel and manipulate luggage and other objects.

7. *In what situations do law enforcement's special needs justify stopping an automobile without reasonable suspicion?*

Warrantless stops of automobiles are permitted at sobriety checkpoints (unless barred within a specific state by its own supreme court) and international borders or when there is reasonable suspicion of a traffic violation or other wrongdoing.

8. *What knowledge must an officer possess in order to conduct a stop-and-frisk search on the streets?*

A reasonable suspicion based on personal observation or information from a reliable informant that an individual is armed and involved in possible criminal activity.

9. *Where can officers search when conducting a warrantless search incident to a lawful arrest?*

Officers can search in the immediate area of the arrestee and do a protective sweep of rooms where the arrestee may have recently been.

10. *What are "exigent circumstances"?*

Urgent situations in which evidence may be destroyed, a suspect may escape, or the public would be endangered if officers took the time to seek a warrant for a search or arrest.

11. *What two elements must be present for a valid consent to permit a warrantless search?*

The person must do it voluntarily and must have the proper authority to consent.

12. *What defines the scope of officers' authority to search containers in automobiles?*

Officers can search any container or closed portion of an automobile for which probable cause exists to justify the search.

13. *What are* Miranda *rights?*

Before custodial interrogation, officers must inform suspects of the right to remain silent, the prosecution's authority to use any of the suspect's statements, the right to the presence of an attorney during questioning, and the right to have an attorney appointed if the suspect cannot afford one.

14. *What is the "public safety" exception?*

Officers can ask questions of suspects in custody without first providing *Miranda* warnings if public safety would be threatened by taking the time to supply the warnings.

15. *How have police officers changed their practices in light of* Miranda?

Officers ask questions before suspects are in custody, use techniques to pretend to befriend or empathize with suspects being questioned, and give suspects misinformation about the existence of evidence demonstrating guilt.

16. *Why was the exclusionary rule created and eventually applied to the states?*

The exclusionary rule was created to deter officers from violating people's rights, and the Supreme Court considers it an essential component of the Fourth and Fifth Amendments.

17. *What are some of the criticisms of the exclusionary rule?*

The rule is criticized as punishing the prosecutor and society rather than the police, imposing excessive costs on society, depriving the legal process of relevant evidence, and permitting some guilty people to go free.

18. *What are the exceptions to the exclusionary rule?*

A "good faith" exception in warrant situations, an "inevitable discovery" exception when evidence would have been discovered by the police anyway, and no application of exclusion in grand jury proceedings and other contexts that do not involve the proof of guilt in a criminal prosecution.

Courts

© Steve Dunwell/Getty Images/Stone

In a democracy, the arrest of a person is but the first part of a complex process designed to separate the guilty from the innocent. Part 3 examines the process by which guilt is determined in accordance with the law's requirements, as well as the processes and underlying philosophies of the punishment that further separates the convicted from the acquitted. Here we look at the work of prosecutors, defense attorneys, bondsmen, probation officers, and judges to understand the contribution each makes toward the ultimate decisions. In the adjudicatory stage, the goals of an administrative system blunt the force of the adversarial process prescribed by law. Although courtroom activities receive the most media attention, most decisions relating to the disposition of a case take place in less public surroundings. After the sentencing, the case recedes even further from the public eye. After studying these chapters, think about whether justice is served by processes that are more like bargaining than like adversarial combat between two lawyers. Also consider whether the punishments our courts hand out are doing the job they are supposed to be doing in punishing offenders.

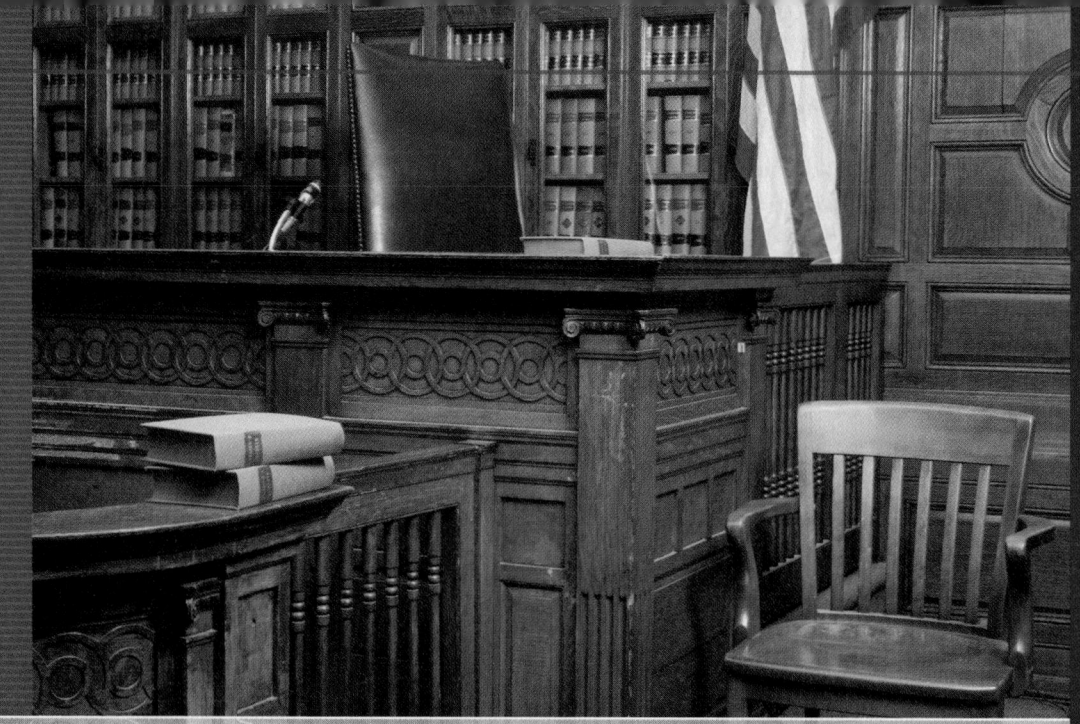

CHAPTER **9**

Courts and Pretrial Processes

LEARNING OBJECTIVES

→ Recognize the structure of the American court system

→ Analyze the qualities that we desire in a judge

→ Identify the ways that American judges are selected

→ Understand the pretrial process in criminal cases

→ Recognize how the bail system operates

→ Understand the context of pretrial detention

On being arrested for a crime, suspects enter the judicial processes that will determine whether they are held in jail until their trials and, ultimately, whether they are guilty and must be punished. The processes of arrest and booking are typically the same for poor people accused of street crimes as for wealthy people accused of white-collar crimes. However, their ability to gain release from jail, while their cases are processed through the courts, often differs.

Police investigators in Pinellas County, Florida, looked closely at an automobile crash on August 26, 2007, to determine who was at fault and whether criminal charges should be filed. A Toyota Supra went out of control, crashed into a palm tree, and left the passenger, a 23-year-old ex-Marine and Iraq War veteran, with paralysis and permanent brain damage. After weeks of interviewing witnesses, calculating the vehicle's speed, and testing the driver for alcohol consumption, the police submitted their report to the prosecutor. Based on the investigation, the prosecutor charged the driver, who was not injured in the crash, with the crime of "reckless driving involving serious bodily injury" (Porter, 2007). The felony was punishable by a sentence of up to five years in prison.

Because the police and prosecutor concluded that the driver was drag racing at the time that he lost control of the vehicle, a warrant

was issued for the driver's arrest in November 2007. As a result, the driver voluntarily turned himself into the Clearwater Police Department. He was photographed, fingerprinted, and searched, just like anyone else who is arrested. However, he was not just like anyone else with respect to the news media attention directed to his case. The criminal defendant being processed for transfer to the Pinellas County Jail was 17-year-old Nick Bollea, the son of wrestling superstar Hulk Hogan and a television celebrity in his own right from his role in his family's reality television series, "Hogan Knows Best" (El-Khoury, 2007).

Bollea was handcuffed and taken to the jail by two police officers. After being processed at the jail, he remained there briefly until his parents posted the $10,000 bail amount required for him to gain release pending the processing of his case through the courts (El-Khoury, 2007).

In May 2008, after several months of plea negotiations between the prosecutor and Bollea's defense attorney, Bollea entered a plea of "no contest" (*nolo contendere*), which permits a defendant to accept punishment for the crime without explicitly admitting guilt. The judge sentenced Bollea to serve an 8-month jail sentence, followed by five years of probation, including three years during which he will be prohibited from obtaining a driver's license and must attend classes for drunken drivers. Immediately after the sentence was announced in the courtroom, officers confiscated his tie and belt as they led him away to begin serving his jail sentence (McCartney, 2008). Bollea had avoided pretrial detention in jail because his family had enough money to pay his bail. However, after being convicted and sentenced to incarceration for less than one year, he was taken back to the very same jail that his wealth had permitted him to avoid in the immediate aftermath of his arrest.

Nick Bollea's cases raises a number of interesting issues about the criminal justice system. Should a 17-year-old adolescent serve a sentence in the same county jail that houses adults who have committed serious offenses? Should judges permit defendants to plead "no contest" rather than "guilty" in an effort to avoid automatic liability in lawsuits filed against them by their victims? These are the kinds of questions that will be addressed in later chapters. For the purposes of this chapter, however, think about the amount of bail and the bail process. Is $10,000 enough as a bail amount for an offense when someone's recklessness has profoundly and permanently injured someone else? Is $10,000 enough as a bail amount for someone from a rich family who can easily pay without any effort? Remember these questions as we later look at the purposes of bail and the way in which bail is set.

For perspective on Nick Bollea's bail, we should compare his situation with that of another defendant. In April 2008, Tracy Tan, age 37, was arrested in Naperville, Illinois, where she worked as a psychic, and charged with defrauding people out of thousands of dollars by using Tarot card readings and fortune-telling to convince them that they were cursed. She was placed in pretrial detention at DuPage County Jail and bail was set at $100,000. However, because DuPage County has a "10 percent bail" system, which we will discuss later in this chapter, she could gain pretrial release by putting up $10,000 and promising to be liable for the remaining $90,000 if she should flee or otherwise fail to appear for her court hearings. Unlike Nick Bollea, Tracy Tan could not pay $10,000 to gain release. Despite being presumptively innocent until the charges against her had been proved, she was destined to sit in jail for at least one month until her first court hearing and then for additional months afterward as her case was processed through the court system (Golz, 2008).

When you look at this comparison, does the bail system seem fair? The wealthy defendant whose reckless actions permanently injured an American war veteran gains pretrial release while a woman merely accused of stealing money must sit in jail. The total bail amount in a case that produced paralysis and permanent brain injuries is only $10,000 while the total bail for someone accused of financial crimes is set at $100,000. Does this make sense?

When defendants are treated differently with respect to bail, the public may begin to think that the bail process clashes with the important American value of equal treatment. Moreover, when defendants cannot gain pretrial release, questions concerning liberty—another important American value—often arise.

Think about the bail amounts. Which one was accused of the most serious crime? Is that the same one who might be most likely to flee? Which one might pose the greatest danger to the community while released on bail? These are not easy questions to answer. No scientific formula can permit accurate predictions about criminal suspects' behavior; judges must make the best decisions they can, case by case.

When people are arrested, they enter the court system, where the decisions of judges, prosecutors, and defense attorneys largely determine their fate. Pretrial decisions can affect the ultimate outcome of a case. If defendants are not released on bail, they might have trouble helping their lawyers prepare arguments and evidence for the defense. In some cases, additional pretrial decisions must be made about the defendant's mental competence. Defendants found to lack the necessary mental competence to stand trial might never be convicted of a crime, even in homicide cases, yet they might still spend years confined in a state institution. Whether or not to perform a pretrial competency evaluation is just one key decision that can affect the defendant's ultimate fate. Important decisions take place in several other pretrial processes as well. These processes include formal events, such as preliminary hearings to determine if enough evidence exists to pursue criminal charges, and informal interactions, such as plea-bargaining discussions that might resolve the case prior to trial.

In this chapter, we examine courts, the setting in which criminal defendants cases are processed. We look at judges and their important role in criminal cases. In particular, we look at pretrial processes that help determine the fates of criminal defendants.

THE STRUCTURE OF AMERICAN COURTS

As we have seen, the United States has a dual court system, with separate federal and state court systems. Other countries have a single national court system, but American rules and traditions permit states to create their own court systems to handle most legal matters, including most crimes.

The federal courts oversee a limited range of criminal cases. For example, they deal with people accused of violating the criminal laws of the national government. Counterfeiting, kidnapping, smuggling, and drug trafficking are examples of federal crimes. But such cases account for only a small portion of the criminal cases that pass through American courts each year. For every offender sentenced to incarceration by federal courts, more than ten offenders are sent to prisons and jails by state courts, because most crimes are defined by state laws (BJS, 2004g). This disparity may grow wider as federal law enforcement agencies increasingly emphasize antiterrorism activities rather than traditional crime-control investigations. The gap is even greater for misdemeanors, because state courts bear primary responsibility for processing the lesser offenses, such as disorderly conduct, that arise on a daily basis.

State supreme courts each interpret their own state's constitution and statutes and ensure that lower courts within the state follow those interpretations. The U.S. Supreme Court oversees both federal and state court systems by interpreting the U.S. Constitution, which protects the rights of defendants in federal and state criminal cases.

The issues of complexity and coordination that the country's decentralized courts face are compounded by a third court system that operates in several

Dick Anthony Heller speaks to reporters outside the U.S. Supreme Court prior to winning his case to strike down Washington, D.C.'s broad prohibition against keeping handguns in private homes for self-protection. Heller's case in 2008 established a limited Second Amendment right to own firearms in federal jurisdictions. Does the Supreme Court possess too much power to strike down laws that are created by the people's elected representatives in city councils, state legislatures, and Congress?

© Roger L. Wollenberg/UPI /Landov

jurisdiction
The geographic territory or legal boundaries within which control may be exercised; the range of a court's authority.

You can learn about all three levels of the federal court system at the federal judiciary's website. To link to this website, go to *The American System of Criminal Justice* 12e companion site at academic.cengage.com/criminaljustice/cole.

trial courts of limited jurisdiction
Criminal courts with trial jurisdiction over misdemeanor cases and preliminary matters in felony cases. Sometimes these courts hold felony trials that may result in penalties below a specified limit.

trial courts of general jurisdiction
Criminal courts with jurisdiction over all offenses, including felonies. In some states, these courts also hear appeals.

appellate courts
Courts that do not try criminal cases but hear appeals of decisions of lower courts.

states. Native Americans have tribal courts, whose authority is endorsed by congressional statutes and Supreme Court decisions. With **jurisdiction** over their own people on tribal land, these tribal courts permit Native American judges to apply their people's cultural values in resolving civil lawsuits and processing certain criminal offenses (Vicenti, 1995).

Both the federal and state court systems have trial and appellate courts. There are three levels of courts: appellate courts, trial courts of general jurisdiction, and trial courts of limited jurisdiction.

Cases begin in a trial court, which handles determinations of guilt and sentencing. **Trial courts of limited jurisdiction** handle only misdemeanors and lawsuits for small amounts of money. Felony cases and all other civil lawsuits are heard in **trial courts of general jurisdiction**. These are the courts in which jury trials take place and judges impose prison sentences. All federal cases begin in the general jurisdiction trial courts, the U.S. district courts.

Cases move to intermediate **appellate courts** if defendants claim that errors by police or the trial court contributed to their convictions. Further appeals can be filed with a state supreme court or the U.S. Supreme Court, depending on which court system the case is in and what kind of legal argument is being made. All states have courts of last resort (usually called "state supreme courts"), and all but a few have an intermediate appellate court (usually called "courts of appeals"). In the federal system, the U.S. Supreme Court is the court of last resort, and the U.S. circuit courts of appeals are the intermediate appellate courts.

Although this basic three-tiered structure operates throughout the United States, the number of courts, their names, and their specific functions vary widely. For example, the federal system has no trial courts of limited jurisdiction. In state systems, 13,000 trial courts of limited jurisdiction handle traffic cases, small claims, misdemeanors, and other less serious matters. These courts handle 90 percent of all criminal cases. The federal system begins with the U.S. district courts, its trial courts of general jurisdiction. In the states, these courts have a variety of names (circuit, district, superior, and others) and are reserved for felony cases or substantial lawsuits. These are the courts in which trials take place, judges rule on evidence, and juries issue verdicts. Figure 9.1 shows the basic structure of the dual court system.

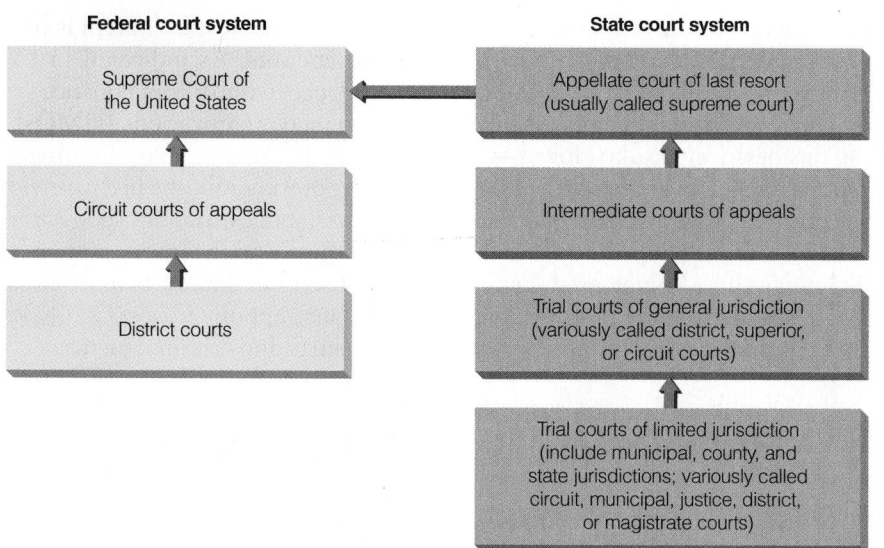

FIGURE 9.1

The dual court system of the United States and routes of appeal
Whether a case enters through the federal or state court system depends on which law has been broken. The right of appeal to a higher court exists in either system.

Some states have reformed their court systems by simplifying the number and types of courts, while others still support a confusing assortment of lower courts. Figure 9.2 contrasts the reformed court structure of Alaska with Georgia's unreformed system. Both follow the three-tiered model, but Georgia has more courts and a more complex system for determining which court will handle which kind of case.

American trial courts are highly decentralized. Local political influences and community values affect the courts in many ways. Local officials determine their resources, residents make up the staff, and operations are managed so as to fit community needs. Only in a few small states is the court system organized on a statewide basis, with a central administration and state funding. In most of the country, the criminal courts operate under the state penal code but are staffed, managed, and financed by county or city government. The federal courts, by contrast, have central administration and funding, although judges in each district help shape their own courts' practices and procedures.

Lower courts, especially at the state level, do not always display the dignity and formal procedures of general jurisdiction trial courts and appellate courts. They are not necessarily courts of record, which keep a detailed account of proceedings. Instead, they may function rather informally. In most urban areas, these courts process seemingly endless numbers of people, and each defendant's "day in court" usually lasts only a few minutes.

This informality may bother the public, who expect their local courts to adhere to the standards that reflect American values of justice. Many people are critical when the courts do not meet these ideals. Because the courts produce the outcomes in criminal cases, especially determinations of guilt and punishment,

 On the website of the National Center for State Courts, you can find an excellent visual presentation of the structure and duties of each court within every state court system. To link to this website, go to *The American System of Criminal Justice* 12e companion site at academic .cengage.com/criminaljustice/cole.

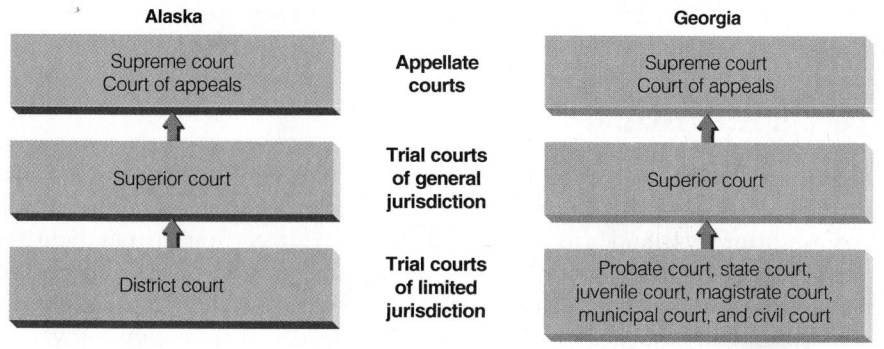

FIGURE 9.2

Court structures of Alaska (reformed) and Georgia (unreformed)
Reformers have called on states to reduce the number of courts, standardize their names, and clarify their jurisdictions.

Source: David B. Rottman, Carol R. Flango, Melissa T. Cantrell, Randall Hansen, and Neil LaFountain, *State Court Organization 1998* (Washington, DC: U.S. Government Printing Office, 2000), 9, 15.

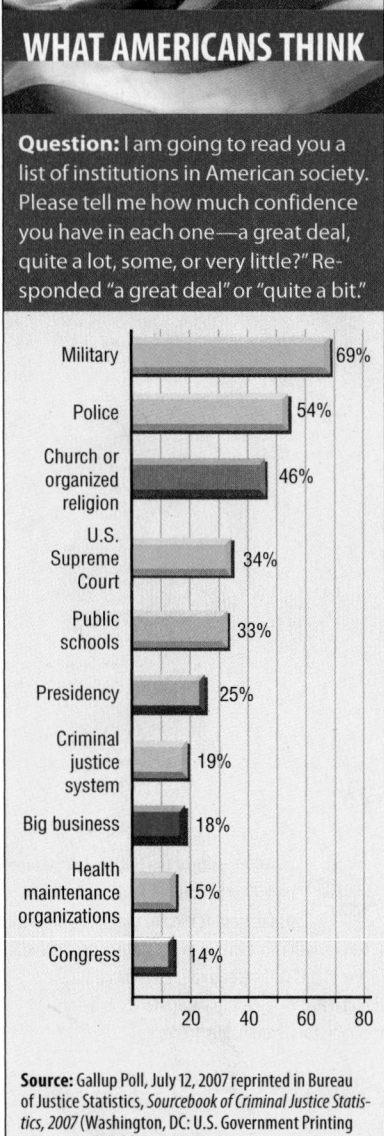

Many states have agencies responsible for management of their court systems. For example, you can learn about Colorado's Office of the State Court Administrator at their website. To link to this website, go to *The American System of Criminal Justice* 12e companion site at academic.cengage.com/criminaljustice/cole.

they are central to people's assessments of whether the justice system is too soft on offenders or unfair in its treatment of defendants. As indicated in "What Americans Think," in 2007, Americans' confidence in the criminal justice system was so low that only Congress, health maintenance organizations (HMOs), and big business were ranked lower—but just barely. Because people demonstrated a relatively high level of confidence in the police, presumably the negative view of the criminal justice system was focused on courts, judges, and lawyers. Although many Americans express dissatisfaction with courts and the justice system, other Americans have volunteered their time in an effort to make courts more effective. As you read the Doing Your Part box about court-appointed special advocates, think about how these volunteers may affect courts and criminal justice.

EFFECTIVE MANAGEMENT OF THE STATE COURTS

Throughout the twentieth century and beyond, reformers attempted to change the structure, administration, and financing of the state courts so the courts can deal more effectively with their huge caseloads. Problems with inadequate resources and the uneven quality of judges hurt the courts' effectiveness (Abrahamson, 2004). There is a need for professional court administrators with expertise and training (Hartley and Bates, 2006). However, people often see the fragmented structure of state courts as the biggest barrier to justice. Proposed solutions include the creation of a unified court system with four goals:

1. Eliminating overlapping and conflicting jurisdictional boundaries
2. Creating a hierarchical and centralized court structure with administrative responsibility held by a chief justice and a court of last resort
3. Having the courts funded by state government instead of local counties and cities
4. Creating a separate civil service personnel system run by a state court administrator

These goals stand at the forefront of the movement to promote the efficiency and fairness of state courts. However, local political interests often resist court reform. Local courts have long been used as a source of jobs to reward people loyal to the political party in power. Centralization of court administration and professionalization of court personnel would eliminate the opportunities to use court jobs in this manner.

checkpoint

1. What is the dual court system?
2. What different categories of courts exist within each court system?
3. What does it mean for courts to be decentralized?
4. What are the main goals of advocates of judicial reform?
   (Answers are at the end of the chapter.)

TO BE A JUDGE

People tend to see judges as the most powerful actors in the criminal justice process. Their rulings and sentencing decisions influence the actions of police, defense attorneys, and prosecutors. If judges treat certain crimes lightly, for example, police and prosecutors may be less inclined to arrest and prosecute people who commit those offenses. Although judges are thought of primarily in connection with trials, they do some of their work—such as signing warrants, setting bail, arraigning defendants, accepting guilty pleas, and scheduling cases—outside the formal trial process.

More than any other person in the system, the judge is expected to embody justice, ensuring the defendant's right to due process and fair treatment. The prosecutor and the defense attorney each represent a "side" in a criminal case. By contrast, the judge's black robe and gavel are symbols of impartiality. Both inside and outside the courthouse, the judge is supposed to act according to a well-defined role. People expect judges to make careful, consistent decisions that uphold the ideal of equal justice for all citizens.

Who Becomes a Judge?

In U.S. society, the position of judge, even at the lowest level of the judicial hierarchy, carries a high status. Many lawyers take a significant cut in pay to assume a position on the bench. Public service, political power, and prestige in the community may matter more than wealth to those who aspire to the judiciary. The ability to control one's own work schedule is an additional attraction for lawyers interested in becoming judges. Unlike private practice attorneys, who often work over 40 hours per week preparing cases and counseling clients, judges can usually control their own working hours and schedules. Although judges face heavy caseloads, they frequently decide for themselves when to go home at the end of the workday.

Historically, the vast majority of judges have been white men with strong political connections. Women and members of minority groups had few opportunities to enter the legal profession prior to the 1960s and thus were seldom considered for judgeships. Although women judges have

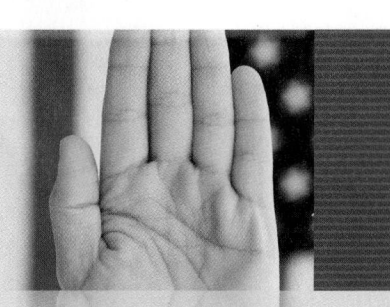

DOING YOUR PART

Court-Appointed Special Advocates

BECAUSE COURTS ARE institutions operated by trained professionals with special expertise in law, imagining how the average citizen can become involved and make a contribution is challenging. Some citizens are summoned to court to serve as jurors, but few others have contact with courts unless they are brought into a case as a defendant, witness, or victim. There is, however, a little known but growing program that permits citizens to make a contribution: CASA, which stands for court-appointed special advocates.

In Boston, Massachusetts, Joanne Beauchamp received a special award in a "Light of Hope" ceremony at the local courthouse. Along with 100 other people, she volunteered her time to serve in the CASA program of the Suffolk County Juvenile Court Probation Department. As in CASA programs at courthouses throughout the country, she spent several hours every week as a court-appointed advocate for children in child abuse and neglect cases. After receiving training on the law of child abuse and neglect, on interviewing, and on advocacy, she became an advocate for children with specific needs. The CASA volunteer advances the best interests of each child by interviewing teachers, foster parents, and others; monitoring compliance with court orders; facilitating contacts with social services agencies; and reporting to the court on the status of the child. About 55,000 CASA volunteers in 948 communities serve more than 200,000 children throughout the nation.

Does CASA give volunteers the opportunity to affect the criminal justice system? This is a valid question, because CASA programs are typically connected not to criminal cases per se but to family courts or probate courts that have jurisdiction over child custody, parental rights, and related matters. However, CASA volunteers clearly do contribute to the criminal justice system. First, they are the "eyes and ears" of the court in supervising the child's best interests. Thus, they may discover information about criminal offenses involving child abuse and neglect. Second, by attempting to protect abused and neglected children, these volunteers try to ensure a better life for them. This will likely help some children to avoid influences and contexts that might lead them to commit crimes later in life.

Sources: Susan W. Miller, "Career Counselor," *Los Angeles Times*, June 9, 2002 (http://www. latimes.com); "SB Child Advocate Honored at 'Light of Hope' Ceremony," *South Boston Online*, May 2000 (http://www .southbostononline.com); "Be the Difference," *Grand Magazine*, April 2007, pp. 54–5; "We Made A Difference," *All You Magazine*, May 4, 2007, p. 89.

Researching the Internet

 For more information on court-appointed special advocates, see the national CASA website. To link to this website, go to *The American System of Criminal Justice* 12e companion site at academic .cengage.com/criminaljustice/cole.

become more numerous, they still face challenges in running for election or being selected by a governor (Williams, 2006; Reid, 2004). In recent decades, political factors in many cities dictated that judges be drawn from specific racial, religious, and ethnic groups as political party leaders sought to gain the support of various segments of the voting public. Currently, 10.1 percent of state judges are members of racial and ethnic minority groups, including 5.9 percent of judges that are

Like all judges, Circuit Court Judge Nikki Clark of Leon County, Florida, is expected to "embody justice," ensuring that the right to due process is respected and that defendants are treated fairly. What qualifications should someone possess in order to assume the important role and responsibilities of a judge?

© Najlah Feanny/Corbis

African American and 2.8 percent that are Latino (American Bar Association, 2008).

Comparing the racial and ethnic makeup of the judiciary with that of the defendants in urban courts raises many questions. Will people believe that decisions about guilt and punishment are being made in an unfair manner if middle-aged white men have nearly all the power to make judgments about people from other segments of society? Will people think that punishment is being imposed on behalf of a privileged segment of society rather than on behalf of the entire, diverse U.S. society?

Within these questions lurks an issue of American values. Americans often claim that equality, fairness, and equal opportunity are important values and, indeed, the equal protection clause in the Fourteenth Amendment of the Constitution demonstrates a formal commitment to use law to combat discrimination. However, the political connections necessary to gain judgeships continue to disadvantage women and members of racial minority groups in many communities. Because judges symbolize the law as well as make important decisions about law, the lack of diversity in the judiciary provides a visible contrast with American values related to equal opportunity.

checkpoint

5. What is the image of the judge in the public's eye?
6. Why might it be important for judges to represent different segments of society?

Functions of the Judge

Although people usually think that the judge's job is to preside at trials, in reality the work of most judges extends to all aspects of the judicial process. Defendants see a judge whenever decisions about their future are being made: when bail is set, pretrial motions are made, guilty pleas are accepted, a trial is conducted, a sentence is pronounced, and appeals are filed (see Figure 9.3). However, judges also perform administrative tasks outside the courtroom. Judges have three major roles: adjudicator, negotiator, and administrator.

FIGURE 9.3

Actions of a trial court judge in processing a felony case

Throughout the process, the judge ensures that legal standards are upheld; he or she maintains courtroom decorum, protects the rights of the accused, meets the requirement of a speedy trial, and ensures that case records are maintained properly.

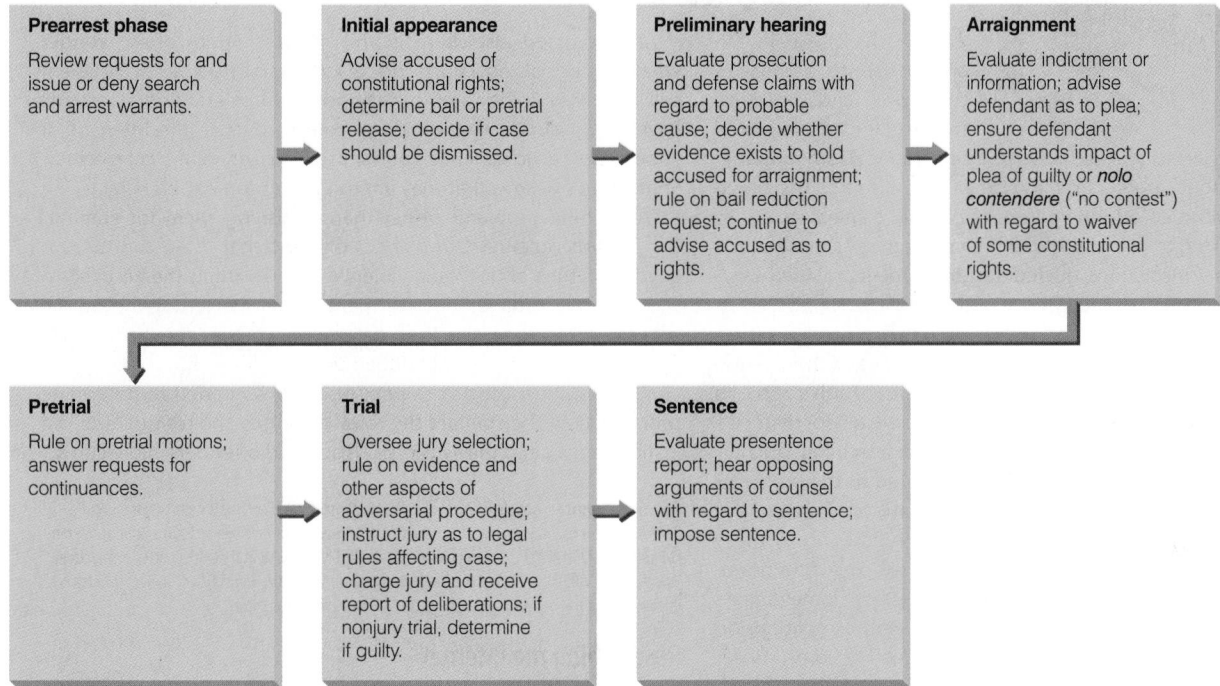

Prearrest phase	**Initial appearance**	**Preliminary hearing**	**Arraignment**
Review requests for and issue or deny search and arrest warrants.	Advise accused of constitutional rights; determine bail or pretrial release; decide if case should be dismissed.	Evaluate prosecution and defense claims with regard to probable cause; decide whether evidence exists to hold accused for arraignment; rule on bail reduction request; continue to advise accused as to rights.	Evaluate indictment or information; advise defendant as to plea; ensure defendant understands impact of plea of guilty or *nolo contendere* ("no contest") with regard to waiver of some constitutional rights.

Pretrial	**Trial**	**Sentence**
Rule on pretrial motions; answer requests for continuances.	Oversee jury selection; rule on evidence and other aspects of adversarial procedure; instruct jury as to legal rules affecting case; charge jury and receive report of deliberations; if nonjury trial, determine if guilty.	Evaluate presentence report; hear opposing arguments of counsel with regard to sentence; impose sentence.

Adjudicator

Judges must assume a neutral stance in overseeing the contest between the prosecution and the defense. They must apply the law so that the rights of the accused are upheld in decisions about detention, plea, trial, and sentence. Judges have a certain amount of discretion in performing these tasks—for example, in setting bail—but they must do so according to the law. They must avoid any conduct that could appear biased (Goldschmidt and Shaman, 1996).

Negotiator

Many decisions that determine the fates of defendants take place outside of public view in the judge's private chambers. These decisions are reached through negotiations between prosecutors and defense attorneys about plea bargains, sentencing, and bail conditions. Judges spend much of their time in their chambers talking with prosecutors and defense attorneys. They often encourage the parties to work out a guilty plea or agree to proceed in a certain way. The judge sometimes acts as referee, keeping both sides on track in accordance with the law. Sometimes the judge takes a more active part in the negotiations, suggesting terms for an agreement or even pressuring one side to accept an agreement.

Administrator

A seldom-recognized function of most judges is managing the courthouse. In urban areas, professional court administrators rather than judges may actually direct the people who keep records, schedule cases, and do the many other jobs

NEW DIRECTIONS in CRIMINAL JUSTICE POLICY

Problem-Solving Courts

IN 1989, A JUDGE in Miami began to emphasize treatment and intensive monitoring of low-level substance abusers as an alternative to incarceration. From these beginnings emerged drug courts and other specialized courts aimed at diverting troubled offenders from traditional criminal sanctions while also seeking to help them with their problems. As these courts spread to other jurisdictions, the federal government provided funding to encourage new developments and to evaluate the success of such programs.

Similar efforts began to surface. In the first years of the twenty-first century, many cities also developed mental health courts. In these courts, judges placed mentally ill people arrested for minor offenses into treatment programs and employment training. Anchorage, Alaska, experimented with a court dedicated to the problems of veterans, some of whom were arrested regularly for drunkenness, substance abuse, and disorderly conducted. In addition to these courts that address minor criminal offenses, New York City developed a parallel court for civil matters that focuses on homelessness and attempts to prevent evictions, encourage employment opportunities, and solve disputes between tenants and landlords. As described by two observers, in these courts "judges are cheerleaders and social workers as much as jurists" (Eaton and Kaufman, 2005).

Research shows that drug courts can be effective in helping substance abusers and keeping them from going to jail (Carey and Finegan, 2004). However, these programs do not always save money for the justice system, because they require funds to monitor, test, and provide services for troubled people (D. C. Gottfredson, Najaka, and Kearley, 2003). Some other kinds of courts are too new to have been fully evaluated.

As discussed elsewhere in this chapter, critics often wonder whether specialized courts place judges into a role of problem solver for which they are not fully prepared. In addition, questions have arisen about whether these courts advance the interests of justice. Domestic violence courts, in particular, cause controversy. Some critics believe that they are too lenient on batterers by trying to solve their problems rather than punishing them for committing acts of violence. Other critics contend that these courts favor alleged victims of domestic violence by pressuring the accused to accept anger management treatment rather than letting the judicial processes take their course to determine whether the individual is actually guilty (Eaton and Kaufman, 2005).

As these new courts develop, research is needed to determine precisely how they impact the roles of judges, the resources of the justice system, and the lives of both accused offenders and victims.

Additional sources: Angela R. Gover, John M. MacDonald, and Geoffrey P. Alpert, "Combating Domestic Violence: Findings from an Evaluation of a Local Domestic Violence Court," *Criminology and Public Policy* 3 (2003): 109–31; Samira Jafari, "Mentally Ill Sent to Mental Health Courts," *Washington Post*, April 25, 2005 (http://www.washingtonpost.com); Matt Volz, "Court Offers Choices to Veterans," *Anchorage News-Miner*, August 8, 2004 (http://www.news-miner.com).

Researching the Internet

You can find more information about drug courts at the combined website of the National Association of Drug Court Professionals and the National Drug Court Institute. To link to this website, go to *The American System of Criminal Justice* 12e companion site at academic.cengage.com/criminaljustice/cole.

---

that keep a system functioning. But even then, judges remain in charge of their own courtroom and staff. In rural areas, where professional court administrators are not usually employed, the judge's administrative tasks may be more burdensome, including responsibility for labor relations, budgeting, and maintenance of the courthouse building.

As administrators, all judges must deal with political actors such as county commissioners, legislators, and members of the state executive bureaucracy. Chief judges in large courts sometimes also use their administrative powers to push other judges to cooperate in advancing the court's goals of processing cases efficiently (Jacob, 1973). For judges whose training as lawyers focused on courtroom advocacy skills, managing a complex organization with a sizable budget and many employees can pose a major challenge (C. E. Smith and Feldman, 2001).

Many observers argue that a fourth role of judges is emerging in some court systems. They see judges acting as "problem solvers" in newly developed courts that seek to address the problems of people arrested for drugs and other charges rather than send these people to jail or prison. As discussed in "New Directions in Criminal Justice Policy," many states and cities have created **drug courts** to

drug courts
Specialized courts that impose drug testing and counseling requirements on substance abusers and monitor their progress instead of sending them immediately to jail or prison.

divert substance abusers away from incarceration. Drug users caught in possession of drugs or for other lesser offenses may be required to appear in drug court regularly over the course of a year so that judges can monitor their progress with frequent drug tests, substance abuse counseling, and plans for education or employment. If these individuals violate the conditions imposed by the judge for drug testing or counseling, then the judge can give them a regular criminal punishment, such as a jail sentence. Other jurisdictions have mental health courts to help mentally ill people arrested for minor offenses (Cowell, Broner, and DuPont, 2004). Other kinds of specialized, problem-solving courts are also emerging, such as domestic violence courts and courts to handle homeless people's problems (Eaton and Kaufman, 2005).

Because judges typically have no training in psychology or social work, critics worry that the development of a problem-solver role will lead judges to make decisions about matters for which they lack expertise. Moreover, some fear that this new role will cause judges to lose sight of their obligation to impose punishment on individuals who have violated criminal laws (Nolan, 2003).

How to Become a Judge

The quality of justice depends to a great extent on the quality of those who make decisions about guilt and punishment. Because judges have the power to deprive a citizen of his or her liberty through a prison sentence, judges should be thoughtful, fair, and impartial. The character and experience of those selected for federal courts and state appellate courts are examined closely (S. Goldman and Slotnick, 1999). Trial judges in state criminal courts undergo less scrutiny. Ironically, these lower courts shape the public's image of a trial judge more than do other courts, because citizens have the most contact with judges there. When a judge is rude or hasty or allows the courtroom to become noisy and crowded, the public may lose confidence in the fairness and effectiveness of the criminal justice process (see the Close Up box on the next page).

Five methods are used to select state trial court judges: gubernatorial appointment, legislative selection, merit selection, **nonpartisan election**, and **partisan election**. Some states combine these methods; for example, in Pennsylvania a judge is initially elected by partisan election, but then at the end of the term there is a nonpartisan election (retention) for a second term. By contrast, federal judges are appointed by the president and confirmed by the U.S. Senate. Many of them are chosen as a result of their support for the president's political party and policy preferences (Epstein and Segal, 2007). Table 9.1 shows the method used in each of the states. All the methods bring up persistent concerns about the desired qualities of judges.

Selection by public voting occurs in more than half the states and has long been part of this nation's tradition. This method of judicial selection embodies the underlying American value of democracy, because it permits the citizens to control the choice of individuals who will be given the power to make decisions in civil and criminal cases. The fulfillment of this American value also helps to ensure that judges remain connected to the community and demonstrate sensitivity to the community's priorities and concerns. The American value of democracy may, however, have detrimental consequences in the judiciary if it pressures judges to follow a community's prejudices rather than make independent decisions using their best judgment in each case.

When lawyers are first elected to serve as judges, they obviously have no prior experience in deciding cases and supervising courthouse operations. Working as a lawyer differs a great deal from working as a judge, especially in the American **adversarial system**, in which lawyers serve as advocates for one party in each case. As a result, judges must "learn on the job." This method

nonpartisan election
An election in which candidates' party affiliations are not listed on the ballot.

partisan election
An election in which candidates openly endorsed by political parties are presented to voters for selection.

 The American Judicature Society, an organization of lawyers and judges dedicated to improving the administration of justice, provides information on methods of judicial selection in each state at their website. To link to this website, go to *The American System of Criminal Justice* 12e companion site at academic.cengage.com/criminaljustice/cole.

adversarial system
Basis of the American legal system in which a passive judge and jury seek to find the truth by listening to opposing attorneys who vigorously advocate on behalf of their respective sides.

CLOSE UP

The Image of Justice

DURING AN ARRAIGNMENT in New York for a defendant charged with assaulting his wife, the judge reportedly said, "What's wrong with that? You've got to keep them in line once in a while." When authorities acted to remove the judge from office, the judge's lawyer said that the judge makes lighthearted comments from the bench but does not misuse his position.

In another New York case, a judge was "censured" (publicly criticized) by the state's judicial conduct commission for walking toward a defendant in the courtroom and saying, "You want a piece of me?" In another case, the same judge said to a police officer, in reference to a disrespectful defendant, "If you are so upset about it, why don't you just thump the shit out of him outside the courthouse because I am not going to do anything about it." Two members of the commission who wanted to remove the judge from office were outvoted by the six other members who thought removal would be too harsh as a punishment.

In California, a judge reportedly indicated to a good-looking defendant that other inmates at the prison would find him attractive. The judge also allegedly called a prosecutor in a drunken-driving case a "hypocrite" who was in all probability guilty of the same offense as the defendant. When a complaint was filed with the state's Commission on Judicial Performance, the judge's attorney claimed that the comments were taken out of context.

Do the statements reportedly made by these judges harm the image of the courts? If so, how? If these statements are improper, what should happen to judges who say such things? If the judges apologize, should they be forgiven and receive another opportunity to behave in a proper manner? Is there any way to make sure that judges always act according to the proper image of their judicial office?

Sources: Drawn from "Court Upholds Removal of Rockland Judge," *New York Times*, March 31, 1999 (Metro News); Richard Marosi, "Hard-Line Judge Is Being Judged Herself," *Los Angeles Times*, May 7, 1999, p. B1; Stephanie Francis Ward, "Confrontation Leads to Censure," *ABA Journal E-Report*, October 13, 2006, http://www.abanet.org/journal/ereport/oc13smack.html.

Researching the Internet

To read about ethical rules for judges, see the website for the Code of Judicial Conduct for judges in Illinois. To link to this website, go to *The American System of Criminal Justice* 12e companion site at academic.cengage.com/criminaljustice/cole.

TABLE 9.1	Methods Used by States to Select Judges

States use different methods to select judges. Note that many judges are initially appointed to fill a vacancy, giving them an advantage if they must run for election at a later date.

Partisan Election	Nonpartisan Election	Gubernatorial Appointment	Legislative Selection	Merit Selection
Alabama	Arizona (some trial courts)	California (appellate)	South Carolina	Alaska
Illinois	Arkansas	Maine	Virginia	Arizona (appellate)
Indiana (trial)	California (trial)	Massachusetts (court of		Colorado
Louisiana	Florida (trial)	last resort)		Connecticut
New Mexico	Georgia	New Hampshire		Delaware
New York (trial)	Idaho	New Jersey		Florida (appellate)
Pennsylvania (initial)	Kentucky			Hawaii
Tennessee (trial)	Michigan			Indiana (appellate)
Texas	Minnesota			Iowa
West Virginia	Mississippi			Kansas
	Montana			Maryland
	Nevada			Massachusetts (trial,
	North Carolina			intermediate appellate)
	North Dakota			Missouri
	Ohio			Nebraska
	Oklahoma (trial)			New York (appellate)
	Oregon			Oklahoma (appellate)
	Pennsylvania (retention)			Rhode Island
	South Dakota (trial)			South Dakota
	Washington			(appellate)
	Wisconsin			Tennessee (appellate)
				Utah
				Vermont
				Wyoming

Source: American Judicature Society, 2008. "Methods of Judicial Selection," http://www.judicialselection.us (accessed May 17, 2008).

seems to counter the notion that judges are trained to "find the law" and apply neutral judgments (M. G. Hall, 1995). In Europe, by contrast, prospective judges receive special training in law school to become professional judges in what is called an **inquisitorial system**. These trained judges must serve as assistant judges and lower court judges before they can become judges in general trial and appellate courts (Provine, 1996). Unlike American judges, these judges are expected to actively question witnesses during court proceedings.

Election campaigns for lower-court judgeships traditionally tended to be low-key contests marked by little controversy. Usually only a small portion of the voters participate, judgeships are not prominent on the ballot, and ethical considerations constrain candidates from discussing controversial issues. Recent research reveals, however, that even lower-level judicial races are becoming more competitive as candidates raise money and seek connections with interest groups (Abbe and Herrnson, 2002; Streb, Frederick, and LaFrance, 2007). In addition, a 2002 decision by the U.S. Supreme Court (*Republican Party of Minnesota v. White*) invalidated Minnesota's ethics rule that forbade judicial candidates from announcing their views on disputed legal or political issues (Gray, 2004). According to the Supreme Court, such rules violate candidates' First Amendment right to freedom of speech. The Court's decision also affects similar rules in other states. Thus, judicial elections might become as controversial and combative as elections for other public offices, as candidates attack each other and openly seek to attract voters to their announced positions on issues. Observers interested in preserving the integrity of courts worry that wide-open elections will ultimately diminish the image and effectiveness of judges, who may begin to look more and more like partisan politicians. Public opinion polls indicate that Americans are divided in their views about judges' honesty and ethics, and these divisions are based, in part, on race and income. It is unclear whether judges' image would improve if merit selection were more widespread (see "What Americans Think" for specific data).

Although the popular election of trial judges may be part of America's political heritage, until recently voters paid little attention to these elections (Brody, 2004). In many cities, judgeships are the fuel for the party machine. Because of the honors and material rewards of a place on the bench, political parties get support—in the form of donated time and money—from attorneys seeking a judgeship. Parties also want judgeships to be elected posts because they can use courthouse staff positions to reward party loyalists. When a party member wins a judgeship, courthouse jobs may become available for campaign workers because the judge chooses clerks, bailiffs, and secretaries.

By contrast, elections for seats on state supreme courts frequently receive statewide media attention. Because of the importance of state supreme courts as policy-making institutions, political parties and interest groups often devote substantial resources to the election campaigns of their preferred candidates (C. S. Thomas, Boyer, and Hrebenar, 2003; Bonneau, 2004). When organized interests contribute tens of thousands of dollars to judicial campaigns, questions sometimes arise about whether the successful candidates who received those contributions will favor the interests of their donors when they begin to decide court cases (Champagne and Cheek, 1996; Reid, 1996).

Some states have tried to reduce the influence of political parties in the selection of judges while still allowing voters to select judges. These states hold nonpartisan elections in which the ballot shows only the names of candidates, not their party affiliations. Nonetheless, political parties are often strongly involved in such elections. In Ohio, for example, the Republican and Democratic political parties hold their own primary elections to choose the judicial candidates whose names will go on the nonpartisan ballot for the general election (Felice and Kilwein, 1992). In other states, party organizations raise and spend money on behalf of candidates in nonpartisan elections. When candidates' party affiliations are not listed on the ballot, voters may not know which party is support-

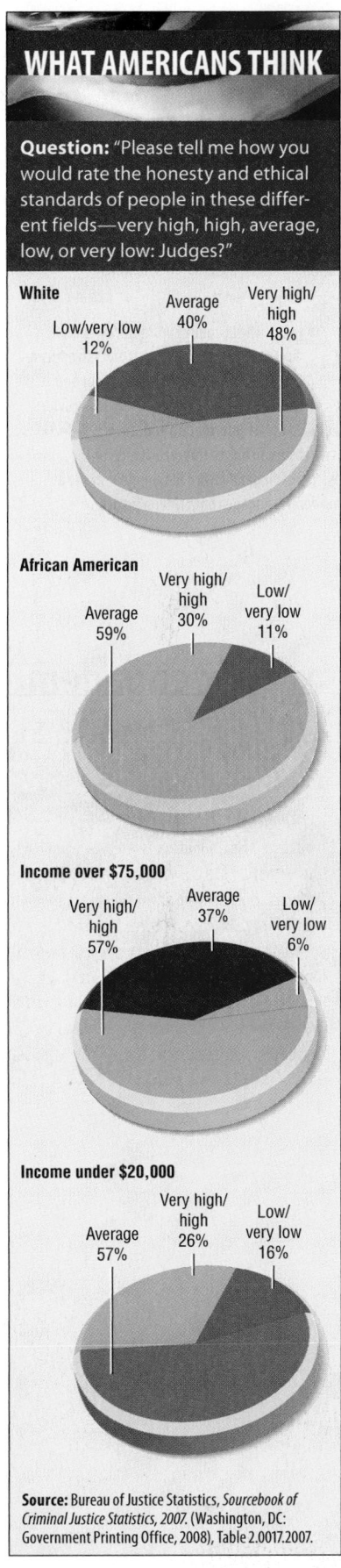

WHAT AMERICANS THINK

Question: "Please tell me how you would rate the honesty and ethical standards of people in these different fields—very high, high, average, low, or very low: Judges?"

White
Low/very low 12%
Average 40%
Very high/high 48%

African American
Very high/high 30%
Low/very low 11%
Average 59%

Income over $75,000
Very high/high 57%
Average 37%
Low/very low 6%

Income under $20,000
Very high/high 26%
Low/very low 16%
Average 57%

Source: Bureau of Justice Statistics, *Sourcebook of Criminal Justice Statistics, 2007.* (Washington, DC: Government Printing Office, 2008), Table 2.0017.2007.

inquisitorial system
Basis of legal system in Europe in which the judge takes an active role in investigating the case and asking questions of witnesses in court.

merit selection
A reform plan by which judges are nominated by a commission and appointed by the governor for a given period. When the term expires, the voters are asked to approve or disapprove the judge for a succeeding term. If the judge is disapproved, the committee nominates a successor for the governor's appointment.

 The League of Women Voters is an organization that attempts to educate the public about government and elections. The League's California branch provides detailed online information about judicial elections at its website. To link to this website, go to *The American System of Criminal Justice* 12e companion site at academic.cengage.com/criminaljustice/cole.

civic engagement
your role in the system

Imagine that a ballot issue was placed before the voters that proposed limiting state appellate judges to no more than 10 years in office. *Make a list of arguments supporting and opposing this proposal.* How would you vote? Then see what Colorado voters did when faced with just such a proposal. To link to this website, go to *The American System of Criminal Justice* 12e companion site at academic.cengage.com/criminaljustice/cole.

ing which candidate, especially in low-visibility elections for local trial judgeships, which do not receive the same level of media attention as elections for state supreme court seats (Lovrich and Sheldon, 1994).

Merit selection, which combines appointment and election, was first used in Missouri in 1940 and has since spread to other states. When a judgeship becomes vacant, a nominating commission made up of citizens and attorneys evaluates potential appointees and sends the governor the names of three candidates, from which the replacement is chosen. After one year, a referendum is held to decide whether the judge will stay on the bench. The ballot asks, "Shall Judge X remain in office?" The judge who wins a majority vote serves out the term and can then be listed on the ballot at the next election.

Merit selection is designed to remove politics from the selection of judges and to allow the voters to unseat judges. However, studies have shown that voters in merit selection states have removed relatively few judges (W. K. Hall and Aspin, 1987). Even so, interest groups sometimes seize the opportunity to mount publicity campaigns during retention elections in order to turn out judges with whom they disagree on a single issue or to open an important court seat so that a like-minded governor can appoint a sympathetic replacement. It may be difficult for judges to counteract a barrage of inflammatory television commercials focusing on a single issue such as capital punishment (Reid, 2000). If merit-selected judges feel intimidated by interest groups that might threaten their jobs at the next retention election, the independence of the judiciary will be diminished.

Despite the support of bar associations, merit selection has not gone unchallenged. Although party politics may have been removed, some argue that it has been replaced by politics within the legal profession. Many lawyers see the system as favoring the selection of "blue bloods" (high-status attorneys with ties to corporations) over the little guy whose clients are regular people with everyday problems (R. A. Watson and Downing, 1969).

In every selection system, critics contend that judges can accumulate too much power and remain beyond public accountability by being automatically reelected or reappointed when the public does not know enough about what judges have done in office. Read "Civic Engagement: Your Role in the System" to consider an approach to this issue. Remember that citizens can affect how the judicial branch is structured through their ability vote on ballot issues or their ability to pressure their representatives in Congress and state legislatures to make new laws about how courts will operate.

checkpoint

7. What are judges' main functions?
8. Why do political parties often prefer that judges be elected?
9. What are the steps in the merit selection process?

FROM ARREST TO TRIAL OR PLEA

At each stage of the pretrial process, key decisions are made that move some defendants to the next stage of the process and filter others out of the system. An innocent person could be arrested based on mistaken identification or misinterpreted evidence (Huff, 2002; Kridler, 1999). However, pretrial processes are meant to force prosecutors and judges to review the available evidence and dismiss unnecessary or unjust charges. These processes are based on the Ameri-

Criminal defendants typically make several court appearances as the judge makes decisions about evidence and the protection of each defendant's due process rights. Here, Michael Mastromarino appears in a New York City courtroom to face charges of stealing body parts from corpses in order to sell human tissue for medical transplants. Does the American system reduce the risk of errors by using a multistep process to examine evidence, protect rights, and determine guilt?

can value of due process. Americans believe that people should be entitled to a series of hearings and other procedural steps in which their guilt is proven before they should be subjected to punishments such as the loss of liberty through incarceration.

Although due process is an important value and is explicitly stated as a right in two different constitutional amendments, the Fifth and the Fourteenth, it can collide with Americans' interest in crime control if errors made by officials in carrying out these steps lead to the release of a guilty offender. For example, errors by judges in preliminary hearings or by police officers in lineups or other procedures can lead to the exclusion of evidence as a remedy for a rights violation. Thus, like other American values, due process can create results that undercut other priorities and objectives.

After arrest, the accused is booked at the police station. This process includes taking photographs and fingerprints, which form the basis of the case record. Usually the defendant must be taken to court for the initial appearance within 48 hours of a warrantless arrest. The purpose of this hearing is for the defendant to hear which charges are being pursued in light of the evidence gathered thus far, be advised of his or her rights, and be given the opportunity to post bail. Sometimes a separate bail hearing is scheduled shortly thereafter, especially when a case includes serious criminal charges. At the initial appearance, the judge also must make sure that probable cause exists to believe that a crime has been committed and that the accused should be prosecuted for the crime.

If the police used an arrest warrant to take the suspect into custody, evidence has already been presented to a judge who believed that it was strong enough to support a finding of probable cause to proceed against the defendant. When an arrest is made without a warrant, the police must, at the initial appearance, present sufficient evidence to persuade the judge to continue the case against the defendant.

Often, the first formal meeting between the prosecutor and the defendant's attorney is the **arraignment**: the formal court appearance in which the charges

arraignment
The court appearance of an accused person in which the charges are read and the accused, advised by a lawyer, pleads guilty or not guilty.

against the defendant are read and the defendant, advised by his or her lawyer, enters a plea of either guilty or not guilty. Most defendants will enter a plea of not guilty, even if they are likely to plead guilty at a later point. This is because, thus far, the prosecutor and defense attorney usually have had little chance to discuss a potential plea bargain. The more serious the charges, the more time the prosecutor and defense attorney will likely need to assess the strength of the other side's case. Only then can plea bargaining begin.

At the time of arraignment, prosecutors begin to evaluate the evidence. The lives of the defendants hinge on this screening process, because their fate depends largely on the prosecutor's discretion (Barnes and Kingsnorth, 1996). If the prosecutor believes the case against the defendant is weak, the charges may simply be dropped. Prosecutors do not wish to waste their limited time and resources on cases that will not stand up in court. A prosecutor may also drop charges if the alleged crime is minor, if the defendant is a first offender, or if the prosecutor believes that the few days spent in jail before arraignment are enough punishment for the alleged offense. Jail overcrowding or the need to work on more serious cases can also influence the decision to drop charges. At times, prosecutors in making these decisions might discriminate against the accused because of race, wealth, or some other factor (Crew, 1991), or they might discriminate against certain victims, such as women who are sexually assaulted by an intimate partner or other acquaintance as opposed to a stranger (Spohn and Holleran, 2001). As cases move through the system, prosecutors' decisions to reduce charges for some defendants greatly affect the punishment eventually applied (J. L. Miller and Sloan, 1994). Thus, individual prosecutors play a major role in deciding which defendants will receive criminal punishment.

As Figure 9.4 shows, prosecutors use their decision-making power to filter many cases out of the system. The 100 cases illustrated are typical felony cases. The percentage of cases varies from city to city, depending on such factors as the effectiveness of police investigations and prosecutors' policies about which cases to pursue. For example, nearly half of those arrested did not ultimately face felony prosecutions. A small number of defendants were steered toward diversion programs. A larger number had their cases dismissed for various reasons including lack of evidence, the minor nature of the charges, or first-time-offender status. Other cases were dismissed by the courts because the police and prosecutors did not present enough evidence to a grand jury or a preliminary hearing to justify moving forward.

FIGURE 9.4
Typical outcomes of 100 urban felony cases
Prosecutors and judges make crucial decisions during the period before trial or plea. Once cases are bound over for disposition, guilty pleas are many, trials are few, and acquittals are rare.

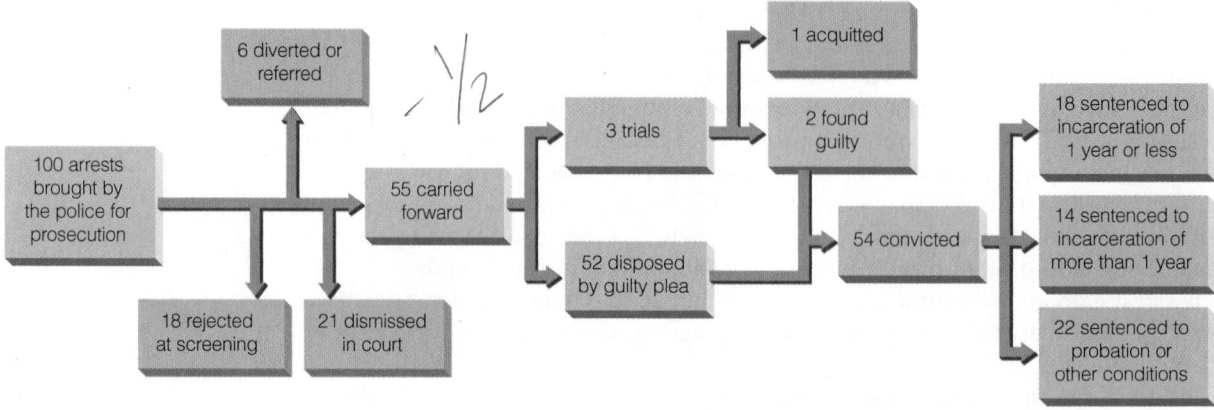

Source: Barbara Boland, Paul Mahanna, and Ronald Stones, *The Prosecution of Felony Arrests, 1988* (Washington, DC: Bureau of Justice Statistics, U.S. Government Printing Office, 1992), 2.

The proportion of cases dropped at the various stages of the pretrial process varies from city to city. In some cities, many cases are dropped before charges are filed. Prosecutors evaluate the facts and evidence and decide which cases are strong enough to carry forward. The others are quickly dismissed. In other cities, formal charges are filed almost automatically on the basis of police reports, but many cases are dismissed when the prosecutor takes the time to examine each defendant's situation closely.

During the pretrial process, defendants are exposed to the informal, assembly-line atmosphere of the lower criminal courts. Often, decisions are quickly made about bail, arraignment, pleas, and the disposition of cases. Moving cases as quickly as possible seems to be the main goal of many judges and attorneys during the pretrial process. Courts throughout the nation face pressures to limit the number of cases going to trial. These pressures may affect the decisions of both judges and prosecutors as well as the defense attorneys who seek to maintain good relationships with them. American courts often have too little money, too few staff members, and not enough time to give detailed attention to each case, let alone a full trial.

In American courts, the defense uses the pretrial period to its own advantage. Preliminary hearings provide an opportunity for defense attorneys to challenge the prosecution's evidence and make **motions** to the court requesting that an order be issued to bring about a specified action. Through pretrial motions, the defense may try to suppress evidence or learn about the prosecutor's case. The defense attorney making the motion must be able to support the claim being made about improper procedures used in the arrest, the insufficiency of the evidence, or the need for exclusion of evidence. Prosecutors also make motions, especially if they have disagreements with the defense about whether and how defense witnesses will be questioned. Judges may decide motions based on the written arguments submitted by each side or they may schedule a motion hearing that will permit each attorney to present arguments about whether the motion should be granted. Decisions on motions can significantly affect the outcome of a case, especially if the motion hearing determines whether key pieces of evidence can be used in court against the defendant.

The large number of cases dismissed during pretrial proceedings need not be viewed as a sign of weakness in the system. Instead, one strength of the system is the power of prosecutors and judges to dismiss charges when a conviction would be either unfair or unlikely. A close look at Figure 9.4 shows that the offenses that a prosecutor decides to pursue have a high rate of conviction. Out of 55 typical cases carried forward, 52 will end with a guilty plea and two of the three defendants who had full trials will be convicted. These examples make it clear that the criminal justice system is effective in producing convictions when a prosecutor, with sufficient evidence, pursues a felony prosecution. In addition, recent research indicates that some of the people whose cases were dismissed will actually receive punishment. In the case of repeat offenders, for example, prosecutors may dismiss criminal charges in favor of probation violation charges that lead the offender to serve time in jail or prison despite not being convicted of a new crime (Kingsnorth, MacIntosh, and Sutherland, 2002). So, the numbers of offenders punished in the process is actually higher than that indicated by Figure 9.4.

motion
An application to a court requesting that an order be issued to bring about a specified action.

 Cable News Network (CNN) took over the courtroom reporting previously broadcast on COURT-TV. Now you can find out detailed information about current criminal trials at CNN's website. To link to this website, go to *The American System of Criminal Justice* 12e companion site at academic.cengage.com/criminaljustice/cole.

checkpoint

10. What are the purposes of preliminary hearings, arraignments, and defense motions?
11. Why and how are cases filtered out of the system?

BAIL: PRETRIAL RELEASE

It is often stated that defendants are presumed innocent until proved guilty or until they enter a guilty plea. However, people who are arrested are taken to jail. They are deprived of their freedom and, in many cases, subjected to miserable living conditions while they await the processing of their cases. The idea that people who are presumed innocent can lose their freedom—sometimes for many months—as their cases work their way toward trial clashes with the American values of freedom and liberty.

On the other hand, government officials also feel an obligation to protect society from harm. A conflict is bound to occur between the American value of individual liberty and the need to keep some criminal suspects in jail in order to protect society from people who are violent or who may try to escape prosecution. Some suspects who are considered threatening to public safety could be held in pretrial detention without causing most Americans to believe that the values of freedom and liberty have been compromised. However, not every person who is charged with a criminal offense need be detained. Thus, bail and other methods of releasing defendants are used on the condition that the accused will appear in court as required.

Bail is a sum of money or property, specified by the judge, that the defendant must present to the court in order to gain pretrial release. The bail will be forfeited if the defendant does not appear in court as scheduled. Although people are generally entitled to a bail hearing as part of their right to due process, there is no constitutional right to release on bail, nor even a right to have the court set an amount as the condition of release. The Eighth Amendment to the U.S. Constitution forbids excessive bail, and state bail laws are usually designed to prevent discrimination in setting bail. They do not guarantee, however, that all defendants will have a realistic chance of being released before trial (Nagel, 1990).

Because the accused is presumed to be innocent, bail should not be used as punishment. The amount of bail should therefore be high enough to ensure that the defendant appears in court for trial—but no higher. But this is not the only purpose of bail. The community must be protected from further crimes that some defendants might commit while out on bail. Except in the recent cases of suspected terrorists, criminal suspects are entitled to a hearing before they are denied bail or bail is set at such a high level that they are certain to be kept in jail despite the fact that they have not yet been convicted. Congress and some of the states have passed laws that permit preventive detention of defendants when the judge concludes that they pose a threat to others or to the community while awaiting trial.

The Reality of the Bail System

The reality of the bail system is far from the ideal. The question of bail may arise at the police station, at the initial court appearance in a misdemeanor case, or at the arraignment in most felony cases. For minor offenses, police officers may have a standard list of bail amounts. For serious offenses, a judge sets bail in court. In both cases, those setting bail may have discretion to set differing bail amounts for different suspects, depending on the circumstances of each case. (See "A Question of Ethics" at the end of this chapter.)

In almost all courts, the amount of bail is based mainly on the judge's view of the seriousness of the crime and of the defendant's record. In part, this emphasis results from a lack of information about the accused. Because bail is typically determined 24 to 48 hours after an arrest, there is little time to conduct a more thorough assessment. As a result, judges in many communities have developed standard rates: so many dollars for such-and-such an offense. In some cases, a

bail
An amount of money specified by a judge that be paid as a condition of pretrial release to ensure that the accused will appear in court as required.

judge may set a high bail if the police or prosecutor want a certain person to be kept off the streets.

Critics of the bail system argue that it discriminates against poor people. Imagine that you have been arrested and have no money. Should you be denied a chance for freedom before trial just because you are poor? What if you have a little money, but if you use it to post bail you will not have any left to hire your own attorney? Professional criminals and the affluent have no trouble making bail; many drug dealers, for instance, can readily make bail and go on dealing while awaiting trial. In contrast, a poor person arrested for a minor violation may spend the pretrial period in jail. Should dangerous, wealthy offenders be allowed out on bail while nonviolent, poor suspects are locked up?

The problems for poor defendants are compounded by the lack of a constitutional right to representation by an attorney at bail hearings (Colbert, 1998). Defendants who cannot afford to hire an attorney may have no one to make arguments on their behalf at the bail hearing. Thus, the prosecutor's arguments in favor of a high bail or a denial of bail may be the only effective arguments presented to the judge. For many poor defendants, bail is set before an attorney has been appointed to represent them in the preparation of their defense.

According to a study of felony defendants in the nation's most populous counties, 57 percent were released before disposition of their cases, 37 percent could not make bail, and 6 percent were detained without bail (Kyckelhahn and Cohen, 2008). Among those for whom bail was set, 20 percent had a bail amount less than $5,000. Figure 9.5 shows the amounts of bail set for various types of felony offenses. Those who cannot make bail must remain in jail awaiting trial, unless they can obtain enough money to pay a bail bondsman's fee. Given the length of time between arraignment and trial in most courts and the hardships of pretrial detention, defendants in many cities depend on bondsmen. In 2004, 23,640 felony suspects in the 75 largest counties could not make bail or use the services of a bail bondsman to gain release (Kyckelhahn and Cohen, 2008).

FIGURE 9.5

Bail amounts for felony defendants by type of offense
The amount of bail varies according to the offense.

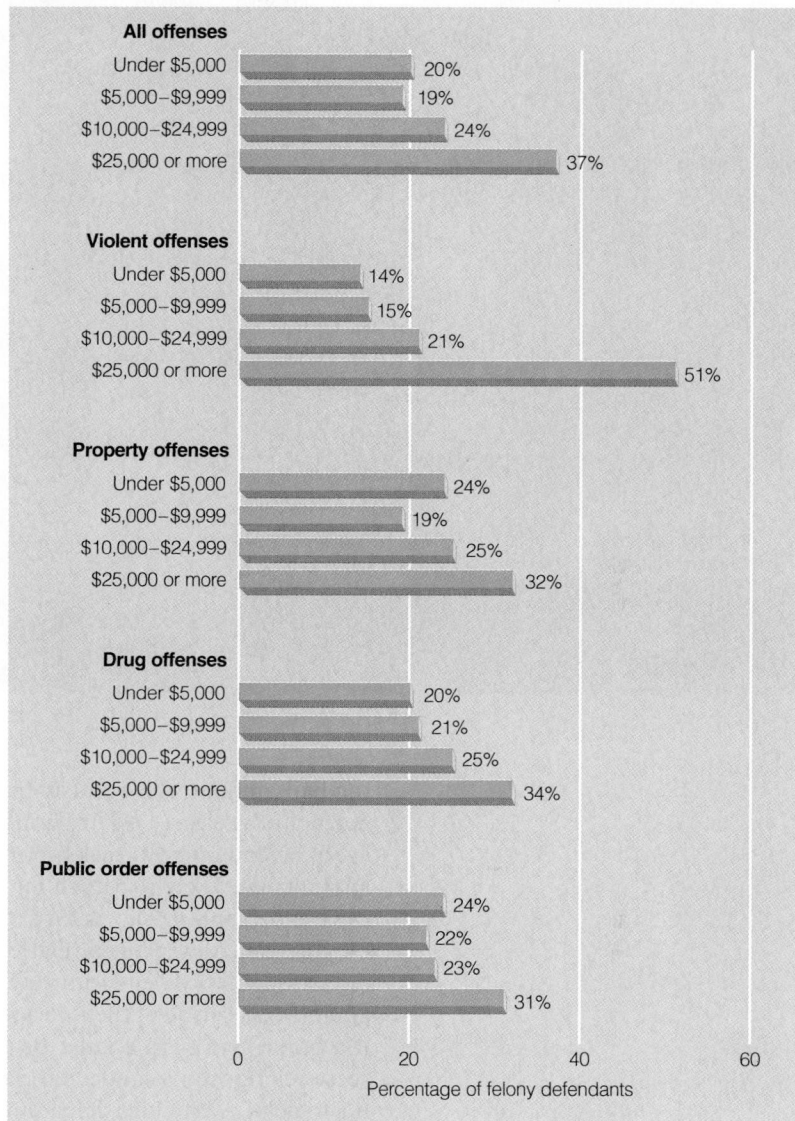

Source: Gerard Rainville and Brian A. Reaves, *Felony Defendants in Large Urban Counties, 2000* (Washington, DC: U.S. Government Printing Office, December 2003).

Bail Bondsmen

The bail bondsman, also called a bail agent, is a key figure in the bail process. Bail bondsmen (or women) are private businesspeople who loan money to defendants who lack the money to make bail. They are licensed by the state and choose their own clients. In exchange for a fee, which may be 5 to 10 percent of

Mackenzie Green is a well-known California bondswoman and bounty hunter. Each year 20 percent of felony defendants out on bail fail to appear for scheduled court hearings. Some forget their court dates or received confusing information on the time and place to appear. Others, however, intentionally skip town. Nearly all of them are eventually found, frequently by bondsmen and their agents. Should such profit-seeking, private businesses be so deeply involved in the criminal justice process?

Left: Courtesy of Thane Plambeck; Right: Courtesy of Mackenzie Green

the bail amount, the bondsman will put up the money (or property) to gain the defendant's release. Again, bondsmen are not obliged to provide bail money for every defendant who seeks to use their services. Instead, they decide which defendants are likely to return for court appearances. If the defendant skips town, the bondsman's money is forfeited.

Bondsmen may build relationships with police officers and jailers to obtain referrals. Many defendants may not know whom to call for help in making bail, and officers can steer them to a particular bondsman. This can lead to corruption if a bondsman pays a jailer or police officer to make such referrals. Moreover, these relationships can lead to improper cooperation, such as a bondsman refusing to help a particular defendant if the police would like to see that defendant remain in jail. In 2006, for example, a bail bondsman in Louisiana was sentenced to prison and provided testimony to bring several judges and other courthouse employees with him for providing a wide range of bribes in the form of gifts, including a Mercedes-Benz automobile, cash, holiday turkeys, vacation weekends, and tickets to shows. In addition, he made more than $35,000 in legal campaign contributions to judges and other local elected officials (Gordon, 2006).

The role of the bondsman poses other ethical questions as well. Is it proper for a private, profit-seeking businessperson to decide who will gain pretrial release and to profit from a person who is "presumed innocent" but is threatened with the loss of his or her freedom? If charges are dropped or a defendant is acquitted, the bondsman still keeps the fee that was paid to make bail. This can be especially costly to poor defendants. Although judges set the bail amount, the bondsmen often actually decide whether certain defendants will gain pretrial release. This ethical issue looms ever larger because the role of bail bondsmen is expanding in many places. In the mid-1990s, only 24 percent of defendants who gained release used the services of a bail bondsman. By 2004, 40 percent

CLOSE UP

Illegal Globally, Bail for Profit Remains in United States

WAYNE SPATH IS A bail bondsman, which means he is an insurance salesman, a social worker, a lightly regulated law enforcement agent, a real estate appraiser—and a for-profit wing of the American justice system.

What he does, which is posting bail for people accused of crimes in exchange for a fee, is all but unknown in the rest of the world. In England, Canada, and other countries, agreeing to pay a defendant's bond in exchange for money is a crime akin to witness tampering or bribing a juror—a form of obstruction of justice.

Mr. Spath, who is burly, gregarious and intense, owns Brandy Bail Bonds, and he sees his clients in a pleasant and sterile office building just down the street from the courthouse here. But for the handcuffs on the sign out front, it could be a dentist's office.

"I've got to run, but I'll never leave you in jail," Mr. Spath said, greeting a frequent customer in his reception area one morning a couple of weeks ago. He turned to a second man and said, "Now, don't you miss court on me."

Other countries almost universally reject and condemn Mr. Spath's trade, in which defendants who are presumed innocent but cannot make bail on their own pay an outsider a nonrefundable fee for their freedom.

"It's a very American invention," John Goldkamp, a professor of criminal justice at Temple University, said of the commercial bail bond system. "It's really the only place in the criminal justice system where a liberty decision is governed by a profit-making business-man who will or will not take your business."

Although the system is remarkably effective at what it does, four states—Illinois, Kentucky, Oregon, and Wisconsin—have abolished commercial bail bonds, relying instead on systems that require deposits to courts instead of payments to private businesses, or that simply trust defendants to return for trial.

Most of the legal establishment, including the American Bar Association and the National District Attorneys Association, hates the bail bond business, saying it discriminates against poor and middle-class defendants, does nothing for public safety, and usurps decisions that ought to be made by the justice system.

Here as in many other areas of the law, the United States goes it alone. American law is, by international standards, a series of innovations and exceptions. From the central role played by juries in civil cases to the election of judges to punitive damages to the disproportionate number of people in prison, the United States has charted a distinctive and idiosyncratic legal path.

Bail is meant to make sure defendants show up for trial. It has ancient roots in English common law, which relied on sworn promises and on pledges of land or property from the defendants or their relatives to make sure they did not flee.

America's open frontier and entrepreneurial spirit injected an innovation into the process: by the early 1800s, private businesses were allowed to post bail in exchange for payments from the de-fendants and the promise that they would hunt down the defendants and return them if they failed to appear.

Commercial bail bond companies dominate the pretrial release systems of only two nations, the United States and the Philippines.

The flaw in the system most often cited by critics is that defendants who have not been convicted of a crime and who turn up for every court appearance are nonetheless required to pay a nonrefundable fee to a private business, assuming they do not want to remain in jail.

"Life is not fair, and I probably would feel the same way if I were a defendant," said Bill Kreins, a spokesman for the Professional Bail Agents of the United States, a trade group. "But the system is the best in world."

The system costs taxpayers nothing, Mr. Kreins said, and it is exceptionally effective at ensuring that defendants appear for court.

Mr. Spath's experience confirms that.

If Mr. Spath considers a potential client a good risk, he will post bail in exchange for a nonrefundable 10 percent fee. In a 35-month period ending in November, his records show, Mr. Spath posted about $37 million in bonds—7,934 of them. That would suggest revenues of about $1.3 million a year, given his fee.

Mr. Spath, who is 62, has seven bail agents working for him, including his daughters Tia and Mia. "It probably costs me 50 grand a month to run this business," he said.

Mr. Spath hounds his clients relentlessly to make sure they appear for court. If they do not, he must pay the court the full amount unless he can find them and bring them back in short order.

Only 434 of his clients failed to appear for a court date over that period, and Mr. Spath straightened out 338 of those cases within the 60 days allowed by Florida law. In the end, he had to pay up only 76 times.

That is a failure rate of less than 1 percent.

Source: From Adam Liptak, "Illegal Globally, Bail for Profit Remains in U.S.," *New York Times*, Jan. 29, 2008.

Researching the Internet

As you consider the possible advantages of permitting bail bondsmen to operate, remember that 40 percent of people arrested have their charges dropped or are found "not guilty." Yet the bondsmen keep the fees paid by these innocent people to avoid being jailed while awaiting trial. Read the summary of an article by a federal judge who is critical of the role of bail bondsmen. To link to this website, go to *The American System of Criminal Justice* 12e companion site at academic.cengage.com/criminaljustice/cole.

of released felony defendants were customers of bondsmen (Liptak, 2008). As you read the Close Up box, consider whether the risks of the private bail bondsman's operation outweigh the benefits for providing fairness and justice.

Despite the problems posed by their role, bondsmen may benefit the criminal justice system. Although bondsmen act in their own interest, they can contribute to the smooth processing of cases. For example, defendants who fail to appear for scheduled court appearances often do so because of forgetfulness and confusion about when and where they must appear. Courthouses in large cities are huge bureaucracies in which changes in the times and locations of hearings are not always communicated to defendants. Bondsmen can help by reminding defendants about court dates, calling defendants' relatives to make sure that the defendant will arrive on time, and warning defendants about the penalties for failing to appear. Indeed, some officials in states that have done away with commercial bail bonds say that they have seen increases in failure-to-appear cases (Liptak, 2008).

Bounty hunters or bail enforcement agents hired by bondsmen find many of the defendants who have skipped out on bail. These independent operators have caused many problems. In highly publicized cases, bounty hunters have broken into the wrong homes, kidnapped innocent people mistaken for wanted criminals, and even shot and killed innocent bystanders (Drimmer, 1997; Liptak, 2008). Bounty hunters' disregard for people's rights and public safety has led to calls for new laws to regulate the activities of bondsmen and the people they hire to hunt for fugitives. Consider the potential problems that can be caused by bounty hunters as you read "Civic Engagement: Your Role in the System."

The justice system may benefit in some ways from the activities of bondsmen. However, court and law enforcement officials could provide the same benefits as well or better if they had the resources, time, and interest to make sure that released defendants return to court. If all courts had pretrial services officers such as those in the federal courts, defendants could be monitored and reminded to return to court without the risks of discrimination and corruption associated with the use of bail bondsmen (Carr, 1993; Marsh, 1994; Peoples, 1995). Data collected by the U.S. Office of Probation and Pretrial Services, which handles processing and monitoring defendants released on bail by the federal courts, indicate low levels of failure-to-appear and rearrest while contributing to a significant decline in the use of bail bondsmen in federal courts (Cadigan, 2007).

civic engagement
your role in the system

Imagine that a candidate for state legislature runs by claiming that she will propose a law to ban bounty hunters from taking people into custody, even when those people have skipped out on bail. *Make a list of the benefits and risks from such a proposed law.* Would you support the law? Then look at a summary of the law in your state and others states at the website of the American Bail Coalition. To link to this website, go to *The American System of Criminal Justice* 12e companion site at academic.cengage.com/criminaljustice/cole.

Learn more about bail bondsmen at the website of their professional association, Professional Bail Agents of the United States. To link to this website, go to *The American System of Criminal Justice* 12e companion site at academic.cengage.com/criminaljustice/cole.

Setting Bail

When the police set bail at the station house for minor offenses, they usually use a standard amount for a particular charge. By contrast, when a judge sets bail, the amount of bail and conditions of release stem from interactions among the judge, prosecutor, and defense attorney, who discuss the defendant's personal qualities and prior record. The prosecutor may stress the seriousness of the crime, the defendant's record, and negative personal characteristics. The defense attorney, if one has been hired or appointed at this point, may stress the defendant's good job, family responsibilities, and place in the community. Like other aspects of bail, these factors may favor affluent defendants over the poor, the unemployed, or people with unstable families. Yet many of these factors provide no clear information about how dangerous a defendant is or whether he or she is likely to appear in court. Moreover, judges may not have accurate information about these factors if pretrial services officers at the court do not carefully investigate the background and circumstances of each defendant (Marsh, 2001).

Research highlights the disadvantages of the poor in the bail process. A study of Hispanic arrestees in the southwestern United States found that those who hired their own attorneys were seven times more likely to gain pretrial release than were those represented by a public attorney (M. D. Holmes et al., 1996). This result may reflect the fact that affluent defendants can more easily come up with bail money, as well as the possibility that private attorneys fight harder for their clients in the early stages of the criminal process (Fender and Brooking, 2004).

The amount of bail may also reflect racial, class, or ethnic discrimination by criminal justice officials. A 1991 study by the State Bail Commission of cases in Connecticut showed that at each step in the process, African American and Hispanic men with clean records were given bail amounts double those given whites. One reason for the difference might be that poor defendants often do not have jobs and a permanent residence, factors that strongly influence bail amounts. The study also recognized that the higher bail might result from the fact that African Americans and Hispanics were more likely to be charged with a felony than were whites. However, the largest disparities in bail were in felony drug cases. In these cases the average bail for African Americans and Hispanics was four times higher than that for whites at the same courthouse (Houston and Ewing, 1991). A study in Nebraska found an impact from gender as well as race. It found that "white females had a bail amount set that was substantially less than that of their white male counterparts" and "[n]on-white males, on the other hand, had a higher bail amount set than the white males" (Turner and Johnson, 2006: 61).

Some claim that bail setting should be guided by six principles:

1. The accused is entitled to release on his or her own recognizance.
2. Nonfinancial alternatives to bail will be used when possible.
3. The accused will receive a full and fair hearing.
4. Reasons will be stated for the decision.
5. Clear and convincing evidence will be offered to support a decision.
6. There will be a prompt and automatic review of all bail determinations.

Many people argue that these principles would hamper the ability of the justice system to deal with offenders and protect society. Others counter that personal freedom is so precious that failure to allow a person every opportunity to gain release creates an even greater injustice.

checkpoint

12. What factors affect whether bail is set and how much money or property a defendant must provide to gain pretrial release?
13. What positive and negative effects does the bail bondsman have on the justice system?

Reforming the Bail System

Studies of pretrial detention in such cities as Philadelphia and New York have raised questions about the need to hold defendants in jail. Criticisms of the bail system focus on judges' discretion in setting bail amounts, the fact that the poor are deprived of their freedom while the affluent can afford bail, the negative aspects of bail bondsmen, and jail conditions for those detained while awaiting trial. To address such criticisms, people have attempted for many years to reform the bail system. Such efforts have led to changes in the number of defendants held in jail. One classic study of 20 cities showed that the release rate in 1962 was 48 percent (W. H. Thomas, 1976: 37–38). A more recent survey found that

TABLE 9.2	Pretrial Release Methods	
Financial Bond		**Alternative Release Options**
Fully secured bail. The defendant posts the full amount of bail with the court.		*Release on recognizance (ROR).* The court releases the defendant on his or her promise to appear in court as required.
Privately secured bail. A bondsman signs a promissory note to the court for the bail amount and charges the defendant a fee for the service (usually 10 percent of the bail amount). If the defendant fails to appear, the bondsman must pay the court the full amount. The bondsman frequently requires the defendant to post collateral in addition to the fee.		*Conditional release.* The court releases the defendant subject to his or her following specific conditions set by the court, such as attendance at drug treatment therapy or staying away from the complaining witness.
Percentage bail. The courts allow the defendant to deposit a percentage (usually 10 percent) of the full bail with the court. The full amount of the bail is required if the defendant fails to appear. The percentage bail is returned after disposition of the case, although the court often retains 1 percent for administrative costs.		*Third-party custody.* The defendant is released into the custody of an individual or agency that promises to ensure his or her appearance in court. No monetary transactions are involved in this type of release.
Unsecured bail. The defendant pays no money to the court but is liable for the full amount of bail should she or he fail to appear.		

Source: Bureau of Justice Statistics, *Report to the Nation on Crime and Justice,* 2nd ed. (Washington, DC: U.S. Government Printing Office, 1988), 76.

 A legal information website describes the various option available for bail. To link to this website, go to *The American System of Criminal Justice* 12e companion site at academic.cengage.com/criminaljustice/cole.

57 percent of felony suspects in the 75 most populous counties were released before disposition of their cases. Only 6 percent were denied bail (Kyckelhahn and Cohen, 2008). The increase in defendants released on bail has occurred, in part, because of the use of certain pretrial release methods (see Table 9.2).

Citation

citation
A written order or summons, issued by a law enforcement officer, often directing an alleged offender to appear in court at a specified time to answer a criminal charge.

What people often call a ticket is more formally known as a **citation**. It is often issued to a person accused of committing a traffic offense or some other minor violation. Depending on the nature of the offense, the citation written out by the officer can also include a summons requiring an appearance in court. By issuing the citation, the officer avoids taking the accused person to the station house for booking and to court for arraignment and setting of bail. Citations are now being used for more serious offenses, in part because the police want to reduce the amount of time they spend booking minor offenders and waiting in arraignment court for their cases to come up.

Release on Recognizance

release on recognizance (ROR)
Pretrial release granted on the defendant's promise to appear in court, because the judge believes that the defendant's ties in the community guarantee that he or she will appear.

Pioneered in the 1960s by the Vera Institute of Justice in New York City, the **release on recognizance (ROR)** approach is based on the assumption that judges will grant releases if the defendant is reliable and has roots in the community. Soon after the arrest, court personnel talk to defendants about their job, family, prior record, and associations. They then decide whether to recommend release.

In the first three years of the New York project, more than 10,000 defendants were interviewed and about 3,500 were released. Only 1.5 percent failed to appear in court at the scheduled time, a rate almost three times better than the rate for those released on bail (Goldfarb, 1965). Programs in other cities have had similar results, although Sheila Maxwell's research raises questions about whether women and property-crime defendants on ROR are less likely than other defendants to appear in court (Maxwell, 1999).

Ten Percent Cash Bail

Although ROR is a useful alternative to bail, not all defendants should be released on their own recognizance. Illinois, Kentucky, Nebraska, Oregon, and Pennsylvania have started bail programs in which the defendants deposit 10 percent of their bail in cash with the court. When they appear in court as required, 90 percent of this amount is returned to them. Begun in Illinois in 1964, this plan is designed to release as many defendants as possible without using bail bondsmen.

Bail Guidelines

To deal with the problem of unequal treatment, reformers have written guidelines for setting bail. The guidelines specify the standards judges should use in setting bail and also list appropriate amounts. Judges are expected to follow the guidelines but deviate from them in special situations. The guidelines take into account the seriousness of the offense and the defendant's prior record, in order to protect the community and ensure that released offenders can be trusted to return for court appearances.

Preventive Detention

Reforms have been suggested not only by those concerned with unfairness in the bail system but also by those concerned with stopping crime (Goldkamp, 1985). Critics of the bail system point to a link between release on bail and the commission of crimes, arguing that the accused may commit other crimes while awaiting trial. A study of the nation's most populous counties found that 21 percent of felony defendants released on bail were rearrested for another crime (Kyckelhahn and Cohen, 2008). To address this problem, legislatures have passed laws permitting detention of defendants without bail.

For federal criminal cases, Congress enacted the Bail Reform Act of 1984, which authorizes **preventive detention**. Under the act, if prosecutors recommend that defendants be kept in jail, a federal judge holds a hearing to determine (1) if there is a serious risk that the person will flee; (2) if the person will obstruct justice or threaten, injure, or intimidate a prospective witness or juror; or (3) if the offense is one of violence or one punishable by life imprisonment or death. On finding that one or more of these factors makes setting bail without endangering the community impossible, the judge can order the defendant held in jail until the case is completed (C. E. Smith, 1990).

preventive detention
Holding a defendant for trial, based on a judge's finding that, if the defendant were released on bail, he or she would flee or would endanger another person or the community.

Obviously, preventive detention provides a particularly powerful clash between important American values. The value placed on liberty for individuals seems to be denied when presumptively innocent individuals remain in jail. On the other hand, the value on all citizens' ability to enjoy the liberty of walking the streets without fear of crime may be advanced by detaining specific individuals who are found to threaten community safety.

Critics of preventive detention argue that it violates the Constitution's due process clause because the accused remains in custody until a verdict is rendered. However, the Supreme Court has ruled that it is constitutional. The preventive detention provisions of the Bail Reform Act of 1984 were upheld in ***United States v. Salerno and Cafero* (1987)**. The justices said that preventive detention was a legitimate use of government power, because it was not designed to punish the accused. Instead, it deals with the problem of people who commit

***United States v. Salerno and Cafero* (1987)**
Preventive detention provisions of the Bail Reform Act of 1984 are upheld as legitimate use of government power designed to prevent people from committing crimes while on bail.

crimes while on bail. By upholding the federal law, the Court also upheld state laws dealing with preventive detention (M. Miller and Guggenheim, 1990).

Supporters of preventive detention claim that it ensures that drug dealers, who often treat bail as a business expense, cannot flee before trial. Research has shown that the nature and seriousness of the charge, a history of prior arrests, and drug use all have a strong bearing on the likelihood that a defendant will commit a crime while on bail.

checkpoint

14. What methods are used to facilitate pretrial release for certain defendants?
15. How did the U.S. Supreme Court rule in cases involving preventive detention?

PRETRIAL DETENTION

People who are not released before trial must remain in jail. Often called "the ultimate ghetto," American jails hold over 600,000 people on any one day. Most are poor, half are in pretrial detention, and the rest are serving sentences (normally of less than a year) or are waiting to be moved to state prison or to another jurisdiction (Clear, Cole, and Reisig, 2008).

Urban jails also contain troubled people, many with drug abuse and mental health problems, whom police have swept off the streets. Michael Welch calls this process, in which the police remove socially offensive people from certain areas, "social sanitation" (Welch, 1994: 262).

Conditions in jails are often much harsher than those in prisons. People awaiting trial are often held in barracks-like cells with sentenced offenders. Thus, a "presumed innocent" pretrial detainee might spend weeks in the same confined space with troubled people or sentenced felons (Beck, Karberg, and Harrison, 2002). The problems of pretrial detention may be even worse in other countries where suspects have no opportunity for bail or face a court system that is disorganized and lacks resources. As you read the "Comparative Perspective" concerning pretrial detention in Russia, ask yourself whether individual U.S. jails could have similar conditions.

Often jails holding pretrial detainees are crowded and have no education or work programs. Some prisoners at the Marion County Jail in Indianapolis must sleep on the floor and spend their days in close quarters with many strangers as they wait days, weeks, or months for their trials or, if after trial, their transfer to a prison. What thoughts and feelings would you experience if you were arrested and detained in jail?

AP Images/Indianapolis Star, Mike Fender

The period just after arrest is the most frightening and difficult time for suspects. Imagine freely walking the streets one minute and being locked in a small space with a large number of troubled and potentially dangerous cell mates the next. Suddenly you have no privacy and must share an open toilet with hostile strangers. You have been fingerprinted, photographed, and questioned—treated like "the criminal" that the police and the criminal justice system consider you to be. You are alone with people whose behavior you cannot predict. You are left to worry and wonder about what might happen. If you are female, you may be placed in a cell by yourself (Steury and Frank, 1990). Given the stressful nature of arrest and jailing, it is little wonder that most jail suicides and psychotic episodes occur during the first hours of detention.

COMPARATIVE PERSPECTIVE

Pretrial Detention in Russia

PRISONERS ALMOST ALWAYS swear they are not guilty. In Russian pretrial detention centers, many inmates insist that they no longer care about proving their innocence. Pretrial detainees spend long periods in unhealthy conditions while investigations of their alleged offense are conducted.

"At first, all I wanted was a fair trial," Pyotr Kuznetsov, 51, said in a dank and stinking cell of Matrosskaya Tishina, one of Moscow's largest and most infamous detention centers.

He said he had been arrested and brutally beaten for stealing less than $5 and had already spent 10 months behind bars awaiting trial. His lice-ridden eighteenth-century cell, built for 30, currently warehouses more than 100 men. The inmates share beds, sleeping in three shifts.

"All I want now is to get out of here, even to a labor camp," Mr. Kuznetsov said. "I've been in prison before, and it is not as bad as this."

Perhaps the most terrifying aspect of the Russian penal system is pretrial detention. Close to 300,000 people awaiting trial are now in jail. There, a death sentence stalks people who have not yet been convicted of a crime.

Unprotected from the TB (tuberculosis) epidemic (as many as 50 percent of Russian prisoners are believed to be infected) and other infectious diseases, many detainees end up spending two, three, and even four years awaiting their day in court in cells as packed as a rush-hour subway car.

The Russian legal system is so torturous that people can find themselves detained for months or years even on minor charges.

Prosecutors are legally required to complete a criminal investigation within two years, but there is no time limit for judges, who can keep a suspect waiting for trial indefinitely. The average stay in detention is 10 months.

In Soviet times, bail was dismissed as a capitalist folly. Today, bail is legal, but it remains a novelty, granted to less than 2 percent of the country's accused—usually to mobsters who have ready cash and connections to a compliant judge.

"Under our system, it is much harder to acquit than find a person guilty," Sergei Pasin, a judge in a Moscow appeals court explained. "Less than 1 percent of all cases end in an acquittal, and that is because before a judge can acquit, he must do a huge amount of work that is not done by the police: requesting information, soliciting expert testimony, etc."

"The fact that time served before trial is subtracted from convicted prisoners' sentences can hardly be viewed as justice," Judge Pasin said. "The predetention centers are a far worse punishment than prison," he said. Prisons and labor camps in Russia are grim, but they are not nearly as overcrowded.

In a report on torture in Russia, Amnesty International said that "torture and ill-treatment occur at all stages of detention and imprisonment," but noted that it was most often reported in pretrial detention.

"Its main purpose appears to be to intimidate detainees and obtain confessions," the report said. Confessions, more than evidence, are a major part of criminal investigations in Russia.

How does the American criminal justice system differ from Russia's? How do those differences affect the conditions of pretrial detention?

Source: Alessandra Stanley, "Russians Lament the Crime of Punishment," *New York Times*, January 1, 1998, p. A1. Copyright © 1998 by the New York Times Co. Reprinted by permission.

The shock of arrest and detention can be made even worse by other factors. Many people are arrested for offenses they committed while under the influence of alcohol or some other substance and may therefore be that much less able to cope with their new situation. Young arrestees who face the risk of being victimized by older, stronger cell mates may sink into depression. Detainees also worry about losing their jobs while in jail, because they do not know if or when they will be released.

Pretrial detention can last a long time. While most felony defendants have their cases adjudicated within six months, other felony defendants can wait more than a year. For example, in 12 percent of felony cases in a recent study the defendants waited for more than one year for their cases to be resolved (Kyckelhahn and Cohen, 2008). If they are held in detention for that time period, they suffer from serious hardships, especially if the charges are eventually dropped or they are found to be not guilty. Thus, the psychological and economic hardships faced by pretrial detainees and their families can be major and prolonged.

Pretrial detention not only imposes stresses and hardships that can reach crisis levels, but it can also affect the outcomes of cases. People who are held in jail can give little help to their defense attorneys. They cannot help find witnesses and perform other useful tasks on their own behalf. In addition, they may feel pressured to plead guilty in order to end their indefinite stay in jail. Even if they believe that they should not be convicted of the crime charged, they may prefer to start serving a prison or jail sentence with a definite endpoint. Some may even gain quicker release on probation or in a community corrections program by pleading guilty, whereas they might stay in jail for a longer period by insisting on their innocence and awaiting a trial.

checkpoint

16. People are detained in jail for many reasons. What categories of people are found in jails?
17. What sources of stress do people face while in jail awaiting trial?

A QUESTION OF ETHICS

ED JOHNSON STOOD in front of Desk Sergeant Janet Sweeney at the Port City Police Station. Johnson was handcuffed and waiting to be booked. He had been caught by Officers Smith and Terrill outside a building in a wealthy neighborhood soon after the police had received a 911 call from a resident reporting that someone had tried to enter her apartment. Johnson was seen smoking a cigarette in an alley behind the building. He was known to the police because he had prior convictions for burglary and was currently out of prison on parole. When approached by the officers, he became angry and argued with them, claiming that he had done nothing wrong. The officers arrested him because of their suspicion that he had attempted to break into the apartment. When placed inside the police cruiser, Johnson exploded in anger, kicking the seat and attempting to kick the window as he accused the officers of unfairly trying to have him sent back to prison.

As Terrill grasped Johnson's arm, Smith went around behind the desk and spoke to Sergeant Sweeney in a soft voice.

"I know we don't have much on this guy, but we know he's a bad guy and we're sick of his attitude. We can't put up with people acting up and trying to damage a patrol vehicle. Let's make sure he isn't getting out of jail right away. He needs some attitude adjustment time by sleeping in a cell, at least for a few days anyway. Who knows? Maybe they'll revoke his parole and take him away. He deserves that."

"Smith, you know I can't do that. You've got nothing on him. There's nothing to tie him to the attempted break-in," said Sweeney.

"Look, forget about the attempted break-in. Can't we charge him for trying to damage police property and interfering with police officers for being so uncooperative? It might not stick but he really did try to damage the vehicle when he threw his fit."

"Yeah. We can't really put up with that kind of crap. Let's make the bail $1,000. I know he can't make that."

Critical Thinking and Analysis

Put yourself in the position of the city attorney and write a memo instructing the police about the following questions: What is the purpose of bail? Was the amount set appropriate in this instance? Should Johnson be held for becoming angry after being arrested based on the police officers' suspicions? Would the case have been handled the same way if Johnson did not have a criminal record? Now step back from your memo and ask yourself whether you would write the same memo if you were in the role of a mayor who is up for reelection or a police chief who has been criticized for being ineffective in controlling crime.

SUMMARY

Recognize the structure of the American court system

- The United States has a dual court system consisting of state and federal courts that are organized into separate hierarchies.

- Trial courts and appellate courts have different jurisdictions and functions.

- Despite resistance from local judges and political interests, reformers have sought to improve state court systems through centralized administration, state funding, and a separate personnel system.

Analyze the qualities that we desire in a judge

- The judge is a key figure in the criminal justice process who assumes the roles of adjudicator, negotiator, and administrator.

- The recent development of specialized courts, such as drug courts and mental health courts, places judges in the role of a problem solver.

Identify the ways that American judges are selected

- State judges are selected through various methods, including partisan elections, nonpartisan elections, gubernatorial appointment, legislative appointment, and merit selection.

- Merit selection methods for choosing judges have gradually spread to many states. Such methods normally use a screening committee to make recommendations of potential appointees who will, if placed on the bench by the governor, later go before the voters for approval or disapproval of their performance in office.

Understand the pretrial process in criminal cases

- Pretrial processes determine the fates of nearly all defendants through case dismissals, decisions defining the charges, and plea bargains, all of which affect more than 90 percent of cases.

- Defense attorneys use motions to their advantage to gain information and delay proceedings to benefit their clients.

Recognize how the bail system operates

- The bail process provides opportunities for many defendants to gain pretrial release, but poor defendants may be disadvantaged by their inability to come up with the money or property needed to secure release. Some preventive detention statutes permit judges to hold defendants considered dangerous or likely to flee.

- Bail bondsmen are private businesspeople who charge a fee to provide money for defendants' pretrial release. Their activities create risks of corruption and discrimination in the bail process, but they may help the system by reminding defendants about court dates and by tracking down defendants who disappear.

- Although judges bear the primary responsibility for setting bail, prosecutors are especially influential in recommending amounts and conditions for pretrial release.

- Initiatives to reform the bail process include release on own recognizance (ROR), police-issued citations, and bail guidelines.

Understand the context of pretrial detention

- Pretrial detainees, despite the presumption of innocence, are held in difficult conditions in jails containing mixed populations of convicted offenders, detainees, and troubled people. The shock of being jailed creates risks of suicide and depression.

QUESTIONS FOR REVIEW

1. Discuss the effects that partisan election of judges may have on the administration of justice. Which system of judicial selection do you think is most appropriate? Why?

2. The judge plays several roles. What are they? In your opinion, do they conflict with one another?

3. What are the methods of securing pretrial release for the accused?

4. What are the criteria used to set bail?

KEY TERMS

adversarial system (p. 331)
appellate courts (p. 324)
arraignment (p. 335)
bail (p. 338)
citation (p. 344)
drug courts (p. 330)
inquisitorial system (p. 333)
jurisdiction (p. 324)
merit selection (p. 334)
motion (p. 337)
nonpartisan election (p. 331)
partisan election (p. 331)
preventive detention (p. 345)
release on recognizance (ROR) (p. 344)
trial courts of general jurisdiction (p. 324)
trial courts of limited jurisdiction (p. 324)
United States v. Salerno and Cafero (1987) (p. 345)

FOR FURTHER READING

Epstein, Lee and Jeffrey Segal. 2007. *Advice and Consent: The Politics of Judicial Appointments.* New York: Oxford University Press. A careful examination of the political factors and processes that influence the selection, nomination, and confirmation of federal judges.

Feeley, Malcolm M. 1983. *Court Reform on Trial.* New York: Basic Books. A study of court reform efforts, such as diversion, speedy trial, bail reform, and sentencing reform. The book illustrates the difficulties involved in attempting to initiate changes within courts.

Goldkamp, John. 1995. *Personal Liberty and Community Safety: Pretrial Release in Criminal Court.* New York: Plenum. An examination of issues surrounding bail and pretrial release.

Slotnick, Elliot E., ed. 2005. *Judicial Politics: Readings from Judicature.* 3rd ed. Washington, DC: Congressional Quarterly Press. A variety of articles about courts, lawyers, and judges, including attention to debates about methods for selecting judges.

Smith, Christopher E. 1997. *Courts, Politics, and the Judicial Process*. 2nd ed. Belmont, CA: Wadsworth. A discussion of the structure and operations of courts, including an examination of methods for selecting judges.

Wice, Paul. 1974. *Freedom for Sale*. Lexington, MA: Lexington Books. A classic survey of bail and its operations.

GOING ONLINE

For an up-to-date list of web links, go to *The American System of Criminal Justice* 12e website: http://academic.cengage.com/criminaljustice/cole.

1. Go the web page for the judiciary of Iowa. Read the section entitled About Our Courts. What are the differences between various kinds of judges in Iowa, including judicial magistrates, associate juvenile judges, associate probate judges, district associate judges, and district court judges?

2. Go online to read Utah's requirements for obtaining a license to work as a bail bondsman. Are these requirements sufficient? Should there be any additional regulations?

3. Read reports from the American Judicature Society on judicial selection at their website. Which form of selection does the organization advocate? Do you agree with the arguments?

CHECKPOINT ANSWERS

1. *What is the dual court system?*

Separate federal and state court systems handling cases in the United States.

2. *What different categories of courts exist within each court system?*

The federal system is made up of the Supreme Court of the United States, circuit courts of appeals, and district courts. State court systems are made up of an appellate court of last resort, intermediate courts of appeals, trial courts of general jurisdiction, and trial courts of limited jurisdiction.

3. *What does it mean for courts to be decentralized?*

Operated and controlled by local communities, not a statewide administration. Most state and county courts are decentralized.

4. *What are the main goals of advocates of judicial reform?*

To create a unified court system with consolidated and simplified structures that has centralized management, full funding by the state, and a central personnel system.

5. *What is the image of the judge in the public's eye?*

That judges carefully and deliberately weigh the issues in a case before making a decision. Judges embody justice and dispense it impartially.

6. *Why might it be important for judges to represent different segments of society?*

So that all segments of society will view the decisions as legitimate and fair.

7. *What are judges' main functions?*

Adjudicator, negotiator, administrator.

8. *Why do political parties often prefer that judges be elected?*

To secure the support of attorneys who aspire to become judges and to ensure that courthouse positions are allocated to party workers.

9. *What are the steps in the merit selection process?*

When a vacancy occurs, a nominating commission is appointed that sends the governor the names of approved candidates. The governor must fill the vacancy from this list. After a short term, a referendum is held to ask the voters whether the judge should be retained.

10. *What are the purposes of preliminary hearings, arraignments, and defense motions?*

Preliminary hearings inform defendants of their rights and determine if there is probable cause. Arraignments involve the formal reading of charges and the entry of a plea. Motions seek information and the vindication of defendants' rights.

11. *Why and how are cases filtered out of the system?*

Cases are filtered out through the discretionary decisions of prosecutors and judges when they believe that there is inadequate evidence to proceed, or when prosecutors believe that their scarce resources are best directed at other cases.

12. *What factors affect whether bail is set and how much money or property a defendant must provide to gain pretrial release?*

Bail decisions are based primarily on the judge's evaluation of the seriousness of the offense and the defendant's prior record. The decisions are influenced by the prosecutor's recommendations and the defense attorney's counterarguments about the defendant's personal qualities and ties to the community.

13. *What positive and negative effects does the bail bondsman have on the justice system?*

Bondsmen help the system by reminding defendants about their court dates and finding them if they fail to appear. However, bondsmen also may contribute to corruption and discrimination.

14. *What methods are used to facilitate pretrial release for certain defendants?*

Bail reform alternatives such as police citations, release on own recognizance (ROR), and 10 percent cash bail.

15. *How did the U.S. Supreme Court rule in cases involving preventive detention?*

Preventive detention did not violate the Constitution's ban on excessive bail because such detentions are not punishment and are merely a way to protect the public.

16. *People are detained in jail for many reasons. What categories of people are found in jails?*

(1) Pretrial detainees for whom bail was not set or those who are too poor to pay the bail amount required, (2) people serving short sentences for misdemeanors, (3) people convicted of felonies awaiting transfer to prison, (4) people with psychological or substance abuse problems who have been swept off the streets.

17. *What sources of stress do people face while in jail awaiting trial?*

The stress of living with difficult and potentially dangerous cell mates; uncertainty about what will happen to their case, their families, their jobs, and their ability to contribute to preparing a defense.

CHAPTER 10

Prosecution and Defense

LEARNING OBJECTIVES

→ Understand the roles of the prosecuting attorney

→ Analyze the process by which criminal charges are filed, and what role the prosecutor's discretion plays in that process

→ Identify those with whom the prosecutor interacts in decision making

→ Understand the day-to-day reality of criminal defense work in the United States

→ Know how counsel is provided for defendants who cannot afford a private attorney

→ Understand the defense attorney's role in the system and the nature of the attorney–client relationship

An extremely rare car, an Enzo Ferrari worth more than $1.3 million, crashed on the Pacific Coast Highway in California in February 2006. At the scene, police officers found Bo Stefan Eriksson, a Swedish businessman whose mouth was bleeding. Eriksson claimed that he was a passenger in the vehicle and that the driver, whom he did not know well, had run away on foot. In investigating the evidence at the scene, the officers concluded that Eriksson had been driving at speeds in excess of 160 miles per hour and had lost control of the vehicle. Further investigation revealed he had previously served a prison term in Sweden for various offenses. In addition, he had leased several luxury vehicles, including the now-destroyed Ferrari, from owners in England who had never authorized him to ship those vehicles to California. Moreover, he stopped making required lease payments on the vehicles and his creditors were not able to find and repossess the vehicles. And to top off the unusual case, a search of his home revealed a .357 Magnum handgun, an item that a former felon is not allowed to possess (Associated Press, 2006).

Local prosecutors sifted through the complex facts in order to make decisions about whether to file criminal charges, what charges to file, and what recommendations to make about bail. The case was assigned to veteran

prosecutor, Tamara Hall, from the Los Angeles County District Attorney's Auto Insurance Fraud Division. She initially charged Eriksson with several felonies, including embezzlement, grand theft, and possession of a gun by a felon as well as two counts of misdemeanor drunken driving. She succeeded in having bail set at $3 million. Although he had not physically harmed anyone in California, the prosecutors were concerned about the risk that he might flee the country and leave the cars' owners with thousands of dollars in costs to repair and recover the luxury vehicles (*Sydney Morning Herald*, 2006).

Ultimately, Eriksson was represented by Jim Parkman, a nationally known criminal defense attorney, who, according to newspaper descriptions, "pokes and prods at the prosecution case with folksy comments and proverbs befitting his Alabama roots" and who was known "for his ability to sway folks in the jury box" (Soble, 2006). Parkman ultimately argued that the U.S. Customs Service had investigated and approved the importation of the luxury cars. By contrast, Deputy District Attorney Hall presented evidence to show that Eriksson set up sham transactions in order to defraud banks that loaned him money for the leases and to steal the vehicles by bringing them to the United States without authorization (KNBC, 2006a).

As the date for the trial approached, Eriksson pleaded "no contest" to one misdemeanor drunken driving charge related to the crash of the Ferrari. As part of the plea agreement, the other drunken driving charge was dropped. The District Attorney's Office decided to try Eriksson in a separate case concerning the gun possession charge, presumably to have the case handled by a prosecutor experienced in such matters. In addition, Deputy District Attorney Hall dropped two felony charges related to Eriksson's possession of the Ferrari that he destroyed in the crash and instead pursued charges concerning two other leased luxury vehicles in his possession for which she felt the evidence of theft and fraud was stronger. She proceeded toward trial with five felony charges for grand theft and fraudulent concealment with intent to defraud, charges that were within her area of expertise in the Auto Fraud Division of the prosecutor's office (KNBC, 2006b).

On the eve of trial, she offered Eriksson a plea deal: if he would plead "no contest" to four of the five felonies, he could receive a prison sentence of 2 years and four months. If he were convicted at trial of all five felony charges, Eriksson faced the possibility of an 11-year prison sentence. Despite the risk, Eriksson and his attorney turned down the deal and decided to fight the charges at trial (KNBC, 2006b).

Newspaper reporters speculated that the outcome of the trial could depend on each attorney's image in the eyes of the jury. Because the businesslike prosecutor Hall would be presenting complicated details of lease contracts and financial transactions, whereas defense attorney Parkman would befriend and charm the jurors, one news article speculated that "courtroom style may trump substance in [the] Ferrari Guy trial" (Soble, 2006). Indeed, on the first day of trial, Parkman tried to endear himself to the jury with his folksy manner. As described in the news, "Speaking in a thick Southern drawl, Parkman told the jury his grandmother had an old saying that was applicable [to the case]. 'No matter how thin you make the pancake, it still has two sides to it.'" (KNBC, 2006b). Clearly, Parkman was intent on convincing the jurors about his client's side to the story.

After a week-long trial and three days of deliberations by the jury, the jurors ultimately told Judge Patricia Schnegg that they were deadlocked 10-to-2 in favor of conviction. Because the jurors did not reach a unanimous decision, Judge Schnegg declared a mistrial—meaning that no resolution could be reached and that the prosecutors must decide either to retry the case in a new trial with a different jury, offer another plea deal, or drop the charges (Associated Press, 2006). The District Attorney's Office initially announced that it would retry Eriksson, but four days later it became clear that behind-the-scenes negotiations between Hall and Parkman had produced a resolution to the case. Eriksson pleaded "no contest" to embezzlement and being a felon in possession of a firearm, thus avoiding trial on any remaining charges. In exchange for accepting responsibility for these crimes, he received a sentence of three years in state prison in November 2006. In addition, his $6 million California home was seized so that the proceeds of its sale could reimburse the banks and lease companies victimized by Eriksson's actions. One of Eriksson's attorneys described the final outcome as "a meeting of the minds" and Hall said that "It was a fair resolution . . . [that was] consistent with the [views of the] majority of jurors" (KNBC, 2006c). Ultimately, Eriksson served only 14 months in prison before he was paroled and immediately deported to Sweden in January 2008 (Soble, 2008).

As illustrated by the Eriksson case, prosecutors and defense attorneys are key decision makers in the criminal justice process. Their decisions, strategies, interactions, and effectiveness determine the fates of individuals facing criminal prosecution. As illustrated by Eriksson's case, prosecutors may shift their decisions about charges and plea agreements depending on how the evidence develops and how jurors are expected to react to that evidence. Defense attorneys must advise their clients and make strategic decisions about whether to plead guilty and what tactics to use during trial. After turning down the first plea bargain offered by the prosecution, defense attorney Parkman succeeded in undercutting the prosecution's case at trial and thereby prevented a guilty verdict and a long sentence. Parkman's success forced Deputy District Attorney Hall to reconsider the strength of the case. Thus the second plea agreement enabled Eriksson to receive a single short prison term for all charges and thereby avoid a retrial as well as a later trial on the gun charge. At the same time, the plea agreement fulfilled the prosecution's goal of sending Eriksson to prison to punish him for breaking the law.

Because of his wealth, the Swedish businessman could afford to hire a well-known defense attorney and fight his case through the entire trial process rather than caving in to the pressure to accept the first plea bargain offered. Many other defendants cannot afford to hire their own attorneys and the American justice system often faces questions about whether these defendants receive equal and fair treatment.

The American system places great power and responsibility in the hands of attorneys for each side in a criminal case. The prosecutor and defense attorney are the most influential figures in determining the outcomes of criminal cases. Their discretionary decisions and negotiations determine people's fates. As we shall see in this chapter, the justice system's ability to handle cases and produce fair results depends on the dedication, skill, and enthusiasm of these lawyers.

THE PROSECUTORIAL SYSTEM

Prosecuting attorneys make discretionary decisions about whether to pursue criminal charges, which charges to make, and what sentence to recommend. They represent the government in pursuing criminal charges against the accused. Except in a few states, no higher authority second-guesses or changes these decisions. Thus, prosecutors are more independent than most other public officials. As with other aspects of American government, prosecution lies mainly in the hands of state and local governments. Because most crimes are violations of state laws, county prosecutors bring charges against suspects in court.

United States attorney
Officials responsible for the prosecution of crimes that violate the laws of the United States; appointed by the president and assigned to a U.S. district court jurisdiction.

state attorney general
A state's chief legal officer, usually responsible for both civil and criminal matters.

prosecuting attorney
A legal representative of the state with sole responsibility for bringing criminal charges; in some states referred to as district attorney, state's attorney, or county attorney.

 The state attorney general in Alaska has responsibility for criminal prosecutions. Learn about this aspect of the attorney general's office on their website. To link to this website, go to *The American System of Criminal Justice* 12e companion site at academic.cengage.com/criminaljustice/cole.

For cases involving violation of federal criminal laws, prosecutions are handled in federal courts by **United States attorneys**. These attorneys are responsible for a large number of drug-related and white-collar crime cases. Appointed by the president, they serve as part of the Department of Justice. One U.S. attorney and a staff of assistant U.S. attorneys prosecute cases in each of the 94 U.S. district courts.

Each state has an elected attorney general, who usually has the power to bring prosecutions in certain cases. A **state attorney general** may, for example, handle a statewide consumer fraud case if a chain of auto repair shops is suspected of overcharging customers. In Alaska, Delaware, and Rhode Island, the state attorney general also directs all local prosecutions.

However, the vast majority of criminal cases are handled in the 2,341 county-level offices of the **prosecuting attorney**—known in various states as the district attorney, state's attorney, commonwealth attorney, or county attorney—who pursues cases that violate state law. The number of prosecutors who work in these offices increased by more than 35 percent from 1990 to 2005, but most of that growth occurred prior to the turn of the century and prosecutorial resources have not increased since 2001 (Perry, 2006). Prosecutors have the power to make independent decisions about which cases to pursue and what charges to file. They also have the power to drop charges and to negotiate arrangements for guilty pleas.

In rural areas the prosecutor's office may consist of merely the prosecuting attorney and a part-time assistant. By contrast, some urban jurisdictions, such as Los Angeles, employ 500 assistant prosecutors and numerous legal assistants and investigators, and organize the office according to various types of crimes. Many assistant prosecutors seek to use the trial experience gained in the prosecutor's office as a means of moving on to a better-paying position in a private law firm.

Politics and Prosecution

Except in a few states, such as Alaska, Connecticut, and New Jersey, prosecutors are typically elected in county or municipal elections, usually for a four-year term; the office thus is heavily involved in local politics. By seeking to please voters, many prosecutors have tried to use their local office as a springboard to higher office—such as state legislator, governor, or member of Congress.

Although the power of prosecutors flows directly from their legal duties, politics strongly influence the process of prosecution. Prosecutors can often mesh their own ambitions with the needs of a political party. The appointment of assistant prosecutors offers a chance to recruit bright young lawyers to the party. Prosecutors may choose certain cases for prosecution in order to gain the favor of voters, or investigate charges against political opponents and public officials to get the attention of the public. Political factors can also cause prosecutors to apply their powers unevenly within a community. Prosecutors' discretionary power can create the impression that some groups or individuals receive harsher treatment, while others receive protection.

The existence of discretionary decision making creates the risk that such decisions will produce discrimination. The limited number of studies of prosecutorial decision making do not present consistent results. However, as summarized by scholars who looked at a number of studies, "a number of studies have found that African American and Hispanic suspects are more likely than white suspects to be charged with a crime and prosecuted fully" (Walker, Spohn, and DeLeone, 2007: 193). In addition, "[t]here also is evidence supporting charges of selective prosecution of racial minorities, especially for drug offenses" (Walker, Spohn, and DeLeone, 2007: 193). Several other studies raise questions about discrimination in specific situations, such as prosecutors' decisions to seek the death penalty (Sorensen and Wallace, 1999). If prosecutors' discretionary decisions produce discriminatory results, these outcomes clearly clash with the American value of equal treatment and fairness. If the criminal justice system is going to fulfill American values concerning equality and fairness, then prosecutors must use their decision-making authority carefully to avoid inequality and injustice.

checkpoint

1.   What are the titles of the officials responsible for criminal prosecution at the federal, state, and local levels of government?
    (Answers are at the end of the chapter.)

The Prosecutor's Influence

Prosecutors exert great influence because they are concerned with all aspects of the criminal justice process (Jacoby, 1995). By contrast, other decision makers play a role in only part of the process. Throughout the entire process—from arrest to final disposition of a case—prosecutors can make decisions that will largely determine the defendant's fate. The prosecutor chooses the cases to be prosecuted, selects the charges to be brought, recommends the bail amount, approves agreements with the defendant, and urges the judge to impose a particular sentence.

Throughout the justice process, prosecutors' links with the other actors in the system—police, defense attorneys, judges—shape the prosecutors' decisions. Prosecutors may, for example, recommend bail amounts and sentences that match the preferences of particular judges. They may make "tough" recommendations in front of "tough" judges, but tone down their arguments before judges who favor leniency or rehabilitation. Likewise, the other actors in the system may adjust their decisions and actions to match the preferences of the prosecutor. For example, police officers' investigation and arrest practices tend to reflect the prosecutor's priorities. Thus, prosecutors influence the decisions of others while also shaping their own actions in ways that reinforce their relationships with police, defense attorneys, and judges.

Prosecutors gain additional power from the fact that their decisions and actions are hidden from public view. For example, a prosecutor and a defense attorney may strike a bargain whereby the prosecutor reduces a charge in exchange for a guilty plea or drops a charge if the defendant agrees to seek psychiatric help. In such instances, decisions are reached in a way that is nearly invisible to the public.

State laws do little to limit or guide prosecutors' decisions. Most laws describe the prosecutor's duties in such vague terms as "prosecuting all crimes and civil actions to which state or county may be party." Such laws do not tell the prosecutor which cases must be prosecuted and which ones dismissed. The prosecutor has significant discretion to make such decisions without direct interference from either the law or other actors in the justice system (Caulfield, 1994). When prosecutors' decisions are challenged, judges generally reject the claim.

Because most local prosecutors are elected, public opinion influences their decisions. If they feel that the community no longer considers a particular act

Michigan's Prosecuting Attorneys Coordinating Council provides extensive information about prosecutors at its website. To link to this website, go to *The American System of Criminal Justice* 12e companion site at academic.cengage.com/criminaljustice/cole.

to be criminal, they may refuse to prosecute or they may try to convince the complainant not to press charges. Public influence over prosecutors can take two forms. First, because most prosecutors are elected, they must keep their decisions consistent with community values in order to increase their chances of gaining reelection. Second, because jurors are drawn from the local community, prosecutors do not want to waste their time and resources pursuing charges about which local jurors are unsympathetic or unconcerned. In some communities, for example, prostitution may be prosecuted actively, while in others it is ignored. About three-fourths of American prosecutors serve counties with populations of fewer than 100,000. There often is only one prosecutor in the community, and he or she may face strong local pressures, especially with regard to victimless crimes such as marijuana smoking, petty gambling, and prostitution. Prosecutors therefore develop policies that reflect community attitudes. As one New York prosecutor has remarked, "We are pledged to enforcement of the law, but we have to use our heads in the process."

checkpoint

2. What are the powers of the prosecuting attorney?

The Prosecutor's Roles

As "lawyers for the state," prosecutors face conflicting pressures to press charges vigorously against lawbreakers while also upholding justice and the rights of the accused. These pressures are often called "the prosecutor's dilemma." In the adversarial system, prosecutors must do everything they can to win a conviction, yet as members of the legal profession they must see that justice is done even if it means that the accused is not convicted. This rule is enshrined in state statutes and lawyers' codes of ethics. For example, the Texas Code of Criminal Procedure states,

"It shall be the primary duty of all prosecuting attorneys, including any special prosecutors, not to convict, but to see that justice is done. They shall not suppress facts or secrete witnesses capable of establishing the innocence of the accused."

As the defendant and defense attorneys listen, prosecutor Steven Lember addresses the New Jersey state court in the manslaughter trial of former NBA basketball star Jayson Williams. Williams was convicted of tampering with evidence in his first trial concerning the shooting of a limo driver at his home. He faced a second trial in 2008 because jurors deadlocked over the original reckless manslaughter charge. What are the prosecutor's responsibilities in conducting a criminal trial?

© Don Murray/Getty Images

Even so, there is always a risk of prosecutor's bias, sometimes called a "prosecution complex." Although they are supposed to represent all the people, including the accused, prosecutors may view themselves as instruments of law enforcement. Thus, as advocates on behalf of the state, their strong desire to close each case with a conviction may keep them from recognizing unfair procedures or evidence of innocence (Weinberg, 2003). A comparison of prosecutors in the United States and Japan, for example, found that American prosecutors often proceed with the assumption that the facts weigh against the defendant, while Japanese prosecutors are more concerned with investigating the case to discover all available facts before making any decisions (D. T. Johnson, 1998).

What happens in the United States if prosecutors make a mistake and it appears that an innocent person may have been convicted? After a trial and the completion of the appellate process, sometimes a defendant has no avenue to gain reconsideration of the conviction (Tucker, 1997). A national commission appointed by U.S. Attorney General Janet Reno recommended in 1999 that prosecutors drop their adversarial posture and cooperate in permitting DNA testing of evidence saved from old cases that had produced convictions before sophisticated scientific tests were developed (Lewis, 1999). Despite the fact that dozens of convicted offenders have been proved innocent in rape and murder cases through after-the-fact DNA testing, some prosecutors have resisted the reexamination of old evidence.

In contrast, when Craig Watkins became the new prosecutor of Dallas County, Texas, in 2007, he received national attention for seeking to reinvestigate cases of offenders convicted by previous prosecutors. Dallas County leads the nation in DNA exonerations. In April 2008, for example, James Woodard was the seventeenth person from Dallas County released from prison when DNA evidence demonstrated that he did not commit the rape and murder for which he had spent 27 years behind bars (Lavandera, 2008). Watkins sent shock waves through the legal community in Texas by proposing that the legislature create a new law that would make it a crime for prosecutors to knowingly hide or suppress evidence that could help a defendant. He made it clear that he thought some past prosecutors in Dallas County should be investigated for possible prosecution under such a law (Lavandera, 2008). Prosecutors are seldom punished for mistakes they made in convicting innocent people, even when there is evidence of possible misconduct, and they remain generally immune from civil lawsuits for their official actions.

Even in those rare circumstances in which prosecutors face criminal misconduct charges for excessive actions in seeking to convict an innocent person, juries do not always convict the prosecutors of crimes. In June 1999 an Illinois jury acquitted seven prosecutors and law enforcement officers of conspiracy and obstruction of justice charges that stemmed from their efforts to convict Rolando Cruz of the gruesome murder of a child. Although Cruz eventually gained release from prison when someone else confessed to the crime, Cruz was not a model citizen and gave inconsistent testimony about his treatment at the hands of police and prosecutors. Thus, jurors were apparently reluctant to convict the prosecutors of crimes for the mistakes that they made in investigating Cruz's case (Possley and Gregory, 1999).

Although all prosecutors must uphold the law and pursue charges against lawbreakers, they can perform these tasks in different ways. Because of their personal values and professional goals, as well as the political climate of their city or county, they may define the prosecutor's role differently than do prosecutors in other places. For example, a prosecutor who believes that young offenders can be rehabilitated would likely define the role differently than one who believes that young offenders should receive the same punishments as adults. One might send juveniles to counseling programs while the other seeks to process

 The Innocence Project, a nationwide organization based at university law schools to investigate claims of innocence by convicted offenders, says that 33 of the convictions involved in the first 74 DNA exonerations included examples of misconduct by prosecutors. See the Project's website for details. To link to this website, go to *The American System of Criminal Justice* 12e companion site at academic.cengage.com/criminaljustice/cole.

them though the adult system of courts and corrections (Sridharan, Greenfield, and Blakley, 2004). A prosecutor with no assistants and few resources for conducting full-blown jury trials may be forced to stress effective plea bargaining, whereas a prosecutor in a wealthier county may have more options when deciding whether to take cases to trial.

Role definition is further complicated by the prosecutor's need to maintain relationships with many other actors—police officers, judges, defense attorneys, political party leaders, and so forth—who may have conflicting ideas about what the prosecutor should do. The prosecutor's decisions affect the ability of the others to perform their duties and achieve their goals. If the prosecutor decides not to prosecute, the judge and jury will not get to decide the case, and police officers may feel that their efforts have been wasted. If the prosecutor decides to launch a campaign against drugs or pornography, this decision will impact both the political and criminal justice arenas. Police may feel that they must redirect their time and energy toward the crimes emphasized by the prosecutor. However, they may also pressure the prosecutor to set new priorities, by declining to devote their efforts to the kinds of crimes the prosecutor wants to concentrate on. Excessive attention to victimless crimes, such as gambling and prostitution, may produce a public backlash if citizens feel that the prosecutor should focus on more serious crimes.

We can see prosecutors as generally following one of four distinct roles:

1. *Trial counsel for the police.* Prosecutors who see their main function in this light believe they should reflect the views of law enforcement in the courtroom and take a crime-fighting stance in public.

2. *House counsel for the police.* These prosecutors believe their main function is to give legal advice so that arrests will stand up in court.

3. *Representative of the court.* Such prosecutors believe their main function is to enforce the rules of due process to ensure that the police act according to the law and uphold the rights of defendants.

4. *Elected official.* These prosecutors may be most responsive to public opinion. The political impact of their decisions is one of their main concerns.

Each of these roles involves a different view of the prosecutor's "clients" as well as his or her own responsibilities. In the first two roles, prosecutors see the police as their primary clients. Take a moment to think about who might be the clients of prosecutors who view themselves as representatives of the court or as elected officials.

checkpoint

3. What are the roles of the prosecutor?

Discretion of the Prosecutor

Because they have such broad discretion, prosecutors can shape their decisions to fit different interests. Their decisions might be based on a desire to impress voters through tough "throw-the-book-at-them" charges in a highly publicized case (Maschke, 1995). Their decisions might stem from their personal values, such as an emphasis on leniency and rehabilitation for young offenders. Prosecutors might also shape their decisions to please local judges by, for example, accepting plea agreements that will keep the judges from being burdened by too many time-consuming trials. Such motives can shape prosecutors' decisions because there is usually no higher authority to tell prosecutors how they

Eliot Spitzer speaks to the news media in 2008 prior to resigning as governor of New York after newspapers reported that he was a customer of a prostitution ring. Those running the prostitution ring were convicted of criminal offenses, but no charges were filed against Spitzer. Is it a fair and appropriate use of prosecutorial discretion to bring charges against the prostitutes and their business managers but not the customers who make use of these illegal services?

© Chris Hondros/Getty Images

must do their jobs. From the time the police turn a case over to the prosecutor, he or she has almost complete control over decisions about charges and plea agreements.

The discretion of American prosecutors sharply contrasts with the situation of prosecutors in European countries such as Germany (see the Comparative Perspective). In Germany, the prosecutors face fewer pressures to win cases and instead bear greater responsibilities for evaluating the evidence and guilt of defendants before deciding whether to drop or pursue charges (Feeney, 1998). By contrast, American prosecutors who have doubts about whether the available evidence actually proves the defendant's guilt may just shrug their shoulders and say, "I'll just let the jury decide" rather than face public criticism for dropping charges. In Japan, prosecutors throughout the country work for a single nationwide agency and are not elected. As such, they must gain approval from superiors for many of their decisions rather than making independent decisions like those of local prosecutors in the United States (D. T. Johnson, 1998).

Although the rate of dismissals varies from place to place, in most cities up to half of all arrests do not lead to formal charges. Prosecutors may decide to drop charges because of factors related to a particular case or because they have a policy of not bringing charges for certain offenses. For example, the U.S. Department of Justice gives its prosecutors guidelines for deciding whether a case should be dismissed or pursued (U.S. Department of Justice, 1980). They include the following:

1. Federal law enforcement priorities

2. The nature and seriousness of the offense

3. The deterrent effect of prosecution

4. The person's culpability (blameworthiness) in connection with the offense

5. The person's history with respect to criminal activity

6. The person's willingness to cooperate in the investigation or prosecution of others

7. The probable sentence or other consequences if the person is convicted

COMPARATIVE PERSPECTIVE

Prosecution in Germany

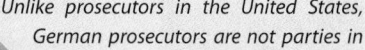

Unlike prosecutors in the United States, German prosecutors are not parties in an adversarial system; rather, they are required to act not only against, but also in favor of, the suspect at any stage of the proceedings. German prosecutors are not elected but are civil servants and thus are relatively immune from public opinion.

German prosecutors are expected to be objective above all, and thus one-third of all fraud cases studied were dismissed because of lack of sufficient evidence even though the suspect had made a confession in the course of police investigation. Another consequence of the rule of objectivity is that prosecutors need not concern themselves with winning every case. In up to 20 percent of all cases studied, the accused was acquitted by the trial judge, usually at the request of the prosecutor.

The Prosecutor's Office as an Investigating Agency

In Germany the prosecutor controls the police investigations of each reported criminal case. Therefore, the prosecutor is often called "head of the preliminary proceedings." However, except in a few sensational cases such as murder, big commercial crime, and, recently, terrorism, prosecutors seldom are in a true supervisory role. Instead, a typical investigatory situation progresses as follows.

An offense will usually be reported to the police, who will then open and register a file. The police lack any discretionary power in deciding whether or not to file a case. They must follow up every suspicion and present all registered offenses—however vague the evidence may be—to the prosecutor, who alone makes the final decision. The police carry out all necessary investigations. If the police feel a case has been thoroughly investigated, they will forward it to the prosecutor, who must decide whether further investigation is necessary. The prosecutor can take over the investigation or can return the case to the police for further inquiries. The law requires the prosecutor to do everything to solve the case—regardless of its seriousness. It does not permit him or her to "filter" out cases, as American prosecutors are authorized to do.

The Prosecutor's Office as a Charging Agency

Calling the prosecutor's office a "charging agency" is something of a misnomer because on the average three out of four cases are dropped. The label refers to the main task of the prosecutor, as it is the prosecutor's decision whether to charge or not. The charging decision involves two distinct considerations: evaluation of evidence and evaluation of guilt.

When prosecutors are *evaluating evidence*, they remain more or less free to make this decision. Some outside control is possible, however, because victims can file a formal complaint against the dismissal of a case. If the complaint is rejected by the attorney general (chief prosecutor of the state), the victim can file a motion for a judicial decision, which would, if successful, force the prosecutor to file a charge. Although this procedure is seldom used, prosecutors nonetheless fear it. As a result, the status of victims may influence prosecutors' decisions. When the prosecutor is *evaluating guilt*, there are significant possibilities of hierarchical control over the decision. According to administrative rules issued by some of the ministries of justice of the states, deputy attorneys must present to their superiors for approval each case they want to dismiss based on minor guilt (mitigation). "In-house" instructions may also attempt to standardize the criteria by which "minor guilt" is defined.

The main task of prosecutors is to determine whether the evidence in a case is sufficient for conviction. As a result, they have large practical discretionary power when they describe whether "probable cause" exists in any given case. The prosecutor's "evaluation of evidence" was examined in two types of cases: petty and serious crimes. It was found that if the damage (monetary value or physical injuries) was considerable or if the suspect had previously been convicted, the prosecutor was less inclined to drop the charge even if the evidence was weak. This situation might be explained by the possibility that the more serious the crime, the more likely the accused is to retain defense counsel, which may hinder police investigation.

The relationship between the suspect and the victim also markedly affects the prosecutor's evaluation of the evidence. Cases involving acquaintances or relatives of the victim rather than stranger-to-stranger cases are more likely to be dismissed if they involve the crimes of theft, robbery, or rape. However, the opposite is true if the crime is fraud or embezzlement, because of the special breach of trust connected with these types of acts.

In summary, then, it seems the prosecutor uses stricter evidentiary rules in *minor* offenses than in *serious* offenses. It may be that even though the evidence might not support a conviction in the more serious cases, the prosecutor still charges the case in order to use the charge itself as a sanction. The latter assumption is supported by the fact that prosecutors tend to regard prior criminal record as an element of proof and therefore charge recidivists more than first offenders. This tendency is in part counterbalanced by the judge, who—stressing the problem of proof more than does the prosecutor—acquits more recidivists than first offenders.

Americans may wonder how the German system, with its requirement of compulsory prosecution, can be efficient. In Germany, caseloads are reduced by decriminalizing some acts, making prosecution contingent on the victim's formal request, turning felonies into misdemeanors, and extending the discretionary power of the prosecutor.

Source: Adapted from Klaus Sessar, "Prosecutorial Discretion in Germany," in *The Prosecutor*, ed. William F. McDonald (Beverly Hills, CA: Sage, 1979), 255–73.

In addition to these formal considerations, decisions to pursue felony charges may also be affected by the staffing levels of individual prosecutor's offices (P. Walker, 1998). If offices lack sufficient resources to pursue all possible cases, prosecutors may establish priorities and then reduce or dismiss charges in cases deemed less important.

If you were a prosecutor, what would you consider the most important factors in deciding whether to pursue a case? Would you have any concerns about the possibility of prosecuting an innocent person? Is there an ethical problem if a prosecutor pursues a case against someone whom the prosecutor thinks is not really guilty of a crime? Read "A Question of Ethics" at the end of the chapter and consider what you would do if you were the prosecutor assigned to the case.

Even after deciding that a case should be prosecuted, the prosecutor has great freedom in deciding what charges to file. In criminal incidents that involve several laws, the prosecutor can bring a single charge or more than one. Suppose that Smith, who is armed, breaks into a grocery store, assaults the proprietor, and robs the cash drawer. What charges can the prosecutor file? By virtue of having committed the robbery, the accused can be charged with at least four crimes: breaking and entering, assault, armed robbery, and carrying a dangerous weapon. Other charges or **counts** can be added, depending on the nature of the incident. A forger, for instance, can be charged with one count for each act of forgery committed. By filing as many charges as possible, the prosecutor strengthens his or her position in plea negotiations. In effect, the prosecutor can use discretion in deciding the number of charges and thus increase the prosecution's supply of "bargaining chips."

The discretionary power to set charges does not give the prosecutor complete control over plea bargaining. Defense attorneys strengthen their position in the **discovery** process, in which the prosecutor discloses information from the case file to the defense. For example, the defense has the right to see any statements made by the accused during interrogation by the police, as well as the results of any physical or psychological tests. This information tells the defense attorney about the strengths and weaknesses of the prosecution's case. The defense attorney may use it to decide whether a case is hopeless or whether it is worthwhile to engage in tough negotiations.

The prosecutor's discretion does not end with the decision to file a certain charge. After the charge has been made, the prosecutor may reduce it in exchange for a guilty plea or enter a notation of *nolle prosequi* (*nol. pros.*). The latter is a freely made decision to drop the charge, either as a whole or as to one or more count. When a prosecutor decides to drop charges, no higher authorities can force him or her to reinstate them. When guilty pleas are entered, the prosecutor uses discretion in recommending a sentence.

To read about the operation of one local prosecutor's office, see the website of the Essex County, New Jersey, prosecutor. To link to this website, go to *The American System of Criminal Justice* 12e companion site at academic .cengage.com/criminaljustice/cole.

count
Each separate offense of which a person is accused in an indictment or an information.

discovery
A prosecutor's pretrial disclosure, to the defense, of facts and evidence to be introduced at trial.

nolle prosequi
An entry made by a prosecutor on the record of a case and announced in court to indicate that the charges specified will not be prosecuted. In effect, the charges are thereby dismissed.

checkpoint

4. How does a prosecutor use discretion to decide how to treat each defendant?

Key Relationships of the Prosecutor

Formal policies and role conceptions alone do not affect prosecutors' decisions (Fridell, 1990). Relationships with other actors in the justice system influence them as well. Despite their independent authority, prosecutors must consider how police, judges, and others will react. They depend on these officials in order to prosecute cases successfully. In turn, the success of police, judges, and correctional officials depends on prosecutors' effectiveness in identifying and convicting lawbreakers. Thus, these officials build exchange relationships in which they cooperate with one another.

Police

Prosecutors depend on the police to provide both the suspects and the evidence needed to convict lawbreakers. Most crimes occur before the police arrive at the scene; therefore, officers must reconstruct the crime on the basis of physical evidence and witnesses' reports. Police must use their training, experience, and work routines to decide whether arrest and prosecution would be worthwhile. Prosecutors cannot control the types of cases brought to them, because they cannot investigate crimes on their own. Thus, the police control the initiation of the criminal justice process through the ways they investigate crimes and arrest suspects. Various factors, such as pressure on police to establish an impressive crime-clearance record, can influence police actions. As a result, such actions can create problems for prosecutors if, for example, the police make many arrests without gathering enough evidence to ensure conviction.

Despite this dependence, prosecutors can influence the actions of the police. For example, prosecutors can return cases for further investigation and refuse to approve arrest warrants. Prosecutors and police have an exchange relationship in which the success of each depends on cooperation with the other.

Police requests for prosecution may be refused for reasons unrelated to the facts of the case. First, prosecutors regulate the workload of the justice system. They must make sure that a backlog of cases does not keep the court from meeting legal time limits for processing criminal cases. To keep cases from being dismissed by the judge for taking too long, prosecutors may themselves dismiss relatively weak or minor cases and focus on those with more serious charges or clear proof of the defendant's guilt. Second, prosecutors may reject police requests for prosecution because they do not want to pursue poorly developed cases that would place them in an embarrassing position in the courtroom. Judges often scold prosecutors if weak cases are allowed to take up scarce courtroom time. Finally, prosecutors may return cases to make sure that police provide high-quality investigations and evidence.

In recent decades, criminal justice officials have expressed concern about coordination between police and prosecutors. Some claim that lack of coordination causes cases to be dismissed or lost. Part of the problem is that lawyers and police have different views of crime and work for different sponsoring organizations. The police often claim that they have made a valid arrest and that there is no reason an offender should not be indicted and tried, but prosecutors look at cases to see if the evidence will result in a conviction. These different perspectives often lead to conflicts.

In response to the need for greater coordination, many jurisdictions have formed police-prosecution teams to work together on cases. This approach is often used for drug or organized-crime investigations and cases in which conviction requires detailed information and evidence. Drug cases require cooperation between the police and prosecutors because without a network of informers, the police cannot catch drug traffickers with evidence that can lead to convictions. Prosecutors can help the police gain cooperation from informants by approving agreements to reduce charges or even to *nolle prosequi* a case. The accused person may then return to the community to gather information for the police.

Victims and Witnesses

Prosecutors depend on the cooperation of victims and witnesses (R. C. Davis, Smith, and Taylor, 2003). Although a case can be prosecuted whether or not a victim wishes to press charges, many prosecutors will not pursue cases in which the key testimony and other necessary evidence must be provided by a victim who is unwilling to cooperate. Prosecutors also need the cooperation of people who have witnessed crimes.

The decision to prosecute is often based on an assessment of the victim's role in his or her own victimization and the victim's credibility as a witness. If a victim has a criminal record, the prosecutor may choose not to pursue the case, in the belief that a jury would not consider the victim a credible witness—despite the fact that the jury will never learn that the victim has a criminal record. In fact, the decision not to prosecute may actually reflect the prosecutor's belief that someone with a criminal record is untrustworthy or does not deserve the protection of the law. In other words, the prosecutor's own biases in sizing up victims may affect which cases he or she pursues. If a victim is poorly dressed, uneducated, or inarticulate, the prosecutor may be inclined to dismiss charges out of fear that a jury would find the victim unpersuasive (Stanko, 1988).

Other characteristics of victims may play a similar role. For example, prosecutors might not pursue cases in which victims are prostitutes who have been raped, drug abusers who have been assaulted by drug dealers, and children who cannot stand up to the pressure of testifying in court. Research indicates that victims' characteristics, such as moral character, behavior at time of incident, and age, influence decisions to prosecute sexual assault cases more than does the actual strength of the evidence against the suspect (J. W. Spears and Spohn, 1997). Prosecutors sometimes also base their decision on whether or not the victim and defendant had a prior relationship. Studies show that prosecutions succeed most when aimed at defendants accused of committing crimes against strangers (Boland et al., 1983). When the victim is an acquaintance, a friend, or even a relative of the defendant, he or she may refuse to act as a witness, and prosecutors and juries may view the offense as less serious. Even if police make an arrest on the scene, a fight between spouses may strike a prosecutor as a weak case, especially if the complaining spouse has second thoughts about cooperating. A high percentage of victims of violent crimes are acquainted with their assailants. That some victims would rather endure victimization than see a friend or relative punished in the justice system creates problems for the prosecution's cases.

Prosecutors and police officers in several American cities express concern about the growth of a "stop snitching" movement that is essentially a means through which drug dealers and other criminals seek to intimidate witnesses into remaining silent. Beatings and murders of witnesses in Baltimore, Philadelphia, Newark, and other cities complicate prosecutors' efforts to gain convictions (Kocieniewski, 2007). Moreover, due to highly publicized "stop snitching" DVDs and T-shirts, the idea of refusing to cooperate with prosecutors and police seems to have become part of the code of behavior by which many young people apparently seek to live. Because prosecutors must rely on witnesses and victims to supply testimony and other evidence against offenders, officials have felt challenged to find ways to counteract the "stop snitching" message that is so widespread and powerful in some neighborhoods.

See the information for victims and witnesses on the website of the Boone County, Indiana, prosecutor's office. To link to this website, go to *The American System of Criminal Justice* 12e companion site at academic.cengage.com/criminaljustice/cole.

Based on the findings of a classic study, Figure 10.1 shows the outcomes of stranger and nonstranger robberies and burglaries in New York City. Note that 88 percent of arrests for robberies by strangers led to conviction, with 68 percent of these on a felony charge. Of those arrested, 65 percent were incarcerated, 32 percent for a year or more. In contrast, when the robbery victim knew the accused person, only 37 percent of those arrested were convicted, only

FIGURE 10.1

Outcomes of stranger and nonstranger robberies and burglaries in New York City
Victims of burglaries and robberies are less likely to pressure for conviction when the offender is known to them. If conviction is successful, the penalties tend to be lower when the offender is not a stranger.

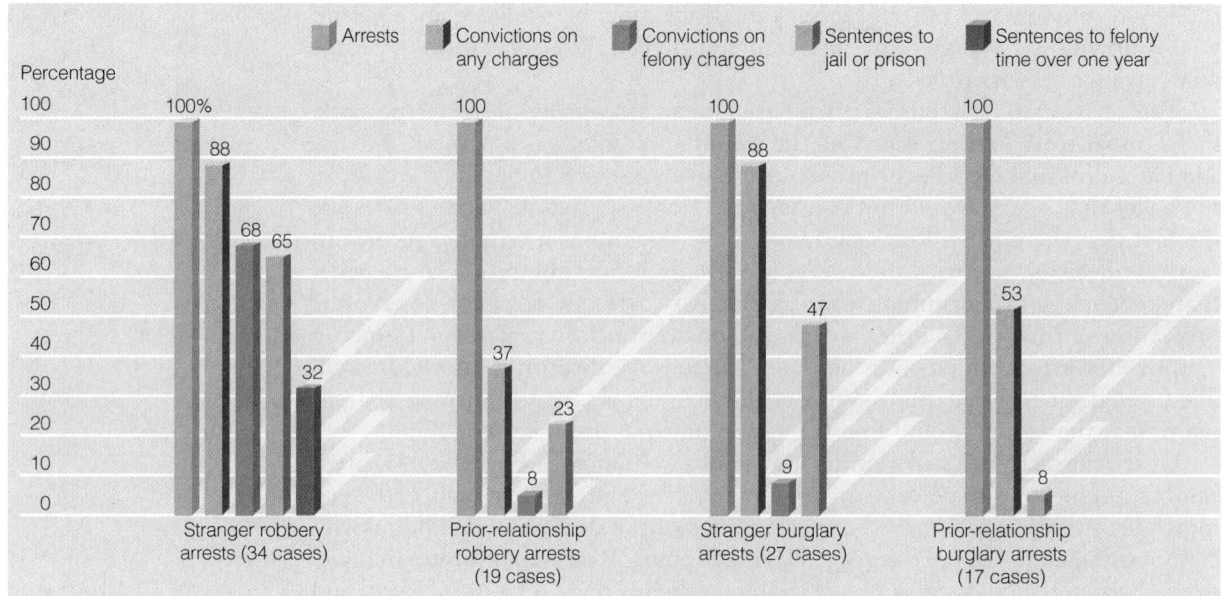

Source: Vera Institute of Justice, *Felony Arrests: Their Prosecution and Disposition in New York City's Courts* (New York: Longman, 1981), 58, 86. Copyright © 1981 by Longman Publishing Group. Reprinted by permission of Vera Institute of Justice.

23 percent incarcerated, and none served more than a year. The same pattern can be seen in burglaries, although the punishments were less severe. Most of the burglars who were strangers were convicted, but only 8 percent on a felony charge. Prosecutors probably bargained these cases down to misdemeanors because the evidence was not strong. As with robberies of acquaintances, the burglars who knew their victims were treated more leniently than those who did not (Vera Institute of Justice, 1981).

In recent years, many people have called for measures that would force prosecutors to make victims more central to the prosecution. Because the state pursues charges against the accused in criminal cases, the victim is often forgotten in the process. The victims' rights movement wants victims to receive a chance to comment on plea bargains, sentences, and parole decisions. In 2004 Congress enacted the Justice for All Act, which included entitlements for victims in federal criminal cases. Victims are entitled to the opportunity to be heard during court proceedings and to confer with the prosecutor. Some people would like to see such provisions added to the U.S. Constitution so that they would apply to all state courts as well as federal courts.

Judges and Courts

The sentencing history of each judge gives prosecutors an idea of how a case might be treated in the courtroom. Prosecutors may decide to drop a case if they believe that the judge assigned to it will not impose a serious punishment. Because prosecutors' offices have limited resources, they cannot afford to waste time pursuing charges in front of a judge who shows a pattern of dismissing those particular cases.

Prosecutors depend on plea bargaining to keep cases moving through the courts. If judges' sentencing patterns are not predictable, prosecutors find it hard to persuade defendants and their attorneys to accept plea agreements. If the defendants and their lawyers are to accept a lesser charge or a promise of a lighter sentence in exchange for a guilty plea, they need to see some basis for believing that the judge will support the agreement. Although some judges will informally approve plea agreements before the plea is entered, other judges believe early judicial action is improper. Because these judges refuse to state their agreement with the details of any bargain, the prosecutor and defense attorney must use the judges' past performance as a guide in arranging a plea that will be accepted in court.

In most jurisdictions, a person arrested on felony charges must receive a preliminary hearing within ten days. For prosecutors, this hearing is a chance to evaluate the testimony of witnesses, assess the strength of the evidence, and try to predict the outcome of the case should it go to trial. After that, prosecutors have several options: recommend that the case be held for trial, seek to reduce the charge to a misdemeanor, or conclude that they have no case and drop the charges. The prosecutor's perception of both the court's caseload and the judge's attitudes greatly influence these decisions. If courts are overwhelmed with cases or if judges do not share the prosecutor's view about the seriousness of certain charges, the prosecutor may drop cases or reduce charges in order to keep the heavy flow of cases moving.

The Community

Studies have shown that the public usually pays little attention to the criminal justice system. Still, the community remains a potential source of pressure that leaders may activate against the prosecutor. The prosecutor's office generally keeps the public in mind when it makes its decisions. Public opinion and the media can play a crucial role in creating an environment that either supports or undermines the prosecutor. Like police chiefs and school superintendents, county prosecutors will likely not be retained if they are out of step with community values.

Public influence is especially important with respect to crimes that are not always fully enforced. Laws on the books may ban prostitution, gambling, and pornography, but a community may nonetheless tolerate them. In such a community the prosecutor will focus on other crimes rather than risk irritating citizens who believe that victimless crimes should not be strongly enforced. Other communities, however, may pressure the prosecutor to enforce morality laws and to prosecute those who do not comply with local ordinances and state statutes. As elected officials, prosecutors must remain sensitive to voters' attitudes.

Prosecutors' relationships and interactions with police, victims, defense attorneys, judges, and the community form the core of the exchange relations that shape decision making in criminal cases. Other relationships, such as those with news media, federal and state officials, legislators, and political party officials, also influence prosecutors' decisions. This long list of influences illustrates that these decisions are not based solely on whether a law was broken. The occurrence of a crime is only the first step in a decision-making process that may vary from one case to the next. Sometimes charges are dropped or reduced. Sometimes plea bargains are negotiated quickly. Sometimes cases move through the system to a complete jury trial. In every instance, relationships and interactions with a variety of actors both within and outside the justice system shape prosecutors' discretionary decisions.

As you read about the Community Prosecution program in "New Directions in Criminal Justice Policy," as well as "Civic Engagement: Your Role in the System," think about how cooperation and coordination among prosecutors, police, and the public can improve by connecting prosecutors more closely with the communities they serve.

**civic engagement
your role in the system**

Imagine that you are a neighborhood leader contacted by the local prosecutor. She wants to start a "community prosecution" program and she needs advice from the community about which activities would be most useful. *Write a short memo that makes four suggestions to the prosecutor and explains how each one will keep citizens involved and address neighborhood problems.* Then go to the website of the Center for Court Innovation to read about the programs at the Red Hook Community Justice Center in one New York neighborhood. To link to this website, go to *The American System of Criminal Justice* 12e companion site at academic.cengage.com/criminaljustice/cole.

NEW DIRECTIONS in CRIMINAL JUSTICE POLICY

Community Prosecution

COMMUNITY PROSECUTION REPRESENTS an initiative to reduce crime and increase the effectiveness of the criminal justice system by bringing prosecutors into closer contact with citizens. This model program in Washington, D.C., gave individual assistant prosecutors responsibility for specific neighborhoods within the city. Some of the prosecutors were assigned exclusively to outreach functions that involved meeting with citizens and working with police to identify and remedy persistent crime problems. Other prosecutors took responsibility for prosecuting cases that arose in their assigned neighborhoods.

By having responsibility for specific neighborhoods, the prosecutors could become well-acquainted with the environment, social problems, crimes, and repeat offenders that burdened the residents of those neighborhoods. The residents could also gain personal familiarity with one or more specific prosecutors assigned to serve them. By contrast, prosecution in most cities is rather impersonal because victims and witnesses must come to the courthouse to meet with prosecutors who may either handle only specific aspects of one case or who have no reason to maintain continuing contacts with the citizens after the case is closed. Under the Community Prosecution model, individual prosecutors would become familiar to residents by working to resolve neighborhood problems and coordinate communications with police and other public service agencies.

According to the Albany, New York, District Attorney's website, "community prosecution is a dynamically proactive approach" that is based on six principles:

1. It gives greater voice to community members in prioritizing and solving problems in neighborhoods.

2. It promotes restorative justice benefiting victims, the community, and offenders.
3. It provides prosecutors a greater opportunity to be proactive in fighting crime.
4. It changes the focus of prosecution to solving problems to ensure that crime problems will not reoccur.
5. It assists with community policing.
6. It helps to get local citizens' groups involved so that they will provide information and evidence to the police.

The advocates of Community Prosecution argue that the initiative is not merely a public relations effort to gain favor with the public. Instead, it is a legitimate strategy for seeking to reduce crime, especially in neighborhoods burdened by the severest problems, and to increase cooperation between citizens and criminal justice officials.

If you were a county prosecutor, would you want to experiment with Community Prosecution? What tasks would you want your assistant prosecutors to perform in the community?

Source: Drawn from Barbara Boland, *Community Prosecution in Washington, D.C.: The U.S. Attorney's Fifth District Pilot Project* (Washington, DC: National Institute of Justice, U.S. Government Printing Office, April 2001); Office of the Albany County District Attorney website (2008), http://www.albanycountyda.com/issues.comm_pros.html.

Researching the Internet

To read about Community Prosecution, see the website of the Kennedy School of Government at Harvard University. To link to this website, go to *The American System of Criminal Justice* 12e companion site at academic.cengage.com/criminaljustice/cole.

---

checkpoint

5. What are the prosecutor's key exchange relationships?

Decision-Making Policies

Despite the many factors that can affect prosecutors' decisions, we can draw some general conclusions about how prosecutors approach their office. Prosecutors develop their own policies on how cases will be handled. These policies shape the decisions made by the assistant prosecutors and thus have a major impact on the administration of justice. In different counties, prosecutors may pursue different goals in forming policies on which cases to pursue, which ones to drop, and which to ones to plea bargain. For example, prosecutors who wish to maintain a high conviction rate will drop cases with weak evidence. Others, concerned about using limited resources effectively, will focus most of their time and energy on the most serious crimes.

Some prosecutors' offices make extensive use of screening and are not inclined to press charges. Guilty pleas are the main method of processing cases in some offices, whereas pleas of not guilty strain the courts' trial resources in others.

FIGURE 10.2
Differences in how prosecutors handle felony cases in two jurisdictions
The discretion of the prosecutor is evident in these two flowcharts. Note that different screening policies seem to be in operation: Cases are referred earlier in the process in Utah than they are in Colorado.

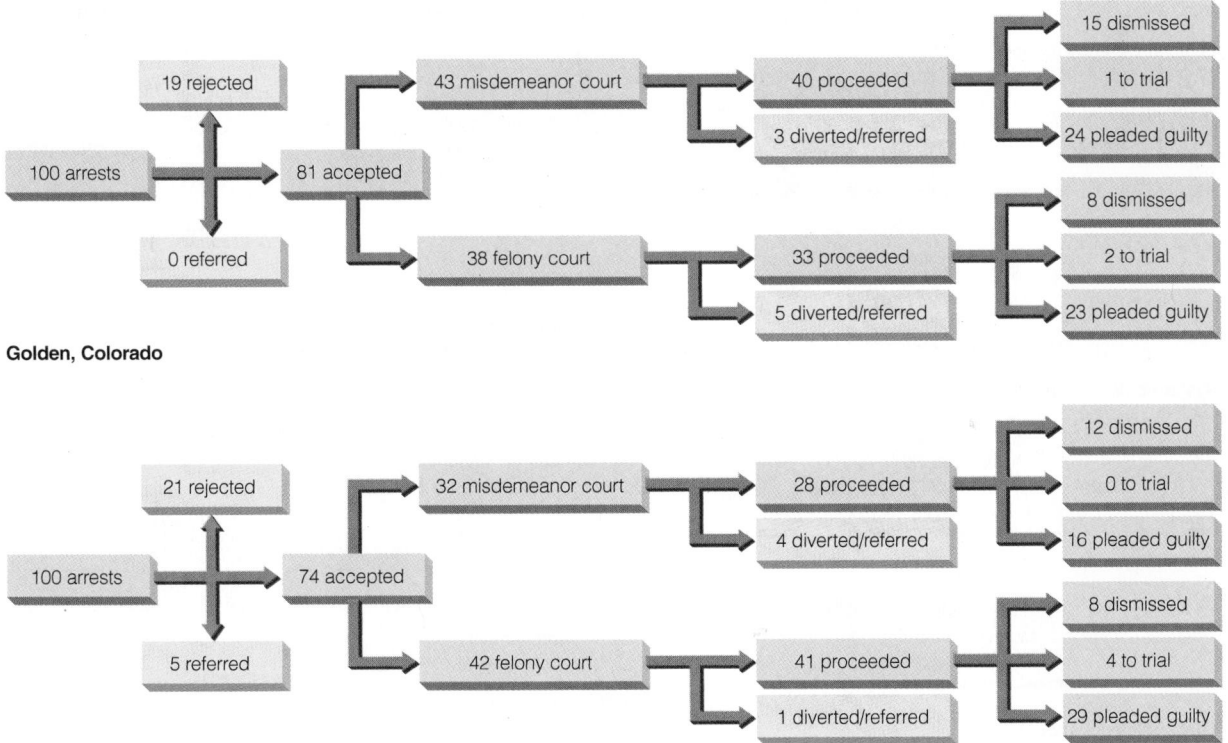

Golden, Colorado

Salt Lake City, Utah

Source: Bureau of Justice Statistics, *Report to the Nation on Crime and Justice*, 2nd ed. (Washington, DC: U.S. Government Printing Office, 1988), 71.

Some offices remove cases—by diverting or referring them to other agencies—soon after they are brought to the prosecutor's attention by the police; in others, disposition occurs as late as the first day of trial. The period from the receipt of the police report to the start of the trial is thus a time of review in which the prosecutor uses discretion to decide what actions should be taken. Figure 10.2 shows how prosecutors handle felony cases in two different jurisdictions.

Implementing Prosecution Policy

Joan Jacoby's classic study analyzed policies that prosecutors use during the pretrial process and how they staff their offices to achieve their goals. On the basis of data from more than 3,000 prosecutors, she describes three policy models: legal sufficiency, system efficiency, and trial sufficiency. The choice of a policy model is shaped by personal aspects of the prosecutor (such as role conception), external factors such as crime levels, and the relationship of prosecution to the other parts of the criminal justice system (Jacoby, 1979).

The policy model adopted by a prosecutor's office affects the screening and disposing of cases. As shown in Figure 10.3, the policy models dictate that prosecutors select certain points in the process to dispose of most of the cases brought to them by the police. Each model identifies the point in the process at which cases are filtered out of the system. A particular model may be chosen to advance specific goals, such as saving the prosecutor's time and energy for the most clear-cut or serious cases. Each model also affects how and when prosecutors interact with defense attorneys in exchanging information or discussing options for a plea bargain.

FIGURE 10.3
Three policy models of prosecutorial case management
Prosecutors develop policies to guide the way their offices will manage cases. These models all assume that a portion of arrests will be dropped at some point in the system so that few cases reach trial.

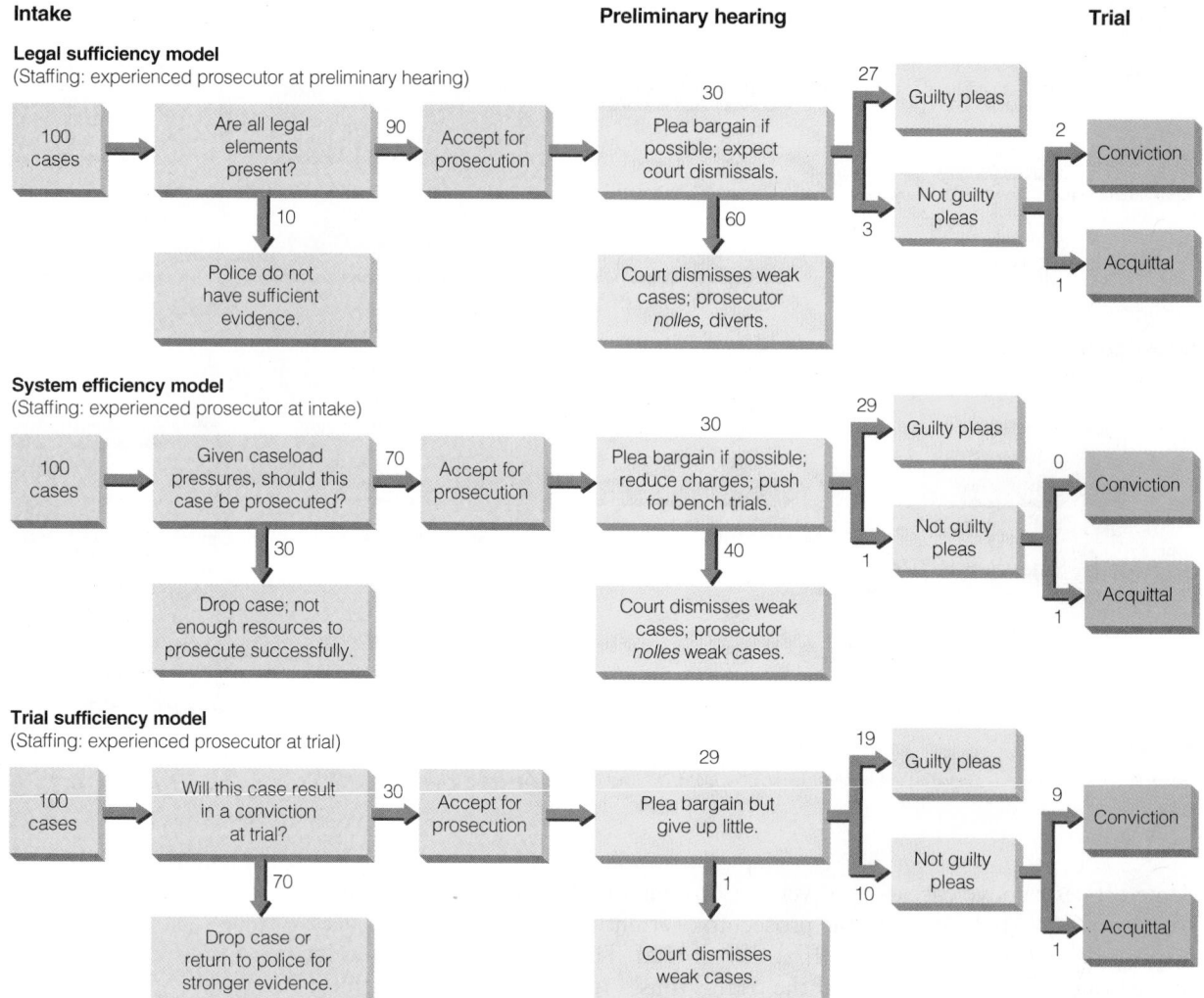

legal sufficiency
The presence of the minimum legal elements necessary for prosecution of a case. When a prosecutor uses legal sufficiency as the customary criterion for prosecuting cases, a great many are accepted for prosecution, but the majority of them are disposed of by plea bargaining or dismissal.

system efficiency
Policy of the prosecutor's office that encourages speedy and early disposition of cases in response to caseload pressures. Weak cases are screened out at intake, and other nontrial alternatives are used a primary means of disposition.

trial sufficiency
The presence of sufficient legal elements to ensure successful prosecution of a case. When a prosecutor uses trial sufficiency as the customary criterion for prosecuting cases, only cases that seem certain to result in conviction at trial are accepted for prosecution. Use of plea bargaining is minimal; good police work and court capacity to go to trial are required.

In the **legal sufficiency** model, prosecutors merely ask whether there is enough evidence to serve as a basis for prosecution. Some prosecutors believe they should pursue any case that likely meets the minimum legal elements of the charge. Prosecutors who use this policy may decide to prosecute a great many cases. As a result, they must have strategies to avoid overloading the system and draining their own resources. Thus, assistant prosecutors, especially those assigned to misdemeanor courts, make extensive use of plea bargains to keep cases flowing through the courts. In this model, judges often dismiss many cases after determining that there is not enough evidence for prosecution to continue.

The **system efficiency** model aims at speedy and early disposition of a case. Each case is evaluated in light of the current caseload pressures. To close cases quickly, the prosecutor might charge the defendant with a felony but agree to reduce the charge to a misdemeanor in exchange for a guilty plea. According to Jacoby's research, this model is usually followed when the trial court is backlogged and the prosecutor has limited resources.

In the **trial sufficiency** model, a case is accepted and charges are made only when there is enough evidence to ensure conviction. For each case the prosecutor asks, "Will this case result in a conviction?" The prosecutor might not correctly predict the likelihood of conviction in every case. However, the prosecutor will make every effort to win a conviction when he or she believes there is evidence to prove that all necessary legal elements for a crime are present. This model requires good police work, a prosecution staff with trial experience, and—because there is less plea bargaining—courts that are not too crowded to handle many trials.

Clearly, these three models lead to different results. Whereas a suspect's case may be dismissed for lack of evidence in a "trial sufficiency" court, the same case may be prosecuted and the defendant pressured to enter a guilty plea in a "legal sufficiency" court.

Case Evaluation

The **accusatory process** is the series of activities that take place from the moment a suspect is arrested and booked by the police to the moment the formal charge—in the form of an indictment or information—is filed with the court. In an indictment, evidence is presented to a grand jury made up of citizens who determine whether to issue a formal charge. In an information, the prosecutor files the charge. Although these two charging processes seem clear-cut (see Figure 10.4), in practice, variations can mix the roles of the city police, prosecutor,

accusatory process
The series of events from the arrest of a suspect to the filing of a formal charge with a court (through an indictment or information).

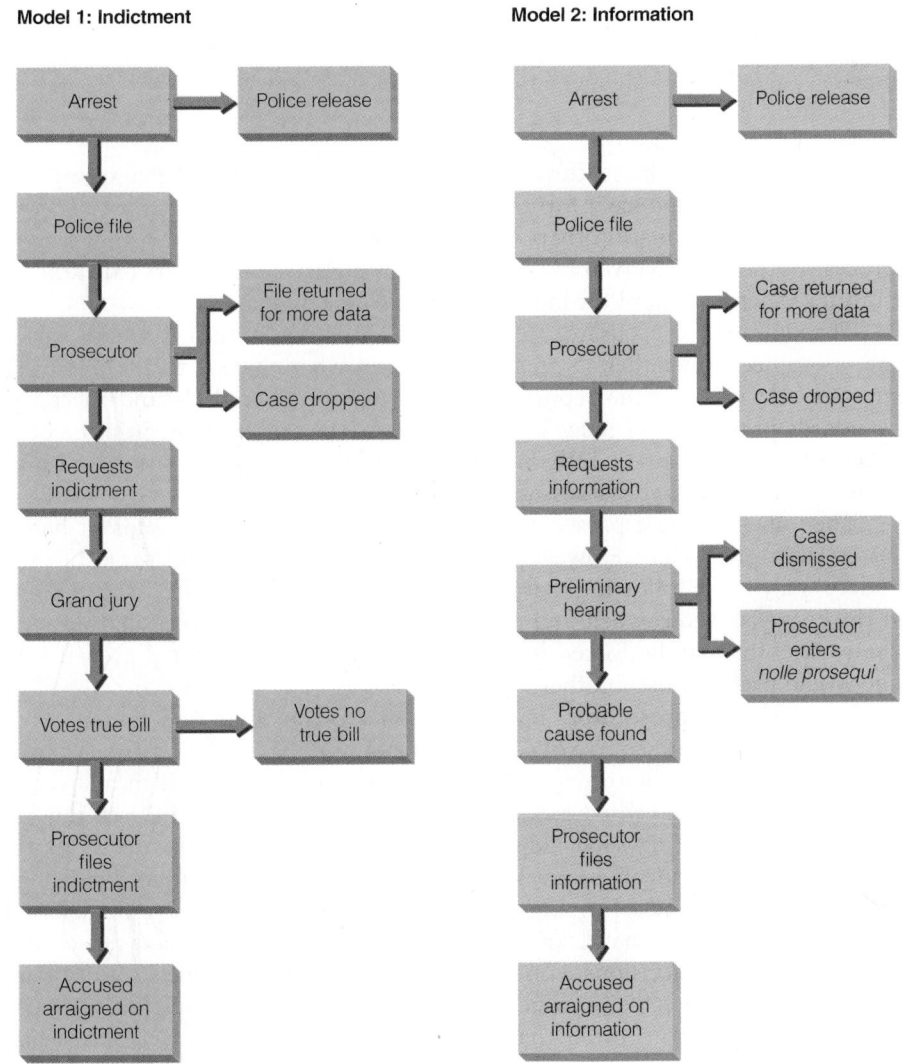

Model 1: Indictment

Model 2: Information

FIGURE 10.4

Two models of the accusatory process
Indictment and information are the two methods used in the United States to accuse a person of a crime. Note the role of the grand jury in an indictment and the preliminary hearing in an information. According to the ideal of due process, each method is designed to spare an innocent person the psychological, monetary, and other costs of prosecution.

FIGURE 10.5

Reasons for declining to prosecute felony cases in four cities

Insufficient evidence was the main reason for declining to prosecute in the four cities studied, but note that the proportions vary.

*Includes diversion and plea to include another case.

Note: Figures may not add up to 100 percent, because of rounding.

Source: Adapted from Bureau of Justice Statistics, *Report to the Nation on Crime and Justice*, 2nd ed. (Washington, DC: U.S. Government Printing Office, 1988), 73.

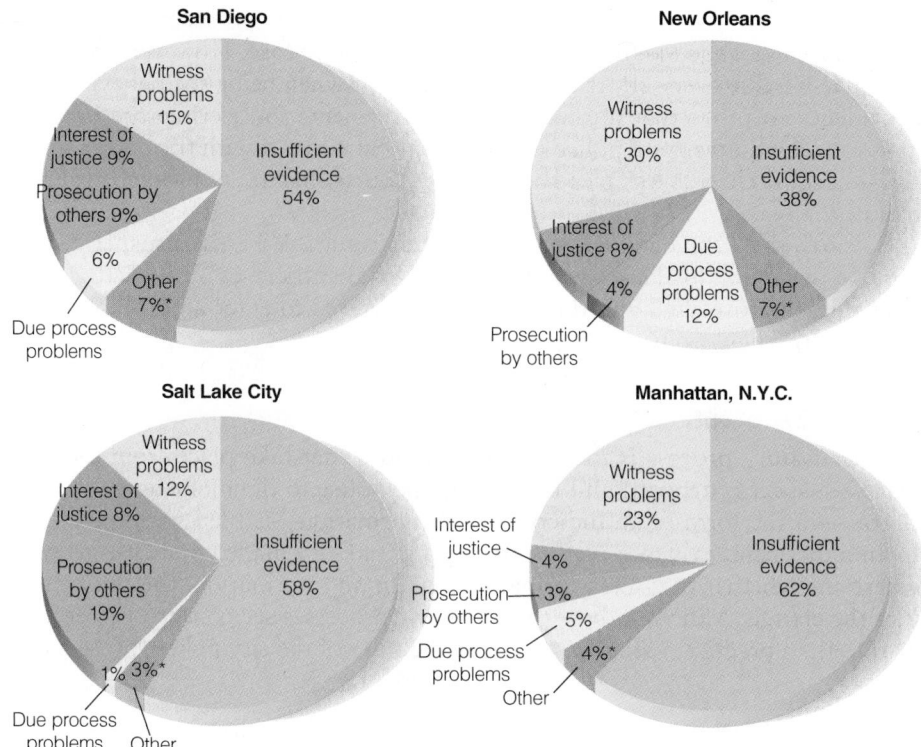

and court. In some places, the prosecutor has full control of the charging decision; in others, the police informally make the decision, which is then approved by the prosecutor; in still others, the prosecutor not only controls the charging process but also is involved in functions such as setting the court calendar, appointing defense counsel for indigents, and sentencing.

Throughout the accusatory process, the prosecutor must evaluate various factors to decide whether to press charges and what charges to file. He or she must decide whether the reported crime will appear credible and meet legal standards in the eyes of judge and jury. Figure 10.5 shows that, in most of the prosecution offices studied, the main reasons for rejecting cases involved problems with evidence and witnesses.

The policy model a prosecutor's office follows will influence his or her decision on a given case. However, the specifics of the case and the office's resources may make following that model impractical or impossible. For example, if the court is overcrowded and the prosecutor does not have enough lawyers, the prosecutor may be forced to use the system efficiency model even if he or she would prefer to use another approach.

In some cases prosecutors may decide that the accused and society would benefit from a certain course of action. For example, a young first-time offender or a minor offender with drug abuse problems may be placed in a diversion program rather than prosecuted in the criminal justice system. In applying their own values in making such judgments, prosecutors may make decisions that run counter to the ideals of law. Prosecutors are, after all, human beings who must respond to some of the most troubling problems in American society. In evaluating cases, they may knowingly or unknowingly permit their personal biases to affect their decisions. For example, a study in Los Angeles County found that men were more likely to be prosecuted than women and that Hispanics were prosecuted more often than African Americans, who were prosecuted more often than whites. The researchers believe that in borderline cases—those

FIGURE 10.6
Typical actions of a prosecuting attorney in processing a felony case
The prosecutor has certain responsibilities at various points in the process. At each point the prosecutor serves as an advocate for the state's case against the accused.

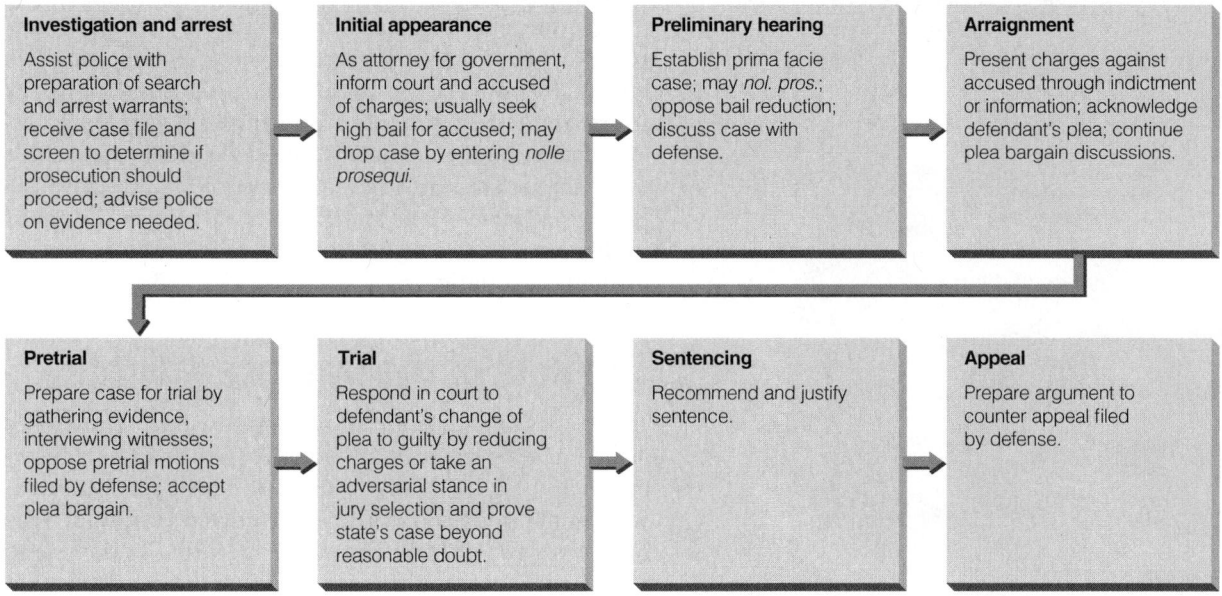

that could either be pursued or dismissed—the scale was often tipped against minorities (Spohn, Gruhl, and Welch, 1987).

Clearly, the prosecutor's established policies and decisions play a key role in determining whether charges will be filed against a defendant. Keep in mind, however, that the prosecutor's decision-making power is not limited to decisions about charges. As shown in Figure 10.6, the prosecutor makes important decisions at each stage, both before and after a defendant's guilt is determined. Because the prosecutor's involvement and influence span the justice process, from seeking search warrants during early investigations to arguing against postconviction appeals, the prosecutor is a highly influential actor in criminal cases. No other participant in the system is involved in so many different stages of the criminal process.

checkpoint

6. What are the three models of prosecution policy, and how do they differ?

THE DEFENSE ATTORNEY: IMAGE AND REALITY

In an adversarial system, the **defense attorney** is the lawyer who represents accused and convicted people in their dealings with the criminal justice system. Most Americans have seen defense attorneys in action on television dramas such as *Boston Legal* and *Law and Order*. In these dramas, defense attorneys vigorously battle the prosecution, and the jury often finds their clients to be not guilty of the crime. Over the course of American history, individual defense attorneys gained public recognition by taking high profile, sensational cases that resulted in jury trials. Defense attorneys are often heroic figures in American literature.

defense attorney
The lawyer who represents accused or convicted offenders in their dealings with criminal justice officials.

Billy Martin, a nationally known defense attorney, has represented such prominent clients as NFL quarterback Michael Vick and former NBA star Jayson Williams. The defense attorney must be persuasive and knowledgeable as well as creative in identifying useful arguments and flaws in the prosecutor's evidence. Could you use your creativity and skills to enthusiastically represent criminal defendants?

AP Images/Ed Pagliarini, Pool

Think of attorney Atticus Finch defending the innocent African American rape suspect in *To Kill a Mockingbird* or various characters in the novels of John Grisham and Scott Turow.

In contrast, most cases are handled by criminal lawyers who must quickly process a large volume of cases for small fees. Rather than adversarial conflict in the courtroom, they process cases through plea bargaining, discretionary dismissals, and other means. In these cases the defense attorney may seem less like the prosecutor's adversary and more like a partner in the effort to dispose of cases as quickly and efficiently as possible through negotiation.

The Role of the Defense Attorney

To be effective, defense attorneys must have knowledge of law and procedure, investigative skills, advocacy experience, and, in many cases, relationships with prosecutors and judges that will help a defendant obtain the best possible outcome. In the American legal system, the defense attorney performs the key function of making sure that the prosecution proves its case in court or has substantial evidence of guilt before a guilty plea is entered.

As shown in Figure 10.7, the defense attorney advises the defendant and protects his or her constitutional rights at each stage of the criminal justice process. The defense attorney advises the defendant during questioning by the police, represents him or her at each arraignment and hearing, and serves as advocate for the defendant during the appeals process if there is a conviction. Without a defense attorney, prosecutors and judges might not respect the rights of the accused. Without knowing the technical details of law and court procedures, defendants have little ability to represent themselves in court effectively.

While filling their roles in the criminal justice system, the defense attorneys also give psychological support to the defendant and his or her family. Relatives are often bewildered, frightened, and confused. The defense attorney is the only legal actor available to answer the question "What will happen next?" In short, the attorney's relationship with the client is crucial. An effective defense requires respect, openness, and trust between attorney and client. If the defendant refuses to follow the attorney's advice, the lawyer may feel obliged to withdraw from the case in order to protect his or her own professional reputation.

Realities of the Defense Attorney's Job

How well do defense attorneys represent their clients? The television image of defense attorneys is usually based on the due process model, in which attorneys are strong advocates for their clients. In reality, the enthusiasm and effectiveness of defense attorneys vary.

Attorneys who are inexperienced, uncaring, or overburdened have trouble representing their clients effectively. The attorney may quickly agree to a plea bargain and then work to persuade the defendant to accept the agreement. The

FIGURE 10.7

Typical actions of a defense attorney processing a felony case

Defense attorneys serve as advocates for the accused. They are obliged to challenge points made by the prosecution and to advise clients about their rights.

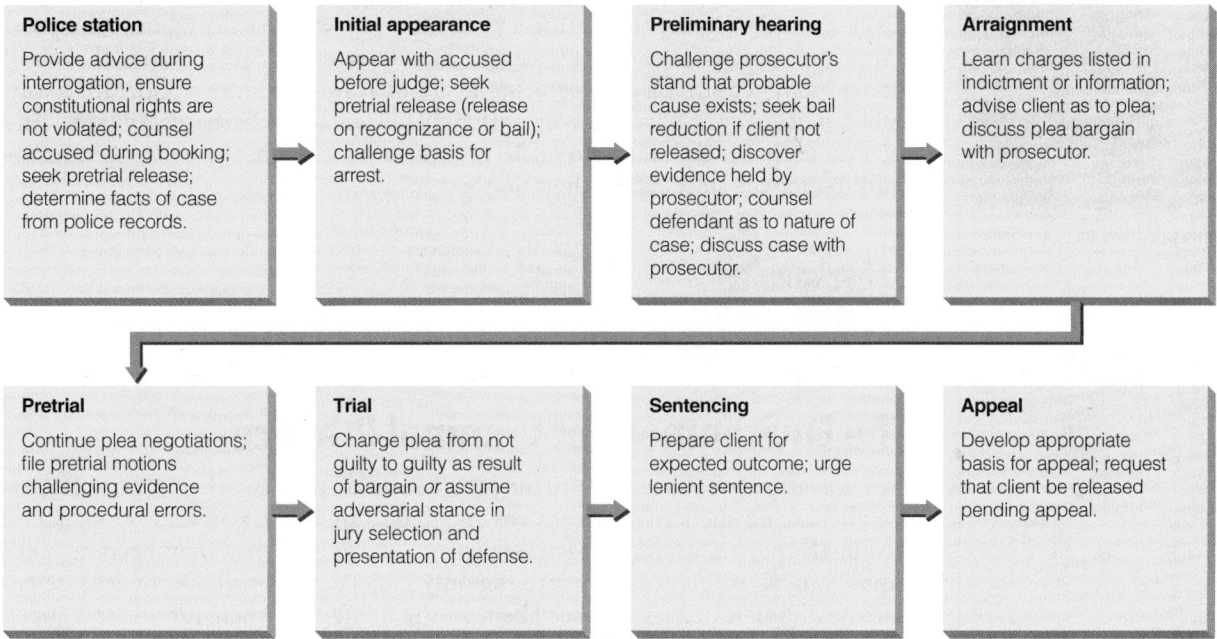

Police station

Provide advice during interrogation, ensure constitutional rights are not violated; counsel accused during booking; seek pretrial release; determine facts of case from police records.

Initial appearance

Appear with accused before judge; seek pretrial release (release on recognizance or bail); challenge basis for arrest.

Preliminary hearing

Challenge prosecutor's stand that probable cause exists; seek bail reduction if client not released; discover evidence held by prosecutor; counsel defendant as to nature of case; discuss case with prosecutor.

Arraignment

Learn charges listed in indictment or information; advise client as to plea; discuss plea bargain with prosecutor.

Pretrial

Continue plea negotiations; file pretrial motions challenging evidence and procedural errors.

Trial

Change plea from not guilty to guilty as result of bargain *or* assume adversarial stance in jury selection and presentation of defense.

Sentencing

Prepare client for expected outcome; urge lenient sentence.

Appeal

Develop appropriate basis for appeal; request that client be released pending appeal.

attorney's self-interest in disposing of cases quickly, receiving payment, and moving on to other cases may cause the attorney to, in effect, work with the prosecutor to pressure the defendant to plead guilty.

Skilled defense attorneys, on the other hand, may also consider a plea bargain in the earliest stages of a case, but their role as an advocate for the defendant will guide them in their use of plea bargaining. An effective defense attorney does not try to take every case all the way to trial. In many cases, a negotiated plea with a predictable sentence will serve the defendant better than a trial spent fending off more serious charges. Good defense attorneys seek to understand the facts of each case and to judge the nature of the evidence in order to reach the best possible outcome for their client. Even in the plea-bargaining process, this level of advocacy requires more time, effort, knowledge, and commitment than some attorneys are willing or able to provide.

The defense attorney's job is all the more difficult because neither the public nor defendants fully understand the attorney's duties and goals. The public often views defense attorneys as protectors of criminals. In fact, the attorney's basic duty is not to save criminals from punishment but to protect constitutional rights, keep the prosecution honest in preparing and presenting cases, and prevent innocent people from being convicted. Surveys indicate that lawyers place much greater emphasis on the importance of right to counsel than does the public. Look at the questions presented in "What Americans Think." Do you think that the public underestimates the necessity of representation by an attorney? Do you agree with the majority of the defense attorneys in the survey or are they too protective of rights for people who might threaten American society?

In performing tasks that ultimately benefit both the defendant and society, the defense attorney must evaluate and challenge the prosecution's evidence. However, defense attorneys can rarely arrange for guilty defendants to go free. Keep in mind that when prosecutors decide to pursue serious charges, they have already filtered out weaker cases. The defense attorney often negotiates the most appropriate punishment in light of the resources of the court, the strength of the evidence, and the defendant's prior criminal record.

Defendants who, like the public, have watched hours of *Law & Order* on television often expect their attorneys to fight vigorous battles against the prosecutor at every stage of the justice process. They do not realize that their best interest may require plea agreements negotiated in a friendly, cooperative way. Public defenders in particular are often criticized because the defendants tend to assume that if the state provided an attorney for them, the attorney must be working for the state rather than on their behalf.

checkpoint

7. How does the image of the defense attorney differ from the attorney's actual role?

The Environment of Criminal Practice

Defense attorneys have a difficult job. Much of their work involves preparing clients and their relatives for the likelihood of conviction and punishment. Although they may know that their clients are guilty, they may become emotionally involved because they are the only judicial actors who know the defendants as human beings and see them in the context of their family and social environment.

Most defense lawyers constantly interact with lower-class clients whose lives and problems are depressing. They sometimes must visit the local jail at all hours of the day and night—far removed from the fancy offices and expensive restaurants of the world of corporate attorneys. As described by one defense attorney, "The days are long and stressful. I spend a good deal of time in jail, which reeks of stale food and body odor. My clients often think that because I'm court-appointed, I must be incompetent" (Lave, 1998: 14).

Defense lawyers must also struggle with the fact that criminal practice does not pay well. Public defenders have relatively low salaries, and attorneys appointed to represent poor defendants are paid small sums. If private attorneys do not demand payment from their clients at the start of the case, they may find that they must persuade the defendants' relatives to pay—because many convicted offenders have no incentive to pay for legal services while sitting in a prison cell. To perform their jobs well and gain satisfaction from their careers, defense attorneys must focus on goals other than money, such as their key role in protecting people's constitutional rights. However, usually being on the losing side can make it hard for them to feel like professionals—with high self-esteem and satisfying work.

Defense attorneys face other pressures as well. If they mount a strong defense and gain an acquittal for their client, the public may blame them for using "technicalities" to keep a criminal on the streets. If they embarrass the prosecution in court, they may harm their prospects for reaching good plea agreements for future clients. Thus, criminal practice can bring major financial, social, and psychological burdens to attorneys. As a result, many criminal attorneys "burn out" after a few years, and few stay in the field past the age of 50.

Relationship to Court Officials

Because plea bargaining is the main method of deciding cases, defense attorneys believe they must maintain close personal ties with the police, prosecutor, judges, and other court officials. Critics point out that daily interaction with the same prosecutors and judges undermines the defenders' independence. When

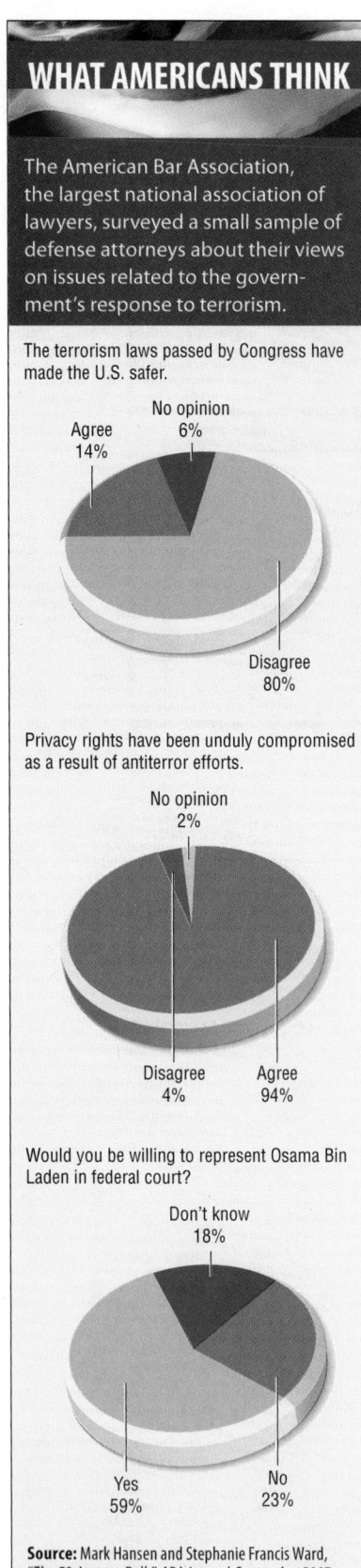

WHAT AMERICANS THINK

The American Bar Association, the largest national association of lawyers, surveyed a small sample of defense attorneys about their views on issues related to the government's response to terrorism.

The terrorism laws passed by Congress have made the U.S. safer.

Agree 14%
No opinion 6%
Disagree 80%

Privacy rights have been unduly compromised as a result of antiterror efforts.

No opinion 2%
Disagree 4%
Agree 94%

Would you be willing to represent Osama Bin Laden in federal court?

Don't know 18%
Yes 59%
No 23%

Source: Mark Hansen and Stephanie Francis Ward, "The 50-Lawyer Poll," *ABA Journal,* September 2007 (http://www.abajournal.com).

the supposed adversaries become close friends as a result of daily contact, the defense attorneys might no longer fight vigorously on behalf of their clients. Also, at every step of the justice process, from the first contact with the accused until final disposition of the case, defense attorneys depend on decisions made by other actors in the system. Even seemingly minor activities such as visiting the defendant in jail, learning about the case from the prosecutor, and setting bail can be difficult unless defense attorneys have the cooperation of others in the system. Thus defense attorneys may limit their activities in order to preserve their relationships with other courthouse actors.

For the criminal lawyer who depends on a large volume of petty cases from poor clients and assumes that they are probably guilty, the incentives to bargain are strong. If the attorney is to be assigned other cases, he or she must help make sure that cases flow smoothly through the courthouse. This requires a cooperative relationship with judges, prosecutors, and others in the justice system.

Despite their dependence on cooperation from other justice system officials to make their work go more smoothly, defense attorneys can sometimes use stubbornness as a tactic. They can, for example, threaten to take a case all the way through trial to test whether the prosecutor is really adamant about not reaching a favorable plea agreement.

Some paying clients may expect their counsel to play the role of combatant in the belief that they are not getting their money's worth unless they hear verbal fireworks in the courtroom. Yet even when those fireworks do occur, one cannot be sure that the adversaries are engaged in a real contest. Studies have shown that attorneys whose clients expect a vigorous defense may engage in a courtroom drama commonly known as the "slow plea of guilty," in which the outcome of the case has already been determined but the attorneys go through the motions of putting up a vigorous fight.

It is often difficult for defendants to understand the benefits of plea bargaining and friendly relationships between defense attorneys and prosecutors. Most cases that are pursued beyond the initial stages are not likely to result in acquittal, no matter how vigorously the attorney presents the defendant's case. In many cases, skilled lawyering simply cannot overcome the evidence of the defendant's guilt. Thus, good relationships can benefit the defendant by gaining a less-than-maximum sentence. At the same time, however, these relationships pose the risk that if the defense attorney and prosecutor are too friendly, the defendant's case will not be presented in the best possible way in plea bargaining or trial.

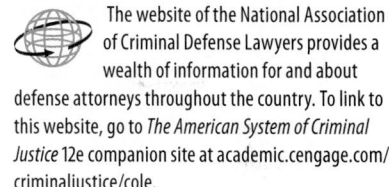

The website of the National Association of Criminal Defense Lawyers provides a wealth of information for and about defense attorneys throughout the country. To link to this website, go to *The American System of Criminal Justice* 12e companion site at academic.cengage.com/criminaljustice/cole.

Relationship to Clients

Some scholars have called defense attorneys "agent-mediators" because they often work to prepare the defendant for the likely outcome of the case—usually conviction (A. Blumberg, 1967). While such efforts may help the defendant gain a good plea bargain and become mentally prepared to accept the sentence, the attorney's efforts are geared to advancing the needs of the attorney and the legal system. By mediating between the defendant and the system—for example, by encouraging a guilty plea—the attorney helps save time for the prosecutor and judge in gaining a conviction and completing the case. In addition, appointed counsel and contract attorneys may have a financial interest in getting the defendant to plead guilty quickly, in that they can receive payment and move on to the next case (K. Armstrong, Davila, and Mayo, 2004).

A more sympathetic view of defense attorneys labels them "beleaguered dealers" who cut deals for defendants in a tough environment (Uphoff, 1992). Defense attorneys face tremendous pressure to manage large caseloads in a difficult court environment. From this perspective, their actions in encouraging clients to plead guilty result from the difficult aspects of their jobs rather than

CLOSE UP

The Public Defender: Lawyer, Social Worker, Parent

EDDIE, A NERVOUS-LOOK-ING heroin abuser with a three-page police record, isn't happy with his lawyer's news about his latest shoplifting arrest.

"The prosecutor feels you should be locked up for a long time," public defender William Paetzold tells Eddie in a closet-sized interview room in Superior Court. Barely big enough for a desk and two chairs, the room is known as "the pit."

Eddie, 34 and wide-eyed with a blond crew cut, twists a rolled-up newspaper in his hands. And as Paetzold goes over the evidence against him for the theft of $90.67 worth of meat from a supermarket, the paper gets tighter and tighter.

"So, you basically walked right through the doors with the shopping carriage?" Paetzold asks, scanning the police report.

"Well, there was another person involved and we really never got out of the store." Eddie replies quickly, now jingling a pocketful of change. Eddie wants to take his case to trial. Paetzold doesn't like his chances with a jury.

"If you're going to base your whole case on that statement about not leaving the store, you're going to lose," he says. "If you lose, you're going to get 5 years."

Paetzold advises Eddie to consider pleading guilty in exchange for a lesser sentence.

Eddie rolls his eyes and grumbles. He thinks he deserves a break because he has been doing well in a methadone clinic designed to wean him from heroin.

"I'm not copping to no time." he says, shifting in his seat. "I'm not arguing the fact that I've been a drug addict my whole life, but I haven't been arrested since I've been in that program. I'm finally doing good and they want to bury me."

Paetzold says he will talk to the prosecutor and see what can be done.

"I'll be waiting upstairs," Eddie says, grabbing his newspaper and walking out past a small crowd of other clients. All are waiting to see either Paetzold or the other public defender seeing clients that morning, Phillip Armentano.

Every client wants individual attention. Many expect Paetzold or Armentano to resolve their case with little or no punishment. And they don't care that the lawyers may have 25 other clients to see that morning demanding the same.

"A lot of what we do is almost like social work," says Armentano. "We have the homeless, the mentally ill, the drug addicts, and the alcoholics. Our job just isn't to try to find people not guilty, but to find appropriate punishment, whether that be counseling, community service, or jail time."

"It's like being a parent," says Paetzold. "These clients are our responsibility and they all have problems and they want those problems solved now."

And like many parents, the lawyers often feel overwhelmed. Too many cases, not enough time or a big enough staff. Those obstacles contribute to another—the stigma that overworked public defenders are pushovers for prosecutors and judges.

"There's a perception that public defenders don't stand up for their clients," Armentano says. "We hear it all the time, 'Are you a public defender or a real lawyer?' There's a mistrust right from the beginning because they view us as part of the system that got them arrested."

With a caseload of more than a thousand clients a year, Paetzold and Armentano acknowledge that they cannot devote as much time to each client as a private lawyer can. But they insist that their clients get vigorous representation.

"Lawyers are competitors, whether you're a public defender or not," Paetzold says. "I think that under the conditions, we do a very good job for our clients."

Source: Steve Jensen, "The Public Defender: He's One Part Lawyer, One Part Social Worker and One Part Parent," *Hartford Courant*, September 4, 1994, p. H1. Reprinted with permission.

Researching the Internet

 For a useful source about various public defender offices, see the public defender website for California. To link to this website, go to *The American System of Criminal Justice* 12e companion site at academic.cengage.com/criminaljustice/cole.

from self-interest. Yet, as described in the Close Up box, some public defenders do maintain a personal interest in their clients.

checkpoint

8. What special pressures do defense attorneys face?

Counsel for Indigents

Since the 1960s, the Supreme Court has interpreted the "right to counsel" in the Sixth Amendment to the Constitution as requiring that the government provide attorneys for indigent defendants who face the possibility of going to prison or jail. Indigent defendants are those who are too poor to afford their own lawyers. The Court has also required that attorneys be provided early in the criminal justice process to protect suspects' rights during questioning and pretrial proceedings. See Table 10.1 for a summary of key rulings on the right to counsel.

Research on felony defendants indicates that 78 percent of those prosecuted in the 75 largest counties and 66 percent of those prosecuted in federal courts received publicly provided legal counsel (Harlow, 2000). The portion of defendants who are provided with counsel because they are indigent has increased greatly in the past three decades.

Many observers debate the quality of counsel given to indigent defendants (Worden, 1991). Ideally, experienced lawyers would be appointed soon after arrest to represent the defendant in each stage of the criminal justice process. However, inexperienced and uncaring attorneys are sometimes appointed. When the appointment occurs after initial court proceedings have already begun, the attorney has no time to prepare the case. Even conscientious attorneys may be unable to provide top-quality counsel if they have heavy caseloads or are not paid enough money to spend the time required to handle the case well.

If they lack the time and desire to interview clients and prepare their cases, appointed counsels may simply persuade defendants to plead guilty, right there in the courtroom during their first and only brief conversation. When the lawyers assigned to provide counsel to poor defendants cooperate with the prosecutor easily, without even asking the defendant about his or her version of events, it is little wonder that convicted offend-

Sean Sullivan, a lawyer who represents indigent clients, carries a heavy caseload under trying conditions. The quality of counsel received by the poor may vary from courthouse to courthouse, depending on the quality of the attorneys, conditions of defense practice, and administrative pressures to reduce caseloads. Should we spend more tax dollars on indigent criminal defense in order to increase resources and quality of representation?

© Ruth Fremson/The New York Times/Redux

TABLE 10.1	The Right to Counsel: Major Supreme Court Rulings	
Case	**Year**	**Ruling**
Powell v. Alabama	1932	Indigents facing the death penalty who are not capable of representing themselves must be given attorneys.
Johnson v. Zerbst	1938	Indigent defendants must be provided with attorneys when facing serious charges in federal court.
Gideon v. Wainwright	1963	Indigent defendants must be provided with attorneys when facing serious charges in state court.
Douglas v. California	1963	Indigent defendants must be provided with attorneys for their first appeal.
Miranda v. Arizona	1966	Criminal suspects must be informed about their right to counsel before being questioned in custody.
United States v. Wade	1967	Defendants are entitled to counsel at "critical stages" in the process, including post-indictment lineups.
Argersinger v. Hamlin	1972	Indigent defendants must be provided with attorneys when facing misdemeanor and petty charges that may result in incarceration.
Ross v. Moffitt	1974	Indigent defendants are not entitled to attorneys for discretionary appeals after their first appeal is unsuccessful.
Strickland v. Washington	1984	To show ineffective assistance of counsel violated the right to counsel, defendants must prove that the attorney committed specific errors that affected the outcome of the case.
Murray v. Giarratano	1989	Death row inmates do not have a right to counsel for habeas corpus proceedings asserting rights violations in their cases.

ers often believe that their interests were not represented in the courtroom. Not all publicly financed lawyers who represent poor defendants ignore their clients' interests. However, the quality of counsel received by the poor may vary from courthouse to courthouse, depending on the quality of the attorneys, conditions of defense practice, and administrative pressure to reduce the caseload.

Ways of Providing Indigents with Counsel

The three main ways of providing counsel to indigent defendants in the United States are (1) the **assigned counsel** system, in which a court appoints a private attorney to represent the accused; (2) the **contract counsel** system, in which an attorney, a nonprofit organization, or a private law firm contracts with a local government to provide legal services to indigent defendants for a specified dollar amount; and (3) **public defender** programs, which are public or private nonprofit organizations with full-time or part-time salaried staff. Figure 10.8 presents the system used in the majority of counties in each of the 50 states. However, many counties use a combination of methods to provide representation. For example, 23 percent of counties use both public defenders and assigned counsel (S. K. Smith and DeFrances, 1996). Counties that have sufficient resources often send cases to assigned counsel when public defenders' caseloads become too large.

assigned counsel
An attorney in private practice assigned by a court to represent an indigent. The attorney's fee is paid by the government with jurisdiction over the case.

contract counsel
An attorney in private practice who contracts with the government to represent all indigent defendants in a county during a set period of time and for a specified dollar amount.

public defender
An attorney employed on a full-time, salaried basis by the government to represent indigents.

FIGURE 10.8

Indigent defense system used by the majority of counties in each state
Some counties use a mixture of methods to provide counsel for indigents; this figure shows only the predominant method per state.

Public defender
Contract
Assigned counsel

Source: Bureau of Justice Statistics, *Bulletin*, September 1988.

Assigned Counsel In the assigned counsel system, the court appoints a lawyer in private practice to represent an indigent defendant. This system is widely used in small cities and in rural areas, but even some city public defender systems assign counsel in some cases, such as in a case with multiple defendants, where a conflict of interest might result if one of them were represented by a public lawyer. But in other cities, such as Detroit, the private bar has been able to insist that its members receive a large share of the cases.

Assigned counsel systems are organized on either an ad hoc system or a co-ordinated basis. In ad hoc assignment systems, private attorneys tell the judge that they are willing to take the cases of indigent defendants. When an indigent requires counsel, the judge either assigns lawyers in rotation from a prepared list or chooses one of the attorneys who are known and present in the court-room. In coordinated assignment systems, a court administrator oversees the appointment of counsel.

Use of the ad hoc system may raise questions about the loyalties of the assigned counsel. Are they trying to vigorously defend their clients or are they trying to please the judges to ensure future appointments? For example, Texas has been criticized for giving judges free rein to assign lawyers to cases without any supervising authority to ensure that the attorneys actually do a good job (Novak, 1999). Additional concerns have arisen in Texas and other states where judges run for election, because lawyers often donate money to judges' political campaigns. Judges may return the favor by supplying their contributors with criminal defense assignments.

The fees paid to assigned defenders are often low compared with what a lawyer might otherwise charge. As described by one attorney, "The level of compensation impacts the level of representation. . . . If an attorney takes [an appointed criminal case], it means they lose the opportunity to take other cases at higher rates" (The Third Branch, 2008). Whereas a private practice attorney might charge clients at rates that exceed $200 per hour, hourly rates for appointed counsel in Cook County (Chicago), Illinois, are merely $40 per hour for in-court tasks and $30 per hour for out-of-court tasks. These same rates have been in place for more than 30 years. Defense attorneys receive the low rate of $40 per hour for out-of-court work in Oklahoma, Oregon, Alabama, South Carolina, and Tennessee. Many other states pay only $50 to $75 per hour (Spangenberg Group, 2007). The average hourly overhead cost for attorneys—the amount they must make just to pay their secretaries, office rent, and tele-phone bills—is $64 (The Third Branch, 2008). If their hourly fees fall short of their overhead costs, then attorneys ac-tually lose money when spending their time on these cases. Look at Table 10.2 to see examples of fees paid to assigned defense counsel.

Low fees discourage skilled attor-neys from taking criminal cases. Low fees may also induce a defense attorney to persuade clients to plead guilty to a lesser charge. Many assigned defenders find that they can make more money by collecting a preparation fee for a few hours work, payable when an indigent client pleads guilty, than by going to trial. Trials are very time-consuming, and appointed attorneys often feel that the fees paid by the state are too low to

TABLE 10.2	Fees Paid to Assigned Counsel in Noncapital Felony Cases.		
State	**Out-of-Court Hourly Rate**	**In-Court Hourly Rate**	**Per-Case Maximum**
Alaska	$50	$60	$4,000 trial; $2,000 plea
Georgia	$40	$60	None
Hawaii	$90	$90	$6,000
Maryland	$50	$50	$3,000
New York	$75	$75	$4,400
North Carolina	$65	$65	None
North Dakota	$65	$65	$2,000
Federal	$100	$100	$7,000

Source: Spangenburg Group, "Rates of Compensation Paid to Court-Appointed Counsel in Non-Capital Felony Cases at Trial: A State-by-State Overview," *American Bar Association Information Program,* June 2007; "Economics of CJA Representation Costly to Attorneys," *The Third Branch (Administrative Office of the U.S. Courts)* vol. 40 (4), April 2008.

cover the amount of time required to prepare for trial, especially when the fee is a flat rate per case or trial rather than an hourly rate. It usually is more profitable to handle many quick plea bargains than to spend weeks preparing for a trial for which the total fee may be capped at $1,000 to $3,000.

Many organizations of judges and lawyers lobby Congress, state legislatures, and county councils to increase the amounts paid to assigned counsel. Courts may also pressure legislators to provide more money for indigent defense. In 2005, for example, the Louisiana Supreme Court ruled that trial judges can prevent prosecutors from proceeding against a defendant if there is not enough money available in the local government budget to pay the defense attorney (Maggi, 2005). Many members of Congress and state legislatures, however, do not wish to spend more money for the benefit of criminal defendants. In addition, even if legislators recognize that funding problems exist, state and local governments may have little ability to increase spending for indigent defense during periods when they face budget problems that affect their responsibilities for all issues, including schools, roads, and health care.

Contract System The contract system is used in a few counties, mainly in western states. Most states using this method do not have large populations. The government contracts with an attorney, a nonprofit association, or a private law firm to handle all indigent cases (Worden, 1994). Some jurisdictions use public defenders for most cases but contract for services in multiple-defendant cases that might present conflicts of interest, in extraordinarily complex cases, or in cases that require more time than the government's salaried lawyers can provide.

The American Bar Association's Standing Committee on Legal Aid and Indigent Defendants provides online access to a variety of studies concerning indigent defense and problems related to fulfillment of the constitutional right to counsel. To link to this website, go to *The American System of Criminal Justice* 12e companion site at academic.cengage.com/criminaljustice/cole.

There are several kinds of contracts (L. Spears, 1991). The most common contract provides for a fixed yearly sum to be paid to the law firm that handles all cases. Some people fear that this method encourages attorneys to cut corners in order to preserve their profits, especially if there are more cases than expected for the year. Other contracts follow a fixed price per case or per hour of work. Still other jurisdictions use a cost-plus contract, in which a new contract is negotiated when the estimated cost of counsel is surpassed. According to Robert Spangenberg and Marea Beeman (1995: 49), "There are serious potential dangers with the contract model, such as expecting contract defenders to handle an unlimited caseload or awarding contracts on a low-bid basis only, with no regard to qualifications of contracting attorneys."

Public Defender The position of public defender developed as a response to the legal needs of indigent defendants. The concept started in Los Angeles County in 1914, when government first hired attorneys to work full-time in criminal defense. The most recent national survey of the 100 most populous counties found that public defender systems handled 82 percent of the 4.2 million indigent criminal cases in 1999, whereas appointed counsel handled 15 percent and contract counsel represented only 3 percent of defendants (DeFrances and Litras, 2000). The public defender system, which is growing fast, is used in 43 of the 50 most populous counties and in most large cities. There are about 20 statewide, state-funded systems; in other states, the counties organize and pay for them. Only two states, North Dakota and Maine, do not have public defenders.

The public defender system is often viewed as better than the assigned counsel system because public defenders are specialists in criminal law. Because they are full-time government employees, public defenders do not sacrifice their clients' cases to protect their own financial interests. Public defenders do face certain special problems, however. Public defenders may have trouble gaining the trust and cooperation of their clients. Criminal defendants may assume that attorneys

CLOSE UP

Public Defender System in Crisis

AS HE SITS in the Boone County jail awaiting next week's sentencing, John Winingar hesitates to say he has received unfair representation from his public defender.

Still, Winingar, 35, arrested nine months ago for robbery and forgery, said there have been problems. He said he usually learns about developments in his case five minutes before he appears before a judge. Budget cuts prohibit his attorney from accepting collect calls, and the direct phone line from the jail to the public defender's office often goes straight to an answering machine.

So he has sent letters. When those phone messages and letters go unanswered, Winingar said he tries to keep in mind that his public defender has a crushing caseload—it's a tough situation for everyone....

The yearly caseload handled by the Missouri Public Defender system has increased from nearly 76,000 in the year 2000 to more than 88,000 in 2005. The legislature approved no new employees to handle the 12,000 new cases, and the department took a half-million dollar budget cut in 2004. Now, each trial division public defender averages 298 cases each year while the state-established limit ... is 235....

... [A consultant's study concluded that] the department's budget would need to increase by $16 million to meet the average per capita spending of the rest of the southern states and Missouri ranks 47th in the nation in per capita spending on indigent defense.

J. Marty Robinson, director of the Missouri State Public Defender system, said the numbers make it easy for lawyers to unintentionally violate Missouri's ethics code for attorneys. "[Clients] are not getting competent, effective, constitutional representation in all cases," said Robinson.....

Source: Meghan Maskery, "Public Defender System 'in Crisis,' Report Finds," *Columbia Missourian*, November 11, 2005 (http://www.columbianmissourian.com).

Researching the Internet

To read about the American Bar Association's recommendations for operating indigent defense systems, see its website. To link to this website, go to *The American System of Criminal Justice* 12e companion site at academic.cengage.com/ criminaljustice/cole.

---

on the state payroll, even with the title "public defender," have no reason to protect the defendants' rights and interests. Lack of cooperation from the defendant may make it harder for the attorney to prepare the best possible arguments for use during hearings, plea bargaining, and trials.

Public defenders may also face heavy caseloads. Public defenders in Kentucky, for example, handled an average of 436 cases in 2007 (Lewis, 2007). Although the Washington State Bar Association recommends that defense attorneys handle no more than 300 cases per year, public defenders in Thurston County, Washington, each had as many as 900 misdemeanor cases per year in 2005 (Associated Press, 2005b). Such heavy caseloads do not allow time for attorneys to become familiar with each case. Public defender programs are most effective when they have enough money to keep caseloads manageable. However, these programs do not control their own budgets and usually are not seen as high priorities by state and local governments (Jaksic, 2007). Thus, gaining the funds to give adequate attention to each defendant's case is difficult. As you read the Close Up box, consider the human consequences, including the risk that justice will be denied, when there is inadequate funding for indigent criminal defense.

Some public defenders' offices try to make better use of limited resources by organizing assignments more efficiently. In some systems, every poor defendant has several public defenders, each handling a different stage or "zone" in the justice process. One attorney may handle all arraignments, another all preliminary hearings, and still another any trial work. No one attorney manages the entire case of any client. Although the zone system may increase efficiency, there is a risk that cases will be processed in a routine way, with no one taking into account special factors. With limited responsibility for a given case, the attorney is less able to advise the defendant about the case as a whole and is unlikely to develop the level of trust needed to gain the defendant's cooperation.

With or without zone systems, overburdened public defenders find it difficult to avoid making routine decisions. One case can come to be viewed as very much like the next, and the process can become routine and repetitive. Overworked attorneys cannot look closely at cases for any special circumstances that would justify a stronger defense.

checkpoint

9. What are the three main methods of providing attorneys for indigent defendants?

Private versus Public Defense

Publicly funded defense attorneys now handle up to 85 percent of the cases in many places, and private defense attorneys have become more and more unusual in many courts. Retained counsel may serve only upper-income defendants charged with white-collar crimes or drug dealers and organized-crime figures who can pay the fees. This trend has made the issue of the quality of representation increasingly important.

Do defendants who can afford their own counsel receive better legal services than those who cannot? Many convicted offenders say "you get what you pay for," meaning that they would have received better counsel if they had been able to pay for their own attorneys. At one time, researchers thought public defenders entered more guilty pleas than did lawyers who had been either privately retained or assigned to cases. However, studies show little variation in case outcomes by various types of defense. For example, in a classic study of plea bargains in nine medium-sized counties in Illinois, Michigan, and Pennsylvania, the type of attorney representing the client appeared to make no difference in the nature of plea agreements (Nardulli, 1986). Other studies also find few differences among assigned counsel, contract counsel, public defenders, and pri-

---

TABLE 10.3   Case Disposition and Types of Defense Attorneys

There are few variations in case disposition among the defense systems used in each jurisdiction. Why do the cities differ in case outcomes?

| Type of Disposition | Detroit, Michigan | | | Denver, Colorado | | Norfolk, Virginia | | Monterey, California | | |
	Public Defender	Assigned Counsel	Private Counsel	Public Defender	Private Counsel	Assigned Counsel	Private Counsel	Public Defender	Assigned Counsel	Private Counsel
Dismissals	11.9%	14.5%	12.8%	21.0%	24.3%	6.4%	10.4%	13.5%	8.9%	3.0%
Trial acquittals	9.5	5.7	10.3	1.8	0.0	3.3	5.2	1.7	1.3	0.0
Trial convictions	22.6	14.5	24.4	5.1	9.5	5.2	2.2	7.1	11.4	18.2
Guilty pleas	54.8	64.9	52.6	72.1	66.2	85.1	81.3	76.8	78.5	78.8
Diversion	1.2	0.3	0.0	0.0	0.0	0.0	0.7	1.0	0.0	0.0
	100.0%	99.9%	100.1%	100.0%	100.0%	100.0%	99.8%	101.1%	101.1%	100.0%
Total number of cases	84	296	78	276	74	329	134	294	79	33

Source: Roger Hanson and Joy Chapper, Indigent Defense Systems, Report to the State Justice Institute (Williamsburg, VA: National Center for State Courts, 1991). Copyright © 1991 by National Center for State Courts.

Released from prison in March 2008 after serving 23 years based on a flawed conviction, Willie Earl Green holds a cell phone for the first time. Green was released after it was discovered that information that had been hidden from his attorneys would have raised serious questions about the testimony of a key witness. In light of such injustices, how can we make sure that defense attorneys are both competent and fully prepared to provide the best representation possible?

AP Images/Nick Ut

vately retained counsel with respect to case outcomes and length of sentence (Hanson and Chapper, 1991). Table 10.3 lists data on the relationship between type of counsel and case results in four cities.

checkpoint

10. Are public defenders more effective than private defense attorneys?

Attorney Competence

The right to counsel is of little value when the counsel is neither competent nor effective. The adequacy of counsel provided to both private and public clients is a matter of concern to defense groups, bar associations, and the courts (Goodpaster, 1986). There are, of course, many examples of incompetent counsel (Gershman, 1993). Even in death penalty cases, attorneys have shown up for court so drunk that they could not stand up straight (Bright, 1994). In other cases, attorneys with almost no knowledge of criminal law have made blunders that have needlessly sent their clients to death row (C. E. Smith, 1997). Lawyers have even fallen asleep during their clients' death penalty trials, yet one Texas judge found no problem with such behavior. He wrote that everyone has a constitutional right to have a lawyer, but "the Constitution does not say that the lawyer has to be awake" (Shapiro, 1997: 27). A divided appellate court later disagreed with this conclusion.

In other cases, the definition of "inadequate counsel" is less clear. What if a public defender's caseload is so large that he or she cannot spend more than a few minutes reviewing the files for most cases? What if, as a deliberate strategy to appear cooperative and thus stay in the judge's good graces, the defense attorney decides not to object to questionable statements and evidence presented by the prosecution? Because attorneys have discretion concerning how to prepare and present their cases, it is hard to define what constitutes a level of performance so inadequate that it violates the defendant's constitutional right to counsel.

The U.S. Supreme Court has examined the question of what requirements must be met if defendants are to receive effective counsel. In two 1984 cases, *United States v. Cronic* and *Strickland v. Washington*, the Court set standards for effective assistance of counsel. Cronic had been charged with a complex mail fraud scheme, which the government had investigated for four and a half years. Just before trial, Cronic's retained lawyer withdrew and a young attorney—who had no trial experience and whose practice was mainly in real estate law—was appointed. The trial court gave the new attorney only 25 days to prepare for the trial, in which Cronic was convicted. The Supreme Court upheld Cronic's conviction on the grounds that, although the new trial counsel had made errors, there was no evidence that the trial had not been a "meaningful" test of the prosecution's case or that the conviction had not been justified.

In *Strickland v. Washington*, the Supreme Court rejected the defendant's claim that his attorney did not adequately prepare for the sentencing hearing in a death penalty case (the attorney sought neither character statements nor a psychiatric examination to present on the defendant's behalf). As it has done in later cases, the Court indicated its reluctance to second-guess a defense attorney's actions. By focusing on whether errors by an attorney were bad enough to make the trial result unreliable and to deny a fair trial, the Court has made it hard for defendants to prove that they were denied effective counsel, even when defense attorneys perform very poorly. As a result, innocent people who were poorly represented have been convicted, even of the most serious crimes (Radelet, Bedeau, and Putnam, 1992).

When imprisoned people are proved innocent and released—sometimes after losing their freedom for many years—we are reminded that the American justice system is imperfect. The development of DNA testing has produced regular reminders of the system's imperfections as new reports surface nearly every month of innocent people released from prison after evidence was reexamined. For example, in May 2008, Levon Jones was released from a North Carolina prison after serving 15 years on death row. He was the 126th person released from a death sentence since 1973 after later investigations unraveled the prosecution's original case. At the time of Jones's release, a federal judge criticized his original defense attorneys for failing to investigate the credibility of the prosecution's star witness—someone who accepted reward money and was coached by police, but who later admitted to lying on the witness stand (Death Penalty Information Center, 2008). Such reminders highlight the importance of having quality legal counsel for criminal defendants. However, because state and local governments have limited funds, concerns about the quality of defense attorneys' work will persist. Think about the importance of defense attorneys in the justice process as you consider "Civic Engagement: Your Role in the System."

civic engagement
your role in the system

Imagine that you must decide how to vote on a ballot issue that proposes denying access to a public defender or appointed counsel for appeals by indigent offenders whose convictions are based on guilty pleas. Should the public pay for an attorney to file an appeal for someone who admitted guilt in an open courtroom proceeding? *Make a list of three arguments favoring and three arguments opposing this ballot issue.* Then read the U.S. Supreme Court's decision concerning such a ballot issue that was passed by voters in Michigan (*Halbert v. Michigan*). To link to this website, go to *The American System of Criminal Justice* 12e companion site at academic.cengage.com/criminal justice/cole.

checkpoint

11.   How has the U.S. Supreme Court addressed the issue of attorney competence?

A QUESTION OF ETHICS

ASSISTANT COUNTY PROSECUTOR Adam Dow entered the office of his boss, County Prosecutor Susan Graham.

"You want to see me?" he said as he closed the door.

"Yes, I do," Graham replied with a flash of anger. "I don't agree with your recommendation to dismiss charges in the Richardson case."

"But the victim was so uncertain in making the identification at the lineup, and the security video from the ATM machine is so grainy that you can't really tell if Richardson committed the robbery."

"Look. We've had six people robbed while withdrawing money at ATM machines in the past month. The community is upset. The banks are upset. The newspapers keep playing up these unsolved crimes. I want to put an end to this public hysteria. Richardson has a prior record for a robbery, and the victim picked him out of the lineup eventually." Graham stared at him coldly. "I'm not going to dismiss the charges."

Dow shifted his feet and stared at the floor. "I'm not comfortable with this case. Richardson may be innocent. The evidence just isn't very strong."

"Don't worry about the strength of the evidence. That's not your problem," said Graham. "We have enough evidence to take the case to trial. The judge said so at the preliminary hearing. So we'll just let the jury decide. Whatever happens, the community will know that we took action against this crime problem."

"But what if he's innocent? The jury could make a mistake in thinking that he's the robber in the grainy videotape. I wouldn't want that on my conscience."

Critical Thinking and Analysis

Should Assistant Prosecutor Dow insist on the certainty of the defendant's guilt before agreeing to take a case forward? Should Prosecutor Graham consider public perceptions when she decides whether to pursue charges against Richardson? Is there an actual risk that an innocent person could be convicted in a jury trial under such circumstances if the prosecutor is reluctant to dismiss questionable charges? Make a list of arguments supporting Graham and a separate list supporting Dow. Whose arguments are the most persuasive?

SUMMARY

Understand the roles of the prosecuting attorney

- American prosecutors, both state and federal, have significant discretion to determine how to handle criminal cases.

- The prosecutor can play various roles, including trial counsel for the police, house counsel for the police, representative of the court, and elected official.

Analyze the process by which criminal charges are filed, and what role the prosecutor's discretion plays in that process

- There is no higher authority over most prosecutors that can overrule a decision to decline to prosecute (*nolle prosequi*) or to pursue multiple counts against a defendant.

- The three primary models of prosecutors' decision-making policies are legal sufficiency, system efficiency, and trial sufficiency.

Identify those with whom the prosecutor interacts in decision making

- Prosecutors' decisions and actions are affected by their exchange relationships with many other important actors and groups, including police, judges, victims and witnesses, and the public.

Understand the day-to-day reality of criminal defense work in the United States

- The image of defense attorneys as courtroom advocates often vastly differs from the reality of pressured, busy negotiators constantly involved in bargaining with the prosecutor over guilty plea agreements.

- Relatively few private defense attorneys make significant incomes from criminal work, but large numbers of private attorneys accept court appointments to handle indigent defendants' cases quickly for relatively low fees.

- Defense attorneys must often wrestle with difficult working conditions and uncooperative clients as they seek to provide representation, usually in the plea-negotiation process.

Know how counsel is provided for defendants who cannot afford a private attorney

- Three primary methods for providing attorneys to represent indigent defendants are appointed counsel, contract counsel, and public defenders.

- Overall, private and public attorneys appear to provide similar quality of counsel with respect to case outcomes.

Understand the defense attorney's role in the system and the nature of the attorney–client relationship

■ The quality of representation provided to criminal defendants is a matter of significant concern, but U.S. Supreme Court rulings have made it difficult for convicted offenders to prove that their attorneys did not provide a competent defense.

QUESTIONS FOR REVIEW

1. What are the formal powers of the prosecuting attorney?

2. How do politics affect prosecutors?

3. What considerations influence the prosecutor's decision about whether to bring charges and what to charge?

4. Why is the prosecuting attorney often cited as the most powerful office in the criminal justice system?

5. What problems do defense attorneys face?

6. How is the defense attorney an agent-mediator?

7. How are defense services provided to indigents?

8. Why might it be argued that publicly financed counsel serves defendants better than does privately retained counsel?

KEY TERMS

accusatory process (p. 371)
assigned counsel (p. 380)
contract counsel (p. 380)
count (p. 363)
defense attorney (p. 373)
discovery (p. 363)
legal sufficiency (p. 370)

nolle prosequi (p. 363)
prosecuting attorney (p. 356)
public defender (p. 380)
state attorney general (p. 356)
system efficiency (p. 370)
trial sufficiency (p. 370)
United States attorney (p. 356)

FOR FURTHER READING

Davis, Angela J. 2007. *Arbitrary Justice: The Power of the American Prosecutor.* New York: Oxford University Press. An examination of prosecutors' discretionary authority and the risks that there are not sufficient controls over prosecutors to prevent errors and excessive use of power.

Delsohn, Gary. 2003. *The Prosecutors: A Year in the Life of a District Attorney's Office.* New York: Dutton. A journalist spent one year observing prosecutors at work. The book focuses on five significant murder cases and describes prosecutors' motives, tactics, and interactions.

Heilbroner, David. 1990. *Rough Justice: Days and Nights of a Young D.A.* New York: Pantheon Books. The author presents the experience of an assistant district attorney learning the ropes in New York's criminal courts.

Humes, Edward. 1999. *Mean Justice: A Town's Terror, a Prosecutor's Power, a Betrayal of Innocence.* New York: Simon & Schuster. An investigative reporter examines prosecutions in one California county in which apparently innocent people were sent to prison for crimes they did not commit.

Lewis, Anthony. 1964. *Gideon's Trumpet.* New York: Vintage. Here is the classic case study of *Gideon v. Wainwright* (1963), the Supreme Court decision that required all states to provide attorneys for indigent defendants facing serious charges.

McIntyre, Lisa J. 1987. *The Public Defender: The Practice of Law in the Shadows of Repute.* Chicago: University of Chicago Press. Here is a case study of the public defender's office in Cook County, Illinois.

Rowland, Judith. 1985. *The Ultimate Violation.* New York: Doubleday. A former San Diego district attorney describes her pioneering legal strategy to prosecute rapists.

Wice, Paul. 2005. *Public Defenders and the American System of Justice.* Westport, CT: Praeger Publishers. A study of public defenders in Newark, New Jersey, based on interviews that gain an insider's view of their jobs and their roles in the criminal justice process.

GOING ONLINE

For an up-to-date list of web links, go to *The American System of Criminal Justice* 12e website: http://academic.cengage.com/criminaljustice/cole.

1. Go to the home pages of the National District Attorneys Association (NDAA) and its affiliate, the American Prosecutors Research Institute (APRI). What purposes does NDAA fulfill for prosecutors across the country? Pay particular attention to the description of the APRI. What are the APRI's goals? How might the institute attempt to influence the development of law and policy?

2. Go to the website of the National Legal Aid and Defender Association. What purposes does the organization fulfill for defense attorneys? How does the organization attempt to influence law and policy?

3. Read a controversial case on prosecutorial immunity that concerns the question of whether a wrongfully convicted man who served two decades in prison is allowed to sue the prosecutors who convicted him. Are there any circumstances in which prosecutors should be vulnerable to be sued for misconduct? If prosecutors can rarely be sued, how can the public hold prosecutors accountable for their actions?

CHECKPOINT ANSWERS

1. *What are the titles of the officials responsible for criminal prosecution at the federal, state, and local levels of government?*

   United States attorney, state attorney general, prosecuting attorney (the prosecuting attorney is also called district attorney, county prosecutor, state's attorney, county attorney).

2. *What are the powers of the prosecuting attorney?*

Decides which charges to file, what bail amounts to recommend, whether to pursue a plea bargain, and what sentence to recommend to the judge.

3. *What are the roles of the prosecutor?*

Trial counsel for the police, house counsel for the police, representative of the court, elected official.

4. *How does a prosecutor use discretion to decide how to treat each defendant?*

The prosecutor can determine the type and number of charges, reduce the charges in exchange for a guilty plea, or enter a *nolle prosequi* (thereby dropping some or all of the charges).

5. *What are the prosecutor's key exchange relationships?*

Police, victims and witnesses, defense attorneys, judges.

6. *What are the three models of prosecution policy, and how do they differ?*

Legal sufficiency: Is there sufficient evidence to pursue a prosecution? System efficiency: What will be the impact of this case on the system with respect to caseload pressures and speedy disposition? Trial sufficiency: Does sufficient evidence exist to ensure successful prosecution of this case through a trial?

7. *How does the image of the defense attorney differ from the attorney's actual role?*

The public often views defense attorneys as protectors of criminals. Defendants believe that defense attorneys will fight vigorous battles at every stage of the process. The defense attorney's actual role is to protect the defendant's rights and to make the prosecution prove its case.

8. *What special pressures do defense attorneys face?*

Securing cases, collecting fees, persuading clients to accept pleas, having to lose most cases, maintaining working relationships with court officers, serving clients in unpleasant surroundings for little money, being negatively viewed by the public.

9. *What are the three main methods of providing attorneys for indigent defendants?*

Assigned counsel, contract system, public defender.

10. *Are public defenders more effective than private defense attorneys?*

Research shows little difference in outcomes.

11. *How has the U.S. Supreme Court addressed the issue of attorney competence?*

The Supreme Court has addressed the issue of "ineffective assistance of counsel" by requiring defendants to prove that the defense attorney made specific errors that affected the outcome of the case.

CHAPTER 11

Determination of Guilt: Plea Bargaining and Trials

LEARNING OBJECTIVES

→ Understand the courtroom workgroup and how it functions

→ Recognize how and why plea bargaining occurs

→ Know how juries are chosen

→ Identify the stages of a criminal trial

→ Understand the basis for an appeal of a conviction

awyers, spectators, and the defendant waited in tense silence as the jurors came back into the courtroom on December 21, 2007. Nearly everyone in the room expected a guilty verdict in one of the most gruesome murder cases covered by Michigan news reporters in recent decades. Stephen Grant, a 37-year-old father of two small children, was charged with first-degree murder for strangling his wife Tara and then cutting her body into many pieces, some of which were scattered in a park. Other body parts were found in the garage of their family home. The Macomb County prosecutor, Eric Smith, who called Grant "evil personified," believed that he could prove that Grant had a

motive for killing his wife because of Grant's sexual relationship with his children's 20-year-old nanny from Germany (Williams, 2008; Associated Press, 2007a).

The case generated national news media attention when Grant reported his wife missing and then later fled to northern Michigan. He was apprehended after a major manhunt in which dozens of law enforcement officers, using dogs and helicopters, tracked him through a snowy state park. When he was caught, he was suffering from hypothermia and frostbite after losing his shoes and jacket in waist-deep snow as he tried to hide from the approaching police officers. After he was caught and

hospitalized, the police taped Grant as he made a detailed confession to the killing (Hackney, Arboscello, and Swickard, 2007).

Prior to his trial, Grant entered a guilty plea to the charge of mutilating a corpse (Associated Press, 2007a). After a judge ruled that Grant's hospital confession could be used at trial, he and his attorney concluded that there was no way that he could avoid conviction on that charge. By pleading guilty, he may have hoped to get a less-than-maximum sentence on that charge by admitting responsibility rather than forcing the court system to use its time and money on a trial.

In contrast, despite the detailed confession, Grant pleaded "not guilty" to the first-degree murder charge. First-degree murder requires proof of premediation—planning and intention in advance. Grant's attorney argued during the trial that Grant killed his wife in the heat of an argument. In Michigan, a conviction for first-degree murder automatically triggers a sentence of life without possibility of parole. A conviction for manslaughter or other lesser homicide, by contrast, could bring a much shorter sentence and the possibility of parole. Thus the attorney used the trial to challenge the prosecutor's claim that Grant had planned the murder and intended to kill his wife.

In the hushed courtroom, the jury's verdict was announced—guilty—but guilty of second-degree murder, not premeditated first-degree murder. The victim's family was shocked and disappointed that such a gruesome murder could lead to a verdict and sentence from which the killer might eventually gain release on parole. Yet, they recognized that jury trials can be unpredictable, especially because criminal juries in most states must reach unanimous conclusions in order to render a guilty verdict. In the words of Alicia Standerfer, the sister of Tara Grant, "Am I happy with the verdict? No, but those 12 people [on the jury] did the best they could" (Associated Press, 2007a).

The American system regards the trial as the best method for determining a defendant's guilt. This is especially true when the defendant can afford to pay for an attorney to mount a vigorous defense. This case occupies the top layer of Samuel Walker's criminal justice wedding cake (see Chapter 3) as one of those relatively few cases that go to trial and command great public attention because a middle-class defendant with the resources to hire an attorney was facing the most severe punishment possible in Michigan's criminal justice process. However, a trial is not a scientific process. Instead of calm, consistent evaluations of evidence, trials involve unpredictable human perceptions and reactions. In discussing the jury's verdict, Prosecutor Smith said, "I think there is premeditation all over this case." But he added, "Jurors are like snowflakes, 12 people from 12 walks of life" (Associated Press, 2007a). Thus his experience had taught him that a mix of citizens drawn from society may react in different ways and reach different conclusions in reacting to the attorneys' presentations of evidence and arguments.

Although Grant's attorney argued that he should receive a sentence of 15 to 25 years in prison, Macomb County Circuit Judge Diane Druzinski ultimately gave Grant a sentence of 50–80 years for the murder and an additional 6–10 years for mutilating the body (Williams, 2008). The length of the sentence virtually guaranteed that Grant would not live long enough to become eligible for parole. Thus the final result satisfied the victim's family and other observers who believed that Grant should have been convicted of first-degree murder.

Because of the high stakes and uncertainty that surround criminal trials, most defendants plead guilty as they get closer to the prospect of being judged by a random group of citizens drawn from the community. Prosecutors also create incentives for guilty pleas by offering reductions in charges and sentences in exchange for admissions of guilt. Even if specific incentives are not offered, defendants may plead guilty in order to demonstrate to the judge that they are taking responsibility for their actions. They may hope that such honesty will lead the judge to soften the sentence. This may have been the motive for Grant's guilty plea for mutilating the corpse.

Even the cases of prominent defendants who can afford to pay top-notch attorneys are often determined by plea bargaining. For example, Baltimore Ravens linebacker Ray Lewis was formally charged with murder and assault for his alleged role in the stabbing deaths of two men during a fight outside a bar in January 2000. However, Lewis was not accused of actually killing the victims. He allegedly participated in the fight and helped two friends who wielded knives to escape in his limousine. In the middle of Lewis's jury trial in June 2000, he pleaded guilty to a misdemeanor charge of obstruction of justice for lying to police about what happened on the night of the killings. Lewis was sentenced to one year on probation (Roedemeier, 2000).

Although trials are relatively unusual, they are important because they provide the reference point for attorneys who must decide whether to seek a plea bargain. In calculating the risks of trial, attorneys use verdicts in other cases to predict how a judge or jury might decide their own clients' cases. Attorneys must ask themselves, "How will jurors react to the evidence I plan to present?" In Lewis's case, the prosecutor apparently had doubts that the jury would issue a guilty verdict for murder and assault. The football player's attorney must have believed that it was better to accept conviction on a minor charge than to take the risk, however slight, that the jury might convict Lewis.

As in other cases resolved through plea bargaining, Lewis's plea negotiations involved *exchange*, the system characteristic discussed in Chapter 3. The prosecutor agreed to drop the serious felony charges and recommend a sentence of probation in exchange for Lewis's guilty plea and his promise to testify against his co-defendants.

In this chapter we discuss plea bargaining and trials as a way to examine the determination of guilt in criminal cases. We also explore the appeals process that occurs when a convicted offender challenges the validity of a criminal conviction. In all of these processes, defendants' fates depend on the interactions and decisions of many individuals in important roles: judges, prosecutors, defense attorneys, and jurors.

THE COURTROOM: HOW IT FUNCTIONS

Criminal cases follow similar rules and processes throughout the nation. However, courts differ in the precise ways they apply those rules and procedures. A study of criminal courts in nine communities in three states shows that similar laws and procedures can produce different results in the treatment of defendants (Eisenstein, Flemming, and Nardulli, 1988). Some courts sentence offenders to longer terms than do others. In some places, court delays and tough bail policies keep many accused people in jail awaiting trial, while in other places defendants are more likely to be released before trial or have their cases resolved quickly. Guilty pleas may make up 90 percent of dispositions in some communities but only 60 percent in others. Such differences can appear even within different courthouses in the same city. How, then, can we explain such differences?

Social scientists are aware that the culture of a community greatly influences how its members behave. The definition of *culture* includes shared beliefs about proper behavior. These beliefs can span entire nations or pertain to smaller communities, including corporations, churches, or neighborhoods. In any community, large or small, the culture can exert a strong effect on people's decisions and behavior.

Researchers have identified a **local legal culture**—values and norms shared by members of a particular court community (judges, attorneys, clerks, bailiffs,

local legal culture
Norms, shared by members of a court community, that center on how cases should be handled and how a participant should behave in the judicial process.

and others)—about how cases should be handled and the way court officials should behave (Church, 1985). The local legal culture influences court operations in three ways:

1. Norms (shared values and expectations) help participants distinguish between our court and other courts. Often a judge or prosecutor will proudly describe how we do the job differently and better than officials in a nearby county or city.

2. Norms tell members of a court community how they should treat one another. For example, one court may see mounting a strong adversarial defense as not in keeping with its norms, but another court may expect that sort of defense.

3. Norms describe how cases *should* be processed. The best example of such a norm is the **going rate**, the local view of the proper sentence based on the defendant's prior record and other factors. The local legal culture also includes attitudes on such issues as whether a judge should take part in plea negotiations, when **continuances**—lawyers' requests for delays in court proceedings—should be granted, and which defendants qualify for a public defender.

Differences among local legal cultures help explain why court decisions often differ even though the formal rules of criminal procedure are basically the same. For example, although judges play a key role in sentencing, the "going rate" concept shows us that sentences also result from shared understandings among the prosecutor, defense attorney, and judge. In one court, shared understandings may mean a court imposes probation on a first-time thief; in other courts, different shared values may send first offenders to jail or prison for the same offense.

going rate
Local court officials' shared view of the appropriate sentence for the offense, based on the defendant's prior record and other case characteristics.

continuance
An adjournment of a scheduled case until a later date.

checkpoint

1. How does the local legal culture affect criminal cases?
   (Answers are at the end of the chapter.)

The Courtroom Workgroup

Television dramas such as *The Practice* or *Boston Legal* present a particular image of the American courtroom. In these shows, prosecutors and defense attorneys lock horns in verbal combat, each side trying to persuade a judge or jury to either convict or acquit the defendant. However, this image of adversarial proceedings does not reflect the actual scene in most American courtrooms. A more realistic portrayal would stress the interactions among the actors, who are guided by the norms and expectations of the local legal culture. Many of these interactions take the form of calm cooperation among the prosecutor, defense attorney, and judge, rather than the battle of adversaries portrayed in fictional accounts (Flemming, Nardulli, and Eisenstein, 1992).

Decisions in criminal cases rely on how the participants interact with each other. We can best understand how criminal justice officials and staff function when we view them as **workgroups**, or groups of people who interact with each other, share certain goals and values, and form relationships that facilitate cooperation. The better the judge, prosecutor, defense attorney, and courtroom staff can function as a workgroup, the more smoothly they can dispose of cases. The workgroup concept is especially important in analyzing urban courts, which have many courtrooms; large numbers of lawyers, judges, and other court personnel; and a heavy caseload.

workgroup
A collection of individuals who interact in the workplace on a continuing basis, share goals, develop norms regarding how activities should be carried out, and eventually establish a network of roles that differentiates the group from others and that facilitates cooperation.

In light of the factors that define the workgroup, we can expect differences among workgroups, from courtroom to courtroom, depending on the strength of these factors in each setting. For example, a rotation system that moves judges among courtrooms in a large courthouse may limit the development of workgroup norms and roles. Although the same prosecutors and defense attorneys may be present every day, the arrival of a new judge every week or month will require them to learn and adapt to new ideas about how cases should be negotiated or tried. When shared norms cannot develop, cases tend to proceed in a relatively formal manner. The actors in such a courtroom have fewer chances to follow agreed-on routines than does a workgroup with a well-developed pattern of interactions.

By contrast, when there are shared expectations and consistent relationships, the business of the courtroom proceeds in a regular but informal manner, with many shared understandings among members easing much of the work (Worden, 1995). Through cooperation, each member can achieve his or her goals as well as those of the group. The prosecutor wants to gain quick convictions, the defense attorney wants fair and prompt resolution of the defendant's case, and the judge wants cooperative agreements on guilt and sentencing. All of these actors want efficient processing of the steady flow of cases that burden their working lives.

Even in the most adversarial cases, courtroom participants form a workgroup that requires constant interaction, cooperation, and negotiation. Do workgroups help or hinder the attainment of justice?

© A. Ramey/PhotoEdit

Each actor in the courtroom workgroup has a specific role with unique duties and responsibilities. If a lawyer moves from the public defender's office to the prosecutor's office and later to a judgeship, each new position calls for a different role in the workgroup because each represents a different sponsoring organization (Eisenstein and Jacob, 1977: 43). One organization, loosely called the court, sends judges; the prosecuting attorney's office sends assistant prosecutors; the public defender's office sends counsel for indigents. In addition, other actors who work in the courtroom contribute to the workgroup's effectiveness. To determine an appropriate plea agreement and sentence, for example, members of the workgroup rely on the probation officer to provide accurate information in the presentence report about the defendant's prior convictions and family history.

Figure 11.1 shows the elements of the courtroom workgroup and the influences that bear on decision making. Note that the workgroup operates in an environment in which decision making is influenced by the local legal culture, recruitment and selection processes, the nature of the cases, and the socioeconomic, political, and legal structures of the broader community.

The crime victim is the missing actor in the courtroom workgroup's processes that produce plea bargains. The workgroup members are interacting together on numerous cases, but each individual victim is only involved in one case. Many victims' rights advocates would like to see victims consulted by the prosecutor as the courtroom workgroup's interactions occur. Some observers believe that consulting with the victims would give the workgroup members more information and enhance the victims' satisfaction with the justice system (O'Hear, 2008). However, the interactions of the workgroup place an emphasis on shared understandings and efficiency—elements that could diminish through slowing their processes in order to consult with an outsider in each individual case.

Judges lead the courtroom team. They ensure that everyone follows procedures correctly. Even though prosecutors and defense attorneys make the key decisions, the judge must approve them. Judges are responsible for coordinating the processing of cases. Even so, each judge can perform this role somewhat

FIGURE 11.1

Model of criminal court decision making

This model ties together the elements of the courtroom workgroup, sponsoring organizations, and local legal culture. Note the effects on decision making. Should any other factors be taken into account?

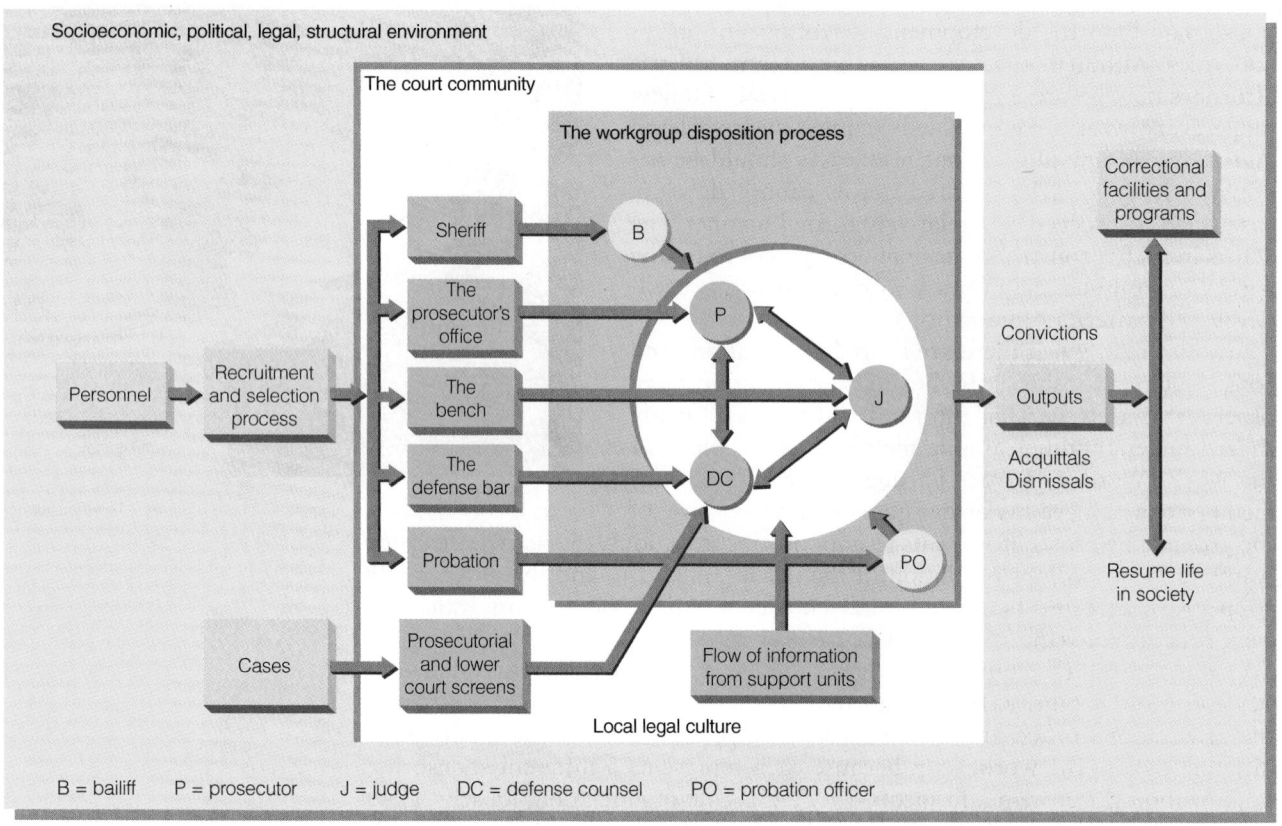

differently. Judges who run a loose administrative ship see themselves as somewhat above the battle. They give other members of the team a great deal of freedom in carrying out their duties and will usually approve group decisions especially when the members of the group have shared beliefs about the court's goals and the community's values. Judges who exert tighter control over the process play a more active role. They anticipate problems; provide cues for other actors; and threaten, cajole, and move the group toward efficient achievement of its goals. Such judges command respect and participate fully in the ongoing courtroom drama.

Because of their position in the justice system, judges can define the level of their involvement in the processing of criminal cases. How they define their role strongly affects interpersonal relations in the courtroom and the way the group performs its task, as measured by the way it disposes of cases. Judges' actions can, for example, pressure defense attorneys to encourage their clients to plead guilty instead of insisting on a trial (D. Lynch, 1999). Whether the judge actively participates in courtroom interactions or supervises from a distance will help define the speed, efficiency, and degree of cooperation involved in disposing cases.

The behavior of defendants greatly affects how they are treated. They are expected to act remorseful, repentant, silent, and submissive. When the defendant admits guilt in public and states that he or she is entering a guilty plea voluntarily, acceptance of the plea can be followed by a brief lecture from the judge about the seriousness of the crime or the harm the defendant has caused the vic-

Read the code of ethics for federal judges and consider how these rules apply to a judges' actions in the courtroom. To link to this website, go to *The American System of Criminal Justice* 12e companion site at academic.cengage.com/criminaljustice/cole.

tim as well as his or her own family. The judge can give a break to a defendant for having cooperated. A defendant who pleads not guilty or whose behavior is inappropriate in other ways may receive a more severe sentence.

checkpoint

2. How does a courtroom workgroup form and operate?

The Impact of Courtroom Workgroups

The classic research of James Eisenstein and Herbert Jacob (1977) on the felony disposition process in Baltimore, Chicago, and Detroit offers important insights into the workgroup's impact on decisions in felony cases. The researchers found that although the same type of felony case was handled differently in each city, the outcomes of the dispositions were remarkably similar. Differences did not stem from the law, rules of procedure, or crime rate. Instead, they emerged from the structure of the courtroom workgroups, the influence of the sponsoring organizations, and sociopolitical factors.

What impact did the courtroom workgroups have on pretrial processes? Eisenstein and Jacob found that the stable courtroom workgroups in Chicago had informal procedures for screening cases. Because of the groups' close links to the trial courtrooms, they felt pressure to screen out many cases and thus spare the resources of the judges and the courts. This led to a very high dismissal rate. In Detroit, also a city with stable workgroups, the prosecutors had discretion to screen cases before they reached the courtroom; hence most of the defendants who appeared at preliminary hearings were sent to trial. Baltimore had less stable workgroups, in part because members were rotated, and sponsoring organizations did not closely supervise assistant prosecutors and defense attorneys. The unstable workgroups lacked all three workgroup criteria: close working relationships, shared values, and reasons to cooperate. As a result, there were fewer guilty pleas, and most defendants were sent on to the grand jury and thence to the trial courts.

The disposition of felony cases results from the interaction of members of the courtroom workgroup. The decisions made by each member are influenced by the policies of their sponsoring organizations. These interactions and policies may vary from courthouse to courthouse. The stability of workgroup interactions can be upset by changes such as a new docket system or changes in the policies and practices of sponsoring organizations.

checkpoint

3. Why are similar cases treated differently in different cities?

PLEA BARGAINING

For the vast majority of cases, plea bargaining—also known as negotiating a settlement, copping a plea, or copping out—is the most important step in the criminal justice process. Few cases go to trial; instead, a negotiated guilty plea arrived at through the interactions of prosecutors, defense lawyers, and judges determines what will happen to most defendants.

Table 11.1 shows the role of plea bargaining in case dispositions in different jurisdictions. Although the percentage of dispositions based on pleas varies from place to place, it is clear that trials are relatively rare events. The differences in percentages also indicate that prosecutors' screening processes vary

TABLE 11.1 Plea Bargaining and Felony Case Dispositions

	75 Most Populous Counties Nationwide (2002)	Alaska Statewide (1999)	Burlington County, New Jersey (2006)	Kitsap County, Washington (2006)	Orange County, New York (2007)
Convicted by Plea	65%	81%	75%	74%	92%
Convicted at Trial	3%	4%	1%	7%	3%
Acquittal/Dismissal/ Diversion	32%	15%	24%	19%	5%

Source: *Orange County (NY) District Attorney's Office 2007 Annual Report* (2008); *Burlington County (NJ) Prosecutor's Office 2006 Annual Report* (2007); *Kitsap County (WA) Prosecuting Attorney Annual Report 2006* (2007); Thomas H. Cohen and Brian A. Reaves, *Felony Defendants in Large Urban Counties, 2002*, Washington, DC: Bureau of Justice Statistics (2002); Teresa White Carns, Larry Cohn, and Susie Mason Dosik, *Alaska Felony Process: 1999*, Anchorage: Alaska Judicial Council (2004).

Republican Congressman Randy "Duke" Cunningham of California faces the press after pleading guilty to bribery for taking $2.4 million from defense contractors. Should officials who violate the public's trust be permitted to gain reduced sentences through plea bargains?

AP Images/Denis Poroy

by jurisdiction. Some prosecutors screen out and dismiss all weak cases prior to charging defendants while others wait until after charges have been filed to dismiss more cases or send defendants into diversion programs. All plea bargains are not based on the same exchanges as illustrated in Table 11.2 from the results of a classic study showing the types of plea bargains made in different cities.

Forty years ago, plea bargaining was not discussed or even acknowledged publicly; it was the criminal justice system's "little secret." Some observers felt that plea bargaining did not accord with American values of fairness. Doubts existed about whether it was constitutional, and it clashed with the image of the courtroom as a place where prosecutors and defense attorneys engage in legal battles as the jury watches "truth" emerge from the courtroom "combat." Yet, a quick resolution of cases through negotiated guilty pleas has been a major means of disposing of criminal cases since at least the 1800s (Vogel, 1999). Researchers began to shed light on plea bargaining in the 1960s, and the U.S. Supreme Court endorsed the process in the 1970s. In *Santobello v. New York* (1971), for example, Chief Justice Warren Burger ruled that prosecutors were obliged to fulfill promises made during plea negotiations. According to Burger, " 'Plea bargaining' is an essential component of the administration of justice. Properly administered, it is to be encouraged." Burger also listed several reasons that plea bargaining was a "highly desirable" part of the criminal justice process:

TABLE 11.2 Types of Plea Concessions in Robbery and Burglary Cases in Five Jurisdictions

Although the percentage of cases ending in a guilty plea is similar in all of the cities (see Table 11.1), there are differences in the types of plea agreements.

Type of Concession	New Orleans	Seattle (King County)	Norfolk	Tucson	Delaware County, PA
Sentence recommendation only	56%	46%	32%	7%	2%
Sentence recommendation plus charge reduction and/ or dismissal	4	42	37	3	31
Charge reduction and/ or dismissal only	40	12	31	90	67

Source: William F. McDonald, *Plea Bargaining: Critical Issues and Common Practices* (Washington, DC: National Institute of Justice, 1985), 7.

- If every case went to trial, federal and state governments would need many times more courts and judges than they now have.

- Plea bargaining leads to the prompt and largely final disposition of most criminal cases.

- Plea bargaining reduces the time that pretrial detainees must spend in jail.

- If they plead guilty to serious charges, they can be moved to prisons with recreational and educational programs instead of enduring the enforced idleness of jails.

- By disposing of cases more quickly than trials would, plea bargaining reduces the amount of time that released suspects spend free on bail. Therefore, the public is better protected from crimes that such suspects may commit while on pretrial release.

- Offenders who plead guilty to serious charges can move more quickly into prison counseling, training, and education programs designed to rehabilitate offenders.

 The American Bar Association's public education office provides an explanation of plea bargaining. To link to this website, go to *The American System of Criminal Justice* 12e companion site at academic.cengage.com/criminaljustice/cole.

In 1976, Justice Potter Stewart revealed the heart and soul of plea bargaining when he wrote in *Blackledge v. Allison* that plea bargaining "can benefit all concerned" in a criminal case. It offers advantages for defendants, prosecutors, defense attorneys, and judges. Defendants can have their cases completed more quickly and know what the punishment will be, instead of facing the uncertainty of a judge's sentencing decision. Moreover, the defendant is likely to receive less than the maximum punishment that might have been imposed after a trial. Prosecutors are not being "soft on crime" when they plea bargain. Instead, they gain an easy conviction, even in cases in which enough evidence may not have been gathered to convince a jury to convict the defendant. They also save time and resources by disposing of cases without having to prepare for a trial. Private defense attorneys as well save the time needed to prepare for a trial. They earn their fee quickly and can move on to the next case. Similarly, plea bargaining helps public defenders cope with large caseloads. Judges, too, avoid time-consuming trials and having to decide what sentence to impose on the defendant. Instead, they often adopt the sentence recommended by the prosecutor in consultation with the defense attorney, provided that it falls within the range of sentences that they deem appropriate for a given crime and offender.

The attraction of plea bargaining for prosecutors and defendants was evident in the 2002 guilty plea of John Walker Lindh, the 21-year-old American captured while fighting with the Taliban in Afghanistan. He faced ten felony charges, including conspiring to kill Americans, and could have been sentenced to three life terms in prison. Instead, he received a 20-year sentence for pleading guilty to two counts, serving as a soldier for the Taliban and carrying a firearm while doing so. As part of the deal, Lindh agreed to cooperate by providing information to the government about the Taliban and the Al-Qaida network (Serrano, 2002). Lindh obviously had an incentive to avoid the risk of spending the rest of his life in prison, especially if he feared that a jury of Americans could not listen objectively to evidence about his involvement with the Taliban. It seems equally apparent that the government was eager to gain information from Lindh and was willing to settle for a lesser sentence in order to obtain that information. The government may also have had doubts about whether the evidence could support convictions on all of the charges. Does this result achieve justice? Such questions are difficult to answer when the evidence is disputed. However, these results spare the system and its decision makers from the risk of expending significant resources on uncertain outcomes.

Defenders of plea bargaining justify the practice by noting that it permits judges, prosecutors, and defense attorneys to individualize justice by agreeing to a plea and punishment that fits the offender and offense. The process also helps

CLOSE UP

Banning Plea Bargaining in Tennessee

IN JANUARY 1997, William Gibbons, District Attorney for Shelby County, Tennessee, which includes the city of Memphis, introduced a policy of refusing to reduce charges of first- and second-degree murder and charges of robbery or rape that involved the use of a deadly weapon. These are generally considered the most violent and harmful of crimes. Under the policy, anyone indicted for these crimes must either plead guilty to the charge specified or go to trial. The operation of the policy raises interesting questions about the impact of bans on plea bargaining.

The District Attorney's Office hoped that the "no deal" policy and the resulting tough sentences for people convicted of these crimes would deter other potential offenders from committing violent crimes. Thus, the ban on plea bargaining was accompanied by a public relations campaign to spread the word about the new policy. The marketing campaign, which would have cost $1 million, was produced through contributions of free advertising and private fund-raising led by a former Memphis mayor, as well as $200,000 in money confiscated from drug dealers by the county sheriff. "No Deal" signs, decals, and bumper stickers were distributed to businesses and neighborhood watch groups.

The District Attorney's Office claims that the ban on plea bargaining "had a positive impact in reducing violent felonies." The Office pointed to a reduction in violent crime in Memphis, yet violent crime throughout the nation declined over the same period time. Can the District Attorney accurately conclude that the reduction in Memphis is due to the plea-bargaining policy rather than reflecting a general social trend?

The District Attorney's Office says that the effectiveness of the new policy stems from cooperation between the prosecutor and local law enforcement agencies. The new policy is largely made possible by a process by which representatives of the District Attorney's Office meet with representatives of the Memphis Police Department and the Shelby County Sheriff's Office to screen cases involving the violent crimes covered by the policy. This early review process helps to insure that the D.A.'s Office has a good case with strong evidence before someone is charged and a proposed indictment is presented to the grand jury.

By filtering out cases for which the most serious charges are not justified and provable, does this review and screening process perhaps fulfill the function served by plea bargaining in other cities? Elsewhere, the plea negotiation process involves discussions between defense attorneys and prosecutors about the provable facts of a case so that both sides can reach agreement about the "going

to encourage the defendant to cooperate and accept the results (O'Hear, 2008). Some argue that plea bargaining is an administrative necessity because courts lack the time and resources to conduct lengthy, expensive trials in all cases. Historical studies cast doubt on the latter justification, however, because during the nineteenth century, when plea bargaining was a regular feature in casework, it existed in courts with relatively few cases (Friedman, 1993; Heumann, 1978). Thus, instead of administrative need, the benefits of plea bargaining for the main participants appear to be the primary driving force behind the practice.

Because plea bargaining benefits all involved, it is little wonder that it existed long before the legal community publicly acknowledged it and that it still exists, even when prosecutors, legislators, or judges claim that they wish to abolish it. In California, for example, voters decided to ban plea bargaining for serious felony cases. Research showed, however, that when plea bargaining was barred in the felony trial courts, it did not disappear. It simply occurred earlier in the justice process, at the suspect's first appearance in the lower-level municipal court (McCoy, 1993). Efforts to abolish plea bargaining sometimes result in bargaining over the charges instead of over the sentence that will be recommended in exchange for a guilty plea. Moreover, if a prosecutor forbids his or her staff to plea bargain, judges may become more involved in negotiating and facilitating guilty pleas that result in predictable punishments for offenders.

As you read the Close Up box concerning the partial ban on plea bargaining in Memphis, Tennessee, consider the impact of the ban. The prosecutor claims that the ban has led to a drop in violent crime because potential criminals know that they will be severely punished under the "no deal" policy. How do we know if this is true? What other consequences might be produced by the ban on plea bargaining?

rate" of punishment for that particular offender and crime. In effect, then, might the Memphis screening process really just produce the same results in "no deal" cases that would have been produced through plea negotiations in other cities?

In reality, the Memphis ban on plea bargaining is not absolute, even for the specified crimes to which it applies. There can be "exceptions based on legal, factual, or ethical grounds [that] must be approved by a supervisor [in the District Attorney's Office] and documented in writing." Does the possibility of exceptions create incentives for defense attorneys to seek special deals for their clients? Does it create opportunities for prosecutors to use discretion to reduce charges against particular defendants or the clients of particular attorneys?

Consider the following results from the "no deal" policy in 2003. Out of 560 "no deal" cases, 319 defendants entered guilty pleas to the offenses charged. Thirty-one defendants had their charges later dismissed, and 120 defendants went to trial, resulting in 106 convictions and 14 acquittals and dismissals. The most interesting number is the 90 defendants who pleaded guilty to lesser charges under the "no deal" system. In explanations given in prior years by the prosecutor's office, such charge reductions were usually the result of the inability of the police to locate crucial witnesses needed for gaining a conviction at trial. In light of those numbers, does the "no deal" policy really live up to its name? Would the public be surprised to learn that a "no deal" policy permits so many plea bargains resulting in reduced charges? Alternatively, in light of how the criminal justice system operates and how much it depends on witnesses and discre-tionary decisions, would it be unrealistic to have a policy in which there were really no charge reductions?

A critic might claim that the screening process and the opportunity to treat cases as exceptions to the "no deal" rule mean that the District Attorney's policy has probably had little impact on the outcomes of criminal cases. Arguably, many of these cases might have produced the same results in a system that relied on plea negotiations. Moreover, proving that any reductions in crime rates are caused by the policy is difficult when similar drops in crimes rates are simultaneously occurring throughout the country in cities that still rely on plea bargaining. Does that mean that the "no deal" policy and the accompanying advertising campaign are primarily a public relations effort to gain support and credit for the District Attorney's Office? Is it possible that the District Attorney honestly believes that the "no deal" policy has positive benefits even if it may have produced little change? What do you think?

Sources: *2007 Annual Report: Shelby County District Attorney* General (2008) (http://www.scdag.com); Thomas D. Henderson, "No Deals Policy," Office of the District Attorney General, 30th Judicial District of Tennessee, 1999 (http://www.scdag.com/nodeals.htm#top); Michael J. Sniffen, "Crime Down for 7th Straight Year," Associated Press report, October 17, 1999.

Researching the Internet

 Go online to read a report by the Alaska Judicial Council about the initial consequences of that state's efforts to ban plea bargaining. To link to this website, go to *The American System of Criminal Justice* 12e companion site at academic.cengage .com/criminaljustice/cole.

Exchange Relationships in Plea Bargaining

Plea bargaining is a set of exchange relationships in which the prosecutor, the defense attorney, the defendant, and sometimes the judge participate. All have specific goals, all try to use the situation to their own advantage, and all tend to see the exchange as a success.

Plea bargaining does not always occur in a single meeting between prosecutor and defense attorney. One study showed that plea bargaining is a process in which prosecutors and defense attorneys interact again and again as they move along in the judicial process. As time passes, the prosecutor's hand may be strengthened by the discovery of more evidence or new information about the defendant's background (Emmelman, 1996). Often the prosecution rather than the defense is in the best position to obtain new evidence (Cooney, 1994). However, the defense attorney's position may gain strength if the prosecutor does not wish to spend time going farther down the path toward a trial.

checkpoint

4. Why does plea bargaining occur?

Tactics of Prosecutor and Defense

Plea bargaining between defense counsel and prosecutor is a serious game in which friendliness and joking may mask efforts to advance each side's cause. Each side tries to impress the other with its confidence in its own case while pointing out weaknesses in the other's. An unspoken rule of openness and candor helps keep the relationship on good terms. Little effort is made to conceal

information that may later be useful to the other side in the courtroom. Studies show that the outcomes of plea bargaining may depend on the relationships between prosecutors and individual attorneys, as well as the defense counsel's willingness to fight for the client (Champion, 1989).

A tactic that many prosecutors bring to plea-bargaining sessions is the multiple-offense indictment. Multiple-offense charges are especially important to prosecuting attorneys in difficult cases in which, for instance, the victim is reluctant to provide information, the value of the stolen item is in question, and the evidence may not be reliable. The police often file charges of selling a drug when they know they can probably convict only for possession. Because the defendants know that the penalty for selling is much greater, they are tempted to plead guilty to the lesser charge rather than risk a severer punishment, even though conviction on the more serious charge is uncertain.

Defense attorneys may threaten to ask for a jury trial if concessions are not made. Their hand is further strengthened if they have filed pretrial motions that require a formal response by the prosecutor. Another tactic is to seek to reschedule pretrial activities in the hope that, with delay, witnesses will become unavailable, media attention will die down, and memories of the crime will diminish by the time of the trial. Rather than resort to such legal tactics, however, some attorneys prefer to bargain on the basis of friendship.

Neither the prosecutor nor the defense attorney is a free agent. Each needs the cooperation of both defendants and judges. Attorneys often cite the difficulty of convincing defendants that they should uphold their end of the bargain. Judges might not sentence the accused according to the prosecutor's recommendation. On the other hand, although their role requires that they uphold the public interest, judges may be reluctant to interfere with a plea agreement. Thus, both the prosecutor and the defense attorney often confer with the judge about the sentence to be imposed before agreeing on a plea. If a particular judge is unpredictable in supporting plea agreements, defense attorneys may be reluctant to reach agreements in that judge's court.

Pleas without Bargaining

Studies show that in many courts, give-and-take plea bargaining does not occur for certain types of cases, yet these cases have as many guilty pleas as they do in other courts (Eisenstein et al., 1988). The term *bargaining* may be misleading in that it implies haggling. Many scholars argue that guilty pleas emerge after the prosecutor, the defense attorney, and sometimes the judge reach an agreement to settle the facts (Utz, 1978). In this view, the parties first study the facts of a case. What were the circumstances of the event? Was it really an assault or was it more of a shoving match? Did the victim antagonize the accused? Each side may hope to persuade the other that provable facts back up its view of the defendant's actions. The prosecution wants the defense to believe that strong evidence proves its version of the event. The defense attorney wants to convince the prosecution that the evidence is not solid and a jury trial would likely result in acquittal.

In some cases, the evidence is strong and the defense attorney has little hope of persuading the prosecutor otherwise. Through their discussions, the prosecutor and defense attorney seek to reach a shared view of the provable facts in the case. Once they agree on the facts, they will both know the appropriate charge, and they can agree on the sentence according to the locally defined going rate. At that point a guilty plea can be entered without any formal bargaining, because both sides agree on what the case is worth in terms of the seriousness of the charge and the usual punishment. This process may be thought of as *implicit plea bargaining* because shared understandings create the expectation that a guilty plea will lead to a less-than-maximum sentence, even without any exchange or bargaining.

The going rates for sentences for particular crimes and offenders depend on local values and sentencing patterns. Often both the prosecutor and the defense attorney belong to a particular local legal culture and thus share an understanding about how cases should be handled. On the basis of their experiences in interacting with other attorneys and judges, they become keenly aware of local practices in the treatment of cases and offenders (Worden, 1995). Thus they may both know right away what the sentence will be for a first-time burglar or second-time robber. The sentence may differ in another courthouse because the local legal culture and going rates can vary.

These shared understandings are important for several reasons. First, they help make plea bargaining more effective, because both sides understand which sentences apply to which cases. Second, they help create a cooperative climate for plea bargaining, even if bad feelings exist between the prosecutor and the defense attorney. The local legal culture dictates how attorneys should treat each other and thereby reach agreements. Third, the shared understandings help maintain the relationship between the attorneys.

checkpoint

5. What is implicit plea bargaining?

Legal Issues in Plea Bargaining

In *Boykin v. Alabama* (1969), the Supreme Court ruled that defendants must state that they made their pleas voluntarily, before judges may accept those pleas. Judges have created standard forms that have questions for the defendant to affirm in open court before the plea is accepted. Trial judges also must learn whether the defendant understands the consequences of pleading guilty and ensure that the plea is not obtained through pressure or coercion.

Can a trial court accept a guilty plea if the defendant claims to be innocent? In *North Carolina v. Alford* (1970), the Court allowed a defendant to enter a guilty plea for the purpose of gaining a lesser sentence, even though he maintained that he was innocent. However, the Supreme Court has stated that trial judges should not accept such a plea unless a factual basis exists for believing that the defendant is in fact guilty (Whitebread and Slobogin, 2000: 689).

Another issue is whether the plea agreement has been fulfilled. If the prosecutor has promised to recommend a lenient sentence, he or she must keep that promise. In *Santobello v. New York* (1971), the Supreme Court "ruled that when a [guilty] plea rests in any significant degree on a promise or agreement of the prosecutor, so that it can be said to be part of the inducement or consideration, such promise must be fulfilled." The Court also decided, in *Ricketts v. Adamson* (1987), that defendants must also keep their side of the bargain, such as an agreement to testify against co-defendants.

May prosecutors threaten to penalize defendants who insist on their right to a jury trial? Yes, according to *Bordenkircher v. Hayes* (1978). Prosecutors may, for example, threaten repeat offenders with life sentences under habitual offender statutes if they do not agree to plead guilty and accept specified terms of imprisonment. A threat of more serious charges, as long as such charges are legitimate and supported by evidence, is not considered improper pressure that makes a guilty plea involuntary and hence invalid. Some scholars criticize this decision as imposing pressures on defendants that are not permitted elsewhere in the justice process (O'Hear, 2006).

Examine the scene in "A Question of Ethics" at the end of the chapter. Are all of the courtroom actors behaving in an honest, ethical manner? Does the description of the courtroom scene raise questions about how plea bargains operate?

Boykin v. Alabama (1969)
Defendants must state that they are voluntarily making a plea of guilty.

North Carolina v. Alford (1970)
A plea of guilty may be accepted for the purpose of a lesser sentence from a defendant who maintains his or her innocence.

Santobello v. New York (1971)
When a guilty plea rests on a promise of a prosecutor, the promise must be filled.

Ricketts v. Adamson (1987)
Defendants must uphold the plea agreement or risk going to trial and receiving a harsher sentence.

Bordenkircher v. Hayes (1978)
A defendant's rights were not violated by a prosecutor who warned that failure to agree to a guilty plea would result in a harsher sentence.

Criticisms of Plea Bargaining

Although plea bargaining is widely used, some critics deplore it. The criticisms are of two main types. The first stresses due process and argues that plea bargaining is unfair because defendants give up some of their constitutional rights, especially the right to trial by jury. The second stresses sentencing policy and points out that plea bargaining reduces society's interest in appropriate punishments for crimes. In urban areas with high caseloads, harried prosecutors and judges are said to make concessions based on administrative needs, resulting in lighter sentences than those required by the penal code.

Plea bargaining also comes under fire because it is hidden from judicial scrutiny. Because the agreement is most often made at an early stage, the judge has little information about the crime and the defendant and thus cannot adequately evaluate the case. Nor can the judge review the terms of the bargain, that is, check on the amount of pressure put on the defendant to plead guilty. The result of bargain justice is that the judge, the public, and sometimes even the defendant cannot know for sure who got what from whom in exchange for what.

Other critics believe that overuse of plea bargaining breeds disrespect and even contempt for the law. They say criminals look at the judicial process as a game or a sham, much like other "deals" made in life.

Critics also contend that it is unjust to penalize people who assert their right to a trial by giving them stiffer sentences than they would have received if they had pleaded guilty. The evidence here is unclear, although it is widely believed that an extra penalty is imposed on defendants who take up the court's time by asserting their right to a trial (Spohn, 1992). Critics note that federal sentencing guidelines also encourage avoidance of trial, because they include a two-point deduction from an offender's base score for a guilty plea—thus lowering the sentence—for "acceptance of responsibility" (McCoy, 1995).

Finally, another concern about plea bargaining is that innocent people will plead guilty to acts they did not commit. Although it is hard to know how often this happens, some defendants have entered guilty pleas when they have not committed the offense (McConville, 2000). For example, the Colorado courts overturned a sentence on the ground that the defendant had been coerced by the judge's statement that he would "put him away forever if he did not accept the bargain" (*People v. Clark*, 1973). Middle-class people might find it hard to understand how anyone could possibly plead guilty when innocent. However, people with little education and low social status may lack the confidence to say "no" to an attorney who pressures them to plead guilty. Poor people may feel especially helpless in the stressful climate of the courthouse and jail. If they lack faith in the system's ability to protect their rights and find them not guilty, they may accept a lighter punishment rather than risk conviction for a serious offense. Think about these criticisms as you examine "Civic Engagement: Your Role in the System."

civic engagement
your role in the system

Imagine that the voters of your state will consider a ballot issue to ban plea bargaining for serious crimes in the trial courts of general jurisdiction. *Make a list of the consequences that you predict if the ballot issue is approved by the voters. Would you vote in favor of the ban?* Then read a brief review that discusses what happened when California voters decided to approve such a ban. To link to this website, go to *The American System of Criminal Justice* 12e companion site at academic.cengage.com/criminaljustice/cole.

checkpoint

6. What issues concerning plea bargaining has the Supreme Court examined?
7. What are the criticisms of plea bargaining?

TRIAL: THE EXCEPTIONAL CASE

Cases not dismissed or terminated through plea bargaining move forward for trial. The seriousness of the charge is probably the most important factor influencing the decision to go to trial. Defendants charged with property crimes rarely demand a trial. However, murder, felonious assault, or rape—all charges that bring long prison terms—are more likely to require judge and jury. In a study of the nation's 75 largest counties, 44 percent of murder cases went to trial, the largest percentage for any crime. For all other crimes, trials occurred in 6 percent of cases or less (Cohen and Reaves, 2006). When the penalty is harsh, many defendants seem willing to risk the possibility of conviction at trial.

Although such statistics suggest consistency in decisions about going to trial, the real practice varies considerably. Note in Table 11.3 the differences in the percentages of defendants going to trial for several offenses in various cities. What might explain the differences from one city to another and for one offense or another? Think about how prosecutors' policies or sentencing practices in different cities can increase or decrease the incentives for a defendant to plead guilty.

Most Americans are familiar with the image of the criminal trial. As portrayed in so many movies and television shows, the prosecutor and defense attorney face off in a tense courtroom conflict. Each attorney attempts to use evidence, persuasion, and emotion to convince a jury of citizens to favor its arguments about the defendant's guilt or innocence.

As we have seen in previous chapters, the trial process is based on the *adversary process*, an open battle between opposing lawyers that is assumed to be the best way to discover the truth. The authors of the Constitution apparently shared this assumption: The Sixth Amendment says the accused shall enjoy a speedy and public trial by an impartial jury in all criminal prosecutions (Langbein, 1992). In theory, each side will present the best evidence and arguments it can muster, and the **jury** will make a decision based on thorough consideration of the available information about the case.

However, because trials are human processes, many factors may keep a trial from achieving its goal of revealing the truth. The rules of evidence can prevent one side from presenting the most useful evidence. One side may have impressive expert witnesses that the other side cannot afford to counter with its own experts. One side's attorney may be more persuasive and likeable, thus swaying the jury in spite of the evidence. The jurors or judge may bring into the courtroom their own prejudices, which cause them to favor some defendants or automatically

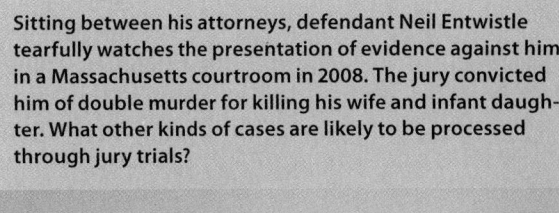

Sitting between his attorneys, defendant Neil Entwistle tearfully watches the presentation of evidence against him in a Massachusetts courtroom in 2008. The jury convicted him of double murder for killing his wife and infant daughter. What other kinds of cases are likely to be processed through jury trials?

AP Images/Brian Snyder, Pool

jury
A panel of citizens selected according to law and sworn to determine matters of fact in a criminal case and to deliver a verdict of guilty or not guilty.

TABLE 11.3	**Percentage of Indicted Cases That Went to Trial, by Offense**				
The percentages of cases that went to trial differ both by offense and by jurisdiction. It seems that the stiffer the possible penalty, the greater the likelihood of a trial.					
Jurisdiction	**Homicide**	**Sexual Assault**	**Robbery**	**Larceny**	**Drug Offenses**
Indianapolis, IN	38%	18%	21%	12%	9%
Los Angeles, CA	29	20	12	5	7
Louisville, KY	57	27	18	10	11
New Orleans, LA	22	18	16	7	7
St. Louis, MO	36	23	15	6	6
San Diego, CA	37	2	12	5	3
Washington, DC	43	32	22	12	10

Source: Adapted from Bureau of Justice Statistics, *Report to the Nation on Crime and Justice*, 2nd ed. (Washington, DC: U.S. Government Printing Office, 1988), 84.

assume the worst about others. Fundamentally, we as a society place great faith in the trial process as the best means for giving complete consideration of a defendant's potential guilt, yet the process does not always work as it should.

Trials determine the fates of very few defendants. Although the right to trial by jury is ingrained in American ideology—it is mentioned in the Declaration of Independence, three amendments to the Constitution, and countless opinions of the Supreme Court—year in and year out fewer than 9 percent of felony cases go to trial. Of these, only about half are jury trials; the rest are **bench trials** presided over by a judge without a jury. In 2004, trials produced only 3 percent of felony convictions in the nation's 75 most populous counties (Kychkelhahn and Cohen, 2008). Defendants may choose a bench trial if they believe a judge will be more capable of making an objective decision, especially if the charges or evidence are likely to arouse emotional reactions in jurors.

Trials take considerable time and resources. Attorneys frequently spend weeks or months preparing evidence, responding to their opponents' motions, planning trial strategy, and setting aside days or weeks to present the case in court. From the perspective of judges, prosecutors, and defense attorneys, plea bargaining is obviously an attractive alternative for purposes of completing cases quickly.

bench trial
Trial conducted by a judge who acts as fact finder and determines issues of law. No jury participates.

Going to Trial

Because the adversary process is designed to get to the truth, the rules of criminal law, procedure, and evidence govern the conduct of the trial. Trials are based on the idea that the prosecution and defense will compete before a judge and jury so that the truth will emerge. Above the battle, the judge sees to it that the rules are followed and that the jury impartially evaluates the evidence and reflects the community's interest (Walpin, 2003). In a jury trial, the jury is the sole evaluator of the facts in a case. Does this adversarial, politically connected, and citizen-juried trial process provide the best mechanism for finding the truth and doing justice in our most serious criminal cases? As you read the Comparative Perspective, consider the French courts' concerns about the American process

COMPARATIVE PERSPECTIVE

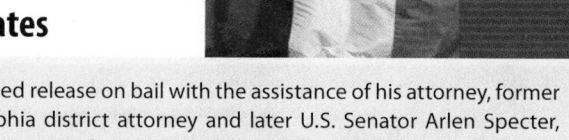

Comparing Trial Processes: France and the United States

IN 1977, HELEN "Holly" Maddux, a 30-year-old woman from a wealthy Texas family, disappeared. She had been living in Philadelphia with her boyfriend, Ira Einhorn, a former hippie leader who had developed a network of friends among prominent people as he ran for mayor and organized artistic events and self-discovery courses. He had even spent one semester as a visiting fellow at Harvard's Kennedy School of Government. Eighteen months after Einhorn claimed that Maddux went out and never returned from a trip to the store, her decomposed remains were found in a trunk in his closet. Einhorn proclaimed his innocence and gained release on bail with the assistance of his attorney, former Philadelphia district attorney and later U.S. Senator Arlen Specter, and the support of prominent Philadelphians who thought this leading advocate of peace and love could never commit a murder.

When Einhorn's trial date approached, he disappeared. Investigators later learned that he had fled the country. Sightings of Einhorn were reported in Ireland and Sweden, but authorities could not find him. When Philadelphia's district attorney became concerned that witnesses' memories might fade over time, Einhorn was tried in absentia in 1993. A trial in absentia means that the trial was conducted even though the defendant was absent. Einhorn was convicted of murder.

Assistant District Attorney Richard DiBenedetto continued to investigate Einhorn's whereabouts, just as he had done for years. In 1997, DiBenedetto directed French police to a house where Einhorn's former Swedish girlfriend resided under an assumed name. The police found a man who said his name was "Mallon," but his fingerprints matched those of Ira Einhorn.

Einhorn hired an attorney to fight his extradition—the process of returning a fugitive to face charges in another jurisdiction. His attorneys argued that the United States has an unfair criminal trial process because it permits defendants to be tried in absentia, it uses the death penalty, and it does not obey the European Convention on Human Rights.

According to an American writer who followed Einhorn's case closely, his attorneys were raising fundamental questions about the fairness of American trials and the justice process (Levy, 1997: 44):

> However, the underlying argument, it would appear, was to urge the French judges to send a message to the "barbarians" in the United States. . . . [They wanted France to] send a message in human rights to the new masters of the world order across the ocean.

The French judges agreed with the attorneys' arguments. The judges refused to send Einhorn back to the United States to stand trial, and he was released from custody. Government officials in the United States protested the decision and its implication that American trial processes are unfair. In an effort to satisfy French criticisms of the trial in absentia, the Pennsylvania legislature passed a special law to give Einhorn a new trial if he were ever returned to the United States. After two additional years of appeals, a French court ordered Einhorn returned to the United States in 1999. He was not transported from France immediately, however, because he was entitled to further appeals in the French courts. Eventually, he was sent to the United States, convicted in a 2002 murder trial, and sentenced to life without parole.

If French judges are so critical of American trial processes that they would permit a suspected murderer to live freely in their country, what does that say about their view of the United States? Moreover, in what ways might French judges view their own trial processes as superior?

Judges in France are not elected officials, and efforts are made to separate the French judiciary from electoral politics. To become a judge in France, law students must take a competitive examination to gain entry into the graduate school for future judges. Based on their performance in graduate school and their achievement on additional tests, they may gain positions at the lower levels of the judiciary, which is a branch of the national civil service. French judges have the protected tenure of civil servants so that, unlike so many American state judges, they never need to worry about running for reelection in order to retain their seats on the bench.

Criminal investigations and trials in France differ fundamentally from those in the United States, because French judges are so deeply involved in each step of the process—from investigation of defendants through jury deliberations after a trial. Rather than a police official or prosecutor, a judge called an "examining magistrate" investigates criminal cases. Critics fear that some examining magistrates might become overly familiar with police and prosecutors and thereby lose their neutral perspective. However, the examining magistrate is positioned to be an independent investigator, unlike American police and elected prosecutors who face political pressure to gain convictions in an adversarial system.

After the investigation is completed, the trial serves as a mechanism to check the quality of the investigation. Trials for serious criminal cases take place in the Courts of Assize. A chief trial judge assumes responsibility for the case. Instead of having adversarial prosecutors and defense attorneys attempting to persuade the jury with carefully phrased and often deceptive questions, the French chief trial judge performs all questioning, and no cross examination of witnesses is permitted. The chief trial judge typically asks many questions about the defendant's background and character, because the trial does not need to focus solely on the evidence about the crime. Because judges control the pretrial investigation and the presentation of evidence in the courtroom, defendants' wealth may not make a difference in how they are treated. Unlike in the United States, where the quality of defense representation sometimes varies depending on whether the defendant can afford to hire his or her own attorney, French judges can ensure that sufficient and proper evidence is presented on behalf of all defendants.

Throughout the trial, the chief judge is joined by two associate judges and nine jurors from the community. Both the prosecution and defense can use peremptory challenges to eliminate a few of the jurors, but they do not engage in the extensive questioning of jurors that can occur in American trials concerning serious crimes.

At the end of the trial, the three judges and nine jurors deliberate in secret. By having judges participate in the jury's verdict, legal professionals can influence the outcome of the case. Such participation may help keep the jurors focused on the relevant facts and law. On the other hand, it may also lead jurors to defer to the legal professionals and thereby fail to express viewpoints that reflect public sentiments about the case. Although judges do not automatically control the verdict, they influence it directly by participating in the vote. The jurors and judges vote by secret ballot. Eight of the 12 must vote in favor of conviction in order for the defendant to be found guilty. Thus, a defendant can be found guilty even when four jurors disagree. A majority vote of the jurors and judges determines the sentence. Thus citizen-jurors have greater direct input into sentencing in France. In the United States, jurors affect the eventual sentence by determining which offenses will be the basis for the conviction. If they want to see a lighter sentence, they can convict of fewer charges or a lesser offense. However, they rarely control the actual sentence, because the judge usually determines it. By contrast, French jurors can vote directly on the sentence, and even outvote the judges in determining the sentence. Thus, community representatives rather than legal professionals may most directly shape criminal punishment in France.

Is the French trial process superior to the processes in the United States? Would American courts benefit from giving judges greater control over criminal investigations, the presentation of evidence, and deliberations about guilt? Would they benefit from giving American jurors the direct authority to determine the sentence for each offender? The Einhorn extradition dispute between France and the United States did not rest solely on the nature of American jury trials. Instead, it seemed to reflect a broader sense that some French judges had doubts about the fairness of the American criminal justice process. The differences between the French and American systems as well as the French criticisms of the American process stem from differences in the respective countries' values and traditions.

Sources: Drawn from Henry J. Abraham, *The Judicial Process*, 6th ed. (New York: Oxford University Press, 1986); Bill Hanna, "Family of Victim Glad Fugitive's Murder Trial Finally under Way," *Fort Worth Star-Telegram*, September 24, 2002 (http://www.star-telegram.com); Steven Levy, "A Guru Goes Free," *Newsweek*, December 15, 1997, p. 44; Robert Moran, "Pennsylvania Governor Signs Provision for Einhorn Retrial," *Philadelphia Inquirer*, January 29, 1998; D. Marie Provine, "Court in the Political Process in France," in *Courts, Law, and Politics in Comparative Perspective* (New Haven, CT: Yale University Press, 1996), 177–248 (http://www.philly.com); Julie Stoiber, "Fugitive Ira Einhorn Loses a Round in Extradition Appeal," *Philadelphia Inquirer*, May 28, 1999 (http://www.philly.com).

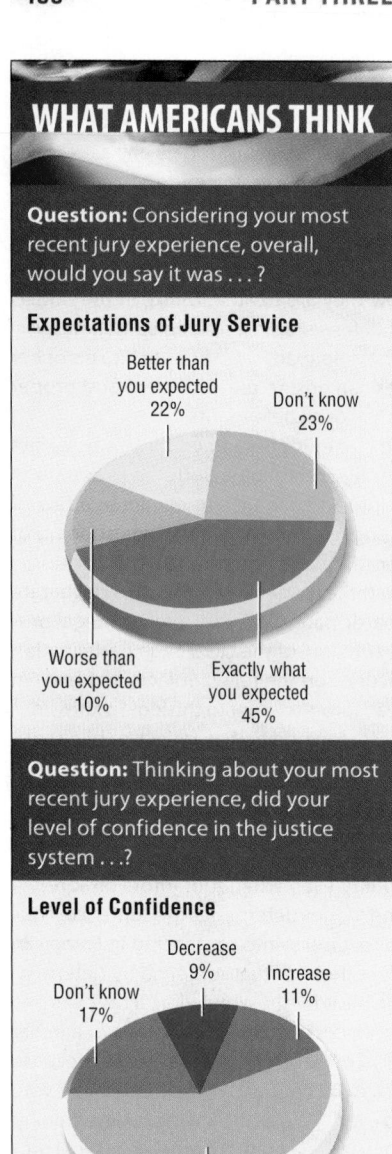

and examine whether the French trial process presents any advantages. Could the American trial process improve by borrowing any elements from France?

The adversary process and inclusion of citizen-jurors in decision making often make trial outcomes difficult to predict. The verdict hinges not only on the nature of the evidence but also on the effectiveness of the prosecution and defense and on the attitudes of the jurors.

Most jury trials worldwide take place in the United States. Common-law countries, such as Australia, Canada, Great Britain, and the United States, are the places that historically have used a group of citizens drawn from the community to determine the guilt of criminal defendants. In civil-law countries, this function is usually performed by a judge or judges, often assisted by two or three nonlawyers serving as assessors. However, a few civil-law countries, including Russia and Spain, have begun to incorporate juries into their legal processes (Thaman, 2000). Japan will introduce criminal jury trials into their system in 2009 (Okada, 2006).

Juries perform six vital functions in the U.S. criminal justice system:

1. Prevent government oppression by safeguarding citizens against arbitrary law enforcement

2. Determine whether the accused is guilty on the basis of the evidence presented

3. Represent diverse community interests so that no one set of values or biases dominates decision making

4. Serve as a buffer between the accused and the accuser

5. Promote knowledge about the criminal justice system by learning about it through the jury duty process

6. Symbolize the rule of law and the community foundation that supports the criminal justice system

As indicated by the responses in "What Americans Think," jury service may help to maintain many jurors' confidence in the justice system.

As a symbol of law, juries demonstrate to the public—and to defendants—that decisions about depriving individuals of their liberty will be made carefully by a group of citizens who represent the community's values. In addition, juries provide the primary element of direct democracy in the judicial branch of government. Through participation on juries, citizens use their votes to determine the outcomes of cases (C. E. Smith, 1994). This branch of government, which is dominated by judges and lawyers, offers few other opportunities for citizens to shape judicial decisions directly. Think about your own views of jury service as you read "Civic Engagement: Your Role in the System."

In the United States, a criminal jury traditionally is composed of 12 citizens, but some states now allow as few as 6 citizens to make up a jury in noncapital

civic engagement
your role in the system

Imagine that you receive a notice to report to jury duty—but it is for the same day that you are supposed to drive four hours to an arena in order to attend a concert by your favorite musical group. A friend says to you, "Don't miss the concert. Just call in and say that you're sick." *Write down your responses to the following questions: Is jury service an important civic duty? Should someone report for jury duty even when it is highly inconvenient? Is jury service a burden to be avoided?* Then see how your responses compare to those of other Americans who were surveyed on this question. To link to this website, go to *The American System of Criminal Justice* 12e companion site at academic.cengage.com/criminaljustice/cole.

FIGURE 11.2

Jury size for felony and misdemeanor trials

All states require 12-member juries in capital cases; six states permit juries of fewer than 12 members in felony cases. Does the smaller number of people on a jury have advantages or disadvantages? Would you rather have your case decided by a 12- or a 6-person jury?

Note: In some states, the number of jurors in misdemeanor cases varies depending on whether it is an aggravated misdemeanor or whether it is in a limited jurisdiction trial court.

Source: David B. Rottman, Carol R. Flango, Melissa T. Cantrell, Randall Hansen, and Neil LaFountain, *State Court Organization 1998* (Washington, DC: U.S. Government Printing Office, 2000), 278–81.

cases. This reform was recommended to modernize court procedures and reduce expenses. It costs less for the court to contact, process, and pay a smaller number of jurors. The Supreme Court in *Williams v. Florida* (1970) upheld the use of small juries. In *Burch v. Louisiana* (1979), the Court ruled that 6-member juries must vote unanimously to convict a defendant, but unanimity is not required for larger juries. Some states permit juries to convict defendants by votes of 10 to 2 or 9 to 3 (see Figure 11.2 for jury size requirements in each state). Critics of the change to 6-person juries charge that the smaller group is less representative of the conflicting views in the community and too quick to bring in a verdict (Amar, 1997).

Williams v. Florida (1970)

Juries of fewer than 12 members are permitted by the U.S. Constitution.

 Alameda County, California, provides information for the public about jury service at their website. To link to this website, go to *The American System of Criminal Justice* 12e companion site at academic.cengage.com/criminaljustice/cole.

checkpoint

8. Approximately what percentage of felony cases reach conclusion through a trial?
9. What are three of the six functions that juries serve for the criminal justice system?
10. What has the Supreme Court decided concerning the size and unanimity requirements of juries?

The Trial Process

The trial process generally follows eight steps:

1. Selection of the jury
2. Opening statements by prosecution and defense
3. Presentation of the prosecution's evidence and witnesses
4. Presentation of the defense's evidence and witnesses
5. Presentation of rebuttal witnesses
6. Closing arguments by each side
7. Instruction of the jury by the judge
8. Decision by the jury

Defense attorney John Thebes presents "real" evidence during the trial of Rev. Gerald Robinson, a Catholic priest, in Toledo, Ohio. Robinson was on trial for the death of Sister Margaret Ann Pahl. Father Robinson was found guilty and sentenced to 15 years to life in prison. Are trials the most effective way to produce accurate determinations of guilt?

AP Images/Andy Morrison, Pool

The details of each step may vary according to each state's rules. Although only a small number of cases go to trial, understanding each step in the process and considering the broader impact of this institution are important.

Jury Selection

The selection of the jury, outlined in Figure 11.3, is a crucial first step in the trial process. Because people always involve their experiences, values, and biases in their decision making, prosecutors and defense attorneys actively seek to identify and select potential jurors who may be automatically sympathetic to their side and to exclude potentially hostile jurors. Lawyers do not necessarily achieve these goals, because the selection of jurors involves the decisions and interactions of prosecutors, defense attorneys, and judges, each of whom has different objectives in the selection process.

Jurors are selected from among the citizens whose names have been placed in the jury pool. The composition of the jury pool tremendously impacts the ultimate composition of the trial jury. In most states, the jury pool is drawn from lists of registered voters and licensed drivers, but research has shown that nonwhites, the poor, and young people register to vote and maintain valid driver's licenses at lower rates than do the rest of the population. As a result, members of these groups are underrepresented on juries (Fukurai, 1996). In many cases, the presence or absence of these groups may make no difference in the ultimate verdict. In some situations, however, members of these groups will likely interpret evidence differently than will their older, white, middle-class counterparts who dominate the composition of juries (Ugwuegbu, 1999). For example, poor people, nonwhites, and young people may be more likely to have had unpleasant experiences with police officers and therefore be less willing to believe that police officers always tell the truth. Today courts may supplement the lists of registered voters and driver's licenses with other lists, such as those for hunting licenses and utility bills, in order to diversify the jury pool (Newman, 1996). Jurors receive minimal financial compensation for their service. In Washington state, they are paid only $10 per day. By contrast, jurors in New York are paid $40 per day. Legislators in many states have proposed increases in daily compensation for jurors. It is hoped that such efforts will make jury service more attractive for poor people who might otherwise avoid participating because they cannot afford to lose pay by missing work (Axtman, 2005b).

Only about 15 percent of adult Americans have ever been called for jury duty. Retired people and homemakers with grown children tend to be overrepresented on juries because

FIGURE 11.3

Jury selection process for a 12-member jury

Potential jurors are drawn at random from a source list. From this pool, a panel is selected and presented for duty. The voir dire examination may remove some, while others will be seated. The 14 jurors selected include two alternates.

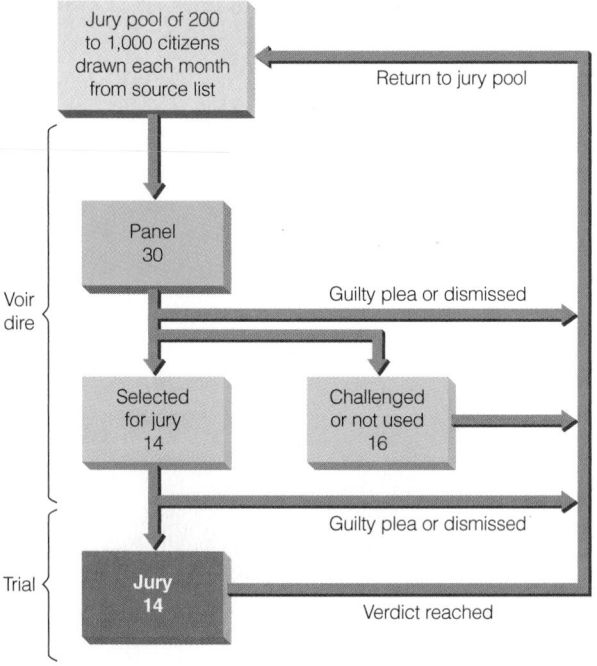

they are less inconvenienced by serving and are often less likely to ask to be excused because of job responsibilities or child-care problems. To make jury duty less onerous, many states have moved to a system called one-day, one-trial, in which jurors serve for either one day or the duration of one trial.

The courtroom process of **voir dire** (which means "to speak the truth") is used to question prospective jurors to screen out those who might be biased or incapable of making a fair decision. Attorneys for each side, as well as the judge, may question jurors about their background, knowledge of the case, and acquaintance with any participants in the case. Jurors will also be asked whether they or their immediate family members have been crime victims or otherwise involved in a criminal case in a manner that may prevent them from making open-minded decisions about the evidence and the defendant. If a juror's responses indicate that he or she will not be able to make fair decisions, an attorney may request a **challenge for cause**. The judge must rule on the challenge, but if the judge agrees with the attorney, then the juror is excused from that specific case. There is usually no limit on the number of jurors that the attorneys may challenge for cause. Nonetheless, identifying all of a juror's biases through brief questioning is not easy (Dillehay and Sandys, 1996).

Although challenges for cause fall ultimately under the judge's control, the prosecution and defense can exert their own control over the jury's composition through the use of **peremptory challenges**. Using these challenges, the prosecution and defense can exclude prospective jurors without giving specific reasons. Attorneys use peremptory challenges to exclude jurors whom they think will be unsympathetic to their arguments (Hoffman, 1999). Attorneys usually use hunches about which jurors to challenge; there is little evidence that they can accurately identify which jurors will be sympathetic or unsympathetic to their side (M. S. White, 1995). Normally, the defense is allowed eight to ten peremptory challenges, and the prosecution six to eight.

The use of peremptory challenges has raised concerns that attorneys can use them to exclude, for example, African American jurors when an African American is on trial (Kennedy, 1997). In a series of decisions in the late 1980s and early 1990s, the Supreme Court prohibited using peremptory challenges to systematically exclude potential jurors because of their race or gender (e.g., *Batson v. Kentucky*, 1986). Jury-selection errors can provide the basis for appeals if a defendant is convicted at trial (Pizzi and Hoffman, 2001). In practice, however, the enforcement of this prohibition on race and gender discrimination falls to the trial judge (C. E. Smith and Ochoa, 1996). If a trial judge is willing to accept flimsy excuses for race-based and gender-based exclusions, then the attorneys can ignore the ban on discrimination (Bray, 1992). As you read the Close Up box, ask yourself whether peremptory challenges have a positive or negative effect on jury selection. Do you think peremptory challenges should be abolished?

 California provides online information about jury selection and service online. To link to this website, go to *The American System of Criminal Justice* 12e companion site at academic.cengage.com/criminaljustice/cole.

voir dire
A questioning of prospective jurors in order to screen out people the judge or attorneys think might be biased or otherwise incapable of delivering a fair verdict.

The Center for Jury Studies monitors developments and reforms affecting jury trials at their website. To link to this website, go to *The American System of Criminal Justice* 12e companion site at academic.cengage.com/criminaljustice/cole.

challenge for cause
Removal of a prospective juror by showing that he or she has some bias or some other legal disability. The number of these challenges permitted to attorneys is potentially unlimited.

peremptory challenge
Removal of a prospective juror without giving any reason. Attorneys are allowed a limited number of such challenges.

checkpoint

11. What is voir dire?
12. What is the difference between a peremptory challenge and a challenge for cause?

Opening Statements

After the jury has been selected, the trial begins. The clerk reads the complaint (indictment or information) detailing the charges, and the prosecutor and the defense attorney may, if they desire, make opening statements to the jury to summarize the position that each side intends to take. The statements are not evidence. The jury is not supposed to regard the attorneys' statements as proving or disproving anything about the case.

CLOSE UP

The Peremptory Challenge Controversy

IN 1987, JIMMY ELEM faced trial on robbery charges in a Missouri state court. During jury selection, the prosecutor used peremptory challenges to exclude two African American men from the jury. Elem's attorney objected, claiming that the prosecutor appeared to be excluding potential jurors because of their race. Under the U.S. Supreme Court's decision in *Batson v. Kentucky* (1986), a trial judge is obligated to ask the prosecutor to provide a nonracial reason for removing jurors when a prosecutor's use of peremptory challenges seems based on racial exclusion. In response to the judge's question, the prosecutor replied,

> I struck [juror] number twenty-two because of his long hair. He had long curly hair. He had the longest hair of anybody on the panel by far. He appeared to me to not be a good juror for that fact, the fact that he had long hair hanging down shoulder length, curly unkempt hair. Also he had a mustache and a goatee type beard. And juror number twenty-four also has a mustache and goatee type beard. Those are the only two people on the jury . . . with the facial hair. . . . And I don't like the way they looked, with the way the hair is cut, both of them. And the mustaches and the beards look suspicious to me.

The trial judge accepted the prosecutor's explanation and the trial moved forward. Elem subsequently filed a habeas corpus action in the federal courts claiming that the prosecutor had used a flimsy, nonsensical excuse to cover the fact that the exclusions were really based on race. The U.S. court of appeals agreed with Elem and declared that peremptory challenges that appear to be based on race are only valid if actually based on reasons related to the individuals' qualifications to be a good juror. The court of appeals did not believe that having curly or long hair affected one's ability to be a good jurist.

Missouri carried the case forward to the U.S. Supreme Court. In a 7-to-2 decision, the Supreme Court reversed and said that prosecutors can put forward silly, superstitious, and implausible reasons as long as the trial judge accepts the exclusion as being based on something other than race or gender. Thus, it is possible to violate the Constitution by using peremptory challenges in a racially discriminatory or sexist manner if the prosecutor or defense attorney can provide some alternative excuse that the judge accepts.

Many attorneys like the peremptory challenge because they believe that they can identify people who are biased and thereby remove them from the jury. Often these attorneys base their decisions on the jurors' facial expressions or body language. However, social science research does not support lawyers' claims that they can use such hunches to tell if a potential juror will be biased.

Although the U.S. Constitution does not say anything about peremptory challenges, Supreme Court Justice Antonin Scalia claims that peremptory challenges should be retained because they are part of a long tradition in the jury-selection process. Others argue that peremptory challenges enhance the legitimacy of the trial process by letting defendants feel they have some influence over the composition of the jury. By contrast, the late Supreme Court Justice Thurgood Marshall indicated that peremptory challenges should be abolished because they were frequently used to discriminate or add bias to the jury. For Marshall, if there is not enough evidence of bias to justify a challenge for cause, then the person should be allowed to serve on the jury. People should not be denied the opportunity to participate in this important aspect of judicial decision making just because one lawyer does not like the expression on their face or the color of their skin.

If you were a state legislator and someone proposed a bill to abolish peremptory challenges in jury selection, how would you vote? Do you think peremptory challenges are helpful or harmful in the trial process?

Researching the Internet

 Go online to read a proposal to abolish peremptory challenges at the APA newsletter's website. To link to this website, go to *The American System of Criminal Justice* 12e companion site at academic.cengage.com/criminaljustice/cole.

Presentation of the Prosecution's Evidence

One of the basic protections of the American criminal justice system is the assumption that the defendant is innocent until proved guilty. The prosecution must prove beyond a reasonable doubt, within the demands of the court procedures and rules of evidence, that the individual named in the indictment committed the crime. This means that the evidence excludes all reasonable doubt; it does not have to determine absolute certainty.

By presenting evidence to the jury, the prosecution must establish a case showing that the defendant is guilty. Evidence is classified as real evidence, demonstrative evidence, testimony, direct evidence, and circumstantial evidence.

Real evidence might include such objects as a weapon, business records, fingerprints, or stolen property. These are real objects involved in the crime. **Demonstrative evidence** is any evidence presented for jurors to see and understand without testimony. Real evidence is one form of demonstrative evidence.

real evidence
Physical evidence such as a weapon, records, fingerprints, stolen property—objects actually involved in the crime.

demonstrative evidence
Evidence that is not based on witness testimony but demonstrates information relevant to the crime, such as maps, x-rays, and photographs; includes real evidence involved in the crime.

Other forms of demonstrative evidence are items not involved in the crime but still used to make points to jurors. These include maps, x-rays, photographs, models, and diagrams.

Most evidence in a criminal trial, however, consists of the **testimony** of witnesses. Witnesses at a trial must be legally competent. Thus the judge may be required to determine whether the witness whose testimony is challenged has the intelligence to tell the truth and the ability to recall what was seen. Witnesses with inadequate intelligence or mental problems can be excluded as unqualified to present testimony. **Direct evidence** refers to eyewitness accounts for example, "I saw John Smith fire the gun." **Circumstantial evidence** requires that the jury infer a fact from what the witness observed: "I saw John Smith walk behind his house with a gun. A few minutes later I heard a gun go off, and then Mr. Smith walked toward me holding a gun." The witness's observation that Smith had a gun and that the witness then heard a gun go off does not provide the direct evidence that Smith fired his gun; yet the jury may link the described facts and infer that Smith fired his gun. After a witness has given testimony, he or she can be cross-examined by counsel for the other side.

Because many cases rely on scientific evidence, especially in the form of experts' testimony about DNA, blood spatters, bullet fragments and trajectories, and the nature of physical injuries, there are concerns that judges and jurors do not fully understand the information presented (Cheng, 2006). Determinations of guilt may hinge on the effectiveness of the presentation of such evidence rather than the accuracy and verifiability of the scientific conclusions. Judges' and jurors' lack of expertise about scientific matters means that there are risks that they cannot effectively question and analyze certain kinds of evidence.

The attorney for each side can challenge the other side's presentation of evidence. If presented evidence violates the rules, reflects untrustworthy hearsay or opinions, or is not relevant to the issues in the case, an attorney will object to the presentation. In effect, the attorney is asking the judge to rule that the opponent's questionable evidence cannot be considered by the jury. See "New Directions in Criminal Justice Policy" to learn about one controversial type of evidence: computer simulations.

After the prosecution has presented all of the state's evidence against the defendant, he or she informs the court that the people's case rests. It is common for the defense then to ask the court to direct the jury to bring forth a verdict of not guilty. Such a motion is based on the defense argument that the state has not presented enough evidence to prove its case. If the motion is sustained by the judge (it rarely is), the trial ends; if it is overruled, the defense presents its evidence.

Presentation of the Defense's Evidence

The defense is not required to answer the case presented by the prosecution. As it is the state's responsibility to prove the case beyond a reasonable doubt, it is theoretically possible—and in fact sometimes happens—that the defense rests its case immediately. Usually, however, the accused's attorney employs one or more of the following strategies: (1) contrary evidence is introduced to rebut or cast doubt on the state's case, (2) an alibi is offered, or (3) an affirmative defense is presented. As discussed in Chapter 4, defenses include self-defense, insanity, duress, and necessity.

When singer R. Kelly was acquitted of child pornography charges by a Chicago jury in June 2008, the defense attorneys used every argument that they could, including arguments that were not consistent with each other, in order to cast doubt on the prosecution's case. The case hinged on whether a VHS tape showed Kelly having sex with a specific underage girl. The defense suggested that the tape showed another man who looked like Kelly, that computer manipulation had made the tape look like Kelly, or that the tape was made with

testimony
Oral evidence provided by a legally competent witness.

direct evidence
Eyewitness accounts.

circumstantial evidence
Evidence, provided by a witness, from which a jury must infer a fact.

 What are the federal rules of evidence? Read the rules online. To link to this website, go to *The American System of Criminal Justice* 12e companion site at academic.cengage.com/criminaljustice/cole.

NEW DIRECTIONS in CRIMINAL JUSTICE POLICY

Computer Simulations in the Courtroom

IN JURY TRIALS, prosecutors and defense attorneys have traditionally attempted to use their words to "paint a picture" for the jurors. Each attorney wants the jurors to envision a specific chain of events. After hearing the same presentations, individual jurors may very well leave the courtroom with quite different perceptions about what happened at the crime scene and whether the defendant played a role. In recent years, attorneys have attempted to use computer technology to present clearer images of events. The advent of realistic computer games has brought with it the development of computer-generated re-creations of crime scenes. If the jury needs to understand how an injury occurred, for example, the prosecution may present a computer-generated film of a person being struck from behind or falling in a manner consistent with the victim's injuries. If a defendant has sufficient money to hire computer experts, the defendant may attempt to develop a computer presentation that re-creates events in a way that absolves him or her of responsibility.

Observers have serious concerns about the use of such computer programs in trials. Such re-creations are available only to those who can afford them. Thus, poor defendants have little hope of using this technology to present their side of the story. In addition, the computer scenes can be developed or manipulated in ways that are not consistent with the available evidence. Jurors may believe the realistic scenes that they watch on the screen despite contrary evidence that they hear from witness testimony. In other words, the image of the re-creation may stick in jurors' minds even when there is strong evidence to show that the re-creation was not accurate.

Should computer-generated re-creations of crimes be shown during trials? How can we reduce the risks that such re-creations will distort reality or otherwise be misused?

Source: Drawn from John McCormick, "Scene of the Crime," *Newsweek*, February 28, 2000, p. 60.

Researching the Internet

 Read about courtroom computer simulations at the Executive Presentation's website. To link to this website, go to *The American System of Criminal Justice* 12e companion site at academic.cengage.com/criminaljustice/cole.

---

models and prostitutes who looked like Kelly and the alleged victim (Streitfeld, 2008). The defense attorneys did not need to prove Kelly's innocence; they just needed to raise questions in the jurors' minds about the accuracy of the prosecution's claims.

A key issue for the defense is whether the accused will take the stand. The Fifth Amendment protection against self-incrimination means that the defendant is not required to testify. The Supreme Court has ruled that the prosecutor may not comment on, nor can the jury draw inferences from, the defendant's decision not to speak in his or her own defense. The decision is not made lightly, because if the defendant does testify, the prosecution may cross-examine him or her. *Cross-examination*, or questioning by the opposing attorney, creates risks for the defendant. The prosecutor may question the defendant not only about the crime but also about his or her past, including past criminal convictions. In R. Kelly's case, he never testified and thereby avoided cross-examination about his past sexual behavior and rumors about his attraction to teenage girls.

Although jurors are not supposed to make assumptions about the defendant's guilt, some of them may do so if the defendant does not testify. For example, when Michael Skakel, a cousin of the Kennedy family, was convicted in 2002 of bludgeoning a girl with a golf club 27 years earlier as a teenager, he never took the witness stand in his own defense. The prosecution gained the conviction based on testimony from several witnesses who claimed that Skakel had told them years earlier about killing a girl with a golf club. Skakel's attorneys used an alibi defense by presenting testimony from witnesses who said that he had been at home watching television with friends at the time of the murder. The defense also sought to cast suspicion on another suspect. The jury, however, accepted the version of events presented by the prosecution's witnesses and, upon conviction, Skakel was given a sentence of 20 years to life (J. Goldman, 2002).

Presentation of Rebuttal Witnesses

When the defense's case is complete, the prosecution may present witnesses whose testimony is designed to discredit or counteract testimony presented on behalf of the defendant. If the prosecution brings rebuttal witnesses, the defense can question them and present new witnesses in rebuttal.

Closing Arguments by Each Side

When each side has completed its presentation of the evidence, the prosecution and defense make closing arguments to the jury. The attorneys review the evidence of the case for the jury, presenting interpretations of the evidence that favor their own side. The prosecutor may use the summation to show how individual pieces of evidence connect to form a basis for concluding that the defendant is guilty. The defense may set forth the applicable law and try to show that (1) the prosecution has not proved its case beyond a reasonable doubt and (2) the testimony raised questions but did not provide answers. Each side may remind the jury of its duty to remain unswayed by emotion and to evaluate the evidence impartially. Some attorneys nonetheless hope that the jurors will react emotionally to benefit their side.

Judge's Instructions to the Jury

The jury decides the facts of the case, but the judge determines the law. Before the jurors depart for the jury room to decide the defendant's fate, the judge instructs them on how the law should guide their decision. The judge may discuss basic legal principles such as proof beyond a reasonable doubt, the legal requirements necessary to show that the prosecution has proved all the elements of the crime, or the rights of the defendant. Specific aspects of the law bearing on the decision such as complicated court rulings on the nature of the insanity defense or the ways certain types of evidence have been gathered may be included in the judge's instructions. In complicated trials, the judge may spend an entire day instructing the jury.

The concept of **reasonable doubt** lies at the heart of the jury system. The prosecution is not required to prove the guilt of the defendant beyond all doubt. Instead, if you as a juror are

> satisfied to a moral certainty that this defendant . . . is guilty of any one of the crimes charged here, you may safely say that you have been convinced beyond a reasonable doubt. If your mind is wavering, or if you are uncertain . . . you have not been convinced beyond a reasonable doubt and must render a verdict of not guilty. (Phillips, 1977: 214)

The experience of listening to the judge may become an ordeal for the jurors, who must hear and understand perhaps two or three hours of instruction on the law and the evidence (Bradley, 1992). It is assumed that somehow jurors will fully absorb these details on first hearing them, so that they will thoroughly understand how they are supposed to decide the case in the jury room (G. P. Kramer and Koenig, 1990). In fact, scholars have concluded that there is "a serious problem [with] . . . the jury's documented difficulty in understanding legal instructions" (Hans and Vidmar, 2008: 228). There are also emerging concerns that jurors—as well as judges and other courtroom actors—can have their thinking and decision making affected by the high degree of stress they may feel about determining someone's fate (Miller, Flores, and Dolezilek, 2007). Not surprisingly, this stress may be particularly powerful in murder cases, especially those concerning the death penalty (Antonio, 2006).

reasonable doubt
The standard used by a juror to decide if the prosecution has provided enough evidence for conviction.

 The American Judicature Society's National Jury Center provides online information about proposed reforms for the jury system on their website. To link to this website, go to *The American System of Criminal Justice* 12e companion site at academic.cengage.com/criminaljustice/cole.

Decision by the Jury

After they have heard the case and received instructions from the judge, the jurors retire to a room where they have complete privacy. They elect a foreperson to run the meeting, and deliberations begin. Until now, the jurors have been passive observers of the trial, unable to question witnesses or discuss the case among themselves; now they can discuss the facts that have been presented. Throughout their deliberations the jurors may be sequestered—kept together day and night, away from the influences of newspapers and conversations with family and friends. If jurors are allowed to spend nights at home, they are ordered not to discuss the case with anyone. The jury may request that the judge reread to them portions of the instructions, ask for additional instructions, or hear portions of the transcript detailing what specific witnesses said.

If the jury becomes deadlocked and cannot reach a verdict, the trial ends with a hung jury and the prosecutor must decide whether to retry the case in front of a new jury. When a verdict is reached, the judge, prosecution, and defense reassemble in the courtroom to hear it. The prosecution or the defense may request that the jury be polled: Each member individually tells his or her vote in open court. This procedure presumably ensures that no juror has felt pressured to agree with the other jurors.

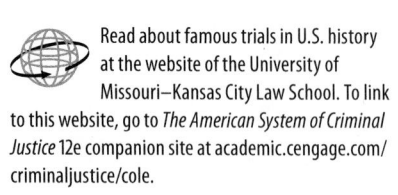

Read about famous trials in U.S. history at the website of the University of Missouri–Kansas City Law School. To link to this website, go to *The American System of Criminal Justice* 12e companion site at academic.cengage.com/criminaljustice/cole.

checkpoint

13. What are the stages in the trial process?
14. What are the kinds of evidence presented during a trial?

Evaluating the Jury System

Early research at the University of Chicago Law School found that, consistent with theories of group behavior, participation and influence in the jury process are related to social status. Men were found to be more active participants than were women, whites more active than minority members, and the better educated more active than those less educated. Much of the discussion in the jury room was not directly concerned with the testimony but rather with trial procedures, opinions about the witnesses, and personal reminiscences (Strodtbeck, James, and Hawkins, 1957). In 30 percent of the cases, a vote taken soon after entering the jury room was the only one necessary to reach a verdict; in the rest of the cases, the majority on the first ballot eventually prevailed in 90 percent of the cases (Broeder, 1959). Because of group pressure, only rarely did a single juror produce a hung jury. Some jurors may doubt their own views or go along with the others if everyone else disagrees with them. Additional studies have upheld the importance of group pressure on decision making (Hastie, Penrod, and Pennington, 1983).

An examination of trials in the 75 largest counties found that 76 percent of jury trials ended in convictions, compared with 82 percent of bench trials (Kyckelhahn and Cohen, 2008). These numbers alone do not reveal whether judges and juries decide cases differently. However, research on trials provides clues about differences between these two decision makers.

Juries tend to take a more liberal view of such issues as self-defense than do judges and are likely to minimize the seriousness of an offense if they dislike some characteristic of the victim (S. J. Adler, 1994: 200–207). For example, if the victim of an assault is a prostitute, the jury may minimize the assault. Perceived characteristics of the defendant may also influence jurors' assessments of guilt (Abwender and Hough, 2001). Judges have more experience with the justice process. They are more likely than juries to convict defendants based on evidence that researchers characterize as moderately strong (Eisenberg et al., 2005). As explained by the premier jury researchers Valerie Hans and Neil Vidmar (2008: 227):

> [T]he jury's distinctive approach of common sense justice, and the judges' greater willingness to convict based on the same evidence, best explain why juries and judges sometimes reach different conclusions. These juror values affect the verdicts primarily in trials in which the evidence is relatively evenly balanced and a verdict for either side could be justified.

In recent years, the American Bar Association and other groups have worked to introduce reforms that might improve the quality of juries' decision making (Post, 2004). For example, some courts now permit jurors to take notes during trials and submit questions that they would like to see asked of witnesses. There are also efforts to make judges' instructions to the jury more understandable through less reliance on legal terminology (Tiersma, 2001). It is hoped that jurors can make better decisions if they have more information and a better understanding of the law and the issues in a case.

checkpoint

15. What factors can make a jury's decision different from that of a judge?

APPEALS

The imposition of a sentence does not mean that the defendant must serve it immediately. He or she typically has the right to appeal. Indigent offenders' right to counsel continues through the first appeal (Priehs, 1999). Some states have limited the right to appeal when defendants plead guilty. For nonviolent crimes, judges sometimes permit newly convicted offenders to remain free as the appeal proceeds.

An **appeal** is based on a claim that one or more errors of law or procedure were made during the investigation, arrest, or trial process (C. E. Smith, 1999b). Such claims usually assert that the trial judge made errors in courtroom rulings or in improperly admitting evidence the police had gathered in violation of some constitutional right. A defendant might base an appeal, for example, on the claim that the judge did not instruct the jury correctly or that a guilty plea was not made voluntarily. Appeals are based on questions of procedure, not on issues of the defendant's guilt or innocence. The appellate court will not normally second-guess a jury. Instead it will check to make sure that the trial followed proper procedures. If the court finds significant errors in the trial, then the conviction is set aside. The defendant may be retried if the prosecutor decides to pursue the case again. Most criminal defendants must file an appeal shortly after trial to have an appellate court review the case; however, many states provide for an automatic appeal in death penalty cases. The quality of defense representation matters a great deal, because the appeal must usually meet short deadlines and carefully identify appropriate issues (Wasserman, 1990).

A case originating in a state court is usually appealed through that state's judicial system. When a state case involves a federal constitutional question,

Chief Judge Judith Kaye of the New York Court of Appeals questions an attorney during oral arguments for the appeal of a murder conviction. The appeals process provides an opportunity to correct errors that occurred in trial court proceedings. What are the advantages or disadvantages of having a group of appeals court judges decide a case together?

AP Images/Mike Groll

appeal
A request to a higher court that it review actions taken in a completed lower court case.

however, a subsequent review may be sought in the federal courts. Even so, state courts decide almost four-fifths of all appeals.

The number of appeals in both the state and federal courts has increased during recent decades. What is the nature of these cases? A classic five-state study by Joy Chapper and Roger Hanson (1989) shows that (1) although a majority of appeals occur after trial convictions, about a quarter result from nontrial proceedings such as guilty pleas and probation revocations; (2) homicides and other serious crimes against people account for more than 50 percent of appeals; (3) most appeals arise from cases in which the sentence is five years or less; and (4) the issues raised at appeal tend to concern the introduction of evidence, the sufficiency of evidence, and jury instructions.

Most appeals do not succeed. In almost 80 percent of the cases Chapper and Hanson examined, the decision of the trial courts was affirmed. Most of the other decisions produced new trials or resentencing; only 9.4 percent of those whose convictions were overturned received acquittals on appeal. Table 11.4 shows the percentage distribution of the outcomes from the appellate process. The appellate process rarely provides a ticket to freedom for someone convicted of a crime.

Habeas Corpus

habeas corpus
A writ or judicial order requesting the release of a person being detained in a jail, prison, or mental hospital. If a judge finds the person is being held improperly, the writ may be granted and the person released or granted a new trial.

After people use their avenues of appeal, they may pursue a writ of habeas corpus if they claim that their federal constitutional rights were violated during the lower-court processes. Known as "the great writ" from its traditional role in English law, a **habeas corpus** petition asks a judge to examine whether an individual is being properly detained in a jail, prison, or mental hospital. If the detention is based on a rights violation or otherwise lacks a legal basis, then the judge will grant the writ of habeas corpus. A successful habeas corpus claim can lead to either an immediate release from government custody or an order for a new trial, which can require criminal defendants to remain in jail until the trial takes place. In the context of criminal justice, convicted offenders often claim that their imprisonment is improper because one of their constitutional rights was violated during the investigation or adjudication of their case. Statutes permit offenders convicted in both state and federal courts to pursue habeas corpus actions in the federal courts (King, Cheesman, and Ostrom, 2007). After first seeking favorable decisions by state appellate courts, convicted offenders can start their constitutional claims anew in the federal trial-level district courts

TABLE 11.4	Percentage Distribution of Alternative Outcomes in Five State Appellate Courts

Although the public thinks defendants exercising their right of appeal will be released, this study shows that 20.6 percent have their convictions reversed, but only a few are acquitted by the appellate court.

Appeal Outcome	Percentage of Appeals
Conviction affirmed	79.4
Conviction reversed	20.6
	100.0
Among Convictions Reversed	
Acquittal	9.4
New trial	31.9
Resentencing	35.3
Other	23.4
	100.0

Source: Joy Chapper and Roger Hanson, *Understanding Reversible Error in Criminal Appeals* (Williamsburg, VA: National Center for State Court, 1989).

and subsequently pursue their habeas cases in the federal circuit courts of appeal and the U.S. Supreme Court.

Only about 1 percent of habeas petitions succeed (Flango, 1994). In a recent study, less than one-half of one percent of noncapital habeas petitioners gained a favorable judicial decision but more than 12 percent of habeas petitioners in death penalty cases demonstrated a rights violation (King, Chessman, and Ostrom, 2007). One reason may be that an individual has no right to be represented by an attorney when pursuing a habeas corpus petition. Few offenders have sufficient knowledge of law and legal procedures to identify and present constitutional claims effectively in the federal courts (Hanson and Daley, 1995). These challenges are especially difficult for offenders in noncapital cases. By contrast, legislatures have enacted statutes to provide extra resources for offenders on death row. Several statutes help to provide representation by lawyers in many capital cases, even though the U.S. Constitution does not give these offenders a constitutional right to counsel for their habeas petitions. In addition, judges may look more closely for rights violations in death penalty cases because the ultimate harm is so significant if an error went undiscovered after review by the judges.

In the late 1980s and early 1990s, the U.S. Supreme Court issued many decisions that made it more difficult for convicted offenders to file habeas corpus petitions (Hoffmann, 2006; C. E. Smith, 1995a). The Court created tougher procedural rules that are more difficult for convicted offenders to follow. The rules also unintentionally created some new problems for state attorneys general and federal trial courts that must now examine the procedural rules affecting cases rather than simply addressing the constitutional violations that the offender claims occurred (C. E. Smith, 1995c). In 1996, Congress passed the Antiterrorism and Effective Death Penalty Act, which placed additional restrictions on habeas corpus petitions. The statute was quickly approved by the U.S. Supreme Court. These reforms were based, in part, on a belief that prisoners' cases were clogging the federal courts (C. E. Smith, 1995b). Ironically, habeas corpus petitions in the federal courts have increased by 50 percent since the passage of the restrictive legislation (Scalia, 2002). By imposing strict filing deadlines for petitions, the legislation may have inadvertently focused more prisoners' attention on the existence of habeas corpus and thereby encouraged them to move forward with petitions in order to meet the deadlines.

Evaluating the Appellate Process

The public seems to believe that many offenders are being let off through the appellate process. Frustrated by the problems of crime, some conservatives have argued that opportunities for appeal should be limited. They claim that too many offenders delay imposition of their sentences and that others seek to evade punishment by filing appeals endlessly. This practice not only increases the workload of the courts but also jeopardizes the concept of the finality of the justice process. However, because 90 percent of accused people plead guilty, the percentage of cases that might be appealed successfully is relatively small.

Consider what follows a defendant's successful appeal, which is by no means a total or final victory. An appeal that results in reversal of the conviction normally means that the case is remanded to the lower court for a new trial. At this point the state must consider whether the procedural errors in the original trial can be overcome and whether the costs of bringing the defendant into court again are justified. Frequently, the prosecutor pursues the case again and gains a new, proper conviction of the defendant. The appeal process sometimes generates new plea negotiations that produce a second conviction with a lesser sentence that reflects the reduced strength of the prosecutor's case. For example, New York City police officer Charles Schwarz was one of the officers charged with participating in a brutal 1997 attack on Haitian immigrant Abner Louima.

Schwarz was accused of escorting Louima to the police restroom where the attack occurred and holding Louima during the attack. After being tried and convicted, then having convictions overturned on appeal, Schwarz faced a fourth trial on federal charges of violating Louima's civil rights. In an unusual Saturday-night session at federal district court, Schwarz's attorney and the prosecution reached a last-minute plea agreement that avoided the necessity of a fourth trial. He pleaded guilty to perjury, a charge for which he had previously been convicted in a jury trial, in exchange for having the prosecutors drop the civil rights charges and recommend that Schwarz serve a sentence of less than five years in prison (Glaberson, 2002). After many months of proclaiming his innocence, Schwarz apparently decided not to take the risk that he might receive a 15-year sentence if convicted by a jury. The prosecution apparently decided not to take the chance that the jury might acquit Schwarz after a long, expensive, and highly publicized trial. Thus, as we saw in Table 11.4, successful appeals do not necessarily result in the defendant being set free.

The appeals process performs the important function of righting wrongs. It also helps to ensure consistency in the application of law by judges in different courts. Beyond that, its presence constantly influences the daily operations of the criminal justice system in that prosecutors and trial judges must consider how their decisions and actions might later be evaluated by a higher court.

checkpoint

16. How does the appellate court's job differ from that of the trial court?
17. What is a habeas corpus petition?

A QUESTION OF ETHICS

LISA DAVIDSON STOOD silently in the courtroom of Judge Helen Iverson. Defense attorney Bill Dixon whispered in Davidson's ear as they waited for Judge Iverson to finish reading Davidson's file. "Are we ready to proceed?" asked the judge.

"Yes, your honor," came the simultaneous replies from both Dixon and the prosecutor standing nearby.

Judge Iverson stared at Davidson momentarily with a serious expression. "Ms. Davidson, you are charged with larceny. Because it is your third offense, I can send you to prison. Do you understand that?"

"Yes, your honor," replied Davidson, her voice quivering.

The judge continued. "Are you pleading guilty to this crime because you are guilty?"

"Yes, your honor."

"Are you pleading guilty of your own free will?" the judge asked.

"Yes, your honor."

"Did anyone threaten you to make you plead guilty?"

"No , your honor."

"Did anyone make any promises to you to induce you to plead guilty?"

Davidson nodded her head. "Yes. Mr. Dixon said that if I plead guilty to this charge then the prosecutor promised that my sentence would be only . . ."

"EXCUSE ME, JUDGE IVERSON," Dixon interrupted in a loud voice. "Could I please have a moment to speak with my client?"

Judge Iverson nodded.

Taking Davidson by the arm, Dixon moved her three feet farther away from the judge's bench. Dixon whispered into Davidson's ear as his hands punched the air with emphatic gestures. A few moments later, they returned to their positions, standing in front of the judge. "We are ready to continue, your honor," said Dixon.

Judge Iverson looked at Davidson once again. "Did anyone promise you anything to induce you to plead guilty?"

Davidson glanced sideways at Dixon before replying. "No, your honor."

"You understand that you are waiving your constitutional right to a trial and you are freely waiving that right?"

"Yes, your honor."

"Then I find you guilty as charged and I will set sentencing for one month from today at 10:00 A.M."

Critical Thinking and Analysis

Write an essay addressing these questions: Should Judge Iverson have accepted the guilty plea? What role did the defense attorney play in staging the guilty plea ceremony? Were there any ethical problems? What would you have done if you were the judge?

SUMMARY

Understand the courtroom workgroup and how it functions

- A court's local legal culture, which defines the going rates of punishment for various offenses, significantly influences the outcomes in criminal cases.

- Courtroom workgroups made up of judges, prosecutors, and defense attorneys who work together can smoothly and efficiently handle cases through cooperative plea-bargaining processes.

Recognize how and why plea bargaining occurs

- Most convictions are obtained through plea bargains, a process that exists because it fulfills the self-interest of prosecutors, judges, defense attorneys, and defendants.

- Plea bargaining is facilitated by exchange relations between prosecutors and defense attorneys. In many courthouses, there is little actual bargaining, as outcomes are determined through the implicit-bargaining process of settling the facts and assessing the going rate of punishment according to the standards of the local legal culture.

- The U.S. Supreme Court has endorsed plea bargaining and addressed legal issues concerning the voluntariness of pleas and the obligation of prosecutors and defendants to uphold agreements.

- Plea bargaining has been criticized for pressuring defendants to surrender their rights and for reducing the sentences imposed on offenders.

Know how juries are chosen

- Americans tend to presume that, through the dramatic courtroom battle of prosecutors and defense attorneys, trials provide the best way to discover the truth about a criminal case.

- Less than 10 percent of cases go to trial, and half of those are typically bench trials in front of a judge, not jury trials.

- Cases typically go to trial because they involve defendants who are wealthy enough to pay attorneys to fight to the very end, or they involve serious disagreements between the prosecutor and defense attorney about the provable facts and the appropriate punishment.

- The U.S. Supreme Court has ruled that juries need not be made up of 12 members, and 12-member juries can, if permitted by state law, convict defendants by a supermajority vote instead of a unanimous vote.

- Juries serve vital functions for society by preventing arbitrary action by prosecutors and judges, educating citizens about the justice system, symbolizing the rule of law, and involving citizens from diverse segments of the community in judicial decision making.

- The jury selection process, especially in the formation of the jury pool and the exercise of peremptory challenges, often creates juries that do not fully represent all segments of a community.

Identify the stages of a criminal trial

- The trial process consists of a series of steps: jury selection, opening statements, presentation of the prosecution's evidence, presentation of the defense's evidence, presentation of rebuttal witnesses, closing arguments, judge's jury instructions, and jury's decision.

- Rules of evidence dictate what kinds of information may be presented in court for consideration by the jury. The types of evidence are real evidence, demonstrative evidence, testimony, direct evidence, and circumstantial evidence.

Understand the basis for an appeal of a conviction

- Convicted offenders can appeal. However, defendants who plead guilty, unlike those convicted through a trial, often have few grounds for an appeal.

- Appeals focus on alleged errors of law or procedure in the investigation by police and prosecutors or in the decisions by trial judges. Relatively few offenders win their appeals, and most of those simply gain an opportunity for a new trial, not release from jail or prison.

- After convicted offenders have used all their appeals, they may file a habeas corpus petition to seek federal judicial review of claimed constitutional rights violations in their cases. Very few petitions succeed.

QUESTIONS FOR REVIEW

1. What is the courtroom workgroup and what does it do?

2. Why does plea bargaining exist?

3. Given that there are so few jury trials, what types of cases would you expect to find adjudicated in this manner? Why?

4. If so few cases ever reach a jury, why are juries such an important part of the criminal justice system?

5. What is the purpose of the appeals process?

KEY TERMS AND CASES

appeal (p. 417)
bench trial (p. 406)
challenge for cause (p. 411)
circumstantial evidence (p. 413)
continuance (p. 394)
demonstrative evidence (p. 412)

direct evidence (p. 413)
going rate (p. 394)
habeas corpus (p. 418)
jury (p. 405)
local legal culture (p. 393)
peremptory challenge (p. 411)
real evidence (p. 412)
reasonable doubt (p. 415)

testimony (p. 413)
voir dire (p. 411)
workgroup (p. 394)
Bordenkircher v. Hayes
(1978) (p. 403)
Boykin v. Alabama
(1969) (p. 403)
North Carolina v. Alford
(1970) (p. 403)

Ricketts v. Adamson
(1987) (p. 403)
Santobello v. New York
(1971) (p. 403)
Williams v. Florida
(1970) (p. 409)

FOR FURTHER READING

Eisenstein, James, Roy Flemming, and Peter Nardulli. 1988. *The Contours of Justice: Communities and Their Courts.* Boston: Little, Brown. A study of nine felony courts in three states. Emphasizes the impact of the local legal culture on court operations.

Geis, Gilbert, and Leigh B. Bienen. 1998. *Crimes of the Century: From Leopold and Loeb to O. J. Simpson.* Boston: Northeastern University Press. An examination of several of the most famous criminal trials in U.S. history.

McCoy, Candace. 1993. *Politics and Plea Bargaining: Victims' Rights in California.* Philadelphia: University of Pennsylvania Press. A study of the abolition of plea bargaining for serious offenses in California's superior courts, with a look at the increase in plea-bargaining activity elsewhere in the criminal justice system.

Pohlman, H. L. 1999. *The Whole Truth? A Case of Murder on the Appalachian Trail.* Amherst: University of Massachusetts Press. An analysis of a highly publicized murder case, including the defendant's and attorneys' considerations about whether to seek a jury trial.

Vidmar, Neil and Valerie P. Hans. 2007. *American Juries: The Verdict.* Amherst, NY: Prometheus Books. A comprehensive review and analysis of current research about juries and jurors' behavior written by the nation's leading authorities on juries.

Wishman, Seymour. 1986. *Anatomy of a Jury.* New York: Times Books. A dramatic account of human interactions within the jury room.

GOING ONLINE

For an up-to-date list of web links, go to *The American System of Criminal Justice* 12e website: http://academic.cengage.com/criminaljustice/cole.

1. Look online at the Texas Rules of Evidence. Read Rule 412 concerning Evidence of Previous Sexual Conduct in Criminal Cases. Why does Texas have this rule? Does the rule make sense to you?

2. Go online to read about the right to a jury in criminal trials in Canada. Can you identify any differences between the jury processes there and in the United States?

3. Read about *jury nullification* online. What is jury nullification? Should jurors be permitted to exercise this power?

CHECKPOINT ANSWERS

1. *How does the local legal culture affect criminal cases?*

   The local legal culture consists of norms that distinguish between our court and other jurisdictions, that stipulate how members should treat one another, and that describe how cases should be processed.

2. *How does a courtroom workgroup form and operate?*

   The courtroom workgroup is made up of judge, prosecutor, defense counsel, and support staff assigned to a specific courtroom. Through the interaction of these members, goals and norms are shared and a set of roles becomes stabilized.

3. *Why are similar cases treated differently in different cities?*

   Several factors can vary in different cities, including the structure of the courtroom workgroup and the influence of sponsoring organizations, which can affect such things as prosecution policies and public defender assignments.

4. *Why does plea bargaining occur?*

   It serves the self-interest of all relevant actors: defendants gain certain, less-than-maximum sentences; prosecutors gain swift, sure convictions; defense attorneys get prompt resolution of cases; judges do not have to preside over as many time-consuming trials.

5. *What is implicit plea bargaining?*

   Implicit plea bargaining occurs when prosecutors and defense attorneys use shared expectations and interactions to settle the facts of a case and reach a resolution based on the going rate for sentences in the local legal culture.

6. *What issues concerning plea bargaining has the Supreme Court examined?*

   The U.S. Supreme Court has examined whether the defendant pleads guilty in a knowing and voluntary way, guilty pleas from defendants who still claim to be innocent, and prosecutors' and defendants' obligations to fulfill their plea agreements.

7. *What are the criticisms of plea bargaining?*

   Concerns about pressures on defendants to surrender their rights and concerns that society's mandated criminal punishments are improperly reduced.

8. *Approximately what percentage of felony cases reach conclusion through a trial?*

   Only about 9 percent of felony cases go to trial; approximately 4 percent are jury trials and 5 percent are bench trials.

9. *What are three of the six functions that juries serve for the criminal justice system?*

   (1) Safeguard citizens against arbitrary law enforcement, (2) determine the guilt of the accused, (3) represent diverse community interests and values, (4) serve as buffer between accused and accuser, (5) become educated about the justice system, and (6) symbolize the law.

10. *What has the Supreme Court decided concerning the size and unanimity requirements of juries?*

Juries can have as few as 6 jurors, except in death penalty cases, in which 12 are required, and convictions can occur through less-than-unanimous verdicts.

11. *What is voir dire?*

The jury selection process in which lawyers and/or judges ask questions of prospective jurors and make decisions about using peremptory challenges and challenges for cause to shape the jury's composition.

12. *What is the difference between a peremptory challenge and a challenge for cause?*

A challenge for cause is based on an indication that a prospective juror cannot make a fair decision. Such challenges must be approved by the judge. A peremptory challenge can be made by the attorney without giving a reason, unless an allegation arises that the attorney is using such challenges to exclude people systematically because of their race or gender.

13. *What are the stages in the trial process?*

Jury selection, attorneys' opening statements, presentation of prosecution's evidence, presentation of defense's evidence, presentation of rebuttal witnesses, closing arguments by each side, judge's instructions to the jury, and jury's decision.

14. *What are the kinds of evidence presented during a trial?*

Real evidence, demonstrative evidence, witness testimony, direct evidence, and circumstantial evidence.

15. *What factors can make a jury's decision different from that of a judge?*

Jurors may discount cases in which they dislike the victims. Jurors may also be more sympathetic to self-defense claims.

16. *How does the appellate court's job differ from that of the trial court?*

Unlike trial courts, which have juries, hear evidence, and decide if the defendant is guilty or not guilty, appellate courts focus only on claimed errors of law or procedure in trial court proceedings. Victory in an appellate court may mean only a chance at a new trial—which often leads to a new conviction.

17. *What is a habeas corpus petition?*

The habeas corpus process may be started after all appeals have been filed and lost. Convicted offenders ask a federal court to review whether any constitutional rights were violated during the course of a case's investigation and trial. If rights were violated, the person's continued detention in prison or jail may be improper.

CHAPTER **12**

Punishment and Sentencing

LEARNING OBJECTIVES

→ Recognize the goals of punishment

→ Identify the types of sentences judges can impose

→ Understand what really happens in sentencing

→ Analyze whether the system treats wrongdoers equally

In April 2008, throngs of onlookers, reporters, and photographers waited in anticipation outside the courthouse as Hollywood actor Wesley Snipes (right), the star of numerous movies, arrived for his sentencing hearing in Ocala, Florida. The federal government had charged Snipes with tax fraud and conspiracy as well as additional charges of failing to file a tax return for a period of six years. Although he made more than $58 million from his acting career during those years, Snipes refused to pay income taxes and claimed that the federal income tax was illegal. The Internal Revenue Service (IRS) had adopted the strategy of prosecuting a select number of prominent people for violating tax laws with the hope that sending a celebrity to prison would scare other Americans and deter them from cheating on their taxes. The government was particularly interested in prosecuting people who were part of the "tax deniers" movement; people who claimed that the government had no authority to collect taxes from them. Snipes had become part of that movement after getting financial advice from two men, Eddie Ray Kahn and Douglas Rosile, who were also charged with criminal offenses in conjunction with the prosecution of Snipes (Johnston, 2008).

Snipes originally faced the possibility of 16 years in prison if he had been convicted of

all charges. Much to the government's dismay, however, the jury acquitted the actor on the most serious fraud and conspiracy charges as well as charges for failing to pay taxes during three years of the six-year period in question. The jurors apparently accepted the defense attorney's argument that Snipes genuinely believed that he was not obligated to pay taxes and therefore he lacked the necessary criminal intent (*mens rea*, discussed in Chapter 4) to be guilty of a crime. With respect to the charges of failing to file a tax return, the jury convicted him of three misdemeanor charges—one for each of the three years prior to him learning that he was the focus of an IRS investigation. The jurors apparently regarded his failure to file a return in the subsequent three years as merely his assertion of his Fifth Amendment right to remain silent and not feel forced to engage in self-incrimination. By contrast, the co-defendants Kahn and Rosile, who helped to advise people to refuse to pay their taxes, were convicted on felony charges (Johnston, 2008).

At the day-long sentencing hearing, the attorneys for Snipes argued that he should receive leniency since he was merely the naïve victim of misguided financial advice from Kahn and Rosile. Snipes arrived at the court with checks totaling $5 million in order to pay the government a portion of the $17 million that he owed in back taxes and interest penalties. In a prepared statement that he read in the courtroom, Snipes said: "I'm very sorry for my mistakes. I acknowledge that I have failed myself and others" (*New York Times*, 2008).

The prosecution argued for the maximum penalty: a total of three years in prison—one year for each of the misdemeanor convictions. They complained that even when Snipes claimed to be "sorry," he never acknowledged his legal duty to pay income taxes, never withdrew his prior assertions that federal taxes are illegal, and did not show any genuine remorse for breaking the law (*New York Times*, 2008).

Ultimately U.S. District Judge William Terrell Hodges demonstrated that he agreed with the prosecution's position. He sentenced Snipes to one year in prison for each misdemeanor conviction and ordered that the sentences be served consecutively, one right after the other for a total of three years in prison plus one additional year of probation afterward. In addition, Snipes was ordered to pay the remaining portion of the $17 million that he owed to the government. In other cases, offenders convicted of multiple charges are often ordered to serve their sentences concurrently, meaning that each year in prison counts as a year toward each sentence. If Snipes had received concurrent sentences, he would have been sent to prison for one year instead of three. Thus Snipes received the maximum penalty possible for the misdemeanor charges (*New York Times*, 2008).

His co-defendants, Kahn and Rosile, received prison sentences of 10 years and four and a half years respectively due to their more serious felony convictions. Throughout the case, Kahn refused to accept that the court had any authority to make decisions about him and he stayed in his jail cell rather than attend many of the court proceedings as a way of demonstrating his view that the government lacked any legal authority to prosecute him for tax law violations (*New York Times*, 2008; Johnston, 2008). In some cases, defendants risk receiving more severe sentences if they show disrespect to the judge or fail to show remorse for their crimes. The severity of Kahn's sentence raises the possibility that his attitude and behavior led to harsher punishment.

The outcome of Wesley Snipes's case brings up many questions about the role of sentencing in the criminal justice system. Did Snipes's sentence achieve justice? Did it appropriately advance society's goals? Which goals? For example, did it compensate the "victim"? Make an example of Snipes? Help him become a law-abiding citizen? Further, was he treated fairly when compared with others who commit similar crimes? Should someone who refuses to accept responsibility or to cooperate receive a maximum sentence? What sentence do you believe

Wesley Snipes deserved? What about his co-defendants? As these questions indicate, criminal behavior may produce a wide variety of punishments, which depend on the goals being pursued by officials who make laws and determine sentences.

The criminal justice system aims to solve three basic issues: (1) What conduct is criminal? (2) What determines guilt? (3) What should be done with the guilty? Earlier chapters emphasized the first two questions. The answers given by the legal system to the first question compose the basic rules of society: Do not murder, rob, sell drugs, commit treason, and so forth. The law also spells out the process for determining guilt or innocence; however, the administrative and interpersonal considerations of the actors in the criminal justice system greatly affect this process. In this chapter we begin to examine the third problem—sanction and punishment. First, we consider the four goals of punishment: retribution, deterrence, incapacitation, and rehabilitation. We then explore the forms punishment takes to achieve its goals. These are incarceration, intermediate sanctions, probation, and death. Finally, we look at the sentencing process and how it affects punishment.

THE GOALS OF PUNISHMENT

Criminal sanctions in the United States have four main goals: retribution (deserved punishment), deterrence, incapacitation, and rehabilitation. Ultimately, all criminal punishment is aimed at maintaining the social order, but the justifications for sentencing speak of the American values of justice and fairness. However, the justice sought by crime victims often conflicts with fairness to offenders.

Punishments reflect the dominant values of a particular moment in history. By the end of the 1960s, for example, the number of Americans who were sentenced to imprisonment decreased because of a widespread commitment to rehabilitating offenders. By contrast, since the mid-1970s record numbers of offenders have been sentenced to prison because of an emphasis on imposing strong punishments for the purposes of retribution, deterrence, and incapacitation (see "What Americans Think"). In the first decade of the twenty-first century, voices are calling for the addition of restorative justice as a fifth goal of the criminal sanction.

Retribution—Deserved Punishment

Retribution is punishment inflicted on a person who has infringed on the rights of others and so deserves to be penalized. The biblical expression "An eye for an eye, a tooth for a tooth" illustrates the philosophy underlying this kind of punishment. Retribution means that those who commit a particular crime should be punished alike, in proportion to the gravity of the offense or to the extent to which others have been made to suffer. Retribution is deserved punishment; offenders must "pay their debts."

Some scholars claim that the desire for retribution is a basic human emotion. They maintain that if the state does not provide retributive sanctions to reflect community revulsion at offensive acts, citizens will take the law into their own hands to punish offenders. Under this view, the failure of government to satisfy the people's desire for retribution could produce social chaos.

This argument may not be valid for all crimes, however. If a rapist is inadequately punished, then the victim's friends, family, and other members of the community may be tempted to exact their own retribution. But what about a

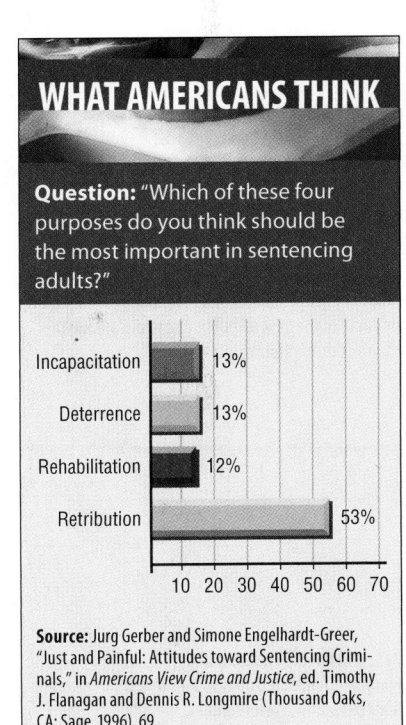

WHAT AMERICANS THINK

Question: "Which of these four purposes do you think should be the most important in sentencing adults?"

Purpose	Percent
Incapacitation	13%
Deterrence	13%
Rehabilitation	12%
Retribution	53%

10 20 30 40 50 60 70

Source: Jurg Gerber and Simone Engelhardt-Greer, "Just and Painful: Attitudes toward Sentencing Criminals," in *Americans View Crime and Justice*, ed. Timothy J. Flanagan and Dennis R. Longmire (Thousand Oaks, CA: Sage, 1996), 69.

retribution
Punishment inflicted on a person who has infringed on the rights of others and so deserves to be penalized. The severity of the sanction should fit the seriousness of the crime.

young adult smoking marijuana? If the government failed to impose retribution for this offense, would the community care? The same apathy may hold true for offenders who commit other nonviolent crimes that only modestly impact society. Even in these seemingly trivial situations, however, retribution may be useful and necessary to remind the public of the general rules of law and the important values they protect.

Since the late 1970s, retribution as a justification for the criminal sanction has aroused new interest, largely because of dissatisfaction with the philosophical basis and practical results of rehabilitation. Using the concept of "just deserts or deserved punishment" to define retribution, some theorists argue that one who infringes on the rights of others *deserves* to be punished. This approach rests on the philosophical view that punishment is a moral response to harms inflicted on society. In effect, these theorists believe that basic morality demands that wrongdoers be punished (von Hirsch, 1976: 49). According to this view, punishment should be applied only for the wrong inflicted and not primarily to achieve other goals such as deterrence, incapacitation, or rehabilitation.

Deterrence

Many people see criminal punishment as a basis for affecting the future choices and behavior of individuals. Politicians frequently talk about being "tough on crime" in order to send a message to would-be criminals. The roots of this approach, called deterrence, lie in eighteenth-century England among the followers of social philosopher Jeremy Bentham.

Bentham was struck by what seemed to be the pointlessness of retribution. His fellow reformers adopted Bentham's theory of utilitarianism, which holds that human behavior is governed by the individual's calculation of the benefits versus the costs of one's acts. Before stealing money or property, for example, potential offenders would consider the punishment that others have received for similar acts and would thereby be deterred.

general deterrence
Punishment of criminals that is intended to provide an example to the general public and to discourage the commission of offenses.

There are two types of deterrence. **General deterrence** presumes that members of the general public, on observing the punishments of others, will conclude that the costs of crime outweigh the benefits. For general deterrence to be effective, the public must be constantly reminded about the likelihood and severity of punishment for various acts. They must believe that they will be caught, prosecuted, and given a specific punishment if they commit a particular crime. Moreover, the punishment must be severe enough that the consequences of committing crimes will impress them. For example, public hanging was once considered to be an effective general deterrent. The prosecution of Wesley Snipes was also intended to advance general deterrence. However, it is not clear that the effect was achieved since the prosecution's failure to convict Snipes of a felony may lead people to believe that they can get away with cheating on their taxes.

specific deterrence
Punishment inflicted on criminals to discourage them from committing future crimes.

By contrast, **specific deterrence** targets the decisions and behavior of offenders who have already been convicted. Under this approach, the amount and kind of punishment are calculated to discourage that criminal from repeating the offense. The punishment must be severe enough to cause the criminal to say, "The consequences of my crime were too painful. I will not commit another crime, because I do not want to risk being punished again."

The concept of deterrence presents obvious difficulties (Stafford and Warr, 1993). Deterrence assumes that all people think before they act. It does not account for the many people who commit crimes while under the influence of drugs or alcohol, or those whose harmful behavior stems from psychological problems or mental illness. Deterrence also does not account for people who act impulsively in stealing or damaging property. In other cases, the low probability of getting caught defeats both general and special deterrence. To be generally deterrent, punishment must be perceived as relatively fast, certain, and severe. But punishment does not always work this way.

Knowledge of the effectiveness of deterrence is limited (Kleck et al., 2005). For example, social science cannot measure the effects of general deterrence, because only those who are *not* deterred come to the attention of researchers. A study of the deterrent effects of punishment would have to examine the impact of different forms of the criminal sanction on various potential lawbreakers. How can we truly determine how many people (if any) stopped themselves from committing a crime because they were deterred by the prospect of prosecution and punishment? Therefore, although legislators often cite deterrence as a rationale for certain sanctions, no one really knows the extent to which sentencing policies based on deterrence achieve their objectives. Because contemporary U.S. society has shown little ability to reduce crime by imposing increasingly severe sanctions, the effectiveness of deterrence for many crimes and criminals should be questioned.

Incapacitation

Incapacitation assumes that society, by means of prison or execution, can keep an offender from committing further crimes. Many people express such sentiments, urging officials to "lock 'em up and throw away the key!" In primitive societies, banishment from the community was the usual method of incapacitation. In early America, offenders often agreed to move away or to join the army as an alternative to some other form of punishment. In contemporary America, imprisonment is the usual method of incapacitation. Offenders can be confined within secure institutions and effectively prevented from committing additional harm against society for the duration of their sentence. Capital punishment is the ultimate method of incapacitation.

Any sentence that physically restricts an offender usually incapacitates the person, even when the underlying purpose of the sentence is retribution, deterrence, or rehabilitation. Sentences based on incapacitation are future oriented. Whereas retribution requires focusing on the harmful act of the offender, incapacitation looks at the offender's potential actions. If the offender is likely to commit future crimes, then a severe sentence may be imposed—even for a relatively minor crime.

For example, under the incapacitation theory, a woman who kills her abusive husband as an emotional reaction to his verbal insults and physical assaults could receive a light sentence. As a one-time impulse killer who felt driven to kill by unique circumstances, she will not likely commit additional crimes. By contrast, someone who shoplifts merchandise and has been convicted of the offense on ten previous occasions may receive a severe sentence. The criminal record and type of crime indicate that he or she will commit additional crimes if released. Thus, incapacitation focuses on characteristics of the offenders instead of characteristics of their offenses.

Does it offend your sense of justice that a person could receive a severer sentence for shoplifting than for manslaughter? This is one of the criticisms of incapacitation. Questions also arise about how to determine the length of sentence. Presumably, offenders will not be released until the state is reasonably sure that they will no longer commit crimes. However, can we accurately predict any person's behavior? Moreover, on what grounds can we punish people for anticipated future behavior that we cannot accurately predict?

In recent years, greater attention has been paid to the concept of **selective incapacitation**, whereby offenders who repeat certain kinds of crimes receive long prison terms. Research has suggested that a relatively small number of offenders commit a large number of violent and property crimes (Clear, 1994: 103). Burglars, for example, tend to commit many offenses before they are caught.

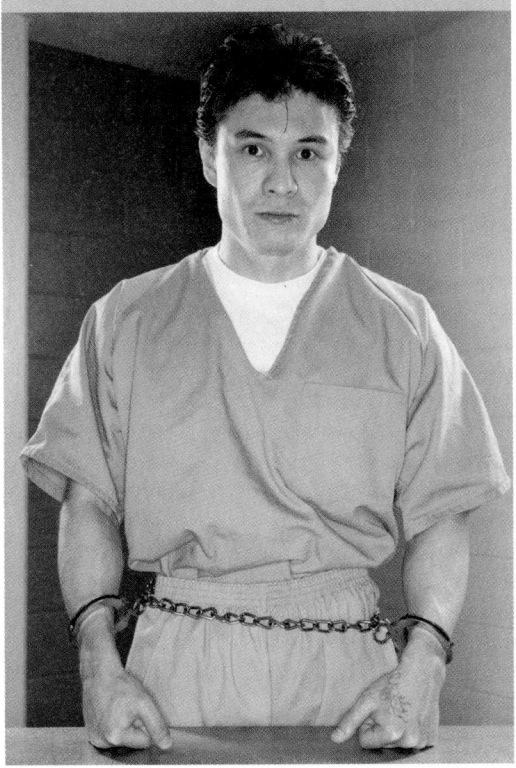

Charlie Chase, considered one of the most dangerous inmates in Massachusetts, is doing time in total isolation in an 8-by-10-foot cinder-block cage. Observers ask if solitary confinement is driving him crazy. If he is ever released, will he be able to adjust to life in free society?

© Stephen Wilkes

incapacitation
Depriving an offender of the ability to commit crimes against society, usually by detaining the offender in prison.

selective incapacitation
Making the best use of expensive and limited prison space by targeting for incarceration those individuals whose detention will do the most to reduce crime in society.

Thus, these "career criminals" should be locked up for long periods (Auerhahn, 1999). Such policies could be costly, however. Not only would correctional facilities have to be expanded, but the number of expensive, time-consuming trials also might increase if longer sentences caused more repeat offenders to plead not guilty. Another difficulty with this policy is that we cannot accurately predict which offenders will commit more crimes upon release.

Rehabilitation

rehabilitation
The goal of restoring a convicted offender to a constructive place in society through some form of vocational or educational training or therapy.

Rehabilitation refers to the goal of restoring a convicted offender to a constructive place in society through some form of training or therapy. Americans want to believe that offenders can be treated and resocialized in ways that allow them to lead a crime-free, productive life upon release. Over the last hundred years, rehabilitation advocates have argued for techniques that they claim identify and treat the causes of criminal behavior. If the offender's criminal behavior is assumed to result from some social, psychological, or biological imperfection, the treatment of the disorder becomes the primary goal of corrections.

Rehabilitation focuses on the offender. Its objective does not imply any consistent relationship between the severity of the punishment and the gravity of the crime. People who commit lesser offenses can receive long prison sentences if experts believe that rehabilitating them will take a long time. By contrast, a murderer might win early release by showing signs that the psychological or emotional problems that led to the killing have been corrected.

According to the concept of rehabilitation, offenders are treated, not punished, and they will return to society when they are "cured." Consequently, judges should not set fixed sentences but rather ones with maximum and minimum terms so that parole boards can release inmates when they have been rehabilitated.

From the 1940s until the 1970s, the goal of rehabilitation was so widely accepted that people generally regarded the treatment and reform of the offender as the only issues worth serious attention. Most assumed that the problems affecting individuals caused crime, and that modern social sciences provided the tools to address those problems. During the past 30 years, however, researchers have questioned the assumptions of the rehabilitation model. Studies of the results of rehabilitation programs have challenged the idea that criminal offenders can be cured (Martinson, 1974). Moreover, scholars no longer take for granted that crime is caused by identifiable, curable problems such as poverty, lack of job skills, low self-esteem, and hostility toward authority. Instead, some argue that we cannot identify the cause of criminal behavior for individual offenders.

Clearly, many legislators, prosecutors, and judges have abandoned the rehabilitation goal in favor of retribution, deterrence, or incapacitation. Yet, in opinion polls, researchers have found public support for rehabilitative programs (Applegate, Cullen, and Fisher, 1997).

restoration
Punishment designed to repair the damage done to the victim and community by an offender's criminal act.

Restorative justice seeks to repair the damage that an offender's criminal act has done to the victim and the community. Here, Susanna Kay Cooper sits next to David Lee Myers as she looks at the photo of his dead wife. Cooper pleaded guilty to vehicular homicide in the death of Elaine Myers, received a 34-month prison sentence, and agreed to enter into talks with the victim's family. How do such meetings advance the idea of justice?

© Rose Howerter/The Oregonian

New Approaches to Punishment

In keeping with the focus on community justice—in policing, prosecution, courts, and corrections—many people are calling for **restoration** (through restorative justice) to be added to the goals of the criminal sanction (Basemore and Umbreit, 1994).

The restorative justice perspective views crime as more than a violation of penal law. The criminal act practically and symbolically denies community. It breaks trust among citizens and requires community members to determine how to counteract the moral message of the crime that the offender is above the law and the victim beneath its reach (Clear and Karp, 1999). Crime victims suffer losses involving damage to property and self. The primary aim of criminal justice should be to repair these losses. Crime also challenges the very essence of community, to the extent that community life depends on a shared sense of trust, fairness, and interdependence. Shifting the focus to restorative justice requires a three-way approach that involves the offender, the victim, and the community (Rodriguez, 2005). This approach may include mediation in which the three actors devise ways that all agree are fair and just for the offender to repair the harm to the victim and community (Walker and Hayaski, 2007). This new approach to criminal justice means that losses suffered by the crime victim are restored, the threat to local safety is removed, and the offender again becomes a fully participating member of the community. The Vermont Reparative Sentencing Boards, described in the Close Up box, exemplify one way of implementing restoration. In addition think about the possible opportunities for citizen involvement in restorative justice programs as you read "Civic Engagement: Your Role in the System."

To see how these goals of punishment might be enacted in real life, consider again the sentencing of Wesley Snipes. Who were the victims of Snipes's crime, and what could he be required to do in order to achieve restorative justice? Table 12.1 shows various hypothetical sentencing statements that the judge might have given, depending on prevailing correctional goals.

As we next consider the ways that the goals are applied though the various forms of punishment, keep in mind the underlying goal—or mix of punishment goals—that justifies each form of sanction.

Read the Frequently Asked Questions section of the website of a restorative justice community center in upstate New York. To link to this website, go to *The American System of Criminal Justice* 12e companion site at academic.cengage.com/criminaljustice/cole.

civic engagement
your role in the system

The mayor of your city asks you to lead a committee to develop a proposal for the creation of restorative justice programs. *Make a list of activities in which citizens can assist in restorative justice processes.* Then look at the array of activities at the Montpelier Community Justice Center in Vermont. To link to this website, go to *The American System of Criminal Justice* 12e companion site at academic.cengage.com/criminaljustice/cole.

TABLE 12.1	The Goals of Punishment

At sentencing, the judge usually gives reasons for the punishments imposed. Here are statements that Judge William Terrell Hodges might have given Wesley Snipes each promoting a different goal for the sanction.

Goal	Judge's Possible Statement
Retribution	I am imposing this sentence because you deserve to be punished for the economic harm caused by violating laws concerning tax evasion. Your criminal behavior is the basis of the punishment. Justice requires that I impose a sanction at a level that illustrates the importance that the community places on obedience to tax laws.
Deterrence	I am imposing this sentence so that your punishment for tax evasion will serve as an example and deter others who may contemplate similar actions. In addition, I hope that this sentence will deter you from ever again committing an illegal act.
Incapacitation	I am imposing this sentence so that you will be incapacitated and hence unable to engage in tax evasion in the free community during the length of this term.
Rehabilitation	The trial testimony and information contained in the presentence report make me believe that there are aspects of your personality that led to the tax evasion. I am therefore imposing this sentence so that you can receive treatment that will rectify your behavior so you will not commit another crime.

CLOSE UP

Restorative Justice in Vermont

ONE NIGHT IN Morrisville, Vermont, Newton Wells went looking for a good time and wound up in an experiment. The 22-year-old college student was charged with assault after nearly driving into two police officers who were breaking up a party. Facing a felony conviction, Wells took a different way out. He pleaded guilty to a lower charge and volunteered to be sentenced by a county "reparative" board. Instead of a judge, a businessman, a counselor, a retired chemistry teacher, and a civil servant issued his punishment.

Restorative justice programs are designed to compensate victims, rehabilitate offenders, and involve the community in a new and direct way in the justice process. Today some Vermont offenders may be sentenced to make public apologies, make restitution, or chop wood for the elderly—to "repair" the community.

Vermont's sentencing boards, typically four to six volunteers, handle misdemeanors and low-grade felonies such as drunken driving and writing bad checks. There are 72 local reparative boards in 45 Vermont towns. Removing the cases from the traditional criminal justice system frees up correctional department resources.

Board members meet with offenders in hour-long sessions, hear explanations and apologies, and tailor the penalties. The idea is to make the punishment relate to the crime, which often occurs in novel ways:

- In Morrisville, college student Wells was ordered to work 30 hours with troubled youths and to meet with the police he menaced so that they could vent their anger about his driving.
- In Rutland, a man who drove 105 mph down a residential street was sentenced to work with brain-injured adults, some of them survivors of high-speed crashes.
- In Hyde Park, a teenager who vandalized a home got 55 hours on a work crew. His job was repairing plaster on an aging opera house.

Panel members get involved in ways they never could if they were serving as jurors. In Rutland, Jack Aicher tells shoplifters they've committed crimes against the "community." Everyone pays higher prices, he says, to cover the store's loss.

Proponents say board sanctions are typically tougher than conventional probation. But offenders opt for the citizen panels to get their sentences concluded quickly. In Vermont, probation can last more than a year and can include special sanctions such as drug tests and rehabilitation programs. Reparative board punishments are concluded within 90 days.

The percentage of nonviolent offenders in the state's eight prisons has dropped from about 50 percent to 28 percent. The decline is ascribed, in part, to the effect of the boards. In Winooski, Vermont, over a five-year period, 82 percent of people who appeared before these boards completed their prescribed tasks. The other 18 percent had their cases sent into the regular criminal justice system. A study released in 2007 that examined more than 9,000 cases handled by local boards between 1998 and 2005 found that these offenders were 23 percent less likely to commit another crime than those sentenced to traditional probation. By handling low-level offenders, the community panels have freed state probation officers to deal with more serious cases. Those probation officers can then monitor criminals serving their sentences in work camps or on furlough rather than in jail, as a way of relieving overcrowding.

Source: Wilson Ring, "Study: Novel Sentencing Program Really Works," *The Barre Montpelier Times Argus*, February 3, 2007 (http://www.timesargus.com); "Volunteer Boards Face Challenges," *WCAX TV Channel 3*, News Scripts, March 2, 2007; USA Today, February 12, 1997 (http://www.usatoday.com).

Researching the Internet

Read about restorative justice at the website of the Centre for Justice and Reconciliation. To link to this website, go to *The American System of Criminal Justice* 12e companion site at academic.cengage.com/criminaljustice/cole.

checkpoint

1. What are the four primary goals of the criminal sanction?
2. What are the difficulties in showing that a punishment acts as a deterrent?
   (Answers are at the end of the chapter.)

FORMS OF THE CRIMINAL SANCTION

Incarceration, intermediate sanctions, probation, and death are the basic ways that the criminal sanction, or punishment, is applied. There is no overarching sentencing law for the United States. The criminal code of each of the states and of the federal government specify the punishments. Each code differs to some extent in the severity of the punishment for specific crimes and in the amount of discretion given judges to tailor the sanction to the individual offender.

Many judges and researchers believe that sentencing structures in the United States are both too severe and too lenient. That is, many offenders who do not warrant incarceration are sent to prison, and many who should receive more restrictive punishment receive minimal probation supervision.

Advocates for more-effective sentencing practices increasingly support a range of punishment options, with graduated levels of supervision and harshness. As Figure 12.1 shows, simple probation lies at one end of this range, and traditional incarceration lies at the other. It is argued that by using this type of sentencing scheme, authorities can reserve expensive prison cells for violent offenders. At the same time, they can use less restrictive community-based programs to punish nonviolent offenders.

As we examine the various forms of criminal sanctions, bear in mind that complex problems are associated with applying these legally authorized punishments. Judges are given wide discretion in determining the appropriate sentence within the parameters of the penal code.

Although these are the sanctions used in the United States, the form and severity of punishment vary across cultures, as seen in the Comparative Perspective on the use of corporal punishment in Singapore (Ripoll-Nunez and Rohner, 2006). As you read that article, consider the reaction in the United States to the flogging of Michael Fay. Why have corporal punishments (inflicting pain on the body of the offender) disappeared in Western countries? Should flogging be reinstituted?

To read detailed descriptions of the procedures and effects of caning in Singapore, look online. To link to this website, go to *The American System of Criminal Justice* 12e companion site at academic.cengage.com/criminaljustice/cole.

Incarceration

Imprisonment is the most visible penalty imposed by U.S. courts. Although less than 30 percent of people under correctional supervision are in prisons and jails, incarceration remains the standard for punishing those who commit serious crimes. Imprisonment is thought to contribute significantly to deterring potential offenders. However, incarceration is expensive. It also creates the problem of reintegrating offenders into society upon release.

In penal codes, legislatures stipulate the type of sentences and the amount of prison time that may be imposed for each crime. Three basic sentencing structures are used: (1) indeterminate sentences (36 states), (2) determinate sentences (14 states), and (3) mandatory sentences (all states). Each type of sentence makes certain assumptions about the goals of the criminal sanction, and each provides judges with varying degrees of discretion (Bureau of Justice Assistance [BJA], 1998: 4; Wool, 2005).

Indeterminate Sentences

When the goal of rehabilitation dominated corrections, legislatures enacted **indeterminate sentences** (often called indefinite sentences). In keeping with the goal of treatment, indeterminate sentencing gives correctional officials and parole boards significant control over the amount of time a prisoner serves. Penal codes with indeterminate sentences stipulate a minimum and a maximum amount of time to be served in prison (for example, 1–5 years, 3–10 years, or 1 year to life). At the time of sentencing, the judge informs the offender about the range of the sentence. The offender also learns that he or she will probably be eligible for parole at some point after the minimum term has been served. The parole board determines the actual release date.

indeterminate sentence
A period, set by a judge, that specifies a minimum and a maximum time to be served in prison. Sometime after the minimum, the offender may be eligible for parole. Because it is based on the idea that the time necessary for treatment cannot be set, the indeterminate sentence is closely associated with rehabilitation.

COMPARATIVE PERSPECTIVE

Corporal Punishment in Singapore

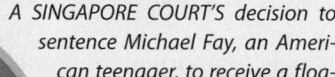

A SINGAPORE COURT'S decision to sentence Michael Fay, an American teenager, to receive a flogging for vandalizing cars with spray paint produced a predictable nod of approval from many Singaporeans, long accustomed to their government's firm hand. For many Americans the punishment seemed unduly harsh, yet others expressed the view that this might be the answer to the U.S. crime problem.

Michael Fay was sentenced to six strokes of the cane; four months in prison; and a $2,230 fine after pleading guilty to two counts of vandalism, two counts of mischief, and one count of possessing stolen property. Canings (floggings) in Singapore are carried out by a jailer trained in martial arts who uses a moistened, 4-foot rattan cane. The offender is stripped, then bound by the hands and feet to a wooden trestle. Pads covering his kidneys and groin are the only protection from the cane. Should he pass out, a doctor will revive him before the caning continues. The wounds generally take two weeks to heal; scarring is permanent.

After Singapore gained independence from Britain, the government imposed increasingly harsh penalties for a range of crimes, culminating in laws that carry a mandatory death penalty for such offenses as armed robbery and drug trafficking. Singapore has dropped some traditional safeguards, such as jury trials, on grounds that guilty criminals were manipulating the system to walk free.

According to Singaporean officials, sentences are intended not just as punishment but also as a deterrent. For example, when an 18-year-old man who was called "educationally subnormal" repeatedly kissed a woman in an elevator, he was charged with molestation. A court sentenced him to six months in prison. When the man's lawyer appealed, Judge Yong Pung How said that "sentences have been too light; they are not having a deterrent effect" and increased the punishment to include three whacks of the rattan cane.

In the United States, by contrast, corporal punishment continues to exist as a form of sanction for misbehavior in some schools, often with the use of a wooden paddle. In 1968, a U.S. court of appeals decision prohibited the use of whipping as punishment for misbehavior by convicted offenders inside prisons (*Jackson v. Bishop*). Although corporal punishment in schools is barred by law in 29 states, it continues to exist in places such as Ohio, where 17 school systems continued to use the practice in 2008. Does it make sense to permit the use of wooden paddles to punish children in schools for misbehavior but to avoid inflicting painful physical punishments on adults who commit crimes? Should the United States follow the example of Singapore?

Source: Adapted from Charles P. Wallace, "Singapore's Justice System: Harsh, Temptingly Effective," *Hartford Courant,* April 4, 1994, p. 1 and Edith Starzyk, "Bill Would Ban Corporal Punishment in Ohio Schools," *Cleveland Plain Dealer,* January 29, 2008 (http://www.cleveland.com).

FIGURE 12.1
Escalating punishments to fit the crime
This list includes generalized descriptions of many sentencing options used in jurisdictions across the country.

PROBATION

Offender reports to probation officer periodically, depending on the offense, sometimes as frequently as several times a month or as infrequently as once a year.

INTENSIVE SUPERVISION PROBATION

Offender sees probation officer three to five times a week. Probation officer also makes unscheduled visits to offender's home or workplace.

RESTITUTION AND FINES

Used alone or in conjunction with probation or intensive supervision and requires regular payments to crime victims or to the courts.

COMMUNITY SERVICE

Used alone or in conjunction with probation or intensive supervision and requires completion of set number of hours of work in and for the community.

SUBSTANCE ABUSE TREATMENT

Evaluation and referral services provided by private outside agencies and used alone or in conjunction with either simple probation or intensive supervision.

Source: Seeking Justice: *Crime and Punishment in America* (New York: Edna McConnell Clark Foundation, 1997), 32–33.

Determinate Sentences

Dissatisfaction with the rehabilitation goal and support for the concept of deserved punishment led many legislatures in the 1970s to shift to **determinate sentences**. With a determinate sentence, a convicted offender is imprisoned for a specific period of time (for example, 2 years, 5 years, 15 years). At the end of the term, minus credited good time (see later discussion), the prisoner is automatically freed. The time of release is tied neither to participation in treatment programs nor to a parole board's judgment concerning the offender's likelihood of returning to criminal activities.

Some determinate-sentencing states have adopted penal codes that stipulate a specific term for each crime category. Others allow the judge to choose a range of time to be served. Some states emphasize a determinate **presumptive sentence**; the legislature or often a commission specifies a term based on a time range (for example, 14 to 20 months) into which most cases of a certain type should fall. Only in special circumstances should judges deviate from the presumptive sentence. Whichever variation is used, however, the offender theoretically knows at sentencing the amount of time to be served. One result of determinate sentencing is that by reducing the judge's discretion, legislatures

Of all correctional measures, incarceration represents the greatest restriction on freedom. These inmates at Alabama's Staton Correctional Facility are part of America's huge incarcerated population. Since 1980, the number of Americans held in prisons and jails has quadrupled. What are the costs to society from having a large population of prisoners?

AP Images/Rob Carr

DAY REPORTING

Clients report to a central location every day where they file a daily schedule with their supervision officer showing how each hour will be spent—at work, in class, at support group meetings, etc.

HOUSE ARREST AND ELECTRONIC MONITORING

Used in conjunction with intensive supervision; restricts offender to home except when at work, school, or treatment.

HALFWAY HOUSE

Residential settings for selected inmates as a supplement to probation for those completing prison programs and for some probation or parole violators. Usually coupled with community service work and/or substance abuse treatment.

BOOT CAMP

Rigorous military-style regimen for younger offenders, designed to accelerate punishment while instilling discipline, often with an educational component.

PRISONS AND JAILS

More-serious offenders serve their terms at state or federal prisons, while county jails are usually designed to hold inmates for shorter periods.

determinate sentence
A sentence that fixes the term of imprisonment at a specific period.

presumptive sentence
A sentence for which the legislature or a commission sets a minimum and maximum range of months or years. Judges are to fix the length of the sentence within that range, allowing for special circumstances.

have tended to limit sentencing disparities and to ensure that terms correspond to those the elected body thinks are appropriate (Griset, 1994).

Mandatory Sentences

mandatory sentence
A sentence determined by statutes and requiring that a certain penalty be imposed and carried out for convicted offenders who meet certain criteria.

Politicians and the public have continued to complain that offenders gain release before serving long enough terms, and legislatures have responded. All states and the federal government now have some form of **mandatory sentences** (often called mandatory minimum sentences), stipulating some minimum period of incarceration that people convicted of selected crimes must serve. The judge may consider neither the circumstances of the offense nor the background of the offender, and he or she may not impose nonincarcerative sentences. Mandatory prison terms are most often specified for violent crimes, drug violations, habitual offenders, or crimes in which a firearm was used. Because mandatory sentences have contributed to expensive state corrections budgets and prison overcrowding, some observers believe that the public has become less supportive of this approach to criminal punishment (see "What Americans Think").

The "three strikes and you're out" laws adopted by 24 states and the federal government provide an example of mandatory sentencing (Schultz, 2000). These laws require that judges sentence offenders with three felony convictions (in some states two or four convictions) to long prison terms, sometimes to life without parole. In California and Georgia, the two states making the greatest use of them, these laws have had the unintended consequences of clogging the courts, lowering rates of plea bargaining, and causing desperate offenders to violently resist arrest (Butterfield, 1996). One early study shows that the law has had little impact on the reduction of rates for serious crime or petty theft (Stolzenberg and D'Alessio, 1997). A later study in California found a reduction in repeat offenders' participation in certain kinds of crimes, but a troubling increase in the violence of third-strike offenses (Iyengar, 2008). This raises the possibility that career criminals who are willing to risk the three-strike ultimate punishment may commit more serious crimes, such as robbery, since the penalty for them will be no greater than that for a lesser felony, such as larceny (Fisman, 2008). The study also raised the possibility that offenders with prior strikes

 For information on mandatory sentencing laws and their impact on individual cases, see the website of the organization called Families Against Mandatory Minimums. To link to this website, go to *The American System of Criminal Justice* 12e companion site at academic.cengage.com/criminaljustice/cole.

Mandatory sentences can impose severe punishments on first offenders or those who commit non-violent crimes if they are convicted of offenses, such as drug crimes, that legislatures treat as especially harmful to society. Here Denise Smith, serving a 10-to-20-year drug sentence in New York, wipes away a tear as she talks about being so far away from her children. Should judges have the power to individualize sentences depending on the prior record of each defendant and circumstances of each crime?

AP Images/Jim McKnight

may be inclined to migrate to other states, thus merely moving their criminal activities to a new location (Iyengar, 2008).

Although legislators may assume that mandatory sentences will be imposed and criminal behavior reduced, the decisions of judges and prosecutors may thwart this intent. California prosecutors vary greatly as to whether they charge under the three-strikes law. There is a much lower use of the law in San Francisco, for example, than in San Diego (Zimring, Hawkins, and Kamin, 2001: 219). Regional voter support for the law may account for the disparity. A study of the impact of the California three-strikes law (Zimring et al., 2001: 62) shows that

- The law does incapacitate habitual offenders for a long time, but no hard evidence proves that it has had a deterrent effect on criminal behavior.

- The law targets repeat felons but captures mostly nonviolent offenders.

- Wide discretion and racial disparity in applying the law raise questions of legality and fairness.

- Prison problems are exacerbated by demand for space, high costs of building and staffing, and escalation of geriatric inmate health care costs.

Use of mandatory minimum sentences expanded significantly during the 1980s as a weapon in the war on drugs. The result has been a significant increase in drug offenders, most for nonviolent offenses, spending very long terms in America's prisons (Gezari, 2008). Research has shown that these are low-level street dealers, mules (who deliver drugs), and addicts rather than the "kingpins" who import and distribute drugs to the market. Across the country, mandatory prison terms are applied more often to African American drug offenders than to their white counterparts (Crawford, 2000).

The Sentence versus Actual Time Served

Regardless of how much discretion judges have to fine-tune the sentences they give, the prison sentences that are imposed may bear little resemblance to the amount of time served. In reality, parole boards in indeterminate-sentencing states have broad discretion in release decisions once the offender has served a minimum portion of the sentence. In addition, offenders can have their prison sentence reduced by earning **good time** for good behavior, at the discretion of the prison administrator.

All but four states have good-time policies (BJA, 1998). Days are subtracted from prisoners' minimum or maximum term for good behavior or for participating in various types of vocational, educational, or treatment programs. Correctional officials consider these policies necessary for maintaining institutional order and reducing crowding. Good-time credit provides an incentive for prisoners to follow institutional rules. Prosecutors and defense attorneys also take good time into consideration during plea bargaining. In other words, they think about the actual amount of time a particular offender is likely to serve.

The amount of good time one can earn varies among the states, usually from five to ten days a month. In some states, once 90 days of good time are earned, they are vested; that is, the credits cannot be taken away as a punishment for misbehavior. Prisoners who then violate the rules risk losing only days not vested.

Judges in the United States often prescribe long periods of incarceration for serious crimes, but good time and parole reduce the amount of time spent in prison. Figure 12.2 shows the estimated time actually served by offenders sent to state prisons versus the average (mean) sentence. The average prison sentence received for violent felony offenders decreased from 10 years in 1994 to about 7.5 years in 2004. The portion of the sentence actually served increased over the same time period from just under half to nearly two-thirds so that the average time served in prison remained stable from 1994 to 2004 (Durose and Langan, 2007: 3).

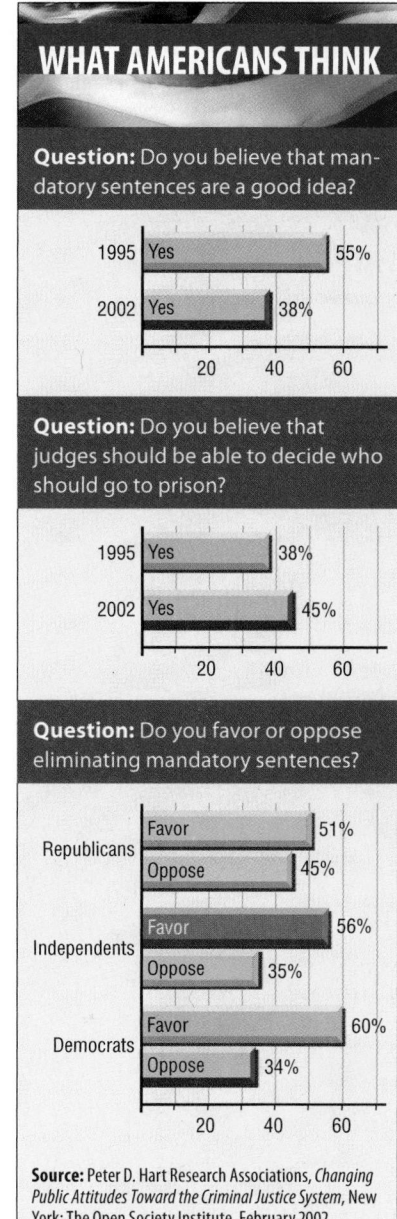

WHAT AMERICANS THINK

Question: Do you believe that mandatory sentences are a good idea?

1995	Yes	55%
2002	Yes	38%

20   40   60

Question: Do you believe that judges should be able to decide who should go to prison?

1995	Yes	38%
2002	Yes	45%

20   40   60

Question: Do you favor or oppose eliminating mandatory sentences?

Republicans	Favor	51%
	Oppose	45%
Independents	Favor	56%
	Oppose	35%
Democrats	Favor	60%
	Oppose	34%

20   40   60

Source: Peter D. Hart Research Associations, *Changing Public Attitudes Toward the Criminal Justice System*, New York: The Open Society Institute, February 2002.

good time
A reduction of an inmate's prison sentence, at the discretion of the prison administrator, for good behavior or participation in vocational, educational, or treatment programs.

FIGURE 12.2
Estimated time served in state prison compared with mean length of sentence
For most crimes, offenders serve two-thirds or less of their mean sentence. Why is there such a difference between the sentence and actual time served?

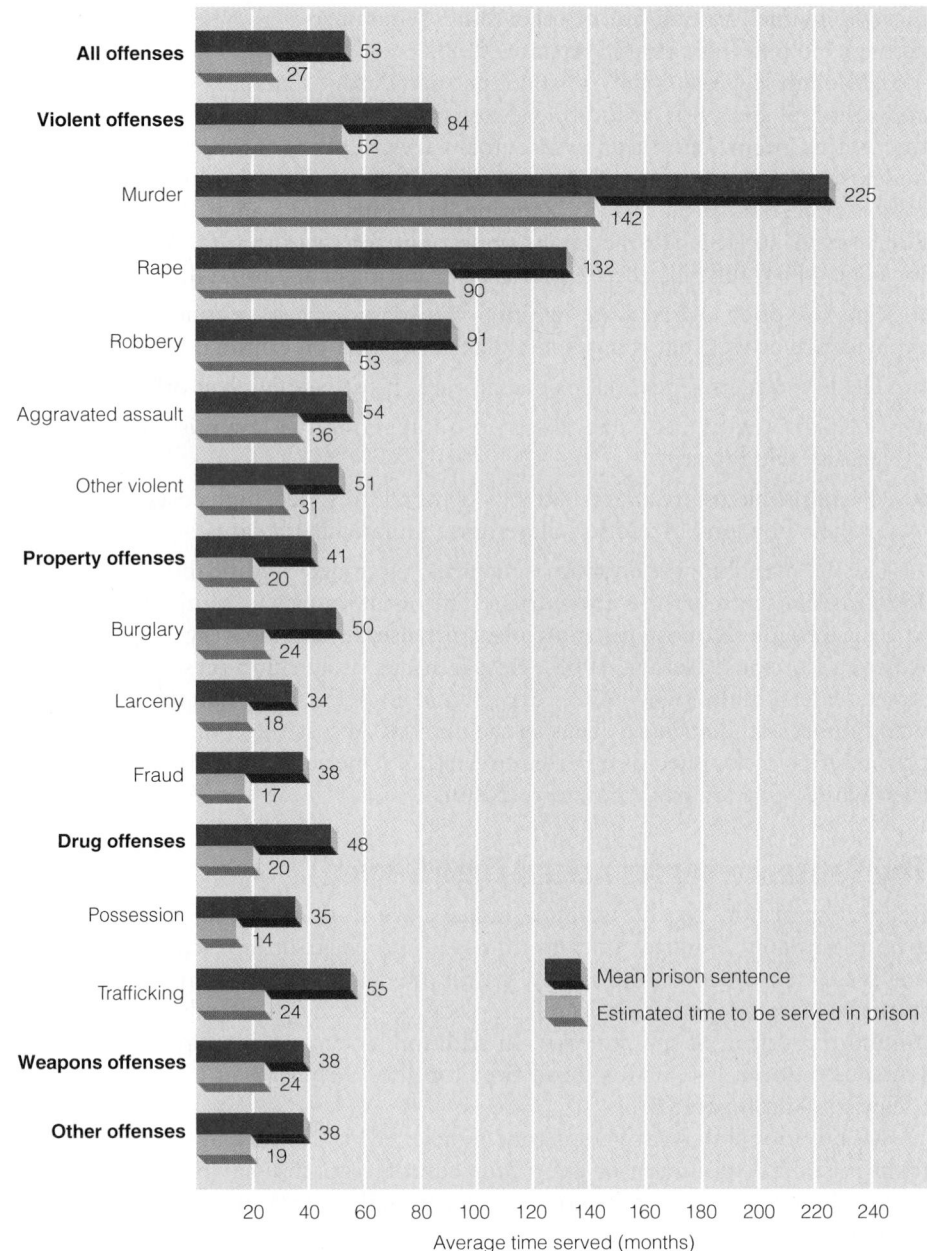

Average time served (months)

Source: Matthew R. Durose and Patrick A. Langan, "Felony Sentences in State Court, 2002," *Bureau of Justice Statistics Bulletin*, December 2004, p. 5

This type of national data often hides the impact of variations in sentencing and releasing laws in individual states. In many states, because of prison crowding and release policies, offenders are serving less than 20 percent of their sentences. In other states, where three-strikes and truth-in-sentencing laws are employed, the average time served will be longer than the national average.

Truth-in-Sentencing

Truth-in-sentencing refers to laws that require offenders to serve a substantial proportion (usually 85 percent for violent crimes) of their prison sentence before being released on parole. These laws have three goals: (1) providing the public with more-accurate information about the actual length of sentences, (2) reducing crime by keeping offenders in prison for longer periods, and (3) achieving a rational allocation of prison space by prioritizing the incarceration of particular classes of criminals (such as violent offenders). Most offenders serve two-thirds or less of their mean sentences. Why is there such a difference between the sentence and actual time served?

Truth-in-sentencing became such a politically attractive idea that the federal government allocated almost $10 billion for prison construction to those states adopting truth-in-sentencing in the 1990s (Donziger, 1996: 24). Critics maintain, however, that truth-in-sentencing will increase prison populations at a tremendous cost. Even relatively small increases in the amount of time served greatly enhance the costs of incarceration (BJS, 1999b: 4–11).

For more information on truth-in-sentencing, see the online report from the U.S. Bureau of Justice Statistics. To link to this website, go to *The American System of Criminal Justice* 12e companion site at academic.cengage.com/criminaljustice/cole.

Intermediate Sanctions

Prison crowding and low levels of probation supervision have spurred interest in the development of **intermediate sanctions**, punishments that are less severe and costly than prison but more restrictive than traditional probation (Morris and Tonry, 1990). Intermediate sanctions provide a variety of restrictions on freedom, such as fines, home confinement, intensive probation supervision, restitution to victims, community service, boot camp, and forfeiture of property. Research shows that if incarceration is reserved for murderers, rapists, those previously incarcerated, and those with a prior sentence for violence, then 29 percent of those who currently occupy expensive prison cells could have been sanctioned in the community (Petersilia and Turner, 1989).

In advocating intermediate punishments, Norval Morris and Michael Tonry (1990: 37) stipulate that these sanctions should not be used in isolation, but rather in combination to reflect the severity of the offense, the characteristics of the offender, and the needs of the community. In addition, intermediate punishments must be supported and enforced by mechanisms that take seriously any breach of the conditions of the sentence. Too often, criminal justice agencies have devoted few resources to enforcing sentences that do not involve incarceration. If the law does not fulfill its promises, offenders may feel that they have "beaten" the system, which makes the punishment meaningless. Citizens viewing the ineffectiveness of the system may develop the attitude that nothing but stiffer sentences will work.

intermediate sanctions
A variety of punishments that are more restrictive than traditional probation but less severe and costly than incarceration.

Probation

The most frequently applied criminal sanction is **probation**, a sentence that an offender serves in the community under supervision. Nearly 60 percent of adults under correctional supervision are on probation. Ideally, under probation, offenders attempt to straighten out their lives. Probation is a judicial act, granted by the grace of the state, not extended as a right. The judge imposes conditions specifying how an offender will behave through the length of the sentence. Probationers may be ordered to undergo regular drug tests, abide by curfews, enroll in educational programs or remain employed, stay away from certain parts of town or certain people, and meet regularly with probation officers. If the conditions of probation are not met, the supervising officer recommends to the court that the probation be revoked and that the remainder of the sentence be served in prison. Probation may also be revoked for commission of a new crime.

Although probationers serve their sentences in the community, the sanction is often tied to incarceration. In some jurisdictions, the court is authorized to modify an offender's prison sentence, after a portion is served, by changing it to probation. This is often referred to as **shock probation** (or split probation): An offender is released after a period of incarceration (the "shock") and resentenced to probation. An offender on probation may be required to spend intermittent periods, such as weekends or nights, in jail. Whatever its specific

probation
A sentence that the offender is allowed to serve under supervision in the community.

shock probation
A sentence in which the offender is released after a short incarceration and resentenced to probation.

terms, a probationary sentence will emphasize guidance and supervision in the community.

Probation is generally advocated as a way of rehabilitating offenders whose crimes are not serious or whose past records are clean. It is viewed as less expensive than imprisonment, and more effective. For example, imprisonment may embitter youthful or first-time offenders and mix them with hardened criminals so that they learn more-sophisticated criminal techniques.

Death

Although other Western democracies abolished the death penalty years ago, the United States continues to use it (Steiker and Steiker, 2006). Capital punishment was imposed and carried out regularly prior to the late 1960s. Amid debates about the constitutionality of the death penalty and with public opinion polls showing opposition to it, the U.S. Supreme Court suspended its use from 1968 to 1976. Eventually the Court decided that capital punishment does not violate the Eighth Amendment's prohibition of cruel and unusual punishments. Executions resumed in 1977 as a majority of states began, once again, to sentence murderers to death.

The numbers of people facing the death penalty increased dramatically from the late 1970s to the early 1990s and then stabilized. As you can see from Figure 12.3, 3,263 people awaited execution in the 36 death penalty states in 2007. The numbers decreased slightly in 2003 when the governor of Illinois commuted the sentences of 167 condemned death row prisoners after it was discovered that flaws in that state's legal processes had led at least a dozen inno-

FIGURE 12.3

People under sentence of death and people executed, 1953–2007

In recent years, 125 or more new offenders have been added to death row each year, but the number of executions has never exceeded 98. What explains this fact?

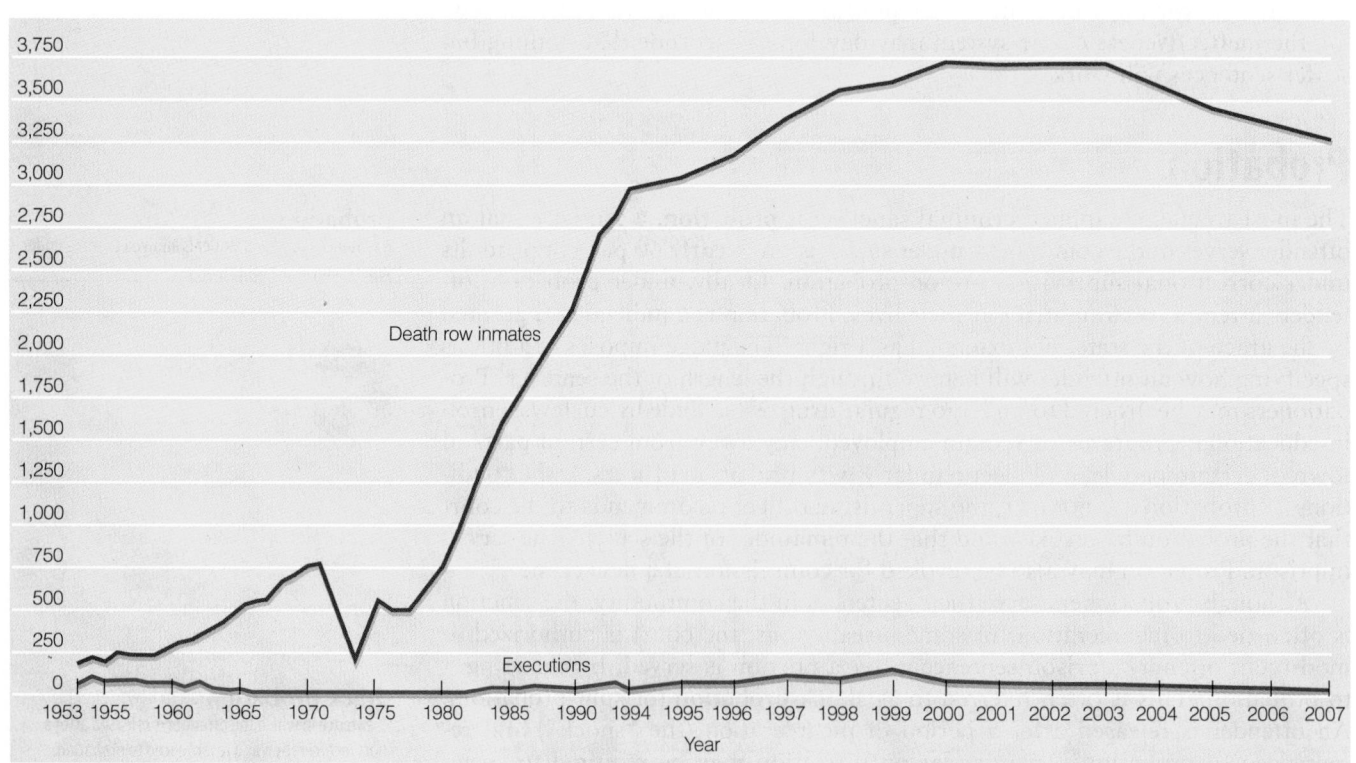

Source: Death Penalty Information Center, *Facts About the Death Penalty*, June 1, 2008 (http://www.deathpenaltyinfo.org).

cent people to be sentenced to death (Flock, 2003). The commutations changed those sentences from death to life in prison.

Although California is the state with the most offenders sentenced to death, two-thirds of those on death row are in the South, with the greatest number of southern condemned prisoners in Florida, Texas, and Alabama (see Figure 12.4). In 1998, 306 people nationwide received death sentences. The number of people added to death row subsequently declined for nine consecutive years, with only 115 sentenced to death in 2006 and 110 in 2007 (Death Penalty Information Center, 2008). Many observers believe that the public has become less support-ive of the death penalty and that juries are more reluctant to impose death sen-tences (Feuer, 2008). Observers further think that this development stems from the publicity each year surrounding the discovery of innocent people on death row by journalists, students, and lawyers reexamining such cases (Sarat, 2005). Twelve innocent people were released from death row in 2003, with another six released in 2004 (Death Penalty Information Center, 2005).

FIGURE 12.4
Death row census, 2007

Many of the inmates on death row are concentrated in certain states. African Americans make up about 13 percent of the U.S. population yet make up 42 percent of the death row population. How might you explain this higher percentage of death sentences in proportion to the population?

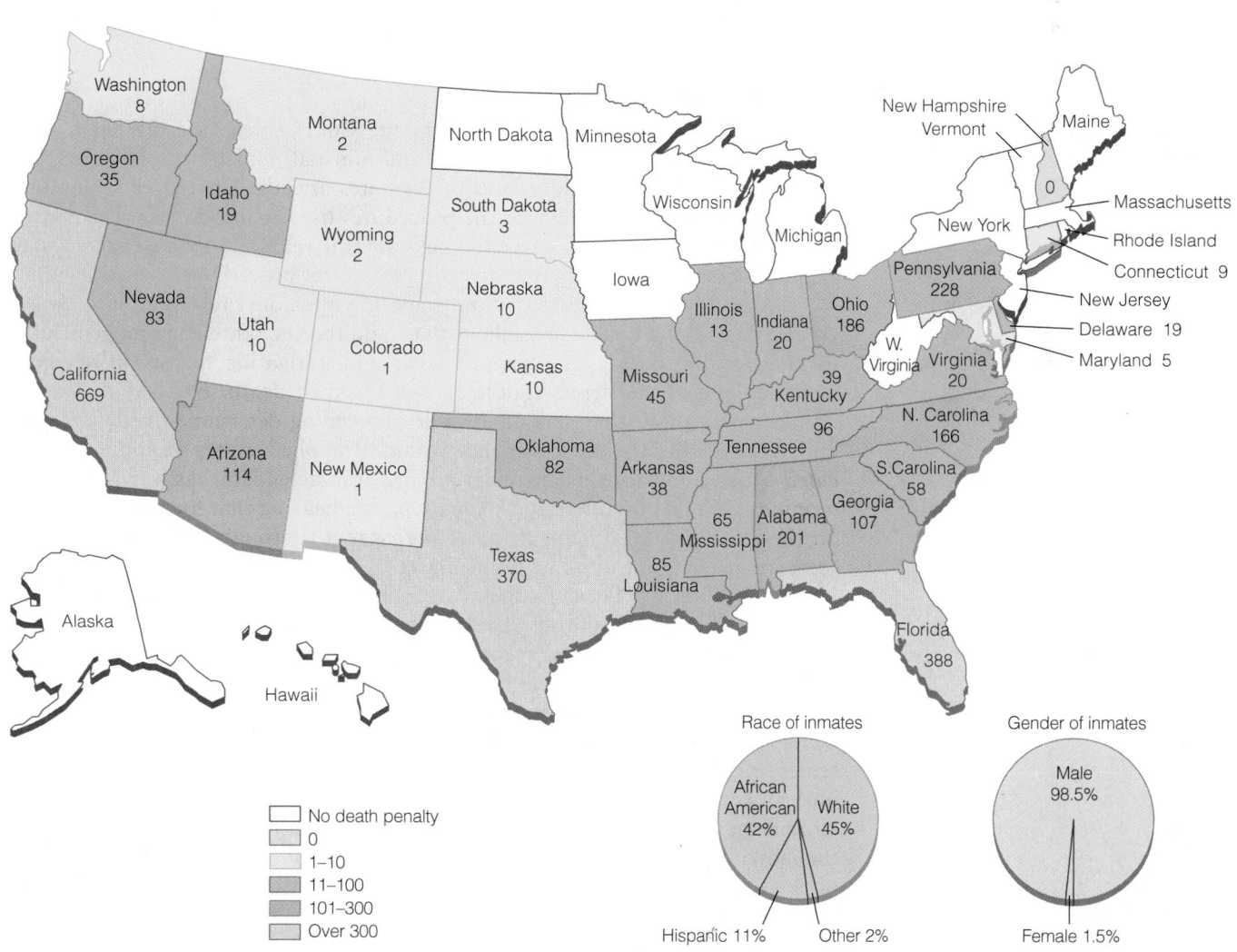

Source: Death Penalty Information Center, *Facts About the Death Penalty*, June 1, 2008 (http://www.deathpenaltyinfo.org).

Articles and information that favor the use of the death penalty can be found online. To link to this website, go to *The American System of Criminal Justice* 12e companion site at academic.cengage.com/criminaljustice/cole.

Despite the number of people currently on death row and the number sentenced to death each year, since 1977 no more than 98 people have been executed in a single year. That number of executions occurred in 1999. Since that time, the number of executions has dropped dramatically. In 2004, for example, only 59 executions took place nationwide. The numbers have subsequently dropped even more with only 53 executions in 2006 and 42 executions in 2007 (Death Penalty Information Center, 2008). This decline is usually attributed to a softening of support for capital punishment among the American public—a trend that appears related to recognition of the risks and flaws that lead to the conviction of innocent (Unnever and Cullen, 2005).

The Death Penalty and the Constitution

Death differs from other punishments in that it is final and irreversible. The Supreme Court has therefore examined the decision-making process in capital cases to ensure that it fulfills the Constitution's requirements regarding due process, equal protection, and cruel and unusual punishment. The Court finds that punishments violate the Eighth Amendment's cruel and unusual punishments clause when they clash with "the evolving standards of decency that mark the progress of a maturing society" (*Trop v. Dulles*, 1958). Because life is in the balance, capital cases must be conducted according to higher standards of fairness and more-careful procedures than are other kinds of cases. Several important Supreme Court cases illustrate this concern.

Key Supreme Court Decisions

Furman v. Georgia (1972)
The death penalty, as administered, constitutes cruel and unusual punishment.

In *Furman v. Georgia* (1972), the Supreme Court ruled that the death penalty, as administered, constituted cruel and unusual punishment. The decision invalidated the death penalty laws of 39 states and the District of Columbia. A majority of justices found that the procedures used to impose death sentences were arbitrary and unfair. Over the next several years, 35 states enacted new capital punishment statutes that provided for better procedures.

The new laws were tested before the Supreme Court in *Gregg v. Georgia* (1976). The Court upheld those laws that required the sentencing judge or jury to take into account specific aggravating and mitigating factors in deciding which convicted murderers should be sentenced to death. Further, the Court decided that, rather than having a single proceeding determine the defendant's guilt and whether the death sentence would be applied, states should use *bifurcated proceedings*. In this two-part process, the defendant has a trial that determines guilt or innocence and then a separate hearing that focuses exclusively on the issue of punishment. It seeks to ensure a thorough deliberation before someone receives the ultimate punishment.

Under the *Gregg* decision, the prosecution uses the punishment-phase hearing to focus attention on the existence of aggravating factors, such as excessive cruelty or a defendant's prior record of violent crimes. The defense may focus on mitigating factors, such as the offender's youthfulness, mental condition, or lack of a criminal record (Kremling et al., 2007). These aggravating and mitigating factors must be weighed before the judge or jury can decide to impose a death sentence. The Supreme Court has ruled that the defendant may not be brought into court for this second hearing wearing chains and shackles. Such visible restraints may influence the jury to favor the death penalty in that they might make the individual seem exceptionally dangerous (*Deck v. Missouri*, 2005). Because of the Court's emphasis on fair procedures and individualized decisions, state appellate courts review trial court procedures in virtually every capital case.

McCleskey v. Kemp (1987)
Rejects a challenge to Georgia's death penalty that was made on the grounds of racial discrimination.

In *McCleskey v. Kemp* (1987), opponents of the death penalty felt that the U.S. Supreme Court dealt a fatal blow to their movement. In this case, the Court rejected a challenge to Georgia's death penalty law, made on the grounds of racial discrimination. Warren McCleskey, an African American, was sentenced to death for killing a white police officer. Before the U.S. Supreme Court, McCleskey's attorney cited research that showed a disparity in the imposition of the death penalty in Georgia, based on the race of the victim and, to a lesser extent, the race of the defendant. Researchers had examined more than two thousand Georgia murder cases and found that defendants charged with killing whites had received the death penalty 11 times more often than had those convicted of killing African Americans. At that time, although 60 percent of homicide victims in Georgia were African Americans, all seven people put to death in that state since 1976 had been convicted of killing white people, and six of the seven murderers were African Americans (Baldus, Woodworth, and Pulaski, 1994).

By a 5–4 vote, the justices rejected McCleskey's assertion that Georgia's capital sentencing practices violated the equal protection clause of the Constitution by producing racial discrimination. The slim majority of justices declared that McCleskey would have to prove that the decision makers acted with a discriminatory purpose in deciding his particular case. The Court also concluded that statistical evidence showing discrimination throughout the Georgia courts did not provide adequate proof. McCleskey was executed in 1991. The decision made it very difficult to prove the existence of racial discrimination in capital cases, but it did not alleviate continuing concerns that death penalty cases can be infected with racial bias (Walker, 2006).

In June 2002, the Supreme Court broke new ground in a way that heartened opponents of the death penalty. In ***Atkins v. Virginia*** (2003) it ruled that execution of the mentally retarded was unconstitutional. Daryl Atkins, who has an IQ of 59, was sentenced to death for killing Eric Nesbitt in a 7-Eleven store parking lot. Lower courts had upheld Atkins's sentence based on *Penry v. Lynaugh* (1989), in which the Supreme Court had upheld execution of the retarded. In that decision it noted that only two states prohibited the death penalty in such cases.

Atkins v. Virginia (2002)
Execution of the mentally retarded is unconstitutional.

Justice John Paul Stevens, writing for the *Atkins* majority, noted that since 1989 there had been a "dramatic shift in the state legislative landscape" and a national consensus had emerged rejecting execution of the retarded. He pointed out that of the 38 death penalty states, the number prohibiting such executions has gone from 2 to 18. The dissenters, Chief Justice Rehnquist and Justices Scalia and Thomas, disputed that there was a real or lasting consensus against executing the retarded. In the absence of an authentic consensus, Justice Scalia said that the majority had merely imposed their own views as constitutional law.

As the majority opinion noted, the characteristics of mentally retarded offenders, people with IQs of less than 70, "undermine the strength of the procedural protections." This point is in keeping with the argument of mental health experts who say their suggestibility and willingness to please leads retarded people to confess. At trial they have problems remembering details, locating witnesses, and testifying credibly in their own behalf.

Three years later the Supreme Court further limited the application of capital punishment. In ***Roper v. Simmons*** (2005), a five-member majority on the Court declared that the execution of individuals who committed murders as juveniles violates the contemporary societal standards of the Eighth Amendment (Bradley, 2006). Previously, the Supreme Court had said that offenders could only be executed for crimes that they committed at age 16 or older (*Stanford v. Kentucky*, 1989). At the time of the decision, the United States was the lone democracy among the handful of countries that permitted the execution of juvenile offenders (Blecker, 2006). Justice Anthony Kennedy's majority opinion claimed that society had moved away from permitting such executions. He noted that 30 states had forbidden the imposition of the death penalty on anyone under the age of 18 and that during the preceding decade only three states had actually

Roper v. Simmons (2005)
Execution of offenders for murders committed before they were 18 years of age is unconstitutional.

executed anyone for crimes committed as juveniles. In dissent, Justice Scalia, on behalf of Chief Justice Rehnquist and Justice Thomas, again asserted that the Court was imposing its own views on society. Justice O'Connor, in a separate dissent, argued that the death penalty may be appropriate for some 17-year-old killers, depending on the maturity of the offender and the circumstances of the crime.

Ring v. Arizona (2002)
Juries, rather than judges, must make the crucial factual decisions regarding whether a convicted murderer should receive the death penalty.

In *Ring v. Arizona* (2002), the Supreme Court ruled that juries, rather than judges, must make the crucial factual decisions regarding whether a convicted murderer should receive the death penalty. The *Ring* decision overturned the law in five states—Arizona, Colorado, Idaho, Montana, and Nebraska—where judges alone had decided whether there were aggravating factors that warrant capital punishment. The decision also raised questions about the procedure in four other states Alabama, Delaware, Florida, and Indiana where the judge chose between life imprisonment or death after hearing a jury's recommendation. The Court's opinion also says that any aggravating factors must be stated in the indictment, thus also requiring a change in federal death penalty laws.

The decision results from the implications of the Court's decision in *Apprendi v. New Jersey* (2000). The Court said that any factor that led to a higher sentence than the statutory maximum must be charged in the indictment and found beyond a reasonable doubt by the jury. In the 7-to-2 majority opinion in *Ring v. Arizona*, Justice Ruth Bader Ginsburg wrote that in view of the *Apprendi* ruling, the right to a jury trial "would be senselessly diminished if it encompassed the fact-finding necessary to increase a defendant's sentence by two years, but not the fact-finding necessary to put him to death."

By 2004 all capital punishment states except Nebraska had authorized the use of lethal injection as the preferred method of execution. However, lethal injection faced close scrutiny and potential challenges from lawyers for condemned offenders. Botched executions occurred, in which needles have popped out of offenders' arms during executions or technicians have misapplied the drugs. Although lethal injection was intended to kill offenders by peacefully rendering them unconscious as they die, the reality can be quite different. For example, during one execution witnessed and described by a journalist, the condemned man continued to gasp and violently gag until death came, some eleven minutes after the drugs were administered (Radelet, 2004).

Baze v. Rees (2008)
Lethal injection has not been shown to violate the Eighth Amendment prohibition on cruel and unusual punishments and thus this method of execution is permissible.

In 2008, the U.S. Supreme Court examined a claim that the use of lethal injection produces unconstitutional "cruel and unusual punishment." By a 7-to-2 vote in *Baze v. Rees* (2008), the justices concluded that the attorneys for the death row inmates had not proven that the use of lethal injection violates the Eighth Amendment. In a separate opinion, Justice John Paul Stevens announced that he had concluded, after more than 30 years on the Supreme Court, that "the death penalty represents 'the pointless and needless extinction of life . . .' [that] is patently excessive and cruel and unusual punishment violative of the Eighth Amendment." By announcing his conclusion that the death penalty itself is unconstitutional, Stevens joined three departed justices—Justice William Brennan, Justice Thurgood Marshall, and Justice Harry Blackmun—who reached the same conclusion in earlier decades but never persuaded a majority of their colleagues to accept their conclusion. Although other opinions indicate that contemporary Justices Ruth Bader Ginsburg, David Souter, and Stephen Breyer may be sympathetic to the view announced by Stevens, it is uncertain if they will find a fifth vote to create a majority on the nine-member court in order to rule that capital punishment is unconstitutional. The future of the death penalty's treatment by the Supreme Court will depend on such factors as which candidate is elected to be president of the United States in November 2008, which justices leave the Court in the near future, and the views of new justices appointed by future presidents. Because Justice Stevens celebrated his 88th birthday in 2008, it is unlikely that he will serve for many more terms.

Continuing Legal Issues

The case law since *Furman* indicates that capital punishment is legal as long as it is imposed fairly. However, opponents argue that certain classes of death row inmates should not be executed, because they are insane, did not have effective counsel, or were convicted by a death-qualified jury. Other issues exist concerning the length of appeals and American compliance with international law.

Execution of the Insane As we have seen, insanity is a recognized defense for commission of a crime. But should people who become mentally disabled after they are sentenced be executed? The Supreme Court responded to this question in 1986 in *Ford v. Wainwright*. In 1974, Alvin Ford was convicted of murder and sentenced to death. Only after he was incarcerated did he begin to exhibit delusional behavior.

Justice Thurgood Marshall, writing for the majority, concluded that the Eighth Amendment prohibited the state from executing the insane—the accused must comprehend both the fact that he had been sentenced to death and the reason for it. Marshall cited the common-law precedent that questioned the retributive and deterrent value of executing a mentally disabled person.

Critics have also raised questions about the morality of treating an offender's mental illness so that he or she can be executed, a policy opposed by the American Medical Association. The Supreme Court has not directly addressed this issue with regard to death row inmates.

Execution for Child Rape Because of the heinous nature of the crime, several states have sought to enact laws permitting use of the death penalty for adults who rape children, even when the children are not murdered. Since the 1970s, capital punishment has been used exclusively for homicide offenses so the use of the ultimate punishment for a sex crime would represent an expansion of the death penalty. In 2008, by a narrow 5-to-4 vote the Supreme Court struck down Louisiana's law applying the death penalty to adults who rape children (*Kennedy v. Louisiana*, 2008). The vote in the case was so close that many observers believe that changes in the Court's composition could lead to a reversal on this issue.

Effective Counsel The effective performance of the defense attorney can be a key factor in determining whether a defendant is sentenced to death (Brewer, 2005). In *Strickland v. Washington* (1984), the Supreme Court ruled that defendants in capital cases had the right to representation that meets an "objective standard of reasonableness." As noted by Justice Sandra Day O'Connor, the appellant must show "that there is a reasonable probability that, but for the counsel's unprofessional errors, the result of the proceeding would be different."

David Washington was charged with three counts of capital murder, robbery, kidnapping, and other felonies, and an experienced criminal lawyer was appointed as counsel. Against his attorney's advice, Washington confessed to two murders, waived a jury trial, pleaded guilty to all charges, and chose to be sentenced by the trial judge. Believing the situation was hopeless, his counsel did not adequately prepare for the sentencing hearing. On being sentenced to death, Washington appealed. The Supreme Court, however, rejected Washington's claim that his attorney was ineffective because he did not call witnesses, seek a presentence investigation report, or cross-examine medical experts on the defendant's behalf. In other words, although his lawyer did not do as good a job as he wanted, Washington nonetheless received a fair trial.

In recent years the public has learned of cases where the defense attorney has seemed incompetent, even to the point of sleeping at trial. In 1999 the *Chicago Tribune* conducted an extensive investigation of capital punishment in Illinois.

Go to the Cornell Law School website to see examples of U.S. Supreme Court cases addressing a variety of death penalty issues. To link to this website, go to *The American System of Criminal Justice* 12e companion site at academic.cengage.com/criminaljustice/cole.

Reporters found that 33 defendants sentenced to death since 1977 were represented by an attorney who had been, or was later, disbarred or suspended for conduct that was "incompetent, unethical, or even criminal." These attorneys included David Landau, who was disbarred one year after representing a Will County defendant sentenced to death, and Robert McDonnell, a convicted felon and the only lawyer in Illinois to be disbarred twice. McDonnell had represented four men who landed on death row (K. Armstrong and Mills, 1999: 1).

In March 2000 a federal judge overturned the conviction of Calvin Jerold Burdine after 16 years on death row. At his 1984 trial, Burdine's defense attorney slept through long portions of the proceedings. As the judge said, "Sleeping counsel is equivalent to no counsel at all" (*New York Times*, March 2, 2000: A19).

These highly publicized cases may have caught the attention of the Supreme Court. In 2003 the Court issued a decision that seemed designed to remind lawyers and judges about the need for competent defense attorneys in capital cases. In *Wiggins v. Smith* (2003), the Court found that the Sixth Amendment right to counsel was violated when a defense attorney failed to present mitigating evidence concerning the severe physical and sexual abuse suffered by the defendant during childhood. It remains to be seen whether the justices create clearer or stricter standards for defense attorneys.

Death-Qualified Juries Should people who are opposed to the death penalty be excluded from juries in capital cases? In *Witherspoon v. Illinois* (1968), the Supreme Court held that potential jurors who have general objections to the death penalty or whose religious convictions oppose its use cannot be automatically excluded from jury service in capital cases. However, it upheld the practice of removing, during *voir dire* (preliminary examination), those people whose opposition is so strong as to "prevent or substantially impair the performance of their duties." Such jurors have become known as "Witherspoon excludables." The decision was later reaffirmed in *Lockhart v. McCree* (1986).

Witherspoon v. Illinois (1968)
Potential jurors who object to the death penalty cannot be automatically excluded from service; however, during voir dire those who feel so strongly about capital punishment that they could not give an impartial verdict may be excluded.

Because society is divided on capital punishment, opponents argue that death-qualified juries do not represent a cross-section of the community. Researchers have also found that juries are likely to be nudged toward believing the defendant is guilty and toward an imposition of the death sentence by the very process of undergoing death qualification (Luginbuhl and Burkhead, 1994: 107).

Mark Costanzo points to research that indicates that death qualification has several impacts. First, those who are selected for jury duty are more conviction prone and more receptive to aggravating factors presented during the penalty phase. A second, subtler impact is that jurors answering the questions about their willingness to vote for a death sentence often conclude that both defenders and prosecutors anticipate a conviction and a death sentence (Costanzo, 1997: 24–25). Think about these arguments as you read "Civic Engagement: Your Role in the System."

civic engagement
your role in the system

Imagine that you have been called to serve as a potential juror in a murder trial in which the prosecution is seeking the death penalty. During pretrial questioning, the prosecutor asks if you would have discomfort in applying the death penalty in any situations. *Make a list of situations in which you might be hesitant to apply the death penalty— consider such things as a lack of physical evidence, a lack of witnesses, two witnesses identifying two completely different people as the alleged murderer, and other situations in which the evidence may not be 100 percent certain.* Then read about Juror Z in the Supreme Court's opinion in *Uttecht v. Brown* (2007). Should Juror Z have been excluded from the jury? To link to this website, go to *The American System of Criminal Justice* 12e companion site at academic.cengage.com/criminaljustice/cole.

Appeals The long appeals process for death penalty cases remains a source of ongoing controversy (Dickson, 2006). The 65 prisoners executed in 2003 were under sentence of death an average of 10 years and 11 months (Bonczar and Snell, 2004). During this waiting period, the state courts review the sentences, as do the federal courts through the writ of habeas corpus.

The late Chief Justice William Rehnquist actively sought to reduce the opportunities for capital punishment defendants to have their appeals heard by multiple courts. In 1996, President Bill Clinton signed the Anti-Terrorism and Effective Death Penalty Act that requires death row inmates to file habeas appeals within one year and requires federal judges to issue their decisions within strict time limits.

Appellate review is a time-consuming and expensive process, but it also makes an impact. From 1977 through 2003, 7,061 people entered prison under sentence of death. During those 26 years, 885 people were executed, 282 died of natural causes, and 2,542 were removed from death row as a result of appellate court decisions and reviews, commutations, or death while awaiting execution (Bonczar and Snell, 2004).

Michael Radelet and his colleagues have examined the cases of 68 death row inmates later released because of doubts about their guilt (Radelet, Lofquist, and Bedau, 1996: 907). This number is equivalent to one-fifth of the inmates executed during the period 1970–1996. Correction of the miscarriage of justice for about one-third of the defendants took four or less years, but it took nine years or longer for another third of the defendants. Had the expedited appeals process and limitations on habeas corpus been in effect at that time, would these erroneous death sentences have been overturned?

International Law The United States is a signatory of the Vienna Convention on Consular Relations, which requires notification of consular officials when a foreign national is arrested. This aspect of international law benefits Americans who are arrested abroad, by enabling the U.S. embassy to help find a lawyer and monitor the prosecution of Americans who face criminal punishment in foreign countries. However, individual prosecutors and police throughout the United States are apparently unaware of the law, because several dozen foreign nationals have been convicted and sentenced to death in the United States without their consular officials being informed. Mexico, Germany, and Paraguay filed complaints against the United States for violating the Vienna Convention in death penalty cases.

Because of this violation of international law, the International Court of Justice in the Hague, Netherlands, ordered the United States in April 2004 to review the death sentences of Mexicans held on American death rows. Although the International Court has no power to force the United States to take action, President George W. Bush announced in February 2005 that the United States will comply with the Vienna Convention in the future. President Bush does not, however, have any means to insure that each county prosecutor throughout the United States follows the Vienna Convention. In light of President Bush's announcement, the Supreme Court decided not to rule in a pending case brought to it by a Mexican citizen on death row in Texas (*Medellin v. Dretke*, 2005). Instead, the majority of justices decided to wait and see how the Texas courts would handle the issue.

The Texas courts subsequently rejected the notion that the treaty was superior to state law and procedure. They also refused to follow President Bush's order to follow the Vienna Convention. When the case returned to the U.S. Supreme Court in 2008, a majority of justices concluded that the president lacked the power to order the states to follow the treaty (*Medellin v. Texas*, 2008). It remains to be seen whether additional issues and arguments based on international law will arise concerning the death penalty.

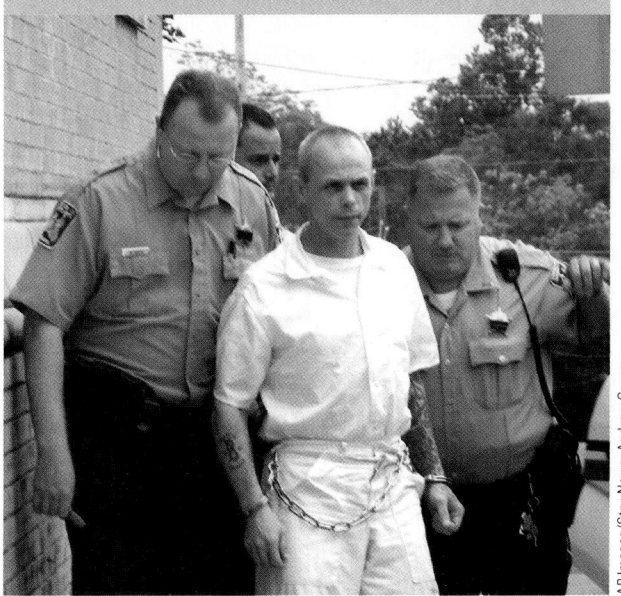

Bobby O'Lee Phillips is escorted by deputies outside the Covington County Courthouse in Alabama after being sentenced to death for committing a murder after he had escaped from jail. Why might a jury or judge believe that capital punishment is appropriate in this case?

AP Images/Star-News, Andrew Garner

The Death Penalty: A Continuing Controversy

Various developments in the twenty-first century appear to indicate a weakening of support for capital punishment in the United States. On January 13, 2000, Governor George Ryan

NEW DIRECTIONS in CRIMINAL JUSTICE POLICY

Should the Death Penalty Be Abolished?

THE APPLICABILITY OF the death penalty has diminished in the twenty-first century. The execution moratorium imposed by Illinois Governor George Ryan in January 2000 reinvigorated debate on the death penalty. His announcement was soon followed by a national poll that found support for the penalty to be the lowest in 19 years, the release of a national study of appeals that found two-thirds of death penalty cases are flawed and overturned by higher courts, and research questioning the quality of counsel given to many defendants. Subsequently, the U.S. Supreme Court reduced the applicability of capital punishment by excluding the mentally retarded and juveniles from executions. In 2007, the New Jersey legislature and governor approved legislation to end capital punishment in that state.

Opponents of capital punishment continue the fight to abolish it. They argue that poor people and minorities receive a disproportionate number of death sentences. They also believe that executing people who are teenage, insane, or mentally retarded is barbaric.

Even the proponents of capital punishment remain dissatisfied with how it is applied. They point to the fact that although more than 3,200 convicted murderers wait on death row, the number of executions since 1976 has never exceeded 98 per year and has declined through the first years of the twenty-first century. The appeals process is a major factor halting this pace, given that it can delay executions for years.

For the Death Penalty

Supporters argue that society should apply swift, severe punishments to killers to address the continuing problems of crime and violence. Execution should occur quite soon after conviction so that the greatest deterrent value will result. They say that justice requires that a person who murders another must be executed. To do less is to denigrate the value of human life.

The arguments for the death penalty include the following:

- The death penalty deters criminals from committing violent acts.
- The death penalty achieves justice by paying killers back for their horrible crimes.

- The death penalty prevents criminals from doing further harm while on parole.
- The death penalty is less expensive than holding murderers in prison for life.

Against the Death Penalty

Opponents believe that the death penalty lingers as a barbaric practice from a less civilized age. They point out that most other developed democracies in the world have ceased to execute criminals. Opponents challenge the death penalty's claims for effectiveness in reducing crime. They also raise concerns about whether the punishment can be applied without errors and discrimination.

The arguments against the death penalty include these:

- No hard evidence proves that the death penalty is a deterrent.
- It is wrong for a government to participate in the intentional killing of citizens.
- The death penalty is applied in a discriminatory fashion.
- Innocent people have been sentenced to death.
- Some methods of execution are inhumane, causing painful, lingering deaths.

What Should U.S. Policy Be?

With more and more people now being sentenced to death row but fewer than 70 individuals executed each year, death penalty policy faces a significant crossroads. Will the United States increase the pace of executions, allow the number of capital offenders in prison to keep growing, or increasingly emphasize sentences of life imprisonment without parole for convicted murderers?

Researching the Internet

 There is much information about the death penalty on the Internet. Compare the perspectives presented at the websites of Pro-Death Penalty and the Death Penalty Information Center. To link to these websites, go to *The American System of Criminal Justice* 12e companion site at academic.cengage.com/criminaljustice/cole.

---

of Illinois, a longtime supporter of the death penalty, called for a moratorium on executions in his state. Ryan said that he was convinced that the death penalty in Illinois was fraught with errors, noting that since 1976, Illinois had executed 12 people yet freed 13 from death row as innocent. Similar calls followed from Kansas Governor Bill Graves, Maryland Governor Paris Glendening, the Louisiana Bar Association, and the Philadelphia City Council. In May 2000 the New Hampshire legislature became the first in more than two decades to vote to repeal the death penalty; however, the governor vetoed the bill. In January 2003, Governor Ryan pardoned four death row inmates and commuted the sentences of 167 to life imprisonment without parole. New York's capital punishment law was declared unconstitutional by its own state courts in 2004. The

New Jersey state legislature and governor eliminated the death penalty in that state in 2007.

Although public opinion polls show that many Americans support the death penalty and more than 100 new death sentences are imposed each year, the number of executions remains low. Recent surveys show the public is divided when respondents are asked to choose between life imprisonment (without parole) and death. As indicated in "What Americans Think," one source of division is conflicting views about whether capital punishment is applied fairly (Saad, 2007). In addition, 2006 was the first year since the beginning this particular survey in 1985 that more Americans favored a sentence of life without parole for murder rather than the death penalty. Does this mean that Americans are ambivalent about carrying out the punishment? What might it say about capital punishment in the next decade? Debate on this important public policy issue has gone on for more than two hundred years, yet there is still no consensus (Unnever, Cullen, and Bartkowski, 2006) (see "New Directions in Criminal Justice Policy").

Both Illinois and Massachusetts appointed commissions to study whether and how death penalty cases could be processed fairly and with little risk that an innocent person would be erroneously convicted. The recommendations from commissions in both states included providing high-quality representation for defendants; using scientific evidence, such as DNA testing, when appropriate; and implementing careful appeals processes. Then Governor Mitt Romney of Massachusetts sought to use his commission report as the basis for proposing the limited use of capital punishment in a state that currently does not use the death penalty.

The criminal sanction takes many forms, and offenders are punished in various ways to serve various purposes. Table 12.2 on page 451 summarizes how these sanctions operate and how they reflect the underlying philosophies of punishment.

WHAT AMERICANS THINK

Question: If you could choose between the following two approaches, which do you think is the better penalty for murder—the death penalty or life imprisonment with absolutely no possibility of parole?

Don't know 5%
Death penalty 47%
Life imprisonment 48%

Source: Gallup Poll, June 1, 2006 (http://www.gallup.com).

 The report of the Massachusetts Governor's Council on Capital Punishment is available online. To link to this website, go to *The American System of Criminal Justice* 12e companion site at academic.cengage.com/criminaljustice/cole.

checkpoint

3. What are the three types of sentences used in the United States?
4. What are thought to be the advantages of intermediate sanctions?
5. What requirements specified in *Gregg v. Georgia* must exist before a death sentence can be imposed?

THE SENTENCING PROCESS

Regardless of how and where the decision has been made—misdemeanor court or felony court, plea bargain or adversarial context, bench or jury trial—judges carry the responsibility for imposing sentences.

Often difficult, sentencing usually involves more than applying clear-cut principles to individual cases. In one case, a judge may decide to sentence a forger to prison as an example to others, even though the offender represents no threat to community safety and probably does not need rehabilitative treatment. In another case, the judge may impose a light sentence on a youthful offender who has committed a serious crime but may be a good risk for rehabilitation if moved quickly back into society. Sentencing requires balancing the scales of justice between a violated society and the fallible but human defendant.

Legislatures establish the penal codes that set forth the sentences judges can impose. These laws generally give judges discretion in sentencing. Judges may combine various forms of punishment in order to tailor the sanction to the

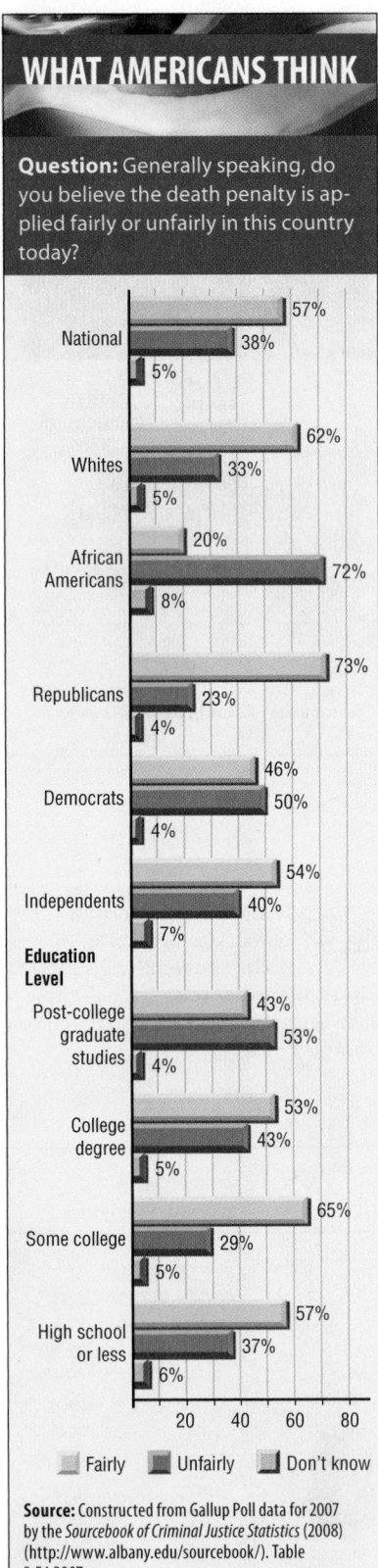

WHAT AMERICANS THINK

Question: Generally speaking, do you believe the death penalty is applied fairly or unfairly in this country today?

National — 57%, 38%, 5%

Whites — 62%, 33%, 5%

African Americans — 20%, 72%, 8%

Republicans — 73%, 23%, 4%

Democrats — 46%, 50%, 4%

Independents — 54%, 40%, 7%

Education Level

Post-college graduate studies — 43%, 53%, 4%

College degree — 53%, 43%, 5%

Some college — 65%, 29%, 5%

High school or less — 57%, 37%, 6%

20 40 60 80

■ Fairly ■ Unfairly ■ Don't know

Source: Constructed from Gallup Poll data for 2007 by the *Sourcebook of Criminal Justice Statistics* (2008) (http://www.albany.edu/sourcebook/). Table 2.54.2007.

offender. The judge may specify, for example, that the prison terms for two charges are to run either concurrently (at the same time) or consecutively (one after the other), or that all or part of the period of imprisonment may be suspended. In other situations, the offender may be given a combination of a suspended prison term, probation, and a fine. The judge may also suspend a sentence as long as the offender stays out of trouble, makes restitution, or seeks medical treatment. Finally, the judge may delay imposing any sentence but retain the power to set penalties at a later date if the offender misbehaves.

Within the discretion allowed by the code, various elements influence the decisions of judges (Johnson, 2006). Social scientists believe that several factors influence the sentencing process: (1) the administrative context of the courts, (2) the attitudes and values of judges, (3) the presentence report, and (4) sentencing guidelines.

The Administrative Context of the Courts

Judges are strongly influenced by the administrative context within which they impose sentences (Johnson, 2005). As a result, differences appear, for example, between the assembly-line style of justice in the misdemeanor courts and the more formal proceedings found in felony courts.

Misdemeanor Courts: Assembly-Line Justice

Misdemeanor or lower courts have limited jurisdiction because they normally can only impose jail sentences of less than one year. These courts hear about 90 percent of criminal cases. Whereas felony cases are processed in lower courts only for arraignments and preliminary hearings, misdemeanor cases are processed completely in the lower courts. Only a minority of cases adjudicated in lower courts end in jail sentences. Most cases result in fines, probation, community service, restitution, or a combination of these punishments.

Because most lower courts are overloaded, they allot minimal time to each case. Judicial decisions are mass-produced because actors in the system share three assumptions. First, any person appearing before the court is guilty, because doubtful cases have presumably been filtered out by the police and prosecution. Second, the vast majority of defendants will plead guilty. Third, those charged with minor offenses will be processed in volume, with dozens of cases being decided in rapid succession within a single hour. The citation will be read by the clerk, a guilty plea entered, and the sentence pronounced by the judge for one defendant after another.

Defendants whose cases are processed through the lower court's assembly line may appear to receive little or no punishment. However, people who get caught in the criminal justice system experience other punishments, whether or not they are ultimately convicted. A person who is arrested, but then released at some point in the process, still incurs various tangible and intangible costs. Time spent in jail awaiting trial, the cost of a bail bond, and days of work lost create an immediate and concrete impact. Poor people may lose their jobs or be evicted from their homes if they fail to work and pay their bills for even a few days. For most people, simply being arrested is a devastating experience. Measuring the psychic and social price of being stigmatized, separated from family, and deprived of freedom is impossible.

Felony Courts

Felony cases are processed and offenders are sentenced in courts of general jurisdiction. Because of the seriousness of the crimes, the atmosphere is more formal and generally lacks the chaotic, assembly-line environment of misdemeanor

TABLE 12.2 The Punishment of Offenders

The goals of the criminal sanction are carried out in a variety of ways, depending upon the provisions of the law, the characteristics of the offender, and the discretion of the judge. Judges may impose sentences that combine several forms to achieve punishment objectives.

Form of Sanction	Description	Purposes
Incarceration	Imprisonment	
Indeterminate sentence	Specifies a maximum and minimum length of time to be served	Incapacitation, deterrence, rehabilitation
Determinate sentence	Specifies a certain length of time to be served	Retribution, deterrence, incapacitation
Mandatory sentence	Specifies a minimum amount of time that must be served for given crimes	Incapacitation, deterrence
Good time	Subtracts days from an inmate's sentence because of good behavior or participation in prison programs	Rewards behavior, relieves prison crowding, helps maintain prison discipline
Intermediate sanctions	Punishment for those requiring sanctions more restrictive than probation but less restrictive than prison	Retribution, deterrence
Administered by the judiciary		
Fine	Money paid to state by offender	Retribution, deterrence
Restitution	Money paid to victim by offender	Retribution, deterrence
Forfeiture	Seizure by the state of property illegally obtained or acquired with resources illegally obtained	Retribution, deterrence
Administered in the community		
Community service	Requires offender to perform work for the community	Retribution, deterrence
Home confinement	Requires offender to stay in home during certain times	Retribution, deterrence, incapacitation
Intensive probation supervision	Requires strict and frequent reporting to probation officer	Retribution, deterrence, incapacitation
Administered institutionally		
Boot camp/shock incarceration	Short-term institutional sentence emphasizing physical development and discipline, followed by probation	Retribution, deterrence, rehabilitation
Probation	Allows offender to serve a sentence in the community under supervision	Retribution, incapacitation, rehabilitation
Death	Execution	Incapacitation, deterrence, retribution

In misdemeanor cases, judges' sentencing decisions may be be influenced by many factors, including the defendant's remorse, the availability of space for new offenders in the county jail, and the defendant's prior record. Here Eric Feltner, a former government official in Missouri, is sentenced to probation and community service for public display of explicit sexual materials. Is it important for judges to impose comparable sentences on offenders who are convicted of the similar crimes?

AP Images/Kelley McCall

TABLE 12.3 Types of Felony Sentences Imposed by State Courts

Although a felony conviction is often equated with a prison sentence, almost a third of felony offenders receive probation.

Most Serious Conviction Offense	Percentage of Felons Sentenced to		
	Prison	Jail	Probation
All offenses	41	28	31
Violent offenses	52	25	23
Murder	91	4	5
Sexual assault	59	23	18
Rape	67	22	11
Other sexual assault	55	23	22
Robbery	71	15	14
Aggravated assault	42	29	29
Other violent	42	35	23
Property offenses	38	28	34
Burglary	46	26	28
Larceny	36	31	33
Motor vehicle	37	39	24
Fraud	31	28	41
Drug offenses	39	27	34
Possession	34	28	38
Trafficking	42	26	32
Weapons offenses	45	28	27
Other offenses	35	35	30

Note: For persons receiving a combination of sanctions, the sentence designation came from the most severe penalty imposed—prison being the most severe, followed by jail and then probation.
Source: Matthew R. Durose and Patrick A. Langan, "Felony Sentences in State Courts, 2002," *Bureau of Justice Statistics Bulletin*, December 2004, p. 2.

courts. Caseload burdens can affect how much time individual cases receive. Exchange relationships among courtroom actors can facilitate plea bargains and shape the content of prosecutors' sentencing recommendations. Sentencing decisions are ultimately shaped, in part, by the relationships, negotiations, and agreements among the prosecutor, defense attorney, and judge. Table 12.3 shows the types of felony sentences imposed for different kinds of offenses.

Attitudes and Values of Judges

All lawyers recognize that judges differ from one another in their sentencing decisions. Administrative pressures, the influence of community values, and the conflicting goals of criminal justice partly explain these differences. Sentencing decisions also depend on judges' attitudes concerning the offender's blameworthiness, the protection of the community, and the practical implications of the sentence (Steffensmeier and Demuth, 2001).

Blameworthiness concerns such factors as offense severity (such as violent crime or property crime), the offender's criminal history (such as recidivist or first timer), and role in commission of the crime (such as leader or follower). For example, a judge might impose a harsh sentence on a repeat offender who organized others to commit a serious crime.

Similar factors, such as dangerousness, recidivism, and offense severity, influence protection of the community. However, protection focuses mostly on the need to incapacitate the offender or deter would-be offenders.

Finally, the practical implications of a sentence can affect judges' decisions. For example, judges may take into account the offender's ability to "do time," as in the case of an elderly person. They may also consider the impact on the offender's family; a mother with children may receive a different sentence than a single woman would. Finally, costs to the corrections system may play a role in sentencing, as judges consider the number of probation officers or prison crowding (Steffensmeier, Kramer, and Streifel, 1993).

presentence report
A report, prepared by a probation officer, that presents a convicted offender's background and is used by the judge in selecting an appropriate sentence.

Presentence Report

Even though sentencing is the judge's responsibility, the **presentence report** has become an important ingredient in the judicial mix. Usually a probation officer investigates the convicted person's background, criminal record, job status, and mental condition to suggest a sentence that is in the interests of both the offender and society. Although the presentence report serves primarily to help the judge select the sentence, it also assists in the classification of proba-

CLOSE UP

Sample Presentence Report

STATE OF NEW MEXICO
Corrections Department Field Service Division
Santa Fe, New Mexico 87501
Date: January 4, 2008
To: The Honorable Manuel Baca
From: Presentence Unit, Officer Brian Gaines
Re: Richard Knight
Evaluation

APPEARING BEFORE YOUR Honor for sentencing is 20-year-old Richard Knight, who on November 10, 2007, pursuant to a Plea and Disposition Agreement, entered a plea of guilty to Aggravated Assault Upon a Peace Officer (Deadly Weapon) (Firearm Enhancement), as charged in Information Number 95-5736900. The terms of the agreement stipulate that the maximum period of incarceration be limited to one year, that restitution be made on all counts and charges whether dismissed or not, and that all remaining charges in the Indictment and DA Files 39780 be dismissed.

The defendant is an only child, born and raised in Albuquerque. He attended West Mesa High School until the eleventh grade, at which time he dropped out. Richard declared that he felt school was "too difficult" and that he decided that it would be more beneficial for him to obtain steady employment rather than to complete his education. The defendant further stated that he felt it was "too late for vocational training" because of the impending 1-year prison sentence he faces, due to the Firearm Enhancement penalty for his offense.

The longest period of time the defendant has held a job has been for 6 months with Frank's Concrete Company. He has been employed with the Madrid Construction Company since August 2007 (verified). Richard lives with his parents who provide most of his financial support. Conflicts between his mother and himself, the defendant claimed, precipitated his recent lawless actions by causing him to "not care about anything." He stressed the fact that he is now once again "getting along" with his mother. Although the defendant contends that he doesn't abuse drugs, he later contradicted himself by declaring that he "gets drunk every weekend." He noted that he was inebriated when he committed the present offense.

In regard to the present offense, the defendant recalled that other individuals at the party attempted to stab his friend and that he and his companion left and returned with a gun in order to settle the score. Richard claimed remorse for his offense and stated that his past family problems led him to spend most of his time on the streets, where he became more prone to violent conduct. The defendant admitted being a member of the 18th Street Gang.

Recommendation

It is respectfully recommended that the defendant be sentenced to 3 years incarceration and that the sentence be suspended. It is further recommended that the defendant be incarcerated for 1 year as to the mandatory Firearm Enhancement and then placed on 3 years probation under the following special conditions:

1. That restitution be made to Juan Lopez in the amount of $622.40.
2. That the defendant either maintain full-time employment or obtain his GED [general equivalency diploma].
3. That the defendant discontinue fraternizing with the 18th Street Gang members and terminate his own membership in the gang.

Researching the Internet

 The United States Probation Office website is designed to inform the bench and bar of the purposes of the presentence investigation report. To link to this website, go to *The American System of Criminal Justice* 12e companion site at academic.cengage.com/criminaljustice/cole.

---

tioners, prisoners, and parolees for treatment planning and risk assessment. In the report, the probation officer makes judgments about what information to include and what conclusions to draw from that information. In some states, however, probation officers present only factual material to the judge and make no sentencing recommendation. Because the probation officers do not necessarily follow evidentiary rules, they may include hearsay statements as well as firsthand information. The Close Up box gives an example of a presentence report.

Although presentence reports are represented as diagnostic evaluations, critics point out that they are not scientific and often reflect stereotypes. John Rosencrance has argued that in actual practice the presentence report primarily serves to maintain the myth of individualized justice. He found that the present offense and the prior criminal record determine the probation officer's final sentencing recommendation (Rosencrance, 1988). He learned that officers begin by reviewing the case and typing the defendant as one who should fit into a particular sentencing category. They then conduct their investigations in ways that help them gather information to buttress their early decision.

The presentence report is one means by which judges ease the strain of decision making. The report lets judges shift partial responsibility to the probation department. Because they can choose from a substantial number of sentencing alternatives, judges often rely on the report for guidance. "A Question of Ethics" at the end of the chapter illustrates some of the difficulties faced by a judge who must impose a sentence with little more than the presentence report to go on.

Sentencing Guidelines

sentencing guidelines
A mechanism to indicate to judges the expected sanction for certain offenses, in order to reduce disparities in sentencing.

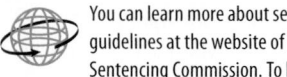
You can learn more about sentencing guidelines at the website of the U.S. Sentencing Commission. To link to this website, go to *The American System of Criminal Justice* 12e companion site at academic.cengage.com/criminaljustice/cole.

Since the 1980s, **sentencing guidelines** have been established in the federal courts and in nearly two dozen state court systems. Such guidelines indicate to judges the expected sanction for particular types of offenses. They are intended to limit the sentencing discretion of judges and to reduce disparity among sentences given for similar offenses (Griffin and Wooldredge, 2006). Although statutes provide a variety of sentencing options for particular crimes, guidelines attempt to direct the judge to more-specific actions that should be taken. The range of sentencing options provided for most offenses is based on the seriousness of the crime and on the criminal history of the offender.

Legislatures—and, in some states and the federal government, commissions—construct sentencing guidelines as a grid of two scores (Tonry, 1993: 140). As shown in Table 12.4, one dimension relates to the seriousness of the offense, and the other to the likelihood of offender recidivism. The offender score is obtained by totaling the points allocated to such factors as the number of juvenile, adult misdemeanor, and adult felony convictions; the number of times incarcerated; the status of the accused at the time of the last offense, whether on probation or parole or escaped from confinement; and employment status or educational achievement. Judges look at the grid to see what sentence a particular offender who has committed a specific offense should receive. Judges may go outside of the guidelines if aggravating or mitigating circumstances exist; however, they must provide a written explanation of their reasons for doing so (J. H. Kramer and Ulmer, 1996).

Sentencing guidelines are to be reviewed and modified periodically in order to include recent decisions. Given that guidelines are constructed on the basis of past sentences, some critics argue that because the guidelines reflect only what has happened, they do not reform sentencing. Others question the choice of characteristics included in the offender scale and charge that some are used to mask racial criteria. However, Lisa Stolzenberg and Steward J. D'Alessio (1994) studied the Minnesota guidelines and found, compared with preguideline decisions, an 18 percent reduction in disparity for the prison/no-prison outcome and a 60 percent reduction in disparity of length of prison sentences.

One impact of guidelines is that sentencing discretion has shifted from the judge to the prosecutor. Prosecutors can choose the charge and plea bargain; therefore, defendants realize that to avoid the harsh sentences specified for some crimes (such as crack cocaine possession or operating a continuing criminal enterprise), they must plead guilty and cooperate. In fact, federal drug laws give prosecutors discretion to ask judges to give sentence reductions for offenders who have "provided substantial assistance in the investigation or prosecution of another person."

Although guidelines make sentences more uniform, many judges object to having their discretion limited in this manner (Weinstein, 1992). However, Peter Rossi and Richard Berk (1997) found a fair amount of agreement between

TABLE 12.4	Minnesota Sentencing Guidelines Grid (presumptive sentence length in months)

The italicized numbers in the grid are the range within which a judge may sentence without the sentence being considered a departure. The criminal history score is computed by adding one point for each prior felony conviction, one-half point for each prior gross misdemeanor conviction, and one-quarter point for each prior misdemeanor conviction.

Severity of Offense (Illustrative Offenses)		Criminal History Score						
		0	1	2	3	4	5	6 or more
Murder, second degree (intentional murder, drive-by shootings)	XI	306 *261–367*	326 *278–391*	346 *295–415*	366 *312–439*	386 *329–463*	406 *346–480[2]*	426 *363–480[2]*
Murder, third degree Murder, second degree (unintentional murder)	X	150 *128–180*	165 *141–198*	180 *153–216*	195 *166–234*	210 *179–252*	225 *192–270*	240 *204–288*
Assault, first degree controlled substance crime, first degree	IX	86 *74–103*	98 *84–117*	110 *94–132*	122 *104–146*	134 *114–160*	146 *125–175*	158 *135–189*
Aggravated robbery, first degree Controlled substance crime, second degree	VIII	48 *41–57*	58 *50–69*	68 *58–81*	78 *67–93*	88 *75–105*	98 *84–117*	108 *92–129*
Felony DWI	VII	36	42	48	54 *46–64*	60 *51–72*	66 *57–79*	72 *62–84[2]*
Controlled substance crime, third degree	VI	21	27	33	39 *34–46*	45 *39–54*	51 *44–61*	57 *49–68*
Residential burglary Simple robbery	V	18	23	28	33 *29–39*	38 *33–45*	43 *37–51*	48 *41–57*
Nonresidential burglary	IV	12	15	18	21	24 *21–28*	27 *23–32*	30 *26–36*
Theft crimes (over $5,000)	III	12	13	15	17	19 *17–22*	21 *18–25*	23 *20–27*
Theft crimes ($5,000 or less) Check forgery ($251–$2,500)	II	12	12	13	15	17	19	21 *18–25*
Sale of simulated controlled substance	I	12	12	12	13	15	17	19 *17–22*

▭ At the discretion of the judge, up to a year in jail and/or other nonjail sanctions can be imposed instead of prison sentences as conditions of probation for most of these offenses. If prison is imposed, the presumptive sentence is the number of months shown.

▭ Presumptive commitment to state prison for all offenses.

Note: First-degree murder has a mandatory life sentence and is excluded from the guidelines by law.
Source: Minnesota Sentencing Guidelines Commission, *Minnesota Sentencing Guidelines and Commentary*, revised August 1, 2008.

the sentences prescribed in the federal guidelines and those desired by the general public.

In 2004 the U.S. Supreme Court decided that aspects of Washington state's sentencing guidelines violated the Sixth Amendment right to trial by jury by giving judges too much authority to enhance sentences based on unproven factual determinations (*Blakely v. Washington*). One year later, the Supreme Court applied the *Blakely* precedent to the federal sentencing guidelines and found a similar violation of the Sixth Amendment when judges enhance sentences based on their own determinations (*United States v. Booker*, 2005). In 2008, the Supreme Court ruled that federal judges are not required to give advance notice to defendants prior to imposing a sentence that is a variance from the sentencing

You can learn more about problems in sentencing, including racial disparities, as well as reform proposals at the website of The Sentencing Project. To link to this website, go to *The American System of Criminal Justice* 12e companion site at academic.cengage.com/criminaljustice/cole.

guidelines (*Irizarry v. United States*, 2008). Observers anticipate that the U.S. Supreme Court must revisit this issue in order to provide guidance about how sentencing guidelines can be properly designed and applied.

checkpoint

6. What are the four factors thought to influence the sentencing behavior of judges?

Who Gets the Harshest Punishment?

Harsh, unjust punishments can occur because of sentencing disparities and wrongful convictions. The prison population in most states contains a higher proportion of African American and Hispanic men than appears in the general population. Are these disparities caused by racial prejudices and discrimination, or are other factors at work? Wrongful conviction occurs when people who are in fact innocent are nonetheless found guilty by plea or verdict. It also includes those cases in which the conviction of a truly guilty person is overturned on appeal because of due process errors. See "New Directions in Criminal Justice Policy" for more on wrongful conviction.

Racial Disparities   *It does happen*

Research on racial disparities in sentencing are inconclusive. Studies of sentencing in Pennsylvania, for example, found that there was a "high cost of being black, young (21–29 years), and male." Sentences given these offenders resulted in a higher proportion going to prison and for longer terms (Steffensmeier, Ulmer, and Kramer, 1998: 789). Although supporting the Pennsylvania results, research in Chicago, Kansas City, Missouri, and Miami found variation among the jurisdictions as to sentence length disparities (Spohn and Holleran, 2000).

Do these disparities stem from the prejudicial attitudes of judges, police officers, and prosecutors? Are African Americans and Hispanics viewed as a "racial threat" when they commit crimes of violence and drug selling, which are thought to be spreading from the urban ghetto to the "previously safe places of the suburbs" (Crawford, Chircos, and Kleck, 1998: 484)? Are enforcement resources distributed so that certain groups face closer scrutiny than faced by other groups?

Scholars have pointed out that the relationship between race and sentencing is complex and that judges consider many defendant and case characteristics. According to this view, judges assess not only the legally relevant factors of blameworthiness, dangerousness, and recidivism risk, but also race, gender, and age characteristics (Steen, Engen, and Gainey, 2005). The interconnectedness of these variables, not judges' negative attitudes, is what culminates in the disproportionately severe sentences given young black men.

Federal sentencing guidelines were adjusted in 2007 and 2008 to address a highly criticized source of racial disparities in prison sentences for offenders convicted of cocaine-related offenses. The federal sentencing guidelines for crack cocaine offenses—which disproportionately affected African American defendants—were adjusted to be more closely aligned with shorter sentences for possessing and selling similar amounts of powder cocaine, crimes more commonly associated with white offenders. The U.S. Sentencing Commission voted to apply these new guidelines retroactively, meaning that offenders currently serving long sentences for crack cocaine offenses were eligible to be resentenced to shorter terms in prisons, which in many cases began to lead to the release of offenders in 2008 who had already served for longer periods than those required under the new sentencing guidelines (Gezari, 2008; The Third Branch, 2008b).

NEW DIRECTIONS in CRIMINAL JUSTICE POLICY

Wrongful Convictions

IN HIS PRESIDENTIAL Address to the American Society of Criminology, C. Ronald Huff explored the problem of wrongful convictions—people who, notwithstanding plea or verdict, are in fact innocent (p. 1). The causes of wrongful convictions include overzealous law enforcement officers and prosecutors, withholding of evidence, false or coerced confessions, perjury, inappropriate use of informants, and ineffective assistance of counsel. The number of wrongful convictions is unknown (Zalman, Smith, and Kiger, 2008). However, if only a 0.5 percent error rate is used, 7,500 people arrested for index crimes were wrongfully convicted in 2000. Huff's policy recommendations include the following:

1. States should enact laws to compensate fairly those who are wrongly convicted.
2. When biological evidence is available for testing, defendants should be able to request and receive such tests. The results should be preserved.
3. When eyewitness identification is involved, the testimony of qualified experts and witnesses should be allowed and judges should give cautionary instructions to juries informing them of the possibility of misidentification.
4. No identification procedure (such as lineups) should be conducted without the presence of counsel for the suspect/accused.
5. Police interrogations of suspects should be recorded in full.
6. Criminal justice officials who engage in unethical or illegal conduct contributing to wrongful conviction should be removed from their position and subjected to appropriate sanctions.
7. Criminal case review commissions should be established to review postappellate claims of wrongful conviction and, when appropriate, refer those cases to the proper courts.

Source: Drawn from C. Ronald Huff, "Wrongful Conviction and Public Policy: The American Society of Criminology 2001 Presidential Address," *Criminology* 40 (2002): 1–18.

Researching the Internet

Read about examples of wrongful convictions and the reasons for errors at the website of Northwestern University's Center on Wrongful Convictions. To link to this website, go to *The American System of Criminal Justice* 12e companion site at academic.cengage.com/criminaljustice/cole.

Wrongful Convictions

A serious dilemma for the criminal justice system concerns people who are falsely convicted and sentenced. Whereas the public expresses much concern over those who "beat the system" and go free, they pay comparatively little attention to those who are innocent, yet convicted. Such cases can be corrected by

© Fort Worth Star-Telegram/MCT /Landov

Thomas McGowan (center) celebrates his release from prison in 2008. After serving over two decades in prison, DNA evidence demonstrated his innocence. One of his lawyers is Barry Scheck (left), a founder of the Innocence Project, which seeks to free wrongly convicted prisoners. How could criminal justice processes be changed to reduce the risks of erroneous convictions?

decisions of the courts or through pardon and clemency decisions by governors (state cases) or the president (federal cases) (Sarat, 2008). But it can be very difficult to achieve correction through either method.

The development of DNA technology has increased the number of people convicted by juries and later exonerated by science. Ronald Huff notes that "because the great majority of cases do not produce biological material to be tested, one can only speculate about the error rate in those cases [without DNA evidence available]" (Huff, 2002: 2). As of June 2008, 218 innocent people had been released from prison after DNA testing excluded them as perpetrators of the rapes and murders for which they had been convicted and imprisoned. Many of these cases are investigated by the Innocence Project at Cardozo Law School in New York City. In May 2008, Levon Jones of North Carolina became the 129th person released from a death sentence since 1973 after a determination that the condemned convict was actually innocent. Many of these exonerations were not based on DNA evidence but rather on the discovery that police and prosecutors had ignored or hidden evidence or that the conviction was based on testimony from an untruthful informant.

Why do wrongful convictions occur? Eyewitness error, unethical conduct by police and prosecutors, community pressure, false accusations, inadequacy of counsel, and plea-bargaining pressures may all contribute to wrongful convictions (Huff, 2002). Beyond the fact that the real criminal presumably remains free in such cases, the standards of our society are damaged when an innocent person has been convicted.

Each year several cases of the conviction of innocent people come to national attention. For example, in Illinois, Northwestern University journalism students uncovered police and prosecution bungling, thus securing the release of four men who had spent nearly 20 years on death row (*New York Times*, March 3, 1999: A1). In 2002, North Carolina and Virginia created commissions to investigate wrongful convictions within those states (Gould, 2004).

Whether from racial discrimination or wrongful convictions, unjust punishments do not serve the ideals of justice. They raise fundamental questions about the criminal justice system and its links to the society it serves.

 Two organizations dedicated to identifying and freeing wrongly convicted prisoners are the Centurion Ministries and the Innocence Project. To link to these websites, go to *The American System of Criminal Justice* 12e companion site at academic.cengage.com/criminaljustice/cole.

A QUESTION OF ETHICS

SEATED IN HER CHAMBERS, Judge Ruth Carroll read the presentence investigation report of the two young men she would sentence when court resumed. She had not heard these cases. As often happens in this overworked courthouse, the cases had been given to her only for sentencing. Judge Harold Krisch had handled the arraignment, plea, and trial.

The co-defendants had held up a convenience store in the early morning hours, terrorizing the young manager and taking $47.50 from the till.

As she read the reports, Judge Carroll noticed that they looked pretty similar. Each offender had dropped out of high school, had held a series of low-wage jobs, and had one prior conviction for which probation was imposed. Each had been convicted of Burglary 1, robbery at night with a gun.

Then she noticed the difference. David Bukowski had pleaded guilty to the charge in exchange for a promise of leniency. Richard Leach had been convicted on the same charge after a one-week trial. Judge Carroll pondered the decisions that she would soon have to make. Should Leach receive a stiffer sentence because he had taken the court's time and resources? Did she have an obligation to impose the light sentence recommended for Bukowski by the prosecutor and the defender?

There was a knock on the door. The bailiff stuck his head in. "Everything's ready, Your Honor."

"Okay, Ben, let's go."

Critical Thinking and Analysis

Write a memo describing how you would determine these sentences. What factors would affect your decision? How would you explain your decision? What would you say to each defendant in your courtroom statement as you announced the sentences?

SUMMARY

Recognize the goals of punishment

- In the United States, the four main goals of the criminal sanction are retribution, deterrence, incapacitation, and rehabilitation.

- Restoration, a new approach to punishment, has not become mainstream yet.

- The goals of the criminal sanction are carried out through incarceration, intermediate sanctions, probation, and death.

Identify the types of sentences that judges can impose

- Penal codes vary as to whether the permitted sentences are indeterminate, determinate, or mandatory. Each type of sentence makes certain assumptions about the goals of the criminal sanction.

- Good time allows correctional administrators to reduce the sentence of prisoners who live according to the rules and participate in various vocational, educational, and treatment programs.

- The U.S. Supreme Court allows capital punishment only when the judge and jury are allowed to take into account mitigating and aggravating circumstances.

- Judges often have considerable discretion in fashioning sentences to take into account factors such as the seriousness of the crime, the offender's prior record, and mitigating and aggravating circumstances.

Understand what really happens in sentencing

- The sentencing process is influenced by the administrative context of the courts, the attitudes and values of the judges, the presentence report, and sentencing guidelines.

Analyze whether the system treats wrongdoers equally

- Many states have formulated sentencing guidelines as a way of reducing disparity among the sentences given offenders in similar situations.

- Harsh, unjust punishments may result from racial discrimination or wrongful convictions.

QUESTIONS FOR REVIEW

1. What are the major differences among retribution, deterrence, incapacitation, and rehabilitation?
2. What is the main purpose of restoration?
3. What are the forms of the criminal sanction?
4. What purposes do intermediate sanctions serve?
5. What has been the Supreme Court's position on the constitutionality of the death penalty?
6. Is there a link between sentences and social class? Between sentences and race?

KEY TERMS AND CASES

determinate sentence (p. 435)
general deterrence (p. 428)
good time (p. 437)
incapacitation (p. 429)
indeterminate sentence (p. 433)
intermediate sanctions (p. 439)
mandatory sentence (p. 436)
presentence report (p. 452)
presumptive sentence (p. 435)
probation (p. 439)
rehabilitation (p. 430)
restoration (p. 430)
retribution (p. 427)
selective incapacitation (p. 429)

sentencing guidelines (p. 454)
shock probation (p. 439)
specific deterrence (p. 428)
Atkins v. Virginia (2002) (p. 443)
Furman v. Georgia (1972) (p. 442)
McCleskey v. Kemp (1987) (p. 442)
Ring v. Arizona (2002) (p. 444)
Roper v. Simmons (2005) (p. 443)
Baze v. Rees (2008) (p. 444)
Witherspoon v. Illinois (1968) (p. 446)

FOR FURTHER READING

Abramsky, Sasha. 2002. *Hard Time Blues: How Politics Built a Prison Nation*. New York: St. Martin's Press. Examines the growth of incarceration in America, through the story of a career criminal with a long history of nonviolent crimes committed to fund his drug habit.

Costanzo, Mark. 1997. *Just Revenge*. New York: St. Martin's Press. Analyzes the costs and consequences of the death penalty. Finds that, when given an option, people give more support for life without parole than for death.

Gaylin, Willard. 1997. *The Killing of Bonnie Garland*. Rev. ed. New York: Simon & Schuster. True story of the murder of a Yale student by her boyfriend and the reaction of the criminal justice system to the crime. Raises important questions about the goals of the criminal sanction and the role of the victim in the process.

Johnson, Robert. 1998. *Death Work*. 2nd ed. Belmont, CA: Wadsworth. A look at those on death row—prisoners and correctional officers—and the impact of capital punishment on their lives.

Scheck, Barry, Peter Neufeld, and Jim Dwyer. 2000. *Actual Innocence*. New York: Doubleday. Describes the harrowing stories of ten men wrongly convicted and the efforts of the Innocence Project to free them.

Tonry, Michael. 1996. *Sentencing Matters*. New York: Oxford University Press. Examination of sentencing reforms over the past quarter century; critiques of the just deserts model, sentencing guidelines, and mandatory penalties.

Zimring, Franklin E., Gordon Hawkins, and Sam Kamin. 2001. *Punishment and Democracy: Three Strikes and You're Out in California*. New York: Oxford University Press. Examines the origins, politics, and impact of the three-strikes law in California.

GOING ONLINE

For an up-to-date list of web links, go to *The American System of Criminal Justice* 12e website: http://academic.cengage.com/criminaljustice/cole.

1. Go to the website of Families Against Mandatory Minimums (FAMM). Click on *The Issue* then read about the history of mandatory sentences and profiles of individuals who are affected. What is the principal characteristic of this type of sentence? What has been its impact according to FAMM?

2. The website of the Death Penalty Information Center contains a wealth of information. At Under the Issues, click the link for Race and examine the data concerning the race of the victim and the race of the offender. Compare intraracial versus interracial punishments (Executions by Race of Victims).

3. Did the Supreme Court make an appropriate decision in *Roper v. Simmons*? Read the majority and dissenting opinions in the case and decide what you think about the issue.

CHECKPOINT ANSWERS

1. *What are the four primary goals of the criminal sanction?*

   Retribution, deterrence, incapacitation, rehabilitation.

2. *What are the difficulties in showing that a punishment acts as a deterrent?*

   It is impossible to show who has been deterred from committing crimes; punishment isn't always certain; people act impulsively rather than rationally; people commit crimes while on drugs.

3. *What are the three types of sentences used in the United States?*

   Determinate, indeterminate, and mandatory sentences.

4. *What are thought to be the advantages of intermediate sanctions?*

   Intermediate sanctions give judges a greater range of sentencing alternatives, reduce prison populations, cost less than prison, and increase community security.

5. *What requirements specified in* Gregg v. Georgia *must exist before a death sentence can be imposed?*

   Judge and jury must be able to consider mitigating and aggravating circumstances, proceedings must be divided into a trial phase and a punishment phase, and there must be opportunities for appeal.

6. *What are the four factors thought to influence the sentencing behavior of judges?*

   The administrative context of the courts, the attitudes and values of judges, the presentence report, and sentencing guidelines.

PART FOUR

Corrections

© Patti McConville/Getty Images/The Image Bank

Throughout history the debate has continued about the most appropriate and effective ways to punish lawbreakers. Over time the corrections system has risen to peaks of excited reform, only to drop to valleys of despairing failure. In Part 4, we examine how the American system of criminal justice now deals with offenders. The process of corrections is intended to penalize the individual found guilty, to impress upon others that violators of the law will be punished, to protect the community, and to rehabilitate and reintegrate the offender into law-abiding society.

Chapters 13 through 16 will discuss how various influences have structured the U.S. corrections system and how offenders are punished.

As these chapters unfold, recall the processes that have occurred before the sentence was imposed and how they are linked to the ways offenders are punished in the correctional portion of the criminal justice system.

CHAPTER 13

Corrections

LEARNING OBJECTIVES

→ Understand how the American system of corrections has developed

→ Understand the roles federal, state, and local governments play in corrections

→ Be familiar with the law of corrections and how it is applied to offenders and correctional personnel

→ Discuss the direction of community corrections

→ Be able to explain why the prison population has more than doubled in the last ten years

In February 2008, a report released by the Pew Center on the States showed that for the first time in history, 1 in 100 American adults were behind bars in prisons (1,596,127) and jails (723,000). Anyone who is at all attentive to public issues knows that the United States has a large and expanding prison population, but the "one in 100" report brought home this fact. The report also noted that the United States incarcerates more of its residents than any other country. China is second with 1.5 million behind bars ("One in 100: Behind Bars in America, 2008," 2008: 3). The United States has less than 5 percent of the world's population, but almost a quarter of the world's prisoners. Closer to home, the United States has 10 times the population of Canada but about 35 times the prison population. Why does this gap exist between American justice and that of the rest of the world?

Over the past 30 years the incarceration rate has quadrupled, even though crime in the United States has been declining for two decades (Liptak, 2008). This increase in the number of offenders incarcerated in prisons and jails has increased the need for new prisons, resulting in a construction boom and increased employment of correctional officers. Correctional budgets have climbed an average of 10 percent annually, and many states have diverted

money from education, welfare, and health programs to meet the soaring needs of corrections.

The incarceration numbers are not spread evenly across American society. For some groups, the impact is startling. For example, while 1 in 30 men between the ages of 20 and 34 are behind bars, for African American males in that age group the ratio is 1 in 9. Gender adds another dimension to the picture. Men are ten times more likely to be in prison or jail but the incarcerated female population is increasing at a brisker pace. For African American women in their mid-30s the incarceration rate has also hit the 1 in 100 mark. Growing older reduces criminal behavior. While 1 in 53 people in their 20s is behind bars, the rate for those over 55 falls to 1 in 837 ("One in 100: Behind Bars in America, 2008," 2008: 3).

The public usually thinks of prisons when it thinks of corrections, however, about 70 percent of persons under supervision are not in prisons or jails, but living in the community on probation or parole.

Corrections refers to the great number of programs, services, facilities, and organizations responsible for the management of people accused or convicted of criminal offenses. In addition to prisons and jails, corrections includes probation, halfway houses, education and work release programs, parole supervision, counseling, and community service. Correctional programs operate in Salvation Army hostels, forest camps, medical clinics, and urban storefronts.

Corrections is authorized by all levels of government, is administered by both public and private organizations, and costs more than $60 billion a year (BJS, 2006: 4). A total of 7.5 million adults and juveniles receive correctional supervision by 750,000 administrators, psychologists, officers, counselors, social workers, and other professionals (BJS, 2007: 1, 8). This chapter will examine (1) the history of corrections, (2) the organization of corrections, (3) the law of corrections, and (4) the policy trends in community corrections and incarceration.

corrections
The variety of programs, services, facilities, and organizations responsible for the management of people who have been accused or convicted of criminal offenses.

DEVELOPMENT OF CORRECTIONS

How did corrections get where it is today? Why are offenders now placed on probation or incarcerated instead of whipped or burned as in colonial times? Over the past two hundred years, ideas about punishment have moved like a pendulum from far in one direction to far in another (Table 13.1). As we review the development of present-day policies, think about how future changes in society may lead to new forms of corrections.

Invention of the Penitentiary

The late eighteenth century stands out as a remarkable period. At that time, scholars and social reformers in Europe and America were rethinking the nature of society and the place of the individual in it. During the **Enlightenment**, as this period was known, philosophers and reformers challenged tradition with new ideas about the individual, about limitations on government, and about rationalism. As the main intellectual force behind the American Revolution, such thinking laid the foundation of American values. The Enlightenment also affected the new nation's views on law and criminal justice. Reformers began to raise questions about the nature of criminal behavior and the methods of punishment.

Prior to 1800, Americans copied Europeans in using physical punishment as the main criminal sanction. Flogging, branding, and maiming served as the primary methods of controlling deviance and maintaining public safety. For more serious crimes, offenders were hanged on the gallows. For example, in the state

Enlightenment
A movement, during the eighteenth century in England and France, in which concepts of liberalism, rationalism, equality, and individualism dominated social and political thinking.

| TABLE 13.1 | **History of Corrections in America** |

Note the extent to which correctional policies have shifted from one era to the next and are influenced by societal factors.

	CORRECTIONAL MODEL					
Colonial (1600s–1790s)	**Penitentiary (1790s–1860s)**	**Reformatory (1870s–1890s)**	**Progressive (1890s–1930s)**	**Medical (1930s–1960s)**	**Community (1960s–1970s)**	**Crime Control (1970s–2000s)**
FEATURES						
Anglican Code	Separate confinement	Indeterminate sentences	Individual case approach	Rehabilitation as primary focus of incarceration	Reintegration into community	Determinate sentences
Capital and corporal punishment, fines	Reform of individual	Parole	Administrative discretion	Psychological testing and classification	Avoidance of incarceration	Mandatory sentences
	Power of isolation and labor	Classification by degree of individual reform	Broader probation and parole	Various types of treatment programs and institutions	Vocational and educational programs	Sentencing guidelines
	Penance	Rehabilitative programs	Juvenile courts			Risk management
	Disciplined routine	Separate treatment for juveniles				
	Punishment according to severity of crime					
PHILOSOPHICAL BASIS						
Religious law	Enlightenment	National Prison Association	The Age of Reform	Biomedical science	Civil rights movement	Crime control
Doctrine of predestination	Declaration of Independence	Declaration of Principles	Positivist school	Psychiatry and psychology	Critique of prisons	Rising crime rates
	Human perfectibility and powers of reason	Crime as moral disease	Punishment according to needs of offender	Social work practice	Small is better	Political shift to the right
	Religious penitence	Criminals as "victims of social disorder"	Focus on the offender	Crime as signal of personal "distress" or "failure"		New punitive agenda
	Power of reformation		Crime as an urban, immigrant ghetto problem			
	Focus on the act					
	Healing power of suffering					

of New York about 20 percent of all crimes on the books were capital offenses. Criminals were regularly sentenced to death for picking pockets, burglary, robbery, and horse stealing (Rothman, 1971: 49). Jails existed throughout the country, but they served only to hold people awaiting trial or to punish people unable to pay their debts. As in England, the American colonies maintained houses of correction, where offenders were sentenced to terms of "hard labor" as a means of turning them from crime (Hirsch, 1992).

With the spread of Enlightenment ideas during the late eighteenth century, such practices began to wane (Foucault, 1977). Before the French Revolution of 1789, European governments tried to control crime by making public spectacles out of punishments such as torture and hanging. They often branded criminals, literally marking their offense for all to see. They also put the dismembered bodies of capital offenders on public display. In the early nineteenth century, such practices were gradually replaced by "modern" penal systems that emphasized fitting the punishment to the individual offender. The new goal was not to inflict pain on the offender's body but to change the individual and set him or her on the right path.

Until the early 1800s, Americans followed the European practice of relying on punishment that was physically painful, such as death, flogging, and branding. Would such punishments be appropriate today?

© Time life Pictures/Mansell/ Getty Images

penitentiary
An institution intended to punish criminals by isolating them from society and from one another so they can reflect on their past misdeeds, repent, and reform.

Clearly, this constituted a major shift in policy. The change from physical (corporal) punishment to correction of the offender reflected new ideas about the causes of crime and the possibility of reforming behavior.

Many people promoted the reform of corrections, but John Howard (1726–1790), sheriff of Bedfordshire, England, was especially influential. His book, *The State of Prisons in England and Wales*, published in 1777, described his observations of the prisons he visited (Howard, 1777/1929). Among generally horrible conditions, the lack of discipline particularly concerned him.

Public response to the book resulted in Parliament's passing the Penitentiary Act of 1779, which called for the creation of a house of hard labor where offenders would be imprisoned for up to two years. The institution would be based on four principles:

1. A secure and sanitary building
2. Inspection to ensure that offenders followed the rules
3. Abolition of the fees charged offenders for their food
4. A reformatory regime

At night prisoners were to be confined to individual cells. During the day they were to work silently in common rooms. Prison life was to be strict and ordered. Influenced by his Quaker friends, Howard believed that the new institution should be a place of industry. More important, it should be a place that offered criminals opportunities for penitence (sorrow and shame for their wrongs) and repentance (willingness to change their ways). In short, the **penitentiary** served to punish and to reform.

Howard's idea of the penitentiary was not implemented in England until 1842, 50 years after his death. Although England was slow to act, the United States applied Howard's ideas much more quickly.

checkpoint

1. What was the Enlightenment and how did it influence corrections?
2. What were the main goals of the penitentiary?
   (Answers are at the end of the chapter.)

Reform in the United States

From 1776 to around 1830, a new revolution occurred in the American idea of criminal punishment. Although based on the work of English reformers, the new correctional philosophy reflected many ideas expressed in the Declaration of Independence, including an optimistic view of human nature and of individual perfectibility. Emphasis shifted from the assumption that deviance was part of human nature to a belief that crime resulted from environmental forces. The new nation's humane and optimistic ideas focused on reforming the criminal.

In the first decades of the nineteenth century, the creation of penitentiaries in Pennsylvania and New York attracted the attention of legislators in other

Eastern State Penitentiary, located outside Philadelphia, became the model for the Pennsylvania system of "separate" confinement. The building was designed to ensure that each offender was separated from all human contact so that he could reflect on his misdeeds. If you designed a prison, what details would it contain?

© The Library Company of Philadelphia

states, as well as investigators from Europe. Even travelers from abroad with no special interest in corrections made it a point to include a penitentiary on their itinerary, much as they planned visits to a southern plantation, a textile mill, or a frontier town. By the mid-1800s, the U.S. penitentiary had become world famous.

The Pennsylvania System

Several groups in the United States dedicated themselves to reforming the institutions and practices of criminal punishment. One of these groups was the Philadelphia Society for Alleviating the Miseries of Public Prisons, formed in 1787. This group, which included many Quakers, was inspired by Howard's ideas. They argued that criminals could best be reformed if they were placed in penitentiaries—isolated from one another and from society to consider their crimes, repent, and reform.

In 1790, the Pennsylvania legislature authorized the construction of two penitentiaries for the solitary confinement of "hardened and atrocious offenders." The first, created out of an existing three-story stone structure in Philadelphia, was the Walnut Street Jail. This 25-by-40-foot building had eight dark cells, each measuring 6 by 8 by 9 feet, on each floor. A yard was attached to the building.

Only one inmate occupied each cell, and no communications of any kind were allowed. From a small, grated window high on the outside wall, prisoners "could perceive neither heaven nor earth."

From this limited beginning, the Pennsylvania system of **separate confinement** evolved. It was based on five principles:

1. Prisoners would not be treated vengefully but should be convinced that through hard and selective forms of suffering they could change their lives.

2. Solitary confinement would prevent further corruption inside prison.

3. In isolation, offenders would reflect on their transgressions and repent.

4. Solitary confinement would be punishment because humans are by nature social animals.

separate confinement
A penitentiary system, developed in Pennsylvania, in which each inmate was held in isolation from other inmates. All activities, including craft work, took place in the cells.

5. Solitary confinement would be economical because prisoners would not need long periods of time to repent, and so fewer keepers would be needed and the costs of clothing would be lower.

The opening of the Eastern Penitentiary near Philadelphia in 1829 culminated 42 years of reform activity by the Philadelphia Society. On October 25, 1829, the first prisoner, Charles Williams, arrived. He was an 18-year-old African American and had been sentenced to two years for larceny. He was assigned to a cell 12 by 8 by 10 feet with an individual exercise yard 18 feet long. In the cell was a fold-up steel bed, a simple toilet, a wooden stool, a workbench, and eating utensils. Light came from an 8-inch window in the ceiling. Solitary labor, Bible reading, and reflection were the keys to the moral rehabilitation that was supposed to occur within the penitentiary. Although the cell was larger than most in use today, it was the only world the prisoner would see throughout the entire sentence. The only other human voice heard would be that of a clergyman who would visit on Sundays. Nothing was to distract the penitent prisoner from the path toward reform.

In the years between Walnut Street and Eastern, other states had adopted aspects of the Pennsylvania system. Separate confinement was introduced by Maryland in 1809, by Massachusetts in 1811, by New Jersey in 1820, and by Maine in 1823.

Within five years of its opening, Eastern endured the first of several outside investigations. The reports detailed the extent to which the goal of separate confinement was not fully observed, physical punishments were used to maintain discipline, and prisoners suffered mental breakdowns from isolation. Separate confinement had declined at Eastern by the 1860s, when crowding required doubling up in each cell, yet it was not abolished in Pennsylvania until 1913 (Teeters and Shearer, 1957).

The New York System

In 1819, New York opened a penitentiary in Auburn that evolved as a rival to Pennsylvania's concept of separate confinement. Under New York's **congregate system**, prisoners were held in isolation at night but worked with other prisoners in shops during the day. They worked under a rule of silence and were even forbidden to exchange glances while on the job or at meals.

Auburn's warden, Elam Llynds, was convinced that convicts were incorrigible and that industrial efficiency should be the overriding purpose of the prison. He instituted a reign of discipline and obedience that include the lockstep and the wearing of prison stripes. He also started a **contract labor system**. By the 1840s, Auburn was producing footwear, barrels, carpets, harnesses, furniture, and clothing.

Seeing the New York approach as a great advance, American reformers copied it throughout the Northeast (see Figure 13.1 on page 470). Advocates said that the inmate production of goods for sale would cover the operating costs. At an 1826 meeting of prison reformers in Boston, the New York system was described in glowing terms:

> At Auburn, we have a more beautiful example still, of what may be done by proper discipline, in a prison well constructed.... The unremitted industry, the entire subordination, and subdued feeling among the convicts have probably no parallel among any equal number of convicts. In their solitary cells, they spend the night with no other book than the Bible, and at sunrise they proceed in military order, under the eye of the turnkey in solid columns, with the lock march to the workshops. (Goldfarb and Singer, 1973: 30)

During this period, advocates of the Pennsylvania and New York plans debated on public platforms and in the nation's periodicals. Advocates of both

 Eastern Penitentiary is today a national historical landmark where visitors are welcome. Learn about current exhibits, events, and links at the website. To link to this website, go to *The American System of Criminal Justice* 12e companion site at academic.cengage.com/criminaljustice/cole.

congregate system
A penitentiary system, developed in Auburn, New York, in which each inmate was held in isolation during the night but worked and ate with other prisoners during the day under a rule of silence.

contract labor system
A system under which inmates' labor was sold on a contractual basis to private employers who provided the machinery and raw materials with which inmates made saleable products in the institution.

 Read about the origins of Auburn State Prison at the website of the New York Correction History Society. To link to this website, go to *The American System of Criminal Justice* 12e companion site at academic.cengage.com/criminaljustice/cole.

TABLE 13.2	Comparison of Pennsylvania and New York (Auburn) Penitentiary Systems			
	Goal	**Implementation**	**Method**	**Activity**
Pennsylvania (separate system)	Redemption of the offender through the well-ordered routine of the prison	Isolation, penance, contemplation, labor, silence	Inmates kept in their cells for eating, sleeping, and working	Bible reading, work on crafts in cell
New York (Auburn) (congregate system)	Redemption of the offender through the well-ordered routine of the prison	Strict discipline, obedience, labor, silence	Inmates sleep in their cells but come together to eat and work	Work together in shops making goods to be sold by the state

systems agreed that the prisoner must be isolated from society and placed on a disciplined routine. They believed that criminality was a result of corruption pervading the community and that the family and the church did not sufficiently counterbalance. Only when offenders were removed from the temptations and influences of society and kept in a silent, disciplined environment could they reflect on their sins and offenses and become useful citizens. The convicts were not inherently depraved; rather, they were victims of a society that had not protected them from vice. While offenders were being punished, they would become penitent and motivated to place themselves on the right path. See Table 13.2 for a comparison of the Pennsylvania and New York systems.

Prisons in the South and West

Scholars tend to emphasize the nineteenth-century reforms in the populous Northeast, neglecting penal developments in the South and the West. Prisons, some following the penitentiary model, were built in four Southern states—Georgia, Kentucky, Maryland, and Virginia—before 1817. Later prisons, such as the ones in Jackson, Mississippi (1842), and Huntsville, Texas (1848), were built on the Auburn model. But further expansion ended with the Civil War. With the exception of San Quentin (1852), the sparse population of the West did not lend itself to the construction of many prisons until the latter part of the nineteenth century.

After the Civil War, southerners began the task of rebuilding their communities and primarily agricultural economy. They lacked funds to build prisons but faced an increasing population of offenders. Given these challenges, a large African American inmate labor force, and the states' need for revenue, southern states developed the **lease system**. Businesses in need of workers negotiated with the state for the labor (logging, agriculture, mining, railroad construction) and care of prisoners. Because these entrepreneurs had no ownership interest in the prisoners, they were exploited worse than they had been as slaves (Rotman, 1995: 176). The prisoner death rate soared.

Settlement in the West did not take off until the California gold rush of 1849. Except in California, the prison ideologies of the East did not greatly influence penology in the West. Prior to statehood, western prisoners were held in territorial facilities or federal military posts and prisons. Until Congress passed the Anticontract Law of 1887, restricting the employment of federal prisoners, leasing programs existed in California, Montana, Oregon, and Wyoming. In 1852 a leasee chose Point San Quentin and, using convict labor, built two prison buildings. In 1858, after reports of deaths, escapes, and brutal discipline, the state of California took over the facility. The Oregon territory had erected a log prison in the 1850s, but it was soon leased to a private company. On joining the Union in 1859, however, the state discontinued the lease system. In 1877 a

lease system
A system under which inmates were leased to contractors who provided prisoners with food and clothing in exchange for their labor. In southern states the prisoners were used as agricultural, mining, logging, and construction laborers.

 The convict lease system in Texas is described online. To link to this website, go to *The American System of Criminal Justice* 12e companion site at academic.cengage.com/criminaljustice/cole.

FIGURE 13.1
Early prisons in the United States

Source: Norman Johnston, *Forms of Constraint: A History of Prison Architecture* (Urbana: University of Illinois, 2000).

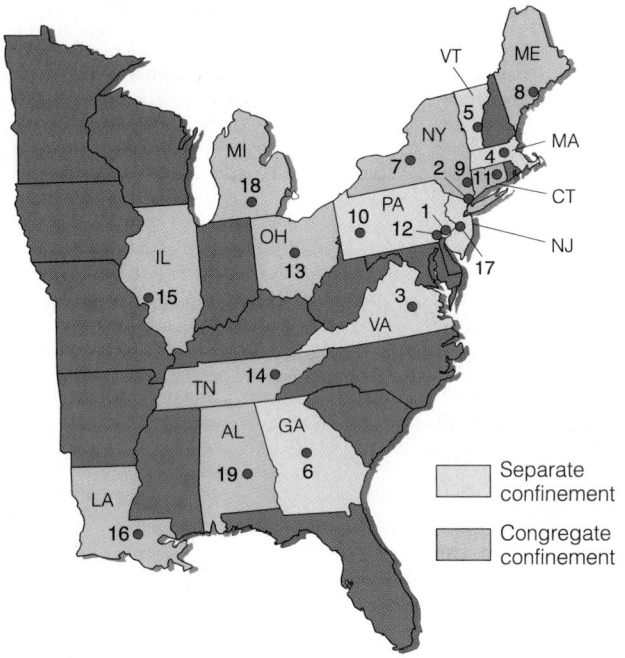

City	Prison	Year built
1. Philadelphia, PA	Walnut Street Jail	1790
2. New York City, NY	Newgate Prison	1797
3. Richmond, VA	Virginia Penitentiary	1800
4. Charlestown, MA	Massachusetts State Prison	1805
5. Windsor, VT	Vermont State Prison	1809
6. Milledgeville, GA	Georgia Penitentiary	1817
7. Auburn, NY	Auburn State Prison	1819
8. Thomaston, ME	Maine State Prison	1823
9. Ossining, NY	Sing Sing	1825
10. Pittsburgh, PA	Western Penitentiary	1826
11. Wethersfield, CT	Connecticut State Prison	1827
12. Cherry Hills, PA	Eastern Penitentiary	1829
13. Columbus, OH	Ohio Penitentiary	1830
14. Nashville, TN	State Prison	1831
15. Alton, IL	State Prison	1833
16. Baton Rouge, LA	State Prison	1835
17. Trenton, NJ	State Prison	1836
18. Jackson, MI	State Prison	1838
19. Wetumpka, AL	State Prison	1841

state prison on the Auburn plan was built, but with labor difficulties and an economic depression in the 1890s, it was turned over to a lessee in 1895 (McKelvey, 1977: 228).

Reformatory Movement

By the middle of the nineteenth century, reformers had become disillusioned with the penitentiary. Neither the Pennsylvania nor the New York systems nor any of their imitators had achieved rehabilitation or deterrence. Most saw this failure as the result of poor administration rather than as a flawed idea. Within 40 years of being built, penitentiaries had become overcrowded, understaffed, and minimally financed. Discipline was lax, brutality was common, and administrators were viewed as corrupt. At Sing Sing Penitentiary in Ossining, New York, for example, investigators in 1870 discovered "that dealers were publicly supplying prisoners with almost anything they could pay for" and that convicts were "playing all sorts of games, reading, scheming, trafficking" (Rothman, 1980: 18).

Cincinnati, 1870

The National Prison Association (the predecessor of today's American Correctional Association) and its 1870 meeting in Cincinnati embodied a new spirit of reform. In its famous Declaration of Principles, the association advocated a new design for penology: that prisons should operate according to a philosophy of inmate change, with reformation rewarded by release. Sentences of indeterminate length would replace fixed sentences, and proof of reformation—rather than mere lapse of time—would be required for a prisoner's release. Classification of prisoners on the basis of character and improvement would encourage the reformation program. Penitentiary practices that had evolved during the first half of the nineteenth century—fixed sentences, the lockstep, rules of silence, and isolation—were now seen as debasing and humiliating and as destroying inmates' initiative.

Elmira Reformatory

The first **reformatory** took shape in 1876 at Elmira, New York, when Zebulon Brockway was appointed superintendent. Brockway believed that diagnosis and treatment were the keys to reform and rehabilitation. He questioned each new inmate in order to explore the social, biological, psychological, and "root cause(s)" of the offender's deviance. An individualized treatment program of work and education was then prescribed. Inmates followed a rigid schedule of work during the day, followed by courses in academic, vocational, and moral subjects during the evening. Inmates who did well achieved early release.

Designed for first-time felons aged 16–30, the approach at Elmira incorporated a **mark system** of classification, indeterminate sentences, and parole. Each offender entered the institution at grade 2, and if he earned nine marks a month for six months by working hard, completing school assignments, and causing no problems, he could be moved up to grade 1—necessary for release. If he failed to cooperate and violated the rules, he would be demoted to grade 3. Only after three months of satisfactory behavior could he reembark on the path toward eventual release. In sum, this system placed "the prisoner's fate, as far as possible, in his own hands" (Pisciotta, 1994: 20).

By 1900 the reformatory movement had spread throughout the nation. However, by the outbreak of World War I in 1914, it was already in decline. In most institutions the architecture, the attitudes of the guards, and the emphasis on discipline differed little from those of the past. Too often, the educational and rehabilitative efforts took a back seat to the traditional emphasis on punishment. Nonetheless, the reformatory movement contributed the indeterminate sentence, rehabilitative programs, and parole. The Cincinnati Principles and the reformatory movement set goals that inspired prison activists well into the twentieth century.

reformatory
An institution for young offenders, emphasizing training, a mark system of classification, indeterminate sentences, and parole.

 The history of Elmira Reformatory is found online. To link to this website, go to *The American System of Criminal Justice* 12e companion site at academic.cengage.com/ criminaljustice/cole.

mark system
A system in which offenders receive a certain number of points at the time of sentencing, based on the severity of their crime. Prisoners can reduce their term and gain release by earning marks to reduce these points through labor, good behavior, and educational achievement.

checkpoint

3. How did the Pennsylvania and the New York systems differ?
4. What was the significance of the Cincinnati Declaration of Principles?

Improving Prison Conditions for Women

Until the beginning of the nineteenth century, female offenders in Europe and North America were treated no differently than men and were not separated from them when they were incarcerated. Only with John Howard's 1777 exposé of prison conditions in England and the development of the penitentiary in Philadelphia did attention begin to focus on the plight of the female offender. Among the English reformers, Elizabeth Gurney Fry, a middle-class Quaker, was the first person to press for changes. When she and other Quakers visited London's Newgate Prison in 1813, they were shocked by the conditions in which the female prisoners and their children were living (Zedner, 1995: 333).

News of Fry's efforts spread to the United States. The Women's Prison Association was formed in New York in 1844 with the goal of improving the

In the 1860s at Wethersfield Prison for Women (Connecticut), the inmates were trained for ironing, laundry work, and cooking; yet time was also spent learning such "ladylike" games as croquet. Should prisons for men and women today be identical to each other?

© Hulton Archive/ Getty Images

treatment of female prisoners and separating them from men. Elizabeth Farnham, head matron of the women's wing at Sing Sing from 1844 to 1848, implemented Fry's ideas until male overseers and legislators thwarted her and she was forced to resign.

The Cincinnati Declaration of Principles did not address the problems of female offenders. It only endorsed the creation of separate treatment-oriented prisons for women. Although the House of Shelter, a reformatory for women, was created in Detroit following the Civil War, not until 1873 did the first independent female-run prison open in Indiana. Within the next 50 years, 13 other states had followed this lead.

Three principles guided female prison reform during this period: (1) the separation of female prisoners from men, (2) the provision of care in keeping with the needs of women, and (3) the management of women's prisons by female staff. "Operated by and for women, female reformatories were decidedly 'feminine' institutions" (Rafter, 1983: 147).

As time passed, the original ideas of the reformers faltered. In 1927 the first federal prison for women opened in Alderson, West Virginia, with Mary Belle Harris as warden. Yet, by 1935 the women's reformatory movement had "run its course, having largely achieved its objective (establishment of separate prisons run by women)" (Rafter, 1983: 165).

checkpoint

5. What principles guided the reform of corrections for women in the nineteenth century?

Rehabilitation Model

In the first two decades of the twentieth century, reformers known as the Progressives attacked the excesses of big business and urban society and advocated government actions against the problems of slums, vice, and crime. The Progressives urged that knowledge from the social and behavioral sciences should replace religious and traditional moral wisdom as the guiding ideas of criminal rehabilitation. They pursued two main strategies: (1) improving conditions in social environments that seemed to be the breeding grounds of crime and (2) rehabilitating individual offenders. By the 1920s, probation, indeterminate sentences, presentence reports, parole, and treatment programs were being promoted as a more scientific approach to criminality.

Although the Progressives were instrumental in advancing the new penal ideas, not until the 1930s did reformers attempt to implement fully what became known as the **rehabilitation model** of corrections. Taking advantage of the new prestige of the social sciences, penologists helped shift the emphasis of corrections. The new approach saw the social, intellectual, or biological deficiencies of criminals as the causes of their crimes. Because most states had in place the essential elements of parole, probation, and the indeterminate sen-

rehabilitation model
A model of corrections that emphasizes the need to restore a convicted offender to a constructive place in society through some form of vocational or educational training or therapy.

tence, incorporating the rehabilitation model meant adding classification systems to diagnose offenders and treatment programs to rehabilitate them.

Because penologists likened the new correctional methods to those used by physicians in hospitals, this approach was often referred to as the **medical model**. Correctional institutions were to be staffed with people who could diagnose the causes of an individual's criminal behavior, prescribe a treatment program, and determine when the offender was cured and could be safely released to the community.

Following World War II, rehabilitation won new followers. Group therapy, behavior modification, counseling, and several other approaches became part of the "new penology." Yet even during the 1950s, when the medical model was at its height, only a small proportion of state correctional budgets went to rehabilitation. What frustrated many reformers was that, even while states adopted the rhetoric of the rehabilitation model, custody remained the overriding goal of most institutions in their actual practices.

Because the rehabilitation model failed to achieve its goals, it became discredited in the 1970s. According to critics of rehabilitation, its reportedly high recidivism rates prove its ineffectiveness. Probably the most thorough analysis of research data from treatment programs was undertaken by Robert Martinson. Using rigorous standards, he surveyed 231 studies of rehabilitation programs, including counseling, group therapy, medical treatment, and educational and vocational training. Martinson summarized his findings by saying, "With few and isolated exceptions, the rehabilitative efforts that have been reported so far have had no appreciable effect on recidivism" (Martinson, 1974: 25). The report had an immediate impact on legislators and policy makers, who took up the cry that "Nothing Works!" As a result of dissatisfaction with the rehabilitation model, new reforms emerged.

medical model
A model of corrections based on the assumption that criminal behavior is caused by biological or psychological conditions that require treatment.

Community Model

The social and political values of particular periods have long influenced correctional goals. During the 1960s and early 1970s, U.S. society experienced the civil rights movement, the war on poverty, and resistance to the war in Vietnam. People challenged the conventional ways of government. In 1967, the President's Commission on Law Enforcement and the Administration of Justice argued that the purpose of corrections should be to reintegrate the offender into the community (President's Commission on Law Enforcement and Administration of Justice, 1967: 7).

Under this model of **community corrections**, the goal of corrections was to reintegrate the offender into the community. Proponents viewed prisons as artificial institutions that hindered offenders from finding a crime-free lifestyle. They argued that corrections should focus on increasing opportunities for offenders to be successful citizens and on providing psychological treatment. Programs were supposed to help offenders find jobs and remain connected to their families and the community. Imprisonment was to be avoided, if possible, in favor of probation, so that offenders could seek education and vocational training that would help their adjustment. The small proportion of offenders who had to be incarcerated would spend a minimal amount of time in prison before release on parole. To promote reintegration, correctional workers were to serve as advocates for offenders in dealing with government agencies providing employment counseling, medical treatment, and financial assistance.

The community model dominated until the late 1970s. It gave way to a new punitiveness in criminal justice, in conjunction with the rebirth of the determinate sentence. Advocates of reintegration claim, as did advocates of previous reforms, that the idea was never adequately tested. Nevertheless, community corrections remains one of the significant ideas and practices in the recent history of corrections.

community corrections
A model of corrections based on the goal of reintegrating the offender into the community.

Crime Control Model

As the political climate changed in the 1970s and 1980s, and with the crime rate at historic levels, legislators, judges, and officials responded with an emphasis on crime control through incarceration and risk containment. The critique of rehabilitation led to changes in the sentencing structures in more than half the states and the abolition of parole release in many.

Compared with the community model, this **crime control model of corrections** is more punitive and makes greater use of incarceration (especially for violent offenders and career criminals), longer sentences, mandatory sentences, and strict supervision of probationers and parolees.

The effect of these get-tough policies is demonstrated by the record number of people incarcerated, the greater amount of time being served, the great number of parolees returned to prison, and the huge size of the probation population. Some advocates point to the crime control policies as the reason for the fall of the crime rate. Others ask whether the crime control policies have really made a difference, considering the smaller number of men in the crime-prone age group and other changes in U.S. society that may have actually reduced the crime rate.

The history of corrections in America reflects a series of swings from one model to another. During this early part of the twenty-first century, the time may be ripe for another look at correctional policy. The language now used in criminal justice journals differs markedly from that found in their pages 30 years ago. The optimism that once suffused corrections has waned. The financial and human costs of the retributive crime control policies of the 1990s are now being scrutinized. Are the costs of incarceration and surveillance justified? Has crime been reduced? Is society safer today than it was, say, 25 years ago? Many researchers think not. Looking to the future, will there be a new direction for corrections? If so, what will be its focus?

crime control model of corrections
A model of corrections based on the assumption that criminal behavior can be controlled by more use of incarceration and other forms of strict supervision.

checkpoint

6. What are the underlying assumptions of the rehabilitation, community, and crime control models of corrections?

ORGANIZATION OF CORRECTIONS IN THE UNITED STATES

The organization of corrections in the United States is fragmented. Each level of government has some responsibility for corrections. The federal government, the 50 states, over 3,047 counties and uncounted municipalities and public and private organizations administer corrections at an annual cost of almost $70 billion (BJS, 2006: 5). State and local governments pay about 90 percent of the cost of all correctional activities in the nation (BJS, 2006: 4).

Federal Correctional System

The correctional responsibilities of the federal government are divided between the Department of Justice, which operates prisons through the Federal Bureau of Prisons, and the Administrative Office of the United States Courts, which covers probation and parole supervision.

Federal Bureau of Prisons

The Federal Bureau of Prisons, created by Congress in 1930, now operates a system of prisons located throughout the nation and houses over 195,000 inmates, supervised by a staff of more than 35,000. Facilities and inmates are classified by security level, ranging from Level 1 (the least secure, camp-type settings such as the Federal Prison Camp at Tyndall, Florida) through Level 5 (the most secure, such as the "super max" penitentiary at Florence, Colorado). Between these extremes are Levels 2 through 4 federal correctional institutions—other U.S. penitentiaries, administrative institutions, medical facilities, and specialized institutions for women and juveniles. The Bureau of Prisons enters into contractual agreements with states, cities, and private agencies to provide community services such as halfway houses, prerelease programs, and electronic monitoring.

Because of the jurisdiction of federal criminal law, prisoners in most federal facilities differ from those in state institutions. Federal prisoners are often a more sophisticated type of criminal, from a higher socioeconomic background, who have committed crimes of extortion, mail fraud, bank robbery, and arson. But since the beginning of the war on drugs in the 1980s, the number of drug offenders has increased and now makes up about 55 percent of the federal inmate population. There are fewer violent offenders in federal prisons than in most state institutions. Interestingly, about 30 percent of federal prisoners are citizens of other countries (Federal Bureau of Prisons, State of the Bureau, 2005: 51).

Federal Probation and Parole Supervision

The Federal Probation and Pretrial Services System, a branch of the Administrative Office of the U.S. Courts, provides probation and parole supervision for federal offenders. The federal judiciary appoints probation officers, who serve the court. The first full-time federal probation officer was appointed in 1927; today 3,842 are assigned to the judicial districts across the country. They assist with presentence investigations but are primarily involved in supervising those on probation and offenders released either on parole or mandatory release. Their average caseload is 70 people.

The Pretrial Services Act of 1982 required pretrial services to be established in each federal judicial district. These services are performed either by probation officers or independently in a separate office of pretrial services. The responsibilities of pretrial services officers are to "collect, verify, and report to the judicial officer information pertaining to the pretrial release of each person charged with an offense" (Administrative Office of the U.S. Courts, 1993).

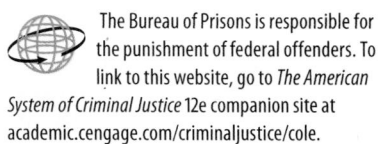

The Bureau of Prisons is responsible for the punishment of federal offenders. To link to this website, go to *The American System of Criminal Justice* 12e companion site at academic.cengage.com/criminaljustice/cole.

State Correctional Systems

Although states vary considerably in how they organize corrections, in all states the administration of prisons falls under the executive branch of state government. This point is important because probation is often part of the judiciary, parole may be separate from corrections, and in most states jails are run by county governments. The differences can be seen in the proportion of correctional employees who work for the state. In Connecticut, Rhode Island, and Vermont, for example, 100 percent are state employees, compared with 47 percent in California. The remaining 53 percent in California work for county or municipal governments.

Community Corrections

Probation, intermediate sanctions, and parole are the three major ways that offenders are punished in the community. States vary in how they carry out these punishments. In many states, probation and intermediate sanctions are

Prisoners in Nevada's Warm Springs Correctional Center play cards in their small cell. Offenders in other states' prisons live under similarly crowded conditions. How should society address the issue of prison overcrowding?

administered by the judiciary, often by county and municipal governments. By contrast, parole is a function of state government. The decision to release an offender from prison is made by the state parole board in those states with discretionary release. Parole boards are a part of either the department of corrections or an independent agency. In states with a mandatory system, the department of corrections makes the release. In all states, a state agency supervises the parolees.

Central to the community corrections approach is a belief in the "least restrictive alternative," the idea that the criminal sanction should be applied only to the minimum extent necessary to meet the community's need for protection, the seriousness of the offense, and society's need for offenders to get their deserved punishment. To this end, probation and parole services are geared to assist and reintegrate the offender into the community.

State Prison Systems

A wide range of state correctional institutions and programs exists for adult felons, including prisons, reformatories, prison farms, forestry camps, and halfway houses. This variety does not exist for women because of the smaller female prisoner population.

States vary considerably in the number, size, type, and location of correctional facilities they have. Louisiana's state prison at Angola, for example, can hold 5,100, whereas specialized institutions house fewer than a hundred inmates. Some states (such as New Hampshire) have centralized incarceration in a few institutions, and other states (such as California, New York, and Texas) have a wide mix of sizes and styles—secure institutions, diagnostic units, work camps, forestry centers, and prerelease centers. For example, Alabama has 13 correctional institutions (prisons), a disciplinary rehabilitation unit, an honor farm, a boot camp, a state cattle ranch, a prison for women, and a youth center for male felons under age 25, in addition to 13 work release centers (Alabama, Department of Corrections, March 20, 2007, http://www.doc.state.al.us/facilities.htm).

State correctional institutions for men are usually classified by level of security: maximum, medium, and minimum. With changes in the number of prisoners and their characteristics, the distinction between maximum and medium security has disappeared in some systems. Crowding has forced administrators to use available space in medium-security institutions to house inmates who actually need maximum-security supervision and facilities.

Forty states have created prisons that exceed maximum security. About 20,000 inmates, are currently held in these "super max" prisons. These institutions are designed to hold the most disruptive, violent, and incorrigible offenders. California's Pelican Bay institution and Connecticut's Northern Correctional Facility are examples of prisons designed to hold the "toughest of the tough." In such institutions, inmates spend up to 23 hours a day in their cells. They are shackled whenever they are out of their cells—during recreation, showers, and telephone calls. All of these measures are designed to send a message to other inmates (Mears, and Watson, 2006: 232–270).

The maximum-security prison (holding about 21 percent of state inmates) is built like a fortress, usually surrounded by stone walls with guard towers and designed to prevent escape. New facilities are surrounded by double rows of chain-link fences with rolls of razor wire in between and along the tops of the fences. Inmates live in cells, each with its own sanitary facilities. The barred doors may be operated electronically so that an officer can confine all prisoners to their cells with the flick of a switch. The purpose of the maximum-security facility is custody and discipline. It maintains a military-style approach to order, with prisoners following a strict routine. Some of the most famous prisons, such as Attica (New York), Folsom (California), Stateville (Illinois), and Yuma (Arizona) are maximum-security facilities.

The medium-security prison (holding 40 percent of state inmates) externally resembles the maximum-security prison, but it is organized somewhat differently and its atmosphere is less rigid. Prisoners have more privileges and contact with the outside world through visitors, mail, and access to radio and television. The medium-security prison usually places greater emphasis on work and rehabilitative programs. Although the inmates may have committed serious crimes, they are not perceived as hardened criminals.

The minimum-security prison (with 33 percent of state inmates) houses the least-violent offenders, long-term felons with clean disciplinary records, and inmates who have nearly completed their term. The minimum-security prison lacks the guard towers and stone walls associated with correctional institutions. Often, chain-link fencing surrounds the buildings. Prisoners usually live in dormitories or even in small private rooms rather than in barred cells. There is more personal freedom: Inmates may have television sets, choose their own clothes, and move about casually within the buildings. The system relies on rehabilitation programs and offers opportunities for education and work release. It also offers reintegration programs and support to inmates preparing for release.

State Institutions for Women

Because only 7 percent of the incarcerated population are women, there are relatively few women's facilities. Although the ratio of arrests is approximately 6 men to 1 woman, the ratio of admissions to state correctional institutions is 18 men to 1 woman. A higher proportion of female defendants is sentenced to probation and intermediate punishments, partly as a result of male offenders' tendency to commit most of the violent crimes. However, the growth rate in number of incarcerated women has exceeded that for men since 1995. From 1995 to 2005, the male population in state and federal prisons increased 34 percent, whereas that of women increased by 57 percent. (BJS, 2006: 4–5). This growth has been particularly acute in the federal system, which, because of the war on drugs, has had to absorb 6,000 female inmates over the past

Information about Washington's Department of Corrections is found online. To link to this website, go to *The American System of Criminal Justice* 12e companion site at academic.cengage.com/criminaljustice/cole.

Learn about Virginia's "super max" prison online. To link to this website, go to *The American System of Criminal Justice* 12e companion site at academic.cengage.com/criminaljustice/cole.

civic engagement
your role in the system

Imagine that you are a member of a fraternity, sorority, church group, or community service organization. You are approached by officials from your state's department of corrections about volunteering your time to work on a public service project in the corrections system. *Make a list of the kinds of contributions that volunteers might be able to make in the corrections system.* Then look at the programs for volunteers in the New Mexico Department of Corrections. To link to this website, go to *The American System of Criminal Justice* 12e companion site at academic.cengage.com/criminaljustice/cole.

twenty years. The increased number of women in prison has significantly affected the delivery of programs, housing conditions, medical care, staffing, and security.

Female offenders are incarcerated in 98 institutions for women and 93 coed facilities (BJS, 2003: 6). Conditions in correctional facilities for women are more pleasant than those of similar institutions for men. Usually the buildings have no gun towers and barbed wire. Because of the small population, however, most states have only one facility, which is often located in a rural setting far removed from urban centers. Thus women prisoners may be more isolated than men from their families and communities. Pressure from women's organizations and the apparent rise in the incidence of crime committed by women may bring about a greater equality in corrections for men and women.

In the United States, the extensive corrections system affects many offenders and imposes significant financial costs on taxpayers.

As you think about the various kinds of correctional institutions, consider whether average citizens can make a contribution to advancing the goals of corrections. Is there a role for citizens in contributing to rehabilitation efforts or in preparing offenders for release? Read "Civic Engagement: Your Role in the System" as you think about this issue.

checkpoint

7. What agencies of the U.S. government are responsible for prisons and probation?
8. What agencies of state government are responsible for incarceration, probation, intermediate sanctions, and parole?

Private Prisons

Corrections is a multibillion-dollar government-funded enterprise that purchases supplies and services from the private sector. Many jurisdictions have long contracted with private vendors to provide specific institutional services and to operate aftercare facilities and programs. Businesses furnish food and medical services, educational and vocational training, maintenance, security, and industrial programs. All of this has been referred to as "the corrections-commerical complex," which we discuss later in this chapter.

One response to prison and jail crowding and rising staff costs has come from private entrepreneurs who argue that they can build and run prisons at least as effectively, safely, and humanely as any level of government can, at a profit and at a lower cost to taxpayers. The management of entire institutions for adult felons under private contract is a relatively new approach in corrections that was launched in the 1980s (Harding, 2001: 265–346).

By the end of 2006, 32 states and the federal system reported a total of almost 114,000 prisoners held in privately operated facilities. Private facilities held 6.2 percent of all state prisoners and 14.4 percent of all federal prisoners. Among the states, Texas, with 18,627 inmates housed in private facilities, and Florida, with 6,350, reported the largest number. Six states had at least 25 percent of their prison population housed in private prisons, led by New Mexico (44 percent), Wyoming (37 percent), Alaska (33 percent), Hawaii (32 percent), Idaho (27 percent), Montana (26.9 percent), and Vermont (23.7 percent). Except for Minnesota, Vermont, and New Jersey, the use of private facilities is concentrated among Southern and Western States (BJS, 2007:19). Of interest is

Families detained for entering the United States illegally are held in a privately run jail in Taylor, Texas, under a contract with U.S. Immigration and Customs Enforcement (ICE). Should private companies be responsible for carrying out the government's detention and punishment functions?

© Pool photo / Charles Reed DHS / The Image Works

the fact that the private prison business has spread overseas to Australia, Great Britain, Brazil, and Denmark (*The Economist*, 2007: 60).

In addition to inmates held for criminal offenses, 17 percent of the estimated 30,000 individuals detained by the Immigration and Customs Enforcement (ICE) agency of the U.S. Department of Homeland Security, are held in private facilities. The increased pressure to enforce immigration laws has been a financial boon to the private prison industry (*San Diego Union-Tribune*, May 11, 2008).

The $1 billion-a-year private prison business is dominated by two companies—Corrections Corporation of America (CCA) and the GEO Group (formerly know as the Wackenhut Corrections Corporation). CCA now operates the fifth-largest correctional system in the United States. It currently manages 72,000 beds in 65 facilities in 19 states and the District of Columbia. This makes up half of all beds under contract. Today, because many states now have excess capacity in their prisons, the growth of the private prison industry is expected to level off somewhat, however, federal detention of aliens by the federal government will undoubtedly increase.

Advocates of privately operated prisons claim that they provide the same level of care as the states but more cheaply and flexibly. Research on private prisons points to the difficulties of measuring the costs and quality of these institutions (Camp and Gaes, 2002: 427–450.) One issue is that many of the "true costs" (fringe benefits, contracting supervision, federal grants) are not taken into consideration. A recent study of 48 juvenile correctional facilities found little difference between private and public facilities in terms of environmental quality (Armstrong and MacKenzie, 2003: 542–563). The Bureau of Justice Statistics found that compared to private prisons a greater proportion of state facilities provide access to work programs, education programs, and counseling programs. But the percentage of private correctional facilities providing education programs had substantially increased since 1995 (BJS, 2003: 6).

Supporters of privatization claim that they can run prisons more cheaply than the state. In 1996 the U.S. General Accounting Office issued a report comparing the costs of public and private prisons. After reviewing five separate

The website for the Corrections Corporation of America is found online. To link to this website, go to *The American System of Criminal Justice* 12e companion site at academic.cengage.com/criminaljustice/cole.

studies, it could not determine whether privatization saved money (*New York Times*, July 13, 1997: D5). Travis Pratt and Jeff Maahs reanalyzed the results of 24 studies and concluded that private prisons were no more cost-effective than public prisons (Pratt and Maahs, 1999: 358–371). When savings can be shown, it appears that they are modest and result primarily from personnel-related costs (Austin and Coventry, 2001: 11).

The profit incentive may result in poor services, as evidenced by a 1995 detainee uprising at an Elizabeth, New Jersey, jail run by Esmore Correctional Services Corporation for the Immigration and Naturalization Service. Undercutting a bid from Wackenhut Corporation by $20 million, Esmore violated the contract by understaffing, abusing detainees, maintaining inadequate physical conditions, and presenting health hazards (*New York Times*, July 23, 1995: 1). In the Northeast Ohio Correctional Center, owned by the Corrections Corporation of America, 20 inmates were stabbed, two of them fatally, during the first ten months of operations (*New York Times*, April 15, 1999: 1).

Political, fiscal, ethical, and administrative issues must be examined before corrections can become too heavily committed to the private ownership and operation of prisons. The political issues, including ethical questions concerning the delegation of social-control functions to people other than state employees, may be the most difficult to overcome. Some people believe that the administration of justice is a basic function of government that should not be delegated. They fear that correctional policy would be skewed because contractors would use their political influence to continue programs not in the public interest. Joseph Hallinan describes the extent to which executives and shareholders of Corrections Corporation of American and U.S. Corrections have funded political campaigns in Indiana, Kentucky, Oklahoma, and Tennessee (Hallinan, 2001: 168–70). Further, some observers fear that the private corporations will press to maintain high occupancy and will "skim off" the best inmates, leaving the most troublesome ones to the public corrections system.

The fiscal value of private corrections cannot yet be demonstrated. However, labor unions have opposed these incursions into the public sector, pointing out that the salaries, benefits, and pensions of workers in private security are lower than those of their public counterparts. Finally, questions have arisen about quality of services, accountability of service providers to corrections officials, and problems related to contract supervision. Opponents cite the many instances in which privately contracted services in group homes, day-care centers, hospitals, and schools have been terminated because of reports of corruption, brutality, or substandard services. Research has shown that staff turnover, escapes, and drug use are problems in private prisons (Camp and Gales, 2002: 427).

A movement for greater government regulation of private prisons is growing. A number of state legislatures have enacted or are considering new laws to ensure that the private prison industry lives up to its contractual obligations. Several members of Congress have introduced bills to prohibit federal inmates from serving their time in private prisons.

The idea of privately run correctional facilities has stimulated much interest among the general public and within the criminal justice community, but the future of this approach is quite uncertain. Further privatization of criminal justice services may ensue, or privatization may become only a limited venture initiated at a time of prison crowding, fiscal constraints on governments, and revival of the free-enterprise ideology. Harding (2001) believes that the future of privatization will revolve around the ability of contracting states to achieve effective public accountability and the ability of the private sector to deliver high-quality correctional services that provide excellent value for the money (Harding, 2001: 265–346).

Incarcerated Immigrants

The United States has experienced an upsurge in the number of noncitizen immigrants, both legal and illegal, during the past twenty years. The number of illegal **aliens** has been estimated at more than 12 million, although, since 2000, about 1 million immigrants per year have legally become residents. According to the U.S. Bureau of the Census 6.9 percent of the total U.S. population are noncitizens (*New York Times*, May 30, 2007).

aliens
Foreign-born noncitizens.

Incarcerated immigrants present a complex jurisdictional and operational situation for corrections. Incarcerated immigrants may be classified into three categories.

1. Illegal immigrants. Some noncitizens are detained by the U.S. Immigration and Customs Enforcement (ICE) branch of the Department of Homeland Security because they have violated immigration laws and are subject to **deportation**. The Bureau of Justice Statistics reported that on December 31, 2006, there were 27,634 detainees under the jurisdiction of ICE. These detainees were held in the sixteen ICE detention centers located around the country (6,079), in private facilities under contract with ICE (3,358), in Federal Bureau of Prisons facilities (592), state prisons (96), local jails (12,482), and other facilities (5,027) (BJS, 2007: 9). This one-day count does not include the more than 300,000 detainees who pass through the system in a year (*New York Times*, March 24, 2008: A15).

deportation
Formal removal by the federal government of an alien from the United States for violation of immigration and other laws.

2. Sentenced illegal immigrants. Some illegal immigrants have been sentenced to prisons and jails for criminal offenses. They must usually serve these sentences before they are handed over to ICE for deportation processing.

3. Sentenced legal immigrants. These are aliens who are legally in the United States and serving time for a criminal conviction. These people may also be subject to deportation upon completion of the sentence if the offense is serious, such as murder, rape, and drug trafficking, and makes the immigrant ineligible for citizenship.

Immigrants in the custody of ICE are not convicted prisoners but are detainees held pursuant to civil immigration laws awaiting disposition of their cases by an administrative judge (Patel and Jawetz, n.d.: 2). According to the U.S. Court of Appeals of the Ninth Circuit (*Jones v. Blanas*, 2004) immigration detainees must be confined under conditions that are less restrictive than those under which criminal pretrial detainees or convicted prisoners are held. In November 2000, the formerly named Immigration and Naturalization Service released the *Detention Operations Manual*, which stipulates detention standards for all facilities holding detainees for more than 72 hours.

The number of sentenced immigrants (legal and illegal) in U.S. prisons and jails is in dispute. The Federal Bureau of Prisons lists 52,820 inmates (26.3 percent of B of P inmates) whose citizenship is other than the United States being held in their facilities (http://www.bop.gov/news/quick.jsp#1). What is lacking is hard data on the number of sentenced immigrants held for criminal convictions in state prisons and local jails. Only 10 percent of the country's jails have access to ICE databases. Some observers have estimated the sentenced immigrant population as about 6.9 percent of the total number of inmates in prisons and jails.

Forty-five percent of alien arrests are for drug and immigration offenses. Scholars have argued that there is little difference between incarceration rates of citizens and noncitizens. In fact, it is pointed out that immigrants have more to lose because conviction prevents them from becoming citizens and makes them deportable.

Immigrant prisoners present problems for correctional officials. In addition to language and cultural barriers their deportation status may cause confusion. Questions arise as to the conditions under which detainees must be held when they are assigned to a non-ICE prison or jail. Second, it is generally assumed that illegal immigrant offenders must complete their criminal sentence before they enter the deportation process, but questions arise concerning their status as they appeal deportation. ICE has a Criminal Alien Program designed to ensure that criminal aliens incarcerated within federal, state, and local facilities are not released into the community before a final order of removal is obtained.

There is also a federal program in which participating jurisdictions can deputize local law enforcement officers to receive training and assist ICE in processing illegal immigrants. The local officers investigate suspects, both on the street and those held in correctional facilities, who they think are illegal immigrants. They work with ICE to increase arrests and expedite the deportation process.

But cracks in this program have developed in Virginia's Prince William County. ICE agents are supposed to pick up suspected illegal aliens from the jail within 72 hours of their release from county custody. Instead, Prince William jail board chairman Patrick Hurd has said that some inmates are waiting as long as four weeks to be transferred, and the already crowded jail is spending $3 million a year in additional transportation and processing costs. Another factor driving up jail costs is that inmates facing county charges, who in the past might have been released on bail, must now be held for ICE. The county picks up the bill (*Washington Post*, April 8, 2008: A01).

States have argued that incarceration of immigrants is costly and that they should be reimbursed by the federal government. The U.S. Department of Justice's State Criminal Alien Assistance Program (SCAAP) reimburses state and local governments for a portion of the incarceration costs. However, a study by the U.S. Government Accountability Office estimates that the reimbursement under SCAAP is only 25 percent of the actual cost (Stana letter, 2006, GAO-65-337R) That study found that 76 percent of the SCAAP criminal aliens were incarcerated in five states: California (40 percent), Texas (15 percent), New York (8 percent), Florida (7 percent), and Arizona (6 percent).

ICE Rapid Repatriation programs in Arizona and New York provide early release of nonviolent, illegal-immigrant inmates from state prisons, and then hand them to ICE for deportation. An Arizona corrections review found that 40 percent of incarcerated illegal immigrants were convicted of violent assaults and were ineligible for early release. Among those who could be released early, 37 percent were convicted of drug or alcohol charges and 18 percent for property crimes (*The Arizona Republic*, April 15, 2008).

In recent years there has been a sharp escalation in the federal crackdown on illegal workers. This is best illustrated by the prosecution and sentencing of 297 Guatemalans arrested in a May 12, 2008, raid on a meat processing plan in Waterloo, Iowa. Ten days later, in unusually swift proceedings, the workers admitted taking jobs using fraudulent Social Security cards and immigration documents. Two hundred and seventy workers were sentenced to five months in prison to be followed by immediate deportation (*New York Times*, May 24, 2008).

With immigration a "hot" political issue, ICE is under pressure to expedite deportations. Immigration officials are scouring prisons, jails, and courts to identify deportable aliens. ICE reported that in the 12-month period ending September 30, 2007, 164,000 criminals had been placed in deportation status, two and a half times as many as in the prior year. (*Washington Post*, February 27, 2008: A01). Julie L. Myers, head of ICE has said that ICE plans to develop a nationwide data base of incarcerated immigrants so as to identify their numbers and plan for their deportation. She told Congress that it would cost $2 billion to find and deport convicted immigrants (*New York Times*, May 24, 2008). Meanwhile incarcerated immigrants contribute to prison and jail crowding, access medical services, and cause instability in the general population of some institutions.

JAILS: DETENTION AND SHORT-TERM INCARCERATION

Most Americans do not distinguish between jails and prisons. **Prisons** are federal and state correctional institutions that hold offenders who are sentenced to terms of more than one year. **Jails** are local facilities for the detention of people awaiting trial and sentenced misdemeanants. Jails are also a holding facility for social misfits—derelicts, junkies, prostitutes, the mentally ill, and disturbers of public order.

prison
An institution for the incarceration of people convicted of serious crimes, usually felonies.

jail
An institution authorized to hold pretrial detainees and sentenced misdemeanants for periods longer than 48 hours. Most jails are administered by county governments; in six jurisdictions, by state governments.

Origins and Evolution

Jails in the United States descend from feudal practices in twelfth-century England. At that time, an officer of the crown, the reeve, was appointed in each shire (what we call a county) to collect taxes, keep the peace, and run the gaol (jail). Among other duties, the *shire reeve* (from which the word *sheriff* evolved) caught and held in custody, until a court hearing determined guilt or innocence, people accused of breaking the law. With the development of the workhouse in the sixteenth century, the sheriff took on added responsibilities for vagrants and the unemployed who were sent there. The sheriff made a living by collecting fees from inmates and by hiring out their labor.

English settlers brought these institutions to the American colonies. After the Revolution, the local community elected law enforcement officials—sheriffs and constables—to run the jail. As in England, the early American jails were used to detain accused people awaiting trial as well as to shelter misfits.

In the 1800s, the jail began to change in response to the penitentiary movement. In addition to shouldering traditional responsibilities, jails now held offenders serving short terms. The development of probation removed some offenders, as did adult reformatories. However, even with these innovations, the overwhelming majority of accused and convicted misdemeanants were held in jail. This pattern continued to modern times.

The Contemporary Jail

Of the 3,376 jails in the United States, 2,700 have a county-level jurisdiction, and most are administered by an elected sheriff. An additional 600 or so municipal jails are in operation. Only in six states—Alaska, Connecticut, Delaware, Hawaii, Rhode Island, and Vermont—does the state administer jails for adults. There are also an estimated 13,500 police lockups (or drunk tanks) and similar holding facilities authorized to detain people for up to 48 hours. The Federal Bureau of Prisons operates 11 jails for detained prisoners only, holding a total of 11,000 inmates. There are 47 privately operated jails, under contract to state or local governments, and they house 2.4 percent of the total jail population (BJS, 2004: 2).

As we have seen, the primary function of jails is to hold people awaiting trial and people who have been sentenced for misdemeanors to terms of less than one year. On a national basis, about 62 percent of jail inmates are unconvicted pretrial detainees, a 20 percent increase over the past decade (Petteruti and Walsh, 2008: 10). In some states, convicted felons may serve more than one year in jail instead of in prison. For 87 percent of the sentenced population, however, stays in jail are less than one month.

Jails and police lockups shoulder responsibility for housing not only criminal defendants and offenders but also those viewed as problems by society. The criminal justice system is thus linked to other government agencies. People with substance abuse and mental problems have become a part of the jail population. They are often reported to the police for their deviant acts, which, although not necessarily illegal, are upsetting to the citizenry (urinating in public, appearing disoriented, shouting obscenities, and so on). Temporary confinement in a lockup or jail may be necessary if no appropriate social service facilities are available. This situation has been likened to a revolving door that shifts these "street people" from the police station to the jail. After an appearance in court, they are often released to the streets to start their cycle through the system all over again.

Ten percent of the national jail population consists of sentenced felons for whom state prisons have no room. They also house people awaiting transportation to prison, such as those convicted of parole or probation violations. This backup of inmates has caused difficulties in some states for judges and jail administrators, who must often put misdemeanants on probation because no jail space is available.

The capacity of jails varies greatly. The 50 largest jurisdictions hold about 30 percent of the nation's jailed inmates. The two jurisdictions with the most inmates, Los Angeles County and New York City, together hold approximately 33,000 inmates in multiple jails, or 4.3 percent of the national total (BJS, 2007: 7). The Los Angeles County Men's Central Jail alone holds more than 6,000 people, but most jails are much smaller, with two-thirds holding fewer than 50 people. However, these small facilities are dwindling in number because of new jail construction and the creation of regional, multicounty facilities.

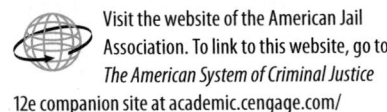 Visit the website of the American Jail Association. To link to this website, go to *The American System of Criminal Justice* 12e companion site at academic.cengage.com/criminaljustice/cole.

Who Is in Jail?

With an estimated 13 million jail admissions and releases per year, more people directly experience jails than experience prisons, mental hospitals, and halfway houses combined. Even if we consider that some people of this total are admitted more than once, probably at least six to seven million people are detained at some time during the year. Nationally, almost 773,000 people, both the convicted and the unconvicted, sit in jail on any one day. However, the number of people held at any one time in jail does not tell the complete story. Many are held for less than 24 hours; others may reside in jail as sentenced inmates for up to one year; a few may await their trial for more than a year (BJS, 2008: 3).

The most recent National Jail Census shows that about 88 percent of inmates are men, most are younger than 30 years old, less than half are white, and most have very little education and incomes (BJS, 2007: 6). An estimated 60 percent of jail inmates have mental health problems. During the last decade, as the country has become more anxious about immigrants—the jailing of people for immigration violations grew by 500 percent (BJS, 2007: 18). The demo-

Direct supervision jails such as the Cayuga County Jail in New York is designed to permit easy supervision of detainees in their cells and in the common area where they spend time during the day. What problems might exist in older jails that were not designed to enable officers to easily keep watch over the entire living area?

graphic characteristics of the jail population differ greatly from those of the national population (Figure 13.2).

Managing Jails

Jail administrators face several problems that good management practices cannot always overcome. These problems include (1) the perceived role of the jail in the local criminal justice system, (2) the inmate population, and (3) fiscal problems.

Role of the Jail

As facilities to detain accused people awaiting trial, jails customarily have been run by law enforcement agencies. We might reasonably expect that the agency that arrests and transports defendants to court should also administer the facility that holds them. Typically, however, neither sheriffs nor deputies have much interest in corrections. They often think of themselves as police officers and of the jail as merely an extension of their law enforcement activities. In some major cities, municipal departments of correction, rather than the police, manage the jails.

Many experts argue that jails have outgrown police administration. Jails no longer are simply holding places but now represent one of the primary correctional facilities. In fact, much correctional work is directed toward jail inmates. Probation officers conduct presentence investigations in jails, alcohol, and drug abusers receive treatment in many facilities, and inmates work toward reintegration or perform community service out of some facilities. Therefore, the effective administration of jails requires skills in offender management and rehabilitation that are not generally included in law enforcement training.

 Locate current statistics about jails online. To link to this website, go to *The American System of Criminal Justice* 12e companion site at academic.cengage.com/criminaljustice/cole and then click on jails at the site.

Inmate Characteristics

The mixture of offenders of widely diverse ages and criminal histories is an often-cited problem in U.S. jails. Because most inmates are viewed as temporary residents, little attempt is made to classify them for either security or

FIGURE 13.2
Characteristics of adult jail inmates in U.S. jails
Compared with the American population as a whole, jails are disproportionately inhabited by men, minorities, the poorly educated, and those with low income.

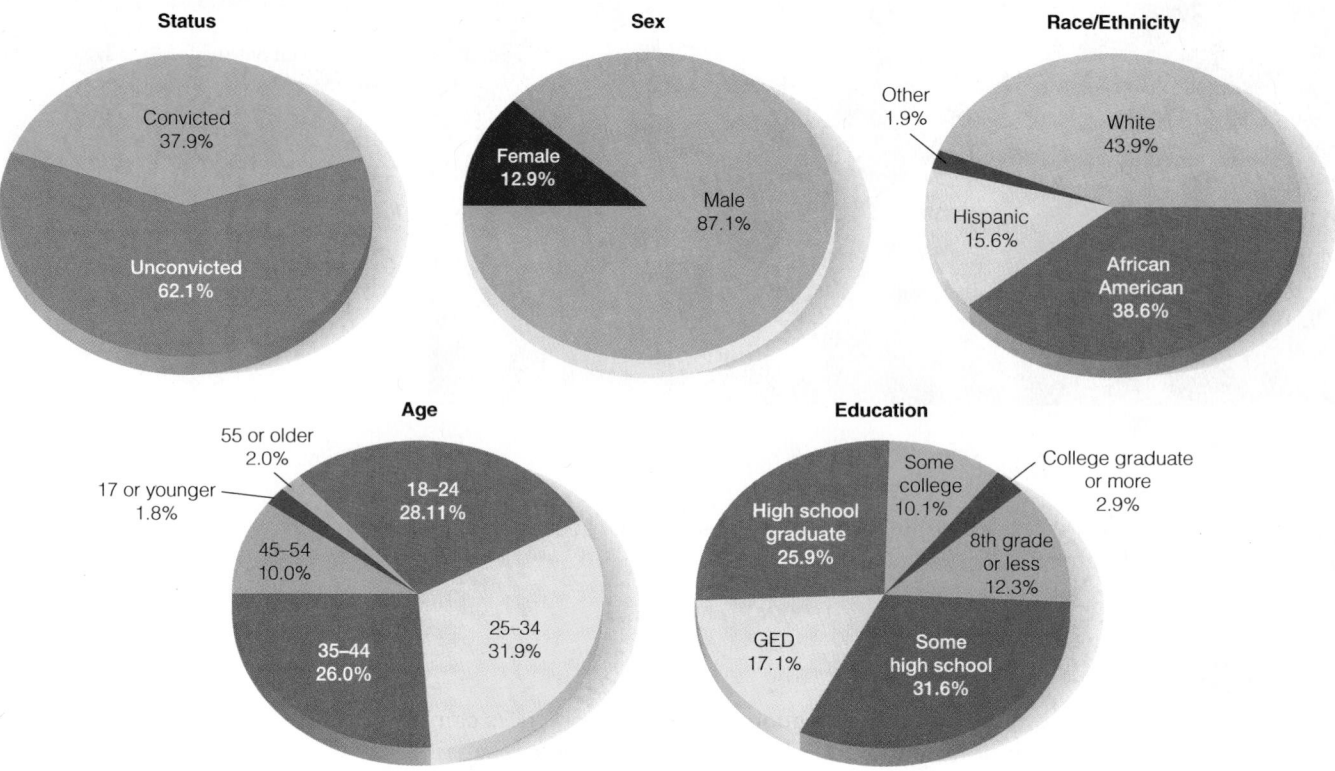

Source: Bureau of Justice Statistics, *Bulletin*, May 2006, p. 8, *Bulletin*, June 2007, p. 6.; Petteruti, A. and N. Walsh, 2008, p. 7.

treatment purposes. Horror stories of the mistreatment of young offenders by older, stronger, and more violent inmates occasionally come to public attention. The physical condition of most jails aggravates this situation, because most are old, overcrowded, and lacking in basic facilities. Many sentenced felons prefer to move on to state prison, where the conditions are likely to be better.

Because of constant inmate turnover and because local control provides an incentive to keep costs down, correctional services are usually lacking in jail. Recreational facilities and treatment programs are not usually found there. Medical services are generally minimal. Such conditions add to the idleness and tensions of the inmates. Suicides and high levels of violence are hallmarks of many jails. In any one year, almost half the people who die while in jail have committed suicide.

Fiscal Problems

Jail helps to control crime but also drains local resources. The tension between these two public interests often surfaces in debates over expenditures for jail construction and operation. Because resources are often insufficient, many jails are overcrowded, lack programs, and do not have enough officers for effective supervision. In some states, multicounty jails have been created to serve an entire region as a means of operating facilities in a cost-efficient way. See "New Directions in Criminal Justice Policy" for one approach to solving these and related problems.

NEW DIRECTIONS in CRIMINAL JUSTICE POLICY

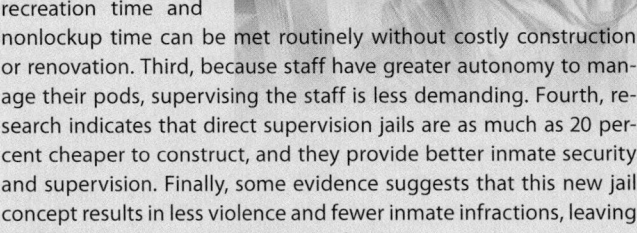

Direct Supervision Jails

TO DEAL WITH jail crowding, violence, and the inefficiency of old construction, many jurisdictions have turned toward the direct supervision jail. This jail is both a design and a set of programs that attempts to use the physical plant to improve the staff's ability to manage and interact with the inmate population and to provide services. Three general concepts are employed: podular design, interaction space, and personal space.

The podular unit, which replaces the old cell blocks, is a living area for a group of inmates. Twelve to 25 individual cells are organized into a unit (the pod) that serves as something like a self-contained mini-jail. Typically the cell doors open into a common living area where the inmates of the pod are allowed to congregate.

The direct supervision jail tends to reinforce interactions of various sorts. For example, inmates have greater freedom to interact socially and recreationally. Further, in traditional jails, bars and doors separate correctional officers from inmates; the direct supervision jail places them in the same rooms with inmates.

The new structure offers several advantages over older jails. First, its flexibility makes it more economical. When jail populations are low, whole pods can be temporarily shut down, saving personnel and operational costs. Second, minimum standards for recreation time and nonlockup time can be met routinely without costly construction or renovation. Third, because staff have greater autonomy to manage their pods, supervising the staff is less demanding. Fourth, research indicates that direct supervision jails are as much as 20 percent cheaper to construct, and they provide better inmate security and supervision. Finally, some evidence suggests that this new jail concept results in less violence and fewer inmate infractions, leaving staff feeling more secure in their work.

Researching the Internet

 Access the article by Towles Biglow, "Comparing the Cost of Direct Supervision and Traditional Jails" online. To link to this website, go to *The American System of Criminal Justice* 12e companion site at academic.cengage.com/criminaljustice/cole. What are the major findings?

As criminal justice policy has become more punitive, jails, like prisons, have become crowded. Surveys have documented population increases averaging 6 percent during each of the past five years. Even with new construction and with alternatives such as release on recognizance programs, diversion, intensive probation supervision, and house arrest with electronic monitoring, the jail population continues to rise. The $4.5 billion annual cost of operating jails is a great financial burden for local governments.

checkpoint

10. What are the functions of jails?
11. What are three of the problems affecting jails?

THE LAW OF CORRECTIONS

Prior to the 1960s, most courts maintained a **hands-off policy** with respect to corrections. Only a few state courts had recognized rights for offenders. Most judges felt that prisoners and probationers did not have protected rights and that courts should not interfere in the operational agencies dealing with probation, prisons, and parole.

Since the 1960s, however, offenders have gained access to the courts to contest correctional officers' decisions and aspects of their punishment that they believe violate basic rights. Judicial decisions have defined and recognized the constitutional rights of probationers, prisoners, and parolees, as well as the need for policies and procedures that respect those rights.

hands-off policy
Judges should not interfere with the administration of correctional institutions.

civic engagement
your role in the system

Imagine that you have been arrested by mistake. In the jail, your cell mates threaten you and you asked to be moved to a different cell. You are not moved. Eventually, you are assaulted and suffer minor injuries. *Make a list of any rights that you believe were violated in this situation and what you would do about it.* Then read about what happened to a jail inmate in California who raised this complaint. To link to this website, go to *The American System of Criminal Justice* 12e companion site at academic.cengage.com/criminaljustice/cole.

Chapter 4 presented an overview of the law in relation to the criminal justice system as a whole. In that discussion, we touched on prisoners' rights. Here, we further explore court decisions in relation to the many aspects of corrections.

Bear in mind that corrections law does not just apply to people who have been convicted of committing crimes. It also applies to people being held in jail while they await the processing of their cases. Many of these people will have charges against them dropped. Others will eventually be found not guilty and released. Also remember that anyone in the United States can be arrested. For example, President George W. Bush and Vice President Dick Cheney were both arrested for drinking and driving before they achieved high positions in government. You do not need to commit a crime to be arrested. You merely need to be subject to a police officer's discretionary decision to make an arrest. This can happen through being misidentified by a witness or from a variety of everyday acts committed by Americans from all segments of society, such as driving after drinking alcohol or forgetting to carry your driver's license. Think about who might be in jail and therefore be affected by corrections law as you consider "Civic Engagement: Your Role in the System."

Constitutional Rights of Prisoners

Cooper v. Pate (1964)
Prisoners are entitled to the protection of the Civil Rights Act of 1871 and may challenge in federal courts the conditions of their confinement.

The U.S. Supreme Court decision in *Cooper v. Pate* (1964) signaled the end of the hands-off policy. The court said that through the Civil Rights Act of 1871 (referred to here as Section 1983), state prisoners were *persons* whose rights are protected by the Constitution. The act imposes *civil liability* on any state or local official who deprives someone of constitutional rights. It allows suits against state officials to be heard in the federal courts. Because of *Cooper v. Pate,* the federal courts now recognize that prisoners may sue state and local officials over such things as brutality by guards, inadequate nutrition and medical care, theft of personal property, and the denial of basic rights.

For news of the current actions of the Supreme Court, see the website On the Docket. To link to this website, go to *The American System of Criminal Justice* 12e companion site at academic.cengage.com/criminaljustice/cole.

The first successful prisoners' rights cases involved the most excessive of prison abuses: brutality and inhumane physical conditions. Gradually, however, prison litigation has focused more directly on the daily activities of the institution, especially on the administrative rules that regulate inmates' conduct. The result has been a series of court decisions concerning the First, Fourth, Eighth, and Fourteenth Amendments to the Constitution. (See Appendix A for the full text of these amendments.)

checkpoint

12. What is the hands-off policy?
13. Why is the case of *Cooper v. Pate* important to the expansion of prisoners' rights?

First Amendment

The First Amendment guarantees freedom of speech, press, assembly, petition, and religion. Many of the restrictions of prison life—access to reading materials, censorship of mail, and rules affecting some religious practices—have been successfully challenged by prisoners in the courts.

Since 1970, courts have extended limited rights of freedom of speech and expression to prisoners. They have required correctional administrators to show why restrictions on these rights must be imposed (Table 13.3). For example, in 1974 the Supreme Court ruled that censorship of mail was permissible only when officials could demonstrate a compelling government interest in maintaining security *(Procunier v. Martinez)*. The result has increased the communication between inmates and the outside world. However, in *Turner v. Safley* (1987), the Court upheld a Missouri ban on correspondence between inmates in different institutions, as a means of combating gang violence and the communication of escape plans.

The First Amendment prevents Congress from making laws respecting the establishment of religion or prohibiting its free exercise. Cases concerning the free exercise of religion have caused the judiciary some problems, especially when the religious practice may interfere with prison routine and the maintenance of order.

The growth of the Black Muslim religion in prisons set the stage for suits demanding that this group be granted the same privileges as other faiths (special diets, access to clergy and religious publications, opportunities for group worship). Attorneys for the Muslims succeeded in winning several important cases that helped to establish for prisoners the First Amendment right to free exercise of religion. These decisions also helped Native Americans, Orthodox Jews, and other prisoners to practice their religions. Court decisions have upheld prisoners' rights to be served meals consistent with religious dietary laws, to correspond with religious leaders, to possess religious literature, to wear a beard if their belief requires it, and to assemble for services. In sum, members of religious minorities have broken new legal ground on First Amendment issues.

TABLE 13.3	**Selected Interpretations of the First Amendment as Applied to Prisoners**
The Supreme Court has made numerous decisions affecting prisoners' rights to freedom of speech and expression and freedom of religion.	
Case	**Decision**
Procunier v. Martinez (1974)	Censorship of mail is permitted only to the extent necessary to maintain prison security.
Turner v. Safley (1987)	Inmates do not have a right to receive mail from one another, and rights can be limited by rules "reasonably related to legitimate penological interests."
Beard v. Banks (2006)	In an effort to promote security and rule compliance, policies that deny magazines, newspapers, and photographs to the most incorrigible inmates are constitutional.
Theriault v. Carlson (1977)	The First Amendment does not protect so-called religions that are obvious shams, that tend to mock established institutions, and whose members lack religious sincerity.
Gittlemacker v. Prasse (1970)	The state must give inmates the opportunity to practice their religion but is not required to provide a member of the clergy.
O'Lone v. Estate of Shabazz (1987)	The rights of Muslim prisoners are not violated when a work assignment makes it impossible for them to attend religious services.
Kahane v. Carlson (1975)	An orthodox Jewish inmate has the right to a diet consistent with his religious beliefs unless the government can show cause why it cannot be provided.
Fulwood v. Clemmer (1962)	The Muslim faith must be recognized as a religion, and officials may not restrict members from holding services.
Cruz v. Beto (1972)	Prisoners who adhere to other than conventional beliefs may not be denied the opportunity to practice their religion.

Fourth Amendment

The Fourth Amendment prohibits unreasonable searches and seizures, but courts have not been active in extending these protections to prisoners. Thus regulations viewed as reasonable to maintain security and order in an institution may be justified. For example, the 1984 decision in ***Hudson v. Palmer*** upheld the right of officials to search cells and confiscate any materials found.

Table 13.4 outlines some of the Supreme Court's Fourth Amendment opinions. They reveal the fine balance between institutional need and the right to privacy. Body searches have been harder for administrators to justify than cell searches, for example. But body searches have been upheld when they are part of a policy clearly related to an identifiable and legitimate institutional need and when they are not intended to humiliate or degrade.

With the increased employment of both male and female correctional officers, courts have ruled that staff members of one sex may not strip search inmates of the opposite sex except in an emergency situation. Here, the

Hudson v. Palmer (1984)
Prison officials have the authority to search cells and confiscate any materials found.

TABLE 13.4	Selected Interpretations of the Fourth Amendment as Applied to Prisoners
The Supreme Court has often considered the question of unreasonable searches and seizures.	
Case	**Decision**
Lanza v. New York (1962)	Conversations recorded in a jail visitor's room are not protected by the Fourth Amendment.
Bell v. Wolfish (1979)	Strip searches, including searches of body cavities after contact visits, may be carried out when need for such searches outweighs the personal rights invaded.
U.S. v. Hitchcock (1972)	A warrantless search of a cell is not unreasonable, and documentary evidence found there is not subject to suppression in court. It is not reasonable to expect a prison cell to be accorded the same level of privacy as a home or automobile.
Lee v. Downes (1981) [U.S. Court of Appeals]	Staff members of one sex may not normally supervise inmates of the opposite sex during bathing, toilet use, or strip searches.
Hudson v. Palmer (1984)	Officials may search cells without a warrant and seize materials found there.

inconvenience of ensuring that the officer is of the same sex as the inmate does not justify the situation. Similar concerns can arise in the supervision of other personal locations, such as showers and bathrooms.

Eighth Amendment

The Constitution's prohibition of cruel and unusual punishments has been tied to prisoners' need for decent treatment and minimum health standards. The courts have applied three principal tests under the Eighth Amendment to determine whether conditions are unconstitutional: (1) whether the punishment shocks the conscience of a civilized society, (2) whether the punishment is unnecessarily cruel, and (3) whether the punishment goes beyond legitimate penal aims.

Federal courts have ruled that, although some aspects of prison life may be acceptable, the combination of various factors—the *totality of conditions*—may determine that living conditions in the institution constitute cruel and unusual punishment. When courts have found brutality, unsanitary facilities, overcrowding, and inadequate food, judges have used the Eighth Amendment to order sweeping changes and even, in some cases, to take over administration of entire prisons or corrections systems. In these cases judges have ordered wardens to follow specific internal procedures and to spend money on certain improvements (Table 13.5).

checkpoint

14. Which amendments to the Bill of Rights have been most influential in expanding prisoners' rights?

Fourteenth Amendment

One word and two clauses of the Fourteenth Amendment are relevant to the question of prisoners' rights. The relevant word is *state*, which is found in several clauses of the Fourteen Amendment. It was not until the 1960s that the Supreme Court ruled that through the Fourteenth Amendment, the Bill of Rights restricts state government actions affecting criminal justice.

As we saw in Chapter 4, the first important clause concerns procedural due process, which requires that government officials treat all people fairly and justly and that official decisions be made according to procedures prescribed by law. The second important clause is the equal protection clause. Assertions that prisoners have been denied equal protection of the law are based on claims of racial, gender, or religious discrimination.

Due Process in Prison Discipline In *Wolff v. McDonnell* (1974), the Supreme Court ruled that basic procedural rights must be present when decisions are made about the disciplining of inmates for serious rule violations. Specifically, prisoners have a right to receive notice of the complaint, to have a fair hearing,

Wolff v. McDonnell (1974)
Basic elements of procedural due process must be present when decisions are made about the disciplining of an inmate.

to confront witnesses, to get help in preparing for the hearing, and to be given a written statement of the decision. However, the Court further stated that prisoners do not have a right to cross-examine witnesses and that the evidence presented by the offender shall not be unduly hazardous to institutional safety or correctional goals. The context of corrections and procedures used in prisons are not the same as those in a formal trial at a courthouse.

As a result of these Supreme Court decisions, some of which are outlined in Table 13.6, prison officials have established rules that provide elements of due process in disciplinary and other proceedings. In many institutions, a disciplinary committee receives the charges, conducts hearings, and decides guilt and punishment. Even with these protections, prisoners are still powerless and may risk further punishment if they challenge the warden's decisions too vigorously.

Equal Protection In 1968 the Supreme Court firmly established that racial discrimination may not be official policy within prison walls (*Lee v. Washington*). Segregation can be justified only as a temporary measure during periods when violence between races is demonstrably imminent. More recent cases concerning equal protection deal with issues concerning female offenders. Although the Supreme Court has yet to rule, state and lower federal courts have considered several cases. In *Pargo v. Elliott* (1995), for example, female inmates in Iowa argued that their equal protection rights were violated because programs and services were not the same as those provided to male inmates. The court ruled that because of differences and needs, identical treatment is not always required for men and women.

TABLE 13.5	Selected Interpretations of the Eighth Amendment as Applied to Prisoners
The Supreme Court is called on to determine whether correctional actions constitute cruel and unusual punishment.	
Case	**Decision**
Ruiz v. Estelle (1975)	Conditions of confinement in the Texas prison system are unconstitutional and remedies must be implemented.
Estelle v. Gamble (1976)	Deliberate indifference to serious medical needs of prisoners constitutes the unnecessary and wanton infliction of pain, and thus violates the Eighth Amendment.
Rhodes v. Chapman (1981)	Double-celling and crowding do not necessarily constitute cruel and unusual punishment. It must be shown that the conditions involve "wanton and unnecessary infliction of pain" and are "grossly disproportionate" to the severity of the crime warranting imprisonment.
Whitley v. Albers (1986)	An innocent prisoner mistakenly shot in the leg during a disturbance does not suffer cruel and unusual punishment if the action was taken in good faith to maintain discipline rather than for the malicious purpose of causing harm.
Wilson v. Seiter (1991)	Prisoners must not only prove that prison conditions are objectively cruel and unusual but also show that they exist because of the deliberate indifference of officials.
Overton v. Bazetta (2003)	Regulations suspending visiting privileges for two years for those prisoners who have "flunked" two drug tests is not a violation of the cruel and unusual punishment clause. The regulations bear a rational relation to legitimate penological objectives.

checkpoint

15. Which two clauses of the Fourteenth Amendment have been interpreted by the Supreme Court to apply to prisoners' rights?

A Change in Judicial Direction?

During the past 30 years, the Supreme Court has been less supportive of expanding prisoners' rights, and a few decisions reflect a retreat. In *Bell v. Wolfish* (1979), the justices took pains to say that prison administrators should be given wide-ranging deference in the adoption and execution of policies. In *Daniels v. Williams* (1986) the concept of deliberate indifference surfaced. Here the Court said that prisoners could sue for damages only if officials had violated rights

TABLE 13.6	Selected Interpretations of the Fourteenth Amendment as Applied to Prisoners

The Supreme Court has issued rulings concerning procedural due process and equal protection.

Case	Decision
Wolff v. McDonnell (1974)	The basic elements of procedural due process must be present when decisions are made concerning the disciplining of an inmate.
Baxter v. Palmigiano (1976)	Although due process must be accorded, an inmate has no right to counsel in a disciplinary hearing.
Vitek v. Jones (1980)	The involuntary transfer of a prisoner to a mental hospital requires a hearing and other minimal elements of due process such as notice and the availability of counsel.
Sandin v. Conner (1995)	Prison regulations do not give rise to protected due process liberty interests unless they place atypical and significant hardships on a prisoner.

 The position of the American Civil Liberties Union on the Prison Litigation Reform Act is found by clicking on "Prisons" on their website. To link to this website, go to *The American System of Criminal Justice* 12e companion site at academic.cengage.com/criminaljustice/cole.

through deliberate actions. This reasoning was extended in *Wilson v. Seiter* (1991), where the Court ruled that a prisoner's conditions of confinement are not unconstitutional unless it can be shown that prison administrators had acted with "deliberate indifference" to basic human needs (Call, 1995: 390–405; Smith, 1993: 187–212).

Many scholars believe that the deliberate-indifference requirement indicates a shift from the use of objective criteria (proof that the inmate suffered conditions protected by the Eighth Amendment) to subjective criteria (the state of mind of correctional officials, namely, deliberate indifference) in determining whether prison conditions are unconstitutional.

In 1996, Congress passed the Prison Litigation Reform Act, making it more difficult for prisoners to file civil rights lawsuits and for judges to make decisions affecting prison operations. For example, the Act:

- Requires that inmates exhaust the prison's grievance procedure before filing a law suit
- Requires judges to dismiss all frivolous law suits
- Requires inmates to pay filing fees
- Specifies that judges' orders affecting prisons must automatically expire after two years unless new hearings are held demonstrating that rights violations continue to exist
- Prohibits prisoners from filing additional civil rights lawsuits if they previously had three lawsuits dismissed as frivolous.

Since the act became law, the number of Section 1983 lawsuits filed in federal courts has dropped dramatically, even though the number of state prisoners has continued to rise (BJS, 2005, Table 5.65).

Impact of the Prisoners' Rights Movement

Although the Supreme Court in recent years reduced its support for the expansion of prisoners' rights, some general changes in American corrections have occurred since the late 1970s. The most obvious are improvements in institutional living conditions and administrative practices. Law libraries or legal assistance is now generally available, communication with the outside is easier, religious practices are protected, inmate complaint procedures have been developed, and due process requirements are emphasized. Prisoners in solitary confinement undoubtedly suffer less neglect than they did before. Although overcrowding is still a major problem, many conditions are much improved and the most brutalizing elements of prison life have diminished. These changes were not entirely the result of court orders, however. They also coincide with the growing influence of college-educated corrections professionals who have sought on their own to improve prisons.

Law and Community Corrections

Although most correctional law concerns prisons and jails, two-thirds of adults under supervision live in the community on probation and parole. However, as with prisoners, offenders in the community are not without rights, and courts have addressed issues concerning due process and searches and seizures.

Conditions of Probation and Parole

Probationers and parolees must live according to conditions specified at the time of their sentencing or parole release. These conditions may interfere with their constitutional rights. The conditions typically limit the right of free association by restricting offenders from contact with their crime partners or victims. However, courts have struck down conditions preventing parolees from exercising their First Amendment rights by giving public speeches and receiving publications.

The case of *Griffin v. Wisconsin* (1987) is a good example of the clash between the Fourth Amendment and community corrections. Learning that Griffin might have a gun, probation officers searched his apartment without a warrant. Noting the practical problems of obtaining a search warrant while a probationer was under supervision, the Supreme Court said that the probation agency must be able to act before the offender damaged himself or society. In Griffin's case the Court felt that the agency had satisfied the Fourth Amendment's reasonableness requirement because a state regulation authorized the warrantless search of probationers' homes.

In a 1998 case, *Pennsylvania Board of Pardons and Parole v. Scott,* a closely divided Court ruled that evidence that would be barred from use by the exclusionary rule by the prosecution in a criminal trial can be used in parole revocation hearings. Operating without a search warrant, officers found guns in the home of a paroled murderer who was barred from owning weapons. The Court upheld revocation of the offender's parole.

Revocation of Probation and Parole

When probationers or parolees do not obey their conditions of release, they may be sent to prison. If the offender commits another crime, probation or parole will likely be revoked. For minor violations of the conditions (such as missing an Alcoholics Anonymous meeting), the supervising officer has discretion as to whether to seek revocation.

The Supreme Court has addressed the question of due process when revocation is being considered. In *Mempa v. Rhay* (1967) the justices determined that a probationer had the right to counsel in revocation and sentencing hearings before a deferred prison sentence could be imposed. Similarly in *Morrissey v. Brewer* (1972) the court ruled that parolees facing revocation must be given a two-step hearing process. In the first stage, a hearing officer determines whether there is probable cause that a violation has occurred. Parolees have the right to be notified of the charges against them, to know the evidence against them, to be allowed to speak on their own behalf, to present witnesses, and to confront the witnesses against them. In the second stage, the revocation hearing, the parolee must receive a notice of charges and the evidence of the violation disclosed, and he or she may cross-examine witnesses. The hearing body determines if the violation is sufficiently severe to warrant revocation. It must give the parolee a written statement outlining the evidence with reasons for the decision.

In the following year the Supreme Court applied the *Morrissey* procedures to probation revocation proceedings in *Gagnon v. Scarpelli* (1973). But in *Gagnon* the Court also looked at the question of the right to counsel. It ruled that there was no absolute requirement. In some cases, however, probationers and parolees might be given attorneys on a case-by-case basis, depending on the complexity of the issues, competence of the offender, and other circumstances.

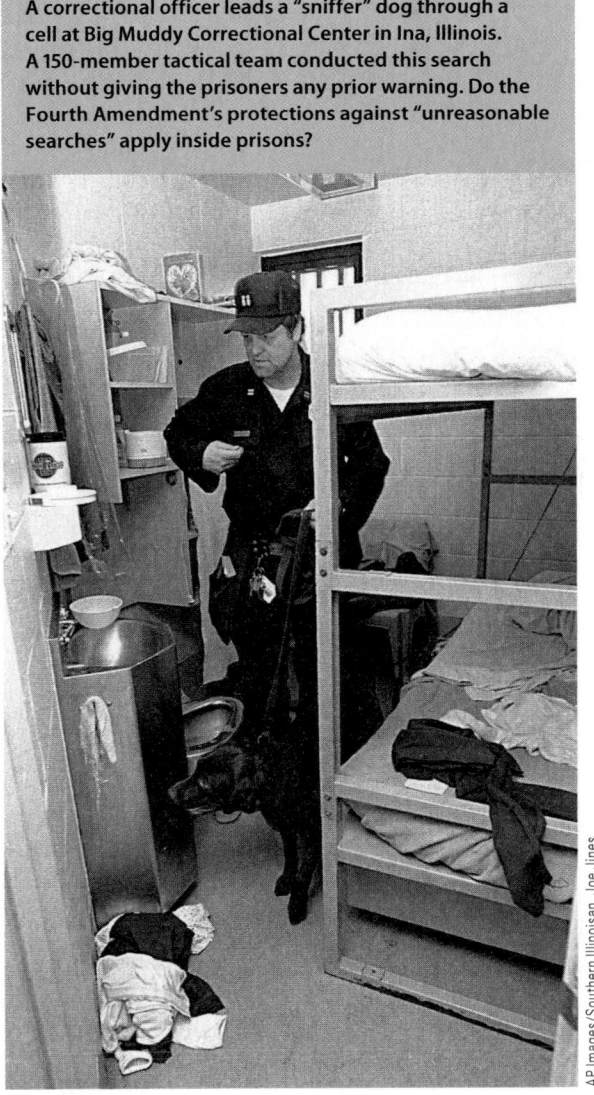

A correctional officer leads a "sniffer" dog through a cell at Big Muddy Correctional Center in Ina, Illinois. A 150-member tactical team conducted this search without giving the prisoners any prior warning. Do the Fourth Amendment's protections against "unreasonable searches" apply inside prisons?

AP Images/Southern Illinoisan, Joe Jines

Mempa v. Rhay (1967)
Probationers have the right to counsel at a combined revocation-sentencing hearing.

Morrissey v. Brewer (1972)
Due process rights require a prompt, informal, two-part inquiry before an impartial hearing officer prior to parole revocation. The parolee may present relevant information and confront witnesses.

Law and Correctional Personnel

Just as law governs relationships among inmates, probationers, and parolees, laws and regulations also define the relationships between correctional administrators and their staff. With the exception of those working for private, nonprofit organizations, correctional personnel are public employees. Here we consider two important aspects of correctional work. First, as public employees all correctional employees are governed by civil service rules and regulations. Second, correctional clients may sue state employees using Section 1983 (Title 42) of the United States Code. We will examine the liability of correctional personnel with regards to these suits.

Civil Service Laws

Civil service laws set the procedures for hiring, promoting, assigning, disciplining, and firing public employees. These laws protect public employees from arbitrary actions by their supervisors. Where correctional personnel can join unions, the collective bargaining process develops rules concerning assignments, working conditions, and grievance procedures. These agreements carry the force of law.

Like their counterparts in the private sector, government employees are protected from discrimination. With the Civil Rights Act of 1964, Congress prohibited employment discrimination based on race, gender, national origin, and religion. Subsequent federal legislation prohibits some forms of age discrimination (Age Discrimination in Employment Act) and discrimination against people with disabilities (Americans with Disability Act). States have their own antidiscrimination laws. All these laws have increased the number of minorities and women who work in corrections.

Unlike many public employees, those who work in corrections are in a difficult position. They must assert authority over persons who have shown that they lack self-control or have little regard for society's rules. Whether in prison, in a probationer's home, or on the street, this responsibility creates pressures and difficult—and sometimes dangerous—situations.

Liability of Correctional Personnel

As noted, in *Cooper v. Pate* (1964) the Supreme Court said that Section 1983—the federal civil rights statute—provides a means for prisoners as well as probationers and parolees, to bring lawsuits against correctional officials. The meaning of Section 1983 was clarified in *Monell v. Department of Social Services for the City of New York* (1978). The court said that individual public employees and their local agency may be sued when a person's civil rights are violated by the agency's "customs and usages." Specifically if an individual can show that harm was caused by employees whose wrongful acts were the result of these "customs, practices, and policies, including poor training and supervision," then the employees as well as their local agencies may be sued. This position was strengthened in *Hope v. Pelzer* (2002). The court denied immunity from suit to Alabama correctional officials who had handcuffed an inmate to a post in the prison yard and denied him adequate water and bathroom breaks. The decision emphasized that a reasonable officer would have known that this was a violation of the Eighth Amendment prohibition on cruel and unusual punishment.

Although huge financial settlements make headlines, and the number of Section 1983 filings are large, few cases come to trial and very few correctional employees must personally pay financial awards to plaintiffs. However, no correctional employee wants to be involved in such legal situations.

CORRECTIONAL POLICY TRENDS

The United States has a large and expanding population under correctional supervision. Since the middle of the 1970s, the United States has fought a war on crime mainly by increasing the severity of sanctions against offenders. This has led to a 500 percent increase in correctional budgets, 4 million people on probation, 2 million incarcerated in prisons and jails, and 770,000 under parole supervision. Some states now spend more on prisons than on higher education. These are staggering figures, especially considering the fact that crime has been decreasing for the past decade. Figure 13.3 shows the tremendous growth in the correctional population since 1980.

Some observers believe that the drop in crime is a result of the harsher arrest and sentencing policies of the past quarter century. Critics say that the "lock 'em up" policies have had little impact on crime and that the fiscal and human costs of current policies severely damage families and communities. Some believe that there now exists a "prison-commercial complex" that encourages increased spending on imprisonment regardless of need. Let's examine community corrections and incarceration policies so as to better understand current practices and future trends.

Community Corrections

Escalating prison growth has captured the public's attention, yet the numbers on probation and parole have actually risen at a faster rate than the incarcerated population has risen. Many factors may explain this growth, including more arrests and successful prosecutions, the lower costs of probation compared with

FIGURE 13.3

Correctional populations in the United States, 1980–December 31, 2007

Although the increase in prison populations receives the most publicity, a greater proportion of correctional growth has occurred in probation and parole.

Sources: Bureau of Justice Statistics, *Bulletin*, November 2006, p. 1; "Prisoners in 2006," December 2007, p. 1; "Probation and Parole in the United States, 2006," December 2007, pp. 1, 3; "Prison Inmates at Midyear 2007," June 2008, p. 1; "Jail Inmates at Midyear 2007," June 2008, p. 1.

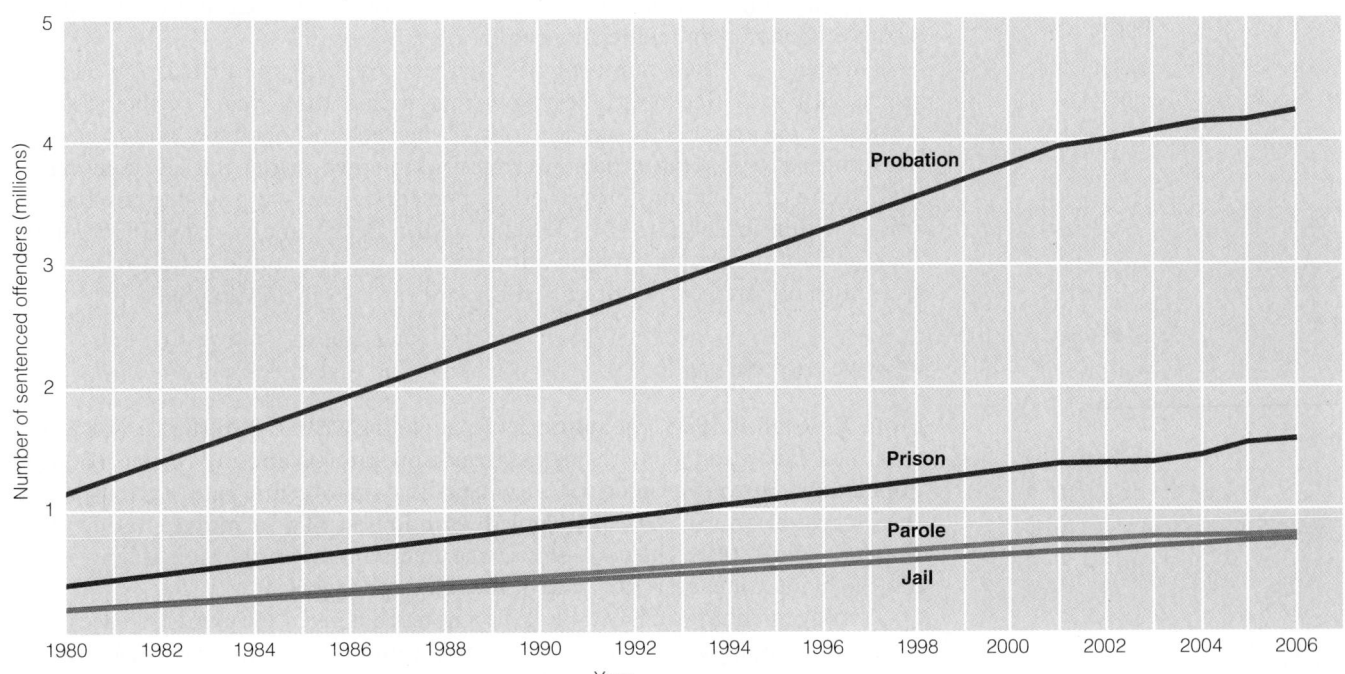

incarceration, prison and jail crowding, and the great numbers of felons now being released from prison.

Probation

People on probation under community supervision now make up 60 percent of the correctional population, yet budgets and staffing have not risen accordingly. In many urban areas, probation caseloads are growing well beyond reasonable management levels: 200- and even 300-person caseloads are no longer unusual. This has led to a deterioration in the quality of supervision. Yet the importance of probation for public safety has never been greater. For example, up to 17 percent of felony arrests in one sample of large urban counties were of people who were on probation at the time of their alleged offense (Reaves and Hart, 1999). As a result, a renewed emphasis on public safety has arisen. Many agencies have seen a resurgence of intensive and structured supervision for selected offenders.

In many respects, then, probation finds itself at a crossroads. Although its credibility is probably as low as it has ever been, its workload is growing dramatically and, in view of the crowding in prison and jails, will probably continue to do so. Under the strain of this workload and on-again, off-again public support, probation faces a serious challenge. Can its methods of supervision and service be adapted successfully to high-risk offenders?

Parole

With the incarcerated population more than quadrupling during the past 30 years, it is not surprising that the number of parolees has also grown. Currently over 650,000 felons are released from prison each year and allowed to live in the community under supervision. In 2006, almost 800,000 offenders were under parole supervision, a threefold increase since 1980 (BJS, 2007: 3). With the massive incarceration binge of recent decades, the number on parole is likely to reach 1 million in the next five years.

Compared with parolees in 1990, today's parolees are older, have served longer sentences, and have higher levels of substance abuse and mental illness; further, more were sentenced for drug violations (Beck, 2000). These characteristics increase reentry problems concerning the renewal of family ties, obtaining a job, and living according to parole rules. Most parolees cannot obtain the assistance necessary to reenter the community successfully.

Further, increased numbers of offenders are being returned to prison as parole violators. Recent studies show that within three years of their release, 68 percent are arrested for a new felony, 47 percent are convicted, and 25 percent are returned to prison for the new crime. Taking revocations for new convictions and "technical violations" together, 52 percent of released prisoners are back in prison within three years (BJS, 2002: 1). Allen Beck's analysis (1997: 10) shows that much of the growth in total admissions to state prisons can be attributed to the return of parolees. We discuss this trend extensively in Chapter 16.

Incarceration

From 1940 until 1973, the number of people incarcerated in the United States remained fairly stable, with an incarceration rate of about 110 per 100,000 population. However, since 1973, when the overall crime rate started to fall, the incarceration rate has quadrupled; standing at 509 at midyear 2007 (BJS, *Bulletin*, June, 2008: 1). As we saw in the chapter opener, the United States now has the highest incarceration rate in the developed world.

A study by the Pew Charitable Trusts notes that given the great increase in the incarcerated population since 1970, "you'd think the nation would have finally run out of lawbreakers to put behind bars." That study goes on to predict that by 2011, 1.7 million men and women will be in prison, an increase of more than

CLOSE-UP

State Highlights, 2011

- By 2011, without changes in sentencing and release policies, Alaska, Arizona, Idaho, Montana, and Vermont can expect to see one new prisoner for every three currently in the system.

- Similarly barring reforms, there will be one new prisoner for every four now in prison in Colorado, Washington, Wyoming, Nevada, South Dakota, and Utah.

- Incarceration rates are expected to spike in Arizona and Nevada from 590 and 540 prisoners per 100,000 residents respectively, to 747 and 640. Particularly worrisome is the growth in the population of young men, the group at highest risk of criminal activity.

- Louisiana, which has the highest incarceration rate among states, with 835 prisoners per 100,000 residents expects that figure to go as high as 859 by 2011.

- Florida is anticipating to cross the 100,000-prisoner threshold within the next five years, becoming the only state other than Texas and California to do so.

- The report projects no growth in Connecticut, Delaware, and New York.

Note: The incarceration data are supplied by the individual states.

Source: *Public Safety, Public Spending: Forecasting America's Prison Population, 2007–2011* (New York: Pew Charitable Trusts, 2007), ii.

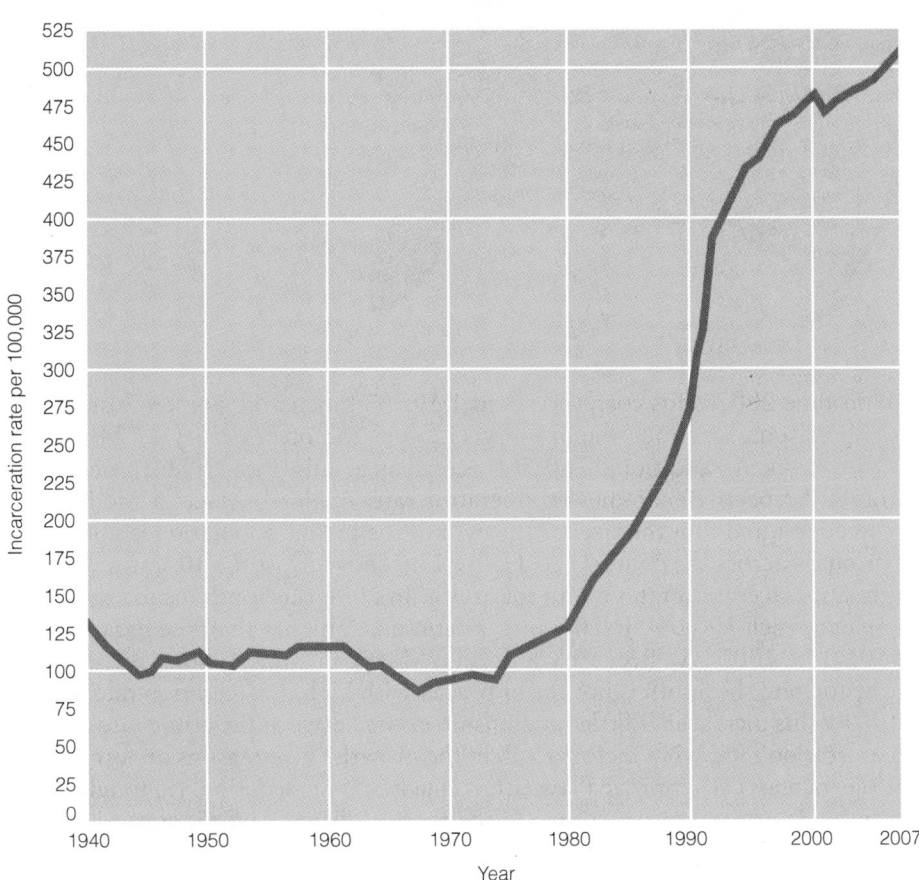

FIGURE 13.4

Incarceration in federal and state prisons per 100,000 population, 1940–2007

Between 1940 and 1973, the incarceration rate held steady. Only since has there been a continuing increase. The rate today has more than quadrupled since 1970.

Sources: Bureau of Justice Statistics, *Bulletin*, November 2004; *Bulletin*, December 2007, p. 21.

192,000 from 2006. Without changes in sentencing or release policies, 10 states can expect one new prison for every three currently in the system (see the Close-up box). This 13 percent jump triples the expected growth in the U.S. population—this during a period of stable or declining crime rates. The cost of these additional prisoners will be over $27 billion (Pew Charitable Trusts, 2007: ii).

Every June and December, a census of the U.S. prison population is taken for the Bureau of Justice Statistics. As shown in Figure 13.4, from a low of 98 per 100,000 population in 1972, the incarceration rate has steadily risen to a high of

FIGURE 13.5

Sentenced prisoners in state institutions per 100,000 population, December 31, 2006

What can be said about the differences in incarceration rates among the states? There are not only regional differences but also differences between adjacent states that seem to have similar socioeconomic and crime characteristics.

*State where prisons and jails form one integrated system. Data include total prison and jail population.

Source: Source: Bureau of Justice Statistics, *Bulletin*, December 2007, p. 21–22.

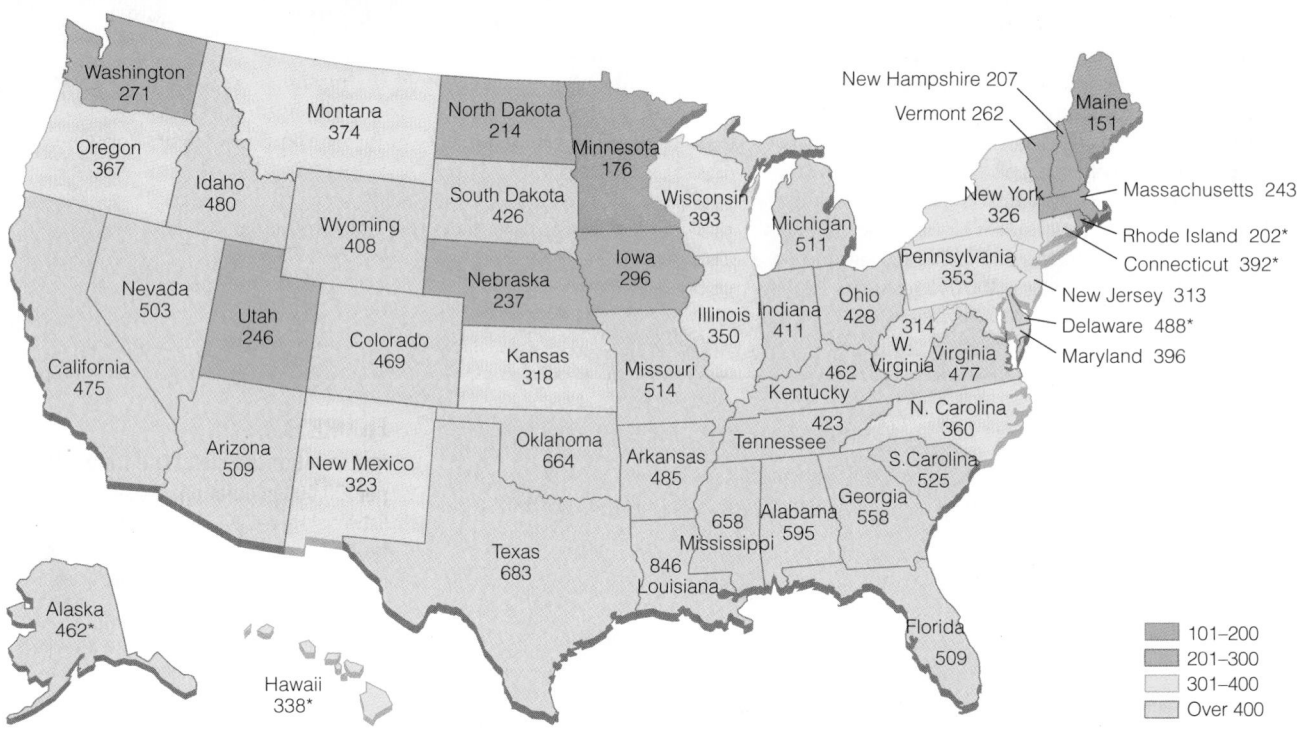

Access the latest data from the annual prison census online. To link to this website, go to *The American System of Criminal Justice* 12e companion site at academic.cengage.com/criminaljustice/cole.

509 in June 2007. This corresponds to 1,595,034 men and women in state and federal prisons, or about one in every 112 men and one in every 1,724 women U.S. residents. An additional 780,581 were in local jails (BJS, 2008: 1). The Comparative Perspective examines incarceration rates in North America and Europe.

Keep in mind that the size and growth of the prison population is not evenly distributed across the country. As Figure 13.5 shows, 7 of the 10 states with the highest incarceration rates are in the South. In 2006 the South incarcerated 547 people for each 100,000 inhabitants, a ratio much higher than the national rate of 501 (BJS, 2007: 21). Because California, Michigan, and Missouri are included in the top ten, the South is not the only area with high incarceration rates.

Why this increase? If little relationship exists between the crime rate and the incarceration rate, what factors explain the growth? Five reasons are often cited for the increase: (1) improved law enforcement and prosecution, (2) tougher sentencing, (3) prison construction, (4) the war on drugs, and (5) state and local politics. None of these reasons should be viewed as a single explanation or as having more impact than the others. In many states, lawmakers must face the budgetary implications of a burgeoning prison population in a period of economic downturn. Various options have been proposed to reduce the population yet maintain community safety.

Increased Arrests and More Likely Incarceration

Some analysts have argued that the billions of dollars spent on the crime problem may be paying off. Not only have arrest rates increased, particularly for some offenses such as drug violations, aggravated assaults, and sexual assaults, but the probability of being sent to prison also has dramatically increased. In addition, the number of offenders returned to prison for parole violations (see Chapter 16) has also increased. Between 1990 and 1998, there was a 54 percent increase in the number of parolees sent back to prison—half of them for a technical violation, the others for a new felony conviction (BJS, 2000: 11). In Texas, 77,000 offenders were admitted to prison in 2004, 46 percent of them were parole or probation violators (*Houston Chronicle*, 2005). Much of the growth in total admissions to state prisons can be attributed to this factor.

Recent studies have also shown that the increase in drug arrests have led to disproportionate rates of incarceration for African Americans. The research points to police tactics of targeting poor, urban, minority areas for enforcement of drug laws even though blacks and whites use illegal drugs at roughly the same rate (*New York Times*, May 6, 2008: A.21).

Tougher Sentencing Practices

Some observers think that a hardening of public attitudes toward criminals is reflected in longer sentences, in a smaller proportion of those convicted getting probation, and in fewer being released at the time of the first parole hearing.

In the past three decades, the states and the federal government have passed laws that increase sentences for most crimes. However, the tougher sentences do not seem to be the main factor keeping offenders in prison for longer periods. Between 1990 and 1998 the mean sentence of new court commitments has actually dropped. Rather, it is the 13 percent increase in the amount of time served that affects the total number of inmates. This increase in time served has resulted from the adoption by states of truth-in-sentencing laws that require offenders to serve most of their sentences in prison, and mandatory minimum laws that limit the discretion of judges (*Unlocking America*, JFA Institute, 2007: 3). The average time served in prison rose from 23 months in 1995 to 30 months in 2002 (BJS, 2006:12). From 1995 to 2003, the number of inmates climbed 76 percent, however, during those years, the number of new admissions grew only 16 percent (BJS, 2004: 6). Keeping people in prison longer seems to account for some of the growth of the incarcerated population.

Prison Construction

The increased rate of incarceration may be related to the creation of additional space in the nation's prisons. Between 1975 and 2000, over 400 prisons were built across the country, at least doubling the number of facilities in each state. Even with the decline in crime rates and tougher economic times in many states, new prison construction continues.

According to organization theorists, available public resources such as hospitals and schools are used to capacity. Prison are no exception. When prison space is limited, judges reserve incarceration for only violent offenders. However, additional prisons may present a variation of the "Field of Dreams" scenario—build them and they will come. As Joseph Davey has noted, "The presence of empty state-of-the-art prison facilities can encourage a criminal court judge to incarcerate a defendant who may otherwise get probation" (1998:84).

Prison construction during the 1990s was a growth industry, building 351 adult facilities that added more than 528,000 beds during the decade (BJS, 2001: 9). The new facilities increased the capacity of state prisons by 81 percent.

For health and security reasons, crowded conditions in existing facilities cannot be tolerated. Many states attempted to build their way out of this dilemma, because the public seemed to favor harsher sentencing policies, which would require more prison space. With many states holding large budget surpluses during the booming economy of the 1990s, legislatures were willing to advance the

COMPARATIVE PERSPECTIVE

Behind Bars in North America and Europe

MOST WESTERN COUNTRIES have put more people behind bars in recent years, but in none has the incarceration rate risen higher than in the United States. The cause of the extraordinary American figure is not higher levels of crime, for the crime rate in the United States is about the same as in western Europe (except for the rate of homicide, which is two to eight times greater in the U.S., mostly because of the ready availability of guns).

The high U.S. rate—which rivals those of former Soviet nations—can be traced primarily to a shift in public attitudes toward crime that began about 30 years ago as apprehension about violence and drugs escalated. Politicians were soon exploiting the new attitudes with promises to get criminals off the streets. Congress and state legislatures, often at the prodding of presidents and governors, promoted "tough on crime" measures, including mandatory sentencing, three-strikes laws, longer sentences, and increased budgets for prison construction.

As a result, the length of sentences, already severe by western European standards, became even more punitive. Consequently, the number of those locked up rose more than fivefold between 1972 and 2008 to more than two million. Most of those sentenced in recent years are perpetrators of nonviolent crimes, such as drug possession, that would not ordinarily be punished by long prison terms in other Western countries.

Source: Adapted from Roger Doyle, "By the Numbers," *Scientific American*, August 1999, p. 25; *One in 100: Behind Bars in America, 2008* (Washington, DC: Pew Center on the States, 2008), p. 35; *World Prison Brief*, London: King's College. Accessed March 5, 2008, from http://www.kcl.ac.uk/dpsta/law/research/icps/worldbrief.

Researching the Internet

Access the article by Marc Mauer of *The Sentencing Project* "Comparative International Rates of Incarceration" online.

To link to this website, go to *The American System of Criminal Justice* 12e companion site at academic.cengage.com/criminaljustice/cole. What are his major findings?

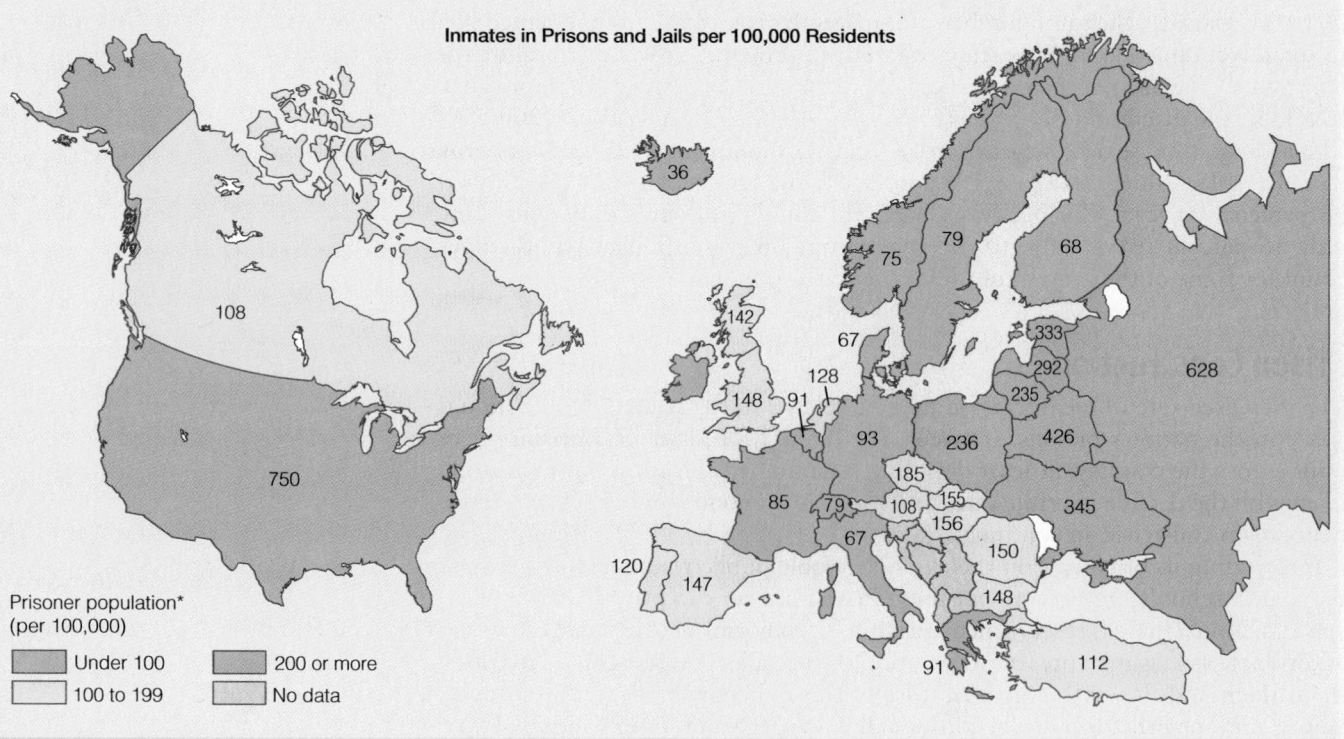

Inmates in Prisons and Jails per 100,000 Residents

Prisoner population* (per 100,000)

- Under 100
- 100 to 199
- 200 or more
- No data

huge sums required for prison expansion. Pressures from contractors, building material providers, and correctional officer unions spurred expansion in many states. Yet many states that tried to build their way out of their crowded facilities found that, as soon as a new prison came on line, it was quickly filled (see the Close Up box).

CLOSE UP

Prison Crowding Defies Easy Fixes

THE PROBLEMS FACING Alabama's overcrowded and underfunded prisons are too big, too complex and too long-lived to be fixed with any single solution, according to experts both inside and outside the system.

After Gov. Bob Riley pushed the early release of more than 4,000 inmates, Alabama's prisons remain nearly as overcrowded as they were when the governor launched the program almost two years ago. With 23,874 inmates jammed into state prisons, work release centers and boot camps, the prison system has almost twice the 12,943 inmates it was designed to house.

Experts point to other steps Alabama must take to get a handle on its overcrowding problem, including reforming sentences, expanding community-based corrections programs, improving supervision of people on parole and probation, and building additional prisons.

A big reason Alabama's prisons are so overcrowded is that the state doles out harsher punishments than most other states. The state has the nation's fifth-highest incarceration rate and the 11th-longest sentences imposed, according to the Bureau of Justice Statistics. It ranks 14th in the country in actual time spent behind bars.

Statistics show that Alabama locks up a large number of drug offenders. Of the states' current prisoners, 43.6 percent committed either a property or a drug offense. Crimes against individuals account for 51.6 percent of inmates. The most common felony for which prisoners are sentenced is drug possession.

It's not just crime that fuels Alabama's prison population. Many of the inmates who leave on parole are destined to return. About a third of those whose paroles have been revoked did not commit new crimes. They violated other terms of their parole.

In exchange for the privilege of parole, released prisoners must keep jobs, maintain contact with parole officers, and stay off drugs. Failure to comply with the rules can result in a parole revocation, sending the parolee back to prison to serve the balance of his original sentence. Reform advocates say the parole board members and officers should have much slower trigger fingers when dealing with these so-called "technical" violations.

Although the number of inmates paroled (4,174) over the last two years has jumped dramatically, new prisoners have arrived almost as fast. Since April 2003 the number of inmates has decreased only 1,083.

"You're going to definitely have to have more prisons built. You're not going to solve this problem simply by having more early releases," said Lynda Flynt, executive director of the Sentencing Commission. "When we're at 185 percent capacity, I don't think that's going to be the solution."

Prisons are the most expensive component of the criminal justice system, however. It is estimated that it would cost Alabama almost a billion dollars to build enough prisons to ensure a bed for every inmate. For a state prison system so short of funds that it doesn't supply napkins to its inmates, that's an almost unthinkable amount of cash, and Department of Corrections spokesman Brian Corbett noted that it doesn't include the money that would be needed to meet future needs.

"The reality is not Dollar One has been budgeted for any new construction," he said. "You want to be tough on crime, and you want to incarcerate people, but you don't want to pay for it."

That leaves legislators and other policymakers to grapple with other options.

If you were a member of the Alabama legislature, would you support the request for an additional 500-bed facility to relieve overcrowding? Why? Why not? What other options are available?

Source: Brendan Kirby, "Prison Crowding Defies Easy Fixes," *Mobile Register*, February 28, 2005 (http://www.al.com/printer/printer.ssf?/base/news/1109587461986).

Researching the Internet

For a different way of dealing with prison crowding, go to the North Carolina Sentencing Commission and Advisory Commission. Search for the word *commission*. To link to this website, go to *The American System of Criminal Justice* 12e companion site at academic.cengage.com/criminaljustice/cole.

The War on Drugs

Crusades against the use of drugs have recurred in American politics since the late 1800s. The latest manifestation began in 1982, when President Ronald Reagan declared another "war on drugs" and asked Congress to set aside more money for drug enforcement personnel and for prison space. This came at a time when the country faced the frightening advent of crack cocaine, which ravaged many communities and increased the murder rate. In 1987, Congress imposed stiff mandatory minimum sentences for federal drug law violations, and many states copied these sentencing laws. The war continues today, with each president urging Congress to appropriate billions more for an all-out law enforcement campaign against drugs.

The war on drugs has succeeded on one front by packing the nation's prisons with drug law offenders, but many scholars believe that is about all it has achieved. With additional resources and pressures for enforcement, the number of people sentenced to prison for drug offenses has increased steadily. In 1980 only 19,000 or about 6 percent of state prisoners had been convicted of drug offenses; by 2003 the number had risen to 250,000. Today, 21 percent of state prisoners are incarcerated for drug offenses, and the percentage in federal prisons is even higher at 54 percent (BJS, 2007: 26). Furthermore, the average state drug sentence has increased from 13 months in 1985 to 47 months in 2000 (BJS, 2003: 5).

State and Local Politics

Incarceration rates vary among the regions and states, but why do states with similar characteristics differ in their use of prisons? Can it be that local political factors influence correctional policies?

One might think that each state would show a certain association between crime rates and incarceration rates—the more crime, the more prisoners. Even when states have similar socioeconomic and demographic characteristics—poverty, unemployment, racial composition, drug arrests—unaccountable variations among their incarceration rates exist. For example, North Dakota and South Dakota have similar social characteristics and crime rates, yet the incarceration rate in South Dakota has risen 477 percent since 1978, compared with a rise of 133 percent in its neighbor (BJS, 2006: 5). One can even find similar and contiguous states—such as Connecticut and Massachusetts, Arizona and New Mexico, or Minnesota and Wisconsin—where the state with the higher crime rate has the lower incarceration rate.

In recent years, scholars have shown that community leaders often promote the siting of prisons in their towns as a means of economic development. However, some studies show that the touted gains are often not realized (King and Mauer, 2004: 453–480). A good example of the impact of prison siting in communities is found in the state of New York, which in the 1970s passed tough drug sentencing laws. Over the next 20 years, the state's prison population increased dramatically. Most of the prisoners ended up in new prisons located in the northern, rural, economically impoverished region of the state. The influx of prisoners brought some jobs to the region. Legislative districts whose economy was tied to prison payrolls soon found that their politics was dominated by the union that represents corrections officers (*New York Times*, December 25, 2005: 18). Across the nation, 21 counties were found in which at least 21 percent of the residents were inmates. In Concho County, Texas, with a population of 4,000, 33 percent of the residents were in prison (*New York Times*, April 30, 2004: A15).

The Bureau of the Census counts prisoners as "residents" of the community where they live. Since state and federal aid such as Medicaid, foster care, and social service block grants are distributed on the basis of population, this has meant that aid for the distressed inner cities where the prisoners come from is diverted to the sparsely populated counties where their former residents are incarcerated. Cook County, Illinois will lose nearly $88 million in federal benefits over the next decade because residents were counted in the 2000 Census in their county of incarceration rather than their county of origin (Lawrence and Travis, 2004: 10).

David Greenberg and Valerie West analyzed variations in the levels of incarceration among the 50 states between 1971 and 1991. They found that the volume of crime in a state accounted for only part of the incarceration rate. Here are the major findings of this research.

1. States with high violent crime rates have higher levels of incarceration.

2. States with higher revenues have higher prison populations.

3. States with higher unemployment and where there is a higher percentage of African Americans have higher prison populations.

4. States with more generous welfare benefits have lower prison populations.

5. States with more conservatives have not only higher incarceration rates, but their rates grew more rapidly than did the rates of states with fewer conservatives.

6. Political incentives for an expansive prison policy transcended Democratic and Republican affiliations

(Greenberg and West, 2001: 633).

It is at the state level that critics point to the operation of a "corrections-commercial complex." They argue that the "punishment industry" influences high incarceration rates during a period of falling levels of crime. Specifically, they point to links among corporations doing business with corrections, government agencies seeking to expand their domain, and legislators promoting tough crime policies that benefit their districts.

Opponents of the "corrections-commercial complex" perspective say that the growth of the prison population has helped to lower crime rates, that felons deserve to be punished severely, and that the links cited above do not exist.

Clearly, doubling of the incarceration rate during the past decade seems to stem from several factors, not just one. Given current public attitudes toward crime and punishment, fear of crime, and the expansion of prison space, incarceration rates will likely remain high (see "What Americans Think"). Perhaps only when the costs of this form of punishment more deeply invade the pockets of taxpayers will attitudes and policies shift, with a greater emphasis being placed on alternatives to incarceration.

Community Safety versus Incarceration

Faced with ever-increasing costs of incarceration many state legislatures are considering budget-cutting proposals that would result in the release of thousands of inmates to parole, halfway houses, or rehabilitation facilities. For example, in 2008:

- Mississippi's governor has signed a law to allow offenders to go free after serving 25 percent of their sentence.

- Rhode Island lawmakers have approved an expansion of "good time," thus saving an estimated $8 billion.

- Kentucky has decided to allow nonviolent, nonsexual offenders to serve up to 180 days of their sentences at home.

- To ease overcrowding and save about $1.1 billion over two years, California's Governor Arnold Schwarzenegger has proposed freeing about 22,000 nonviolent, nonsexual offenders 20 months earlier than their scheduled release date.

- New Jersey, South Carolina, and Vermont were examining plans to funnel drug-addicted offenders into treatment, which is cheaper than imprisonment (*USA Today*, April 4, 2008).

Legislators are faced with the hard task of reducing prison costs while ensuring community safety. This is particularly true in a state such as Michigan which has one of the largest and most costly ($2 billion per year, 50,000 inmates) prison systems, mainly because of its "truth in sentencing" law (*Washington Post*, May 5, 2008: A01). Michigan faces serious long-term economic problems. Corrections now takes 20 cents of every tax dollar in the state's general fund and employs nearly one of every three state government workers (*The Detroit News*, April 14, 2008).

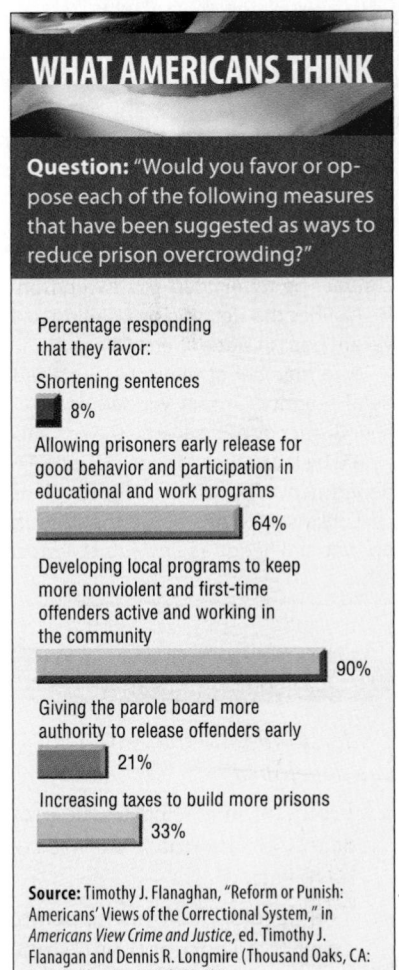

WHAT AMERICANS THINK

Question: "Would you favor or oppose each of the following measures that have been suggested as ways to reduce prison overcrowding?"

Percentage responding that they favor:

Shortening sentences
8%

Allowing prisoners early release for good behavior and participation in educational and work programs
64%

Developing local programs to keep more nonviolent and first-time offenders active and working in the community
90%

Giving the parole board more authority to release offenders early
21%

Increasing taxes to build more prisons
33%

Source: Timothy J. Flanaghan, "Reform or Punish: Americans' Views of the Correctional System," in *Americans View Crime and Justice*, ed. Timothy J. Flanagan and Dennis R. Longmire (Thousand Oaks, CA: Sage Publication, 1996), 88, 192.

A report by the Pew Center on the States addressed the issue of reducing incarceration costs while maintaining public safety. The report argues that "states are paying a high cost for corrections—one that may not be buying them as much in public safety as it should" (Riordan, 2008: 1). According to Pew Center, some states are attempting to protect public safety and reap corrections savings by holding lower-risk offenders accountable in less-costly settings and using intermediate sanctions for parolees and probationers who violate conditions of their release. These include a mix of community-based programs such as day reporting centers, treatment facilities, electronic monitoring, and community services. These tactics have been adopted in a number of states including Kansas and Texas (Riordan, 2008). It will be interesting to follow this policy trend to see if legislators are willing to risk the political consequences of being labeled as "soft on crime."

checkpoint

16. What are five explanations for the great increase in the incarcerated population?
17. Why might additional construction only aggravate the problem?

A QUESTION OF ETHICS

YOU ARE A state senator. For the past 15 years, your legislative district has benefited from the construction of two 500-bed facilities operated by American Prison Services (APS), Inc. Local residents of this poor, rural district have been hired as correctional officers and merchants have profited by sales to the institution. With a downturn in the economy, the state is facing a fiscal crisis. The governor has proposed that the APS contract be terminated and two prisons in your district be closed. He justifies this decision by pointing to the declining crime rate and vacant beds in state-operated prisons.

As a member of the state legislature you have always stood for fiscal integrity—in fact, you supported construction of the prisons in your district by APS because they promised that operating expenses would be lower than at state facilities. The governor's budget for the department of corrections is now before the legislature.

Lobbyists for APS argue that their facilities should continue to operate as a hedge against future corrections needs. They also point to the benefits that have come to your district. Further, they remind you of the campaign contributions they made to help you get elected. The local chamber of commerce supports the APS position. Opposing APS, the union representing the state correctional officers say that their members shouldn't suffer to satisfy a private company that is no longer needed. The governor is a member of your party and his operatives press you to support his budget. A major prison reform group argues that if the space is not needed the private facilities should be closed. They say that to keep them open while there are vacancies in state institutions is another example of the "corrections-commercial complex."

Critical Thinking and Analysis

Legislative debate on the future of the APS contract is strident. Each side puts forth strong arguments and pressure on you is intense. How will you vote? Is this an ethical question? How will you explain your decision to your constituents, to your party's leadership?

SUMMARY

Understand how the American system of corrections has developed

- From colonial days to the present, the methods of criminal sanctions that are considered appropriate have varied.

- The development of the penitentiary brought a shift away from corporal punishment.

- The Pennsylvania and New York systems were competing approaches to implementing the ideas of the penitentiary.

- The Declaration of Principles of 1870 contained the key elements for the reformatory and rehabilitation models of corrections.

- Three principles guided female prison reform during the nineteenth century: (1) separation from male prisoners, (2) care specialized to women's needs, and (3) management by female staff.

- Although based on the social sciences, the rehabilitative model failed to reduce recidivism.

- The community model of corrections tried to provide psychological treatment and increase opportunities for offenders to be successful citizens.

- The crime control model emphasized incarceration, long and mandatory sentencing, and strict supervision.

Understand the roles federal, state, and local governments play in corrections

- The administration of corrections in the United States is fragmented in that various levels of government are involved.

- The correctional responsibilities of the federal government are divided between the Federal Bureau of Prisons (of the U.S. Department of Justice), and the Administrative Office of the U.S. Courts.

- In all states, the administration of prisons falls under the executive branch of state government.

- Private prisons may or may not become accepted as a way to address overcrowding.

- Jails, which are administered by local government, hold people awaiting trial and hold sentenced offenders.

- Jail administrators face several problems: (1) the perceived role of the jail in the local criminal justice system, (2) the inmate population, and (3) fiscal problems.

Be familiar with the law of corrections and how it is applied to offenders and correctional personnel

- Until the 1960s the courts held a "hands-off" policy with respect to corrections.

- The rights of offenders are found in the First, Fourth, Eighth, and Fourteenth Amendments to the U.S. Constitution.

- The prisoners' rights movement, through lawsuits in the federal courts, has brought many changes to the administration and conditions of U.S. prisons.

- Decisions of the Supreme Court have affected community corrections through rules governing probation and parole revocation.

Discuss the direction of community corrections

- The growth of prisons has attracted public attention but the numbers of offenders on probation and parole have risen at a faster rate.

- Probation is faced with the challenge of supervising high-risk offenders.

- Increasing numbers of offenders are being returned to prison as parole violators.

Be able to explain why the prison population has more than doubled in the last ten years

- Prison populations have more than doubled during the past decade; there has also been a great increase in facilities and staff to administer them.

QUESTIONS FOR REVIEW

1. What were the major differences between the New York and Pennsylvania systems in the nineteenth century?

2. What are some of the pressures that administrators of local jails face?

3. What types of correctional programs does your state support? What government agencies run them?

4. Why do some state legislators consider private prisons an attractive option for corrections?

5. What Supreme Court decisions are the most significant for corrections today? What effects has each had on correctional institutions? On probation and parole?

6. What explanations might be given for the increased use of incarceration during the past two decades?

KEY TERMS

aliens (p. 481)
community corrections (p. 473)
congregate system (p. 468)
contract labor system (p. 468)
corrections (p. 464)
crime control model of corrections (p. 474)
deportation (p. 481)
Enlightenment (p. 464)
hands-off policy (p. 487)
jail (p. 483)
lease system (p. 469)
mark system (p. 471)
medical model (p. 473)

penitentiary (p. 466)
prison (p. 483)
reformatory (p. 471)
rehabilitation model (p. 472)
separate confinement (p. 467)
Cooper v. Pate (1964) (p. 488)
Hudson v. Palmer (1984) (p. 489)
Mempa v. Rhay (1967) (p. 493)
Morrissey v. Brewer (1972) (p. 493)
Wolff v. McDonnell (1974) (p. 490)

FOR FURTHER READING

Bostworth, Mary. 2002. *The U.S. Federal Prison System.* Thousand Oaks, CA: Sage Publications. A useful reference book on the Bureau of Prisons.

Braman, Donald. 2004. *Doing Time on the Outside: Incarceration and Family Life in Urban America.* Ann Arbor: University of Michigan Press. Examines the impact of incarceration on the personal relationships vital to family and community life.

Clear, Todd R., George F. Cole and Michael D. Reisig. 2009. *American Corrections*, 8th ed. Belmont, CA: Thomson Wadsworth. An overview of American corrections.

Davey, Joseph Dillion. 1998. *The Politics of Prison Expansion: Winning Elections by Waging War on Crime*. Westport, CT: Praeger. Examines increases in the crime rate and increases in the incarceration rate at the state level. Finds that political factors have influenced prison expansion since 1972.

Foucault, Michel. 1977. *Discipline and Punish*. Translated by Alan Sheridan. New York: Pantheon. Describes the transition of the focus of correctional punishment from the body of the offender to the reform of the individual.

Herivel, Tara and Paul Wright (eds.). *Prison Profiteers*. New York: New Press, 2007. An interesting collection of essays examining the role that private prison companies play in corrections. Asks the question, "Who makes money from mass incarceration?"

Jacobson, Michael. 2005. *Downsizing Prisons*. New York: NYU Press. Examines specific ways that states have begun to transform their prison systems. Offers policy solutions and strategies that can increase public safety as well as save money.

Mauer, Marc, and Meda Chesney-Lind, eds. 2002. *Invisible Punishment: The Collateral Consequences of Mass Imprisonment*. New York: New Press. An outstanding collection of articles examining the impact of incarceration on individuals, families, and communities.

Rothman, David J. 1971. *The Discovery of the Asylum: Social Order and Disorder in the New Republic*. Boston: Little, Brown. Rothman notes that, before the nineteenth century, deviants were cared for in the community. Urbanization and industrialization brought this function to government institutions.

———. 1980. *Conscience and Convenience*. Boston: Little, Brown. Argues that conscience activated the Progressives to reform corrections, yet the new structures for rehabilitation operated for the convenience of administrators.

Tonry, Michael. *Thinking About Crime: Sense and Sensibility in American Penal Culture*. New York: Oxford University Press, 2004. Makes the case that the United States has a punishment system that no one would knowingly have chosen and shows how it can be changed to do more good and less harm.

GOING ONLINE

For an up-to-date list of web links, go to *The American System of Criminal Justice* 12e companion site at academic .cengage.com/criminaljustice/cole.

1. Write a short paper describing the organization, staffing, and facilities of the department of corrections in your state. You can access this information by using a search engine to find the website of your state's department of corrections.

2. Go to the website of the Bureau of Justice Statistics. Click on "publications" and then access the bulletin, "Prisoners in 2006." How many prisoners were held in your state on December 31, 2006? What was the incarceration rate? Compare the numbers and rates of two adjacent states. Can you explain differences among the three states?

3. Using Internet search engines seek sites on *prison reformers*, then read about Elizabeth Fry. What were conditions like in British prisons? What did Fry try to accomplish?

CHECKPOINT ANSWERS

1. *What was the Enlightenment and how did it influence corrections?*

A period in the late eighteenth century when philosophers rethought the nature of society and the place of the individual in the world. New ideas about society and government arose from the Enlightenment.

2. *What were the main goals of the penitentiary?*

(1) secure and sanitary building, (2) systematic inspection, (3) abolition of fees, and (4) a reformatory regime.

3. *How did the Pennsylvania and New York systems differ?*

The Pennsylvania system of separate confinement held inmates in isolation from one another. The New York congregate system kept inmates in their cells at night, but they worked together in shops during the day.

4. *What was the significance of the Cincinnati Declaration of Principles?*

It advocated indeterminate sentences, rehabilitation programs, classifications based on improvements in character, and release on parole.

5. *What principles guided the reform of corrections for women in the nineteenth century?*

Separation of women prisoners from men, care in keeping with women's needs, women's prisons staffed by women.

6. *What are the underlying assumptions of rehabilitation, community, and crime control models of corrections?*

Rehabilitation model: criminal behavior is the result of a biological, psychological, or social deficiency; clinicians should diagnose the problem and prescribe treatment; when cured, the offender may be released. *Community model*: the goal of corrections is to reintegrate the offender into the community, so rehabilitation should be carried out in the community rather than in prison if possible; correctional workers should serve as advocates for offenders in their dealings with government agencies. *Crime control model*: criminal behavior can be controlled by greater use of incarceration and other forms of strict supervision.

7. *What agencies of the U.S. government are responsible for prisons and probation?*

The Federal Bureau of Prisons of the Department of Justice, and the Administrative Office of the U.S. Courts, which handles probation.

8. *What agencies of state government are responsible for incarceration, probation, intermediate sanctions, and parole?*

Incarceration (prisons): department of corrections. *Probation*: judiciary or executive branch department. *Intermediate sanctions*: judiciary, probation department, department of corrections. *Parole*: executive agency.

9. *What are the arguments in favor of and against privately run prisons?*

In favor: costs are lower, yet conditions are the same or better than prisons run by the government. *Opposed*: incarceration should be a function of government, not an enterprise for private profit. Private interests can skew public policy.

10. *What are the functions of jails?*

Holding of alleged offenders before trial and incarceration of offenders sentenced to short terms.

11. *What are three of the problems affecting jails?*

High population turnover, lack of services, scarce resources.

12. *What is the hands-off policy?*

Judges' belief that prisoners do not have protected rights and that the courts should not become involved in the administration of prisons.

13. *What is the case of* Cooper v. Pate *important to the expansion of prisoners' rights?*

Cooper v. Pate allowed state prisoners to sue the federal courts in order to challenge conditions of confinement and other rights issues in prisons.

14. *Which amendments to the Bill of Rights have been most influential in expanding prisoners' rights?*

First Amendment concerning speech and religion; Eighth Amendment concerning prison conditions.

15. *Which two clauses of the Fourteenth Amendment have been interpreted by the Supreme Court to apply to prisoners' rights?*

The due process and equal protection clauses.

16. *What are five explanations for the great increase in the incarcerated population?*

Increased arrests and more likely incarceration, tougher sentencing, prison construction, the war on drugs, state and local politics.

17. *Why might additional construction only aggravate the problem?*

New prison beds will quickly become filled because judges will be less hesitant to sentence people to prison and because the correctional bureaucracy needs the space to be used.

CHAPTER 14

Community Corrections: Probation and Intermediate Sanctions

LEARNING OBJECTIVES

→ Understand the philosophical assumptions that underlie community corrections

→ Understand how probation evolved, and how probation sentences are implemented today

→ Be familiar with the types of intermediate sanctions and how are they administered

→ Recognize the key issues facing community corrections at the beginning of the twenty-first century

Fresh out of rehab, Lindsay Lohan was accused of driving under the influence in May 2007 and police found what they believed to be cocaine in the car. Witnesses said that the 20-year-old celebrity actress was driving down Hollywood's Sunset Boulevard when her Mercedes convertible jumped the curb and smashed into a set of trees. Ms. Lohan left the scene and ended up in a Los Angeles hospital where police arrested her. Later they impounded her car and discovered illegal narcotics, primarily cocaine.

This was Lohan's third car wreck in the past two and a half years. In January 2007 she had checked into a rehabilitation facility for alcohol abuse, however, paparazzi cameras have since caught her drinking.

On August 23, Lindsay Lohan pleaded guilty to two counts of being under the influence of cocaine, no contest to two counts of driving with a blood-alcohol level above 0.08 percent, and one count of reckless driving. Two counts of driving under the influence were dropped.

The judge sentenced Lohan to 96 hours in jail, the mandatory minimum for a second drunken-driving offense, 10 days of community service, 36 months probation, completion of an 18-month drug treatment program, fines of several hundred dollars, and attendance at a three-day county coroner program in which

she'll visit a morgue and talk to victims of drunken drivers (*Washington Post*, August 23, 2007).

Was Lohan's sentence lenient? Should she have been given more jail time? Deputy District Attorney Danete Meyers, who presented the case, said Lohan's sentence was "the same that would happen with respect to anyone else. And as long as that happens, justice is done" (*Washington Post*, August 23, 2007). The sentence is a good example of community corrections—probation and intermediate sanctions.

Since the early nineteenth century, supervision in the community has been recognized as an appropriate punishment for some offenders. Probation was developed in the 1840s and parole followed in the 1870s. By the 1930s every state and the federal government used these forms of community corrections to either punish offenders without incarceration (probation) or to supervise offenders in the community after leaving prison (parole). Intermediate sanctions were developed in the 1980s when people saw the need for punishments that were less restrictive than prison but more restrictive than probation.

In years to come, community corrections can be expected to play a much greater role in the criminal justice system. As shown in Figure 14.1, already two-thirds of offenders are under correctional supervision in the community. This portion is likely to increase as states try to deal with the high costs of incarceration. Probation and intermediate sanctions appear to many criminal justice experts to be less expensive and just as effective as imprisonment.

COMMUNITY CORRECTIONS: ASSUMPTIONS

Community corrections seeks to keep offenders in the community by building ties to family, employment, and other normal sources of stability and success. This model of corrections assumes that the offender must change, but it also recognizes that factors within the community that might encourage criminal behavior (unemployment, for example) must also change.

Four factors are usually cited in support of community corrections:

1. Many offenders' criminal records and current offenses are not serious enough to warrant incarceration.

2. Community supervision is cheaper than incarceration.

3. Rates of **recidivism**, or returning to crime, for those under community supervision are no higher than for those who go to prison.

4. Ex-inmates require both support and supervision as they try to remake their lives in the community.

Community corrections is based on the goal of finding the "least restrictive alternative"—punishing the offender only as severely as needed to protect the community and to satisfy the public. Advocates call for programs to assist offenders in the community so they will have opportunities to succeed in law-abiding activities and to reduce their contact with the criminal world. Surveys have found there is support for community-based punishments for some types of offenders (see "What Americans Think").

FIGURE 14.1

Percentage of people in each category of correctional supervision

Although most people think of corrections as prisons and jails, in fact almost three-quarters of offenders are supervised within the community.

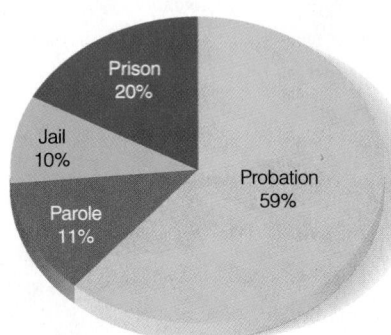

Source: Bureau of Justice Statistics, *Bulletin,* "Probation and Parole in the United States, 2006," December 2007, p. 3.

recidivism
A return to criminal behavior.

Checkpoint

1. What are the four main assumptions underlying community corrections? (Answers are at the end of the chapter.)

PROBATION: CORRECTION WITHOUT INCARCERATION

As we have seen, probation is the conditional release of the offender into the community, under the supervision of correctional officials. Although probationers live at home and work at regular jobs, they must report regularly to their probation officers. They must also abide by specific conditions, such as submitting to drug tests, obeying curfews, and staying away from certain people or parts of town. Although probation is used mainly for lesser offenses, states are increasingly using probation for more serious felonies, as shown in Figure 14.2.

Probation can be combined with other sanctions, such as fines, restitution, and community service. Fulfillment of these other sanctions may, in effect, become a condition for successful completion of probation. The sentencing court retains authority over the probationer, and if he or she violates the conditions or commits another crime, the judge can order the entire sentence to be served in prison.

The number of probationers now under supervision is at a record high and is still rising. Much has been written about overcrowded prisons, but the adult probation population has also been increasing—by 2.2 percent a year since 1995, a total of almost 1 million (30 percent) additional probationers (BJS, 2007: 1). Today, more than 4.2 million offenders are on probation, yet probation budgets in many states have been cut and caseloads increased as resources are diverted to prisons.

Although probation offers many benefits that cause it to be chosen over incarceration, the public often sees it as merely a "slap on the wrist" for offenders. With caseloads in some urban areas of as high as 300 offenders per officer, probation officers cannot provide the level of supervision necessary to ensure compliance and proper behavior by probationers.

WHAT AMERICANS THINK

Question: "It has been proposed that nonviolent offenders be given community-based punishments rather than serve time in prison. Do you strongly support, somewhat support, somewhat oppose, or strongly oppose this proposal?

Somewhat oppose 8%
Don't know 2%
Somewhat support 34%
Strongly oppose 10%
Strongly support 45%

Source: Based on telephone interviews with a national adult sample conducted by Penn, Schoen, and Berland Associates, June 10–13, 2000. Data provided by the Roper Center for Public Opinion Research, University of Connecticut.

Origins and Evolution of Probation

The historical roots of probation lie in the procedures for reprieves and pardons of early English courts. Probation first developed in the United States when John Augustus, a Boston boot maker, persuaded a judge in the Boston Police Court in 1841 to give him custody of a convicted offender for a brief period and then helped the man to appear rehabilitated by the time of sentencing.

Massachusetts developed the first statewide probation system in 1880, and by 1920, 21 other states had followed suit. The federal courts were authorized to hire probation officers in 1925. By the beginning of World War II, 44 states had probation systems.

Probation began as a humanitarian effort to allow first-time and minor offenders a second chance. Early probationers were expected not only to obey the law but also to behave in a morally acceptable fashion. Officers sought to provide moral leadership to help shape probationers' attitudes and behavior with respect to family, religion, employment, and free time.

By the 1940s, the development of psychology led probation officers to shift their emphasis from moral leadership to therapeutic counseling. This shift brought three important changes. First, the

The American Probation and Parole Association is a national organization concerned with community corrections. To link to this website, go to *The American System of Criminal Justice* 12e companion site at academic .cengage.com/criminaljustice/cole.

FIGURE 14.2

Felony sentences to probation in state courts

Although many people believe that probation is mainly used for those convicted of misdemeanors, 28 percent of convicted felons were sentenced to probation. Shown here are the percentages of felony offenders sentenced to probation, listed by the type of offense.

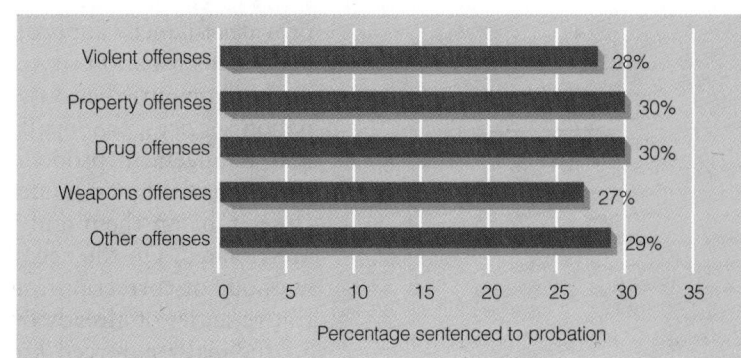

Violent offenses — 28%
Property offenses — 30%
Drug offenses — 30%
Weapons offenses — 27%
Other offenses — 29%

Percentage sentenced to probation

Source: Bureau of Justice Statistics, *Bulletin*, July 2007, p. 3.

officer no longer primarily acted as a community supervisor charged with enforcing a particular morality. Second, the officer became more of a clinical social worker whose goal was to help the offender solve psychological and social problems. Third, the offender was expected to become actively involved in the treatment. The pursuit of rehabilitation as the primary goal of probation gave the officer extensive discretion in defining and treating the offender's problems. Officers used their judgment to evaluate each offender and develop a treatment approach to the personal problems that presumably had led to crime.

During the 1960s, a new shift occurred in probation. Rather than counseling offenders, probation officers provided them with concrete social services such as assistance with employment, housing, finances, and education. This emphasis on reintegrating offenders and remedying the social problems they faced was consistent with federal efforts to wage a "war on poverty." Instead of being a counselor or therapist, the probation officer served as an advocate, dealing with private and public institutions on the offender's behalf.

In the late 1970s, the orientation of probation changed again as the goals of rehabilitation and reintegration gave way to "risk management." This approach, still dominant today, seeks to minimize the probability that an offender will commit a new offense. Risk management reflects two basic goals. First, in accord with the deserved-punishment ideal, the punishment should fit the offense, and correctional intervention should neither raise nor lower the level of punishment.

Second, according to the community protection criterion, the amount and type of supervision are determined according to the risk that the probationer will return to crime.

community justice
A model of justice that emphasizes reparation to the victim and the community, approaching crime from a problem-solving perspective, and citizen involvement in crime prevention.

Today there is a growing interest in probation's role as part of **community justice**, a philosophy that emphasizes restorative justice (see Chapter 12), reparation to the victim and the community, problem-solving strategies instead of adversarial procedures, and increased citizen involvement in crime prevention. By breaking away from traditional bureaucratic practices, community justice advocates hope to develop a more flexible and responsive form of local justice initiatives—and many see probation leading the way.

Checkpoint

2. Who was John Augustus, and what did he do?
3. What is the main goal of probation today?

Organization of Probation

As a form of corrections, probation falls under the executive branch, and people usually see it as a concern of state government. However, in about 25 percent of the states, probation falls to county and local governments. Further, in many states it is administered locally by the judiciary. The state sets the standards and provides financial support and training courses, but about two-thirds of all people under probation supervision are handled by locally administered programs.

In many jurisdictions, although the state is formally responsible for all probation services, the locally elected county judges are in charge. This seemingly odd arrangement produces benefits as well as problems. On the positive side, having probationers under the supervision of the court permits judges to keep closer tabs on them and to order incarceration if the conditions of probation are violated. On the negative side, some judges know little about the goals and methods of corrections, and the probation responsibility adds to the administrative duties of already overworked courts.

Judicially enforced probation seems to work best when the judge and the supervising officer have a close relationship. Proponents of this system say that judges need to work with probation officers whom they can trust, whose presentence reports they can accurately evaluate, and on whom they can rely to report on the success or failure of individual cases.

For the sake of their clients and the goals of the system, probation officers need direct access to corrections and other human services agencies. However, these agencies are located within the executive branch of government. Several states have combined probation and parole services in the same agency to coordinate resources and services better. Others point out, however, that probationers differ from parolees. Parolees already have served prison terms, frequently have been involved in more serious crimes, and often have been disconnected from mainstream society. By contrast, most probationers have not developed criminal lifestyles to the same degree and do not have the same problems of reintegration into the community.

Probation Services

Probation officers play roles similar to both the police and social workers. In addition to assisting the judiciary with presentence investigations (see Chapter 12), probation officers supervise clients to keep them out of trouble and enforce the conditions of the sentence. This law enforcement role involves discretionary decisions about whether to report violations of probation conditions. Probation officers are also expected to play a social worker role by helping clients obtain the housing, employment, and treatment services they need. The potential conflict between the roles is great. Not surprisingly, individual officers sometimes emphasize one role over the other.

A continuing issue for probation officers is the size of their caseloads. How many clients can one officer effectively handle? In the 1930s the National Probation Association recommended a 50-unit caseload, and in 1967 the President's Commission on Law Enforcement and Administration of Justice reduced it to 35. However, today the national average for adult supervision is about 150, but some urban caseloads exceed 300. The oversized caseload is usually cited as one of the main obstacles to successful probation. However, the field's most effective advocate for probation and parole supervision, the American Probation

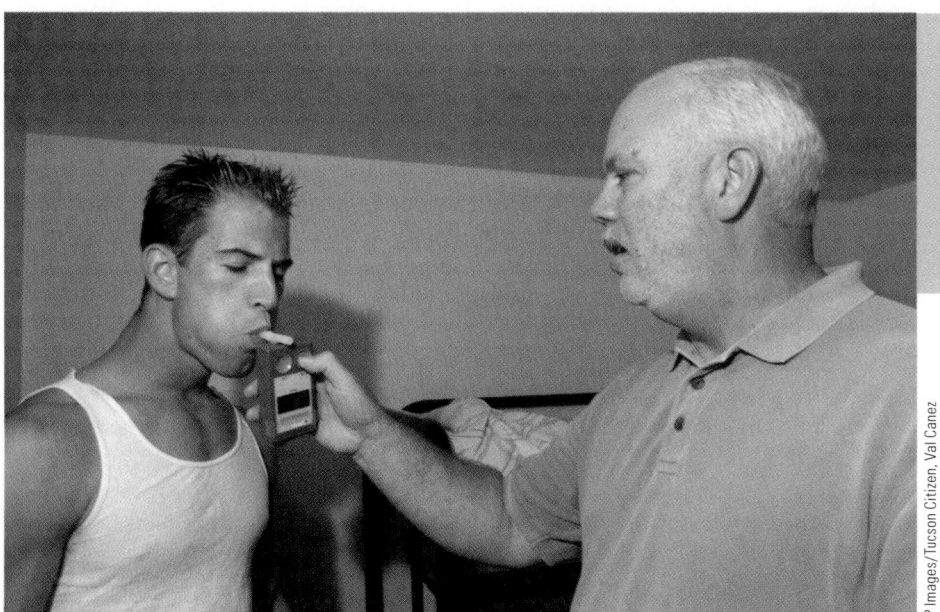

Jonathan Cady blows into a Breathalyzer for probation officer Scott Greene in Cady's home in Tucson, Arizona. Frequent alcohol and drug testing is a condition of probation for many offenders. Administering these tests has become part of the officer's supervisory role. How difficult is it to monitor the behavior of offenders in the community?

AP Images/Tucson Citizen, Val Canez

civic engagement
your role in the system

Imagine that the voters of your state are presented with a ballot issue seeking approval of a new law that would mandate probation and drug treatment for nonviolent drug offenders instead of sending such individuals to prison or jail. *Make a list of the results and consequences likely to be produced by such a law. Would you vote to favor the ballot issue?* Then look to see the results of California's ballot issue in 2000 on this very subject. To link to this website, go to *The American System of Criminal Justice* 12e companion site at academic.cengage.com/criminaljustice/cole. For a look at one probation organization's approach to adult field services, look online. When you reach the home page, type "adult field services" in the search function. To link to this website, go to *The American System of Criminal Justice* 12e companion site at academic.cengage.com/criminaljustice/cole.

and Parole Association, has been unable to uncover a link between caseload size and the effectiveness of supervision (Papparozzi and Hinzman, 2005: 23–25).

During the past decade, probation officials have developed methods of classifying clients according to their service needs, the element of risk they pose to the community, and the chance that they will commit another offense. Risk classification fits the deserved-punishment model of the criminal sanction in that the most serious cases receive the greatest restrictions and supervision. If probationers live according to the conditions of their sentence, the level of supervision is gradually reduced.

Several factors affect how much supervision serious cases actually receive. Consider the "war on drugs." It has significantly increased probation levels in urban areas because large numbers of people convicted of drug sales or possession are placed on probation. Many of these offenders have committed violent acts and live in inner-city areas marked by drug dealing and turf battles to control drug markets. Under these conditions, direct supervision can be dangerous for the probation officer. In some urban areas, probationers are merely required to telephone or mail reports of their current residence and employment. In such cases, it is hard to see how any goal of the sanctions—deserved punishment, rehabilitation, deterrence, or incapacitation—is being realized. If none of these objectives is being met, the offender is "getting off." As you look at "Civic Engagement: Your Role in the System," consider whether you believe probation serves the interests of society.

Checkpoint

4. What are the major tasks of probation officers?

Revocation and Termination of Probation

Probation ends in one of two ways: (1) the person successfully completes the period of probation, or (2) the probationary status is revoked because of misbehavior. In 2006, a national survey of probationers found that 57 percent of adults released from probation successfully completed their sentences, while only 18 percent had been reincarcerated (BJS, 2007: 2). Revocation of probation can occur for either a **technical violation** or a new arrest.

Technical violations occur when a probationer fails to meet the conditions of a sentence by, for instance, violating curfew, failing a drug test, or using alcohol. Officers have discretion as to whether or not they bring this fact to the attention of the judge. Table 14.1 presents the reasons presented to the court for revocation of probation.

Probation officers and judges have widely varying notions of what constitutes grounds for revoking probation (see "A Question of Ethics"). Once the officer calls a violation to the attention of the court, the probationer may be arrested or summoned for a revocation hearing. Because the contemporary emphasis is on avoiding incarceration except for flagrant and continual violation of the conditions of probation, most revocations today occur because of a new arrest or conviction.

As discussed in Chapter 13, in two cases, *Mempa v. Rhay* (1967) and *Gagnon v. Scarpelli* (1973), the U.S. Supreme Court extended the right to due

technical violation
The probationer's failure to abide by the rules and conditions of probation (specified by the judge), resulting in revocation of probation.

process by requiring that, before probation can be revoked, the offender is entitled to a preliminary and a final hearing and a right to counsel in some cases. When a probationer is taken into custody for violating the conditions of probation, a preliminary hearing must be held to determine whether probable cause exists to believe that the incident occurred. If there is a finding of probable cause, a final hearing, where the revocation decision is made, is mandatory. At these hearings, the probationer has the right to cross-examine witnesses and to be given notice of the alleged violations and a written report of the proceedings. The Court ruled, though, that the probationer does not have an automatic right to counsel. This decision is to be made on a case-by-case basis. At the final hearing, the judge decides whether to continue probation or to impose tougher restrictions, such as incarceration.

For those who successfully complete probation, the sentence ends. Ordinarily the probationer is then a free citizen again, without obligation to the court or to the probation department.

Probation officers often require the assistance of police officers in bringing a client to court for possible revocation of probation. In Tampa, Florida, police and probation officers cooperate in rounding up violators. Do probation officers need the same training as police officers or should they receive a different kind of training in order to do their jobs effectively?

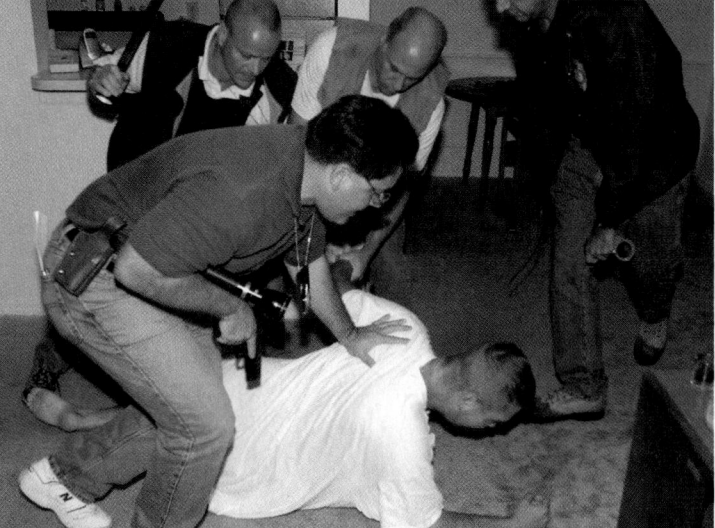

AP Images/Chris O'Meara

TABLE 14.1   Reasons for Probation Revocation Hearings

Before probation can be revoked, a hearing must be held to evaluate the charges.

Outcome*	Total	Severity of Original Offense	
		Felony	Misdemeanor
Charges Not Sustained	3.5%	3.7%	3.5%
Supervision Reinstated			
With new conditions	41.9%	46.0%	33.9%
Without new conditions	28.6	26.8	30.5
Incarcerated	29.1%	34.4%	18.9%
Other Outcomes			
Bench warrant issued/declared absconder	2.7%	1.7%	4.7%
Residential treatment/diversion order	1.6	2.1	0.7
Supervision level reduced	1.6	1.7	1.7
Other	1.6	2.3	0.3
Hearing Not Completed	24.0%	20.2%	32.4%
Number of probationers	455,221	299,941	141,075

*Details exceed the total because some probationers had more than one disciplinary hearing, whereas others had a single hearing with more than one reason.

Source: U.S. Department of Justice, Bureau of Justice Statistics, *Special Report* (Washington, DC: Government Printing Office, December 1997, p. 10).

checkpoint

5. What are the grounds for probation revocation?
6. What rights does a probationer have while revocation is being considered?

Assessing Probation

Probation is at a crossroads. Some critics see probation as nothing more than a slap on the wrist, an absence of punishment. Yet the importance of probation for public safety has never been greater: At the end of 2006, 49 percent of probationers had been convicted of a felony, yet three out of five felony probationers see their officer no more than once a month at best (BJS, 2007: 4). While probation suffers from poor credibility in the public's eyes, its workload is growing dramatically and, in view of the crowding of prisons and jails, will probably continue to do so.

Although the recidivism rate for probationers is lower than the rate for those who have been incarcerated, researchers question whether this is a direct result of supervision or an indirect result of the maturing of the offenders. Most offenders placed on probation do not become career criminals, their criminal activity is short-lived, and they become stable citizens as they obtain jobs and get married. Most of those who are arrested a second time do not repeat their mistake again.

What rallies support for probation is its relatively low cost: Keeping an offender on probation instead of behind bars costs roughly $1,000 a year, (a savings of more than $20,000 a year). However, these savings might not satisfy community members who hear of a sex offender on probation who repeats his crime.

In recent years as prisons have become overcrowded, increasing numbers of felony offenders have been placed on probation. Half of all convicted felons receive probation and more than 75 percent of probationers abuse drugs or alcohol. These factors present new challenges for probation, because officers can no longer assume that their clients pose little threat to society and that they have the skills to lead productive lives in the community.

To offer a viable alternative to incarceration, probation services need the resources to supervise and assist their clients appropriately. The new demands on probation have brought calls for increased electronic monitoring and for risk-management systems that provide different levels of supervision for different kinds of offenders.

INTERMEDIATE SANCTIONS IN THE COMMUNITY

Dissatisfaction with the traditional means of probation supervision, coupled with the crowding and high cost of prisons, has resulted in a call for intermediate sanctions. These are sanctions that restrict the offender more than does simple probation and that constitute actual punishment for more serious offenders.

Many experts have supported the case for intermediate sanctions. For example, as Norval Morris and Michael Tonry relate, "Prison is used excessively; probation is used even more excessively; between the two is a near vacuum of purposive and enforced punishments" (Morris and Tonry, 1990: 3). Seventy percent of convicted felons are incarcerated, the severest sentence, while 28 percent receive probation, the least severe. Hence all convicted felons receive either the severest or the most lenient of possible penalties (BJS, 2007: 2). Morris and Tonry urge that punishments be created that are more restrictive than probation yet match the severity of the offense and the characteristics of the offender, and that can be carried out while still protecting the community.

We can view intermediate sanctions as a continuum—a range of punishments that vary in levels of intrusiveness and control, as shown in Figure 14.3. Probation plus a fine or community service may be appropriate for minor offenses, while six weeks of boot camp followed by intensive probation supervision

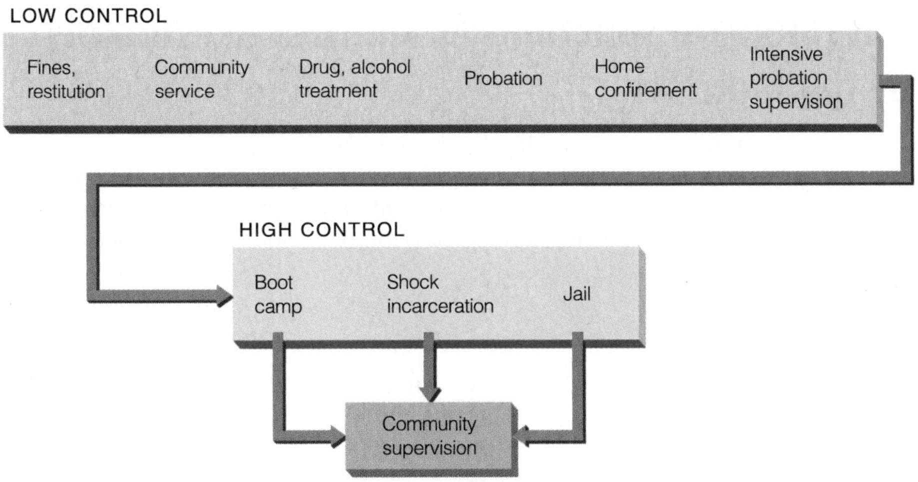

LOW CONTROL

| Fines, restitution | Community service | Drug, alcohol treatment | Probation | Home confinement | Intensive probation supervision |

HIGH CONTROL

| Boot camp | Shock incarceration | Jail |

Community supervision

FIGURE 14.3
Continuum of intermediate sanctions
Judges may use a range of intermediate sanctions, from those imposing a low level of control to those imposing a high level.

might be right for serious crimes. But some question whether offenders will be able to fulfill the conditions added to probation. Moreover, if prisons are overcrowded, is incarceration a believable threat if offenders fail to comply?

As seen in Table 14.2 a sentence to probation is often tied to additional intermediate sanctions such as community service, restitution, and alcohol or drug treatment.

Across the country, corrections employs many types of intermediate sanctions. They can be divided into (1) those administered primarily by the judiciary (fines, restitution, and forfeiture), (2) those primarily administered in the community with a supervision component (home confinement, community service, day reporting centers, and intensive probation supervision), and (3) those that are administered inside institutions and followed by community supervision (boot camp). Furthermore, sanctions may be imposed in combination—for example, a fine and probation, or boot camp with community service and probation.

The Community Corrections Association of Pennsylvania provides information about the state's programs. To link to this website, go to *The American System of Criminal Justice* 12e companion site at academic.cengage.com/criminaljustice/cole.

TABLE 14.2   Conditions of Probation Sentence Most Often Received in the 75 Largest Urban Counties

Percentage whose sentence to probation includes:

	Community Service	Restitution	Treatment
All Felonies	16%	13%	30%
Violent Offenses	22	15	22
Property Offenses	19	32	9
Drug Offenses	14	2	49
Public Order Offenses	11	7	8
Misdemeanors	14	16	15

Source: BJS, *Bulletin*, February 2006, p. 34.

Checkpoint

7. What is the main argument for intermediate sanctions?
8. What is meant by a continuum of sanctions?

Intermediate Sanctions Administered Primarily by the Judiciary

The judiciary administers many kinds of intermediate sanctions. Here we discuss three of them—fines, restitution, and forfeiture. Because all three involve the transfer of money or property from the offender to the government or crime victim, the judiciary is considered the proper body not only to impose the sanction but also to collect what is due.

Fines

fine
A sum of money to be paid to the state by a convicted person as punishment for an offense.

Fines are routinely imposed for offenses ranging from traffic violations to felonies. Studies have shown that the fine is used widely as a criminal sanction and that nationally well over $1 billion in fines have been collected annually. Yet, judges in the United States make little use of fines as the sole punishment for crimes more serious than motor vehicle violations. Instead, fines typically are used in conjunction with other sanctions, such as probation and incarceration; for example, two years of probation and a $500 fine.

Many judges cite the difficulty of collecting fines as the reason that they do not make greater use of this punishment. They note that offenders tend to be poor, and many judges fear that fines will be paid from the proceeds of additional illegal acts. Other judges are concerned that relying on fines as an alternative to incarceration will let affluent offenders "buy" their way out of jail while forcing the poor to serve time.

In contrast, fines are used extensively in Europe, are enforced, and are normally the sole sanction for a wide range of crimes. In Germany, 81 percent of all sentenced offenders must pay a fine, including 73 percent of those convicted of crimes of violence. In Sweden, fines are used in 91 percent of cases; in England, 47 percent of indictable offenses (roughly equivalent to an American felony) (Tonry, 1998: 698). To deal with the concern that fines exact a heavier toll on the poor than on the wealthy, Sweden and Germany have developed the day fine, which bases the penalty on offender's income (see the Comparative Perspective). The day fine has been tested in Arizona, Connecticut, Iowa, New York, and Washington.

Restitution

restitution
Repayment—in the form of money or service—by an offender to a victim who has suffered some loss from the offense.

Restitution is repayment by an offender to a victim who has suffered some form of financial loss from the crime. It is reparative in that it seeks to repair the harm done. In the Middle Ages, restitution was a common way to settle a criminal case. The offender was ordered to pay the victim or do the victim's work. The growth of the modern state saw the decline of such punishments based on "private" arrangements between offender and victim. Instead, the state prosecuted offenders, and punishments focused on the wrong the offender had done to society.

Victim restitution has remained a part of the U.S. criminal justice system, though it is largely unpublicized. In many instances, restitution derives from informal agreements between the police and offenders at the station, during plea bargaining, or in the prosecutor's sentence recommendation. Only since the late 1970s has restitution been institutionalized, usually as one of the conditions of probation.

As with fines, convicted offenders differ in their ability to pay restitution, and the conditions inevitably fall more harshly on less affluent offenders who cannot easily pay. Someone who has the "good fortune" to be victimized by an affluent criminal might receive full compensation, while someone victimized by a poor offender might never receive a penny. As a demonstration that courts

COMPARATIVE PERSPECTIVE

Day Fines in Germany: Could the Concept Work in the United States?

MONETARY SANCTIONS ARE used extensively in Europe in part because of the existence of the day-fine system. Under this system the amount of the fine is related not only to the seriousness of the crime but also to the offender's income. Could a day-fine system work in the United States?

Modern implementation of fines related to the income of the offender began with creation of the day-fine system in Finland in 1921, followed by its development in Sweden (1931) and Denmark (1939). The Federal Republic of Germany instituted day fines in 1975. Since then, the way offenders are punished has greatly changed, so that now more than 80 percent of those convicted receive a fine-alone sentence.

Judges determine the amount of the day fine through a two-stage process. First, judges relate the crime to offense guidelines, which state the minimum and maximum number of day-fine units for each offense. For example, theft may be punished by a day fine of 10–50 units. Judges choose the number of units by considering the culpability of the offender and by examining the offender's motivation and the circumstances surrounding the crime. Second, the value of these units is determined. The German day fine is calculated as the cost of a day of freedom: the amount of income an offender would have forfeited if incarcerated for a day. One day-fine unit is

equal to the offender's average net daily income (considering salary, pensions, welfare benefits, interest, and so on), without deductions for family maintenance, so long as the offender and the offender's dependents have a minimal standard of living. Finally, the law calls for publication of the number of units and their value for each day fine set by the court so that the sentencing judgment is publicly known.

For example, say a judge is faced with two defendants who have separately been convicted of theft. One defendant is a truck driver who earns an average of 100 Euros per day and the other is a business manager whose earnings average 300 Euros per day. The judge uses the guidelines and decides that the circumstances of the theft and the criminal record of each offender are the same. The judge decides that 40 day-fine units should be assessed to each. By multiplying these units by the average daily income for each, the truck driver's fine is 4,000 Euros and the manager's fine is 12,000 Euros.

Since the day-fine system was introduced in Germany, there has been an increase in the use of fines and a decrease in short-term incarceration. The size of fines has also increased, reflecting the fact that affluent offenders are now being punished at levels corresponding to their financial worth. Likewise, fines for poor offenders have remained relatively low. These results have been accomplished without an increase in the default rate.

Some Americans believe that day fines would be more equitable than the current system of low fines for all, regardless of wealth. Others believe that to levy higher fines against rich people than poor people is unjust because the wealthy person is being penalized for working hard for a high income. What do you think?

---

can collect monetary sanctions, Colorado collected $20 million in restitution in 2004. A corps of investigators work with probation officers monitoring cases, collecting restitution and working out payment plans if necessary (*The Denver Post*, January 3, 2005).

Restitution is more easily imposed when the "damage" inflicted can be easily measured—value of property destroyed or stolen, or medical costs, for instance. But what should be the restitution for the terror of an attempted rape?

Forfeiture

With passage of two laws in 1970—the Racketeer Influenced and Corrupt Organizations Act (RICO) and the Continuing Criminal Enterprise Act (CCE)—Congress resurrected forfeiture, a criminal sanction that had lain dormant since the American Revolution. Through amendments in 1984 and 1986, Congress improved ways to implement the law. Similar laws are now found in most states, particularly to deal with trafficking in controlled substances and with organized crime.

Forfeiture is government seizure of property and other assets derived from or used in criminal activity. Assets seized by federal and state agencies through forfeiture can be quite considerable. For example, the Drug Enforcement Administration alone annually seizes assets (including cash, real estate, vehicles, vessels, and airplanes) valued at more than a half billion dollars (BJS, 1999: 378).

A potential buyer examines property seized by federal officials from Congressman Randy "Duke" Cunningham after his conviction for taking bribes. The property items were presumably obtained through illegal funds and they were to be sold at auction. Should law enforcement agencies be permitted to keep or sell the property that they seize from criminal offenders?

AP Images/Ric Francis

Forfeiture is controversial. Critics argue that confiscating property without a court hearing violates citizens' constitutional rights. Concerns have also been raised about the excessive use of this sanction, because forfeited assets often go into the budget of the law enforcement agency taking the action.

In a 1993 opinion, the Supreme Court ruled that the Eighth Amendment's ban on excessive fines requires that the seriousness of the offense be related to the property that is taken (*Austin v. United States*). The ruling places limits on the government's ability to seize property and invites the judiciary to monitor the government's forfeiture activities when convicted offenders challenge them.

Critics argue that ownership of the seized property is often unclear. For example, in Hartford, Connecticut, a woman's home was seized because her grandson, unbeknownst to her, was using it as a base for selling drugs. Under the Civil Asset Forfeiture Reform Act passed by Congress in 2000, property cannot be seized if owners demonstrate their innocence by a preponderance of evidence (*Lansing State Journal*, April 14, 2000: 6A).

checkpoint

9.   How do fines, restitution, and forfeiture differ?
10. What are some of the problems of implementing these sanctions?

Intermediate Sanctions Administered in the Community

One basic argument for intermediate sanctions is that probation, as traditionally practiced, is inadequate for the large numbers of offenders whom probation officers must supervise today. Probation leaders have responded to this criticism by developing new intermediate sanction programs and expanding old ones. Four of these are: home confinement, community service, day reporting centers, and intensive supervision probation.

Home Confinement

With technological innovations that provide for electronic monitoring, **home confinement**, in which offenders must remain at home during specific periods, has gained attention. Offenders under home confinement (often called "house arrest") may face other restrictions such as the usual probation rules against alcohol and drugs as well as strictly monitored curfews and check-in times (see the Close-Up box).

Some offenders are allowed to go to a place of employment, education, or treatment during the day but must return to their homes by a specified hour. Those supervising home confinement may telephone offenders' homes at various times of the day or night to speak personally with offenders to make sure they are complying.

Home confinement offers a great deal of flexibility. It can be used as a sole sanction or in combination with other penalties. It can be imposed at almost any point in the criminal justice process: during the pretrial period, after a short term in jail or prison, or as a condition of probation or parole. In addition, home confinement relieves the government of the responsibility to provide the offender with food, clothing, and housing, as it must do in prisons. Home confinement programs have grown and proliferated.

The development of electronic monitoring equipment has made home confinement an enforceable sentencing option. The number of offenders currently being monitored is difficult to estimate, because the equipment manufacturers consider this privileged information. However, the best estimates are that about 17 different companies provide electronic monitoring of nearly 100,000 offenders (Conway, 2001: 7–9).

Two basic types of electronic monitoring devices exist. Passive monitors respond only to inquiries; most commonly, the offender receives an automated telephone call from the probation office and is told to place the device on a receiver attached to the phone. Active devices send continuous signals that a receiver picks up; a computer notes any break in the signal.

Despite favorable publicity, certain legal, technical, and correctional issues must be addressed before home confinement with electronic monitoring can become a standard punishment. First, some criminal justice scholars question its constitutionality. Monitoring may violate the Fourth Amendment's protection against unreasonable searches and seizures. The issue is a clash between the constitutionally protected reasonable expectation of privacy and the invasion of one's home by surveillance devices. Second, technical problems with the monitoring devices are still extensive, often giving erroneous reports that the offender is home. Third, offender failure rates may prove to be high. Being one's own warden is difficult, and visits by former criminal associates and other enticements may become problematic for many offenders (Renzema, 1992: 41). Some observers believe that four months of full-time monitoring is about the limit before a violation will occur (Clear and Braga, 1995: 435). Finally, some observers point out that only offenders who own telephones and can afford the $25–$100 per week these systems cost to rent are eligible. In addition, confinement to the home is no guarantee that crimes will not occur. Many crimes—child abuse, drug sales, and assaults, to name a few—commonly occur in offenders' residences.

A probation officer fits an electronic monitor to a client sentenced to home confinement. The device allows the officer to ensure that the sentence is being obeyed. Does home confinement and monitoring actually impose punishment on offenders?

© Bob Daemmrich/The Image Works

home confinement
A sentence requiring the offender to remain inside his or her home during specified periods.

 Private companies provide electronic monitoring equipment and services. To link to this website, go to *The American System of Criminal Justice* 12e companion site at academic.cengage.com/criminaljustice/cole.

CLOSE UP

Long Arm of the Law Has Man by the Ankle

THE ELECTRONIC LEASH is always on, fastened 24-7 to Johnnie Whichard's left ankle, a little waterproof black box with a transmitter inside, helping authorities to keep track of him. Whichard did the crime, a minor one, and now he's doing the time—and so what if he's not behind bars? He's an inmate just the same, confined to a rented four-room duplex most hours when he's not at work painting houses. And even then, on the job, he's a prisoner. Can't do this, can't do that—a straitjacket of rules.

In fact, said Whichard, 32, he gets so frustrated at times that he thinks the jail terms he served over the years were easier in some ways than the electronically monitored probation he's on now. Not that he'd prefer a cell over the ankle transmitter that he has been wearing for the past seven weeks. But it can be stressful, he said, being out in the free world most days, seeing it up close, and not being able to live in it.

Whichard's days are governed by rigid itineraries preapproved by authorities, each day purposeful and all but devoid of whim and spontaneity, with the ankle gadget, phone calls, and on-site spot-checks helping to keep him in line.

Whichard, a recovering alcoholic, can't remember how many times he was arrested for beer-and-rum-fueled mayhem, including accidentally shooting a man in the buttocks, an act that landed him in state prison for 13 months in the mid-1990s. He also has served some shorter stretches in county jails.

For his current tussle with the police, he pleaded guilty to resisting arrest and wound up in Montgomery County's (Maryland) Community Accountability, Reintegration and Treatment Program, which is known as CART, but might as well be called Big Brother.

The daily itineraries of three dozen electronically monitored probationers are filed in CART's computer. If a man with an ankle transmitter is approved to leave home at 6:00 A.M. for a job, say, at Wal-Mart, he had better not step out the door early.

There's a base unit mounted in Whichard's home, connected by a phone line to the computer. If the ankle transmitter moves out of range of the base before it's supposed to, the computer knows it, and someone at CART immediately gets a fax, a page, and an email. The same thing happens if the probationer is late getting home from work. During the day at work, he gets random phone calls and visits from a caseworker.

It's hard to fool Big Brother. Like a few other CART probationers whose jobs keep them moving, Whichard is monitored on the road by satellite through a global positioning system (GPS) device that he carries on his belt. It gives CART a minute-by-minute report of his locations, superimposed by computer on a street map, as he motors along, watching the free world go by. If his ankle transmitter moves more than 50 feet from the positioning device, CART is notified.

Whichard is allowed a few hours a week to buy groceries and attend religious services. He also gets six hours a week for leisure activities away from home, but there's so much planning involved—detailed itineraries, a two-day wait for approval—that he rarely bothers.

"It's a lot of getting used to," he says of the routine, which exhausts him—the monitoring, the itineraries, Alcoholics Anonymous meetings, the drug tests, the sessions with a mental health counselor.

"Sometimes I want to go sit outside the house and rest," he says. "I can't sit outside."

Source: Adapted from Paul Duggan, "Long Arm of the Law Has Man by the Ankle," *Washington Post,* March 28, 2005, p. B1.

Researching the Internet

 Michigan's system of electronically monitoring offenders in the community is described online. To link to this website, go to *The American System of Criminal Justice* 12e companion site at academic.cengage.com/criminaljustice/cole.

Variations in the use of electronic monitoring may alleviate some of these problems. For instance, after a time some offenders might be allowed to go to work or simply to leave home for restricted periods of the day; others might be allowed to maintain employment for their entire sentence. Whatever the details, such monitoring centers on using the offender's residence as the place of punishment.

Community Service

community service
A sentence requiring the offender to perform a certain amount of unpaid labor in the community.

A **community service** sentence requires the offender to perform a certain amount of unpaid labor in the community. Community service can take a variety of forms, including assisting in social service agencies, cleaning parks and roadsides, or helping the poor. The sentence specifies the number of hours to be worked and usually requires supervision by a probation officer. Judges can tailor community service to the skills and abilities of offenders. For example, less educated offenders might pick up litter along the highway, while those with schooling might teach reading in evening literacy classes. Many judges order community service when an offender cannot pay a fine. The offender's effort to make reparation to the community harmed by the crime also serves a symbolic function.

Remember that community services programs require contact between citizens in the community and the offenders fulfilling their sentences. Do the members of the public want offenders providing services to their community organizations? Do they want to be involved in supervising offenders in various contexts? As you read "Civic Engagement: Your Role in the System," think about your own willingness to interact with offenders in the community.

Although community service has many supporters, some labor unions and workers criticize it for possibly taking jobs away from law-abiding citizens. In addition, some experts believe that if community service is the only sanction, it may be too mild a punishment, especially for upper-class and white-collar criminals.

Day Reporting Centers

Another intermediate sanction option is the **day reporting center**—a community correctional center to which the offender must report each day to carry out elements of the sentence. Designed to ensure that probationers follow the employment and treatment stipulations attached to their sentence, day reporting centers also increase the likelihood that offenders and the general public will consider probation supervision to be credible.

Most day reporting centers incorporate multiple correctional methods. For example, in some centers offenders must be in the facility for eight hours or report for drug urine checks before going to work. Centers that have a rehabilitation component carry out drug and alcohol treatment, literacy programs, and job searches. Others provide contact levels equal to or greater than intensive supervision programs, in effect, creating a community equivalent to confinement.

So far, there are few evaluations of these programs, and initial studies suggest that day reporting does not result in lower rearrest rates than do other intensive supervision methods (Marciniak, 2001: 34–39). One problem common to a newly established program is that strict eligibility requirements result in small numbers of cases entering the program. But some evidence is promising: Evaluation of jail-run day-reporting centers find that program participants have lower levels of drug use and absconding. However, because participants were carefully screened for acceptance, applicability may be limited to low-risk cases (Porter, Lee, and Lutz, 2002).

In 2006, 1980s pop singer Boy George (center) swept the streets of New York City as part of his community service sanction after pleading guilty to drug possession. Such sanctions can provide benefits to the community. There may also be a "shaming" effect if offenders are embarrassed to be seen in public fulfilling a criminal punishment. Can you think of creative and effective ways to expand the use of community service sanctions?

© Dennis Van Tine/Landov

civic engagement
your role in the system

If you were asked to contribute your time to help make a correctional community service program succeed, what could you do to contribute? *Make a list of things that you could do to help such a program succeed.* Then look at the description of a volunteer opportunity related to a correctional community service program. To link to this website, go to *The American System of Criminal Justice* 12e companion site at academic.cengage.com/criminaljustice/cole.

checkpoint

11. What are some of the problems of home confinement?
12. What goes on at a day reporting center?

day reporting center
A community correctional center where an offender reports each day to comply with elements of a sentence.

intensive supervision probation (ISP)

Probation granted under conditions of strict reporting to a probation officer with a limited caseload.

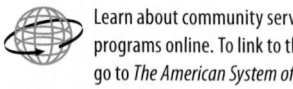

Learn about community service programs online. To link to this website, go to *The American System of Criminal Justice* 12e companion site at academic.cengage.com/criminaljustice/cole.

Intensive Supervision Probation (ISP)

Intensive supervision probation (ISP) is a means of dealing with offenders who need greater restrictions than traditional community-based programs can provide. Jurisdictions in every state have programs to intensively supervise such offenders. ISP uses probation as an intermediate form of punishment by imposing conditions of strict reporting to a probation officer who has a limited caseload.

ISP programs are of two general types: probation diversion and institutional diversion. *Probation diversion* puts offenders under intensive surveillance who are thought to be too risky for routine supervision. *Institutional diversion* selects low-risk offenders sentenced to prison and provides supervision for them in the community. Daily contact between the probationer and the probation officer may cut rearrest rates. Such contact also gives the probationer greater access to the resources the officer can provide, such as treatment services in the community. Offenders have incentives to obey rules, knowing that they must meet with their probation officers daily and in some cases must speak with them even more frequently. Additional restrictions—electronic monitoring, alcohol and drug testing, community service, and restitution—often are imposed on offenders as well.

ISP programs have been called "old-style" probation because each officer has only 20 clients and requires frequent face-to-face contact. Nonetheless, some people question how much of a difference constant surveillance can make to probationers with numerous problems. Such offenders frequently need help to get a job, counseling to deal with emotional and family situations, and a variety of supports to avoid drug or alcohol problems that may have contributed to their criminality. Yet ISP may be a way of getting the large number of drug-addicted felons into treatment.

Because it presents a "tough" image of community supervision and addresses the problem of prison crowding, ISP has become popular among probation administrators, judges, and prosecutors. Most ISP programs require a specific number of monthly contacts with officers, performance of community service, curfews, drug and alcohol testing, and referral to appropriate job-training, education, or treatment programs.

Observers have warned that ISP is not a "cure" for the rising costs and other problems facing corrections systems. Ironically, ISP can also increase the number of probationers sent to prison. All evaluations of ISP find that, probably because of the closer contact with clients, probation officers uncover more violations of rules than they do in regular probation. Therefore, ISP programs often have higher failure rates than do regular probation, even though their clients produce fewer arrests (Tonry and Lynch, 1996: 116).

Another surprising finding is that when given the option of serving prison terms or participating in ISP, many offenders have chosen prison. In New Jersey, 15 percent of offenders withdrew their applications for ISP once they learned the conditions and requirements. Similarly, when offenders in Marion County, Oregon, were asked if they would participate in ISP, one-third chose prison instead (Petersilia, 1990: 24). Apparently some offenders would rather spend a short time in prison, where conditions differ little from their accustomed life, than a longer period under demanding conditions in the community. To these offenders, ISP does not represent freedom, because it is so intrusive and the risk of revocation seems high.

Despite problems and continuing questions about its effectiveness, ISP has rejuvenated probation. Some of the most effective offender supervision has been carried out by these programs. As with regular probation, the size of a probation officer's caseload, within reasonable limits, is often less important for preventing recidivism than is the quality of supervision and assistance provided to probationers. If ISP is properly implemented, it may improve the quality of supervision and services that foster success for more kinds of offenders.

checkpoint _____

13. How does intensive supervision probation differ from traditional probation?

Intermediate Sanctions Administered in Institutions and the Community

Among the most publicized intermediate sanctions are the **boot camps**. Often referred to as *shock incarceration*, these programs vary, but all are based on the belief that young offenders (usually 14- to 21-year-olds) can be "shocked" out of their criminal ways.

Boot camps put offenders through a 30-to-90-day physical regimen designed to develop discipline and respect for authority. Like the Marine Corps, most programs emphasize a spit-and-polish environment and keep the offenders in a disciplined and demanding routine that seeks ultimately to build self-esteem. Most camps also include education, job-training programs, and other rehabilitation services. On successful completion of the program, offenders are released to the community. At this point probation officers take over, and the conditions of the sentence are imposed.

Boot camps proliferated in the late 1980s and by 1995 states and the Federal Bureau of Prisons operated 93 camps for adults and 30 for juveniles. At their peak, boot camps had more than 7,000 offenders. By 2000, about one-third of the camps had closed and the decline in boot camp operations has continued. In January 2005, the Federal Bureau of Prisons announced that its remaining boot camps would be phased out over six months. Further, the public uproar following the death of teenager Martin Anderson caused Florida to scrap its system of juvenile boot camps. Anderson died after being pummeled by a group of guards at a Panama City boot camp. He had been sent to the camp for joyriding in his grandmother's automobile (*Miami Herald*, April 27, 2006).

boot camp
A short-term institutional sentence, usually followed by probation, that puts the offender through a physical regimen designed to develop discipline and respect for authority. Also referred to as shock incarceration.

Military-type drills and physical workouts are part of the regimen at most boot camps, such as this one in Massachusetts. Evaluations of boot camps have reduced the initial optimism about this approach. Boot camps have been closed in many states. What are the potential shortcomings of boot camps as punishment?

© Joel Stettenheim/Corbis

CLOSE UP

After Boot Camp, A Harder Discipline

NELSON COLON MISSES waking up to the blast of reveille. He sometimes yearns for those 16-hour days filled with military drills and 9-mile runs. He even thinks fondly of the surly drill instructors who shouted in his face.

During his four months at New Jersey's boot camp, Mr. Colon adapted to the rigors of military life with little difficulty. He says it was a lot easier than what he faces now. He is back in his old neighborhood, trying to stay away from old friends and old ways.

So far, Colon, at age 18, has managed to stay out of trouble since he graduated with the camp's first class of 20 cadets in June. Yet each day, he said, he fears he will be pulled back onto the corner, only two blocks away, where he was first arrested for selling drugs at age 15.

A 10:00 P.M. curfew helps keep Colon off the streets. His parole officer checks in with him almost daily, sometimes stopping by at 11:00 to make sure he is inside. He is enrolling in night classes to help him earn his high school equivalency certificate, and he plans on attending Narcotics Anonymous meetings.

His biggest problems are the same ones that tens of thousands of Camden residents confront daily. Camden's unemployment rate exceeds 20 percent. There are few jobs in this troubled city, particularly for young men who have dropped out of high school. Colon has found work as a stock clerk in a sneaker store, but it is miles away at a shopping center on a busy highway, and he has no transportation there.

Selling drugs paid a lot more than stacking shoe boxes, and it did not require commuting. Mr. Colon says he pushes those thoughts of easy money out of his head and tries to remember what the boot camp's drill instructors told him over and over again.

"They used to tell us, 'It's up to you.' You have to have self-accountability. You have to be reliable for your own actions, not because some person wanted you to do it. They taught us not to follow, to lead. That was one of the most important things."

Colon said his immediate goal was to find a job that he could get to more easily, and then save enough to get as far away from Camden as possible. "I want to get out of here," he said.

"The people's mentality here is real petty. Life isn't nothing to them. The other night, they killed one of the guys I grew up with. They shot him a couple of times. My old friends came around and knocked on my door at one o'clock in the morning to tell me." He said it was his eighth childhood friend to die.

Source: Adapted from *New York Times*, September 3, 1995, p. B1.

Researching the Internet

 For more on *boot camps*, access the article "Inmates' Attitude Change During Incarceration: A Comparison of Boot Camp with Traditional Prison," by Doris Layton MacKenzie and Claire Souryal. Google "Claire Souryal" and find the article that is Chapter 12 of the book, *Correctional Boot Camps: Military Basic Training or a Model for Corrections*.

Evaluations of boot camp programs have reduced the initial optimism about such approaches. Critics suggest that the emphasis on physical training ignores young offenders' real problems. Some point out that, like the military, boot camp builds esprit de corps and solidarity, characteristics that can improve the leadership qualities of the young offender and therefore enhance a criminal career. In fact, follow-up studies of boot camp graduates show they do no better after release from the program than do other offenders. Research has also been found that, like intensive supervision probation, boot camps do not automatically reduce prison crowding. A National Institute of Justice summary of the boot camp experiment noted that they failed to reduce recidivism or prison populations (National Institute of Justice, 2003: 9).

Defenders of boot camps argue that the camps are accomplishing their goals; the failure lies in the lack of educational and employment opportunities in the participants' inner-city communities (see the Close Up box). A national study found that few boot camp graduates received any aftercare assistance on returning to their communities (Bourque, Han, and Hill, 1996). Because boot camps have been popular with the public, which imagines that strict discipline and harsh conditions will instill positive attitudes in young offenders, some camps are likely to continue operating whether or not they are more effective than probation or prison. Some criminal justice experts believe the entire boot camp experiment has been a cynical political maneuver. As Franklin Zimring pointed out more than a decade ago, "Boot camps are rapidly becoming yesterday's enthusiasm" (*Newsweek*, February 21, 1994:26).

checkpoint

14. What are some typical activities at a boot camp?

Implementing Intermediate Sanctions

Although the use of intermediate sanctions has spread rapidly, three major questions have emerged about their implementation: (1) Which agencies should implement the sanctions? (2) Which offenders should be admitted to these programs? (3) Will the "community corrections net" widen as a result of these policies so that more people will come under correctional supervision?

As in any public service organization, administrative politics is an ongoing factor in corrections. In many states, agencies compete for the additional funding needed to run the programs. The traditional agencies of community corrections, such as probation offices, could receive the funding, or the new programs could be contracted out to nonprofit organizations. Probation organizations argue that they know the field, have the experienced staff, and—given the additional resources—could do an excellent job. They correctly point out that a great many offenders sentenced to intermediate sanctions are also on probation. Critics of giving this role to probation services argue that the established agencies are not receptive to innovation. They say that probation agencies place a high priority on the traditional supervision function and would not actively help to solve the offenders' problems.

The different types of offenders who are given intermediate sanctions prompt a second issue in the implementation debate. One school of thought focuses on the seriousness of the offense and the other on the problems of the offender. If offenders are categorized by the seriousness of their offense, they may be given such close supervision that they will not be able to abide by the sentence. Sanctions for serious offenders may accumulate to include, for example, probation, drug testing, addiction treatment, and home confinement. As the number of sentencing conditions increases, even the most willing probationers find fulfilling every one of them difficult.

Some agencies want to accept into their intermediate sanctions program only those offenders who will succeed. These agencies are concerned about their success ratio, especially because of threats to future funding if the program does not reduce recidivism. Critics point out that this strategy leads to "creaming," taking the most promising offenders and leaving those with worse problems to traditional sanctions.

The third issue concerns **net widening**, a process in which the new sanction increases instead of reduces the control over offenders' lives. This can occur when a judge imposes a more intrusive sentence than usual. For example, rather than merely giving an offender probation, the judge might also require that the offender perform community service. Critics of intermediate sanctions argue that they have created the following:

net widening
Process in which new sentencing options increase instead of reduce control over offenders' lives.

- *Wider nets.* Reforms increase the proportion of individuals in society whose behavior is regulated or controlled by the state.

- *Stronger nets.* By intensifying the state's intervention powers, reforms augment the state's capacity to control individuals.

■ *Different nets.* Reforms transfer jurisdictional authority from one agency or control system to another.

The creation of intermediate sanctions have been advocated as a less costly alternative to incarceration and a more effective alternative to probation. But how have they been working? Michael Tonry and Mary Lynch have discouraging news: "Few such programs have diverted large numbers of offenders from prison, saved public monies or prison beds, or reduced recidivism rates" (Tonry and Lynch, 1996: 99). With incarceration rates still at record highs and probation caseloads increasing, intermediate sanctions will probably play a major role in corrections through the first decades of this century. However, correctional reform has always had its limitations, and intermediate sanctions may not achieve the goals of their advocates (Cullen, Wright, and Applegate, 1996: 69).

---

checkpoint

15.   What are three problems in the implementation of intermediate sanctions?

THE FUTURE OF COMMUNITY CORRECTIONS

In 1995 there were 3.7 million Americans under community supervision; by 2006 this figure had grown to over 5 million (BJS, 2007: 2). Despite this tremendous growth, community corrections still lacks public support. Community corrections suffers from the image of being "soft on crime." As a result, some localities provide adequate resources for prisons and jails but not for community corrections.

Community corrections also faces the challenge that offenders today require closer supervision. The crimes, criminal records, and drug problems of these offenders are often worse than those of lawbreakers of earlier eras. Nationally, 30 percent of convicted felons are sentenced to probation with no jail or prison time, and about one-fourth of these have been found guilty of violent crimes (BJS, 2007: 3). These people are supervised by probation officers whose caseloads number in the hundreds. Such officers, and their counterparts in parole, cannot provide effective supervision and services to all their clients.

Community corrections also faces even greater caseload pressures than in the past. With responsibility for about three-fourths of all offenders under correctional supervision, community corrections needs an infusion of additional resources. To succeed, public support for community corrections is essential, but it will come only if citizens believe that offenders are being given appropriate punishments. Opinion polls have shown that the public will support community sanctions only if offenders are strictly supervised. Allowing offenders to "roam free on the streets" with minimal supervision undermines community corrections and raises the question as to why these offenders are not incarcerated (Turner et al., 1997: 6–26).

Citizens must realize that policies designed to punish offenders in the community yield not mere "slaps on the wrists" but meaningful sanctions, even while these policies allow offenders to retain and rebuild their ties to their families and society. Joan Petersilia argues that too many crime control policies focus solely on the short term. She believes that long-term investments in community corrections will pay off for both the offender and the community (Petersilia, 1996: 21–29). But, again, before new policies can be put in place, public opinion must shift toward support of community corrections.

A QUESTION OF ETHICS

AS YOU LOOK over the Recommendation for Revocation Report sent to you by Officer Sawyer, you are struck by the low-level technical violations used to justify sending James Ferguson, a minor drug offender, to prison. Sawyer cites Ferguson's failure to attend all the drug treatment sessions, to complete his community service, and to pay a $500 fine. You call Sawyer in to discuss the report.

"Bill, I've looked over your report on Ferguson and I'm wondering what's going on here. Why isn't he fulfilling the conditions of his probation?"

"I'm really not sure, but it seems he just doesn't want to meet the conditions. I think he's got a bad attitude, and I don't like the guys he hangs around with. He's always mouthing off about the 'system' and says I'm on his case for no reason."

"Well, let's look at your report. You say that he works for Capital Services cleaning offices downtown from midnight till 8:00 A.M. yet has to go to the drug programs three mornings a week and put in ten hours a week at the Salvation Army Thrift Store. Is it that he isn't trying or does he have an impossible situation?"

"I think he could do it if he tried, but also, I think he's selling cocaine again. Perhaps he needs to get a taste of prison."

"That may be true, but do you really want to revoke his probation?"

Critical Thinking and Analysis

What's going on here? Is Sawyer recommending revocation because of Ferguson's attitude and the suspicion that he is selling drugs again? Do the technical violations warrant prison?

SUMMARY

Understand the philosophical assumptions that underlie community corrections

- Community corrections is based on four assumptions: (1) many offenders' records and offenses do not warrant incarceration, (2) community supervision is cheaper than incarceration, (3) recidivism of those under community supervision is no higher than those who go to prison, (4) ex-inmates require support and supervision to remake their lives in the community.

- Community supervision through probation, intermediate sanctions, and parole is a growing part of the criminal justice system.

Understand how probation evolved, and how probation sentences are implemented today

- Probation began as a humanitarian effort to allow first-time and minor offenders a second chance.

- Probation is imposed on more than half of offenders. People with this sentence live in the community according to conditions set by the judge and under the supervision of a probation officer.

Be familiar with the types of intermediate sanctions and how they are administered

- Intermediate sanctions are designed as punishments that are more restrictive than probation and less restrictive than prison.

- The range of intermediate sanctions allows judges to design sentences that incorporate one or more of these punishments.

- Some intermediate sanctions are implemented by courts (fines, restitution, forfeiture), others in the community (home confinement, community service, day reporting centers, intensive supervision probation), and others in institutions and the community (boot camps).

Recognize the key issues facing community corrections at the beginning of the twenty-first century

- Despite tremendous growth, community sanctions lack public support.

- Some offenders require closer supervision with attendant higher costs.

- Caseload pressures often limit supervision effectiveness.

- The use of community sanctions is expected to grow during the next decade, in spite of the problems implementing these sanctions.

QUESTIONS FOR REVIEW

1. What is the aim of community corrections?
2. What is the nature of probation, and how is it organized?
3. What is the purpose of intermediate sanctions?
4. What are the primary forms of intermediate sanctions?
5. What problems confront parolees upon their release?

KEY TERMS AND CASES

boot camp (p. 525)
community justice (p. 512)
community service (p. 522)
day reporting center (p. 523)
fine (p. 518)
home confinement (p. 521)

intensive supervision probation (ISP) (p. 524)
net widening (p 527)
recidivism (p. 510)
restitution (p. 518)
technical violation (p. 514)

FOR FURTHER READING

Anderson, David. 1998. *Sensible Justice: Alternatives to Prison*. New York: The New Press. A comprehensive review of the arguments for alternatives to incarceration. Develops a politically feasible case for expanded use of alternatives.

Byrne, James M., Arthur J. Lurigio, and Joan Petersilia. 1992. *Smart Sentencing; The Emergence of Intermediate Sanctions*. Newbury Park, CA: Sage. A collection of papers exploring various issues in the design and implementation of intermediate sanctions programs.

Clear, Todd R. and Harry Dammer. 2000. *The Offender in the Community*, Belmont, CA: Wadsworth. A comprehensive description of community corrections issues and programs.

Morris, Norval, and Michael Tonry. 1990. *Between Prison and Probation: Intermediate Punishments in a Rational Sentencing System*. New York: Oxford University Press. Urges development of a range of intermediate punishments that can be used to sanction offenders more severely than probation but less severely than incarceration.

Tonry, Michael, and Kate Hamilton, eds. 1995. *Intermediate Sanctions in Overcrowded Times*. Boston: Northeastern University Press. Summaries of research on intermediate sanctions in the United States and England.

 GOING ONLINE

For an up-to-date list of web links, go to *The American System of Criminal Justice* 12e companion site at academic.cengage.com/criminaljustice/cole.

1. Go to the website of the New York State Probation Officers association. Click on "Research Info" and then access the probation officers' salaries for the last few years. Are you surprised by the salaries for probation officers? Do these officers receive adequate pay for the kind of work they do?

2. Go to the Carolina Correctional Services website. Write a short paper describing one of the services they provide.

3. Access the report, "Case Classification and Community Corrections: A National Survey of the State of the Art," by D. J. Hubbard, L. F. Travis, and E. J. Latessa. What is the purpose of case classification. How is it used? What are its limitations?

CHECKPOINT ANSWERS

1. *What are the four main assumptions underlying community corrections?*

   Many offenders' crimes and records do not warrant incarceration; community supervision is cheaper; recidivism rates for those supervised in the community are no higher than for those who serve prison time; ex-inmates require support and supervision as they try to remake their lives in the community.

2. *Who was John Augustus, and what did he do?*

   A Boston boot maker who became the first probation officer by taking responsibility for a convicted offender before sentencing; called the father of probation.

3. *What is the main goal of probation today?*

   Risk management.

4. *What are the major tasks of probation officers?*

   To assist judges by preparing presentence reports and to provide assistance and supervision to offenders in the community.

5. *What are the grounds for probation revocation?*

   An arrest for a new offense or a technical violation of the conditions of probation that were set by the judge.

6. *What rights does a probationer have while revocation is being considered?*

   Right to a preliminary and final hearing, right to cross-examine witnesses, right to notice of the alleged violations, and right to a written report of the proceedings. Right to counsel is determined on a case-by-case basis.

7. *What is the main argument for intermediate sanctions?*

   Judges need a range of sentencing options that are less restrictive than prison and more restrictive than simple probation.

8. *What is meant by a continuum of sanctions?*

   A range of punishments reflecting different degrees of intrusiveness and control over the offender.

9. *How do fines, restitution, and forfeiture differ?*

   A fine is a sum of money paid to the government by the offender. Restitution is a sum of money paid to the victim by the offender. Forfeiture is the taking by the government of assets derived from or used in criminal activity.

10. *What are some of the problems of implementing these sanctions?*

    Most offenders are poor and cannot pay, and the courts do not always allocate resources for collection and enforcement.

11. *What are some of the problems of home confinement?*

    Home confinement may violate the Fourth Amendment's protections against unreasonable searches, monitoring devices have technical problems, and failure rates are high because offenders cannot tolerate home confinement for very long.

12. *What goes on at a day reporting center?*

    Drug and alcohol treatment, job searches, educational programs, and sometimes just offenders reporting in.

13. *How does intensive supervision probation differ from traditional probation?*

    In ISP the offender is required to make stricter and more frequent reporting to an officer with a much smaller caseload.

14. *What are some typical activities at a boot camp?*

Boot camps maintain a spit-and-polish environment and strict discipline, involve offenders in physical activity, and provide educational, vocational, and rehabilitative services.

15. *What are three problems in the implementation of intermediate sanctions?*

Deciding which agencies should implement the sanctions, deciding which offenders should be admitted to these programs, and the possible widening of the community corrections net.

CHAPTER **15**

Incarceration and Prison Society

LEARNING OBJECTIVES

→ Understand the three models of corrections that have predominated since the 1940s

→ Understand how a prison is organized

→ Understand how a prison is governed

→ Understand the role of correctional officers in a prison

→ Discuss what it is like to be in prison

→ Understand the special needs and problems of incarcerated women

→ Learn about programs and services that are available to prisoners

→ Understand the nature of prison violence

We're crowded into the department of corrections' bus, 20 convicts en route to the state prison. I'm handcuffed to two other men, the chains gleaming dully at wrists and ankles. The man on my right lifts his hand to smoke, the red eye of his cigarette burning through the darkness of the van. When he exhales, the man at my left coughs, the sound in his lungs suggesting that he's old, maybe sick. I want to ask what he's in for. But I don't speak, restrained by my fear, a feeling that rises cold up the back of my spine. For a long time no one else speaks either, each man locked in his own thoughts. It's someone up front, a kid, his voice brittle with fear, who speaks first. "What's it like down there—in the joint? Is it as bad as they say?"

"Worse," someone answers. "Cell blocks are dirty. Overcrowded. Lousy chow. Harassment. Stabbings."

"How do you live there?"

"You don't exactly live. You go through the motions. Eat, sleep, mind your own business. Do drugs when you can get them. Forget the world you came from."

This description of the "way in" was written by an inmate who was incarcerated in the Arizona penal system for seven years. It conveys much of the anxiety not only of the new "fish" but also of the old con. What is it like to be

incarcerated? What does it mean to the inmates, the guards, and the administrators? Are the officers in charge or do the prisoners "rule the joint"? This chapter explores the lives of the incarcerated, both in prison and as they face release into the community.

As we examine the social and personal dimensions of prison life, imagine visiting a foreign land and trying to learn about its culture and daily activities. The prison may be located in the United Sates, but the traditions, language, and relationships are unlike anything you have experienced. In the Close Up, Michael Santos, a long-term prisoner, describes his entry to the U.S. Federal Penitentiary in Atlanta.

THE MODERN PRISON: LEGACY OF THE PAST

American correctional institutions have always been more varied than movies or novels portray them to be. Fictional depictions of prison life are typically set in a fortress, the "big house"—the maximum-security prisons where the inmates are

CLOSE UP

One Man's Walk through Atlanta's Jungle

Michael G. Santos

I WAS NOT expecting to receive the southern hospitality for which Atlanta is famous when the bus turned into the penitentiary's large, circular drive, but neither did I expect to see a dozen uniformed prison guards—all carrying machine guns—surround the bus when it stopped. A month in transit already had passed by the time we made it to the U.S. Penitentiary (USP) in Atlanta, the institution that would hold me (along with over two thousand other felons) until we were transferred to other prisons, we were released, or we were dead.

I left the jail in Tacoma, Washington, on the first of August, but I didn't see the huge gray walls that surround USP Atlanta until the first of September. That month was spent in a bus operated by the U.S. Marshal Service as it moved across the country, picking up federal prisoners in local jails and dropping them off at various Bureau of Prison facilities.

As I crossed the country, I listened to tales from numerous prisoners who sat beside me on the bus. There wasn't much to discuss except what was to come. Each of us was chained at the hands and feet. There were neither magazines to read nor music playing. Mostly people spoke about a riot that had taken place behind USP Atlanta's walls a few months earlier. A lot of the men had been to prison before, and Atlanta would be nothing new. Those prisoners only talked about reuniting with old friends, explaining prison routine, or sat like stone-cold statues waiting for what was to come. I'd never been confined before, so it was hard to tune out the stories that others were telling. While I was listening, though, I remember telling myself that I would survive this sentence. No matter what it took, I would survive.

I was in my early twenties, younger than perhaps every other prisoner on the bus. Pimples spotted my face as I began my term, but I was certain my black hair would be white by the time I finished. I had been sentenced to 45 years by a U.S. district court judge in Tacoma on charges related to cocaine trafficking. I was expected to serve close to 30 years before release. It was hard then—just as it is hard now—to believe the sentence was real. The best thing I could do, I reasoned, was to stay to myself. I'd heard the same rumors that every suburban kid hears about prison. I was anxious about what was to come, but I was determined to make it out alive and with my mind intact. Now it was all to begin!

After the bus stopped, the guards began calling us off by last name and prison number. It is not easy to walk with a 12-inch chain connected to each ankle, and wrists bound to a chain that runs around the waist, but when my name was called, I managed to wobble through the bus's aisle, hop down the steps, and then begin the long march up the stairs leading to the fortress. As I was moving to the prison's doors, I remember glancing over my shoulder, knowing it would be the last time I'd see the world from the outside of prison walls for a long time.

Once inside the institution, the guards began unlocking my chains. About 50 other prisoners arrived with me that day, so the guards had plenty of chains to unlock, but their work didn't stop there. They also had to squeeze us through the dehumanizing admissions machine. The machine begins with photographs, fingerprints, and interrogations. Then comes the worst part, the strip search, where each prisoner stands before a prison official, naked, and responds to the scream: "Lift up your arms in the air! Let me see the back of your hands! Run your fingers through your hair! Open your mouth! Stick your tongue out! Lift your balls! Turn around! Bend over! Spread your ass! Wider! Lift the bottom of your feet! Move on!" The strip search, I later learned, is a ritual Atlanta's officers inflict on prisoners every time they have contact with anyone from outside the walls, and sometimes randomly as prisoners walk down the corridor.

tough and the guards are just as tough or tougher. Although big houses predominated in much of the country during the first half of the twentieth century, many prisons were built on another model. In the South, for instance, prisoners worked outside at farm labor, and the massive walled structures were not so common.

The typical big house of the 1940s and 1950s was a walled prison with large, tiered cell blocks, a yard, shops, and industrial workshops. The prisoners, in an average population of about 2,500 per institution, came from both urban and rural areas, were usually poor, and outside the South, were predominantly white. The prison society was essentially isolated; access to visitors, mail, and other communication was restricted. Prisoners' days were strictly structured, with rules enforced by the guards. A basic division stood between inmates and staff; rank was observed and discipline maintained. In the big house, few treatment programs existed; custody was the primary goal.

During the 1960s and early 1970s, when the rehabilitation model prevailed, many states built new prisons and converted others into "correctional institutions." Treatment programs administered by counselors and teachers became a major part of prison life, although the institutions continued to give priority to the custody goals of security, discipline, and order.

There was a lot of hatred behind those walls. Walking through the prison must be something like walking through a jungle, I imagined, not knowing whether others perceive you as predator or prey, knowing that you must remain always alert, watching every step, knowing that the wrong step may be the one that sucks you into the quicksand. The tension is ever present; I felt it wrapped all over, under and around me. I remember it bothering me that I didn't have enough hatred, because not hating in the jungle is a weakness. As the serpents slither, they spot that lack of hatred and salivate over a potential target.

Every prisoner despises confinement, but each must decide how he or she is going to do the time. Most of the men run in packs. They want the other prisoners either to run with them or run away from them. I wasn't interested in doing either. Instead of scheming on how I could become king of the jungle, I thought about ways that I could advance my release date. Earning academic credentials, keeping a clean record, and initiating projects that would benefit the communities both inside and outside of prison walls seemed the most promising goals for me to achieve. Yet working toward such goals was more dangerous than running with the pack; it didn't take me long to learn that prisoners running in herds will put forth more energy to cause others to lose than they will to win themselves. Prison is a twisted world, a menagerie.

I found that a highly structured schedule would not only move me closer to my goals but also would limit potential conflicts inside the prison. There is a pecking order in every prison, and prisoners vying for attention don't want to see others who are cutting their own path. I saw that bullies generally look for weaker targets, so I began an exercise routine that would keep me physically strong. If I were strong, I figured, others would be more reluctant to try me. Through discipline, I found, I could develop physical strength. Yet

I've never figured out how to develop the look of a killer, or the hatred off which that look feeds.

I don't know whether the strategies I have developed for doing time are right for everyone. But they are working for me. Still, I know that I may spend many more years in prison. The only fear I have—and as I'm working on my eighth year, it's still here—is that someone will try me and drag me into an altercation that may jeopardize my spotless disciplinary record. I've been successful in avoiding the ever-present quicksand on my walk through the jungle so far, but I know that on any given day, something may throw me off balance, or I may take a wrong step. And one wrong step in this jungle can drown me in quicksand, sucking me into the abysmal world of prison forever. That wrong step also could mean the loss of life, mine or someone else's.

In prison, more than anywhere else I know, understanding that some things are beyond an individual's sphere of control is vital. No matter how much preparation is made, the steel and concrete jungle is a dangerous place in which to live.

Source: Written for this book in 1995 by Michael G. Santos. In 2008 he was in his 21st year of a 45-year sentence for drug trafficking. With good time reductions he should be released in 2013.

Researching the Internet

Michael Santos is now incarcerated at the Federal Prison Camp, Taft, California. While in prison, he has completed his bachelor's and master's degrees. He is the author of *About Prison* (Belmont, CA: Wadsworth, 2004) and three other books. You can contact him online. To link to this website, go to *The American System of Criminal Justice* 12e companion site at academic.cengage.com/criminaljustice/cole.

The civil rights movement of the early 1960s profoundly affected prisoners, especially minority inmates. Prisoners demanded their constitutional rights as citizens and greater sensitivity to their needs. As discussed in Chapter 13, the courts began to take notice of the legal rights of prisoners. As inmates gained more legal services, the traditional judicial hands-off policy evaporated. Suddenly, administrators had to respond to the directives of the judiciary and run the institutions according to constitutional mandates.

During the past 30 years, as the population of the United States has changed, so has the prison population. The number of African American and Hispanic inmates has greatly increased. More inmates come from urban areas, and more have been convicted of drug-related and violent offenses. Incarcerated members of street gangs, which are often organized along racial lines, frequently regroup inside prison and contribute to elevated levels of violence. Another major change has been the rising number of correctional officers joining public employee unions, along with the use of collective bargaining to improve working conditions, safety procedures, and training.

Now the focus of corrections has shifted to crime control, which emphasizes the importance of incarceration. As a result, the number of people in prison greatly increased. Some politicians argue that offenders have it too "cushy" and that prisoners should return to the strict regimes found in the early twentieth century. Many states have removed educational and recreational amenities from institutions.

Although today's correctional administrators seek to provide humane incarceration, they must struggle with limited resources and shortages of cell space. Thus, the modern prison faces many of the difficult problems that confront other parts of the criminal justice system: racial conflicts, legal issues, limited resources, and growing populations. Despite these challenges, can prisons still achieve their objectives? The answer to this question depends, in part, on how we define the goals of incarceration.

checkpoint

1. How does today's prison differ from the "big house" of the past?
   (Answers are at the end of the chapter.)

GOALS OF INCARCERATION

Citing the nature of inmates and the need to protect staff and the community, most people consider security the dominant purpose of a prison. High walls, razor wire, searches, checkpoints, and regular counts of inmates serve the security function: Few inmates escape. More importantly, such features set the tone for the daily operations. Prisons are expected to be impersonal, quasi-military organizations where strict discipline, minimal amenities, and restrictions on freedom carry out the punishment of criminals.

Three models of incarceration have predominated since the early 1940s: the custodial, rehabilitation, and reintegration models. Each is associated with one style of institutional organization.

custodial model
A model of incarceration that emphasizes security, discipline, and order.

1. The **custodial model** assumes that prisoners have been incarcerated for the purpose of incapacitation, deterrence, or retribution. It emphasizes security, discipline, and order as they subordinate the prisoner to the authority of the warden. Discipline is strict, and most aspects of behavior are regulated. Having prevailed in corrections before World War II, this model still dominates most maximum-security institutions.

2. The *rehabilitation model*, which reached its height during the 1950s (see Chapter 13) emphasizes treatment programs designed to reform the offender. According to this model, security and housekeeping activities are viewed primarily as preconditions for rehabilitative efforts. Because all aspects of the organization should be directed toward rehabilitation, professional treatment specialists have a higher status than do other employees. Since the rethinking of the rehabilitation goal in the 1970s, treatment programs still exist in most institutions, but few prisons conform to this model today.

3. The **reintegration model** is linked to the structures and goals of community corrections. Recognizing that prisoners will be returning to society, this model emphasizes maintaining the offenders' ties to family and community as a method of reform. Prisons following this model gradually give inmates greater freedom and responsibility during their confinement, moving them to halfway houses or work release programs before giving them community supervision.

reintegration model
A model of a correctional institution that emphasizes maintaining the offender's ties to family and community as a method of reform, recognizing that the offender will be returning to society.

Although one can find correctional institutions that conform to each of these models, most prisons are mainly custodial. Nevertheless, treatment programs do exist, and because almost all inmates return to society at some point, even the most custodial institutions must prepare them for their reintegration. See "What Americans Think" for a look at how the public views the goals of incarceration.

Much is asked of prisons. As Charles Logan notes, "We ask them to correct the incorrigible, rehabilitate the wretched, deter the determined, restrain the dangerous, and punish the wicked" (Logan, 1993: 19). Because prisons are expected to pursue many different and often incompatible goals, they are almost doomed to fail as institutions. Logan believes the mission of prisons is confinement. He argues that the basic purpose of imprisonment is to punish offenders fairly and justly through lengths of confinement proportionate to the seriousness of their crimes. He summarizes the mission of prison as follows: "to keep prisoners—to keep them in, keep them safe, keep them in line, keep them healthy, and keep them busy—and to do it with fairness, without undue suffering, and as efficiently as possible" (Logan, 1993: 21). If the purpose of prisons is punishment through confinement under fair and just conditions, what are the implications of this purpose for correctional managers?

checkpoint

2. What three models of prison have predominated since the 1940s?

PRISON ORGANIZATION

The prison's physical features and function set it apart from almost every other institution and organization in modern society. It is a place where a group of employees manage a group of captives. Prisoners must live according to the rules of their keepers, and their movements are sharply restricted. Unlike managers of other government agencies, prison managers

■ Cannot select their clients

■ Have little or no control over the release of their clients

■ Must deal with clients who are there against their will

■ Must rely on clients to do most of the work in the daily operation of the institution—work they are forced to do and for which they receive little, if any, compensation

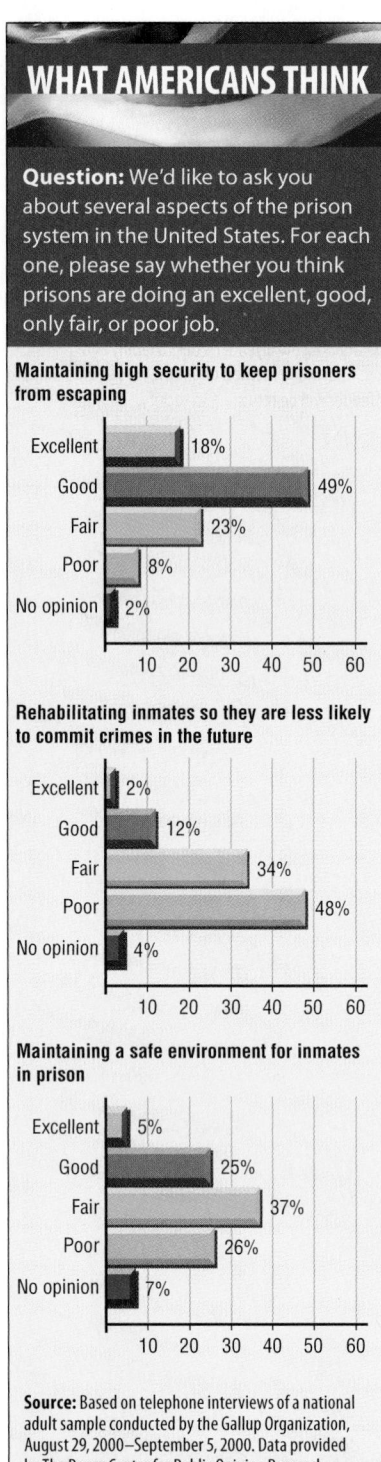

■ Must depend on the maintenance of satisfactory relationships between clients and staff

Given these unique characteristics, how should a prison be run? What rules should guide administrators? As the description just given indicates, wardens and other key personnel are asked to perform a difficult job, one that requires skilled and dedicated managers.

Most prisons are expected to fulfill goals related to keeping (custody), using (working), and serving (treating) inmates. Because individual staff members are not equipped to perform all functions, separate lines of command organize the groups of employees that carry out these different tasks. One group is charged with maintaining custody over the prisoners, another group supervises them in their work activities, and a third group attempts to treat them.

The custodial employees are the most numerous. They are normally organized along military lines, from warden to captain to officer, with accompanying pay differentials down the chain of command. The professional personnel associated with the using and serving functions, such as industry supervisors, clinicians, and teachers, are not part of the custodial structure and have little in common with its staff. All employees are responsible to the warden, but the treatment personnel and the civilian supervisors of the workshops have their own salary scales and titles. Figure 15.1 presents the formal organization of staff responsibilities in a typical prison.

The multiple goals and separate lines of command often cause ambiguity and conflict in the administration of prisons. For example, the goals imposed on prisons are often contradictory and unclear. Conflict between different groups of staff (custodial versus treatment, for instance), as well as between staff and inmates, presents significant challenges for administrators.

How, then, do prisons function? How do prisoners and staff try to meet their own goals? Although the U.S. prison may not conform to the ideal goals of

FIGURE 15.1

Formal organization of a prison for adult felons
Prison staff are divided into various sections consistent with the goals of the organization. Custodial employees are the most numerous.

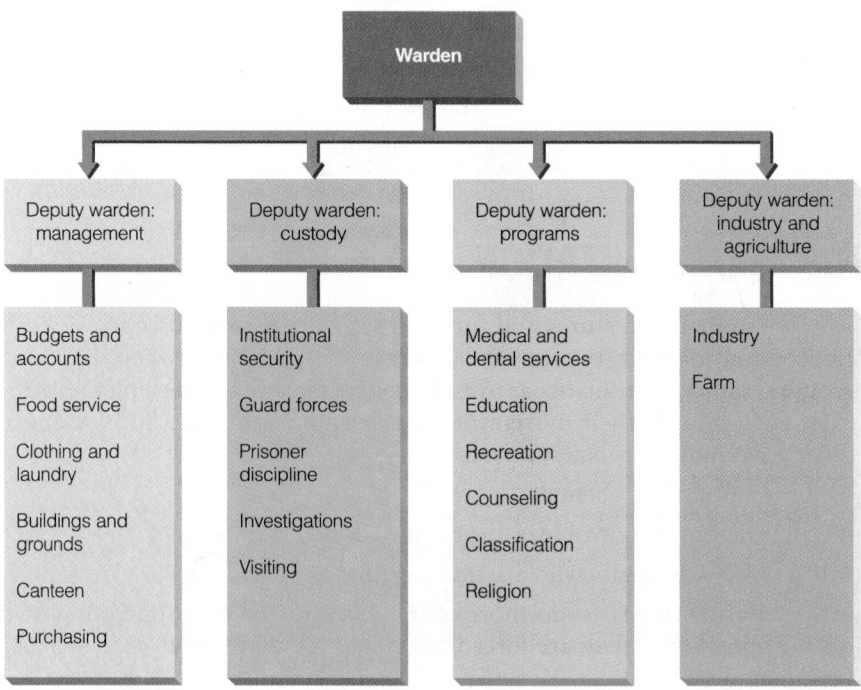

corrections and the formal organization may bear little resemblance to the on-going reality of the informal relations, order is kept and a routine is followed.

checkpoint

3. How do prisons differ from other organizations in society?
4. What are the multiple goals pursued in today's prisons?
5. What problems do these goals present to administrators?

GOVERNING A SOCIETY OF CAPTIVES

Much of the public believes that prisons are operated in an authoritarian manner. In such a society, correctional officers give orders and inmates follow orders. Strictly enforced rules specify what the captives may and may not do. Staff members have the right to grant rewards and to inflict punishment. In theory, any inmate who does not follow the rules could be placed in solitary confinement. Because the officers have a monopoly on the legal means of enforcing rules and can be backed up by the state police and the National Guard if necessary, many people believe that no question should arise as to how the prison is run.

But what quality of life should be maintained in prison? According to John DiIulio, a good prison is one that "provides as much order, amenity, and service as possible given the human and financial resources" (DiIulio, 1987: 12). *Order* is here defined as the absence of individual or group misconduct that threatens the safety of others—for example, assault, rapes, and other forms of violence or insult. *Amenities* include anything that enhances the comfort of the inmates, such as good food, clean cells, and recreational opportunities. *Service* includes programs designed to improve the lives of inmates: vocational training, remedial education, and work opportunities. Here, too, we expect inmates to be engaged in activities during incarceration that will make them better people and enhance their ability to lead crime-free lives upon release.

If we accept the premise that well-run prisons are important for the inmates, staff, and society, what are the problems that correctional administrators must address? The correctional literature points to four factors that make governing prisons different from administering other public institutions: (1) the defects of total power, (2) the limitation on the rewards and punishments officials can use, (3) the co-optation of correctional officers by inmates, and (4) the strength of inmate leadership. After we review each of these research findings, we shall ask what kind of administrative systems and leadership styles ensure that prisons remain safe and humane and serve inmates' needs.

The Defects of Total Power

Imagine a prison society that comprises hostile and uncooperative inmates ruled by force. Prisoners can be legally isolated from one another, put under continuous surveillance, and physically abused until they cooperate. Although all of these things are possible, such practices would probably not be countenanced for long because the public expects correctional institutions to be run humanely.

In reality, the power of officers is limited, because many prisoners have little to lose by misbehaving, and unarmed officers have only limited ability to force compliance with rules. Perhaps more important is the fact that forcing people to follow commands is an inefficient way to make them carry out complex tasks; efficiency is further diminished by the ratio of inmates to officers (typically 9 to 1 in federal prisons and 4.5 to 1 in state prisons) and by the potential danger.

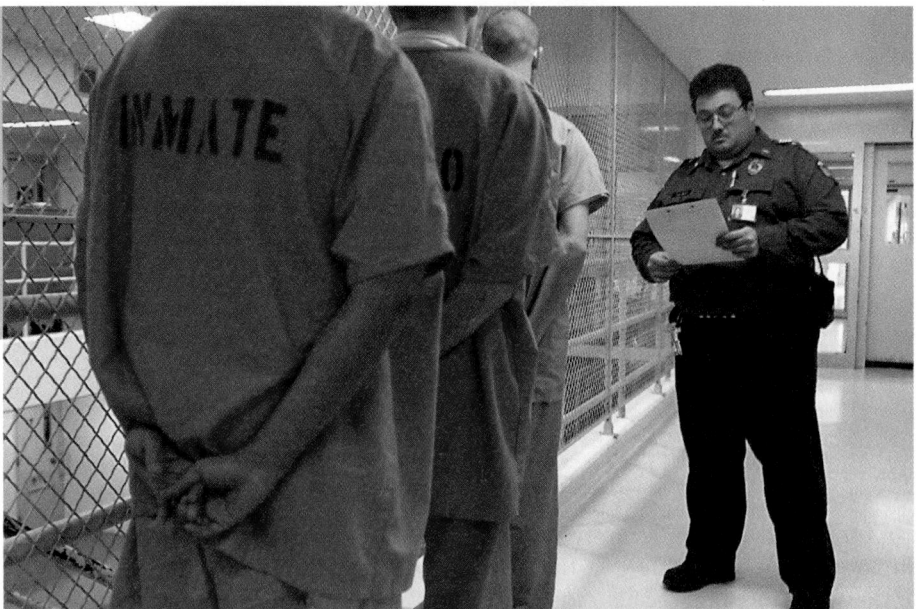

Sgt. John Thomas checks the list of offenders that he must supervise in moving to a different area within the correctional assessment center in Lexington, Oklahoma. Officers face significant challenges in maintaining order and safety while outnumbered by prisoners, especially when many prisons are understaffed. What qualities and skills do corrections officers need in order to be effective?

AP Images/J. Pat Carter

Rewards and Punishments

Correctional officers often rely on rewards and punishments to gain cooperation. To maintain security and order among a large population in a confined space, they impose extensive rules of conduct. Instead of using force to ensure obedience, however, they reward compliance and punish rule violators by granting and denying privileges.

To promote control, officers may follow any of several policies. One is to offer cooperative prisoners rewards such as choice job assignments, residence in the honor unit, and favorable parole reports. Inmates who do not break rules are given good time. Informers may also be rewarded, and administrators may ignore conflict among inmates on the assumption that it keeps prisoners from uniting against authorities.

The system of rewards and punishments has some deficiencies. One is that the punishments for rule breaking do not represent a great departure from the prisoners' usual circumstances. Because inmates are already deprived of many freedoms and valued goods—heterosexual relations, money, choice of clothing, and so on—not being allowed to attend, say, a recreational period does not carry much weight. Further, inmates receive authorized privileges at the start of the sentence that are taken away only if rules are broken, but they receive few rewards for progress or exceptional behavior. However, as an inmate approaches release, opportunities for furloughs, work release, or transfer to a halfway house can serve as incentives to obey rules.

Gaining Cooperation: Exchange Relationships

One way that correctional officers obtain inmate cooperation is by tolerating minor rule infractions in exchange for compliance with major aspects of the custodial regime. The correctional officer plays the key role in these exchange relationships. Officers and prisoners remain in close association both day and night—in the cell block, workshop, dining hall, recreation area, and so on. Although the formal rules require a social distance between officers and inmates, the physical closeness makes them aware that each relies on the other. The officers need the cooperation of the prisoners so that they will look good to their superiors, and the inmates count on the officers to relax the rules or occasionally look the other way. For example, officers in a Midwestern prison told researcher Stan Stojkovic that flexibility in rule enforcement was especially important as it related to the ability of prisoners to cope with their environment. As one officer said, "Phone calls are really important to guys in this place. . . . You cut off their calls and they get pissed. So what I do is give them a little extra and they are good to me." Yet the officers also told Stojkovic that they would be crazy to intervene to stop illicit sex or drug use (Stojkovic, 1990: 214).

Correctional officers must be careful not to pay too high a price for the cooperation of their charges. Under pressure to work effectively with prisoners, officers may be blackmailed into doing illegitimate favors in return for cooperation. Officers who establish sub-rosa, or secret, relationships can be manipulated by prisoners into smuggling contraband or committing other illegal acts. At the end of this chapter, "A Question of Ethics" presents a dilemma that correctional officers frequently face.

Inmate Leadership

In the traditional prison of the big-house era, administrators enlisted the inmate leaders to help maintain order. Inmate leaders had been "tested" over time so that they were neither pushed around by other inmates nor distrusted as stool pigeons. Because the staff could rely on them, they served as the essential communications link between staff and inmates. Their ability to acquire inside information and gain access to higher officials brought inmate leaders the respect of other prisoners and special privileges from officials. In turn, they distributed these benefits to other prisoners, thus bolstering their own influence within the prison society.

Prisons seem to function more effectively now than they did in the recent past. Although prisons are more crowded, riots and reports of violence have declined. In many prisons, the inmate social system may have reorganized, so that correctional officers again can work through prisoners respected by fellow inmates. Yet, some observers contend that when wardens maintain order in this way, they enhance the positions of some prisoners at the expense of others. The leaders profit by receiving illicit privileges and favors, and they increase their influence by distributing benefits.

Further, descriptions of the contemporary maximum-security prison raise questions about administrators' ability to run prisons in this way. In most of today's institutions, prisoners are divided by race, ethnicity, age, and gang affiliation, so that no single leadership structure exists.

The Challenge of Governing Prisons

The factors of total power, rewards and punishments, exchange relationships, and inmate leadership exist in every prison and must be managed. How they are managed greatly influences the quality of prison life. John DiIulio's research (1987) challenges the common assumption of many correctional administrators that "the cons run the joint." Instead, successful wardens have made their prisons function well by applying management principles within the context of their own style of leadership. Prisons can be governed, violence can be minimized, and services can be provided to the inmates if correctional executives and wardens exhibit leadership. Governing prisons is an extraordinary challenge, but it can be and has been effectively accomplished. The Close Up box on page 542 describes the unique management practices of Warden Dennis Luther.

checkpoint

6. What four factors make the governing of prisons different from administering other public institutions?

CLOSE UP

A Model Prison

IN THE WOODS outside of Bradford, Pennsylvania, stands the Federal Correctional Institution, McKean. Opened in 1989 as a medium-security facility, it houses more than one thousand male inmates. Until he retired in July 1995, Dennis Luther was McKean's warden, an administrator who, during this 16 years in prison work, gained a reputation for unorthodox policies.

At a time when politicians were railing against "country club" prisons and the need to "make 'em bust rocks," Warden Luther ran an institution that earned a 99.3 accreditation rating from the American Correctional Association, the highest in the Bureau of Prisons. Although badly overcrowded and with an increasing number of violent offenders, McKean cost taxpayers $15,370 a year for each inmate, well below the federal average of $21,350. Amazingly in six years there were no escapes, no murders, no suicides, and only three serious assaults against staff and six recorded against inmates.

How did Warden Luther do it? According to Luther, each prison has its own culture, which is often violent and abusive, based on gangs. The staff in such institutions feel they cannot change it. At McKean, Warden Luther set out to build a different type of culture, one based on unconditional respect for the inmates as people. As he says, "If you want people to behave responsibly and treat you with respect, then you treat other people that way." This credo has been translated into 28 beliefs, the product of Luther's years of experience. These "Beliefs about the Treatment of Inmates" are posted all over the institution to remind both staff and inmates alike of their responsibilities. They include the following:

1. Inmates are sent to prison as punishment and not for punishment.
2. Correctional workers have a responsibility to ensure that inmates are returned to the community no more angry or hostile than when they were committed.
3. Inmates are entitled to a safe and humane environment while in prison.
4. You must believe in man's capacity to change his behavior. . . .
10. Be responsive to inmate requests for action or information. Respond in a timely manner and respond the first time an inmate makes a request. . . .
12. It is important for staff to model the kind of behavior they expect to see duplicated by inmates. . . .
14. There is an inherent value in self-improvement programs such as education, whether or not these programs are related to recidivism. . . .
18. Staff cannot, because of their own insecurities, lack of self-esteem, or concerns about their masculinity, condescend or degrade inmates. . . .
26. Inmate discipline must be consistent and fair. . . .

Merely posting the "Beliefs" in prominent places will not create a superior prison culture. The credo must be put into practice. Here are some examples:

1. *Front-Line Staff.* To get front-line staffers to treat inmates with respect, top managers must treat staffers with respect. As Luther has said, "Line-level people have good ideas, not only about how to do their job, but about how to do your job better." With this in mind he created the Line Staff Advisory Board, a rotating group of frontline workers who meet with him to talk through complaints, suggestions, and rumors.
2. *"Management By Walking Around."* Through contact with staff and inmates in the dining hall, on the yard, and in the cell blocks, a warden becomes a visible presence who can hear suggestions and complaints. Often he or she can nip problems before they fester and explode. This presence sets an example of the extent to which the warden is concerned about the problems of inmates and staff.
3. *Inmate Involvement.* Regular "town hall" meetings with inmates provide opportunities for two-way communications. Proposed changes in regulations or procedures are first brought to the inmates for comment. For example, items to be offered in the commissary would be discussed.
4. *Inmate Benefit Fund.* The Inmate Benefit Fund (IBF) was created to generate money inmates could use to purchase items for which taxpayer dollars were not available. Using their own funds, inmates could order items from Bradford stores and restaurants that would ease their stay in McKean. Orders were placed with the IBF and delivered to the institution for a modest handling charge. With 2,000 inmates, substantial sums were generated by these surcharges. The inmates could use these funds to purchase additional educational and recreational programs for the population. Besides helping inmates gain access to these programs, the IBF spending contributed to the local economy.
5. *Education.* McKean has a higher percentage of inmates enrolled in classes than does almost any other federal prison. Luther believes that prison time should be spent preparing offenders for their return to the community. Courses are taught by staff members of the prison's education department, professors from neighboring colleges, and inmates. The inmates teach Adult Continuing Education courses and act as mentors and tutors.

Luther expects inmates to be responsible, and he holds them to a higher standard than found in most prisons. After a few minor incidents, the warden ordered "closed movement" during evening hours. This restricted inmate activity and was meant to be permanent. A group of inmates asked if he would restore "open movement" if the prison was incident-free for 90 days. Luther agreed and the prison has remained "open." Inmates who meet the standards receive rewards. Weekly inspections are held in each cell block, and inmates who score high are given additional privileges. Those whose disciplinary record is clean and excel in the programs can earn their way to the "honor unit." Those who show consistently good behavior are allowed to attend supervised picnics on Family Day.

Dennis Luther is convinced that his methods will work in any prison, even those plagued by violence, overcrowding, and gangs.

Many staff members feel the same way. They believe that McKean is a shining example of the difference good management can make.

Source: Drawn from Tom Peters, *Liberation Management* (New York: Knopf, 1992), 247–55; Robert Worth, "A Model Prison," *Atlantic Monthly*, November 1995, pp. 38–44.

Researching the Internet

 Access the article by Michael Montgomery, "Leadership in a Correctional Environment," in the August 2006 issue of

Corrections Today. You will find this online. To link to this website, go to *The American System of Criminal Justice* 12e companion site at academic.cengage.com/criminaljustice/cole. Click on the *Corrections Today* archive for 2006. What special factors influence leadership in a correctional environment?

CORRECTIONAL OFFICERS: THE LINCHPIN OF MANAGEMENT

A prison is simultaneously supposed to keep, use, and serve its inmates. The achievement of these goals depends heavily on the performance of its correctional officers. Their job is not easy. Not only do they work long and difficult hours with a hostile client population, but their superiors also expect them to do so with few resources or punishments at their disposal. Most of what they are expected to do must be accomplished by gaining and keeping the cooperation of the prisoners.

The Officer's Role

Over the past 30 years, the correctional officer's role has changed greatly. No longer responsible merely for "guarding," the correctional officer is now considered a crucial professional who has the closest contact with the prisoners and performs a variety of tasks. Officers are expected to counsel, supervise, protect, and process the inmates under their care. But the officer also works as a member of a complex bureaucratic organization and is expected to deal with clients impersonally and to follow formal procedures. Fulfilling these contradictory role expectations is difficult in itself, and the physical closeness of the officer and inmate over long periods exacerbates this difficulty.

Recruitment of Officers

Employment as a correctional officer is neither glamorous nor popular. The work is thought to be boring, the pay is low, and career advancement is minimal. Studies have shown that one of the primary incentives for becoming involved in correctional work is the security that civil service status provides. In addition, because most correctional facilities are located in rural areas, prison work often is better than other available employment. Because correctional officers are recruited locally, most of them are rural and white, in contrast to the majority of prisoners who come from urban areas and are often either African American or Hispanic (Figure 15.2). Yet some correctional officers see their work as a way of helping people, often the people most in need in U.S. society.

Much of the work of correctional officers involves search and counting. Such officers have a saying, "We're all doing time together, except guards are doing it in eight-hour shifts." What are the professional rewards—if any—of working as a corrections officer?

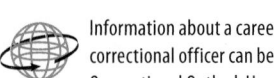 Information about a career as a correctional officer can be found at the Occupational Outlook Handbook website. To link to this website, go to *The American System of Criminal Justice* 12e companion site at academic .cengage.com/criminaljustice/cole.

Today, because they need more well-qualified correctional officers, most states recruit quality personnel. Salaries have been raised so that the yearly average entry-level pay runs from $16,000 in some southern and rural states to over $30,000 in states such as Massachusetts and New Jersey ("Wages and Benefits Paid to Correctional Employees," 2003: 8–26). In addition to their salaries, most officers can earn overtime pay, supplementing base pay by up to 30 percent. However, low salaries in a competitive economy, the massive increase in the prison population, and a tougher, more violent class of prisoners are thought to have contributed to a shortage of correctional officers (*New York Times*, April 21, 2001: A1). In 2008, officials in Texas sought to address their shortage of corrections officers by proposing a 20 percent pay increase. At the time, Texas had 3,000 vacant position for correction personnel. Under the new salary proposal, starting salaries for corrections officers would rise to $30,000 (*Austin American-Statesman*, August 14, 2008).

Special efforts have been made to recruit women and minorities. Today approximately 30 percent of correctional officers are members of minority groups and 23 percent are women (Camp, 2003: 158). How do these increases in the number of minority and female officers shape the work environment among correctional officers? Dana Britton found in her study that African American male and female officers are less satisfied with their jobs than are white male officers. She also found that African American and Hispanic male officers felt they were more effective working with the inmates than did their white counterparts. And female correctional officers were also found to be more contented with their work than male officers with their own (Britton, 1990: 85–105). Contrary to the assumption of some male officers that women cannot handle the job, Denise Jenne and Robert Kersting ("Aggression and Women Correctional Officers in Male Prisons," 1996: 442–460) found that female officers tended to respond to violent situations as aggressively as their male coworkers. In some states, male prisoners raised the issue of privacy when female officers were assigned to cell-block duty; courts have upheld inmate objections with regard to women supervising shower and toilet facilities (Pogrebin and Poole, 1997: 41–57).

Most states now have training programs for correctional officers. Ted Conover compares his experience as a "newjack" (recruit) at the Corrections Academy of the State of New York to that of the military's basic training (Conover, 2000: 12–56). During the typical six-week programs, recruits receive at least a rudimentary knowledge of job requirements and correctional rules. The classroom work, however, often bears little resemblance to problems confronted in the cell block or on the yard. Therefore, on completing the course, the new officer is placed under the supervision of an experienced officer. On the job, the new officer experiences real-life situations and learns the necessary techniques and procedures. Through encounters with inmates and officers, the recruit becomes socialized to life behind the walls and gradually becomes part of that subculture (Crouch and Marquart, 1994: 301).

FIGURE 15.2

Racial/ethnic composition of correctional officers and inmates, adult systems, nationwide

Although the racial/ethnic composition of correctional officers does not equal the racial/ethnic composition of the inmate population, great strides have been made during the past quarter century.

Source: Camille Graham Camp, *Corrections Yearbook, 2002* (Middletown, CT: Criminal Justice Institute, 2003), 158.

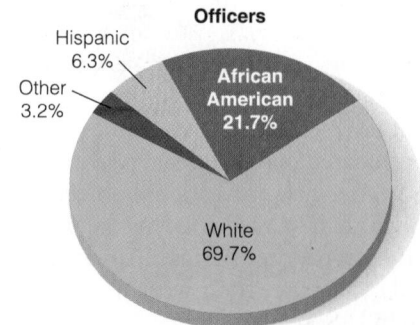
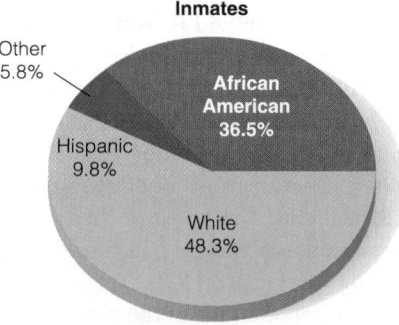

For most correctional workers, being a custodial officer is a dead-end job. Although officers who perform well may be promoted to higher ranks such as correctional counselor, few ever move into administrative positions. However, in some states and in the Federal Bureau of Prisons, people with college degrees can move up the career ladder to management positions.

The Association of Oregon Correctional Employees maintains a website. To link to this website, go to *The American System of Criminal Justice* 12e companion site at academic .cengage.com/criminaljustice/cole.

Use of Force

When and how can force be used? Although corporal punishment and the excessive use of force are not permitted, correctional officers use force in many situations. They often confront inmates who challenge their authority or are attacking other inmates. Though unarmed and outnumbered, officers must maintain order and uphold institutional rules. Under these conditions they feel justified in using force.

When and how much force may be used? All correctional agencies now have formal policies and procedures with regard to the legitimate use of force. In general these policies allow only levels of force necessary to achieve legitimate goals. Officers violating these policies may face an inmate lawsuit and dismissal. There are five situations in which the use of force is legally acceptable:

1. *Self-defense*: If officers are threatened with physical attack, they may use a level of force that is reasonable to protect themselves from harm.

2. *Defense of third persons*: As in self-defense, an officer may use force to protect an inmate or another officer. Again, only reasonably necessary force may be used.

3. *Upholding prison rules*: If prisoners refuse to obey prison rules, officers may need to use force to maintain safety and security. For example, if an inmate refuses to return to his or her cell it may be necessary to use handcuffs and forcefully transfer the prisoner.

4. *Prevention of a crime*: Force may be used to stop a crime, such as theft or destruction of property, from being committed.

5. *Prevention of escapes*: Officers may use force to prevent escapes, because they threaten the well-being of society and order within correctional institutions. Although escape from a prison is a felony, officials may not shoot the fleeing inmate at will as in the past. Today, agencies differ as to their policies toward escapees. Some limit the use of deadly force to prisoners thought to be dangerous, while others require warning shots. However, officers in Nebraska and Texas may face disciplinary action if they fail to use deadly force. Although the U.S. Supreme Court has limited the ability of police officers to shoot fleeing felons, the rule has not been applied to correctional officers.

Correctional departments have detailed sets of policies on the use of force. However, correctional officers face many challenges to self-control and professional decision making. Inmates often "push" officers in subtle ways such as moving slowly, or they use verbal abuse to provoke officers. Correctional officers are expected to run a "tight ship" and maintain order, often in situations where they are outnumbered and dealing with troubled people. In confrontational situations they must defuse hostility yet uphold the uphold the rules—a difficult task at best.

checkpoint

7. Why are correctional officers called the "linchpin of management"?
8. Name three of the five legally acceptable reasons for the use of force.

WHO IS IN PRISON?

The age, education, and criminal history of the inmate population influence how correctional institutions function. What are the characteristics of inmates in our nation's prisons? Do most offenders have long records of serious offenses, or are many of them first-time offenders who have committed minor crimes? Do some inmates have special needs that dictate their place in prison? These questions are crucial to an understanding of the work of wardens and correctional officers.

Data on the characteristics of prisoners are limited. The Bureau of Justice Statistics reports that a majority of prisoners are men, aged 25 to 44, and members of minority groups. Approximately 40 percent of state prisoners have not completed their high school education (Figure 15.3).

Recidivists and those convicted of violent crimes make up a overwhelming portion of the prison population. Research shows that 44 percent of prisoners are rearrested within the first year after release. Within three years, approximately 25 percent of all released inmates will return to prison (BJS, 2002: 3). Most of today's prisoners have a history of persistent criminality. Four additional factors affect correctional operations: the increased number of elderly

FIGURE 15.3

Sociodemographic and offense characteristics of state prison inmates
These data reflect the types of people found in state prisons. What do they indicate about the belief that many offenders do not "need" to be incarcerated?

Sources: Bureau of Justice Statistics: *Education and Correctional Population* (Washington, DC: U.S. Government Printing Office, January 2003, p. 2); *Bulletin*, December 2007, p. 25.

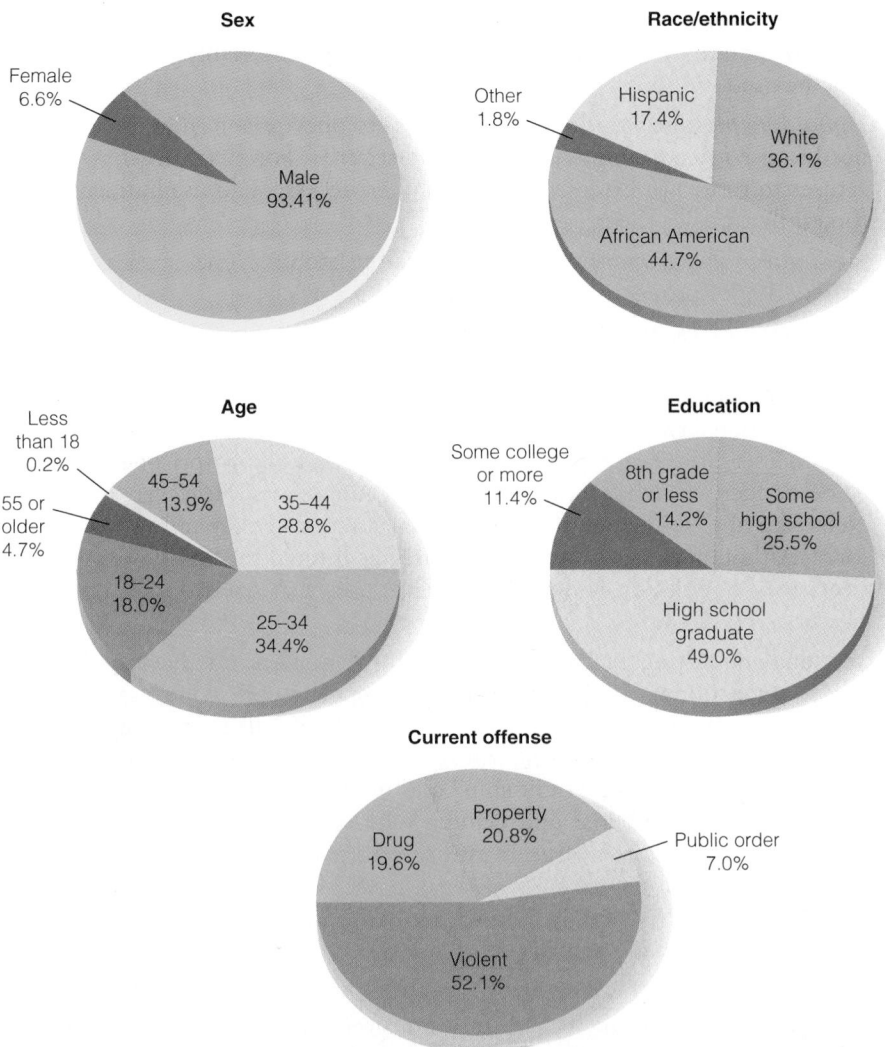

prisoners, the many prisoners with HIV/AIDS, the thousands of prisoners who are mentally ill, and the increase in long-term prisoners.

Elderly Prisoners

Correctional officials have only recently become aware of issues arising from the increasing number of inmates older than age 55. In 2006, state prisons held more than 65,000 offenders over 55 years old (BJS, 2007: 25). The elderly inmate population nationwide is rising—33 percent from 2000 to 2005—faster than the 9 percent growth in the number of prisoners overall (*USA Today*, September 29, 2007.). A number of states have created "geriatric prisons" designed to hold older inmates classified according to need: geriatric, wheelchair users, and long-term care.

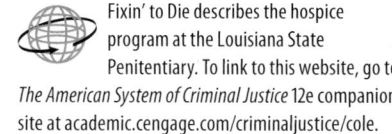

Fixin' to Die describes the hospice program at the Louisiana State Penitentiary. To link to this website, go to *The American System of Criminal Justice* 12e companion site at academic.cengage.com/criminaljustice/cole.

To some extent, the prison population is growing older because it reflects the aging of the overall citizenry, but more so because sentencing practices have changed. Consecutive lengthy sentences for heinous crimes, long mandatory minimum sentences, and life sentences without parole mean that more people who enter prison will spend most or all the rest of their lives behind bars.

Elderly prisoners have security and medical needs that differ from those of the average inmate. For example, they can't climb into top bunks. In many states, special sections of the institution have been designated for this older population so they will not have to mix with the younger, tougher inmates. New York has opened a dementia unit within the state prison in Fishkill (*Washington Post*, May 29, 2007: 12). Elderly prisoners are more likely to develop chronic illnesses such as heart disease, stroke, and cancer. The costs for maintaining an elderly inmate averages about $69,000 per year, triple the average cost for other prisoners (*Pittsburgh Post-Gazette*, March 6, 2005).

Ironically, while in prison the offender will benefit from much better medical care and live a longer life than if he or she were discharged. As one Georgia inmate has said, "You have to wonder why they haven't. . . . let them go home? What can an 80-year-old man in a wheelchair do? Run?" (*USA Today*, September 29, 2007). See "New Directions in Criminal Justice Policy" for more on the release of the elderly.

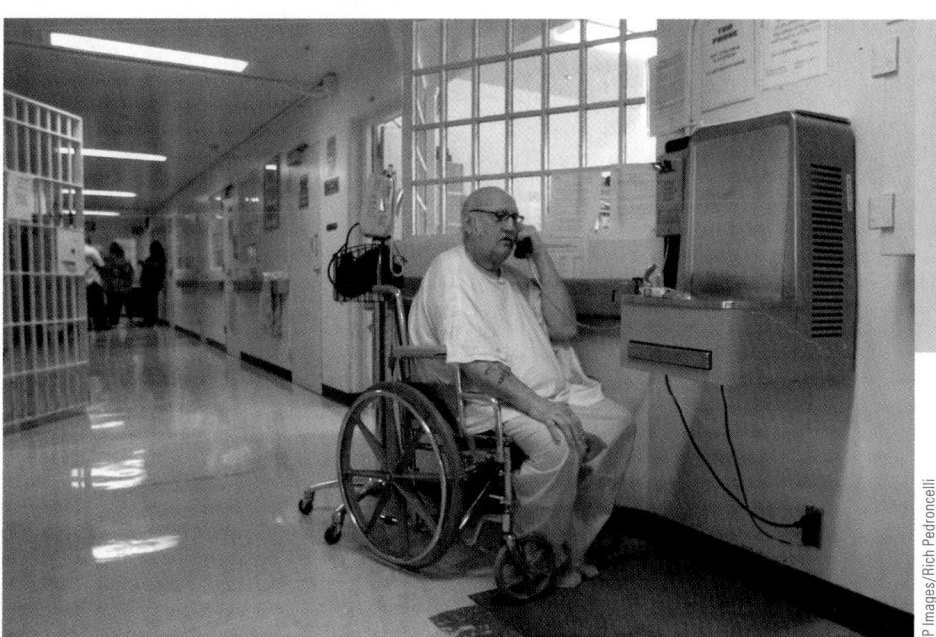

AP Images/Rich Pedroncelli

Ron Anderson, serving time for involuntary manslaughter in the California Department of Corrections Medical Facility, makes a collect phone call. The imposition of long mandatory sentences is increasing the population of elderly prisoners whose medical needs create significant financial burdens for government budgets. Are there less expensive ways to punish elderly and infirm offenders?

NEW DIRECTIONS in CRIMINAL JUSTICE POLICY

Release of the Elderly

SEVERE SENTENCING laws, including mandatory minimums, have resulted in a major increase in the number of prisoners older than age 55. Research has shown that age is the most reliable predictor of recidivism. As people get older, most become less dangerous. People older than 60 years of age commit only 1 percent of serious crime. Incarceration of the elderly costs more than three times that of holding younger inmates, because of health issues.

The Project for Older Prisoners (POPS) was organized at Tulane Law School in 1989 to cull low-risk geriatric inmates from overcrowded prisons so that they can live in the community. Chapters of POPS are now found at law schools in Louisiana, Maryland, Michigan, North Carolina, Virginia, and the District of Columbia.

POPS is meticulous in selecting candidates for release. Prisoners must acknowledge their guilt, have an exemplary record while incarcerated, and meet age and medical criteria. POPS then considers supporting the prisoner for a pardon, commutation, parole release, or some other alternative to incarceration such as a halfway house. Given the size of the elderly prison population across the nation, the more than two hundred geriatric inmates who have secured release through POPS is small; however, their recidivism rate is zero.

Many states and the federal government are considering legislation that will deal with the problem of elderly prisoners in overcrowded times. Programs such as POPS are one answer. What are others?

Researching the Internet

 Learn more about the Project for Older Prisoners online. To link to this website, go to *The American System of Criminal Justice* 12e companion site at academic.cengage.com/criminaljustice/cole.

Prisoners with HIV/AIDS

Follow the latest regarding HIV in prison at the Correctional HIV Consortium. To link to this website, go to *The American System of Criminal Justice* 12e companion site at academic.cengage.com/criminaljustice/cole.

In the coming years, AIDS is expected to be the leading cause of death among men aged 35 and younger. With 52 percent of the adult inmate population younger than age 35, correctional officials must cope with the problem of HIV as well as AIDS and related health issues. In 2006, there were 22,676 HIV-positive inmates (1.8 percent of the prison population) and 5,674 offenders with AIDS. The rate of confirmed AIDS cases in state and federal prisons is two and a half times higher than the rate in the total U.S. population. In 2005, 167 AIDS-related inmate deaths were recorded in state and federal prisons. Although AIDS is the next leading cause of death in prison behind "natural causes" and suicide, the actual number of deaths has substantially decreased since 1995 (BJS, 2008). Because many inmates who are HIV infected are undiagnosed, these numbers underestimate the scope of the problem.

The high incidence of HIV/AIDS among prisoners can be traced to increased incarceration of drug offenders. Many of these inmates engaged in intravenous drug use, shared needles, and/or traded sex for drugs or money. Male homosexual activity is also a major way that HIV is transmitted. But rates of HIV/AIDS are higher among female prisoners (2.4 percent) than male prisoners (1.7 percent) (BJS, 2006: 4). Some argue that government has a compelling interest to educate prisoners about the risk of unprotected sex or drug use in prison and even beyond the walls (Merianos, Marquart, and Damphousse, 1997: 298–314). In many correctional facilities HIV/AIDS prevention programs are in place.

To deal with offenders who have AIDS symptoms or who test positive for the virus, prison officials can develop policies on methods to prevent transmission of the disease, housing of those infected, and medical care for inmates with the full range of symptoms. Administrators are confronting a host of legal, political, medical, budgetary, and attitudinal factors as they decide what actions the institution should take.

Mentally Ill Prisoners

Mass closings of public hospitals for the mentally ill began in the 1960s. At the time new psychotropic drugs made treating patients in the community seem a more humane alternative to long-term hospitalization. It also promised to be less expensive. Soon, however, people saw that community treatment works only if patients take their medication. Widespread homelessness was the most public sign that the community treatment approach had its shortcomings. With the expansion of prisons and the greater police emphasis on public order offenses, many mentally ill individuals are now arrested and incarceration. These inmates tend to catch a revolving door from homelessness to incarceration and then back to the streets.

Currently far more mentally ill are in the nation's jails and prisons (191,000) than in state hospitals (62,000) (BJS, 2001: 3; Human Rights Watch, 2003: 1). The incarceration rate of the mentally ill is four times that of the general population. The prison has become the largest psychiatric facility in some states. For example, New York City's Riker's Island houses three thousand mentally ill inmates (*The New York Times Sunday Magazine*, May 23, 1999: 42). Over the past ten years, the mentally ill portion of Connecticut's prison population has gone from 24 to 40 percent (*Hartford Courant*, May 23, 1999: A1). In Los Angeles, 50 percent of those entering the county jail are identified as mentally ill (*New York Times*, March 5, 1998: A26).

Correctional workers are usually unprepared to deal with the mentally ill. Cell-block officers, for instance, often do not know how to respond to disturbed inmates. Although most corrections systems have mental health units that segregate the ill, many inmates with psychiatric disorders live among other prisoners in the general population, where they are teased and otherwise exploited.

The availability and type of prison mental health treatment programs vary. The two most common types involve therapy/counseling or dispensing medications. One in eight inmates in state prisons receives counseling services, and approximately one in ten receives psychotropic medications (BJS, 2001: 3). Although some inmates benefit from the regular medication and therapy they receive, others suffer as the stress of confinement deepens their depressions, intensifies delusions, or leads to mental breakdown. Many commit suicide.

Visit the Mental Health Consortium in Corrections online. To link to this website, go to *The American System of Criminal Justice* 12e companion site at academic.cengage.com/criminaljustice/cole.

Long-Term Prisoners

More prisoners in the United States serve longer sentences than do prisoners in other Western nations. One survey found that nearly 310,000 prisoners are currently serving at least 20-year sentences. Of these inmates, about 10 percent are serving "natural life," which means there is no possibility of parole (Camp, 2003: 40–41). The number of inmates serving natural life has nearly tripled since 1992 and they now make up 10 percent of all prisoners (*New York Times*, May 12, 2004: A15). These long-term prisoners are often the same people who will become elderly offenders, with all the attendant problems. Each life sentence costs taxpayers an estimated $1 million (Mauer, King, and Young, 2004: 3). The "get tough" policies of the last 30 years—three strikes, mandatory minimums, truth-in-sentencing—have altered the composition of the lifer population, which now includes more nonviolent offenders (Mauer, et al., 2004: 13).

Studies show substantial differences in the way the long-termer responds to incarceration. Some, but not others, experience severe stress, depression, and other health problems (Maue, 2001: 8). Such emotional stress tends to take place earlier rather than later in the sentence as these inmates lose contact with their families.

Long-term prisoners are generally not seen as control problems. They are charged with disciplinary infractions about half as often as are short-term inmates. They do, nonetheless, present challenges for administrators who must find ways of making long terms livable. Experts suggest that administrators follow three main principles: (1) maximize opportunities for the inmate to exercise choice in living circumstances, (2) create opportunities for meaningful living, and (3) help the inmate maintain contact with the outside world (Flanagan, T. J. ed., *Long-Term Imprisonment*, Thousand Oaks, CA: Sage, 1995: 256).

Many long-term inmates will eventually be released after spending their prime years incarcerated. Will offenders be able to support themselves when they return to the community at age 50, 60, or 70?

The contemporary inmate population presents several challenges to correctional workers. Resources may not be available to provide rehabilitative programs for most inmates. Even if the resources exist, the goal of maintaining a safe and healthy environment may tax the staff's abilities. These difficulties are multiplied still further by AIDS and the increasing numbers of elderly and long-term prisoners. The contemporary corrections system must also deal with a different type of inmate, one who is more prone to violence, and with a prison society where racial tensions are great. How well it meets this correctional challenge will greatly affect American society.

checkpoint

9. What are the major characteristics of today's prisoners?

THE CONVICT WORLD

inmate code
The values and norms of the prison social system that define the inmates' idea of the model prisoner.

Inmates of a maximum-security prison do not serve their time in isolation. Rather, prisoners form a society with traditions, norms, and a leadership structure. Some choose to associate with only a few close friends; others form cliques along racial or "professional" lines. Still others serve as the politicians of the convict society; they attempt to represent convict interests and distribute valued goods in return for support. Just as there is a social culture in the free world, there is a prisoner subculture on the "inside." Membership in a group provides mutual protection from theft and physical assault, the basis of wheeling and dealing activities, and a source of cultural identity (Irwin, 1980).

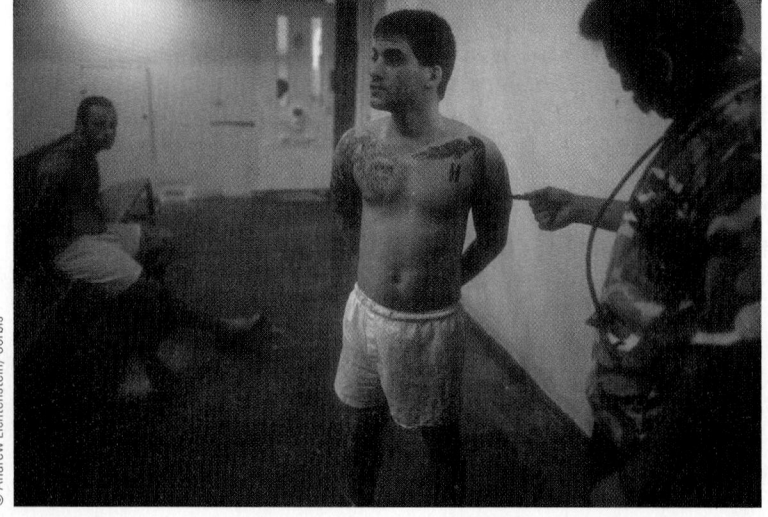

Contemporary prison society is divided along racial, ethnic, and gang subgroups. There is no longer an inmate code to which all prisoners subscribe. Here an officer inspects a prisoner for evidence of new tattoos, especially those displaying gang symbols—a violation of prison rules. As a correctional officer, how would you deal with members of white supremacist gangs or other gangs based on racial and ethnic divisions and conflicts?

© Andrew Lichtenstein/Corbis

As in any society, the convict world has certain norms and values. Often described as the **inmate code**, these norms and values develop within the prison social system and help to define the inmate's image of the model prisoner. As Robert Johnson notes, "The public culture of the prison has norms that dictate behavior 'on the yard' and in other public areas of the prison such as mess halls, gyms, and the larger program and work sites" (Johnson, 2002: 100). Prison is an ultramasculine world. The culture breathes masculine toughness and insensitivity, impugning softness, and emphasizes the use of hostility and manipulation in one's relations with fellow inmates and staff. It makes caring and friendly behavior, especially with respect to the staff, look servile and silly (Sabo, Kupers, and London, 2001: 7).

Former inmate Chuck Terry, says that male prisoners must project an image of "fearlessness in the way they walk, talk and socially interact" (Terry, 1997: 26). Because showing emotion is seen as a weakness, inmates must suppress expressions of their true feelings.

The code also emphasizes the solidarity of all inmates against the staff. For example, inmates should never inform on one another, pry into one another's affairs, "run off at the mouth," or put another inmate on the spot. They must be tough and not trust the officers or the principles for which the guards stand. Further, guards are "hacks" or "screws"; the officials are wrong and the prisoners are right.

Some sociologists believe that the code emerges within the institution as a way to lessen the pain of imprisonment (Sykes, 1958); others believe that it is part of the criminal subculture that prisoners bring with them (Irwin, and Cressey, 1962: 142–155). The inmate who follows the code can be expected to enjoy a certain amount of admiration from other inmates as a "right guy" or a "real man." Those who break the code are labeled "rat" or "punk" and will probably spend their prison life at the bottom of the convict social structure, alienated from the rest of the population and targeted for abuse (Sykes, 1958: 84).

A single, overriding inmate code probably does not exist in today's prisons. Instead, convict society has divided itself along racial lines (Irwin, 1980). The level of adherence to the inmate code also differs among institutions, with greater modifications to local situations found in maximum-security prisons. Still, the core commandments described by Sykes 50 years ago remain. For a somewhat different perspective, see the Close Up box.

In a changing society that has no single code of behavior accepted by the entire population, the tasks of administrators become much more difficult. They must be aware of the different groups, recognize the norms and rules that members hold, and deal with the leaders of many cliques rather than with a few inmates who have risen to top positions in the inmate society.

checkpoint

10. What are the key elements of the inmate code?
11. Why is it unlikely that a single, overriding inmate code exists in today's prisons?

Adaptive Roles

On entering prison, a newcomer ("fish") is confronted by the question, "How am I going to do my time?" Some decide to withdraw and isolate themselves. Others decide to become full participants in the convict social system. The choice, influenced by prisoners' values and experiences, helps determine strategies for survival and success.

Most male inmates use one of four basic role orientations to adapt to prison: "doing time," "gleaning," "jailing," and functioning as a "disorganized criminal" (Irwin, 1970: 67).

Doing Time

Men "doing time" view their prison term as a brief, inevitable break in their criminal careers, a cost of doing business. They try to serve their terms with the least amount of suffering and the greatest amount of comfort. They avoid trouble by living by the inmate code, finding activities to fill their days, forming friendships with a few other convicts, and generally doing what they think is necessary to survive and to get out as soon as possible.

CLOSE UP

Survival Tips for Beginners

TJ Granack

OKAY, SO YOU just lost your case. Maybe you took a plea bargain. Whatever. The point is you've been sentenced. You've turned yourself over to the authorities and you're in the county jail waiting to catch the next chain to the R Units (receiving) where you'll be stripped and shaved and photographed and processed and sent to one of the various prisons in your state.

So what's a felon to do? Here are some survival tips that may make your stay less hellish:

1. *Commit an Honorable Crime.* Commit a crime that's considered, among convicts, to be worthy of respect. I was lucky. I went down for first-degree attempted murder, so my crime fell in the "honorable" category. Oh, goodie. So I just had to endure the everyday sort of danger and abuse that comes with prison life.
2. *Don't Gamble.* Not cards, not chess, not the Super Bowl. And if you do, don't bet too much. If you lose too much, and pay up (don't even think of doing otherwise), then you'll be known as rich guy who'll be very popular with the vultures.
4. *Never Loan Anyone Anything.* Because if you do, you'll be expected to collect one way or another. If you don't collect, you will be known as a mark, as someone without enough heart to take back his own. . . .
6. *Make No Eye Contact.* Don't look anyone in the eye. Ever. Locking eyes with another man, be he a convict or a guard, is considered a challenge, a threat, and should therefore be avoided.

7. *Pick Your Friends Carefully.* When you choose a friend, you've got to be prepared to deal with anything that person may have done. Their reputation is yours, and the consequences can be enormous.
8. *Fight and Fight Dirty.* You have to fight, and not according to Marquis of Queensbury rules, either. If you do it right, you'll only have to do it once or twice. If you don't, expect regular whoopings and loss of possessions. . . .
10. *Mind Your Own Business.* Never get in the middle of anyone else's discussion/argument/confrontation/fight. Never offer unsolicited knowledge or advice.
11. *Keep a Good Porn Collection.* If you don't have one, the boys will think you're funny. . . .
14. *Don't Talk to Staff, Especially Guards.* Any prolonged discussions or associations with staff makes you susceptible to rumor and suspicion of being a snitch.
15. *Never Snitch.* Or even appear to snitch. And above all, avoid the real thing. And if you do, you'd better not get caught.

Source: Drawn from TJ Granack, "Welcome to the Steel Hotel: Survival Tips for Beginners," in *The Funhouse Mirror*, ed. Robert Gordon Ellis (Pullman: Washington State University Press, 2000), 6–10.

Researching the Internet

 See the survival tips for beginners that are presented online. To link to this website, go to *The American System of Criminal Justice* 12e companion site at academic.cengage.com/criminaljustice/cole.

Gleaning

Inmates who are "gleaning" try to take advantage of prison programs to better themselves and improve their prospects for success after release. They use the resources at hand: libraries, correspondence courses, vocational training, schools. Some make a radical conversion away from a life of crime.

Jailing

"Jailing" is the choice of those who cut themselves off from the outside and try to construct a life within the prison. These are often "state-raised" youths who have spent much of their lives in institutional settings and who identify little with the values of free society. These are the inmates who seek power and influence in the prison society, often becoming key figures in the politics and economy of prison life.

Disorganized Criminal

A fourth role orientation—the "disorganized criminal"—describes inmates who cannot develop any of the other three orientations. They may be of low intelligence or afflicted with psychological or physical disabilities, and they find functioning in prison society difficult. They are "human putty" to be manipulated by others. These are also the inmates who cannot adjust to prison life and who develop emotional disorders, attempt suicide, and violate prison rules (Adams, 1992: 275–359).

As these roles suggest, prisoners are not members of an undifferentiated mass. Individual convicts choose to play specific roles in prison society. The roles they choose reflect the physical and social environment they have experienced and also influence their relationships and interactions in prison. How do most prisoners serve their time? Although the media generally portray prisons as violent, chaotic places, research shows that most inmates want to get through their sentence without trouble. As journalist Pete Earley found in his study of Leavenworth, roughly 80 percent of inmates try to avoid trouble and do their time as easily as possible (Early, 1992: 44).

checkpoint

12. What are the four role orientations found in adult male prisons?

The Prison Economy

In prison, as outside, individuals want goods and services. Although the state feeds, clothes, and houses all prisoners, amenities are scarce. Prisoners are deprived of everything but bare necessities. Their diet and routine are monotonous and their recreational opportunities scarce. They experience a loss of identity (due to uniformity of treatment) and a lack of responsibility. In short, the prison is relatively unique in having been deliberately designed as "an island of poverty in the midst of a society of relative abundance" (Williams and Fish, 1974: 40).

The number of items that a prisoner can purchase or receive through legitimate channels differs from state to state and from facility to facility. For example, inmates in some prisons may have televisions, civilian clothing, and hot plates. Not all prisoners enjoy these luxuries, nor do they satisfy lingering desires for a variety of other goods. Some state legislatures have decreed that amenities will be prohibited and that prisoners should return to Spartan living conditions.

Recognizing that prisoners do have some needs that are not met, prisons have a commissary or "store" from which inmates may periodically purchase a limited number of items—toilet articles, tobacco, snacks, and other items—in exchange for credits drawn on their "bank accounts." The size of a bank account depends on the amount of money deposited on the inmate's entrance, gifts sent by relatives, and amounts earned in the low-paying prison industries.

However, the peanut butter, soap, and cigarettes of the typical prison store in no way satisfy the consumer needs and desires of most prisoners. Consequently, an informal, underground economy is a major element in prison society. Many items taken for granted on the outside are highly valued on the inside. For example, talcum powder and deodorant become more important because of the limited bathing facilities. Goods and services unique to prison can take on exaggerated importance inside prison. For example, unable to get alcohol, offenders may seek a similar effect by sniffing glue. Or to distinguish themselves from others, offenders may pay laundry workers to iron a shirt in a particular way, a modest version of conspicuous consumption.

Many studies point to the pervasiveness of this economy. When David Kalinich (Kalinich, 1980) studied the State Prison of Southern Michigan in Jackson, he learned that a market economy provides the goods (contraband) and services not available or not allowed by prison authorities. Mark Fleisher (Fleisher, 1989: 151) found an inmate running a "store" in almost every cell block in the U.S. Penitentiary at Lompoc, California. Food stolen (from the kitchen) for late-night snacks, homemade wine, and drugs (marijuana) were available in these "stores." As a principal feature of prison culture, this informal economy reinforces the norms and roles of the social system and influences the nature of interpersonal relationships. The extent of the underground economy and its ability to produce desired goods and services—food, drugs, alcohol, sex, preferred living conditions—vary according to the scope of official surveillance, the demands of the consumers, and the opportunities for entrepreneurship. Inmates' success as "hustlers" determines the luxuries and power they can enjoy.

Because real money is prohibited and a barter system is somewhat restrictive, the standard currency of the prison economy is cigarettes. They are not contraband, are easily transferable, have a stable and well-known standard of value, and come in "denominations" of singles, packs, and cartons. Furthermore they are in demand by smokers. Even those who do not smoke keep cigarettes for prison currency. As more prisons become "nonsmoking," cans of tuna fish or bars of soap have emerged as a new form of currency.

Certain positions in the prison society enhance opportunities for entrepreneurs. For example, inmates assigned to work in the kitchen, warehouse, and administrative office steal food, clothing, building materials, and even information to sell or trade to other prisoners. The goods may then become part of other market transactions. Thus, the exchange of a dozen eggs for two packs of cigarettes may result in the reselling of the eggs in the form of egg sandwiches made on a hot plate for five cigarettes each. Meanwhile, the kitchen worker who stole the eggs may use the income to get a laundry worker to starch his shirts, to get drugs from a hospital orderly, or to pay a "punk" for sexual favors.

Economic transactions can lead to violence when goods are stolen, debts are not paid, or agreements are violated. Disruptions of the economy can occur when officials conduct periodic "lockdowns" and inspections. Confiscation of contraband can result in temporary shortages and price readjustments, but gradually business returns. The prison economy, like that of the outside world, allocates goods and services, rewards and sanctions, and it is closely linked to the society it serves.

checkpoint

13. Why does an underground economy exist in prison?
14. Why are prison administrators wary of the prison economy?

WOMEN IN PRISON

Most studies of prisons have been based on institutions for men. How do prisons for women differ, and what are the special problems of female inmates? Women constitute only 7.2 percent (about 112,000) of the entire U.S. prison population (BJS, 2007: 5). However, the growth rate in the number of incarcerated women has exceeded that of men since 1981. In fact, from 1995 to 2005, the population of men in state and federal prisons increased 34 percent, whereas that of women increased by 57 percent (BJS, 2006: 4). The war on drugs has had a decided impact on the prison population with the large proportion of drug offenders making up the largest category in women's prisons (Kruttschnitt, and Gartner, 2003: 7). This growth is particularly acute in the federal system, which has had to absorb an additional six thousand female drug offenders during the past 20 years (BJS, 2004: 5). The increased number of women in prison has significantly affected the delivery of programs, housing conditions, medical care, staffing, and security. As you read "Civic Engagement: Your Role in the System," think about how society should treat women prisoners, particularly in light of the fact that nearly all of them will eventually gain release.

Life in the nation's 98 confinement facilities for women and 93 coed facilities both resembles and differs from that in institutions for men (BJS, 2003: 6). Women's prisons are smaller, with looser security and less structured relationships; the underground economy is not as well developed; and female prisoners seem less committed to the inmate code. Women also serve shorter sentences than do men, so their prison society is more fluid as new members join and others leave.

Many women's prisons have the outward appearance of a college campus, often seen as a group of "cottages" around a central administration/dining/program building. Generally these facilities lack the high walls, guard towers, and cyclone fences found at most prisons for men. In recent years, however, the trend has been to upgrade security for women's prisons by adding barbed wire, higher fences, and other devices to prevent escapes.

These characteristics of correctional facilities for women are offset by geographic remoteness and inmate heterogeneity. Few states operate more than one institution for women, so inmates are generally far from children, families, friends, and attorneys. In many institutions, the small numbers of inmates limit the extent to which the needs of individual offenders can be recognized and treated. Housing classifications are often so broad that dangerous or mentally ill inmates are mixed with women who have committed minor offenses and have no psychological problems. Similarly, available rehabilitative programs are often not used to their full extent, because correctional departments fail to recognize women's problems and needs.

In most respects, we can see incarcerated women, like male prisoners, as disadvantaged losers in this complex and competitive society. However the two groups differ with regard to types of offenses, length of sentences, patterns of drug use, and correctional history. A Bureau of Justice Statistics survey found that 32 percent of female prisoners were sentenced for violent offenses (compared with 49 percent of male prisoners), and 30 percent for drug-related offenses (versus 20 percent of men) (BJS, 2003: 10). Overall, women receive shorter maximum sentences than do men. Half of the women had a maximum sentence of five years or less, whereas half of the men had a sentence of ten years or less (BJS, 2000). Figure 15.4 summarizes some characteristics of female prisoners.

civic engagement
your role in the system

Imagine that your fraternity, sorority, church group, or other social service organization has been asked to participate in programs to help women prisoners prepare for successful reentry into society. *Make a list of needs that women prisoners are likely to have and what measures volunteer groups could take to provide assistance with reentry and success in society.* Then compare your responses with the activities of the Women's Prison Association. To link to this website, go to *The American System of Criminal Justice* 12e companion site at academic.cengage.com/criminaljustice/cole.

 Hollywood's depiction of female prisoners may be understood by reading the reviews of the many films about them, which are available online. To link to this website, go to *The American System of Criminal Justice* 12e companion site at academic.cengage.com/criminaljustice/cole.

checkpoint

15. What accounts for the neglect of facilities and programs in women's prisons?

The Subculture of Women's Prisons

Studies of the subculture of women's prisons have been less extensive than those of male convict society. Further, just as there have been few ethnographic studies of men's prisons during the past two decades, there have been few such studies of women's prisons—in fact, far fewer even than those of men's prisons.

Much early investigation of separate women's prisons focused on types of social relationships among female offenders. As in all types of penal institutions, same-sex relationships were found, but unlike in male prisons, such relationships among women appeared more voluntary than coerced. Perhaps more importantly, scholars reported that female inmates tended to form pseudofamilies in which they adopted various roles—father, mother, daughter, sister—and interacted as a unit, rather than identifying with the larger prisoner subculture (Girshick, 1999; Propper, 1982: 127–139). Esther Hefferman views these "play" families as a "direct, conscious substitution for the family relationships broken by imprisonment, or . . . the development of roles that perhaps were not fulfilled in the actual home environment" (Hefferman, 1972: 41–42). She also notes the economic aspect of the play families and the extent to which they are formed to provide for their members. Such cooperative relationships help relieve the tensions of prison life, assist the socialization of new inmates, and permit individuals to act according to clearly defined roles and rules.

FIGURE 15.4

Characteristics of female inmates in state prisons

Like their male counterparts, women inmates in state prisons are typically young, have little education, are members of minority groups, and are incarcerated for a serious offense.

Sources: Bureau of Justice Statistics, *Special Report*, December 1999, p. 7; *Bulletin*, July 2003, p. 10.

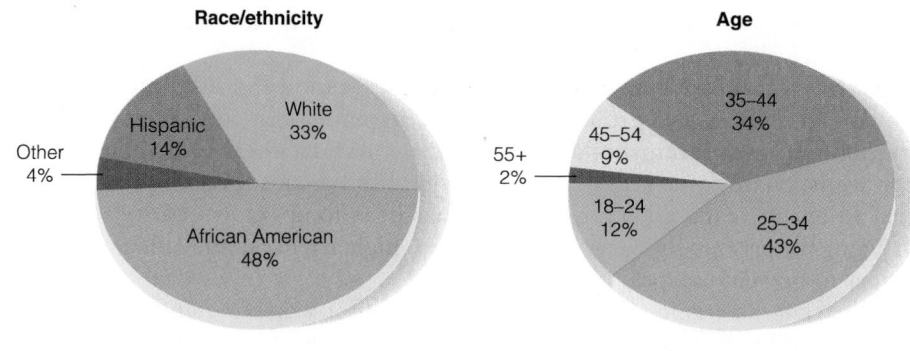

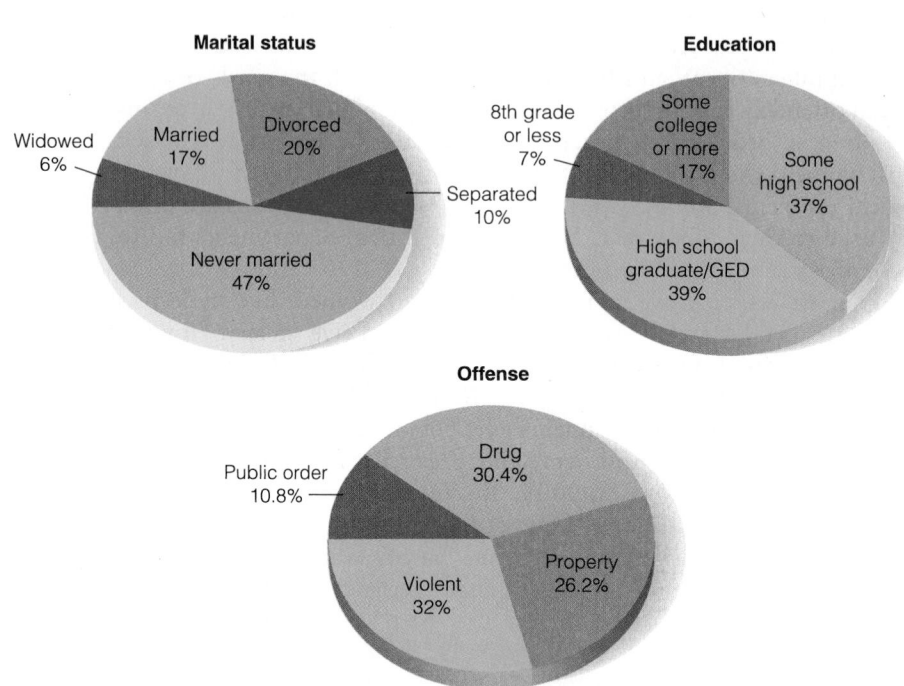

In discussing the available research on women in prison, we need to consider the most recent shifts in prison life. Just as the subculture of male prisons has changed since the pioneering research of the 1950s, the climate of female prisons has undoubtedly changed. Kimberly Greer (Greer, 2000: 442–468) found support for the idea that prisons for women are less violent, involved less gang activity, and do not have the racial tensions existing in men's prisons; however, the respondents indicated that their interpersonal relationships may be less stable and less familial than in the past. They reported higher levels of mistrust among women and greater economic manipulation.

In one of the few recent studies of prison culture, Barbara Owen (1998) (Owen, 1998) found that the inmates at the Central California Women's Facility, holding over 4,500 women, developed various styles of doing time. Based on the in-prison experience, these styles correspond to the day-to-day business of developing a program of activities and settling into a routine. She observed that the vast majority wanted to avoid "the mix"—"behavior that can bring trouble and conflict with staff and other prisoners." A primary feature of "the mix" is anything for which one can lose good time or can result in being sent to administrative segregation. Being in "the mix" was related to "'homo-secting,' involvement in drugs, fights, of 'being messy,' that is, being involved in conflict and trouble." Owen found that most women want to do their time and go home, but some "are more at home in prison and do not seem to care if they 'lost time'"(Owen, 1998: 179).

Male versus Female Subcultures

Comparisons of male and female prisons are complicated by the nature of the research: Most studies have been conducted in single-sex institutions, and most follow theories and concepts first developed in male prisons. However, the following facts may explain the differences in subculture:

- Nearly half of male inmates but only a third of female inmates are serving time for violent offenses.
- There is less violence in prisons for women than in prisons for men.
- Women show greater responsiveness to prison programs than do men.
- Men's prison populations are divided by security level, but most women serve time in facilities where the entire population is mixed.
- Men tend to segregate themselves by race; this is less true with women.
- Men rarely become intimate with their keepers, but many women share their lives with officers.

A major difference between the two types of prisons relates to interpersonal relationships. Male prisoners act for themselves and are evaluated by others according to how they adhere to subcultural norms. As James Fox (1982) noted in his comparative study of one women's prison and four men's prisons, men believe they must demonstrate physical strength and consciously avoid any mannerisms that might imply homosexuality. To gain recognition and status within the convict community, the male prisoner must strictly adhere to these values. Men form cliques, but not the family networks found in prisons for women. Male norms stress autonomy, self-sufficiency, and the ability to cope with one's own problems, and men are expected to "do their own time." Fox found little sharing in the men's prisons (Fox, 1982).

Women place less emphasis on achieving status or recognition within the prisoner community. Fox writes that women are also less likely "to impose severe restrictions on the sexual (or emotional) conduct of other members" (1982: 100). As noted previously, in prisons for women, close ties seem to exist among small groups akin to extended families. These family groups provide emotional support and share resources.

Some have ascribed the differences between male and female prisoner subcultures to the nurturing, maternal qualities of women. Critics charge that such an analysis stereotypes female behavior and imputes a biological basis to personality where none exists. Of importance as well is the issue of inmate–inmate violence in male and female institutions. The few data that exist indicate that women are less likely to engage in violent acts against other inmates than are men (Kruttschnitt and Krmopotich, 1990: 371). It will be interesting to see whether such gender-specific differences continue to be found among prisoners as society comes to view women and men as equals.

checkpoint

16. How do the social relationships among female prisoners differ from those of their male counterparts?

Issues in the Incarceration of Women

As noted, the number of incarcerated women has greatly increased over the past ten years. Under pressures for equal opportunity, states seem to believe that they should run women's prisons as they do prisons for men, with the same policies and procedures. Joycelyn Pollock (Pollock, 1998) believes that when prisons emphasize parity and use a male standard, women lose. She says that with the increased number of women in prison and more equality in programming, there are also more security measures and formalistic approaches to supervision.

Departments of corrections have been playing "catch up" to meet the challenge of crowded facilities, sexual misdconduct by officers, as well as demands for education and training, medical services, and methods for dealing with the problems of mothers and their children. We next examine each of these issues and the policy implications they pose for the future.

Sexual Misconduct

As the number of female prisoners has increased, cases of sexual misconduct by male correctional officers have escalated. As a result of an investigation of sexual misconduct by officers in the women's prisons of five states—California, Georgia, Illinois, Michigan, and New York—Human Rights Watch reported that male officers had raped, sexually assaulted, and abused female inmates. Guards had also "used their near total authority to provide or deny goods and privileges to female prisoners to compel them to have sex or, in other cases, to reward them for having done so" (*New York Times*, December 27, 1996: A18).

Monetary civil judgments awarded to women for mistreatment while in prison have grown. Officials in California, Georgia, and the District of Columbia have reached out-of-court settlements in class-action suits brought on behalf of women who said they were sexually harassed or assaulted by guards while incarcerated.

To deal with the problem of sexual abuse in prison, all but eight states have enacted statutes prohibiting sexual misconduct with correctional clients. While some of these laws are directed at correctional officers, several states are revising their statutes to include anyone who supervises offenders (Criminal Justice Research Reports, 2001: 87). Beyond the new laws, corrections faces a great need for the implementation of effective sexual harassment policies, the training of officers, and tougher screening of recruits.

Some institutions have programs to permit mothers in prison to spend time with their children. Here Yolanda Hall enjoys the swing with her daughter during Mother's Day activities at the California Institution for Women. Should society be more concerned about the impact on children when they have little contact with their incarcerated mothers?

Educational and Vocational Training Programs

A major criticism of women's prisons is that they lack the variety of vocational and educational programs available in male institutions. Critics also charge that existing programs tend to conform to sexual stereotypes of "female" occupations—cosmetology, food service, housekeeping, sewing. Such training does not correspond to the wider employment opportunities available to women in today's world. Both men's and women's facilities usually offer educational programs so inmates can become literate and earn general equivalency diplomas (GEDs). There are questions about whether the few work assignments available for incarcerated women actually teach the prisoners any marketable job skills (American Correctional Association, 1990).

Research conducted in the 1970s by Ruth Glick and Virginia Neto (1977) documented and confirmed that fewer programs were offered in women's than in men's institutions and that the existing programs lacked variety. Morash and her colleagues noted changes during the 1980s, but they too found that gender stereotypes shaped vocational programs (Morash, Haarr, and Rucker, 1994: 197–221). The American Correctional Association (1990) reported that the few work assignments available for incarcerated women do teach marketable job skills (American Correctional Association, 1990).

To get a good job, workers must have the education necessary to meet the needs of a complex workplace. However, the educational level of most female offenders limits their access to these occupations. In some institutions less than half of the inmates have completed high school. Some corrections systems assign these women to classes so they can earn a GED, and other inmates can do college work through correspondence study or courses offered in the institution.

Medical Services

Women's prisons lack proper medical services. Because of their socioeconomic status and limited access to preventive medical care, women typically have more serious health problems than do men. Compared with men, they have a higher incidence of asthma, drug abuse, diabetes, and heart disorders, and many women also have gynecological problems (BJS, 2008). Although a higher percentage of women than men report receiving medical services in prison, women's institutions are less likely than men's to have a full-time medical staff or hospital facilities.

HIV, tuberculosis, drug addiction, and mental illness affect female prisoners more than they do male inmates. A national survey revealed that a higher percentage of female than male state prison inmates (2.9 percent versus 1.9 percent) tested positive for HIV. In addition, nearly 24 percent of women in state prisons are mentally ill, and 60 percent used drugs during the month before entering prison (BJS, 2004: 3; BJS, 1999: 3).

Pregnant women also need special medical and nutritional resources. About 25 percent of incarcerated women are pregnant on admission or have given birth during the previous year. However, less than half received prenatal care, and only 15 percent receive special diets and counseling (Woodridge and Masters, 1993: 195). Pregnancies raise numerous issues for correctional policy, including special diets, abortion rights, access to delivery rooms and medical personnel, and length of time that newborns can remain with incarcerated mothers. Many pregnant inmates have characteristics (older than 35, history of drug abuse, prior multiple abortions, and sexually transmitted diseases) that indicate the potential for a high-risk pregnancy requiring special medical care. Many prison systems are attempting to address this problem by allowing nursing infants to stay with their mothers, creating in-prison nurseries, instituting counseling programs, and improving standards of medical care (Wooldredge and Masters, 1993).

Saying that corrections must "defuse the time bomb," Leslie Acoca (1998) (Acoca, 1998: 49–69) argues that failure to provide female inmates with basic preventive and medical treatments such as immunizations, breast cancer screenings, and management of chronic diseases "is resulting in the development of more serious health problems that are exponentially more expensive to treat." She says that poor medical care for the incarcerated merely shifts costs to overburdened community health care systems after release.

Mothers and Their Children

Of greatest concern to incarcerated women is the fate of their children. Over 65 percent of women inmates are mothers, and approximately 45 percent have two or more minor children. Thus on any given day, 115,500 children—two-thirds of whom are under ten years old—have mothers who are in jail or prison. Roughly half of these children do not see their mothers the entire time that the prison sentence is being served (BJS, 2000: 1).

Because about 65 percent of incarcerated mothers were single caretakers of minor children before they entered prison, they do not have partners to take care of the children. Nearly 78 percent of these children are cared for by relatives, while 10 percent are in state-funded foster care (Acoca, 1997: 44–55).

Imprisoned mothers have difficulty maintaining contact with their children. Because most states have only one or two prisons for women, mothers may be

Chicago Legal Advocacy for Incarcerated Mothers assists families of female prisoners. To link to this website, go to *The American System of Criminal Justice* 12e companion site at academic.cengage.com/criminaljustice/cole.

incarcerated 150 miles or more away. Transportation is thus difficult, visits are short and infrequent, and phone calls uncertain and irregular. When the children do visit the prison, the surroundings are strange and intimidating. In some institutions, children must conform to the rules governing adult visitations: strict time limits and no physical contact.

Other correctional facilities, however, seek ways to help mothers maintain links to their children. For example, the Dwight Correctional Center in Illinois schedules weekend retreats, similar to camping trips, for women and their children. In some states, children can meet with their mothers at almost any time, for extended periods, and in playrooms or nurseries that allow contact. Some states transport children to visit their mothers; some institutions even let children stay overnight with their mothers. A few prisons have family visitation programs that let the inmate, her legal husband, and her children be together, often in a mobile home or apartment, for up to 72 hours.

The future of women's correctional institutions is hard to predict. More women are being sent to prison now, and more have committed the violent crimes and drug offenses that used to be more typical of male offenders. Will these changes affect the adaptive roles and social relationships that differentiate women's prisons from men's? Will women's prisons need to become more security conscious and to enforce rules through more formal relationships between inmates and staff? These important issues need further study.

checkpoint

17. What are some of the problems encountered by female prisoners in maintaining contact with their children?
18. How are children cared for while their mothers are incarcerated?

PRISON PROGRAMS

Modern correctional institutions differ from those of the past in the number and variety of programs provided for inmates. Early penitentiaries included prison industries; educational, vocational, and treatment programs were added when rehabilitation goals became prevalent. During the last 35 years, as the public has called for harsher punishment of criminals, legislators have gutted prison educational and treatment programs as "frills" that only "coddled" inmates. In addition, the great increase in the number of prisoners has limited access to those programs that are still available. Yet, respondents to one survey support some prison programs (see "What Americans Think").

Administrators argue that programs help them deal with the problem of time on the prisoners' hands. They know that the more programs prisons offer, the less likely that inmate idleness will turn into hostility—less cell time means fewer tensions. Evidence suggests that inmate education and jobs may positively affect the running of prisons, as well as reduce recidivism (*New York Times,* July 16, 1995: E.3).

classification
The process of assigning an inmate to a category specifying his or her needs for security, treatment, education, work assignment, and readiness for release.

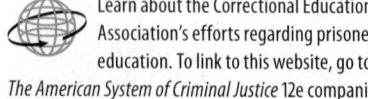

Learn about the Correctional Education Association's efforts regarding prisoner education. To link to this website, go to *The American System of Criminal Justice* 12e companion site at academic.cengage.com/criminaljustice/cole.

Classification of Prisoners

Determining the appropriate program for an individual prisoner usually involves a process called **classification.** A committee—often comprising the heads of the security, treatment, education, and industry departments—evaluates the inmate's security level, treatment needs, work assignment, and, eventually, readiness for release.

Classification decisions are often based on the institution's needs rather than those of the inmates. For example, inmates from the city may be assigned to farm work because that is where they are needed. Further, certain popular programs may remain limited, even though the demand for them is great. Thus inmates may find that the few places in, for example, a computer course are filled and that there is a long waiting list. Prisoners are often angered and frustrated by the classification process and the limited availability of programs. Release on parole can depend on a good record of participation in these programs, yet entrance for some inmates is blocked.

checkpoint

19. Why are prison programs important from the standpoint of prison administrators?
20. How are inmates assigned to programs?

Educational Programs

Surveys have shown that programs offering academic courses are the most popular in corrections systems. Offenders constitute one of the most undereducated groups in the U.S. population. In many systems, all inmates who have not completed eighth grade are assigned full-time to prison school. Many programs provide remedial help in reading, English, and math. They also permit prisoners to earn their GED. As you read, "Civic Engagement: Your Role in the System," think about the resources required for presenting successful education programs.

In 1995 there were an estimated 350 college-degree programs across the nation. However, since that time funding for such programs has come under attack. The Comprehensive Crime Control Act of 1994 bans federal funding to prisoners for postsecondary education (Buruma, 2005: 36–41). Some state legislatures have passed similar laws, under pressure from people who argue that tax dollars should not be spent on the tuition of prisoners.

Studies have shown that prisoners assigned to education programs tend to avoid committing crimes after release (Andrews and Bonta, 1994). However, it is unclear whether education helps to rehabilitate these offenders or whether the types of prisoners ("gleaners") assigned to education programs tend to be those motivated to avoid further crimes. See "Doing Your Part" for more on prisoner education.

Vocational Education

Vocational education programs attempt to teach offenders a marketable job skill. Unfortunately, too many programs train inmates for trades that already have an adequate labor supply or in which new methods have made the skills taught obsolete.

Offenders often lack the attitudes necessary to obtain and keep a job—punctuality, accountability, deference to supervisors, cordiality to coworkers. Therefore most prisoners need to learn not only a skill but also how to act in the work world.

Yet another problem is perhaps the toughest of all. In many states, the law bars ex-felons from practicing certain occupations including nurse, beautician, barber, real estate salesperson, chauffeur, worker where alcoholic beverages are sold, cashier, and insurance salesperson. Unfortunately, some prison vocational

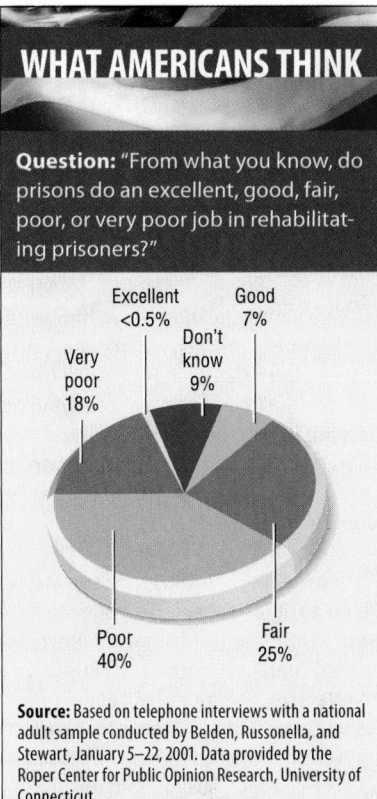

WHAT AMERICANS THINK

Question: "From what you know, do prisons do an excellent, good, fair, poor, or very poor job in rehabilitating prisoners?"

Excellent <0.5%
Good 7%
Don't know 9%
Very poor 18%
Poor 40%
Fair 25%

Source: Based on telephone interviews with a national adult sample conducted by Belden, Russonella, and Stewart, January 5–22, 2001. Data provided by the Roper Center for Public Opinion Research, University of Connecticut.

Companies are finding that prison labor can be more efficient than outsourcing to low-wage countries elsewhere in the world. Prisoners at the Wabash Valley Correctional Facility assemble yo-yos as part of a joint venture between the Indiana Department of Corrections' prison industry program and the Flambeau Products Corporation. Are these prisoners doing jobs that otherwise would provide wages for law-abiding citizens?

AP Images/Tribune-Star, Jim Avelis

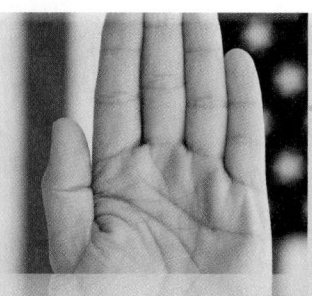

DOING YOUR PART

Mentor to Prisoners

Dr. R. Bruce McPherson

ABOUT TEN YEARS before the late Dr. R. Bruce McPherson retired as Professor of Education at the University of Illinois at Chicago, a colleague asked him to send a copy of one of his published articles to her brother, incarcerated at the Federal Correctional Institution, Butner, North Carolina. That initial contact led to a visit to the prison and a friendship. The brother was studying at the college level, and McPherson became interested as to how these courses were made available to prisoners. He contacted the administrator for all Bureau of Prison educational programs, who alerted supervisors at half a dozen prisons with strong college programs of McPherson's interest in visiting, observing, and assisting inmates with their education.

From 1987 to 2004, Professor McPherson was a teacher, mentor, and friend to 18 prisoners. He believed that his most effective contributions were to four men with long sentences who are still incarcerated but are especially prepared for release. He argued that the criminal justice system has no effective, commonsensical means of assessing the readiness of prisoners for release and acting on that knowledge.

Ten of the 18 have been released and McPherson remained in close touch with eight, all of whom are doing well. One runs a clothing store and plans to purchase it soon, one is a corporate manager, another works for a major airline, another is studying at a fine university, another has published two books and aspires to a literary career, another married and is now a salesman, and another works as a union painter and part-time evangelist.

Bruce McPherson was a provider of books, a mentor and tutor as college courses were selected and completed and degrees attained, an advocate, an advice giver, an editor, an information provider, and—perhaps most important—a friend. He was distressed that in 1994 Congress banned federal funding (Pell Grants) to prisoners for postsecondary education. This decision has all but eliminated college courses in state and federal prisons, yet research shows that participation in educational programs is one of the best predictors of inmate success in the community upon release.

Professor McPherson said that he considered all of these men and women as his students.

I learned never to overestimate or underestimate my impact on them. Inmates need strong contacts with mainstream citizens who will befriend them, help them in practical ways, serve as role models and give them faith in themselves and hope for a decent, productive life after prison. A part of my contribution remains with those who now live among us. My heart remains with those who are still incarcerated.

McPherson believed that education, coupled with attention to religious/spiritual needs, typically proves to be the strongest force in rehabilitation and atonement. He said, "If I could design a prison, I would have the chapel and the classroom at its core."

Researching the Internet

 Learn more about opportunities for Missouri's program for volunteers in corrections online. To link to this website, go to *The American System of Criminal Justice* 12e companion site at academic .cengage.com/criminaljustice/cole.

programs actually train inmates for jobs they can never hold.

Prison Industries

 Prison industries, which trace their roots to the early workshops of New York's Auburn Penitentiary, are intended to teach work habits and skills that will assist prisoners' reentry into the outside workforce. In practice, institutions rely on prison labor to provide basic food, maintenance, clerical, and other services. In addition, many prisons contain manufacturing facilities that produce goods, such as office furniture and clothing, to be used in correctional and other state institutions.

The prison industries system has had a checkered career. During the nineteenth century, factories were established in many prisons, and inmates manufactured items that were sold on the open market. With the rise of the labor movement, however, state legislatures and Congress passed laws restricting the sale of prison-made goods so that they would not compete with those made by free workers. In 1979, Congress lifted restrictions on the interstate sale of prison-made products and urged correctional administrators to explore with the private sector possible improvements for prison industry programs. Industrial programs would relieve idleness, allow inmates to earn wages that they could save until release, and reduce the costs of incarceration.

The Federal Bureau of Prisons and some states have developed industries, but generally their products are not sold on the free market and the percentage of prisoners employed varies greatly. For example, in North Carolina and Utah more than 20 percent of prisoners work in prison industries, while in most states 5 percent or less do (Camp and Camp, 1999: 96). In 2002, about 3.5 percent of the prisoners in the United States produced goods and services worth $1.5 billion (*Today*, July 6, 2004: 1).

Although the idea of employing inmates sounds attractive, the inefficiencies of prison work may offset its economic value. Turnover is great because many inmates are transferred among several institutions or released over a two-year period. Many prisoners have little education and lack steady work habits, making it difficult for them to perform many of the tasks of modern production. An additional cost to efficiency is the need to stop production periodically to count heads and to check that tools and materials have not been stolen.

farm work because that is where they are needed. Further, certain popular programs may remain limited, even though the demand for them is great. Thus inmates may find that the few places in, for example, a computer course are filled and that there is a long waiting list. Prisoners are often angered and frustrated by the classification process and the limited availability of programs. Release on parole can depend on a good record of participation in these programs, yet entrance for some inmates is blocked.

checkpoint

19. Why are prison programs important from the standpoint of prison administrators?
20. How are inmates assigned to programs?

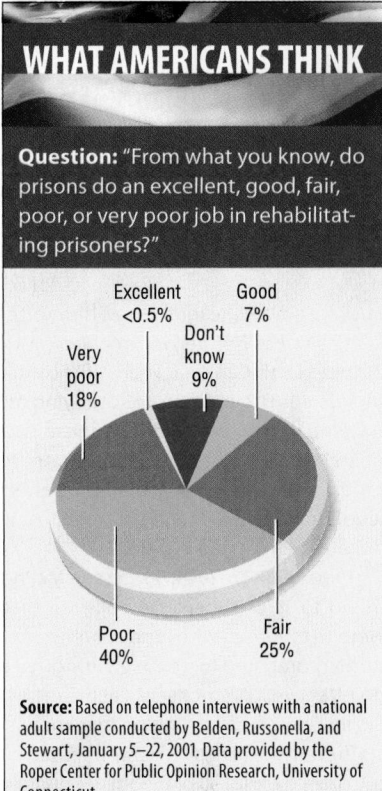

WHAT AMERICANS THINK

Question: "From what you know, do prisons do an excellent, good, fair, poor, or very poor job in rehabilitating prisoners?"

- Excellent <0.5%
- Good 7%
- Don't know 9%
- Very poor 18%
- Poor 40%
- Fair 25%

Source: Based on telephone interviews with a national adult sample conducted by Belden, Russonella, and Stewart, January 5–22, 2001. Data provided by the Roper Center for Public Opinion Research, University of Connecticut.

Educational Programs

Surveys have shown that programs offering academic courses are the most popular in corrections systems. Offenders constitute one of the most undereducated groups in the U.S. population. In many systems, all inmates who have not completed eighth grade are assigned full-time to prison school. Many programs provide remedial help in reading, English, and math. They also permit prisoners to earn their GED. As you read, "Civic Engagement: Your Role in the System," think about the resources required for presenting successful education programs.

In 1995 there were an estimated 350 college-degree programs across the nation. However, since that time funding for such programs has come under attack. The Comprehensive Crime Control Act of 1994 bans federal funding to prisoners for postsecondary education (Buruma, 2005: 36–41). Some state legislatures have passed similar laws, under pressure from people who argue that tax dollars should not be spent on the tuition of prisoners.

Studies have shown that prisoners assigned to education programs tend to avoid committing crimes after release (Andrews and Bonta, 1994). However, it is unclear whether education helps to rehabilitate these offenders or whether the types of prisoners ("gleaners") assigned to education programs tend to be those motivated to avoid further crimes. See "Doing Your Part" for more on prisoner education.

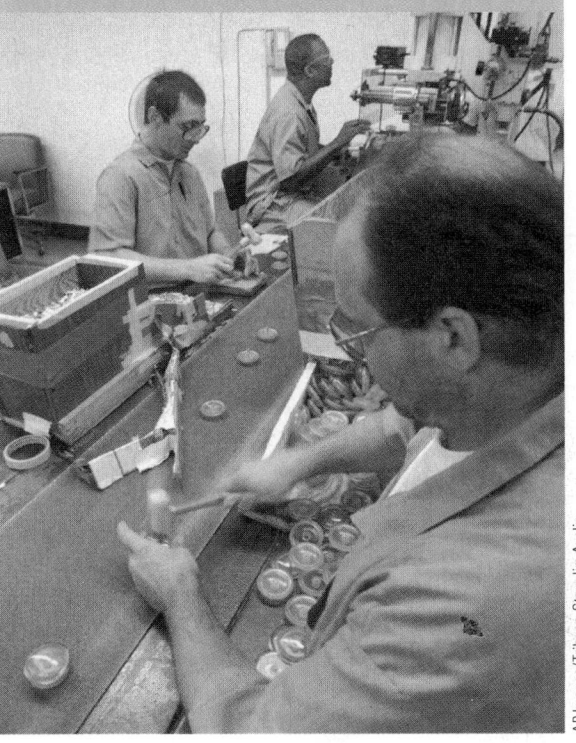

Companies are finding that prison labor can be more efficient than outsourcing to low-wage countries elsewhere in the world. Prisoners at the Wabash Valley Correctional Facility assemble yo-yos as part of a joint venture between the Indiana Department of Corrections' prison industry program and the Flambeau Products Corporation. Are these prisoners doing jobs that otherwise would provide wages for law-abiding citizens?

Vocational Education

Vocational education programs attempt to teach offenders a marketable job skill. Unfortunately, too many programs train inmates for trades that already have an adequate labor supply or in which new methods have made the skills taught obsolete.

Offenders often lack the attitudes necessary to obtain and keep a job—punctuality, accountability, deference to supervisors, cordiality to coworkers. Therefore most prisoners need to learn not only a skill but also how to act in the work world.

Yet another problem is perhaps the toughest of all. In many states, the law bars ex-felons from practicing certain occupations including nurse, beautician, barber, real estate salesperson, chauffeur, worker where alcoholic beverages are sold, cashier, and insurance salesperson. Unfortunately, some prison vocational

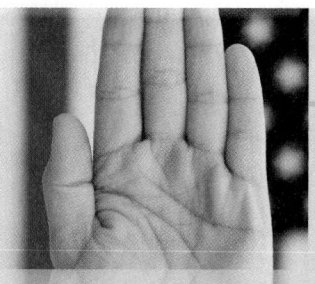

DOING YOUR PART

Mentor to Prisoners

Dr. R. Bruce McPherson

ABOUT TEN YEARS before the late Dr. R. Bruce McPherson retired as Professor of Education at the University of Illinois at Chicago, a colleague asked him to send a copy of one of his published articles to her brother, incarcerated at the Federal Correctional Institution, Butner, North Carolina. That initial contact led to a visit to the prison and a friendship. The brother was studying at the college level, and McPherson became interested as to how these courses were made available to prisoners. He contacted the administrator for all Bureau of Prison educational programs, who alerted supervisors at half a dozen prisons with strong college programs of McPherson's interest in visiting, observing, and assisting inmates with their education.

From 1987 to 2004, Professor McPherson was a teacher, mentor, and friend to 18 prisoners. He believed that his most effective contributions were to four men with long sentences who are still incarcerated but are especially prepared for release. He argued that the criminal justice system has no effective, commonsensical means of assessing the readiness of prisoners for release and acting on that knowledge.

Ten of the 18 have been released and McPherson remained in close touch with eight, all of whom are doing well. One runs a clothing store and plans to purchase it soon, one is a corporate manager, another works for a major airline, another is studying at a fine university, another has published two books and aspires to a literary career, another married and is now a salesman, and another works as a union painter and part-time evangelist.

Bruce McPherson was a provider of books, a mentor and tutor as college courses were selected and completed and degrees attained, an advocate, an advice giver, an editor, an information provider, and—perhaps most important—a friend. He was distressed that in 1994 Congress banned federal funding (Pell Grants) to prisoners for postsecondary education. This decision has all but eliminated college courses in state and federal prisons, yet research shows that participation in educational programs is one of the best predictors of inmate success in the community upon release.

Professor McPherson said that he considered all of these men and women as his students.

> I learned never to overestimate or underestimate my impact on them. Inmates need strong contacts with mainstream citizens who will befriend them, help them in practical ways, serve as role models and give them faith in themselves and hope for a decent, productive life after prison. A part of my contribution remains with those who now live among us. My heart remains with those who are still incarcerated.

McPherson believed that education, coupled with attention to religious/spiritual needs, typically proves to be the strongest force in rehabilitation and atonement. He said, "If I could design a prison, I would have the chapel and the classroom at its core."

Researching the Internet

Learn more about opportunities for Missouri's program for volunteers in corrections online. To link to this website, go to *The American System of Criminal Justice* 12e companion site at academic.cengage.com/criminaljustice/cole.

programs actually train inmates for jobs they can never hold.

Prison Industries

Prison industries, which trace their roots to the early workshops of New York's Auburn Penitentiary, are intended to teach work habits and skills that will assist prisoners' reentry into the outside workforce. In practice, institutions rely on prison labor to provide basic food, maintenance, clerical, and other services. In addition, many prisons contain manufacturing facilities that produce goods, such as office furniture and clothing, to be used in correctional and other state institutions.

The prison industries system has had a checkered career. During the nineteenth century, factories were established in many prisons, and inmates manufactured items that were sold on the open market. With the rise of the labor movement, however, state legislatures and Congress passed laws restricting the sale of prison-made goods so that they would not compete with those made by free workers. In 1979, Congress lifted restrictions on the interstate sale of prison-made products and urged correctional administrators to explore with the private sector possible improvements for prison industry programs. Industrial programs would relieve idleness, allow inmates to earn wages that they could save until release, and reduce the costs of incarceration.

The Federal Bureau of Prisons and some states have developed industries, but generally their products are not sold on the free market and the percentage of prisoners employed varies greatly. For example, in North Carolina and Utah more than 20 percent of prisoners work in prison industries, while in most states 5 percent or less do (Camp and Camp, 1999: 96). In 2002, about 3.5 percent of the prisoners in the United States produced goods and services worth $1.5 billion (*Today*, July 6, 2004: 1).

Although the idea of employing inmates sounds attractive, the inefficiencies of prison work may offset its economic value. Turnover is great because many inmates are transferred among several institutions or released over a two-year period. Many prisoners have little education and lack steady work habits, making it difficult for them to perform many of the tasks of modern production. An additional cost to efficiency is the need to stop production periodically to count heads and to check that tools and materials have not been stolen.

Rehabilitative Programs

Rehabilitative programs seek to treat the personal defects thought to have brought about the inmate's criminality. Most people agree that rehabilitating offenders is a desirable goal, but they disagree a great deal on the amount of emphasis that these programs should receive.

Reports in the 1970s cast doubt on the ability of treatment programs to stem recidivism. They also questioned the ethics of requiring inmates to participate in rehabilitative programs in exchange for the promise of parole (Martinson, R. "What Works? Questions and Answers About Prison Reform," *The Public Interest*, Spring, 1974; p. 25). Supporters of treatment programs argue that certain programs, if properly run, work for certain offenders (Andrews, et al., 1990; Palmer, 1992). A national survey found support for rehabilitative programs (see "What Americans Think").

Most corrections systems still offer a range of psychological, behavioral, and social services programs. How much they are used seems to vary according to the goals of the institution and the attitudes of the administrators. Nationally, little money is spent on treatment services, and these programs reach only 5 percent of the inmate population. Therefore, although rehabilitative programs remain a part of correctional institutions, their emphasis has diminished. Incarceration's current goal of humane custody implies no effort to change inmates.

Medical Services

Most prisons offer medical services through a full-time staff of nurses, augmented by part-time physicians under contract to the corrections system. Nurses take care of routine health care and dispense medicines from a secure in-prison pharmacy; regularly scheduled visits to the prison by doctors can enable prisoners to obtain checkups and diagnoses. For cases needing a specialist, surgery, or emergency medical assistance, prisoners must be transported to local hospitals under close supervision by correctional staff. The aim is for the prison system to be able to provide a range of medical assistance to meet the various needs of the population as a whole.

While inmates' needs for health care echo those of the general population, prisoners pose two special needs, one due to poverty and the other to aging. Because prisoners as a group are very poor, they often bring to the prison years of neglect of their general health. Other consequences of being poor, such as an inadequate diet and poor hygiene, also affect the general health of the prison population. As we have seen, by far the most extraordinary health problem in contemporary corrections is the burgeoning number of elderly prisoners. Elderly inmates have more complicated and more numerous health problems overall, and they eventually reach an age where they cannot productively participate in prison assignments. Some prison systems have formed nursing and hospice facilities where younger inmates can care for the elderly as they spend their last days on earth behind bars.

civic engagement
your role in the system

Imagine that your instructor assigns a class project: you must start a program to send books to prisoners in order to help them advance their education and increase their chances of being productive citizens after release. *Write a memo on what books the prisoners would want and need as well as what problems and challenges might hinder the program.* Then compare your ideas with the experience of the Prison Book Program in Massachusetts. To link to this website, go to *The American System of Criminal Justice* 12e companion site at academic.cengage.com/criminaljustice/cole.

 Visit the website of Prison Blues, which features a line of denim jeans, shirts, and jackets made by the inmates at Eastern Oregon Correctional Institution. To link to this website, go to *The American System of Criminal Justice* 12e companion site at academic.cengage.com/criminaljustice/cole.

 For information on medical services for prisoners in Louisiana, see online. To link to this website, go to *The American System of Criminal Justice* 12e companion site at academic.cengage.com/criminaljustice/cole.

checkpoint

21. Why have legislatures and the general public been so critical of educational and rehabilitative programs in prisons?
22. What problems are encountered in vocational training programs?
23. Why have legislatures restricted prison industries?

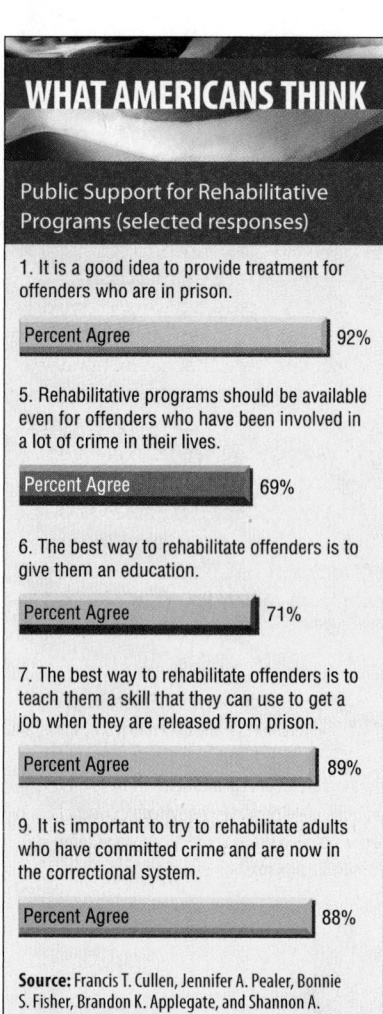

VIOLENCE IN PRISON

Prisons provide a perfect recipe for violence. They confine in cramped quarters a thousand men, some with histories of violent behavior. While incarcerated, these men are not allowed contact with women and live under highly restrictive conditions. Sometimes these conditions spark collective violence, as in the riots at Attica, New York (1971), Santa Fe, New Mexico (1980), Atlanta, Georgia (1987), Lucasville, Ohio (1993), and Florence, Colorado (2008).

Although prison riots are widely reported in the news, few people know the level of everyday interpersonal violence in U.S. prisons. For example, each year about 34,000 inmates are physically attacked by other inmates. In 2003 the homicide rate was 4 per 100,000 inmates, which is substantially lower than it was in 1980 (54 homicides per 100,000). Similarly, the suicide rate among state prisoners was 16 per 100,000 inmates in 2003, which is also lower than the rate reported in 1980 (34 suicides per 100,000 inmates) (BJS, 2005: 1).

Although the reductions over 20 years demonstrate progress, there are still great numbers of prisoners who live in a state of constant uneasiness, always on the lookout for people who might demand sex, steal their few possessions, or otherwise harm them. In any case, some researchers suggest that the level of violence varies by offender age, institutional security designation, and administrative effectiveness (Maitland and Sluder, 1998: 55). Read the Close Up box for a discussion of the problem of prison rape.

Assaultive Behavior and Inmate Characteristics

For the person entering prison for the first time, the anxiety level and fear of violence is especially high. One fish asked, "Will I end up fighting for my life?" Gary, an inmate at Leavenworth, told Pete Earley, "Every convict has three choices, but only three. He can fight (kill someone), he can hit the fence (escape), or he can fuck (submit)" (Earley, 1992: 55). Inmates who are victimized are significantly more likely than others to be depressed and experience symptoms associated with posttraumatic stress such as nightmares. Even if a prisoner is not assaulted, the potential for violence permeates the environment of many prisons, adding to the stress and pains of incarceration.

When officers must remove an uncooperative or violent prisoner from a cell, trained cell extraction teams must overwhelm the prisoner through the use of force while also limiting the risk of injury to themselves. Such events are often filmed to prevent false claims by prisoners that officers used excessive force. Are there additional precautions that these officers should take in order to avoid injuries to themselves or to the prisoner?

CLOSE UP

On Prison Rape

THE PROBLEM OF sexual assault in prison receives little attention from policy makers and the public. There are no reliable national data on prison rape; only a few small-scale studies indicate the scope of the problem. If these findings reflect the national picture, then at least 140,000 prisoners have been raped. Prison rape is a crime hidden by a curtain of silence.

Victims of prison rape tend to be young, physically small, first-timers who are gay, have "feminine" characteristics, or were convicted of sexual offense against a minor. Not only are such attacks traumatic, but the victim also becomes a target for further exploitation.

Although the characteristics of prison rapists are somewhat less clear, Human Rights Watch found certain patterns. The perpetrators tend to be young, if not always as young as their victims—generally younger than 35 years old. Frequently larger or stronger than their victims, they are generally more assertive, physically aggressive, and more at home in the prison environment. They are "street smart"—often gang members—and have typically been convicted of more-violent crimes than their victims have.

Incidents occasionally come to public attention when the victim goes to the press or to court. For example, Edward Dillard, a 120-pound inmate serving time for assault at California's Corcoran State Prison, was repeatedly raped by Wayne Robertson, a 230-pound sexual predator serving life without parole for a murder conviction.

Dillard had previously clashed with Robertson and placed his name on a list of known enemies with whom he should not share a cell. Yet Dillard was moved into Robertson's cell, where he was raped numerous times over a weekend. On Monday Robertson was taken to a hearing, and when he returned Dillard ran out and refused to reenter the cell.

Dillard's case is one of the few to come to both criminal and civil trials. In court papers he charged that prison guards set up the rape. Robertson backed up the complaint saying that Robert Decker, a correctional officer, agreed to place Dillard with him so that he "could show Mr. Dillard 'how to do his time.'" Although Decker and three other officers were charged with aiding and abetting sodomy, they were acquitted at trial. Dillard is now out of prison and is pursuing a civil suit against the four.

In the age of AIDS, rape can be a death penalty. Kenneth Spruce, an Arkansas prisoner serving time on a fraudulent check conviction, was raped by 20 inmates in one year and contracted AIDS as a result. He sued prison officials, charging cruel and unusual treatment. Warden Willis Sargent testified that prisoners bore the responsibility for fighting off sexual advances, by letting others know they are "not going to put up with that." A Federal District Court found that even if the warden knew of the risks to Spruce, his actions did not amount to "deliberate indifference," the legal standard holding him accountable.

Some correctional departments are taking steps to train correctional officers to prevent inmate rape, to bring criminal charges against the perpetrators, and to provide medical and psychological care for the victim. But these initiatives are the exception. Prison rape remains a crime for which the victims receive little sympathy or remedy.

Sources: Drawn from Stephen Donaldson, "The Rape Crisis behind Bars," *New York Times*, December 29, 1993; Human Rights Watch, "No Escape: Male Rape in U.S. Prisons (http://www.hrw.org/reports/2001/prison/report1.html); Tamar Lewin, "Little Sympathy or Remedy for Inmates Who Are Raped," *New York Times*, April 15, 2001, p. A1; *Prison Journal* 80 (December 2000) [special issue on prison sexuality].

Researching the Internet

 Learn more about prison rape at the website of Stop Prison Rape, a national nonprofit organization. To link to this website, go to *The American System of Criminal Justice* 12e companion site at academic.cengage.com/criminaljustice/cole.

Violent behavior in prisons is related in large part to the characteristics of the inmates. Christopher Innes and Vicki Verdeyen suggest that violent offenders can be divided into those who (1) have learned to be violent, (2) cannot regulate their violence, because of mental disabilities, and (3) are violent and have severe personality disorders (Innes and Verdeyen 1997: 1). Three characteristics underlie these behavioral factors: age, attitudes, and race.

Age

Young men aged 16–24, both inside and outside prison, are more prone to violence than are their elders (Simon, 1993: 263). Not surprisingly, 96 percent of adult prisoners are men, with an average age at the time of admission of 27. There is also evidence that younger inmates are more likely to be victimized than are older inmates.

Besides greater physical strength, young men also lack the commitments to career and family that can restrict antisocial behavior. In addition, many have difficulty defining their position in society. Thus they interpret many things as challenges to their status.

"Machismo," the concept of male honor and the sacredness of one's reputation as a man, requires physical retaliation against those who insult one's honor. Some have argued that many homosexual rapes are not sexual but political attempts to impress on the victim the aggressor's male power and to define the target as passive or "feminine" (Rideau and Wikberg, 1992: 79). Some inmates adopt a preventive strategy of trying to impress others with their bravado, which may result in counterchallenges and violence. The potential for violence among such prisoners is clear.

Attitudes

One sociological theory of crime suggests that a subculture of violence exists among certain socioeconomic groups and ethnic gangs. In this subculture, found in the lower class and in its value system, violence is "tolerable, expected, or required" (Wolfgang and Ferracuti, 1967: 263). Arguments are settled and decisions are made by the fist rather than by verbal persuasion. Many inmates bring these attitudes into prison with them.

Race

Race has become a major divisive factor in today's prisons. Racist attitudes, common in the larger society, have become part of the "convict code," or implicit rules of life. Forced association—having to live with people one would not likely associate with on the outside—exaggerates and amplifies racial conflict. Violence against members of another race may be how some inmates deal with the frustrations of their lives. The shouting of racial slurs against black inmates by a group of white supremacists celebrating Adolf Hitler's birthday, is cited as the basis of a riot at the U.S. Penitentiary, Florence, Colorado, in 2008 that resulted in the death of two inmates and a brawl involving up to 200 (*Rocky Mountain News*, April 22, 2008).

Prisoner–Prisoner Violence

Although prison folklore may attribute violence to brutal guards, most prison violence occurs between inmates. The Bureau of Justice Statistics reports that the rate of prisoner–prisoner assault is 28 attacks per 1,000 inmates (BJS, 2003: 10). But official statistics likely do not reflect the true amount of prisoner–prisoner violence, because many inmates who are assaulted do not make their victimization known to prison official. Instead many spend years in fear of harm. Some inmates request segregation, others lock themselves in, and some are hermits by choice.

Prison Gangs

For more on prison gangs, go online. To link to this website, go to *The American System of Criminal Justice* 12e companion site at academic.cengage.com/criminaljustice/cole.

Racial or ethnic gangs (also referred to as "security threat groups") are now linked to acts of violence in most prison systems. Gangs make it difficult for wardens to maintain control. By continuing their street wars inside prison, gangs make some prisons more dangerous than any American neighborhood. Gangs are organized primarily to control an institution's drug, gambling, loan-sharking, prostitution, extortion, and debt-collection rackets. In addition, gangs protect their members from other gangs and instill a sense of macho camaraderie.

Contributing to prison violence is the "blood-in, blood-out" basis for gang membership: A would-be member must stab a gang's enemy to be admitted and, once in, cannot drop out without endangering his own life. Given the racial and ethnic foundation of gangs, violence between them can easily spill into the general prison population. Some institutions have programs that offer members "a way out" of the gang. Often referred to as "deganging," these programs educate members and eventually encourage them to renounce their gang membership. Critics say that for many this supposed change is only a "way of getting out of lock-down status; proponents counter with 'So what? Their behavior within the prison setting has been modified'" (Carlson, 2001: 13).

Prison gangs exist in the institutions of most states and the federal system. In Illinois as much as 60 percent of the prison population belongs to gangs (Hallinan, 2001: 95). The Florida Department of Corrections has identified over 200 street gangs operating in their prisons (Davitz, 1998). A study by the American Correctional Association found more than 46,000 gang members in the federal system and in the prisons of at least 35 states (American Correctional Association, 1994: 21).

Although prison gangs are small, they are tightly organized and have even arranged the killing of opposition gang leaders housed in other institutions. Administrators say that prison gangs, like organized crime groups, tend to pursue their "business" interests, yet they are also a major source of inmate–inmate violence as they discipline members, enforce orders, and retaliate against other gangs.

The racial and ethnic basis of gang membership has been documented in several states. Beginning in the late 1960s, a Chicano gang—the Mexican Mafia—whose membership had known each other in Los Angeles—took over the rackets in San Quentin. In reaction, other gangs were formed, including a rival Mexican gang, La Nuestra Familia; CRIPS (Common Revolution in Progress); the Texas Syndicate; the Black Guerrilla Family; and the Aryan Brotherhood (Table 15.1). Gang conflict in California prisons became so serious in the 1970s that attempts were made to break up the gangs by dividing members among several institutions. As of 2002, however, California had the largest number of prison gang members (5,342), followed by Texas (5,262). Data from 41 different jurisdictions shows that nearly 5 percent of inmates are validated gang members (Camp, 2003: 37).

Many facilities segregate rival gangs by housing them in separate units of the prison or moving members to other facilities. Administrators have also set up intelligence units to gather information on gangs, particularly about illegal acts both in and outside of prison. In some prisons, however, these policies

TABLE 15.1   Characteristics of Major Prison Gangs

These gangs were founded in the California prison system during the late 1960s and 1970s. They have now spread across the nation and are viewed as major security threat groups in most corrections systems.

	Name	Makeup	Origin	Characteristics	Enemies
	Aryan Brotherhood	White	San Quentin, 1967	Apolitical. Most in custody for crimes such as robbery.	CRIPS, Bloods, BGF
	Black Guerrilla Family (BGF)	African American	San Quentin, 1966	Most politically oriented. Antigovernment.	Aryan Brotherhood, EME
	Mexican Mafia (EME)	Mexican American/Hispanic	Duel Vocational Center, Los Angeles, late 1950s	Ethnic solidarity, control of drug trafficking.	BGF, NF
	La Nuestra Familia (NF)	Mexican American/Hispanic	Soledad, 1965	Protect young, rural Mexican Americans.	EME
	Texas Syndicate	Mexican American/Hispanic	Folsom, early 1970s	Protect Texan inmates in California.	Aryan Brotherhood, EME, NF

Source: Florida Department of Corrections, "Major Prison Gangs" (http://www.dc.state.fl.us/pub/gangs/prison.html).

created a power vacuum within the convict society that newer groups with new codes of behavior soon filled.

Prison Rape

Much of the mythology of prison life revolves around sexual assaults. Typically the perpetrators are thought to be physically strong, African American, an experienced con serving a sentence for a violent offense. Victims are portrayed as young, white, physically weak, mentally challenged, effeminate, and first-time nonviolent offenders (Austin, et al., 2006).

As noted in the Close Up box, prison rape is a crime hidden by a curtain of silence. Inmate–inmate and inmate–staff sexual contact is prohibited in all prisons, however it exists and much of it is hidden from authorities. Sexual violence ranges from unwanted touching to nonconsensual sex. When incidents are reported, correctional officers say that it is difficult to distinguish between consensual sexual acts and rapes. Most officers have not caught inmates in the act, and only a few said they ignored violations when they discovered them (Eigenberg, 2000: 415–433).

In September 2004, President Bush signed the Prison Rape Elimination Act into law. The Act establishes a zero tolerance standard for the incidence of rape in prison and requires the Department of Justice's Bureau of Justice Statistics to conduct annual surveys in the nation's prisons and jails to measure the incidence of rape. The law also requires the Attorney General to provide a list of institutions ranked according to the incidence of prison rape.

Until recently there has been no reliable data on prison sexual assaults. In 2006, the Bureau of Justice Statistics released nationwide statistics based on reports by *prison administrators*. The research found 1,865 allegations of inmate-on-inmate sexual assaults among state prison inmates, a rate of 1.5 attacks per 1,000 inmates. Perpetrators of substantiated incidents tended to be male (85.7 percent), black (42 percent) or white (42 percent). Victims were more likely to be male (84.8 percent), under the age of 30 (57 percent), and white (78 percent). The report also showed that sexual violence involves a single victim (95 percent) and one assailant (93 percent). Gang rapes involving four or more perpetrators constituted only 1.5 percent of known incidents (BJS, 2006: 6).

A second survey, published in 2007 based on reports by *inmates*, found a higher incident rate of inmate to inmate nonconsensual acts in state and federal prisons (56 per 1,000). Inmates also reported an estimated 85 incidents of unwilling sexual contacts with staff members per 1,000 inmates, and 82 "willing" incidents of sexual contact with staff members per 1,000. An estimated 0.8 percent of inmates nationwide reported being injured by the sexual victimization. Injuries included anal or vaginal tearing, knife or stab punctures, broken bones, bruises, black eyes and other less serious injuries (BJS, 2007: 1, 3).

How are we to interpret the results of these two surveys. Both show that sexual victimization is a serious problem, but why are the incident rates so different? It might be that administrators are unaware of the higher, nonreported levels of violence in their facilities. It may also be that many allegations by inmates are false. The 2007 BJS report notes that efforts were made to reassure inmates that their responses would be confidential, however some inmates may not have felt confident in reporting their experiences. On the other hand about one-quarter of the incidents reported to administrators in the 2006 survey were unfounded.

For victims of prisoner–prisoner violence there are few options. According to the "inmate code" one should "stand and fight" your own battles. For many victims this is not feasible. Alternatively, some may seek the protection of a gang or stronger inmate to whom the victim is beholding. Others may try to fade into the shadows. Still others may seek protective custody. Each option has it pluses and minuses, none provide victims the ability to serve their time without constantly looking over their shoulder.

Protective Custody

For many victims of prison violence, protective custody offers the only way to escape further abuse. About 5,000 state prisoners are in protective custody (Camp and Camp, 2001: 26). Life is not pleasant for these inmates. Often they are let out of their cells only briefly to exercise and shower. Inmates who ask to "lock up" have little chance of returning to the general prison population without being viewed as a weakling—a snitch or a punk—to be preyed on. Even when they are transferred to another institution, their reputations follow them through the grapevine.

---

checkpoint

24. Which inmate characteristics are thought to be factors in prison violence?
25. Why are gangs such as threat to prison order?

Prisoner–Officer Violence

The mass media have focused on riots in which guards are taken hostage, injured, and killed. However, violence against officers typically occurs in specific situations and against certain individuals. Yearly, inmates assault more than 18,000 staff members (BJS, 2003: 10). Correctional officers do not carry weapons within the institution, because a prisoner might seize them. However, prisoners do manage to obtain lethal weapons and can use the element of surprise to injure an officer. In the course of a work day, an officer may encounter situations that require the use of physical force against an inmate—for instance, breaking up a fight or moving a prisoner to segregation. Because such situations are especially dangerous, officers may enlist others to help them minimize the risk of violence. The officer's greatest fear is unexpected attacks, such as a missile thrown from an upper tier or an officer's "accidental" fall down a flight of stairs. The need to constantly watch against personal attacks adds stress and keeps many officers at a distance from the inmates.

Officer–Prisoner Violence

A fact of life in many institutions is unauthorized physical violence by officers against inmates. Stories abound of guards giving individual prisoners "the treatment" when supervisors are not looking. Many guards view physical force as an everyday, legitimate procedure. In some institutions, authorized "goon squads" composed of physically powerful officers use their muscle to maintain order.

Perhaps the worst cases of officer–prisoner violence in recent years have occurred at the California State Prison at Corcoran. Between 1989 and 1995, 43 inmates were wounded and 7 killed by officers firing assault weapons—the most killings in any prison. Guards even instigated fights between rival gang members. During those "gladiator days," tower guards often shot the gladiators after they had been ordered to stop fighting. Each shooting was justified by state-appointed reviewers (*Los Angles Times*, July 5, 1998: 1).

Correctional officers are expected to follow departmental rules in their dealings with prisoners, yet supervisors generally cannot observe staff–prisoner confrontations directly. Further, prisoner complaints about officer brutality are often not believed until the officer involved gains a reputation for harshness. Even in this case, wardens may feel they must support their officers in order to retain their officers' support.

Decreasing Prison Violence

Five factors contribute to prison violence: (1) inadequate supervision by staff members, (2) architectural design that promotes rather than inhibits victimization, (3) the easy availability of deadly weapons, (4) the housing of violence-prone prisoners near relatively defenseless people, and (5) a general high level of tension produced by close quarters. The physical size and condition of the prison and the relations between inmates and staff also affect violence.

The Effect of Architecture and Size

The fortress-like prison certainly does not create an atmosphere for normal interpersonal relationships, and the size of the larger institutions can create management problems. The massive scale of the mega-prison, which may hold up to 3,000 inmates, provides opportunities for aggressive inmates to hide weapons, dispense private "justice," and engage more or less freely in other illicit activities.

The size of the population in a large prison may also result in some inmates' "falling through the cracks"—being misclassified and forced to live among more violent offenders.

Much of the emphasis on the "new generation prisons"—small housing units, clear sight lines, security corridors linking housing units—is designed to limit these opportunities and thus prevent violence.

The Role of Management

The degree to which inmate leaders are allowed to take matters into their own hands can affect the level of violence among inmates. When administrators run a tight ship, security measures prevent sexual attacks in dark corners, the making of "shivs" and "shanks" (knives) in the metal shop, and open conflict among inmate groups. A prison must afford each inmate defensible space, and administrators should ensure that every inmate is secure from physical attack.

Effective prison management can decrease the level of assaultive behavior by limiting opportunities for attacks. Wardens and correctional officers must therefore recognize the types of people with whom they are dealing, the role of prison gangs, and the structure of institutions. John DiIulio argues that no group of inmates is "unmanageable [and] no combination of political, social, budgetary, architectural, or other factors makes good management impossible" (DiIulio, 1991: 12). He points to such varied institutions as the California Men's Colony, New York City's Tombs and Rikers Island, the Federal Bureau of Prisons, and the Texas Department of Corrections under the leadership of George Beto. At these institutions, good management practices have resulted in prisons and jails where inmates can "do time" without fearing for their personal safety. Wardens who exert leadership can manage their prisons effectively, so that problems do not fester and erupt into violent confrontations.

In sum, prisons must be made safe places. Because the state puts offenders there, it has a responsibility to prevent violence and maintain order. To exclude violence from prisons, officials may have to limit movement within institutions, contacts with the outside, and the right of inmates to choose their associates. Yet these measures may run counter to the goal of producing men and women who will be accountable when they return to society.

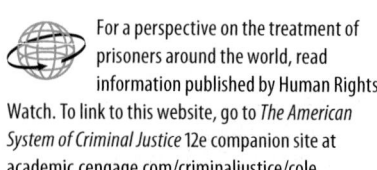

For a perspective on the treatment of prisoners around the world, read information published by Human Rights Watch. To link to this website, go to *The American System of Criminal Justice* 12e companion site at academic.cengage.com/criminaljustice/cole.

checkpoint

26. What seven factors are thought to contribute to prison violence?

A QUESTION OF ETHICS

AFTER THREE YEARS of daily contact, correctional officer Bill Mac-Leod and Jack Douglas, who was serving a 3–5 year sentence, knew each other very well. They were both devoted to the Red Sox and the Celtics. Throughout the year they would chat about the fortunes of their teams and the outlook ahead. MacLeod got to know and like Douglas. They were about the same age and had come from similar backgrounds. Why they were now on opposite sides of the cell bars was something that MacLeod could not figure out.

One day Douglas called MacLeod and said that he needed money because he had lost a bet gambling on the Red Sox. Douglas said that his wife would send him the money but that it couldn't come through the prison mail to him in cash. And a check or money order would show on his commissary account.

"The guy wants cash. If he doesn't get it, I'm dead." Douglas took a breath and then rushed on with his request. "Could you bring it in for me? She'll mail the money to you at home. You could just drop the envelope on my bed."

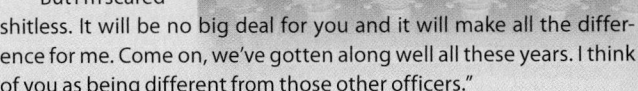

"You know the rules. No gambling and no money," said MacLeod.

"But I'm scared shitless. It will be no big deal for you and it will make all the difference for me. Come on, we've gotten along well all these years. I think of you as being different from those other officers."

Critical Thinking and Analysis

Ask a classmate to engage in a role-playing scenario. Continue the conversation between MacLeod and Douglas. What should Mac-Leod do? Is this kind of request likely to be a one-time occurrence with Douglas? What if MacLeod's sergeant finds out? What if other inmates learn about it? How is the issue likely to be resolved?

SUMMARY

Understand the three models of incarceration that have predominated since the 1940s

- (1) The custodial model emphasizes the maintenance of security, (2) the rehabilitation model views security and housekeeping activities as mainly a framework for treatment efforts, and (3) the reintegration model recognizes that prisoners must be prepared for their return to society.

Understand how a prison is organized

- Most prisons are expected to fulfill goals related to keeping (custody), using (working), and serving (treating) inmates. The formal organization of prisons is designed to achieve these goals.

Understand how a prison is governed

- The public's belief that the warden and officers have total power over the inmates is outdated.

- Good management through effective leadership can maintain the quality of prison life as measured by levels of order, amenities, and services.

- Four factors make managing prisons different from administering other public institutions: defects of total power, limited use of rewards and punishments, exchange relationships, and strength of inmate leadership.

Understand the role of correctional officers in a prison

- Correctional officers, because they are constantly in close contact with the prisoners, are the real linchpins

in the prison system. The effectiveness of the institution lies heavily on their shoulders.

- Prison administrators must deal with the special needs of some groups, including elderly prisoners, prisoners with HIV/AIDS, mentally ill prisoners, long-term prisoners, and immigrants.

Discuss what it is like to be in prison

- Inmates do not serve their time in isolation but are members of a subculture with its own traditions, norms, and leadership structure. Such norms are often called the inmate code.

- Today's prisons, unlike those of the past, do not have a uniform inmate code but several, in part because of the influence of gangs.

- Inmates deal with the pain of incarceration by assuming an adaptive role and lifestyle.

- To meet their needs for goods and services not provided by the state, prisoners run an underground economy.

Understand the special needs and problems of incarcerated women

- Women make up only a small portion of the inmate population. This is cited as the reason for the limited programs and services available to female prisoners.

- Social relationships among female inmates differ from those of their male counterparts. Women tend to form pseudofamilies in prison. Many women experience the added stress of being responsible for their children on the outside.

Learn about the programs and services that are available to prisoners

- Educational, vocational, industrial, and treatment programs are available in prisons. Administrators believe that these programs are important for maintaining order.

Understand the nature of prison violence

- Violence in prison depends on such things as administrative effectiveness, the architecture and size of prisons, and inmate characteristics such as age, attitudes, and race.

- Violence occurs between prisoners, often through gangs, and between prisoners and guards.

QUESTIONS FOR REVIEW

1. How do modern prisons differ from those in the past?

2. What are the characteristics of prisons that make them different from other institutions?

3. What must a prison administrator do to ensure successful management?

4. What is meant by an adaptive role? Which roles are found in male prison society? In female prison society?

5. How does the convict society in institutions for women differ from that in institutions for men?

6. What are the main forms of prison programs, and what purposes do they serve?

7. What are forms and causes of prison violence?

KEY TERMS

custodial model (p. 536)   inmate code (p. 550)
reintegration model (p. 537)   reintegration model (p. 560)

FOR FURTHER READING

Aday, Ronald. 2003. *Aging Prisoners: Crisis in American Corrections*. Westport, CT: Praeger. Addresses the challenges and issues that local, state, and federal governments must face in dealing with the great increase in the number of elderly prisoners.

Conover, Ted. 2000. *Newjack: Guarding Sing Sing*. New York: Random House. Denied permission to write about the lives of correctional officers, Conover became one himself and served a year at Sing Sing. The book provides an officer's view of a maximum-security institution.

DiIulio, John J., Jr. 1987. *Governing Prisons*. New York: Free Press. A critique of the sociological perspective on inmate society. DiIulio argues that governance by correctional officers is the key to the maintenance of good prisons and jails.

Earley, Pete. 1992. *The Hot House: Life inside Leavenworth Prison*. New York: Bantam Books. An eyewitness account of daily life in the United States Penitentiary in Leavenworth, Kansas, written by the first journalist given unlimited access to a maximum-security institution of the Federal Bureau of Prisons.

Johnson, Robert. 2002. *Hard Time: Understanding and Reforming the Prison*. 3rd ed. Belmont, CA: Wadsworth. A significant contribution to understanding prison society.

Lamb, Wally and Carolyn Adams Goodwin. 2003. *Couldn't Keep It to Myself: Testimonies from Our Imprisoned Sisters*. New York: HarperCollins. A collection of vivid life portraits written by inmates housed at a maximum-security prison for women.

Santos, Michael G. 2006. *Inside: Life Behind Bars in America*. New York: St. Martin's Press. Capturing the voices of his fellow prisoners, Santos makes the tragic and inspiring stories of men—from the toughest gang leaders to the richest Wall Street criminals—come alive.

GOING ONLINE

For an up-to-date list of web links, go to *The American System of Criminal Justice* 12e companion site at academic .cengage.com/criminaljustice/cole.

1. Go to the website of the Massachusetts Department of Corrections roster of prison gangs. Read about the gangs represented in Massachusetts prisons. How should officials address the problem of multiple, diverse gangs within prisons?

2. Access the article by Reginal A. Wilkinson, "The Future of Adult Corrections," *Correctional Management Quarterly*, 1997. Choose one of the issues that the author says that corrections will face in the future. Write a short paper about that problem. What must correctional leaders do to deal with that problem?

3. Go to website for "My Place." Write a short paper describing the role that My Place plays for women prisoners upon their release. What problems do these women face?

CHECKPOINT ANSWERS

1. *How does today's prisons differ from the "big house" of the past?*

The characteristics of the inmate population have changed, more inmates are from urban areas and have been convicted for drug-related or violent offenses, the inmate population is fragmented along racial and ethnic lines, prisoners are less isolated from the outside world, and correctional officers have used collective bargaining to improve their working conditions.

2. *What three models of prison have predominated since the 1940s?*

The custodial, rehabilitation, and reintegration models.

3. *How do prisons differ from other organizations in society?*

It is a place where a group of workers manages a group of captives.

4. *What are the multiple goals pursued in today's prisons?*

Keeping (custody), using (working), serving (treatment).

5. *What problems do these goals present to administrators?*

The goals often mean the administration of prisons is marked by ambiguity and conflict.

6. *What four factors make the governing of prisons different from administering other public institutions?*

The defects of total power, a limited system of rewards and punishments, exchange relations between correctional officers and inmates, and the strength of inmate leadership.

7. *Why are correctional officers called the "linchpin of management"?*

They are in daily contact with the inmates.

8. *Name three of the five legally acceptable reasons for the use of force.*

Self-defense, defense of third person, upholding prison rules, prevention of crime, prevention of escapes.

9. *What are the major characteristics of today's prisoners?*

Today's prisoners are largely men in their late twenties to early thirties with less than a high school education. They are disproportionately members of minority groups.

10. *What are the key elements of the inmate code?*

The values and norms of prison society that emphasize inmate solidarity.

11. *Why is it unlikely that a single, overriding inmate code exists in today's prisons?*

The prison society is fragmented by racial and ethnic divisions.

12. *What are the four role orientations found in adult male prisons?*

Doing time, gleaning, jailing, and functioning as a disorganized criminal.

13. *Why does an underground economy exist in prison?*

To provide goods and services not available through regular channels.

14. *Why are prison administrators wary of the prison economy?*

The prison economy is responsible for the exploitation of prisoners by other prisoners and has the potential for conflict and violence.

15. *What accounts for the neglect of facilities and programs in women's prisons?*

The small number of female inmates compared with the number of male inmates.

16. *How do the social relationships among female prisoners differ from those of their male counterparts?*

Men are more individualistic and their norms stress autonomy, self-sufficiency, and the ability to cope with one's own problems. Women share more with one another.

17. *What are some of the problems encountered by female prisoners in maintaining contact with their children?*

The distance of prisons from homes, intermittent telephone privileges, and unnatural visiting environment.

18. *How are children cared for while their mothers are incarcerated?*

Children are either with relatives or in foster care.

19. *Why are prison programs important from the standpoint of prison administrators?*

Programs keep prisoners busy and reduce security problems.

20. *How are inmates assigned to programs?*

Classification by a committee according to the needs of the inmate or of the institution.

21. *Why have legislatures and the general public been so critical of educational and rehabilitation programs in prisons?*

They are thought to "coddle" prisoners and give them resources not available to law-abiding citizens.

22. *What problems are encountered in vocational training programs?*

Too many programs train inmates for trades for which there is already an adequate labor supply or in which the skills are outdated. They are inefficient because of the low education level and poor work habits of the prisoners. Production has to be stopped for periodic head counts and checks on tools and materials.

23. *Why have legislatures restricted prison industries?*

Pressures from labor unions whose members make competing products at higher wages.

24. *Which inmate characteristics are thought to be factors in prison violence?*

Age, attitudes, and race.

25. *Why are gangs such a threat to prison order?*

Gang wars continue on the inside.

26. *What seven factors are thought to contribute to prison violence?*

Inadequate supervision, architectural design, availability of weapons, housing of violence-prone inmates with the defenseless, the high level of tension of people living in close quarters, the physical size and condition of the prison, and the role of management.

CHAPTER 16

Reentry into the Community

LEARNING OBJECTIVES

→ Understand the nature of the "reentry problem"

→ Learn about the origins of parole and the way it operates today

→ Comprehend the mechanisms for the release of felons to the community

→ Understand the problems parolees face during their reentry

→ Understand how ex-offenders are supervised in the community

→ Learn how civil disabilities block successful reentry

During his last night in the Texas State Prison, Huntsville, Angel Coronado was unable to sleep. Rather, he thought about the next morning when he would be released from prison after three years, two years of which he served in administrative segregation. Coronado, 20 years old, with a limited education, had been brought up in Donna, Texas, on the Mexican border. At 12, he snorted cocaine and as a teenager soon fell in with a local gang. When he was 17, he ran over a friend while drunken driving and was given a three-year prison sentence.

The next morning Coronado was given a new set of clothes, one hundred dollars "gate money," instructions as to when he should report to his parole officer, and a bus ticket to Donna. Carrying his few belongings in a plastic bag he joined about 20 other parolees on a Greyhound bus heading south. As the bus left Huntsville some parolees cheered. There were high fives and some pointed their middle finger at the prison. Coronado was quiet. He said that he hoped to land a job, but knows that he lacks the skills to get more than the minimum wage. He is also concerned about his first encounter with the gang members he left behind. As he says, "I may go out with them, but I know I must follow the parole rules. I can't go back to prison" (Johnson, 2002: 1A).

HUNTSVILLE

Angel Coronado is typical of the more than 650,000 adult felons who leave state and federal prisons each year (about 1,780 daily). With the great expansion of incarceration during the past three decades, the number of offenders now returning to the community has increased dramatically. Ex-prisoners are mostly male, 47 percent from minority groups, and mainly unskilled. Many have alcohol and drug problems, about one-third of state inmates have a physical or mental impairment (Maruschak, 2008,). Some are "churners" who have already served terms for prior offenses and are being let out again. About two-thirds will return to a few metropolitan areas in their states, where they will live in poor, inner-city neighborhoods (Lynch and Sabol, 2001: 16). Some researchers believe this leads to further instability in areas that already have high levels of crime, drug abuse, and other social problems (Clear, et al., 2003: 33–63). About a third of parolees will return to prison, often within a year of their release.

In this chapter we examine the mechanisms by which prisoners are released from incarceration and their supervision in the community. We will discuss the many problems facing parolees as they reenter society.

PRISONER REENTRY

Prisoner reentry has become an important public issue. The sudden flood of offenders leaving prison and the fact that more than 40 percent will return to prison, either because of a new crime or a parole violation, raise serious questions as to how the criminal justice system deals with the reentry of ex-felons (BJS, 2007). What is the crux of this problem?

Jeremy Travis and Joan Petersilia point to several factors that seem to have contributed to the reentry problem (Travis and Petersilia, 2001: 291–313). They argue that beginning in the 1970s the power of parole boards to decide whether a prisoner was "ready" to be released was abolished in mandatory release states and severely restricted in discretionary release states. This means that more inmates are automatically leaving prison, ready or not, when they meet the requirements of their sentence. It also means that there has been little or no pre-release planning so that the new parolee has a job, housing, and a supportive family when he or she hits the streets.

A second factor contributing to the reentry problem is the curtailing of prison education, job training, and other rehabilitation programs designed to prepare inmates for their return to the community.

Finally, Travis and Petersilia note that the profile of returning prisoners has changed in ways that pose new challenges to successful reentry. In particular the conviction offense and time served is different than it was 30 years ago. Now, about 40 percent of prisoners released to parole were incarcerated for a drug offense—up from 12 percent in 1985. While the average time served has also increased by almost a half year since 1990, some drug and violence offenders are exiting prison after very long terms, perhaps 20 or more years. The longer time in prison means a longer period the prisoner has been absent from family and friends.

How prepared, then, are prisoners to live as law-abiding citizens? Successful prisoner reentry requires that parole and services focus on linking offenders with community institutions—churches, families, self-help groups, and assistance programs. As emphasized by Joan Petersilia, "We must share the responsibility for transitioning offenders *with* the community." Ultimately successful reentry is crucial for family and neighborhood stability as well as public safety (*When Prisoners Come Home: Parole and Prisoner Reentry*, New York: Oxford University Press, 2003:3).

The reentry problem has stimulated action by Congress and the states to provide assistance to parolees and to reduce the staggering amount of recidivism among them. The Second Chance Act of 2007, signed into law by President Bush on April 9, 2008, is designed to ensure the safe and successful return of prisoners to the community. The Act provides federal grants to states and communities to support reentry initiatives focused on employment, housing, substance abuse and mental health treatment, and children and family services.

checkpoint

1. What three factors underlie the prisoner reentry problem?
   (answers are at the end of the chapter)

RELEASE AND SUPERVISION

Except for the 7 percent of offenders who die in prison, all inmates will eventually be released to live in the community. Currently about 77 percent of felons will be released on parole and will remain under correctional supervision for a specific period of time. About 19 percent are released at the expiration of their sentence, having "maxed out," and are free to live in the community without supervision.

Parole is the conditional release of an offender from incarceration but not from the legal custody of the state. Thus offenders who comply with parole conditions and do not violate the law receive an absolute discharge from supervision at the end of their sentences. If a parolee breaks a rule, parole can be revoked and the person returned to a correctional facility. Parole rests on three concepts:

1. *Grace*: The prisoner could be kept incarcerated but the government extends the privilege of release.

2. *Contract*: The government enters into an agreement with the prisoner whereby the prisoner promises to abide by certain conditions in exchange for being released.

parole
The conditional release of an inmate from incarceration under supervision after a part of the prison sentence has been served.

Carolyn Aselton (left) is the sister of Hartford Police Office Brian Asleton, who was murdered in 1999. Here, she read a statement to the Connecticut Parole Board during a hearing for Jose Gonzalez (center left). The board unanimously rejected a request for early release for Gonzalez, who is serving an 8-year sentence for his part in the killing. How much influence should crime victims have over parole decisions?

AP Images/Douglas Healey

3. *Custody*: Even though the offender is released from prison, he or she is still under supervsion by the government. Parole is an extension of correctional programs into the community.

Only felons are released on parole; adult misdemeanants are usually released immediately after they have finished serving their sentences. Today about 800,000 people are under parole supervision, a threefold increase since 1980 (BJS, 2007: 4).

The Origins of Parole

ticket of leave
A system of conditional release from prison, devised by Captain Alexander Maconochie and first developed in Ireland by Sir Walter Crofton.

Parole in the United States evolved during the nineteenth century from the English, Australian, and Irish practices of conditional pardon, apprenticeship by indenture, transportation of criminals from one country to another, and the issuance of **tickets of leave**. These were all methods of moving criminals out of prison as a response to overcrowding, labor shortages, and the cost of incarceration.

A key figure in developing the concept of parole in the nineteenth century was Captain Alexander Maconochie, an administrator of British penal colonies in Tasmania and elsewhere in the South Pacific. A critic of definite prison terms, Maconochie devised a system of rewards for good conduct, labor, and study. Under his classification procedure, prisoners could pass through stages of increasing responsibility and freedom: (1) strict imprisonment, (2) labor on government chain gangs, (3) freedom within a limited area, (4) a ticket of leave or parole resulting in a conditional pardon, and (5) full restoration of liberty. Like modern correctional practices, this procedure assumed that prisoners should be prepared gradually for release. The roots of the American system of parole can be seen in the transition from imprisonment to conditional release to full freedom.

Maconochie's idea of requiring prisoners to earn their early release caught on first in Ireland. There, Sir Walter Crofton built on Maconochie's idea that an offender's progress in prison and a ticket of leave were linked. Prisoners who graduated through Crofton's three successive levels of treatment were released on parole under a series of conditions. Most significant was the requirement that parolees submit monthly reports to the police. In Dublin, a special civilian inspector helped releasees find jobs, visited them periodically, and supervised their activities.

checkpoint

2. In what countries did the concept of parole first develop?
3. What were the contributions of Alexander Maconochie and Sir Walter Crofton?

The Development of Parole in the United States

In the United States, parole developed during the prison reform movement of the latter half of the nineteenth century. Relying on the ideas of Maconochie and Crofton, American reformers such as Zebulon Brockway of the Elmira State Reformatory in New York began to experiment with the concept of parole. After New York adopted indeterminate sentences in 1876, Brockway started to release prisoners on parole. Under the new sentencing law, prisoners could be released when their conduct showed they were ready to return to society.

As originally implemented, the parole system in New York did not require supervision by the police. Instead, volunteers from citizens' reform groups assisted with the parolee's reintegration into society. As parole became more common and applied to larger numbers of offenders, states replaced the volunteer supervisors with correctional employees.

Many individuals and groups in the United States opposed the release of convicts before they had completed the entire sentence that they had earned by their crimes. However, the use of parole continued to spread. By 1900, twenty states had parole systems; and by 1932, forty-four states and the federal government had them (Friedman, 1993: 304). Today every state has some procedure for the release of offenders before the end of their sentences.

Although it has been used in the United States for more than a century, parole remains controversial. To many people, parole allows convicted offenders to avoid serving the full sentence they deserve. Public pressure in the 1970s to be tougher on criminals has led half the states and the federal government to restructure their sentencing laws and release mechanisms (Petersilia, 1999: 479).

RELEASE MECHANISMS

From 1920 to 1973 there was a nationwide sentencing and release policy. During this period, all states and the federal government used indeterminate sentencing, authorized discretionary release by parole boards, and supervised prisoners after release. They did this all in the interest of the rehabilitation of offenders.

The critique of rehabilitation in the 1970s led to determinate sentencing as the public came to view the system as "soft" on criminals. By 2002, 16 states had abolished discretionary release by parole boards. Another five states had abolished discretionary release for certain offenses (Petersilia, 2003: 65).

Further, in some states that kept discretionary release, parole boards have been reluctant to grant it. In Texas, for example, 57 percent of all cases considered for parole release in 1988 were approved; by 1998 that figure had dropped to just 20 percent (Fabelo, 1999).

There are now five basic mechanisms for people to be released from prison: (1) discretionary release, (2) mandatory release, (3) probation release, (4) other conditional release, and (5) expiration release. Figure 16.1 shows the percentage of felons released by the various mechanisms. Read the Comparative Perspective to learn about parole release in Japan.

 The Oklahoma Pardon and Parole Board provides information to the public about its responsibilities. To link to this website, go to *The American System of Criminal Justice* 12e companion site at academic.cengage.com/criminaljustice/cole.

discretionary release
The release of an inmate from prison to conditional supervision at the discretion of the parole board within the boundaries set by the sentence and the penal law.

Discretionary Release

States retaining indeterminate sentences allow **discretionary release** by the parole board within the boundaries set by the sentence and the penal law. As a conditional release to parole supervision, this approach lets the parole board assess the prisoner's readiness for release within the minimum and maximum terms of the sentence. In reviewing the prisoner's file and asking questions, the parole board focuses on the nature of the offense, the inmate's behavior, and his or her participation in rehabilitative programs. This process places great faith in the ability of parole board members to predict the future behavior of offenders (see the Close Up box).

FIGURE 16.1

Methods of release from state prison
Felons are released from prison to the community, usually under parole supervision, through various means depending on the law.

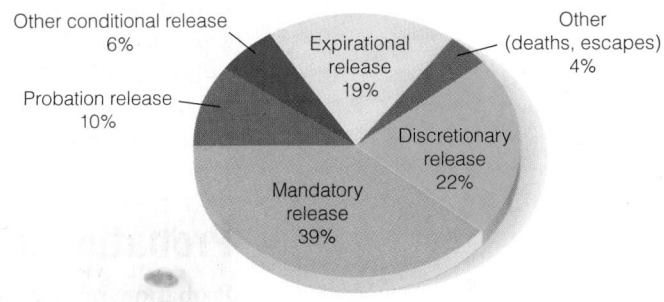

Other conditional release 6%
Probation release 10%
Mandatory release 39%
Expirational release 19%
Other (deaths, escapes) 4%
Discretionary release 22%

Source: Bureau of Justice Statistics, *Bulletin*, November 2006, p. 8.

COMPARATIVE PERSPECTIVE

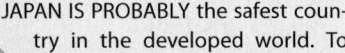

Parole Release in Japan

JAPAN IS PROBABLY the safest country in the developed world. To understand why Japan's crime rate is so low, we might talk to a short, squat man with rumpled clothes, a gentle smile, and big, leathery hands who once crushed his neighbor's head with a hammer.

This 62-year-old man, who killed his neighbor after robbing him of money, is on parole after 15 years in prison. No one in his family ever visited him. His wife and son have told him never to return to their village. His three daughters have even refused to see him. "I have four grandchildren—I think," he said. He has never even seen their pictures.

More than any other developed country, Japan has resolved to "just say no" to crime. Japanese society ostracizes offenders and demands that they not just be caught but that they also confess and show remorse. But, as in the United States, few Japanese offenders die in prison; almost all are released on parole to live under supervision in the community.

Aftercare programs have been available for Japanese offenders since the 1880s. But not until the 1950s were all elements of community treatment for ex-offenders—probation, parole, and aftercare—brought together on a national basis.

Today, decisions to release offenders from prison and place them under supervision in the community are made by eight regional parole boards (RPBs). Sitting in panels of three, the members review applications for parole from prisons and training schools. They also have the authority to revoke an individual's parole on the recommendation of a local office.

The service units of the RPBs coordinate parole. One-third of the sentence must be served. The warden, not the inmate, files the application; he thus clearly uses parole to manage prisoners. The prison directly helps select parolees by sending information to the RPB for parole.

A parole officer visits the home specified in the inmate's job/living plan. The officer checks the situation over and recommends changes, if necessary. The report goes to the prison and the RPB. Sometimes the inmate has to revise and submit another plan.

Then the regional parole board looks at the inmate's character, behavior, and other circumstances. A board member interviews the inmate. Parole conditions are set partly by law and partly by administrative actions. For example, Parker (1986: 53–54) writes that parolees must (1) maintain a fixed residence and pursue a lawful occupation, (2) refrain from associating with persons having criminal or delinquent tendencies, (3) maintain good behavior, (4) obtain advance permission from a parole supervisor before changing a place of residence or traveling for an extended period, and (5) comply with any special conditions imposed by the parole board at the time of release.

Japanese probation, parole, and aftercare focus on community. Unpaid volunteers do the supervision; private organizations administer aftercare, paid only partly by governmental subsidies.

The Japanese public largely believes that people can correct themselves. Repentant offenders tend to get out; others end up in prison. "Rehabilitation" is a way to earn the right to be reincluded in society.

Sources: Adapted from Elmer H. Johnson, *Japanese Corrections: Managing Convicted Offenders in an Orderly Society* (Carbondale: Southern Illinois University Press, 1996), 266–67, 294; Nicholas D. Kristof, "Japanese Say No to Crime: Tough Methods at a Price," *New York Times*, May 14, 1995, p. 1; L. Craig Parker, Jr., *Parole and the Community Based Treatment of Offenders in Japan and The United States* (New Haven, CT: University of New Haven Press, 1986), 53–54.

Mandatory Release

mandatory release
The required release of an inmate from incarceration to community supervision upon the expiration of a certain period, as specified by a determinate-sentencing law or parole guidelines.

Mandatory release occurs after an inmate has served time equal to the total sentence minus good time, if any, or to a certain percentage of the total sentence as specified by law. Mandatory release is found in federal jurisdictions and states with determinate sentences and good time provisions (see Chapter 12). Without a parole board to make discretionary decisions, mandatory release is a matter of bookkeeping to check the correct amount of good time and other credits and make sure the sentence has been accurately interpreted. The prisoner is conditionally released to parole supervision for the rest of the sentence.

Probation Release

probation release
The release of an inmate from incarceration to probation supervision, as required by the sentencing judge.

Probation release occurs when a sentencing judge requires a period of post-custody supervision in the community. Probation release is often tied to shock incarceration, a practice in which first-time offenders are sentenced to a short

CLOSE UP

A Roomful of Strangers

AFTER THREE YEARS, three months, and four days in Stanhope Correctional Facility, Ben Brooks was ready to go before the Board of Parole. He awoke with butterflies in his stomach, realizing that at nine o'clock he was to walk into the hearing room to confront a roomful of strangers. As he lay on his bunk he rehearsed the answers to the questions he thought the board members might ask: "How do you feel about the person you assaulted? What have you done with your time while incarcerated? Do you think you have learned anything here that will convince the board that you will follow a crime-free life in the community? What are your plans for employment and housing?" According to prison scuttlebutt, these were the types of questions asked, and you had to be prepared to answer that you were sorry for your past mistakes, had taken advantage of the prison programs, had a job waiting for you, and planned to live with your family. You had to "ring bells" with the board.

At breakfast, friends dropped by Ben's table to reassure him that he had it made. As one said, "Ben, you've done everything they've said to do. What else can they expect?" That was the problem, What did they expect?

At eight-thirty, Officer Kearney came by the cell. "Time to go, Ben." They walked out of the housing unit and down the long prison corridors to a group of chairs outside the hearing room.

Other prisoners were already seated there. "Sit here, Ben. They'll call when they're ready. Good luck." At ten minutes past nine the door opened and an officer called, "First case, Brooks." Ben got up, walked into the room. "Please take a seat, Mr. Brooks," said the African American man seated in the center at the table. Ben knew he was Reverend Perry, a man known as being tough but fair. To his left was a white man, Mr. MacDonald, and to his right a Hispanic woman, Ms. Lopez. The white man led the questioning.

"Mr. Brooks. You were convicted of armed robbery and sentenced to a term of 6–10 years. Please tell the board what you have learned during your incarceration." Ben paused and then answered hesitantly, "Well, I learned that to commit such a stupid act was a mistake. I was under a lot of pressure when I pulled the robbery and now am sorry for what I did."

"You severely injured the woman you held up. What might you tell her if she were sitting in this room today?"

"I would just have to say, I'm sorry. It will never happen again."

"But this is not the first time you have been convicted. What makes you think it will never happen again?"

"Well this is the first time I was sent to prison. You see things a lot differently from here."

Ms. Lopez spoke up. "You have a good prison record—member of the Toastmaster's Club, gotten your high school equivalency diploma, kept your nose clean. Tell the board about your future plans should you be released."

"My brother says I can live with him until I get on my feet, and there is a letter in my file telling you that I have a job waiting at a meat-processing plant. I will be living in my hometown but I don't intend to see my old buddies again. You can be sure that I am now on the straight and narrow."

"But you committed a heinous crime. That woman suffered a lot. Why should the board believe that you won't do it again?"

"All I can say is that I'm different now."

"Thank you Mr. Brooks," said Reverend Perry. "You will hear from us by this evening." Ben got up and walked out of the room. It had only taken eight minutes, yet it seemed like hours. Eight minutes during which his future was being decided. Would it be back to the cell or out on the street? It would be about ten hours before he would receive word from the board as to his fate.

Researching the Internet

 For more on this subject, see the Community Resources for Justice website. To link to this website, go to *The American System of Criminal Justice* 12e companion site at academic .cengage.com/criminaljustice/cole.

---

period in jail ("the shock") and then allowed to reenter the community under supervision. Since 2000, releases to probation have increased from 6 to 10 percent.

Other Conditional Release

Because of the growth of prison populations, many states have devised ways to get around the rigidity of mandatory release. They place inmates in the community through furloughs, home supervision, halfway houses, emergency release, and other programs (BJS, 2000: 95–104; Griset, 1995: 307). These types of **other conditional release** also avoid the appearance of the politically sensitive label "discretionary parole."

other conditional release
A term used in some states to avoid the rigidity of mandatory release by placing convicts under supervision in various community settings.

An increasing number of offenders are leaving prison at the expiration of their sentences. They have "maxed out" and leave without the requirement of parole supervision. What is their future?

AP Images/Joseph Kaczmarek

Expiration Release

expiration release
The release of an inmate from incarceration, without any further correctional supervision; the inmate cannot be returned to prison for any remaining portion of the sentence for the current offense.

An increasing percentage of prisoners receive an **expiration release**. These inmates are released from any further correctional supervision and cannot be returned to prison for their current offense. Such offenders have served the maximum court sentence, minus good time—they have "maxed out."

checkpoint

4. How do discretionary release, mandatory release, other conditional release, and expiration release differ?

Impact of Release Mechanisms

Parole release mechanisms do more than simply determine the date at which a particular prisoner will be sent back into the community. Parole release also has an enormous impact on other parts of the system, including sentencing, plea bargaining, and the size of prison populations.

One important effect of discretionary release is that an administrative body—the parole board—can shorten a sentence imposed by a judge. Even in states that have mandatory release, various potential reductions built into the sentence mean that the full sentence is rarely served. Good time, for example, can reduce punishment even if there is no parole eligibility. Consider the role of citizens from the community who serve on parole boards in many states as you read "Civic Engagement: Your Role in the System."

To understand the impact of release mechanisms on criminal punishment, we must compare the amount of time actually served in prison with the sentence specified by the judge. In some jurisdictions, up to

60 percent of felons sentenced to prison are released to the community after their first appearance before a parole board. Eligibility for discretionary release is ordinarily determined by the minimum term of the sentence minus good time and jail time.

Although states vary considerably, on a national basis felony inmates serve an average of two years and three months before release. Some offenders who receive long sentences actually serve a smaller proportion of such sentences than do offenders given shorter sentences. For example, the average robbery offender is given a term of 91 months and serves 58 percent of the term before being released after 53 months. By contrast, the average aggravated assault offender is given a

FIGURE 16.2

Estimated time to be served by adults convicted of selected crimes

The data indicate that the average felony offender going to prison for the first time spends about two years in prison. How would you expect the public to react to that fact?

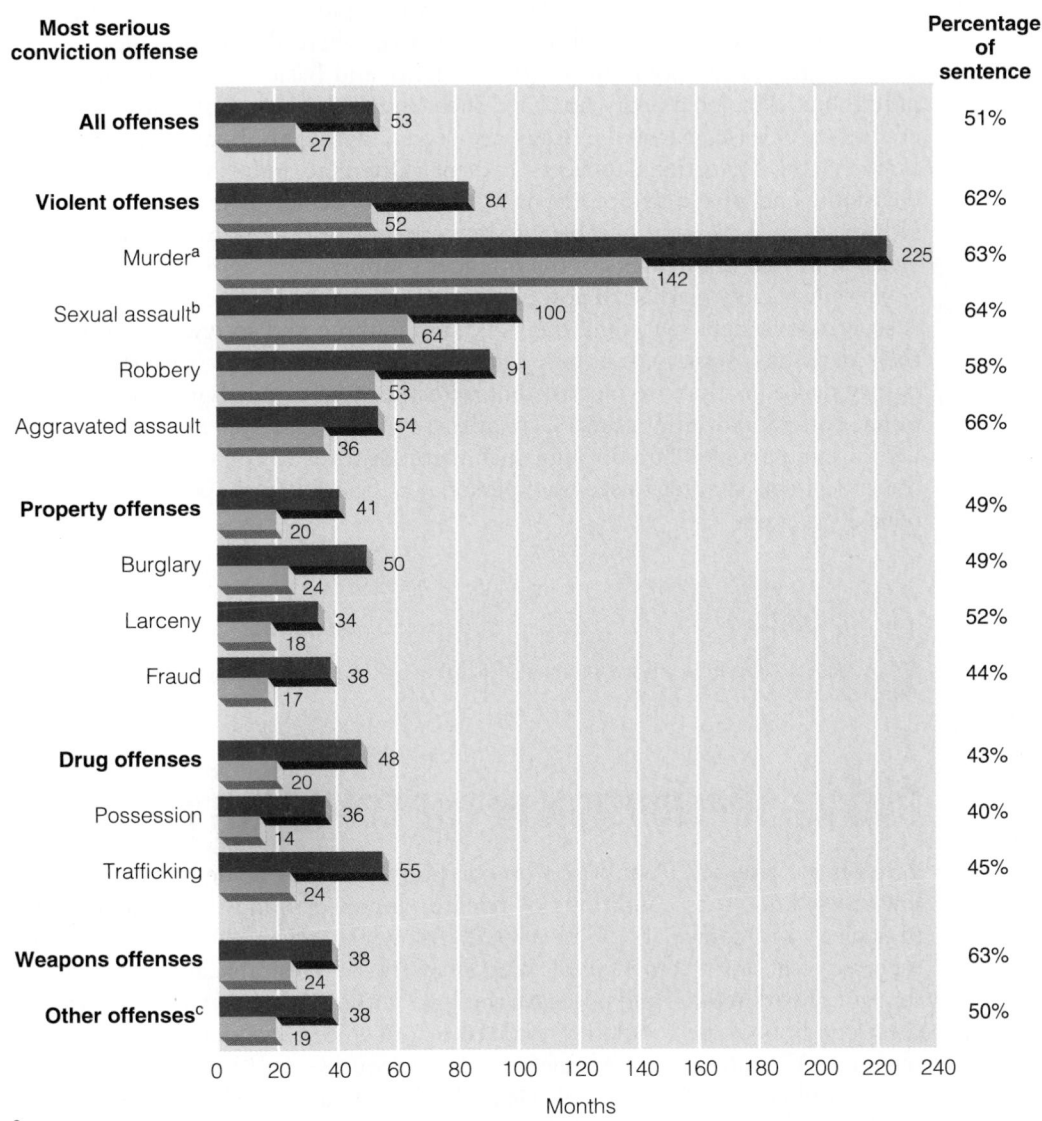

Most serious conviction offense	Mean prison sentence	Average time served	Percentage of sentence
All offenses	53	27	51%
Violent offenses	84	52	62%
Murder[a]	225	142	63%
Sexual assault[b]	100	64	64%
Robbery	91	53	58%
Aggravated assault	54	36	66%
Property offenses	41	20	49%
Burglary	50	24	49%
Larceny	34	18	52%
Fraud	38	17	44%
Drug offenses	48	20	43%
Possession	36	14	40%
Trafficking	55	24	45%
Weapons offenses	38	24	63%
Other offenses[c]	38	19	50%

Months (0 20 40 60 80 100 120 140 160 180 200 220 240)

[a]Includes nonnegligent manslaughter

[b]Includes rape

[c]Composed of nonviolent offenses such as receiving stolen property and vandalism

■ Mean prison sentence
▨ Average time served

Source: Bureau of Justice Statistics, *Bulletin*, December 2004, p. 5.

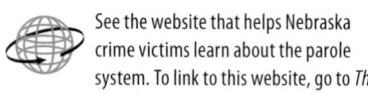

See the website that helps Nebraska crime victims learn about the parole system. To link to this website, go to *The American System of Criminal Justice* 12e companion site at academic.cengage.com/criminaljustice/cole.

term of 54 months but serves 66 percent of the term, 36 months. Figure 16.2 shows the average time served and the percentage of the sentence for selected offenses.

Supporters of discretion for the paroling authority argue that parole benefits the overall system. Discretionary release mitigates the harshness of the penal code. If the legislature must establish exceptionally strict punishments as a means of conveying a "tough on crime" image to frustrated and angry voters, parole can effectively permit sentence adjustments that make the punishment fit the crime. Everyone convicted of larceny may not have done equivalent harm, yet some legislatively mandated sentencing schemes may impose equally strict sentences. Early release on parole can be granted to an offender who is less deserving of strict punishment, such as someone who voluntarily makes restitution, cooperates with the police, or shows genuine regret. Discretionary release is also an important tool for reducing prison populations, in states with overcrowded prisons and budget deficits.

A major criticism of discretionary release is that it shifts responsibility for many primary criminal justice decisions from a judge, who holds legal procedures uppermost, to an administrative board, where discretion rules. Judges know a great deal about constitutional rights and basic legal protections, but parole board members may not have such knowledge. In most states with discretionary release, parole hearings are secret, with only board members, the inmate, and correctional officers present. Often no published criteria guide decisions, and prisoners are given no reason for denial or granting of parole. However, an increasing number of states permit oral or written testimony by victims, as well as members of the offender's family.

Should society place such power in the hands of parole boards? Because there is so little oversight regarding their decision making and so few constraints on their decisions, some parole board members will make arbitrary or discriminatory decisions that are inconsistent with the values underlying our constitutional system and civil rights. Generally, the U.S. legal system seeks to avoid determining people's fate through such methods. See "A Question of Ethics" at the end of this chapter to see how personal attitudes can shape the decision to release on parole.

checkpoint

5. How does parole release influence the rest of the criminal justice system?

PAROLE SUPERVISION IN THE COMMUNITY

conditions of release
Conduct restrictions that parolees must follow as a legally binding requirement of being released.

Parolees are released from prison on condition that they abide by laws and follow rules, known as **conditions of release**, designed to aid their readjustment to society and control their movement. As in probation, the parolee may be required to abstain from alcohol, keep away from undesirable associates, maintain good work habits, and not leave the state without permission. If they violate these conditions, they could be returned to prison to serve out the rest of their sentence. All states except Maine have some requirement for postprison supervision, and nearly 80 percent of released prisoners are subject to some form of conditional community supervision release (Petersilia, 1999: 489.).

The restrictions are justified on the ground that people who have been incarcerated must readjust to the community so that they will not fall back into preconviction habits and associations. The strict enforcement of these rules may

Grace Bernstein, an administrative law judge at the Harlem Parole Reentry Court in New York City, conducts a hearing to discuss and resolve issues related to parolees under supervision in the community. Should parolees be given second chances if they violate conditions of release, such as rules about curfews or consumption of alcohol?

create problems for parolees who cannot fulfill all of the demands placed on them. For example, it may be impossible for a parolee to be tested for drugs, attend an Alcoholics Anonymous meeting, and work full-time while also meeting family obligations.

The day they come out of prison, parolees face a staggering array of problems. In most states, they are given only clothes, a token amount of money, a list of rules governing their conditional release, and the name and address of the parole officer to whom they must report within 24 hours. Although a promised job is often a condition for release, an actual job may be another matter. Most former convicts are unskilled or semiskilled, and the conditions of release may prevent them from moving to areas where they could find work. If the parolee is African American, male, and younger than 30, he belongs to the largest category of unemployed workers in the country. Figure 16.3 shows the characteristics of parolees.

Parolees have the added handicap of former convict status. In most states, laws prevent former prisoners from working in certain types of establishments— where alcohol is sold, for example—thus ruling out many jobs. In some states, the fact of having served time is taken as a fact of "a lack of good moral character and trustworthiness" required to obtain a license to be employed as a barber, for example. In many trades, workers must belong to a union, and unions often have restrictions on the admission of new members. Finally, many parolees, as well as other ex-convicts, face a significant dilemma. If they are truthful about their backgrounds, many employers will not hire them. If they are not truthful, they can be fired for lying if the employer ever learns about their conviction. Some problems that parolees encounter when they reenter the community are illustrated in the Close Up box. As you read about Jerome Washington's experience, ask yourself what problems you might encounter after a long term in "max."

Other reentry problems plague parolees. For many, the transition from the highly structured life in prison to open society is too difficult to manage. Many

FIGURE 16.3.
Personal Characteristics of Parolees
Prison releasees tend to be men in their thirties who have an inadequate education and were incarcerated for a nonviolent offense.

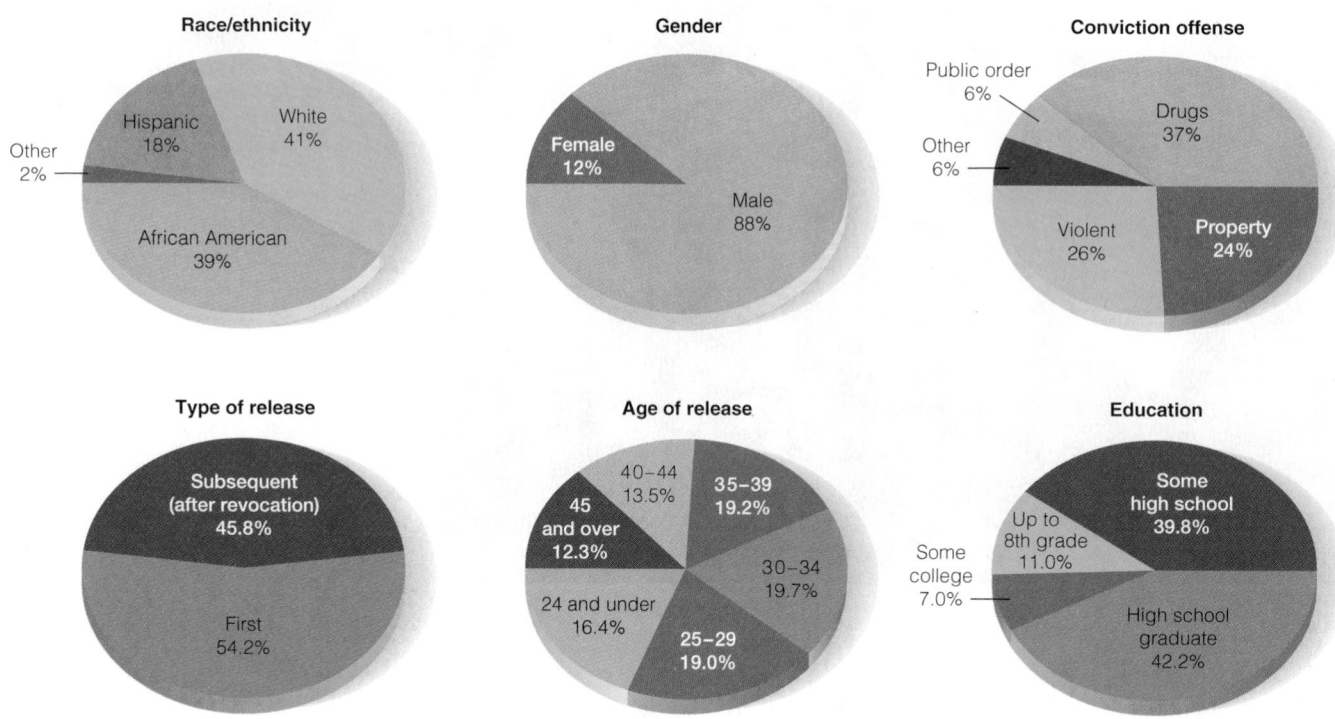

Race/ethnicity
- Other 2%
- Hispanic 18%
- White 41%
- African American 39%

Gender
- Female 12%
- Male 88%

Conviction offense
- Public order 6%
- Other 6%
- Drugs 37%
- Violent 26%
- Property 24%

Type of release
- Subsequent (after revocation) 45.8%
- First 54.2%

Age of release
- 40–44 13.5%
- 45 and over 12.3%
- 24 and under 16.4%
- 35–39 19.2%
- 30–34 19.7%
- 25–29 19.0%

Education
- Some high school 39.8%
- Up to 8th grade 11.0%
- Some college 7.0%
- High school graduate 42.2%

Source: Bureau of Justice Statistics, *Special Report*, October, 2001, p. 7; *Bulletin*, November 2007, p. 6.

just do not have the social, psychological, and material resources to cope with the temptations and complications of modern life. For these parolees, freedom may be short-lived as they fall back into forbidden activities such as drinking, using drugs, and stealing.

Community Programs Following Release

There are various programs to assist parolees. Some help prepare offenders for release while they are still in prison; others provide employment and housing assistance after release. Together, the programs are intended to help the offender progress steadily toward reintegration into the community. Penologists agree that there should be pre- and postrelease programs to assist reentry, yet as Petersilia notes more than 90 percent of prisoners do not now participate in such programs (Petersilia, 2003: 98) Although reentry programs are available in prisons in all states, relatively few inmates have access to them.

Among the many programs developed to help offenders return to the community, three are especially important: work and educational release, furloughs,

Angel Orkmon begins her day opening the cash drawer as a receptionist in an Indianapolis hotel. Orkmon, serving a three-year sentence for forgery, is one of about 5,000 Indiana residents on work release. These programs ease reentry into the community. Should the government assist offenders in finding jobs?

© Todd Bigelow/ Aurora Photos

CLOSE UP

Returning to America

RETURNING TO AMERICA after living in France, China, Swaziland, or the high Himalayas is one thing, but returning to America after serving sixteen years and three months in maximum security, mostly in Attica, is something altogether different.

In 1972 when I went to prison, Richard M. Nixon was president and politicians were still thought to be ethical; . . . the Supreme Court was reasonably balanced; the Vietnam War was winding down, but the weekly body count was still news. The HIV virus was unknown and free sex had more fans than the Super Bowl. Although everybody was not living the American Dream, and some people felt that life was hopeless, most were optimistic about their future and many had a strong commitment to social activism. People cared, and even the most disadvantaged could still dream without fear of having nightmares.

Soon after I got out I was with my brother Freddy. We were standing at Columbus Circle, a major hub, a New York City crossroads. Freddy was my guide. He asked where I'd like to go; what I'd like to do; what I'd like to see. Did I want to meet new people, or just hang out, drift from place to place? Suddenly, life was a smorgasbord, a cornucopia of enticements and alluring temptations. I didn't know where to start, what to do first. Prison was my immediate reference point and, there, decisions related to physical movement were made by the guards, not by me. "We can't stand here all day," my brother said, over and over.

"Go slow," I told myself as I recalled a number of prisoners who shortly after release returned to prison with new convictions, and new sentences. They tried to make everything happen at once, all at the same time. Like children, they wanted instant gratification. Played all their cards at the same time, swung before the ball got to the plate, struck out and found themselves back in a cell where their only landscape was the sun setting against the prison wall.

I decided to do life the same way I did prison. Nothing fancy. One step at a time, one day at a time, and most of all, don't forget to breathe.

Freddy was supportive and sensitive. He understood that I needed to relearn the rhythm of the streets, tune in on the city, explore my new freedom and tune out on prison. I had no preference which direction we'd walk, or which street we'd take. Freddy didn't seem to have any preference either. He just started off, leaving me to stay where I was or to catch up. I learned a quick but important lesson. It was this kind of small, ordinary decision—often taken for granted and overlooked—that I missed most in prison. Now, by just walking off and letting me decide what to do, Freddy was tuning me in again to this level of free choice.

The morning after my release found me in Harlem. I was staying with Bert, a long-time family friend. I awoke at dawn. There was no excitement. No stage fright or butterflies to signal the first day of the rest of my life. Looking up from sleep I could have dreamed my release from prison the day before. The sky was as gray as a prison sky—the same sky I had seen for the past sixteen years and three months.

Not long after I went to prison, I woke in the middle of the night and sat up on the side of the bed. The cell was so quiet I could hear cockroaches foraging in my garbage.

"When I get out of prison," I said to myself, "sex can wait." Thinking of what I would most like to do, I said, "I'm going to eat strawberries! Big! Fresh! Red strawberries!" And that became my mantra for the rest of the time I was in prison.

On the day I was released, Kathrin, a friend, a sister, my confidante, came to pick me up. She was there with her camera, taking photos of me as I walked through the last gate to freedom. She drove me to the house where she lived with her husband and son, and fed me steamed shrimp, French champagne, and strawberries!

Source: Excerpts from "Time After Time," from Iron House: Stories from the Yard, pp.155–163 copyright 1994 Jerome Washington; used with permission of QED Press, Fort Bragg, California. (Jerome Washington, a writer, died April 20, 2002.)

Researching the Internet

To learn about reentry services offered to parolees, go to the website of the California Division of Parole. To link to this website, go to *The American System of Criminal Justice* 12e companion site at academic.cengage.com/criminaljustice/cole.

---

and residential programs. Although similar in many ways, each offers a specific approach to helping formerly incarcerated individuals reenter the community.

Work and Educational Release

Programs of **work and educational release**, in which inmates are released from correctional institutions during the day to work or attend school, were first established in Vermont in 1906. However, the Huber Act, passed by the Wisconsin legislature in 1913, is usually cited as the model on which such programs

work and educational release
The daytime release of inmates from correctional institutions so they can work or attend school.

are based. By 1972, most states and the federal government had instituted these programs, yet in 2002 only one-third of prisons operated them for fewer than 3 percent of U.S. inmates (Petersilia, 2003: 99).

Although most work and educational release programs are justifiable in terms of rehabilitation, many correctional administrators and legislators also like them because they cost relatively little. In some states a portion of the inmate's earnings from work outside may be deducted for room and board. One problem with these programs is that they allegedly take jobs from free citizens, a complaint often given by organized labor.

Furloughs

furlough
The temporary release of an inmate from a correctional institution for a brief period, usually one to three days, for a visit home. Such programs help maintain family ties and prepare inmates for release on parole.

Isolation from loved ones is one of the pains of imprisonment. Although correctional programs in many countries include conjugal visits, only a few U.S. corrections systems have used them. Many penologists view the **furlough**—the temporary release of an inmate from a correctional institution for a visit home—as a meaningful approach to inmate reintegration.

Furloughs are thought to offer an excellent means of testing an inmate's ability to cope with the larger society. Through home visits, the inmate can renew family ties and relieve the tensions of confinement. Most administrators also feel that furloughs are good for prisoners' morale. The general public, however, does not always support the concept. Public outrage is inevitable if an offender on furlough commits another crime or fails to return. Correctional authorities are often nervous about using furloughs, because they fear being blamed for such incidents.

Halfway Houses

halfway house
A correctional facility housing convicted felons who spend a portion of their day at work in the community but reside in the halfway house during nonworking hours.

As its name implies, the **halfway house** is a transitional facility for soon-to-be released inmates that connects them to community services, resources, and support. Usually, felons work in the community but reside in the halfway house during nonworking hours. Halfway houses range from secure institutions in the community, with programs designed to assist inmates who are preparing for release on parole, to group homes where parolees, probationers, or others diverted from the system live with minimal supervision and direction. Some halfway houses deliver special treatment services, such as programs designed to deal with alcohol, drug, or mental problems.

**civic engagement
your role in the system**

Imagine that the state proposes to purchase a motel near your house to use as a prerelease center for offenders on parole as they reenter the community. *Make a list of arguments that you would make either for or against the creation of this prerelease center.* Then look at one community's experience with a prerelease center. To link to this website, go to *The American System of Criminal Justice* 12e companion site at academic.cengage .com/criminaljustice/cole.

Residential programs have problems. Few neighborhoods want to host halfway houses or treatment centers for convicts. Community resistance has significantly impeded the development of community-based correctional facilities and even has forced some successful facilities to close. Many communities, often wealthier ones, have blocked placement of halfway houses or treatment centers within their boundaries. One result of the NIMBY ("not in my backyard") attitude is that many centers are established in deteriorating neighborhoods inhabited by poor people, who lack the political power and resources to block unpopular programs. Consider your views on these issues as you read "Civic Engagement: Your Role in the System."

In the 1970s, during the community corrections era, halfway houses were found across the nation. However, a 1999 survey by the American Correctional Association (American Correctional Association, 2000) found only 55 halfway houses being operated by ten state agencies. That year fewer than 20,000 inmates (0.04 percent of all inmates released that year) were served by such residential programs. At a time when there is such a great need to assist offenders returning to their communities, funding for residential support services has been deleted from most state budgets.

checkpoint

6. What are three programs designed to ease the reentry of offenders into the community?

Parole Officer: Cop or Social Worker?

After release, a parolee's principal contact with the criminal justice system is through the parole officer, who has the dual responsibility of providing surveillance and assistance. Thus, parole officers are asked to play two different, some might say incompatible, roles: cop and social worker. Whereas parole was originally designed to help offenders make the transition from prison to the community, supervision has shifted ever more toward surveillance, drug testing, monitoring curfews, and collecting restitution. Safety and security have become major issues in parole services.

The Parole Officer as Cop

In their role as cop, parole officers have the power to restrict many aspects of the parolee's life, to enforce the conditions of release, and to initiate revocation proceedings if parole conditions are violated. Like other officials in the criminal justice system, the parole officer has extensive discretion in low-visibility situations. In many states, parole officers have the authority to search the parolee's house without warning, to arrest him or her without the possibility of bail for suspected violations, and to suspend parole pending a hearing before the board. This authoritarian component of the parole officer's role can give the ex-offender a sense of insecurity and hamper the development of mutual trust.

The parole officer is responsible for seeing that the parolee follows the conditions imposed by the parole board. Typically the conditions require the parolee to follow the parole officer's instructions; permit the officer to visit the home and place of employment; maintain employment; not leave the state without permission; not marry without permission; not own a firearm; not possess, use, or traffic in narcotics; not consume alcohol to excess; and comply with all laws and be a good citizen.

Parole officers are granted law enforcement powers so as to protect the community from offenders who are coming out of prison. However, because these powers diminish the possibility for the officer to develop a close relationship with the client, they can weaken the officer's other role of assisting the parolee's readjustment to the community.

The Parole Officer as Social Worker

Parole officers must act as social workers by helping the parolee find a job and restore family ties. Officers channel parolees to social agencies, such as psychiatric, drug, and alcohol clinics, where they can obtain help. As caseworkers, officers work to develop a relationship that allows parolees to confide their frustrations and concerns.

Because parolees are not likely to do this if they are constantly aware of the parole officer's ability to send them back to prison, some researchers have suggested that parole officers' conflicting responsibilities of cop and social worker

The Delancey Street Foundation provides residential and employment assistance to ex-prisoners in San Francisco and at five other sites. To link to this website, go to *The American System of Criminal Justice* 12e companion site at academic.cengage.com/criminaljustice/cole.

Learn how the Fortune Society helps ex-offenders. To link to this website, go to *The American System of Criminal Justice* 12e companion site at academic.cengage.com/criminaljustice/cole. Click on "About Us" to learn about the mission, history, and services of the organization.

should be separated. Parole officers could maintain the supervisory aspects of the position, and other personnel—perhaps a separate parole counselor—could perform the casework functions. Another option would be for parole officers to be charged solely with social work duties, while local police check for violations.

The Parole Bureaucracy

Although parole officers have smaller caseloads than do probation officers, parolees require more extensive services. One reason is that parolees, by the very fact of their incarceration, have generally committed much more serious crimes. Another reason is that parolees must make a difficult transition from the highly structured prison environment to a society in which they have previously failed to live as law-abiding citizens. It is exceptionally difficult for a parole officer to monitor, control, and assist clients who may have little knowledge of or experience with living successfully within society's rules.

The parole officer works within a bureaucratic environment. Like most other human services organizations, parole agencies are short on resources and expertise. Because the difficulties faced by many parolees are so complex, the officer's job is almost impossible. As a result, parole officers frequently must classify parolees and give priority to those most in need. For example, most parole officers spend extra time with the newly released. As the officer gains greater confidence in the parolee, the level of supervision can be adjusted to "active" or "reduced" surveillance. Depending on how the parolee has functioned in the community, he or she may eventually be allowed to check in with the officer periodically instead of submitting to regular home visits, searches, and other intrusive monitoring.

checkpoint

7. What are some of the rules most parolees must follow while under supervision in the community?
8. What are the major tasks of parole officers?

Adjustments to Life Outside Prison
General Adjustments

With little preparation, the ex-offender moves from the highly structured, authoritarian life of the institution into a world that is filled with temptations and complicated problems. Suddenly, ex-convicts who are unaccustomed to undertaking even simple tasks such as going to the store for groceries are expected to assume pressing, complex responsibilities. Finding a job and a place to live are not the only problems the newly released person faces. The parolee must also make significant social and psychological role adjustments. A male ex-convict, for example, is suddenly required to become not only a parolee but also an employee, a neighbor, a father, a husband, and a son. The expectations, norms, and social relations in the free world are very different from those learned in prison. The relatively predictable inmate code is replaced by society's often unclear rules of behavior—rules that the offender had failed to cope with during his or her previous life in free society. The Close Up box describes the frustrations experienced by a builder who has tried to employ parolees.

CLOSE-UP

Seeking the Key to Employment for Ex-Cons

OVER THE PAST two years, Peter Santos has hired 40 ex-convicts to help him build and renovate apartments in Newark, New Jersey; 36 did not last, many of them doing unacceptably sloppy work or simply disappearing within a few weeks—or a few days—on the job.

One worker, Ronald O'Reilly, 41, had spent more than half his life in prison for burglary, drug sales, and weapons possession, yet Mr. Santos gave him not just a job but a cheap apartment and the furnishings to make the place feel like home. He even paid to repair Mr. O'Reilly's neglected teeth. "I gave him my all," Mr. Santos said. "I really thought Ron would be different."

But within five months, Mr. O'Reilly had rekindled his love affair with crack cocaine. He stopped coming to work, ceased paying his $300 monthly rent, and by the time he was evicted, had not only sold off the contents of the apartment, but also the items in an adjacent storage space that belonged to his patron. He was arrested soon after and charged with sexual assault.

The situation epitomizes the way Newark's two leading problems, crime and unemployment, are intertwined with the huge number of ex-convicts in the city. Some 2,300 men and women pour into the city from prison each year, and 65 percent are rearrested within five years. One in six adult residents has a criminal record.

With Newark's unemployment rate stubbornly stuck at twice the state average of 4.9 percent—and criminal history and lack of education leaving many chronically unemployable—Mayor Cory A. Booker has tried to make prisoner reentry a signature issue, aware that his twin promises of safety and economic vitality depend on it.

Mayor Booker has recruited 50 local companies to hire ex-convicts screened by the city's workforce-development agency, rewarding them with tax breaks, and persuaded 300 lawyers, who had volunteered on his election campaign to donate their services to felons facing legal obstacles to employment. He is selling city land to developers willing to employ former prisoners on their construction sites.

But many of Mayor Booker's initiatives have been stymied. He has lobbied legislators to take down some of the barriers ex-offenders face—like rules preventing those with criminal records from working at the Port of Newark—but many are loath to appear to be soft on crime. A threadbare municipal budget upended the idea of providing sanitation jobs to parolees.

Meanwhile, Mr. Santos, the local developer, did not give up after Mr. O'Reilly shirked his job and stole his property. Instead, he gave another ex-convict, Rahman Parker, the keys to the apartment. He has promised, too, to replace the stolen furnishings.

Mr. Parker, a recovering addict who most recently spent five months in the county jail for possession of heroin, is 35, a quiet man with big hands. He has been doing demolition work, painting, and carpentry for Mr. Santos for the last year and a half. Mr. Santos says he will help Mr. Parker fix his teeth, just as he did for Mr. O'Reilly.

"I think Mr. Parker will be different," says Mr. Santos.

Researching the Internet

 Read the press release describing a study of Massachusetts recidivists by the Urban Institute. What were the major problems the parolees faced in the community? How did these problems lead to their reincarceration? What might be done to reduce recidivism? You can find a summary of the report online. To link to this website, go to *The American System of Criminal Justice* 12e companion site at academic.cengage.com/criminaljustice/cole.

Source: From Andrew Jacobs, "Seeking the Key to Employment of Ex-Cons," *New York Times*, April 27, 2008, p. 31.

Today's parolees face even greater obstacles in living a crime-free life than did parolees released prior to 1990. Since that time, Congress and many state legislatures have imposed new restrictions on ex-felons. These include denial of many things for those convicted of even minor drug crimes: welfare benefits such as food stamps, access to public housing, receipt of student loans, and, in some states, voting rights. Studies have found that returning inmates often face so many restrictions after long periods of incarceration that the conditions amount to more years of "invisible punishment" (Mauer and Chesney-Lind, 2002: 1). As emphasized by Jeremy Travis (Travis, 2002: 15–36), the effects of these policies impact not only the individual parolee, but also their families and communities.

The Texas Department of Criminal Justice operates Project RIO (Re-Integration of Offenders), which helps ex-prisoners find employment. To link to this website, go to *The American System of Criminal Justice* 12e companion site at academic.cengage.com/criminaljustice/cole.

checkpoint

9. What are some of the major problems faced by parolees?

Sexual-offender registration laws have made it increasingly difficult for many parolees to adjust to the community. Residents of some neighborhoods, such as these in Placentia, California, have protested the renting or sale of property to paroled sex offenders. To what extent have these laws resulted in all parolees being labeled as "dangerous"?

AP Images/Francis Specker

Public Opinion

News accounts of brutal crimes committed by ex-offenders on parole fuel a public perception that parolees are a threat to the community. The murder of 12-year-old Polly Klaas by a parolee in California and the rape and murder of 7-year-old Megan Kanka by a paroled sex offender in New Jersey spurred legislators in more than 35 states and the federal government to enact "sexual offender notification" laws. These laws require that the public be notified of the whereabouts of "potentially dangerous" sex offenders. In some states, paroled sex offenders must register with the police, while in others, the immediate neighbors must be informed. Many states now have publicly accessible sex offender websites listing the names and addresses of those registered.

The impact of these laws have had several unintended consequences. Incidents have occurred in which parolees have been "hounded" from communities, where the media have televised the parolee's homecoming, where homes have been burned, and where neighbors have assaulted parolees they erroneously thought were sex offenders. In some states, the legislation was written so broadly that minor, nonpredatory, consensual acts, such as two teenagers charged with indecent exposure for being caught engaged in sexual acts in a parked car, are included in the notification mandate. Real estate agents have also found it difficult to sell property in neighborhoods where registered sex offenders live.

The fact of repeat violence fuels a public perception that parolees represent a continuing threat to the community. Although the new laws are directed primarily at people who have committed sex offenses against children, some fear that the community will target all parolees. This preoccupation with potential parolee criminality makes it even more difficult for ex-offenders to successfully reenter society. "What Americans Think" presents public attitudes on the availability of criminal records of ex-offenders.

Revocation of Parole

Always hanging over the ex-inmate's head is the potential revocation of parole for committing a new crime or violating the conditions of release. The public tends to view the high number of revocations as a failure of parole. Corrections officials point to the great number of parolees who are required to be drug-free, be employed, and pay restitution—conditions that are difficult for many to fulfill. Yet, as shown in "What Americans Think," there is strong support for sending parolees who fail drug tests back to prison.

As discussed in Chapter 13, the Supreme Court ruled in **Morrissey v. Brewer (1972)**, that if the parole officer alleges that a technical violation occurred, a two-step revocation proceeding is required. In the first stage a hearing determines whether there is probable cause to believe the conditions have been violated. The parolee has the right to be notified of the charges, to be informed of the evidence, to be heard, to present witnesses, and to confront the witnesses. In the second stage, the parole authority decides if the violation is severe enough to warrant return to prison.

Despite the increase in the number of parolees supervised, the percentage of those who are returned to prison because of a technical violation or conviction for a new offense has remained at about 39 percent (BJS, 2007: 7). However,

Morrissey v. Brewer (1972)
Due process rights require a prompt, informal inquiry before an impartial hearing officer before parole may be revoked. The parolee may present relevant information and confront witnesses.

the percentage of violators returned to prison varies by state, accounting for more than half of prison admissions in California (67 percent), Utah (55 percent), and Louisiana (53 percent), but less than 10 percent in Alabama and Florida. As shown in Table 16.1, 70 percent of parole violators were returned to prison because of an arrest or conviction for a new offense. The percentage of parolees returned for technical violations also varies. For example 17 percent of California's prison population (29,000 beds) consists of inmates who were returned for a technical violation. In the state of Washington, only 1 percent was returned for technical violations (Austin, 2001: 319). As seen in "What Americans Think," much of the public believes that those who recidivate should not be released on parole.

checkpoint

10. What are "offender notification laws"?
11. What two conditions can result in the revocation of parole?
12. What does the U.S. Supreme Court require during the revocation process?

The Reentry Problem

The rising number of parolees returned to prison is a problem that has only recently come to the attention of policy makers. One underrecognized impact of the incarceration policies of the 1980s and 1990s was that more prisoners in prison means that, eventually, more prisoners will be let out. There is now a sudden flood of offenders leaving prison—about 650,000 per year—and probably about a third will return to prison, often within a year of their release. The recidivism rate demonstrates a failure of the criminal justice system to deal with the reentry problems of ex-felons. What is at the crux of this problem?

Jeremy Travis and Joan Petersilia (2001: 291–313) point to several factors that seem to have contributed to the reentry problem. They argue that beginning in the 1970s the power of parole boards to decide whether a prisoner was "ready" to be released was abolished in mandatory release states and severely restricted in discretionary release states. This means that more inmates are automatically leaving prison, ready or not, when they meet the requirements of their sentence. It also means that there has been little or no prerelease planning so that the new parolee has a job, housing, and a supportive family when he or she hits the streets. There is also an increasing percentage of prison releasees who "max out" and hence are not on parole because they served their full sentences in prison.

A second factor believed to contribute to the recidivism rate is the curtailment of prison education, job training, and other rehabilitation programs designed to prepare inmates for reentry into the community. Even with these programs, housing and related services in the community are usually not available. This lack of housing and services is thought to increase the recidivism rate (Metrux, and Culhane, 2004: 139–160).

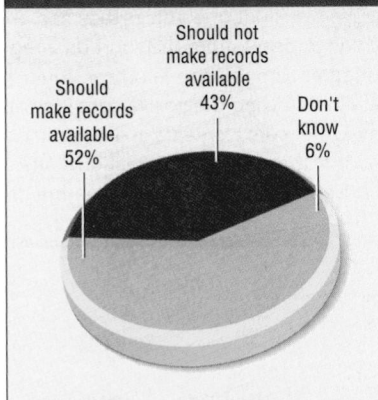

WHAT AMERICANS THINK

Question: "Some people think that if a person convicted of a crime serves his or her sentence and then does not violate the law for a period such as five years, government agencies SHOULD NOT make that criminal record available to employers or licensing agencies. Other people believe employers and licensing agencies SHOULD have access to such records and be able to consider the fact of a conviction in the hiring or licensing process. What do you think?

Should make records available 52%
Should not make records available 43%
Don't know 6%

Source: Bureau of Justice Statistics, *Sourcebook of Criminal Justice Statistics, 2001* (Washington, DC: Government Printing Office, 2002), Table 2.55.

TABLE 16.1	Reasons for Revocation Among Parole Violators in State Prison

An increasing number of parolees are being returned to prison because of new arrests or technical violations. What factors might be causing this increase?

Reason for Revocation	
Arrest/conviction for new offense	69.9%
Drug-related violations	16.1
Positive test for drug use	7.9
Possession of drugs	6.6
Failure to report for drug testing	2.3
Failure to report for drug treatment	1.7
Absconders	22.3%
Failure to report/absconded	18.6
Left jurisdiction without permission	5.6
Other reasons	17.8%
Possession of gun(s)	3.5
Failure to report for counseling	2.4
Failure to meet financial obligations	2.3
Failure to maintain employment	1.2
Maintained contact with known offenders	1.2

Source: Bureau of Justice Statistics, *Special Report*, October 2001, p. 14.

NEW DIRECTIONS IN CRIMINAL JUSTICE POLICY

Reentry Courts

COURTS PLAY ONLY a marginal role in the reentry to the community of former prisoners. Traditionally, a judge's responsibility ends when the defendant is sentenced; prison administrators and parole officers are the ones to prepare prisoners for release and supervise their transition as members of the community. Officials, however, are considering policy alternatives that can deal with the reentry crisis, in which so many ex-prisoners are returned to prison because of new offenses or technical violations.

One suggestion for dealing with this problem is the creation of "reentry courts," patterned after drug courts. Judges would maintain active oversight of parolees they had originally sentenced. Parolees would appear before the court on a regular basis so that the judge, together with the parole officer, could assess the ex-inmates' progress in following the parole conditions and adjusting to life in society. Other core elements of the reentry court include (1) the involvement of the judge and correctional officials in assessing the needs of a prisoner prior to release and in building linkages to family, social services, housing, and work opportunities that would support reintegration; (2) the provision of supportive services such as substance abuse treatment, job training, and family assistance; and (3) a system of sanctions and rewards to encourage positive behavior.

The failure of so many ex-prisoners to succeed on parole has only recently been recognized as a serious problem requiring policy changes. Proponents of reentry courts point to the success of drug courts and say that with continuing judicial oversight and supportive services a greater percentage of ex-felons succeed on parole.

Skeptics are concerned that this is only the latest "enthusiasm" to strike corrections and that the supportive services will not be funded so as to make reentry viable.

Researching the Internet

 To learn more about reentry courts, go to the website of the U.S. Department of Justice, Office of Justice Programs. To link to this website, go to *The American System of Criminal Justice* 12e companion site at academic.cengage.com/criminal justice/cole.

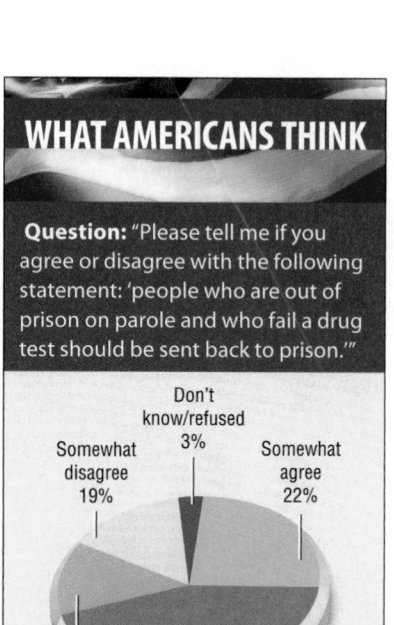

WHAT AMERICANS THINK

Question: "Please tell me if you agree or disagree with the following statement: 'people who are out of prison on parole and who fail a drug test should be sent back to prison.'"

Don't know/refused 3%
Somewhat disagree 19%
Somewhat agree 22%
Strongly disagree 12%
Strongly agree 43%

Source: Telephone interviews with a national adult sample by Beldon, Russonello, and Stewart, January 5–22, 2001. Data provided by the Roper Center for Public Opinion Research, University of Connecticut.

Finally, Travis and Petersilia note that the profile of returning prisoners has changed in ways that pose new challenges to successful reentry. In particular the conviction offense and time served is different than it was 20 years ago. Now, more than a third of prisoners released to parole are incarcerated for a drug offense—up from 12 percent in 1985. While the average time served has also increased by almost a half year since 1990, some drug and violence offenders are exiting prison after very long terms, perhaps 20 or more years. The longer time in prison means a longer period the prisoner has been absent from family and friends. See "New Directions in Criminal Justice Policy" for a look at one way proposed to alleviate the problem of reentry.

checkpoint

13.   Why are recidivism rates high?

THE FUTURE OF PRISONER REENTRY

Parole has been under attack since the 1970s as a symbol of leniency whereby criminals are "let out" early. Public outrage is heightened when the media report the gruesome details of violent crimes committed by parolees. Calls by legislators for the abolition of parole have been politically popular. Some people argue that without parole, criminals would serve longer terms and there would be greater honesty in sentencing. Where discretionary release has been retained, many boards have limited the number of prisoners granted parole.

Correctional experts argue that parole plays an important role in the criminal justice system, given that early release from prison must be earned. Discretionary release enables parole boards to individualize punishment, place offenders in treatment programs, and provide incentives for early release. Neither mandatory nor expiration release provides the tools to prepare felons to reenter the community, because the parole date is based solely on the sentence minus good time.

As prison populations rise, demands that felons be allowed to serve part of their time in the community have mounted. These demands do not come from the public, which typically believes that all offenders should serve their full sentences. Instead, they come from legislators and correctional officials who recognize that the money and facilities to incarcerate all offenders for the complete terms of their sentences are lacking. Although many offenders are not successfully integrated into the community, most will end up back in free society whether or not they serve their full sentences. Parole and community programs represent an effort to address the inevitability of their return. Even if such programs do not prevent all offenders from leaving the life of crime, they do help some to turn their lives around.

CIVIL DISABILITIES OF EX-FELONS

Once a person has been released from prison, paid a fine, or completed parole or probation, the debt to society—in theory—has been paid and the punishment has ended. For many offenders, however, a criminal conviction is a lifetime burden. In most states, certain civil rights are forfeited forever, some fields of employment are closed, and some insurance or pension benefits may be denied. It does not matter if an ex-convict successfully obtains steady employment, raises a family, and contributes time to community organizations.

The **civil disabilities** of ex-felons include loss of the right to vote and to hold public office. In all but two states convicted felons are disenfranchised while incarcerated. In 33 states, they may reapply for the right to vote only when they are off parole. Seven states bar them for life from voting. Nationally, an estimated 5.3 million Americans are barred from voting because of felony convictions

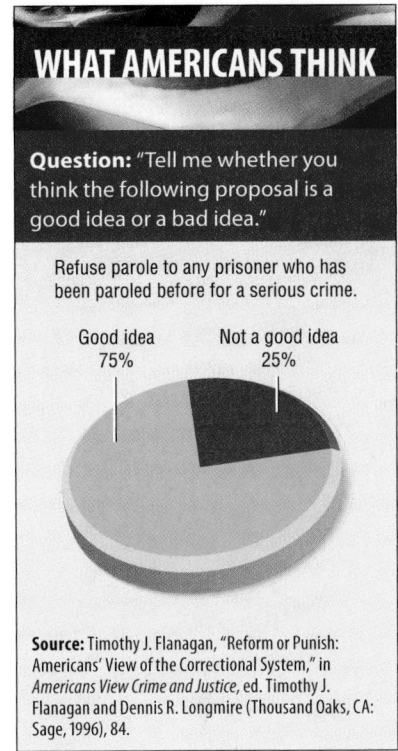

WHAT AMERICANS THINK

Question: "Tell me whether you think the following proposal is a good idea or a bad idea."

Refuse parole to any prisoner who has been paroled before for a serious crime.

Good idea
75%

Not a good idea
25%

Source: Timothy J. Flanagan, "Reform or Punish: Americans' View of the Correctional System," in *Americans View Crime and Justice*, ed. Timothy J. Flanagan and Dennis R. Longmire (Thousand Oaks, CA: Sage, 1996), 84.

civil disabilities
Legal restrictions that prevent released felons from voting, serving on juries, and holding public office.

William Harrington instructs a class at the Watkins Pre-Release Center in South Carolina. Prisoners with substance abuse problems spend their final 60 days in prison in the Center's programs. What do prisoners need to be taught in order to prepare them for release into the community?

AP Images//Mary Ann Chastain

(The Sentencing Project, 2008). This includes 1.4 million African American men (13 percent of all black men). In five states that bar ex-offenders from voting, as many as one-fourth of African American men are permanently forbidden to vote (The Sentencing Project, 2008). Researchers have shown that Al Gore would have won the presidency in 2000 if felons had been allowed to vote (Uggen and Manza, 2001).

Voting may be the most notable civil disability of ex-prisoners, but other legal barriers directly affect those trying to make it after a term in prison. For example, in many states, felons are not allowed to serve on juries, maintain parental rights, and have access to public employment. In most states, ex-felons are prohibited from obtaining a license to practice a trade or profession. For example, Marc LaCloche was taught barbering during the 11 years he served in New York prisons. Upon release his application for a state barbering license was rejected on the grounds that his "criminal history indicates a lack of good moral character and trustworthiness required for licensure" (Haberman, 2005).

Critics of civil disability laws point out that, upon fulfilling the penalty imposed for a crime, the former offender should be assisted to full reintegration into society. They argue that it is counterproductive for the government to promote rehabilitation with the goal of reintegration while at the same time preventing offenders from fully achieving that goal. Supporters of these laws respond that they are justified by the possibility of recidivism and the community's need for protection.

Between these two extremes is the belief that not all people convicted of felonies should be treated equally. In other words, to be protected, society needs to place restrictions only on certain individuals.

PARDON

pardon
An action of the executive branch of state or federal government excluding the offense and absolving the offender from the consequences of the crime.

References to **pardon** are found in ancient Hebrew law. In medieval Europe, the church and monarchies exercised the power of clemency. Pardon later became known as the "royal prerogative of mercy" in England.

I. Lewis "Scooter" Libby (center) leaves a Washington, D.C. courthouse escorted by his attorneys in 2007. Libby, the chief of staff for Vice President Dick Cheney, was convicted of four felonies for lying to investigators concerning leaks to the news media that revealed the identity of an undercover CIA agent. President Bush commuted Libby's sentence to spare him from serving 30 months in prison, but he did not issue a full pardon to erase Libby's criminal record. Was this an appropriate use of the president's powers to reduce or eliminate criminal punishments?

© Mark Wilson/ Getty Images

In the United States, the president or the state governor may grant clemency in individual cases. In each state, the executive receives recommendations from the state's board of pardons (often combined with the board of parole) concerning individuals who are thought to be deserving of the act. Pardons serve three main purposes: (1) to remedy a miscarriage of justice, (2) to remove the stigma of a conviction, and (3) to mitigate a penalty. Although full pardons for miscarriages of justice are rare, from time to time society hears the story of some individual who has been released from prison after the discovery that he or she was incarcerated by mistake. The more typical activity of pardons boards is to erase the criminal records of first-time offenders—often young people—so they may enter those professions whose licensing procedures keep out former felons, may obtain certain types of employment, and in general will not have to bear the stigma of a single mistake.

checkpoint

14. What is a civil disability? Give three examples.
15. What purposes does pardoning serve?

A QUESTION OF ETHICS

THE FIVE MEMBERS of the parole board questioned Jim Allen, an offender with a long history of sex offenses involving teenage boys. Now approaching 45 and having met the eligibility requirement for a hearing, Allen respectfully answered the board members.

Toward the end of the hearing, Richard Edwards, a dentist who had recently been appointed to the board, spoke up: "Your institutional record is good, you have a parole plan, a job has been promised, and your sister says she will help you. All of that looks good, but I just can't vote for your parole. You haven't attended the behavior modification program for sex offenders. I think you're going to repeat your crime. I have a 13-year-old son, and I don't want him or other boys to run the risk of meeting your kind."

Allen looked shocked. The other members had seemed ready to grant his release.

"But I'm ready for parole. I won't do that stuff again. I didn't go to that program because electroshock to my private area is not going to help me. I've been here 5 years of the 7-year max and have stayed out of trouble. The judge didn't say I was to be further punished in prison by therapy."

After Jim Allen left the room, the board discussed his case. "You know, Rich, he has a point. He has been a model prisoner and has served a good portion of his sentence," said Brian Lynch, a long-term board member. "Besides we don't know if Dr. Hankin's program works."

"I know, but can we really let someone like that out on the streets?"

Critical Thinking and Analysis

Are the results of the behavior-modification program for sex offenders relevant to the parole board's decision? Is the purpose of the sentence to punish Allen for what he did or for what he might do in the future? Would you vote for his release on parole? Would your vote be the same if his case had received media attention?

SUMMARY

Understand the nature of the "reentry problem"

■ The successful reentry of ex-prisoners to the community has become a pressing problem.

■ About 650,000 felons are released to the community each year.

■ Preventing recidivism by assisting parolees to become law-abiding citizens requires government effort.

Learn about the origins of parole and the way it operates today

■ Parole in the United States evolved during the nineteenth century from the English, Australian, and Irish practices of conditional pardon, apprenticeship by indenture, transportation, and the issuance of tickets of leave.

- The ideas of Captain Alexander Maconochie, Sir Walter Crofton, and Zebulon Brockway played a major role in the development of parole.

Comprehend the mechanisms for the release of felons to the community

- Conditional release from prison on parole is the primary method by which inmates return to society. While on parole, they remain under correctional supervision.

- There are five types of release: discretionary, mandatory, probation, other conditional release, and expiration release.

- Parole boards exercise the discretion to consider various factors in making the decision to release.

- Parolees are released from prison on the condition that they do not again violate the law and that they live according to rules designed both to help them adjust to society and to control their movements.

- Parole officers are assigned to assist ex-inmates making the transition to society and to ensure that they follow the conditions of their release.

Understand the problems parolees face during their reentry

- Upon release, offenders face a number of problems, such as finding housing and employment and renewing relationships with family and friends.

- Community corrections assumes that reentry should be a gradual process through which parolees should be assisted. Work and educational release, halfway houses, and furloughs are geared to ease the transition.

Understand how ex-offenders are supervised in the community

- Each releasee is assigned a parole officer whose role is part cop and part social worker.

- The parole officer's work combines supervision and assistance.

- Parole may be revoked for commission of a crime or for violating the rules governing their supervision.

Learn how civil disabilities block successful reentry

- Society places restrictions on many ex-felons. State and federal laws prevent offenders from entering certain professions and occupations.

- Voting rights and the right to hold public office are often denied to ex-felons.

- A small number of offenders obtain pardons for their crime and have their civil rights reinstated, usually after successfully completing their time on parole.

QUESTIONS FOR REVIEW

1. What are the basic assumptions of parole?
2. How do discretionary release, mandatory release, probation release, other conditional release, and expiration release differ?
3. What is the role of the parole officer?
4. What problems confront parolees upon their release?

KEY TERMS

civil disabilities (p. 595)
conditions of release (p. 584)
discretionary release (p. 579)
expiration release (p. 582)
furlough (p. 588)
halfway house (p. 588)
mandatory release (p. 580)
other conditional release (p. 581)
pardon (p. 596)
parole (p. 577)
probation release (p. 580)
ticket of leave (p. 578)
work and educational release (p. 587)
Morrissey v. Brewer (1972) (p. 592)

FOR FURTHER READING

Gonnerman, Jennifer. 2004. *Life on the Outside: The Prison Odyssey of Elaine Bartlett*. New York: Farrar, Straus & Giroux. The struggle of Elaine Bartlett to adjust to "life on the outside": conforming to parole rules, finding a job and apartment, reclaiming her role as head of the household.

Mauer, Marc and Meda Chesney-Lind, eds. 2002. *Invisible Punishment: The Collateral Consequences of Mass Imprisonment*. New York: The New Press. A collection of articles exploring the far-reaching consequences of incarceration policies on prisoners, ex-felons, families and communities.

Petersilia, Joan. 2003. *When Prisoners Come Home: Parole and Prisoner Reentry*. New York: Oxford University Press. A major analysis of the reentry problem with implications for community safety.

Simon, Jonathan. 1993. *Poor Discipline: Parole and Social Control of the Underclass*. Chicago: University of Chicago Press. Explores the use of parole to control poor and disadvantaged members of society.

Stanley, David T. 1976. *Prisoners Among Us*. Washington, DC: Brookings Institution. Still the only major published account of discretionary parole-release decision making.

GOING ONLINE

For an up-to-date list of web links, go to *The American System of Criminal Justice* 12e companion site at academic.cengage.com/criminaljustice/cole.

1. Access New Jersey's Megan's Law informational website on the Internet. Describe the requirements imposed on released sex offenders. What is the process of neighborhood notification? What are the likely advantages and disadvantages of this policy?

2. Explore the impact of disenfranchisement laws in the United States. What reforms does the Sentencing Project hope will be enacted?

3. Enter the keyword *parole* into a search engine to find the website of an attorney offering services to inmates at release hearings. What services are offered? Do you think an attorney would be helpful?

CHECKPOINT ANSWERS

1. *What three factors underlie the prisoner reentry problem?*

   Changes in the powers of parole boards, reduction in programs designed to assist ex-prisoners, and the changing profile of those being released from prison.

2. *In what countries did the concept of parole first develop?*

   England, Australia, Ireland

3. *What were the contributions of Alexander Maconochie and Sir Walter Crofton?*

   Captain Alexander Maconochie developed a classification procedure through which prisoners could get increasing responsibility and freedom. Sir Walter Crofton linked Maconochie's idea of an offender's progress in prison to the ticket of leave and supervision in the community.

4. *How do discretionary release, mandatory release, probation release, other conditional release, and expiration release differ?*

   Discretionary release is the release of an inmate from incarceration to conditional supervision at the discretion of the parole board within the boundaries set by the sentence and the penal law. Mandatory release is the required release of an inmate from incarceration to community supervision upon the expiration of a certain period as specified by a determinate sentencing law. Probation release is the release to probation supervision, as required by the sentencing judge. Other conditional release is the release of an inmate who has received a mandatory sentence from incarceration to a furlough, halfway house, or home supervision by correctional authorities attempting to deal with a crowding problem. Expiration release is the release of an inmate from incarceration without any further correctional supervision; the inmate cannot be returned to prison for any remaining portion of the sentence for the current offense.

5. *How does parole release influence the rest of the criminal justice system?*

   Parole release affects sentencing, plea bargaining, and the size of prison populations.

6. *What are three programs designed to ease the reentry of offenders into the community?*

   Work and educational release programs, halfway houses, and furlough programs.

7. *What are some of the rules most parolees must follow while under supervision in the community?*

   Make required reports to parole officer, do not leave the state without permission, do not use alcohol or drugs, maintain employment, attend required treatment programs.

8. *What are the major tasks of parole officers?*

   Surveillance and assistance.

9. *What are some of the major problems faced by parolees?*

   Finding housing and employment, having a shortage of money, and reestablishing relationships with family and friends.

10. *What are "offender notification laws"?*

    Laws requiring certain types of parolees (usually sex offenders) to notify police or residents that they are living in the community.

11. *What two conditions can result in the revocation of parole?*

    (1) Arrest for a new crime; (2) technical violation of one or more of the conditions of parole.

12. *What does the U.S. Supreme Court require during the revocation process?*

    A two-step hearing process. The first stage determines if there is probable cause to believe the conditions of parole have been violated. In the second stage, a decision is made as to whether the violation is severe enough to warrant a return to prison.

13. *Why are recidivism rates high?*

    Many parolees have been away from society for long periods of time. There is a lack of prerelease preparation, counseling, and services.

14. *What is a civil disability? Give three examples.*

    Ex-felons may forfeit certain civil rights such as the right to vote, to serve on juries, and to hold public office. Ex-felons are restricted from certain types of employment as well.

15. *What purposes does pardoning serve?*

    To remedy a miscarriage of justice, to remove the stigma of a conviction, to mitigate a penalty.

PART FIVE

The Juvenile Justice System

AP Images/Robert Caplin

CHAPTER 17
Juvenile Justice

Crimes committed by juveniles are a serious national problem. The Uniform Crime Reports reveal that just under one-quarter of all arrests for index crimes are suspects younger than 18 years of age. Children who are charged with crimes, who have been neglected by their parents, or whose behavior is otherwise judged to require official action enter the juvenile justice system, an independent process that is interrelated with the adult system.

Many of the procedures used in handling juvenile problems are similar to those used with adults, but the overriding philosophy of juvenile justice is somewhat different, and the state may intrude into the lives of children to a much greater extent. In recent years, political and legal moves have been made to reduce the differences in the procedures of the two systems.

CHAPTER 17

Juvenile Justice

LEARNING OBJECTIVES

→ Recognize the extent of youth crime in the United States

→ Understand how the juvenile justice system developed and the assumptions on which it was based

→ Identify what determines the jurisdiction of the juvenile justice system

→ Understand how the juvenile justice system operates

→ Analyze some of the problems facing the American system of juvenile justice

Lonely, depressed, and afraid, Shaquanda Cotton found herself locked up in the Ron Jackson State Juvenile Correctional Complex in Brownwood, Texas. Confined in close quarters with teenagers who were violent, repeat offenders, she faced the prospect of being incarcerated for seven years. The sentence that she faced was more than twice as long as the average prison sentence served by adult felons who are convicted of aggravated assault. Indeed, her sentence was just a few months shorter than the average served by adults convicted of the serious crime of rape (Durose and Langan, 2004). Yet her crime consisted of merely shoving a hall monitor at her high school. The despair that she felt eventually led to an unsuccessful suicide attempt.

As a high school freshman in Paris, Texas, 14-year-old Shaquanda arrived at her school 20 minutes early on the morning of September 30, 2005. After being told by a school aide that it was too early to enter the school, she pushed the aide aside and the aide pushed Shaquanda back. During the altercation, both Shaquanda and the school aide received minor injuries (Richards, 2006).

Shaquanda was charged with felony assault on a public servant. She was offered a lesser sentence by the prosecution in exchange for a plea of guilty, but she maintained that she was

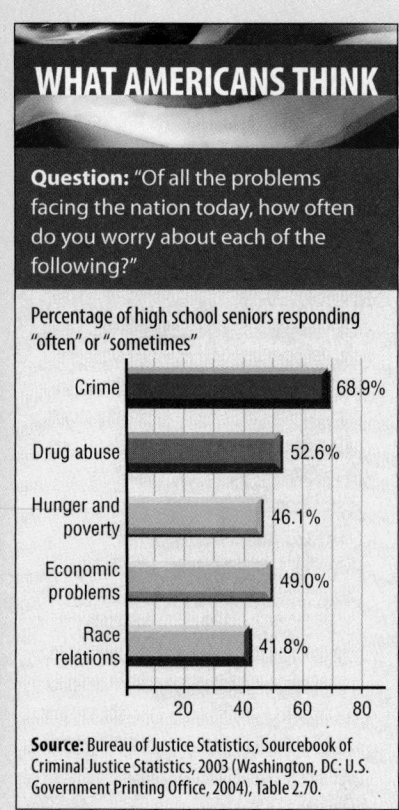

WHAT AMERICANS THINK

Question: "Of all the problems facing the nation today, how often do you worry about each of the following?"

Percentage of high school seniors responding "often" or "sometimes"

Crime	68.9%
Drug abuse	52.6%
Hunger and poverty	46.1%
Economic problems	49.0%
Race relations	41.8%

20   40   60   80

Source: Bureau of Justice Statistics, Sourcebook of Criminal Justice Statistics, 2003 (Washington, DC: U.S. Government Printing Office, 2004), Table 2.70.

innocent of any crime. After a trial in which the jury took a mere ten minutes to deliberate and reach a verdict, Shaquanda was found guilty of felony assault. At the urging of the prosecutor, Lamar County Judge Chuck Superville sentenced her to an indeterminate term of incarceration of no more than seven years, at which time she would be 21 years old and therefore no longer under the jurisdiction of the Texas Youth Commission.

When the *Chicago Tribune* ran a story about her long sentence, it aroused a nationwide storm of controversy about the harshness of her punishment. One source of controversy was the perception that racial discrimination may have affected Shaquanda's case. She was an African American teenager sentenced to seven years of incarceration for pushing a school aide. Yet the same judge who imposed that sentence had just weeks earlier sentenced a 14-year-old white girl to probation for the more serious felony of arson when she burned down her family's house. As more newspapers and websites focused on the story, the supervisor of the Texas youth prison system ordered Shaquanda's release after only one year of imprisonment (Witt, 2007a).

If Shaquanda had not received widespread media attention, however, she would likely still be locked up. Indeed, very few juvenile justice cases receive attention from the news media and the public so there are likely other "Shaquandas" out there facing years of confinement for acts that would not be treated so seriously if committed by adults. At the same time, there are many other juveniles like the girl sentenced to probation for arson who would have received much harsher sentences if they had been adults. What do these inconsistent outcomes indicate about the nature of the juvenile justice system? In this chapter, we will examine this important question.

Although the juvenile justice system is separate from the adult criminal justice system, the key values of freedom, fairness, and justice undergird both systems. The formal processes of each differ mainly in emphasis, not in values. Although different, the systems are interrelated. One cannot separate the activities and concerns of policing, courts, and corrections from the problems of youth. With juveniles committing a significant portion of criminal offenses, officials in the adult system must pay serious attention to the juvenile system as well.

YOUTH CRIME IN THE UNITED STATES

In Denver, a child visiting the zoo was hit by a bullet intended by one teenager for another. Sixteen-year-old Jeff Weise shot ten people in Red Lake, Minnesota. A British tourist was killed while at a rest stop; a 13-year-old boy was one of the suspects. Such dramatic criminal acts make headlines. Are these only isolated incidents, or is the United States facing a major increase in youth crime?

The juvenile crime incidents just described are rare. In a nation with 74 million people younger than age 18, about 1.6 million arrests of juveniles occur each year, 74,000 of which (just over 4.5 percent) are for violent crimes (FBI, 2006: Table 41). After rising from 1988 through 1994, the juvenile violent crime rate has dropped by half since 1994 to the lowest levels since 1985 (FBI, 2004b: Table 41). Yet when American high school seniors are asked to identify the two or three most serious problems they worry about, they cite crime and drugs, as shown in "What Americans Think."

Youth crimes range from UCR Index Crimes (for example murder, rape, robbery, assault) to "youthful crimes" such as curfew violations, loitering, and being a runaway (see Figure 17.1). About 1 in 50 people in the younger than 18 cohort is taken into police custody each year and about 1.5 million are processed by juvenile courts (FBI, 2006). Most juvenile crimes are committed by

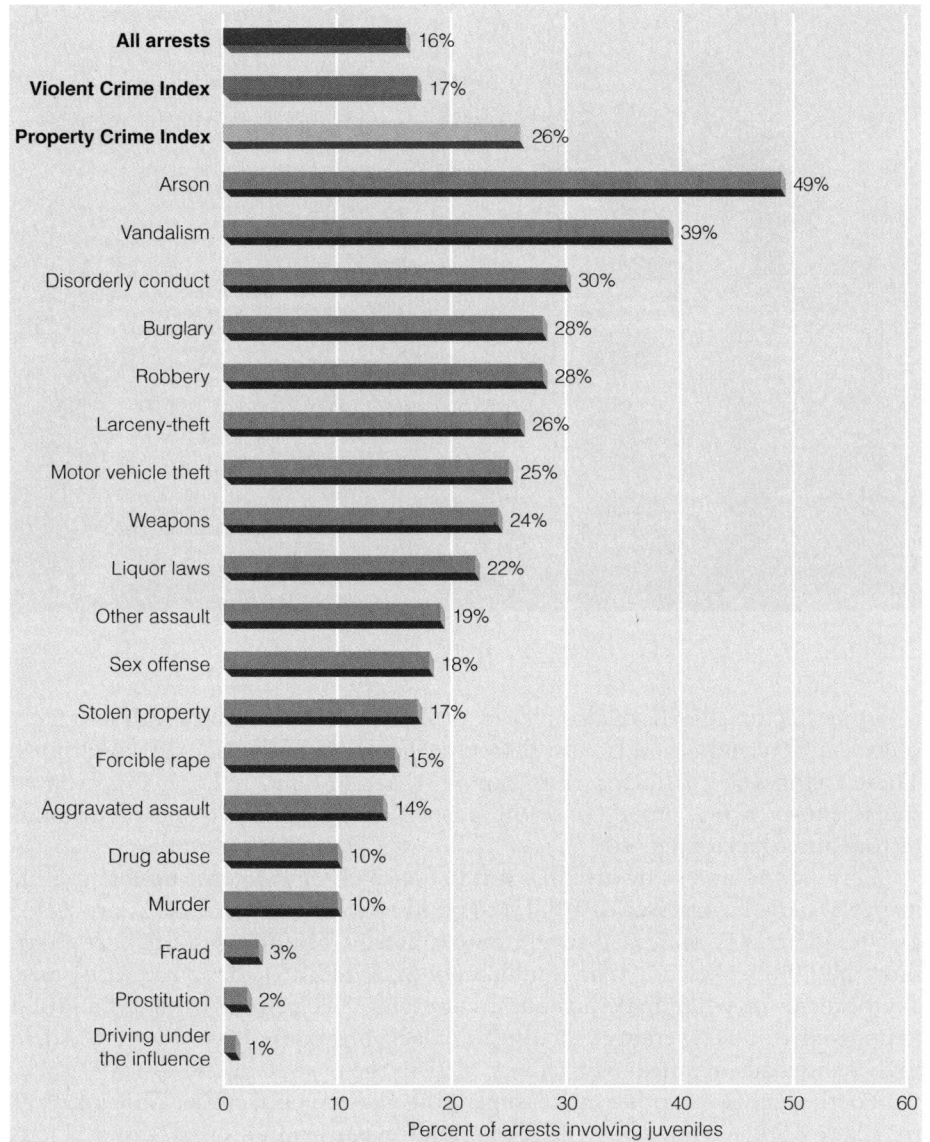

FIGURE 17.1
Percentage of arrests of people younger than 18 years old (rounded)
Juveniles are arrested for a wide range of offenses. For some offenses such as arson, vandalism, motor vehicle theft, and burglary, juveniles account for a larger proportion of arrests than the percentage of juveniles in the general population would suggest.

Source: FBI, *Uniform Crime Reports* (Washington, DC: U.S. Government Printing Office, 2007), Table 41.

young men; only 29 percent of arrestees younger than 18 years of age are female (FBI, 2006). Some researchers have estimated that one boy in three will be arrested by the police at some point before his 18th birthday.

Criminologists have tried to explain the rise of the "epidemic" of violent youth crime that erupted in the mid-1980s, reaching its peak in 1993. Among the explanations, two seem most promising. One explanation uses a "cohort" approach, arguing that during the 1980s the increase in violence was due to an increase in the prevalence of exceptionally violent individuals—so-called "super predators." Critics of this approach say that the birth cohort that peaked during the early 1990s was not at all exceptional with respect to involvement in violence in their younger years (Cook and Laub, 2002: 2).

A second explanation focuses on environmental factors during the epidemic period that influenced the rise in violent youth crime. Scholars holding this position point to the impact of the drug trade, especially crack cocaine and the related increase in gun carrying and use by youths. Alfred Blumstein (1996) suggests that as more juveniles, particularly inner-city minority men, were recruited into the drug trade, they armed themselves with guns and used those firearms in battles over market turf.

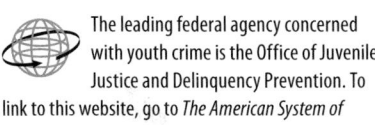 The leading federal agency concerned with youth crime is the Office of Juvenile Justice and Delinquency Prevention. To link to this website, go to *The American System of Criminal Justice* 12e companion site at academic .cengage.com/criminaljustice/cole.

Youthful members of the Pico Norte 19th Street gang pose and flash gang signs in El Paso, Texas. Gangs can draw youths into serious criminal activities. What kinds of programs might lure young people away from the attractions of the image of toughness, solidarity, respect, and power that youths may believe to be offered by gang membership?

© Hector Mata/AFP/Getty Images

To learn more about research on gangs, including profiles of different gangs, see the website of the National Gang Research Center. To link to this website, go to *The American System of Criminal Justice* 12e companion site at academic.cengage.com/criminaljustice/cole.

Other factors may have also played a role—violent crime by youth was most prevalent in neighborhoods with deteriorating social and economic conditions. These changes led to increases in family instability and reductions in shared social expectations about behavior, particularly in minority neighborhoods (Strom and MacDonald, 2007).

Certainly, drug use by juveniles has had a significant impact on the juvenile justice system. From 1985 to 2004, the number of drug offense cases processed by juvenile courts increased from approximately 75,000 cases per year to almost 200,000 cases per year (Stahl, 2008). In addition, drug-use cases have skyrocketed for white male juveniles, increasing 341 percent from 1984–2004 (compared to a 32 percent increase for black juveniles). This has resulted in higher caseloads handled by juvenile courts in the past 20 years.

Youth gangs are another factor explaining violent youth crime. Gangs such as the Black P Stone Nation, CRIPS (Common Revolution in Progress), and Bloods first came to police attention in the 1970s. The National Youth Gang Survey estimates that there are now more than 21,500 gangs with 731,500 members involved in over a half a million serious crimes (OJJDP, 2004: 1). Gangs are a primary source of fear and peril in many neighborhoods. Especially where gang members are armed, the presence of the gang can destabilize neighborhood life. Youth gangs are not restricted to large cities—crackdowns on violence in cities can sometimes force gang behavior into suburban areas (Sanchez and Giordano, 2008). To deal with the problem of youth gangs and guns, Boston developed Operation Ceasefire, as described in "New Directions in Criminal Justice Policy." Other cities have created innovative programs to deal with gang violence—in Chicago, people calling themselves "violence interrupters" try to stop gang violence before it occurs. In this model, violence is treated like a quickly spreading disease with citizens trying to stop the spread of violence through intervention techniques (Kotlowitz, 2008). In Los Angeles, police officers in gang units are on the street all day—looking for gang members and aggressively enforcing the law (Mozingo, 2008).

Although juvenile delinquency, neglect, and dependency have been concerns since the nation's early decades, not until the early twentieth century did a separate system to deal with these problems evolve. The contemporary juvenile justice system has gone through a major shift of emphasis as well. The rest of the

NEW DIRECTIONS in CRIMINAL JUSTICE POLICY

Operation Ceasefire

AS IN OTHER large U.S. cities, Boston witnessed a dramatic increase in youth homicide in the early 1990s. From 1990 to 1995, the average number of juvenile homicide victims per year nearly doubled from that in the 1980s. Operation Ceasefire was initiated to determine the extent of the crime problem in Boston and develop possible solutions.

Criminal justice officials and researchers began Operation Ceasefire by gathering data on youth homicides in Boston and attempting to identify a root cause. This group determined that most youth violence was the result of a small group of highly active violent offenders who were also gang members.

Operation Ceasefire was designed to minimize conflicts between gangs as a method of reducing violence. Police and youth workers notified gang members that violence would not be tolerated in the city, and those arrested for such offenses would receive harsh punishments. In addition, illegal drug markets were targeted by police to reduce the number of illegal guns on the street.

The Boston program ran from 1996 through 2000, during which researchers recorded a 63 percent decrease in the homicide rate, a 32 percent decrease in the number of "shots fired" calls to police, and a 25 percent decrease in gun assaults.

Some researchers have argued that juvenile crime was declining across the country during this time period, and Operation Ceasefire may not have had a significant impact in and of itself. While there is still some debate over the effectiveness of Ceasefire, the community networks that were created to deal with the problem of violent youth crime have helped to serve thousands of youth in need of intervention.

Other cities in the United States have attempted to implement programs similar to Operation Ceasefire, but those programs have struggled. The strong ties in Boston between police, researchers, youth workers, clergy, and others helped to create a unique and apparently successful program. The efforts by reformers in Boston underscored the need for careful analysis of crime problems and careful planning of responsive interventions.

Source: Adapted from Anthony A. Braga and Christopher Winship, "Creating an Effective Foundation to Prevent Youth Violence: Lessons Learned from Boston in the 1990s." *Rappaport Institute Policy Brief* #PB-2005-5, Kennedy School of Government at Harvard University (September 26, 2005).

Researching the Internet

 For more on Boston's youth violence issues, go to the website of the Harvard Youth Violence Prevention Center. To link to this website, go to *The American System of Criminal Justice* 12e companion site at academic.cengage.com/criminal justice/cole.

Read the questions that teenagers are asked in the Boston Youth Survey. Is there additional information that researchers should seek in order to understand the causes and nature of youth violence?

chapter explores the history of juvenile justice, the process it follows today, and some of the problems associated with it.

---

checkpoint

1. What might explain the epidemic of violent crime committed by juveniles in the 1990s? (Answers are at the end of the chapter.)

THE DEVELOPMENT OF JUVENILE JUSTICE

The system and philosophy of juvenile justice that began in the United States during the social reform period of the late nineteenth century was based on the idea that the state should act as a parent in advancing the interest of the child. This view remained unchallenged until the 1960s, when the Supreme Court ushered in the juvenile rights period. With the rise in juvenile crime in the 1980s, the juvenile justice system shifted again to one focusing on the problem of controlling youth crime. Today people are again reexamining the philosophy and processes of the juvenile justice system.

The idea that children should be treated differently from adults originated in the common law and in the chancery courts of England. The common law had long prescribed that children younger than seven years of age were incapable of felonious intent and were therefore not criminally responsible. Children aged 7

parens patriae
The state as parent; the state as guardian and protector of all citizens (such as juveniles) who cannot protect themselves.

to 14 could be held accountable only if it could be shown that they understood the consequences of their actions.

The English chancery courts, established during the Middle Ages, heard only civil cases, mainly concerning property. However, under the doctrine of *parens patriae*, which held the king to be the father of the realm, the chancery courts exercised protective jurisdiction over all children, particularly those involved in questions of dependency, neglect, and property. At this time the criminal courts, not a separate juvenile court, dealt with juvenile offenders. In legitimizing the actions of the state on behalf of the child, however, the concept of *parens patriae* laid the groundwork for the development of juvenile justice.

Table 17.1 outlines the shifts in how the United States has dealt with the problems of youth. These shifts fall into six periods of American juvenile justice history. Each was characterized by changes in juvenile justice that reflected the social, intellectual, and political currents of the time. During the past two hundred years, population shifts from rural to urban areas, immigration, developments in the social sciences, political reform movements, and the continuing problem of youth crime have all influenced how Americans have treated juveniles.

checkpoint

2. Until what age were children exempt from criminal responsibility under common law?
3. What was the jurisdiction of the English chancery court?
4. What is meant by the doctrine of *parens patriae*?

TABLE 17.1   Juvenile Justice Developments in the United States

Period	Major Developments	Causes and Influences	Juvenile Justice System
Puritan 1646–1824	Massachusetts Stubborn Child Law (1646)	A Puritan view of child as evil B Economically marginal agrarian society	Law provides A Symbolic standard of maturity B Support for family as economic unit
Refuge 1824–1899	Institutionalization of deviants; House of Refuge in New York established (1825) for delinquent and dependent children	A Enlightenment B Immigration and industrialization	Child seen as helpless, in need of state intervention
Juvenile court 1899–1960	Establishment of separate legal system for juveniles; Illinois Juvenile Court Act (1899)	A Reformism and rehabilitative ideology B Increased immigration, urbanization, large-scale industrialization	Juvenile court institutionalized legal irresponsibility of child
Juvenile rights 1960–1980	Increased "legalization" of juvenile law; *Gault* decision (1967); Juvenile Justice and Delinquency Prevention Act (1974) calls for deinstitutionalization of status offenders	A Criticism of juvenile justice system on humane grounds B Civil rights movement by disadvantaged groups	Movement to define and protect rights as well as to provide services to children
Crime control 1980–2005	Concern for victims, punishment for serious offenders, transfer to adult court of serious offenders, protection of children from physical and sexual abuse	A More-conservative public attitudes and policies B Focus on serious crimes by repeat offenders	System more formal, restrictive, punitive; increased percentage of police referrals to court; incarcerated youths stay longer periods
"Kids are different" 2005–present	Elimination of death penalty for juveniles, focus on rehabilitation, states increasing age of transfer to adult court	A *Roper v. Simmons* (2005) B Scientific evidence on youth's biological, emotional, and psychological development	Recognition that juveniles are less culpable than adults

Sources: Adapted from Barry Krisberg, Ira M. Schwartz, Paul Litsky, and James Austin, "The Watershed of Juvenile Justice Reform," *Crime and Delinquency* 32 (January 1985): 5–38; U.S. Department of Justice, *A Preliminary National Assessment of the Status Offender and the Juvenile Justice System* (Washington, DC: U.S. Government Printing Office, 1980), 29.

The Puritan Period (1646–1824)

The English procedures were maintained in the American colonies and continued into the nineteenth century. The earliest attempt by a colony to deal with problem children was passage of the Massachusetts Stubborn Child Law in 1646. With this law, the Puritans of the Massachusetts Bay Colony imposed the view that the child was evil and they emphasized the need of the family to discipline and raise youths. Those who would not obey their parents were dealt with by the law.

The Refuge Period (1824–1899)

As the population of American cities began to grow during the early 1800s, the problem of youth crime and neglect became a concern for reformers. Just as the Quakers of Philadelphia had been instrumental during the same period in reforming correctional practices, other groups supported changes toward the education and protection of youths. These reformers focused their efforts primarily on the urban immigrant poor, seeking to have parents declared "unfit" if their children roamed the streets and were apparently "out of control." Not all such children were engaged in criminal acts, but the reformers believed that children would end up in prison if their parents did not discipline them and train them to abide by the rules of socity. The state would use its power to prevent delinquency. The solution was to create institutions where these children could learn good work and study habits, live in a disciplined and healthy environment, and develop "character."

During the nineteenth century, reformers were alarmed by the living conditions of inner-city youths. Reformers in Chicago ushered in the juvenile justice system. Would it have been better to permit youthful offenders to receive the same punishments as adult offenders?

© Topham/The Image Works

The first of these institutions was the House of Refuge of New York, which opened in 1825. This half-prison, half-school housed destitute and orphaned children as well as those convicted of crime (Friedman, 1993: 164). Similar facilities followed in Boston, Philadelphia, and Baltimore. Children were placed in these homes by court order usually because of neglect or vagrancy. They often stayed until they were old enough to be legally regarded as adults. The houses were run according to a strict program of work, study, and discipline.

Some states created "reform schools" to provide the discipline and education needed by wayward youth in a "homelike" atmosphere, usually in rural areas. The first, the Lyman School for Boys, opened in Westboro, Massachusetts, in 1848. A similar Massachusetts reform school for girls opened in 1855 for "the instruction . . . and reformation, of exposed, helpless, evil disposed and vicious girls" (Friedman, 1993: 164). Institutional programs began in New York in 1849, Ohio in 1850, and Maine, Rhode Island, and Michigan in 1906.

Despite these reforms, children could still be arrested, detained, tried, and imprisoned. Even in states that had institutions for juveniles, the criminal justice process for children was the same as that for adults.

The Juvenile Court Period (1899–1960)

With most states providing services to neglected youth by the end of the nineteenth century, the problem of juvenile criminality became the focus of attention. Progressive reformers pushed for the state to provide individualized care and treatment to deviants of all kinds—adult criminals, the mentally ill, juvenile delinquents. They urged adoption of probation, treatment, indeterminate sentences, and parole for adult offenders and succeeded in establishing similar programs for juveniles.

Referred to as the "child savers," these upper-middle-class reformers sought to use the power of the state to "save" children from a life of crime (Platt, 1977). They shared a concern about the role of environmental factors on behavior and a belief that benevolent state action could solve social problems. They also believed the claim of the new social scientists that they could treat the problems underlying deviance.

Reformers wanted a separate juvenile court system that could address the problems of individual youths by using flexible procedures that, as one reformer said, "banish entirely all thought of crime and punishment" (Rothman, 1980: 213). They put their idea into action with the creation of the juvenile court.

Passage of the Juvenile Court Act by Illinois in 1899 established the first comprehensive system of juvenile justice. The act placed under one jurisdiction cases of dependency, neglect, and delinquency ("incorrigibles and children threatened by immoral associations as well as criminal lawbreakers") for children younger than 16. The act had four major elements:

1. A separate court for delinquent, dependent, and neglected children.

2. Special legal procedures that were less adversarial than those in the adult system.

3. Separation of children from adults in all portions of the justice system.

4. Programs of probation to assist the courts in deciding what the best interest of the state and the child entails.

Activists such as Jane Addams, Lucy Flower, and Julia Lathrop, of the settlement house movement; Henry Thurston, a social work educator; and the National Congress of Mothers successfully promoted the juvenile court concept. By 1904, ten states had implemented procedures similar to those of Illinois. By 1917, all but three states provided for a juvenile court.

The philosophy of the juvenile court derived from the idea that the state should deal with a child who broke the law much as a wise parent would deal with a wayward child. The doctrine of *parens patriae* again helped legitimize the system. Procedures would be informal and private, records would be confidential, children would be detained apart from adults, and probation and social workers would be appointed. Even the vocabulary and physical setting of the juvenile system were changed to emphasize diagnosis and treatment instead of findings of guilt. The term "criminal behavior" was replaced by "delinquent behavior" when referring to the acts of children. The terminology reflected the underlying belief that these children could be "cured" and returned to society as law-abiding citizens.

Because procedures were not to be adversarial, lawyers were unnecessary. The main professionals attached to the system were psychologists and social workers, who could determine the juvenile's underlying behavioral problem. These reforms, however, took place in a system in which children lacked the due process rights held by adults.

While the creation of the juvenile court was a positive development for juveniles in general, some contemporary researchers criticize the tendency for these reformers to hold different standards for girls and boys. For example, girls found guilty of the status offense of "promiscuity" were frequently incarcerated until adulthood (age 18) for their own protection. Boys were rarely charged with this type of offense.

The Juvenile Rights Period (1960–1980)

Until the early 1960s, few questioned the sweeping powers of juvenile justice officials. When the U.S. Supreme Court expanded the rights of adult defendants, however, lawyers and scholars began to criticize the extensive discretion given

FIGURE 17.2

Major decisions by the U.S. Supreme Court regarding the rights of juveniles

Since the mid-1960s, the Supreme Court has gradually expanded the rights of juveniles but has continued to recognize that the logic of the separate system for juvenile offenders justifies differences from some adult rights.

Note: For discussion of death penalty cases, see Chapter 12.

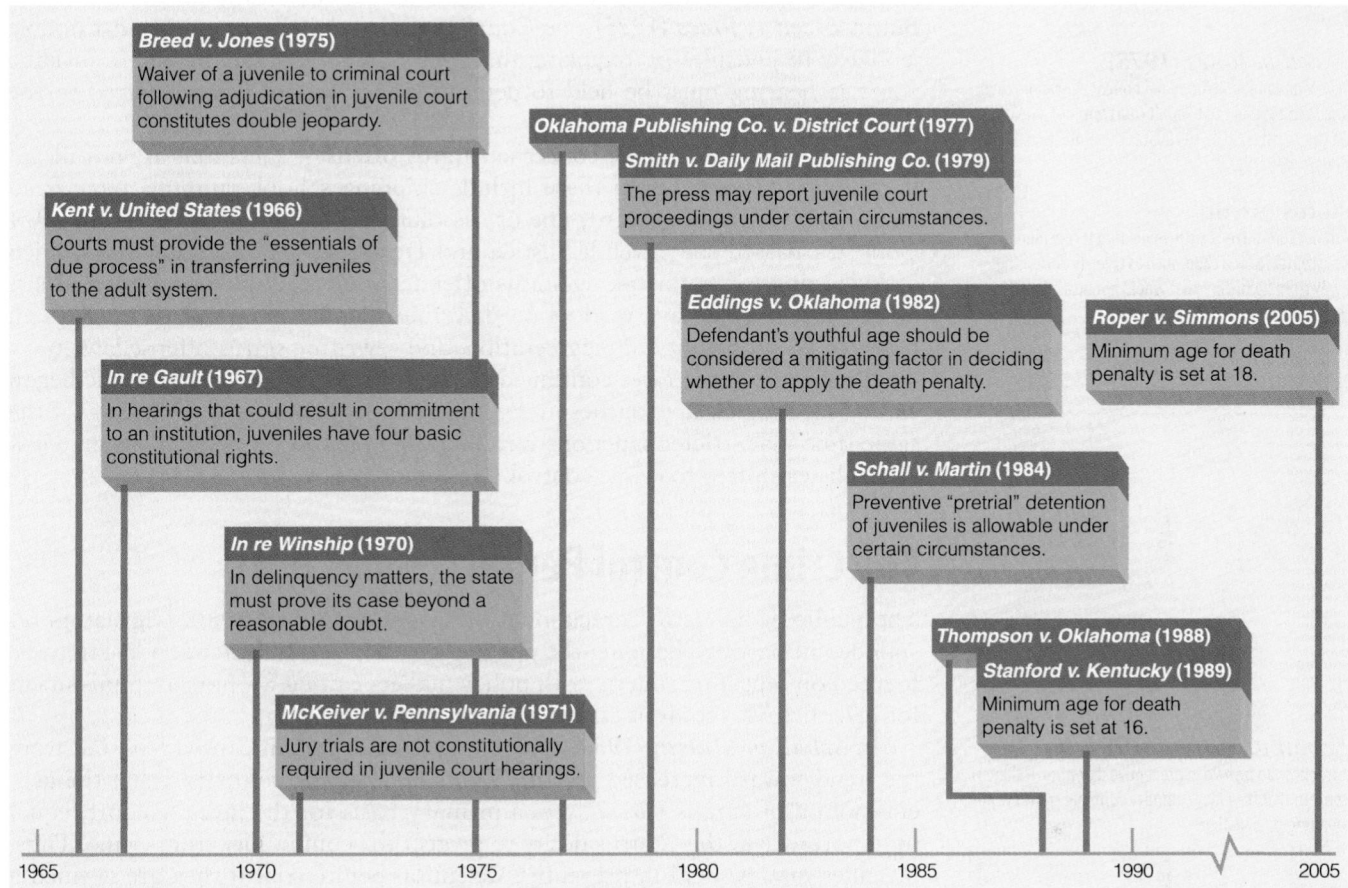

Sources: Office of Juvenile Justice and Delinquency Prevention, *1999 National Report* (Washington, DC: U.S. Government Printing Office, 1999), 90–91; *Roper v. Simmons*, 000 U.S. 03-633 (2005).

to juvenile justice officials. In a series of decisions (Figure 17.2), the U.S. Supreme Court expanded the rights of juveniles.

In the first of these cases, *Kent v. United States* (1966), the Supreme Court ruled that juveniles had the right to counsel at a hearing at which a juvenile judge may waive jurisdiction and pass the case to the adult court.

In re Gault (1967) extended due process rights to juveniles. Fifteen-year-old Gerald Gault had been sentenced to six years in a state training school for making a prank phone call. Had he been an adult, the maximum punishment for making such a call would have been a fine of $5 to $50 or imprisonment for two months at most. Gault was convicted and sentenced in an informal proceeding without being represented by counsel. The justices held that a child in a delinquency hearing must be given certain procedural rights, including notice of the charges, right to counsel, right to confront and cross-examine witnesses, and protection against self-incrimination. Writing for the majority, Justice Abe Fortas emphasized that due process rights and procedures have a place in juvenile justice: "Under our Constitution the condition of being a boy does not justify a kangaroo court."

The precedent-setting *Gault* decision was followed by a series of cases further defining the rights of juveniles. In the case of **In re Winship (1970)**, the

In re Gault (1967)
Juveniles have the right to counsel, to confront and examine accusers, and to have adequate notice of charges when confinement is a possible punishment.

In re Winship (1970)
The standard of proof beyond a reasonable doubt applies to juvenile delinquency proceedings.

McKeiver v. Pennsylvania (1971)
Juveniles do not have a constitutional right to a trial by jury.

Breed v. Jones (1975)
Juveniles cannot be found delinquent in juvenile court and then transferred to adult court without a hearing on the transfer; to do so violates the protection against double jeopardy.

status offense
Any act committed by a juvenile that is considered unacceptable for a child, such as truancy or running away from home, but that would not be a crime if it were committed by an adult.

Court held that proof must be established "beyond a reasonable doubt" and not on "a preponderance of the evidence" before a juvenile may be classified as a delinquent for committing an act that would be a crime if it were committed by an adult. The Court was not willing to give juveniles every due process right, however: It held in *McKeiver v. Pennsylvania* (1971) that "trial by jury in the juvenile court's adjudicative stage is not a constitutional requirement." But in *Breed v. Jones* (1975), the Court extended the protection against double jeopardy to juveniles by requiring that, before a case is adjudicated in juvenile court, a hearing must be held to determine if it should be transferred to the adult court.

Another area of change concerned **status offenses**—acts that are not illegal if committed by an adult; these include skipping school, running away from home, or living a "wayward, idle or dissolute life" (Feld, 1993: 203). In 1974 Congress passed the Juvenile Justice and Delinquency Prevention Act, which included provisions for taking status offenders out of correctional institutions. Since then, people have worked on diverting such children out of the system, reducing the possibility of incarceration, and rewriting status offense laws.

As juvenile crime rates continued to rise during the 1970s, the public began calling for tougher approaches in dealing with delinquents. In the 1980s, at the same time that stricter sanctions were imposed on adult offenders, juvenile justice policies shifted to crime control.

The Crime Control Period (1980–2005)

The public demands to "crackdown on crime" began in 1980. Legislators responded in part by changing the juvenile system. Greater attention began to be focused on repeat offenders, with policy makers calling for harsher punishment for juveniles who commit crimes.

Schall v. Martin (1984)
Juveniles can be held in preventive detention if there is concern that they may commit additional crimes while awaiting court action.

In *Schall v. Martin* (1984), the Supreme Court significantly departed from the trend toward increased juvenile rights. The Court confirmed that the general notion of *parens patriae* was a primary basis for the juvenile court, equal in importance to the Court's desire to protect the community from crime. Thus, juveniles may be held in preventive detention before trial if they are deemed a "risk" to the community.

The *Schall* decision reflects the ambivalence permeating the juvenile justice system. On one side are the liberal reformers, who call for increased procedural and substantive legal protections for juveniles accused of crime. On the other side are conservatives devoted to crime control policies and alarmed by the rise in juvenile crime.

Crime control policies brought many more juveniles to be tried in adult courts. As noted by Alex Kotlowitz, "the crackdown on children has gone well beyond those accused of violent crimes" (1994: 40). Data from the National Juvenile Court Data Archive show that delinquency cases waived to the adult criminal courts increased 83 percent from 1987 to 1994 (OJJDP, 2006: 186). In addition, some claim increased penalties on juvenile offenders disproportionately affect minority youth more than white youth (Feld, 1999; 2003).

"Kids Are Different" (2005–present)

Some observers believe that a new period in juvenile justice may be developing. In *Roper v. Simmons* (2005), the case discussed in Chapter 12, the United States Supreme Court ruled that executions were unconstitutional for crimes committed by those younger than 18 years of age. This important ruling arguably signaled a new era of juvenile justice. In *Roper*, the Court focused on the issue of culpability, and decided that juveniles were less culpable than adults due to a number of different factors related to physical and emotional development involving the growth and maturation process of the human brain (MacArthur Foundation, 2007b). Additional research into the development of juveniles indicates that intellectual maturity occurs at age 16, but other factors (such as relating to impulsiveness) are not fully developed until early adulthood (ages 24–26). This growing recognition of the developmental differences of teens provides a basis for new programs and proposed laws designed to re-emphasis treating juveniles differently than adults for purposes of treatment and punishment.

Current program trends aimed at helping juvenile offenders are rooted in the principles of rehabilitation and the prevention of delinquency. Such programs are not yet widespread or fully developed. For example, there are few low-cost substance abuse programs for juveniles outside of correctional institutions— therefore, a poor juvenile must be incarcerated to receive such assistance without significant financial expenses. Reducing drug use before it accelerates delinquency would seem to be the key to keeping juveniles crime-free and thus there is increasing interest in developing more programs that are accessible to youths in the community. Research is also focusing on the relationship between parents and children, and how parenting programs may help to keep kids out of the juvenile court (MacArthur Foundation, 2007a).

Once a popular method of trying juveniles, the use of judicial **waiver**, the process to waive juvenile court jurisdiction in order to move juveniles into adult court for prosecution and punishment, declined dramatically in 2001, reaching the lowest number of waived cases since 1985 (OJJDP, 2006: 186). This decrease in waiver mirrors the decrease in juvenile crime during that period (OJJDP, 2006: 64). Recent changes in a few states indicate that waiver is becoming less popular. Several states are considering the abolition of juvenile waiver by increasing their minimum age for adult trial to 18. The state of Colorado has recently abolished the use of "life without parole" as a sentence for juvenile offenders, setting a maximum sentence of 40 years for the most serious juvenile offenders.

The current movement for more lenient treatment of juveniles is still in its infancy. It is unknown how states will react to changes reflected in *Roper v. Simmons*, and there is still considerable support for the "get tough" stance toward older juveniles. In California, for example, legislators are attempting to count juvenile convictions as "strikes" under their "Three Strikes and You're Out" law mandating long sentences (*People v. Nguyen*, 2008). Opponents point out this violates the spirit of the *parens patriae* philosophy (Juvenile Law Center, 2008). In many places, the juvenile court, where the use of discretion and the desire to rehabilitate were previously uppermost goals, employs a system of rules and procedures similar to those in adult courts.

In spite of the increasingly tough policies directed at juvenile offenders in the late twentieth century, changes that occurred during the juvenile rights period continue to affect the system profoundly. Lawyers are now routinely present at court hearings and other stages of the process, adding a note of formality that was not present 30 years ago. Status offenders seldom end up in secure, punitive environments such as training schools. The juvenile justice system looks more like the adult justice system than it did, but it remains less formal. Its stated intention is also less harsh: to keep juveniles in the community whenever possible.

The United States has been criticized by other countries for our harsh treatment of juveniles; however, treatment of juvenile crime differs around the world. As an example, read the Comparative Perspective to examine how Norway deals with youth crime.

waiver
Procedure by which the juvenile court waives its jurisdiction and transfers a juvenile case to the adult criminal court.

COMPARATIVE PERSPECTIVE

The Hidden Juvenile Justice System in Norway

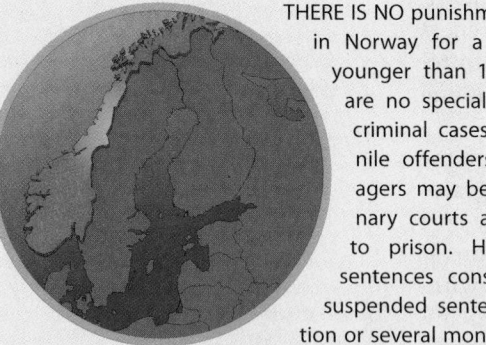

THERE IS NO punishment for crimes in Norway for a child who is younger than 15. Thus, there are no special courts to try criminal cases against juvenile offenders. Older teenagers may be tried in ordinary courts and sentenced to prison. However, most sentences consist of only a suspended sentence or probation or several months in an open prison.

In practice, the prosecutor transfers the juvenile case directly to a division of the "social office," the *barnevern*—literally, child protection. After a trial the judge may also refer the child to this office. Police evidence is turned over to the social workers, not for prosecution, but for "treatment."

The usual first step in treatment is that the *barnevern* takes emergency custody of the child and places the child in a youth home. If the parents or guardians do not give consent, the child welfare committee will consider arguments against placement. Here the question is the appropriate treatment for the child.

The *barnevern* is most often associated in the public mind with handling of cases of child abuse and neglect. In such a case, the board will turn over custody of the child to the social workers for placement in a foster home or youth home. Once the custody is removed from the parents, the burden of proof is on the parents to retain custody. Social workers are well aware of numerous such cases of recovering alcoholics who, even after recovery, have been unable to retain custody of their children.

In contrast to the U.S. juvenile court, the Norwegian model is wholly dominated by the social worker. The function of the judge is to preside over the hearing and to maintain proper legal protocol, but the child welfare office presents the evidence and directs the case. The five laypeople who constitute the [social welfare committee] are advised by the child welfare office well before the hearing of the "facts" of the case. Before the hearing, the youth will have been placed in a youth home or mental institution "on an emergency basis"; the parents' rights to custody will have already been terminated.

The hearing is thus a mere formality after the fact. There is overwhelming unanimity among members of the board and between

checkpoint

5. What was the function of a House of Refuge?
6. What were the major elements of the Illinois Juvenile Court Act of 1899?
7. What was the main point of the *In re Gault* decision?
8. How did the decline in juvenile crime in the 1990s affect juvenile justice policy?

THE JUVENILE JUSTICE SYSTEM

Juvenile justice operates through a variety of procedures in different states; even different counties within the same states vary. Because the offenses committed by juveniles are mostly violations of state laws, there is little federal involvement in the juvenile justice system. Despite internal differences, the juvenile justice system is characterized by two key factors: (1) the age of clients and (2) the categories of cases under juvenile court jurisdiction.

Age of Clients

Age normally determines whether a person is processed through the juvenile or adult justice system. The upper age limit for original juvenile court jurisdiction varies from 16–18. In 39 states and the District of Columbia, it is the 18th birthday; in 10 states, the 17th; and in the remaining 2 states, the 16th. In 45 states, judges have the discretion to transfer juveniles to adult courts through a waiver hearing. Figure 17.3 shows the age at which juveniles can be transferred to adult court.

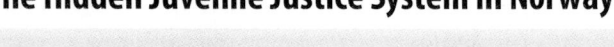

The website for the National Center for Juvenile Justice provides information on the differences in the juvenile justice systems in various states. To link to this website, go to *The American System of Criminal Justice* 12e companion site at academic.cengage.com/criminaljustice/cole.

the board and social worker administrators. The arguments of the clients and of their lawyers seem to "fall on deaf ears."

Proof of guilt brought before the committee will generally consist of a copy of the police report of the offenses admitted by the accused and a school report written by the principal after he or she has been informed of the lawbreaking. Reports by the *barnevern*-appointed psychologist and social worker are also included. The *barnevern*, in its statement, has summarized the reports from the point of view of its arguments (usually for placement). Otherwise, the reports are ignored.

The hearing itself is a far cry from standard courtroom procedure. The youth and his or her parents may address the board briefly. The attorney sums up the case for a return to the home. Expert witnesses may be called and questioned by the board concerning, for instance, their treatment recommendations.

Following the departure of the parties, the *barnevern* office presents what amounts to "the case for the prosecution." There is no opportunity to rebut the testimony and no opportunity for cross-examination.

Placement in an institution is typically for an indefinite period. No notice of the disposition of the matter is given to the press. This absence of public accountability may serve more to protect the social office than the child.

Children receive far harsher treatments than do adults for similar offenses. For instance, for a young adult first offender the typical penalty for thievery is a suspended sentence. A child, however, may languish in an institution for years for the same offense.

A *barnevern*'s first work ought to be to create the best possible childhood. However, the *barnevern* also has a control function in relation to both the parents and the child, and the controller often feels a stronger duty to the community than to the parents and child. The institutionalization of children with behavioral problems clearly reflects this social control function. Approximately half of the children under care of the child welfare committee were placed outside the home and the other half placed under protective watch.

The system of justice for children accused of crimes is therefore often very harsh. This is in sharp contrast to the criminal justice system for adults, which is strikingly lenient. Where punishment is called *treatment*, however, the right of the state can almost become absolute. The fact that the state is represented by social work administrators creates a sharp ethical conflict for those whose first duty is to the client.

What we see in Norway is a process of juvenile justice that has not changed substantially since the 1950s. Due to flaws within the system, including the lack of external controls, the best intentions of social workers "have gone awry." Where care and protection were intended, power and secrecy have prevailed. Juvenile justice in Norway today is the justice of America yesterday.

Source: Condensed from Katherine Van Wormer, "The Hidden Juvenile Justice System in Norway: A Journey Back in Time," *Federal Probation*, March 1990, pp. 57–61.

FIGURE 17.3

The youngest age at which juveniles may be transferred to adult criminal court by waiver of juvenile jurisdiction

The waiver provisions of states vary greatly, and no clear regional or other factor explains the differences.

Legend:
- No specific age
- 10 years
- 12 years
- 13 years
- 14 years
- 15 years

Source: National Center for Juvenile Justice, *State Juvenile Justice Profiles 2006* (http://www.ncjj.org).

Categories of Cases under Juvenile Court Jurisdiction

delinquent
A child who has committed an act that if committed by an adult would be a criminal act.

PINS
Acronym for "person(s) in need of supervision," a term that designates juveniles who are either status offenders or thought to be on the verge of trouble.

Four types of cases fall under the jurisdiction of the juvenile justice system: delinquency, status offenses, neglect, and dependency. Mixing together young criminals and children who suffer from their parents' inadequacies dates from the earliest years of juvenile justice.

Delinquent children have committed acts that if committed by an adult would be criminal—for example, auto theft, robbery, or assault. Juvenile courts handle about 1.6 million delinquency cases each year, 74 percent involving male delinquents, and 29 percent involving African Americans. Among the criminal charges brought before the juvenile court, 24 percent are for crimes against the person, 36 percent for property offenses, 12 percent for drug law violations, and 28 percent for public order offenses (Stahl, Finnegan, and Kang, 2007). Table 17.2 shows the distribution of delinquency cases that are referred to juvenile court.

Recall that status offenses are acts that are illegal only if they are committed by juveniles. Status offenders have not violated a penal code; instead they are charged with being ungovernable or incorrigible: as runaways, truants, or **PINS** (persons in need of supervision). Status offenders make up about 10 percent of the juvenile court caseload. Although female offenders account for only 26 percent of delinquency cases, they make up 44 percent of the status offense cases (Stahl, 2008).

Some states do not distinguish between delinquent offenders and status offenders; they label both as juvenile delinquents. Those judged to be ungovernable and those judged to be robbers may be sent to the same correctional institution.

Beginning in the early 1960s, many state legislatures attempted to distinguish status offenders and to exempt them from a criminal record. In states that have decriminalized status offenses, juveniles who participate in these activities may now be classified as dependent children and placed in the care of child-protective agencies.

Juvenile justice also deals with problems of neglect and dependency—situations in which children are viewed as being hurt through no fault of their own because their parents have failed to provide a proper environment for them. People see the state's proper role as acting as a parent to a child whose own parents are unable or unwilling to provide proper care. Illinois, for example, defines a **neglected child** as one who is receiving inadequate care because of some action or inaction of his or her parents. This may include not being sent to school, not receiving medical care, being abandoned, living in an injurious environment, or not receiving some other care necessary for the child's well-being. A **dependent child** either has no parent or guardian or is receiving inadequate care because of the physical or mental disability of the parent. The law governing neglected and dependent children is

TABLE 17.2	Distribution of Delinquency Cases Referred to Juvenile Court	
About 90 percent of the juvenile court caseload involves criminal charges against youths.		
Percentage of Total Cases Referred, 2004		
24%	**Crimes against persons**	
	Homicide	Less than 1%
	Forcible rape	Less than 1%
	Robbery	1%
	Aggravated assault	3
	Simple assault	17
	Other personal offenses	2
	Other violent sex offenses	1
36%	**Property crimes**	
	Burglary	6%
	Larceny/theft	17
	Motor vehicle theft	2
	Arson	Less than 1%
	Vandalism	6
	Trespassing	3
	Stolen property offenses	1
	Other property offenses	1
12%	**Drug violations**	
28%	**Public order offenses**	
	Weapons offenses	2%
	Obstruction of justice	13
	Disorderly conduct	7
	Liquor law violations	2
	Nonviolent sex offenses	1
	Other public order offenses	2

Source: Office of Juvenile Justice and Delinquency Prevention, *Delinquency Cases in Juvenile Courts, 2004* (Washington, DC: U.S. Government Printing Office, February 2008).

broad and includes situations in which the child is viewed as a victim of adult behavior.

Nationally about 75 percent of the cases referred to the juvenile courts are delinquency cases, 20 percent of which are status offenses. Twenty percent are dependency and neglect cases, and about 5 percent involve special proceedings, such as adoption. The system, then, deals with both criminal and noncriminal cases. Often juveniles who have done nothing wrong are categorized, either officially or in the public mind, as delinquents. In some states little effort is made in detention facilities or in social service agencies to separate the classes of juveniles prior to their judicial hearings.

neglected child
A child who is receiving inadequate care because of some action or inaction of his or her parents.

dependent child
A child who has no parent or guardian or whose parents cannot give proper care.

checkpoint

9. What are the jurisdictional criteria for the juvenile court?

THE JUVENILE JUSTICE PROCESS

Underlying the juvenile justice system is the philosophy that police, judges, and correctional officials should focus primarily on the interests of the child. Prevention of delinquency is the system's justification for intervening in the lives of juveniles who are involved in either status or criminal offenses.

In theory at least, juvenile proceedings are to be conducted in a nonadversarial environment. The juvenile court is to be a place where the judge, social workers, clinicians, and probation officers work together to diagnose the child's problem and select a treatment program to attack that problem.

Juvenile justice is a bureaucracy based on an ideology of social work. It is staffed primarily by people who think of themselves as members of the helping professions. Not even the recent emphasis on crime control and punishment has removed the treatment philosophy from most juvenile justice arenas. However, political pressures and limits on resources may stymie the implementation of this philosophy by focusing on the punishment of offenders rather than the prevention of delinquency, even though the public is willing to pay more for prevention programs and rehabilitation than continued use of incarceration (Nagin et al., 1997).

Like the adult system, juvenile justice functions within a context of exchange relationships between officials of various government and private agencies that influence decisions. The juvenile court must deal not only with children and their parents, but also with patrol officers, probation officers, welfare officials, social workers, psychologists, and the heads of treatment institutions all of whom have their own goals, perceptions of delinquency, and concepts of treatment.

Figure 17.4 outlines the sequence of steps that are taken from the point of police investigation through to correctional disposition. As you examine this figure, compare the procedures with those of the criminal justice system for adults. Note the various options available to decision makers and the extensive discretion that they may exercise.

Police Interface

Many police departments, especially in cities, have special juvenile units. The juvenile officer is often selected and trained to relate to youths, knows much about relevant legal issues, and is sensitive to the special needs of young offenders. This officer also serves as an important link between the police and other

FIGURE 17.4

The juvenile justice system
Decision makers have more options for the disposition of juvenile offenders, compared with options in the criminal justice system for adults.

Source: National Advisory Commission on Criminal Justice Standards and Goals, *Report of the Task Force on Juvenile Justice and Delinquency Prevention* (Washington, DC: Law Enforcement Assistance Administration, 1976).

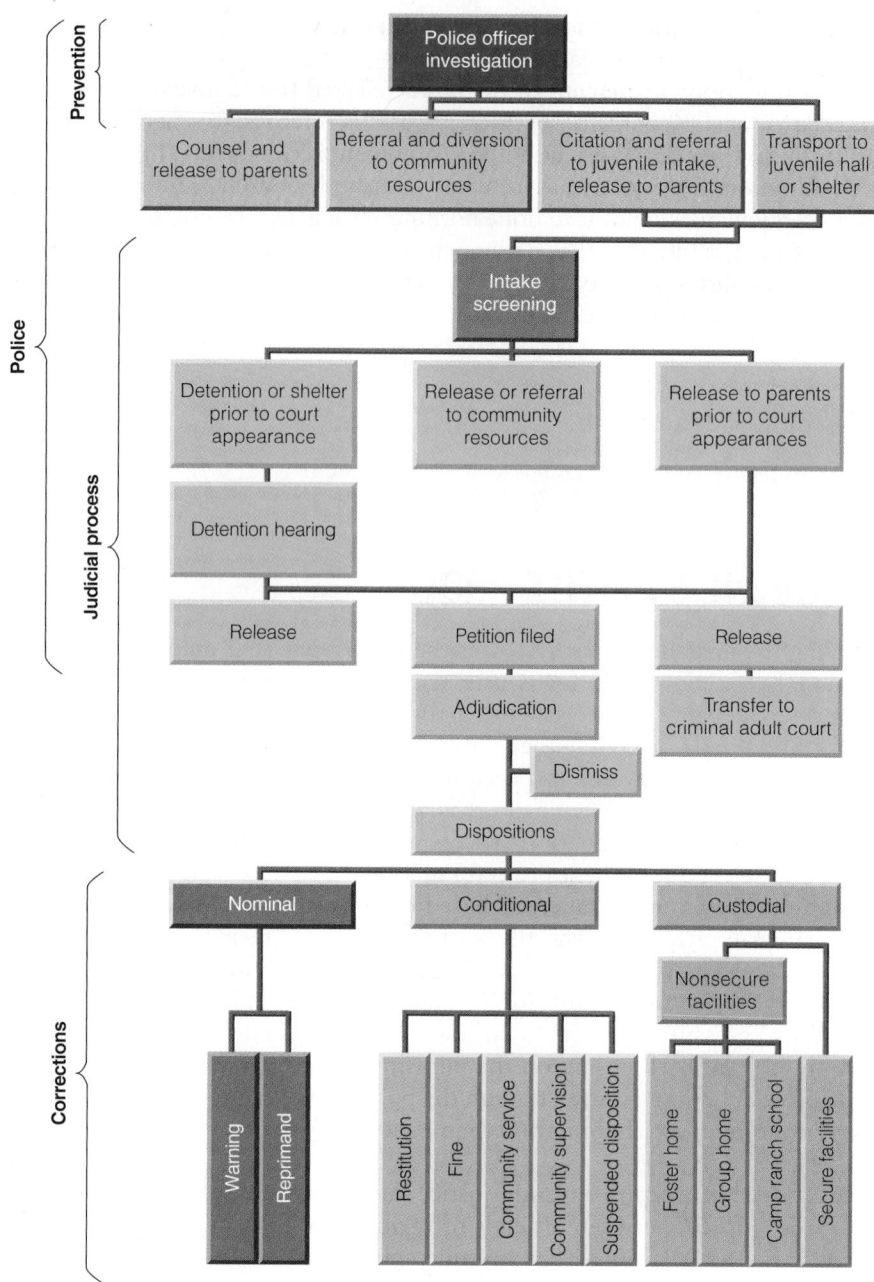

You can find information on school resource officers at the website of the Center for Prevention of School Violence. To link to this website, go to *The American System of Criminal Justice* 12e companion site at academic .cengage.com/criminaljustice/cole.

community institutions, such as schools and other organizations serving young people. Some communities hire *school resource officers*, who provide counseling and a security presence in school buildings.

Most complaints against juveniles are brought by the police, although an injured party, school officials, and even the parents can initiate them as well. The police must make three major decisions with regard to the processing of juveniles:

1. Whether to take the child into custody

2. Whether to request that the child be detained following apprehension

3. Whether to refer the child to court

The police exercise enormous discretion in these decisions. They do extensive screening and make informal assessments in the street and at the station house. In communities and neighborhoods where the police have developed close relationships with the residents or where policy dictates, the police may deal with violations by giving warnings to the juveniles and notifying their parents. Figure 17.5 shows the disposition of juveniles taken into police custody.

Initial decisions about what to do with a suspected offender are influenced by such factors as the predominant attitude of the community; the officer's attitude toward the juvenile, the juvenile's family, the offense, and the court; and the officer's conception of his or her own role. The disposition of juvenile cases at the arrest stage also relies on the seriousness of the offense, the child's prior record, and his or her demeanor. To summarize, several key factors influence how the police dispose of a case of juvenile delinquency:

1. The seriousness of the offense

2. The willingness of the parents to cooperate and to discipline the child

3. The child's behavioral history as reflected in school and police records

4. The extent to which the child and the parents insist on a formal court hearing

5. The local political and social norms concerning dispositions in such cases

6. The officer's beliefs and attitudes

In dealing with juveniles, police often confront issues concerning the *Miranda* warnings and the *Mapp* unreasonable search and seizure rulings. Although the language of these decisions is not explicit, most jurisdictions now provide the *Miranda* protections. But questions remain as to the ability of juveniles to waive these rights. In 1979, the Supreme Court ruled in *Fare v. Michael C.* that a child may waive his or her rights to an attorney and to protections against self-incrimination. But the Court said that juvenile court judges must evaluate the totality of circumstances under which the minor made these decisions, to ensure that they were voluntary.

On the issue of unreasonable searches and seizures prohibited by the Fourth Amendment, the Court has not been as forthcoming. State courts interpreted *Gault* to extend these provisions, but in 1985 the Supreme Court ruled in *New Jersey v. T. L. O.* that school officials can search students and their lockers. The justices recognized that children do have Fourth Amendment rights, yet a search could be viewed as reasonable if (1) it is based on a suspicion of lawbreaking and (2) it is required to maintain order, safety, and discipline in the school.

Faced with problems of drug use and students carrying weapons in the public schools, administrators have taken steps to enforce rules so as to increase security. This has led to conflicts concerning the right to privacy versus school safety. In 1995 the Supreme Court said certain students, such as athletes, could be subject to random drug testing. The case, ***Vernonia School District v. Acton*** (1995), concerned a seventh grader's parents who refused to sign a urinalysis consent form. As a result their son, James Acton, was kept off of the football team. The court ruled that the testing was constitutional in the interest of ensuring a safe learning environment even though the student had not exhibited suspicious behavior. The Supreme Court later expanded school officials' authority to impose drug testing by permitting schools to require students to submit to random drug testing in order to participate in nonsports extracurricular activities, such as band and choir (*Board of Education v. Earls*, 2002).

Although young people commit many serious crimes, the juvenile function of police work is concerned largely with order maintenance. In most incidents of this sort, the law is ambiguous, and blame cannot easily be assigned. Many

FIGURE 17.5

Disposition of juveniles taken into police custody

The police have discretion in the disposition of juvenile arrest cases. What factors can influence how a case is disposed?

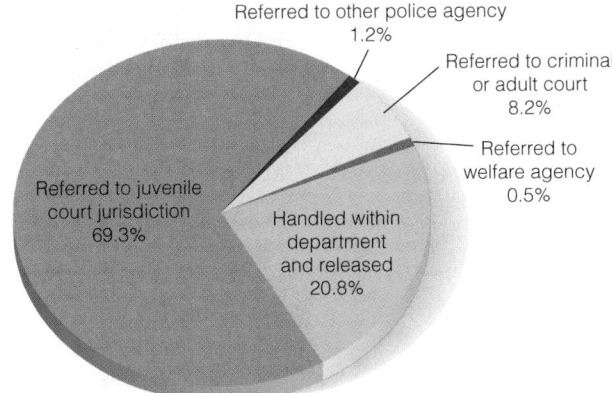

Source: Federal Bureau of Investigation, *Uniform Crime Reports 2006*. (Washington, DC: U.S. Government Printing Office, 2007), Table 68.

Fare v. Michael C. (1979)

By examining the totality of circumstances, trial court judges must evaluate the voluntariness of juveniles' waiving their rights to an attorney and to protections against self-incrimination.

New Jersey v. T. L. O. (1985)

School officials may search a student if they have a reasonable suspicion that the search will produce evidence that a school rule or a criminal rule has been violated.

Vernonia School District v. Acton (1995)

To ensure a safe learning environment, school officials may require random drug testing of students involved in extracurricular school sports teams..

offenses committed by juveniles that involve physical or monetary damage are minor infractions: breaking windows, hanging around the business district, disturbing the peace, public sexual behavior, and shoplifting. Here the function of the investigating officer is not so much to solve crimes as to handle the often legally uncertain complaints involving juveniles. The officer seeks both to satisfy the complainant and to keep the youth from future trouble. Given this emphasis on settling cases within the community—instead of strictly enforcing the law—the police power to arrest is a weapon that can be used to deter juveniles from criminal activity and to encourage them to conform to the law.

Intake Screening at the Court

The juvenile court processing of delinquency cases begins with a referral in the form of a petition, not an arrest warrant as in the adult system. When a petition is filed, an intake hearing is held, over which a hearing officer presides. During this stage, the officer determines whether the alleged facts are sufficient for the juvenile court to take jurisdiction or whether some other action would be in the child's best interest.

diversion
The process of screening children out of the juvenile justice system without a decision by the court.

Nationally, 43 percent of all referrals are disposed of at this stage, without formal processing by a judge. **Diversion** is the process of screening children out of the system without a decision by the court (Stahl et al., 2007). In 47 percent of these cases, the charges are dismissed; another one-third or so are diverted to an informal probation, 6 percent are placed in a mental health facility or other treatment facility, and 21 percent are dealt with through some agreed-on alternative sanction (OJJDP, 2003b: 2).

Pretrial Procedures

When a decision is made to refer the case to the court (57 percent of cases), the court holds an initial hearing. Here, the juveniles are informed of their rights and told that if a plea is given it must be voluntary.

detention hearing
A hearing by the juvenile court to determine if a juvenile is to be detained or released prior to adjudication.

If the juvenile is to be detained pending trial, most states require a **detention hearing**, which determines if the youth is to be released to a parent or guardian or to be held in a detention facility until adjudication. Some children are detained to keep them from committing other crimes while awaiting trial. Others are held to protect them from the possibility of harm from gang members or parents. Still others are held because if released they will likely not appear in court as required. Nationally, about 20 percent of all delinquency cases involve detention between referral to the juvenile court and disposition of the case (Stahl et al., 2007).

The conditions in many detention facilities are poor; abuse is often reported. In some rural areas, juveniles continue to be detained in adult jails even though the federal government has pressed states to hold youths in separate facilities. In 2003, the city of Baltimore, Maryland, unveiled a new juvenile detention facility, meant to expedite juvenile cases and centralize services to delinquent youth. The new facility was recently termed a "monstrosity," with poor lines of sight (meaning officers cannot easily observe and supervise the juvenile detainees), overcrowding, and increasing rates of violence within its walls (Bykowicz, 2008).

Based on the belief that detaining youth accelerates their delinquent behaviors, some jurisdictions have attempted to stem the tide of rising numbers of juveniles in detention. The city of Indianapolis has implemented a program to increase the use of diversion and send more youths home to live with their families while awaiting trial. This attempt has reduced both the number of incarcerated youth and delinquency rates (Murray, 2008).

Transfer (Waiver) to Adult Court

In 1997, an 11-year-old boy named Nathaniel Abraham shot and killed a man outside a convenience store in Pontiac, Michigan. At the time, Michigan law specified no minimum age for transfer of a juvenile to adult court. Nathaniel's case was waived to adult court and he stood trial for the homicide. The jury, however, refused to charge him with the crime of homicide in the first degree, which would have necessitated incarceration in an adult prison. Instead, they found him guilty of second-degree homicide, allowing the judge to use his discretion to place Nathaniel in a juvenile facility. Abraham's case attracted national attention because it highlighted the difficulty of deciding what to do with children and teens who commit offenses as serious as those committed by the most violent adult offenders. As you read "Civic Engagement: Your Role in the System," consider how you might react if you were a juror in regular criminal court considering the case of a youthful defendant.

One of the first decisions to be made after a juvenile is referred is whether a case should be transferred to the criminal (adult) justice system. In 45 states, juvenile court judges may waive their jurisdiction. This means that after considering the seriousness of the charge, the age of the juvenile, and the prospects of rehabilitation, the judge can transfer the case to adult court. In 29 states, certain violent crimes such as murder, rape, and armed robbery are excluded by law from the jurisdiction of the juvenile courts (NIJ, 1997). In 1970, only three states allowed prosecutors the authority to decide whether to file in adult or juvenile court. Today, 15 states give prosecutors the authority to do so (Snyder & Sickmund, 2006). Critics question whether prosecutors will "make better informed and more appropriate 'criminal adulthood' decisions than would judges in an adversarial waiver hearing" (Feld, 2004: 599). See "What Americans Think" for a look at public attitudes about transferring juveniles to the adult court.

Since a "tougher" approach to juvenile crime took hold in the 1970s, the number of cases transferred has increased dramatically. Several states expanded their ability to transfer juveniles by excluding certain crimes from juvenile court jurisdiction, or lowering their minimum age for transfer to adult court. Several states specify no minimum age for certain offenses (note the number of states in Figure 17.3 that can waive a juvenile regardless of his or her age).

However, waived cases still represent less than 1 percent (about 9,000) of delinquency cases. The likelihood of waiver varies by offense, offender age, and offender race. In all, violent offenders make up the majority of those transferred to adult court (43 percent), followed by property offenders (33 percent), drug offenders (15 percent) and public order offenders (9 percent). In addition, African American youths are more likely to be waived than white youth, although this is partially due to differences in offending patterns (Stahl et al., 2007). A study of 40 large urban counties found that nearly two-thirds of juvenile felony defendants in adult court were charged with a violent crime, compared with one-quarter of adult defendants (BJS, 2003g: 1).

One result of the increased use of the waiver is that more juveniles are being sent to adult state prisons. Between 1985 and 1997, the number doubled—from 3,400 to 7,400 (BJS, 2000f). Through 2005, the number of youths in prison aged 17 or younger declined only to increase again in 2006 (BJS, 2007b: 4). Sixty-nine percent of inmates younger than age 18 are in prison for violent offenses (BJS, 2000h: 1).

Supporters of waiving juveniles to adult court argue that serious crime deserves a serious punishment. Critics of the policies claim that waiver subverts the intent of the juvenile justice system, and exposes juvenile offenders to harsh

civic engagement
your role in the system

Imagine that you were a juror in the case of Nathaniel Abraham. *Make a list of arguments favoring and opposing convicting him as an adult defendant. How do you think you would vote during the jury's deliberations?* Then read about a study that indicates jurors may become biased in favor of conviction when they learn that a youthful defendant in adult court has been sent there by the juvenile court. To link to this website, go to *The American System of Criminal Justice* 12e companion site at academic.cengage.com/criminaljustice/cole.

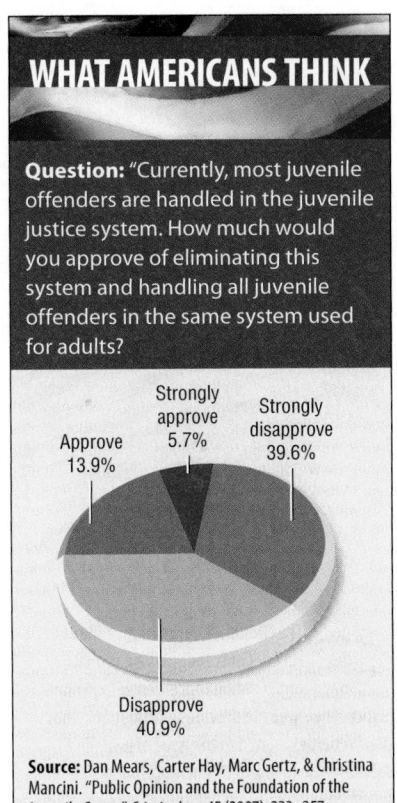

WHAT AMERICANS THINK

Question: "Currently, most juvenile offenders are handled in the juvenile justice system. How much would you approve of eliminating this system and handling all juvenile offenders in the same system used for adults?

- Strongly approve 5.7%
- Strongly disapprove 39.6%
- Approve 13.9%
- Disapprove 40.9%

Source: Dan Mears, Carter Hay, Marc Gertz, & Christina Mancini. "Public Opinion and the Foundation of the Juvenile Court." *Criminology* 45 (2007): 223–257.

Alex King, age 13, is escorted into a Florida courtroom where he and his 14-year-old brother Derek were convicted of beating their father to death with a baseball bat as he slept. They were sentenced to, respectively, 7- and 8-year sentences of imprisonment. Should youthful offenders who commit such serious crimes always be tried as adults and given the same punishments as adults?

AP Images/Phil Coale

conditions in adult prisons—where they are susceptible to physical and sexual victimization (DeJong and Merrill, 2000). In addition, those juveniles tried in adult courts are more likely to reoffend after release (MacArthur Foundation, 2007c). There is also evidence that increased use of waiver has had no effect on juvenile crime rates (Steiner and Wright, 2006; Steiner, Hemmons, and Bell, 2006).

Transferring juveniles to be tried in the adult criminal courts remains controversial. Many states now place on the youth the burden of proving that he or she is amenable to treatment in the juvenile instead of the adult court. Further, research has shown that offenders transferred to adult court were rearrested more frequently upon release than similar offenders handled by the juvenile court (Winner et al., 1997). Thus, the question remains about the benefits, if any, of juvenile waiver.

The National Council of Juvenile and Family Court Judges is a national organization concerned with juvenile justice. Their website provides information about their activities related to the issue of juvenile delinquency. To link to this website, go to *The American System of Criminal Justice* 12e companion site at academic.cengage.com/criminaljustice/cole.

Adjudication

Juvenile courts deal with almost 1.6 million delinquency cases each year (Stahl et al., 2007). *Adjudication* is the trial stage of the juvenile justice process. If the child has not admitted to the charges and the case has not been transferred to the adult court, an adjudication hearing is held to determine the facts in the case and, if appropriate, label the juvenile as "delinquent."

The Supreme Court's decision in *Gault* and other due process rulings mandated changes that have altered the philosophy and actions of the juvenile court.

Contemporary juvenile proceedings are more formal than those of the past, although still more informal than adult courts. The parents and child must receive copies of petitions with specific charges; counsel may be present, and free counsel can be appointed if the juvenile cannot pay; witnesses can be cross-examined; and a transcript of the proceedings must be kept.

As with other Supreme Court decisions, local practice may differ sharply from the procedures spelled out in the high court's rulings. Juveniles and their parents often waive their rights in response to suggestions from the judge or probation officer. The lower social status of the offender's parents, the intimidating atmosphere of the court, and judicial hints that the outcome will be more favorable if a lawyer is not present are reasons the procedures outlined in *Gault* might not be followed. The litany of "getting treatment," "doing what's right for the child," and "working out a just solution" may sound enticing, especially to people who are unfamiliar with the intricacies of formal legal procedures. In practice, then, juveniles still lack many of the protections given to adult offenders. Some of the differences between the juvenile and adult criminal justice systems are listed in Table 17.3.

The increased concern about crime has given prosecuting attorneys a more prominent part in the system. In keeping with the traditional child-saver philosophy, prosecuting attorneys rarely appeared in juvenile court prior to the *Gault* decision. Now that a defense attorney is present, the state often uses legal counsel as well. In many jurisdictions, prosecutors are assigned to deal specifically with juvenile cases. Their functions are to advise the intake officer, administer diversion programs, negotiate pleas, and act as an advocate during judicial proceedings.

TABLE 17.3   The Adult and Juvenile Criminal Justice Systems

Compare the basic elements of the adult and juvenile systems. To what extent does a juvenile have the same rights as an adult? Are the different decision-making processes necessary because a juvenile is involved?

	Adult System	Juvenile System
Philosophical assumptions	Decisions made as result of adversarial system in context of due process rights	Decisions made as result of inquiry into needs of juvenile within context of some due process elements
Jurisdiction	Violations of criminal law	Violations of criminal law, status offenses, neglect, dependency
Primary sanctioning goals	Retribution, deterrence, rehabilitation	Retribution, rehabilitation
Official discretion	Widespread	Widespread
Entrance	Official action of arrest, summons, or citation	Official action, plus referral by school, parents, other sources
Role of prosecuting and defense attorneys	Required and formalized	Sometimes required; less structured; poor role definition
Adjudication	Procedural rules of evidence in public jury trial required	Less formal structure to rules of evidence and conduct of trial; no right to public trial or jury in most states
Treatment programs	Run primarily by public agencies	Broad use of private and public agencies
Application of Bill of Rights amendments		
Fourth: Unreasonable searches and seizures	Applicable	Applicable
Fifth: Double jeopardy	Applicable	Applicable (re: waiver to adult court)
Self-incrimination	Applicable (*Miranda* warnings)	Applicable
Sixth: Right to counsel	Applicable	Applicable
Public trial	Applicable	Applicable in less than half of states
Trial by jury	Applicable	Applicable in less than half of states
Fourteenth: Right to treatment	Not applicable	Applicable

Juvenile proceedings and court records have traditionally remained closed to the public to protect the child's privacy and potential for rehabilitation. As such, judges in the adult courts usually do not have access to juvenile records. This means that people who have already served time on juvenile probation or in institutions are erroneously perceived to be first offenders when they are processed for crimes as adults. Some people argue that adult courts should have access to juvenile records and that young criminals should be treated more severely than adults to deter them from future illegal activity.

Disposition

If the court makes a finding of delinquency, the judge will schedule a dispositional hearing to decide what action should be taken. Typically, before passing sentence the judge receives a predispositional report prepared by a probation officer. Similar to a presentence report, it serves to assist the judge in deciding on a disposition that is in the best interests of the child and is consistent with the treatment plan developed by the probation officer.

The court finds most juveniles to be delinquent at trial, because the intake and pretrial processes normally filter out cases in which a law violation cannot be proved. Besides dismissal, four other choices are available: (1) probation, (2) alternative dispositions, (3) custodial care, and (4) community treatment.

Juvenile court advocates have traditionally believed that rehabilitation is the only goal of the sanction imposed on young people. For most of the twentieth century, judges sentenced juveniles to indeterminate sentences so that correctional administrators could decide when release was appropriate. As in the adult criminal justice system, indeterminate sentences and unbridled discretion in juvenile justice have faced attack during the last three decades. Several states have tightened the sentencing discretion of judges, especially with regard to serious offenses. The state of Washington, for example, has adopted a determinate sentencing law for juveniles. In other states, a youth can be transferred more readily than before to the adult court for adjudication and sentencing. Jurisdictions such as the District of Columbia, Colorado, Florida, and Virginia have passed laws requiring mandatory sentences for certain offenses committed by juveniles.

The concept of restorative justice has been extended to juveniles. At the Red Hook Youth Court in New York, a 15-year-old arrested for spraying graffiti sits before a jury of his peers and a 16-year-old acting as the judge. The court deals with minor offenses, often where formal charges have not yet been brought. Officials say that 85 percent of the offenders complete restitution, ranging from community service to letters of apology. Is this an effective way to deal with youthful offenders?

© Joe Tabacca

Corrections

Many aspects of juvenile corrections resemble those of adult corrections. Both systems, for example, mix rehabilitative and retributive sanctions. However, juvenile corrections differs in many respects from the adult system. Some of the differences flow from the *parens patriae* concept and the youthful, seemingly innocent people with whom the system deals. At times, the differences show up in formal operational policies, such as contracting for residential treatment. At other times, the differences appear only in the style and culture of an operation, as they do in juvenile probation.

One predominant aim of juvenile corrections is to avoid unnecessary incarceration. When children are removed from their homes, they are inevitably damaged emotionally, even when the home life is harsh and abusive, because they are forced to abandon the only environment they know. Further, placing children in institutions has labeling effects; the children may perceive themselves as bad because they have received punitive treatment, and children who see themselves as "bad" may behave that way. Finally, treatment is believed to be more effective when the child is living in a normal, supportive home environment. For these reasons, noninstitutional forms of corrections are seen as highly desirable in juvenile justice and have proliferated in recent years. See "Doing Your Part" for a novel program emphasizing restorative justice for minor violations.

Probation

In 63 percent of cases, the juvenile delinquent is placed on probation and released to the custody of a parent or guardian (Stahl et al., 2007). Often the judge orders that the delinquent undergo some form of education or counseling. The delinquent can also be required to pay a fine or make restitution while on probation.

Juvenile probation operates in much the same way that adult probation does, and sometimes the same agency carries it out. In two respects, however, juvenile probation can differ markedly from adult probation. First, juvenile probation officers have smaller caseloads. Second, the juvenile probation officer is often infused with the sense that the offender is worthwhile and can change and that the job is valuable and enjoyable. Such attitudes make for greater creativity than adult probation officers usually exhibit. For example, a young offender can be

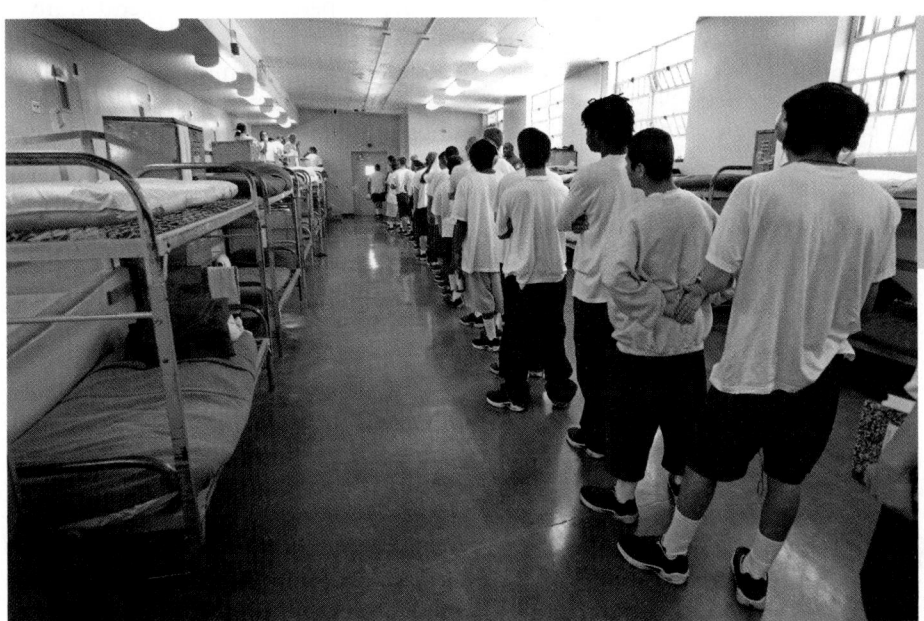

Youths in a sex offender treatment program walk in a single-file line to the exercise yard at California's Close Youth Correctional Facility. Do such crowded, stark surroundings provide the best environment for implementing effective treatment programs for juvenile offenders?

AP Images/Steve Yeater

DOING YOUR PART

Teen Court

TIM NADON, a social studies teacher at Plymouth High School in Michigan, volunteers his time to arrange for his students to serve as jurors in criminal cases. Very few of his students are actually old enough to be called for jury duty at the local courthouse. Instead, they serve as jurors in a Teen Court program that enables them to determine appropriate punishments for their peers who have committed misdemeanors and petty offenses. More than six hundred Teen Court programs exist throughout the United States. The defendants are teenagers who have committed a variety of lesser offenses, including theft, minor assault, vandalism, alcohol possession, truancy, and traffic violations.

The defendants must be first offenders who agree to plead guilty. Juvenile probation officers can then refer them to the local Teen Court where a jury of teenage volunteers, who have been trained in the Teen Court's processes and goals, will determine their punishments. In many Teen Courts, teenagers who have gained experience as jurors later serve as "attorneys" in these cases, either arguing for specific punishments as "prosecutors" or serving as "defense attorneys" who support the defendant's explanation for why the offenses occurred. The jury carefully questions the defendant and then reaches a unanimous decision about punishment.

Punishments often emphasize restorative justice by requiring community service and restitution. Defendants may also be required to write letters of apology to victims and essays that will force them to think about and learn from their experiences. An adult volunteer, often a local attorney, serves as the "judge" who ensures that the proceedings remain serious and that fair procedures are followed.

These courts are relatively informal in the sense that they do not follow formal trial rules, but they are serious affairs in which the defendant and other participants are expected to be well-dressed and respectful of the process.

Sources: Drawn from Sheri Hall, "Teen Court Changes Venue," *Detroit Free Press*, August 21, 2002 (http://www.freep.com); Sharon J. Zehner, "Teen Court," *FBI Law Enforcement Bulletin*, March 1997 (http://www.fbi.gov/publications).

Researching the Internet

The Teen Court program in Knox County, Illinois, provides detailed information about its operations on its website. To link to this website, go to *The American System of Criminal Justice* 12e companion site at academic.cengage.com/criminaljustice/cole.

paired with a "big brother" or "big sister" from the community.

Intermediate Sanctions

Although probation and commitment to an institution are the system's two main dispositional options, intermediate sanctions served in the community now account for 15 percent of adjudicated juvenile cases (Stahl et al., 2007). Judges have wide discretion to warn, to fine, to arrange for restitution, to order community service, to refer a juvenile for treatment at either a public or a private community agency, or to withhold judgment.

Judges sometimes suspend judgment—that is, continue a case without a finding—when they wish to put a youth under supervision but are reluctant to apply the label "delinquent." The judge holds off on giving a definitive judgment but can give one should a youth misbehave while under the informal supervision of a probation officer or parents.

Custodial Care

Of those juveniles declared delinquent, 22 percent are placed in public or private facilities. The placement rate of juveniles over time has decreased from about one in three adjudicated juveniles in 1989, to about one in five juveniles in 2004 (Stahl et al., 2007) The national incarceration rate per 100,000 juveniles aged 10–18 is 307—this includes juveniles held both prior to trial and as a sentence of incarceration. Like the adult incarceration rate, these rates vary widely among the states, with the highest rate in the District of Columbia (625) and the lowest in Vermont (72) (Sickmund et al., 2006: 201). Nationally, 69 percent of incarcerated juveniles are held in public facilities, with the remainder in private facilities (Sickmund et al., 2006: 218). See "What Americans Think" for a picture of attitudes toward prisons for juveniles.

Policy makers are concerned about the overrepresentation of incarcerated African American juveniles. One study (Figure 17.6) found that the disproportionate confinement of minority juveniles often stems from disparity at the early stages of case processing. Thus, if more African American juveniles are detained than others, more of them will likely be adjudicated in juvenile court, and more placed in residential facilities. Some research suggests that juvenile court actors have biased perceptions of minority juveniles, and thus they receive more severe treatment at all levels of the juvenile justice system (Leiber and Mack, 2003). Others have indicated the importance of examining both race and gender when analyzing court outcomes, as girls are generally treated more leniently than boys in the justice system (Guevara, Herz, and Spohn, 2006).

Institutions for juvenile offenders are classified as either nonsecure or secure. *Nonsecure* placements (foster homes, group homes, camps, ranches, or

FIGURE 17.6

Representation of African American juveniles in the juvenile justice system compared with their proportion of the population

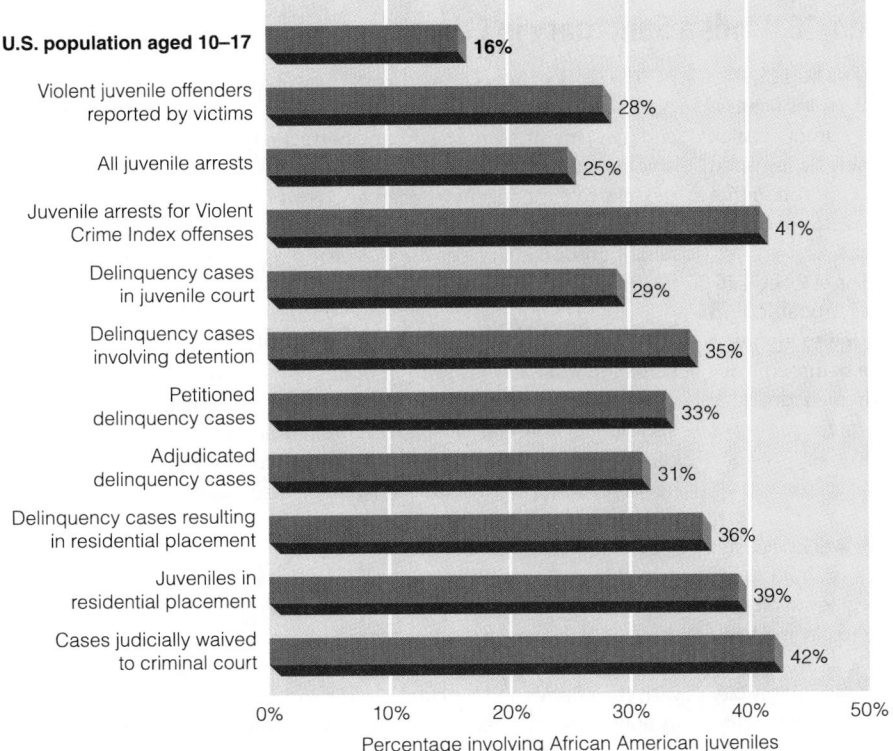

Source: M. Sickmund, "Juveniles in Corrections," in *National Report Series Bulletin* (Washington, DC: Office of Juvenile Justice and Delinquency Prevention, June 2004), 12.

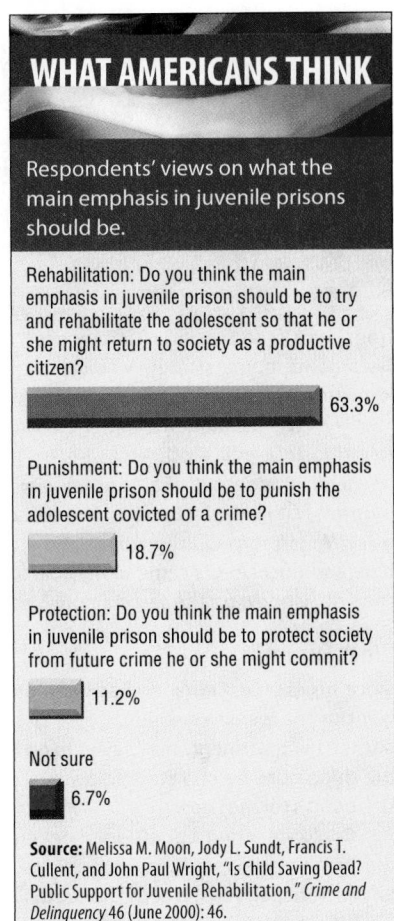

WHAT AMERICANS THINK

Respondents' views on what the main emphasis in juvenile prisons should be.

Rehabilitation: Do you think the main emphasis in juvenile prison should be to try and rehabilitate the adolescent so that he or she might return to society as a productive citizen?

63.3%

Punishment: Do you think the main emphasis in juvenile prison should be to punish the adolescent covicted of a crime?

18.7%

Protection: Do you think the main emphasis in juvenile prison should be to protect society from future crime he or she might commit?

11.2%

Not sure

6.7%

Source: Melissa M. Moon, Jody L. Sundt, Francis T. Cullen, and John Paul Wright, "Is Child Saving Dead? Public Support for Juvenile Rehabilitation," *Crime and Delinquency* 46 (June 2000): 46.

schools) include a significant number of nonoffenders youths referred for abuse, neglect, or emotional disturbance. *Secure* facilities, such as reform schools and training schools, deal with juveniles who have committed serious violations of the law and have serious personal problems. Most secure juvenile facilities are small, designed to hold 40 or fewer residents. However, many states have at least one facility holding two hundred or more hard-core delinquents who are allowed limited freedom. Because the residents are younger and somewhat more volatile than adults, behavioral control is often an everyday issue, and fights and aggression are common. Poor management practices, such as those described in "A Question of Ethics" at the end of this chapter, can lead to difficult situations.

Boot camps for juvenile offenders saw a growth spurt in the early 1990s. By 1997, more than 27,000 teenagers were passing through 54 camps in 34 states annually. However, as with boot camps for adults, the results have not been promising. A national study shows that recidivism among boot camp attendees ranges from 64 percent to 75 percent, slightly higher than for youths sentenced to adult prisons (*New York Times*, January 2, 2000: WK3). States are rethinking their policies, with many closing their programs.

A national survey of public custodial institutions in 1999 showed that 36 percent of juveniles were incarcerated for violent offenses, 60 percent used drugs regularly, and 50 percent said that a family member had been in prison at some time in the past. Also, 88 percent of the residents were male, only 30 percent had grown up in a household with both parents, and the percentages of African Americans (40 percent)

FIGURE 17.7

Juveniles in public facilities: Types of offenses

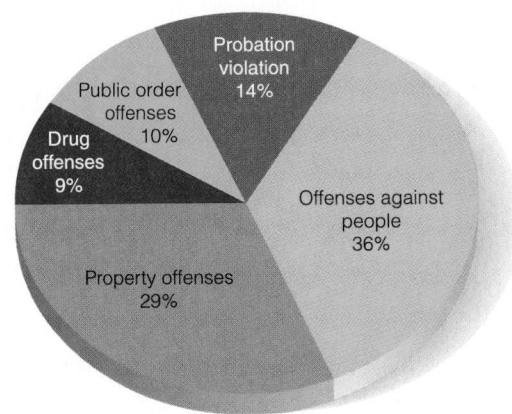

Source: M. Sickmund, "Juveniles in Corrections," in *National Report Series Bulletin* (Washington, DC: Office of Juvenile Justice and Delinquency Prevention, June 2004), 6.

CLOSE UP

Fernando, 16, Finds a Sanctuary in Crime

FERNANDO MORALES WAS glad to discuss his life as a 16-year-old drug dealer. He had recently escaped from Long Lane School, a [Connecticut] correctional institution that became his home after he was caught with $1,100 worth of heroin known as P.

"The Five-O caught me right here with the bundles of P," he said, referring to a police officer, as he stood in front of a boarded-up house on Bridgeport's East Side. "They sentenced me to eighteen months, but I jetted after four. Three of us got out a bathroom window. We ran through the woods and stole a car. Then we got back here and the Five-O's came to my apartment, and I had to jump out the side window on the second floor."

What Future?

Since his escape, Fernando has been on the run for weeks. He still went to the weekly meetings of his gang, but he was afraid to go back to his apartment, afraid even to go to a friend's place to pick up the three guns he had stashed away. "I would love to get my baby Uzi, but it's too hot now."

"Could you bring a photographer here?" he asked. "I want my picture in the newspaper. I'd love to have me holding a bundle right there on the front page so the cops can see it. They're going to bug out."

The other dealers on the corner looked on with a certain admiration. They realized that a publicity campaign might not be the smartest long-term career move for a fugitive drug dealer—"Man, you be the one bugging out," another dealer told him—but they also recognized the logic in Fernando's attitude. He was living his life according to a common assumption on these streets: There is no future.

When you ask the Hispanic teenagers selling drugs here what they expect to be doing in five years, you tend to get a lot of bored shrugs. Occasionally they'll talk about being back in school or being a retired drug dealer in a Porsche. But the most common answer is the one that Fernando gave without hesitation or emotion: "Dead or in jail."

The story of how Fernando got that way is a particularly sad one, but the basic elements are fairly typical in the lives of drug dealers and gang members in any urban ghetto. He has grown up amid tenements, housing projects, torched buildings, and abandoned factories. His role models have been adults who use "the city" and "the state" primarily as terms for the different types of welfare checks. His neighborhood is a place where 13-year-olds know by heart the visiting hours at local prisons.

The Family: A Mother Leaves, a Father Drinks

Fernando Morales was born in Bridgeport, Connecticut, and a few months after his birth his mother moved out. Since then he has occasionally run into her on the street. Neither he nor his relatives can say exactly why she left or why she didn't take Fernando and her other son with her—but the general assumption is that she was tired of being hit by their father.

The father, Bernabe Morales, who was 24 years old and had emigrated from Puerto Rico as a teenager, moved the two boys in with his mother at the P. T. Barnum public housing project. Fernando lived there until the age of 8, when his grandmother died. . . .

After that Fernando and his brother Bernard lived sometimes with their father and his current girlfriend, sometimes with relatives in Bridgeport or Puerto Rico. They eventually settled with their father's cousin, Monserrate Bruno, who already had ten children living in her two-bedroom apartment. . . .

His father, by all accounts, was a charming, generous man when sober but something else altogether when drinking or doing drugs. He was arrested more than two dozen times, usually for fighting or drugs, and spent five years in jail while Fernando was growing up. He lived on welfare, odd jobs, and money from selling drugs, a trade that was taken up by both his sons.

The "Industry": Moving Up in the Drug Trade

Fernando's school days ended two years ago, when he dropped out of ninth grade. School was corny," he explained. "I was smart,

and Hispanics (18 percent) were greater than the percentages of those groups in the general population (OJJDP, 1999: 195). The Close Up box (see above) tells the story of Fernando, whose background matches this profile. Figure 17.7 shows the types of offenses of juveniles in public correctional facilities.

With the elimination of the death penalty as a punishment for juvenile offenders through the Supreme Court's decision in *Roper v. Simmons* (2005), some juvenile offenders receive "life without possibility of parole" (LWOP) for homicide offenses. Referring to this sentence as "a slower form of [the] death [penalty]," some argue that the juvenile justice system must always take age and juveniles' incomplete mental development into account, even for homicide offenses, to avoid giving youths the same sentences imposed on the most serious adult offenders (Feld, 2008).

I learned quick, but I got bored. I was just learning things when I could be out making money."

Fernando might have found other opportunities—he had relatives working in fast-food restaurants and repair shops, and one cousin tried to interest him in a job distributing bread that might pay $700 a week—but nothing with such quick rewards as the drug business flourishing on the East Side.

He had friends and relatives in the business, and he started as one of the runners on the street corner making sales or directing buyers to another runner holding the marijuana, cocaine, crack, or heroin. The runners on each block buy their drugs—paying, for instance, $200 for 50 bags of crack that sell for $250—from the block's lieutenant, who supervises them and takes the money to the absentee dealer called the owner of the block.

By this winter Fernando had moved up slightly on the corporate ladder." I'm not the block lieutenant yet, but I have some runners selling for me," he explained as he sat in a bar near the block. Another teenager came in with money for him, which he proudly added to a thick wad in his pocket. "You see? I make money while they work for me."

Fernando still worked the block himself, too, standing on the corner watching for cars slowing down, shouting "You want P?" or responding to veteran customers for crack who asked, "Got any slab, man?" Fernando said he usually made between $100 and $300 a day, and that the money usually went as quickly as it came.

He had recently bought a car for $500 and wrecked it making a fast turn into a telephone pole. He spent money on gold chains with crucifixes, rings, Nike sneakers, Timberland boots, an assortment of Russell hooded sweatshirts called hoodies, gang dues, trips to New York City, and on his 23-year-old girlfriend.

His dream was to get out of Bridgeport. "I'd be living fat somewhere. I'd go to somewhere hot, Florida or Puerto Rico or somewhere, buy me a house, get six blazing girls with dope bodies." In the meantime, he tried not to think about what his product was doing to his customers.

"Sometimes it bothers me. But see, I'm a hustler. I got to look out for myself. I got to be making money. Forget them. If you put that in your head, you're going to be caught out. You going to be a sucker. You going to be like them." He said he had used marijuana, cocaine, and angel dust himself, but made a point of never using crack or heroin, the drugs that plagued the last years of his father's life....

The Gangs: "Like a Family" of Drug Dealers

"I cried a little, that's it," was all that Fernando would say about his father's death. But he did allow that it had something to do with his subsequent decision to join a Hispanic gang named Neta. He went with friends to a meeting, answered questions during an initiation ceremony, and began wearing its colors, a necklace of red, white, and blue beads.

"It's like a family, and you need that if you've lost your own family," he said. "At the meetings we talk about having heart, trust, and all that. We don't disrespect nobody. If we need money, we get it. If I need anything they're right there to help me."

Neta is allied with Bridgeport's most notorious gang, the Latin Kings, and both claim to be peaceful Hispanic cultural organizations opposed to drug use. But they are financed at least indirectly by the drug trade, because many members like Fernando work independently in drug operations, and the drug dealers' disputes can turn into gang wars....

"I like guns, I like stealing cars, I like selling drugs, and I like money," he said. "I got to go to the block. That's where I get my spirit at. When I die, my spirit's going to be at the block, still making money. Booming...."

"I'll be selling till I get my act together. I'm just a little kid. Nothing runs through my head. All I think about is doing crazy things. But when I be big, I know I need education. If I get caught and do a couple of years, I'll come out and go back to school. But I don't have that in my head yet. I'll have my little fun while I'm out."

Source: John Tierney, *New York Times*, April 13, 1993, pp. Al, B6. Copyright © 1993 by The New York Times Company. Reprinted by permission.

Researching the Internet

 Read about the problem of youth gangs at the website of the National Youth Violence Prevention Resource Center. To link to this website, go to *The American System of Criminal Justice* 12e companion site at academic.cengage.com/criminaljustice/cole.

Institutional Programs

Because of the emphasis on rehabilitation that has dominated juvenile justice for much of the past 50 years, a wide variety of treatment programs has been used. Counseling, education, vocational training, and an assortment of psychotherapy methods have been incorporated into the juvenile correctional programs of most states. Unfortunately, research has raised many questions about the effectiveness of rehabilitation programs in juvenile corrections. For example, incarceration in a juvenile training institution primarily seems to prepare many offenders for entry into adult corrections. John Irwin's (1970) concept of the state-raised youth is a useful way of looking at children who come in contact with institutional life at an early age, lack family relationships and structure, become accustomed to living in a correctional facility, and cannot function in

Staff member Vincent Vaielua (left) talks to a youth at an evening reporting center run by the Pierce County Juvenile Court in Tacoma, Washington. Many courts develop community programs in an effort to avoid confining youthful offenders in juvenile corrections institutions. What are the potential advantages and benefits of emphasizing community-based programs?

AP Images/ Elaine Thompson

civic engagement
your role in the system

Imagine that you have been asked to serve as a mentor to a youth who has been released from a juvenile detention facility. *Make a list of the things that you would say and do to attempt to be a positive influence for a delinquent youth. Write a brief statement describing what you think you might be able accomplish.* Then read about the mentoring experiences of students at the University of Southern California. To link to this website, go to *The American System of Criminal Justice* 12e companion site at academic.cengage.com/criminaljustice/cole.

aftercare
Juvenile justice equivalent of parole, in which a delinquent is released from a custodial sentence and supervised in the community.

other environments. Current recommendations focus on the importance of prevention, and keeping juvenile offenders away from incarceration during the first signs of problem behavior (Hoge, Guerra, and Boxer, 2008).

Aftercare

The juvenile equivalent of parole is known as **aftercare.** Upon release, the offender is placed under the supervision of a juvenile parole officer who assists with educational, counseling, and treatment services. Quality aftercare is associated with lower rates of recidivism after release from incarceration, and many have blamed the failure of boot camps on poor aftercare postrelease (Kurlychek and Kempinen, 2006). As with the adult system, juveniles may be returned to custodial care should they violate the conditions of their parole. As you read "Civic Engagement: Your Role in the System," consider how people in the community may be able to contribute to the success of aftercare.

Community Treatment

In the past decade, treatment in community-based facilities has become much more common. Today many private, nonprofit agencies contract with states to provide services for troubled youths. Community-based options include foster homes, in which juvenile offenders live with families, usually for a short period, and group homes, often privately run facilities for groups of 12–20 juvenile offenders. Each group home has several staff personnel who work as counselors or houseparents during 8- or 24-hour shifts. Group home placements provide individual and group counseling, allow juveniles to attend local schools, and offer a more structured life than most of the residents have received in their own homes. However, critics suggest that group homes often are mismanaged and may do little more than "warehouse" youths.

checkpoint

10. What three discretionary decisions do the police make with regard to processing juveniles?
11. What are the costs and benefits of trying juveniles in adult court?
12. What is the purpose of diversion?
13. What are five sentencing dispositions available to the judge?

PROBLEMS AND PERSPECTIVES

Much of the criticism of juvenile justice has emphasized the disparity between the treatment ideal and the institutionalized practices of an ongoing bureaucratic system. Commentators have focused on how the language of social reformers has disguised the day-to-day operations that lack the elements of due process and in which custodial incarceration is all too frequent. Other criticisms claim that the juvenile justice system does not control juvenile crime.

The juvenile court, in both theory and practice, is a remarkably complex institution that must perform a wide variety of functions. The juvenile justice system must play such a range of roles that goals and values will inevitably collide.

In many states, the same judges, probation officers, and social workers are asked to deal with both neglected children and young criminals. Although departments of social services usually deal primarily with cases of neglect, the distinction between the criminal and the neglected child is often not maintained.

In addition to recognizing that the juvenile system has organizational problems, society must acknowledge that little is known about the causes of delinquency and its prevention or treatment. Over the years, people have advanced various social and behavioral theories to explain delinquency. One generation looked to slum conditions as the cause of juvenile crime, and another pointed to the affluence of the suburbs. Psychologists sometimes point to masculine insecurity in a matriarchal family structure, and some sociologists note the peer group pressures of the gang. This array of theories has led to an array of proposed—and often contradictory—treatments. In such confusion, those interested in the problems of youth may despair. What is clear is that we need additional research on the causes of delinquency and the treatment of juvenile offenders.

Youth gangs pose unique problems to those making decisions in the juvenile justice system. Gangs are responsible for a significant amount of delinquency in communities, and these gangs also thrive in correctional institutions (particularly adult institutions). How does the presence and behavior of youth gangs affect juvenile justice policy? Recent research has indicated gang members are more likely than nongang members to carry guns, thereby also increasing the likelihood of severe or lethal violence among these groups. Gang members are also more likely to receive longer sentences, given that gang membership and weapon ownership can increase the severity of punishment for juveniles (Melde, 2009).

In recent years, juveniles have been engaging in delinquent behavior online. The phenomenon of "cyberbullying" involves the use of computers, cell phones, and other electronic devices by youth to mistreat and harm their peers. Approximately one-third of adolescents have been bullied online, whereas approximately 20 percent of youth admit to cyberbullying others (Hinduja and Patchin, 2009; Patchin and Hinduja, 2006). Although additional inquiry is necessary, cyberbullying has been correlated with traditional bullying and various forms of school violence (Hinduja and Patchin, 2007).

What trends may foretell the future of juvenile justice? The conservative crime control policies that hit the adult criminal justice system—with their emphasis on deterrence, retribution, and getting tough—have also influenced juvenile justice in the past 20 years. One can point to growing levels of overcrowding in juvenile institutions, increased litigation challenging the abuse of children in training schools and detention centers, and higher rates of minority youth incarceration. All of these problems have emerged during a period of declining youth populations and fewer arrests of juveniles. With a renewed focus on juvenile crime under the philosophy that "kids are different," the juvenile justice system may be embarking on a less severe path to dealing with juvenile offenders.

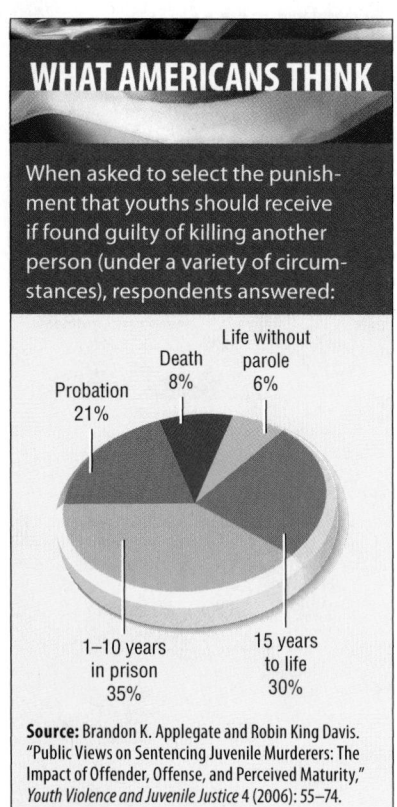

WHAT AMERICANS THINK

When asked to select the punishment that youths should receive if found guilty of killing another person (under a variety of circumstances), respondents answered:

Probation 21%

Death 8%

Life without parole 6%

1–10 years in prison 35%

15 years to life 30%

Source: Brandon K. Applegate and Robin King Davis. "Public Views on Sentencing Juvenile Murderers: The Impact of Offender, Offense, and Perceived Maturity," *Youth Violence and Juvenile Justice* 4 (2006): 55–74.

On the other hand, future developments and events might ultimately lead to a continuation of the crime control orientation in many states. We must wait to see if we are truly moving into a new era that focuses on juveniles' developmental differences from adults. For example, the Supreme Court's ban on the execution of offenders for crimes committed prior to the age of 18 is not necessarily permanent. *Roper v. Simmons* was decided on a 5-to-4 vote of the Supreme Court's justices. Thus a change in the Court's composition through the retirement or death of one of the five justices in the *Roper* majority may lead to the reinstatement of the death penalty for juveniles in some states if the replacement justice votes to reverse the *Roper* decision in a future case.

Such a change may seem primarily symbolic because only a small number of offenders who committed crimes as juveniles were actually executed in the decades prior to *Roper*. Between 1973 and 2000, 17 juvenile offenders were executed, mostly in the state of Texas. All but one of these offenders were age 17 at the time of their offense (Sickmund, 2004). In addition, there does not appear to be strong public opinion supporting the death penalty for juvenile offenders (Applegate & Davis, 2006) (see "What Americans Think" regarding attitude toward punishment).

Yet, even if a reversal of the *Roper* decision does not lead to many executions of youthful murderers, a new Supreme Court decision would weaken the "kids are different" message that the Court announced in *Roper*. As a result, a future increase in youth crime or highly publicized gang violence could lead policy makers to turn back toward crime control priorities or otherwise slow the current trend toward reemphasizing treatment and rehabilitation for youthful offenders. In recent decades, the United States has not shown a consistent, firm commitment to the original rehabilitative goals of the juvenile justice system. Thus it remains to be seen which priorities will shape the system's approach to punishing youthful offenders in the future.

A QUESTION OF ETHICS

RESIDENTS OF THE Lovelock Home had been committed by the juvenile court because they were either delinquent or neglected. All 25 boys, aged 12 to 16, were streetwise, tough, and interested only in getting out. The institution had a staff of social services professionals who tried to deal with the educational and psychological needs of the residents. Because state funding was short, these services looked better in the annual report than to an observer visiting Lovelock. Most of the time the residents watched television, played basketball in the backyard, or just hung out in one another's rooms.

Joe Klegg, the night supervisor, was tired from the eight-hour shift that he had just completed on his "second job" as a convenience store manager. The boys were watching television when he arrived at seven. Everything seemed calm. It should have been, because Joe had placed a tough 15-year-old, Randy Marshall, in charge. Joe had told Randy to keep the younger boys in line. Randy used his muscle and physical presence to intimidate the other residents. He knew that if the home was quiet and there was no trouble, he would be rewarded with special privileges such as a "pass" to go see his girlfriend. Joe wanted no hassles and a quiet house so that he could doze off when the boys went to sleep.

Critical Thinking and Analysis

Does the situation at Lovelock Home raise ethical questions, or does it merely raise questions of poor management practices? What are the potential consequences for the residents? For Joe Klegg? What is the state's responsibility?

SUMMARY

Recognize the extent of youth crime in the United States

- Crimes committed by juveniles have increased since 1980 even though crimes of violence in general have decreased.

Understand how the juvenile justice system developed and the assumptions on which it was based

- The history of juvenile justice comprises six periods: Puritan, Refuge, juvenile court, juvenile rights, crime control, and "kids are different."

- Creation of the juvenile court in 1899 established a separate juvenile justice system.

- The *In re Gault* decision by the U.S. Supreme Court in 1967 brought due process to the juvenile justice system.

Identify what determines the jurisdiction of the juvenile justice system

- The juvenile system handles cases based on the ages of youths who are affected by delinquency, dependency, and neglect.

Understand how the juvenile justice system operates

- Decisions by police officers and juvenile intake officers dispose of a large portion of the many cases that are never referred to the court.

- In juvenile court, most cases are settled through a plea agreement.

- After conviction or plea, a disposition hearing is held. Before passing sentence, the judge reviews the offense and the juvenile's social history.

- Possible dispositions of a juvenile case include suspended judgment, probation, community treatment, or institutional care.

- Juvenile court jurisdiction may be waived so that youths can be tried in the adult criminal justice system, but this appears to be decreasing in recent years.

- Options for juvenile corrections include probation, alternative dispositions, custodial care, institutional programs, aftercare, and community treatment.

Analyze some of the issues facing the American system of juvenile justice

- Juvenile justice faces issues of racial disparities in punishment, criminal activity by gangs, and new behavioral problems, such as cyberbullying, that involve computers.

- It remains to be seen whether the current move toward increased rehabilitation will continue or whether crime control policies will be a primary priority.

QUESTIONS FOR REVIEW

1. What are the major historical periods of juvenile justice in the United States?

2. What is the jurisdiction of the juvenile court system?

3. What are the major processes in the juvenile justice system?

4. What are the sentencing and institutional alternatives for juveniles who are judged delinquent?

5. What due process rights do juveniles have?

KEY TERMS AND CASES

aftercare (p. 630)
delinquent (p. 616)
dependent child (p. 617)
detention hearing (p. 620)
diversion (p. 620)
neglected child (p. 617)
parens patriae (p. 608)
PINS (p. 616)
status offense (p. 612)
waiver (p. 613)
Breed v. Jones (1975) (p. 612)

Fare v. Michael C. (1979) (p. 619)
In re Gault (1967) (p. 611)
In re Winship (1970) (p. 611)
McKeiver v. Pennsylvania (1971) (p. 612)
New Jersey v. T. L. O. (1985) (p. 619)
Schall v. Martin (1984) (p. 612)
Vernonia School District v. Acton (1995) (p. 619)

FOR FURTHER READING

Ayers, William. 1997. *A Kind and Just Parent: The Children of Juvenile Court.* Boston: Beacon Press. Examination of the lives of offenders in the Chicago juvenile court system through the eyes of one of their teachers.

Decker, Scott H., and Barick Van Winkle. 1996. *Life in the Gang: Families, Friends, and Violence.* New York: Cambridge University Press. Follows the life of a juvenile gang in St. Louis for a year, documenting their trouble with the law. Examines juvenile justice efforts to deal with family and community problems.

Feld, Barry C. 1999. *Bad Kids: Race and the Transformation of the Juvenile Court.* New York: Oxford University Press. Examination of the shifts in policies regarding youth crime and the juvenile justice system in the context of race issues in U.S. society.

Greenwood, Peter W. 2005. *Changing Lives: Delinquency Prevention as Crime-Control Policy.* Chicago: University of Chicago Press. A thorough review of research on juvenile delinquency as well as an examination of the effectiveness of various treatments and programs.

Klein, Malcolm W. 1996. The *American Street Gang: Its Nature, Prevalence, and Control.* New York: Oxford University Press. A study of street gangs in the American city. Advocates the need for investment in jobs, schools, and social services to serve the needs of the poor and to discourage the growth of gangs.

Kotlowitz, Alex. 1992. *There Are No Children Here: The Story of Two Boys Growing Up in the Other America.*

New York: Anchor. True story of two boys growing up in a Chicago housing project surrounded by street gangs, gunfire, violence, and drugs.

Kupchik, Aaron. 2006. *Judging Juveniles: Prosecuting Adolescents in Adult and Juvenile Courts*. New York: New York University Press. A study that provides a critical examination of the prosecution of juveniles in adult court.

Tannenhaus, David S. 2004. *Juvenile Justice in the Making*. New York: Oxford University Press. An excellent history of the development and implementation of juvenile justice in Chicago.

GOING ONLINE

For an up-to-date list of web links, go to *The American System of Criminal Justice* 12e companion site at academic .cengage.com/criminaljustice/cole.

1. Go to the federal government's website that lists juvenile justice statistics.

2. Read about juvenile corrections. What are the trends in juveniles being held in custody? Can you tell from data available at the website whether these trends are caused by changes in the crime rates or by changes in custody policies?

3. Read the Bureau of Justice Assistance report *Juvenile Drug Courts: Strategies in Practice*. What are the pros and cons of this approach? How well would a drug court for juveniles work in your community?

4. Read an online report from the Center on Juvenile and Criminal Justice on the risks juveniles experience when incarcerated with adults. Should juveniles ever be held in adult jails or prisons?

CHECKPOINT ANSWERS

1. *What might explain the "epidemic" of violent crime committed by juveniles in the 1990s?*

   Two theories: (1) The presence of a large number of violent super predators in the age cohort; (2) juveniles, armed with guns, recruited into the inner-city drug trade.

2. *Until what age were children exempt from criminal responsibility under common law?*

   Age seven.

3. *What was the jurisdiction of the English chancery court?*

   Chancery courts had protective jurisdiction over children, especially those involved in cases concerning dependency, neglect, and property.

4. *What is meant by the doctrine of* parens patriae?

   The state acting as parent and guardian.

5. *What was the function of a House of Refuge?*

   To provide an environment where neglected children could learn good work and study habits, live in a disciplined and healthy environment, and develop character.

6. *What were the major elements of the Illinois Juvenile Court Act of 1899?*

   A separate court for delinquent, dependent, and neglected children; special legal procedures that were less adversarial than those in the adult system; separation of children from adults throughout the system; programs of probation to assist judges in deciding what is in the best interest of the state and the child.

7. *What was the main point of the* In re Gault *decision?*

   Procedural rights for juveniles, including notice of charges, right to counsel, right to confront and cross-examine witnesses, and protection against self-incrimination.

8. *How did the decline in juvenile crime in the 1990s affect juvenile justice policy?*

   A decrease in the use of judicial waiver to move youthful offenders from juvenile court to adult court.

9. *What are the jurisdictional criteria for the juvenile court?*

   The age of the juvenile, usually younger than 16 or 18, and the type of case: delinquency, status offense, neglect, or dependency.

10. *What three discretionary decisions do the police make with regard to processing juveniles?*

    (1) Whether to take the child into custody, (2) whether to request that the child be detained, (3) whether to refer the child to court.

11. *What are the costs and benefits of trying juveniles in adult court?*

    Costs: youth tried as adults receive longer sentences, are likely to be incarcerated with criminal (and potentially abusive) adults, and are more likely to recidivate post-release than youth not transferred. Benefits: sends "get tough" message to juvenile offenders

12. *What is the purpose of diversion?*

    To avoid formal proceedings when the child's best interests can be served by treatment in the community.

13. *What are five sentencing dispositions available to the judge?*

    Suspended judgment, probation, community treatment, institutional care, judicial waiver to an adult court.

APPENDIX A

Constitution of the United States: Criminal Justice Amendments

The first ten amendments to the Constitution, known as the Bill of Rights, became effective on December 15, 1791.

I. Congress shall make no law respecting an establishment of religion, or prohibiting the free exercise thereof; or abridging the freedom of speech, or of the press, or the right of the people peaceably to assemble, and to petition the Government for a redress of grievances.

IV. The right of the people to be secure in their persons, houses, papers, and effects, against unreasonable searches and seizures, shall not be violated, and no warrants shall issue but upon probable cause, supported by oath or affirmation, and particularly describing the place to be searched, and the persons or things to be seized.

V. No person shall be held to answer for a capital or otherwise infamous crime, unless on a presentment or indictment of a grand jury, except in cases arising in the land or naval forces or in the militia when in actual service in time of war or public danger; nor shall any person be subject for the same offense to be twice put in jeopardy of life or limb; nor shall be compelled in any criminal case to be a witness against himself, nor be deprived of life, liberty, or property, without due process of law; nor shall private property be taken for public use without just compensation.

VI. In all criminal prosecutions the accused shall enjoy the right to a speedy and public trial, by an impartial jury of the State and district wherein the crime shall have been committed, which district shall have been previously ascertained by law, and to be informed of the nature and cause of the accusation; to be confronted with the witnesses against him; to have compulsory process for obtaining witnesses in his favor, and to have the assistance of counsel for his defense.

VIII. Excessive bail shall not be required, nor excessive fines imposed, nor cruel and unusual punishments inflicted.

The Fourteenth Amendment became effective on July 28, 1868.

XIV. SECTION 1. All persons born or naturalized in the United States, and subject to the jurisdiction thereof, are citizens of the United States and of the State wherein they reside. No State shall make or enforce any law which shall abridge the privileges or immunities of citizens of the United States; nor shall any State deprive any person of life, liberty, or property, without due process of law; nor deny to any person within its jurisdiction the equal protection of the laws.

APPENDIX B
Understanding and Using Criminal Justice Data

When it comes to numbers, criminal justice is somewhat like baseball. Both require a wealth of quantitative data to answer a variety of questions. Casual baseball fans want to know who has the highest batting average in the league or how many runs a certain pitcher gives up per game. More-serious fans might want information that can help them judge whether statistics on various events (home runs, stolen bases, sacrifice bunts) support one or more of the manager's strategies.

Similarly, people interested in criminal justice need quantitative data to describe events as well as to make inferences about trends or about the impact of different policies. They want to know, for example, how much crime there is; whether crime is on the increase and which types of crimes are increasing or decreasing; whether strong gun control laws are linked to a decrease in violent crime; or what effects correctional policies have on the likelihood that criminals will break the law in the future.

Researchers constantly gather, analyze, and disseminate quantitative information that fosters an understanding of the dimensions of crime and the workings of the criminal justice system. As a student in this course and as an informed citizen, you need to be able to read about these data intelligently and to make valid inferences about them.

In this text, as in most criminal justice books and articles, quantitative data often are reported in graphs and tables that organize the information and highlight certain aspects of it. The way the information is presented reflects the writer's choices about what is important in the raw data that underlie the graphic display. So that you can better interpret and use quantitative information, this appendix provides some pointers on reading graphic presentations and on interpreting raw data.

READING GRAPHS AND TABLES

Writers use graphs and tables to organize information so that key factors stand out. Although you may be tempted to try to take in the meaning of such displays in a quick glance, you will need to *analyze* what is being presented so that you do not misinterpret the material.

To begin, read the title and descriptive caption carefully to find out what the data do and do not represent. For example, consider the title of Figure B.1: "Violent crime trends measured by UCR and NCVS." The title tells you that the data presented pertain to *violent* crime (not all crime) and that the *sources* of the information are reports to police (Uniform Crime Reports) and victimization surveys (National Crime Victimization Survey). Knowing where the data come from is important, because different means of data collection have their own strengths and weaknesses. So what this figure presents is not a directly observed picture of crime trends, but a picture that has been filtered through two

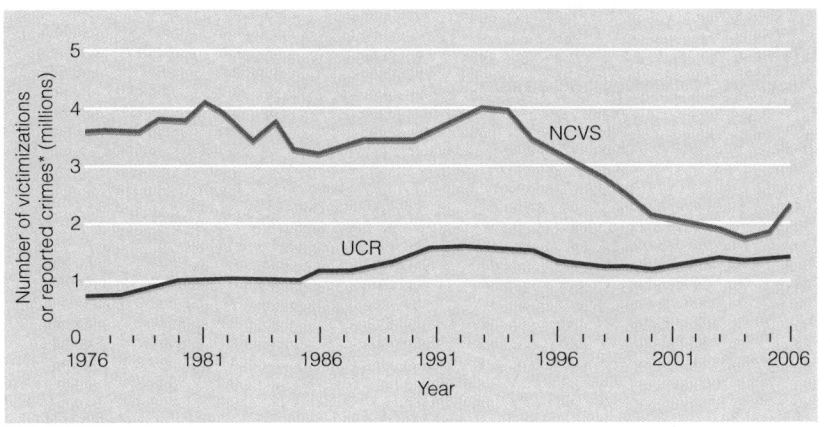

Source: Bureau of Justice Statistics, *Highlights from Twenty Years of Surveying Crime Victims,* August 1993, p. 4.

FIGURE B.1

Violent crime trends measured by UCR and NCVS

Note that these data are for the number of violent victimizations reported, not for the victimization rate from 1976 to 2006.

*Includes NCVS violent crimes of rape, robbery, aggravated assault, and simple assault and UCR violent crimes of murder and nonnegligent manslaughter, forcible rape, robbery, and aggravated assault.

distinct methods of measuring crime. (These measures of crime are described in Chapter 1.) In general, always note the sources of the data before drawing conclusions from a graphic display.

After reading the title and caption, study the figure itself. Note that the graph compares the number of crimes from 1976 to 2006 as reported by the two types of surveys. As indicated in the caption, the data are presented in terms of the *number* of victimizations, not the relative *frequency* of crime (a crime *rate*). For this reason you need to be cautious in making inferences about what the data show about crime trends. In baseball, a graph showing an increase in the number of home runs hit over a certain period would not prove that home runs were becoming more common if, during the same period, new teams were added to the league. More teams and more games being played would naturally lead to an increase in the total number of home runs. Similarly, given the increases in the U.S. population over the 30-year period of the data, part of the increase in the *number* of crimes can be attributed to the greater number of Americans.

Also note that the data show what has happened over three decades. Even though the lines in the graph depict trends during that period, they do *not* in themselves forecast the future. There are statistical procedures that could be used to predict future trends based on certain assumptions, but such projections are not a part of this figure.

A final caution about graphic display in general: The form in which data are presented can affect or even distort your perception of the content. For example, a graph showing incarceration rates in the United States from 1940 to 2004 could be drawn with a shorter or longer time line (see Figure B.2). Figure B.2a shows the graph in normal proportions. If the time line is made shorter in relation to the incarceration rate scale, as in Figure B.2b, the changes in incarceration rates will appear to be more drastic than if the line is longer, as in Figure B.2c. By the same token, the height chosen for the vertical axis affects the appearance of the data and can influence the way the data are interpreted. How does your impression of the same data change when you compare Figure B.2d with B.2e?

Although much more could be said about interpreting graphical displays, these brief comments alert you to the need to carefully review data presented in graphic form. In criminal justice, as in baseball, you need to actively question and think about the information you encounter, in order to become a serious student of the game.

FIGURE B.2

Incarceration rates in the United States, 1940–2004

The panels of this graph are intentionally distorted to show the effects of varying the dimensions of graphs.

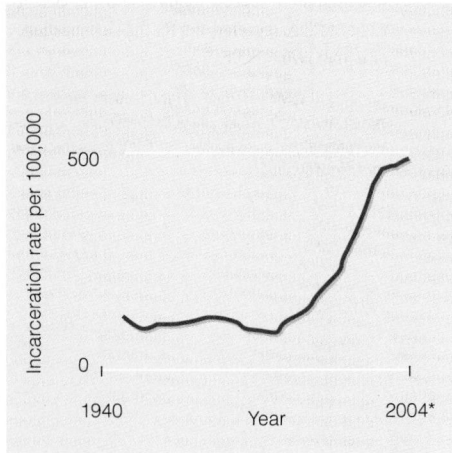

a

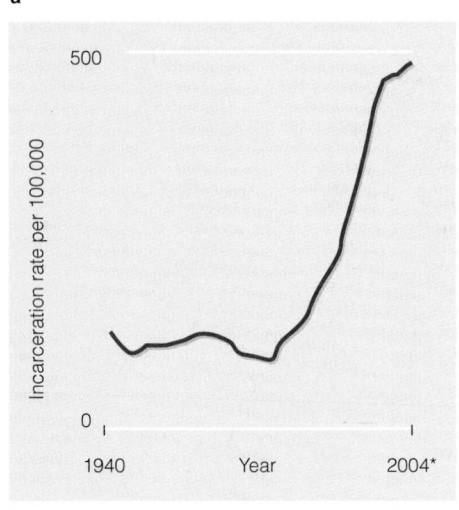

b

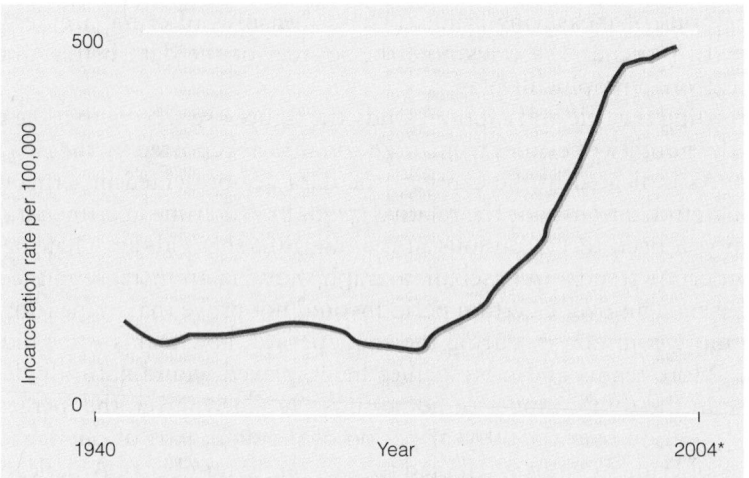

c

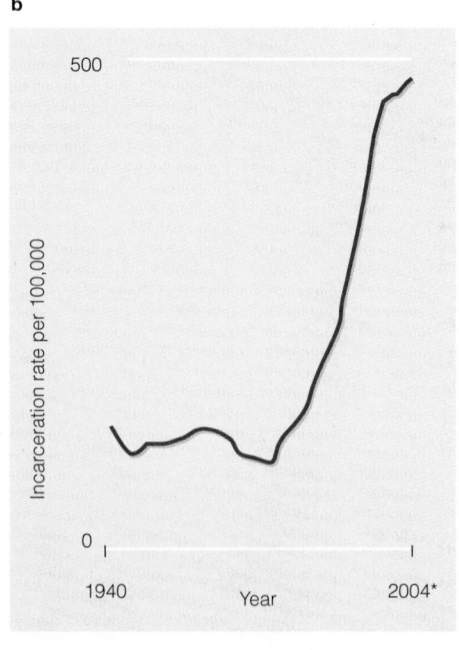

d

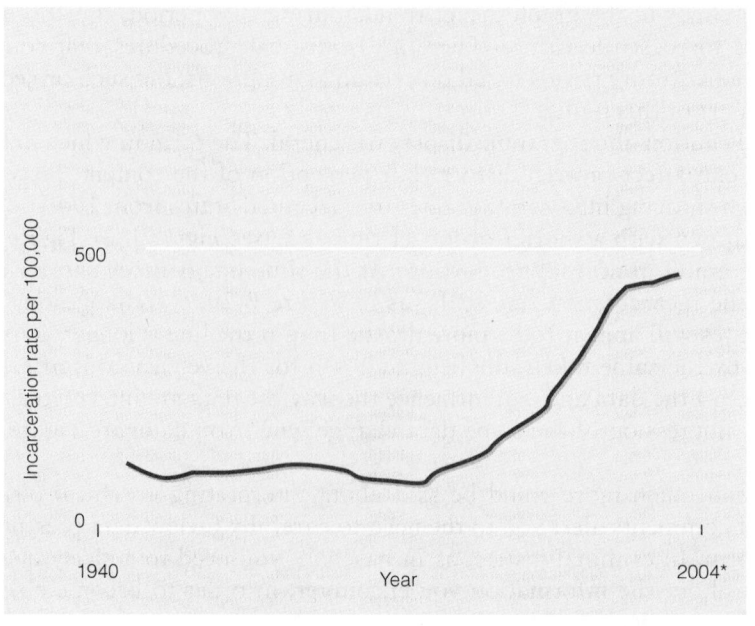

e

* Rate as of June 2004.

Sources: Bureau of Justice Statistics, *Bulletin:* June 1997; August 1998; August 2001; August 2002; November 2004, April 2005.

THREE TYPES OF GRAPHS

You will find three types of graphs in this book: bar graphs, pie graphs (or pie charts), and line graphs. All three are represented in Figure B.3. Each graph displays information concerning public opinion about crime.

Figure B.3a is a bar graph. Bar graphs compare quantities organized in different categories. In this case, each bar represents the percentage of teenage poll respondents ranking the indicated problem as "the most important problem facing people your age." The lengths of the bars (or their heights, when a bar graph is oriented vertically) allow for a visual comparison of the quantities associated with each category of response. In this case, you can readily see that when the data were collected in May 2004, the crime-related problem of drugs ranked as the number one concern, just ahead of social pressure to fit in. The problem of school violence lagged well behind with respect to the number of teens who saw it as the most important problem. The creator of a graph of this type needs to take care that the sizes of the bars are visually proportionate to the quantities they represent. A bar graph that is drawn unscrupulously or carelessly can make the difference in quantities appear larger or smaller than it really is. Intentionally or not, graphs that appear in the mass media often exaggerate some effect in this way. The lesson here is to go beyond looking at the shape of the graph. Use the scales provided on the axes to directly compare the numbers being depicted and verify your visual impression.

Figure B.3b is a pie graph. Pie graphs show the relative sizes of the parts of a single whole. Usually these sizes are reported as percentages. In this case, respondents were asked in 2007 if there was more, less, or about the same amount of crime in their home areas as there was one year earlier. The whole consists of all the responses taken together, and the portions of the "pie" represent the percentage of respondents who chose each option. The pie graph indicates that a slim majority (51 percent) of respondents in the survey believed that crime had increased. The same data could have been reported in a bar graph, but it would not have been as clear that a single whole was divided into parts.

FIGURE B.3

Crime: In the nation, in our neighborhood

Crime remains one of the most important problems facing Americans. Most Americans say that crime has increased in their neighborhood in the past year.

a. Survey of teenagers (2004): What is the most important problem facing people your age—that is, the thing which concerns you the most?

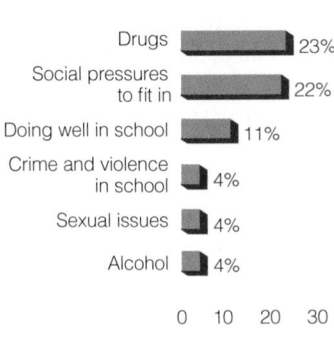

b. Is there more crime in your area than there was a year ago, or less? (Survey of adults, 2007).

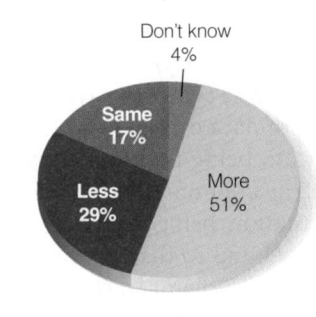

c. Is there more crime in your area than there was a year ago, or less? (Survey of adults, 1972–2007).

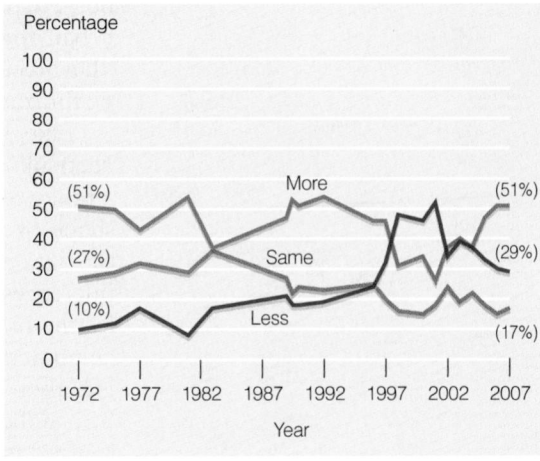

Note: Less frequent responses omitted.

Source: *Sourcebook of Criminal Justice Statistics, 2007* (Washington, DC: U.S. Bureau of Justice Statistics, 2008).

Whenever data are presented as percentages of a whole—whether in a pie graph, a table, or another display—the percentages should add up to 100 percent. Often, however, the sum may be slightly over or under 100 because of what is known as *rounding error*. Rounding error can occur when percentages are rounded to the nearest whole number. For instance, suppose the percentage of "more crime" responses was calculated as 51.6 percent. The figure might be reported as 52 percent. Unless rounding of the other percentages compensated for the error, the total of the reported percentages would add up to 101 percent. Where rounding error occurs, the figure or table will usually have a note indicating this fact.

Figure B.3c is a line graph. Line graphs show the relationship between two or more variables. The variables in question are indicated by the labels on the vertical axis and the longitudinal (horizontal) axis of the graph. In this case, the variable on the vertical axis is the percentage of people who say that crime has been increasing, decreasing, or staying about the same in the past year. The variable on the longitudinal axis is time, reported as years when the survey question was asked. In 1972, for instance, 51 percent of respondents said that crime had been increasing in the past year. Drawing a line through the points that show the percentage associated with each response for each year allows for a graphic presentation of how opinions have changed over time. The same data could have been presented in a table, but this would have made it harder to see the direction of change in opinion. Line graphs are especially well suited to showing data about trends.

ANALYZING TABLES

All these points about graphic presentations in general apply also to tables. When you see a table, read the title and descriptive information carefully, note the source of the data, and be aware of how the presentation itself affects your perception of the content.

Tables relate two or more variables by organizing information in vertical columns and horizontal rows. In Table B.1, the columns give data about victimization rates for two categories of crime: violent crime and personal theft. The rows of the table show categories of victims organized by sex, age, race, Hispanic origin, household income, and so forth. Reading down a column allows you to compare information about personal theft, for example, for different types of victims. By inspecting each column in turn, you can see that the rates for both types of crime victimization are higher for Hispanics than for non-Hispanics, for people aged 16–19 than for those in other age groups, for urban than for rural groups, and so on. Reading across a row, for example, "Divorced/separated," allows you to compare the different categories of crime victimization for the same type of victim.

Like other types of data displays, tables often require close study beyond the particular information being highlighted by the writer. When you come across a table, read down the columns and across the rows to discover for yourself the shape of the information being reported. Be careful, however, to notice how the data are organized and to distinguish between the data themselves and any inferences you draw from them. In this case, for example, you might be struck by the higher victimization rates reported by people who have never married compared with the rates reported by those who are married. Before you speculate about why this is so, note that the data for marital status are not broken out by age. People under age 25 are more likely than those who are older to be victimized (see the data under "age"). Because these younger people are far more likely than older ones to be unmarried, the difference in victimization rates for married and unmarried people may be largely accounted for by age rather than

TABLE B.1	Who are the Victims of Violent Crimes and Personal Theft?

NCVS data help clarify the characteristics of crime victims.

	Victims	Rate per 1,000 persons age 12 or older	
		Violence*	Personal Theft**
Sex	Male	26	0.4
	Female	19	1.1
Age	12–15	52	1.5
	16–19	53	1.4
	20–24	43	1.6
	25–34	26	1.0
	35–49	18	0.5
	50–64	10	0.3
	65 or older	2	0.5
Race	White	21.5	0.6
	African American	29	1.7
	Other race	16	0.9
	Two or more races	68	2.7
Hispanic origin	Hispanic	24	1.1
	Non-Hispanic	22	0.7
Household income	Less than $7,000	50	1.2
	$7,000–$14,999	31	1.1
	$15,000–$24,999	26	0.7
	$25,000–$34,999	25	0.8
	$35,000–$49,999	21	0.7
	$50,000–$74,999	23	0.5
	$75,000 or more	17.5	1.0
Marital Status	Never married	41.6	1.4
	Married	10	0.3
	Divorced/separated	35	0.7
	Widowed	3.5	0.8
Region	Northeast	21	1.1
	Midwest	24	1.0
	South	21	0.5
	West	25	0.6
Residence	Urban	28	1.3
	Suburban	21	0.7
	Rural	19	0.3

*Rounded
**Personal theft includes only purse snatching and pocket picking.
Source: Bureau of Justice Statistics, *National Crime Victimization Survey* (September 2004): 7, 8.

by marital status. The table does not provide enough information to tell to what extent this might be the case.

In summary, data are presented in tables and graphs so they can be more easily grasped. But before you decide that you have truly understood the information, read the item and accompanying commentary attentively and be aware of the ways the writer has chosen to organize and display the data. By working with graphic presentations and posing questions to yourself as you read them, you also make the important information easier to remember.

UNDERSTANDING RAW DATA

Data that you see in graphs and tables have already been sifted and organized. As a student of criminal justice, you also encounter raw (or "whole") data. For example, the *Sourcebook of Criminal Justice Statistics, 2007* reports that there were 17,034 homicides in the category of "murder and non-negligent manslaughter" in the United States in 2006. These are the killings that result from intentional criminal acts that we typically describe in crime data as "murders." Data often are expressed in terms of the *rate* at which an event occurs for a certain number of people in the population. The murder rate in 2006 was 5.7 murders per 100,000 people in the United States. The formula for determining the rate is:

$$\frac{\text{Number of murders}}{\text{Total U.S. population}} \times 100,000 = \text{Rate per } 100,000$$

For some purposes, the total figures (the raw data) are needed; for other purposes, percentages are more informative; and for still other purposes, expressing data as a rate is most useful. To illustrate this point, consider the following example of data about incarceration in two different states.

On June 30, 2004, 48,591 offenders were held in the prisons of Michigan and 36,745 in the prisons of Louisiana. How does incarceration in these states compare? Knowing the number of prisoners does not allow you to draw many conclusions about incarceration in these states. If, however, the numbers are expressed as a rate, the difference in the sizes of the two state populations would be taken into consideration and a much clearer picture would result.

Although Louisiana has fewer prisoners than Michigan, the incarceration rate in Louisiana (814 prisoners per 100,000 population) is considerably higher than in Michigan (480 per 100,000). On a national basis, the number of incarcerated people on June 30, 2004, represents a rate of 486 prisoners for every 100,000 U.S. residents, so the rate in Louisiana was significantly higher than in the United States as a whole. In fact, Louisiana has the highest incarceration rate in the country.

SOURCES OF CRIMINAL JUSTICE DATA

To a large extent, criminal justice researchers depend on data collected and analyzed by agencies of the government. Many of these sources are cited throughout this book. In particular, the Bureau of Justice Statistics of the U.S. Department of Justice produces the *Sourcebook of Criminal Justice Statistics,* an annual compilation of data on most aspects of crime and justice; the *Bulletin,* which regularly publishes issues focusing on a single topic related to police, courts, and corrections; and the *Special Report,* a publication that presents findings from specific research projects. The National Institute of Justice, also an arm of the U.S. Department of Justice, publishes *Research in Brief* summary versions of major research studies. *Crime in the United States,* published each August by the Department of Justice, contains data collected through the FBI's Uniform Crime Reports system. All of these documents are available online. To reach these sites, go to "Web Links" on *The American System of Criminal Justice* 12e companion site at academic.cengage.com/criminaljustice/cole.

The libraries of most colleges and universities hold these publications in the government documents or reference section. Ask your librarian to help you find them. If you would like to get on the mailing list to receive the free publications of the Bureau of Justice Statistics, fill out the form on the last page of the *Bulletin*. You can also access most of these publications through the Internet, as noted earlier.

Glossary

accusatory process The series of events from the arrest of a suspect to the filing of a formal charge with a court (through an indictment or information).

adjudication The process of determining whether the defendant is guilty or not guilty.

administrative regulations Rules made by government agencies to implement specific public policies in areas such as public health, environmental protection, and workplace safety.

adversarial system Basis of the American legal system in which a passive judge and jury seek to find the truth by listening to opposing attorneys who vigorously advocate on behalf of their respective sides.

affidavit Written statement of fact, supported by oath or affirmation, submitted to judicial officers to fulfill the requirements of probable cause for obtaining a warrant.

aftercare Juvenile justice equivalent of parole, in which a delinquent is released from a custodial sentence and supervised in the community.

aggressive patrol A patrol strategy designed to maximize the number of police interventions and observations in the community.

aliens Foreign-born noncitizens.

anomie A breakdown in and disappearance of the rules of social behavior.

appeal A request to a higher court that it review actions taken in a completed lower court case.

appellate courts Courts that do not try criminal cases but hear appeals of decisions of lower courts.

arraignment The court appearance of an accused person in which the charges are read and the accused, advised by a lawyer, pleads guilty or not guilty.

arrest The physical taking of a person into custody on the grounds that probable cause exists to believe that he or she has committed a criminal offense. Police may use only reasonable physical force in making an arrest.

The purpose of the arrest is to hold the accused for a court proceeding.

assigned counsel An attorney in private practice assigned by a court to represent an indigent. The attorney's fee is paid by the government with jurisdiction over the case.

Atkins v. Virginia (2002) Execution of the mentally retarded is unconstitutional.

bail An amount of money specified by a judge that be paid as a condition of pretrial release to ensure that the accused will appear in court as required.

Barron v. Baltimore (1833) The protections of the Bill of Rights apply only to actions of the federal government.

Baze v. Rees (2008) Lethal injection has not been shown to violate the Eighth Amendment prohibition on cruel and unusual punishments and thus this method of execution is permissible.

bench trial Trial conducted by a judge who acts as fact finder and determines issues of law. No jury participates.

biological explanations Explanations of crime that emphasize physiological and neurological factors that may predispose a person to commit crimes.

boot camp A short-term institutional sentence, usually followed by probation, that puts the offender through a physical regimen designed to develop discipline and respect for authority. Also referred to as shock incarceration.

Bordenkircher v. Hayes (1978) A defendant's rights were not violated by a prosecutor who warned that failure to agree to a guilty plea would result in a harsher sentence.

Boykin v. Alabama (1969) Defendants must state that they are voluntarily making a plea of guilty.

Breed v. Jones (1975) Juveniles cannot be found delinquent in juvenile court and then transferred to adult court without a hearing on the transfer; to do so violates the protection against double jeopardy.

case law Court decisions that have the status of law and serve as precedents for later decisions.

challenge for cause Removal of a prospective juror by showing that he or she has some bias or some other legal disability. The number of these challenges permitted to attorneys is potentially unlimited.

Chimel v. California (1969) Supreme Court decision that endorsed warrantless searches for weapons and evidence in the immediate vicinity of people who lawfully are arrested.

circumstantial evidence Evidence, provided by a witness, from which a jury must infer a fact.

citation A written order or summons, issued by a law enforcement officer, often directing an alleged offender to appear in court at a specified time to answer a criminal charge.

civil disabilities Legal restrictions that prevent released felons from voting, serving on juries, and holding public office.

civil forfeiture The confiscation of property by the state because it was used in or acquired through a crime. In recent years the police have used civil forfeiture to seize property that they believe was purchased with drug profits.

civil law Law regulating the relationships between or among individuals, usually involving property, contract, or business disputes.

classical criminology A school of criminology that views behavior as stemming from free will, that demands responsibility and accountability of all perpetrators, and that stresses the need for punishments severe enough to deter others.

classification The process of assigning an inmate to a category specifying his or her needs for security, treatment, education, work assignment, and readiness for release.

clearance rate The percentage rate of crimes known to the police that they believe they have solved through an arrest; a statistic used to measure a police department's productivity.

common law The Anglo-American system of uncodified law, in which judges follow precedents set by earlier decisions when they decide new but similar cases. The substantive and procedural criminal law was originally developed in this manner but was later codified—set down in codes—by state legislatures.

community corrections A model of corrections based on the goal of reintegrating the offender into the community.

community justice A model of justice that emphasizes reparation to the victim and the community, approaching crime from a problem-solving perspective, and citizen involvement in crime prevention.

community service A sentence requiring the offender to perform a certain amount of unpaid labor in the community.

conditions of release Conduct restrictions that parolees must follow as a legally binding requirement of being released.

congregate system A penitentiary system, developed in Auburn, New York, in which each inmate was held in isolation during the night but worked and ate with other prisoners during the day under a rule of silence.

constitution The basic laws of a country or state defining the structure of government and the relationship of citizens to that government.

continuance An adjournment of a scheduled case until a later date.

contract counsel An attorney in private practice who contracts with the government to represent all indigent defendants in a county during a set period of time and for a specified dollar amount.

contract labor system A system under which inmates' labor was sold on a contractual basis to private employers who provided the machinery and raw materials with which inmates made saleable products in the institution.

control theories Theories holding that criminal behavior occurs when the bonds that tie an individual to society are broken or weakened.

Cooper v. Pate (1964) Prisoners are entitled to the protection of the Civil Rights Act of 1871 and may challenge in federal courts the conditions of their confinement.

corrections The variety of programs, services, facilities, and organizations responsible for the management of people who have been accused or convicted of criminal offenses.

count Each separate offense of which a person is accused in an indictment or an information.

crime A specific act of commission or omission in violation of the law, for which a punishment is prescribed.

crime control model A model of the criminal justice system that assumes freedom is so important that every effort must be made to repress crime; it emphasizes efficiency, speed, finality, and the capacity to apprehend, try, convict, and dispose of a high proportion of offenders.

crime control model of corrections A model of corrections based on the assumption that criminal behavior can be controlled by more use of incarceration and other forms of strict supervision.

crime without victims Offenses involving a willing and private exchange of illegal goods or services that are in strong demand. Participants do not feel they are being harmed, but these crimes are prosecuted on the ground that society as a whole is being harmed.

criminogenic Factors thought to bring about criminal behavior in an individual.

custodial model A model of incarceration that emphasizes security, discipline, and order.

cybercrime Offenses that involve the use of one or more computers.

dark figure of crime A metaphor referring to the dangerousness dimension of crime that is never reported to the police.

day reporting center A community correctional center where an offender reports each day to comply with elements of a sentence.

defense attorney The lawyer who represents accused or convicted offenders in their dealings with criminal justice officials.

delinquent A child who has committed an act that if committed by an adult would be a criminal act.

demonstrative evidence Evidence that is not based on witness testimony but demonstrates information relevant to the crime, such as maps, x-rays, and photographs; includes real evidence involved in the crime.

dependent child A child who has no parent or guardian or whose parents cannot give proper care.

deportation Formal removal by the federal government of an alien from the United States for violation of immigration or other laws.

detention hearing A hearing by the juvenile court to determine if a juvenile is to be detained or released prior to adjudication.

determinate sentence A sentence that fixes the term of imprisonment at a specific period.

differential response A patrol strategy that assigns priorities to calls for service and chooses the appropriate response.

direct evidence Eyewitness accounts.

directed patrol A proactive form of patrolling that directs resources to known high-crime areas.

discovery A prosecutor's pretrial disclosure, to the defense, of facts and evidence to be introduced at trial.

discretion The authority to make decisions without reference to specific rules or facts, using instead one's own judgment; allows for individualization and informality in the administration of justice.

discretionary release The release of an inmate from prison to conditional supervision at the discretion of the parole board within the boundaries set by the sentence and the penal law.

discrimination Differential treatment of individuals or groups based on race, ethnicity, sexual orientation, or economic status, instead of on their behavior or qualifications.

disparity The unequal treatment of one group by the criminal justice system, compared with treatment accorded other groups.

diversion The process of screening children out of the juvenile justice system without a decision by the court.

double jeopardy The subjecting of a person to prosecution more than once in the same jurisdiction for the same offense; prohibited by the Fifth Amendment.

drug courts Specialized courts that impose drug testing and counseling requirements on substance abusers and monitor their progress instead of sending them immediately to jail or prison.

dual court system A system consisting of a separate judicial structure for each state in addition to a national structure. Each case is tried in a court of the same jurisdiction as that of the law or laws broken.

due process model A model of the criminal justice system that assumes freedom is so important that every effort must be made to ensure that criminal justice decisions are based on reliable information; it emphasizes the adversarial process, the rights of defendants, and formal decision-making procedures.

Enlightenment A movement, during the eighteenth century in England and France, in which concepts of liberalism, rationalism, equality, and individualism dominated social and political thinking.

entrapment The defense that the police induced the individual to commit the criminal act.

Escobedo v. Illinois (1964) Police cannot refuse access to an attorney for arrested suspects who ask to see one.

exchange A mutual transfer of resources; a balance of benefits and deficits that flow from behavior based on decisions about the values and costs of alternatives.

exclusionary rule The principle that illegally obtained evidence must be excluded from a trial.

exigent circumstances When there is a threat to public safety or the risk that evidence will be destroyed, officers may search, arrest, or question suspects without obtaining a warrant or following other usual rules of criminal procedure.

expiration release The release of an inmate from incarceration, without any further correctional supervision; the inmate cannot be returned to prison for any remaining portion of the sentence for the current offense.

Fare v. Michael C. (1979) By examining the totality of circumstances, trial court judges must evaluate the voluntariness of juveniles' waiving their rights to an attorney and to protections against self-incrimination.

federalism A system of government in which power is divided between a central (national) government and regional (state) governments.

felonies Serious crimes usually carrying a penalty of incarceration for more than one year or the death penalty.

filtering process A process by which criminal justice officials screen out some cases while advancing others to the next level of decision making.

fine A sum of money to be paid to the state by a convicted person as punishment for an offense.

Florida v. J. L. (2000) Police officers may not conduct a stop-and-frisk search based solely on an anonymous tip.

frankpledge A system in old English law in which members of a tithing, a group of ten families, pledged to be responsible for keeping order and bringing violators of the law to court.

fundamental fairness A legal doctrine supporting the idea that so long as a state's conduct maintains basic standards of fairness, the Constitution has not been violated.

furlough The temporary release of an inmate from a correctional institution for a brief period, usually one to three days, for a visit home. Such programs help maintain family ties and prepare inmates for release on parole.

Furman v. Georgia (1972) The death penalty, as administered, constitutes cruel and unusual punishment.

general deterrence Punishment of criminals that is intended to provide an example to the general public and to discourage the commission of offenses.

Gideon v. Wainwright (1963) Indigent defendants have a right to counsel when charged with serious crimes for which they could face six months or more incarceration.

going rate Local court officials' shared view of the appropriate sentence for the offense, based on the defendant's prior record and other case characteristics.

"good faith" exception When police act in honest reliance on a warrant, the evidence seized is admissible even if the warrant is later proved to be defective.

good time A reduction of an inmate's prison sentence, at the discretion of the prison administrator, for good behavior or participation in vocational, educational, or treatment programs.

grand jury A body of citizens that determines whether the prosecutor possesses sufficient evidence to justify the prosecution of a suspect for a serious crime.

habeas corpus A writ or judicial order requesting the release of a person being detained in a jail, prison, or mental hospital. If a judge finds the person is being held improperly, the writ may be granted and the person released or granted a new trial.

halfway house A correctional facility housing convicted felons who spend a portion of their day at work in the community but reside in the halfway house during nonworking hours.

hands-off policy Judges should not interfere with the administration of correctional institutions.

home confinement A sentence requiring the offender to remain inside his or her home during specified periods.

Hudson v. Palmer (1984) Prison officials have the authority to search cells and confiscate any materials found.

identity theft The theft of social security numbers, credit card numbers, and other information in order to secure loans, withdraw bank funds, and purchase merchandise while posing as someone else, the unsuspecting victim, who will eventually lose money in these transactions.

incapacitation Depriving an offender of the ability to commit crimes against society, usually by detaining the offender in prison.

inchoate offense Conduct that is criminal even though the harm that the law seeks to prevent has been merely planned or attempted but not done.

incident-driven policing A reactive approach to policing emphasizing a quick response to calls for service.

incorporation The extension of the due process clause of the Fourteenth Amendment to make binding on state governments the rights guaranteed in the first ten amendments to the U.S. Constitution (the Bill of Rights).

indeterminate sentence A period, set by a judge, that specifies a minimum and a maximum time to be served in prison. Sometime after the minimum, the offender may be eligible for parole. Because it is based on the idea that the time necessary for treatment cannot be set, the indeterminate sentence is closely associated with rehabilitation.

indictment A document returned by a grand jury as a "true bill" charging an individual with a specific crime on the basis of a determination of probable cause from evidence presented by a prosecuting attorney.

indigent defendants People facing prosecution who do not have enough money to pay for their own attorneys and court expenses.

"inevitable discovery" exception Improperly obtained evidence can be used when it would later have inevitably been discovered without improper actions by the police.

information A document charging an individual with a specific crime. It is prepared by a prosecuting attorney and presented to a court at a preliminary hearing.

inmate code The values and norms of the prison social system that define the inmates' idea of the model prisoner.

inquisitorial system Basis of legal system in Europe in which the judge takes an active role in investigating the case and asking questions of witnesses in court.

In re Gault (1967) Juveniles have the right to counsel, to confront and examine accusers, and to have adequate notice of charges when confinement is a possible punishment.

In re Winship (1970) The standard of proof beyond a reasonable doubt applies to juvenile delinquency proceedings.

intensive supervision probation (ISP) Probation granted under conditions of strict reporting to a probation officer with a limited caseload.

intermediate sanctions A variety of punishments that are more restrictive than traditional probation but less severe and costly than incarceration.

internal affairs unit A branch of a police department that receives and investigates complaints alleging violations of rules and policies on the part of officers.

jail An institution authorized to hold pretrial detainees and sentenced misdemeanants for periods longer than 48 hours. Most jails are administered by county governments; in six jurisdictions, by state governments.

jurisdiction The geographic territory or legal boundaries within which control may be exercised; the range of a court's authority.

jury A panel of citizens selected according to law and sworn to determine matters of fact in a criminal case and to deliver a verdict of guilty or not guilty.

Kyllo v. United States (2001) Law enforcement officials cannot examine a home with a thermal-imaging device unless they obtain a warrant.

labeling theories Theories emphasizing that the causes of criminal behavior are not found in the individual but in the social process that labels certain acts as deviant or criminal.

latent fingerprints Impressions from the ridges on the fingertips that are left behind on objects due to natural secretions from the skin or contaminating materials, such as ink, blood, or dirt, that were present on the fingertips at the time of their contact with the objects.

law enforcement The police function of controlling crime by intervening in situations in which the law has clearly been violated and the police need to identify and apprehend the guilty person.

law enforcement intelligence Information, collected and analyzed by law enforcement officials, concerning criminal activities and organizations, such as gangs, drug traffickers, and organized crime.

learning theories Theories that see criminal behavior as learned, just as legal behavior is learned.

lease system A system under which inmates were leased to contractors who provided prisoners with food and clothing in exchange for their labor. In southern states the prisoners were used as agricultural, mining, logging, and construction laborers.

legal responsibility The accountability of an individual for a crime because of the perpetrator's characteristics and the circumstances of the illegal act.

legal sufficiency model The presence of the minimum legal elements necessary for prosecution of a case. When a prosecutor uses legal sufficiency as the customary criterion for prosecuting cases, a great many are accepted for prosecution, but the majority of them are disposed of by plea bargaining or dismissal.

less-lethal weapons Weapons such as pepper spray and air-fired beanbags or nets that intend to incapacitate a suspect without inflicting serious injuries.

life course theories Theories that identify factors affecting the start, duration, nature, and end of criminal behavior over the life of an offender.

line functions Police components that directly perform field operations and carry out the basic functions of patrol, investigation, traffic, vice, juvenile, and so on.

local legal culture Norms, shared by members of a court community, that center on how cases should be handled and how a participant should behave in the judicial process.

mala in se Offenses that are wrong by their very nature.

mala prohibita Offenses prohibited by law but not wrong in themselves.

mandatory release The required release of an inmate from incarceration to community supervision upon the expiration of a certain period, as specified by a determinate-sentencing law or parole guidelines.

mandatory sentences A sentence determined by statutes and requiring that a certain penalty be imposed and carried out for convicted offenders who meet certain criteria.

Mapp v. Ohio (1961) Evidence obtained through illegal searches by state and local police must be excluded from use at trial.

mark system A system in which offenders receive a certain number of points at the time of sentencing, based on the severity of their crime. Prisoners can reduce their term and gain release by earning marks to reduce these points through labor, good behavior, and educational achievement.

McCleskey v. Kemp (1987) Rejects a challenge to Georgia's death penalty that was made on the grounds of racial discrimination.

McKeiver v. Pennsylvania (1971) Juveniles do not have a constitutional right to a trial by jury.

medical model A model of corrections based on the assumption that criminal behavior is caused by biological or psychological conditions that require treatment.

Mempa v. Rhay (1967) Probationers have the right to counsel at a combined revocation-sentencing hearing.

mens rea "Guilty mind" or blameworthy state of mind, necessary for legal responsibility for a criminal offense;

criminal intent, as distinguished from innocent intent.

merit selection A reform plan by which judges are nominated by a commission and appointed by the governor for a given period. When the term expires, the voters are asked to approve or disapprove the judge for a succeeding term. If the judge is disapproved, the committee nominates a successor for the governor's appointment.

Miranda v. Arizona (1966) Before questioning a suspect held in custody, police officers must inform the individual of the right to remain silent and the right to have an attorney present during questioning.

misdemeanors Offenses less serious than felonies and usually punishable by incarceration of no more than one year, probation, or intermediate sanctions.

money laundering Moving the proceeds of criminal activities through a maze of businesses, banks, and brokerage accounts in order to disguise their origin.

Morrissey v. Brewer (1972) Due process rights require a prompt, informal, two-part inquiry before an impartial hearing officer prior to parole revocation. The parolee may present relevant information and confront witnesses.

motions An application to a court requesting that an order be issued to bring about a specified action.

National Crime Victimization Surveys (NCVS) Interviews of samples of the U.S. population conducted by the Bureau of Justice Statistics to determine the number and types of criminal victimization and thus the intent of unreported as well as reported crime.

National Incident-Based Reporting System (NIBRS) A reporting system in which the police describe each offense in a crime incident, together with data describing the offender, victim, and property.

neglected child A child who is receiving inadequate care because of some action or inaction of his or her parents.

net widening Process in which new sentencing options increase instead of reduce control over offenders' lives.

New Jersey v. T. L. O. (1985) School officials may search a student if they have a reasonable suspicion that the search will produce evidence that a school rule or a criminal rule has been violated.

Nix v. Williams (1984) Decision in which the Supreme Court created the "inevitable discovery" exception to the exclusionary rule.

nolle prosequi An entry made by a prosecutor on the record of a case and announced in court to indicate that the charges specified will not be prosecuted. In effect, the charges are thereby dismissed.

nonpartisan election An election in which candidates' party affiliations are not listed on the ballot.

North Carolina v. Alford (1970) A plea of guilty may be accepted for the purpose of a lesser sentence from a defendant who maintains his or her innocence.

occupational crime Criminal offense committed through opportunities created in a legal business or occupation.

open fields doctrine Officers are permitted to search and to seize evidence, without a warrant, on private property beyond the area immediately surrounding the house.

order maintenance The police function of preventing behavior that disturbs or threatens to disturb the public peace or that involves face-to-face conflict among two or more people. In such situations, the police exercise discretion in deciding whether a law has been broken.

organized crime A framework for the perpetration of criminal acts—usually in fields, such as gambling, drugs, and prostitution—providing illegal services that are in great demand.

other conditional release A term used in some states to avoid the rigidity of mandatory release by placing convicts under supervision in various community settings.

pardon An action of the executive branch of state or federal government excluding the offense and absolving the offender from the consequences of the crime.

parens patriae The state as parent; the state as guardian and protector of all citizens (such as juveniles) who cannot protect themselves.

parole The conditional release of an inmate from incarceration under supervision after a part of the prison sentence has been served.

partisan election An election in which candidates openly endorsed by political parties are presented to voters for selection.

penitentiary An institution intended to punish criminals by isolating them from society and from one another so they can reflect on their past misdeeds, repent, and reform.

peremptory challenge Removal of a prospective juror without giving any reason. Attorneys are allowed a limited number of such challenges.

PINS Acronym for "person(s) in need of supervision," a term that designates juveniles who are either status offenders or thought to be on the verge of trouble.

plain view doctrine Officers may examine and use as evidence, without a warrant, contraband or evidence that is in open view at a location where they are legally permitted to be.

plea bargain A defendant's plea of guilty to a criminal charge with the reasonable expectation of receiving some consideration from the state for doing so, usually a reduction of the charge. The defendant's ultimate goal is a penalty lighter than the maximum punishment formally warranted by the original charge.

political crime An act, usually done for ideological purposes, that constitutes a threat against the state (such as treason, sedition, or espionage) or a criminal act by a state.

positivist criminology A school of criminology that views behavior as stemming from social, biological, and psychological factors. It argues that punishment should be tailored to the individual needs of the offender.

Powell v. Alabama (1932) An attorney must be provided to a poor defendant facing the death penalty.

presentence report A report, prepared by a probation officer, that presents a convicted offender's background and is used by the judge in selecting an appropriate sentence.

presumptive sentence A sentence for which the legislature or a commission sets a minimum and maximum range of months or years. Judges are to fix the length of the sentence within that range, allowing for special circumstances.

preventive detention Holding a defendant for trial, based on a judge's finding that, if the defendant were released on bail, he or she would flee or would endanger another person or the community.

preventive patrol Making the police presence known, in order to deter crime and to make officers available to respond quickly to calls.

prison An institution for the incarceration of people convicted of serious crimes, usually felonies.

proactive Acting in anticipation, such as an active search for potential offenders that is initiated by the police without waiting for a crime to be reported. Arrests for crimes without victims are usually proactive.

probable cause Reliable information indicating that evidence will likely be found in a specific location or that a specific person is likely to be guilty of a crime.

probation A sentence that the offender is allowed to serve under supervision in the community.

probation release The release of an inmate from incarceration to probation supervision, as required by the sentencing judge.

problem-oriented policing An approach to policing in which officers routinely seek to identify, analyze, and respond to the circumstances underlying the incidents that prompt citizens to call the police.

procedural criminal law Law defining the procedures that criminal justice officials must follow in enforcement, adjudication, and corrections.

procedural due process The constitutional requirement that all people be treated fairly and justly by government officials. An accused person can be arrested, prosecuted, tried, and punished only in accordance with procedures prescribed by law.

prosecuting attorney A legal representative of the state with sole responsibility for bringing criminal charges; in some states referred to as district attorney, state's attorney, or county attorney.

psychological explanations Explanations of crime that emphasize mental processes and behavior.

public defender An attorney employed on a full-time, salaried basis by the government to represent indigents.

"public safety" exception When public safety is in jeopardy, police may question a suspect in custody without providing the *Miranda* warnings.

reactive Acting in response, such as police activity in response to notification that a crime has been committed.

real evidence Physical evidence such as a weapon, records, fingerprints, stolen property—objects actually involved in the crime.

reasonable doubt The standard used by a juror to decide if the prosecution has provided enough evidence for conviction.

reasonable expectation of privacy Standard developed for determining whether a government intrusion of a person or property constitutes a search because it interferes with individual interests that are normally protected from government intrusion.

reasonable suspicion A police officer's belief, based on articulable facts, that criminal activity is taking place, so that intruding on an individual's reasonable expectation of privacy is necessary.

recidivism A return to criminal behavior.

reformatory An institution for young offenders, emphasizing training, a mark system of classification, indeterminate sentences, and parole.

rehabilitation The goal of restoring a convicted offender to a constructive place in society through some form of vocational or educational training or therapy.

rehabilitation model A model of corrections that emphasizes the need to restore a convicted offender to a constructive place in society through some form of vocational or educational training or therapy.

reintegration model A model of a correctional institution that emphasizes maintaining the offender's ties to family and community as a method of reform, recognizing that the offender will be returning to society.

release on recognizance (ROR) Pretrial release granted on the defendant's promise to appear in court, because the judge believes that the defendant's ties in the community guarantee that he or she will appear.

restitution Repayment—in the form of money or service—by an offender to a victim who has suffered some loss from the offense.

restoration Punishment designed to repair the damage done to the victim and community by an offender's criminal act.

retribution Punishment inflicted on a person who has infringed on the rights of others and so deserves to be penalized. The severity of the sanction should fit the seriousness of the crime.

Ricketts v. Adamson (1987) Defendants must uphold the plea agreement or risk going to trial and receiving a harsher sentence.

Ring v. Arizona (2002) Juries, rather than judges, must make the crucial factual decisions regarding whether a convicted murderer should receive the death penalty.

Roper v. Simmons (2005) Execution of offenders for murders committed before they were 18 years of age is unconstitutional.

Santobello v. New York (1971) When a guilty plea rests on a promise of a prosecutor, the promise must be fulfilled.

Schall v. Martin (1984) Juveniles can be held in preventive detention if there is concern that they may commit additional crimes while awaiting court action.

search Officials' examination of and hunt for evidence in or on a person or place in a manner that intrudes on reasonable expectations of privacy.

seizure Any use by the police of their authority to deprive people of liberty or property.

selective incapacitation Making the best use of expensive and limited prison space by targeting for incarceration those individuals whose detention will do the most to reduce crime in society.

self-incrimination The act of exposing oneself to prosecution by being forced to respond to questions whose answers may reveal that one has committed a crime. The Fifth Amendment protects defendants against compelled self-incrimination. In any criminal proceeding, the prosecution must prove the charges by means of evidence other than the involuntary testimony of the accused.

sentencing guidelines A mechanism to indicate to judges the expected sanction for certain offenses, in order to reduce disparities in sentencing.

separate confinement A penitentiary system, developed in Pennsylvania, in which each inmate was held in isolation from other inmates. All activities, including craft work, took place in the cells.

service The police function of providing assistance to the public, usually in matters unrelated to crime.

shock probation A sentence in which the offender is released after a short incarceration and resentenced to probation.

specific deterrence Punishment inflicted on criminals to discourage them from committing future crimes.

social conflict theories Theories that assume criminal law and the criminal justice system are primarily a means of controlling the poor and the have-nots.

social process theories Theories that see criminality as normal behavior. Everyone has the potential to become a criminal, depending on (1) the influences that impel one toward or away from crime and (2) how one is regarded by others.

social structure theories Theories that attribute crime to the existence of a powerless lower class that lives with poverty and deprivation and often turns to crime in response.

socialization The process by which the rules, symbols, and values of a group or subculture are learned by its members.

sociological explanations Explanations of crime that emphasize the social conditions that bear on the individual as causes of criminal behavior.

state attorney general A state's chief legal officer, usually responsible for both civil and criminal matters.

status offense Any act committed by a juvenile that is considered unacceptable for a child, such as truancy or running away from home, but that would not be a crime if it were committed by an adult.

statutes Laws passed by legislatures. Statutory definitions of criminal offenses are found in penal codes.

stop Government officials' interference with an individual's freedom of movement for a duration that can be measured in minutes.

stop-and-frisk search Limited search approved by Supreme Court in *Terry v. Ohio* that permits officers to pat down clothing of people on the streets if there is reasonable suspicion of dangerous criminal activity.

strict liability An obligation or duty that when broken is an offense that can be judged criminal without a showing of *mens rea*, or criminal intent; usually applied to regulatory offenses involving health and safety.

subculture The symbols, beliefs, and values shared by members of a subgroup of the larger society.

substantive criminal law Law defining acts that are subject to punishment and specifying the punishments for such offenses.

sworn officers Police employees who have taken an oath and been given powers by the state to make arrests and use necessary force, in accordance with their duties.

system A complex whole consisting of interdependent parts whose operations are directed toward goals and are influenced by the environment within which they function.

system efficiency Policy of the prosecutor's office that encourages speedy and early disposition of cases in response to caseload pressures. Weak cases are screened out at intake, and other non-trial alternatives are used a primary means of disposition.

technical violation The probationer's failure to abide by the rules and conditions of probation (specified by the judge), resulting in revocation of probation.

***Tennessee v. Garner* (1985)** Deadly force may not be used against an unarmed and fleeing suspect unless necessary to prevent the escape and unless the officer has probable cause to believe that the suspect poses a significant threat of death or serious injury to the officers and others.

***Terry v. Ohio* (1968)** Supreme Court decision endorsing police officers' authority to stop and frisk suspects on the street when there is reasonable suspicion that they are armed and involved in criminal activity.

testimony Oral evidence provided by a legally competent witness.

theory of differential association The theory that people become criminals because they encounter more influences that view criminal behavior as normal and acceptable than influences that are hostile to criminal behavior.

ticket of leave A system of conditional release from prison, devised by Captain Alexander Maconochie and first developed in Ireland by Sir Walter Crofton.

totality of circumstances test Flexible test established by the Supreme Court for identifying whether probable cause exists to justify the issuance of a warrant.

trial courts of general jurisdiction Criminal courts with jurisdiction over all offenses, including felonies. In some states, these courts also hear appeals.

trial courts of limited jurisdiction Criminal courts with trial jurisdiction over misdemeanor cases and preliminary matters in felony cases. Sometimes these courts hold felony trials that may result in penalties below a specified limit.

trial sufficiency The presence of sufficient legal elements to ensure successful prosecution of a case. When a prosecutor uses trial sufficiency as the customary criterion for prosecuting cases, only cases that seem certain to result in conviction at trial are accepted for prosecution. Use of plea bargaining is minimal; good police work and court capacity to go to trial are required.

Uniform Crime Reports Annually published statistical summary of crimes reported to the police, based on voluntary reports to the FBI by local, state, and federal law enforcement agencies.

United States attorney Officials responsible for the prosecution of crimes that violate the laws of the United States; appointed by the president and assigned to a U.S. district court jurisdiction.

***United States v. Drayton* (2002)** Police officers are not required to inform people of their right to decline when police ask for consent to search.

***United States v. Salerno and Cafero* (1987)** Preventive detention provisions of the Bail Reform Act of 1984 are upheld as legitimate use of government power designed to prevent people from committing crimes while on bail.

USA Patriot Act A federal statute passed in the aftermath of the terrorist attacks of September 11, 2001, that broadens government authority to conduct searches and wiretaps and that expands the definitions of crimes involving terrorism.

***Vernonia School District v. Acton* (1995)** To ensure a safe learning environment, school officials may require random drug testing of students involved in extracurricular school sports teams.

victimology A field of criminology that examines the role the victim plays in precipitating a criminal incident and the impact of crimes on victims.

visible crime An offense against persons or property that is committed primarily by members of the lower social classes. Often referred to as "street crime" or "ordinary crime," this type of offense is the one most upsetting to the public.

voir dire A questioning of prospective jurors in order to screen out people the judge or attorneys think might be biased or otherwise incapable of delivering a fair verdict.

waiver Procedure by which the juvenile court waives its jurisdiction and transfers a juvenile case to the adult criminal court.

warrant A court order authorizing police officials to take certain actions; for example, to arrest suspects or to search premises.

Williams v. Florida (1970) Juries of fewer than 12 members are permitted by the U.S. Constitution.

Witherspoon v. Illinois (1968) Potential jurors who object to the death penalty cannot be automatically excluded from service; however, during voir dire those who feel so strongly about capital punishment that they could not give an impartial verdict may be excluded.

Wolff v. McDonnell (1974) Basic elements of procedural due process must be present when decisions are made about the disciplining of an inmate.

work and educational release The daytime release of inmates from correctional institutions so they can work or attend school.

workgroup A collection of individuals who interact in the workplace on a continuing basis, share goals, develop norms regarding how activities should be carried out, and eventually establish a network of roles that differentiates the group from others and that facilitates cooperation.

working personality A set of emotional and behavioral characteristics developed by a member of an occupational group in response to the work situation and environmental influences.

References

Abadinsky, H. 1997. *Probation and Parole*. 6th ed. Upper Saddle, NJ: Prentice-Hall.

———. 2003. *Organized Crime*. 7th ed. Belmont, CA: Wadsworth.

Abbe, O. G., and P. S. Herrnson. 2002. "How Judicial Election Campaigns Have Changed." *Judicature* 85: 286–95.

ABC News. 2004. "Suspect Says Hunters Shot at Him First." November 23. http://abcnews.go.com.

Abrahamson, S. S. 2004. "The State of the State Courts." *Judicature* 87: 241–42.

Abrams, J. 2000. "Congress Passes Asset Forfeiture Bill." *Topeka Capital Journal*, April 12. http://cjonline.com/stories/.

Abramsky, S. 1999. "When They Get Out." *Atlantic Monthly*, June, pp. 30–36.

Abwender, D. A., and K. Hough. 2001. "Interactive Effects of Characteristics of Defendant and Mock Juror on U.S. Participants: Judgment and Sentencing Recommendations." *Journal of Social Psychology* 141: 603–16.

Acoca, L. 1997. "Hearts on the Ground: Violent Victimization and Other Themes in the Lives of Women Prisoners." *Corrections Management Quarterly* 1 (Spring): 44–55.

———. 1998. "Defusing the Time Bomb: Understanding and Meeting the Growing Health Care Needs of Incarcerated Women in America." *Crime and Delinquency* 44 (January): 49–69.

Adams, K. 1992. "Adjusting to Prison Life." In *Crime and Justice: A Review of Research*, vol. 16, ed. M. Tonry. Chicago: University of Chicago Press, 275–359.

———. 1999. "What We Know about Police Use of Force." In *Use of Force by Police: Overview of National and Local Data*. Washington, DC: U.S. Government Printing Office.

Adang, O. M. J., and J. Mensink. 2004. "Pepper Spray: An Unreasonable Response to Suspect Verbal Resistance." *Policing: International Journal of Police Strategies and Management* 27: 206–19.

Adler, F. 1975. Sisters in Crime: The Rise of the New Female Criminal. New York: McGraw-Hill.

Adler, S. J. 1994. *The Jury: Disorder in the Court*. New York: Doubleday.

Administrative Office of the U.S. Courts. 1993. *Guide to Judiciary Policies and Procedures: Probation Manual*, vol. 10. [mimeograph]

———. 2005. "Need for DNA Testing Taxes Courts." *The Third Branch* 37 (February): 3.

Alabama, Department of Corrections, March 20, 2007. http://www.doc.state.al.us/map.asp.

Alarid, L. F., J. M. Marquart, V. S. Burton, Jr., and S. J. Cuvelier. 1996. "Women's Roles in Serious Offenses: A Study of Adult Felons." *Justice Quarterly* 13 (September): 431–54.

Albanese, J. 1991. "Organized Crime: The Mafia Myth." In *Criminology: A Contemporary Handbook*, ed. J. Sheley. Belmont, CA: Wadsworth, 201–18.

Alpert, G. 2007. "Eliminate Race as the Only Reason for Police-Citizen Encounters." *Criminology & Public Policy* 6 (4): 671–8.

Alexander, R., Jr. 1993. "The Demise of State Prisoners' Access to Federal Habeas Corpus." *Criminal Justice Policy Review* 6: 55–70.

Alley, M. E., E. M. Bonello, and J. A. Schafer. 2002. "Dual Responsibilities: A Model for Immersing Midlevel Managers in Community Policing." In *The Move to Community Policing: Making Change Happen*, ed. M. Morash and J. Ford. Thousand Oaks, CA: Sage, 112–25.

Alonso-Zaldivar, R. 2002. "Police Officers Face New Hazard: Assault by Air Bag." *Los Angeles Times*, August 7, p. 24.

Amar, A. R. 1997. *The Constitution and Criminal Procedure: First Principles*. New Haven, CT: Yale University Press.

American Bar Association. 2008. *National Database on Judicial Diversity in State Courts*. http://www.abanet.org/judind/diversity/national.html (accessed May 17, 2008).

American Correctional Association. 1990. *The Female Offender: What Does the Future Hold?* Alexandria, VA: Kirby Lithographic Company.

———. 1994. *Gangs in Correctional Facilities: A National Assessment*. Laurel, MD: American Correctional Association.

———. 2000. *Vital Statistics in Corrections*. Lanham, MD: American Correctional Association.

American Society of Neuroradiology. 2003. "MRI Technology Shows Promise in Detecting Human Truth and Deception." Press release, May 5. http://www.asnr.org.

Anderson, G., R. Litzenberger, and D. Plecas. 2002. "Physical Evidence of Police Officer Stress." *Policing* 25: 399–420.

Anderson, L. 1999. "Attacks Spur Call to Force Medications." *Chicago Tribune*, June 1, p. 1.

Andrews, D. A., and J. Bonta. 1994. *The Psychology of Criminal Behavior*. Cincinnati, OH: Anderson.

Andrews, D. A., I. Zinger, R. D. Hoge, J. Bonta, P. Gendreau, and F. T. Cullen. 1990. "Does Correctional Treatment Work? A Clinically Relevant and Psychologically Informed Meta-Analysis." *Criminology* 28: 369–404.

Anglen, R. 2008. "Judge Rules for Taser in Cause-of-Death Decisions." *Arizona Republic*, May 2. http://www.azcentral.com.

Antonio, M. E. 2006. "Jurors' Emotional Reactions to Serving on a Capital Jury." *Judicature* 89: 282–88.

Applegate, B. K., F. T. Cullen, and B. S. Fisher. 1997. "Public Support for Correctional Treatment: The Continuing Appeal of the Rehabilitative Ideal." *Prison Journal* 77: 237–58.

Applegate, B. K. and R. K. Davis. 2006. "Public Views on Sentencing Juvenile Murderers: The Impact of Offender, Offense, and Perceived Maturity." Youth Violence and Juvenile Justice 4: 55–74.

Arax, M., and M. Gladstone. 1998. "State Thwarted Brutality Probe in Corcoran Prison, Investigators Say." *Los Angeles Times*, July 5, p. 1.

Arballo, J. 2007. "SWAT Teams Deal in High Risk." *The Press-Enterprise*, October 19. http://www.pe.com

Archibold, R. 2007. "Officials See a Spread in Activity of Gangs." *New York Times*, February 8. http://www.nytimes.com.

Arena, K. and K. Bohn. 2008. "Rape Victim Pushes for Expanded DNA Database." CNN.COM, May 12. http://www.cnn.com.

Armstrong, G. S., and D. L. MacKenzie. 2003. "Private versus Public Juvenile Facilities: Do Differences in Environmental Quality Exist?" *Crime and Delinquency* 49 (October): 542–63.

Armstrong, G. S. and M. L. Griffin. 2007. "The Effect of Local Life Circumstances on Victimization of Drug-Involved Women." *Justice Quarterly* 24 (1): 80–105.

Armstrong, K., F. Davila, and J. Mayo. 2004. "Public Defender Profited While His Clients Lost." *Seattle Times*, April 12. http://www.seattletimes.com.

Armstrong, K., and S. Mills. 1999. "Death Row Justice Derailed." *Chicago Tribune*, November 14, 15, p. 1.

Arnold, N. 2008. "Madison Murder Prompts Look at 911 Procedures." WBAY-TV, May 5. http://www.wbay.com.

Associated Press. 2005a. "Deputies Will Be Disciplined for Wild Shootout." *Pasadena Star News*, June 9. http://www.pasadenastarnews.com.

———. 2005b. "Panel Faults County's Public Defender Load." *Seattle Post-Intelligencer*, November 23, 2005. http://seattlepi.nwsource.com.

———. 2006. "Mistrial Declared in Ferrari Crash Case." *Washington Post*, November 3. http://www.washingtonpost.com.

———. 2007a. Grant Convicted of 2nd-Degree Murder." ClickonDetroit.com. December 21. http://www.clickondetroit.com.

———. 2007b. "Vick Is Indicted on State Dogfighting Charges." *New York Times*, September 26. http://www.nytimes.com.

———. 2008. "Ex-Gitmo Prosecutor Alleges Politics." *New York Times*, April 28. http://www.nytimes.com.

Auerhahn, K. 1999. "Selective Incapacitation and the Problem of Prediction." *Criminology* 37: 703–34.

Austin, J. 2001. "Prisoner Reentry: Current Trends, Practices, and Issues." *Crime and Delinquency* 47 (July): 314–33.

Austin, J., and G. Coventry. 2001. "Emerging Issues on Privatizing Prisons." *Corrections Forum* 10 (December): 11.

Axtman, K. 2005a. "Houston Grapples with Gang Resurgence." *Christian Science Monitor*, April 29, pp. 2–3.

———. 2005b. "A New Motion to Make Jury Service More Attractive." *Christian Science Monitor*, May 23, pp. 2–3.

———. 2005c. "Why Tolerance Is Fading for Zero Tolerance in Schools." *Christian Science Monitor*, March 31, pp. 1, 4.

Baker, A. 2008a. "11 Years of Police Gunfire, in Painstaking Detail." *New York Times*, May 8. http://www.nytimes.com.

———. A. 2008b. "Police Data Shows Increase in Street Stops." *New York Times*, May 6. http://www.nytimes.com.

Baldus, D. C., G. Woodworth, and C. A. Pulaski. 1994. *Equal Justice and the Death Penalty: A Legal and Empirical Analysis.* Boston: Northeastern University Press.

Bandy, D. 1991. "$1.2 Million to Be Paid in Stray-Bullet Death." *Akron Beacon Journal*, December 3, p. B6.

Barnes, C. W., and R. Kingsnorth. 1996. "Race, Drug, and Criminal Sentencing: Hidden Effects of the Criminal Law." *Journal of Criminal Justice* 24: 39–55.

Basemore, G., and M. S. Umbreit. 1994. Foreword to *Balanced and Restorative Justice: Program Summary*. Washington, DC: Office of Juvenile Justice and Delinquency Prevention, U.S. Government Printing Office.

Bast, C. M. 1995. "Publication of the Name of a Sexual Assault Victim: The Collision of Privacy and Freedom of the Press." *Criminal Law Bulletin* 31: 379–99.

Bayley, D. H. 1986. "The Tactical Choice of Police Patrol Officers." *Journal of Criminal Justice* 14: 329–48.

———. 1994. *Police for the Future*. New York: Oxford University Press.

———. 1998. *What Works in Policing?* New York: Oxford University Press.

Beck, A. 1997. "Growth, Change, and Stability in the U.S. Prison Population, 1980–1995." *Corrections Management Quarterly* 8 (January): 1–14.

———. 2000. "State and Federal Prisoners Returning to the Community: Findings from the Bureau of Justice Statistics." Paper presented at the First Reentry Courts Initiative Cluster Meeting, Washington, DC, April 13.

Beck, A. J., J. C. Karberg, and P. M. Harrison. 2002. "Prison and Jail Inmates at Mid-Year 2001." Bureau of Justice Statistics *Bulletin*, April.

Becker, Howard S. 1963. *Outsiders: Studies in the Sociology of Deviance*. New York: Free Press.

Bell, D. 1967. *The End of Ideology*. 2nd. rev. ed. New York: Collier.

Belluck, P. 1998. "44 Officers Are Charged After Ohio Sting Operation." *New York Times*, January 22. http://www.nytimes.com.

———. 1999a. "As More Prisons Go Private, States Seek Tighter Controls," *New York Times*, April 15, p. 1.

———. 1999b. "Death Row Lessons and One Professor's Mission," *New York Times*, March 6, p. A1.

———. 2001. "Desperate for Prison Guards, Some States Even Rob Cradles." *New York Times*, April 21, p. A1.

———. 2005. "DNA Test Leads, at Last, to Arrest in Cape Cod Case." *New York Times*, April 16. http://www.nytimes.com.

Bermudez, E. 2008. "Are Crime and Immigration Linked?" *The Oregonian*, May 4. http://www.oregonlive.com.

Bershard, L. 1985. "Discriminatory Treatment of the Female Offender in the Criminal Justice System." *Boston College Law Review* 26: 389–438.

Bichler, G., and L. Gaines. 2005. "An Examination of Police Officers' Insights into Problem Identification and Problem Solving." *Crime and Delinquency* 51: 53–74.

BJS (Bureau of Justice Statistics). 1988. *Report to the Nation on Crime and Justice*. 2nd ed. Washington, DC: U.S. Government Printing Office.

———. 1997a. *Police Use of Force*. Washington, DC: U.S. Government Printing Office.

———. 1997b. Press release, November 22.

———. 1998a. *Bulletin*, January.

———. 1998b. *Bulletin*, June.

———. 1998c. Crime and Justice in the United States and in England and Wales, 1981–1996. Washington, DC: U.S. Government Printing Office.

———. 1999a. *American Indians and Crime*. Washington, DC: U.S. Government Printing Office.

———. 1999b. *Special Report*, January.

———. 1999c. *Special Report*, July.

———. 1999d. *Special Report*, December.

———. 2000a. *Bulletin*, April.

———. 2000b. *Bulletin*, August.

———. 2000c. Census of State and Federal Correctional Facilities, 2000. Washington, DC: U.S. Government Printing Office.

———. 2000d. *Correctional Populations in the United States, 1997*. Washington, DC: U.S. Government Printing Office.

———. 2000e. Law Enforcement Management and Administration Statistics (LEMAS) Survey, 1999. Washington, DC: U.S. Government Printing Office.

———. 2000f. Press release, February 27.

———. 2000g. *Sourcebook of Criminal Justice Statistics, 1999*. Washington, DC: U.S. Government Printing Office.

———. 2000h. *Special Report*, February.

———. 2000i. *Special Report*, May.

———. 2000j. *Special Report*, August.

———. 2001a. *Bulletin*, July.

———. 2001b. *Bulletin*, August.

———. 2001c. *Sourcebook of Criminal Justice Statistics, 2000*. Washington, DC: U.S. Government Printing Office.

———. 2001d. *Special Report*, January 2001.

———. 2001e. *Special Report*, July 2001.

———. 2002a. *Bulletin*, June.

———. 2002b. Special Report, May.

———. 2002c. *Special Report*, June.

———. 2003a. *Bulletin*, June.

———. 2003b. *Bulletin*, July.

———. 2003c. *Bulletin*, August.

———. 2003d. Census of State and Federal Correctional Facilities, 2000. Washington, DC: U.S. Government Printing Office.

———. 2003e. Criminal Victimization in the United States——Statistical Tables, 2002. Washington, DC: U.S. Government Printing Office.

———. 2003f. *Sourcebook of Criminal Justice Statistics, 2002*. Washington, DC: U.S. Government Printing Office.

———. 2003g. Special Report, May.

———. 2004a. *Bulletin*, January.

———. 2004b. *Bulletin*, May.

———. 2004c. *Bulletin*, July.

———. 2004d. *Bulletin*, November.

———. 2004e. *Bulletin*, December.

———. 2004f. "Criminal Victimization." http://www.ojp.usdoj.gov/bjs/cvictgen.htm.

———. 2004g. *Sourcebook of Criminal Justice Statistics, 2003*. Washington, DC: U.S.

Government Printing Office. BJS. 2004h. *Special Report,* July.

———. 2005. "Law Enforcement Statistics—2000." http://www .ojp.usdoj.gov/bjs/lawenf.htm.

———. 2006. Criminal Victimization in the United States, 2005—Statistical Tables." NCJ 215244.

———. 2007a. *Sourcebook of Criminal Justice Statistics— 2006.* http://www.albany.edu/ sourcebook.

———. 2007b. *Sourcebook of Criminal Justice Statistics— 2007c,* Table 2.34.2007, http:// www.albany.edu/sourcebook/.

———. 2007c. "Prison and Jail Inmates at Midyear" Bureau of Justice Statistics *Bulletin* (June). Washington, DC: U.S. Department of Justice.

———. 2008. *Employment and Earnings Bulletin,* vol. 55 (January). http://www.bls.gov.

Blair, J. 2000. "Boot Camps: An Idea Whose Time Came and Went," *New York Times,* January 2, p. WK3.

Blecker, R. 2006. "'A Poster Child for Us'." *Judicature* 89 (5): 297–301.

Bloch, P., and D. Anderson. 1974. *Policewomen on Patrol: First Report.* Washington, DC: Police Foundation.

Blonston, G. 1993. "'Explosion' in Crime Powerful—But False Statistics: Most Americans Are Safer Than a Decade Ago." *San Jose Mercury News,* October 24, p. 1A.

Blumberg, A. 1967. "The Practice of Law as a Confidence Game." *Law and Society Review* 1: 11–39.

Blumberg, M. 1989. "Controlling Police Use of Deadly Force: Assessing Two Decades of Progress." In *Critical Issues in Policing,* ed. G. Dunham and G. Alpert. Prospect Heights, IL: Waveland Press.

Blumenson, E., and E. Nilsen. 1998. "The Drug War's Hidden Economic Agenda." *The Nation.* March 9, p. 11.

Blumstein, A. 1996. "Youth Violence, Guns, and Illicit Drug Markets." In *NIJ Research Preview.* Washington, DC: National Institute of Justice, U.S. Government Printing Office.

Boland, B., E. Brady, H. Tyson, and J. Bassler. 1983. *The Prosecution of Felony Arrests.*

Washington, DC: Bureau of Justice Statistics, U.S. Government Printing Office.

Bonczar, T. P., and T. L. Snell. 2004. "Capital Punishment, 2003." Bureau of Justice Statistics *Bulletin,* November.

Bonne, J. 2001. "Meth's Deadly Buzz." *MSNBC News Special Report,* February. http:// msnbc.msn.com.

Bonneau, C. W. 2004. "Patterns of Campaign Spending and Electoral Competition in State Supreme Court Elections." *Justice System Journal* 25 (1): 21–38.

Bontrager, S., W. Bales and T. Chiricos. 2005. "Race, Ethnicity, Threat and the Labeling of Convicted Felons." *Criminology* 43 (3): 589–622.

Bourque, B. B., M. Han, and S. M. Hill. 1996. "A National Survey of Aftercare Provisions for Boot Camp Graduates." In *Research in Brief.* Washington, DC: National Institute of Justice, U.S. Government Printing Office.

Bowers, F. 2002. "The Intelligence Divide: Can It Be Bridged?" *Christian Science Monitor,* October 8, p. 2.

Bowker, L. H. 1982. "Victimizers and Victims in American Correctional Institutions." In *Pains of Imprisonment,* ed. R. Johnson and H. Toch. Beverly Hills, CA: Sage.

Bradley, C. 1992. "Reforming the Criminal Trial." *Indiana Law Journal* 68: 659–64.

Bradley, C. M. 2006. "The Right Decision on the Juvenile Death Penalty." *Judicature* 89 (5): 302–5.

Braga, A. A. 1999. "Problem-Oriented Policing in Violent Crime Places: A Randomized Controlled Experiment." *Criminology* 37: 541–80.

Braga, A. A. and G. L. Pierce. 2005. "Disrupting Illegal Firearms Markets in Boston: The Effects of Operation Ceasefire on the Supply of Handguns to Criminals." *Criminology & Public Policy* 4: 717–48.

Brandl, S. 1993. "The Impact of Case Characteristics of Detectives' Decision Making." *Justice Quarterly* 10 (September): 395–415.

Brandl, S., and Frank, J. 1994. "The Relationship between Evidence, Detective Effort, and the Disposition of Burglary

and Robbery Investigations." *American Journal of Police* 13: 149–68.

Brandon, K. 1999. "Legal Abortions Tied to Decline in Crime." *Hartford Courant,* August 8, p. A5.

Bray, K. 1992. "Reaching the Final Chapter in the Story of Peremptory Challenges." *U.C.L.A. Law Review* 40: 517–55.

Brennan, P. A., S. A. Mednick, and J. Volavka. 1995. "Biomedical Factors in Crime." In *Crime,* ed. J. Q. Wilson and J. Petersilia. San Francisco: ICS Press.

Brennan, P. K. 2006. "Sentencing Female Misdemeanants: An Examination of the Direct and Indirect Effects of Race/Ethnicity." *Justice Quarterly* 23 (1): 60–95.

Brewer, T. W. 2005. "The Attorney-Client Relationship in Capital Cases and Its Impact on Juror Receptivity to Mitigation Evidence." *Justice Quarterly* 22 (3): 340–63.

Bridges, K. L. 2004. "The Forgotten Constitutional Right to Present a Defense and Its Impact on the Acceptance of Responsibility-Entrapment Debate." *Michigan Law Review* 103: 367–96.

Bright, S. B. 1994. "Counsel for the Poor: The Death Sentence Not for the Worst Crime but for the Worst Lawyer." *Yale Law Journal* 103: 1850.

Britt, C. 2000. "Social Context and Racial Disparities in Punishment Decisions." *Justice Quarterly* 17: 707–32.

Britton, D. M. 1997. "Political Attacks on the Judiciary." *Judicature* 80: 165–73.

Brody, D. C. 2004. "The Relationship between Judicial Performance Evaluations and Judicial Elections." *Judicature* 87: 168–77, 192.

Broeder, D. W. 1959. "The University of Chicago Jury Project." *Nebraska Law Review* 38:774–803.

Brooks, R., D. R. Santschi, C. Chambers and J. Asbury. 2007. "Officer Dies in Drug Raid." *The Press-Enterprise,* October 19. http://www.pe.com.

Brown, M. K. 1981. *Working the Street.* New York: Russell Sage Foundation.

Brown, R. A. and J. Frank. 2006. "Race and Officer Decision

Making: Examining Differences in Arrest Outcomes between Black and White Officers." *Justice Quarterly* 23: 96–126.

Bruce, M. 2003. "Contextual Complexity and Violent Delinquency among Black and White Males." *Journal of Black Studies* 35: 65–98.

Buentello, S. 1992. "Combating Gangs in Texas." *Corrections Today* 54 (July): 58–60.

Bureau of Justice Assistance (BJA). 1998. *1996 National Survey of State Sentencing Structures.* Washington, DC: U.S. Government Printing Office.

Bureau of Labor Statistics. 2005. "Labor Force Statistics from the Current Population Survey." U.S. Department of Labor. http://www.bls.gov/cps/ home.htm.

Buruma, I. 2005. "What Teaching a College-Level Class at a Maximum Security Correctional Facility Did for the Inmates—and for Me." *The New York Times Magazine,* February 20, pp. 36–41.

Bushway, S. D., and A. M. Piehl. 2001. "Judging Judicial Discretion: Legal Factors and Racial Discrimination in Sentencing." *Law and Society Review* 35: 733–64.

Business Wire. 2001a. "Study Shows Iris Recognition Technology Is Superior among Biometrics; Britain's National Physical Laboratory Publishes Performance Evaluation of Seven Biometric Systems." May 17. Lexis-Nexis.

———. 2001b. "WorldNet Technologies, Creators of a State of the Art Weapons Detection System, Signs Consulting Deal with NuQuest." November 27. Lexis-Nexis.

Butterfield, F. 1995a. "Idle Hands within the Devil's Own Playground." *New York Times,* July 16, p. E3.

———. 1995b. "More Blacks in Their 20's Have Trouble with the Law." *New York Times,* October 5, p. A18.

———. 1996. "Three Strikes Rarely Invoked in Courtrooms." *New York Times,* September 10, p. A1.

———. 1998a. "Decline in Violent Crimes Is Linked to Crack Market." *New York Times,* December 18, p. A16.

———. 1998b. "Prisons Replace Hospitals for the Nation's Mentally Ill." *New York Times,* March 5, p. A26.

———. 1999. "Rethinking the Strong Arm of the Law." *New York Times,* April 4, p. WK1.

———. 2000. "Often, Parole Is One Stop on the Way Back to Prison." *New York Times,* November 29, p. A1.

———. 2004. "Almost 10% of All Prisoners Are Now Serving Life Terms," *New York Times,* May 12, p. A15.

Bykowicz, J. 2008. "Juvenile Center Home to Despair." Baltimore Sun, (May 25). http://baltimoresun.com.

Bynum, T., and S. Varano. 2002. "The Anti-Gang Initiative in Detroit: An Aggressive Enforcement Approach to Gangs." In *Policing Gangs and Youth Violence,* ed. Scott H. Decker. Belmont, CA: Wadsworth, 214–38.

Cadigan, T. P. 2007. "Pretrial Services in the Federal System: Impact of the Pretrial Services Act of 1982." *Federal Probation* 71 (2): 10–15.

Calhoun, F. 1990. *The Lawmen.* Washington, DC: Smithsonian Institution.

Call, J. E. 1995. "Prison Overcrowding Cases in the Aftermath of *Wilson v. Seiter.*" *Prison Journal* 75 (September): 390–405.

Callahan, L. A., M. A. McGreevy, C. Cirincione, and H. J. Steadman. 1992. "Measuring the Effects of the Guilty But Mentally Ill (GBMI) Verdict." *Law and Human Behavior* 16: 447–62.

Callahan, R. 2002. "Scientists: Liars Are Betrayed by Their Faces." Associated Press Wire Service, January 2.

Camp, C. G. 2003. *Corrections Yearbook, 2002.* Middletown, CT: Criminal Justice Institute.

Camp, C. G., and G. M. Camp. 1999. *Corrections Yearbook, 1999.* Middletown, CT: Criminal Justice Institute.

———. 2001. *Corrections Yearbook, 2000.* Middletown, CT: Criminal Justice Institute.

Camp, D. D. 1993. "Out of the Quagmire: After *Jacobson v. United States:* Toward a More Balanced Entrapment Standard." *Journal of Criminal Law and Criminology* 83: 1055–97.

Camp, S. D., and G. G. Gales. 2002. "Growth and Quality of U.S. Private Prisons: Evidence from a National Survey." *Criminology and Public Policy* 1: 427–50.

Cancino, J. M., and R. Enriquez. 2004. "A Qualitative Analysis of Officer Peer Retaliation: Preserving the Police Culture." *Policing: International Journal of Police Strategies and Management* 27: 320–40.

Carey, S. M., and M. W. Finegan. 2004. "A Detailed Cost Analysis in a Mature Drug Court Setting." *Journal of Contemporary Criminal Justice* 20: 315–38.

Carlson, P. M. 2001. "Prison Interventions: Evolving Strategies to Control Security Threat Groups." *Corrections Management Quarterly* 5 (Winter): 10–22.

Carlson, T. 1995. "Safety , Inc." *Policy Review,* Summer, pp. 67–73.

Carr, J. G. 1993. "Bail Bondsmen and the Federal Courts." *Federal Probation* 57 (March): 9–14.

Carr, P. J., and L. Napolitano and J. Keating. 2007. "We Never Call the Cops and Here Is Why: A Qualitative Examination of Legal Cynicism in Three Philadelphia Neighborhoods." *Criminology* 45: 445–80.

Carroll, L. 1974. *Hacks, Blacks, and Cons: Race Relations in a Maximum Security Prison.* Lexington, MA: Lexington Books.

Carter, C. J. 2002. "Army Officer, Four Others Indicted." Associated Press Wire Service, July 3.

Casey, M. 1999. "Defense Lawyers for Poor Clients May Get Pay Raise." *New York Times,* April 11, p. 5.

Cassell, P., and R. Fowles. 1998. "Handcuffing the Cops? A Thirty-Year Perspective on *Miranda*'s Harmful Effects on Law Enforcement." *Stanford Law Review* 50: 1055–145.

Catalano, S. M. 2004. "Criminal Victimization 2003." In *National Crime Victimization Survey.* Washington, DC: Bureau of Justice Statistics, U.S. Government Printing Office, September.

———. 2007. *Intimate Partner Violence in the United States.* Washington, DC: U.S. Bureau of Justice Statistics.

Cauffman, E., L. Steinberg, and A. R. Piquero. 2005. "Psychological, Neuropsychological, and Physiological Correlates of Serious Antisocial Behavior in Adolescence: The Role of Self-Control." *Criminology* 43: 133–76.

Caulfield, S. L. 1994. "Life or Death Decision: Prosecutorial Power vs. Equality of Justice." *Journal of Contemporary Criminal Justice* 5: 233–47.

CBS News. 2004a. "Deer Hunt Dispute Turns Deadly." November 22. http://www.cbsnews.com.

———. 2004b. "John Hinckley Wants More Freedom." November 8. http://www.cbsnews.com.

———. 2008a. "Captured Marine's Wife Refused to Help Him," April 11. http://www.cbsnews.com.

———. 2008b. "Murdered Pregnant Women: The Racial Divide." April 11. http://www.cbsnews.com.

CBS2-TV. 2008. "City Council Approves 19.8M Burge Settlement." CBS2-TV Chicago, January 9. http://www.cbs2chicago.com.

Center for Corporate Policy. 2005. "Corporate Crime and Abuse: Tracking the Problem." http://www.corporatepolicy.org/issues/crimedata.htm.

Chaddock, G. R. 2002. "Sniper Revives Prospects for Gun-Tracking Moves." *Christian Science Monitor,* October 17, p. 1.

Champagne, A., and K. Cheek. 1996. "PACs and Judicial Politics in Texas." *Judicature* 80: 26–29.

Champion, D. J. 1989. "Private Counsels and Public Defenders: A Look at Weak Cases, Prior Records, and Leniency in Plea Bargaining." *Journal of Criminal Justice* 17: 253–63.

Chapman, S. G. 1970. *Police Patrol Readings.* 2nd ed. Springfield, IL: Thomas.

Chapper, J. A., and R. A. Hanson. 1989. *Understanding Reversible Error in Criminal Appeals.* Williamsburg, VA: National Center for State Courts.

"Charging Common Criminals under Terrorism Laws Doesn't Fit in America's Justice Values." 2003. *Asheville Citizen-Times,* July 23. http://www.citizentimes.com.

Chavez, P. 2005. "Shooting Raises Racial Tension in L.A." *Sacramento Union,* February 21. http://www.sacunion.com.

Cheesman, F., R. A. Hanson, and B. J. Ostrom. 1998. "To Augur Well: Future Prison Population and Prisoner Litigation." Paper presented at the Federal Judicial Center, Washington, DC, May 20.

Cheng, E. K. 2006. "Should Judges Do Independent Research on Scientific Issues?" *Judicature* 90: 58–61.

Chermak, S. M. 1995. *Victims in the News: Crime and the American News Media.* Boulder, CO: Westview Press.

Chermak, S., and E. McGarrell. 2004. "Problem-Solving Approaches to Homicide: An Evaluation of Indianapolis Violence Reduction Partnership." *Criminal Justice Policy Review* 15: 161–92.

Cheung, H. 2007. "LAPD's Dart-Firing, License Plate Reading, Video Streaming Car." *TG Daily,* August 22. http://www.tgdaily.com.

Chiricos, T. G., and W. D. Bales. 1991. "Unemployment and Punishment: An Empirical Assessment." *Criminology* 29: 701–24.

Chiricos, T. G., and C. Crawford. 1995. "Race and Imprisonment: A Contextual Assessment of the Evidence." In *Ethnicity, Race, and Crime: Perspectives across Time and Place,* ed. D. F. Hawkins. Albany: State University of New York Press.

Chiricos, T. G., S. Escholz, and M. Gertz. 1997. "Crime, News, and Fear of Crime." *Social Problems* 44: 342–57.

Chiricos, T., K. Padgett, and M. Gertz. 2000. "Fear, TV News, and the Reality of Crime." *Criminology* 38: 755–85.

Christensen, P. H. 2008. "Crime Prevention Takes Teamwork." *Spokesman Review,* April 17. http://www.spokesmanreview.com.

Christopher, R. L. 1994. "Mistake of Fact in the Objective Theory of Justification." *Journal of Criminal Law and Criminology* 85: 295–332.

Church, T. W. 1985. "Examining Local Legal Culture." *American Bar Foundation Research Journal* 1985 (Summer): 449.

Clear, T. R. 1994. *Harm in American Penology*. Albany: State University of New York Press.

Clear, T. R., and A. A. Braga. 1995. "Community Corrections." In *Crime*, ed. J. Q. Wilson and J. Petersilia. San Francisco: ICS Press, 421–44.

Clear, T., G. Cole and M. Reisig. 2008. *American Corrections*, 8th ed. Belmont, Calif.: Cengage.

Clear, T., and D. Karp. 1999. *Community Justice: Preventing Crime and Achieving Justice*. New York: Westview Press.

Clear, T. R., and E. J. Latessa. 1993. "Probation Officers' Roles in Intensive Supervision: Surveillance vs. Treatment." *Justice Quarterly* 10 (3): 441–60.

Clear, T., D. R. Rose, E. Waring, and K. Scully. 2003. "Coercive Mobility and Crime: A Preliminary Examination of Concentrated Incarceration and Social Disorganization." *Justice Quarterly*, 20 (March): 33–63.

CNN. 2004a. "Boston Police Accept 'Full Responsibility' in Death of Red Sox Fan." October 22. http://www.cnn.com.

———. 2004b. "Police Review Policy after Tasers Used on Kids." November 14. http://www.cnn.com.

———. 2005a. "Autopsy: Toddler Hit Twice by LAPD." August 3. http://www.cnn.com.

———. 2005b. "Pregnant Woman: 'Maternal Instinct' Helped Kill Attacker." February 14. http://www.cnn.com.

———. 2005c. "Rapper Lil' Kim Gets 366 Days in Prison." July 6. http://www.cnn.com.

——— 2008. "Pregnant Marine Missing from North Carolina Base." January 9. http://www.cnn.com.

———. 2007. "Astronaut Granted Bond on Attempted Murder Charge." CNN.com, February 6. http://www.cnn.com.

Cohen, L. E., and M. Felson. 1979. "Social Change and Crime Rates: A Routine Activ-

ity Approach." *American Sociological Review* 44: 588–608.

Cohen, M., T. R. Miller, and S. B. Rossman. 1990. "The Costs and Consequences of Violent Behavior in the United States." Paper prepared for the Panel on the Understanding and Control of Violent Behavior, National Research Council, National Academy of Sciences, Washington, DC.

Cohen, T. H. and B. A. Reaves. 2006. *Felony Defendants in Large Urban Counties, 2002*. Washington, DC: Bureau of Justice Statistics. NCJ 210818

Colbert, D. 1998. "Thirty-five Years after *Gideon*: The Illusory Right to Counsel at Bail Proceedings." *University of Illinois Law Review* 1998: 1–58.

Cole, D. 1999. *No Equal Justice: Race and Class in American Criminal Justice*. New York: New Press.

Collins, J. 2005. *Preventing Identity Theft in Your Business: How to Protect Your Business, Customers, and Employees*. New York: Wiley.

Commission on Accreditation for Law Enforcement Agencies. 1989. *Standards for Law Enforcement Accreditation*. Fairfax, VA:

"Concern Mounts over Anti-Terrorism Law." 2005. *Michigan Daily*, April 7. http://www.michigandaily.com.

Conover, T. 2000. *Newjack: Guarding Sing Sing*. New York: Random House.

Constanzo, M. 1997. *Just Revenge*. New York: St. Martin's Press.

Consumer Reports. n.d. "Will Your Cell Phone Reach 911?" http://www.consumerreports.org.

Conway, P. 2001. "The 2001 Electronic Monitoring Survey." *Journal of Electronic Monitoring* 14 (Winter–Spring): 7–9.

Cook, P. J., and J. H. Laub. 2002. "After the Epidemic: Recent Trends in Youth Violence in the United States." In *Crime and Justice: A Review of Research*, vol. 29, ed. Michael Tonry. Chicago: University of Chicago Press.

Cooney, M. 1994. "Evidence as Partisanship." *Law and Society Review* 28: 833–58.

COURT TV. 2002a. "Blake Judge May Reconsider Bail." May 2. http://www.courttv.com.

———. 2002b. "Police: 'Physical and Significant Circumstantial Evidence' against Robert Blake in Wife's Killing." April 19. http://www.courttv.com.

———. 2003a. "Blake Ordered to Stand Trial but Granted Bail." March 13. http://www.courttv.com.

———. 2003b. "In Secret Recording, Blake Accuses Wife of Lying to Him about Pregnancy." February 26. http://www.courttv.com.

———. 2005. "Actor Robert Blake Acquitted of His Wife's Murder." March 17. http://www.courttv.com.

Coutts, L., and F. Schneider. 2004. "Police Officer Performance Appraisal Systems: How Good Are They?" *Policing: International Journal of Police Strategies and Management* 27: 67–81.

Cowell, A. J., N. Broner, and R. DuPont. 2004. "The Cost-Effectiveness of Criminal Justice Diversion Programs for People with Serious Mental Illness Co-occurring with Substance Abuse." *Journal of Contemporary Criminal Justice* 20: 292–315.

Crawford, C. 2000. "Gender, Race, and Habitual Offender Sentencing in Florida." *Criminology* 38 (February): 263–80.

Crawford, C., T. Chiricos, and G. Kleck. 1998. "Race, Racial Threat, and Sentencing of Habitual Offenders." *Criminology* 36 (August): 481–512.

Crew, B. K. 1991. "Race Differences in Felony Charging Sentencing: Toward an Integration of Decision-Making and Negotiation Models." *Journal of Crime and Justice* 14: 99–122.

Criminal Justice Research Reports. 2001. July–August, p. 87.

Crouch, B. M., and J. M. Marquart. 1994. "On Becoming a Prison Guard." *In The Administration and Management of Criminal Justice Organizations*, 2nd ed., ed. S. Stojokovic, J. Klofas, and D. Kalinich. Prospect Heights, IL: Waveland Press.

Cullen, F. T., L. Cao, J. Frank, R. H. Langworthy, S. L. Browning, R. Kopache, and T. J. Stevenson. 1996. "'Stop or I'll Shoot': Racial Differences in Support for Police Use of

Deadly Force on Fleeing Felons." *American Behavioral Scientist* 39 (February): 449–60.

Cullen, F. T., T. Leming, B. Link, and J. Wozniak. 1985. "The Impact of Social Supports in Police Stress." *Criminology* 23: 503–22.

Cullen, F. T., J. P. Wright, and B. K. Applegate. 1996. "Control in the Community: The Limits of Reform?" In *Choosing Correctional Options that Work: Defining the Demand and Evaluating the Supply*, ed. A. T. Harland. Thousand Oaks, CA: Sage, 69–116.

Cunningham, W. C., J. J. Strauchs, and C. W. Van Meter. 1990. *Private Security Trends, 1970 to the Year 2000*. Boston: Butterworth-Heinemann.

Daly, K. 1998. "Gender, Crime, and Criminology." In *The Handbook of Crime and Punishment*, ed. M. Tonry. New York: Oxford University Press, 85–108.

Daly, K., and M. Chesney-Lind. 1988. "Feminism and Criminology." *Justice Quarterly* 5: 497–538.

Davitz, T. 1998. "The Gangs Behind Bars." *Insight on the News*, September 28.

Davey, J. D. 1998. *The Politics of Prison Expansion: Winning Elections by Waging War on Crime*. Westport, CT: Praeger.

Davies, T. Y. 1983. "A Hard Look at What We Know (and Still Need to Learn) about the 'Costs' of the Exclusionary Rule: The NIJ Study and Other Studies of 'Lost' Arrests." *American Bar Foundation Research Journal* 1983: 611–90.

Davis, A. 2001. "Laptop Computers in Police Cars Keep Officers Informed, on Streets." *Arkansas Democrat-Gazette*, February 24, p. B3.

Davis, M., R. Lundman, and R. Martinez, Jr. 1991. "Private Corporate Justice: Store Police, Shoplifters, and Civil Recovery." *Social Problems* 38: 395–408.

Davis, R. C., B. E. Smith, and B. Taylor. 2003. "Increasing the Proportion of Domestic Violence Arrests That Are Prosecuted: A Natural Experiment in Milwaukee." *Criminology and Public Policy* 2: 263–82.

Dawson, M., and R. Dinovitzer. 2001. "Victim Cooperation and the Prosecution of Domestic Violence in a Specialized Court." *Justice Quarterly* 18: 593–622.

Death Penalty Information Center. 2005. "Facts about the Death Penalty." May 25. http://www.deathpenaltyinfo.org.

———. 2008a. "Cases of Innocence: 1973–Present." http://www.deathpenaltyinfo.org.

———. 2008b. "Facts About the Death Penalty." June 1. http://www.deathpenaltyinfo.org.

Decker, S., R. Wright, A. Redfern, and D. Smith. 1993. "A Woman's Place Is in the Home: Females and Residential Burglary." *Justice Quarterly* 10 (March): 143–62.

DeFrances, C. J. 2002. "Prosecutors in State Courts, 2001." *Bureau of Justice Statistics Bulletin,* May.

DeFrances, C. J., and J. Litras. 2000. "Indigent Defense Services in Large Counties, 1999." *Bureau of Justice Statistics Bulletin,* November.

DeJong, C. and E. S. Merrill. 2000. "Getting 'Tough on Crime': Juvenile Waiver and the Criminal Court. *Ohio Northern University Law Review* 27: 175–96.

DeJong, C., S. Mastrofski, and R. Parks. 2001. "Patrol Officers and Problem Solving: An Application of Expectancy Theory." *Justice Quarterly* 18: 31–61.

Dewan, S. 2005. "Jurors in Boy's Murder Trial Consider if Zoloft Is to Blame." *New York Times,* February 15, http://www.nytimes.com.

———. 2007. "An SOS for 911 Systems in Age of High-Tech." *New York Times,* April 6. http://www.nytimes.com.

Dewan, S., and B. Meier. 2005. "Boy Who Took Antidepressant Is Convicted in Killings." *New York Times,* February 16. http://www.nytimes.com.

Dickerson, B. 2008. "Hard Lemonade, Hard Price." *Detroit Free Press,* April 28. http://www.freep.com.

Dickson, B. E. 2006. "Effects of Capital Punishment on the Justice System: Reflections of a

State Supreme Court Justice." *Judicature* 89 (5): 278-281.

Diggs, D. W., and S. L. Peiper. 1994. "Using Day Reporting Centers as an Alternative to Jail." *Federal Probation* 58 (March): 9–13.

DiIulio, J. J., Jr. 1987. *Governing Prisons.* New York: Free Press.

———. 1991. *No Escape: The Future of American Corrections.* New York: Basic Books.

———. 1993. "Rethinking the Criminal Justice System: Toward a New Paradigm." In *Performance Measures for the Criminal Justice System.* Washington, DC: Bureau of Justice Statistics, U.S. Government Printing Office.

———. 1994. "The Question of Black Crime." *The Public Interest,* Fall, pp. 3–32.

Dill, F. 1975. "Discretion, Exchange, and Social Control: Bail Bondsmen in Criminal Courts." *Law and Society Review* 9: 644–74.

Dillehay, R. C., and M. R. Sandys. 1996. "Life under *Wainwright v. Witt:* Juror Dispositions and Death Qualification." *Law and Human Behavior* 20: 147–65.

Dodd, T., S. Nicholas, D. Povey, and A. Walker. 2004. "Crime in England and Wales 2003/2004." *Home Office Statistical Bulletin,* July.

Dodge, J., and M. Pogrebin. 2001. "African-American Policewomen: An Exploration of Professional Relationships." *Policing* 24: 550–2.

Donohue, J. J., and S. D. Levitt. 1998. "The Impact of Race on Policing, Arrest Patterns, and Crime." American Bar Foundation Working Paper #9705 (Revision).

Donziger, S. R., ed. 1996. *The Real War on Crime: The Report of the National Criminal Justice Commission.* New York: HarperCollins.

Dority, B. 2005. "The USA Patriot Act Has Decimated Many Civil Liberties." In *Homeland Security: Current Controversies,* ed. Andrea Nakaya. Detroit: Thomson/Gale, 130–6.

Drimmer, J. 1997. "America' s Least Wanted: We Need New Rules to Stop Abuses." *Washington Post,* September 21, p. C6.

Dugan, L. 1999. "The Effect of Criminal Victimization on a Household's Moving Decision." *Criminology* 37: 903–30.

Dugdale, R. 1910. The Jukes: Crime, Pauperism, Disease, and Heredity. 4th ed. New York: Putnam.

Durose, M. R., and P. A. Langan. 2003. "Felony Sentences in State Courts, 2000." Bureau of Justice Statistics *Bulletin,* June.

Durose, M. R., E. L. Schmitt, and P. Langan. 2005. *Contacts between Police and the Public: Findings from the 2002 National Survey.* Washington, DC: Bureau of Justice Statistics, U.S. Government Printing Office, April.

Durose, M. R. and P.A. Langan. 2007. "Felony Sentences in State Courts, 2004." Bureau of Justice Statistics *Bulletin,* July. NCJ 215646.

Durose, M. R., E. L. Smith and P. A. Langan. 2007. "Contacts Between Police and the Public, 2005." Bureau of Justice Statistics *Special Report* (April). NCJ 215243.

Dwyer, J., P. Neufeld, and B. Scheck. 2001. *Actual Innocence: When Justice Goes Wrong and How to Make It Right.* New York: New American Library.

Earley, P. 1992. The Hot House: *Life inside Leavenworth Prison.* New York: Bantam Books.

Eaton, L., and L. Kaufman. 2005. "In Problem-Solving Court, Judges Turn Therapist." *New York Times,* April 26. http://www.nytimes.com.

Editor. 2003. "Wages and Benefits Paid to Correctional Employees." *Correctional Compendium,* January 28, pp. 8–26.

Egan, T. 1999. "A Drug Ran Its Course, Then Hid with Its Users." *New York Times,* September 19, p. A1. Eggen, D., and J. Stockwell. 2005. "10,000 Fugitives Are Captured in Huge Dragnet." *Washington Post,* April 15, p. A1.

Eichenwald, K. 2006. "On the Web, Pedophiles Extend Their Reach." *New York Times,* August 21. http://www.nytimes.com.

Eigenberg, H. 2000. "Correctional Officers, and their Perceptions

of Homosexuality, Rape, and Prosecution in Male Prisons." *Prison Journal* 80 (December): 415–33.

Eisenberg, T., P. Hannaford-Agor, V. P. Hans, N. L. Mott, G. T. Munsterman, S. J. Schwab, and M. T. Wells. 2005. "Judge-Jury Agreement in Criminal Cases: A Partial Replication of Kalven and Zeisel's *The American Jury. Journal of Empirical Legal Studies* 2: 171–206.

Eisenstein, J., R. B. Flemming, and P. F. Nardulli. 1988. *The Contours of Justice: Communities and Their Courts.* Boston: Little, Brown.

Eisenstein, J., and H. Jacob. 1977. *Felony Justice: An Organizational Analysis of Criminal Courts.* Boston: Little, Brown.

Eitle, D. J. 2000. "Regulatory Justice: A Re-Examination of the Influence of Class Position on the Punishment of White-Collar Crime." *Justice Quarterly* 17: 809–35.

El-Khoury, T. 2007. "Hulk Hogan's Son Charged in Serious Wreck." *St. Petersburg Times,* November 7. http://blogs.tampabay.com.

Elliott, J., and B. Murphy. 2005. "Parole, Probation V iolators Add to Crowding." *Houston Chronicle,* January 20. http://www.chron.com/cs/CDA/ printstory.mpl/metropolitan/3000503.

Emmelman, D. S. 1996. "Trial by Plea Bargain: Case Settlement as a Product of Recursive Decisionmaking." *Law and Society Review* 30: 335–60.

Engber, D. 2005. "Does the FBI Have Your Fingerprints?" *Slate,* April 22. http://slate.msn.com/id/2117226.

Engel, R. S., and J. Calnon. 2004. "Examining the Influence of Drivers' Characteristics during Traffic Stops with Police: Results from a National Survey." *Justice Quarterly* 21: 49–90.

Engel, R. S., J. M. Calnon, and T. J. Bernard. 2002. "Theory and Racial Profiling: Shortcomings and Future Directions in Research." *Justice Quarterly* 19: 249–73.

Epstein, L. and J. Segal. 2007. *Advice and Consent: The Politics of Judicial Appointments.* New York: Oxford University Press.

Estrich, S. 1998. *Getting Away with Murder: How Politics Is Destroying the Criminal Justice System*. Cambridge, MA: Harvard University Press.

Fabelo, T. 1999. *Biennial Report to the 76th Texas Legislature*. Austin, TX: Criminal Justice Policy Council.

FBI (Federal Bureau of Investigation). 2002. *National Press Release: Crime Trends, 2001 Preliminary Figures*. June 24. http://www.fbi.gov.

———. 2004a. *Crime in the United States—2003*. Washington, DC: U.S. Government Printing Office.

———. 2004b. Uniform Crime Reports 2003. Washington, DC: U.S. Government Printing Office.

———. 2005. Uniform Crime Reports 2004—Preliminary Report. Washington, DC: U.S. Government Printing Office.

———. 2007. *Crime in the United States, 2006*, Washington, DC: U.S. Government Printing Office.

———. 2006. "FBI Cyber Action Teams: Traveling the World to Catch Cyber Criminals." March 6. www.fbi.gov.

———. 2007a. *Crime in the United States, 2006*. http://www.fbi.gov.

———. 2007b. "Law Enforcement Officers Killed and Assaulted," 2006. http://www.fbi.gov.

———. 2008. "Cyber Solidarity: Five Nations, One Mission." March 18. http://www.fbi.gov.

Federal Bureau of Prisons. 2000. "State of the Bureau: Accomplishments and Goals." Washington, DC: U.S. Government Printing Office.

Feeney, F. 1998. *German and American Prosecution: An Approach to Statistical Comparison*. Washington, DC: Bureau of Justice Statistics, U.S. Government Printing Office.

Feinberg, M. E., M. T. Greenwood, and D. W. Osgood. 2004. "Readiness, Functions, and Perceived Effectiveness in Community Prevention Coalitions: A Study of Communities That Care." *American Journal of Community Psychology* 33: 163–77.

Felch, J. and M. Dolan. 2008. "DNA Matches Aren't Always a Lock." *Los Angeles Times*, May 4. http://www.latimes.com.

Feld, B. C. 1993. "Criminalizing the American Juvenile Court." In *Crime and Justice: A Review of Research*, vol. 17, ed. M. Tonry. Chicago: University of Chicago Press, 197–280.

Feld, B. C. 1999. Bad Kids: Race and the Transformation of the Juvenile Court. New York: Oxford University Press.

———. 2003. "The Politics of Race and Juvenile Justice: The 'Due Process Revolution' and the Conservative Reaction." *Justice Quarterly* 20: 765–800.

———. 2004. "Editorial Introduction: Juvenile Transfers." *Criminology and Public Policy* 3 (November): 599–603.

———. 2008. "A Slower Form of Death: Implications of Roper v. Simmons for Juveniles Sentenced to Life without Parole." *Notre Dame Journal of Law, Ethics & Public Policy* 22: 101–58.

Felice, J. D., and J. C. Kilwein. 1992. "Strike One, Strike Two . . .: The History and Prospect for Judicial Reform in Ohio." *Judicature* 75: 193–200.

Felson, R. B., and J. Ackerman. 2001. "Arrest for Domestic and Other Assaults." *Criminology* 39: 655–75.

Feuer, A. 2004. "$3 Million Deal in Police Killing of Diallo in '99." *New York Times*, January 7. http://www.nytimes.com.

———. 2005a. "Detectives' Lawyers Know the Spotlight." *New York Times*, March 19. http://www.nytimes.com.

———. 2005b. "Fewest Added to Death Row Since 1976." 2005. *Washington Post*, April 26, p. A9.

———. 2008. "An Aversion to the Death Penalty, but No Shortage of Cases." *New York Times*, March 10. http://www.nytimes.com.

Fender, B. F. and C. Brooking. 2004. "A Profile of Indigent Defense and Presentencing Jail Time in Mississippi." *Justice System Journal* 25 (2): 209–25.

Fields, G. 2008. "Murder Spike Poses Quandary." *Wall Street Journal*, May 6. http://online.wsj.com.

Finn, M. A. 2002. "Police Handling of the Mentally Ill in Domestic Violence Situations." *Criminal Justice and Behavior* 29: 278–307.

Fishbein, D. H. 1990. "Biological Perspectives in Criminology." *Criminology* 28:27–72.

Fisman, R. 2008. "Going Down Swingin: What If Three-Strikes Laws Make Criminals Less Likely to Repeat Offend—But More Violent When They Do?" Slate.com, March 20. http://www.slate.com.

Flanagan, T. J., ed. 1995. *Long-Term Imprisonment*. Thousand Oaks, CA: Sage.

Flango, V. E. 1994. *Habeas Corpus in State and Federal Courts*. Williamsburg, VA: National Center for State Courts.

Fleisher, M. 1989. *Warehousing Violence*. Newbury Park, CA: Sage.

Flemming, R. B., P. F. Nardulli, and J. Eisenstein. 1992. *The Craft of Justice: Politics and Work in Criminal Court Communities*. Philadelphia: University of Pennsylvania Press.

Flock, J. 2003. "'Blanket Commutation' Empties Illinois Death Row." CNN, January 13. http://www.cnn.com.

Flynn, K. 1999. "Record Payout in Settlements against Police." *New York Times*, October 1. http://www.nytimes.com.

Forman, J., Jr. 2004. "Community Policing and Youth as Assets." *Journal of Criminal Law and Criminology* 95: 1–49.

Foucault, M. 1977. *Discipline and Punish*. Trans. A. Sheridan. New York: Pantheon.

Fox, J. G. 1982. *Organizational and Racial Conflict in Maximum Security Prisons*. Lexington, MA: Lexington Books.

Frank, J., S. G. Brandl, F. T. Cullen, and A. Stichman. 1996. "Reassessing the Impact of Race on Citizens' Attitudes toward the Police: A Research Note." *Justice Quarterly* 13 (June): 320–34.

Friday, P. C., S. Metzger, and D. Walters. 1991. "Policing Domestic Violence: Perceptions, Experience, and Reality." *Criminal Justice Review* 16: 198–213.

Fridell, L. 1990. "Decision Making of the District Attorney: Diverting or Prosecuting Intrafamilial Child Sexual Abuse Offenders." *Criminal Justice Policy Review* 4:249–67.

Friedman, L. M. 1993. *Crime and Punishment in American History*. New York: Basic Books.

Friedrichs, D. O. 1996. *Trusted Criminals: White-Collar Crime in Society*. Belmont, CA: Wadsworth.

Fritsch. J. 2000. "The Diallo Verdict: 4 Officers in Diallo Shooting Are Acquitted of All Charges." *New York Times*, February 26, p. A13.

Frohmann, L. 1997. "Convictability and Discordant Locales: Reproducing Race, Class, and Gender Ideologies in Prosecutorial Decision-making." *Law and Society Review* 31: 531–56.

Frye, S. 2005. "Judge To Hit List Kid: 'Don't Come Back.'" *The Oakland Press*, August 26. http://www.theoaklandpress.com.

Fukurai, H. 1996. "Race, Social Class, and Jury Participation: New Dimensions for Evaluating Discrimination in Jury Service and Jury Selection." *Journal of Criminal Justice* 24: 71–88.

Fyfe, J. 1993. "Police Use of Deadly Force: Research and Reform." In *Criminal Justice: Law and Politics*, 6th ed., ed. G. F. Cole. Belmont, CA: Wadsworth.

Fyfe, J., D. A. Klinger, and J. M. Flavin, 1997. "Differential Policy Treatment of Male-on-Female Spousal Violence." *Criminology* 35 (August): 454–73.

Gallup Poll. 2002. June 11. http://www.gallup.com.

____. 2008. "Gallup's Pulse of Democracy: Crime." http://www.gallup.com.

Gannon, M. 2006. "Crime Statistics in Canada, 2005." *Juristat* 26 (4): 1–23 [Canadian Centre for Justice Statistics]

Garcia, M. 2005. "N.Y. Using Terrorism Law to Prosecute Street Gang." *Washington Post*, February 1, p. A3.

Garner, J., and E. Clemmer. 1986. *Danger to Police in Domestic Disturbances: A New Look*. Washington, DC: Bureau of Justice Statistics, U.S. Government Printing Office.

Garner, J. H., and C. D. Maxwell. 1999. "Measuring the Amount of Force by and against the Police in Six Jurisdictions." In *Use of Force by the Police*. Washington, DC: National Institute of Justice, U.S. Government Printing Office.

Garner, J. H., C. D. Maxwell, and C. G. Heraux. 2002. "Characteristics Associated with the Prevalence and Severity of Force Used by the Police." *Justice Quarterly* 19: 705–46.

Garner J., T. Schade, J. Hepburn, and J. Buchanan. 1995. "Measuring the Continuum of Forced Used by and against the Police." *Criminal Justice Review* 20 (Autumn): 146–68.

Garvey, C. 2002. "Risk Assessment: Looking for Chinks in the Armor." In *Readings in Security Management,* ed. Robert McCrie. New York: ASIS International, 99–104.

Geller, W. A., and Morris, N. 1992. "Relations between Federal and Local Police." In *Modern Policing*, ed. M. Tonry and N. Morris. Chicago: University of Chicago Press, 231–348.

German, M. and J. Stanley. 2007. *What's Wrong with Fusion Centers?* New York: American Civil Liberties Union.

Geroux, B. 2007. "Vick Dogfighting Trial Set for April 2." *Richmond Times-Dispatch*. November 28, http://www.inrich.com.

Gershman, B. L. 1993. "Themes of Injustice: Wrongful Convictions, Racial Prejudice, and Lawyer Incompetence." *Criminal Law Bulletin* 29: 502–15.

Gesch, C. B., S. M. Hammond, S. H. Hampson, A. Eves, and M. J. Crowder. 2002. "Influence of Supplementary Vitamins, Minerals, and Essential Fatty Acids on the Antisocial Behavior of Young Adult Prisoners." *British Journal of Psychiatry* 181: 22–28.

Gest, T. 2001. *Crime and Politics: Big Government's Erratic Campaign for Law and Order*. New York: Oxford University Press.

Gezari, V. M. 2008. "Cracking Open." *Washington Post*, June 1. http://www.washingtonpost.com.

Giacomazzi, A. L., S. Riley, and R. Merz. 2004. "Internal and External Challenges to Implementing Community Policing: Examining Comprehensive Assessment Reports from Multiple Sites." *Criminal Justice Studies* 17: 223–37.

Gill, M. S. 1997. "Cybercops Take a Byte out of Computer Crime." *Smithsonian,* May, pp. 114–24.

Giordano, P. C., M. A. Longmore, R. D. Schroeder, and P. M. Seffrin. 2008. "A Life-Course Perspective on Spirituality and Desistance From Crime." *Criminology* 46 (1): 99–131.

Girshick, L. B. 1999. *No Safe Haven: Stories of Women in Prison*. Boston: Northeastern University Press.

Glaberson, W. 2002. "On Eve of Trial, Ex-Officer Agrees to Perjury Term in Louima Case." *New York Times*, September 22, p. 1.

Glanz, J. and D. Rohde. 2006. "Panel Faults U.S.-Trained Afghan Police." *New York Times*, December 4. http://www.nytimes.com.

Glick, R. M., and V. V. Neto. 1977. *National Study of Women's Correctional Programs*. Washington, DC: U.S. Government Printing Office.

Glueck, S., and E. Glueck. 1950 *Unraveling Juvenile Delinquency*. New York: Commonwealth Fund.

Goddard, H. H. 1902. *The Kallikak Family*. New York: Macmillan.

Goldfarb, R. L. 1965. *Ransom: A Critique of the American Bail System*. New York: Harper & Row.

Goldfarb, R. L., and L. R. Singer. 1973. *After Conviction*. New York: Simon & Schuster.

Goldkamp, J. S. 1985. "Danger and Detention: A Second Generation of Bail Reform." *Journal of Criminal Law and Criminology* 76: 1–75.

Goldman, J. 2002. "Skakel Is Found Guilty of 1975 Moxley Murder." *Los Angeles Times,* June 8. http://www.latimes.com.

Goldman, S., and E. Slotnick. 1999. "Clinton's Second Term Judiciary: Picking Judges under Fire." *Judicature* 82: 264–85.

Goldman, S., E. Slotnick, G. Gryski, G. Zuk, and S. Schiavoni. 2003. "W. Bush Remaking the Judiciary: Like Father Like Son?" *Judicature* 86: 282–309.

Goldschmidt, J., and J. M. Shaman. 1996. "Judicial Disqualifications: What Do Judges Think?" *Judicature* 80: 68–72.

Goldstein, H. 1977. *Policing a Free Society*. Cambridge, MA: Ballinger.

———. 1979. "Improving Policing: A Problem-Oriented Approach." *Crime and Delinquency* 25: 236–57.

———. 1990. *Problem-Oriented Policing*. New York: McGraw- Hill.

Golz, J. 2008. "Businessman Won't Pay Psychic's Bail." *Naperville Sun*, April 20. http://suburbanchicagonew.com/napervillesun/news/.

Goode, E. 2002. "Jobs Rank Low As Risk Factors for Suicide." *New York Times*, November 12. www.nytimes.com.

Goodman, J. 1994. *Stories of Scottsboro*. New York: Random House.

Goodpaster, G. 1986. "The Adversary System, Advocacy, and Effective Assistance of Counsel in Criminal Cases." *New York University Review of Law and Social Change* 14: 57–92.

Goolkasian, G. A., R. W. Geddes, and W. DeJong. 1989. "Coping with Police Stress." In *Critical Issues in Policing*, ed. R.G. Dunham and G. P. Alpert. Prospect Heights, IL: Waveland Press, 489–507.

Gordon, J. 2005. "In Patriots' Cradle, the Patriot Act Faces Scrutiny." *New York Times,* April 24. http://www.nytimes.com.

Gordon, M. 2006. "Disgraced Bondsman Candid on Eve of Jail." *New Orleans Times-Picayune*, October 27. http://www.nola.com.

Gottfredson, D. C., S. S. Najaka, and B. Kearley. 2003. "Effectiveness of Drug Treatment Courts: Evidence from a Randomized Trial." *Criminology and Public Policy* 2: 171–96.

Gottfredson, M., and T. Hirschi. 1990. *A General Theory of Crime*. Stanford, CA: Stanford University Press.

Gould, J. B. 2004. "After Further Review: A New Wave of Innocence Commissions." *Judicature* 88: 126–31.

Graham, B. L. 1995. "Judicial Recruitment and Racial Diversity on State Courts." In *Courts and Justice*, ed. G. L. Mays and P. R. Gregware. Prospect Heights, IL: Waveland Press.

"Grand Jury Ruling Sparks Police Shootings," 1996. *USA Today*, December 5. http://www.usatoday.com.

Gray, C. 2004. "The Good News in Republican Party of Minnesota v. White." *Judicature* 87: 271–72.

Green, G. S. 1997. *Occupational Crime*. 2nd ed. Belmont, CA: Wadsworth.

Greenberg, D. F., and V. West. 2001. "State Prison Populations and their Growth, 1971–1991." *Criminology* 39 (August): 615–54.

Greene, J. A. 1999. "Zero Tolerance: A Case Study of Police Policies and Practices in New York City." *Crime and Delinquency* 45 (April): 171–87.

Greenhouse, L. 2007. "In Steps Big and Small, Supreme Court Moved Right." *New York Times*, July 1. http://www.nytimes.com.

———. 2008. "Justices Accept Question of Prosecutors as Lawyers or Managers." *New York Times*, April 15. http://www.nytimes.com.

Greenwood, P., J. M. Chaiken, and J. Petersilia. 1977. *Criminal Investigation Process*. Lexington, MA: Lexington Books.

Greer, K. R. 2000. "The Changing Nature of Interpersonal Relationships in a Women's Prison." *Prison Journal* 80 (December): 442–68.

Grennan, S. A. 1987. "Findings on the Role of Officer Gender in Violent Encounters with Citizens." *Journal of Police Science and Administration* 15: 78–85.

Griffin, T. and J. Wooldredge. 2006. "Sex-Based Disparities in Felony Dispositions Before and Versus After Sentencing Reform in Ohio." *Criminology* 44(4): 893–923.

Griset, P. L. 1994. "Determinate Sentencing and the High Cost of Overblown Rhetoric: The New York Experience." *Crime and Delinquency* 40 (4): 532–48.

———. 1995. "The Politics and Economics of Increased Correctional Discretion over Time Served: A New York Case Study." *Justice Quarterly* 12 (June): 307–23.

Guevara, L., D. Herz and C. Spohn. 2006. "Gender and

Juvenile Justice Decision Making: What Role Does Race Play?" Feminist Criminology 1: 258–82.

Haarr, R. N., and M. Morash. 1999. "Gender, Race and Strategies of Coping with Occupational Stress in Policing." Justice Quarterly 16: 303–36.

Haberman, C. 2005. "He Did Time, So He's Unfit to Do Hair." New York Times, March 4. http://www.query.nytimes.com/mem/tnt.html?tntget=2005/03/04/nyregion.html.

Hackett, D. P., and J. M. Violanti, eds. 2003. Police Suicide: Tactics for Prevention. Springfield, IL: Thomas.

Hackney, Arboscello and Swickard, 2007. "Fatigue, Frostbite Catch Up to Him," Detroit Free Press, March 5, 1A.

Hagan, F. E. 1997. Political Crime: Ideology and Criminality. Needham Heights, MA: Allyn and Bacon.

Hagan, J., and R. D. Peterson. 1995. "Criminal Inequality in America: Patterns and Consequences." In Crime and Inequality, ed. J. Hagan and R. D. Peterson. Stanford, CA: Stanford University Press, 14–36.

Haghighi, B., and J. Sorensen. 1996. "America's Fear of Crime." In Americans View Crime and Justice, ed. T. Flanaghan and D. R. Longmire. Thousand Oaks, CA: Sage, 16–30.

Hall, J. 1947. General Principles of Criminal Law. 2nd ed. Indianapolis: Bobbs-Merrill.

Hall, M. G. 1995. "Justices as Representatives: Elections and Judicial Politics in the United States." American Politics Quarterly 23: 485–503.

Hall, W. K., and L. T. Aspin. 1987. "What Twenty Years of Judicial Retention Elections Have Told Us." Judicature 70: 340–47.

Hallinan, J. T. 2001. Going Up the River: Travels in a Prison Nation. New York: Random House.

Hambling, D. 2005. "Police Toy with 'Less Lethal' Weapons." April 30. http://www.newscientist.com.

Hamilton, P. 2007. "Truth Gets in Way of Tribune Story." The Paris News (March 18). http://theparisnews.com.

Hanlon, M. 2007. "Run Away the Ray-Gun is Coming: We Test U.S. Army's New Secret Weapon." The Daily Mail, September 18. http://www.dailymail.co.uk.

Hans, V., and N. Vidmar. 1986. Judging the Jury. New York: Plenum Press.

Hans, V. P. and N. Vidmar. 2008. "The Verdict on Juries." Judicature 91: 226–30.

Hanson, R. A., and J. Chapper. 1991. Indigent Defense Systems. Williamsburg, VA: National Center for State Courts.

Hanson, R. A., and H. W. K. Daley. 1995. Challenging the Conditions of Prisons and Jails: A Report on Section 1983 Litigation. Washington, DC: Bureau of Justice Statistics, U.S. Government Printing Office.

Harding. R. 2001. "Private Prisons." In Crime and Justice: A Review of Research, vol. 27, ed. M. Tonry. Chicago: University of Chicago Press, 265–346.

Harkin, T. 2005. "Confronting the Meth Crisis." Press release, February 7. http://harkin.senate.gov. Harlow, C. 2000. "Defense Counsel in Criminal Cases." Bureau of Justice Statistics Bulletin, November.

Hartley, R., S. Madden and C. Spohn. 2007. "Prosecutorial Discretion: An Examination of Substantial Assistance Departures in Federal Crack-Cocaine and Powder-Cocaine Cases." Justice Quarterly 24 (3): 382–407.

Hartley, R. E. and K. Bates. 2006. "Meeting the Challenge of Educating Court Managers." Judicature 90 (2): 81–8.

Hastie, R., S. Penrod, and N. Pennington. 1983. Inside the Jury. Cambridge, MA: Harvard University Press.

Hathaway, W. 2002. "A Clue to Antisocial Behavior: Study Finds Gene Marker for which Abused Children May Become Troubled Adults." Hartford Courant, August 2, p. A17.

Hauser, C. 2008. "A Precinct's Hard Road Back." New York Times, February 24. http://www.nytimes.com.

Hays, C. L. 2004. "5 Months in Jail, and Stewart Vows, 'I'll Be Back'." New York Times, July 17, p. A1. Heffernan, E. 1972. Making It in Prison. New York: Wiley.

Hegsted, M. 2005. "Sniper's Conviction Upheld." Potomac News, April 23. http://www.potomacnews.com.

Helms, M. 2004. "Of Crime and Culture." Minnesota Public Radio Online News and Feature, November 25. http://news.minnesota.publicradio.org.

Henizmann, D. and S. St. Clair. 2008. "Gunman Was Top Scholar with 'No Record of Trouble.'" Detroit Free Press, February 15. http://www.freep.com.

Henning, P. J. 1993. "Precedents in a Vacuum: The Supreme Court Continues to Tinker with Double Jeopardy." American Criminal Law Review 31:1–72.

Hensley, T. R. , J. A. Baugh and C. E. Smith. 2007. "The First-Term Performance of Chief Justice John Roberts." Idaho Law Review 43: 625–42.

Herbert, S. 1996. "Morality in Law Enforcement: Chasing "Bad Guys" with the Los Angeles Police Department." Law and Society Review 30: 799–818.

Heredia, C. 2007. "Officer Shortage to Persist in '08, Police Chief Says." San Francisco Chronicle, February 10. http://www.sfgate.com.

Herrnstein, R. J. 1995. "Criminogenic Traits." In Crime, ed. J. Q. Wilson and J. Petersilia. San Francisco: ICS Press.

Heumann, M. 1978. Plea Bargaining. Chicago: University of Chicago Press.

Hickey, T. J. 1993. "Expanding the Use of Prior Act Evidence in Rape and Sexual Assault." Criminal Law Bulletin 29: 195–218.

———. 1995. "A Double Jeopardy Analysis of the Medgar Evers Murder Case." Journal of Criminal Justice 23: 41–51.

Hickman, M. J. 2003. "Tribal Law Enforcement, 2000." Bureau of Justice Statistics Fact Sheet (January). NCJ 197936.

Hickman, M. J., and B. A. Reaves. 2001. Local Police Departments, 1999. Washington, DC: Bureau of Justice Statistics, U.S. Government Printing Office.

———. 2006. Local Police Departments, 2003." (May) Washington, DC: U.S. Bureau of Justice Statistics. NCJ 210118.

Hicks, N. 2005. "Bill Aims to Gut Police Liability in High-Speed Chases." Lincoln Journal Star, February 6. http://www.journalstar.com.

Hillsman, S. T., J. L. Sichel, and B. Mahoney. 1983. Fines in Sentencing. New York: Vera Institute of Justice.

Hinduja, S. 2004. "Perceptions of Local and State Law Enforcement Concerning the Role of Computer Crime Investigative Teams." Policing: International Journal of Police Strategies and Management 27: 341–57.

———. 2007. "Neutralization Theory and Online Software Piracy: An Empirical Analysis." Ethics and Information Technology 9(3): 187–204.

Hinduja, S. and J. Patchin. 2007. "Offline Consequences of Online Victimization: School Violence and Delinquency." Journal of School Violence 6(3): 89–112.

Hinduja, S. and J. W. Patchin. 2009. Bullying Beyond the Schoolyard: Preventing and Responding to Cyberbullying. Thousand Oaks, CA: Sage Publications (Corwin Press).

Hinton, H. L., Jr. 2002. "Considerations for Investing Resources in Chemical and Biological Preparedness." In Terrorism: Are We Ready?, ed. Diana Miller. Huntington, NY: Nova Science, 21–31.

Hirsch, A. J. 1992. The Rise of the Penitentiary. New Haven, CT: Yale University Press.

Hirschi, T. 1969. Causes of Delinquency. Berkeley: University of California Press.

Ho, N. T. 2000. "Domestic Violence in a Southern City: The Effects of a Mandatory Arrest Policy on Male-Versus-Female Aggravated Assault Incidents." American Journal of Criminal Justice 25: 107–18.

Ho, T. 1998. "Retardation, Criminality, and Competency to Stand Trial among Mentally Retarded Criminal Defendants: Violent versus Non-violent Defendants." Journal of Crime and Justice 21: 57–70.

Hoctor, M. 1997. "Domestic Violence as a Crime against the

State." *California Law Review* 85 (May): 643–700.

Hoffman, M. 1999. "Abolish Peremptory Challenges." *Judicature* 82: 202–4.

Hoffmann, H. L. 2006. "Rehnquist and Federal Habeas Corpus," in C. Bradley, ed. *The Rehnquist Legacy*. New York: Cambridge University Press.

Hoge, R. D., N. G. Guerra and P. Boxer. 2008. *Treating the Juvenile Offender*. New York: Guilford Press.

Holmes, M. D. 2000. "Minority Threat and Police Brutality: Determinants of Civil Rights Criminal Complaints in U.S. Municipalities." *Criminology* 38: 343–67.

Holmes, M. D., H. M. Hosch, H. C. Daudistel, D. A. Perez, and J. B. Graves. 1996. "Ethnicity, Legal Resources, and Felony Dispositions in Two Southwestern Jurisdictions." *Justice Quarterly* 13: 11–29.

Holmes, O. W., Jr. 1881. *The Common Law*. Boston: Little, Brown.

Holmes, S. A. 1996. "With More Women in Prison, Sexual Abuse by Guards Becomes Greater Concern," *New York Times*, December 27, p. A18.

Horne, P. 2006. "Policewomen: Their First Century and the New Era." *The Police Chief*, vol. 73 (9). September. http://policechiefmagazine.org

Horney, J., and C. Spohn. 1991. "Rape Law Reform and Instrumental Change in Six Urban Jurisdictions." *Law and Society Review* 25: 117–53.

Houston, B., and J. Ewing. 1991. "Justice Jailed." *Hartford Courant,* June 16, p. A1.

Howard, J. 1929. *The State of Prisons in England and Wales*. London: J. M. Dent. Originally published in 1777.

Howlett, D. 2004. "Chicago Plans Advanced Surveillance." September 9. http://www.usatoday.com.

Huebner, B. M. 2005. "The Effect of Incarceration on Marriage and Work Over the Life Course." *Justice Quarterly* 22 (3): 281–301.

Huff, C. R. 2002. "Wrongful Conviction and Public Policy: The American Society of Criminology 2001 Presidential Address." *Criminology* 40: 1–18.

Huff, C. R., and M. Meyer. 1997. "Managing Prison Gangs and Other Security Threat Groups." *Corrections Management Quarterly* 1 (Fall): 10–8.

Hughes, K. A. 2006. "Justice Expenditures and Employment in the United States, 2003. Bureau of Justice Statistics *Bulletin*, NCJ 212260, April.

Human Rights Watch. 2003. *Ill-Equipped: U.S. Prisons and Offenders with Mental Illness*. New York: Human Rights Watch.

Hunt, G., S. Riegel, T. Morales, and D. Waldorf. 1993. "Changes in Prison Culture: Prison Gangs and the Case of the Pepsi Generation." *Social Problems* 40: 398–409.

Hurtado, p. 2005. "Lil' Kim Takes the Stand, Denies Perjury Charges." *Newsday*, March 11, p. A18.

Ianni, F. A. J. 1973. *Ethnic Succession in Organized Crime*. Washington, DC: U.S. Government Printing Office.

Innes, C. A., and V. D. Verdeyen. 1997. "Conceptualizing the Management of Violent Inmates." *Corrections Management Quarterly* 1 (Fall): 1–9.

International Association of Chiefs of Police. 1998. *The Future of Women in Policing: Mandates for Action*. Alexandria, VA: Author.

Internet Crime Complaint Center. 2008. *2007 Internet Crime Report*. Washington, DC. U.S. Department of Justice.

Iribarren, C. J., J. H. Markovitz, D. R. Jacobs, P. J. Schreiner, M. Daviglus, and J. R. Hibbeln. 2004. "Dietary Intake of n-3, n-6 Fatty Acids and Fish: Relationship with Hostility in Young Adults—the CARDIA Study." *European Journal of Clinical Nutrition* 58: 24–31.

Irwin, J. 1970. *The Felon*. Englewood Cliffs, NJ: Prentice-Hall.

———. 1980. *Prisons in Turmoil*. Boston: Little, Brown.

Irwin, J., and D. Cressey. 1962. "Thieves, Convicts, and the Inmate Culture." *Social Problems* 10: 142–55.

Ith, I. 2001. "Taser Fails to Halt Man with Knife; Seattle Officer Kills 23-Year-Old." *Seattle Times,* November 28, p. A1.

Iyengar, R. 2008. "I'd Rather Be Hanged for a Sheep Than a Lamb: The Unintended Consequences of 'Three-Strikes' Laws." National Bureau of Economic Research Working Paper No. 13784. February.

Jacob, H. 1973. *Urban Justice*. Boston: Little, Brown.

Jacobs, J. B., and C. Panarella. 1998. "Organized Crime." In *The Handbook of Crime and Punishment*, ed. M. Tonry. New York: Oxford University Press, 159–77.

Jacobs, J. B., C. Panarella, and J. Worthington. 1994. *Busting the Mob: United States v. Cosa Nostra*. New York: New York University Press.

Jacoby, J. 1979. "The Charging Policies of Prosecutors." In *The Prosecutor*, ed. W. F. McDonald. Beverly Hills, CA: Sage.

———. 1995. "Pushing the Envelope: Leadership in Prosecution." *Justice System Journal* 17: 291–307.

Jaksic, V. 2007. "Public Defenders, Prosecutors Face a Crisis in Funding." *National Law Journal*. March 27. http://www.law.com.

Jenne, D. L., and R. C. Kersting. 1996. "Aggression and Women Correctional Officers in Male Prisons." *Prison Journal* 76: 442–60.

Johnson, B. D. 2005. "Contextual Disparities in Guidelines Departures: Courtroom Social Contexts, Guidelines Compliance, and Extralegal Disparities in Criminal Sentencing." *Criminology* 43 (3): 761–96.

———. 2006. "The Multilevel Context of Criminal Sentencing: Integrating Judge- and County-Level Influences." *Criminology* 44(2): 259–98.

Johnson, D. T. 1998. "The Organization of Prosecution and the Possibility of Order." *Law and Society Review* 32: 247–308.

Johnson, K. 2002. "From Extreme Isolation, Waves of Felons are Freed." *USA Today*, December 12, p. 1A.

Johnson, R. 2002. *Hard Time: Understanding and Reforming the Prison*. 3rd ed. Belmont, CA: Wadsworth.

Johnson, S. P. 2007. "The Prosecution of Lee Harvey Oswald," *South Texas Law Review* 48: 667–93.

Johnston, D. C. 2008. "Wesley Snipes Cleared of Serious Tax Charges." *New York Times*, February 2. http://www.nytimes.com.

Jonsson P. 2003. "How Did Eric Rudolph Survive?" *Christian Science Monitor*, June 4, http://www.csmonitor.com.

Jordan, J. 2002. "Will Any Woman Do? Police, Gender and Rape Victims." *Policing* 25: 319–44.

Kadlec, D. 2002. "WorldCon." *Time Magazine*, July 8, pp. 20–6.

Kalinich, D. B. 1980. *Power, Stability, and Contraband*. Prospect Heights, IL: Waveland Press.

Kampeas, R. 2001. "Terror Attacks Bring Profound Changes in FBI Focus, Challenges for New Director." Associated Press News Service, October 27.

Kane, R. J. 2005. "Compromised Police Legitimacy As a Predictor of Violent Crime in Structurally Disadvantaged Communities." *Criminology* 43: 469–98.

Kappeler, V. E., M. Blumberg, and G. W. Potter. 1996. *The Mythology of Crime and Criminal Justice*. 2nd ed. Prospect Heights, IL: Waveland Press.

Karmen, A. 2001. *Crime Victims*. 4th ed. Belmont, CA: Wadsworth.

Karnowski, S. 2008. "City's I-35W Bridge Response Generally Praised." Associated Press, April 22. http://www.twincities.com.

Katel, P. 1994. "The Bust in Boot Camps." *Newsweek*, February 21, p. 26.

Kates, B. 2003. "We Get $5-a-Head for Security." *New York Daily News*, November 24. http://www.nydailynews.com.

Keller, S. J. 2007. "Judge Rules Provision in Patriot Act to Be Illegal." *New York Times*, September 27. http://www.nytimes.com.

Kelling, G. L. 1985. "Order Maintenance, the Quality of Urban Life, and Police: A Line of Argument." In *Police Leadership in America*, ed. W. A. Geller. New York: Praeger.

———. 1991. *Foot Patrol*. Washington, DC: National Institute of Justice, U.S. Government Printing Office.

———. 1992. "Measuring What Matters: A New Way of

Thinking about Crime and Public Order." *City Journal* 2 (Spring): 21–31.

Kelling, G. L., and C. M. Coles. 1996. *Fixing Broken Windows: Restoring and Reducing Crime in Our Communities*. New York: Free Press.

Kelling, G. L., and M. Moore. 1988. "The Evolving Strategy of Policing." In *Perspectives on Policing*, no. 13. Washington, DC: National Institute of Justice, U.S. Government Printing Office.

Kelling, G. L., T. Pate, D. Dieckman, and C. E. Brown. 1974. *The Kansas City Preventive Patrol Experiments: A Summary Report*. Washington, DC: Police Foundation.

Kennedy, R. 1997. *Race, Crime, and the Law*. New York: Pantheon.

Kenney, D. J., and J. O. Finckenauer. 1995. *Organized Crime in America*. Belmont, CA: Wadsworth.

Kenworthy, T. 1998. "Michael Kennedy Dies in Accident on Aspen Slopes." *Washington Post,* January 1, p. A1.

Kerlikowske, R. G. 2004. "The End of Community Policing: Remembering the Lessons Learned," *FBI Law Enforcement Bulletin* 73 (April): 6–11.

Kerry, J. S. 1997. *The New War*. New York: Simon & Schuster.

Kim, R., and D. Walsh. 2005. "Finger Suspect to Be Extradited to San Jose; Attorney Says Anna Ayala Wants to Clear Her Name." *San Francisco Chronicle*, April 26. http://www.sfgate.com.

Kimberly, J. 2003. "House Passes Crime Lab Bill." *Houston Chronicle*, May 2. http://www.houstonchronicle.com.

King, N. J. 1994. "The Effects of Race-Conscious Jury Selection on Public Confidence in the Fairness of Jury Proceedings: An Empirical Puzzle." *American Criminal Law Review* 31: 1177–202.

King, N. J., F. Cheesman and B. Ostrom. 2007. *Habeas Litigation in the U.S. District Courts*. Williamsburg, VA: National Center for State Courts.

King, R. S., M. Mauer, and T. Huling. 2004. "An Analysis of the Economics of Prison Siting in Rural Communities." *Criminology and Public Policy* 3 (July): 453–80.

Kingsnorth, R., R. MacIntosh, and S. Sutherland. 2002. "Criminal Charge or Probation Violation? Prosecutorial Discretion and Implications for Research in Criminal Court Processing." *Criminology* 40: 553–77.

Kirkpatrick, D. D. 2005a. "Alito Memos Supported Expanding Police Powers." *New York Times*, November 29. http://www.nytimes.com.

———. 2005b. "In Secretly Taped Conversations, Glimpses of the Future President." *New York Times*, February 20. http://www.nytimes.com.

Klaus, P. A. 2004. "Crime and the Nation's Households, 2003." Bureau of Justice Statistics *Bulletin,* October.

Kleck, G., B. Sever, S. Li and M. Gertz. 2005. "The Missing Link in General Deterrence Research." *Criminology* 43 (3): 623–59.

Klein, D. 1973. "The Etiology of Female Crime: A Review of the Literature." Issues in Criminology 8(2): 3–30.

Kleinknecht, W. 1996. *The New Ethnic Mobs: The Changing Face of Organized Crime in America*. New York: Free Press.

Klockars, C. B. 1985. "Order Maintenance, the Quality of Urban Life, and Police: A Different Line of Argument." In *Police Leadership in America*, ed. W. A. Geller. New York: Praeger.

Klofas, J., and J. Yandrasits. 1989. "'Guilty but Mentally Ill' and the Jury Trial: A Case Study." *Criminal Law Bulletin* 24: 423–43.

KNBC. 2006a. "Jury Deliberations Begin in Eriksson Case." KNBC.COM, November 2. http://www.knbc.com.

———. 2006b. "Opening Statements Delivered in Eriksson Trial." KNBC.COM, October 23. http://www.knbc.com.

———. 2006c. "Stefan Eriksson Sentenced After No Contest Plea." KNBC.COM, November 7. http://www.knbc.com.

Knox, G. W. 2000. "A National Assessment of Gangs and Security Threat Groups (STGs) in Adult Correctional Institutions: Results of the 1999 Adult Corrections Survey." *Journal of Gang Research* 7: 1–45.

Kocieniewski, D. 2007. "So Many Crimes, and Reasons Not to Cooperate." *New York Times*, December 30. http://www.nytimes.com.

Kolbert, E. 1999. "The Perils of Safety." *New Yorker,* March 22, p. 50.

Koper, C. 1995. "Just Enough Police Presence: Reducing Crime and Disorderly Behavior by Optimizing Patrol Time in Crime Hot Spots." *Justice Quarterly* 12 (December): 649–72.

Kotlowitz, A. 1994. "Their Crimes Don't Make Them Adults." *The New York Times Magazine,* February 13, p. 40.

———. 2008. "Blocking the Transmission of Violence." *New York Times Magazine*, May 4. http://www.nytimes.com.

Kramer, G. P., and D. M. Koenig. 1990. "Do Jurors Understand Criminal Justice Instructions? Analyzing the Results of the Michigan Juror Comprehension Project." *University of Michigan Journal of Law Reform* 23: 401–37.

Kramer, J. H., and J. T. Ulmer. 1996. "Sentencing Disparity and Departures from Guidelines." *Justice Quarterly* 13 (March): 81.

Krane, J. 2003. "Concerns about Citizen Privacy Grow as States Create MATRIX Database." *Boston Globe*, September 24. http://www.boston.com.

Krauss, C. 1994. "No Crystal Ball Needed on Crime." *New York Times*, November 13, sec. 4, p. 4.

Kremling, J., M. D. Smith, J. K. Cochran, B. Bjerregaard and S. J. Fogel. 2007. "The Role of Mitigating Facts in Capital Sentencing Before and After *McKoy v. North Carolina*." *Justice Quarterly* 24(3): 357–81.

Kridler, C. 1999. "Sergeant Friday, Where Are You?" *Newsweek*, May 17, p. 14.

Krimmel, J. T. 1996. "The Performance of College-Educated Police: A Study of Self-Rated Performance Measures." *American Journal of Policing* 15: 85–96.

Kristof, N. 2005. "When Rapists Walk Free." *New York Times*, March 5. http://www.nytimes.com.

Kruttschnitt, C. and K. Carbone-Lopez. 2006. "Moving Beyond the Stereotypes: Women's Subjective Accounts of Their Violent Crime. *Criminology* 44 (2): 321–51.

Kruttschnitt, C., and S. Krmpotich. 1990. "Aggressive Behavior among Female Inmates: An Exploratory Study." *Justice Quarterly* 7 (June): 371–89.

Kurlychek, M. and C. Kempinen. 2006. "Beyond Boot Camp: The Impact of Aftercare on Offender Re-entry." *Criminology & Public Policy,* 5: 363–88.

Kurtz, H. 1997. "The Crime Spree on Network News." *Washington Post,* August 12, p. 1.

Kyckelhahn, T. and T. H. Cohen. 2008. "Felony Defendants in Large Urban Counties, 2004." Bureau of Justice Statistics *Bulletin* (April) NCJ221152.

Labaton, S. 2002. "Downturn and Shift in Population Feed Boom in White-Collar Crime." *New York Times*, June 2, pp. 1, 22.

Laffey, M. 1998. "Cop Diary *New Yorker*, August 10, pp. 36–9.

———. 1999. "Cop Diary ." *New Yorker*, February 1, pp. 29–32.

Langbein, J. H. 1992. "On the Myth of Written Constitutions: The Disappearance of the Criminal Jury Trial." *Harvard Journal of Law and Public Policy* 15: 119–27.

Langworthy, R. H., T. Hughes, and B. Sanders. 1995. *Law Enforcement Recruitment Selection and Training: A Survey of Major Police Departments*. Highland Heights, IL: Academy of Criminal Justice Sciences.

Laub, J. H., and R. J. Sampson. 2003. *Shared Beginnings, Divergent Lives: Delinquent Boys to Age 70*. Cambridge, MA: Harvard University Press.

Lauritsen, J., and N. White. 2001. "Putting Violence in Its Place: The Influence of Race, Ethnicity, Gender, and Place on the Risk for Violence." *Criminology and Public Policy* 1: 37–59.

Lavandera, E. 2008. "Cleared by DNA, Man Tries to Reclaim His Life." CNN.COM, May 16. http://www.cnn.com.

Lave, T. R. 1998. "Equal before the Law." *Newsweek,* July 13, p. 14.

"Law Enforcement Solution." 2002. October 10. http://www.cisco.com.

Lear, E. T. 1995. "Contemplating the Successive Prosecution Phenomenon in the Federal System." *Journal of Criminal Law and Criminology* 85: 625–75.

LeDuff, C. 1999. "Jury Decides Hospitalized Killer in Cannibalism Case Can Go Free." New York Times, April 22, p. B1.

Lee, M. S., and J. T. Ulmer. 2000. "Fear of Crime among Korean Americans in Chicago Communities." *Criminology* 38: 1173–206.

Leiber, M. J. and K. Y. Mack. 2003. "The Individual and Joint Effects of Race, Gender, and Family Status on Juvenile Justice Decision-Making." *Journal of Research in Crime and Delinquency* 40: 34-70.

Leo, R. A. 1996a. "The Impact of *Miranda* Revisited." *Journal of Criminal Law and Criminology* 86: 621–92.

———. 1996b. " Miranda's Revenge: Police Interrogation as a Confidence Game." *Law and Society Review* 30: 259–88.

Leonard, J. 2002. "Dropping 'Nonlethal' Beanbags as Too Dangerous." *Los Angeles Times,* June 3, p. 1.

Leopold, J. 2002, "Bush and Harken." *The Nation,* July 18. http://www.thenation.com.

Leovy, J., and N. Lee. 2005. "Grieving Police Provide Account of Fatal Standoff." *Los Angeles Times,* July 12. http://www.latimes.com.

Lersch, K. M. 2002. "Are Citizen Complaints Just Another Measure of Officer Productivity? An Analysis of Citizen Complaints and Officer Activity Measures." *Police Practices and Research* 3: 135–47.

Lersch, K. M., and L. Kunzman. 2001. "Misconduct Allegations and Higher Education in a Southern Sheriff's Department." *American Journal of Criminal Justice* 25: 161–72.

Levine, J. P. 1992. Juries and Politics. Belmont, CA: Wadsworth.

Levy, P. 2007. "4 Dead, 20 Missing After Dozens of Vehicles Plummet Into River." *Minneapolis Star Tribune,* August 2. http://www.startribune.com.

Levy, S. 1997. "A Guru Goes Free." *Newsweek,* December 15, p. 44.

Lewis, E. 2007. *Realizing Justice: Defender Caseload Report 2007.* Frankfort, KY: Kentucky Department of Public Advocacy.

Lewis, N. 1999. "Prosecutors Urged to Allow Appeals on DNA." *New York Times,* September 28, p. 14.

Lichtblau, E. 2008a. "F.B.I. Made 'Blanket' Demands for Phone Records." *New York Times,* March 13. http://www.nytimes.com.

———. 2008b. "F.B.I. Says Records Demands Are Curbed." *New York Times,* March 6. http://www.nytimes.com.

Lightfoot, E., and M. Umbreit. 2004. "An Analysis of State Statutory Provisions for Victim-Offender Mediation." *Criminal Justice Policy Review* 15: 418–36.

Lighty, T. 2005. "Prosecutors Boast of 'a Hit on the Mob.'" *Chicago Tribune,* April 25, p. 1.

Liptak, A. 2007. "Judge Voids F.B.I. Tool Granted by Patriot Act." *New York Times,* September 7. http://www.nytimes.com.

———. 2008. "Illegal Globally, Bail for Profit Remains in U.S." *New York Times,* January 29. http://www.nytimes.com.

Liptak, A., N. Lewis, and B. Weiser. 2002. "After Sept. 11, a Legal Battle on the Limits of Civil Liberty." *New York Times,* August 4, pp. 1, 16.

Lipton, E. 2005a. "Nominee Says U.S. Agents Abused Power after 9/11." *New York Times,* February 3. http://www.nytimes.com.

———. 2005b. "Trying to Keep the Nation's Ferries Safe from Terrorists." *New York Times,* March 19. http://www.nytimes.com.

Liska, A. E., and S. F. Messner. 1999. *Perspectives on Crime and Deviance.* 3rd ed. Upper Saddle River, NJ: Prentice-Hall.

Lithwick, D., and J. Turner. 2003. "A Guide to the Patriot Act, Part 4." *Slate,* September 11. http://slate.msn.com.

Logan, C. 1992. "Well Kept: Comparing Quality of Confinement in Private and Public Prisons." *Journal of Criminal Law and Criminology* 83 (Fall): 577–613.

———. 1993. "Criminal Justice Performance Measures in Prisons." In *Performance Measures for the Criminal Justice System.* Washington, DC: Bureau of Justice Statistics, U.S. Government Printing Office, 19–60.

Logan, C., and J. J. DiIulio, Jr. 1993. "Ten Deadly Myths about Crime and Punishment in the United States." In *Criminal Justice: Law and Politics,* ed. G. F. Cole. Belmont, CA: Wadsworth, 486–502.

Lombroso, C. 1968 [1912]. *Crime: Its Causes and Remedies.* Montclair, NJ: Patterson Smith.

Lorentzen, A. 2002. "Trooper Who Had Stopped Bank Suspect Kills Self." *Seattle Times,* September 28. http://www.seattletimes.com.

Love, M., and S. Kuzma. 1996. *Civil Disabilities of Convicted Felons.* Washington, DC: Office of the Pardon Attorney, U.S. Government Printing Office.

Loviglio, J. 2002. "Judge Reverses Himself, Will Allow Fingerprint-Analysis Testimony." *Associated Press Wire Service,* March 13. Lexis-Nexis.

Lovrich, N. P., and C. H. Sheldon. 1994. "Is Voting for State Judges a Flight of Fancy or a Reflection of Policy and Value Preferences?" *Justice System Journal* 16: 57–71.

Luginbuhl, J., and M. Burkhead. 1994. "Sources of Bias and Arbitrariness in the Capital Trial." *Journal of Social Issues* 7: 103–112.

Lundman, R., and R. Kaufman. 2003. "Driving While Black: Effects of Race, Ethnicity, and Gender on Citizen Self-Reports of Traffic Stops and Police Actions." *Criminology* 41: 195–220.

Lupica, M. 2007. "Vick's Biggest Move Yet." *New York Daily News,* July 29. www.nydailynews.com.

Lynch, D. 1999. "Perceived Judicial Hostility to Criminal Trials: Effects on Public Defenders in General and on Their Relationships with Clients and Prosecutors in Particular." *Criminal Justice and Behavior* 26: 217–34.

Lynch, J. 1995. "Crime in International Perspective." In *Crime,* ed. J. Q. Wilson and J. Petersilia. San Francisco: ICS Press, 11–38.

Lynch, J., and W. J. Sabol. 2001. *Prisoner Reentry in Perspective.* Washington, DC: Urban Institute.

Lynem, J. N. 2002. "Guards Call for Higher Wages, More Training: Industry Faces Annual Staff Turnover Rate of up to 300%." *San Francisco Chronicle,* August 22, p. B3.

Maag, C. 2008. "Police Shooting of Mother and Infant Exposes a City's Racial Tension," *New York Times,* January 30. http://www.nytimes.com.

MacArthur Foundation. 2007a. "Creating Turning Points for Serious Adolescent Offenders: Research on Pathways to Desistance" (Issue Brief 2, MacArthur Foundation Research Network on Adolescent Development and Juvenile Justice). Philadelphia, PA: MacArthur Foundation.

———. 2007b. "Less Guilty by Reason of Adolescence" (Issue Brief 3, MacArthur Foundation Research Network on Adolescent Development and Juvenile Justice). Philadelphia, PA: MacArthur Foundation.

———. 2007c "The Changing Borders of Juvenile Justice: Transfer of Adolescents to Adult Criminal Court" (Issue Brief 5, MacArthur Foundation Research Network on Adolescent Development and Juvenile Justice). Philadelphia, PA: MacArthur Foundation

MacCoun, R. J., A. Saiger, J. P. Kahan, and P. Reuter. 1993. "Drug Policies and Problems: The Promises and Pitfalls of Cross-National Comparisons." In *Psychoactive Drugs and Human Harm Reduction: From Faith to Science,* ed. N. Heather, E. Nadelman, and P. O'Hare. London: Whurr.

Maggi, L. 2005. "Courts Look at Indigent Defense." *New Orleans Times-Picayune,* April 14. http://www.nola.com.

Maitland, A. S., and R. D. Sluder. 1998. "Victimization and Youthful Prison Inmates: An Empirical Analysis." *Prison Journal* 78: 55–73.

Manchester, J. 2003. "Beyond Accommodation: Reconstructing the Insanity Defense to Provide an Adequate Remedy for PostPartum Psychotic Women." *Journal of Criminal Law and Criminology* 93: 713–53.

Mann, C. R. 1993. *Unequal Justice: A Question of Color.* Bloomington: Indiana University Press.

Manning, P. K. 1971. "The Police: Mandate, Strategies, and Appearances." In *Crime and Justice in American Society,* ed. J. D. Douglas. Indianapolis, IN: Bobbs-Merrill, 149–93.

———. 1977. *Police Work.* Cambridge, MA: MIT Press.

Mansnerus, L. 2002. "High Court in New Jersey Strictly Limits Auto Searches." *New York Times,* August 5. http://www.nytimes.com.

Marciniak, L-M. 2001. "The Addition of Day Reporting to Intensive Supervision Probation: A Comparison of Recidivism Rates." *Federal Probation* 64 (June): 34–9.

Margasak, L. 2007. "Ill-Trained, Underpaid Guard Terror Targets." Associated Press, May 29. http://news.aol.com.

———. 2006. "Guards Say Homeland Security HQ Insecure." Associated Press, March 6. http://www.sfgate.com.

Markon, J. 2008. "FBI, ATF Battle for Control of Cases." *Washington Post,* May 10. http://www.washingtonpost.com.

Markon, J. and J. Mummolo. 2007. "Vick: 'I'm Totally Responsible' Vick Pleads Guilty to Dogfighting Charges." *Washington Post,* August 28. http://www.washingtonpost.com.

Marsh, J. R. 1994. "Performing Pretrial Services: A Challenge in the Federal Criminal Justice System." *Federal Probation* 58 (December): 3–10.

———. 2001. "Reducing Unnecessary Detention: A Goal or Result of Pretrial Services?" *Federal Probation,* December, pp. 16–9.

Martin, S. E. 1991. "The Effectiveness of Affirmative Action." *Justice Quarterly* 8: 489–504.

———. 2005. "Women Officers on the Move." In *Critical Issues in Policing,* 5th ed., ed. Roger G Dunham and Geoffrey P. Alpert. Long Grove, IL: Waveland Press.

Martinson, R. 1974. "What Works? Questions and Answers about Prison Reform." *The Public Interest,* Spring, p. 25.

Maruschak, L., and A. Beck. 2001. *Medical Problems of Inmates, 1997.* Washington, DC: Bureau of Justice Statistics, U.S. Government Printing Office.

Maschke, K. J. 1995. "Prosecutors as Crime Creators: The Case of Prenatal Drug Use." *Criminal Justice Review* 20: 21–33.

Mask, T., and F. Witsil. 2005. "The Face of Terrorism: A Bullied Teen?" *Detroit Free Press,* March 26. http://www.freep.com.

Maske, M. 2007. "Falcons' Vick Indicted in Dogfighting Case." *Washington Post,* July 18, p. E1.

Mastrofski, S. D., M. D. Reisig, and J. D. McCluskey. 2002. "Police Disrespect Toward the Public: An Encounter-Based Analysis." *Criminology* 40: 519–52.

Mastrofski, S. D., J. J. Willis, and J. B. Snipes. 2002. "Styles of Patrol in a Community Policing Context." In *The Move to Community Policing: Making Change Happen,* ed. M. Morash and J. Ford. Thousand Oaks, CA: Sage, 81–111.

Maudsley, H. 1974. *Responsibility in Mental Disease.* London, England: Macmillan.

Maue, F. R. 2001. "An Overview of Correctional Mental Health Issues." *Corrections Today* 63 (August, 2001): 6–10.

Mauer, M. 1999. *Race to Incarcerate.* New York: New Press.

Mauer, M., and M. Chesney-Lind, eds. 2002. *Invisible Punishment: The Collateral Consequences of Mass Imprisonment.* New York: New Press.

Mauer, M., R. S. King, and M. C. Young. 2004. *The Meaning of "Life": Long Prison Sentences in Context.* Washington, DC: The Sentencing Project.

Maxwell, S. R. 1999. "Examining the Congruence between Predictors of ROR and Failures to Appear." *Journal of Criminal Justice* 27: 127–41.

Maxwell, S. R., and C. Maxwell. 2000. "Examining the 'Criminal Careers' of Prostitutes within the Nexus of Drug Use, Drug Selling, and Other Illicit Activities." *Criminology* 38: 787–809.

Mayhew, P., and J. J. M. van Dijk. 1997. *Criminal Victimisation in Eleven Industrial Countries.* The Hague, Netherlands: Dutch Ministry of Justice.

McCartney, A. 2008. "Hulk Hogan's Son Sentenced to 8 Months for Crash." Associated Press, ABC News, May 9. http://www.abcnews.go.com.

McConville, M. 2000. "Plea Bargaining: Ethics and Politics." In *The Judicial Role in Criminal Proceedings,* ed. Sean Doran and John Jackson. Oxford, England: Hart, 67–91.

McCoy, C. 1986. "Policing the Homeless." *Criminal Law Bulletin* 22 (May–June): 263.

———. 1993. *Politics and Plea Bargaining: Victims' Rights in California.* Philadelphia: University of Pennsylvania Press.

———. 1995. "Is the Trial Penalty Inevitable?" Paper presented at the annual meeting of the Law and Society Association, Phoenix, Arizona, June.

McDivitt, J., and R. Miliano. 1992. "Day Reporting Centers: An Innovative Concept in Intermediate Sanctions." In *Smart Sentencing: The Emergence of Intermediate Sanctions,* ed. J. M. Byrne, A. J. Lurigio, and J. Petersilia. Newbury Park, CA: Sage, 152–65.

McGarrell, E., S. Chermak, A. Weiss, and J. Wilson. 2001. "Reducing Firearms Violence through Directed Police Patrol." *Criminology and Public Policy* 1: 119–48.

McGeehan, P. 2007. "New York Plan for DNA Data in Most Crimes." *New York Times,* May 14. http://www.nytimes.com.

McGuire, D. 2004. "Study: Online Crime Costs Rising." *Washington Post,* May 25. http://www.washingtonpost.com.

McKelvey, B. 1977. *American Prisons.* Montclair, NJ: Patterson Smith.

McKinley, James C. 2008. "North Carolina: Arrest Warrant Issued for Marine." *New York Times,* January 30. http://www.nytimes.com.

McMahon, P. 2002. "311 Lightens Load for Swamped 911 Centers." *USA Today,* March 5. http://www.usatoday.com.

McNulty, T. L., and P. E. Bellair. 2003. "Explaining Racial and Ethnic Differences in Adoles-cent Violence: Structural Disadvantage, Family Well-Being, and Social Capital." *Justice Quarterly* 20: 1–31.

Mears, T. 1998. "Place and Crime." *Chicago-Kent Law Review* 73:669.

Meier, B. 2004. "A Drug on Trial: Justice and Science; Boy's Murder Case Entangled in Fight over Antidepressants." *New York Times,* August 23. http://www.nytimes.com.

Meier, R. F., and T. D. Miethe. 1993. "Understanding Theories of Criminal Victimization." In *Crime and Justice: A Review of Research,* ed. M. Tonry. Chicago: University of Chicago Press.

Melde, C., F. Esbensen and T. J. Taylor. 2009. "'May Piece Be with You': A Typological Examination of the Fear and Victimization Hypothesis of Adolescent Weapon Carrying." *Justice Quarterly* (forthcoming).

Melekian, B. 1990. "Police and the Homeless." *FBI Law Enforcement Bulletin* 59:1–7.

Menard, S. 2000. "The 'Normality' of Repeat Victimization from Adolescence through Early Adulthood." *Criminology* 17: 541–74.

Mentzer, A. 1996. "Policing in Indian Country: Understanding State Jurisdiction and Authority." *Law and Order* (June): 24–9.

Merianos, D. E., J. W. Marquart, and K. Damphousse. 1997. "From the Outside In: Using Public Health Data to Make Inferences about Older Inmates." *Crime and Delinquency* 43 (July): 298–314.

Messerschmidt, J. W. 1993. *Masculinities and Crime: Critique and Reconceptualization of Theory.* Lanham, MD: Rowman & Littlefield.

Messner, S. F., and R. Rosenfeld. 2001. *Crime and the American Dream.* 3rd ed. Belmont, CA: Wadsworth.

Messner, S. F., S. Galea, K. J. Tardiff, M. Tracy, A. Bucciarelli, T. M. Piper, V. Frye, D. Vlahov. 2007. "Policing, Drugs, and the Homicide Decline in New York City in the 1990s." *Criminology* 45: 385–413.

Metraux, S., and D. P. Culhane. 2004. "Homeless Shelter Use and Reincarceration following

Prison Release." *Criminology and Public Policy* 3 (March): 139–60.

Meyer, C., and T. Gorman. 2001. "Criminal Faces in the Crowd Still Elude Hidden ID Camera Security." *Los Angeles Times,* February 2, p. 1.

"Michigan State Police Drop Out of Anti-Terrorism Network." 2005. *Detroit Free Press,* March 7. http://www.freep.com.

Miethe, T. D. 1995. "Fear and Withdrawal from Urban Life." *Annals of the American Academy of Political and Social Science* 539 (May): 14–27.

Miller, J. L., and J. J. Sloan. 1994. "A Study of Criminal Justice Discretion." *Journal of Criminal Justice* 22: 107–23.

Miller, M., and M. Guggenheim. 1990. "Pretrial Detention and Punishment." *Minnesota Law Review* 75: 335–426.

Miller, M. K., D. M. Flores and A. N. Dolezilek. 2007. "Addressing the Problem of Courtroom Stress." *Judicature* 91: 60–9.

Milloy. 2000. "Judge Frees Texas Inmate Whose Lawyer Slept at Trial," *New York Times,* March 2, p. A19.

Mintz, H. 2005. "Prosecutors Must Prove Finger Suspect Planned to Falsely Accuse Wendy's." *San Jose Mercury News,* April 22. http://www.mercurynews.com.

Monkkonen, E. H. 1981. *Police in Urban America, 1869–1920.* Cambridge, England: Cambridge University Press.

———. 1992. "History of the Urban Police." In *Modern Policing,* ed. M. Tonry and N. Morris. Chicago: University of Chicago Press, 547–80.

Moore, M. 1992. "Problem- Solving and Community Policing." In *Modern Policing,* ed. M. Tonry and N. Morris. Chicago: University of Chicago Press, 99–158.

Moore, M., and G. L. Kelling. 1983. "T o Serve and to Protect: Learning from Police History." *The Public Interest,* Winter, p. 55.

Moran, R. 2002. *Executioner's Current: Thomas Edison, George Westinghouse, and the Invention of the Electric Chair.* New York: Knopf.

Morash, M., and J. K. Ford, eds. 2002. *The Move to Commu-*

nity Policing: Making Change Happen. Thousand Oaks, CA: Sage.

Morash, M., J. K. Ford, J. P. White, and J. G. Boles. 2002. "Directing the Future of Community-Policing Initiatives." In *The Move to Community Policing: Making Change Happen,* ed. M. Morash and J. Ford. Thousand Oaks, CA: Sage, 277–88.

Morash, M., R. N. Haarr, and L. Rucker. 1994. "A Comparison of Programming for Women and Men in the U.S. Prisons in the 1980s." *Crime and Delinquency* 40 (April): 197–221.

Morris, N. 1982. *Madness and the Criminal Law.* Chicago: University of Chicago Press.

Morris, N., and M. Tonry. 1990. *Between Prison and Probation: Intermediate Punishments in a Rational Sentencing System.* New York: Oxford University Press.

Moses, P. 2005. "Corruption? It Figures: NY Police Department's Crime Stats and the Art of Manipulation." *Village Voice,* March 29. http://www.villagevoice.com.

Mosher, C., T. Miethe, and D. Phillips. 2002. *The Mismeasure of Crime.* Thousand Oaks, CA: Sage.

"The Most Stress Related Occupations." 2006. *Consumer Awareness Journal* (September). http://www.consumer-awareness-journal.com.

Mozingo, J. 2008. "L.A. police Aggressively Target Hard-Core Gangs." *Los Angeles Times* (May 1). http://www.latimes.com.

MSNBC News. 2005. "Girl Killed Sister for Hamburger, Police Say." February 15. http://www.msnbc.com.

Mueller, R.S. 2008. "Statement of FBI Director Before the House Judiciary Committee," (April 23) http://www.fbi.gov.

Munson, L. 2008. "Vick at Leavenworth But Isn't in Prison Drug Program." www.Espn.com, March 8.

Murphy, P. V. 1992. "Organizing for Community Policing." In *Issues in Policing: New Perspectives,* ed. J. W. Bizzack. Lexington, KY: Autumn Press, 113–28.

Murray, J. 2008. "Transforming Juvenile Justice". *Indianapolis*

Star (May 27). http://www.indystar.com.

Nadelmann, E. A. 1993. *Cops across Borders: The Internationalization of U.S. Criminal Law Enforcement.* University Park: Pennsylvania State University Press.

Nagel, R. F. 1990. "The Myth of the General Right to Bail." *The Public Interest,* Winter, pp. 84–97.

Nagin, D. S. 1998. "Criminal Deterrence Research at the Outset of the Twenty-First Century." In *Crime and Justice,* vol. 23, ed. M. Tonry. Chicago: University of Chicago Press, 1–42.

Nagin, D. S., G. Pogarsky and D. P. Farrington. (1997). Adolescent mothers and the criminal behavior of their children, *Law and Society Review,* 31: 137–62.

Nagin, D. S., A. R. Piquero, E. S. Scott, and L. Steinberg. 2006. "Public Preferences for Rehabilitation Versus Incarceration of Juvenile Offenders: Evidence from a Contingent Valuation Survey." *Criminology & Public Policy* 5: 627–52.

Nalla, M. 2002. "Common Practices and Functions of Corporate Security: A Comparison of Chemical, Financial, Manufacturing, Service, and Utility Industries." *Journal of Security Administration* 25: 33–46.

Nardulli, P. F. 1986. "Insider Justice: Defense Attorneys and the Handling of Felony Cases." *Journal of Criminal Law and Criminology* 79: 379–417.

National Legal Aid and Defender Association. 1999. "Full-Court Press on Federal CJA Rate Increase." Press release, April 21.

NBC News. 2002. "Sheriff Larry Waldie Discusses the Rescue of the Two Girls Kidnapped in California." *Today Show* transcript, August 2. Lexis-Nexis.

NBC4 News. 2005. "Mother of Girl Shot by Police Surprised at Cocaine Report." NBC4 TV, August 4. http://www.nbc4.tv.news.

New York Times. 2008. "Wesley Snipes Gets 3 Years for Not Filing Tax Returns." April 25. http://www.nytimes.com.

Newman, T. C. 1996. "Fair Cross-Section and Good Intention: Representation in Federal

Juries." *Justice System Journal* 18: 211–32.

News Channel 8. 2005. "Court Upholds Murder Conviction of Tulsa Man." February 9. http://www.ktul.com.

Nicholas, S. C. Kershaw and A. Walker. "Crime in England and Wales, 2006/7." 2007. *Home Office Statistical Bulletin.* (London: UK Home Office). http://www.homeoffice.gov.uk.

Niesse, M. 2004. "Audit: Atlanta Hedged Crimes in '96 Bid." *Washington Post,* February 20. http://www.washingtonpost.com.

NIJ (National Institute of Justice). 1996. *Victim Costs and Consequences: A New Look.* Washington, DC: U.S. Government Printing Office.

———. 1997. *Research in Brief,* January.

Noble, R. K. 2006. "All Terrorism Is Local, Too." *New York Times,* August 13. http://www.nytimes.com.

Nolan, J. 2003. "Redefining Criminal Courts: Problem-Solving and the Meaning of Justice." *American Criminal Law Review* 40: 1541–66.

Novak, V. 1999. "The Cost of Poor Advice." *Time,* July 5, p. 38.

Ogletree, C. J., Jr., M. Prosser, A. Smith, and W. Talley, Jr. 1995. *Beyond the Rodney King Story: An Investigation of Police Misconduct in Minority Communities.* Boston: Northeastern University Press.

Ogunwole, S. U. 2006. *We the People: American Indians and Alaska Natives in the United States.* Washington, DC: U.S. Census Bureau (February). CENSR-28.

O'Harrow, R. 2008. "Centers Tap Into Personal Databases." *Washington Post,* April 2. http://www.washingtonpost.com.

O'Hear, M. M. 2006. "The End of *Bordenkircher*: Extending the Logic of *Apprendi* to Plea Bargaining." *Washington University Law Review* 84: 835–49.

———. 2008a. "Plea Bargaining and Procedural Justice." *Georgia Law Review* 42: 407–15.

O'Hear, M. M. 2008b. "Plea Bargaining and Victims: From Consultation to Guidelines." *Marquette Law Review* (forthcoming). Available at http://ssrn.com/abstract=1005373.

OJJDP (Office of Juvenile Justice and Delinquency Prevention). 1999. *Juvenile Offenders and Victims: 1999 National Report*. Washington, DC: U.S. Government Printing Office.

———. 2002. http://www.ojjdp.ncjrs.org/ojstatbb/html.

———. 2003a. *Bulletin*, June.

———. 2003b. *Juveniles in Court*, June.

———. 2004. *Fact Sheet*, April.

Okada, Y. 2006. "Lay Participation in Japanese Criminal Trials and Citizens' Attitudes Toward the Legal Profession." Paper presented at the annual meeting of the American Society of Criminology. Los Angeles, CA.

Olivares, K., V. Burton, and F. Cullen. 1996. "The Collateral Consequences of a Felony Conviction: A National Study of State Legal Codes Ten Years Later." *Federal Probation* 60: 10–8.

Oliver, W. M. 2002."9-11, Federal Crime Control Policy, and Unintended Consequences." *ACJS Today* 22 (September–October): 1–6.

Orson, D. 2008. "White Sentenced in Police Corruption Trial." WNPR-Connecticut Public Radio, April 29. http://www.cpbn.org.

Owen, B. 1998. *"In the Mix": Struggle and Survival in a Woman's Prison*. Albany: State University of New York Press.

Owen, B., and B. Bloom. 1995. "Profiling Women Prisoners: Findings from National Surveys and a California Sample." *Prison Journal* 75 (June): 165–85.

Packer, H. L. 1968. *The Limits of the Criminal Sanction*. Stanford, CA: Stanford University Press.

Palmer, T. 1992. *The Re-Emergence of Correctional Intervention*. Newbury Park, CA: Sage.

Pankratz, H. 2005. "Crime-Victim Project Pays Off." *Denver Post*, January 3. http://www.denverpost.com.

Parker, L. C., Jr. 1986. *Parole and the Community Based Treatment of Offenders in Japan and the United States*. New Haven, CT: University of New Haven Press.

Patchin, J. and S. Hinduja. 2006. "Bullies Move Beyond the Schoolyard: A Preliminary Look at Cyberbullying." *Youth Violence and Juvenile Justice* 4 (2): 148–69.

Pate, A. M., and E. H. Hamilton. 1991. *The Big Six: Policing America's Large Cities*. Washington, DC: Police Foundation.

Paulson, T. 2004. "'Brain Fingerprinting' Touted as Truth Meter." *Seattle Post-Intelligencer*, March 1. http://www.brainwavescience.com.

Peoples, J. M. 1995. "Helping Pretrial Services Clients Find Jobs." *Federal Probation* 59 (March): 14–18.

"Perdue OKs Bill to Expand Use." 2008. *Augusta (GA) Chronicle*, May 8. http://chronicle.augusta.com.

Perito, R. M. 1999. "Managing U.S. Participation in International Police Operations." In *Civilian Police and Multinational Peacekeeping: Workshop Series*. Washington, DC: National Institute of Justice, U.S. Government Printing Office, 9–11.

Perkins, D. B., and J. D. Jamieson. 1995. "Judicial Probable Cause Determinations after *County of Riverside v. McLaughlin*." *Criminal Law Bulletin* 31: 534–46.

Perry, S. W. 2006. "Prosecutors in State Courts, 2005." Bureau of Justice Statistics *Bulletin*, July. NCJ 213799.

Petersilia, J. 1990. "When Probation Becomes More Dreaded than Prison." *Federal Probation*, March, p. 24.

———. 1996. "A Crime Control Rationale for Reinvesting in Community Corrections." *Perspectives* 20 (Spring): 21–9.

———. 1998. "Probation and Parole." In *The Handbook of Crime and Punishment*, ed. M. Tonry. New York: Oxford University Press, 563–88.

———. 1999. "Parole and Prisoner Reentry in the United States." In *Prisons*, ed. M. Tonry and J. Petersilia. Chicago: University of Chicago Press, 479–529.

———. 2003. *When Prisoners Come Home: Parole and Prisoner Reentry*. New York: Oxford University Press.

Petersilia, J., and S. Turner. 1989. "Reducing Prison Admissions:

The Potential of Intermediate Sanctions." *The Journal of State Government* 62 (2): 65–9.

———. 1993. "Intensive Probation and Parole." In *Crime and Justice*, vol. 17, ed. M. Tonry. Chicago: University of Chicago Press, 281–336.

Peterson, J. L., and M. J. Hickman. 2005. "Census of Publicly Funded Forensic Crime Laboratories, 2002." Bureau of Justice Statistics *Bulletin*, February, p. 1.

Phillips, S. 1977. *No Heroes, No Villains*. New York: Random House.

Pisciotta, A. W. 1994. *Benevolent Repression: Social Control and the American Reformatory-Prison Movement*. New York: New York University Press. Pittsburg Post-Gazette. 2005. March 6. http://www.post-gazette.com/pg/pg05065/467032.stm.

Pizzi, W. T., and M. B. Hoffman. 2001. "Jury Selection Errors on Appeal." *American Criminal Law Review* 38: 1391–442.

Platt, A. 1977. *The Child Savers*. 2nd ed. Chicago: University of Chicago Press.

Pochna, P. 2002. "Computers on Patrol; Cops Linking Up with National Data Network." *Bergen County (NJ) Record*, March 16, p. A1.

Pogrebin, M. R., and E. D. Poole. 1997. "The Sexualized Work Environment: A Look at Women Jail Officers." *Prison Journal* 77 (March): 41–57.

Pollock, J. M. 1998. *Counseling Women in Prison*. Thousand Oaks, CA: Sage.

Porter, S. 2007. "Bollea Arrested for Reckless Driving." *Clearwater Citizen*, November 7. http://www.tbnweekly.com.

Possley, M., and T. Gregory. 1999. "DuPage 5 W in Acquittal." *Chicago Tribune*, June 5, p. 1.

Post, L. 2004. "ABA Wants to Transform Way Jurors Do their Jobs." *New Jersey Law Journal*, August 16, p. 1.

PR Newswire. 2001. "Ion Track Instruments Unveils New Technology to Aid in Fight against Terrorism and Drug Trafficking." March 22. Lexis-Nexis.

———. 2002. "As Homeland Security Bill Approaches House Vote, It Still Neglects

Problems with Massive Private Security Industry." July 24. Lexis-Nexis.

Pratt, T. C., and J. Maahs. 1999. "Are Private Prisons More Cost Effective Than Public Prisons? A Meta-Analysis of Evaluation Research Studies." *Crime and Delinquency* 45 (July): 358–71.

President's Commission on Law Enforcement and the Administration of Justice. 1967. *The Challenge of Crime in a Free Society*. Washington, DC: U.S. Government Printing Office.

Press, E. 2006. "Do Immigrants Make Us Safer?" *New York Times Magazine*, December 3, pp. 20–4.

Preston, J. 2005. "Rape Victims' Eyes Were Covered, but a Key Clue Survived." *New York Times*, April 28. http://www.nytimes.com.

Priehs, R. 1999. "Appointed Counsel for Indigent Criminal Appellants: Does Compensation Influence Effort?" *Justice System Journal* 21: 57–79.

Proctor, B. D., and J. Dalaker. 2003. "Poverty in the United States: 2002." In *U.S. Census Bureau Current Population Reports*. Washington, DC: U.S. Government Printing Office.

Propper, A. 1982. "Make Believe Families and Homosexuality among Imprisoned Girls." *Criminology* 20: 127–39.

Provine, D. M. 1996. "Courts in the Political Process in France." In *Courts, Law, and Politics in Comparative Perspective*, ed. H. Jacob, E. Blankenburg, H. Kritzer, D. M. Provine, and J. Sanders. New Haven, CT: Yale University Press, 177–248.

Prussel, D., and K. Lonsway. 2001. "Recruiting Women Police Officers." *Law and Order* 49 (July): 91–6.

Purser, B. 2005. "Houston County, Georgia E-911 Able to Pinpoint Cell Phones." *Macon (GA) Telegraph*, February 10, p. 6.

Pyle, R. 2002. "Swaggering Mafia Boss John Gotti Dies in Prison Hospital." *Seattle Times*, June 11. http://www.seattletimes.com.

Radelet, M. L. 2004. "Post-*Furman* Botched Executions." http://www.deathpenaltyinfor

.org/article.php?scid=8&did =478.

Radelet, M. L., H. A. Bedeau, and C. E. Putnam. 1992. *In Spite of Innocence*. Boston: Northeastern University Press.

Radelet, M. L., W. S. Lofquist, and H. A. Bedau. 1996. "Prisoners Released from Death Rows Since 1970 Because of Doubts about Their Guilt." *Thomas M. Cooley Law Review* 13: 907–66.

Rafter, N. H. 1983. "Prisons for Women, 1790–1980." In *Crime and Justice,* 5th ed., ed. M. Tonry and N. Morris. Chicago: University of Chicago Press.

Rainville, G., and B. A. Reaves. 2003. *Felony Defendants in Large Urban Counties*. Washington, DC: U.S. Government Printing Office.

Rand, M. and Catalano, S. 2007. "Criminal Victimization, 2006." Bureau of Justice Statistics *Bulletin* (December). NCJ 219413.

Randolph, E. D. 2001. "Inland Police Like New Weaponry." *Riverside (CA) Press-Enterprise,* November 24, p. B4.

Rankin, B. and D. O. Ledbetter. 2007. "Vick's Sentence: 23 Months." *Atlanta Journal-Constitution,* December 11, p. 1.

Reaves, B. A. 1992. *State and Local Police Departments, 1990*. Washington, DC: Bureau of Justice Statistics, U.S. Government Printing Office.

———. 2001. *Felony Defendants in Large Urban Counties, 1998: State Court Processing Statistics*. Washington, DC: Bureau of Justice Statistics, U.S. Government Printing Office.

Reaves, B. A. 2006. "Federal Law Enforcement Officers, 2004." Bureau of Justice Statistics *Bulletin.* July. NCJ 212750.

Reaves, B. A., and A. L. Goldberg. 2000. *Local Police Departments, 1997*. Washington, DC: Bureau of Justice Statistics, U.S. Government Printing Office.

Reaves, B. A., and T. C. Hart. 1999. *Felony Defendants in Large Urban Counties, 1996: State Court Case Processing Statistics*. Washington, DC: Bureau of Justice Statistics, U.S. Government Printing Office.

———. 2000. *Law Enforcement Management and Administrative Statistics, 1999*. Washington, DC: Bureau of Justice Statistics, U.S. Government Printing Office.

Reaves, B. A., and M. J. Hickman. 2002. "Police Departments in Large Cities, 1999–2000." Bureau of Justice Statistics *Special Report,* May.

———. 2004. *Law Enforcement Management and Administrative Statistics, 2000: Data for Individual State and Local Agencies with 100 or More Officers*. Washington, DC: Bureau of Justice Statistics, U.S. Government Printing Office, April.

Redfern, C. 2004. "Man Found Innocent of Attempted Murder." *Santa Cruz (CA) Sentinel,* April 24. http://www.baumhed lundlaw.com/SSRIs/Zoloft%20 -%20Santa%20Cruz%20man %20aquitted.htm.

Regoli, R. M., J. P. Crank, and R.G. Culbertson. 1987. "Rejoinder—Police Cynicism: Theory Development and Reconstruction." *Justice Quarterly* 4: 281–86.

Regoli, R. M., and J. D. Hewitt. 1994. *Criminal Justice*. Englewood Cliffs, NJ: Prentice- Hall.

Reibstein, L. 1997. "NYPD Black and Blue." *Newsweek,* June 2, p. 66.

Reichers, L. M., and R. R. Roberg. 1990. "Community Policing: A Critical Review of Underlying Assumptions." *Journal of Police Science and Administration* 17: 105–14.

Reid, T. V. 1996. "PAC Participation in North Carolina Supreme Court Elections." *Judicature* 80: 21–5.

———. 2000. "The Politicization of Judicial Retention Elections: The Defeat of Justices Lamphier and White." In *Research on Judicial Selection 1999*. Chicago: American Judicature Society, 45–72.

———. 2004. "Assessing the Impact of a Candidate's Sex in Judicial Campaigns and Elections in North Carolina." *Justice System Journal* 25 (2): 183–207.

Reilly, M. 2004a. "Ex-Net Convicted of Cover-Up of Shooting." *Newark Star-Ledger,* May 1. http://www.nj.com.

———. 2004b. "Prosecutor: We'll Retry Williams on Key Charge." *Newark Star-Ledger,* May 22. http://www.nj.com.

Reiman, J. 1996. . . . *And the Poor Get Prison: Economic Bias in American Criminal Justice*. Boston: Allyn and Bacon.

Reisig, M. D. 2002. "Citizen Input and Police Service: Moving beyond the "Feel Good" Community Survey." In *The Move to Community Policing: Making Change Happen,* ed. M. Morash and J. Ford. Thousand Oaks, CA: Sage, 43–60.

Reisig, M. D., W. Bales, C. Hay and X. Wang. 2007. "The Effect of Racial Inequality on Black Male Recidivism." *Justice Quarterly* 24 (3): 408–34.

Reisig, M. D., K. Holtfreter, and M. Morash. 2006. "Assessing Recidivism Risk Across Female Pathways to Crime." *Justice Quarterly* 23 (3): 384–405.

Reisig, M. D., J. D. McCluskey, S. D. Mastrofski, and W. Terrill. 2004. "Suspect Disrespect toward the Police." *Justice Quarterly* 21: 241–68.

Reiss, A. J., Jr. 1988. *Private Employment of Public Police*. Washington, DC: National Institute of Justice, U.S. Government Printing Office.

———. 1992. "Police Organization in the Twentieth Century." In *Crime and Justice: A Review of Research,* vol. 15, ed. M. Tonry and N. Morris. Chicago: University of Chicago Press, 51–97.

Reitzel, J. D., N. L. Piquero, and A. R. Piquero. 2005. "Problem-Oriented Policing." In *Critical Issues in Policing,* 5th ed., ed. Roger G. Dunham and Geoffrey P. Alpert. Long Grove, IL: Waveland, 419–32.

Renzema, M. 1992. "Home Confinement Programs: Development, Implementation, and Impact." In *Smart Sentencing: The Emergence of Intermediate Sanctions,* ed. J. M. Byrne, A. J. Lurigio, and J. Petersilia. Newbury Park, CA: Sage, 41–53.

Reston, M. and D. Kelly. 2007. "Rialto Officer Dies After Being Shot In a Struggle." October 19. http://www.latimes .com.

Rich, E. 2006. "Immigration Enforcement's Shift in the Work-

place." *Washington Post,* April 16, p. C6.

Richards, C., 2006. "Student Sent to TYC for Shoving Aide." The Paris (TX) News. March 12. http://www.lamarcountyattorney.com.

Richey, W. 2006. "US Creates Terrorist Fingerprint Database." *Christian Science Monitor,* December 27, pp. 1, 4.

———. 2007. "U.S. Gov't Broke Padilla Through Intense Isolation, Say Experts." *Christian Science Monitor,* August 14. http://www.csmonitor.com.

Richtel, M. 2002. "Credit Card Theft Online as Global Market." *New York Times,* May 13. http://www.nytimes.com.

Rideau, W., and R. Wikberg. 1992. *Life Sentences: Rage and Survival behind Bars*. New York: Times Books.

Ring, W. 2005. "Backlogs in Labs Undercut DNA's Crime-Solving Value." *Lansing (MI) State Journal,* April 28, p. A3.

Ripoll-Nunez, K. J. and R. P. Rohner. 2006. "Corporal Punishment in Cross-Cultural Perspective: Directions for a Research Agenda." *Cross-Cultural Research* 40 (2): 220–49.

Roane, K. R., and D. Morrison. 2005. "The CSI Effect." *U.S. News and World Report,* April 25. http://www.usnews.com.

Roberg, R., and S. Bonn. 2004. "Higher Education and Policing: Where Are We Now?" *Policing: International Journal of Police Strategies and Management* 27: 469–86.

Robinson, A. L. 2000. "The Effect of a Domestic Violence Policy Change on Police Officers' Schemata." *Criminal Justice and Behavior* 27: 600–24.

Robinson, P. H. 1993. "Foreword: The Criminal-Civil Distinction and Dangerous Blameless Offenders." *Journal of Criminal and Criminology* 83: 693–717.

Rodriguez, N. 2005. "Restorative Justice, Communities, and Delinquency: Whom Do We Reintegrate?" *Criminology and Public Policy* 4: 103–30.

Roedemeier, C. 2000. "Linebacker Pleads Guilty to Lesser Charge, Avoids Jail Time." Associated Press News Service, June 5.

Rosen, L. 1995. "The Creation of the Uniform Crime Report: The Role of Social Science."

Social Science History 19 (Summer): 215–38.

Rosenbaum, J. L. 1989. "Family Dysfunction and Female Delinquency." *Crime and Delinquency* 35:31–44.

Rosencrance, J. 1988. "Maintaining the Myth of Individualized Justice: Probation Presentence Reports." *Justice Quarterly* 5: 235.

Rosenfeld, R., R. Fornango and A. F. Rengifo. 2007. "The Impact of Order-Maintenance Policing on New York City Homicide and Robbery Rates, 1988-2001." *Criminology* 45: 355–83.

Rossi, P. H., and R. A. Berk. 1997. *Just Punishments: Federal Guidelines and Public Views Compared.* New York: Aldine DeGruyter.

Rothman, D. J. 1971. *The Discovery of the Asylum: Social Order and Disorder in the New Republic.* Boston: Little, Brown.

———. 1980. *Conscience and Convenience.* Boston: Little, Brown.

Rotman, E. 1995. "The Failure of Reform." In *Oxford History of the Prison,* ed. N. Morris and D. J. Rothman. New York: Oxford University Press.

Rottman, D. B., C. R. Flango, M. T. Cantrell, R. Hansen, and N. LaFountain. 2000. *State Court Organization 1998.* Washington, DC: U.S. Department of Justice.

Rousey, D. C. 1984. "Cops and Guns: Police Use of Deadly Force in Nineteenth-Century New Orleans." *American Journal of Legal History* 28: 41–66.

Ryan, H. 2004. "Williams Cleared of Aggravated Manslaughter in Driver's Shooting." COURT TV, April 30. http://www.courttv.com.

———. 2005. "Judge Sentences Scott Peterson to Death for Killing His Wife and Unborn Son." COURT TV, March 16. http://www.courttv.com.

Saad, L. 2004. "U.S. Crime Problem Less Troubling to Americans." Gallup News Service, November 9. http://www.gallup.com.

———. 2007. "Racial Disagreement Over Death Penalty Has Varied Historically." *The Gallup Poll Report.* July 30. http://www.gallup.com.

Sabo, D., T. A. Kupers, and W. London. 2001. "Gender and the Politics of Punishment." In *Prison Masculinities,* ed. D. Sabo, T. A. Kupers, and W. London. Philadelphia: Temple University Press, 3–18.

Sample, L. L., and T. M. Bray. 2003. "Are Sex Offenders Dangerous?" *Criminology and Public Policy* 3 (November): 59–82.

Sampson, R. J., and J. H. Laub. 1993. *Crime in the Making: Pathways and Turning Points through Life.* Cambridge, MA: Harvard University Press.

Sampson, R. J., and J. L. Lauritsen. 1997. "Racial and Ethnic Disparities in Crime and Criminal Justice in the United States." In *Crime and Justice,* vol. 21, ed. M. Tonry. Chicago: University of Chicago Press, 311–74.

Sampson, R. J., J. D. Morenoff and S. Raudenbush. 2005. "Social Anatomy of Racial and Ethnic Disparities in Violence." *American Journal of Public Health* 95: 224–32.

Sampson, R., and S. Raudenbush. 2001. "Disorder in Urban Neighborhoods: Does It Lead to Crime?" *NIJ Research in Brief,* February, pp. 1–6.

Samuelson, R. J. 1999. "Do We Care about Truth?" *Newsweek,* September 6, p. 76.

Sanchez, C. E. and M. Giordano. 2008. "Gang Activity in Suburbs Acknowledged." *Nashville Tennessean* (April 28) http://tennessean.com.

Santos, F. 2008. "Crimes in White Plains Decline to Record Lows." *New York Times,* January 25. http://www.nytimes.com.

Sarat, A. 2005. "Innocence, Error and the 'New Abolitionism': A Commentary." *Criminology and Public Policy* 4: 45–54.

———. 2008. Memorializing Miscarriages of Justice: Clemency Petitions in the Killing State." *Law and Society Review* 42 (1): 183–224.

Saulny, S. and M. Davey. 2008. "Gunman Slays 6 at N. Illinois University." *New York Times,* February 15. http://www.nytimes.com.

Savage, D. G. 2008. "Supreme Court to Hear Challenge to D.C. Gun Law." March 17. http://www.latimes.com.

Scalia, J. 2002. "Prisoners Petitions Filed in U.S. District Courts, 2000, with Trends 1980–2000." Bureau of Justice Statistics *Special Report,* January.

Schafer, J. A. 2002. "The Challenge of Effective Organizational Change: Lessons Learned in Community-Policing Implementation." In *The Move to Community Policing: Making Change Happen,* ed. M. Morash and J. Ford. Thousand Oaks, CA: Sage, 243–63.

Scheingold, S. A. 1995. *Politics, Public Policy, and Street Crime.* Philadelphia: Temple University Press.

Schmidt, J., and E. H. Steury. 1989. "Prosecutorial Discretion in Filing Charges in Domestic Violence Cases." *Criminology* 27: 487–510.

Schmitt, E. and D. Rohde. 2007. "Reports Assail State Department on Iraq Security." *New York Times,* October 23. http://www.nytimes.com.

Schmitt, R. B. 2008. "FBI Is Called Slow to Join the Terrorism Fight." *Los Angeles Times,* May 9. http://www.latimes.com.

Schultz, D. 2000. "No Joy in Mudville Tonight: The Impact of Three Strikes Laws on State and Federal Corrections Policy, Resources, and Crime Control." *Cornell Journal of Law and Public Policy* 9: 557–83.

Schwartz, J. 2006. "All Smiles as Shuttle Ends a Nearly Perfect Mission." *New York Times,* July 18. http://www.nytimes.com.

———. 2007a. "Ex-Astronaut to Enter a Plea of Insanity on Assault Charges." *New York Times,* August 29. http://www.nytimes.com.

———. 2007b. "From Spaceflight to Attempted Murder Charge." *New York Times,* February 7. http://www.nytimes.com.

Scott, E. J. 1981. *Calls for Service: Citizen Demand and Initial Police Response.* Washington, DC: U.S. Government Printing Office.

Security Industry Association. 2000. "Economic Crime Cost Reaches $200 Billion in 2000." *Research Update,* January, p. 1.

Sentencing Project. 2001. "U.S. Continues to Be World Leader in Rate of Incarceration." Press release, August.

Seron, C., J. Pereira and J. Kovath. 2006. "How Citizens Assess Just Punishment for Police Misconduct." *Criminology* 44: 925–60.

Serrano, R. 2002. "Lindh Pleads Guilty, Agrees to Aid Inquiry." *Los Angeles Times,* July 16, p. 1.

Shane, S. and R. Nixon. 2007. "In Washington, Contractors Take On Biggest Role Ever." *New York Times,* February 4. http://www.nytimes.com.

Shapiro, B. 1997. "Sleeping Lawyer Syndrome." *The Nation,* April 7, pp. 27–9.

Sheridan, M. and S. S. Hsu. 2006. "Localities Operate Intelligence Centers to Pool Terror Data." *Washington Post,* December 31. http://www.washingtonpost.com.

Sherman, L. W. 1983. "Patrol Strategies for Police." In *Crime and Public Policy,* ed. J. Q. Wilson. San Francisco: ICS Press, 149–54.

———. 1990. "Police Crackdowns: Initial and Residual Deterrence." In *Crime and Justice,* ed. M. Tonry and N. Morris. Chicago: University of Chicago Press, 1–48.

———. 1995. "The Police." In *Crime,* ed. J. Q. Wilson and J. Petersilia. San Francisco: ICS Press, 327–48.

———. 1998. "Police." In *Handbook of Crime and Punishment,* ed. M. Tonry. New York: Oxford University Press, 429–56.

Sherman, L. W., and R. A. Berk. 1984. "The Specific Effects of Arrest for Domestic Assault." *American Sociological Review* 49: 261–72.

Sherman, L. W., and E. G. Cohn. 1986. "Citizens Killed by Big City Police: 1970–84." Unpublished manuscript, Crime Control Institute, Washington, DC, October.

Sherman, L. W., P. R. Gartin, and M. E. Buerger. 1989. "Hot Spots of Predatory Crime: Routine Activities and the Criminology of Place." *Criminology* 27: 27–55.

Sherman, L. W., and D. P. Rogan. 1995a. "Effects of Gun Seizures on Gun Violence: 'Hot Spots' Patrol in Kansas City." *Justice Quarterly* 12 (December): 673–93.

———. 1995b. "Deterrent Effects of Police Raids on Crack Houses: A Randomized Controlled Experiment." *Justice Quarterly* 12 (December): 755–81.

Sherman, L. W., J. D. Schmidt, D. P. Rogan, P. R. Gartin, E. G. Cohn, D. J. Collins, and A. R. Bacich. 1991. "From Initial Deterrence to Long-Term Escalation: Short Custody Arrest for Poverty Ghetto Domestic Violence." *Criminology* 29: 821–50.

Sherman, L. W., and D. A. Weisburd. 1995. "General Deterrent Effects of Police Patrol in Crime 'Hot Spots': A Randomized Controlled Trial." *Justice Quarterly* 12 (December): 625–48.

Shover, N. 1998. "White-Collar Crime." In *The Handbook of Crime and Punishment*, ed. M. Tonry. New York: Oxford University Press, 133–58.

Sichel, J. L. 1978. *Expectations Which Have Shaped Women's Role in Policing New York City*. Washington, DC: National Institute of Justice, U.S. Government Printing Office.

Sickmund, M. 2004. "Juveniles in Corrections." In *National Report Series Bulletin*. Washington, DC: Office of Juvenile Justice and Delinquency Prevention, June.

Silverman, E. 1999. *NYPD Battles Crime*. Boston: Northeastern University Press.

Simon, L. M. S. 1993. "Prison Behavior and the Victim–Offender Relationships among Violent Offenders." *Justice Quarterly* 10 (September): 489–506.

Simon, R. 1975. *Women and Crime*. Lexington, MA: D. C. Heath.

Skogan, W. G. 1990. *Disorder and Decline: Crime and the Spiral of Decay in America*. New York: Free Press.

———. 1995. "Crime and Racial Fears of White Americans." *Annals of the American Academy of Political and Social Science* 539 (May): 59–71.

Skogan, W. G., and M. G. Maxfield. 1981. *Coping with Crime*. Newbury Park, CA: Sage.

Skolnick, J. H. 1966. *Justice without Trial: Law Enforcement in a Democratic Society*. New York: Wiley.

Skolnick, J. H., and D. H. Bayley. 1986. *The New Blue Line*. New York: Free Press.

Skolnick, J. H., and J. J. Fyfe. 1993. *Above the Law: Police and Excessive Use of Force*. New York: Free Press.

Slobodzian, J.A. 2008. "TV Footage Shows Police Beating Suspects." *Philadelphia Inquirer*, May 7. http://www.philly.com.

Slocum, L., S. S. Simpson, and D. A. Smith. 2005. "Strained Lives and Crime: Examining Intra-Individual Variation in Strain and Offending in a Sample of Incarcerated Women." 43 (4): 1067–110.

Smith, A. B., and H. Pollack. 1972. *Crimes and Justice in a Mass Society*. New York: Xerox.

Smith, C. E. 1990. United States Magistrates in the Federal Courts: Subordinate Judges. New York: Praeger.

———. 1993. "Justice Antonin Scalia and Criminal Justice Cases." *Kentucky Law Journal* 81: 187–212.

———. 1994. "Imagery , Politics, and Jury Reform." *Akron Law Review* 28: 77–95.

———. 1995a. "The Constitution and Criminal Punishment: The Emerging Visions of Justices Scalia and Thomas." *Drake Law Review* 43: 593–613.

———. 1995b. "Federal Habeas Corpus Reform: The State's Perspective." *Justice System Journal* 18: 1–11.

———. 1995c. "Judicial Policy Making and Habeas Corpus Reform." *Criminal Justice Policy Review* 7: 91–114.

———. 1997. The Rehnquist Court and Criminal Punishment. New York: Garland.

———. 1999a. "Criminal Justice and the 1997–98 U.S. Supreme Court Term." *Southern Illinois University Law Review* 23: 443–67.

———. 1999b. *Law and Contemporary Corrections*. Belmont, CA: Wadsworth.

———. 2004. "The Bill of Rights after September 11th: Principles or Pragmatism?" *Duquesne Law Review* 42: 259–91.

Smith, C. E., C. DeJong, and J. D. Burrow. 2002. *The Supreme Court, Crime, and the Ideal of Equal Justice*. New York: Peter Lange.

Smith, C. E., and H. Feldman. 2001. "Burdens of the Bench: State Supreme Courts' Non-Judicial Tasks." *Judicature* 84: 304–9.

Smith, C. E., and J. Hurst. 1996. "Law and Police Agencies' Policies: Perceptions of the Relative Impact of Constitutional Law Decisions and Civil Liabilities Decisions." Paper given at the annual meeting of the American Society of Criminology, Chicago.

———. 1997. "The Forms of Judicial Policy Making: Civil Liability and Criminal Justice Policy." *Justice System Journal* 19: 341–54.

Smith, C. E., and R. Ochoa. 1996. "The Peremptory Challenge in the Eyes of the Trial Judge." *Judicature* 79: 185–89.

Smith, S. K., and C. J. DeFrances. 1996. "Indigent Defense." Bureau of Justice Statistics *Bulletin*, February.

Snyder, H. N. and M. Sickmund. 2006. Juvenile Offenders and Victims: 2006 National Report. Washington, DC: U.S. Department of Justice.

Soble, A. 2006. Courtroom Style May Trump Substance in Ferrari Guy Trial." *Malibu Surfside News*, October 26. http://malibusurfsidenews.com.

———. 2008. "Malibu Ferrari Crash Driver Deported to Sweden." *Malibu Surfside News*, January 30. http://www.malibusurfsidenews.com.

Solomon, A. L., J. W. L. Osborne, S. F. LoBuglio, J. Mellow and D.A. Mukamal. 2008. *Life After Lockup: Improving Reentry from Jail to the Community*. Washington, DC: The Urban Institute.

Sorenson, J. R., and D. H. Wallace. 1999. "Prosecutorial Discretion in Seeking Death: An Analysis of Racial Disparity in the Pretrial Stages of Case Processing in a Midwestern County." *Justice Quarterly* 16: 561–78.

Sorensen, J. R., J. M. Marquart, and D. E. Brock. 1993. "Factors Related to Killings of Felons by Police Officers: A Test of the Community Violence and Conflict Hypotheses." *Justice Quarterly* 10: 417–40.

Souryal, S. S., D. W. Potts, and A. I. Alobied. 1994. "The Penalty of Hand Amputation for Theft in Islamic Justice." *Journal of Criminal Justice* 22: 249–65.

Spangenberg Group. 2003. "Rates of Compensation Paid to Court-Appointed Counsel in Non-capital Felony Cases at Trial: A State-by-State Overview." American Bar Association Bar Information Program, August 2003.

Spangenberg, R. L., and M. L. Beeman. 1995. "Indigent Defense Systems in the United States." *Law and Contemporary Problems* 58: 31–49.

Sparrow, M. K., M. H. Moore, and D. M. Kennedy. 1990. *Beyond 911: A New Era for Policing*. New York: Basic Books.

Spears, J. W., and C. C. Spohn. 1997. "The Effect of Evidence Factors and Victim Characteristics on Prosecutors' Charging Decisions in Sexual Assault Cases." *Justice Quarterly* 14: 501–24.

Spears, L. 1991. "Contract Counsel: A Different Way to Defend the Poor—How It's Working in North Dakota." *American Bar Association Journal on Criminal Justice* 6: 24–31.

Spelman, W. G., and D. K. Brown. 1984. *Calling the Police: Citizen Reporting of Serious Crime*. Washington, DC: Police Executive Research Forum.

Spencer, C. 2000. "Nonlethal Weapons Aid Lawmen: Police Turn to Beanbag Guns, Pepper Spray to Save Lives of Defiant Suspects." *Arkansas Democrat-Gazette*, November 6, p. B1.

Spitzer, S. 1975. "Toward a Marxian Theory of Deviance." *Social Problems* 22:638–51.

Spohn, C. 1992. "An Analysis of the 'Jury Trial Penalty' and Its Effect on Black and White Offenders." *The Justice Professional* 7: 93–97.

Spohn, C., J. Gruhl, and S. Welch. 1987. "The Impact of the Ethnicity and Gender of Defendants on the Decision to Reject or Dismiss Felony Charges." *Criminology* 25: 175–91.

Spohn, C., and D. Holleran. 2000. "The Imprisonment Penalty Paid by Young, Unemployed Black and Hispanic Male Offenders." *Criminology* 38: 281–306.

———. 2001. "Prosecuting Sexual Assault: A Comparison of Charging Decisions in Sexual Assault Cases Involving Strangers, Acquaintances, and Intimate Partners." *Justice Quarterly* 18: 651–85.

Sridharan, S., L. Greenfield, and B. Blakley. 2004. "A Study of Prosecutorial Certification Practice in Virginia." *Criminology and Public Policy* 3: 605–32.

Staba, D. 2007. "Killer of 3 Women in Buffalo Area Is Given a Life Term." *New York Times*, August 15. http://www.nytimes.com.

Stafford, M. C., and M. Warr. 1993. "A Reconceptualization of General and Specific Deterrence." *Journal of Research in Crime and Delinquency* 30 (May): 123–35.

Stahl, A. 2008a. "Petitioned Status Offense Cases in Juvenile Court." (OJJDP Fact Sheet #FS-200802). Washington, DC: U.S. Department of Justice.

———. 2008b. "Drug Offense Cases in Juvenile Courts," 1985–2004. Washington, DC: U.S. Department of Justice.

Stahl, A., T. Finnegan, and W. Kang. 2007b. "Easy Access to Juvenile Court Statistics: 1985–2004." http://ojjdp.ncjrs.gov/ojstabb/ezajcs.

Stahl, M. B. 1992. "Asset Forfeiture, Burden of Proof, and the War on Drugs." *Journal of Criminal Law and Criminology* 83: 274–337.

Stanford, M. R., and B. L. Mowry. 1990. "Domestic Disturbance Danger Rate." *Journal of Police Science and Administration* 17: 244–49.

Stanko, E. 1988. "The Impact of Victim Assessment on Prosecutors' Screening Decisions: The Case of the New York District Attorney's Office." In *Criminal Justice: Law and Politics*, 5th ed., ed. G. F. Cole. Pacific Grove, CA: Brooks/Cole.

"State and Local Fusion Centers." 2008. U.S. Department of Homeland Security. http://www.dhs.gov/xinfoshare.programs/.

Statistics Canada. 2004. "The Daily." July 28. http://www.statcan.ca.

Stecklow, S., J. Singer, and A. O. Patrick. 2005. "Watch on the Thames." *Wall Street Journal*, July 8. http://www.wsj.com.

Steen, S., R.L. Engen and R. R. Gainey. 2005. "Images of Danger and Culpability: Racial Stereotyping, Case Processing, and Criminal Sentencing." *Criminology* 43 (2): 435–68.

Steffensmeier, D., and S. Demuth. 2001. "Ethnicity and Judges' Sentencing Decisions: Hispanic-Black-White Comparisons." *Criminology* 39: 145–78.

Steffensmeier, D., J. Kramer, and C. Streifel. 1993. "Gender and Imprisonment Decisions." *Criminology* 31: 411–46.

Steffensmeier, D., J. Schwartz, H. Zhong, and J. Ackerman. 2005. "An Assessment of Recent Trends in Girls' Violence Using Diverse Longitudinal Sources: Is the Gender Gap Closing?" *Criminology* 43 (2): 355-406.

Steffensmeier, D., J. Ulmer, and J. Kramer. 1998. "The Interaction of Race, Gender, and Age in Criminal Sentencing: The Punishment Cost of Being Young, Black, and Male." *Criminology* 36: 763–97.

Steiker, C. and J. Steiker. 2006. "The Shadow of Death: The Effect of Capital Punishment on American Criminal Law and Policy." *Judicature* 89 (5): 250–3.

Steinberg, J. 1999. "The Coming Crime Wave Is Washed Up." *New York Times*, January 3, p. 4WK.

Steiner, B., C. Hemmens, and V. Bell. 2006. "Legislative Waiver Reconsidered: General Deterrent Effects of Statutory Exclusion Laws Enacted Post-1979." *Justice Quarterly* 23: 34–59.

Steiner, B. and E. Wright. 2006. "Assessing the Relative Effects of State Direct File Waiver Laws on Violent Juvenile Crime: Deterrence or Irrelevance?" *The Journal of Criminal Law and Criminology* 96: 1451–77.

Steinman, M. 1988. "Anticipating Rank and File Police Reactions to Arrest Policies Regarding Spouse Abuse." *Criminal Justice Research Bulletin* 4: 1–5.

Steury, E. 1993. "Criminal Defendants with Psychiatric Impairment: Prevalence, Probabilities, and Rates." *Journal of Criminal Law and Criminology* 84: 352–76.

Steury, E., and N. Frank. 1990. "Gender Bias and Pretrial Release: More Pieces of the Puzzle." *Journal of Criminal Justice* 18: 417–32.

Steward, D., and M. Totman. 2005. *Racial Profiling: Don't Mind If I Take a Look, Do Ya? An Examination of Consent Searches and Contraband Hit Rates at Texas Traffic Stops*. Austin: Texas Justice Coalition.

Stoddard, E. R. 1968. "The Informal 'Code' of Police Deviancy: A Group Approach to Blue-Coat Crime." *Journal of Criminal Law, Criminology, and Police Science* 59: 204–11.

Stojkovic, S. 1990. "Accounts of Prison Work: Corrections Officers' Portrayals of Their Work Worlds." *Perspectives on Social Problems* 2: 211–30.

Stolberg, S. G. 2006. "Senate Passes Legislation to Renew Patriot Act." *New York Times*, March 3. http://www.nytimes.com.

Stolzenberg, L., and S. J. D'Alessio. 1994. "Sentencing and Unwarranted Disparity: An Empirical Assessment of the Long-Term Impact of Sentencing Guidelines in Minnesota." *Criminology* 32: 301–10.

———. 1997. "Three Strikes and You're Out: The Impact of California's New Mandatory Sentencing Law on Serious Crime Rates." *Crime and Delinquency* 43: 457–69.

Streb, M. J., B. Frederick and C. LaFrance. 2007. "Contestation, Competiton, and the Potential for Accountability in Intermediate Appellate Court Elections." *Judicature* 91 (2): 70–78.

Streitfeld, D. 2008. "R. Kelly Is Acquitted in Child Pornography Case." *New York Times*, June 14. http://www.nytimes.com.

Strodtbeck, F., R. James, and G. Hawkins. 1957. "Social Status in Jury Deliberations." *American Sociological Review* 22: 713–19.

Strom, K. J. and J. M. MacDonald. 2007. "The Influence of Social and Economic Disadvantage on Racial Patterns in Youth Homicide over Time." *Homicide Studies* 11: 50–69.

Stroshine, M. S. 2005. "Information Technology Innovations in Policing." In *Critical Issues in Policing*, 5th ed., ed. R. G. Dunham and G. P. Alpert. Long Grove, IL: Waveland Press, 172–83.

Stucky, T. D., K. Heimer, and J. B. Lang. 2005. "Partisan Politics, Electoral Competition and Imprisonment: An Analysis of States over Time." *Criminology* 43 (February): 211–48.

Sullivan, J. and M. Purdy. 1995. "A Prison Empire: How It Grew," *New York Times*, July 23, p. 1.

Sullivan, K. M. 2003. "Under a Watchful Eye: Incursions on Personal Privacy." In *The War on Our Freedoms: Civil Liberties in an Age of Terrorism*," ed. R. C. Leone and G. Anrig, Jr. New York: Public Affairs, 128–46.

"Survey Estimates Shoplifting Costs Retailers Billions." 2007. *Security Beat*, December 4. http://www.securitysolutions.com/news/shoplifting-costs-billions-index.html.

Sutherland, E. H. 1947. *Criminology*. 4th ed. Philadelphia: Lippincott.

———. 1949. *White-Collar Crime*. New York: Holt, Rinehart, and Winston.

———. 1950. "The Sexual Psychopath Laws." *Journal of Criminal Law and Criminology* 40 (January–February): 543–54.

Swartz, J. 2004. "Inmates vs. Outsourcing." *USA Today*, July 6, p. 1.

Sydney Morning Herald. 2006. "Supercar Crash: $7.5m Bail Set." SMH.COM.AU, April 18. http://www.smh.com.au.

Sykes, G. M. 1958. *The Society of Captives*. Princeton, NJ: Princeton University Press.

Taifa, N. 2002. Testimony on Behalf of American Civil Liberties Union of the National Capital Area concerning Proposed Use of Surveillance Cameras, before the Joint Public Oversight Hearing Committee on the Judiciary, Council of the District of Columbia, June 13. http://www.dcwatch.com.

Tanveer, K. 2002. "Pakistani Council Doles out Brutal Punishment: Gang Rape." *Lansing (MI) State Journal*, July 4, p. 2A.

Tark, J., and G. Kleck. 2004. "Resisting Crime: The Effects

of Victim Action on the Outcomes of Crimes." *Criminology* 42: 861–909.

Teeters, N. K., and J. D. Shearer. 1957. *The Prison at Philadelphiaʼs Cherry Hill*. New York: Columbia University Press.

Terrill, W. 2005. "Police Use of Force: A Transactional Approach." *Justice Quarterly* 22: 107–38.

Terrill, W., E. A. Paoline, III, and P. K. Manning. 2003. "Police Culture and Coercion." *Criminology* 41: 1003–34.

Terry, C. 1997. "The Function of Humor for Prison Inmates." *Journal of Contemporary Criminal Justice* 13: 23-40.

Terry, D. 1996. "After 18 Years in Prison, 3 Are Cleared of Murders." *New York Times,* July 3, p. A8.

Thaman, S. C. 2000. "The Separation of Questions of Law and Fact in the New Russian and Spanish Jury Verdicts." In *The Judicial Role in Criminal Proceedings,* ed. Sean Doran and John Jackson. Oxford, England: Hart, 51–63.

The Third Branch. 2008a. "Economics of CJA Regulations Costly to Attorneys." Administrative Office of the U.S. Courts. Vol 40 (4), April. http://www.uscourts.gov.

———. 2008b. "National Summits Help Federal Courts Prepare for Sentence Reduction Requests." Administrative Office of the U.S. Courts. Vol 40 (2), February, pp. 1–3, 6. http://www.uscourts.gov.

Thomas, C. S., M. L. Boyer, and R. J. Hrebenar. 2003. "Interest Groups and State Court Elections." *Judicature,* 87: 135–44.

Thomas, C. W. 2002. "A 'Real Time' Statistical Profile of Private Prisons for Adults." http://web.crim.ufl.edu/pcp/census.

Thomas, W. H., Jr. 1976. *Bail Reform in America*. Berkeley: University of California Press.

Thompson, R. A. 2001. "Police Use of Force against Drug Suspects: Understanding the Legal Need for Policy Development." *American Journal of Criminal Justice* 25: 173–97.

Thurman, Q., J. Zhao, and A. Giacomazzi. 2001. *Community Policing in a Community Era*. Los Angeles: Roxbury.

Tiersma, P. 2001. "The Rocky Road to Legal Reform: Improving the Language of Jury Instructions." *Brooklyn Law Review* 66:1081–119.

Toch, H. 1976. *Peacekeeping: Police, Prisons, and Violence*. Lexington, MA: Lexington Books.

Tonry, M. 1993. "Sentencing Commissions and Their Guidelines." In *Crime and Justice,* vol. 17, ed. M. Tonry. Chicago: University of Chicago Press.

———. 1995. *Malign Neglect: Race, Crime, and Punishment in America*. New York: Oxford University Press.

———. 1998a. "Intermediate Sanctions." In *Handbook of Crime and Punishment,* ed. M. Tonry. New York: Oxford University Press, 683–711.

———. 1998b. Introduction to *Handbook of Crime and Punishment,* ed. M. Tonry. New York: Oxford University Press, 22–3.

Tonry, M., and M. Lynch. 1996. "Intermediate Sanctions." In *Crime and Justice,* vol. 20, ed. M. Tonry. Chicago: University of Chicago Press, 99–144.

Torriero, E. A., and R. Manor. 2002. "Andersen Convicted; Most Work Will Cease." *Seattle Times,* June 16. http://www .seattletimes.com.

Travis, J. 2002. "Invisible Punishment: An Instrument of Social Exclusion." In *Invisible Punishment: The Collective Consequences of Mass Imprisonment,* ed. M. Mauer and M. Chesney-Lind. New York: New Press, 15–36.

Travis, J., and J. Petersilia. 2001. "Reentry Reconsidered: A New Look at an Old Question." *Crime and Delinquency,* July, pp. 291–313.

"The Trial." 2004. *Newark Star-Ledger,* February 8. http:// www.nj.com.

Tucker, J. 1997. *May God Have Mercy*. New York: Norton.

Turner K. B. and J. B. Johnson. 2006. "The Effect of Gender on the Judicial Pretrial Decision of Bail Amount Set." *Federal Probation* 70 (1): 56–62.

Turner, M. G., F. T. Cullen, J. L. Sundt, and B. K. Applegate. 1997. "Public Tolerance for Community-Based Sanctions." *Prison Journal* 77 (March): 6–26.

"Turnpike Shootings to be Reenacted," 1999. *New York Times,* April 9. http://www.nytimes .com.

Tyler, T. R., and C. J. Wakslak. 2004. "Profiling and Police Legitimacy: Procedural Justice, Attributions of Motive, and Acceptance of Police Authority." *Criminology* 42: 253–81.

"Typical Drug User Is Profiled by U.S.," 1999. *New York Times,* September 9, p. A14.

Twyman, A. S. 2005. "Police Policy on Mentally Ill Questioned." *Philadelphia Inquirer,* April 18. http://www.philly.com.

Uchida, C. 2005. "The Development of the American Police: An Historical Overview." In *Critical Issues in Policing,* ed. R. G. Dunham and G. P. Alpert. Long Grove, IL: Waveland Press, 20–40.

Uchida, C., and T. Bynum. 1991. "Search Warrants, Motions to Suppress and 'Lost Cases': The Effects of the Exclusionary Rule in Seven Jurisdictions." *Journal of Criminal Law and Criminology* 81: 1034–66.

Uggen, C., and J. Manza. 2002. "Democratic Contradiction? Political Consequences of Felon Disenfranchisement Law in the United States." *American Sociological Review* 67: 777–803.

Ugwuegbu, D. 1999. "Racial and Evidential Factors in Juror Attributions of Legal Responsibility." In *The Social Organization of Law,* 2nd ed., ed. M. P. Baumgartner. San Diego: Academic Press.

University of Pittsburgh Medical Center. 2005. "Lead in Environment Causes Violent Crime, Reports University of Pittsburgh Researcher at AAAS." *UPMC News Release,* February 18. http://news bureau. upmc.com.

Unnever, J., and F. T. Cullen. 2005. "Executing the Innocent and Support for Capital Punishment: The Implications for Public Policy." *Criminology and Public Policy* 4:3–38.

Unnever, J. D., F. T. Cullen and J. P. Bartkowski. 2006. "Images of God and Public Support for Capital Punishment: Does a Close Relationship with a Loving God Matter?" *Criminology* 44 (4): 835–66.

Uphoff, R. J. 1992. "The Criminal Defense Lawyer: Zealous Advocate, Double Agent, or Beleaguered Dealer?" *Criminal Law Bulletin* 28: 419–56.

U.S. Census Bureau. 2007. "Historical Poverty Tables," Table 2 at http://www.census.gov/hhes/ www/poverty/histpov/hstpov2 .html.

U.S. Department of Justice. 1980. *Principles of Prosecution*. Washington, DC: U.S. Government Printing Office.

———. 2003. *Correctional Boot Camps: Lessons from a Decade of Research*. Washington, DC: National Institute of Justice, U.S. Government Printing Office.

———. 2004. "Local Physician Pleads Guilty in Multi-Million Dollar Motorized Wheelchair Fraud Scheme and Forfeits $1.6 million to U.S." Press release, April 1. http:// www.usdoj.gov/usao/txs/ releases.

———. 2008. "Foreign National Sentenced to Nine Years in Prison for Hotel Business Center Computer Fraud Scheme." Press Release. April 11. http:// www.usdoj.gov.

U.S. Department of State. 2004. *Country Reports on Human Rights Practices*. http://www .state.gov.

U.S. Marshals Service. 2008. "U.S. Marshals: Facts and Figures." January 30. ttp://www.usmar shals.gov/duties/factsheets/ facts.pdf.

U.S. Office of Juvenile Justice and Deliquency Prevention Programs. 2006. National Juvenile Court Data Archive. http:// ojjdp.ncjrs.org/ojstatbb/njcda/.

U.S. President's Commission on Law Enforcement and Administration of Justice. 1967. *The Challenge of Crime in a Free Society*. Washington, DC: U.S. Government Printing Office.

USA Today. 2008. "UNC Suspect Charged in Duke Killing," March 13. http://usatoday.com.

Utz, P. 1978. *Settling the Facts*. Lexington, MA: Lexington Books.

Valencia-Martinez, A. 2006. "Futuristic Gadgets Arm LAPD Car." *Los Angeles Daily News,* July 31. http://www.dailynews .com.

Varano, S. P., J. D. McCluskey, J. W. Patchin, and T. S. Bynum. 2004. "Exploring the Drug-Homicide Connection." *Journal of Contemporary Criminal Justice* 20: 369–92.

Vaughn, M. S. 2001. "Assessing the Legal Liabilities in Law Enforcement: Chiefs' Views." *Crime and Delinquency* 47: 3–27.

Vera Institute of Justice. 1981. *Felony Arrests: Their Prosecution and Disposition in New York City's Courts.* New York: Longman.

Vicenti, C. N. 1995. "The Reemergence of Tribal Society and Traditional Justice Systems." *Judicature* 79: 134–41.

Vila, B., and D. J. Kenney. 2002. "Tired Cops: The Prevalence and Potential Consequences of Police Fatigue." *National Institute of Justice Journal* 248: 16–21.

Vogel, M. 1999. "The Social Origins of Plea Bargaining: Conflict and the Law in the Process of State Formation, 1830–1860." *Law and Society Review* 33: 161–246.

von Hirsch, A. 1976. *Doing Justice.* New York: Hill and Wang.

Wade, N. 2006. "Wider Use of DNA Lists Is Urged in Fighting Crime." *New York Times,* May 12. http://www.nytimes.com.

Wakeling, S., M. Jorgensen and S. Michaelson. 2001. "Policing American Indian Reservations." *National Institute of Justice Journal* (January), pp. 2–7.

Walker, L. and L. A. Hayashi. 2007. "Pono Kaulike: A Hawaii Criminal Court Provides Restorative Justice Practices for Healing Relationships." *Federal Probation* 71 (3): 18–24.

Walker, P. 1998. "Felony and Misdemeanor Defendants Filed in the U.S. District Courts during Fiscal Years 1990–95: An Analysis of the Filings of Each Offense Level." *Journal of Criminal Justice* 26: 503–11.

Walker, R. N. 2006. "How the Malfunctioning Death Penalty Challenges the Criminal Justice System." *Judicature* 89 (5): 265–9.

Walker, S. 1984. "'Broken Windows' and Fractured History: The Use and Misuse of History in Recent Police Patrol Analysis." *Justice Quarterly* 1 (March): 79–82.

———. 1993. *Taming the System: The Control of Discretion in Criminal Justice 1950–1990.* New York: Oxford University Press.

———. 1999. *The Police in America.* 3rd ed. New York: McGraw-Hill.

———. 2001. *Sense and Nonsense about Crime and Drugs: A Policy Guide.* 5th ed. Belmont, CA: Wadsworth

Walker, S., C. Spohn and M. DeLeone. 2007. *The Color of Justice: Race, Ethnicity, and Crime in America*, 4th ed. Belmont, CA: Thomson Wadsworth.

Walker, S., and K. B. Turner. 1992. "A Decade of Modest Progress: Employment of Black and Hispanic Police Officers, 1983–1992." Omaha: Department of Criminal Justice, University of Nebraska at Omaha.

Walker, S., and B. Wright. 1995. "Citizen Review of the Police, 1994: A National Survey." In *Fresh Perspectives.* Washington, DC: Police Executive Research Forum.

Walpin, G. 2003. "America's Adversarial and Jury Systems: More Likely to Do Justice?" *Harvard Journal of Law and Public Policy* 26: 175–87.

Walsh, W. 1989. "Private/Public Police Stereotypes: A Different Perspective." *Security Journal* 1: 21–27.

Walsh, W. F., and G. F. Vito. 2004. "The Meaning of Compstat." *Journal of Contemporary Criminal Justice* 20:51–69.

Warr, M. 1993. "Fear of Victimization." *The Public Perspective,* November–December, pp. 25–28.

Warren, J. 2005. "State Is Joining the Shift on Prisons." *Los Angeles Times,* March 27. http://www.latimes.com.

Warren, P., D. Tomaskovic-Devey, W. Smith, M. Zingraff, and M. Mason. 2006. "Driving While Black: Bias Processes and Racial Disparity in Police Stops." *Criminology* 44 (3): 709–38.

Wasserman, D. T. 1990. *A Sword for the Convicted: Representing Indigent Defendants on Appeal.* New York: Greenwood Press.

Watson, G. 1999. "Prisons Struggling to Deal with Mental Illness." *Hartford Courant,* May 23, p. A1.

Watson, R. A., and R. G. Downing. 1969. *The Politics of the Bench and Bar: Judicial Selection under the Missouri Nonpartisan Court Plan.* New York: Wiley.

Weil, M., and P. Dvorak. 2002. "Authorities Link Virginia Shooting to Sniper Case." *Washington Post,* October 15, p. 1.

Weinberg, S. 2003. "Unbecoming Conduct." *Legal Affairs,* November–December, pp. 28–33.

Weinstein, J. B. 1992. "A Trial Judge's Second Impression of the Federal Sentencing Guidelines." *Southern California Law Review* 66: 357.

Weisburd, D. A., and L. Green. 1995. "Measuring Immediate Spatial Displacement: Methodological Issues and Problems." In *Crime and Place: Crime Prevention Studies,* vol. 4, ed. D. A. Weisburd and J. E. Eck. Monsey, New York: Criminal Justice Press.

Weisburd, D., S. D. Mastrofski, A. M. McNally, R. Greenspan and J. J. Willis. 2003. "Reforming to Preserve: Compstat and Strategic Problem Solving in American Policing." *Criminology and Public Policy* 2: 421–56.

Weitzer, R. 2002. "Incidents of Police Misconduct and Public Opinion." *Journal of Criminal Justice* 30: 397–408.

Welch, M. 1994. "Jail Overcrowding: Social Sanitation and the Warehousing of the Urban Underclass." In *Critical Issues in Crime and Justice,* ed. A. Roberts. Thousand Oaks, CA: Sage, 249–74.

WFSB. 2007. "New Haven Detectives Plead Guilty: Men Charged with Stealing Money." WFSB-TV, October 5. http://www.wfsb.com.

"What Was She Thinking?" 2005. *XXL Magazine,* July. http://xxlmag.com/Features/2005/july/lil-kim/.

White, J. 2004. *Defending the Homeland.* Belmont, CA: Thomson/Wadsworth.

White, M. S. 1995. "The Nonverbal Behaviors in Jury Selection." *Criminal Law Bulletin* 31: 414–45.

Whitebread, C. H., and C. Slobogin. 2000. *Criminal Procedure: An Analysis of Cases and Concepts.* 4th ed. Westbury, NY: Foundation Press.

Widom, C. S. 1995. *Victims of Childhood Sexual Abuse: Later Criminal Consequences.* Washington, DC: U.S. Dept. of Justice, Office of Justice Programs, National Institute of Justice.

Wilbanks, W. 1987. *The Myth of a Racist Criminal Justice System.* Pacific Grove, CA: Brooks/Cole.

"Williams' Co-defendant Pleads Guilty to Tampering." 2002. *Seattle Times,* August 22. http://www.seattletimes.com.

Williams, H., and P. V. Murphy. 1990. "The Evolving Strategy of Police: A Minority View." In *Perspectives on Policing,* no. 13. Washington, DC: National Institute of Justice, U.S. Government Printing Office.

Williams, H., and A. M. Pate. 1987. "Returning to First Principles: Reducing the Fear of Crime in Newark." *Crime and Delinquency* 33 (January): 53–9.

Williams, L. 2008. "Detroit-Area Man Gets 50 to 80 Years in Prison for Killing, Dismembering His Wife." *International Business Times,* February 21. http://ibtimes.com.

Williams, M. S. 2006. "The Process of Becoming a Judge for Women and Men." *Judicature* 90 (3): 104–13.

Williams, V., and M. Fish. 1974. *Convicts, Codes, and Contraband.* Cambridge, MA: Ballinger.

Willis, J. J., S. D. Mastrofski, and D. Weisburd. 2004. "Compstat and Bureaucracy: A Case Study of Challenges and Opportunities for Change." *Justice Quarterly* 21: 463–96.

Willott, S., C. Griffin, and M. Torrance. 2001. "Snakes and Ladders: Upper-Middle Class Male Offenders Talk about Economic Crime." *Criminology* 39: 441–66.

Wilson, J. Q. 1968. *Varieties of Police Behavior.* Cambridge, MA: Harvard University Press.

Wilson, J. Q., and B. Boland. 1979. *The Effect of the Police on Crime.* Washington, DC: U.S. Government Printing Office.

Wilson, J. Q., and R. Herrnstein. 1985. *Crime and Human Nature.* New York: Simon & Schuster.

Wilson, J. Q., and G. L. Kelling. 1982. "Broken Windows: The Police and Neighborhood Safety." *Atlantic Monthly,* March, pp. 29–38.

Wilson, M. 2007. "Lives Intersect Violently on a Busy City Street." *New York Times,* March 16. http://www.nytimes.com.

———. 2008. "Judge Acquits Detectives in 50-Shot Killing of Bell." *New York Times,* April 26. http://www.nytimes.com.

Winerip, M. 1999. "Bedlam in the Streets." *The New York Times Sunday Magazine,* May 23, p. 42.

Winick, B. J. 1995. "Reforming Incompetency to Stand Trial and Plead Guilty." *Journal of Criminal Law and Criminology* 85: 571–624.

Winkeljohn, M. 2002. "A Random Act of Hate: Duckett's Attack Linked to Racism." *Atlanta Journal and Constitution,* August 4, p. E1.

Winner, L., L. Lanza-Kaduce, D. M. Bishop, and C. E. Frazier. 1997. "The Transfer of Juveniles to Criminal Court: Reexamining Recidivism over the Long Term." *Crime and Delinquency* 43 (October): 549–63.

Witt, H. 2007a. "To Some in Paris, Sinister Past Is Back." *Chicago Tribune* (March 12). http://chicagotribune.com.

———. 2007b. "Texas Denies Teen's Appeal of Conviction." *Chicago Tribune* (July 6). http://chicagotribune.com.

Wolfgang, M. E., and F. Ferracuti. 1967. *The Subculture of Violence.* London: Tavistock.

Wool, J. 2005. "Beyond *Blakely*: Implications of the *Booker* Decision for State Sentencing Systems." *Policy and Practice Review* (Vera Institute of Justice), February, pp. 1–7.

Wooldredge, J. D., and K. Masters. 1993. "Confronting Problems Faced by Pregnant Inmates in State Prisons." *Crime and Delinquency* 39 (April): 195–203.

Worden, A. p. 1991. "Privatizing Due Process: Issues in the Comparison of Assigned Counsel, Public Defenders, and Contracted Indigent Defense Counsel." *Justice System Journal* 15: 390–418.

———. 1993. "The Attitudes of Women and Men in Policing: Testing Conventional and Contemporary Wisdom." *Criminology* 31 (May): 203–24.

———. 1994. "Counsel for the Poor: An Evaluation of Contracting for Indigent Criminal Defense." *Justice Quarterly* 10: 613–37.

———. 1995. "The Judge's Role in Plea Bargaining: An Analysis of Judges' Agreement with Prosecutors' Sentencing Recommendations." *Justice Quarterly* 12: 257–78.

Worrall, J. L. and T. V. Kovandzic. 2007. "COPS Grants and Crime Revisited." *Criminology* 45: 159–90.

Worth, R. F. 2001. "73 Tied to Genovese Family Are Indicted, Officials Say." *New York Times,* December 6, p. A27.

Wright, J. P., and F. Cullen. 2000. "Juvenile Involvement in Occupational Delinquency." *Criminology* 38: 863–96.

Xiong, N. 1997. "Private Prisons: A Question of Savings," *New York Times,* July 13, D5.

Yang, S. S. 1990. "The Unique Treatment Needs of Female Substance Abusers: The Obligation of the Criminal Justice System to Provide Parity Services." *Medicine and Law* 9: 1018–27.

Yardley, W. 2006. "DNA Samples Link 4 Murders in Connecticut." *New York Times,* June 8. http://www.nytimes.com.

Yardley, W., and S. Stowe. 2005. "A Contrite Rowland Gets a Year for Accepting $107,000 in Gifts." *New York Times,* March 19. http://www.nytimes.com.

Zagaris, B. 1998. "U.S. International Cooperation against Transnational Organized Crime." *Wayne Law Review* 44 (Fall): 1401–64.

Zalman, M. and B. Smith. 2007. "The Attitudes of Police Executives Toward Miranda and Interrogation Policies." *The Journal of Criminal Law and Criminology* 97: 873–942.

Zalman, M., B. W. Smith and A. Kiger. 2008. "Officials' Estimates of the Frequency of 'Actual Innocence' Convictions." *Justice Quarterly* 25 (1): 72–99.

Zedner, L. 1995. "Wayward Sisters." In *The Oxford History of Prisons,* ed. N. Morris and D. J. Rothman. New York: Oxford University Press, 329–61.

Zernike, K. 2007. "Violent Crime in Cities Shows Sharp Surge," *New York Times,* March 9. http://www.nytimes.com.

Zhao, J. S., N. He, and N. Loverich. 2003. "Community Policing: Did It Change the Basic Functions of Policing in the 1990s? A National Follow-Up Study." *Justice Quarterly* 20: 697–724.

Zhao, J. S., N. P. He, N. Loverich, and J. Cancino. 2003. "Marital Status and Police Occupational Stress." *Journal of Crime and Justice* 26: 23–46.

Zimmer, L. 1987. "Operation Pressure Point: The Disruption of Street-Level Trade on New York's Lower East Side." Occasional paper from the Center for Research in Crime and Justice, New York University School of Law.

Zimring, F. E., G. Hawkins, and S. Kamin. 2001. *Punishment and Democracy: Three Strikes and You're Out in California.* New York: Oxford University Press.

Cases Cited

Adams v. Williams, 407 U.S. 143 (1972).

Aguilar v. Texas, 378 U.S. 108 (1964).

Apprendi v. New Jersey, 500 U.S. 466 (2000).

Argersinger v. Hamlin, 407 U.S. 25 (1972).

Arizona v. Evans, 514 U.S. 1 (1995).

Atkins v. Virginia, 122 S. Ct. 2242 (2002).

Atwater v. City of Lago Vista, 532 U.S. 318 (2001).

Austin v. United States, 61 LW 4811 (1993).

Barron v. Baltimore, 32 U.S. 243 (1833).

Batson v. Kentucky, 476 U.S. 79 (1986).

Baxter v. Palmigiano, 425 U.S. 308 (1976).

Baze v. Rees, 128 S.Ct. 1520 (2008).

Beard v. Banks, 548 U.S. 521 (2006).

Bell v. Wolfish, 441 U.S. 520 (1979).

Bennis v. Michigan, 116 S. Ct. 994 (1996).

Blackledge v. Allison, 431 U.S. 71 (1976).

Blake v. Los Angeles, 595 F. 2d 1367 (1979).

Blakely v. Washington, 124 S. Ct. 2531 (2004).

Board of Education v. Earls, 536 U.S. 822 (2002).

Bond v. United States, 529 U.S. 334 (2000).

Bordenkircher v. Hayes, 343 U.S. 357 (1978).

Boykin v. Alabama, 395 U.S. 238 (1969).

Breed v. Jones, 421 U.S. 519 (1975).

Breihaupt v. Abram, 352 U.S. 432 (1957).

Brendlin v. California, 127 S.Ct. 2400 (2007).

Brewer v. Williams, 430 U.S. 387 (1977).

Brown v. Mississippi, 297 U.S. 281 (1936).

Bumper v. North Carolina, 391 U.S. 543 (1968).

Burch v. Louisiana, 441 U.S. 130 (1979).

California v. Acevedo, 500 U.S. 565 (1991).

Carroll v. United States, 267 U.S. 132 (1925).

Chimel v. California, 395 U.S. 752 (1969).

City of Indianapolis v. Edmond, 531 U.S. 32 (2000).

Coolidge v. New Hampshire, 403 U.S. 443 (1971).

Cooper v. Oklahoma, 116 S. Ct. 1373 (1996).

Cooper v. Pate, 378 U.S. 546 (1964).

Cruz v. Beto, 450 U.S. 319 (1972).

Cupp v. Murphy, 412 U.S. 291 (1973).

Daniels v. Williams, 474 U.S. 327 (1986).

Dawson v. State, 274 Ga. 327 (2001).

Deck v. Missouri, 125 S. Ct. 2007 (2005).

Delaware v. Prouse, 440 U.S. 648 (1979).

Dickerson v. United States, 530 U.S. 428 (2000).

Douglas v. California, 372 U.S. 353 (1963).

Durham v. United States, 214 F. 2d 862 (D.C. Cir. 1954).

Eddings v. Oklahoma, 455 U.S. 104 (1982).

Escobedo v. Illinois, 378 U.S. 478 (1964).

Estelle v. Gamble, 429 U.S. 97 (1976).

Fare v. Michael C., 442 U.S. 707 (1979).

Fierro v. Gomez, 865 F. Supp. 1387 (N.D. Cal. 1994).

Flippo v. West Virginia, 528 U.S. 11 (1999).

Florida v. J. L., 529 U.S. 266 (2000).

Ford v. Wainwright, 477 U.S. 399 (1986).

Foster v. Florida, 537 U.S. 990 (2002).

Fulwood v. Clemmer, 206 F. Supp. 370 (D.C. Cir. 1962).

Furman v. Georgia, 408 U.S. 238 (1972).

Gagnon v. Scarpelli, 411 U.S. 778 (1973).

Gideon v. Wainwright, 372 U.S. 335 (1963).

Gittlemacker v. Prasse, 428 F. 2d 1 (1970).

Graham v. Connor, 490 U.S. 396 (1989).

Gregg v. Georgia, 428 U.S. 153 (1976).

Griffin v. Wisconsin, 483 U.S. 868 (1987).

Griggs v. Duke Power Company, 401 U.S. 424 (1971).

Hamdi v. Rumsfeld, 542 U.S. 507 (2004).

Harris v. New York, 401 U.S. 222 (1971).

Heath v. Alabama, 474 U.S. 82 (1985).

Hester v. United States, 265 U.S. 57 (1924).

Hope v. Pelzer, 536 U.S. 730 (2002).

Hudson v. Palmer, 468 U.S. 517 (1984).

Illinois v. Caballes, 125 S. Ct. 834 (2005).

Illinois v. Gates, 462 U.S. 213 (1983).

Illinois v. Krull, 480 U.S. 340 (1987).

Illinois v. Lidster, 540 U.S. 419 (2004).

Illinois v. Rodriguez, 497 U.S. 177 (1990).

Illinois v. Wardlow, 528 U.S. 119 (2000).

Immigration and Naturalization Service v. Lopez-Mendoza, 468 U.S. 1032 (1984).

In re Gault, 387 U.S. 9 (1967).

In re Winship, 397 U.S. 358 (1970).

Irizarry v. United States, 128 S.Ct. 2198 (2008).

Jackson v. Bishop, 404 F.2d 471 (8th Cir. 1968).

Jacobson v. United States, 503 U.S. 540 (1992).

Johnson v. Zerbst, 304 U.S. 458 (1938).

Kahane v. Carlson, 527 F. 2d 592 (2d Cir. 1975).

Kansas v. Hendricks, 117 S. Ct. 2072 (1997).

Kent v. United States, 383 U.S. 541 (1966).

Knowles v. Iowa, 525 U.S. 113 (1998).

Kyllo v. United States, 533 U.S. 27 (2001).

Lanza v. New York, 370 U.S. 139 (1962).

Lawrence v. Texas, 539 U.S. 558 (2003).

Lee v. Downes, 641 F. 2d 1117 (4th Cir. 1981).

Lee v. Washington, 390 U.S. 333 (1968).

Lewis v. United States, 116 S. Ct. 2163 (1996).

Lockhart v. McCree, 476 U.S. 162 (1986).

Mapp v. Ohio, 367 U.S. 643 (1961).

Maryland v. Garrison, 480 U.S. 79 (1987).

Maryland v. Wilson, 519 U.S. 408 (1997).

Massiah v. United States, 377 U.S. 201 (1964).

McCleskey v. Kemp, 478 U.S. 1019 (1987).

McKeiver v. Pennsylvania, 403 U.S. 528 (1971).

Medellin v. Dretke, 125 S. Ct. 2088 (2005).

Mempa v. Rhay, 389 U.S. 128 (1967).

Michigan Department of State Police v. Sitz, 496 U.S. 440 (1990).

Michigan v. Long, 463 U.S. 1032 (1983).

Minnesota v. Dickerson, 508 U.S. 366 (1993).

Miranda v. Arizona, 384 U.S. 436 (1966).

M'Naughten's Case, 8 Eng. Rep. 718 (1843).

Monell v. Department of Social Services of the City of New York, 436 U.S. 658 (1978).

Montana v. Egelhoff, 116 S. Ct. 2013 (1996).

Morrissey v. Brewer, 408 U.S. 471 (1972).

Muehler v. Mena, 125 S. Ct. 1465 (2005).

Murray v. Giarratano, 492 U.S. 1 (1989).

Nelson v. Campbell, 124 S. Ct. 2117 (2004).

New Jersey v. T. L. O., 105 S. Ct. 733 (1985).

New York v. Belton, 453 U.S. 454 (1981).

New York v. Class, 475 U.S. 321 (1986).

New York v. Quarles, 467 U.S. 649 (1984).

Nix v. Williams, 467 U.S. 431 (1984).

North Carolina v. Alford, 400 U.S. 25 (1970).

Oklahoma Publishing Co. v. District Court, 430 U.S. 308 (1977).

Oliver v. United States, 466 U.S. 170 (1984).

O'Lone v. Estate of Shabazz, 482 U.S. 342 (1987).

Overton v. Bazetta, 539 U.S. 126 (2003).

Pargo v. Elliott, 69 F.3d 280 (8th Cir. 1995).

Pennsylvania Board of Pardons and Parole v. Scott, 524 U.S. 357 (1998).

Pennsylvania v. Muniz, 496 U.S. 582 (1990).

Penry v. Lynaugh, 492 U.S. 302 (1989).

People v. Clark, 183 Colo. 201 (1973).

People v. Nguyen, California Supreme Court, #07-416 (2008).

Powell v. Alabama, 287 U.S. 45 (1932).

Procunier v. Martinez, 416 U.S. 396 (1974).

Queen v. Dudley and Stephens, 14 Q.B.D. 273 (1884).

Rasul v. Bush, 542 U.S. 466 (2004).

Republican Party of Minnesota v. White, 122 S. Ct. 2528 (2002).

Rhodes v. Chapman, 452 U.S. 337 (1981).

Ricketts v. Adamson, 481 U.S. 1 (1987).

Ring v. Arizona, 122 S. Ct. 2428 (2002).

Robinson v. California, 370 U.S. 660 (1962).

Roper v. Simmons, 125 S. Ct. 1183 (2005).

Ross v. Moffitt, 417 U.S. 660 (1974).

Ruiz v. Estelle, 503 F. Supp. 1265 (S.D. Tex. 1980).

Rumsfeld v. Padilla, 542 U.S. 426 (2004).

Sandin v. Conner, 115 S. Ct. 2293 (1995).

Santobello v. New York, 404 U.S. 260 (1971).

Schall v. Martin, 467 U.S. 253 (1984).

Scott v. Harris, 127 S.Ct. 1769 (2007).

Scott v. Illinois, 440 U.S. 367 (1979).

Silveira v. Lockyer, 312 F. 3d 1052 (9th Cir. 2002).

Sitz v. Department of State Police, 506 N.W. 2d 209 (Mich. 1993).

Skinner v. Oklahoma, 316 U.S. 535 (1942).

Smith v. Daily Mail Publishing Co., 443 U.S. 97 (1979).

South Dakota v. Opperman, 428 U.S. 364 (1976).

Spinelli v. United States, 393 U.S. 410 (1969).

Stanford v. Kentucky, 492 U.S. 361 (1989).

State v. Russell, 477 N.W. 2d 886 (Minn. 1991).

Strickland v. Washington, 466 U.S. 686 (1984).

Tennessee v. Garner, 471 U.S. 1 (1985).

Terry v. Ohio, 392 U.S. 1 (1968).

Theriault v. Carlson, 339 F. Supp 375 (N.D. Ga. 1972).

Thompson v. Oklahoma, 108 S. Ct. 1687 (1988).

Thornburgh v. Abbott, 490 U.S. 401 (1989).

Trop v. Dulles, 356 U.S. 86 (1958).

Turner v. Safley, 482 U.S. 78 (1987).

United States v. Bajakajian, 118 S. Ct. 2028 (1998).

United States v. Booker, 125 S. Ct. 738 (2005).

United States v. Brawner, 471 F. 2d 969 (D.C. Cir. 1972).

United States v. Calandra, 414 U.S. 338 (1974).

United States v. Cronic, 444 U.S. 654 (1984).

United States v. Drayton, 122 S. Ct. 2105 (2002).

United States v. Emerson, 270 F. 3d 203 (5th Cir. 2001).

United States v. Hitchcock, 992 F. 2d 1107 (CA9 1972).

United States v. Leon, 468 U.S. 897 (1984).

United States v. Robinson, 414 U.S. 218 (1973).

United States v. Salerno and Cafero, 481 U.S. 739 (1987).

United States v. Ursery, 116 S. Ct. 2135 (1996).

United States v. Wade, 388 U.S. 218 (1967).

Uttecht v. Brown, 127 S. Ct. 2218 (2007).

Vernonia School District v. Acton, 515 U.S. 646 (1995).

Vitek v. Jones, 445 U.S. 480 (1980).

Warden v. Hayden, 387 U.S. 294 (1967).

Weeks v. United States, 232 U.S. 383 (1914).

Whitley v. Albers, 475 U.S. 312 (1986).

Whren v. United States, 517 U.S. 806 (1996).

Wiggins v. Smith, 539 U.S. 510 (2003).

Williams v. Florida, 399 U.S. 78 (1970).

Wilson v. Seiter, 111 S. Ct. 232 (1991).

Wisconsin v. Mitchell, 113 S. Ct. 2194 (1993).

Witherspoon v. Illinois, 391 U.S. 510 (1968).

Wolf v. Colorado, 338 U.S. 25 (1949).

Wolff v. McDonnell, 418 U.S. 539 (1974).

Wyoming v. Houghton, 526 U.S. 295 (1999).

Name Index

Abadinsky, H., 22
Abbe, O. G., 333
Abraham, H. J., 407
Abraham, N., 621
Abrahamson, S. S., 326
Abrams, J., 123
Abu Ali, A. O., 309
Abwender, D. A., 416
Ackerman, J., 189
Acoca, L., 559
Acton, J., 619
Adams, K., 246, 247, 552
Adang, O. M., 249
Addams, J., 610
Adler, F., 70
Adler, S. J., 416
Aicher, J., 432
Albanese, J., 22
Alito, S., 151
Alley, M. E., 235
Al-Marri, A., 309
al-Muhajir, A., 309
Alobied, A. I., 126
Alpert, G., 106
Alpert, G. P., 330
Amar, A. R., 409
Anderson, D., 206
Anderson, G., 211
Anderson, M., 525
Anderson, R., 547
Andrews, D. A., 561, 563
Andrews, S., 190
Anglen, R., 267
Antonio, M. E., 415
Applegate, B. K., 430, 528, 564, 632
Arballo, J., 201
Arboscello, C., 392
Archibold, R., 22
Arena, K., 261
Armentano, P., 378
Armstrong, D. S., 479
Armstrong, G. S., 50
Armstrong, K., 377, 446
Arnold, N., 214
Aselton, B., 577
Aselton, C., 577
Aspin, L. T., 334
Atkins, D., 443
Audi, N., 130
Auerhahn, K., 430
Augustus, J., 511
Austin, J., 480, 568, 593, 608
Axtman, K., 14, 271, 410

Baca, M., 453
Baker, A., 216, 232, 248
Baldus, D. C., 443
Baldwin, L., 205
Bales, W., 107
Bandy, D., 124
Barnes, C. W., 336
Bartkowski, J. P., 449
Basemore, G., 431
Bast, C. M., 131
Bates, K., 326
Baugh, J. A., 151
Bayley, D. H., 181, 218, 220, 223, 224, 234, 235, 237
Bazelon, D., 138
Beauchamp, J., 327
Beccaria. C., 59
Beck, A. J., 346, 496
Becker, H. S., 67
Bedau, H. A., 386, 447
Beeman, M. L., 382
Bell, D., 22
Bell, S, 243, 247, 248, 249
Bell, V., 622
Bellair, P. E., 105
Belluck, P., 262
Bentham, J., 428
Berk, R. A., 189, 454
Bermudez, E.., 236
Bernard, A., 177
Bernard,T. J., 106
Bernstein, G., 585
Beto, G., 570
Bichler, G, 228
bin Laden, O., 376
Black, C., 19
Blackmun, H., 150, 444
Blakley, B., 360
Blecker, R., 443
Bloch, P., 206
Blonston, G., 6
Blumberg, A., 377
Blumberg, M., 53, 249
Blumenthal, R., 108
Blumstein, A., 38, 605
Bohn, K., 261
Boland, B., 231, 232, 365, 368
Bollea, N., 322
Bonczar, T. P., 446, 447
Bonello, E. M., 235
Bonilla, D., 58
Bonn, S., 203
Bonne, J., 105
Bonneau, C. W., 333
Bonta, J., 561

Bontrager, S., 107
Booker, C. A., 591
Bourque, B. B., 526
Bowers, F., 238
Boxer, P., 630
Boyer, M. L., 333
Bradley, C., 415
Bradley, C. M., 443
Brady, J., 15
Brady, S., 15
Braga, A. A., 234, 521, 607
Brand, G., 100
Brandl, S., 222, 223
Brandon, K., 37
Bratton, W., 250
Bray, K., 411
Brennan, P. A., 61
Brennan, P. K., 109
Brennan, W., 150, 444
Brewer, T. W., 445
Breyer, S., 444
Bridges, K. L., 133
Bright, S. B., 385
Britton, D. M., 544
Brock, D. E., 247
Brockway, Z., 471, 578
Brody, D. C., 333
Broeder, D. W., 416
Broner, N., 331
Brooking, C., 343
Brooks, B., 581
Brooks, R., 201
Brown, D. K., 229, 230
Brown, F., 97, 98, 99, 100
Brown, M. K., 211
Brown, R. A., 204
Brownback, S., 9
Bruce, M., 105
Bryant, K., 131
Bueno, J., 122
Buerger, M. E., 228
Bukowski, D., 458
Burdine, C. J., 446
Burger, W., 144, 312, 398
Burkhead, M., 446
Burrow, J. D., 106
Burton, V., 121
Buruma, I., 561
Bush, G. W., 56, 84, 92, 103, 117, 309, 447, 488
Bushway, S. D., 107
Butterfield, F., 38, 106, 436
Bykowicz, J., 620
Bynum, T., 232, 312

Cadigan, T. P., 342
Cady, J., 513

Cairns, V., 99, 100
Calhoun, F., 165
Call, J. E., 492
Callahan, L. A., 138
Callahan, R., 265
Calnon, J. M., 106
Camp, C. G., 544, 562, 567, 569
Camp, D. D., 133
Camp, G. M., 562, 569
Camp, S. D., 479, 480
Cancino, J., 211
Cancino, J. M., 251
Canto, M., 152
Cantrell, M. T., 137, 325, 409
Carbone-Lopez, K., 70
Carey, S. M., 330
Carlson, D. K., 194
Carlson, P. M., 567
Carlson, T., 276
Carns, T. W., 398
Carr, J. G., 342
Carr, P. J., 210
Carrera, S., Jr., 201
Carroll, R., 458
Carson, E., 4, 5
Carter, C. J., 20
Carter, J., 135
Cassell, P., 305
Catalano, S. M., 36, 37, 188
Cauffman, E., 61
Caulfield, S. L., 357
Chaddock, G. R., 260
Chaiken, J. M., 223
Champagne, A., 333
Champion, D. J., 402
Chapman, S. G., 218
Chapper, J. A., 384, 385, 418
Chase, C., 429
Chavez, P., 247
Cheek, K., 333
Cheesman, F., 418, 419
Cheney, D., 103, 488, 596
Cheng, E. K., 413
Chermak, S. M., 53, 234
Chertoff, M., 84, 278
Chesney-Lind, M., 591
Cheung, H., 259
Chiricos, T. G., 53, 107, 109, 456
Christensen, P. H., 196
Christenson, T., 100
Christopher, R. L., 135
Church, T. W., 394

Clark, N., 328
Clark, T. C., 311
Clear, T., 346, 429, 431, 576
Clear, T. R., 521
Clemmer, E., 189
Clinton, B., 446
Cohen, L. E., 228
Cohen, M., 231
Cohen, T. H., 339, 344, 345, 347, 398, 405, 406, 416
Cohn, E. G., 248
Cohn, L., 398
Colbert, D., 339
Cole, D., 102
Cole, G., 346
Coleman, C., 110
Coleridge, J. D., Lord, 134
Coles, C. M., 19, 54, 168, 196
Collins, J., 24, 259
Colon, N., 526
Comparet-Cassini, J., 152
Conover, T., 544
Conway, P., 521
Cook, P. J., 605
Cooney, M., 401
Cooper, M., 243
Cooper, S. K., 430
Cooperman, A., 244
Coopman, J., 227
Corbett, B., 501
Coronado, A., 575–576
Costanzo, M., 446
Cotton, S., 603–604
Coutts, L., 215
Coventry, G., 480
Cowell, A. J., 331
Crank, J. P., 210
Crawford, C., 109, 437, 456
Cressey, D., 551
Crew, B. K., 336
Crofton, W., 578
Crouch, B. M., 544
Cruz, R., 359
Culbertson, R. G., 210
Culhane, D. P., 593
Cullen, F., 21, 121
Cullen, F. T., 212, 248, 430, 442, 449, 528, 564
Cullent, F. T., 627
Cunningham, R., 398
Cunningham, W. C., 276, 277

677

Subject Index

THE CRIMINAL JUSTICE SYSTEM

CRIME

ENTRY INTO THE SYSTEM

Reported and observed crime

Investigation

Arrest

Charges filed

Released without prosecution

Released without prosecution

Unsolved crime or no arrest

Initial appearance

Charges dropped or dismissed

PROSECUTION AND PRETRIAL SERVICES

Bail or detention hearing

Charges dropped or dismissed

Grand jury

Refusal to indict

Charge dismissed

New trial granted

Acquitted

Found guilty

Trial

Guilty plea

Appeal

Misdemeanors

Felonies

Gather information

Gather information

Preliminary hearing

Arraignment

Reduction of charge

ADJUDICATION

Plea bargain

Acquitted

Found guilty

Guilty plea

Preliminary hearing

Arraignment

Charge dismissed

Plea bargain

Trial
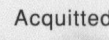